MODERN COMPLEX LITIGATION

Second Edition

by

JAY TIDMARSH
Professor of Law
Notre Dame Law School

ROGER H. TRANGSRUD
James F. Humphreys Professor of
Complex Litigation and Civil Procedure
The George Washington University Law School

FOUNDATION PRESS
2010

THOMSON REUTERS™

© 1998 FOUNDATION PRESS
© 2010 By THOMSON REUTERS/FOUNDATION PRESS
195 Broadway, 9th Floor
New York, NY 10007
Phone Toll Free 1–877–888–1330
Fax (212) 367–6799
foundation–press.com
Printed in the United States of America

ISBN 978–1–58778–537–5

Mat #40135345

MODERN COMPLEX LITIGATION

Second Edition

by

JAY TIDMARSH
Professor of Law
Notre Dame Law School

ROGER H. TRANGSRUD
James F. Humphreys Professor of
Complex Litigation and Civil Procedure
The George Washington University Law School

FOUNDATION PRESS
2010

THOMSON REUTERS

© 1998 FOUNDATION PRESS
© 2010 By THOMSON REUTERS/FOUNDATION PRESS
195 Broadway, 9th Floor
New York, NY 10007
Phone Toll Free 1–877–888–1330
Fax (212) 367–6799
foundation–press.com

Printed in the United States of America

ISBN 978–1–58778–537–5

Mat #40135345

To Jan

— J.T.

To Lisa, Amy, and David

— R.H.T.

PREFACE

This book is the successor edition to our casebook, *Complex Litigation and the Adversary System*, written in 1998. In the intervening twelve years, much has changed in the field of complex litigation and in the way that we view the field. As a result, rather than merely updating our prior book, we completely revised it. Although still following the same general structure — proceeding from issues of aggregation to issues of pretrial, trial, and remedy — this book is thoroughly reorganized and thoroughly up to date. Sixty-three principal cases (out of a total of 143) that we use in this book were decided since we published our prior edition. We have likewise included hundreds of post-1998 cases and dozens of post-1998 law-review articles, books, and other secondary literature. The notes have been revamped and significantly shortened. Because of our emphasis on currency and our new organization, we decided to signal the break from the past by giving this edition a new title: *Modern Complex Litigation.*

Despite these many changes, the basic goals for this casebook remain the same as they were for the last one: to serve as an educational tool for students learning about complex civil litigation for the first time; to provide a resource for judges, lawyers, and academics struggling with the intractable problems these cases create; and to defend a thesis about the proper roles of — and limitations on — judges, lawyers, and parties involved in large-scale adjudication in our democratic society. We meet none of these goals perfectly. But we hope that we convey to each of you the great enthusiasm and respect that we have for this most difficult and important subject.

I

Briefly stated, our perspective is this: Complex litigation tests the limits of the adversarial system. In complex litigation, the adversarial process functions poorly, if at all; there are so many parties, documents, facts, and/or issues that the lawyers, the litigants, and the jury are simply incapable of performing the tasks which the adversarial process has traditionally assigned to them. To overcome this dysfunction and to preserve the opportunity for rational adjudication, the judge must of necessity step in. The shift toward increased judicial power, however, has at least two untoward effects. First, the judge handling complex litigation adopts a role foreign to adversarial theory and to the notions of party autonomy which underlie that theory. Second, as long as the traditional judicial role remains unchanged in routine litigation, the judge handling complex litigation creates a conflict with one of the bedrock principles of modern procedure: the like procedural treatment of all lawsuits. It is no exaggeration to say that complex litigation presents the critical test for the continued viability of the adversarial system and the modern American procedural system set up around adversarial norms.

In consequence, the critical questions of complex litigation, and the questions which this book seeks to address, are: (1) How important are adversarial process and party autonomy? (2) How important is the like procedural treatment of cases? and (3) Under what circumstances is it desirable or even essential to depart from adversarial and equalitarian procedure? Although we are on record in our other writings as answering (1) "Important," (2) "Important," and (3) "Not many," we let the materials shape the questions, rather than force the readers to accept our conclusions.

We also believe that by framing the issues in these terms, readers can gain new perspectives on fields such as Civil Procedure, Federal Courts, Conflict of Laws, and Mass Torts. A course in complex litigation can act as a bridge linking and synthesizing these fields, and our materials are intended to show the interconnection of procedure and substance in several specific categories of modern civil litigation.

II

A word of caution is in order regarding our editing of cases. First, we deleted most citations to other cases, to secondary materials, and to the record. When we deleted such citations, we did not signify that fact with ellipses. We did, however, mark with ellipses any deletions of textual material, including on occasion some significant arguments that were less central to the reasons that we chose the case or were edited out for space considerations. Second, we used brackets to signify the addition of language not found in the original source. Third, in the excerpts we used, we tended to "correct" citation forms to conform to the *Bluebook* style, even when the source used another citation form. In some instances, we used brackets to indicate what we added or omitted, but as a rule we did not. Third, in order to maintain a consistent style throughout the book, we tended to delete some italics found in the opinions or to insert others. Finally, on very rare occasions, and only when absolutely necessary for comprehension of the edited material, we blended two or more paragraphs into one. In short, readers should not assume that the cases in the book are a verbatim reproduction of the language, citation style, or the full range of the arguments in the sources themselves; readers should always go to the original source to obtain precise text. We took great care in the editing process, however, to ensure that each selection, as nearly as possible, retained its original flavor and style.

We also tried to use gender-inclusive language wherever possible. Sometimes this proved awkward, so we tended to use "she" to refer to the hypothetical judge, "he" to refer to the hypothetical lawyer, and either pronoun to refer to hypothetical parties.

III

A word about your authors is also in order. Both of us have experience as practicing lawyers in complex litigation. You should know that one of authors was lead counsel for the United States for a period of time in the *Agent Orange* and *Triana DDT* litigation, and the other author worked as an associate in the *MGM Grand Hotel Fire* litigation and was involved in aspects of the *Ortiz* litigation as a consultant. One of us has also been involved in a federally funded study that examined a number of mass-tort class actions (including *Amchem*, *Ortiz*, and *Silicone Gel Breast Implants*). All these cases are discussed at various points in the book.

IV

We tried to make the book as current as possible. Some developments as recent as March, 2010 are captured in the book. But we have no illusions: In a field evolving as rapidly as complex civil litigation, the book will be out of date before it arrives in the bookstores. Should you ever wish to share with us any recent developments, or should you wish to share any questions or thoughts about the materials in this book, please feel free to contact us.

Notre Dame, Indiana
Washington, D.C.
April, 2010

ACKNOWLEDGMENTS

We gratefully acknowledge the contributions of the people who helped to make this book possible. At the risk of neglecting others, we especially thank:

• Our deans — Nell Newton and Patty O'Hara of Notre Dame Law School and Fred Lawrence of the George Washington University Law School— who provided us with support, encouragement, and a sabbatical (for one of us) to finish this project. Our law schools and universities also gave us research grants that helped to bring this book to completion.

• Our colleagues, whose conversations about civil procedure and complex litigation are always insightful.

• Our research librarians — Dwight King, Leslie Lee, Patti Ogden, Scott Pagel, Lucy Payne, and Warren Rees — who helped with either the predecessor edition or with this one, and who are simply the best.

• Our research assistants — Jesse Schoemer and John Schoenig at Notre Dame, and John Dundon, Macey Harrington-Woodard, Neil Marchand, and Wrede Smith at George Washington— who provided research, editorial assistance, and technical advice.

• Our administrative and technical staffs — Debi McGuigan Jones and Dan Manier at Notre Dame, and Frances Arias at George Washington — who did everything we asked of them, and more. A special thanks to Debi, who also proved to be a fabulous proofreader.

• Our students, who put up with handouts and half-finished thoughts.

• The authors and publishers that permitted us to reprint excerpts of copyrighted works. They are:

American Law Institute, Complex Litigation: Statutory Recommendations and Analysis (1994). Reprinted with permission.

American Law Institute, Principles of the Law of Aggregate Litigation (2009). Reprinted with permission.

American Bar Association, ABA Report to the House of Delegates from the Commission on Mass Torts (1989). Reprinted with permission.

Bacigal, Ronald J., The Limits of Litigation: The Dalkon Shield Controversy (1990), reprinted with permission of Carolina Academic Press, copyright © 1990.

Cecil, Joe S., & Willging, Thomas E., Accepting Daubert's Invitation: Defining a Role for Court-Appointed Experts in Assessing Scientific Validity, 43 Emory L.J. 995 (1994), reprinted with permission of Emory Law Journal, copyright © 1994.

Chayes, Abram, The Role of the Judge in Public Law Litigation, 89 Harv. L. Rev. 1281 (1976), reprinted with permission of the author, copyright © 1976.

Cover, Robert M., For James Wm. Moore: Some Reflections on a Reading of the Rules, 84 Yale L.J. 718 (1975). Reprinted with permission of The Yale Law Journal Company and Fred B. Rothman & Company from *The Yale Law Journal*, copyright © 1975, Vol. 84, pages 718-740.

Elliott, E. Donald, Managerial Judging and the Revolution of Procedure, 53 U. Chi. L. Rev. 306 (1986), reprinted with permission of University of Chicago Law Review, copyright © 1986.

Fuller, Lon L., The Forms and Limits of Adjudication, 92 Harv. L. Rev. 353 (1978), reprinted with permission of John J. Roche, Trustee, Lon L. Fuller Trust, copyright © 1978.

Hazard, Geoffrey C., Jr., Ethics in the Practice of Law (1978), reprinted with permission of Yale University Press, copyright © 1978.

Horowitz, Irwin A. & Bordens, Kenneth S., The Consolidation of Plaintiffs: The Effects of Number of Plaintiffs on Jurors' Liability Decisions, Damage Awards, and Cognitive Processing of Evidence The Effects of Outlier Presence, Plaintiff Population Size, and Aggregation of Plaintiffs on Simulated Jury Decisions, 85 J. Applied Psychol. 909 (2000), reprinted with permission of the American Psychological Association and the authors, copyright © 2000.

Juenger, Friedrich K., Mass Disasters and the Conflict of Laws, 1989 U. Ill. L. Rev. 105, reprinted with permission of the Illinois Law Review, copyright © 1989.

Langbein, John, The German Advantage in Civil Procedure, 52 U. Chi. L. Rev. 823 (1985), reprinted with permission of University of Chicago Law Review, copyright © 1985.

Maitland, F.W., Equity, (A.H. Chaylor & W.J. Whittaker eds., 2d ed. 1936), reprinted with permission of Cambridge University Press, copyright © 1936.

McGovern, Francis E., An Analysis of Mass Torts for Judges, 73 Tex. L. Rev. 1821 (1995), reprinted with permission of Texas Law Review Association and the author, copyright © 1995. Permission applies only to the English version.

Posner, Richard A., Economic Analysis of Law (7th ed. 2007), reprinted with permission of the author, copyright © 2007.

Rawls, John, A Theory of Justice (1971), reprinted by permission of the publisher, Cambridge, Mass.: The Belknap Press of Harvard University Press, Copyright ©1971, 1999 by the President and Fellows of Harvard College.

Resnik, Judith, Managerial Judges, 96 Harv. L. Rev. 374 (1982), reprinted with permission of Harvard Law Review Association and the author, copyright © 1982.

Rosenberg, David, Class Actions for Mass Torts: Doing Individual Justice by Collective Means, 62 Ind. L.J. 561, 562-67 (1987), reprinted with permission of Indiana Law Journal, copyright © 1987.

Saltzburg, Steven A., Lawyers, Clients, and the Adversary System, 37 Mercer L. Rev. 647 (1985), copyright © 1984 Mercer Law Review.

Schwarzer, William W, Judicial Federalism in Action: Coordination of Litigation in State and Federal Courts, 78 Va. L. Rev. 1689 (1992), reprinted with permission of Virginia Law Review Association and Fred B. Rothman & Co., copyright © 1992.

Subrin, Stephen N., How Equity Conquered Common Law: The Federal Rules of Civil Procedure in Historical Perspective, 135 U. Pa. L. Rev. 909 (1987), reprinted with permission of author, copyright © 1987.

Tidmarsh, Jay, Unattainable Justice, 60 Geo. Wash. L. Rev. 1683 (1992), reprinted with permission of George Washington Law Review, copyright © 1992.

Trangsrud, Roger H., Mass Trials in Mass Tort Cases: A Dissent, 1989 U. Ill. Rev. 69, reprinted with permission of the University of Illinois Law Review, copyright © 1989.

Trangsrud, Roger H., Joinder Alternatives in Mass Tort Litigation, 70 Cornell L. Rev. 779 (1985), reprinted with permission of the author, copyright © 1984.

Weinstein, Jack B., Individual Justice in Mass Tort Litigation (1995), reprinted with permission of the author, copyright © 1995.

Zeisel, Hans, & Callahan, Thomas, Split Trials and Time Saving: A Statistical Analysis, 76 Harv. L. Rev. 1606 (1963), reprinted with permission of Harvard Law Review Association, copyright © 1963.

Except for permitting us to reproduce excerpts of their work in this book, all copyright holders have retained all rights in their works.

SUMMARY OF CONTENTS

CHAPTER THREE: Aggregation and Jurisdiction in a Federal System 249

TABLE OF CONTENTS

TABLE OF CASES

Principal authorities appear in bold typeface.
References are to page number.

TABLE OF AUTHORITIES

Principal authorities appear in bold typeface.
References are to page number.

CHAPTER ONE

AN OVERVIEW OF COMPLEX LITIGATION

At this point in your legal education, you have become steeped enough in the American system of civil procedure to take many of its features for granted. You have become accustomed to the dual system of federal and state courts. The complicated layers of rules — constitutional, statutory, common law, and code-based — that govern the way in which these courts resolve disputes no longer mystify you.

A central feature of the American system is its adversarial approach to adjudication: The parties (or, typically, their lawyers) are in charge of tasks such as identifying the issues at stake, discovering the evidence to bolster claims and defenses, and presenting evidence and arguments to the decision maker (either judge or jury). Although Americans place great faith in this process, we also appreciate that unrestrained adversarialism is not always desirable. We want substantial justice to be done; we want to make sure that the parties get a hearing on the merits of their dispute and are not hogtied by an adversary using procedural technicalities to his or her advantage.

Because we are familiar with what we know, it is easy to forget that our adversarial system is not the only available option. In fact, in civil litigation, our system has significant costs and drawbacks that we could avoid if we chose other methods of handling disputes. Of course, those methods have their own costs and drawbacks.

The ultimate goals of this book are to identify the problems that our procedural choices have created, and to see whether different sets of choices might lead to a more sensible, more just, and more efficient litigation system. The vehicle that we will use to explore these issues is complex civil litigation. Judges and scholars first recognized the phenomenon of complex civil litigation about sixty years ago. Although no precise definition of "complex litigation" exists, for now we will use an intuitive definition:

Complex civil litigation involves cases which are "bigger" or "more complicated" than the typical suit for which our adversarial procedures work tolerably well. The *Microsoft* antitrust litigation, *Brown v. Board of Education*, and the thousands of asbestos cases clogging court dockets are paradigms of complex civil litigation. At first blush, these cases have little in common. On reflection, however, all share a common feature: They have thrown the American procedural system — an adversarial system originally designed for a far simpler type of lawsuit — into crisis.

The rise of complex civil litigation has many causes, but several lie at the fore. The first is the growth of substantive bodies of law that regulate institutions with the capacity to inflict widespread harm. Antitrust and securities law, constitutional-rights litigation, mass torts, and employment discrimination are just a few examples of new substantive fields (or, at least, old fields turned to new uses). Such lawsuits can threaten the future of important economic or political entities, and thus create high stakes that to some extent justify and inevitably create a "no stone unturned" mentality in litigation. A second factor is the concentration of power in corporate and government institutions; as a result, the potential that illegal overreaching will have broad consequences has increased. Third, our own perceptions about the legitimacy of challenging established entities has changed; we have become, in Professor Hazard's words, more willing to put "authority in the dock." *See* Geoffrey C. Hazard, Jr., *Authority in the Dock*, 69 B.U. L. REV. 469 (1989). Finally, after the adoption of the Federal Rules of Civil Procedure in 1938, our procedural rules have tended to focus resolving cases on their factual merits. Issues and facts are sorted out during a discovery stage rather than at a pleading stage; and the rules provide wide latitude in the joinder of parties and claims in a single suit. The combined effect of these rules is to make big lawsuits easier to bring, costlier to litigate, and harder to dispose of at an early stage.

In this chapter we lay the foundation for the doctrines and details of complex litigation that we examine in the succeeding chapters. We begin with a brief history of Anglo-American procedure that places modern-era complex litigation in context. We then explore theoretical arguments that underpin the present procedural system and inform the possible solutions for complex cases. Finally, we provide some comparative context for our study by exploring the ways in which other modern legal systems have crafted procedural regimes that hold certain advantages (and contain certain drawbacks) for addressing the problems of complex litigation.

This book often returns to the historical, theoretical, and comparative insights of this chapter. They lie at the heart of the phenomenon we call complex civil litigation, and the subject cannot be understood without them.

A. A SHORT HISTORY OF AMERICAN CIVIL PROCEDURE

The Norman conquest of 1066 is a good point at which to mark the beginning of Anglo-American civil procedure. Before then, the English judicial "system" was largely a hodgepodge of local courts that employed processes that relied heavily on divine intervention to obtain the proper results. Judges threw litigants into the water (on the view that the water would reject the wrongdoer), listened as an alleged wrongdoer and others chosen on his behalf precisely recited an oath (on the view that God would trip the tongue of a liar), and presided over a battle between champions selected by the litigants (on the view that God would grant victory to the righteous). With their genius for administration, the early Norman kings consolidated royal power in part by asserting authority over the most significant disputes of the day — breaches against the king's peace and disputes over land (land then being the most important form of wealth). Within the next hundred years, an administrative process evolved into a judicial one. The common-law courts had been established.

1. The Common Law

The Normans sometimes resolved disputes by means of a device that used Anglo-Saxon and possibly Norman elements: calling together witnesses familiar with the events and asking their views on how to resolve the matter. Thus was the modern jury system begun. This new approach was, in the words of historian S.F.C. Milsom, "a larger change than it sounds." No longer did courts preside over "the ritual formulation of a question to be put to an oracle beyond the need of human guidance"; they were "now in some way responsible for the answer." The "rational nature of this new form of trial" required "consideration of the actual facts," which in turn "require[d] the expression, for the first time, of rules of law." S.F.C. MILSOM, HISTORICAL FOUNDATIONS OF THE COMMON LAW 42 (2d ed. 1981).

This approach presented complications. Relying on human judgment, the jury system was fallible. One response to fallibility would have been to do what the Romans had done — develop a body of legal principles that constrained decision-making. Another response — the one the English adopted — was to develop a series of procedural strictures that confined as narrowly as possible the questions left open to the jury's judgment, and hence confined the jury's opportunity to make a mistake. As a result, for centuries English common lawyers focused on the procedural mechanisms for asserting this claim or that defense rather than on the substance of the claims or defenses.

a. The Writ System. The procedural system that the common law devised had two principal components. The first was the writ system. A writ contained a royal command that a particular person do something or else show cause to the king why he could not do it. During the first century of Norman rule, a number of these writs ordered royal officials either to investigate alleged errors in the local courts or actually to resolve certain claims, particularly disputes over land ownership. As more time passed and permanent royal courts were established, the writ became the formal piece of parchment that authorized one of the king's courts to hear a dispute. Without a writ, a royal court had — to use an anachronistic term

— no jurisdiction over the controversy. The disputants were left to whatever local procedures and remedies were available.

Writs could be obtained only from the chancellor, who was the king's most senior advisor and, in the early days, also a cleric trained in Roman law. In the beginning, no particular subject matter automatically entitled a person to a writ; obtaining a writ depended upon being able to convince the chancellor that the conduct at issue was of concern to the Crown. Over time, however, the subject matter and language of the writs became systematized. Systematization, however, did not mean inflexibility. During the thirteenth century the Chancery (i.e., the office of the chancellor) created new writs to cover factual circumstances that slipped between the cracks of existing writs, and existing writs were stretched to cover conduct that had previously been handled only in local courts. Indeed, in 1250, Henry de Bracton, the author of one of England's first legal treatises, stated with confidence that "there will be as many formulas for writs as there are kinds of action; . . . for it is the king's duty to provide an adequate remedy to redress every wrong." HENRY DE BRACTON, OF THE LAWS AND CUSTOMS OF ENGLAND f. 413b (George E. Wodbine ed., Samuel E. Thorne trans., Harvard Univ. Press 1968) (ca. 1258).

History proved Bracton wrong. The thirteenth century saw efforts by the nobility to thwart the king's increasing power. One manifestation of that struggle was the effort to prevent the Chancery from issuing new types of writs. The matter was more or less settled in 1285 by the Statute of Westminster, which allowed the Chancery to issue new writs only "*in consimili casu*" (i.e., in cases similar to those for which writs already existed). Under the authority of this statute the Chancery devised new writs with close analogues to existing writs, and Parliament occasionally authorized others. But the rapid growth of the jurisdiction of the king's courts halted.

During the fourteenth century the judges of the three royal courts (the Exchequer, the King's Bench, and the Court of Common Pleas) succeeded in winning a further degree of independence from the Crown. Common-law judges frequently quashed writs issued by the Chancery because of their failure to conform to the scope of existing writs. "The common law is therefore beginning to retire to a definite and limited field, resigns its flexibility, and declines to be drawn into attempts to remove its own defects: that will henceforth be the province of Parliament. Still later, when Parliament fails to keep pace with the needs of litigants, it will be the Chancellor who will take up the task." THEODORE F.T. PLUCKNETT, A CONCISE HISTORY OF THE COMMON LAW 159 (5th ed. 1956).[*]

Rather than developing systematic theories of property, contract, tort, or crime, the common law remained a group of independent, loosely

---

[*] One limit on the calcification of the common-law courts was competition among themselves for cases (and the lucrative fees sometimes associated with them). On occasion, this competition led the courts to establish new remedies. *See* Daniel Klerman, *Jurisdictional Competition and the Evolution of the Common Law*, 74 U. CHI. L. REV. 1179 (2007).

associated writs, each of which dealt with specific dimensions of these subjects. As Sir Henry Maine once observed, "[s]o great is the ascendancy of the Law of Actions in the infancy of the Courts of Justice, that substantive law has at first the look of being gradually secreted in the interstices of procedure." HENRY MAINE, DISSERTATION ON EARLY LAW AND CUSTOMS 389 (1886). The simple reality is that medieval English lawyers did not conceive of law in the substantive terms that we do today. There were writs and procedures to handle this type of harm and different ones to handle that type of harm, but rarely did the common law stop to consolidate substantive or procedural issues that, with the benefit of hindsight, we can see to be conceptually linked.

The need for reform, however, was more apparent in retrospect than it was at the time. For the most part, the writs were sufficient to cover the types of disputes which were common to the age; and local courts filled in many remaining gaps. But the times finally began to run ahead of the forms of action. Despite the emergence of English mercantilism, it was not until the seventeenth century that the common law generally enforced contracts. Likewise, the common law never developed doctrines dealing with most of the aspects of uses and trusts, in spite of their frequent employment from the fifteenth century forward.

b. Common-Law Procedure. The second major feature the of common law was its peculiar procedural system. Just as the history of the writ system reflects a transition from flexibility to rigidity, so does the history of common-law procedure.

The centerpiece of common-law procedure was the pleading system. By the fourteenth century, the purpose of pleading was plain: to constrain, as much as possible, the opportunity for the fallible jury to make an error. The point of pleading was to narrow the case to a single determinable issue. A centuries-long fascination with the issue of pleading (e.g., whether a claim of self-defense was a plea that could be made in response a writ of trespass) had the eventual effect of establishing the doctrines of substantive law (e.g., self-defense is a defense to a claim for battery), but it was never the intention of the medieval lawyers to do so. "There was no substantive law to which pleading was adjective. These were the terms in which the law existed and in which lawyers thought." MILSOM, *supra*, at 59.

It is nearly impossible to describe in brief fashion the intricacies of common-law pleading, but several generalizations can be made. First, the rules of pleading did not always give the parties a good sense of the case that they would face at trial. The opening plea made clear the form of action under which the plaintiff was proceeding. Typically, however, facts could be pleaded with great generality, and were often fictional. Aside from the pleadings, no court-sanctioned process permitted the parties to discover before trial the relevant evidence in the possession of an opponent or other persons.

Second, the pleadings after the plaintiff's opening declaration generally proceeded through a series of responses and counter-responses. In general, the defendant had several choices in responding: Filing a dilatory plea for defects such as a misjoinder of parties, another pending action, and so forth; filing a special demurrer for formal defects in the declaration; pleading the general issue (in effect, stating "I did not do it"); setting up a special plea ("I did it, but I was justified because . . ."); or making a general demurrer ("I did it, but my action as alleged in the plaintiff's plea was not a wrong in law"). If the defendant pleaded the general issue, the issue was joined and the trial determined whether the defendant did the thing alleged in the complaint. For special pleas and demurrers, further pleading occurred; over the centuries, layers of technicalities encrusted these pleadings. If the litigants avoided the traps of these technicalities, the special plea also resulted in a trial, limited only to the issue of whether the facts justified the plea. On the other hand, demurrers led to a judicial decision.

In spite of these similarities, each form of action varied in its particulars (procedures among writs varied on important matters such as the process available to compel the defendant's attendance, the mode of trial, and the permitted defensive pleas). Each form of action had its own procedures that a lawyer needed to master. Pleading was a game — a very serious game — in which specialists in the art of pleading thrived on an opponent's miscues.

The third general feature was the severity with which the system responded to miscues. As Professor Plucknett explained:

> The lawyers had a maxim that they would tolerate a "mischief" (a failure of substantial justice in a particular case) rather than an "inconvenience" (a breach of legal principle). . . .[T]he real question which [common-law lawyers] had to face was how the future of the law should be developed. Was it to be a system of strict rule, mainly procedural, or was there to be a broader principle of conscience, reason, natural justice, equity? Plainly there were two points of view on this matter in the reign of Edward II [1307-27 — ED.], but it must have been fairly evident by the middle of the century that the stricter party had won. [PLUCKNETT, *supra*, at 680.]

By the fifteenth century, when pleading moved from an oral to a written process, wrong pleading choices were often fatal. Suppose that a plaintiff obtained a writ of trespass, but the defendant's wrong actually fit within the writ of trespass on the case. Too bad — the judge threw the case out, despite the existence of a perfectly good claim. Or suppose that the defendant was alleged to have injured the plaintiff in a way that arguably was not a legal wrong, and that the defendant also did not do the act alleged. The pleading system put the defendant to an irrevocable choice: either demur or plead the general issue. If he chose the former, the alleged facts were conclusively established; if he chose the latter, he could never again contest the issue of legal liability. In this system, parties often had to abandon valid legal positions. Even more startling was the common law's response to missteps during pleading. If a lawyer who claimed self-defense pleaded the general issue rather than correctly entering a special plea in justification, he could not use self-defense to justify his conduct; the only issue at trial would be whether he had hit the plaintiff. As Professor

Millar observed, "[a] mingling of logic and illogic, not untinctured by tricklings of medieval scholasticism, appears throughout the whole discipline [of common-law pleading]. . . . Except in the simplest cases, the plaintiff can never be quite sure that his demand will attain the stage of trial, the defendant that some inadvertence will not see him cast *in toto*." ROBERT W. MILLAR, CIVIL PROCEDURE OF THE TRIAL COURT IN HISTORICAL PERSPECTIVE 34, 36 (1952).

Trial was usually to the jury, which was initially the persons who were familiar with the facts and who provided information to the judge. At an early point, juries also began to give advice to the judge, and eventually rendered verdicts. By the fifteenth century, juries ceased to be witnesses to the event, and instead rendered verdicts based on the testimony of others. Lawyers now examined the witnesses. By the sixteenth century, cross-examination seems to have become a widely accepted practice.

In its mature form, the trial was the pride of the common-law system. "In the *viva voce* examination and cross-examination of witnesses in open court, with their demeanor and mode of speech directly appreciable by the organs of decision, is present the method that yields all those advantages of orality, immediacy, and publicity to which contemporary Continental reform is already beginning to aspire." MILLAR, *supra*, at 36. These positive qualities of jury trial blinded many to the inequities caused by the rigid pleading system that preceded the trial.

Finally, the remedies available at common law were limited. This limit derived both from the nature of writs and from the jury system itself. Common-law writs typically involved retrospective controversies for which an award of money or a declaration of property rights was the appropriate remedy. Moreover, as an ad hoc body, the jury was ill-suited to the task of issuing and enforcing an injunction. Hence, as a general matter, injunctions, accountings, and other complex remedies were unavailable at common law.

This history remains relevant to our present procedural situation, and to complex litigation. One lesson is the legacy of the jury system. Although we can disagree with the way in which it implemented the insight, the common law correctly understood that the use of a group of lay decision-makers required development of pretrial devices to narrow issues and facts for trial; and it also required the clear separation of pretrial from trial. Moreover, common-law procedure demonstrates the evils of overly technical and non-uniform procedural rules: Lawyers can become so caught up in the game of procedural manipulation that they fail to appreciate the effect of their efforts on the substantive law and the merits of a dispute. Next, the history of the common law also shows the dangers of a system in which the discretion to overlook procedural missteps in the search for substantive justice is squeezed out and ultimately eliminated.

Despite its limitations, common-law procedure had some advantages. In its mature form, it was certain and precise, it narrowed issues, and it led to speedy and dispositive trials. It is unlikely that these advantages alone would have saved the common law from significant procedural reform long before the nineteenth century. What tamped down reform efforts was the rise of a parallel system of procedure that promised all the advantages that common-law procedure lacked. Of course, that system also suffered from all the defects that common-law procedure avoided.

2. The Rise of Equity

Tracing the roots of equity is difficult, but they certainly lie in the days before the common law hardened. During the twelfth and thirteenth century parties often bypassed their common-law remedies and appealed directly to the king, his Parliament, or his chancellor for relief. Since the chancellor already had the responsibility for issuing writs and was trained in Roman and canon law, most requests landed in the Chancery. When a writ covered (or could cover) the petitioner's claim, however, the plaintiff bore the burden of persuading the chancellor to hear the claim directly.

F.W. MAITLAND, EQUITY

4-6 (A.H. Chaylor & W.J. Whittaker eds., 2d ed. 1936)

[T]he petitioner . . . complains that for some reason or another he can not get a remedy in the ordinary course of justice and yet he is entitled to a remedy. He is poor, he is old, he is sick, his adversary is rich and powerful, will bribe or intimidate jurors, or has by some trick or some accident acquired an advantage of which the ordinary courts with their formal procedure will not deprive him. . . . Gradually in the course of the fourteenth century petitioners, instead of going to the king, will go straight to the Chancellor, will address their complaints to him and adjure him to do what is right for the love of God and in the way of charity. Now one thing the Chancellor may do in such a case is to invent a new writ and so to provide the complainant with a means of bringing an action in a court of law. But in the fourteenth century the courts of law have become very conservative and are given to quashing writs which differ in material points from those already in use. But another thing that the Chancellor can do is to send for the complainant's adversary and examine him concerning the charge that is made against him. Gradually a procedure is established. The Chancellor, having considered the petition, or "bill" as it is called, orders the adversary to come before him and answer the complaint. The writ whereby he does so is called a subpoena . . . . Then when he comes before the Chancellor he will have to answer on oath, and sentence by sentence, the bill of the plaintiff. This procedure is rather like that of the ecclesiastical courts and the canon law than like that of our old English courts of law. . . . [T]he Chancellor will decide questions of fact as well as questions of law.

I do not think that in the fourteenth century the Chancellors considered that they had to administer any body of substantive rules that differed from the ordinary law of the land. They were administering the law but they were administering it in cases which escaped the meshes of the ordinary courts. . . . However, this sort of thing can not well be permitted. The law courts will not have it and parliament will not have it. . . . And so the Chancellor is warned off the field of common law — he is not to hear cases which might go to the ordinary courts, he is not to make himself a judge of torts and contracts, of property in lands and goods.

But then just at this time it is becoming plain that the Chancellor is doing some convenient and useful works that could not be done, or could not easily be done by the courts of the common law. . . .

We ought not to think of common law and equity as of two rival systems. Equity was not a self-sufficient system, at every point it presupposed the existence of common law. Common law was a self-sufficient system. I mean this: that if the legislature had passed a short act saying "Equity is hereby abolished," we might still have got on fairly well . . . . On the other hand, had the legislature said, "Common law is hereby abolished," this decree if obeyed would have meant anarchy. . . .

For this reason, I do not think that any one has expounded or ever will expound equity as a single, consistent system, an articulate body of law. It is a collection of appendixes between which there is no very close connexion. . . .

In my view equity has added to our legal system, together with a number of detached doctrines, one novel and fertile institution, namely the trust; and three novel and fertile remedies, namely the decree for specific performance, the injunction, and the judicial administration of estates.

Although it operated over a restricted range, equity had a number of advantages over the common law that made parties seek to push the boundaries of equity jurisdiction outward. The advantages included:

- the injunction, because "there were matters which could best be settled by securing the prompt personal attendance of parties, and giving them direct personal commands to act or to desist in certain matters";

- better rules regarding discovery and the admissibility of evidence, because "the common law was slow to admit the evidence of parties and witnesses," while "the canonists [i.e., the chancellors in equity and their adjuncts] were using the written deposition" with success;

- the absence of a jury, because "[e]specially in the fifteenth century there were complaints that juries were packed, bribed, intimidated, partial and difficult to obtain within any reasonable space of time";

- better substantive rules, because "the substantive rules of the common law, defensible enough when considered purely from a technical point of view, seemed unjust to the unlearned who had to suffer from them, and so we need not be surprised that there grew up a desire for more equitable rules";

- better procedural rules, because "there were cases which could not be satisfactorily handled by the common law with its writs, its delays, its pleadings, its limited resources in the finding of facts and the awarding of judgment, and its weakness in the face of disorder and corruption."

THEODORE F.T. PLUCKNETT, A CONCISE HISTORY OF THE COMMON LAW 177-78 (5th ed. 1956).

A number of influences shaped the procedural system in equity. One was canon law, which "was impatient of pedantry and inclined to place substance before form." *Id.* at 685. Another was the fact that, until the nineteenth century, only the chancellor of his chief assistant, the Master of the Rolls, could enter a final decision. The chancellor was a powerful and busy person, and could not afford the time to travel the countryside, empanel juries, and hear evidence in an ever increasing number of suits.

Thus, the procedural system in equity was in many regards the opposite of common-law procedure. There was no jury trial; the chancellor found the facts. Indeed, there was no "trial" at all, at least in the common-law sense. Equity proceeded piecemeal, taking evidence on and then determining one issue after another until some resolution occurred. As with the common law, pleadings in equity were important, and they were often lengthy. But many of the technical pleading traps of the common law did not exist. The chancellor, after all, was supposed to get to the equity of the matter; and, since there was no jury, there was no need of pleading devices designed to prevent multiple-issue confusion. In particular, one of the common law's strongest issue-narrowing devices — restrictive rules of party joinder — did not exist, for complete justice required the joinder of all interested persons. Without stringent issue-narrowing devices, however, equitable disputes were often sprawling affairs (at least compared to common-law disputes).

Equity also differed from common law in its use of discovery devices to obtain relevant information. The chancellor had a staff of assistants, known as masters, who collected most of the information. Borrowing from the canon law's administrative and inquisitorial process of subpoena and deposition, the chancellor or his masters drafted questions for witnesses, whose responses were reduced to writing. Relevant documents were taken or copied down. All the information — as well as the parties' written arguments — were collected for the chancellor, who read it and rendered a decision in due course. The chancellor heard no live testimony.

Without a jury, a final, trial-like event bringing the case to closure was unnecessary. If the chancellor did not have enough information to judge a particular case, he could reopen the record to obtain it. Even after the judgment, the parties could always request reconsideration.

It was often said that the chancellor worked only on the conscience of the litigants. In other words, the chancellor's judgments took the form of injunctions directed to the parties. Thus arose the remedial distinction that many first-year law students learn: Law provides damages and equity provides injunctions. Although the distinction was not ironclad in practice, it roughly describes the remedial realm of each system.

Equity's flexibility, its pretrial discovery, its lack of a final trial event, and its commitment to substantive justice over procedural technicality created a strong contrast to the common-law process. The weaknesses of the common law were the strengths of equity. The converse was also true.

1 WILLIAM HOLDSWORTH, A HISTORY OF ENGLISH LAW

423-28 ((A.L. Goodhart & H.G. Hanbury eds., 7th rev. ed. 1956)

As soon as the business of the court of Chancery began to increase complaints begin to be heard of its defective organization. . . .

It was said in a debate in Parliament in 1623 that 35,000 subpoenas had been issued in one year. This may have been an exaggeration; but it is probable that over 20,000 were issued. It was thus obvious that the work was too much for the Chancellor and the Master of the Rolls. . . . The result was a constantly increasing arrear of causes, and long delays in the administration of justice. This evil was aggravated by the suspicions entertained, not without reason, that the justice when administered was not always pure. Bacon's confession of corruption showed that the Lord Chancellor himself could not always be trusted . . . .

The official staff of the court of Chancery was recruited and paid upon exactly the same plan as the official staffs of the courts of common law; and the same results ensued. The officials were appointed for life, and paid by fees upon the business done. . . . It followed that all those who, from their experience of the court, were most competent to reform it, were the most interested in maintaining it in its existing condition. . . .

. . . There were several reasons why this system of appointing and paying officials produced much worse effects in the case of the court of Chancery than in the case of the courts of common law.

Firstly, a suit in equity very often lasted very many years. . . . Obviously this gave the officials a great chance of increasing their revenues. . . .

Secondly, the fact that the procedure of the court was wholly written afforded another chance to the official of making money. The suitor was not in a position to object to being compelled to pay for unnecessary copies of unduly lengthened documents . . . .

Thirdly the practice of the court was unsettled, and many of the Chancellors were not competent to settle it. No trouble was taken to distinguish suits which were merely frivolous from those which were real. "Of ten bills," said Norburie, "Hardly three have any colour or shadow of just complaint." Everything was referred to the Masters. Counsel made needless interlocutory motions. . . . During this period the rules of equity were so vague that enormous scope was left to those who desired to persuade a weak or a corrupt Chancellor. . . .

A tale related by Sir John Bramston in his Autobiography is perhaps the best illustration of the effects of the abuses upon the ordinary litigant. He tells us that during the civil war his grandmother had begun a suit in Chancery to recover some tithes to which she was entitled. She died, and he continued the action. The amount in dispute was £4. "It cost, to recover that £4, £200 at least. . . ."

Charles Synge Christopher, PROGRESS IN THE ADMINISTRATION OF JUSTICE DURING THE VICTORIAN PERIOD

Reprinted in 1 SELECT ESSAYS IN ANGLO-AMERICAN LEGAL HISTORY 516, 528-29 (Ass'n of Am. Law Schools ed., 1907)

. . . At the beginning of January 1839, 556 causes and other matters were waiting to be heard by the Chancellor and Vice-Chancellor. . . . If, as seemed possible to skilled observers of the day, the Chancellor should prove unable to do more than keep pace with his appellate work, it would be — so they calculated — six years before the last on the list came on for hearing even in its first stage; if a second hearing was required, thirteen or more years would elapse before this was reached; while, if on the final hearing the master's report was successfully objected to, the long process must begin *de novo*. "*No man, as things now stand*," says in 1839 Mr. George Spence, the author of the well-known work on the equitable jurisdiction of the Court of Chancery, "*can enter into a Chancery suit with any reasonable hope of being alive at its termination, if he has a determined adversary.*"

———

In retrospect, one solution to the weaknesses of common law and equity would have been to combine the two systems, picking the best features of both. Such an approach would hardly have been novel; in the rest of the world, nothing like the division between law and equity existed. Moreover, in the early centuries, the main difference between the systems was procedural rather than substantive. Consultation between law and equity occurred: Common-law judges sometimes sat as commissioners in equitable matters, and some chancellors (such as Thomas More) were common lawyers. Indeed, during the fifteenth and sixteenth centuries, there were opportunities when law and equity could have merged.

Unfortunately, there were to be no shortcuts through history. Slowly but surely, the scope of equity's jurisdiction increased as the common law refused to incorporate equitable notions. Equity began to plug the gaps in the substantive law as well. The chancellor took over the field of uses and trusts, and remade the law of mortgages. He enforced ordinary contracts, eventually spurring the common law to do likewise. The chancellor asserted a jurisdiction to remedy frauds, mistakes, accidents, and forgeries with which the common law was procedurally unable (or in later years unwilling) to deal.

The growing disparity in jurisdiction, remedy, procedure, and philosophy made compromise increasingly difficult. As Professor Plucknett has observed:

> Adjudication, like most other questions of human conduct, depends upon a nice balance between law and equity, rule and exception, tradition and innovation. Each of these different principles became exaggerated when it became the badge of an institution, with the result that law and equity instead of being complementary, became rivals in a political upheaval.

Theodore F.T. Plucknett, A Concise History of the Common Law 681 (5th ed. 1956). This upheaval had little to do with legal differences as such. Although a minor part of the rebellions that dethroned two monarchs in the seventeenth century, common law and equity were important symbols in the battle. The common law represented independence from the Crown; its fixed writs, remedies, and procedures, as well as its jury process, were a buffer against the royal prerogative. Common-law judges and lawyers were powerful actors in Parliament, which was the seat of political opposition to the Crown; the chancellor was a minister of the Crown. Equity's gap-filling in the common law was seen as an effort to increase royal power, and equity's discretion gave further power a royal servant who was thought (often with reason) to be subject to royal influence and corruption.

During the eighteenth century, equity finally emerged as an institution whose power equaled or exceeded that of common-law courts — a victory that was remarkable in view of the triumph of Parliament over the Crown. The reason was simple: "Against Chancery [the common lawyers] had suffered a defeat which was well deserved; their own justice was an inferior product to that of the chancellors." Plucknett, *supra*, at 197. Harmonious relations between law and equity were restored (for instance, the chancellors sometimes referred matters to law for jury trial and law sometimes invoked Chancery jurisdiction to obtain pretrial discovery).

By then, however, equity had stopped being equitable in spirit. As a mature concept of substantive law developed during the sixteenth century, it became more difficult to hold to the notion that equity was implementing the same sense of justice as law and that the deficiencies of the common law were merely procedural. English lawyers began to recognize that the substantive principles of law and equity were different as well.

This realization had an indelible effect on equity. In the early phases of equity, the chancellor's decision in one case did not act as a precedent for subsequent cases; each case was determined on its own equities. As equity came to be seen as a system of positive law, it needed to decide whether it would continue to abide by a single principle of equity, or develop a more "law-like" set of substantive principles. *See* WILLIAM LAMBARDE, ARCHEION 46 (Charles H. McIlwain & Paul L. Ward ed. 1957) (1591). With his famous dictum in *Cook v. Fountain*, 36 Eng. Rep. 984 (1676), Lord Nottingham, the chancellor often called the "Father of Modern Equity," strongly committed equity to the course of fixed, law-like doctrine as opposed to broad equitable discretion. With that change, the idea of two systems held in equipoise by their correlative strengths and weaknesses collapsed:

> The discussion about the relative importance in a legal system of certainty and abstract justice is unending: but it begins at a definite stage of development, namely when the law is first seen as a system of substantive rules prescribing results upon given states of fact. In England this discussion was at once institutionalized: certainty resided in the common law courts, justice in the chancellor's equity. But there were calls for the regularization of equity itself. . . . The dialogue between certainty and justice, law and morals, had been acted out in real life; and the end of it was two systems of certainty, two systems of law. [MILSOM, *supra*, at 94-95.]

3. American Civil Procedure After the Revolution

American dissatisfaction with the Crown never manifested itself in comparable dissatisfaction with the English legal system. With necessary accommodations to account for differing political circumstances colonial governments essentially replicated the English system of courts. After the Revolution, some of the former colonies changed aspects of their procedure or judicial structure. Georgia, for example, extended jury trial to suits in equity. Some states simplified the common-law pleading; some also allowed limited pretrial discovery. Generally, however, American courts accepted the structure of English law and procedure without serious question.

a. Early Efforts at Reform. By the early nineteenth century, however, dissatisfaction with English pleading rules was growing. The most momentous result of this dissatisfaction was New York's adoption in 1848 of the Field Code (named after its principal proponent, David Dudley Field). The Field Code (1) abolished the common-law forms of action; (2) eliminated the distinction between procedural rules for law and those for equity; (3) allowed the more generous joinder or related causes of action and multiple parties; and (4) simplified pleadings by requiring the parties only to allege the facts supporting each element of a cause of action or defense. Like the common law, but unlike equity, the Field Code in general provided no opportunity to discover information before trial. Often called "code pleading," this new system had spread to twenty-seven states by the turn of the twentieth century.

Reform efforts in the United States arose principally at the state level. The United States Constitution permitted Congress to create federal trial courts, which Congress immediately did in 1789. But in the procedural area, federal courts were followers, not leaders. In suits in equity, Congress provided the Supreme Court with rule-making power as early as 1792; but it was not exercised until 1822, and even then the Supreme Court adopted an incomplete group of rules whose gaps were filled in by the traditional equity procedures of each state. In common-law cases, Congress required federal courts to use the procedures that a state court in the same locality would have used in 1789. A principal problem with this "static conformity" was federal and state practice split further and further apart as state courts reformed their procedures after 1789. Congress finally passed the Conformity Act of 1872, which substituted "dynamic conformity" for static conformity: In common-law cases, a federal court was to use the same procedural rules as a state court in the same locality. *See* RICHARD H. FALLON ET AL., HART & WECHSLER'S THE FEDERAL COURTS AND THE FEDERAL COURT SYSTEM 533-39 (6th ed. 2009) (describing the development of federal procedure up to 1938).

Code pleading was not a panacea for all the ills of American procedure. The Field Code was hardly a model of simplicity and flexibility. In its original form it had nearly 400 sections, and it was incomplete at that. The New York Legislature added many new sections in an effort to clarify ambiguities in the original code. In 1876 it replaced the Field Code with the infamous Throop Code, which was called "reactionary in spirit. . . . Its requirements ran into the most minute and trivial details of practice." CHARLES M. HEPBURN, THE HISTORICAL DEVELOPMENT OF CODE PLEADING IN AMERICA AND ENGLAND (1897). More and more amendments were added to the Throop Code, so that by 1895, the New York code of civil procedure had expanded to more than 3,400 sections! Moreover, the lack of discovery often left the parties as much in the dark about their opponents' claims as the system of common-law pleading that it had replaced.

Another problem with code pleading was that its penalties for mispleading could be as severe as they had been at common law. Unless the pleader stated the ultimate facts on each element of a cause of action, an opponent could successfully file a demurrer and get the cause of action or defense thrown out. An intricate body of law sprang up around what constituted "ultimate facts," as opposed to mere evidentiary facts and conclusions of law that were not supposed to be pleaded.

Another dominant feature of the American legal system at the turn of the twentieth century was the degree of its adversarialism. Just as the English common-law system had departed from continental Europe in its use of juries, it departed from the continental approach in its allocation of responsibility between judges and lawyers. The continental approach — as well as equity in its early days — was inquisitorial in nature: The judge was responsible for obtaining the factual information and selecting the arguments needed to make a decision. In contrast, the common law, and equity in its mature form, were adversarial: The lawyers had principal responsibility for obtaining the facts, choosing the arguments, and presenting the case to the judge and jury, who were expected to remain passive, neutral, and unbiased. In England, the adversarial approach was tempered by the division of legal work between barristers and solicitors. Solicitors owed principal loyalty to the client, and barristers, who appeared in court, had a long tradition of independence from the interests of their clients. In the United States, however, lawyers combined the functions of solicitors and barristers; like solicitors they were principally devoted to advancing the interests of their clients.

Roscoe Pound, who began the call for procedural reform in whose shadow we still live, proposed a solution he argued would simultaneously check the adversarial system's potential for abuse and stop the system's downward spiral into rigidity and technicality that had haunted our procedural history for centuries. Beginning with an excerpt from his call to arms at the 1906 convention of the American Bar Association, we study Pound's efforts to work out the terms of his solution.

ROSCOE POUND, THE CAUSES OF POPULAR DISSATISFACTION WITH THE ADMINISTRATION OF JUSTICE

29 A.B.A. REP. 395 (1906), *reprinted in* 35 F.R.D. 273, 275, 281 (1964)

The most important and most constant cause of dissatisfaction with all law at all times is to be found in the necessarily mechanical operation of legal rules. This is one of the penalties of uniformity. Legal history shows an oscillation between wide judicial discretion on the one hand and strict confinement of the magistrate by minute and detailed rules upon the other hand. From time to time more or less reversion to justice without law becomes necessary in order to bring the public administration of justice into touch with changed moral, social or political conditions. But such periods of reversion result only in new rules or changed rules. In time the modes of exercising discretion become fixed, the course of judicial action becomes stable and uniform, and the new element, whether custom or equity or natural law becomes as rigid and mechanical as the old. This mechanical action of the law may be minimized, but it cannot be obviated. . . .

A no less potent source of irritation lies in our American exaggeration of the common law contentious procedure. The sporting theory of justice . . . is so rooted in the profession in America that most of us take it for a fundamental legal tenet. . . . So far from being a fundamental fact of jurisprudence, it is peculiar to Anglo-American law; and it has been strongly curbed in modern English practice. With us, it is not merely in full acceptance, it has been developed and its collateral possibilities have been cultivated to the furthest extent. Hence in America we take it as a matter of course that a judge should be a mere umpire, to pass upon objections and hold counsel to the rules of the game, and that the parties should fight out their own game in their own way without judicial interference. We resent such interference as unfair, even when in the interest of justice. The idea that procedure must of necessity be wholly contentious disfigures our judicial administration at every point.

ROSCOE POUND, THE DECADENCE OF EQUITY

5 COLUM. L. REV. 20, 36 (1905)

Ihering has told us that we must fight for our law. No less must we fight for equity. Law must be tempered with equity, even as justice with mercy. And if, as some assert, mercy is part of justice, we may say equally that equity is part of law, in the sense that it is necessary to the working of any legal system.

ROSCOE POUND, SOME PRINCIPLES OF PROCEDURAL REFORM

4 ILL. L. REV. 388, 400, 402-03 (1910)

To go back, now to the immediate problem, how shall we make the rules of procedure, rules to help litigants, rules to assist them in getting through the courts, not rules to be made, in the trenchant phrase of Professor Wigmore, "instruments of stratagem for the bar and of logical exercitation for the judiciary?" First of all, I venture to think, we shall do this by making it unprofitable to raise questions of procedure for any purpose except to develop the merits of the cause to the full. . . . Hence I should propose as the first principles of procedural reform the two following:

I. It should be for the court, in its discretion, not the parties, to vindicate rules of procedure intended solely to provide for the orderly dispatch of business, saving of public time, and maintenance of the dignity of tribunals; and such discretion should be reviewable only for abuse.

II. Except as they exist for the saving of public time and maintenance of the dignity of tribunals, so that the parties should not be able to insist as of right upon enforcement of them, rules of procedure should exist only to secure to all parties a fair opportunity to meet the case against them and a full opportunity to present their own case; and nothing should depend on or be obtainable through them except the securing of such opportunity.

Next in importance to the two principles just stated, but second to them only, I should put the following:

III. A practice act should deal only with the general features of procedure and prescribe the general lines to be followed, leaving details to be fixed by rules of court, which the courts may change from time to time as actual experience of their application and operation dictates.

―――――――

Pound's efforts bore important fruit in 1912, when the Supreme Court revised the Federal Equity Rules for the first time in seventy years. These Rules sought to combine the best aspects of common law and equity.

Technical forms of pleadings were abolished; a "short and plain statement" of jurisdiction, and a "short and simple statement of the ultimate facts upon which the plaintiff asks relief" usually sufficed for the plaintiff, while an answer which "in short and simple terms set out his defense" and specifically admitted or denied the plaintiff's allegations sufficed for the defendant. Joinder of all claims against a defendant was permitted; joinder of parties and actions by class representatives were also allowed in some cases. A system of pretrial disclosure permitted discovery of documents, interrogatories, and, in "good and exceptional" instances, depositions. The Equity Rules followed the common-law tradition in one important respect, requiring that the testimony of witnesses be taken in open court. *See* 226 U.S. 627, 649-73 (1912). They did not, however, affect the federal courts' larger common-law jurisdiction, for which the Conformity Act of 1872 still required the use of state procedure.

If these rules sound vaguely familiar, they should. They became the model for the Federal Rules of Civil Procedure.

b.   The World Created by the Federal Rules of Civil Procedure. The work of the next generation of procedural reformers was to persuade Congress to repeal the Conformity Act and allow the federal courts to promulgate rules of procedure in all cases. *See* Stephen B. Burbank, *The Rules Enabling Act of 1934*, 130 U. PA. L. REV. 1015 (1982), Congress eventually enacted the Rules Enabling Act of 1934, 48 Stat. 1064 (codified as subsequently amended at 28 U.S.C. § 2072). The Rules Enabling Act permitted the Supreme Court to "unite the general rules prescribed by it for cases in equity with those in actions at law so as to secure one form of civil action and procedure for both." It also mandated that "[s]aid rules shall neither abridge, enlarge, nor modify the substantive rights of any litigant."

In 1938, the Federal Rules of Civil Procedure emerged. The Rules' structure was heavily influenced by the ideas of Pound, and by the legwork of Charles Clark (who was the leading proponent of the highly simplified pleading system known as "notice pleading") and Anson Sunderland (who developed the discovery system). The Rules abolished the distinction between law and equity. Pleadings were barebones; discovery was wide-open. More than one-third of the Federal Rules (including many of the most significant ones) called for the exercise of judicial discretion. Even as they sought to cure one set of procedural ills, however, the Rules created the procedural conditions for the rise of modern complex litigation.

STEPHEN N. SUBRIN, HOW EQUITY CONQUERED COMMON LAW: THE FEDERAL RULES OF CIVIL PROCEDURE IN HISTORICAL PERSPECTIVE

135 U. PA. L. REV. 909, 922-25, 974 (1987)

. . . The underlying philosophy of, and procedural choices embodied in, the Federal Rules were almost universally drawn from equity rather than common law. The expansive and flexible aspects of equity are all implicit in the Federal Rules. Before the rules, equity procedure and jurisprudence historically had applied to only a small percentage of the totality of litigation. Thus the drafters made an enormous change: in effect the tail of historic adjudication was now wagging the dog.

The result is played out in the Federal Rules in a number of different but interrelated ways: ease of pleading; broad joinder; expansive discovery; greater judicial power and discretion; flexible remedies; latitude for lawyers; control over juries; reliance on professional experts; reliance on documentation; and disengagement of substance, procedure, and remedy. This combination of procedural factors contributes to a procedural system and view of the law that markedly differs from either a combined common law and equity system or the nineteenth century procedural code system. The norms and attitudes borrowed from equity define our current legal landscape: expansion of legal theories, law suits, and, consequently, litigation departments; enormous litigation costs; enlarged judicial discretion; and decreased jury power. . . .

When one looks at the disgruntlement over unwieldy cases, uncontrolled discovery, unrestrained attorney latitude, and judicial discretion, . . . the pattern is clear. These are not the complaints about the rigor and inflexibility associated with the common law, but the opposite. The symptoms sound like what one would expect from an all-equity procedural system. The praise for modern litigation as a creator of new rights essential for a humane society is also consonant with this diagnosis.

The Federal Rules of Civil Procedure also inverted the federal-state relationship on procedural issues. Until 1938, except for its small equity docket, federal courts looked to state law for their procedural rules. Now they looked to federal law. Even more significantly, states did the same. Many states adopted the Federal Rules of Civil Procedure as their own. This inverse "dynamic conformity" was voluntary, and not every state went along; but even in states that did not adopt the Federal Rules *in toto*, the Rules' orientation toward liberal discovery, wide-open discovery, discretion, and "on the merits" decision-making often exercised an important influence. *See* John B. Oakley, *A Fresh Look at the Federal Rules in State Courts*, 3 NEV. L.J. 354 (2003) (updating a prior survey on the influence of the Federal Rules on state rules of procedure).

Although influential, the original Federal Rules were hardly perfect. They have been frequently tweaked, with the most sweeping amendments occurring in 1946, 1966, 1970, 1983, and 1993. (The Federal Rules also underwent a major stylistic facelift in 2007.) Most major amendments in the past twenty-five years had their origin in the phenomenon of complex litigation — in the desire to do something about the way in which complex litigation was straining the capacity of the procedural system.

With a knowledge of history, the Rules' imperfections are evident. As Professor Subrin suggests, it is not so easy to abolish the difference between law and equity. First of all, there is the problem that a jury right exists for some claims but not for others. The procedural needs in a jury-tried case, however, are different from those in a suit without a jury. Second, as a practical matter, how do you merge a system with a tradition of technical pleading, no pretrial discovery, a final trial event, and an adversarial process with a system with a tradition of liberal pleading, written pretrial discovery, a continuous trial, and an inquisitorial process? The hope was to take the best of both systems — the "on their merits" orientation and discretion of equity, and the final trial event of the common law. Isn't there an equal risk that, by combining the two systems, the worst of each system will emerge? Remember that common-law procedure functioned tolerably well for routine cases, and that equity was intended to handle the cases with which the common law dealt rather poorly. Might not the adoption of equity-inspired procedures complicate every case — even the routine?

Third, there is the danger of an even more rapid descent into technicality after the initial set of reforms had taken effect. For instance, Joseph Story, the highly regarded nineteenth-century scholar and Supreme Court justice, strongly opposed the merger of law and equity because he believed that law would lose the beauty of its certainty and equity the beauty of its justice. Story overstated the case, but he had a point. As a single set of procedural rules emerges over time, what keeps the merged system from going down the same road to rigidity which neither the common law nor equity had been able to avoid? Will a "new equity" need to spring up as a competitor to the merged system?

And fourth, the merged system of the Federal Rules of Civil Procedure retained the adversarial approach of the common law and the mature equity system. Is it ever possible to avoid a focus on procedural questions, and to come to the substance of the case, when lawyers locked in a struggle for supremacy have an incentive to use every available tool to gain an advantage? Isn't that a special problem in complex cases, in which the stakes of the litigation make even a tiny advantage valuable?

Although he was not speaking specifically of the Federal Rules of Civil Procedure or the problems of modern complex litigation, Learned Hand once offered a skeptical appraisal of Americans' ability to escape their history and their very character:

> The truth is that no rules in the end will help us. We shall succeed in making our results conform with our professions only by a change of heart in ourselves. It is hard to expect lawyers who are half litigants to forgo the advantages which come from obscuring the case and supporting contentions which they know to be false. . . .
>
> And still at times I can have the hope that in America time may at length mitigate our fierce individualism . . . . If through some such conversion we can be taught to abate the intensity of our own wills, to subject our desires to what has been laid down for us, even when we dislike or distrust it, then in this which seems so trivial and minor a

detail, the management of our private disputes, we may succeed. But not, I fear, short of something like that; we are made all of a piece, and the cloven hoof will show however well the bestial heart be covered.

Learned Hand, *The Deficiencies of Trials to Reach the Heart of the Matter*, in LECTURES ON LEGAL TOPICS 1921-1922 87, 104, 106 (1926).

These are the questions that our procedural history poses for the modern American system of procedure — and especially for complex litigation, in which the deficiencies and successes of our present approach to litigation reveal themselves most dramatically.

B. THEORETICAL PERSPECTIVES ON COMPLEX LITIGATION

The last section described the principal events that led us to choose an equity-based but adversarial approach. We did not, however, examine whether this approach is justified as a theoretical matter. Put differently, we might approach the design of the American procedural system by asking what the fundamental norms of a procedural system are, and whether those norms require or limit our procedural options. Exploring whether all procedural systems possess fundamental norms, which inevitably also requires us to engage in some comparative analysis, is critical to the procedural enterprise generally. But it is particularly crucial to complex litigation. If complex litigation involves the cases in which our procedural system does not work well, such norms might help us to appreciate the constraints on procedural solutions designed to ameliorate complexity.

JOHN RAWLS, A THEORY OF JUSTICE

58, 235-39 (1971)

This impartial and consistent administration of laws and institutions, whatever their substantive principles, we may call formal justice. If we think of justice as always expressing a kind of equality, then formal justice requires that, in their administration laws and institutions should apply equally (that is, in the same way) to those belonging to the classes defined by them . . . .

. . . [W]e can say that, other things equal, one legal order is more justly administered than another if it more perfectly fulfills the precepts of the rule of law. It will provide a more secure basis for liberty and a more effective means for organizing cooperative schemes. Yet because these precepts guarantee only the impartial and regular administration of rules, whatever these are, they are compatible with injustice. They impose rather weak constraints on the basic structure, but ones that are not by any means negligible.

Let us begin with the precept that ought implies can. This precept identifies several obvious features of legal systems. First of all, the actions which the rules of law require and forbid should be of a kind which men can reasonably be expected to do and to avoid. . . . The rule of law also implies the precept that similar cases be treated similarly. . . .

Finally, there are those precepts defining the notion of natural justice. These are guidelines intended to preserve the integrity of the judicial process. If laws are directives addressed to rational persons for their guidance, courts must be concerned to apply and to enforce these rules in an appropriate way. A conscientious effort must be made to determine whether an infraction has taken place and to impose the correct penalty. Thus a legal system must make provisions for conducting orderly trials and hearings; it must contain rules of evidence that guarantee rational procedures of inquiry. While there are variations in these procedures, the rule of law requires some form of due process: that is, a process reasonably designed to ascertain the truth, in ways consistent with the other ends of the legal system, as to whether a violation has taken place and under what circumstances. For example, judges must be independent and impartial, and no man may judge his own case. Trials must be fair and open, but not prejudiced by public clamor. The precepts of natural justice are to insure that the legal order will be impartially and regularly maintained.

RICHARD A. POSNER, ECONOMIC ANALYSIS OF LAW

593-94 (7th ed. 2007)

The objective of a procedural system, viewed economically, is to minimize the sum of two types of cost. The first is the cost of erroneous judicial decisions. Suppose the expected cost of a particular type of accident is $100 and the cost to the potential injurer of avoiding it is $90 (the cost of avoidance by the victim, we will assume, is greater than $100). If the potential injurer is subject to either a negligence or a strict liability standard, he will avoid the accident — assuming the standard is administered accurately. But suppose that in 15 percent of the cases in which an accident occurs, the injurer can expect to avoid liability because of erroneous factual determinations by the procedural system. Then the expected cost of the accident to the injurer will fall to $85, and since this is less than the cost of avoidance to him ($90), the accident will not be prevented. The result will be a net social loss of $10 — or will it?

We must not ignore the cost of operating the procedural system. Suppose that to reduce the rate of erroneous failures to impose liability from 15 percent to below 10 percent would require an additional investment in procedure of $20 per accident. Then we should tolerate the 15 percent probability of error, because the cost of error ($10) is less than the cost necessary to eliminate it ($20).

This type of cost comparison is implicit in . . . *Mathews v. Eldridge*, [424 U.S. 319 (1976),] which held that in deciding how much process is due to someone complaining that the government has deprived him of property the courts should consider the value of the property, the probability of erroneous deprivation because the particular procedural safeguard sought was omitted, and the cost of the safeguard. In Hand Formula terms, due process is denied when $B < PL$, where B is the cost of the procedural safeguard, P is the probability of error if the safeguard is denied, and L is the magnitude of the loss if the error materializes.

Of course, as with the Hand Formula itself, it is rarely possible (or at least efforts are not made) to quantify the terms. But the formula is valuable even when used qualitatively rather than quantitatively.

Frank I. Michelman, THE SUPREME COURT AND LITIGATION ACCESS FEES: THE RIGHT TO PROTECT ONE'S RIGHTS — PART I

1973 DUKE L.J. 1153, 1172-73

I have been able to identify four discrete, though interrelated, types of [procedural] values, which may be called dignity values, participation values, deterrence values, and (to choose a clumsily neutral term) effectuation values. *Dignity values* reflect concern for the humiliation or loss of self-respect which a person might suffer if denied the opportunity to litigate. *Participation values* reflect an appreciation of litigation as one of the modes in which persons exert influence, or have their wills "counted," in societal decisions they care about. *Deterrence values* recognize the instrumentality of litigation as a mechanism for influencing or constraining individual behavior in ways thought socially desirable. *Effectuation values* see litigation as an important means through which persons are enabled to get, or are given assurance of having, whatever we are pleased to regard as rightfully theirs.

Notes

1.   Professor Rawls, Judge Posner, and Professor Michelman state three different visions of the role of procedure in society. Professor Rawls's interest is the creation of a just political society, and he briefly sketches the qualities that the ways in which the legal procedures can contribute to such a society. His view is that procedure must aid rational adjudication, which is a building block of the just society. Judge Posner takes as his starting point the ideal of efficiency, and describes the ways in which the litigation system can act as a drag on efficient legal rules. His view is that procedure should work to minimize the total costs of litigation, thus reducing people's incentives to engage in inefficient behavior. Judge Posner gives rational adjudication an economic spin, both explaining its importance and imposing constraints on it. Professor Michelman is like Professor Rawls in specifying moral criteria for fair procedure, but also like Judge Posner in recognizing that procedural rules should, at least in part, induce socially beneficial

behavior (although his deterrence values do not necessarily match up perfectly with Judge Posner's focus on efficient behavior). In another way, however, Professor Michelman's views are different from those of the others. Both Professor Rawls and Judge Posner see procedure as an instrument to achieve other, more fundamental goods (whether a just or an efficient society). Professor Michelman believes that certain procedural principles have intrinsic moral value — that dignity, participation, and effectuation are important in their own right, worthy of protection even when their invocation thwarts rational adjudication or efficiency.

2. Thinking about procedure in terms of justice, economics, and the intrinsic value of process are three common approaches. *See* Robert G. Bone, *The Process of Making Process: Court Rulemaking, Democratic Legitimacy, and Procedural Efficiency*, 87 GEO. L.J. 887 (1999). As we examine specific issues that arise in complex litigation, we will see how these theoretical approaches sometimes suggest different prescriptions. It is not too early to ask yourself which approach(es) you prefer.

3. Professor Rawls, Judge Posner, and Professor Michelman do not capture all the possible values that a procedural system might advance. For instance, Professor Mashaw argues that three procedural values — individual dignity, equality, and tradition — are better value theories for due process than efficiency. Jerry L. Mashaw, *The Supreme Court's Due Process Calculus for Administrative Adjudication in* Mathews v. Eldridge*: Three Factors in Search of a Value*, 44 U. CHI. L. REV. 28 (1976). Professor Bush identifies resource allocation, social justice, protecting fundamental rights, maintaining public order, advancing human relations, legitimacy, and ease of administration as the objects of a civil-justice system. Robert A. Bush, *Dispute Resolution Alternatives and Achieving the Goals of Civil Justice: Jurisdictional Principles for Process Choice*, 1984 WIS. L. REV. 893. *See also* John R. Allison, *Ideology, Prejudgment, and Process Values*, 28 NEW ENG. L. REV. 657 (1994) (dividing process values into instrumental values of accuracy, efficacy, efficiency, and fairness and non-instrumental values of individual dignity, heuristic goals, and institutional legitimacy).

4. Procedural theory is controversial on several scores. One criticism of procedural theory is that it implicitly recognizes a distinction between procedural and substantive justice. Perhaps that distinction does not exist. Rather "justice" is an aggregate of substantive and procedural elements that merge "in a single whole greater than the sum of its parts." Michel Rosenfeld, *Deconstruction and Legal Interpretation*, in DECONSTRUCTION AND THE POSSIBILITY OF JUSTICE 187 (1992).

5. Note the effect that this conclusion has on the debate about procedure. In essence, it says that we cannot think about procedure independently of the substance of the controversy. It further implies that procedural rules might vary according to the aims of the substantive law they serve. Rather than there being a single set of procedural rules, there might be one set of rules for product-liability cases, another for civil rights cases, and so forth. This may sound like a radical proposal, but as we saw in the last section of this chapter, we had substance-specific procedures for

most of the last millennium. Only in the last few decades we have tried to divorce procedure from substance through a uniform set of rules that applies to all bodies of substantive law.

A set of rules that applies equally across substantive fields of law is called "trans-substantive." Theorists have debated the wisdom of trans-substantive rules. Without trans-substantivity, every procedural rule is to some extent contingent on its substantive context; the ability to analyze procedural rules independently of substantive policy diminishes. The most famous critique of trans-substantivism belongs to Professor Cover:

> The fine tuning of remedial and procedural instruments for implementing substantive preferences . . . is severely retarded once procedural norms are codified in a trans-substantive structure. . . . It is extraordinary that our legal system holds a divided view of procedure: Our norms for minimal process, expressed in the constitutional rubric of procedural due process, are generally conceded to constitute a substance-sensitive calibrated continuum in which the nature of the process due is connected to the nature of the substantive interest to be vindicated; yet our primary set of norms for optimal procedure, the procedure available in our courts of general jurisdiction, is assumed to be largely invariant with substance. It is by no means intuitively apparent that the procedural needs of a complex antitrust action, a simple automobile negligence case, a hard-fought school integration suit, and an environmental class action to restrain the building of a pipeline are sufficiently identical to be usefully encompassed in a single set of rules which makes virtually no distinctions among such cases in terms of available process. . . .

> [T]he manipulation of procedural tools to effectuate substantive objectives is by no means undesirable and often seems necessary. . . . [C]ourts, in applying the Federal Rules of Civil Procedure or any subsequently enacted similar body of rules, [should] not forsake their responsibility to justify substantive impact in terms of substantive values. . . .

> [Of course, one] cannot re-invent a procedural system for every case. And the question of what is to be presumptively or generally available may be best settled by rule. But where the only or primary issues at stake are substantive, justifications in substantive terms may be necessary.

Robert M. Cover, *For Wm. James Moore: Some Reflections on a Reading of the Rules*, 84 YALE L.J. 718, 732-35, 737 (1975). Granting Professor Rawls his assumption that there is such a thing as formal justice, is trans-substantivism one of those irreducible elements that a just legal system cannot eliminate? Rawls himself says that "similar cases [should] be treated similarly." For a partial defense of trans-substantivism, arguing that some like cases must be treated procedurally alike, see Jay Tidmarsh, *Unattainable Justice: The Form of Complex Litigation and the Limits of Judicial Power*, 60 GEO. WASH. L. REV. 1683 (1992).

Trans-substantivism is one of the critical arguments that can be made against a number of otherwise attractive solutions to various problems in complex litigation. We often recur to the idea in this book.

6. A different criticism of procedural theory emerges from the recent rise of comparative procedural work. As transnational litigation and regional federations have increased, it has become vital to understand the working of other procedural systems. As you might expect, procedural systems vary on almost every point imaginable. *See*, *e.g.*, INTERNATIONAL CIVIL PROCEDURE (Shelby R. Grubbs ed., 2003). Unless we are willing to adjudge some procedural rules normatively wrong, procedural theory operates at a such high level of abstraction that it does not affect the design of actual procedural systems. Look, for example, at the norms suggested by Professor Rawls, Judge Posner, and Professor Michelman. Do they give you guidance on specific questions such as how much detail a complaint should contain or whether a jury should determine the facts?

7. One of the fundamental design issues in a procedural system is the choice of an adversarial (or party-driven) system or an inquisitorial (or judicially-driven) system. Does procedural theory help in this choice? (And if not, what good is theory?) The following articles present arguments in favor of either the inquisitorial or the adversarial system of justice.

John H. Langbein, THE GERMAN ADVANTAGE IN CIVIL PROCEDURE

52 U. CHI. L. REV. 823, 826, 830-35, 843-46, 848-50 (1985)

There are two fundamental differences between German and Anglo-American civil procedure, and these differences lead in turn to many others. First, the court rather than the parties' lawyers takes the main responsibility for gathering and sifting evidence, although the lawyers exercise a watchful eye over the court's work. Second, there is no distinction between pretrial and trial, between discovering evidence and presenting it. Trial is not a single continuous event. Rather, the court gathers and evaluates evidence over a series of hearings, as many as the circumstances require. . . .

From the standpoint of comparative civil procedure, the most important consequence of having judges direct fact-gathering in this episodic fashion is that German procedure functions without the sequence rules to which we are accustomed in the Anglo-American procedural world. The implications for procedural economy are large. The very concepts of "plaintiff's case" and "defendant's case" are unknown. In our system those concepts function as traffic rules for the partisan presentation of evidence to a passive and ignorant trier. By contrast, in German procedure the court ranges over the entire case, constantly looking for the jugular — for the issue of law or fact that might dispose of the case. Free of constraints that arise from party presentation of evidence, the court investigates the dispute in the fashion most likely to narrow the inquiry. A major job of counsel is to guide the search by directing the court's attention to particularly cogent lines of inquiry. . . .

Part of what makes our discovery system so complex is that, on account of our division into pretrial and trial, we have to discover for the entire case. We investigate everything that could possibly come up at trial, because once we enter the trial phase we can seldom go back and search for further evidence. By contrast, the episodic character of German fact-gathering largely eliminates the danger of surprise; if the case takes an unexpected turn, the disadvantaged litigant can count on developing his response in another hearing at a later time. Because there is no pretrial discovery phase, fact-gathering occurs only once; and because the court establishes the sequence of fact-gathering according to criteria of relevance, unnecessary investigation is minimized. . . .

The episodic character of German civil procedure — Benjamin Kaplan called it the "conference method" of adjudication — has other virtues: It lessens tension and theatrics, and it encourages settlement. Countless novels, movies, plays, and broadcast serials attest to the dramatic potential of the Anglo-American trial. . . . German civil proceedings have the tone not of the theatre, but of a routine business meeting — serious rather than tense. When the court inquires and directs, it sets no stage for advocates to perform. The forensic skills of counsel can wrest no material advantage, and the appearance of a surprise witness would simply lead to the scheduling of a further hearing. . . .

In this business-like system of civil procedure the tradition is strong that the court promotes compromise. The judge who gathers the facts soon knows the case as well as the litigants do, and he concentrates each subsequent increment of fact-gathering on the most important issues still unresolved. As the case progresses the judge discusses it with the litigants, sometimes indicating provisional views of the likely outcome. He is, therefore, strongly positioned to encourage a litigant to abandon a case that is turning out to be weak or hopeless, or to recommend settlement . . .

Adversary control of fact-gathering in our procedure entails a high level of conflict between partisan advantage and orderly disclosure of the relevant information. Marvin Frankel put this point crisply when he said that "it is the rare case in which either side yearns to have the witnesses, or anyone, give *the whole truth*." . . .

When we cross the border into German civil procedure, we leave behind all traces of this system of partisan preparation, examination, and cross-examination of witnesses. German law distinguishes parties from witnesses. A German lawyer must necessarily discuss the facts with his client, and based on what his client tells him and on what the documentary record discloses, the lawyer will nominate witnesses whose testimony might turn out to be helpful to his client. As the proofs come in, they may reveal to the lawyer the need to nominate further witnesses for the court to examine. But the lawyer stops at nominating; virtually never will he have occasion for out-of-court contact with a witness. Not only would such contact be a serious ethical breach, it would be self-defeating. "German judges are given to marked and explicit doubts about the reliability of the testimony of witnesses who previously have discussed the case with counsel or who have consorted unduly with a party."

No less a critic than Jerome Frank was prepared to concede that in American procedure the adversaries "sometimes do bring into court evidence which, in a dispassionate inquiry, might be overlooked." That is a telling argument for including adversaries in the fact-gathering process, but not for letting them run it. German civil procedure . . . totally avoids the distortions incident to our partisan witness practice. . . .

Equality of representation. The German system gives us a good perspective on another great defect of adversary theory, the problem that the Germans call "'Waffenungleichheit" — literally, inequality of weapons, or in this instance, inequality of counsel. . . . The simple truth is that very little in our adversary system is designed to match combatants of comparable prowess, even though adversarial prowess is a main factor affecting the outcome of litigation. Adversary theory thus presupposes a condition that adversary practice achieves only indifferently. . . . Disparity in the quality of legal representation can make a difference in Germany, too, but the active role of the judge places major limits on the extent of the injury that bad lawyering can work on a litigant. In German procedure both parties get the same fact-gatherer — the judge. . . .

Prejudgment. Perhaps the most influential justification for adversary domination of fact-gathering has been an argument put forward by Lon Fuller: Nonadversarial procedure risks prejudgment — that is, prematurity in judgment. . . .

[Fuller's argument] obtains much of its force from the all-or-nothing contrast that so misdescribes German civil procedure. In a system like the German, which combines judicial fact-gathering with vigorous and continuing adversarial efforts in nominating lines of factual inquiry and analyzing factual and legal issues, the adversaries perform just the role that Fuller lauds, helping hold the decision in suspension while issues are framed and facts explored.

In German procedure counsel oversees and has means to prompt a flagging judicial inquiry . . . . [In addition,] the decision-maker does his own investigating in most of life's decisions, [so] it seems odd to despair of prematurity only when that normal mode of decision-making is found to operate in a courtroom. . . .

Depth. Fuller's concern about prematurity shades into a different issue: How to achieve appropriate levels of depth in fact-gathering. Extra investment in search can almost always turn up further proofs that would be at least tenuously related to the case. Adversary domination of fact-gathering privatizes the decision about what level of resources to invest in the case. . . .

[German fact-gathering] does indeed contrast markedly with the inclination of American litigators "to leave no stone unturned, provided, of course, they can charge by the stone." The primary reason that German courts do less fact-gathering than American lawyers is that the Germans eliminate the waste. . . .

Because German procedure places upon the judge the responsibility for fact-gathering, the danger arises that the job will not be done well. The American system of partisan fact-gathering has the virtue of its vices: It aligns responsibility with incentive. Each side gathers and presents proofs according to its own calculation of self-interest. This privatization is an undoubted safeguard against official sloth. After all, who among us has not been treated shabbily by some lazy bureaucrat in a government department? And who would want to have that ugly character in charge of one's lawsuit?

The answer to that concern in the German tradition is straightforward: The judicial career must be designed in a fashion that creates incentives for diligence and excellence. The idea is to attract very able people to the bench, and to make their path of career advancement congruent with the legitimate interests of the litigants.

The career judiciary.   The distinguishing attribute of the bench in Germany (and virtually everywhere else in Europe) is that the profession of judging is separate from the profession of lawyering. Save in exceptional circumstances, the judge is not an ex-lawyer like his Anglo-American counterpart. Rather, he begins his professional career as a judge. . . .

The work of a German judge is overseen and evaluated by his peers throughout his career, initially in connection with his tenure review, and thereafter for promotion through the several levels of judicial office and salary grades.

Stephen A. Saltzburg, LAWYERS, CLIENTS, AND THE ADVERSARY SYSTEM

37 MERCER L. REV. 647, 654-56, 658-59, 687, 697-99 (1986)

. . . [T]hose who attack the adversary system as failing in a search for truth attack a straw man, the purple prose of appellate courts notwithstanding. The goal of the adversary system is to apply the substantive legal principles so that those who have rights may claim them and those who have liabilities must face them. This the adversary system endeavors to do, while simultaneously announcing that it is an imperfect process. . . .

The American adversary process entrusts the decision whether to bring claims and to make defenses to the litigants who seek to claim substantive rights and defenses or to impose liability. The desire to win is the motivating consideration that prompts litigants to seek out, develop, and offer evidence and to bring relevant and persuasive legal doctrines and precedents to a decisionmaker's attention. . . . In order to win, litigants have the motivation to gather the most persuasive evidence, put forth the best theories available to them, and develop evidence and theories that will enable them to respond to their adversaries. The result is that the decisionmaker hears the strongest argument that each litigant who is trying to win can muster to support a finding of fact or an evaluation of fact and the most devastating response each adversary can make to that argument.

This incentive system is similar, of course, to other free enterprise concepts that govern economic thinking. The notion is that people who stand to gain or lose from a transaction are likely to be motivated to act more effectively than those who are indifferent to the transaction. . . .

Assuming that the litigants act according to society's highest expectations so that they produce the best evidence and theories for consideration by a competent decisionmaker, it would seem that every chance exists that the substantive law will be applied in an appropriate way. Decisionmakers will make errors, but these errors are inevitable. The adversary process would not appear to exacerbate the problems of dealing with uncertainty in examining and evaluating past events. . . .

The greatest problem facing the adversary system is that lawyers and their clients may want to win so badly that they will violate the rules that govern their conduct in litigation or other tasks. The desire to win has led, and surely will lead, some individuals to risk criminal penalties, disbarment, and disgrace to prevail in a dispute or venture. . . .

The advantages some litigants have over others is [also] cause for concern. It is doubtful, however, that a reasonable way to handicap the judicial process in order to promote greater equality exists. The greater a person's wealth, the more litigation that person can afford. Money can enable some litigants to hire better investigators, better experts, and better lawyers. This ability can increase the chance that the wrong person will win in litigation. . . .

. . . [Nevertheless, the] adversary system has some attributes that might equalize the litigation more than many people realize. The jury, for instance, generally will not be exceptionally wealthy. Corporations and other entities cannot sit on juries. When an individual litigates against an entity with greater resources, the jury might take the disparity in resources into account when it evaluates the evidence and arguments offered by opposing parties. Thus, the guarantee of trial by jury is one way of assuring that those litigants with political power, social influence, and wealth must argue their case before members of the community who most often lack these advantages.

Other aspects of the adversary system might have an equalizing effect. For example, trial judges may impose time limits on opening statements or closing arguments and may exclude cumulative evidence. . . . That one may hire many lawyers and gather an incredible amount of evidence does not necessarily mean that he can use the talent and evidence.

. . . In the courtroom, each side has an equal chance to examine and cross-examine witnesses and to explain its theories to the jury. A wealthy litigant who . . . offers much more evidence than an opponent may find that . . . the more evidence that is offered, the stronger the cross-examination by the opponent.   The adversary system provides cross-examination in response to examination; one opening statement in response to another; one side's argument in response to another's.   The process treats all litigants equally and does not permit a wealthy litigant to obtain advantages easily.

Equality is promoted only if the lawyers for less wealthy litigants are capable and if the lawyers for more wealthy litigants do not take unfair advantage.

GEOFFREY C. HAZARD, JR., ETHICS IN THE PRACTICE OF LAW

121-23, 128-29, 131-35 (1978)

The theory of adjudication in the adversary system, as usually stated, has two linked components.   One is that party presentation will result in the best presentation, because each party is propelled into maximum effort in investigation and presentation by the prospect of victory . . . .   The other component of the theory is more complex and has to do with the psychology of decisionmaking.   It runs essentially as follows: Proof through evidence requires hypothesis; hypothesis requires a preliminary mind-set; if an active judge-interrogator develops the proof, his preliminary mind-set too easily can become his final decision; therefore, it is better to have conflicting preliminary hypotheses and supporting proofs presented by the parties so that the judge's mind can be kept open until all the evidence is at hand.

In this version of the adversary theory, the role of the advocate is central to adjudication, because the advocate is a necessary orchestrator of the proof to be offered by a party. . . .   There are other interpretations of the adversary system, however, that attach much less significance to the role of the advocate as an instrument for developing proofs.   One of these interpretations emphasizes the importance of party participation, the idea being that a party's presentation of the case on his behalf gives him a sense of involvement and control in the decision procedure. . . . .

There is still another and more radical theory of the adversary system.   On this view, trials are not quests for truth in a serious objective or empirical sense, and cannot be. . . .   [I]n the cases that go to trial the evidence is hopelessly ambiguous according to any concept of rational proof, and decision necessarily involves important elements of intuition, predisposition, and bias.   On this analysis, a trial is necessarily theatre or ritual to an important extent.

The adversary system has a strange status in the American legal tradition.   [I]t is one derivative of fundamental theories of political liberty. . . . In [some] respects, the adversary system stands with freedom of speech and the right of assembly as a pillar of our constitutional system. . . .

Paradoxically, the primary benefit of the system is often said to be the promotion of truth. For every instance in which truth is suppressed or distorted by the adversary system, it is thought there are more instances in which the system uncovers truth that otherwise would not have been uncovered. There is no practicable way to test this claim. It is worth considering, however, whether the situation would really be much better if we gave up the adversary system in favor of the interrogative system. . . . In our political culture, the interrogative system of trial could well turn out to resemble Congressional hearings.

The real value of the adversary system thus may not be its contribution to truth but its contribution to the ideal of individual autonomy. This is the rationale underlying many rules that obscure the truth, such as the privilege against self-incrimination and the rule that private premises may not be searched without a warrant. . . .

As the situation stands, the advocate is supposed to be both the champion of his client and a gatekeeper having a duty to prevent his client from contaminating the courtroom. In principle, these responsibilities are compatible. The duty to the court simply limits the ways in which a lawyer can champion his client's cause. In practice, however, the duties have come to be in perhaps uncontrollable conflict. . . .

In the American system, . . . the advocate['s] relationship to his client's cause is . . . dependent and intimate. In litigation involving "repeat business" clients, the advocate or his firm usually is also counsel under retainer to the client. In litigation involving "one shot" clients, such as plaintiff's injury claims, the lawyer's fee is usually contingent on the outcome. . . .

. . . The trial lawyer can become completely immersed in his lawsuits, to the point where they become his identity and their outcome the sole criterion of his professional stature. Indeed, it is often only with difficulty that a modern trial specialist can maintain distance between himself and his craft. The whole tendency of his work leads him to hold, with Vince Lombardi, that winning is not the most important thing but the only thing. And the result can be that he becomes incapacitated to give his client detached advice about the prospects of ultimate victory and the advisability of settling through compromise. The problem can be especially severe in "big" cases for and against big corporations, because one such case can for several years be the vocation of a good part of a firm or agency's litigation staff. . . .

. . . The system as it exists expresses a number of strongly held beliefs and ideals. One is that justice should be free. It is this proposition that supports the rule that the loser in litigation does not have to pay the winner's expenses. From this in turn follows the contingent fee system and the lack of inhibitions on running up an opposing party's costs, with the corresponding impairment of the advocate's gatekeeper function. Another belief is that entry into the legal profession should be relatively democratic. From this proposition it follows that admission is relatively easy, levels of training uneven, and professional esprit de corps weak. From this it follows that the images of professional lawyers are fuzzy and the potential for self-policing correspondingly low. Another is that litigation should secure not only justice under law but natural and popular justice. From this it follows that litigation often has inherently political, redistributive, and sometimes subversive characteristics, which infuse not only the merits of the controversies but the way they are prosecuted or defended. . . .

Perhaps the problem is this: We can have a system that does not charge user fees, lets everyone play, seeks both law and common justice, and is subject to few inhibitions in style. We can also have a system in which a trial is a serious search for the truth or at least a ceremony whose essential virtue is solemnity. But we probably cannot have both. So long as the advocate in the American system is supposed to be at once a champion in forensic roughhouse and a guardian of the temple of justice, he can fulfill his responsibilities only if he combines extraordinary technical skill with an unusually disciplined sense of probity. That seems to be asking too much of any profession.

Notes

1.   Some form of inquisitorial process exists in most civil-law countries, including countries in continental Europe. The inquisitorial system does not introduce new players into the litigation enterprise, but the roles assigned to lawyers, parties, and decision-maker(s) are different from those in the adversarial model. Professor Langbein suggests that the use of the judge to gather facts is an advantage of the German system. Do you agree? With inquisitorial fact-finding come a decreased need for juries, reduced need for rules of evidence, a different trial process, and an enlarged judicial bureaucracy. You might like some of these features more than others, but you pretty much have to take them as a package — unless you can imagine a hybrid adversarial-inquisitorial process.

2.   At one time, the Ecuadoran inquisitorial system, which is based on the Napoleonic Code (by way of the Andres Bello Code of Chile), removed more power from the lawyers, who are unable to examine witnesses or even suggest follow-up questions during a hearing. *See* Jose R. Bustamonte, *Trial and Court Procedures in Ecuador, in* TRIAL AND COURT PROCEDURES WORLDWIDE 205 (1991). Are there principled reasons why the German and most other civil systems stop short of this point?

3.   At the peak of their commitments to Communist principles, courts in the former Soviet Union and in China introduced other players into the litigation process. In the Soviet Union, the official was known as the procurator, who often exercised a commanding influence over the judge, the lawyers, and the parties. The procurator, a member of the Communist Party, ensured that judges dispensed justice in a manner consistent with the public interest (in other words, the Party's ideology). *See* MARY ANN GLENDON ET AL., COMPARATIVE LEGAL TRADITIONS (1985); *cf.* Stephen C. Thaman, *Reform of the Procuracy and Bar in Russia*, 3 PARKER SCH. J. E.

EUR. L. 1 (1996) (discussing changes in the procuracy after the break-up of the Soviet Union). During the reign of Mao, China also used procurators, as well as a "people's lawyer" who sought to avoid trial by bringing every dispute to the settlement that best advanced the state's interests. *See* SHAO-CHUAN LENG, JUSTICE IN COMMUNIST CHINA (1967).

4. Professors Saltzburg and Hazard suggest that adversarial adjudication better advances certain societal goals in the United States. Professor Hazard also suggests that adversarial process might be required by political or moral theories of liberty, autonomy, or democracy, at least in a society that ascribes to such values. Do you agree?

5. Approaching the question from a different direction, Professor Damaška explained the world's procedural systems with two political, rather than theoretical, variables: the organization of authority in a state and the extent to which a state manages social interactions. MIRJAN DAMAŠKA, THE FACES OF JUSTICE AND STATE AUTHORITY (1986). With respect to the first variable, Professor Damaška identified two organizational structures: a hierarchical, bureaucratic structure and a "coordinate" structure in which power is diffused widely to autonomous decision-makers. With respect to the second variable, he identified two opposing types of state: an activist (or "policy-implementing") state that actively manages social interactions to achieve some ideal of the good and a reactive (or "conflict-solving") state that is laissez-faire, merely resolving disputes about citizens' private orderings. He then mapped the variables onto a 2x2 matrix:

Type of State

		Policy-implementing	Conflict-solving
Organization of Authority	Hierarchical	(1)	(2)
	Coordinate	(3)	(4)

Professor Damaška argues that certain procedural consequences flow from each of these four paradigms, and demonstrates that these predicted features are reflected in the procedural systems in use around the world. The predicted procedural features in Box (1) correspond to socialist civil procedure; the predicted features in Box (2) correspond to the procedures found in civil-law countries; the predicted features in Box (4) correspond to common-law procedure; and the predicted features in Box (3) correspond to procedures employed in complex cases in the United States.

If Professor Damaška is right, politics more than theory determines procedural design; procedure reflects the political and institutional commitments of a society. Professor Damaška's work also suggests that, until a society is willing to change these commitments, the ability to effect successful procedural change in that society is limited. Finally, Professor Damaška's argument suggests that using a single, uniform set of rules for complex and routine litigation is unlikely to be successful.

6.   The relevance of these insights to complex litigation is two-fold. First, if complex litigation involves a breakdown in the adversarial system, and if we wish to adjudicate the dispute, then we must envision alternative procedures with which to replace the ordinary rules. Studying other systems gives us a sense about the benefits and drawbacks of moving away from adversarial process. Second, these insights help us to think about whether there exist fundamental procedural norms that we cannot abandon as we explore whether and how to accommodate the needs of complex cases.

The book often returns to theoretical concerns, the lessons of history, and the guidance of comparative law. You cannot adequately understand the challenges that complex litigation poses for the American procedural system without these perspectives.

C. THE MEANING OF COMPLEX LITIGATION

At the beginning of this chapter, we loosely defined complex litigation as those cases that the American adversarial system is poorly equipped to handle. Relying on the historical, theoretical, and comparative insights of the past two sections, we now refine this meaning into a precise definition.

The definition of complex litigation might seem to be a mere matter of semantics. But knowing what "complex litigation" is vital. As you proceed through this book, you will notice that the phrase "complex litigation" has a magical quality; when a judge believes that a case is "complex," procedural innovation often replaces procedural conservatism. Innovation might lead to a different result than the result that would have occurred under traditional procedures. An advocate wants to make sure that the judge applies the most favorable procedural rules; and that goal often requires a lawyer to convince a judge that the case is (or is not) "complex."

As we move from a more intuitive to a more formal definition, we discover the multiplicity of definitions on offer. We begin with two that are the most famous. Professor Fuller was seeking to justify the adversarial system, not to define a phenomenon still in its infancy at the time that he wrote. His article, posthumously published, was written in the 1950s. Nowhere does he mention complex litigation. Nonetheless, his concept of "polycentrism" is often regarded as a good proxy for "complex litigation." Responding to Professor Fuller a generation later, Professor Chayes coined the phrase "public law litigation," which others regard as another good proxy for "complex litigation." The tensions between their views still form the heart of the debate over the meaning of and solutions to complex litigation. Once we explore these differences, we examine other definitions, including the one that serves to organize this book.

Lon L. Fuller, THE FORMS AND LIMITS OF ADJUDICATION

92 HARV. L. REV. 353, 363, 381-86, 388-95, 397-98 (1978)

III. ADJUDICATION AS A FORM OF SOCIAL ORDERING

Adjudication, contract, and elections are three ways of reaching decisions, of settling disputes, of defining men's relations to one another. Now I submit that the characteristic feature of each of these forms of social ordering lies in the manner in which the affected party participates in the decision reached. This may be presented graphically as follows:

Form of Social Ordering	Mode of Participation by the Affected Party
Contract	Negotiation
Elections	Voting
Adjudication	Presentation of proofs and reasoned arguments

It is characteristic of these three ways of ordering men's relations that though they are subject to variation — they present themselves in different "forms" — each contains certain intrinsic demands that must be met if it is to function properly. We may distinguish roughly between "optimum conditions," which would lift a particular form of order to its highest expression, and "essential conditions," without which the form of order ceases to function in any significant sense at all. . . .

Now much of this paper will be concerned in carrying through with [an] analysis of the optimum and essential conditions for the functioning of adjudication. This whole analysis will derive from one simple proposition, namely, that the distinguishing characteristic of adjudication lies in the fact that it confers on the affected party a particular form of participation in the decision, that of presenting proofs and reasoned arguments for a decision in his favor. Whatever heightens the significance of this participation lifts adjudication toward its optimum expression. Whatever destroys the meaning of that participation destroys the integrity of adjudication itself. . . .

VI. THE FORMS OF ADJUDICATION

. . .

2. Is an Adversary Presentation Necessary to Adjudication?

The Lawyer's Role as Advocate in Open Court

. . . In a very real sense it may be said that the integrity of the adjudicative process itself depends upon the participation of the advocate.

This becomes apparent when we contemplate the nature of the task assumed by any arbiter who attempts to decide a dispute without the aid of partisan advocacy. . . .

The Lawyer as a Guardian of Due Process

The lawyer's highest loyalty is at the same time the most intangible. It is a loyalty that runs, not to persons, but to procedures and institutions. The lawyer's role imposes on him a trusteeship for the integrity of those fundamental processes of government and self-government upon which the successful functioning of our society depends. . . .

3.   May the Arbiter Act on His Own Motion in Initiating the Case?

Certainly it is true that in most of the practical manifestations of adjudication the arbiter's function has to be "promoted" by the litigant and is not initiated by itself. But is this coy quality of waiting to be asked an essential part of adjudication?

It would seem that it is not. . . . Yet I think that most of us would consider such a case exceptional and would not be deterred by it from persisting in the belief that the adjudicative process should normally not be initiated by the tribunal itself. There are, I believe, sound reasons for adhering to that belief. . . . [I]t is generally impossible to keep even the bare initiation of proceedings untainted by preconceptions about what happened and what its consequences should be. In this sense, initiation of the proceedings by the arbiter impairs the integrity of adjudication by reducing the effectiveness of the litigant's participation through proofs and arguments. . . .

4.   Must the Decision Be Accompanied by a Statement of the Reasons for It?

We tend to think of the judge or arbitrator as one who decides and who gives reasons for his decision. Does the integrity of adjudication require that reasons be given for the decision rendered? I think the answer is, not necessarily. . . . [But by] and large it seems clear that the fairness and effectiveness of adjudication are promoted by reasoned opinions. Without such opinions the parties have to take it on faith that their participation in the decision has been real, that the arbiter has in fact understood and taken into account their proofs and arguments. A less obvious point is that, where a decision enters into some continuing relationship, if no reasons are given the parties will almost inevitably guess at reasons and act accordingly. Here the effectiveness of adjudication is impaired, not only because the results achieved may not be those intended by the arbiter, but also because his freedom of decision in future cases may be curtailed by the growth of practices based on a misinterpretation of decisions previously rendered.

5. May the Arbiter Rest His Decision on Grounds Not Argued by the Parties?

Obviously the bond of participation by the litigant is most secure when the arbiter rests his decision wholly on the proofs and argument actually presented to him by the parties. In practice, however, it is not always possible to realize this ideal. . . . If the ideal of a perfect congruence between the arbiter's view of the issues and that of the parties is unattainable, this is no excuse for a failure to work toward an achievement of the closest approximation of it. We need to remind ourselves that if this congruence is utterly absent . . . then the adjudicative process has become a sham, for the parties' participation in the decision has lost all meaning . . . .

6. Qualifications and Disqualifications of the Arbiter . . .

I shall merely suggest that the problem of securing a properly qualified and impartial arbiter be tried by the same touchstone that has been used throughout — what will preserve the efficacy and meaning of the affected party's participation through proofs and arguments? Obviously, a strong emotional attachment by the arbiter to one of the interests involved in the dispute is destructive of that participation. In practice, however, another kind of "partiality" is much more dangerous. I refer to the situation where the arbiter's experience of life has not embraced the area of the dispute, or, worse still, where he has always viewed that area from some single vantage point. Here a blind spot of which he is quite unconscious may prevent him from getting the point of testimony or argument. . . .

VII. THE LIMITS OF ADJUDICATION

1. Introduction

Attention is now directed to the question, What kinds of tasks are inherently unsuited to adjudication? The test here will be that used throughout. If a given task is assigned to adjudicative treatment, will it be possible to preserve the meaning of the affected party's participation through proofs and arguments?

2. Polycentric Tasks and Adjudication

. . .

. . . [S]uppose in a socialist regime it were decided to have all wages and prices set by courts which would proceed after the usual forms of adjudication. It is, I assume, obvious that here is a task that could not successfully be undertaken by the adjudicative method. The point that comes first to mind is that courts move too slowly to keep up with a rapidly changing economic scene. The more fundamental point is that the forms of adjudication cannot encompass and take into account the complex repercussions that may result from any change in prices or wages. . . . In such a case it is simply impossible to afford each affected party a meaningful participation through proofs and arguments. It is a matter of capital importance to note that it is not merely a question of the huge number of possibly affected parties, significant as that aspect of the thing may be. A more fundamental point is that each of the various forms that award might take (say, a three-cent increase per pound, a four-cent increase, a five-cent increase, etc.) would have a different set of repercussions and might require in each instance a redefinition of the "parties affected."

We may visualize this kind of situation by thinking of a spider web. A pull on one strand will distribute tensions after a complicated pattern throughout the web as a whole. Doubling the original pull will, in all likelihood, not simply double each of the resulting tensions but will rather create a different complicated pattern of tensions. This would certainly occur, for example, if the doubled pull caused one or more of the weaker strands to snap. This is a "polycentric" situation because it is "many centered" — each crossing of strands is a distinct center for distributing tensions. . . .

It should be carefully noted that a multiplicity of affected persons is not an invariable characteristic of polycentric problems. . . . [R]apid changes with time are not an invariable characteristic of such problems. On the other hand, in practice polycentric problems of possible concern to adjudication will normally involve many affected parties and a somewhat fluid state of affairs. . . .

Now, if it is important to see clearly what a polycentric problem is, it is equally important to realize that the distinction involved is often a matter of degree. There are polycentric elements in almost all problems submitted to adjudication. A decision may act as a precedent, often an awkward one, in some situation not foreseen by the arbiter. . . . In lesser measure, concealed polycentric elements are probably present in almost all problems resolved by adjudication. It is not, then, a question of distinguishing black from white. It is a question of knowing when the polycentric elements have become so significant and predominant that the proper limits of adjudication have been reached. . . .

If problems sufficiently polycentric are unsuited to solution by adjudication, how may they in fact be solved? So far as I can see, there are only two suitable methods: *managerial direction* and *contract* (or reciprocity).

Abram Chayes, THE ROLE OF THE JUDGE IN PUBLIC LAW LITIGATION

89 HARV. L. REV. 1281, 1282-84, 1288-90, 1292-94, 1296-98, 1302, 1315-16 (1976)

In our received tradition, the lawsuit is a vehicle for settling disputes between private parties about private rights. The defining features of this conception of civil adjudication are:

(1) The lawsuit is *bipolar*. Litigation is organized as a contest between two individuals or at least two unitary interests diametrically opposed, to be decided on a winner-takes-all basis.

(2) Litigation is *retrospective*. The controversy is about an identified set of completed events: whether they occurred and if so, with what consequences for the legal relations of the parties.

(3) *Right and remedy are interdependent.* The scope of the relief is derived more or less logically from the substantive violation under the general theory that the plaintiff will get compensation measured by the harm caused by the defendant's breach of duty — in contract by giving plaintiff the money he would have had absent the breach; in tort by paying the value of the damage caused.

(4) The lawsuit is a *self-contained* episode. The impact of the judgment is confined to the parties. If plaintiff prevails there is a simple compensatory transfer, usually of money, but occasionally the return of a thing or the performance of a definite act. If defendant prevails, a loss lies where it has fallen. In either case, entry of judgment ends the court's involvement.

(5) The process is *party-initiated* and *party-controlled*. The case is organized and the issues defined by exchanges between the parties. Responsibility for fact development is theirs. The trial judge is a neutral arbiter of their interactions who decides questions of law only if they are put in issue by an appropriate move of a party. . . .

Whatever its historical validity, the traditional model is clearly invalid as a description of much current civil litigation in the federal district courts. Perhaps the dominating characteristic of modern federal litigation is that lawsuits do not arise out of disputes between private parties about private rights. Instead, the object of litigation is the vindication of constitutional or statutory policies. The shift in the legal basis of the lawsuit explains many, but not all, facets of what is going on "in fact" in federal trial courts. For this reason, although the label is not wholly satisfactory, I shall call the emerging model "public law litigation." . . .

II. THE PUBLIC LAW LITIGATION MODEL

A. *The Demise of the Bipolar Structure*

Joinder of parties, which was strictly limited at common law, was verbally liberalized under the codes to conform with the approach of equity calling for joinder of all parties having an "interest" in the controversy. The codes, however, did not at first produce much freedom of joinder. . . . The proponents of "efficiency" argued for a more informal and flexible approach, to the end that the courts should not have to rehear the same complex of events. This argument ultimately shifted the focus of the lawsuit from legal theory to factual context — the "transaction or occurrence" from which the action arose. This in turn made it easier to view the set of events in dispute as giving rise to a range of legal consequences all of which ought to be considered together.

This more open-ended view of the subject matter of the litigation fed back upon party questions and especially intervention. Here, too, the sharp constraints dictated by the right-remedy nexus give way. And if the right to participate in litigation is no longer determined by one's claim to relief at the hands of another party or one's potential liability to satisfy the claim, it becomes hard to draw the line determining those who may participate so as to eliminate anyone who is or might be significantly (a weasel word) affected by the outcome — and the latest revision of the Federal Rules of Civil Procedure has more or less abandoned the attempt. . . .

B. *The Triumph of Equity*

One of the most striking procedural developments of this century is the increasing importance of equitable relief. . . . [T]he old sense of equitable remedies as "extraordinary" has faded. . . .

At this point, right and remedy are pretty thoroughly disconnected. The form of relief does not flow ineluctably from the liability determination, but is fashioned ad hoc. In the process, moreover, right and remedy have been to some extent transmuted. The liability determination is not simply a pronouncement of the legal consequences in a way that accommodates the range of interests involved. . . .

At the same time, the breadth of interests that may be affected by public law litigation raises questions about the adequacy of the representation afforded by a plaintiff whose interest is narrowly traditional.

C. *The Changing Character of Factfinding*

. . .

In public law litigation, . . . factfinding is principally concerned with "legislative" rather than "adjudicative" fact. And "fact evaluation" is perhaps a more accurate term than "factfinding." The whole process begins to look like the traditional description of legislation: Attention is drawn to a "mischief," existing or threatened, and the activity of the parties and court is directed to the development of on-going measures designed to cure that mischief. . . .

The courts, it seems, continue to rely primarily on the litigants to produce and develop factual materials, but a number of factors make it impossible to leave the organization of the trial exclusively in their hands. With the diffusion of the party structure, fact issues are no longer sharply drawn in a confrontation between two adversaries, one asserting the affirmative and the other the negative. The litigation is often extraordinarily complex and extended in time, with a continuous and intricate interplay between factual and legal elements. It is hardly feasible and, absent a jury, unnecessary to set aside a contiguous block of time for a "trial stage" at which all significant factual issues will be presented. The scope of the fact investigation and the sheer volume of factual material that can be exhumed by the discovery process pose enormous problems of organization and assimilation. All these factors thrust the trial judge into an active role in shaping, organizing and facilitating the litigation. We may not yet have reached the investigative judge of the continental systems, but we have left the passive arbiter of the traditional model a long way behind.

D. *The Decree*

The centerpiece of the emerging public law model is the decree. It differs in almost every relevant characteristic from relief in the traditional model of adjudication, not the least in that it *is* the centerpiece. The decree seeks to adjust future behavior, not to compensate for past wrong. It is deliberately fashioned rather than logically deduced from the nature of the legal harm suffered. It provides for a complex, on-going regime of performance rather than a simple, one-shot, one-way transfer. Finally, it prolongs and deepens, rather than terminates, the court's involvement with the dispute. . . .

E. *A Morphology of Public Law Litigation*

The public law litigation model portrayed in this paper reverses many of the crucial characteristics and assumptions of the traditional concept of adjudication:

(1) The scope of the lawsuit is not exogenously given but is shaped primarily by the court and parties.

(2) The party structure is not rigidly bilateral but sprawling and amorphous.

(3) The fact inquiry is not historical and adjudicative but predictive and legislative.

(4) Relief is not conceived as compensation for past wrong in a form logically derived from the substantive liability and confined in its impact to the immediate parties; instead, it is forward looking, fashioned ad hoc on flexible and broadly remedial lines, often having important consequences for many persons including absentees.

(5) The remedy is not imposed but negotiated.

(6) The decree does not terminate judicial involvement in the affair: its administration requires the continuing participation of the court.

(7) The judge is not passive, his function limited to analysis and statement of governing legal rules; he is active, with responsibility not only for credible fact evaluation but for organizing and shaping the litigation to ensure a just and viable outcome.

(8) The subject matter of the lawsuit is not a dispute between private individuals about private rights, but a grievance about the operation of public policy. . . .

IV. SOME THOUGHTS ON LEGITIMACY

More fundamentally, our transformed appreciation of the whole process of making, implementing, and modifying law in a public law system points to sources other than professional method and role for the legitimacy of the new model lawsuit. As we now begin to see it, that process is plastic and fluid. Popular participation in it is not alone through the vote or by representation in the legislature. And judicial participation is not by way of sweeping and immutable statements of *the* law, but in the form of a continuous and rather tentative dialogue with other political elements — Congress and the executive, administrative agencies, the profession and the academics, the press and wider publics. Bentham's "judge and company" has become a conglomerate. In such a setting, the ability of a judicial pronouncement to sustain itself in the dialogue and the power of judicial action to generate assent over the long haul become the ultimate touchstones of legitimacy. . . .

In my view, judicial action only achieves such legitimacy by responding to, indeed by stirring, the deep and durable demand for justice in our society.

Notes

1.   Professor Fuller's article is perhaps the most famous effort to derive the structure of the adversarial system from fundamental norms. Professor Chayes was aware of Professor Fuller's article. Indeed, the "bipolar" model that Professor Chayes critiqued was essentially the adjudicatory model that Professor Fuller advocated. Thus, Professor Chayes's article, which is one of the most cited articles of all time, is an extended realpolitik response to Professor Fuller's normative claims. In one sense, the articles pass like ships in the night — the one operating at the level of philosophical inquiry, the other describing the facts on the ground. But each article poses a hard question for the other: Do Professor Chayes's observations about public-law litigation prove that Professor Fuller's claim about the nature of adjudication is wrong? Does Professor Fuller's claim demonstrate that Professor Chayes's public-law model is illegitimate? *Cf.* Robert G. Bone, *Lon Fuller's Theory of Adjudication and the False Dichotomy Between Dispute Resolution and Public Law Models of Litigation*, 75 B.U. L. REV. 1273 (1995) (arguing that the views can be reconciled).

2.   Professor Fuller's idea of polycentrism has sometimes been taken as a shorthand definition for complex litigation: many-sided disputes in which a multiplicity of variables makes adversarial adjudication impossible. Because he does not believe that adjudication can handle the dispute, he believes only two solutions for such disputes exist, a political solution or a contractually negotiated one. Professor Chayes's definition of public-law litigation is also sometimes taken as a shorthand definition of complex litigation: disputes in which the judge, in the decidedly non-adversarial posture of an active participant, takes control of the case. For Professor

Chayes, that control manifested itself principally in the negotiated remedy, which he believed lay at the center of public-law litigation. If Professor Chayes is right about the need to resolve these disputes through negotiation, hasn't Professor Fuller's prediction come true?

3.   The public-law model proposed by Professor Chayes has enjoyed significant praise and come under significant criticism over the years. One common thread is to ask whether the public-law judge shifts the adversarial process too much (or not enough) in the direction of the inquisitorial process. Professor Fiss assays a different criticism:

> A judge deeply involved in the reconstruction of a school system or prison is likely to lose much of his distance from the organization. He is likely to identify with the organization he is reconstructing, and this process of identification is likely to deepen as the enterprise of organizational reform moves through several cycles of supplemental relief, drawn out over a number of years. There is, however, a deeper and more pervasive threat to judicial independence, one that turns . . . on the desire of the judge represented by the very attempt to give a remedy, any remedy — the desire to be efficacious.

> Judges are not all powerful. They can decree some results but not all. Some results depend on forces beyond their control. . . . Judges realize that practical success vitally depends on the preferences, the will of the body politic.

> This perception of dependence has obvious and important implications for the remedy: no judge is likely to decree more than he thinks he has the power to accomplish. . . . He will strive to lessen the gap between declaration and actualization. He will tailor the right to fit the remedy.

Owen M. Fiss, *Foreword: The Forms of Justice*, 93 HARV. L. REV. 1, 53-54 (1979).

4.   Since Professor Chayes's article, others have noted an expansion of and shift in the role of the public-law judge. *See* Judith Resnik, *Managerial Judges*, 96 HARV. L. REV. 374 (1982) (arguing that non-adversarial judging had moved from the remedial phase to the pretrial phase); William B. Rubenstein, *A Transactional Model of Adjudication*, 89 GEO. L.J. 371 (2002) (arguing that the public-law model has been replaced by a newer model that focuses even more explicitly on negotiated solutions); Charles F. Sabel & William H. Simon, *Destabilization Rights: How Public Law Litigation Succeeds*, 117 HARV. L. REV. 1015 (2004) (arguing that public-law litigation has evolved in ways that enhance democratic accountability). This change in judicial role does not respond directly to Professor Fuller's criticism that the new-found role is not legitimate. One response to Professor Fuller is to argue that the adversarial system is not normatively required, and a judge can depart from it when necessary. But that response raises two additional questions: How do we decide when departures from adversarial process are "necessary," and how do we justify maintaining two systems of justice (one for the "ordinary" case and one for the "complex" one)?

The following sources seek to define complex litigation more precisely. To what extent do these definitions adequately answer these two questions?

MANUAL FOR COMPLEX AND MULTIDISTRICT LITIGATION

7-9 (1970)

0.1 *Definitions.*

"Complex litigation," as used in this Manual, includes one or more related cases which present unusual problems and which require extraordinary treatment, including but not limited to the cases designated as "protracted" and "big." . . .

0.22   *Classes of potentially complex cases.*

Cases in the following classification may require special treatment in accordance with the procedures in this Manual: (a) antitrust cases; (b) cases involving a large number of parties or an unincorporated association of large membership; (c) cases involving requests for injunctive relief affecting the operations of a large business entity; (d) patent, copyright, and trademark cases; (e) common disaster cases; (f) individual stockholders', stockholders' derivative, and stockholders' representative actions; (g) products liability cases; (h) cases arising as a result of prior or pending Government litigation; (i) multiple or multidistrict litigation; (j) class actions or potential class actions; or (k) other cases involving an unusual multiplicity or complexity of factual issues.

AMERICAN LAW INSTITUTE, COMPLEX LITIGATION: STATUTORY RECOMMENDATIONS AND ANALYSIS

7 (1994)

"Complex litigation" has no fixed definition, and the term sometimes is used to refer to litigation that concerns complex issues even if the dispute takes place only between two parties in a single forum. As used in this Project, however, "complex litigation" refers exclusively to multiparty, multiforum litigation; it is characterized by related claims dispersed in several forums and often involving events that occurred over long periods of time. . . . Repeated relitigation of the common issues in a complex case unduly expends the resources of attorney and client, burdens already overcrowded dockets, delays recompense for those in need, results in disparate treatment for persons harmed by essentially identical or similar conduct, and contributes to the negative image many people have of the legal system. . . .

Complex cases may arise under state or federal law and in the courts of either system. They are generated by a variety of circumstances — from a single mass disaster such as the collapse of a Hyatt Hotel skywalk, from myriad individual contacts with a hazardous product such as asbestos, or from allegations of antitrust violations committed by one of the world's largest corporations or a number of small ones. The claims in a complex case may accrue all at once as in an air crash, or they may be latent for generations and mature at different times, as in the case of DES. . . . But complex cases share two defining characteristics: they all involve the potential for relitigation of identical or nearly identical issues, and consequently, they all involve the enormous expenditure of resources.

MANUAL FOR COMPLEX LITIGATION, THIRD

3 (1995)

What is complex litigation? . . . A functional definition of complex litigation recognizes the need for management in the sense used here — judicial management with the participation of counsel — does not simply arise from complexity, but is its defining characteristic: The greater the need for management, the more "complex" is the litigation. Clearly, litigation involving many parties in numerous related cases — especially if pending in different jurisdictions — requires management and is complex, as is litigation involving large numbers of witnesses and documents and extensive discovery. On the other hand, litigation raising difficult and novel questions of law, though challenging to the court, may require little or no management, and therefore may not be complex as that term is used here.

Notes

1.   The foregoing definitions or descriptions of complex litigation were arranged in chronological order. The *Manual for Complex and Multidistrict Litigation*, published in 1970, was the direct predecessor of the *Manual for Complex Litigation (Second)*, published in 1985. The *Manual (Second)* is the direct predecessor of the *Manual, Third*, published in 1995; it was followed by the *Manual for Complex Litigation, Fourth*, published in 2004. The *Manual* is the Bible of case-management techniques for judges and practitioners. Two editions of the *Manual* (the original *Manual*, and the *Manual, Third*) provided definitions of complex litigation. The definitions, however, are different. The *Manual (Second)* intentionally declined to define complex litigation. The *Manual, Fourth* also eschewed a definition, noting only that "the term 'complex litigation' [is not] susceptible to any bright-line definition." How can someone write a manual describing what to do in complex litigation without first defining what complex litigation is?

2.   The ALI's definition of "complex litigation" recognizes that the phrase's meaning shifts the nature of the problem being studied shifts. Do the various conflicting efforts to define "complex litigation" suggest that this

approach is best? Note that the ALI's definition keys into a particular problem — expensive relitigation of similar claims and issues. Does that problem explain why we need to move away from adversarial process in complex cases and tolerate different (or non-trans-substantive) rules of procedure for routine and complex cases? Consider whether the following definition does a better job answering these questions.

Jay Tidmarsh, UNATTAINABLE JUSTICE: THE FORM OF COMPLEX LITIGATION AND THE LIMITS OF JUDICIAL POWER

60 GEO. WASH. L. REV. 1683, 1801 (1992)

It is now possible to provide a formal definition of complex litigation: Litigation in an adversarial system in which the judicial power necessary to overcome the dysfunction of the lawyers, the jury, or the parties results in procedural disparities that cause substantively disparate outcomes among similarly situated parties, claims, or transactions. The definition contains three essential elements. The first element is dysfunction — the inability of the lawyers, jury, or parties to fulfill the responsibilities for rational adjudication assigned to them by the adversarial system. The second element is curative judicial power — the ability of the judge to establish procedures that remedy this dysfunction and thus allow rational adjudication, albeit in a manner inconsistent with the adversarial model. The third element is that like cases are treated unalike because of the tendency of the selected procedures to cause the nature and quality of evidence, and consequently the substantive outcome, to vary (1) among persons who have experienced the same or similar factual occurrences, (2) among cases seeking recovery under the same legal theory, or (3) among legal theories constituting a party's claim or defense.

Notes

1. The idea of dysfunction is central to our understanding of complex litigation. Every litigation system expects certain players to perform certain roles. In the adversarial system, the roles of gathering facts and developing arguments are performed by lawyers; the role of rational decision-making is performed by the judge (and sometimes the jury); and the role of complying with the remedy is performed by the parties. Under this definition, at least one party cannot perform the assigned task. The desire to adjudicate cases rationally provides the reason for the judicial departures from adversarial process that Professor Chayes and others have observed, and the reason that complex cases are treated differently from routine ones.

2. "Dysfunction" can arise in different ways. First, when lawyers vigorously representing their clients do not bring together all interested

parties in one proceeding, and when that decision means that those left out of the case will either be unable to secure a remedy comparable to those who have been joined or else disrupt the remedy obtained by others, we have "structural complexity." Next, the voluminous nature of a case may make it impossible for a lawyer adequately to gather the relevant facts and organize the relevant issues into arguments. When this dysfunction occurs during the pretrial process, we have "pretrial complexity." When this type of dysfunction occurs during the trial process, or when the volume or technicality of the evidence makes it impossible for a decision-maker to decide rationally, we have "trial complexity." When the courts are unable to declare or the parties are unable to implement the remedy, "remedial complexity" exists. A single case can be — but need not be — complex in more than one way.

These four types of dysfunction provide the organizational structure for this casebook. Part One of the book examines issues of structural complexity, Part Two examines pretrial complexity, Part Three examines trial complexity, and Part Four examines remedial complexity.

3. This definition also requires that the dysfunction is curable by the non-adversarial application of judicial power, but that this application of power causes the unequal treatment of like cases. These qualifications return us to Professor Fuller. Even if we do not accept the full thrust of Professor Fuller's argument — that the adversarial system is demanded by the form of adjudication — we might still think that the adversarial system is better than any other. If so, is the same procedural treatment of like cases (in other words, trans-substantivism) a fundamental procedural norm? Are there limits on our ability to depart from adversarial and trans-substantive process, so that some complex cases lie beyond the bounds of adjudication?

These are the questions that the remainder of this book explores, as we examine the specific ways in which complexity affects procedural and remedial doctrines. But the answers to these questions lie in this chapter — in the history of procedure, in its theory, and in its many manifestations in the world.

PART ONE

STRUCTURAL COMPLEXITY

One of the lawyers' primary tasks in the prosecution or defense of a lawsuit is the selection of parties to be joined and the forum in which to file the case. The plaintiff's lawyer exercises the greatest influence over this process. The plaintiff is often said to be "master of the complaint" who enjoys the "venue privilege" — in other words, the plaintiff makes the initial decisions about party structure, legal theories, and forum. Within narrow parameters, a defendant can sometimes alter these choices.

In making these choices, lawyers are guided by two considerations. The first is the panoply of restrictions found in the constitutions, statutes, and codes of procedure regulating state and federal courts. The second is the adversarial system's ethical command to represent a client's interests with zeal. Lawyers seek to find the combination of claims, parties, and court that meets their obligation to secure the best outcome for their clients. Typically there will be trade-offs. For instance, a plaintiff's attorney might believe that the best chance of recovery lies in state court, but the best legal theory lies within the exclusive jurisdiction of the federal courts. Hence, the attorney needs to decide whether the state forum or the federal claim is more important. Conversely, those defending a lawsuit try to thwart the plaintiff's choices.

But the choices that best protects clients' interests may not match the interests of society in efficiently allocating access to the courts. Whether this adversarial approach to selection of parties, theories, and forum should continue to be maintained is the main theme of Part One. The vehicle through which we will be exploring this theme is complex litigation. Complex litigation often involves hosts of potential parties and claims. In these multi-party cases, certain lawyers are simply unable to represent their clients with the degree of diligence upon which the adversarial system insists. There are various reasons for this "lawyer dysfunction," but they can generally be grouped into two categories:

(1) When individual plaintiffs wish to sue a defendant separately and the defendant's assets are insufficient to pay the total claims against it,

the plaintiffs who obtain early judgments will recover in full and later plaintiffs will take nothing. The decisions of the early-filing lawyers make it impossible for later-filing lawyers to obtain any meaningful remedy for their clients.

(2) When a plaintiff seeks a remedy that might have an adverse effect on nonparties and does not join these nonparties, one of two results will occur: (a) The nonparties will be barred from later challenging the remedy, so that the rights of the nonparties will effectively have been determined in a lawsuit in which they had no representation; or (b) The nonparties will not be barred from a later challenge, so that either the original plaintiffs lose the rights that they had previously secured, or the original defendants are possibly subject to inconsistent obligations. The first outcome is unfair to nonparties; the second is unfair to either the original plaintiffs or the original defendants.

A third category of cases that does not necessarily involve lawyer dysfunction also tests the adversarial assumption. In these cases, large numbers of plaintiffs are injured by the same or similar event, but for tactical or practical reasons they wish to sue in different forums at different times. Thus, the same factual and legal issues are litigated in hundreds of forums across the country — an expensive and inefficient proposition.

You might think that the proper response to dysfunction and inefficiency is to aggregate all the parties into a single proceeding that resolves all claims, defenses, and issues once and for all. But aggregation also poses numerous challenges and pitfalls. This Part explores the benefits and costs of aggregation. Chapter Two examines the four principal approaches, both direct and indirect, to aggregation: joinder, consolidation, stays or antisuit injunctions, and preclusion. Chapter Three explores the limits that our federal system imposes on the ability of these devices to achieve their full potential. Chapter Four examines the most powerful — and most controversial — aggregation device generally in use: the class action. Chapter Five examines another powerful aggregation device of more limited utility: bankruptcy. Chapter Six studies the procedural and substantive law (or laws) which a court can choose to resolve a case that has been aggregated. The answer to this last question has an important effect on the ability to aggregate litigation.

Throughout this Part, we examine whether the adversarial assumption of party control over the litigation's structure is appropriate, and whether it is wise to entrust judges with discretion to override the parties' choices. In effect, we explore the legitimate boundaries of adjudication.

CHAPTER TWO

AGGREGATION AND LITIGANT AUTONOMY

Complex litigation often involves numerous plaintiffs, numerous defendants, and numerous claims and defenses. Sometimes all the claims arise out of a discrete event, and all or most of the parties live in a discrete geographical area. Typically, however, the parties are geographically dispersed, and the claims are often temporally dispersed as well. When multiplied over the number of possible claims and claimants, the repetitive relitigation of common factual and legal issues is inefficient, and possibly financially crippling for the defendant(s). In addition, individual litigation sometimes works an injustice, either to nonparties whose rights are foreclosed by earlier litigation, to plaintiffs who see later litigation undo the rights they previously vindicated, or to defendants who are subject to inconsistent obligations from multiple lawsuits. Whether to reduce inefficiency or to avoid an injustice to a party or nonparty, the need for a mechanism to prevent relitigation seems apparent.

This chapter examines the four principal methods to aggregate related cases. Two aggregation devices — joinder and consolidation — directly bring related cases together. The other two devices — antisuit injunctions and preclusion — indirectly accomplish the same result. This chapter focuses primarily on joinder and consolidation; under the present law, preclusion and antisuit injunctions are useful only over a narrow range of cases presenting unique circumstances.

Before we examine the four devices in detail, however, we provide some readings on the expected consequences of aggregated, as opposed to individual, litigation. Aggregation is not a value-neutral decision. (Nor, for that matter, is individual litigation.) Certain substantive consequences can be anticipated when related claims are joined together. Certain losses in the right of autonomous control over litigation — a right sometimes summed up with the line that "every person deserves his or her day in court" — also occur.

A. PERSPECTIVES ON AGGREGATION
AND LITIGANT AUTONOMY

Assume that a defendant has engaged in conduct that has injured 100 people across the country. Assume as well that the claims are large enough that each plaintiff is likely to sue. One option — the default option in the American legal system — is to leave the decision about whether and where to sue in the hands of each plaintiff. Plaintiffs who wish to join together and bring an aggregated suit can do so; plaintiffs who prefer to go it alone are also free to do so. In other words, each plaintiff is master of his or her complaint. Plaintiffs in this world have a high degree of litigant autonomy. The opposing option is to require that all similarly situated plaintiffs aggregate their cases in one forum. This option affords litigants precious little autonomy.

Assume as well that both options involve exactly the same costs, exactly the same delays, and exactly the same outcome. Which of the approaches do you prefer? Now suppose that individual litigation will cost $1,000,000 more than aggregated litigation. Does this fact change your preference for individual or aggregated treatment? Suppose that individual litigation involves a 50% chance of recovery for each plaintiff, but aggregated litigation increases the expected recovery for plaintiff to 60%. Does aggregation's potential to change litigation outcomes affect your preference?

These thought experiments are intended to test how much you value litigant autonomy. The following readings examine the experiment's assumptions — that autonomy is valuable; that aggregated treatment yields savings in litigation costs; and that aggregating related cases can affect the outcomes of cases — and provide helpful information with which you can evaluate the aggregation devices that this chapter describes.

Irwin A. Horowitz & Kenneth S. Bordens, THE CONSOLIDATION OF PLAINTIFFS: THE EFFECTS OF NUMBER OF PLAINTIFFS ON JURORS' LIABILITY DECISIONS, DAMAGE AWARDS, AND COGNITIVE PROCESSING OF EVIDENCE

85 J. APPLIED PSYCHOL. 909, 911-12, 916-17 (2000)

We recruited 135 individuals from jury rolls. There were 61 men and 74 women. The participants ranged in age from 20 to 67 years . . . .

The trial, produced on videotape, involved claims by railroad workers of repetitive stress injuries, specifically carpal tunnel syndrome (CTS), allegedly caused by repetitive actions across a number of different tasks. . . .

The trial had several versions. In the base version, 10 plaintiffs were aggregated for trial. Each plaintiff claimed CTS, but the plaintiffs performed few job tasks in common. . . . The plaintiffs all had similar claims but lived and worked in geographically disparate parts of the "Big Mountain" Railway network, which ranges from the Deep South to the Middle West. All of the tasks involved some repetitive motion, and all plaintiffs had been examined and tested for CTS. All plaintiffs claimed that Big Mountain Railroad had been negligent in not adequately providing for worker safety and not warning the workers that their jobs entailed the risk of CTS.

In addition to the 10-plaintiff version, there were four other versions of the trial in which 6 of the original 10 plaintiffs, 4 of the original 10, and 2 of the original 10 were consolidated for trial in four different combinations . . . . Finally, 4 of the original 10 plaintiffs were given individual trials. . . .

We pretested the strength of the evidence for each plaintiff, and 35 third-year law students did not find any plaintiff's case to be any more or less meritorious than any other was. Each plaintiff and his supervisor testified as to the nature of the complaints and the job requirements. . . . Defendants' counsel also required each plaintiff to testify as to nonwork-related afflictions that could have either caused or contributed to their complaints. Smoking, alcohol consumption, and diabetes or previous injuries were most prevalent.

However, the bulk of the testimony came from four expert witnesses, two for each side. . . . After the testimony and closing statements were concluded, jurors were provided with written instructions from the judge, a procedure that is not uncommon in this type of trial.

In summary, mock jurors saw a trial in which the only variable was the number of plaintiffs consolidated for trial. All other complexity factors (e.g., strength of evidence, technicality of the language) were constant for all plaintiffs. . . .

Discussion

The results of this study on the effects of number of plaintiffs on liability and awards suggest that within the context of a close trial involving repetitive stress injuries, an increase in information load had a significant impact on verdicts and information processing. With respect to liability verdicts, 1 or 2 plaintiffs were less likely to prevail than when the plaintiffs were aggregated in a 4-, 6-, or 10-plaintiff group.

Compensatory awards followed a somewhat different pattern. The fulcrum in this study was the 4-plaintiff aggregation. Lower awards were assigned in the 1- and 2-plaintiff conditions, and awards appeared to reach their zenith in the 4-plaintiff condition and then begin to show decrements in the 6- and 10-plaintiff configurations. . . . The recognition data collected in this study suggest that when the number reaches 4, jurors have difficulty distinguishing among various plaintiffs. . . .

. . . We theorize that jurors in the 10-plaintiff condition, because they are attending to a larger aggregation, may use 1 or 2 modal plaintiffs as anchors and assign awards on that basis. . . . Jurors may focus on those plaintiffs with modest injuries and apply that metric to the entire group. . . .

The results of the present study also clearly show that judgment of liability is directly related to the amount of compensation awarded to the plaintiffs. . . . As numbers of plaintiffs increased, the amount of responsibility attributed to the defendant also increased significantly. The crucial judgment, then—and this finding does not surprise us—was the degree of responsibility attributed to the defendant and the plaintiffs.

. . . [J]urors were less likely to entertain alternative constructions of the evidence as the number of plaintiffs increased. This follows previous findings that indicate that increasing levels of information load lead to simplified strategies . . . .

. . . In addition, greater numbers of plaintiffs degraded the jurors' ability to understand the expert witnesses and to correctly recognize what work task the plaintiffs performed and how they differed from other plaintiffs. It is not surprising that a blending effect occurred as the aggregated number reached four and higher.

How do the present results inform the issue of juror competence in complex civil trials? . . . [J]urors were not judging the evidence pertaining to these plaintiffs on merits alone. Furthermore, there is no gainsaying the finding that jurors reasoned holistically, using evidence pertaining to liability to decide damage awards. . . .

Finally, generalization is circumscribed by the fact that all jury analogue studies have their limitations, and this is no exception. The fact that the jurors did not deliberate limits the heuristic value; the jury's collective and transactive memory may be of some help in decision making. We did, however, use a representative sample of real-world jurors, and the trial was as realistic as one can hope for using a videotaped presentation.

David Rosenberg, CLASS ACTIONS FOR MASS TORTS: DOING INDIVIDUAL JUSTICE BY COLLECTIVE MEANS

62 IND. L.J. 561, 562-67 (1987)

. . . [B]ureaucratic justice is most strikingly antithetical to notions of individual justice because it legitimates the aggregation and averaging of circumstances and interests of affected individuals in pursuit of the collective benefits from process efficiency, outcome consistency, and the maximum production of substantive goods. These goals are implemented through "public law" procedures which combine claims for uniform and summary treatment according to classifications based on a set of salient, if partial, common variables relating to the individuals involved. . . .

Nowhere do class actions seem a more alien force than in the torts system, which epitomizes the individual justice tradition. The hallmark of this system — at least as a formal matter — is its adherence to the "private law" mode of case-by-case, particularized adjudication.   Attention is lavished on the particular details of each claim to ensure that the norms of liability and remedy are tailored to the specific facts of the defendant's conduct and its causal relationship to the plaintiff's injury. Every effort is made to avoid (or at least minimize) the erroneous redistribution of wealth that occurs when innocent defendants are held liable or deserving plaintiffs denied compensation.

In mass tort cases involving claims for personal injury, which pose daunting problems of causation and remedy, the price of individual justice is notoriously high. . . .

The case-by-case mode of adjudication magnifies this burden by requiring the parties and courts to reinvent the wheel for each claim. The merits of each case are determined de novo even though the major liability issues are common to every claim arising from the mass tort accident, and even though they may have been previously determined several times by full and fair trials. These costs exclude many mass tort victims from the system and sharply reduce the recovery for those who gain access. Win or lose, the system's private law process exacts a punishing surcharge from defendant firms as well as plaintiffs.

These costs of litigation, which are borne directly by the parties, also cast a broad array of shadow prices that have widespread indirect effects. The redundant adjudication of mass tort claims thus consumes vast quantities of public resources, raising the price of access for other, sporadic, types of tort claims. Moreover, even though most of the claims arising from mass accidents are eventually settled on the basis of recovery patterns projected from relatively few trials, the settlement calculus will reflect the costs of redundant, de novo, particularized adjudication, as well as the incentives of each party to increase the litigation expenses for the other. These conditions generally disadvantage claimants. Because defendant firms are in a position to spread the litigation costs over the entire class of mass accident claims, while plaintiffs, being deprived of the economies of scale afforded by class actions, can not, the result will usually be that the firms will escape the full loss they have caused and, after deducting their attorneys' shares, the victims will receive a relatively small proportion of any recovery as compensation. As a consequence, the tort system's primary objectives of compensation and deterrence are seriously jeopardized. . . .

Individual justice critiques . . . have little power when the primary purpose of tort liability is taken to be the utilitarian objective of maximizing welfare by deterring socially inappropriate risk-taking. The aggregation and averaging techniques of bureaucratic justice are not only consistent with the social welfare justification for tort liability — at least, when defendant firms are not on the whole under or overcharged — but they also produce the positive benefits of lower administrative costs. . . . [I]ndividual justice arguments . . . ignore not only the realities of claimant dependency and powerlessness in individual actions, but they also fail to recognize the existence of collectivizing forces operating in the mass accident context, particularly the class-wide nature of the risk ex ante, which exerts a unifying influence over the security interests (deterrence) and protective responses (insurance) of the potential accident victims. . . . [G]iven such ex ante conditions, bureaucratic justice . . . provides better opportunities for achieving individual justice than does the tort system's private law, disaggregative processes.

Francis E. McGovern, AN ANALYSIS OF MASS TORTS FOR JUDGES

73 TEX. L. REV. 1821, 1822, 1838, 1840-43 (1995)

When confronted by mass torts, many judges perceive an alluring commonality among cases that may lead them to make a critical shift in the balance of policies underlying tort law and civil procedure. Faced with seemingly repetitive trials and an unending queue of mass tort plaintiffs, some judges have decided that efficiency concerns call for a more collective rather than individual treatment of claims. More importantly, many of these same judges believe that fairness concerns — making sure that each individual receives some compensation in a reasonable period of time — also lead to a more collective approach. Thus, the balance of policies — between efficiency and corrective justice — shifts in the context of mass torts and leads to more nontraditional aggregative solutions to mass tort issues.

This shift, however, creates a Catch-22 that has not become obvious until recently: The more successful judges become at dealing "fairly and efficiently" with mass torts, the more and larger the mass tort filings become. The creation of devices that speed the resolution of the case in front of the court also encourages more traditionally successful plaintiffs, more traditionally unsuccessful plaintiffs, and more plaintiffs who traditionally did not enter the tort system at all to take advantage of the new techniques. . . .

What should the appropriate role for the judge be in confronting mass torts? The traditional model of the judge as an umpire, ruling on the issues as they are served by the adversaries, has been criticized as too limited. An alternative approach — the judge as a manager — has been suggested as superior. In this latter role, the judge should actively learn the details of the litigation and channel the efforts of the court and counsel to resolve the litigation more efficiently. . . .

Both approaches have strengths and weaknesses. The traditional approach promotes the tort-law value of individual treatment. Regardless of the judge's intention, however, isolated judicial decisions inevitably have effects on the other cases addressing the mass tort. Thus, a judge can easily exacerbate the problem by ignoring the realities of the mass tort world. In addition, counsel for plaintiffs and defendants typically encourage those judges who are favorable to their particular strategic position to make even more extreme decisions. In this manner, judge-shopping has developed into a fine art, and the incentives for judges to be viewed as gurus of mass torts have become strong. . . .

The management model, however, also has problems in its implementation. . . . Attempting to resolve a complex social problem with courts rather than with legislatures is viewed as counterproductive. Judges who take it upon themselves to control a mass tort and achieve a global solution, at least outside of bankruptcy, have been subject to substantial criticisms. The rules of civil procedure were arguably not designed to contemplate this type of litigation resolution. . . .

A third emerging judicial strategy focuses on the concept of maturity. This approach assumes that a life cycle exists for mass torts — mass torts go through various stages in their evolution — and that different judicial strategies should be used at different stages of the life cycle. At the early stages of the litigation, judges should take a more traditional approach; at the later stages, once the full dimensions of the tort are recognized, a more activist model is appropriate. . . .

The cyclical theory of mass tort litigation contemplates an initial stage in the litigation during which there are inherent advantages for the defendant in available resources, information, law, strategy, and public opinion. . . . During this initial stage of the cycle, the defendant tends to win the cases it chooses to try and is often able to settle lawsuits quietly with little impact on other cases. Plaintiffs have to be particularly tenacious to overcome these barriers and establish the vitality of their claims.

If, however, the plaintiffs are able to achieve success, either by jury verdicts or major settlements, the cycle proceeds into a second phase. Here, the plaintiffs have the advantage. Their success suggests that they have discovered sufficient information and expertise to present a credible case on liability, causation, and damages; have surmounted legal obstacles or made new, more favorable law; and have developed a second-generation offensive strategy to counter the previously successful approach of the defense. This shift in momentum drives all parties to excess. Once there is a popular consensus that a particular series of outcomes is inevitable, a herd instinct generates an overabundance of support for those outcomes. The pendulum eventually swings much further than is warranted by the rational circumstances. The most significant ramification of this second phase is the creation of a heightened demand for litigation: filings of new cases increase dramatically. . . .

Typically, a third phase in the cycle develops as the plaintiffs' attorneys push the envelope of viability of existing cases and select new, marginal cases to litigate. At the same time, the defendant develops its second-generation defensive strategy to overcome its earlier lack of success and launches a counterattack on unfavorable law, evidence, and public opinion. As a result, the defendant has proportionately more success in the third phase than in the second. Even if a liability finding seems preordained by the plaintiffs' previous success, plaintiffs may receive lower verdict amounts.

The theory suggests that although subsequent cycles do occur, depending on the idiosyncracies of the particular litigation, eventually a rough equilibrium of case values ensues as the cases become more routinized and the parties' contentions become more defined. . . . Eventually, the litigation becomes a mature mass tort. . . . Typically at the mature stage, little or no new evidence will be developed, significant appellate review of any novel legal issues has been concluded, and at least one full cycle of trial strategies has been exhausted.

Once a mass tort has matured, the second judicial strategy of case management has a substantially greater chance of acceptability and success. Sufficient information is available, even in the litigation process, to make informed decisions, and a greater chance exists that the affected public will receive global resolutions more favorably.

Notes

1.   Professors Horowitz and Bordens have designed other experiments to determine the effect of aggregation on jury decision-making. In another study, they found that, in comparison to individual trials, juries awarded higher punitive damages in 4-plaintiff aggregated trials when an "outlier" with a very strong claim was present and when the jury was made aware that other persons who were not plaintiffs had been injured. The same tendency was noted with respect to compensatory damages, but the effect was not statistically significant. The presence of an "outlier," however, made outcomes more unpredictable, with more defense verdicts, than the individual-litigation condition. Their ultimate conclusion was that "a plaintiff with a relatively weak case is [definitely] helped by aggregation; conversely, a plaintiff with quite a strong case . . . appears to be better served by being disaggregated, particularly with reference to punitive damages." Irwin A. Horowitz & Kenneth S. Bordens, *The Effects of Outlier Presence, Plaintiff Population Size, and Aggregation of Plaintiffs on Simulated Civil Jury Decisions*, 12 LAW & HUM. BEHAV. 209, 226 (1988).

The studies by Horowitz and Bordens show that more information, and information about more potential victims, influence decision-making. On the assumption that the decisions reached in the individual-trial condition are more accurate, aggregation makes jury decision-making less accurate. But is that assumption correct? Or does the focus on individual cases distort decision-making? On one reading, the findings of the Horowitz and Bordens studies suggest that trying to apply the same law to one-victim and multi-victim cases is itself the problem.

2.   Even if individual litigation leads to more accurate outcomes in particular cases, Professor Rosenberg points out that individual litigation imposes substantial costs. In Chapter One (*supra* p. 22), we saw that the economically preferable procedure minimizes the sum of the costs of inaccurate judgments *and* the costs of litigation. If the benefits of aggregated litigation are great enough, a loss in accuracy is something that

we might tolerate. Of course, to balance the costs, we also need a way to value the costs and benefits on each side in a particular case.

3.   In discussing the benefits of aggregated litigation, it is important to consider net benefits. Aggregated litigation also imposes certain costs that individual litigation does not. As we will see in Parts Two and Three, aggregated litigation sometimes requires the use of costly devices to handle complex pretrial and trial issues. Moreover, although it is a difficult matter to quantify, litigant autonomy is lost in aggregated litigation. How much is a litigant's right to control the principal decisions affecting his or her suit worth? Professor Hensler's study of tort cases in the 1980s suggests that, whatever the theoretical answer, the answer on the ground is "not very much." Relying on surveys of tort litigants, she found that two-thirds of tort plaintiffs met their lawyers four or fewer times; and about half had four or fewer phone conversations with their lawyers. Only 18% of plaintiffs felt that they had "a lot" of control over their lawsuits; 26% felt that they had "some" control; 18% thought they had "a little" control, and 38% felt they had "not much" control. *See* Deborah R. Hensler, *Resolving Mass Toxic Torts: Myths and Realities*, 1989 U. ILL. L. REV. 89. Hensler went on to note that, in both routine and mass litigation, plaintiffs with small claims tended to be overcompensated by the tort system, and plaintiffs with large claims tended to be undercompensated.

4.   Professor McGovern adds another consideration into the balance: the timing of aggregation. Put into the terms we have been discussing, McGovern's point is that, if we aggregate in the infancy of mass litigation, we will likely have an inaccurate (and defendant-favoring) outcome. If we aggregate in the adolescence of mass litigation, we will likely have inaccurate (but now plaintiff-favoring) outcomes. If we wait until maturity to aggregate, we will have the information from which to make accurate assessments of each case's merits and settlement values. Therefore, we need to have the patience to suffer some early erroneous judgments, as well as some early repetitive litigation costs, because the payoff down the road is more accuracy at less cost.

5.   In a sense, the point of these readings is to show that the decision to aggregate — whether made by plaintiffs, defendants, or the court — is not value neutral. Whether and when we choose to aggregate litigation has a significant effect on the outcome of litigation, as well as the efficiency with which it is conducted. With these ideas in mind, we now turn to the methods by which aggregation can occur.

B. AGGREGATION THROUGH JOINDER RULES

The most common way in which aggregation of related claims and parties occurs is joinder — the process by which litigants consciously choose to bring related claims and add related parties to one proceeding. Joinder begins from a simple base: one claim asserted by one plaintiff against one defendant. The rules of joinder then determine which additional claims and which additional parties can be added to the base claim. The more liberal the rules of joinder, the more aggregation a legal system can accomplish.

The Federal Rules of Civil Procedure, which operate in federal courts and are representative of the joinder approach in most state courts, evince a liberal attitude toward joinder. Rules 8(d)(2) and 18(a) allow a plaintiff to add any legal theory or claim — indeed, even unrelated claims — to the base claim. These Rules also evince a high regard for plaintiff autonomy: A plaintiff is not required to assert such additional theories or claims (although, under the rules of preclusion, a plaintiff might lose the right to assert some claims in future litigation by failing to assert them in the present case). The plaintiff is "master of the complaint," able to choose which claims to bring.

To a large extent, this same attitude carries over to the joinder of parties. This section begins by looking at Rule 20, the basic rule by which plaintiffs join plaintiffs and defendants. Under Rule 20, the liberal attitude toward joinder is tempered by the idea of litigant autonomy: Aside from possible preclusion consequences, plaintiffs generally suffer no penalty from failing to join other plaintiffs or defendants in their individual lawsuits and no penalty from refusing to agree to join another plaintiff's case. As we see, however, this basic orientation toward plaintiff autonomy in making joinder decisions has some exceptions of consequence to complex litigation. After examining Rule 20, this section then examines the joinder rules that provide defendants a limited opportunity to modify the claim and party structure that the plaintiff creates; rules and statutes that permit, in limited circumstances, the involuntary joinder of additional parties; and rules and statutes that allow a person not joined by any party to intervene and participate in the suit.

1. Voluntary Joinder of Plaintiffs and Defendants Under Rule 20

MOSLEY V. GENERAL MOTORS CORP.

497 F.2d 1330 (8th Cir. 1974)

■ ROSS, Circuit Judge.

Nathaniel Mosley and nine other persons joined in bringing this action individually and as class representatives alleging that their rights guaranteed under 42 U.S.C. § 2000e et seq. and 42 U.S.C. § 1981 were denied by General Motors and Local 25, United Automobile, Aerospace and Agriculture Implement Workers of America [Union] by reason of their color and race. Each of the ten named plaintiffs had, prior to the filing of the complaint, filed a charge with the Equal Employment Opportunity Commission [EEOC] asserting the facts underlying these claims. Pursuant thereto, the EEOC made a reasonable cause finding that General Motors, Fisher Body Division and Chevrolet Division, and the Union had engaged in unlawful employment practices in violation of Title VII of the Civil Rights Act of 1964. Accordingly, the charging parties were notified by EEOC of their right to institute a civil action in the appropriate federal district court, pursuant to § 706(e) of Title VII, 42 U.S.C. § 2000e-5(e).

In each of the first eight counts of the twelve-count complaint, eight of the ten plaintiffs alleged that General Motors, Chevrolet Division, had engaged in unlawful employment practices by: "discriminating against Negroes as regards promotions, terms and conditions of employment"; "retaliating against Negro employees who protested actions made unlawful by Title VII of the Act and by discharging some because they protested said unlawful acts"; "failing to hire Negro employees as a class on the basis of race"; "failing to hire females as a class on the basis of sex"; "discharging Negro employees on the basis of race"; and "discriminating against Negroes and females in the granting of relief time." Each additionally charged that the defendant union had engaged in unlawful employment practices "with respect to the granting of relief time to Negro and female employees" and "by failing to pursue 6a grievances." The remaining two plaintiffs made similar allegations against General Motors, Fisher Body Division. All of the individual plaintiffs requested injunctive relief, back pay, attorneys fees and costs. Counts XI and XII of the complaint were class action counts against the two individual divisions of General Motors. They also sought declaratory and injunctive relief, back pay, attorneys fees and costs.

General Motors moved to strike portions of each count of the twelve-count complaint . . . The district court ordered that "insofar as the first ten counts are concerned, those ten counts shall be severed into ten separate causes of action," and each plaintiff was directed to bring a separate action based upon his complaint, duly and separately filed. . . .

In reaching this conclusion on joinder, the district court followed the reasoning of *Smith v. North American Rockwell Corp.*, 50 F.R.D. 515 (N.D. Okla. 1970), which, in a somewhat analogous situation, found there was no right to relief arising out of the same transaction, occurrence or series of transactions or occurrences, and that there was no question of law or fact common to all plaintiffs sufficient to sustain joinder under Federal Rule of Civil Procedure 20(a). Similarly, the district court here felt that the plaintiffs' joint actions against General Motors and the Union presented a variety of issues having little relationship to one another; that they had only one common problem, i.e. the defendant; and that as pleaded the joint actions were completely unmanageable. Upon entering the order, and upon application of the plaintiffs, the district court found that its decision involved a controlling question of law as to which there is a substantial ground for difference of opinion and that any of the parties might make application for appeal under 28 U.S.C. § 1292(b). We granted the application to permit this interlocutory appeal and for the following reasons we affirm in part and reverse in part.

Appeal from interlocutory order

[The court began by quoting the then-extant language of Federal Rule 20(a), which was stylistically revised in 2007. The operative language in Rule 20(a) remains the same. — ED.]

Additionally, Rule 20(b) and Rule 42(b) vest in the district court the discretion to order separate trials or make such other orders as will prevent delay or prejudice. In this manner, the scope of the civil action is made a matter for the discretion of the district court, and a determination on the question of joinder of parties will be reversed on appeal only upon a showing of abuse of that discretion. . . . To determine whether the district court's order was proper herein, we must look to the policy and law that have developed around the operation of Rule 20.

Abuse of discretion standard

The purpose of the rule is to promote trial convenience and expedite the final determination of disputes, thereby preventing multiple lawsuits. . . . Single trials generally tend to lessen the delay, expense and inconvenience to all concerned. Reflecting this policy, the Supreme Court has said:

> Under the Rules, the impulse is toward entertaining the broadest possible scope of action consistent with fairness to the parties; joinder of claims, parties and remedies is strongly encouraged.

United Mine Workers of Am. v. Gibbs, 383 U.S. 715, 724 (1966).

Permissive joinder is not, however, applicable in all cases. The rule imposes two specific requisites to the joinder of parties: (1) a right to relief must be asserted by, or against, each plaintiff or defendant relating to or arising out of the same transaction or occurrence, or series of transactions or occurrences; and (2) some question of law or fact common to all the parties must arise in the action.

In ascertaining whether a particular factual situation constitutes a single transaction or occurrence for purposes of Rule 20, a case by case approach is generally pursued. . . . No hard and fast rules have been established under the rule. However, construction of the terms "transaction or occurrence" as used in the context of Rule 13(a) counterclaims offers some guide to the application of this test. For the purposes of the latter rule,

> "Transaction" is a word of flexible meaning. It may comprehend a series of many occurrences, depending not so much upon the immediateness of their connection as upon their logical relationship.

Moore v. N.Y. Cotton Exchange, 270 U.S. 593, 610 (1926). Accordingly, all "logically related" events entitling a person to institute a legal action against another generally are regarded as comprising a transaction or occurrence. . . . The analogous interpretation of the terms as used in Rule 20 would permit all reasonably related claims for relief by or against different parties to be tried in a single proceeding. Absolute identity of all events is unnecessary.

This construction accords with the result reached in *United States v. Mississippi*, 380 U.S. 128 (1965), a suit brought by the United States against the State of Mississippi, the election commissioners, and six voting registrars of the State, charging them with engaging in acts and practices hampering and destroying the right of Negro citizens of Mississippi to vote. The district court concluded that the complaint improperly attempted to hold the six county registrars jointly liable for what amounted to nothing more than individual torts committed by them separately against separate applicants. In reversing, the Supreme Court said:

> But the complaint charged that the registrars had acted and were continuing to act as part of a statewide system designed to enforce the registration laws in a way that would inevitably deprive colored people of the right to vote solely because of their color. On such an allegation the joinder of all the registrars as defendants in a single suit is authorized by Rule 20(a) of the Federal Rules of Civil Procedure. . . . These registrars were alleged to be carrying on activities which were part of a series of transactions or occurrences the validity of which depended to a large extent upon "[questions] of law or fact common to all of them."

Here too, then, the plaintiffs have asserted a right to relief arising out of the same transactions or occurrences. Each of the ten plaintiffs alleged that he had been injured by the same general policy of discrimination on the part of General Motors and the Union. Since a "state-wide system designed to enforce the registration laws in a way that would inevitably deprive colored people of the right to vote" was determined to arise out of the same series of transactions or occurrences, we conclude that a company-wide policy purportedly designed to discriminate against Negroes in employment similarly arises out of the same series of transactions or occurrences. Thus the plaintiffs meet the first requisite for joinder under Rule 20(a).

The second requisite necessary to sustain a permissive joinder under the rule is that a question of law or fact common to all the parties will arise in the action. The rule does not require that all questions of law and fact raised by the dispute be common. Yet, neither does it establish any qualitative or quantitative test of commonality. . . .

The right to relief here depends on the ability to demonstrate that each of the plaintiffs was wronged by racially discriminatory policies on the part of the defendants General Motors and the Union. The discriminatory character of the defendants' conduct is thus basic to each plaintiff's recovery. The fact that each plaintiff may have suffered different effects from the alleged discrimination is immaterial for the purposes of determining the common question of law or fact. Thus, we conclude that the second requisite for joinder under Rule 20(a) is also met by the complaint.

For the reasons set forth above, we conclude that the district court abused its discretion in severing the joined actions. The difficulties in ultimately adjudicating damages to the various plaintiffs are not so overwhelming as to require such severance. If appropriate, separate trials may be granted as to any particular issue after the determination of common questions.

The judgment of the district court disallowing joinder of the plaintiffs' individual actions is reversed and remanded with directions to permit the plaintiffs to proceed jointly.

Notes

1. Perhaps the most important word in Rule 20 is "may," which appears in both Rule 20(a)(1) (joinder of plaintiffs) and Rule 20(a)(2) (joinder of defendants). In one important sense, the word has the same meaning in both contexts: A plaintiff is not *required* to join any additional plaintiffs or defendants. Although plaintiffs who fail to join potential defendants might suffer issue-preclusive consequences in later litigation (*see infra* p. 210), the decision not to join is a matter of choice.

In another important sense, however, the word "may" has different meanings in the two contexts. In the context of joining other plaintiffs, it is understood that the decision to join a lawsuit belongs to each plaintiff; if you are a plaintiff, and you want to join your case with that of another victim, you cannot do so unless the other victim consents. Indeed, the idea that each potential plaintiff must consent to joinder is so ingrained in Rule 20 that it is difficult to find cases that discuss nonconsensual joinder of plaintiffs. In *Cle-Ware Rayco, Inc. v. Perlstein*, 401 F. Supp. 1231 (S.D.N.Y. 1975), a court refused to grant an injunction in a trademark case unless the owner of the trademark was made an additional plaintiff. The owner was already a third-party defendant, on the original plaintiff's motion, the court made the owner a plaintiff and issued the injunction. It was not clear from the opinion, however, whether the owner consented to joinder. In *Lyne v. Arthur Andersen & Co.*, 1991 WL 247576 (N.D. Ill. Nov. 12, 1991), ten individually joined plaintiffs sought either to maintain their case as a class action or, in the alternative, to force the joinder of seven additional plaintiffs that did not consent to joinder. After refusing to certify a class, the court refused to require the requested joinder:

> In considering a Rule 20 motion, the court should examine whether permissive joinder of a party comports with fundamental fairness. . . . When plaintiffs invoke Rule 20 to bring in additional plaintiffs, the additional plaintiffs usually want to participate in the litigation. . . . All prospective class members have been contacted about this action. If any of the seven unnamed prospective class members desired to participate in this litigation, they could have joined with plaintiffs voluntarily or petitioned to intervene. There is nothing fundamentally fair about joining plaintiffs who have expressed no interest in participating in this litigation. [1991 WL 247576, at *3.]

On the other hand, for obvious reasons, the word "may" contains no comparable notion that additional defendants must consent to joinder. Here, the choice of which defendants to join belongs to the plaintiff(s) alone.

2. *Mosley* is the leading case on the issue of voluntary (or permissive) joinder of plaintiffs. It takes a generous view of Rule 20(a) when some issues are common, common pretrial and trial proceedings can achieve economy, and the plaintiffs consent to joinder. For a comparable case, see Alexander v. Fulton County, 207 F.3d 1303 (11th Cir. 2000). Even though *Mosley* is the "leading" case, do not think that it reflects the only attitude about Rule 20 joinder. For a few cases refusing to permit Rule 20 joinder

of plaintiffs, see Grayson v. K-Mart Corp., 849 F. Supp. 785 (N.D. Ga. 1994) (refusing to permit the joinder of eleven store managers allegedly fired due to age discrimination when they did not allege that their firings resulted from a company-wide policy); Johnson v. Indopco, Inc., 846 F. Supp. 670 (N.D. Ill. 1994) (not permitting the joinder of two plaintiffs allegedly denied promotions due to racial and/or sexual discrimination); Saval v. BL Ltd., 710 F.2d 1027 (4th Cir. 1983) (denying joinder of four owners of the same model of car in a case alleging breaches of a federal warranty statute).

3.   Why did the plaintiffs in *Mosley* want to join together? (Hint: Recall some of the ways that joinder can affect the outcome of the case.) Aside from trying to increase the odds of victory, might the plaintiffs' lawyer have been motivated by the prospect of a larger fee (or at least as large a fee with less effort)? To convince a court that joinder is proper, a plaintiffs' lawyer must talk about how much more efficient the joined case will be. But there is a gap between what the law is, when the plaintiffs' lawyer will seek the benefit of that law, and how the lawyer will argue for the application of that law. Put differently, plaintiffs' lawyers will achieve efficiency only when it is in their (or their clients') interests to do so. Is this result inevitable in an adversarial system that entrusts joinder decisions to the plaintiffs? Would it be better to scrap Rule 20's permissive approach and task courts with creating the most efficient party structure?

4.   If the chance of skewing the outcome in their favor is the plaintiffs' motivation for joinder, should the defendant(s) be able to argue that the plaintiffs' structure is so unfair to them that it cannot be maintained? *See Alexander*, 207 F.3d 1303 (suggesting that, on appropriate facts, the prejudicial effect of the joint adjudication of disparate claims and the potential for jury confusion might affect the scope of Rule 20(a)).

This question is part of a larger concern. The critical provisions that *Mosley* interprets are the "transaction or occurrence" and "common question" clauses now contained in Rules 20(a)(1)(A) and -(B). *Mosley* says that these provisions are to be construed to achieve the economical and efficient resolution of disputes. Should any factors other than economy and efficiency also influence the interpretation of Rule 20(a)?

5.   Aside from unfairness to the defendant(s), factors that sometimes influence a court's interpretation are the effects of joinder on subject-matter jurisdiction and, relatedly, on the proper management of complex litigation. The following two cases explore these issues.

IN RE PREMPRO PRODUCTS LIABILITY LITIGATION

591 F.3d 613 (8th Cir. 2010)

■ BRIGHT, Circuit Judge.

The plaintiffs, women and next-of-kin of deceased women, sued a number of manufacturers of hormone replacement therapy drugs, asserting the drugs caused breast cancer. The defendants, manufacturers of hormone replacement therapy drugs ("manufacturers"), removed the cases to federal court. The plaintiffs moved to remand to state court on the grounds that complete diversity of citizenship was lacking, thereby depriving the court of subject matter jurisdiction. The district court concluded that the plaintiffs' claims were misjoined to defeat diversity jurisdiction, dropped the non-diverse plaintiffs, and dismissed these cases. Plaintiffs appeal, and we reverse the district court's orders denying plaintiffs' motions to remand and granting the manufacturers' motions to dismiss duplicative cases.

I. BACKGROUND

[Hormone replacement therapy ("HRT") drugs is used in the treatment of menopausal symptoms. The Women's Health Initiative ("WHI"), a group focused on defining the risks and benefits of strategies that could reduce heart disease, cancer, and fractures in post-menopausal women, began studying the effects of HRT drugs in the 1990s. In 2002, an independent data and safety monitoring board revealed that the number of cases of breast cancer in one HRT group had crossed the boundary established as a signal of increased risk. The independent board recommended that the trial be ended early based on an increased breast cancer risk.]

This case concerns three lawsuits. The *Kirkland* suit was brought by 57 women who each alleged injuries resulting from their use of HRT medications. The *Kirkland* plaintiffs alleged they each developed breast cancer after taking HRT drugs that were manufactured, marketed, and sold by one or more of eleven manufacturers. Fourteen *Kirkland* plaintiffs are citizens of the same state as at least one of the manufacturers. Three of those fourteen plaintiffs asserted claims against manufacturers with the same citizenship. For example, Nancy States is a citizen of Pennsylvania, the same state as Wyeth Pharmaceuticals, Inc., a company that manufactured and marketed HRT drugs she took.

The *Jasperson* suit was brought by Rick Jasperson, as trustee of the next-of-kin of six decedents who used HRT drugs. The Jasperson plaintiffs alleged that in each case, the next-of-kin sustained injuries when a woman family member developed breast cancer as a result of taking HRT drugs that were manufactured, marketed, and sold by one or more of six defendants. One of the six decedents, Elizabeth Mendelson, was a citizen of New Jersey, the same state as Pharmacia Corporation, Wyeth, and Pharmacia & Upjohn Company, companies that manufactured and marketed HRT drugs that Mendelson took.

The *Allen* suit was brought by 60 women who also alleged they each developed breast cancer as a result of HRT medications manufactured, marketed, and sold by one or more of eight defendants. Five *Allen* plaintiffs are citizens of the same state as at least one of the defendants. Three of these five plaintiffs asserted claims against manufacturers who were citizens of the same state. For example, Rachel Epstein is a citizen of New York, the same state as Pfizer, a company that manufactured and marketed HRT drugs that she took. . . .

The *Kirkland, Jasperson,* and *Allen* plaintiffs filed suits for damages in Minnesota state court in July 2008. . . . The plaintiffs asserted state law claims for negligence, strict liability, breach of implied warranty, breach of express warranty, fraud, negligent misrepresentation, and statutory violations of [various Minnesota consumer-protection acts].

The manufacturers removed all three cases to the United States District Court for the District of Minnesota. In the manufacturers' removal petitions, they argued diversity jurisdiction existed under the fraudulent misjoinder doctrine. They alleged that the plaintiffs joined their claims together against the manufacturers to defeat diversity jurisdiction. The manufacturers argued that the plaintiffs' claims were fraudulently misjoined, stating that those claims did not arise out of the same transaction or occurrence, a requirement for joinder under Federal Rule of Civil Procedure 20(a).

The plaintiffs filed motions to remand the cases to state court for lack of subject matter jurisdiction, asserting that complete diversity between the plaintiffs and defendants did not exist. Before the plaintiffs' motions were addressed, the litigation came before the United States Judicial Panel on Multidistrict Litigation ("MDL"). The *Kirkland* and *Jasperson* cases were transferred to the Eastern District of Arkansas and assigned to an MDL judge. Plaintiffs requested that the MDL court rule on their pending motions to remand to state court. . . .

On December 29, 2008, . . .the court denied in part plaintiffs' motions to remand the *Kirkland* and *Jasperson* cases to state court, concluding that the plaintiffs were misjoined. The court stated that there was no reason for the joinder of the non-diverse plaintiffs other than to defeat diversity jurisdiction . . . The court concluded that the plaintiffs had failed to properly join under Rule 20 because "[t]he only thing common among Plaintiffs is that they took an HRT drug-but not necessarily the same HRT drug. Plaintiffs are residents of different states and were prescribed different HRT drugs by different doctors, for different lengths of time, in different amounts, and they suffered different injuries."

The court granted four of the *Kirkland* and *Jasperson* plaintiffs' motions to remand because those plaintiffs had asserted claims against a defendant who was from the same state. The court denied 59 *Kirkland* and *Jasperson* plaintiffs' motions to remand because the plaintiffs were not asserting claims against manufacturers from the same state. The court granted the manufacturers' motions to dismiss as to these 59 plaintiffs. The court dropped the 59 plaintiffs from the lawsuit and dismissed their claims, because they duplicated previously-filed California claims. . . .

In February 2009, the United States Judicial Panel on MDL transferred the *Allen* case to the same MDL court for coordinated proceedings with other pending HRT cases. On February 10, 2009, plaintiffs refiled their motions to remand the *Allen* case to state court. The court denied the motions on that same day, stating that the plaintiffs were improperly joined under Rule 20 . . . . The court granted three of the *Allen* plaintiffs' motions to remand because those women had asserted claims against a manufacturer who was from the same state.   The court granted the manufacturers' motions to dismiss as to the remaining 57 plaintiffs . . . because of their duplicative cases. . . .

II. DISCUSSION

On appeal, the plaintiffs argue the district court erred in denying their motions to remand by applying a discredited theory known as "fraudulent misjoinder" when it concluded they were improperly joined to defeat diversity jurisdiction.

"We review the district court's denial of the remand motion de novo."

A defendant may remove a state law claim to federal court only if the action originally could have been filed there. Diversity jurisdiction under 28 U.S.C. § 1332 requires an amount in controversy greater than $75,000 and complete diversity of citizenship among the litigants. "Complete diversity of citizenship exists where no defendant holds citizenship in the same state where any plaintiff holds citizenship."

After removal, a plaintiff may move to remand the case to state court, and the case should be remanded if it appears that the district court lacks subject matter jurisdiction. 28 U.S.C. § 1447(c). The defendant bears the burden of establishing federal jurisdiction by a preponderance of the evidence. All doubts about federal jurisdiction should be resolved in favor of remand to state court.

Courts have long recognized fraudulent joinder as an exception to the complete diversity rule. Fraudulent joinder occurs when a plaintiff files a frivolous or illegitimate claim against a non-diverse defendant solely to prevent removal. When determining if a party has been fraudulently joined, a court considers whether there is any reasonable basis in fact or law to support a claim against a nondiverse defendant.

A more recent, somewhat different, and novel exception to the complete diversity rule is the fraudulent misjoinder doctrine which one appellate court and several district courts have adopted. Fraudulent misjoinder

> occurs when a plaintiff sues a diverse defendant in state court and joins a viable claim involving a nondiverse party, or a resident defendant, even though the plaintiff has no reasonable procedural basis to join them in one action because the claims bear no relation to each other. In such cases, some courts have concluded that diversity is not defeated where the claim that destroys diversity has "no real connection with the controversy" involving the claims that would qualify for diversity jurisdiction.

The Eleventh Circuit first considered and adopted the fraudulent misjoinder doctrine in *Tapscott v. MS Dealer Serv. Corp.*, 77 F.3d 1353, 1360 (11th Cir. 1996). *Tapscott* concerned a putative class action filed in Alabama state court. In the initial complaint, one Alabama plaintiff sued four defendants, one of whom was an Alabama resident. The first amended complaint added sixteen named plaintiffs and twenty-two named defendants. The plaintiffs then amended their complaint again, naming four additional plaintiffs, all Alabama residents, and three named defendants. One of those defendants, Lowe's Home Centers, was a North Carolina resident.

The initial complaint and first amended complaint alleged fraud violations arising from the sale of automobile service contracts. The second amended complaint alleged fraud violations arising from the sale of extended service contracts in connection with the sale of retail products. The result of the amended complaints and joinder under Rule 20 was to create two distinct groups of plaintiffs and defendants: the non-diverse "automobile class" and the diverse "merchant class."

Lowe's Home Centers removed the case to federal court and moved to sever the claims against it from the claims against the automobile class defendants. . . .

On appeal, the Eleventh Circuit Court of Appeals affirmed the district court's denial of the plaintiffs' motion to remand. The court held there was misjoinder under Rule 20 because there was "no real connection" between the two sets of alleged transactions. . . . The only similarity between the two classes was that both classes violated particular fraud provisions in the Alabama state code. The Eleventh Circuit cautioned that "mere misjoinder" is not fraudulent misjoinder. However, the plaintiffs' joinder of these two groups of unrelated defendants was "so egregious as to constitute fraudulent joinder." Therefore, the Eleventh Circuit reasoned that the district court did not err in concluding the plaintiffs attempted to defeat diversity jurisdiction by misjoinder.

Courts' reactions to *Tapscott* have been mixed. Some district courts have adopted the doctrine as a means of ensuring defendants their statutory right of removal to the federal courts and precluding plaintiffs from preventing removal to federal court.

Other courts have criticized *Tapscott*, arguing that questions of joinder under state law do not implicate federal subject matter jurisdiction, federal jurisdiction is to be narrowly construed, and the fraudulent misjoinder doctrine has created an unpredictable and complex jurisdictional rule.

. . . We make no judgment on the propriety of the doctrine in this case, and decline to either adopt or reject it at this time. Rather, on the record in this case, we conclude that even if we adopted the doctrine, the plaintiffs' alleged misjoinder in this case is not so egregious as to constitute fraudulent misjoinder.

Rule 20(a)(1), Federal Rules of Civil Procedure, allows multiple plaintiffs to join in a single action if (i) they assert claims "with respect to or arising out of the same transaction, occurrence, or series of transactions or occurrences;" and (ii) "any question of law or fact common to all plaintiffs will arise in the action."[6] In construing Rule 20, the Eighth Circuit has

---

6. Whether the federal or state rules on joinder apply has also received conflicting results post-*Tapscott*. . . . However, we decline to address this choice

provided a very broad definition for the term "transaction." As stated in *Mosley v. General Motors Corp.*, 497 F.2d 1330 (8th Cir. 1974):

> "Transaction" is a word of flexible meaning. It may comprehend a series of many occurrences, depending not so much upon the immediateness of their connection as upon their logical relationship. . . .

Id. at 1333; *see also* 7 CHARLES A. WRIGHT ET AL., FEDERAL PRACTICE AND PROCEDURE § 1653, at 415 (3d ed. 2001) (explaining that the transaction/ occurrence requirement prescribed by Rule 20(a) is not a rigid test and is meant to be "read as broadly as possible whenever doing so is likely to promote judicial economy.").

After considering the Rule 20 joinder standards, we conclude that the manufacturers have not met their burden of establishing that plaintiffs' claims are egregiously misjoined. Plaintiffs' claims arise from a series of transactions between HRT pharmaceutical manufacturers and individuals that have used HRT drugs. Plaintiffs allege the manufacturers conducted a national sales and marketing campaign to falsely promote the safety and benefits of HRT drugs and understated the risks of HRT drugs. Plaintiffs contend their claims are logically related because they each developed breast cancer as a result of the manufacturers' negligence in designing, manufacturing, testing, advertising, warning, marketing, and selling HRT drugs. Some of the plaintiffs allege to have taken several HRT drugs made by different manufacturers.

Furthermore, given the nature of the plaintiffs' claims, this litigation is likely to contain common questions of law and fact. . . . One such common question might be the causal link between HRT drugs and breast cancer. Causation for all of the plaintiffs' claims will likely focus on the 2002 WHI study suggesting a link between HRT drugs and breast cancer and whether the manufacturers knew of the dangers of HRT drugs before the publication of that study.

Based on the plaintiffs' complaints, we cannot say that their claims have "no real connection" to each other such that they are egregiously misjoined. *See Tapscott*, 77 F.3d at 1371. This is unlike *Tapscott* where the alleged transactions concerning the automobile class were wholly distinct from the transactions involving the merchant class and there was "no real connection" between the two sets of transactions. Here, there may be a palpable connection between the plaintiffs' claims against the manufacturers as they all relate to similar drugs and injuries and the manufacturers' knowledge of the risks of HRT drugs.

Furthermore, the manufacturers have presented no evidence that the plaintiffs joined their claims to avoid diversity jurisdiction. . . . Without any evidence that the plaintiffs acted with bad faith, we decline to conclude they egregiously misjoined their claims.

of law issue because the standards for joinder under Fed. R. Civ. P. 20 and Minn. R. Civ. P. 20.01 are identical in all significant respects, and application of the state joinder rules does not affect our analysis. Therefore, for purposes of this case only, we apply the federal rules in addressing the misjoinder allegation.

We clarify that we make no judgment on whether the plaintiffs' claims are properly joined under Rule 20. It may be that the plaintiffs' claims are not properly joined, and it has been suggested that the proper procedure may be for the manufacturers to argue that to the state court.[8] However, it is not clear that the joinder is so egregious and grossly improper under the broadly-interpreted joinder standards that it warrants an adoption and application of the fraudulent misjoinder doctrine. Therefore, absent evidence that plaintiffs' misjoinder borders on a "sham," *see Tapscott*, 77 F.3d at 1360, we decline to apply *Tapscott* to the present case.

III. CONCLUSION

. . . We reverse the district court's orders and judgments granting in part and denying in part plaintiffs' motions to remand to state court and instruct the district court to remand all of the cases to Minnesota state court for lack of diversity jurisdiction. Because the district court lacked jurisdiction to act in this matter, we also vacate the district court's orders granting the manufacturers' motions to dismiss the duplicative cases.

IN RE AVANDIA MARKETING, SALES PRACTICES AND PRODUCTS LIABILITY LITIGATION

2008 WL 2078917 (E.D.Pa. May 14, 2008)

■ RUFE, District Judge.

Presently before the Court is the procedural issue whether to permit multiple, unrelated plaintiffs to file a single complaint in this MDL ["multidistrict litigation" — ED.], provided the plaintiffs seeking to make such a consolidated filing are domiciled in the same federal judicial district. Counsel for the parties have briefed the question and have addressed it in oral argument on May 9, 2008, and the matter is ready for decision without prejudice.

Under Federal Rule of Civil Procedure 20(a)(1), "[p]ersons may join in one action as plaintiffs if: (A) they assert any right to relief . . . with respect to or arising out of the same transaction, occurrence or series of transactions or occurrences; and (B) any question of law or fact common to all plaintiffs will arise in the action." Courts charged with managing multi-district litigation have, in the preliminary discovery stages of such cases, and in a provisional fashion, taken a rather expansive view of the conditions that would justify joinder, and have permitted joinder of plaintiffs domiciled in the same jurisdiction for the purpose of consolidated filing in the interest of court efficiency and limiting expense and inconvenience to parties. As plaintiffs' counsel have argued, in this case,

---

8. Considering the uncertainty surrounding the propriety of the joinder of plaintiffs' claims, the preferable course of action may have been for defendants to challenge the misjoinder in state court before it sought removal.

to permit consolidated filings by plaintiffs domiciled in the same jurisdiction, at least during the early stages of fact discovery, would appear to promote the aim of "conserv[ing] the resources of the parties, their counsel and the judiciary" which this MDL was in part centralized to accomplish. The decision to provisionally and for a limited purpose permit joinder will be evaluated in the near future to determine whether "such joinder proves to be inefficient or prejudicial to any parties;" if such is found to be the case, a corrective order may issue. . . .

[Therefore,] [m]ulti-party complaints including multiple, unrelated personal injury plaintiffs who each are domiciled in the same federal judicial district shall be permitted. This ruling is made without prejudice.

. . . Unrelated plaintiffs domiciled in different federal judicial districts shall not be permitted to jointly file a single complaint. Except for the first-named plaintiff, each plaintiff (and his or her derivative claimants, if any) named in a complaint currently pending or subsequently filed in, or transferred or removed to, this MDL which includes multiple, unrelated plaintiffs domiciled in different federal judicial districts shall be severed from the complaint, pursuant to Fed.R.Civ.P. 21 . . . .

. . . Multi-plaintiff actions permitted by this Order shall not be deemed joined for trial absent a Court order issued after duly-noticed motion filed by plaintiff's counsel.

Notes

1.   Consider as well the following three cases. First, in *In re Silica Products Liability Litigation*, 398 F. Supp. 2d 563 (S.D. Tex. 2005), cases ranging from 1 plaintiff to 4,280 plaintiffs, and from 6 defendants to 134 defendants, were filed in state court. Most of the cases involved some non-diverse plaintiffs and defendants on each side of the case. The defendants removed to federal court. Accepting *arguendo* the "fraudulent joinder" principle, the court severed the cases of plaintiffs whose injuries arose from distinct exposures to silica in different lines of work. But the court refused to find that each plaintiff's joinder of the non-diverse defendants was egregious. As a result, it remanded most cases to state court. Second, in *In re Orthopedic Bone Screw Products Liability Litigation*, 1995 WL 428683 (E.D. Pa. July 17, 1995), the court permitted plaintiffs to join under Rule 20 as long as each joined plaintiff received a medical device made by the same manufacturer at the same medical facility. Acknowledging that Rule 20(a) should be read liberally to promote judicial economy and efficiency, the court nonetheless thought that Rule 20(a) "requires at a minimum that the central facts of each plaintiff's claim arise on a somewhat individualized basis out of the same set of circumstances." *Id.* at *2. Third, in *In re Norplant Contraceptive Prods. Liab. Litig.*, 168 F.R.D. 579 (E.D. Tex. 1996) the judge rejected the joinder limitations imposed in *Bone Screw*, but did require that every plaintiff in a given case be represented by the same lawyer and also have received the medical device in the same state.

One way to think about the results in cases like *Prempro, Avandia, Bone Screw, Silica Products,* and *Norplant* is to ask what the court was trying to accomplish. In some cases, the issue is subject-matter jurisdiction. If a court is trying to capture the economies of scale from aggregation in a single federal forum, treating the claims as improperly joined under Rule 20(a) overcomes the jurisdiction-frustrating joinder decisions of some plaintiffs' lawyers. In other cases, the issue is how best to resolve a large number of claims over which a court has subject-matter jurisdiction. As long as keeping the cases together holds out the promise of a more efficient resolution, there is a reason to treat the plaintiffs' claims as closely enough related to meet the terms of Rule 20(a)(1).

Does this explanation make sense? If so, it proves a point that *Mosley* made (*supra* pp. 62-63): that the "transaction or occurrence" and "common question" requirements of Rule 20(a) are flexible in meaning. It also proves a point that we made (*supra* p. 35): that courts, when confronted by cases that they regard as complex, fashion doctrine to achieve the resolution that they regard as appropriate on the facts. Of course, the result in *Prempro* serves as a reminder that flexibility in fashioning doctrines applicable to complex cases is not unlimited.

2.   Rule 20(a) concerns not only the joinder of plaintiffs (Rule 20(a)(1)) but also the joinder of defendants (Rule 20(a)(2)). Cases discussing the scope of the "transaction or occurrence" and "common question" requirements in the context of joining defendants are not common, but neither are they rare. When analyzing the plaintiffs' joinder of defendants, courts sometimes appear to show heightened sensitivity to the possible unfairness that the plaintiffs' joinder choice might cause the defendants. *See* Intercon Research Assocs., Ltd. v. Dresser Indus., Inc., 696 F.2d 53 (7th Cir. 1982); Desert Empire Bank v. Ins. Co. of N. Am., 623 F.2d 1371, 1375 (9th Cir. 1980); *cf.* Sprint Comms. Co. v. Theglobe.com, Inc, 233 F.R.D. 615, 617 (D. Kan. 2006) (stating that joinder of competitors was not "inherently unfair" when their joinder advanced the efficient disposition of the case). Cases never explicitly state, however, that Rule 20(a)(2) imposes a heightened standard of fairness.

3.   One of the principal ways in which plaintiffs attempt to increase their chances of winning is to choose the most hospitable court for their claims. In *Prempro,* for instance, the plaintiffs evidently believed that their best forum was Minnesota state court. They tried to structure their case to avoid federal court; in particular, they used Minnesota's joinder rules to join non-diverse plaintiffs and defendants that they hoped (correctly, for the most part) would avoid federal diversity jurisdiction. We examine the details of federal subject-matter jurisdiction in the next chapter. But it should be evident that in the real world the rules of joinder and those of subject-matter jurisdiction fit hand in glove, and that clever plaintiffs can often use the combination of these rules to obtain the best forum from their viewpoint — even if, from the viewpoint of efficiently resolving disputes, that choice of forum is suboptimal.

4. As *Prempro* says, the doctrine of "fraudulent misjoinder" (sometimes called "procedural misjoinder") has divided the courts. *Prempro* shows some of the major issues with which courts are struggling: whether the doctrine exists; if so, what standard should apply to determine misjoinder (egregiousness or something less stringent); and whether Rule 20(a) or the comparable state rule of joinder is the relevant text for determining misjoinder. For an analysis of the varying positions on these issues, see Geffen v. Gen. Elec. Co., 575 F. Supp. 2d 865 (N.D. Ohio 2008).

5. In light of the ways in which plaintiffs can game joinder to achieve a favorable result, would it be better if judges had a sua sponte power to join parties when it served the interests of economy and efficiency? Rule 21 provides that, "on its own, the court may at any time . . . add or drop a party." How much power does this give a federal judge to reshape the case that the plaintiff(s) have created? There is surprisingly little authority on the issue. Most cases decided under Rule 21 involve dropping, rather than adding, parties. A judge can drop parties only when their joinder violates the relevant joinder rules or the complaint states no claim against them; Rule 21 creates no roving commission to prune a case to its most efficient package. *See* 7 CHARLES ALAN WRIGHT ET AL., FEDERAL PRACTICE AND PROCEDURE § 1683 (3d ed. 2001).

Among the cases involving the addition of parties, nearly all involve motions made by existing parties rather than sua sponte orders of the court. It is fairly clear that a federal court can on its own require the joinder of a real party in interest under Rule 17 or a party whose joinder is required under Rule 19(a). *Id.* § 1687. But joinder under these rules is limited, and Rule 21 serves simply as the vehicle by which their requirements can be enforced. The critical issue is whether a federal court can add parties that the plaintiff(s) declined (or were unable) to join when the court believes that joinder would yield a fairer or more efficient litigation unit. In *Lanehart v. Devine*, 102 F.R.D. 592 (D. Md. 1984), a court added 550 plaintiffs that, but for amount of damages, were identically situated to the original seven plaintiffs. In *Lanehart*, however, the original plaintiffs requested the joinder, and it appears that the additional plaintiffs might have consented to join. In *Du Shane v. Conlisk*, 583 F.2d 965 (7th Cir. 1978), a court of appeals affirmed the sua sponte post-trial joinder of a new party whose presence was necessary to provide the plaintiff with the relief to which he was entitled. Because the joined party was a required party under Rule 19(a), *Du Shane* appears to create no general power of judicial joinder. *Du Shane* is nonetheless significant for its citation to the All Writs Act, 28 U.S.C. § 1651, as support for the district court's decision. The Act, which provides federal courts with a power to issue "issue all writs necessary or appropriate in aid of their respective jurisdictions," could arguably serve as a basis for a broad judicial-joinder power. *Cf.* City of Syracuse v. Onondaga County, 464 F.3d 297 (2d Cir. 2006) (holding that the district court had power under Rules 19 and 21 to grant a motion seeking the joinder of an additional party; declining to decide the scope of the joinder power under the All Writs Act). In this book you will have numerous opportunities to consider the breadth of the All Writs power in complex litigation; suffice it to say for now that its precise contours are unclear, but it creates no "wild card" power for judges to do whatever they wish in complex cases. Nor has it yet been used to create a roving judicial-joinder power.

The most analogous case takes a dim view of a sua sponte joinder power under Rule 21. In *Pan American World Airways, Inc. v. United States District Court for the Central District of California*, 523 F.2d 1073 (9th Cir. 1975), a district judge before whom a number of airplane-crash cases was pending ordered that notice of the lawsuits be given to the personal representatives of all crash victims. Notice was not the same as joinder, but the judge hoped that the notice would induce the estates of other victims to file suit in his court. The airline refused to provide the passenger lists, and sought a writ of mandamus. The court of appeals found that Rule 21 did not give the judge the power to order notice. The court noted that Rule 21 "incorporate[s] standards to be found elsewhere. The only standards for proper joinder relevant to this case are Rules 19 and 20." It first held that "Rule 19 is inapplicable." Next, although acknowledging that "Rule 21 has been used to join potential plaintiffs who meet the requirements of Rule 20 and who subsequently consent to be joined," the court held that Rule 21 could not be used in a way that "will effectively transform the present action into an [unwieldy] pseudo-class-action not authorized by Rule 23" and "circumvent the requirements of that rule." 523 F.2d at 1079-80.

2. Expanding the Lawsuit

Although plaintiff(s) establish the basic claim and party structure, defendants and the court have limited powers to expand on the choices that the plaintiff(s) have made. In this section, we explore those powers. Once again, the basic issue is the same: To what extent do the rules establishing the litigation structure require, or at least provide incentives for, packaging complex litigation in its fairest and most efficient way?

a. Counterclaims, Crossclaims, and Third-Party Claims

Defendants have some power to assert new claims and to add new parties to the litigation. Although the power is limited, in some cases its use can significantly complicate the litigation.

LASA PER L'INDUSTRIA DEL MARMO SOCIETÀ PER AZIONI OF LASA, ITALY V. ALEXANDER

414 F.2d 143 (6th Cir. 1969)

■ PHILLIPS, Circuit Judge.

It has been said that the doctrine of ancillary jurisdiction providing for joinder of claims in the federal courts is "the child of necessity and the sire of confusion." The confusion in pleadings that can arise out of cross-claims, counterclaims and a third-party complaint, all involving the same construction project, is demonstrated by the present appeal.

The complicated procedural problems with which we are confronted arose out of the building of a new City Hall at Memphis, Tennessee.

The complaint was filed by an Italian corporation which had a contract with a subcontractor to furnish marble for the City Hall. Recovery is sought against the subcontractor, the prime contractor, its surety, and the City of Memphis for a balance alleged to be due for marble and labor.

Filed in the action were a series of counterclaims, cross-claims and a third-party complaint which are described in detail in the opinion of the District Court.

[The following additional facts are taken verbatim from the dissenting opinion:

[The City of Memphis built a City Hall. Southern Builders, Inc. was the principal or prime contractor with the City for this project; and it furnished to the City a statutory bond for performance and payment of labor and materials. The surety in this bond was the Continental Casualty Company.

[Southern Builders, Inc., the above-named contractor for the building of the City Hall, then entered into a contract with Alexander Marble and Tile Company, under which Alexander was to supply all marble and anchoring devices, and install the marble used in the building.

[Alexander, the subcontractor, then entered into a contract with plaintiff- appellee, LASA Per L'Industria Del Marmo Società Per Azioni of Lasa, Italy, in which LASA agreed to supply to Alexander all of the marble specified at a certain contract price.

[LASA, alleging that the marble had been supplied as agreed, and that there was an unpaid balance of $127,240.80, filed a complaint against Alexander, with whom it had contracted to deliver the marble, Southern Builders, the principal contractor, Continental Casualty Company, the surety for the performance and payment of all labor and materials, and the City of Memphis.

[To the original complaint of LASA, Alexander filed an answer and counterclaim in which it contended that LASA had failed to ship the marble as agreed; that it had threatened to cease shipments; and that, under duress, the price had been greatly increased; that much of the marble arrived late, was broken, or of the wrong type, and that LASA had failed to ship all of the marble it was obligated to furnish. Alexander, by this counterclaim, sued LASA for overpayment of the contract price and for damages in the amount of $350,000 for failure to ship the marble as agreed.

[Furthermore, to the original complaint of LASA, the principal contractor, Southern Builders, and the surety for performance, Continental Casualty, filed answers and a counterclaim. They averred that Southern Builders was obligated to pay just and valid claims for labor and materials only, and that LASA had no such claims; that nothing was owed LASA for marble delivered and installed on the job. They denied that LASA had shipped the marble as agreed, and, by its counterclaim, Southern Builders sued LASA for its failure to ship the marble as agreed with the subcontractor, Alexander. Up to this point no question is raised with regard to the right of LASA to commence suit; with regard to the right of Alexander to file an answer and counterclaim against LASA; or with regard to the right of Southern Builders and Continental Casualty to file answers; and for Southern Builders to file its counterclaim against LASA for damages for failure to deliver the marble as it had agreed with Alexander.

[Now comes the pleading that gives rise to the controversy in this suit. After Alexander had filed its answer and counterclaim against LASA, and Southern Builders and Continental Casualty had filed answers, and Southern Builders had filed its counterclaim against LASA, Alexander filed a cross-claim against Southern Builders, Continental Casualty, and the City of Memphis. Further, Alexander filed a cross-claim against A. L. Aydelott and Associates, and against Aydelott individually. Aydelott was the architect for the City Hall. Upon the filing of Alexander's cross-claim against Southern Builders, Continental Casualty, and the City of Memphis, and its cross-claim against Aydelott, Southern Builders and Aydelott filed motions to dismiss such cross-claims; and the District Court . . . dismissed them; and, from the order of dismissal, Alexander appeals.

[In one count of its cross-claim against Southern Builders, Continental Casualty, and the City of Memphis, Alexander, claiming damages in the amount of $158,061.75, alleged that Southern Builders, upon the insistence of the architect, A. L. Aydelott, wrongfully hindered Alexander in the performance of the subcontract by failing properly to prepare the concrete base for the marble; by failing to install metal support angles; by insisting that Alexander work in inclement weather; by further insisting that Alexander install the marble in accordance with Aydelott's improper specifications; and by wrongfully refusing to pay over funds due to Alexander for work performed. Alexander further alleged, in a second count in his cross-claim, that Southern Builders, under the insistence of Aydelott, and, necessarily cooperating with him, wrongfully terminated the subcontract, wrongfully forced Alexander off the job altogether; brought in another subcontractor who was allowed to finish the job not in accordance with the specifications and at an inflated price, all of which was wrongfully charged to the account of Alexander. In the same count in its cross-claim against Southern Builders, Alexander alleged that Southern Builders and Aydelott wrongfully injured the business reputation of Alexander by publicly blaming Alexander for many ills not its fault, and which were the fault of Southern Builders and Aydelott. In this count, Alexander asked for an additional amount of $250,000 for punitive damages, or a total, claimed in its cross-claim, of $408,061.75 with interest and costs.

[Alexander further proceeded to file a third-party complaint — a cross-claim, as above mentioned, against the architect, A. L. Aydelott, claiming that Aydelott wrongfully and illegally induced Southern Builders to breach its contract with Alexander and, for such allegedly wrongful conduct, claimed from Aydelott treble damages in the amount of $750,000.]

. . . The third-party complaint was treated by the District Court as a cross-claim against the architect as was the counterclaim of the prime contractor against Alexander.

Construing Rules 13(g) and 13(h), Fed. R. Civ. P., the District Court dismissed the two cross-claims and the third-party complaint, holding that they do not arise out of the same transaction or occurrence that is the subject matter of the original action or of a counterclaim therein.

We reverse.

In the cross-claim of Alexander which was dismissed by the District Court, Alexander sues all cross-defendants for a balance of $158,061.75 alleged to be due under Alexander's subcontract with the prime contractor. In the second count of the same pleading Alexander sues the prime contractor for $250,000 in actual and punitive damages, averring that the prime contractor failed to prepare properly the concrete base upon which marble pieces were to be affixed and to install correct metal support angles in the concrete base; that the prime contractor required Alexander to work on marble installation in the most inclement cold and rainy weather, contrary to specifications; that the prime contractor terminated Alexander's subcontract without justification and brought in a new subcontractor at a highly inflated price, the cost of which was charged wrongfully to Alexander; and that the prime contractor damaged Alexander's business reputation and publicly blamed Alexander for many ills which were the fault of the prime contractor or the architect.

In its third-party complaint against the architect, treated by the District Court as a cross-claim under Rule 13(h) . . . , Alexander sued the architect for actual and punitive damages, alleging that the architect negligently provided improper specifications and insisted that they be followed; negligently failed to require the prime contractor to perform its work properly; wrongfully directed Alexander to install marble in inclement weather; willfully refused to approve Alexander's estimates for work done; influenced the prime contractor to terminate Alexander's subcontract and to bring in a new subcontractor at an inflated price and with preferred treatment through modified specifications; and wrongfully and maliciously injured Alexander's business reputation.

The prime contractor's cross-claim against Alexander, which also was dismissed by the District Court, seeks to hold Alexander liable for unliquidated damages for delays, faulty materials and workmanship and the failure of Alexander generally to conform to specifications. The count of the cross-claim of the prime contractor for indemnity against Alexander in the event of judgment for the plaintiff against the prime contractor was not dismissed.

After the dismissal of these claims there remain in the case now pending in the District Court the amended complaint, the answer and counterclaim of Alexander, the answer and counterclaim of the prime contractor, and the answer of the surety and the cross-claim by the prime contractor against Alexander for indemnity. Trial on these pleadings has been delayed pending disposition of the present appeal.

Under the Federal Rules of Civil Procedure the rights of all parties generally should be adjudicated in one action. Rules 13 and 14 are remedial and are construed liberally. Both Rules 13 and 14 are "intended to avoid circuity of action and to dispose of the entire subject matter arising from one set of facts in one action, thus administering complete and evenhanded justice expeditiously and economically." The aim of these rules "is facilitation not frustration of decisions on the merits." . . .

The District Court held that no part of Alexander's cross-claim against the prime contractor, his third-party complaint against the architect or of the prime contractor's cross-claim against Alexander for breach of contract arose out of the transaction or occurrence that is the subject matter of the original action or the two counterclaims. With deference to the well-written opinion of the District Judge, we disagree.

In 1A BARRON & HOLTZOFF, FEDERAL PRACTICE & PROCEDURE (Wright ed.) § 424, at 653, the rule is stated as follows:

> It is the theory of the rule that the defendant's right against the third party is merely the outgrowth of the same aggregate or core of facts which is determinative of the plaintiff's claim. In this view, the court which has jurisdiction over the aggregate of facts which constitutes the plaintiff's claim needs no additional ground of jurisdiction to determine the third-party claim which comprises the same core of facts. It is in this sense that the court is said to have ancillary jurisdiction over the third-party claim.

In *Moore v. N. Y. Cotton Exchange*, 270 U.S. 593, 609-610 (1926), the Supreme Court construed the words "arising out of the transaction which is the subject matter of the suit" in Equity Rule 30, precursor of Rule 13, Fed. R. Civ. P. The Court said:

> "Transaction" is a word of flexible meaning. It may comprehend a series of many occurrences, depending not so much upon the immediateness of their connection as upon their logical relationship.

The words "transaction or occurrence" are given a broad and liberal interpretation in order to avoid a multiplicity of suits.

Our reading of the pleadings in this case convinces us that there is a "logical relationship" between the cross-claims (including the third party complaint against the architect) and the "transaction or occurrence" that is the subject matter of the complaint and the two pending counterclaims. Although different subcontracts are involved, along with the prime contract and specifications, all relate to the same project and to problems arising out of the marble used in the erection of the Memphis City Hall. The recurring question presented by the various pleadings is directed to the principal issue of who is responsible for the marble problems which arose on this job. Blame is sought to be placed upon plaintiff as furnisher of the marble, upon Alexander as subcontractor, upon the prime contractor and upon the architect. Many of the same or closely related factual and legal issues necessarily will be presented under the complaint, counterclaims and cross-claims in the resolution of these issues. It seems apparent that some of the same evidence will be required in the hearing on the cross-claims and in the hearing or hearings with respect to the complaint and the two pending counterclaims.

We understand it to be the purpose of Rule 13 and the related rules that all such matters may be tried and determined in one action and to make it possible for the parties to avoid multiplicity of litigation. The intent of the rules is that all issues be resolved in one action, with all parties before one court, complex though the action may be.

In support of the decision of the District Court it is argued that, since a jury trial has been demanded, the complications and confusions of the cross-claims are such that it would be impossible to try the numerous issues before the jury in an orderly manner. The short answer to this contention is that the District Judge is authorized by Rule 42(b) to order separate trials on any cross-claim, counterclaim, other claim or issues. If on the trial of this case the District Court concludes that separate trials on one or more of the counterclaims, cross-claims or issues would be conducive to expedition and economy, Rule 42(b) provides a practical solution to this problem.

Reversed and remanded for further proceedings not inconsistent with this opinion.

■ McALLISTER, Senior Circuit Judge (dissenting). . . .

The proofs in LASA's suit and in Alexander's and Southern Builders' counterclaims against LASA would be entirely different from the proofs in Alexander's cross-claim against Southern Builders and its cross-claim against Aydelott.

The proofs in LASA's suit would consist of evidence showing a balance due on the contract to deliver marble. The proofs in Alexander's counterclaims and Southern Builders' counterclaims against LASA would consist of evidence showing breach of LASA's contract to deliver the marble. . . .

The proofs in Alexander's cross-claim against Southern Builders and Aydelott would consist of evidence of repeated, malicious, wrongful conduct in terminating Alexander's contract, and in forcing Alexander off the job and maliciously ruining its business reputation by abuse, harassment, and public blame.

The proofs in Alexander's cross-claim against Aydelott would consist only of evidence that Aydelott wrongfully and maliciously ruined Alexander's business reputation. . . .

The legal issue in the original claim filed by LASA is: Whether the contract is valid, and whether, under the contract, there is a balance due. The counterclaims of Alexander and Southern Builders are based on breach of contract by LASA. The only issue with regard to LASA's obligations under its agreement with Alexander and with regard to its breach of the agreement set forth in the counterclaims is determinable by the law of contract.

The only legal issue in Alexander's cross-claim against Southern Builders and its third-party claim against the architect, Aydelott, is whether Southern Builders and Aydelott are guilty of malicious, wrongful conduct which resulted in damages to Alexander. This issue is determinable by the law of torts.

There is, therefore, no identity of legal issues in the original claims of LASA and Alexander's and Southern Builders' counterclaims — all founded on contract and breach of contract — and Alexander's cross-claim against Southern Builders and its third-party claim against Aydelott — all founded in tort.

Notes

1. The complicated facts of this case work best if we imagine LASA as a wizened Italian stonecutter, suddenly thrown into a "who shot John" maelstrom over the City Hall fiasco. All the old stonecutter wants is his money, yet the operation of Rules 13(a), 13(g), 13(h), and 14(a) makes him slug it out in a multiparty affair in which, for the most part, he has no interest. And his legal fees mount by the day. Unfortunately, the facts generate less sympathy for LASA. LASA was a large corporation employing modern methods to hew its desirable marble from the ground. Nonetheless, the bevy of counterclaims, crossclaims, and third-party claims in *LASA* make a valuable point. There is a danger that the litigation's tail will wag the dog, and there is a chance that simple cases will turn into complex ones that expand beyond the means or the objectives of the original litigants.

2. Counterclaims and crossclaims do not necessarily add new parties to the case; they assert claims against those already parties. Counterclaims assert claims against opposing parties, and crossclaims assert claims against coparties. But Rule 13(h) allows the party asserting a counterclaim or crossclaim (typically, a defendant) the joinder of additional parties to the counterclaim or crossclaim, as long as the joinder meets the terms of either Rule 19 (*see infra* p. 91) or Rule 20 (*see supra* p. 60).

In contrast, a third-party claim involves the assertion of a claim against a nonparty, *see* Fed. R. Civ. P. 14(a)(1), and this nonparty (now called the "third-party defendant") can now assert claims either against existing parties or another nonparty (often called a "fourth-party defendant"), *see* Fed. R. Civ. P. 14(a)(2), -(3), -(5).

3. The circumstances under which a party can assert a counterclaim, a crossclaim, and a third-party claim differ, and the preclusive effect of failing to assert them also differ.

(a) Counterclaims come in two flavors: compulsory and permissive. Aside from a couple of exceptions mentioned in Rule 13(a)(2), parties "must" assert compulsory counterclaims, which "arise[ ] out of the transaction or occurrence that is the subject matter of the opposing party's claim" and do not require the joinder of a third party over whom the court lacks jurisdiction. *See* Fed. R. Civ. P. 13(a)(1). Rule 13(a) does not in words state the consequence to a party that fails to assert a compulsory counterclaim, but the common-law "compulsory counterclaim rule" dictates that the party will be barred from ever bringing the claim in future litigation. In contrast, a party "may" assert a permissive counterclaim, which is "any claim that is not compulsory." *See* Fed. R. Civ. P. 13(b). If the party fails to assert such a claim, the party is not precluded from bringing it in a later case.

Given the difference in preclusive effect, it is important to know whether a counterclaim is compulsory or permissive. As with Rule 20(a), Rule 13(a) uses the phrase "transaction or occurrence" to define compulsory counterclaims. Interpreting the meaning of this phrase in Rule 13(a) poses the same issues as it did in Rule 20(a); and for the most part, courts have cashed out the meaning in a similar way. Indeed, *Moore v. New York Cotton Exchange*, 270 U.S. 593 (1926), which *Mosley* cited to determine the meaning of "transaction or occurrence" in Rule 20(a) (*see supra* p. 62), was a case involving the counterclaim rule that was the precursor to Rule 13(a). *Moore*'s held that the "transaction" requirement is met when there exists a "logical relationship" between the original claim and counterclaim, *see* 270 U.S. at 610; this latter phrase has in turn been understood to focus on the similarity of the evidence between the claims and the efficiency that could be achieved from joint handling of the claims. *See* Peter Farrell Supercars, Inc. v. Monsen, 82 Fed. Appx. 293 (4th Cir. 2003); *In re* Price, 42 F.3d 1068, 1073 (7th Cir. 1994); 6 CHARLES ALAN WRIGHT ET AL., FEDERAL PRACTICE AND PROCEDURE § 1410 (2d ed. 1990).

(b) With respect to crossclaims, a party "may" assert those claims that "arise[ ] out of the transaction or occurrence that is the subject matter of the original action or of a counterclaim." The "transaction or occurrence" language is the same as that of Rules 13(a) and 20(a), and, as *LASA* shows, it has generally been interpreted with comparable liberality when inclusion of the crossclaim advances the fair and efficient disposition of the dispute. *See* 6 WRIGHT ET AL., *supra*, § 1432. Rule 13(g), however, differs in one significant regard from Rule 13(a): The standard view is that, in light of Rule 13(g)'s use of the word "may," a party who fails to assert a crossclaim does not lose the right to assert such a claim in future litigation. *Id.* § 1431.

(c) Third-party claims, which allow the defendant to add a new party, have a standard that is more restrictive than "transaction or occurrence": The claim must allege that the third-party defendant "is or may be liable to" the defendant for any liability that the defendant owes on a claim. As in *LASA*, third-party practice generally involves claims for indemnity or contribution. Within this parameter, as with joinder of parties under Rules 20(a) and counterclaims and crossclaims under Rules 13(a), (b), and (g), courts permit impleader under Rule 14(a) with liberality and with an eye toward the economical and expeditious resolution of disputes. *Id.* § 1442. Nonetheless, the decision whether to take advantage of this opportunity remains with the defendant. Under Rule 14(a), defendants "may" assert third-party claims; like crossclaims, no preclusive effect attaches against a defendant that chooses to assert the indemnity or contribution claim in a separate lawsuit. *Id.* § 1446.

4. *LASA* speaks of "ancillary jurisdiction" over the crossclaim at issue in the case. This doctrine jurisdiction deals with the following situation: Suppose that a federal court has subject-matter jurisdiction over the original claim(s) filed in the case but would not have jurisdiction over the counterclaim, crossclaim, or third-party claim if it had been brought as a separate suit.   Does the court have subject-matter jurisdiction over counterclaim, crossclaim, or third-party claim because it is "ancillary" to a claim lying within federal jurisdiction. The traditional answer was "yes," as long as a logical relationship existed between the jurisdiction-satisfying original claim(s) and jurisdictionally insufficient ancillary claim(s).   In a rough sense, this rule meant that compulsory counterclaims, crossclaims, and third-party claims fell within federal jurisdiction; permissive counterclaims did not.

Today, ancillary jurisdiction is a part of the doctrine known as "supplemental jurisdiction," which is codified at 28 U.S.C. § 1367. We briefly examine § 1367 in the next chapter. *See infra* pp. 294-95.

5. Once a claim is properly stated under Rules 13(a), 13(b), 13(g), or 14(a), the party asserting the claim can then assert any other claim — whether related or unrelated — against an opposing party. Fed. R. Civ. P. 18(a); Lehman v. Revolution Portfolio LLC, 166 F.3d 389 (1st Cir. 1999).

6. Despite the apparent ability of parties to file just about any type of counterclaim, crossclaim, or third-party claim, Rules 13 and 14 have a couple of gaps that do not permit in express language the assertion of some types of claims that parties in unique circumstances might wish to assert. One example is the failure of Rules 13 and 14 to provide for a third-party defendant's assertion of a crossclaim against the original defendant. As a general matter, courts have allowed the assertion of such claims; they appeal to the liberal spirit of the joinder rules that avoids the "strained" and "nonsensical" result a literal reading of the Rules might require. Thomas v. Barton Lodge II, Ltd., 174 F.3d 636, 652 (5th Cir. 1999); *but see* Asher v. Unarco Material Handling, Inc., 2008 WL 130858 (E.D. Ky. Jan. 10, 2008) (not permitting an original defendant to assert a crossclaim against a third-party defendant brought into the litigation by another defendant).

7. Thematically, this section shows that the assertion of claims under Rules 13 and 14 can make a case more complicated; that the goal of obtaining the fair and efficient resolution of cases runs throughout the joinder rules; and that, for the most part, achieving this goal relies on the defendant(s) — whose self-interest will not always lead to the realization of the goal. Moreover, it shows that, despite the power of defendant(s) to reshape the case to some degree, each plaintiff's power to establish the structure of his or her lawsuit remains preeminent.   In the following sections, we explore other limitations on this power.

b. Interpleader

Interpleader developed at law and in equity to handle a specific problem. Suppose that a person possessed a tangible thing (like property or money) to which other persons claimed title. The person holding the thing (the "stakeholder") claimed no interest in it, but faced the unhappy prospect that each of the individuals who claimed title would separately sue the stakeholder at common law for the thing (or its monetary equivalent). Even if the first claimant won the first lawsuit, the second claimant was not bound by that judgment, and could still sue the stakeholder. Thus, the stakeholder faced the prospect of multiple judgments — even though, as a matter of logic, the stakeholder was responsible to only one claimant. Building on a modest common-law remedy, equity created a more general remedy that allowed a stakeholder to sue (or "interplead") all interested parties in one suit. These parties then litigated their entitlement to the thing, and the decree deciding ownership bound all the joined parties.

Although interpleader has been liberalized in various ways over the years, this basic concept remains the heart of interpleader. In most cases, interpleader turns the tables, and allows the underlying defendant (the stakeholder) in the dispute to join preemptively all potential plaintiffs. The stakeholder makes a voluntary decision whether to interplead potential plaintiffs and which potential plaintiffs to interplead; the stakeholder cannot be forced to interplead, or to interplead everyone with an interest in the case. Nonetheless, because the decree cannot bind claimants that the stakeholder does not join, the stakeholder had an obvious incentive to interplead all claimants. Thus, interpleader presents an intriguing opportunity to attain the complete and efficient adjudication of an entire controversy in a single suit, even as it carves an exception into the usual principle that plaintiffs are masters of their own complaints.

There are two distinct forms of interpleader: rule interpleader under Federal Rule 22 and statutory interplader under 28 U.S.C. §§ 1335 and 2361. The following case, involving statutory interpleader, shows both the promise and the limits of interpleader as an aggregation device.

STATE FARM FIRE & CASUALTY CO. V. TASHIRE

386 U.S. 523 (1967)

■ MR. JUSTICE FORTAS delivered the opinion of the Court.

[A Greyhound bus collided with a pickup truck driven by Ellis Clark and owned by Kenneth Glasgow, who was a passenger in the truck. The accident killed two passengers on the bus and injured thirty-three; most were American, and 11 were Canadians. The accident occurred in Shasta County, California. Greyhound was a California corporation. Clark, Glasgow, and the bus driver were residents of Oregon. Clark had a $20,000 automobile-insurance policy, issued by State Farm, an Illinois corporation.

[Four passengers filed suit in California state court against Greyhound, Clark, Glasgow, and the bus driver. State Farm filed an action in the nature of interpleader in a federal court in the District of Oregon, paying the $20,000 proceeds of the policy into the court and joining as defendants Greyhound, Clark, Glasgow, the bus driver, and all of the bus's passengers.

[The district court then exercised its powers under 28 U.S.C. § 2361 and enjoined prosecution of further proceedings against Clark and State Farm. Greyhound requested that the injunction be broadened to encompass actions brought against it or its driver. The court granted the request, although it still permitted the filing (but not the prosecution) of such cases in other courts. In effect, as long as it remained in force, the injunction pushed the litigation of all suits against Clark, State Farm, Greyhound, and Greyhound's driver into the interpleader proceeding.]

On interlocutory appeal, the Court of Appeals for the Ninth Circuit reversed. The court . . . concluded that interpleader was not available in the circumstances of this case. It held that in States like Oregon which do not permit "direct action" suits against insurance companies until judgments are obtained against the insured, the insurance companies may not invoke federal interpleader until the claims against the insured, the alleged tortfeasor, have been reduced to judgment. Until that is done, said the court, claimants with unliquidated tort claims are not "claimants" within the meaning of § 1335, nor are they "persons having claims against the plaintiff" within the meaning of Rule 22 of the Federal Rules of Civil Procedure.[3] In accord with that view, it directed dissolution of the temporary injunction and dismissal of the action. . . . Although we reverse the decision of the Court of Appeals upon the [§ 1335] question, we direct a substantial modification of the District Court's injunction for reasons which will appear.

I.

[The Court's held that 28 U.S.C. § 1335, which requires only minimal diversity in statutory interpleader, was constitutional.]

II.

We do not agree with the Court of Appeals that, in the absence of a state law or contractual provision for "direct action" suits against the

---

3. We need not pass upon the Court of Appeals' conclusions with respect to the interpretation of interpleader under Rule 22 . . . . First, as we indicate today, this action was properly brought under § 1335. Second, State Farm did not purport to invoke Rule 22. Third, State Farm could not have invoked it in light of venue and service of process limitations. Whereas statutory interpleader may be brought in the district where any claimant resides (28 U.S.C. § 1397), Rule interpleader based upon diversity of citizenship may be brought only in the district where all plaintiffs or all defendants reside (28 U.S.C. § 1391 (a)). And whereas statutory interpleader enables a plaintiff to employ nationwide service of process (28 U.S.C. § 2361), service of process under Rule 22 is confined to that provided in Rule 4. . . .

insurance company, the company must wait until persons asserting claims against its insured have reduced those claims to judgment before seeking to invoke the benefits of federal interpleader. That may have been a tenable position under the 1926 and 1936 interpleader statutes. These statutes did not carry forward the language in the 1917 Act authorizing interpleader where adverse claimants "may claim" benefits as well as where they "are claiming" them. In 1948, however, in the revision of the Judicial Code, the "may claim" language was restored. Until the decision below, every court confronted by the question has concluded that the 1948 revision removed whatever requirement there might previously have been that the insurance company wait until at least two claimants reduced their claims to judgments. The commentators are in accord.

Considerations of judicial administration demonstrate the soundness of this view which, in any event, seems compelled by the language of the present statute, which is remedial and to be liberally construed. Were an insurance company required to await reduction of claims to judgment, the first claimant to obtain such a judgment or to negotiate a settlement might appropriate all or a disproportionate slice of the fund before his fellow claimants were able to establish their claims. The difficulties such a race to judgment pose for the insurer, and the unfairness which may result to some claimants, were among the principal evils the interpleader device was intended to remedy.[15]

III.

The fact that State Farm had properly invoked the interpleader jurisdiction under § 1335 did not, however, entitle it to an order both enjoining prosecution of suits against it outside the confines of the interpleader proceeding and also extending such protection to its insured, the alleged tortfeasor. Still less was Greyhound Lines entitled to have that order expanded so as to protect itself and its driver, also alleged to be tortfeasors, from suits brought by its passengers in various state or federal courts. Here, the scope of the litigation, in terms of parties and claims, was vastly more extensive than the confines of the "fund," the deposited proceeds of the insurance policy. In these circumstances, the mere existence of such a fund cannot, by use of interpleader, be employed to accomplish purposes that exceed the needs of orderly contest with respect to the fund.

There are situations, of a type not present here, where the effect of interpleader is to confine the total litigation to a single forum and proceeding. One such case is where a stakeholder, faced with rival claims to the fund itself, acknowledges — or denies — his liability to one or the other of the claimants. In this situation, the fund itself is the target of the

---

15. The insurance problem envisioned at the time was that of an insurer faced with conflicting but mutually exclusive claims to a policy, rather than an insurer confronted with the problem of allocating a fund among various claimants whose independent claims may exceed the amount of the fund. . . .

claimants. It marks the outer limits of the controversy. It is, therefore, reasonable and sensible that interpleader, in discharge of its office to protect the fund, should also protect the stakeholder from vexatious and multiple litigation. In this context, the suits sought to be enjoined are squarely within the language of 28 U.S.C. § 2361, which provides in part:

> "In any civil action of interpleader or in the nature of interpleader under section 1335 of this title, a district court may issue its process for all claimants and enter its order restraining them from instituting or prosecuting *any proceeding* in any State or United States court *affecting the property, instrument or obligation involved in the interpleader action . . . .*" (Emphasis added.)

But the present case is another matter. Here, an accident has happened. Thirty-five passengers or their representatives have claims which they wish to press against a variety of defendants: the bus company, its driver, the owner of the truck, and the truck driver. The circumstance that one of the prospective defendants happens to have an insurance policy is a fortuitous event which should not of itself shape the nature of the ensuing litigation. For example, a resident of California, injured in California aboard a bus owned by a California corporation should not be forced to sue that corporation anywhere but in California simply because another prospective defendant carried an insurance policy. And an insurance company whose maximum interest in the case cannot exceed $20,000 and who in fact asserts that it has no interest at all, should not be allowed to determine that dozens of tort plaintiffs must be compelled to press their claims — even those claims which are not against the insured and which in no event could be satisfied out of the meager insurance fund — in a single forum of the insurance company's choosing. There is nothing in the statutory scheme, and very little in the judicial and academic commentary upon that scheme, which requires that the tail be allowed to wag the dog in this fashion.

State Farm's interest in this case, which is the fulcrum of the interpleader procedure, is confined to its $20,000 fund. That interest receives full vindication when the court restrains claimants from seeking to enforce against the insurance company any judgment obtained against its insured, except in the interpleader proceeding itself. To the extent that the District Court sought to control claimants' lawsuits against the insured and other alleged tortfeasors, it exceeded the powers granted to it by the statutory scheme.

We recognize, of course, that our view of interpleader means that it cannot be used to solve all the vexing problems of multiparty litigation arising out of a mass tort. But interpleader was never intended to perform such a function, to be an all-purpose "bill of peace."[17] Had it been so intended, careful provision would necessarily have been made to insure that a party with little or no interest in the outcome of a complex controversy

---

17. There is not a word in the legislative history suggesting such a purpose. *See* S. Rep. No. 558, 74th Cong., 1st Sess. (1935). . . .

should not strip truly interested parties of substantial rights — such as the right to choose the forum in which to establish their claims, subject to generally applicable rules of jurisdiction, venue, service of process, removal, and change of venue. None of the legislative and academic sponsors of a modern federal interpleader device viewed their accomplishment as a "bill of peace," capable of sweeping dozens of lawsuits out of the various state and federal courts in which they were brought and into a single interpleader proceeding. . . .

In light of the evidence that federal interpleader was not intended to serve the function of a "bill of peace" in the context of multiparty litigation arising out of a mass tort, of the anomalous power which such a construction of the statute would give the stakeholder, and of the thrust of the statute and the purpose it was intended to serve, we hold that the interpleader statute did not authorize the injunction entered in the present case. Upon remand, the injunction is to be modified consistently with this opinion.

IV.

The judgment of the Court of Appeals is reversed, and the case is remanded to the United States District Court for proceedings consistent with this opinion.

Notes

1.   The § 1335 interpleader remedy combines a number of different aggregation concepts that we have explored and will explore in this chapter. First, it permits a person holding an interpleader stake to join on a mandatory basis all parties that might have a claim to the stake. Second, it provides for an antisuit injunction, so that claimants cannot continue to prosecute cases in other courts. We will examine the antisuit injunction in detail shortly (*see infra* p. 170), but *Tashire* well demonstrates its basic idea — by enjoining litigation elsewhere, a judge can effectively channel litigants to bring suit in his or her court. As *Tashire* describes, § 1335 interpleader also overcomes subject-matter-jurisdiction and personal-jurisdiction hurdles that we will examine in the next chapter. In addition, it finds a way to marry the self-interest of the defendant with the social interest in achieving optimal aggregation. In terms of aggregation, interpleader is one of the most effective devices that we have.

2.   Despite its effectiveness, interpleader has numerous drawbacks. The most significant is its limited utility. To explain, begin with the fact that there are two forms of interpleader — rule and statutory — with slightly different standards. Rule interpleader, permitted under Federal Rule 22, allows a person against whom "claims that may expose [the person] to double or multiple liability" to bring suit against the various claimants and force the claimants to interplead. The circumstances under which a person can be exposed to double or multiple liability are few.

Traditionally, the circumstances involved a piece of property in which more than one person claimed an interest. It has never expanded beyond that setting. Statutory interpleader, permitted under 28 U.S.C. § 1335, contains a slightly different standard; it requires that the stakeholder have money, property, an insurance policy, or a legal instrument "of the value of $500 or more" that "[t]wo or more adverse claimants . . . are claiming or may be entitled to claim." Again, however, a specific *res* that is the subject of multiple claims is the touchstone of liability. The requirement of a *res* ill fits the standard large-scale case, in which multiple plaintiffs seek an *in personam* judgment rather than title to a particular piece of property.

3. It is possible to come up with a creative argument for interpleader in some of these cases. Suppose that a defendant has assets worth $10 million, but the total claims against the defendant amount to $20 million. If we conceive of the defendant's entire assets as a *res*, then might that defendant be able to use Rule 22 or § 1335 to interplead all claimants? (This argument is a variant of the limited-fund theory that we encounter later in this book (*see infra* pp. 391-92; p. 395, Note 9; p. 506).)

Thus far, no court has been willing to be so creative with interpleader. One reason is the occasionally invoked rule that interpleader is unavailable to one who seeks protection from his own wrong. For instance, in *Farmers Irrigating Ditch & Reservoir Co. v. Kane*, 845 F.2d 229 (10th Cir. 1988), an impecunious tortfeasor whose conduct caused severe flooding to numerous individuals attempted to pay into the court what it claimed to be virtually all its assets. The court declined to authorize interpleader:

> Our attention has not been directed to any case where a tortfeasor in a multi-claim tort can admit liability, tender into court a minimal amount of money with the representation that such is all he has, force the claimants to prorate the amount deposited, and then obtain an order discharging him from any further liability for his tort. . . . . It is the general rule that a party seeking interpleader must be free from blame in causing the controversy, and where he stands as a wrongdoer with respect to the subject matter of the suit or any of the claimants, he cannot have relief by interpleader. [845 F.2d at 232.]

But see Paula J. McDermott, Note, *Can Statutory Interpleader Be Used as a Remedy by the Tortfeasor in Mass Tort Litigation?*, 90 DICK. L. REV. 439 (1985) (arguing to overturn this requirement); Holcomb v. Aetna Life Ins. Co., 228 F.2d 75 (10th Cir. 1955) (refusing to deny interpleader until allegations of bad faith had been established at trial).

A second problem with an adventurous "limited-fund interpleader" is its conflict with the bankruptcy and class actions. If a party's assets are insufficient to satisfy all claimants, then the party is insolvent. Because the law of bankruptcy has crafted a complex scheme to balance the interests of debtors and creditors, there is a strong argument that debtors should not use interpleader as a backdoor debt-resolution device. Similarly, the Supreme Court has placed significant restrictions on the "limited-fund" theory as a way to obtain class certification under Fed. R. Civ. P. 23(b)(1)(B). *See* Ortiz v. Fibreboard Corp., 527 U.S. 815 (1999) (*infra* p.

506). Using interpleader as an end-run around those restrictions presents evident problems.

4.   A high-water mark for the use of "limited-fund interpleader" is *Aetna Casualty & Surety Co. v. Ahrens*, 414 F. Supp. 1235 (S.D. Tex. 1975), a case in which 300 oyster-loving patrons of an insolvent (or marginally solvent) restaurant contracted food poisoning.   The district court was sympathetic to the argument that the restaurant's assets and insurance proceeds constituted a limited fund that justified interpleader of all the poisoned patrons who had filed state-court actions, but ultimately declined to afford it dispositive weight:

> [T]he possibility of improvement in financial condition, viewed together with the recognition that many tortfeasors face comprehensive insolvency whenever their assets are levied against with substantial adverse judgments, causes this Court to conclude that solvency alone, or its absence, cannot justify expanding interpleader jurisdiction. [*Id.* at 1246.]

The court went on, however, to hold that insolvency "remains as a factor to be considered." *Id.*   After considering all of the factors it thought relevant — including the fact that, unlike *Tashire*, the insurance funds were the bulk of the available assets; the desire of all the insureds for interpleader; the duplication and expense of multiple state and federal trials; the possibility that state actions would frustrate the "orderly, uniform manner" of contesting liability in the federal interpleader proceeding; the possibility that early judgments in state court could interfere with an orderly distribution of assets; and the degree to which interpleader would frustrate the plaintiffs' choice of forum — the court preliminarily enjoined the state proceedings pending further evidence on the issues of insolvency and frustration of plaintiffs' chosen forum.   *See also In re* Enron Corp. Sec., Derivative & "ERISA" Litig., 2006 WL 1663383 (S.D. Tex. 2006) (stating that interpleader is proper when claims asserted against layered insurance policies might exhaust the proceeds and prejudice the ability of some defendants to obtain a share).

5.   Even if the lack of a *res* is surmountable, interpleader has other drawbacks.   First, under 28 U.S.C. § 1335(a)(2), a statutory-interpleader plaintiff must either deposit the assets in dispute into court or post a bond for their value.   Since this requirement is a part of the jurisdictional statute, courts have held that the deposit or bond requirement cannot be waived.   *See* 7 CHARLES A. WRIGHT ET AL., FEDERAL PRACTICE AND PROCEDURE § 1716 (3d ed. 2001).   In many cases, it is impossible to pay in all of the assets of the corporation; even if it were, payment of all assets would effectively be equivalent to a bankruptcy liquidation without the protections of the bankruptcy code.   Likewise, a bond might be very costly to post.   This problem does not necessarily apply to a plaintiff invoking interpleader under Rule 22, which has no comparable provision; the court has discretion to decide whether deposit or a bond is appropriate.   *Id.*

Nevertheless, an equally thorny problem exists for interpleader: It is not clear that Rule 22's standard — exposure to "double or multiple liability" — can be met. Because a mass tortfeasor's liability is limited to its available assets, and because the inequitable distribution of those assets in no way results in double or multiple liability to the tortfeasor, rule interpleader may be unavailable in the mass tort context.

A third problem, nettlesome in both statutory and rule interpleader, is the difficulty of identifying and joining all, or even most, of the potential claimants against the wrongdoer's assets. Since the reason to interpret interpleader liberally in the case of mass wrongdoing is to assure that the assets will be fairly distributed, the inability to join all victims undercuts the value of interpleader.

6. Statutory and rule interpleader have significant differences, including different standards; different rules of subject-matter jurisdiction, personal jurisdiction, and venue; and different limitations on the scope of antisuit injunctions. For a full discussion, see JAY TIDMARSH & ROGER H. TRANGSRUD, COMPLEX LITIGATION AND THE ADVERSARY SYSTEM 418-19 (1998). In nearly all circumstances, these differences make statutory interpleader a more broadly useful aggregation device.

7. *Tashire* contrasted interpleader with equity's bill of peace, which sounded, from the Court's description, like a promising aggregation device for eliminating repetitive litigation. The bill of peace was a precursor to the class action. As a result, many states have decided that their modern class-action rules supplanted the bill of peace. *See, e.g.*, Baughman v. Am. Tel. & Tel. Co., 378 S.E.2d 599 (S.C. 1989). The few states that retain the bill of peace (or its remedial equivalent) limit its use to situations such as the frivolous relitigation of decided claims or the consolidation of existing cases. *See, e.g., In re* Rolleston, 651 S.E.2d 739 (Ga. 2007); Am. Bankers Ins. Co. of Fla. v. Booth, 830 So. 2d 1205 (Miss. 2002). Those limits, plus the limits of subject-matter jurisdiction, personal jurisdiction, and venue, make the bill of peace fairly ineffective as an all-purpose aggregation device.

c. Joinder of Required Parties Under Rule 19

Another method through which the initial shape of the plaintiff's case can be altered is joinder under Rule 19. Under Rule 19, some nonparties whose presence in the case is essential "must be joined" even when none of the existing parties has thought to or been able to join them. The first task of Rule 19 is to identify exactly who these "persons required to be joined if feasible" are. Because of our commitment to litigant autonomy, evidenced in the permissive joinder approach of Rule 20, the circumstances under which a nonparty can be forced to join a case are limited; otherwise, the exception of required joinder swallows the rule of permissive joinder. Rule 19(a) takes up the task of identifying those subject to required joinder.

In many situations, the required party is joined and the case proceeds along its way. Nonetheless, due to various constraints on a court's authority — such as subject-matter jurisdiction, personal jurisdiction, venue, and various immunity doctrines — in some cases a court will not be able to adjudicate the claims asserted by or against a required party. What is the court to do when joinder of a required party is not feasible? One option is to limp along without the required party. The other is to dismiss the case, on the view that the presence of the required party is so essential that the court is better off denying the plaintiff's claim *in toto* rather than proceeding in the required party's absence. Rule 19(b) states the guidelines under which a court makes the determination of whether to proceed without the required party or dismiss the case due to the party's absence.

The following two cases describe the operation of Rules 19(a) and -(b). As you consider the cases, ask whether Rule 19 is calibrated in such a way as to make the aggregation of claims in complex litigation more likely, or whether the rule is neutral — or even harmful — to the effort to aggregate related claims in one proceeding.

TEMPLE V. SYNTHES CORP.

498 U.S. 5 (1990)

■ PER CURIAM.

Petitioner Temple, a Mississippi resident, underwent surgery in October 1986 in which a "plate and screw device" was implanted in his lower spine. The device was manufactured by respondent Synthes, Ltd. (U.S.A.) (Synthes), a Pennsylvania corporation. Dr. S. Henry LaRocca performed the surgery at St. Charles General Hospital in New Orleans, Louisiana. Following surgery, the device's screws broke off inside Temple's back.

Temple filed suit against Synthes in the United States District Court for the Eastern District of Louisiana. The suit, which rested on diversity jurisdiction, alleged defective design and manufacture of the device. . . . [Subsequently] Temple filed suit against the doctor and the hospital in Louisiana state court.

Synthes did not attempt to bring the doctor and the hospital into the federal action by means of a third-party complaint, as provided in Federal Rule of Civil Procedure 14(a). Instead, Synthes filed a motion to dismiss Temple's federal suit for failure to join necessary parties pursuant to Federal Rule of Civil Procedure 19. Following a hearing, the District Court ordered Temple to join the doctor and the hospital as defendants within twenty days or risk dismissal of the lawsuit. According to the court, the most significant reason for requiring joinder was the interest of judicial economy. The court relied on this Court's decision in Provident Tradesmens Bank & Trust Co. v. Patterson, 390 U.S. 102 (1968), wherein we recognized that one focus of Rule 19 is "the interest of the courts and the public in complete, consistent, and efficient settlement of controversies." When Temple failed to join the doctor and the hospital, the court dismissed the suit with prejudice.

Temple appealed, and the United States Court of Appeals for the Fifth Circuit affirmed. . . .

In his petition for certiorari to this Court, Temple contends that it was error to label joint tortfeasors as indispensable parties under Rule 19(b) and to dismiss the lawsuit with prejudice for failure to join those parties. We agree. . . . It has long been the rule that it is not necessary for all joint tortfeasors to be named as defendants in a single lawsuit. . . . Nothing in the 1966 revision of Rule 19 changed that principle. The Advisory Committee Notes to Rule 19(a) explicitly state that "a tortfeasor with the usual 'joint-and-several' liability is merely a permissive party to an action against another with like liability." . . . There is nothing in Louisiana tort law to the contrary. . . .

The opinion in *Provident Bank* does speak of the public interest in limiting multiple litigation, but that case is not controlling here. There, the estate of a tort victim brought a declaratory judgment action against an insurance company. We assumed that the policyholder was a person "who, under § (a), should be joined if 'feasible[,]'" . . . and went on to discuss the appropriate analysis under Rule 19(b), because the policyholder could not be joined without destroying diversity. After examining the factors set forth in Rule 19(b), we determined that the action could proceed without the policyholder; he therefore was not an indispensable party whose absence required dismissal of the suit.

Here, no inquiry under Rule 19(b) is necessary, because the threshold requirements of Rule 19(a) have not been satisfied. As potential joint tortfeasors with Synthes, Dr. LaRocca and the hospital were merely permissive parties. The Court of Appeals erred by failing to hold that the District Court abused its discretion in ordering them joined as defendants and in dismissing the action when Temple failed to comply with the court's order. For these reasons, we grant the petition for certiorari, reverse the judgment of the Court of Appeals for the Fifth Circuit, and remand for further proceedings consistent with this opinion.

REPUBLIC OF THE PHILIPPINES V. PIMENTEL

553 U.S. 851 (2008)

■ JUSTICE KENNEDY delivered the opinion of the Court.

This case turns on the interpretation and proper application of Rule 19 of the Federal Rules of Civil Procedure and requires us to address the Rule's operation in the context of foreign sovereign immunity.

This interpleader action was commenced to determine the ownership of property allegedly stolen by Ferdinand Marcos when he was the President of the Republic of the Philippines. Two entities named in the suit invoked sovereign immunity. They are the Republic of the Philippines and the Philippine Presidential Commission on Good Governance, referred to in turn as the Republic and the Commission. They were dismissed, but the interpleader action proceeded to judgment over their objection. Together with two parties who remained in the suit, the Republic and the

Commission now insist it was error to allow the litigation to proceed. Under Rule 19, they contend, the action should have been dismissed once it became clear they could not be joined as parties without their consent.

The United States Court of Appeals for the Ninth Circuit, agreeing with the District Court, held the action could proceed without the Republic and the Commission as parties. Among the reasons the Court of Appeals gave was that the absent, sovereign entities would not prevail on their claims. We conclude the Court of Appeals gave insufficient weight to the foreign sovereign status of the Republic and the Commission, and that the court further erred in reaching and discounting the merits of their claims.

I

A

. . . [A]fter the case was in the Court of Appeals and before it came here, the text of [Rule 19] changed. The Rules Committee advised the changes were stylistic only, *see* Advisory Committee's Notes on 2007 Amendment to Fed. R. Civ. P. 19 (2008); and we agree. These are the three relevant stylistic changes. First, the word "required" replaced the word "necessary" in subparagraph (a). Second, the 1966 Rule set out factors in longer clauses and the 2007 Rule sets out the factors affecting joinder in separate lettered headings. Third, the word "indispensable," which had remained as a remnant of the pre-1966 Rule, is altogether deleted from the current text. Though the word "indispensable" had a lesser place in the 1966 Rule, it still had the latent potential to mislead.

As the substance and operation of the Rule both pre- and post-2007 are unchanged, we will refer to the present, revised version. . . .

B

In 1972, Ferdinand Marcos, then President of the Republic, incorporated Arelma, S.A. (Arelma), under Panamanian law. Around the same time, Arelma opened a brokerage account with Merrill Lynch, Pierce, Fenner & Smith Inc. (Merrill Lynch) in New York, in which it deposited $2 million. As of the year 2000, the account had grown to approximately $35 million.

[A class action (the *Pimentel* litigation) was filed against Marcos and his estate on behalf of some 9,539 victims of human-rights abuses. In 1996, the *Pimentel* class obtained a judgment of almost $2 billion, which remained uncollected. The class sought to satisfy part of the judgment out of the Merrill Lynch account. Competing claimants for this money included the Republic, the Commission, Arelma, and the estate of a person from whom Marcos had allegedly stolen the "Yamashita Treasure." In 1991, the Commission asked the Sandiganbayan, a Philippine court, to declare forfeited to the republic any property Marcos had obtained through the misuse of his office. That litigation was pending in the Sandiganbayan.

[The present lawsuit began when Merrill Lynch filed an interpleader action under 28 U.S.C. § 1335, in which Merrill Lynch asked the court to the parties to whom the Arelma account should be distributed. Defendants included the *Pimentel* class, the Republic, the Commission, Arelma, and the "Yamashita Treasure" estate.]

. . . [T]he Republic and the Commission asserted sovereign immunity under the Foreign Sovereign Immunities Act of 1976 (FSIA), 28 U.S.C. § 1604. They moved to dismiss pursuant to Rule 19(b), based on the premise that the action could not proceed without them. . . .

[The district court allowed the action to proceed, and the Court of Appeals for the Ninth Circuit affirmed.] Dismissal of the interpleader suit, [the Court of Appeals] held, was not warranted under Rule 19(b) because, though the Republic and the Commission were required ("necessary") parties under Rule 19(a), their claim had so little likelihood of success on the merits that the interpleader action could proceed without them. One of the reasons the court gave was that any action commenced by the Republic and the Commission to recover the assets would be barred by [the applicable] 6-year statute of limitations for claims involving the misappropriation of public property. The court thus found it unnecessary to consider whether any prejudice to the Republic and the Commission might be lessened by some form of judgment or interim decree in the interpleader action. The court also considered the failure of the Republic and the Commission to obtain a judgment in the Sandiganbayan . . . . The court further found it relevant that allowing the interpleader case to proceed would serve the interests of the *Pimentel* class, which, at this point, likely has no other available forum in which to enforce its judgment against property belonging to Marcos. . . .

III

We turn to the question whether the interpleader action could proceed in the District Court without the Republic and the Commission as parties.

Subdivision (a) of Rule 19 states the principles that determine when persons or entities must be joined in a suit. The Rule instructs that nonjoinder even of a required person does not always result in dismissal. Subdivision (a) opens by noting that it addresses joinder "if Feasible." Where joinder is not feasible, the question whether the action should proceed turns on the factors outlined in subdivision (b). The considerations set forth in subdivision (b) are nonexclusive, as made clear by the introductory statement that "[t]he factors for the court to consider include." Fed. R. Civ. P. 19(b). The general direction is whether "in equity and good conscience, the action should proceed among the existing parties or should be dismissed." The design of the Rule, then, indicates that the determination whether to proceed will turn upon factors that are case specific, which is consistent with a Rule based on equitable considerations. This is also consistent with the fact that the determination of who may, or must, be parties to a suit has consequences for the persons and entities affected by the judgment; for the judicial system and its interest in the integrity of its processes and the respect accorded to its decrees; and for society and its concern for the fair and prompt resolution of disputes. For these reasons, the issue of joinder can be complex, and determinations are case specific.

Under the earlier Rules the term "indispensable party" might have implied a certain rigidity that would be in tension with this case-specific approach. The word "indispensable" had an unforgiving connotation that did not fit easily with a system that permits actions to proceed even when some persons who otherwise should be parties to the action cannot be joined. As the Court noted in *Provident [Tradesmens Bank & Trust Co. v. Patterson*, 390 U.S. 102, 117 n.12 (1968)], the use of "indispensable" in Rule 19 created the "verbal anomaly" of an "indispensable person who turns out to be dispensable after all." Though the text has changed, the new Rule 19 has the same design and, to some extent, the same tension. Required persons may turn out not to be required for the action to proceed after all.

In all events it is clear that multiple factors must bear on the decision whether to proceed without a required person. This decision "must be based on factors varying with the different cases, some such factors being substantive, some procedural, some compelling by themselves, and some subject to balancing against opposing interests." [*Provident Bank*, 390 U.S.] at 119.

IV

We turn to Rule 19 as it relates to this case. The application of subdivision (a) of Rule 19 is not contested. The Republic and the Commission are required entities because "[w]ithout [them] as parties in this interpleader action, their interests in the subject matter are not protected." In re Republic of Philippines, 309 F.3d [1143, 1152 (9th Cir. 2002)]; *see* Fed. R. Civ. P. 19(a)(1)(B)(i). All parties appear to concede this. The disagreement instead centers around the application of subdivision (b), which addresses whether the action may proceed without the Republic and the Commission, given that the Rule requires them to be parties.

We have not addressed the standard of review for Rule 19(b) decisions. The case-specific inquiry that must be followed in applying the standards set forth in subdivision (b), including the direction to consider whether "in equity and good conscience" the case should proceed, implies some degree of deference to the district court. In this case, however, we find implicit in the District Court's rulings, and explicit in the opinion of the Court of Appeals, errors of law that require reversal. Whatever the appropriate standard of review, a point we need not decide, the judgment could not stand.

The Court of Appeals erred in not giving the necessary weight to the absent entities' assertion of sovereign immunity. The court in effect decided the merits of the Republic and the Commission's claims to the Arelma assets. Once it was recognized that those claims were not frivolous, it was error for the Court of Appeals to address them on their merits when the required entities had been granted sovereign immunity. The court's consideration of the merits was itself an infringement on foreign sovereign immunity; and, in any event, its analysis was flawed. We discuss these errors first in the context of how they affected the Court of Appeals' analysis under the first factor of Rule 19(b). We then explain that the outcome suggested by the first factor is confirmed by our analysis under the other provisions of Rule 19(b). The action may not proceed.

A

As to the first Rule 19(b) factor — the extent to which a judgment rendered in the person's absence might prejudice that person or the existing parties, Fed. R. Civ. P. 19(b)(1) — the judgment of the Court of Appeals is incorrect.

In considering whether the Republic and the Commission would be prejudiced if the action were to proceed in their absence, the Court of Appeals gave insufficient weight to their sovereign status. The doctrine of foreign sovereign immunity has been recognized since early in the history of our Nation. It is premised upon the "perfect equality and absolute independence of sovereigns, and th[e] common interest impelling them to mutual intercourse." . . .

The District Court and the Court of Appeals failed to give full effect to sovereign immunity when they held the action could proceed without the Republic and the Commission. Giving full effect to sovereign immunity promotes the comity interests that have contributed to the development of the immunity doctrine.

Comity and dignity interests take concrete form in this case. The claims of the Republic and the Commission arise from events of historical and political significance for the Republic and its people. The Republic and the Commission have a unique interest in resolving the ownership of or claims to the Arelma assets and in determining if, and how, the assets should be used to compensate those persons who suffered grievous injury under Marcos. There is a comity interest in allowing a foreign state to use its own courts for a dispute if it has a right to do so. The dignity of a foreign state is not enhanced if other nations bypass its courts without right or good cause. Then, too, there is the more specific affront that could result to the Republic and the Commission if property they claim is seized by the decree of a foreign court. . . .

The Court of Appeals accordingly erred in undertaking to rule on the merits of the Republic and the Commission's claims. There may be cases where the person who is not joined asserts a claim that is frivolous. In that instance a court may have leeway under both Rule 19(a)(1), defining required parties, and Rule 19(b), addressing when a suit may go forward nonetheless, to disregard the frivolous claim. Here, the claims of the absent entities are not frivolous; and the Court of Appeals should not have proceeded on the premise that those claims would be determined against the sovereign entities that asserted immunity.

The Court of Appeals determined that the claims of the Republic and the Commission as to the assets would not succeed because a suit would be time barred in New York. This is not necessarily so. If the Sandiganbayan rules that the Republic owns the assets or stock of Arelma because Marcos did not own them and the property was forfeited to the Republic under Philippine law, then New York misappropriation rules might not be the applicable law. . . . We need not seek to predict the outcomes. It suffices that the claims would not be frivolous. . . .

. . . [T]the decision to proceed in the absence of the Republic and the Commission ignored the substantial prejudice those entities likely would incur. This most directly implicates Rule 19(b)'s first factor, which directs consideration of prejudice both to absent persons and those who are parties. We have discussed the absent entities. As to existing parties, we do not discount the *Pimentel* class' interest in recovering damages it was awarded pursuant to a judgment. Furthermore, combating public corruption is a significant international policy. . . . This policy does support the interest of the *Pimentel* class in recovering damages awarded to it. But it also underscores the important comity concerns implicated by the Republic and the Commission in asserting foreign sovereign immunity. The error is not that the District Court and the Court of Appeals gave too much weight to the interest of the *Pimentel* class, but that it did not accord proper weight to the compelling claim of sovereign immunity.

Based on these considerations we conclude the District Court and the Court of Appeals gave insufficient weight to the likely prejudice to the Republic and the Commission should the interpleader proceed in their absence.

B

As to the second Rule 19(b) factor — the extent to which any prejudice could be lessened or avoided by relief or measures alternative to dismissal, Fed. R. Civ. P. 19(b)(2) — there is no substantial argument to allow the action to proceed. No alternative remedies or forms of relief have been proposed to us or appear to be available. If the Marcos estate did not own the assets, or if the Republic owns them now, the claim of the *Pimentel* class likely fails; and in all events, if there are equally valid but competing claims, that too would require adjudication in a case where the Republic and the Commission are parties. *See* State Farm Fire & Cas. Co. v. Tashire, 386 U.S. 523 (1967) [*supra* p. 84].

C

As to the third Rule 19(b) factor — whether a judgment rendered without the absent party would be adequate, Fed. R. Civ. P. 19(b)(3) — the Court of Appeals understood "adequacy" to refer to satisfaction of the

Pimentel class' claims. But adequacy refers to the "public stake in settling disputes by wholes, whenever possible." *Provident Bank,* 390 U.S. at 111. This "social interest in the efficient administration of justice and the avoidance of multiple litigation" is an interest that has "traditionally been thought to support compulsory joinder of absent and potentially adverse claimants." Going forward with the action without the Republic and the Commission would not further the public interest in settling the dispute as a whole because the Republic and the Commission would not be bound by the judgment in an action where they were not parties.

D

As to the fourth Rule 19(b) factor — whether the plaintiff would have an adequate remedy if the action were dismissed for nonjoinder, Fed. R. Civ. P. 19(b)(4) — the Court of Appeals made much of what it considered the tort victims' lack of an alternative forum should this action be dismissed. This seems to assume the plaintiff in this interpleader action was the *Pimentel* class. It is Merrill Lynch, however, that has the statutory status of plaintiff as the stakeholder in the interpleader action. . . .

Merrill Lynch, as the stakeholder, makes the point that if the action is dismissed it loses the benefit of a judgment allowing it to disburse the assets and be done with the matter. Dismissal of the action, it urges, leaves it without an adequate remedy, for it "could potentially be forced . . . to defend lawsuits by the various claimants in different jurisdictions, possibly leading to inconsistent judgments." A dismissal of the action on the ground of nonjoinder, however, will protect Merrill Lynch in some respects. . . . As matters presently stand, in any later suit against it Merrill Lynch may seek to join the Republic and the Commission and have the action dismissed under Rule 19(b) should they again assert sovereign immunity. Dismissal for nonjoinder to some extent will serve the purpose of interpleader, which is to prevent a stakeholder from having to pay two or more parties for one claim.

Any prejudice to Merrill Lynch in this regard is outweighed by prejudice to the absent entities invoking sovereign immunity. Dismissal under Rule 19(b) will mean, in some instances, that plaintiffs will be left without a forum for definitive resolution of their claims. But that result is contemplated under the doctrine of foreign sovereign immunity.

V

The Court of Appeals' failure to give sufficient weight to the likely prejudice to the Republic and the Commission should the interpleader proceed in their absence would, in the usual course, warrant reversal and remand for further proceedings. In this case, however, that error and our further analysis under the additional provisions of Rule 19(b) lead us to conclude the action must be dismissed. This leaves the *Pimentel* class, which has waited for years now to be compensated for grievous wrongs, with no immediate way to recover on its judgment against Marcos. And it leaves Merrill Lynch, the stakeholder, without a judgment.

The balance of equities may change in due course. One relevant change may occur if it appears that the Sandiganbayan cannot or will not issue its ruling within a reasonable period of time. Other changes could result when and if there is a ruling. If the Sandiganbayan rules that the Republic and the Commission have no right to the assets, their claims in some later interpleader suit would be less substantial than they are now. If the ruling is that the Republic and the Commission own the assets, then they may seek to enforce a judgment in our courts; or consent to become parties in an interpleader suit, where their claims could be considered; or file in some other forum if they can obtain jurisdiction over the relevant persons. . . . The present action, however, may not proceed.

* * * * *

The judgment of the Court of Appeals for the Ninth Circuit is reversed, and the case is remanded with instructions to order the District Court to dismiss the interpleader action.

It is so ordered.

■ JUSTICE STEVENS, concurring in part and dissenting in part.

. . . I believe the appropriate disposition of this case is to reverse and remand for further proceedings. The District Court and the Ninth Circuit erred by concluding that the . . . statute of limitations provides a virtually insuperable obstacle to petitioners' recovery of the Arelma . . . assets, and I therefore agree that this Court should reverse. I would not, however, give near-dispositive effect to the Republic of the Philippines (Republic) and the Philippine Presidential Commission on Good Governance's (Commission) status as sovereign entities, as the Court does in ordering outright dismissal of the case.

In my judgment, the Court of Appeals should either order the District Judge to stay further proceedings pending a reasonably prompt decision of the Sandiganbayan or order the case reassigned to a different District Judge to conduct further proceedings. There is, of course, a risk of unfairness in conducting such proceedings without the participation of petitioners. But it is a risk that they can avoid by waiving their sovereign immunity, and the record provides a basis for believing that they would do so if the case proceeded before a different judge. . . .

■ [The opinion of JUSTICE SOUTER, concurring in part and dissenting in part, is omitted.]

Notes

1. *Temple* shows that increased efficiency is in itself an insufficient reason to require the joinder of additional parties to a case. Put slightly

differently, efficiency is an insufficient reason to overcome inefficient joinder decisions that plaintiffs make under the aegis of Rule 20(a). Recall that the requirements of Rule 20(a) were interpreted in such a way as to permit the efficient packaging of parties. *See supra* pp. 62-63. When a plaintiff is either unwilling or unable to effectuate this packaging, Rule 19 is not an automatic end run around the plaintiff's chosen structure.

From the standpoint of the present structure of our joinder rules, this result must the rule; otherwise, joinder (permissive in some cases, required in the rest) would turn solely on the issue of efficiency. But two questions emerge. First, why isn't the efficient packaging of litigation a sufficient reason to require the joinder of those whom the plaintiff does not or cannot join? Second, if efficiency is an insufficient reason to require joinder, then what is a sufficient reason?

2. The first question comes to the heart of our joinder system. We do not generally require transactionally related claims brought by or against additional parties — in other words, claims in which efficiency gains are likely — to be filed in one case. The desire to preserve litigant (especially plaintiff) autonomy to shape the strongest case in the litigant's best forum is one reason. The adversarial system's preference for decentralized decisions — in which the court plays the role of neutral arbiter rather than promoter of socially desirable outcomes — is another. Third, recall the outcome-determinative thesis of Professors Horowitz and Bordens and the maturity thesis of Professor McGovern (*supra* pp. 52-54, 56-58). Deciding whether and when to join additional parties has real-world effects that skew outcomes in relation to individual litigation. Should we entrust such decisions to courts? Next, consider the practical problems of joinder. When only a few parties might be added, as in *Temple*, the problem of identifying and joining other parties is not too difficult, but the efficiency gains in such cases are also likely to be fairly modest. The cases in which real efficiency gains are possible are those in which potential plaintiffs and defendants are geographically and temporally dispersed. But how are litigants and courts to identify and effect the joinder of such parties?

Finally, and relatedly, as joinder rules start to sweep larger and larger numbers of cases together, problems of jurisdiction, venue, and immunity become greater obstacles to resolving the cases in a single forum. Chapter Three examines jurisdictional issues in more detail, but *Pimentel* highlights an obvious downside to broad joinder: Due to doctrines such as jurisdiction and sovereign immunity, which are not typically oriented toward efficiency, it is not always possible to achieve the most efficient level of joinder. The problem then is to decide what to do in such situations. Dismiss the cases (even though no other court may be able to effect a more efficient packaging)? Limp along with an inefficient package? Find some middle ground between these alternatives?

Perhaps you can now understand — whether or not you agree with — our system's inclination to leave joinder decisions principally to the parties.

3. In answering the second question, Rule 19 shows that our system does not always leave joinder decisions to the parties. Indeed, Rule 19(a)

requires joinder in three circumstances. As a general matter, Rule 19(a)(1)(A) protects the plaintiff's interest in obtaining complete relief; Rule 19(a)(1)(B)(ii) protects the defendant's interest in not being whipsawed by multiple individual judgments; and Rule 19(a)(1)(B)(i) protects nonparties whose interests might be effectively damaged by a lawsuit conducted in their absence. Does any single principle unite these three situations? Or are they three completely distinct reasons to permit joinder?

4.   Take a second look at *Pimentel*. The Court does not pause long on the issue whether the Republic of the Phillippines and the Commission are required parties under Rule 19(a) because the parties agreed that they were. Their argument was that, if the Republic and the Commission were not joined, Merrill Lynch would give away money that might be theirs to the *Pimentel* class — a classic Rule 19(a)(1)(B)(i) problem. As nonparties, however, the Republic and the Commission weren't bound by Merrill Lynch's interpleader action; if Merrill Lynch gave their money to someone else, they could still sue Merrill Lynch for the money (the likeliest theory being a tort for conversion). In Parts IV.C. and IV.D of the opinion, Merrill Lynch and the Court assumed that such subsequent lawsuits were possible. If this was true, then no Rule 19(a)(1)(B)(i) problem existed.

Thus, the reason to join the Republic and the Commission wasn't Rule 19(a)(1)(B)(i); it was Rule 19(a)(1)(B)(ii). In theory, Merrill Lynch should pay out the proceeds of the brokerage account only once; but in practice, if it cannot join all claimants against the account in one case, it might end up paying out the proceeds multiple times. It was this fear — a fear of multiple judgments regarding the same assets — that motivated Merrill Lynch to file an interpleader action in the first place. As long as Merrill Lynch was solvent and could satisfy all judgments, the risk of harm from multiple suits fell on Merrill Lynch, not the Republic or the Commission. Preventing this harm is the point of Rule 19(a)(1)(B)(ii), not Rule 19(a)(1)(B)(i). The Court and the parties were imprecise on the matter.

The imprecision did not matter in *Pimentel*. As the case shows, Rules 19(a)(1)(B)(i) and -(ii) often operate as flip sides of the same coin. If the first judgment effectively limits a nonparty's remedies in subsequent litigation, then Rule 19(a)(1)(B)(i) is the proper provision to invoke. If the first judgment does not limit such remedies, then Rule 19(a)(1)(B)(ii) is the proper provision. Either way, joinder is required if feasible.

5.   Once a court identifies the parties whose joinder is required, the issue turns to the feasibility of joinder. If the required parties can be joined, they are joined. If they cannot be joined — usually due to issues of jurisdiction, venue, or immunity — then Rule 19(b), which is the focus of *Pimentel*, comes into play. By definition, one or more party whose joinder is required cannot be joined, and the issue is now whether to dismiss the case or limp along without a party that ideally ought to be present. Rule 19(b)'s stated test for making the decision to dismiss or not to dismiss — "equity and good conscience" — is supplemented by the four factors listed in Rule 19(b) and analyzed in *Pimentel*. Rather than simply applying each factor, as *Pimentel* does, it is possible to reconfigure the factors by analyzing

the harms to the plaintiffs, the defendants, the absent Rule 19(a) parties, and the court system that will be incurred if the case went forward and balancing them against the harms that the same players will suffer if the case were dismissed. *See* Provident Tradesmens Bank & Trust Co. v. Patterson, 390 U.S. 102, 109-11 (1968) (suggesting such an analysis of interests in applying the Rule 19(b) issue). Because the interest of the court system in efficient adjudication is nowhere mentioned in Rule 19(a) or (b), should it even be a relevant consideration?

Pimentel emphasizes the sovereignty interests of the Republic and the Commission. At some points (especially in Part IV.A, analyzing the first Rule 19(b) factor), the Court highlights the affront to those interests if Merrill Lynch's interpleader action proceeded without them. In other parts of the opinion (Parts IV.C and IV.D, analyzing the third and fourth Rule 19(b) factors), the Court assumes that the Republic and Commission would not be bound by the interpleader judgment and could still recover from Merrill Lynch in another proceeding — in which case, it is difficult to see how the interpleader proceeding poses any risk of harm to their sovereign interests. Can you reconcile this apparent inconsistency in the Court's reasoning? Adopting the interest analysis from *Provident Tradesmens*, does *Pimentel* give too much weight to the absent parties' interests, and not enough weight to the interests of Merrill Lynch, the *Pimentel* class, and a federal court that wants its judgment enforced?

In cases in which another forum (such as a state court) exists, dismissal under Rule 19(b) poses an inconvenience to a plaintiff that must re-file the case in a less preferable forum, as well as a loss in the plaintiff's autonomy to choose the forum. These harms are hardly inconsequential. But at least the plaintiff can bring the case somewhere. In cases like *Pimentel*, a dismissal under Rule 19(b) means that the plaintiff has no remedy anywhere. On the facts of *Pimentel*, that result isn't awful; Merrill Lynch just keeps on holding the money for now. The really disadvantaged group is the *Pimentel* class. Is there ever a reason to dismiss a case when the result is an abject failure of a remedy anywhere?

The reality is that Rule 19 sometimes operates in a way that bars any remedy. That reality creates a real-world dynamic that can make courts reluctant to construe the provisions of Rule 19(a) broadly — for if they do, they know that the chances are that, by virtue of the operation of Rule 19(b), they will dismiss some meritorious cases.

6.   In sum, Rule 19 impinges on plaintiff autonomy, doesn't necessarily foster efficient packaging of litigation, and can leave some plaintiffs without remedy. Are you convinced that the harms identified in Rule 19 are of such great moment that their prevention is worth these costs? At a minimum, should the harm to the plaintiff's interests even be counted, given that the plaintiff, by choosing the federal forum, has signaled a willingness to incur these harms? Isn't Rule 19's solicitude for the harm to plaintiffs' interests paternalistic? Would Rule 19 be more palatable if it required the joinder of the parties identified in Rule 19(a) when joinder was feasible, but did not

include the Rule 19(b) option of dismissing the case when joinder of Rule 19(a) parties was infeasible?

7.   Finally, from the viewpoint of complex litigation, how relevant — either positively or negatively — is Rule 19? We started this chapter with the idea that, in some cases, the inability to aggregate related parties in one case fomented complexity. Rule 19(a) is a device that can force related parties into one case. But does it force aggregation in the cases of concern to us: complex cases? As we have seen, efficiency — which is one reason we would like to foster aggregation — is an insufficient basis for invoking Rule 19. What about "limited fund" cases, in which a defendant's assets are insufficient to satisfy all claimants? Such cases arguably fit within the terms of Rule 19(a)(1)(B)(i), which requires the joinder of parties whose interests will be impaired by the present case. A few cases hint at the possible use of Rule 19 in this situation, but all are distinguishable because they involve competing claims against a defined object. *See, e.g.*, Belcher v. Prudential Ins. Co. of Am., 158 F. Supp. 2d 777, 779 (S.D. Ohio 2001) (an absent claimant to a limited fund such as insurance proceeds is a required party under Rule 19(a)(1)(B)(ii)); Makah Indian Tribe v. Verity, 910 F.2d 555 (9th Cir. 1990) (absent tribes with a stake in the allocation of fishing rights are required parties under Rule 19(a)). There are no cases in which the "limited fund" theory has been applied to require joinder merely because a defendant's assets are inadequate to satisfy all potential persons with claims against the defendant. Moreover, you might have noticed Rule 19(d), which renders Rule 19 inapplicable in cases subject to Rule 23, the important class-action aggregation mechanism that we consider in Chapter Four. Therefore, at least so far, parties and courts have not really utilized Rule 19 as a joinder mechanism in complex litigation.

Perhaps that is a good thing. If claims are temporally dispersed, Rule 19 can never aggregate all the claims; at most, it can aggregate the claims of groups of people whose claims arise during the pendency of the suit. If the claims are geographically dispersed, the chances are high that no single federal court will have subject-matter jurisdiction, personal jurisdiction, and venue over all the joined parties. That fact would provoke a Rule 19(b) crisis, possibly forcing the dismissal of such cases from federal courts (and all state court that similarly interpreted comparable rules they might have on the books). Moreover, as we have mentioned, the headache of locating and giving notice to each potential required party is great, and joinder might also have outcome-skewing effects of the kinds suggested by Professors Horowitz, Bordens, and McGovern.

Indeed, Rule 19 provides a lens into both the promise and the problems of joining all related claimants in one case.

d. Intervention

A different approach to joinder is to allow the plaintiff to set the initial party and claim structure, and then to permit others that have related claims or might otherwise be affected by the litigation to intervene in the litigation if they wish. This approach denies the original plaintiff full autonomy in structuring his or her case, but advances the autonomy of others who want to participate in the case. It also does not demand the most efficient aggregation of the litigation, but it allows a more efficient packaging than an alternative that gave the plaintiff absolute autonomy over structural decisions.

Rule 24 details the circumstances in which nonparties can seek to intervene in a case. As you read the following materials, consider whether Rule 24 is a helpful compromise between autonomy and efficiency in complex cases, or a device with little promise for achieving the degree of aggregation that complex litigation requires.

GRUTTER V. BOLLINGER

188 F.3d 394 (6th Cir. 1999)

■ DAUGHTREY, Circuit Judge.

Before us are two cases in which proposed defendant-intervenors were denied intervention under Federal Rule of Civil Procedure 24(a) and (b), in actions brought against the University of Michigan contesting the use of an applicant's race as a factor in determining admission. . . . [W]e find in both instances that the district courts erred in denying intervention under Rule 24(a).

PROCEDURAL AND FACTUAL BACKGROUND

In each of the cases before the court, a group of students and one or more coalitions appeal the denial of their motion to intervene in a lawsuit brought to challenge a race-conscious admissions policy at the University of Michigan. The named plaintiffs in *Gratz v. Bollinger* are two white applicants who were denied admission to the College of Literature, Arts and Science. They allege that the College's admissions policy violates the Equal Protection Clause of the Fourteenth Amendment, 42 U.S.C. § 1981 and § 1983, and 42 U.S.C. §§ 2000d *et seq.* The plaintiffs seek compensatory and punitive damages, injunctive relief forbidding continuation of the alleged discriminatory admissions process, and admission to the College. The intervenors are 17 African-American and Latino/a individuals who have applied or intend to apply to the University, and the Citizens for Affirmative Action's Preservation (CAAP), a nonprofit organization whose stated mission is to preserve opportunities in higher education for African-American and Latino/a students in Michigan. The intervenors claim that the resolution of this case directly threatens the access of qualified African-American and Latino/a students to public higher education and that the University will not adequately represent their interest in educational opportunity. The district court denied their motion for intervention as of right, holding that the plaintiffs did not have a substantial interest in the litigation and that the University could adequately represent the proposed intervenors' interests. The district court also denied the proposed intervenors' alternative motion for permissive intervention.

The named plaintiff in *Grutter v. Bollinger* is a white woman challenging the admissions policy of the University of Michigan Law School [on the same legal grounds]. . . . The proposed intervenors are 41 students and three pro-affirmative action coalitions. As described by the district court:

> [The] individual proposed intervenors include 21 undergraduate students of various races who currently attend [various undergraduate institutions], all of whom plan to apply to the law school for admission; five black students who currently attend [local high schools] and who also plan to apply to the law school for admission; 12 students of various races who currently attend the law school; a paralegal and a Latino graduate student at the University of Texas at Austin who intend to apply to the law school for admission; and a black graduate student at the University of Michigan who is a member of the Defend Affirmative Action Party.

The plaintiff opposed the motion to intervene, but the defendants, various officials of the Law School and the University, did not oppose the motion. The district court denied the motion to intervene as of right on the basis that the intervenors failed to show that their interests would not be adequately represented by the University. The district court also denied the proposed intervenors' alternative motion for permissive intervention.

DISCUSSION

The proposed intervenors in each of these cases contend principally that the district court erred by denying their motion to intervene as of right. . . . In this circuit, proposed intervenors must establish four elements in order to be entitled to intervene as a matter of right: (1) that the motion to intervene was timely; (2) that they have a substantial legal interest in the subject matter of the case; (3) that their ability to protect that interest may be impaired in the absence of intervention; and (4) that the parties already before the court may not adequately represent their interest. *See* Jansen v. City of Cincinnati, 904 F.2d 336, 340 (6th Cir. 1990). A district court's denial of intervention as of right is reviewed de novo, except for the timeliness element, which is reviewed for an abuse of discretion. The district court held in each of these cases that the motion for intervention was timely, and the plaintiffs do not contest this finding on appeal. We will therefore consider the motions timely and need address only the three remaining elements.

Substantial Legal Interest

The proposed intervenors must show that they have a substantial interest in the subject matter of this litigation. However, in this circuit we subscribe to a "rather expansive notion of the interest sufficient to invoke intervention of right." Mich. State AFL-CIO v. Miller, 103 F.3d 1240, 1245 (6th Cir. 1997). For example, an intervenor need not have the same standing necessary to initiate a lawsuit. We have also "cited with approval decisions of other courts 'reject[ing] the notion that Rule 24(a)(2) requires a specific legal or equitable interest.'" *Miller*, 103 F.3d at 1245. "The inquiry into the substantiality of the claimed interest is necessarily fact-specific." *Id.*

The proposed intervenors argue that their interest in maintaining the use of race as a factor in the University's admissions program is a sufficient substantial legal interest to support intervention as of right. Specifically, they argue that they have a substantial legal interest in educational opportunity, which requires preserving access to the University for African-American and Latino/a students and preventing a decline in the enrollment of African-American and Latino/a students. The district court in *Grutter* "assumed without deciding" that the proposed intervenors do have a significant legal interest in this case and that their ability to protect that interest may be impaired by an adverse ruling in the underlying case. The district court in *Gratz*, however, determined that the proposed intervenors did not have a direct and substantial interest which is "legally protectable" and that they therefore failed to establish this required element. We conclude that Sixth Circuit precedent requires a finding to the contrary. . . .

The *Gratz* district court's opinion relies heavily on the premise that the proposed intervenors do not have a significant legal interest unless they have a "legally enforceable right to have the existing admissions policy construed." We conclude that this interpretation results from a misreading of this circuit's approach to the issue. . . . For example, in *Miller*, the Michigan Chamber of Commerce sought to intervene in a suit by labor unions challenging an amendment to Michigan's Campaign Finance Act, Mich. Comp. Laws Ann. §§ 169.201-.282 (1996), which extended the application of statutory restrictions on corporate political expenditures so that they applied to unions as well as to corporations. The majority found that the Chamber of Commerce did have a substantial legal interest by virtue of its role in the political process that resulted in the adoption of the contested amendments. The Chamber of Commerce was therefore allowed to intervene as of right, although the Chamber had no legal "right" to the enactment of the challenged legislation. We believe that the district court's attempt to distinguish *Miller* . . . on the sole basis that [it] involved challenges to legislation, was misguided. The case law of this circuit does not limit the finding of a substantial interest to cases involving the legislative context, any more than it limits such a finding to cases involving a consent decree. Neither a legislative context nor the existence of a consent decree is dispositive as to whether proposed intervenors have shown that they have a significant interest in the subject matter of the underlying case. We find that the interest implicated in the case now before us is even more direct, substantial, and compelling than the general interest of an organization in vindicating legislation that it had previously supported. This case is, if anything, a significantly stronger case for intervention than *Miller* and many of the cases on which *Miller* relied.

Even if it could be said that the question raised is a close one, "close cases should be resolved in favor of recognizing an interest under Rule 24(a)." *Miller*, 103 F.3d at 1247. The proposed intervenors have enunciated a specific interest in the subject matter of this case, namely their interest in gaining admission to the University, which is considerably more direct and substantial than the interest of the Chamber of Commerce in *Miller* — a much more general interest. We therefore hold that the district court erred in *Gratz* in failing to rule that the proposed intervenors have established that they have a substantial legal interest in the subject matter of this case.

Impairment

"To satisfy this element of the intervention test, a would-be intervenor must show only that impairment of its substantial legal interest is possible if intervention is denied. This burden is minimal." *Miller*, 103 F.3d at 1247. As noted above, the district court in *Grutter* "assumed without deciding" that the proposed intervenors met this element. The district court in *Gratz*, however, determined that because "the proposed intervenors . . . failed to articulate the existence of a substantial legal interest in the subject matter of the instant litigation, it necessarily follows that the proposed intervenors cannot demonstrate an impairment of any interest." The proposed intervenors in *Gratz* continue to argue on appeal that a decision in favor of the plaintiff will adversely affect their interest in educational opportunity by diminishing their likelihood of obtaining admission to the University and by reducing the number of African-American and Latino/a students at the University.

As we have now decided, the district court erred in determining that the proposed intervenors did not have a substantial interest in the subject matter of this case. Consequently, we must likewise conclude that the district court erred in its analysis of the impairment element as well. There is little room for doubt that access to the University for African-American and Latino/a students will be impaired to some extent and that a substantial decline in the enrollment of these students may well result if the University is precluded from considering race as a factor in admissions. Recent experiences in California and Texas suggest such an outcome. The probability of similar effects in Michigan is more than sufficient to meet the minimal requirements of the impairment element.

Inadequate Representation

Finally, the prospective intervenors must show that the existing defendant, the University, may not adequately represent their interests. However, the proposed intervenors are "not required to show that the representation will in fact be inadequate." *Miller*, 103 F.3d at 1247. Indeed, "[i]t may be enough to show that the existing party who purports to seek the same outcome will not make all of the prospective intervenor's arguments." *Id.*

As a preliminary matter, there is some dispute about the relevant standard for determining whether this element has been met when the existing defendant is a governmental entity. The district court in *Gratz* mentioned that the plaintiff relied on Hopwood v. State of Texas, 21 F.3d 603 (5th Cir. 1994), for the proposition that a stronger showing of inadequacy is required when a governmental agency is involved as the existing defendant. On reconsideration, however, the district court made clear that it had simply noted the plaintiff's argument in regard to the higher *Hopwood* standard but had not applied this higher standard. In *Grutter*, by contrast, the district court does appear to have applied the more demanding *Hopwood* standard. However, this circuit has declined to endorse a higher standard for inadequacy when a governmental entity in involved. For example, in *Miller*, where the defendants included the Secretary of State and the Attorney General, this court clearly stated that the proposed intervenors were required only to show that the representation *might* be inadequate. The district court in *Grutter* therefore erred in applying the higher standard articulated by the Fifth Circuit in *Hopwood*.

The proposed intervenors insist that there is indeed a possibility that the University will inadequately represent their interests, because the University is subject to internal and external institutional pressures that may prevent it from articulating some of the defenses of affirmative action that the proposed intervenors intend to present. They also argue that the University is at less risk of harm than the applicants if it loses this case and, thus, that the University may not defend the case as vigorously as will the proposed intervenors. The district court in *Gratz*, however, found that the proposed intervenors did not identify any specific separate or additional defenses that they will present that the University will not present. The district court in *Grutter* also found that the proposed intervenors failed to show that the University would not adequately represent their interests.

We conclude that the district court erred in each of these cases. The Supreme Court has held, and we have reiterated, that the proposed intervenors' burden in showing inadequacy is "minimal." *See* Trbovich v. United Mine Workers, 404 U.S. 528, 538 n.10 (1972). The proposed intervenors need show only that there is a *potential* for inadequate representation. The proposed intervenors in these two cases have presented legitimate and reasonable concerns about whether the University will present particular defenses of the contested race-conscious admissions policies. We find persuasive their argument that the University is unlikely to present evidence of past discrimination by the University itself or of the disparate impact of some current admissions criteria, and that these may be important and relevant factors in determining the legality of a race-conscious admissions policy. We must therefore conclude that the proposed intervenors have articulated specific relevant defenses that the

University may not present and, as a consequence, have established the possibility of inadequate representation.

CONCLUSION

For the reasons set out above, we find that the proposed intervenors have shown that they have a substantial legal interest in the subject matter of this matter, that this interest will be impaired by an adverse determination, and that the existing defendant, the University, may not adequately represent their interest. Hence, the proposed intervenors are entitled to intervene as of right and the district court's decision in each of these cases denying the motion for intervention as of right cannot be sustained. While this determination renders moot the question of permissive intervention under Rule 24(b), we do not believe that the denial of intervention on a permissive basis was erroneous. . . .

■ STAFFORD, District Judge, dissenting. . . .

There is nothing in the record of either case to suggest that the University of Michigan will not zealously defend its voluntarily-adopted admissions policies, will not present all relevant evidence in support of its admissions policies, will not resist unspecified pressures that could temper its ability to defend its admissions policies, or will not raise all defenses or make all arguments that the prospective intervenors may raise or make. Because I do not think that we should substitute our judgment for the informed judgment of the two respective trial judges who determined that, based on the record before them, intervention was not merited, I must respectfully dissent.

COALITION TO DEFEND AFFIRMATIVE ACTION V. GRANHOLM

501 F.3d 775 (6th Cir. 2007)

■ COLE, Circuit Judge.

Before us are two appeals challenging a district court's order denying intervention under Federal Rule of Civil Procedure 24(a) and (b) to (1) the Michigan Civil Rights Initiative committee (the "MCRI"), (2) the American Civil Rights Foundation (the "ACRF"), and (3) Toward a Fair Michigan's ("TAFM," collectively, the "proposed intervenors"). Each wishes to intervene in an action brought against (1) Jennifer Granholm, the Governor of Michigan, and (2) the Regents of the University of Michigan, the Board of Trustees of Michigan State University, and the Board of Governors of Wayne State University (collectively, the "Universities"), seeking to invalidate and permanently enjoin from enforcement a recently enacted amendment to Michigan's constitution that outlaws, among other things, sex- and race-based preferences in public education, public employment, and public contracting. Mich. Const., art. 1, § 26. The amendment was the result of the Michigan voters' approval, in November 2006, of Proposal 06-2 ("Proposal 2"), a statewide ballot initiative. For the following reasons, we affirm the district court's denial of intervention to the proposed intervenors.

I. BACKGROUND

From approximately July 2004 through December 2004, the MCRI, with the assistance of paid agents, solicited signatures in support of placing a statewide ballot initiative, which would later become Proposal 2, on Michigan's November 2006 general election ballot. Proposal 2 has been characterized as "anti-affirmative action," because, if approved, it would amend Michigan's constitution to prohibit the state from granting "preferential treatment to, any individual or group on the basis of race, sex, color, ethnicity, or national origin in the operation of public employment, public education, or public contracting." Mich. Const., art. 1, § 26. . . . [O]n November 7, 2006, Michigan voters approved Proposal 2, with approximately 57.9% of voters favoring it. After its approval, Proposal 2 was scheduled to go into effect on December 23, 2006.

The day after the election, however, on November 8, the Coalition to Defend Affirmative Action, Integration and Immigrant Rights, and Fight for Equality By Any Means Necessary, along with other organizations and individuals (collectively, the "Plaintiffs"), filed suit in the Eastern District of Michigan against Governor Granholm and the Universities, seeking a declaratory judgment that the amendment was invalid and a permanent injunction against its enforcement. "In their amended complaint, [P]laintiffs contended that Proposal 2 violates two federal constitutional provisions (the First and Fourteenth Amendments), three federal civil rights statutes (Title VI, Title VII [,] and Title IX)[,] and one presidential order (Executive Order 11246)." . . .

On December 14, . . . the MCRI and the ACRF jointly moved to intervene as well. . . .

On December 18, TAFM and Eric Russell, a white applicant to the University of Michigan Law School, jointly moved to intervene in the lawsuit. . . . On December 19, the district court entered a preliminary injunction . . . enjoining the application of Proposal 2 to the Universities' admissions and financial-aid policies until July 1, 2007, and dismissed the Universities' cross-claim. . . .

On December 27, 2006, the district court granted Eric Russell's motion to intervene but denied the MCRI's, the ACRF's, and TAFM's motions both as of right and by permission. The next day, . . . the MCRI, the ACRF, and TAFM all appealed the denials of their motions to intervene.

On December 29, 2006, . . . a panel of this Court stayed the district court's preliminary injunction pending appeal, allowing article I, section 26 of the Michigan Constitution to take immediate effect. The merits appeal of the district court's preliminary injunction is still pending before this Court.

II. ANALYSIS

. . .

A. *Intervention as of Right*

. . . We have explained that a proposed intervenor must establish four factors before being entitled to intervene: (1) the motion to intervene is timely; (2) the proposed intervenor has a substantial legal interest in the subject matter of the case; (3) the proposed intervenor's ability to protect their interest may be impaired in the absence of intervention; and (4) the parties already before the court cannot adequately protect the proposed intervenor's interest. Grutter v. Bollinger, 188 F.3d 394, 397-98 (6th Cir. 1999). Acknowledging that Rule 24 should be "broadly construed in favor of potential intervenors," the district court nevertheless held that none of the proposed intervenors met any of the four factors.

"We review de novo motions to intervene as of right, except for the timeliness element, which is reviewed for an abuse of discretion." Northland Family Planning Clinic, Inc. v. Cox, 487 F.3d 323, 344 (6th Cir. 2007) (citing *Grutter*, 188 F.3d at 398). . . .

We begin by addressing whether the proposed intervenors have a substantial legal interest in the litigation. Because we conclude that none do, we need not address the remaining factors.

1. *Substantial Legal Interest*

"The proposed intervenors must show that they have a substantial interest in the subject matter of this litigation." Although we have noted that this Circuit "has opted for a rather expansive notion of the interest sufficient to invoke intervention of right," Mich. State AFL-CIO v. Miller, 103 F.3d 1240, 1245 (6th Cir. 1997), this does not mean that any articulated interest will do. Of course, establishing a substantial legal interest "is necessarily fact-specific."

a. *The MCRI and the ACRF*

According to the MCRI and the ACRF, "they were at the forefront of the protracted campaign to adopt Proposal 2 and are committed to ensuring its constitutionality and timely implementation." The MCRI, headed by Jennifer Gratz, the lead plaintiff in Gratz v. Bollinger, 539 U.S. 244 (2003), is registered with the Michigan Secretary of State as the official ballot-question committee for Proposal 2, and was, by all accounts, the driving force behind the controversial solicitation of signatures necessary to place Proposal 2 on the ballot. The ACRF is a public-interest corporation dedicated to eradicating sex and race preferences throughout the United States. Ward Connerly, an ACRF board member, was instrumental in the passage of Proposition 209 in California . . . . Indeed, by design, Proposal 2 tracks the language of Proposition 209. The MCRI and the ACRF worked together, expending labor and funds, to see that Proposal 2 found its way on Michigan's November 2006 general election ballot and to see that the Michigan voters approved Proposal 2. The district court recognized that "[i]t would not be unreasonable to posit that [Proposal 2] would not have reached the ballot without their efforts."

Both the MCRI and the ACRF argue that as groups substantially involved in the process leading to the adoption of the challenged amendment, they have a legal interest in the subject matter of this lawsuit. They rely primarily on our decisions in *Grutter* and *Miller* . . . . We, however, conclude that our precedent requires a contrary conclusion. Since the district court denied the proposed intervenors motions back in December, we decided *Northland Family Planning,* which is directly on point and controls our disposition.

In *Northland Family Planning,* six health-care facilities and four physicians filed suit against various Michigan officials, seeking to invalidate and enjoin the enforcement of the Legal Birth Definition Act, which "prohibit[ed] the practice colloquially referred to as partial-birth abortions." Like Proposal 2, the Legal Birth Definition Act became law after a successful proposal by a citizen initiative petition. Prior to the district court holding the Act unconstitutional (which we affirmed), a group called "Stand Together to Oppose Partial-Birth-Abortion" ("STTOP") moved to intervene in the litigation under Federal Rule of Civil Procedure 24(a) and (b). Similar to the MCRI and the ACRF, "STTOP is a ballot-question committee, which was formed to promote the passage and continued viability of the Legal Birth Definition Act." . . .

In affirming the denial of STTOP's motion to intervene, we held that an organization involved in the process leading to the adoption of a challenged law, does not have a substantial legal interest in the subject matter of a lawsuit challenging the legality of that already-enacted law, unless the challenged law regulates the organization or its members. In so holding, we drew a distinction between cases involving challenges "to the procedure required to pass a particular rule, as opposed to the government's subsequent enforcement of the rule after its enactment." . . . [W]e further explained, "in a challenge to the constitutionality of an already-enacted statute, as opposed to the process by which it is enacted, the public interest in its enforceability is entrusted for the most part to the government, and the public's legal interest in the legislative process becomes less relevant." . . .

Like STTOP's relationship to the Legal Birth Definition Act, the MCRI was created and continues to exist for the purpose of passing and upholding Proposal 2. The ACRF's goals are, of course, more national, but for the purposes of this case, its relationship to Proposal 2 and interest in the underlying litigation is identical to the MCRI's. . . . *Northland Family Planning* compels us to hold that the MCRI's and the ACRF's status as organizations involved in the process leading to the adoption of Proposal 2 is insufficient to provide them with a substantial legal interest in a lawsuit challenging the validity of those portions of Michigan's constitution amended by Proposal 2.

This is not to say that all organizations that advocate for the passage of a law lack a substantial legal interest in a suit challenging the government's subsequent enforcement of that law. Indeed, we have held that where a group is "regulated by the new law, or, similarly, whose members are affected by the law, may likely have an ongoing legal interest in its enforcement after it is enacted." [*Northland Family Planning*, 487 F.3d] at 345; *accord, e.g., Grutter*, 188 F.3d at 401 (holding that proposed intervenors, who were applicants to the University of Michigan, had a substantial legal interest in the school's admissions process); *Miller*, 103 F.3d at 1247 (holding that the Michigan Chamber of Commerce had a substantial legal interest where it was regulated by at least three of the four statutory provisions challenged by plaintiffs). Where, however, an organization has only a general ideological interest in the lawsuit-like seeing that the government zealously enforces some piece of legislation that the organization supports — and the lawsuit does not involve the regulation of the organization's conduct, without more, such an organization's interest in the lawsuit cannot be deemed substantial.

Here, the MCRI and the ACRF have only a general ideological interest in seeing that Michigan enforces Proposal 2. Each group asserts that its mission to enforce civil-rights laws at all levels of government will be impeded if not granted intervention. . . . This, however, amounts to only a generic interest shared by the entire Michigan citizenry. An "interest so generalized will not support a claim for intervention as of right." *Miller*, 103 F.3d at 1246. Thus, the MCRI's and the ACRF's cognizable legal interests extend only to suits challenging the legislative process by which Proposal 2 was approved. . . . As we aptly explained in *Northland Family Planning*, "[w]ithout these sorts of limitations of the legal interest required for intervention, Rule 24 would be abused as a mechanism for the over-politicization of the judicial process."

The MCRI and the ACRF point out, however, that in *Grutter* we reversed a district court's denial of intervention as of right to the Citizens for Affirmative Action's Preservation ("CAAP"), "a nonprofit organization whose stated mission was to preserve the opportunities in higher education for African-American and Latino/a students in Michigan." In *Grutter*, we held that CAAP had a substantial legal interest in a lawsuit challenging the constitutionality of the University of Michigan's race-conscience admissions policy. The MCRI and the ACRF contend that CAAP, like them, had only an ideological interest in the lawsuit . . . .

The MCRI and the ACRF misidentify CAAP's interest in *Grutter*. Although CAAP certainly had a general ideological aversion to the elimination of the University of Michigan's race-conscience admissions policy, its members were also directly affected by the challenged policy. At the time of the litigation, CAAP was a coalition consisting of minority students and civil-rights groups, among others, premised on preserving affirmative action in higher education. Indeed, consistent with the makeup of its members, the district court treated CAAP's interests as identical to the proposed minority-student intervenors in that lawsuit, who, like Eric Russell, no doubt had a substantial legal interest in the litigation. . . .

Thus, we hold that the MCRI and the ACRF lack a substantial legal interest in the outcome of this case and affirm the district court's denial of their joint motion to intervene as of right. Accordingly, as mentioned, we need not address the remaining intervention-as-of-right elements.

b. *TAFM*

TAFM's contention that it is entitled to intervene as of right is even less compelling. We have little trouble concluding that TAFM is without a substantial legal interest in the outcome of this case. TAFM took no position in favor or against Proposal 2 before, during, or after the November 2006 election, and instead sought only to "promote an educated decision on the question by Michigan citizens through civil and informed discourse." By all accounts, neither TAFM nor its members are regulated by the challenged constitutional amendment. At best, TAFM has only an ideological interest in seeing that Proposal 2 is enforced. . . .

B. *Permissive Intervention*

. . . "The denial of permissive intervention should be reversed only for clear abuse of discretion by the trial judge."

In denying the proposed intervenors permissive intervention, the district court explained that, "in cases of this importance, [the district courts] are mere way stations on the judicial road to resolution by courts beyond," and that granting intervention to the proposed intervenors "will inhibit, not promote, a prompt resolution. . . ." The district court expressed further concern that the proposed intervenors would "seek to file more claims, amend pleadings even further, and inject issues that may not lead directly to a resolution of the issues circumscribed by the present pleadings." This, coupled with the district court's conclusions that the proposed intervenors lacked a substantial legal interest in the lawsuit, and that the proposed intervenors were adequately represented by existing parties, was a sufficient analysis of the relevant criteria required by Rule 24(b). We cannot say that we are "left with a definite and firm conviction[ ]" that the district court acted outside its discretion when it denied permissive intervention to the MCRI, the ACRF, and TAFM. . . .

■ KENNEDY, Circuit Judge, concurring in part and dissenting in part.

I concur with the majority's disposition with regard to appellant TAFM. I cannot, however, agree that *Northland Family Planning* "compels us to hold that the MCRI's and the ACRF's status . . . is insufficient to provide them with a substantial legal interest" in this case. . . .

. . . *Northland Family Planning* is distinguishable because (1) the challenged state law in that case was enacted by the legislature, rather than by the citizens through constitutional amendment as here, and (2) the groups here have raised reasons why they cannot rely on the office of the Michigan Attorney General to vigorously advocate the constitutionality of Proposal 2. . . .

There are good reasons to conclude . . . that the sponsors of a constitutional amendment, like Proposal 2 in this case, have a greater interest in defending the measure than the group that sought to intervene in *Northland Family Planning*. . . . When the government has passed a law, it can be trusted to administer it. When, as here, however, government did not pass the law, but rather the citizens of the state amended their constitution in a general election (arguably because their elected officials would not accede to their will), that presumption does not arise. . . .

I would [also find] that (1) the district court abused its discretion when it determined that the motion to intervene was not timely, (2) the ability of MCRI and ACRF to protect its substantial legal interest may be impaired in the absence of intervention, and (3) that the Attorney General, as well as the other parties in the case, might not adequately represent that interest.

Notes

1.   In both *Grutter* and *Coalition to Defend Affirmative Action*, the nonparties wished to intervene as defendants. You might think it odd that a nonparty would willingly become a defendant, but in public-law litigation, an entity that wants its views heard must intervene on whichever side it supports. It is also common for parties to seek to intervene as plaintiffs. *See, e.g.*, Cook v. Boorstin, 763 F.2d 1462 (D.C. Cir. 1985).

2.   For purposes of preventing relitigation of common issues, intervention as plaintiffs is more critical. Intervention provides a vehicle for some claimants to enter a case, but it is far from the silver bullet of aggregation. To begin with, a putative intervenor must have a claim or interest; thus, when injuries are temporally dispersed, intervention by those not yet injured is unlikely. Next, when claims are geographically dispersed, those with claims elsewhere must find out about the case. Finally, in all circumstances, the putative intervenors must choose to enter the case. But what incentive do they have to do so? If they had wanted to join the case and if the existing plaintiffs were willing to have them, they putative intervenors could have joined as co-plaintiffs under Rule 20(a)(1). They did not do so, perhaps because (1) they perceived that they were best served by going it alone, (2) they had sufficiently distinct interests or litigation strategies that they wished to remain separate from the plaintiff(s), or (3) the plaintiff(s) believed that the putative intervenors' interests and strategies were so distinct that the existing plaintiff(s) refused to join with the putative intervenors.

If either of the first two situations is true, it is unlikely that putative intervenors will intervene; intervention will occur only when the present case threatens to do more harm to the putative intervenors than they can gain from litigating separately. In the third situation, putative intervenors have an incentive to join, but intervention is likely to pull the case in a different direction — a result that damages the autonomy of the original plaintiff(s) and likely eats into the efficiency gains that joint treatment might otherwise obtain. *Cf.* Smuck v. Hobson, 408 F.2d 175, 179 (D.C. Cir. 1969) ("The decision whether intervention of right is warranted thus involves an accommodation between two potentially conflicting goals: to achieve judicial economies of scale by resolving related issues in a single lawsuit, and to prevent the single lawsuit from becoming fruitlessly complex or unending."); Bethune Plaza, Inc. v. Lumpkin, 863 F.2d 525 (7th Cir. 1988) (arguing that allowing broad intervention of right "would turn the court into a forum for competing interest groups, submerging the ability of the original parties to settle their own dispute (or have the court resolve it expeditiously)"); Edward J. Brunet, *A Study in the Allocation of Scarce Judicial Resources: The Efficiency of Federal Intervention Criteria*, 12 GA. L. REV. 701, 746 (1978) (arguing that intervention is likely to lead to greater efficiency in many instances, but noting "the possibility that judges might allow potentially counter-productive intervention").

Of course, sometimes none of these three scenarios applies, and the original plaintiff(s) welcome the intervenors into the case. *See, e.g., Cook,* 763 F.2d 1462. Our point is not that intervention is completely ineffective as an aggregation tool, only that it is incomplete and unlikely to achieve, on its own, the socially desirable level of aggregation.

3.   Even if a putuative intervenor wants to intervene and intervention is socially desirable, the putative intervenor must meet the criteria for intervention. Rule 24 provides for two forms of intervention: intervention of right under Rule 24(a) and permissive intervention under Rule 24(b). Because courts have more discretion in permitting permissive intervention and also have more discretion to limit the rights of permissive intervenors to participate fully, *see* 7C CHARLES ALAN WRIGHT ET AL., FEDERAL PRACTICE AND PROCEDURE §§ 1913, 1922 (3d ed. 2007), persons generally prefer to be intervenors of right. Nevertheless, because it "plainly dispenses with any requirement that the intervenor shall have a direct personal or pecuniary interest in the subject if the litigation," *see* SEC v. United States Realty & Improvement Co., 310 U.S. 434, 459 (1940), permissive intervention is a viable option for persons that fail to meet the Rule 24(a) criteria but are interested in participating in a case. *But see* City of Herriman v. Bell, 590 F.3d 1176, 1184 (10th Cir. 2010) ("[T]o intervene under Rule 24(b) the proposed intervenor must have a claim or defense that shares at least some aspect with a claim or defense presented in the main action.").

4.   *Grutter* and *Coalition to Defend Affirmative Action* list the four elements for Rule 24(a)(2) intervention of right: timeliness, an "interest relating to the property or transaction that is the subject of the action," a practical impairment or impeding of the intervenor's "ability to protect its interest," and inadequate representation by existing parties. The first and last elements create obstacles to intervention only occasionally. Arguments over the propriety of intervention of right, however, usually revolve around

the second and third elements — whether the putative intervenor has a cognizable "interest" and whether the existing litigation "as a practical matter impair[s] or impede[s]" that interest.

(a) Courts construe the timeliness element flexibly, with factors such as the length of the delay in requesting intervention, the reasons for the delay, and the prejudice to the parties caused by the delay often influencing their decisions. *See* 7C WRIGHT ET AL., *supra*, § 1916.

(b) *Grutter* and *Coalition to Defend Affirmative Action* show the slipperiness of trying to define the "interests" that justify intervention. As both cases say, the presumption is to treat the concept broadly, in order to allow liberal intervention. Perhaps the most famous description of the liberal approach is found in Nuesse v. Camp, 385 F.2d 694, 700 (D.C. Cir. 1967):

> [T]he "interest" test is primarily a practical guide to disposing of lawsuits by involving as many apparently concerned persons as is compatible with efficiency and due process.

One reason why there has not been more clarity about the meaning of "interest" is that the Supreme Court seems to be of two minds. In *Cascade Natural Gas Corp. v. El Paso Natural Gas Co.*, 386 U.S. 129 (1967), the acquisition of one natural-gas supplier by another was found to have violated the antitrust laws. During divestiture hearings, the State of California, a distributor of the acquired company's natural gas, and a large consumer sought to intervene to assure that the acquired company be restored as an effective competitor. The Court held that the State and the user could intervene under a since-abrogated intervention rule. It then allowed the distributor to intervene under Rule 24(a)(2). On the other hand, in *Donaldson v. United States*, 400 U.S. 517 (1971), the Court refused to permit the target of an Internal Revenue Service investigation to intervene in an enforcement proceeding in which the Service sought the target's employment records. "What is obviously meant" by Rule 24(a)(2), the Court said, "is a significantly protectable interest." 400 U.S. at 531. Since the target could protect his interest in a subsequent trial, there was no reason to "unwarrantedly cast doubt upon and stultify the Service's every investigatory move." *Donaldson* did not cite *Cascade*. Can you reconcile the results? *See* Diamond v. Charles, 476 U.S. 54, 68 (1986) (citing both cases favorably in dicta).

One possible distinction between the cases is that in *Donaldson*, another forum existed to protect the putative intervenor's rights, while in *Cascade*, no other forum existed. Another distinction is that in *Cascade*, the plaintiff, the United States, was dragging its feet, even though the Court had, in a prior opinion, ordered "divestiture without delay." United States v. El Paso Natural Gas Co., 376 U.S. 651, 662 (1964). On this distinction, *Donaldson*'s narrow view of "interest" is correct, and *Cascade*'s willingness to permit intervention should "be regarded as an extraordinary case, occasioned by the Court's 'splenetic displeasure' with the government's lack of diligence in seeking relief." United States v. Hooker Chems. & Plastics Corp., 749 F.2d 968, 986 n.15 (2d Cir. 1984) (Friendly, J.).

It is also possible to reconcile *Cascade* with *Donaldson* along the following principle: that the term "interest" should be interpreted either broadly or narrowly depending on the public interest involved in permitting intervention. *See* Tachiona v. Mugabe, 186 F. Supp. 2d 383 (S.D.N.Y. 2002). One problem with this reconciliation is that any effort "to deduce from those cases rules applicable to ordinary private litigation is fraught with great risks." 7C WRIGHT ET AL., *supra*, §1908.1. Moreover, the language of Rule 24(a)(2) speaks in terms of the putative intervenor's "interest," not the public interest.

(c) The third element for Rule 24(a)(2) intervention is a practical impairment of the interest. The seminal case is *Atlantis Development Corp. v. United States*, 379 F.2d 818 (5th Cir. 1967), in which the court held that the stare decisis effect of a judgment was a sufficient practical impairment to justify intervention. In *Atlantis*, however, the claims of the intervening parties and the plaintiffs involved the same transaction. Should other stare decisis effects constitute an impairment for Rule 24(a)(2) purposes? For instance, could a tort plaintiff intervene in an unrelated tort case merely because the case might unfavorably decide legal issues relevant to the tort plaintiff's case? Moreover, many courts hold to the view that district court judgments have no stare decisis effect. Threadgill v. Armstrong World Indus., Inc., 928 F.2d 1366, 1371 (3d Cir. 1991). In *Bethune Plaza*, 863 F.2d 525, the court took a cautious view, holding that only the stare-decisis effect of an appellate court decision might support intervention — and even then, only in some cases. *See also* FDIC v. Jennings, 816 F.2d 1488, 1492 (10th Cir. 1987) (stare-decisis effect not enough to justify intervention when plaintiff's and putative intervenor's theories of liability differed, intervenor would inject new issues into trial, and intervention would make a complicated suit less manageable).

(d) As *Grutter* mentions, the putative intervenor's burden to show inadequate representation is "minimal." Trbovich v. United Mine Workers, 404 U.S. 528, 538 n.10 (1972). In *Trbovich*, a union member sought to intervene in a case brought by the Secretary of Labor to set aside a union election. The union member wanted the same relief as the Secretary, but the Supreme Court pointed out that the Secretary's obligation to consider the public interest in addition to union members' interests made the Secretary's representation of the union member inadequate. Despite its minimal nature, the adequacy element occasionally trips up a putative intervenor that cannot show how his or her interests diverge from those that the government is vindicating. *See, e.g., Hooker*, 749 F.2d 968; Edwards v. City of Houston, 78 F.3d 983, 1005 (5th Cir. 1996).

5.   Because the "interest" and "impairment" language of both rules is nearly identical, is every person who is entitled to intervene under Rule 24(a)(2) also a required party under Rule 19(a)(1)(B)(i)? In *Eldredge v. Carpenters 46 Northern California Counties JATC*, 662 F.2d 534 (9th Cir. 1981), the Ninth Circuit found that the 4,500 signatory employers to a collective bargaining agreement were not required parties in a case alleging that an apprenticeship program established by the agreement was

discriminatory. Because the employers had "ceded whatever legally protectable interest they may have had in selecting apprentices" to the program, the court found no "interest" under Rule 19(a). The court then noted that employers might wish to consider intervening under Rule 24. 662 F.2d at 538. If the employers had no "interest" for purposes of Rule 19(a), how could they have had an "interest" for purposes of Rule 24(a)? Consider the discussion in *Smuck v. Hobson*:

> The phrasing of Rule 24(a)(2) as amended parallels that of Rule [19(a)(1)(B)(i)] concerning joinder. But the fact that the two rules are entwined does not imply that an "interest" for the purpose of one is precisely the same as for the other. The occasions upon which a petitioner should be allowed to intervene under Rule 24 are not necessarily limited to those situations when the trial court should compel him to become a party under Rule 19. [408 F.2d at 178.]

6. Permissive intervention requires that the putative intervenor make a timely application and that the intervenor's "claim or defense . . . shares with the main action a common question of law or fact." In deciding whether to grant intervention, Rule 24(b)(3) requires a court to consider "whether the intervention will unduly delay or prejudice the adjudication of the original parties' rights." The court's decision is also informed by matters such as the delay in the request for intervention, the desire to avoid a multiplicity of suits, the often-opposing desire to ensure that the original parties receive a fair hearing on their original claims, other forums in which the intervenor's rights can be determined, and other means (including amicus participation) by which the intervenor's interests can be protected or otherwise aired. *See* 7C WRIGHT ET AL., *supra*, § 1913.

7. An even more limited form of participation, for which the Federal Rules of Civil Procedure do not specifically provide, is amicus curiae (literally, "friend of the court") status. Unlike an intervenor, an amicus does not become a party, and typically does not become involved in discovery. *See* United States v. Mich., 940 F.2d 143, 163-66 (6th Cir. 1991); *but see* Hoptowit v. Ray, 682 F.2d 1237, 1260 (9th Cir. 1982) (amicus participated in discovery, trial, and appeal). Rather, the amicus provides input (usually by brief) on legal issues. A judge can, and often does, limit amicus participation just to the issues raised by the parties. *See* Richardson v. Ala. State Bd. of Educ., 935 F.2d 1240, 1247 (11th Cir. 1991); *but see* Michel v. Anderson, 14 F.3d 623 (D.C. Cir. 1994) (court would consider jurisdictional arguments made by amicus but not by parties). Amicus participation tends to be more common at the appellate level. *See* Fed. R. App. P. 29.

The precise requirements for amicus participation have changed over time. Initially, an amicus needed to show an interest in the litigation. *See* N. Sec. Co. v. United States, 191 U.S. 555 (1903). Furthermore, the concept of a "friend" of the court was thought to imply a degree of neutrality that excluded obviously interested partisans from amicus participation. *See* Funbus Sys., Inc. v. Cal. Pub. Util. Comm'n, 801 F.2d 1120, 1124-25 (9th Cir. 1986); Village of Elm Grove v. Py, 724 F. Supp. 612 (E.D. Wis. 1989).

The modern trend has been to care less about the precise interests or the neutrality of an amicus, and to focus instead on whether the information supplied by the amicus "is timely, useful, or otherwise necessary to the administration of justice." *United States v. Michigan*, 940 F.2d at 165; *see* Linda Sandstrom Simard, *An Empirical Study of Amici Curiae in Federal Court: A Fine Balance of Access, Efficiency, and Adversarialism*, 27 REV. LITIG. 669 (Summer 2008).

3. A Preliminary Assessment

Joinder is the principal procedural mechanism by which courts are able to adjudicate related disputes in a single forum. The rules are structured to permit joinder on a liberal scale: The federal system and the systems of most state courts stand ready to determine all claims by or against all parties whose lawsuits arise out of the same "transaction or occurrence." This phrase has been consistently interpreted to permit joinder as long as joint treatment is efficient. Thus, the joinder rules are capacious enough to allow the aggregation needed in complex litigation.

But this potential for aggregation is not fully realized, for two distinct reasons. First, even though the system *permits* such broad joinder, it does not *require* such joinder. The joinder system also values litigant — especially plaintiff — autonomy highly. For the most part, therefore, the parties — especially plaintiff(s) — determine the party structure. Leaving such structural issues in the hands of the parties is an approach highly consonant with the adversarial model of American litigation. But adversaries are likely to be motivated not by the social interest in efficiency but by their private interests in achieving the best outcome. In some instances, social and the private interests will converge, and optimal aggregation will occur. In other instances, it will not. No joinder rule permits courts, in all situations, to override adversarial jousting and fill in the gaps of party joinder to achieve optimal aggregation.

A second reason is factual: Joining everyone in one case is not always possible. Claims might be geographically dispersed; in this situation, rules of venue and jurisdiction (both personal and subject-matter) might make aggregation in one forum impossible. (*See infra* pp. 134-39, 249-340.) In other situations claims are temporally dispersed, so that those receiving injuries at an earlier date will file suit, while those that have not yet received injuries cannot yet join the case. The problem of these "future plaintiffs" is particularly acute in certain mass torts involving exposure to substances whose alleged health effects are manifested years later.

Although the law of joinder is limited, it is not the only means by which aggregation can occur. In the rest of this chapter, we examine other methods by which the American system responds, directly or indirectly, to the problem of repetitive litigation. Chapter Four examines the class-action device, which is one of the most potent aggregation devices available in the American system and which deserves special consideration. Only after we have studied how these approaches supplement the joinder system can we render a full appraisal of the American approach to aggregation.

As we continue to chase this Holy Grail of aggregation, however, it is always worth asking whether the price of its attainment is too high. Optimal aggregation can frustrate litigant autonomy to structure a case in a litigant's best interests. As Section A of this chapter showed, decisions about whether we aggregate and when we aggregate influence the outcomes attained by litigants. Are the benefits of aggregation worth the costs? Does a cost-benefit analysis ignore other values that are not easily captured in the utility-maximizing balance? The joinder materials that we have examined raise these issues throughout; so will the materials on other aggregation mechanisms to which we now turn.

C. AGGREGATION THROUGH CONSOLIDATION AND TRANSFER

The idea behind consolidation and transfer is to allow plaintiffs to file their cases wherever they wish, and against whom they wish — and then to consolidate or transfer the cases in a single forum after the fact. To the extent that consolidation and transfer are effective tools, they operate to reduce the repetitive litigation of related claims that are dispersed across different courtrooms and courthouses. But consolidation and transfer devices have limitations, especially when cases are dispersed among the court systems of the various states or between the federal and state systems. Consolidation and transfer are also of modest assistance when claims are temporally dispersed.

We begin with the easier situation: the consolidation of cases filed in one district. We then move to the more difficult situation of transferring cases filed in different districts. In the latter context we encounter one of complex litigation's signature mechanisms: the multidistrict transfer.

1. Intradistrict Consolidation

On the federal level, the principal rule describing the power of a federal court to consolidate cases is Rule 42(a), which permits a court to order consolidation when "actions before the court involve a common question of law or fact." Although Rule 42(a) states no standard for consolidation aside from the existence of a common question, Rule 42(a)(3) permits the court to "issue any other order to avoid unnecessary cost or delay." That language suggests that achieving the same goal also applies to consolidation.

By its plain terms, Rule 42(a) permits only the consolidation of two or more cases that are already pending in the same court. In that sense, it provides a limited power. But this power is also the first necessary piece in solving the consolidation puzzle. With litigation that is not geographically dispersed, it is likely that the plaintiffs in most or all of the related cases will file their cases in one court. Moreover, the interdistrict consolidation mechanisms that we will study shortly transfer cases from multiple courts into a single court; and it does little good to transfer related cases into one court if the cases cannot be consolidated once they arrive in that court.

At first blush, the desirability of intradistrict consolidation seems so obvious that it is hard to imagine any reasons to oppose it. Reconsider that view after reading the following cases.

JOHNSON V. CELOTEX CORP.

899 F.2d 1281 (2d Cir. 1990)

■ CARMAN, Judge.

. . . This appeal is one of many which arises from thousands of cases filed against manufacturers and producers of asbestos, resulting in unparalleled litigation in American tort law. [Two plaintiffs, Johnson and Higgins, filed separate suits in the United States District Court for the Southern District of New York. Both suits alleged injuries due to asbestos exposure. Among the eleven defendants sued were Celotex Corporation and Owens-Illinois, Inc., both of whom manufactured asbestos products.

[Judge Sifton, before whom both cases were pending, ordered] that *Higgins* and *Johnson* be consolidated for trial. Plaintiff Higgins, a chipper and caulker, whose work included chipping off welded sections to prepare for repair work of others, was alleged to have died because of exposure to asbestos while at the Brooklyn Navy Yard from approximately 1946 to 1966. Appellee-plaintiff, John Johnson (plaintiff), an electrician's helper, alleged that he had contracted lung disease while working at the Brooklyn Navy Yard from 1942 to 1945 by inhaling asbestos fibers during this employment. [In 1985 Johnson was diagnosed as suffering from a benign asbestos-related lung condition.]

The Court declined to trifurcate or bifurcate the trial to separate issues of causation and compensatory damages from issues of liability and punitive damages. Appellants' motions to have separate juries consider claims of liability and punitive damages in *Johnson*, apart from claims in *Higgins*, were denied. . . . Eight defendants settled and one filed a petition in bankruptcy prior to trial. The *Higgins* and *Johnson* cases proceeded to trial against defendants Celotex, Owens-Illinois and Raymark Industries, Inc. (Raymark). The jury rendered a verdict for the plaintiffs in both cases. In *Higgins*, plaintiff was awarded $1 million in compensatory damages and $3 million in punitive damages, divided equally among Celotex, Raymark and Owens-Illinois. In *Johnson* compensatory damages were $350,000 (Celotex 12.5%, Raymark 12.5%, Owens-Illinois 5.0%, seven settling co-defendants 10% each), and punitive damages were assessed as follows: Celotex $1 million, Raymark $1 million and Owens-Illinois $800,000. Plaintiff Ann Marie Johnson was awarded $30,000 for loss of services.

[After trial, it was discovered that the court had no subject-matter jurisdiction over Higgins' claim, and it was dismissed. In addition, Raymark filed for bankruptcy protection, which stayed the proceedings as to Raymark. On appeal, Celotex and Owens-Illinois] contend the trial court abused its discretion in consolidating the *Johnson* and *Higgins* cases. . . .

Rule 42(a) of the Federal Rules of Civil Procedure empowers a trial judge to consolidate actions for trial when there are common questions of law or fact to avoid unnecessary costs or delay. . . .

The trial court has broad discretion to determine whether consolidation is appropriate. In the exercise of discretion, courts have taken the view that considerations of judicial economy favor consolidation. However, the discretion to consolidate is not unfettered. Considerations of convenience and economy must yield to a paramount concern for a fair and impartial trial. When exercising its discretion, the court must consider:

> [W]hether the specific risks of prejudice and possible confusion [are] overborne by the risk of inconsistent adjudications of common factual and legal issues, the burden on parties, witnesses and available judicial resources posed by multiple lawsuits, the length of time required to conclude multiple suits as against a single one, and the relative expense to all concerned of the single-trial, multiple-trial alternatives.

[Hendrix v. Raybestos-Manhattan, Inc., 776 F.2d 1492, 1495 (11th Cir. 1985)] When considering consolidation, a court should also note that the risks of prejudice and confusion may be reduced by the use of cautionary instructions to the jury and verdict sheets outlining the claims of each plaintiff.

In the instant case, the court properly exercised its discretion in consolidating these two cases for trial. Courts in the Southern and Eastern Districts of New York have used the criteria outlined in an unreported Maryland district court case, In re All Asbestos Cases Pending in the United States District Court for the District of Maryland, (D. Md. Dec. 16, 1983) (en banc) as a guideline in determining whether to consolidate asbestos exposure cases. . . . [T]he criteria included: "(1) common worksite; (2) similar occupation; (3) similar time of exposure; (4) type of disease; (5) whether plaintiffs were living or deceased; (6) status of discovery in each case; (7) whether all plaintiffs were represented by the same counsel; and (8) type of cancer alleged. . . ." *In re Maryland Asbestos Cases* at 3. *Johnson* and *Higgins* had the following characteristics: (1) common worksite; (2) similar occupation to the extent that both workers were exposed to asbestos in a bystander capacity (they worked in trades that did not involve direct handling of asbestos products); (3) Johnson's period of exposure was from 1942 to 1945 while Higgins' exposure was from approximately 1946 to 1966; (4) Johnson contended that he suffered from asbestosis and asbestosis-related pleural disease while it was alleged that Higgins died as a result of asbestosis and lung disease; (5) Johnson was living and Higgins was deceased; (6) *Johnson* and *Higgins* were both ready for trial; and (7) all plaintiffs were represented by the same counsel. Instructions were given throughout the trial and in the charge to caution the jury to consider each plaintiff's claims individually. Two separate verdict forms were provided to the jury, one for *Johnson*, the other for *Higgins*.

An appellate court will not disturb a trial court's decision to consolidate unless a clear abuse of discretion is shown. In the instant case, the trial court was well within its discretion to consolidate the two cases and the court acted throughout in a manner which ensured that each plaintiff's claim was considered separately. . . .

[T]he judgment of the district court is affirmed.

■ [The opinion of MAHONEY, Circuit Judge, concurring in part and dissenting in part, is omitted.]

MALCOLM V. NATIONAL GYPSUM CO.

995 F.2d 346 (2d Cir. 1993)

■ McLAUGHLIN, Circuit Judge.

Keene Corporation appeals from a final judgment of the United States District Courts for the Eastern and Southern Districts of New York (Charles P. Sifton, Judge) awarding plaintiff Roberta Kranz, as the executrix of the estate of Lee Lewis, $226,038.49 for personal injury, wrongful death, and loss of consortium. . . . The claims arose from Lewis's exposure to asbestos products manufactured by Keene's subsidiary, the Baldwin-Ehret-Hill Company ("BEH"). For the reasons stated below, we reverse and remand for a new trial.

BACKGROUND

The Explosion Of Asbestos Litigation

One of the greatest challenges facing both state and federal courts is the crush of tort suits arising from the extensive use of asbestos as flame-retardant insulation throughout much of this century. Asbestos litigation today constitutes the largest mass toxic tort in the United States. *See* In re Joint E. & S. Dists. Asbestos Litig., 125 F.R.D. 60, 63 (E.D.N.Y. 1989) (hereinafter "*Drago*"). To date, more than 200,000 asbestos cases have been filed by injured persons and their heirs, and as many as 250,000 additional cases may be filed in years to come. . . .

In New York, the Chief Judges of the Second Circuit, the Southern District, and the Eastern District transferred all cases filed in either district to the district judge in this action for purposes of discovery. We commend Judge Sifton for his masterful stewardship of these cases. Eventually, the cases approached the Rubicon of either settling or going to trial. To facilitate settlements and provide for manageable trials, the cases were "subdivided by the location in which the plaintiff suffered primary exposure."

The Consolidation Here

In the instant action, 600 cases were consolidated. The thread upon which all 600 cases hung was that each plaintiff had been exposed to asbestos in one or more of over 40 power-generating stations, or "powerhouses" as they are called, in New York State.

Forty-eight were selected from the 600 cases for trial on a reverse-bifurcated basis, i.e. damages to be tried first and then liability. The damages trial began on April 1, 1991. Each of the 48 plaintiffs had named as defendants between 14 and 42 manufacturers or distributors of asbestos-containing products. Of these, 25 appeared at trial as direct defendants. Several of the defendants impleaded third-party defendants. For example, on March 18, 1991, 13 days before the trial began, Judge Sifton allowed defendant Owens-Corning Fiberglas Corporation to implead over 200 companies. Some of the third-party defendants, in turn, impleaded fourth-party defendants.

During the four-month damages trial, evidence of the debilitating diseases and/or deaths of all 48 plaintiffs was presented to the jury. Often, the plaintiffs themselves would testify to the devastating consequences suffered as a result of asbestos-related disease. Where, as in Kranz-Lewis's case, a particular victim had died prior to trial, evidence regarding his disease and death was presented by family members. A parade of medical doctors testified on the etiologies and pathologies of the asbestos-related diseases suffered by each of the plaintiffs. Economists testified concerning the present value of past and future income streams, and the dollar value of ordinary household services.

In addition, detailed testimony for each victim was necessary concerning his degree of impairment, specific medical history, emotional state, and medical prognosis. Further complicating matters, the jury had to sift through each victim's medical history to determine whether factors other than asbestos, such as smoking, were responsible, in whole or part, for his physical complaints. . . . Claims by spouses and children presented extensive plaintiff-specific evidence.

After four months of such evidence, the jury returned verdicts for 45 of the plaintiffs for an aggregate of over $94 million. Kranz-Lewis's damages were calculated as $1,682,795, including $1,250,000 for "Pain, Suffering and Other Non-Economic Losses to Decedent."

The liability portion of the trial began on September 11, 1991. During this phase, the jury was presented with a dizzying amount of evidence regarding each victim's work history. Where a victim, like Lewis, had died before trial, the sites where he had worked during his career, the types of asbestos-containing products with which he had been involved, and the identity of the manufacturers or distributors of the asbestos products to which he may have been exposed were reconstructed through the testimony of family members and co-workers.

The testimony of just one plaintiff illustrates the cosmic sweep of the factual data that the jury had to absorb. That plaintiff, Hubert Feeley, testified that from 1953 until 1974, he worked in "'hundreds of' buildings; "could not keep track of all of them;" used "[p]ipe covering, block cement, asbestos cloth, all different sorts of cement;" worked for "[t]wenty-five or so" employers; travelled as an asbestos worker to Alaska, Egypt, Wyoming, Minnesota, West Virginia, Connecticut, White Plains and New Jersey; worked in "[o]ffice buildings, high-rises, shopping centers, [and] state office buildings" including the Chase Manhattan Building, the Exxon Building and the Holiday Inn; and worked in at least seven powerhouses throughout the greater New York area. He also testified that he used at least ten different products while working for one of his many employers. He candidly testified on direct examination that "of the hundreds of buildings [he had] worked on," "[m]aybe eight or nine were powerhouses." Finally, the longest period that he could recall working at any one powerhouse was "about six months." . . .

After three months, plaintiffs rested on December 4, 1991. For the next three months, the defendants presented their case. The district court and the lawyers valiantly attempted to maintain the identity of each claim throughout the trial. The jury was instructed on several occasions to consider each case separately and each juror was given a notebook for this purpose. Thanks to the effective settlement techniques of the district judge and a special master, only two plaintiffs remained by the time the jury rendered its liability verdict. It concluded that appellant Keene Corporation was 9% liable for the Kranz-Lewis damages.

Following the verdict, Keene moved for judgment as a matter of law, a new trial, or other post-verdict relief, contending, *inter alia*, that the district court's decision to consolidate the 48 cases for trial constituted prejudicial error. The district judge rejected this argument without extended discussion; and, after molding the verdict in accordance with various New York statutes to add interest and to reflect different degrees of fault among defendants, entered a judgment for Kranz against Keene for $226,038.29.

DISCUSSION

Addressing the complaints of hundreds of thousands of severely injured asbestos plaintiffs, while safeguarding the rights of the defendants, all the while searching for equitable resolutions in each case, is a herculean task. Many of the asbestos victims suffered exposure for decades and at many different worksites. Finding an appropriate forum to resolve all these claims with minimal delay is the goal. Faced with this challenge, district judges throughout the country have reacted with commendable ingenuity. Pre-trial consolidation for the purposes of discovery, the appointment of special masters to expedite settlement, and, especially, the liberal use of consolidated trials have ameliorated what might otherwise be a sclerotic backlog of cases. . . .

The benefits of efficiency can never be purchased at the cost of fairness. As we recently stated:

> [W]e are mindful of the dangers of a streamlined trial process in which testimony must be curtailed and jurors must assimilate vast amounts of information. The systemic urge to aggregate litigation must not be allowed to trump our dedication to individual justice, and we must take care that each individual plaintiff's — and defendant's — cause not be lost in the shadow of a towering mass litigation.

In re Brooklyn Navy Yard Asbestos Litig., 971 F.2d 831, 853 (2d Cir. 1992); *see also* Arnold v. Eastern Air Lines, Inc., 712 F.2d 899, 906 (4th Cir. 1983) (en banc) ("considerations of convenience may not prevail where the inevitable consequence to another party is harmful and serious prejudice"); Baker v. Waterman S.S. Corp., 11 F.R.D. 440, 441 (S.D.N.Y. 1951) ("a fair and impartial trial to all litigants" is the foremost concern when considering consolidation); Cain v. Armstrong World Indus., 785 F. Supp. 1448, 1457 (S.D. Ala. 1992) (new trial warranted where "[a]s the evidence unfolded . . . it became more and more obvious . . . that a process had been unleashed that left the jury the impossible task of being able to carefully sort out and distinguish the facts and law of thirteen plaintiffs' cases that varied greatly in so many critical aspects").

To strike the appropriate balance as to consolidation *vel non*, "[c]ourts in the Southern and Eastern Districts of New York have used [a standard set of] criteria . . . as a guideline in determining whether to consolidate asbestos exposure cases." Johnson [v. Celotex Corp. 899 F.2d 1281, 1285 (2d Cir. 1990)]. These criteria include: "(1) common worksite; (2) similar occupation; (3) similar time of exposure; (4) type of disease; (5) whether plaintiffs were living or deceased; (6) status of discovery in each case; (7) whether all plaintiffs were represented by the same counsel; and (8) type of cancer alleged. . . ." *Id.* (quoting In re All Asbestos Cases Pending in the United States Dist. Court for the Dist. of Md., slip op. at 3 (D. Md. Dec. 16, 1983) (en banc)). As in *Johnson*, we again conclude that the test furnishes a useful guideline to evaluate consolidation of asbestos cases.

(1) *Worksite*

Plaintiffs did not all work at the same worksite. Rather, their only worksite similarity was that each was alleged to have suffered some part of his asbestos exposure at one or more of over 40 power-generating plants throughout New York State. Judge Sifton apparently selected the 48 cases based on his conclusion that, in each case, the plaintiff had suffered "primary" exposure in such powerhouses. . . .

The work history evidence of [plaintiffs] dispels the notion that they shared primary exposure at the 40-odd power plants. Indeed, the record contains evidence of over 250 worksites. Thus, not only was there no common worksite in this case, but any contention that there was a common type of worksite must be viewed with a skeptical eye.

(2) *Similar Occupation*

This inquiry is significant because a worker's exposure to asbestos must depend mainly on his occupation. . . . The occupations of the plaintiffs in this case ranged from plumbers to machinists to carpenters to boilermakers to sheet-metal workers.

(3) *Times of Exposure*

The third factor similarly does not support a finding of commonality. The time frame that the jury was required to consider was enormous: a period involving exposures in intervals that began as early as the 1940's and ended as late as the 1970's. While some plaintiffs suffered asbestos exposure over periods of up to 30 years, others had much shorter periods of exposure, undercutting the benefit of efficiency, and increasing the likelihood of prejudice . . . .

(4) *Disease Type*

Not all plaintiffs alleged the same type of disease. Rather, of the 48 plaintiffs, 28 suffered from asbestosis, 10 suffered from lung cancer, and 10 from mesothelioma. The significance of this disparity is obvious. When the plaintiffs suffer from the same disease, the economy derived by not rehashing the etiology and pathology of the particular disease will be great, while the concomitant prejudice will be minimal. Here, by contrast, the jury was required to hear testimony about three different diseases. The opportunity for prejudice is particularly troubling where, as here, asbestosis sufferers, who may under certain circumstances expect close to normal life spans, are paired for trial with those suffering from terminal cancers, such as mesothelioma and lung cancer.

(5) *The Living & The Dead*

Some victims in this case were still living during trial. Others had already died. . . . The significance of this factor is evident. *Drago*, 125 F.R.D. at 65-66 ("[T]he presence of wrongful death claims and personal injury actions in a consolidated trial is somewhat troublesome. . . . [T]he dead plaintiffs may present the jury with a powerful demonstration of the fate that awaits those claimants who are still living.").

(6) *Discovery Status*

Keene does not argue that any of the 48 cases was not ready for trial. We note however, the absence of any express finding of readiness in the district court's decision rejecting a challenge to consolidation. Query: were the 200 third-party defendants that were impleaded two weeks before the trial ready for the trial?

(7) *Counsel*

Plaintiffs were represented by five law firms, each of which played an active role throughout the trial.

(8) *Cancer*

Two different types of cancer were alleged: lung cancer, and mesothelioma, a cancer of the lining of the wall of the chest. Each required distinct testimony regarding its etiology, pathology, and consequences.

In addition to the foregoing eight factors, courts contemplating consolidation must also take into account the number of cases affected. In re New York Asbestos Litig., 145 F.R.D. 644, 653 (S.D.N.Y. 1993) (consolidating twelve cases). Here, the maelstrom of facts, figures, and witnesses, with 48 plaintiffs, 25 direct defendants, numerous third-and-fourth party defendants, and evidence regarding culpable non-parties and over 250 worksites throughout the world was likely to lead to jury confusion. Kranz quite properly emphasizes the number of precautions the district court took to assure that each case maintained its identity. We conclude, however, that the sheer breadth of the evidence made these precautions feckless in preventing jury confusion.

Plaintiff contends that even if the consolidation was not warranted, the decision below should nevertheless be affirmed because Keene can show no prejudice arising from it. We disagree. At trial, Keene did not dispute that Lewis was exposed to a wide array of asbestos-containing products; rather, Keene disputed exposure to *its* products. Also, Keene readily conceded that it was known early on that massive, prolonged, and *direct* exposure to pure asbestos dust was dangerous; but Keene vehemently disputed that *bystander* exposure, such as that suffered by Mr. Lewis, was known to be dangerous when Lewis was allegedly exposed to Keene's products.

We are concerned that the jury's ability to focus on this distinction may have been compromised in this case. While the evidence regarding Lewis's exposure to Keene's products was vague, minimal, and heavily circumstantial when compared to the extensive evidence regarding the products of defendant Owens-Corning Fiberglas, the jury apportioned an equal 9% liability to each defendant. This is hard to explain. We conclude that under the unique circumstances of this case, there is an unacceptably strong chance that the equal apportionment of liability amounted to the jury throwing up its hands in the face of a torrent of evidence. . . .

While district courts need not perform any specific rituals or recite any incantations before ordering cases to be consolidated, they must in every instance consider whether the "actions involv[e] a common question of law or fact." Only then can all be assured that innovative and creative efforts to provide compensation to deserving plaintiffs do not violate Federal Rule of Civil Procedure 42(a), which is designed to achieve efficiency without compromising a litigant's right under the Seventh Amendment to a jury trial.

We do not wish to be understood as condemning all consolidations of asbestos cases. Our holding today is narrow and amounts to little more than a caution that it is possible to go too far in the interests of expediency and to sacrifice basic fairness in the process. In ordering consolidation we repeat the counsel of Talleyrand, "Pas trop de zele" — not too much zeal.

Accordingly, the judgment of the district court is reversed, and the matter remanded for a new trial.

■ WALKER, Circuit Judge, dissenting. . . .

Consolidated trials are an indispensable means of resolving the thousands of asbestos claims flooding our state and federal courts, as well as claims arising from other types of mass torts. I agree that trial courts should not employ consolidated trials where they pose substantial risks of prejudice . . . However, by overturning the consolidated trial here, where indisputably substantial common issues of fact and law prevailed, without a substantial showing of prejudice, I think the majority errs, while sending the wrong message to courts faced with the difficult task of administering such claims in a manner that is fair to all parties involved.

Notes

1. *Malcolm* cites *Cain*, which held that the consolidation of thirteen asbestos cases was too many, and *New York Asbestos Litigation*, which held that the consolidation of twelve asbestos plaintiffs was not too many. *See also* In re Asbestos Litig., 173 F.R.D. 81 (S.D.N.Y. 1997) (permitting consolidation and distinguishing *Malcolm* in an asbestos case involving five plaintiffs and six defendants). Do these cases suggest that, unless a very high degree of factual overlap among related cases exists, the maximum carrying capacity of the consolidation device is somewhere around a dozen cases? If so, consolidation will be a useful device when small numbers of claimants file suit in a single court, but will be less helpful as the number of related cases rises. In other words, consolidation is least helpful as an aggregation tool when it is most needed.

2. One aspect of *Johnson* and *Malcolm* deserves attention: They both involved consolidation for trial purposes. It is possible to argue for a looser, more aggregation-friendly standard during pretrial, in which the problem of jury confusion is absent and joint discovery can achieve economies of scale. (Just because cases are consolidated for pretrial purposes, they need not be consolidated for trial.) But consider *In re: Repetitive Stress Injury Litigation*, 11 F.3d 368 (2d Cir. 1993), *reh'g*, 35 F.3d 637 (2d Cir. 1994). A district court's *pretrial* consolidation order consolidated forty-four cases, filed against two defendants, that alleged various repetitive-stress injuries from the use of the defendants' machines.

The Second Circuit treated the defendants' immediate appeal of this order as a petition for a writ of mandamus. Although a writ of mandamus "is an extraordinary measure and should be done sparingly, to redress a 'clear abuse of discretion,' or 'to confine an inferior court to a lawful exercise of its prescribed authority,'" *id.* at 373, the court found the relief warranted after applying the six-factor test from *Johnson* and *Malcolm*:

> . . . [T]he sole common fact among these cases is a claim of injury of such generality that it covers a number of different ailments for each of which there are numerous possible causes other than the tortious conduct of one of the defendants. As a class, the plaintiffs presumably have the usual wide variety of individual health conditions and problems that are found in any similar sample of persons and that might be relevant to the claimed injuries. The defendants manufacture or distribute a variety of mechanical devices with differing propensities, if any, to cause the harm alleged. With regard to issues of law, the plaintiffs come from a variety of jurisdictions and rely for their claims on the laws of different states. [*Id.*]

The court of appeals also thought that the failure of the Judicial Panel on Multidistrict Litigation to order the consolidation of repetitive-stress cases under 28 U.S.C. § 1407 (a statute about which we learn more shortly) was significant. *See* In re Repetitive Stress Injury Prods. Liab. Litig., 1992 WL 403023 (J.P.M.L. 1992). After noting that the district court could assign all related cases to one judge for coordinated handling, the court concluded:

> . . . Our differences with the district court are more than philosophical. The burden is on the party seeking aggregation of discovery or other proceedings to show common factual or legal issues warranting it. A party may not use aggregation as a method of increasing the costs of its adversaries — whether plaintiffs or defendants — by forcing them to participate in discovery or other proceedings that are irrelevant to their case. It may be that such increased costs would make settlement easier to achieve, but that would occur only at the cost of elemental fairness. [11 F.3d at 374.]

3. Earlier in the chapter, we encountered the same "common question of law or fact" language in the joinder rules, especially Rules 20(a) and 24(b). There we saw that the "common question" language was read in light of concerns for efficiency and fairness. The same concerns appear to inform Rule 42(a). But should the concerns be weighed exactly the same in the two situations? Put differently, does Rule 42(a) pose unique constraints or permit additional flexibility in comparison to joinder — or should a court treat the consolidation question exactly as if the plaintiffs were seeking to join cases? Rule 20(a) contains a "transaction or occurrence" requirement not present in Rule 42(a), although Rule 42(a)'s the implicit requirements of convenience and fairness map onto the "transaction or occurrence" requirement quite well. *See* 9A CHARLES A. WRIGHT & ARTHUR R. MILLER, FEDERAL PRACTICE AND PROCEDURE § 2382 (3d ed. 2008) (describing differences between Rule 42(a) and joinder).

4. As *Malcolm* states, a critical issue under Rule 42(a) is whether consolidation will make it impossible for the factfinder — especially a jury — to distinguish among numerous plaintiffs, defendants, evidence, and claims. We examine some devices to reduce jury confusion and increase jury comprehension in Chapter Ten. The probable success of those devices

might well determine the success of a motion for consolidation. Procedure is a seamless web, in which late-in-the-day issues such as trial procedure affect early-in-the-day decisions on aggregation. Since most cases settle during pretrial, however, should possible difficulties at trial determine whether consolidation for pretrial purposes is appropriate?

5. For a consolidation under a state rule equivalent to Rule 42(a), see ACandS, Inc. v. Godwin, 667 A.2d 116 (Md. 1995) (trial consolidation of six asbestos cases against six defendants was proper). *Godwin* arose out of one of the largest consolidations in history; the Circuit Court for Baltimore City consolidated 8,555 asbestos cases against 150 manufacturers for pretrial handling. For trial, however, the Circuit Court consolidated groups of only five to ten cases at a time. *Godwin*, 667 A.2d at 119-20.

6. "Consolidation" is a word of flexible meaning. It is "generally used in three different contexts: (1) when several actions are stayed while one is tried, and the judgment in the case tried will be conclusive as to the others; (2) when several actions are combined and lose their separate identities, becoming a single action with a single judgment entered; and (3) when several actions are tried together, but each suit retains its separate character, with separate judgments entered." Schnabel v. Lui, 302 F.3d 1023, 1035 (9th Cir. 2002). Although Rule 42(a) can be read as authorizing either of the second or third types of consolidation, the usual view is that Rule 42(a) authorizes only the third. *Id.*; *see* Johnson v. Manhattan Ry., 289 U.S. 479, 496-97 (1933) ("[C]onsolidation is permitted as a matter of convenience and economy in administration, but does not merge the suits into a single cause, or change the rights of the parties, or make those who are parties in one suit parties in another"). Thus, consolidated cases do not lose their individual identities; the court must enter separate orders and judgments in each of the consolidated cases.

For a detailed analysis of the jurisdictional and procedural consequences of consolidating litigation, see Joan Steinman, *The Effects of Case Consolidation on the Procedural Rights of Litigants: What They Are, What They Might Be — Part 1: Justiciability and Jurisdiction (Original and Appellate)*, 42 UCLA L. REV. 717 (1995), and *Part 2: Non-Jurisdictional Matters*, 42 UCLA L. REV. 967 (1995).

7. Courts enjoy a sua sponte power to order consolidation. *See* Devlin v. Transp. Commc'ns Int'l Union, 175 F.3d 121, 130 (2nd Cir. 1999) ("A district court can consolidate related cases under Federal Rule of Civil Procedure 42(a) sua sponte."); Disher v. Citigroup Global Markets, Inc., 487 F. Supp. 2d 1009, 1013-14 (S.D. Ill. 2007) ("A court may order consolidation sua sponte and, if need be, over the objections of parties."). Consolidation is usually accomplished by the order of a single judge; it does not require the action of each judge before whom a case is pending.

In other ways, however, consolidation falls well short of the mark as an aggregation device. It does not force nonparties into the consolidated litigation. It does not permit the consolidation of cases pending in different federal districts. *See* 9A WRIGHT ET AL., *supra*, § 2382. Nor does it permit a federal court to order the consolidation of federal and state cases. *Id.*

Therefore, we turn to other consolidation devices to see whether they can overcome some or all of these obstacles to aggregation.

2. Interdistrict Transfers

When cases are spread among different districts, federal courts have two principal devices to effect the cases' consolidation in a single district. The first is the § 1404(a) transfer. The second is the § 1407(a) multidistrict transfer. This subsection examines § 1404(a), which states in full: "For the convenience of parties and witnesses, in the interest of justice, a district court may transfer any civil action to any other district or division where it might have been brought." As we now see, § 1404(a) has some significant limits as an aggregation device. Nonetheless, it is helpful to study § 1404 transfer and its limits before considering the benefits, as well as the limits, of the more useful § 1407 transfer, which the next subsection examines.

IN RE JOINT EASTERN AND SOUTHERN DISTRICTS ASBESTOS LITIGATION

769 F. Supp. 85 (E. & S.D.N.Y. 1991)

■ WEINSTEIN, District Judge.

Some 700 asbestos cases in which workers were allegedly exposed to asbestos while working in New York state powerhouses were consolidated for trial and settlement by Judge Charles P. Sifton. Some of these cases were pending in the Southern District of New York and others were pending in the Eastern District of New York. After Judge Sifton, a judge of the Eastern District of New York, was designated by the Chief Judge of the Court of Appeals to sit in the Southern District of New York, he was designated by the Chief Judges of the Eastern and Southern District courts of New York to supervise all asbestos cases in the districts. The first forty-eight of these cases are on trial before Judge Sifton. . . .

All 700 cases are before Judge Jack B. Weinstein for purposes of settlement. . . .

Several third-party defendants have moved to dismiss defendant Owens Corning Fiberglas' (OCF) third-party contribution claims against them on the ground that . . . the order of consolidation previously entered must be vacated because actions pending in different districts cannot be consolidated. . . .

. . . Presently, over 30,000 asbestos personal injury cases are pending in federal courts nationwide. Extraordinary steps, such as this large consolidation, are necessary to cope with the current judicial asbestos emergency. . . .

Nevertheless, it is asserted that prior cases deny power to consolidate cases pending in different districts. *See, e.g.*, Town of Warwick v. N.J. DEP,

647 F. Supp. 1322, 1324-25 (S.D.N.Y. 1986); Facen v. Royal Rotterdam Lloyd S.S. Co., 12 F.R.D. 443, 443 (S.D.N.Y. 1952).   One 1936 case addressed the problem not of consolidation, but of the power to try a case pending in one district within the geographical confines of another. *See* In re Associated Gas, 83 F.2d 734, 737 (2d Cir. 1936) (Manton, C.J.). . . .

We do not need to decide whether these precedents apply to consolidation of related mega-mass tort cases pending before the courts in different districts in the same circuit. Nor need we decide whether Section 1407 of Title 28, empowering the Multidistrict Panel to transfer cases, exhausts the power of the courts within the same circuit to consolidate cases pending in different districts for trial. The matter is easily resolved by applying Section 1404 of Title 28 to transfer all the related cases to a single district within the circuit. . . .

. . . Factors relevant to a [§ 1404] transfer determination include convenience of parties and witnesses, the relative ease of access to the sources of proof, the availability of process to subpoena witnesses if necessary, considerations of trial efficiency and the interests of the law in the "just, speedy and inexpensive determination" of actions. Fed. R. Civ. P. 1.

In view of the context of asbestos cases, in particular the enormous burden they place on the courts, the plaintiffs' need for prompt relief, and defendants' need to reduce transaction costs, transfer of the Southern District cases to the Eastern District will serve the interests of justice. Consolidation of these legally and factually similar asbestos claims will afford litigants an opportunity to prosecute the cases efficiently and expeditiously. It will avoid needless duplication in proof and decrease wasteful expenditures of time, energy and money. Availability of evidence, process, witnesses and other aspects of convenience weigh heavily in favor of the transfer.

Venue is proper in the Eastern District because each third-party defendant conducts business in the district sufficient to support a finding of residency and because a "substantial part of the events or omissions giving rise to the claim" occurred in the district. 28 U.S.C. § 1391(a). . . .

A judge sitting by designation in a district has authority to transfer cases from that district. This general power is particularly useful in the instant litigation. The pool of attorneys and witnesses is exactly the same in the Eastern and Southern Districts, and their main courthouses are in the City of New York within semaphore flag distance of each other. Consolidation is appropriate and necessary both for judicially efficiency and to provide effective justice to the litigants. Breaking up the consolidated powerhouse cases at this point in the litigation would be wasteful of both court and litigant resources. *Cf.* 28 U.S.C. § 1406 (transfer from "wrong" district to proper district "in the interests of justice").

All consolidated powerhouse cases pending in the Southern District are transferred to the Eastern District.

Notes

1.   To start with the nomenclature, the court that enters the transfer order is called the "transferor court." The court to which the case is transferred is called the "transferee court."

2.   In *Eastern and Southern Districts*, Judge Weinstein hints that § 1404 is not the only power that a transferor court can tap for interdistrict transfers. He first suggests that such a power might exist in Rule 42, which has generally been held not to contain such a power. *See supra* p. 133, Note 7. Then he alludes to the possibility that district courts may enjoy some (inherent?) power to transfer cases within a circuit even if transfer is not authorized under § 1407. He ultimately avoids the question, however, by resolving the case under § 1404. You might nonetheless wish to keep Judge Weinstein's suggestion of alternative sources of power in mind as you examine the limits of §§ 1404 and 1407.

3.   In *Eastern and Southern Districts*, was a § 1404 transfer appropriate? In what ways was the case *after* transfer more convenient for the witnesses or the parties than *before* transfer? Was proof more accessible in Brooklyn than in Manhattan? Was testimony easier or cheaper to obtain? Was the availability of process different? *See* 15 CHARLES A. WRIGHT ET AL., FEDERAL PRACTICE AND PROCEDURE § 3854 (3d ed. 2007) (transfers to nearby transferee forums are not usually "in the interest of justice"). Does *Eastern and Southern Districts* reduce to the holding that a case can be transferred whenever it can be aggregated more efficiently elsewhere? If it does, then has a plaintiff's right of forum selection been effectively abolished? *Cf.* Norwood v. Kirkpatrick, 349 U.S. 29, 32 (1955) ("[P]laintiff's choice of forum is . . . to be considered" but is not dispositive under § 1404).

4.   The right of plaintiffs to select the forum raises an interesting interpretive problem for § 1404: the weight to be given to the "interest of justice" factor. Linguistically, the "interest of justice" clause seems to qualify (and therefore be subordinate to) the "convenience of parties and witnesses" clause. On this reading, convenience is always a necessary element for § 1404 transfers; considerations of justice then act as a further restriction on convenient transfers. On an alternate reading, however, the "interest of justice" clause is an independent clause; thus, even if transfer is not more convenient, a case can be transferred as long as transfer is just. *Eastern and Southern Districts* seems to adopt the latter reading. *See* N.Y. Cent. R.R. v. United States, 200 F. Supp. 944, 946-47 (S.D.N.Y. 1961) (Friendly, J.) (raising issue whether a transfer in "the interest of justice" is possible when the transfer achieves no "convenience"); Heller Fin., Inc. v. Midwhey Powder Co., 883 F.2d 1286, 1293 (7th Cir. 1989) (suggesting that the "interest of justice" factor has independent status).

On either reading, what types of considerations inform the "interest of justice" requirement? As we noted, the plaintiff's right to a forum is one factor. Among the others are "ensuring speedy trials, trying related litigation together, and having a judge who is familiar with the applicable law try the case." *Id.* The availability of a jury familiar with community norms that the law might expect the jury to apply and the likelihood of jury prejudice in the transferor court can also matter. For a general discussion of relevant concerns, see 15 WRIGHT ET AL., *supra*, § 3854.

5. The final clause of § 1404(a) — that transfer can occur only to "to any other district or division where it might have been brought" — contains an important restriction. *Hoffman v. Blaski*, 363 U.S. 335 (1960), held that this clause permits transfer only to a district court in which venue would have been proper if the case had originally been filed there. Subsequent amendments to 28 U.S.C. § 1391, which is the basic venue statute, have somewhat tempered the effect of *Hoffman v. Blaski*; these amendments opened up more venues in which a case could have been filed originally, and therefore opened up more districts to which the case could be transferred under § 1404. Even with these amendments, however, § 1391 often creates no single venue in which all cases in a multiparty controversy can be filed. In these cases, *Hoffman v. Blaski* prevents the aggregation of related cases in a single forum. Moreover, the liberalization of § 1391 has a downside: It provides more districts in which plaintiffs that want to avoid aggregation can file, and more districts in which defendants that want to frustrate aggregation can seek to have cases transferred. *Cf.* In re Fine Paper Antitrust Litig., 685 F.2d 810 (3d Cir. 1982) (despite *Hoffman v. Blaski*, permitting transfer to a district in which case could not originally have been brought after the parties that had made transfer impossible settled and venue in the transferee forum existed for all remaining parties).

6. Transfers under § 1404(a) have certain features that seem desirable in an aggregation device, as well as some features that seem less desirable.

(a) *Desirable Aggregation Features of § 1404 Transfer.* Transfer under § 1404 has two desirable dimensions as an aggregation device. First, when a case is transferred under § 1404, the transfer is effective for all purposes — pretrial, trial, and post-trial. After transfer, the case quite literally behaves as if it had been filed in the transferee forum. Second, any party can seek transfer, *see Hoffman v. Blaski* , 363 U.S. 335 (defendant), and Ferens v. John Deere Co., 494 U.S. 516 (1990) (plaintiff); and, as *Eastern and Southern Districts* shows, the court can order transfer sua sponte.

Providing the defendant and the court a significant opportunity to affect the plaintiff's chosen party and court structure makes transfer a useful adjunct to the system of party joinder, which, as we have seen, generally gives defendants and courts little opportunity to affect potentially aggregation-frustrating joinder decisions by plaintiffs. Indeed, it is arguably the critical antidote. But transfer works as an antidote only if defendants and courts apply it in such a way that aggregation of related litigation becomes the principal goal of using § 1404 in complex litigation. How likely is that? Does giving the plaintiffs the privilege to set the initial party and court structure, giving the defendants the right to seek transfer, and giving the courts discretion to referee the parties' efforts to manipulate forum selection seem like the best formula for securing the correct level of aggregation in complex litigation?

Note that the answer to these last questions depends to some extent on the capacity of the court to which related cases are transferred to handle the cases on a consolidated basis. As we saw in the previous subsection, consolidation has important limits.

(b) *Undesirable Aggregation Features of § 1404 Transfer.* In other ways, § 1404 is not an ideal aggregation device. We have already described *Hoffman v. Blaski*'s barrier to aggregation. Second, a transfer order must issue from the transferor court; a party seeking transfer of numerous related cases bears the burden of obtaining an order from each transferor court. Given the flexibility of § 1404's criteria, there is no guarantee that each transferor judge can or will grant a transfer motion. Third, a court cannot transfer a case to a district that lacks territorial jurisdiction over the parties. *See* Sunbelt Corp. v. Noble, Denton & Assocs., 5 F.3d 28 (3d Cir. 1993); 15 WRIGHT ET AL., *supra*, § 3845. (In the following chapter, we examine in more detail the limits that territorial jurisdiction imposes on aggregation. *See infra* p. 250.) Fourth, § 1404 transfers an entire "action" from one district to another, rather than just the claims that are related to cases in another forum. *See* In re Orthopedic Bone Screw Prods. Liab. Litig. (MDL No. 1014), 79 F.3d 46, 47 (7th Cir. 1996). In some cases, however, it makes little sense to transfer an entire action. For instance, in a medical product-liability case, a plaintiff often joins both the manufacturer and the physician. It may be convenient for cases against the manufacturer to be aggregated in one district, but inconvenient for the doctor to have the case shipped off to another part of the country. Might it be possible to overcome this defect by severing the transferable portion of the action under Federal Rule of Civil Procedure 42(b), and transfer only that portion? *See Sunbelt*, 5 F.3d 28 (raising the possibility of severance); 15 WRIGHT ET AL., *supra*, § 3845 (collecting cases).

A final set of limitations on § 1404 transfer is the inability of § 1404 to address the problems of temporal dispersion or geographical dispersion between state and federal courts. Evidently, § 1404 can do nothing about the claims of nonparties that have not yet filed suit in any court; the statute allows the transfer of *cases*, not *potential claims*. Similarly, § 1404 operates only among the federal courts; a federal court cannot use § 1404 to transfer a case from state court to federal court. Likewise, although a number of states have legislation akin to § 1404 that permits intrastate transfer of cases, a state court in one state cannot use § 1404 or any comparable device to transfer a case to the courts of another state. In 1991 the National Conference of Commissioners on Uniform State Laws proposed a Uniform Transfer of Litigation Act to allow participating states to transfer cases between them "to serve the fair, effective, and efficient administration of justice and the convenience of the parties and witnesses." This transfer was to be made after considering "all relevant factors." The two specific factors mentioned in the Act were "the interest of each plaintiff in selecting a forum and the public interest in securing a single litigation and disposition of related matters." Unif. Transfer of Litig. Act, § 104, 14 U.L.A. 189 (Supp. 1999). The American Law Institute has also proposed federal legislation that would establish a mechanism by which cases could be transferred among state courts or between state and federal courts. AM. L. INST., COMPLEX LITIGATION §§ 4.02, 5.01 (1994). So far, however, no state has enacted the Uniform Act, nor has Congress enacted the ALI proposal.

The inability of § 1404 to reach across the state-federal divide, or to provide state courts with a state-to-state transfer power, is less problematic if another set of devices can handle those situations. In the next section of this chapter, we explore one possible set of devices to remedy the problem: stays and antisuit injunctions. As we will see, however, these devices are of limited assistance in the aggregation context. Moreover, the inability of § 1404 to deal with nonparties is less problematic if another set of devices can handle these situations. In the final section of this chapter, we explore another device — preclusion doctrine — that might remedy the nonparty problem. Again, we will find that preclusion provides only a very narrow solution in some nonparty situations. Therefore, § 1404 must be seen as a helpful but ultimately bounded solution to aggregation.

7.   When a case raises federal-law issues, the transferee court can apply the law of the transferee circuit to the case. In re Korean Air Lines Disaster of Sept. 1, 1983, 829 F.2d 1171 (D.C. Cir. 1987), *aff'd on other grounds* sub nom. Chan v. Korean Air Lines, 490 U.S. 122 (1989). When a case raises state-law issues, however, the transferee court must apply the law of the transferor court. *Ferens*, 494 U.S. 516; Van Dusen v. Barrack, 376 U.S. 612 (1964). Both rules present difficulties. On federal-law issues, a switch in circuit might well be case-dispositive, if the law in the transferor and transferee circuits are markedly different. On the likely assumption that the plaintiff filed the case in the circuit with more favorable law, the transfer raises serious issues about failing to respect the plaintiff's forum choice.   On state-law issues, the transfer of numerous cases to the transferee court means that the court will need to resolve the cases under the laws of numerous states.   This fact complicates the aggregation of related cases, making single-venue aggregation far less efficient and desirable. Moreover, the difficulty of having a judge unfamiliar with the relevant state law decide the case has sometimes been cited as a factor in § 1404 decisions. *See* 15 WRIGHT ET AL., *supra*, § 3854. We return to some of these considerations in Chapter Six, which concerns choice-of-law issues.

8.   Transfer orders under § 1404 are appealable after entry of final judgment. Some interesting questions of appellate jurisdiction arise when the transferor and transferee forums are located in different circuits. The circumstances under which interlocutory review or mandamus is available to review a decision on § 1404 transfer also varies somewhat among the circuits. *See* 15 WRIGHT ET AL., *supra*, § 3855.

3. Multidistrict Transfers Under § 1407

Enacted in 1968, 28 U.S.C. § 1407 creates an entity called the Judicial Panel on Multidistrict Litigation, which is composed of seven federal judges. The Panel has the power to order the transfer of cases for "coordinated or consolidated pretrial proceedings" to a single transferee forum that is chosen by the Panel; the Panel does not itself handle transferred cases. The Panel can exercise this power on its own initiative, or on the motion of any party in any of the cases.

Section 1407(a) establishes four requirements for a multidistrict (or "MDL") transfer: (1) "civil actions involving one or more common questions of fact are pending in different districts"; (2) transfer "will be for the convenience of the parties"; (3) transfer "will be for the convenience of the . . . witnesses"; and (4) transfer "will promote the just and efficient conduct of such actions." The influence of both Rule 42(a) and § 1404(a) is evident in § 1407(a), but § 1407 contains unique features not present in either Rule 42(a) or § 1404(a). Most important, once coordinated pretrial proceedings conclude, § 1407 directs the Panel to remand transferred cases back to their transferor forums for trial. Moreover, the Panel can "separate any claim, cross-claim, counterclaim, or third-party claim and remand any of such claims before the remainder of the action is filed." 28 U.S.C. § 1407(a). Finally, although the statute does not clearly provide for this event, the Panel has authority to transfer related cases (called "tag-along actions") that are filed after the initial transfer order is entered. *See* Rules 1, 12-13 of the Rules of Procedure for the Judicial Panel on Multidistrict Litigation.

Obviously, MDL transfer does not overcome all of the barriers to single-venue aggregation. For instance, it applies only to actions pending in federal court, thus allowing nonparties and those with claims in state court to escape its reach. Nor does its text appear to permit consolidation for trial purposes. In other ways, however, § 1407 seems to be — and is — the most useful aggregation device that we have encountered so far. A single, centralized decision-maker makes the aggregation decision; that decision-maker has sua sponte transfer authority; the device reaches every federal case; the Panel's power to transfer tag-along cases ameliorates to some degree the problem of temporal dispersion; the Panel can aggregate just those claims deserving of consolidated treatment, throwing back the rest; and the district to which the case is transferred need not be either a district in which the case might originally have been brought or a district in which territorial jurisdiction over the parties exists.

Multidistrict transfer is a commonly used device in complex litigation. In the first forty years of § 1407's existence, parties sought MDL treatment approximately 2,000 times. On average, this number translates to about 50 MDL requests per year, but the annual number of requests has been rising in recent years. Although the Panel does not grant all requests for MDL treatment, the chances that litigators who handle complex litigation will eventually become involved in an MDL proceeding are high.

Have we found at last the single-venue aggregation device that we have been seeking? Should it be expanded to overcome its present limitations? Or does it already go too far to destroy the plaintiffs' adversarial right to choose the parties, the claims, and the forum?

IN RE ASBESTOS AND ASBESTOS INSULATION
MATERIAL PRODUCTS LIABILITY LITIGATION

431 F. Supp. 906 (J.P.M.L. 1977)

■ PER CURIAM.

This litigation consists of 103 actions pending in nineteen districts. . . .

The 103 actions have been brought by workers who were exposed to asbestos dust in the course of their employment, or by persons associated with those workers, either as co-workers or as members of the family. Many diverse types of vocational exposure are involved in these actions.

Plaintiffs in most of the actions are or were workers at plants which produce asbestos products (the factory worker actions), or tradesmen who work with a variety of asbestos products (the tradesman actions). A majority of the tradesmen are installers of insulation products containing asbestos. Ninety-four of the actions are tradesman actions and nine of the actions are factory worker actions.

Six of the actions were brought as class actions on behalf of employees at three different plants that manufacture or once manufactured asbestos products. Three of the actions in the Eastern District of Texas were brought as class actions on behalf of employees at a PPG Industries plant in Tyler, Texas. Class certification has been denied in these three actions. The other three purported class actions are pending in the District of New Jersey. Two are brought on behalf of employees of Raybestos Manhattan, Inc. at a now defunct plant in Passaic, New Jersey. The other action is brought on behalf of employees at a Johns-Manville, Inc. plant in Manville, New Jersey. Class certification is still pending in the New Jersey actions.

There are a total of 80 defendants in the 103 actions. The majority of the defendants are manufacturers or distributors of various asbestos products. Johns-Manville is a defendant in 91 of the actions. Seven other defendant corporations are named in more than 50 actions, seven others are named in more than 30 actions, and ten others are named in ten or more actions.

The complaints in the actions generally allege that the defendants wrongfully caused the plaintiffs to be exposed to asbestos dust and asbestos fibers over a period of time, as a result of which the plaintiffs have contracted or are in danger of contracting asbestosis, mesothelioma, or other disorders. Alleged liability is based on the principles of strict liability, negligence, and/or breach of warranties of merchantability and/or fitness. It is also alleged that the defendants knew or should have known of the dangers to persons exposed to asbestos products, but that defendants failed to warn the plaintiffs of these dangers; failed to provide adequate precautions, safety devices, or wearing apparel to prevent exposure; and/or failed to establish reasonable standards for exposure.

Pursuant to 28 U.S.C. § 1407(c)(i) and Rule 8, R.P.J.P.M.L., the Panel issued an order to show cause why all these actions should not be transferred to a single district for coordinated or consolidated pretrial proceedings. All except one of the 55 respondents to the Panel's order to show cause oppose transfer in this litigation. The primary arguments presented by the parties in opposition to transfer are the following:

(1) Many of the actions have been pending for several years and are well advanced in discovery. In several actions a discovery cutoff date or a trial date has been set. Transfer would merely delay the progress of discovery or the trial of those actions.

(2) In several districts, arrangements for voluntarily sharing the common aspects of discovery have been made among the parties to the actions pending within those districts. Transfer would cause unnecessary additional expenses which can be avoided by voluntary coordination of efforts among the parties.

(3) There is a lack of commonality among the parties in these actions.

(a) There is considerable variation in named defendants from action to action. No defendant or category of defendants is a party to all actions. Defendants include manufacturers of asbestos products, distributors of asbestos products, insurance companies, doctors, suppliers of raw asbestos fibers, trade associations, trade unions, and the United States of America.

(b) The plaintiffs are not a homogeneous group. They include insulation workers involved in the installation or removal of insulation products, workers in factories manufacturing asbestos products, co-workers, members of workers' families, and persons living in the proximity of asbestos manufacturing facilities.

(4) Although a common thread among these actions is exposure to some type of asbestos or asbestos product, the circumstances of exposure are predominantly individual to each action. The variables include the following:

(a) type of vocational exposure (e.g. — miner, transporter, factory worker, or tradesman);

(b) products to which exposed;

(c) conditions of exposure;

(d) duration and intensity of exposure;

(e) safety precautions taken by the worker;

(f) medical, personal, employment, and family history of the worker over the long periods of exposure involved (up to 50 years).

Regarding the factory workers and tradesmen, the two basic types of vocational exposure involved, the exposure of factory workers was to 100% raw asbestos, while the exposure of tradesmen was to products which generally contain about 15% asbestos.

(5) The question of causation is an individual issue. Several different types of disorders are alleged, including asbestosis, lung cancer, peritoneal mesothelioma, mesothelioma of the lining of the stomach or gastric organs,

cancer of the esophagus, cancer of the colon, and cancer of the rectum. The question of whether particular disorders may be attributable to exposure to a particular type of asbestos is a matter of dispute among medical authorities. Causation of an individual's disability by asbestos exposure will necessarily be related to the individual factors of length, intensity, and type of vocational exposure, and to the physical characteristics of the person. A considerable amount of technical medical evidence such as diagnoses, x-rays and tissue microscopies will be involved in each action. This evidence is of an individual nature.

Significant differences in causation will exist between the factory worker actions and the tradesman actions. Medical and scientific knowledge concerning the two types of exposure is different. The tradesmen will have been exposed to a wider variety of asbestos products, and will need to prove which products caused their disabilities.

(6) The liability of each defendant in each action is predominantly an individual question. The variables will include the defendants' knowledge at a particular time of the health risks involved in exposure to asbestos, the adequacy of any product testing by the defendant manufacturers, the sufficiency of any warnings or directions for use of products, and the issue of assumption of risk by the plaintiffs. Other variables will include the materials used, the method of manufacture, and the period of production.

(7) Although a common aspect among these actions is the state of medical and scientific knowledge at a particular time regarding the health hazards posed by exposure to asbestos, this knowledge can be readily discerned from literature which is easily available in most medical libraries. The common need for this literature is therefore not a significant justification for transfer.

(8) Local issues will predominate in the discovery process. The medical, personnel, and product use records of each individual will be found locally. Liability in these actions will be based on state substantive law. As a result, transfer would not promote the parties' and witnesses' convenience regarding discovery.

(9) There is not a significant possibility of inconsistent or overlapping class action determinations since any certifiable class could include only those persons who were exposed to asbestos in a specific plant or in the service of a particular employer. The classes alleged to date are properly restricted, and do not overlap in any respect.

Although we recognize the existence of some common questions of fact among these actions, we find that transfer under Section 1407 would not necessarily serve the convenience of the parties and witnesses or promote the just and efficient conduct of the litigation. . . .

The virtually unanimous opposition of the parties to transfer, though a very persuasive factor in our decision to deny transfer in this litigation, is not by itself determinative of the question of transfer under Section 1407. In an appropriate situation, the Panel has the power to order transfer in multidistrict litigation even if all parties are opposed to transfer.

We are, however, persuaded by the parties' arguments in this particular litigation. On the basis of the record before us, the only questions of fact common to all actions relate to the state of scientific and medical knowledge at different points in time concerning the risks of exposure to asbestos. The pertinent literature on this subject is readily available. Many factual questions unique to each action or to a group of actions already pending in a single district clearly predominate, and therefore transfer is unwarranted. Furthermore, many of these actions already are well advanced. Some of the actions have been pending for up to four years, and trial dates or discovery cutoff dates have been set in several actions. Under these circumstances, transfer would not further the purposes of Section 1407.

It is therefore ordered that the order to show cause regarding the [103] actions . . . be, and the same hereby is, vacated.

In re Asbestos Products Liability Litigation (No. VI)

771 F. Supp. 415 (J.P.M.L. 1991)

■　Judge NANGLE, Chairman, delivered the opinion of the Panel, in which Judges POLLAK, WOODWARD, MERHIGE and ENRIGHT joined.[*]

On January 17, 1991, the Panel issued an order to show cause why all pending federal district court actions not then in trial involving allegations of personal injury or wrongful death caused by asbestos should not be centralized in a single forum under 28 U.S.C. § 1407. . . . [T]he parties to the 26,639 actions pending in 87 federal districts . . . are subject to the Panel's order.[2] . . .

Supporting transfer are plaintiffs in approximately 17,000 actions (including a core group of more than 14,000 plaintiffs represented by over 50 law firms) and 30 defendants (24 of which are named in more than 20,000 actions). Opposing transfer are plaintiffs in at least 5,200 actions and 454 defendants. The positions of those parties that have expressed a preference with respect to transferee district are varied. Many parties suggest centralization in what amounts to their home forum. The Eastern District of Pennsylvania is the district either expressly favored or not objected to in the greatest number of pleadings. The Eastern District of Texas, which is the choice of the aforementioned core group of 14,000 plaintiffs, is also the district that has generated the most opposition from defendants. . . . Some parties' forum recommendations are expressed in the

---

[*]　Judges Dillin and Pollack did not participate in the decision of this matter.

2.　. . . [A]s of March 31, 1991, nearly 31,000 actions were pending in federal districts. Based on Panel communications with courts throughout the country, the approximately 4,000 pending actions not embraced by the present order likely include actions that, as of January 17, 1991, were overlooked, in trial or already at least partially tried but not yet statistically closed because, inter alia, claims against one or more defendants were stayed under the Bankruptcy Code.

form of a suggested individual transferee judge or transferee judge structure.

. . . [T]he Panel finds that the actions in this litigation involve common questions of fact relating to injuries or wrongful death allegedly caused by exposure to asbestos or asbestos containing products, and that centralization under § 1407 in the Eastern District of Pennsylvania will best serve the convenience of the parties and witnesses and promote the just and efficient conduct of this litigation.

DISCUSSION

Any discussion of § 1407 transfer in this docket must begin with the recognition that the question does not arise in a vacuum. Indeed, the impetus for the Panel's order to show cause was a November 21, 1990 letter signed by eight federal district judges responsible for many asbestos actions in their respective districts. These judges, citing the serious problem that asbestos personal injury litigation continues to be for the federal judiciary, requested that the Panel act on its own initiative to address the question of § 1407 transfer. Furthermore, as the title of this docket suggests, this is the sixth time that the Panel has considered transfer of asbestos litigation. On the five previous occasions (1977, 1980, 1985, 1986 and 1987) that the Panel considered the question, it denied transfer in each instance.

The Panel's constancy is not as dramatic as a mere recitation of the denials might suggest, however. The 1986 and 1987 dockets considered by the Panel involved only five and two actions, respectively. The 1985 Panel decision pertained not to personal injury/wrongful death asbestos actions but rather to property damage claims of school districts that incurred significant costs in removing asbestos products from school buildings. The denial in the 1980 Panel docket was based almost exclusively on the movants' failure to offer any distinctions that would warrant a disposition different from the Panel's first asbestos decision in 1977.

It is only in the 1977 decision, pertaining to 103 actions in nineteen districts, that the Panel offered any detailed analysis of its asbestos litigation reasoning with respect to asbestos personal injury/wrongful death actions. . . .

Many of the parties presently opposing transfer in this docket rely on the facts and reasoning of the Panel's 1977 transfer decision. They insist that the situation that warranted denial then not only still prevails but has been magnified by the greatly increased number of actions and parties in federal asbestos personal injury/wrongful death litigation — more than 30,000 pending federal actions now, as opposed to the 103 actions subject to the Panel's 1977 decision. In our view, it is precisely this change that now leads us to conclude that centralization of all federal asbestos personal injury/wrongful death actions, in the words of 28 U.S.C. § 1407(a), "will be for the convenience of parties and witnesses and will promote the just and efficient conduct of such actions." In short, we are persuaded that this litigation has reached a magnitude, not contemplated in the record before us in 1977, that threatens the administration of justice and that requires a new, streamlined approach.

The Panel is not the first to reach such a conclusion. Just this past March 1991, the Judicial Conference Ad Hoc Committee on Asbestos Litigation . . . stated as follows:

> The committee . . . has concluded that the situation has reached critical dimensions and is getting worse. What has been a frustrating problem is becoming a disaster of major proportions to both the victims and the producers of asbestos products, which the courts are ill-equipped to meet effectively. . . .
>
> It is a tale of danger known in the 1930s, exposure inflicted upon millions of Americans in the 1940s and 1950s, injuries that began to take their toll in the 1960s, and a flood of lawsuits beginning in the 1970s. On the basis of past and current filing data, and because of a latency period that may last as long as 40 years for some asbestos related diseases, a continuing stream of claims can be expected. . . . Predictions have been made of 200,000 asbestos disease deaths before the year 2000 and as many as 265,000 by the year 2015.
>
> The most objectionable aspects of asbestos litigation can be briefly summarized: dockets in both federal and state courts continue to grow; long delays are routine; trials are too long; the same issues are litigated over and over; transaction costs exceed the victims' recovery by nearly two to one; exhaustion of assets threatens and distorts the process; and future claimants may lose altogether. . . .

Conclusions similar to those of the Judicial Conference Asbestos Committee have also been reached by judges actively involved in asbestos litigation. In perhaps the most recent comprehensive review of asbestos litigation, Judge Jack B. Weinstein (E.D.N.Y.) observed:

> The large number of asbestos lawsuits pending throughout the country threatens to overwhelm the courts and deprive all litigants, in asbestos suits as well as other civil cases, of meaningful resolution of their claims. . . .
>
> The heyday of individual adjudication of asbestos mass tort lawsuits has long passed. The reasons are obvious: the complexity of asbestos cases makes them expensive to litigate; costs are exacerbated when each individual has to prove his or her claim de novo; high transaction costs reduce the recovery available to successful plaintiffs; and the sheer number of asbestos cases pending nationwide threatens to deny justice and compensation to many deserving claimants if each claim is handled individually. The backlog is eroding a fundamental aspiration of our judicial system to provide equality of treatment for similarly situated persons.
>
> Overhanging this massive failure of the present system is the reality that there is not enough available from traditional defendants to pay for current and future claims. Even the most conservative estimates of future claims, if realistically estimated on the books of

many present defendants, would lead to a declaration of insolvency — as in the case of some dozen manufacturers already in bankruptcy.

Given the dimensions of the perceived problem in federal asbestos litigation, it is not surprising that no ready solution has emerged. The Judicial Conference Asbestos Committee concluded that the only true solution lies in Congressional legislation. Nevertheless, it stressed that "at the same time, or failing congressional action, the federal judiciary must itself act now to achieve the best performance possible from system under current law." . . .

It is against this backdrop that the Panel's decision and role in this litigation must be understood. First of all, our decision to order transfer is not unmindful of the fact that the impact of asbestos litigation varies from district to district, and that in some courts asbestos personal injury actions are being resolved in a fashion indistinguishable from other civil actions. It is not surprising, therefore, that parties and courts involved in such actions might urge that inclusion of their actions in multidistrict proceedings is inappropriate. The Panel, however, must weigh the interests of all the plaintiffs and all the defendants, and must consider multiple litigation as a whole in the light of the purposes of the law. It is this perspective that leads us to conclude that centralization in a single district of all pending federal personal injury and wrongful death asbestos actions is necessary.

Much of the argument presented to the Panel in response to its order to show cause is devoted to parties' differing (and often inconsistent) visions of § 1407 proceedings: 1) some plaintiffs see centralized pretrial proceedings as a vehicle leading to a single national class action trial or other types of consolidated trials on product defect, state of the art and punitive damages, while many defendants staunchly oppose such a trial, favor a reverse bifurcation procedure where actual damages and individual causation are tried before liability, and hope to use § 1407 proceedings to effect the severance of claims for punitive damages through a transferee court order directing that, upon the return of any case to its transferor district, such claims not be tried until claims for compensatory damages have been resolved in all federal cases; 2) some parties hope to persuade the transferee court to establish case deferral programs for plaintiffs who are not critically ill, or who have been exposed to asbestos but do not presently show any signs of impairment (i.e., pleural registries), while many plaintiffs assert that such procedures are unfair or unconstitutional; 3) in response to the pressing concern about transaction costs in this litigation, some defendants consider § 1407 transfer necessary in order to provide a single federal forum in which limits on plaintiffs' contingent fees can be addressed, while some plaintiffs maintain that transfer is necessary to prevent the depletion of defendants' limited insurance coverage by defense costs incurred in multiple districts; 4) some plaintiffs and defendants urge that transfer is necessary in order to develop through discovery proceedings nationwide product data bases on all asbestos products and corporate histories of all asbestos defendants, while other plaintiffs and defendants contend that such efforts would be of no utility and are simply designed to shift liability; 5) some plaintiffs are suggesting that defendants' finances are so fragile as to require limited fund class action determinations pursuant to Fed.R.Civ.P. 23(b)(1)(B), while other plaintiffs resist any attempt to restrict their right to pursue punitive damages; 6) some parties anticipate that a single transferee court would speed up case disposition and purge meritless claims, while others expect a system of spacing out claims so as not to overwhelm currently solvent defendants' cash flow and drive them into bankruptcy; and 7) some parties contend that single transferee court is necessary for the purpose of exploring the opportunities for global settlements or alternative dispute resolution mechanisms, while other parties assert that such hopes are utopian at best as long as i) more than twice as many asbestos cases remain pending in state courts as in federal courts, and ii) currently stayed claims against bankrupt defendants cannot be addressed by the transferee court.[6]

We enumerate these issues not for the purpose, as some parties seemingly misunderstand, of passing on their merits. The language of the first sentence of paragraph (b) of § 1407 is quite clear about the proper forum for resolution of such issues — "coordinated or consolidated pretrial proceedings shall be conducted by a judge or judges to whom such actions are assigned" by the Panel. The Panel has neither the power nor the disposition to direct the transferee court in the exercise of its powers and discretion in pretrial proceedings. In re Plumbing Fixture Cases, 298 F. Supp. 484, 489 (J.P.M.L. 1968).

6.   . . . Transfer under § 1407 of an action containing claims against a defendant in bankruptcy has no effect on the automatic stay provisions of the Bankruptcy Code (11 U.S.C. § 362). Claims that have been stayed in the transferor court remain stayed in the transferee court. The Panel, however, has never considered the pendency of such stayed claims in an action to be an impediment to transfer of the action. 28 U.S.C. § 1407(a) authorizes the Panel to transfer only "civil actions" and not claims. . . . To have allowed the pendency of claims against a single bankrupt defendant to preclude the transfer of actions containing claims actively being litigated against common nonbankrupt defendants would have frustrated the essential purpose of § 1407.

Some parties have urged the Panel to treat the bankruptcy reorganizations themselves as "civil actions" appropriate for transfer under § 1407 to the transferee district. The reorganization proceedings are not subject to our order to show cause, and this question is therefore not ripe for a Panel decision. We have not addressed this question before and would be reluctant to do so until: 1) the transferee court determines that other alternatives, such as coordination with the concerned bankruptcy courts, are insufficient to accomplish the goals of § 1407; and 2) other suggested means of transferring the bankruptcy reorganizations or relevant portions thereof have been fully explored by the transferee court and the concerned bankruptcy courts.

Finally, we note that to the extent that state court actions and bankruptcy proceedings are excluded from the ambit of the Panel's transfer decision, transfer will nonetheless have the salutary effect of creating one federal court with which such proceedings can be coordinated, to the extent deemed desirable by the concerned courts. Indeed, state court judges have communicated to the Panel that coordination among state courts and a single transferee court for the federal actions is an objective worthy of pursuit.

We cite these issues only as illustrations of 1) the types of pretrial matters that need to be addressed by a single transferee court in order to avoid duplication of effort (with concomitant unnecessary expenses) by the parties and witnesses, their counsel, and the judiciary, and in order to prevent inconsistent decisions; and 2) why, at least initially, all pending federal personal injury or wrongful death asbestos actions not yet in trial must be included in § 1407 proceedings. For example, if, as some courts, parties and commentators have suggested, there are insufficient funds to fairly compensate all deserving claimants, this should be determined before plaintiffs in lightly impacted districts go to trial and secure recoveries (often including punitive damages) at the possible expense of deserving plaintiffs litigating in districts where speedy trial dates have not been available. Similarly, if there are economies to be achieved with respect to remaining national discovery, pretrial rulings or efforts at settlement, these should be secured before claims against distinct types or groups of defendants are separated out of the litigation. Finally, because many of the arguments of parties seeking exclusion from transfer are intertwined with the merits of their claims or defenses and affect the overall management of this litigation, we are unwilling, on the basis of the record presently before us, to carve out exceptions to transfer. We prefer instead to give the transferee court the opportunity to conduct a substantive review of such contentions and how they affect the whole proceedings.

It may well be that on further refinement of the issues and close scrutiny by the transferee court, some claims or actions can be remanded in advance of the other actions in the transferee district. Should the transferee court deem remand of any claims or actions appropriate, the transferee court can communicate this to the Panel, and the Panel will accomplish remand with a minimum of delay. *See* Rule 14, R.P.J.P.M.L.[8] We add that for those parties urging that resolution of this litigation lies primarily in the setting of firm, credible trial dates, § 1407 transfer may serve as a mechanism enabling the transferee court to develop a nationwide roster of senior district and other judges available to follow actions remanded back to heavily impacted districts, for trials in advance of when such districts' overburdened judges may have otherwise been able to schedule them.

We remain sensitive to the concerns of some parties that § 1407 transfer will be burdensome or inconvenient. We note that since § 1407 transfer is primarily for pretrial, there is usually no need for the parties and witnesses to travel to the transferee district for depositions or otherwise. Furthermore, the judicious use of liaison counsel, lead counsel and steering committees will eliminate the need for most counsel ever to travel to the transferee district. And it is most logical to assume that prudent counsel will combine their forces and apportion their workload in

---

8.   Those parties who may seek early remand of their actions or claims are reminded of . . . Panel Rule 14(d)'s expression of the Panel's reluctance to order remand absent a suggestion of remand from the transferee judge . . . . [Note that former Rule 14, cited by the Panel, is now Rule 7.6. — ED.]

order to streamline the efforts of the parties and witnesses, their counsel, and the judiciary, thereby effectuating an overall savings of cost and a reduction of inconvenience to all concerned. Hopefully, combining such practices with a uniform case management approach will, in fact, lead to sizeable reductions in transaction costs (and especially in attorneys' fees).

In a docket of this size and scope, no district emerges as the clear nexus where centralized pretrial proceedings should be conducted. The Panel has decided to centralize this litigation in the Eastern District of Pennsylvania before Judge Charles R. Weiner. We note that: 1) more asbestos personal injury or wrongful death actions are pending in that district than any other; 2) the court there has extensive experience in complex litigation in general and asbestos litigation in particular; and 3) the court has graciously expressed its willingness to assume the responsibility for this massive undertaking. Furthermore, in the person of Judge Weiner the Panel finds a judge thoroughly familiar with the issues in asbestos litigation, a track record of accomplishment and successful innovation, and, on the basis of pleadings before the Panel in which an opinion was expressed, a selection to which the majority of responding plaintiffs and defendants either expressly agree or are not opposed.

Many parties have suggested that the dynamics of this litigation make it impractical, if not impossible, for one single judge to discharge the responsibilities of transferee judge, while other parties have emphasized that more than a single transferee judge would dilute the judicial control needed to effectively manage the litigation. Varying suggestions have been made that the Panel appoint additional transferee judges to handle specific issues (e.g., class or limited fund determinations, discovery, settlement, claims administration, etc.), to deal with separate types of claims or defendants (e.g., maritime asbestos actions, railroad worker actions, friction materials actions, tire workers actions, etc.), or to divide the litigation along regional or circuit lines (helping to insure uniformity of decisions within each circuit pertaining, inter alia, to state law questions involved in the actions). Each of these suggestions has merit, as long as one judge has the opportunity to maintain overall control.

Section 1407(b) contemplates that multidistrict litigation may be conducted by "a judge or judges." It further expressly provides that "upon request of the panel, a circuit judge or a district judge may be designated and assigned temporarily for service in the transferee district by the Chief Justice of the United States of the United States or the chief judge of the circuit, as may be required, in accordance with the provisions of chapter 13 of this title." And the Panel has long expressed its willingness to appoint additional transferee judges in litigations whose size and complexity make it difficult for the original transferee judge to handle § 1407 proceedings alone. We emphasize our intention to do everything within our power to provide such assistance in this docket. Before making any specific appointments, however, we deem it advisable to allow the transferee judge to make his own assessment of the needs of this docket and communicate his preferences to us.

The Panel is under no illusion that centralization will, of itself, markedly relieve the critical asbestos situation. It offers no panacea. Only through the combined and determined efforts of the transferee judge and his judicial colleagues, of the many attorneys involved in asbestos matters, and of the parties, can true progress be made toward solving the "asbestos mess." This order does offer a great opportunity to all participants who sincerely wish to resolve these asbestos matters fairly and with as little unnecessary expense as possible.

Finally, in light of the Panel's disposition in this docket, it is necessary to remind parties and counsel of their continuing responsibility with respect to transfer of potential tag-along actions . . . . Panel Rule 13(e) [now Rule 7.5(e) — ED.] provides as follows:

> Any party or counsel in actions previously transferred under Section 1407 or under consideration by the Panel for transfer under Section 1407 shall notify the Clerk of the Panel of any potential "tag-along actions" in which that party is also named or in which that counsel appears.

It is therefore ordered that, pursuant to 28 U.S.C. § 1407, the actions listed on the following Schedule A that are pending as of the date of this order, are not in trial, and are pending outside the Eastern District of Pennsylvania, be, and the same hereby are, transferred to the Eastern District of Pennsylvania and, with the consent of that court, assigned to the Honorable Charles R. Weiner for coordinated or consolidated pretrial proceedings with the actions on Schedule A that remain pending in that district and are not in trial.

[Schedule A is omitted.]

Notes

1.   The *Asbestos (No. VI)* consolidation of 26,000 cases was by far the largest number of individual actions transferred into one consolidated MDL proceeding. The fewest number of transferred actions was two. In re: Toys "R" Us — Delaware, Inc., Fair and Accurate Credit Transactions Act (FACTA) Litig., 581 F. Supp. 2d 1377 (J.P.M.L. 2008); In re CBS Licensing Antitrust Litig., 328 F. Supp. 511 (J.P.M.L. 1971).

2.   Are you convinced that the MDL transfer in *Asbestos (No. VI)* was warranted by the text of § 1407(a)? The Panel spent little time analyzing the factors of common questions (exactly what questions of law or fact were common to *all* 26,000 cases?), convenience of the parties, and convenience of the witnesses. It focused principally on the "just and efficient conduct" factor, but it failed to demonstrate how transfer would lead to a more just and efficient outcome. The opinion seems to say, "We have to do something because the present situation is unjust and inefficient. We hope that by transferring these 26,000 cases to one forum, the transferee judge can figure out how to conduct this litigation more justly and efficiently. But we don't pretend to know how the transferee judge will accomplish this task."

How can the Panel determine whether MDL treatment is just and efficient without providing some sense of how the transferee judge might conduct the litigation after transfer?

In terms of the fair and efficient adjudication of the controversy, didn't it make more sense to consolidate the cases earlier than 1991? One factual difference between the first and sixth *Asbestos Products* decisions was that, by 1991, many of the parties consented to transfer. Did that fact alone make an MDL proceeding fair and efficient? A second factual difference was that, by 1991, numerous asbestos manufacturers had declared bankruptcy, and it was obvious that there were insufficient assets to meet all the claims that could be asserted against remaining defendants. Should some measure of equality of treatment enter into the Panel's calculus? If so, what about the state asbestos cases and the cases of those not yet injured by asbestos? Wouldn't the aggregation and settlement of pending federal cases potentially leave these claimants worse off? Or would it make state-court claimants with cases that were ready for trial better off? Should the Panel aggregate some cases when doing so does not eliminate the problem of inequitable treatment among similarly situated claimants?

3. The *Asbestos (No. VI)* MDL proceeding has been no panacea for asbestos litigation, but it has enjoyed some success. The number of new asbestos filings in federal court fluctuates, but remains high. *See Workload of the Courts*, 41 THIRD BRANCH No. 1 (Jan. 2009), *available at* http://www.uscourts.gov/ttb/2009-01/article02.cfm. In 2009, the MDL proceeding was still going strong, with more than 99,000 cases, containing 3.3 million claims, now part of the proceeding. In re Asbestos Prods. Liab. Litig. (No. VI), 256 F.R.D. 151, 152 n.2 (E.D. Pa. 2009). (To give some sense of the magnitude, there are about 260,000 civil cases, give or take a few thousand, pending in the federal courts at any given time). The 99,000 present cases are not, for the most part, the same as the 20,000 original cases. Judge Weiner, his colleagues, and his successor as the MDL judge have worked hard to resolve cases, mostly through settlements. Indeed, much of the time in the first decade of the MDL proceeding was spent in efforts to craft global settlements, although these ultimately fell through in the Supreme Court. *See infra* pp. 493-520.

As of 2008, the *Asbestos (No. VI)* MDL proceeding had resolved more than 77,000 cases; only 1,375 actions or claims had returned to their originating district for trial or completion of settlement proceedings. *See* In re: Asbestos Prods. Liab. Litig. (No. VI), 560 F. Supp. 2d 1367, 1369 (J.P.M.L. 2008). The number of asbestos trials during these years has been few indeed. At one point, Judge Weiner suggested that his reluctance to recommend remand of cases for trial arose from his concern that trials would upset settlement efforts and also might force some defendants into bankruptcy, which would hurt other plaintiffs. Judge Weiner also tried to prioritize the cases, so that the most serious injuries were handled first. In re: Asbestos Prods. Liab. Litig. (No. VI), 1996 WL 539589 (E.D. Pa. Sept. 16, 1996). Even when cases are remanded, the Panel, acting on the recommendation of the transferee judge, has declined to remand punitive damage claims. *See* In re Collins, 233 F.3d 809, 812 (3rd Cir. 2000) (noting that "[t]he continued hemorrhaging of available funds deprives current and future victims of rightful compensation").

Some asbestos plaintiffs have objected to these measures, arguing that the MDL proceeding is the legal equivalent of a black hole from which cases do not emerge. Indeed, some have argued that transfer into the *Asbestos (No. VI)* MDL deprives litigants of their Seventh Amendment right to jury trial. Thus far, neither the Panel nor the transferee judge has been sympathetic. *See* In re: Asbestos Prods. Liab. Litig. (No. VI), 170 F. Supp. 2d 1348, 1349 (J.P.M.L. 2001) (rejecting the argument that "the way in which [*Asbestos (No. VI)*] is being administered effectively denies [plaintiffs] their constitutional right to a jury trial"); *Asbestos (No. VI)*, 1996 WL 359389 (denying plaintiffs' motion for the transferee judge to suggest to the Panel that thousands of asbestos cases be remanded).

Do these facts suggest that the decision to multidistrict the asbestos litigation was correct? Does it concern you that one judge has the power to determine the fate of thousands of cases — including the power to thwart a trial in the forum of the plaintiffs' choice? Do you have a better solution?

4.   So far, all of the cases in this section have been asbestos cases. That was an advertent editorial choice. We wanted to show how different doctrines — Rule 42(a), § 1404(a), and § 1407 — all played out in essentially the same situation. Asbestos litigation has posed the most intractable aggregation problem in American history. Because it involves massive numbers of cases, geographical dispersion across the country, temporal dispersion over numerous decades, and jurisdictional dispersion among the federal and state courts, the asbestos crisis provides an excellent vehicle for comparing and contrasting consolidation and transfer doctrines, and for testing their limits. On the other hand, because it is so intractable, the asbestos situation is *sui generis*, so the limits of consolidation and transfer devices in asbestos litigation do not necessarily mean that the devices are equally limited in their effectiveness in other litigation. For instance, in a securities-fraud action in which all injuries have already occurred, federal law governs the dispute, and federal jurisdiction exists over all the claims, the MDL process can be a very effective mechanism for consolidating cases. The following case is a recent example of the Panel's approach to MDL transfer in a non-asbestos context.

IN RE VIOXX PRODUCTS LIABILITY LITIGATION

360 F. Supp. 2d 1352 (J.P.M.L. 2005)

■   WM. TERRELL HODGES, Chairman.

This litigation presently consists of 148 actions pending in 41 federal districts and listed on the attached Schedule A. Before the Panel are two motions, pursuant to 28 U.S.C. § 1407, that taken together seek centralization for coordinated or consolidated pretrial proceedings of all but one of these actions. Plaintiff in one Eastern Louisiana action seeks centralization of this litigation in the Eastern or Western Districts of Louisiana. Defendant Merck & Co., Inc. (Merck) moves for centralization of this litigation in either the District of Maryland, the Southern District of Indiana, or the Northern District of Illinois. Merck also agrees with some plaintiffs that the District of New Jersey would be an appropriate transferee district. AmerisourceBergen Corp., a wholesaler defendant, supports centralization in the Maryland district. Most responding plaintiffs agree that centralization is appropriate, although some plaintiffs suggest alternative transferee districts, including the Northern District of Alabama, the Central or Northern Districts of California, the District of Delaware, the Southern District of Illinois, the District of Minnesota, the Eastern District of Missouri, the District of New Jersey, the Eastern or Southern Districts of New York, the Northern or Southern Districts of Ohio, the Western District of Oklahoma, the Eastern District of Pennsylvania, and the Southern or Western Districts of Texas.

The Panel has been notified of nearly 300 potentially related actions pending in multiple federal districts. In light of the Panel's disposition of this docket, these actions will be treated as potential tag-along actions.

The three arguments in opposition to Section 1407 centralization can be summarized as follows: plaintiffs in two actions oppose inclusion of their actions in MDL-1657 proceedings, because motions to remand their actions to state court are pending; plaintiffs in some Southern Texas actions along with plaintiffs in one third-party payor action pending in the Southern District of New York oppose these actions' inclusion in MDL-1657, arguing that individual questions of fact in their actions predominate over any common questions of fact and/or that discovery is already underway in these actions; and plaintiffs in one action pending in the Eastern District of New York oppose inclusion of their action in 1407 proceedings, since it involves additional claims relating to a different prescription medication not involved in other MDL-1657 actions.

On the basis of the papers filed and hearing session held, the Panel finds that the actions in this litigation involve common questions of fact, and that centralization under Section 1407 in the Eastern District of Louisiana will serve the convenience of the parties and witnesses and promote the just and efficient conduct of the litigation. All actions focus on alleged increased health risks (including heart attack and/or stroke) when taking Vioxx, an anti-inflammatory drug, and whether Merck knew of these increased risks and failed to disclose them to the medical community and consumers. Centralization under Section 1407 is necessary in order to eliminate duplicative discovery, avoid inconsistent pretrial rulings, and conserve the resources of the parties, their counsel and the judiciary.

The pendency of a motion to remand to state court is not a sufficient basis to avoid inclusion in Section 1407 proceedings. We note that motions to remand in two actions, one action each in the District of Kansas and the Eastern District of Missouri, as well as in any other MDL-1657 actions can be presented to and decided by the transferee judge.

Nor are we persuaded by the arguments of some opposing Texas plaintiffs and the New York third-party payor plaintiffs. We point out that transfer under Section 1407 has the salutary effect of placing all actions in this docket before a single judge who can formulate a pretrial program that: 1) allows discovery with respect to any non-common issues to proceed concurrently with discovery on common issues; and 2) ensures that pretrial proceedings will be conducted in a manner leading to the just and expeditious resolution of all actions to the overall benefit of the parties. We note that the MDL-1657 transferee court can employ any number of pretrial techniques — such as establishing separate discovery and/or motion tracks — to efficiently manage this litigation. In any event, we leave the extent and manner of coordination or consolidation of these actions to the discretion of the transferee court. It may be, on further refinement of the issues and close scrutiny by the transferee judge, that some claims or actions can be remanded to their transferor districts for trial in advance of the other actions in the transferee district. But we are unwilling, on the basis of the record before us, to make such a determination at this time. Should the transferee judge deem remand of any claims or actions appropriate, procedures are available whereby this may be accomplished with a minimum of delay. *See* Rule 7.6. We are confident in the transferee judge's ability to streamline pretrial proceedings in these actions, while concomitantly directing the appropriate resolution of all claims.

The Panel is persuaded, however, that claims involving a prescription drug other than Vioxx in one Eastern District of New York action do not share sufficient questions of fact with claims relating to Vioxx to warrant inclusion of these non-Vioxx claims in MDL-1657 proceedings.

Given the geographic dispersal of constituent actions and potential tag-along actions, no district stands out as the geographic focal point for this nationwide docket. Thus we have searched for a transferee judge with the time and experience to steer this complex litigation on a prudent course. By centralizing this litigation in the Eastern District of Louisiana before Judge Eldon E. Fallon, we are assigning this litigation to a jurist experienced in complex multidistrict products liability litigation and sitting in a district with the capacity to handle this litigation.

It is therefore ordered that, pursuant to 28 U.S.C. § 1407, the actions listed on the attached Schedule A and pending outside the Eastern District of Louisiana are transferred to the Eastern District of Louisiana and, with the consent of that court, assigned to the Honorable Eldon E. Fallon for coordinated or consolidated pretrial proceedings with the actions pending there and listed on Schedule A.

It is further ordered that claims in Dominick Cain, et al. v. Merck & Co., Inc., et al., E.D. New York, C.A. No. 1:01-3441, against Pharmacia Corp., Pfizer Inc., and G.D. Searle & Co. relating to a prescription medication other than Vioxx are simultaneously separated and remanded to the Eastern District of New York.

[Schedule A omitted.]

Notes

1. The Panel's opinions often contain a great deal of boilerplate, with little extended discussion of the nuances of the cases being considered for transfer. For many years, most of the Panel's decisions were unpublished. Even today, the Panel's opinions are notoriously short, rarely running for more than two to three pages. Usually the opinions begin with a quick recital of the number of pending actions, the facts of the case, and the positions of the parties. When transfer is ordered, conclusory and formulaic statements — like the ones found in *Vioxx* that (1) "the actions in this litigation involve common questions of fact, and that centralization under Section 1407 . . . will best serve the convenience of the parties and witnesses and promote the just and efficient conduct of this litigation," and (2) "[c]entralization under Section 1407 is necessary in order to eliminate duplicative discovery, avoid inconsistent pretrial rulings, and conserve the resources of the parties, their counsel and the judiciary" — often follow. (If you doubt that these statements are formulaic, look at these cases that involve very different legal theories but use language virtually identical to that quoted above: In re Land Rover LR3 Tire Wear Prods. Liab. Litig., 598 F. Supp. 2d 1384 (J.P.M.L. 2009) (products liability); In Re Wachovia Corp. Pick-A-Payment Mortgage Mktg. & Sales Practices Litig., 598 F. Supp. 2d 1383 (J.P.M.L. 2009) (consumer fraud and deceptive sales practices); In re Regions Morgan Keegan Sec., Derivative & Employee Ret. Income (ERISA) Litig., 598 F. Supp. 2d 1379 (J.P.M.L. 2009) (securities fraud and ERISA liability); and In re Aftermarket Auto. Lighting Prods. Antitrust Litig., 598 F. Supp. 2d 1366 (J.P.M.L. 2009) (antitrust).) As in *Vioxx*, there then ensues a paragraph or so plugging the facts of the case into the formulas. Finally, the Panel's opinion concludes with a brief discussion of the appropriate transferee district and judge.

Denials of MDL treatment are often even more perfunctory. For example, in one recent opinion, after a quick three sentences noting the fact of the defendant's § 1407 motion and the lack of any opposition from the plaintiffs, the Panel denied transfer with only this explanation:

> After considering all argument of counsel, we find that Section 1407 centralization would not necessarily serve the convenience of the parties and witnesses or further the just and efficient conduct of this litigation. Inasmuch as this litigation involves only two actions, which are pending in adjacent districts, the proponents of centralization have failed to persuade us that any common questions of fact are sufficiently complex and/or numerous to justify Section 1407 transfer in this docket at this time. Alternatives to transfer exist that can minimize whatever possibilities there might be of duplicative discovery and/or inconsistent pretrial rulings. The proximity of these two actions may make coordination by the parties and the courts feasible.

In re: U.S.A. Exterminators, Inc., Fair Labor Standards Act (FLSA) Litig., 588 F. Supp. 2d 1378, 1379 (J.P.M.L. 2008).

Therefore, even though *Vioxx* provides some window into the thought process of the Panel and the factors that it considers important, you need to read the decision with a large grain of salt. To this day, two of the most revealing decisions of the Panel remain the first and sixth *Asbestos Products* decisions that were previously discussed (*supra* pp. 141, 144). For another thoughtful, and very early, opinion laying out the wide range of factors that ought to guide the Panel, see In re "East of the Rockies" Concrete Pipe Antitrust Cases, 302 F. Supp. 244, 253 (J.P.M.L. 1969) (Weigel, J., concurring).

2.   Given the terseness of the Panel's decisions, it is not easy to analyze the circumstances under which transfer occurs. Begin, however, with a few basic propositions. First, the moving party has the burden of proving that a § 1407 transfer is appropriate. In re Chiropractic Antitrust Litig., 483 F. Supp. 811 (J.P.M.L. 1980). Second, there is no appellate review of any kind when the Panel denies transfer. 28 U.S.C. § 1407(e). Third, all other orders of the Panel may occur only by extraordinary writ in the court of appeals encompassing the place in which the Panel's hearing on a transfer order takes place, or (with respect to post-transfer orders) in the court of appeals encompassing the transferee circuit. *Id.* Predictably, such writs are nearly impossible to obtain. *See* In re Collins, 233 F.3d 809 (3rd Cir. 2000); In re Ivy, 901 F.2d 7 (2d Cir. 1990).

3.   The first statutory requirement for MDL treatment is the existence of "one or more common questions of fact." By limiting itself just to factual issues, § 1407 is different from Rules 20(a), 24(b), and 42(a), all of which permit joinder or consolidation based on common factual *or* legal issues. The Panel has made it clear that common questions of law are not a ground for transfer, although common questions of fact that underlie common questions of law can serve as the basis for MDL transfer. *See* In re Air Fare Litig., 322 F. Supp. 1013 (J.P.M.L. 1971); In re Fourth Class Postage Regulations, 298 F. Supp. 1326 (J.P.M.L. 1969); *but see* In re Pharmacy Benefit Plan Adm'rs Pricing Litig., 206 F. Supp. 2d 1362, 1363 (J.P.M.L. 2002) ("[W]hile these five actions clearly share common legal questions and, perhaps, a few factual questions, unique questions of fact predominate over any common questions of fact."); In re Kugel Mesh Hernia Patch Prods. Liab. Litig., 493 F Supp. 2d 1371, 1373 (J.P.M.L. 2007) ("Transfer under Section 1407 does not require a complete identity or even a majority of common factual *or legal* issues as a prerequisite to transfer.") (emphasis added).

The quotations from *Pharmacy Benefit Plan* and *Kugel Mesh* raises another important issue, on which the Panel has taken a somewhat wavering position: the comparative number or weight of common questions of fact in relation to non-common questions. Here, the issue of commonality merges with the later factors of convenience, justice, and efficiency. If there truly is only one common question of fact, it is difficult to see how transfer would be convenient, fair, or efficient. So the critical issue is how many, or how weighty, the common issues of fact must be in relation to the non-common issues. As *Kugel Mesh* says, the question is not a simple matter of majority rule. As *Pharmacy Benefit Plan* shows, the Panel sometimes suggests that common factual questions should "predominate." It usually does so in a back-handed way, particularly in opinions in which it orders transfer and rejects the argument of parties opposing MDL treatment that the common issues do not predominate. *See, e.g.*, In re Diet Drugs (Phentermine, Fenfluramine, Dexfenlfuramine) Prods. Liab. Litig., 990 F. Supp. 834, 836 (J.P.M.L. 1998). Sometimes, however, the Panel uses "predominance" in a positive fashion, as a reason to permit transfer. *See* In re RadioShack Corp. "ERISA" Litig., 528 F. Supp. 2d 1348, 1349 (J.P.M.L. 2007) (centralizing cases when "common factual questions clearly predominate over any unique questions of fact"). And sometimes, as in *Pharmacy Benefit Plan*, the Panel uses a lack of predominance in a negative fashion, as a reason to deny MDL treatment. Indeed, the first case in which the Panel denied MDL treatment due to a lack of common questions was its first asbestos decision, which we have already studied and which used the lack of "predominance" of common issues as a reason to deny transfer. In re Asbestos & Asbestos Insulation Material Prods. Liab. Litig., 431 F. Supp. 906 (J.P.M.L. 1977) (*supra* p. 144). Typically, however, when the Panel denies MDL transfer, it eschews the language of "predominance" altogether, and uses language like that used in *U.S.A. Exterminators*: that the common factual questions are "not sufficiently complex and/or numerous." 588 F. Supp. 2d at 1379; *see also* In re Circuit City Stores, Inc., Restocking Fee Sales Practices Litig., 528 F. Supp. 2d 1363, 1364 (J.P.M.L. 2007) ("[T]he proponents of centralization have failed to persuade us that any common questions of fact are sufficiently complex and/or numerous to justify Section 1407 transfer.").

Is the upshot of this analysis that words such as "predominance," "sufficient complexity," and "numerosity" are conclusory labels, and the phrase "one or more common questions of fact" is a fact-bound inquiry that depends on the presence of factual issues that by significance or by number merit joint resolution, despite the costs to litigant autonomy that the MDL process entails? If so, the commonality question cannot be divorced from the later questions of convenience, fairness, and efficiency. *Cf.* In re Air Crash off Long Island, N.Y., on July 17, 1996, 965 F. Supp. 5, 8 (S.D.N.Y. 1997) (stating that "a practical application of the policies behind and limitations of consolidated multidistrict litigation should minimize the difficulty of resolving" whether an issue is sufficiently common to justify resolution in the transferee court).

For what it is worth, the Panel has been criticized for finding common questions of fact too readily. *See* Blake M. Rhodes, Comment, *The Judicial Panel on Multidistrict Litigation: Time for Rethinking*, 140 U. PA. L. REV. 711 (1991). On the other hand, it has been criticized for making the "common questions of fact" requirement too stringent. *See* Mark Hermann & Pearson Bownas, *An Uncommon Focus on "Common Questions": Two Problems with the Judicial Panel on Multidistrict Litigation's Treatment of the "One or More Common Questions of Fact" Requirement for Centralization*, 82 TUL. L. REV. 2297 (2008).

4. Turning then to the second and third criteria mentioned in § 1407—convenience to parties and convenience to witnesses — the Panel does not often discuss these issues in detail. As *Vioxx* shows, the convenience factors that the Panel most often mentions in its formulaic transfer orders are reducing discovery costs and conserving the parties' resources. The Panel is clear that inconvenience to individual litigants is irrelevant as long as, on balance, more convenience is achieved from consolidation. *See, e.g.*, In re West of the Rockies Concrete Pipe Antitrust Cases, 303 F. Supp. 507, 509 (J.P.M.L. 1969) (burdens to local defendants of litigating in distant forum "will be offset by the savings from and convenience of coordinated or consolidated pretrial proceedings directed by the transferee judge"). One commentary has suggested that "the Panel has largely eliminated this [convenience] guideline as a determinative standard." Wilson W. Herndon & Ernest R. Higginbotham, *Complex Multidistrict Litigation — An Overview of 28 U.S.C.A. § 1407*, 31 BAYLOR L. REV. 33, 43 (1979).

5. The fourth requirement of § 1407 is the need for an MDL transfer to advance "the just and efficient conduct of such actions." Again, *Vioxx* describes the kinds of factors that the Panel regards as relevant to this inquiry: eliminating duplicative discovery, preventing inconsistent rulings, and conserving party and judicial resources. Our reading of many Panel opinions suggests a few factors that put flesh on these general principles:

- As we have described, the significance and importance of common issues of fact matter.

- So do the number and location of cases; MDL transfer is more likely when there are more cases and they are geographically dispersed.

- Also important are the number of lawyers and, relatedly, the ability of the various lawyers to create informal structures to coordinate and share information.

- The age and progress of the cases; the panel is less likely to order transfer when cases are at vastly different stages of litigation, especially when some are nearing trial.

- The position of the parties regarding transfer is relevant; when most parties consent to transfer, transfer becomes more likely.

- Multiple requests for preliminary or permanent injunctive relief can lead the Panel to order an MDL transfer when the requested injunctions would subject the defendant to inconsistent standards.

- The existence of overlapping class actions; when two or more of the cases subject to transfer both involve requests for class certification, transfer is used to avoid the problem of dueling classes.

6. On this last factor — the relevance of class actions — it is true that the presence of dueling class actions makes the case a near shoo-in for MDL treatment. *Toys "R" Us*, 581 F. Supp. 2d at 1377 (ordering MDL transfer when, among other factors, "there is a risk of inconsistent rulings on class certification"); In re Epogen and Aranesp Off-Label Marketing and Sales Practices Litig., 545 F. Supp. 2d 1365, 1366 (J.P.M.L. 2008) (same); *see* In

re: Hip & Knee Implant Marketing Litig., 572 F. Supp. 2d 1379, 1379 (J.P.M.L. 2008) (refusing to consolidate cases when the class actions in two cases involved, respectively, only California citizens and only New York citizens, so that there "appears to be no risk of inconsistent class certification rulings"); In re: Chrysler LLC 2.7 Liter V-6 Engine Oil Sludge Prods. Liab. Litig., 598 F. Supp. 2d 1372 (J.P.M.L. 2009) (consolidating five cases, even though class actions did not overlap, due to common discovery). But the relevance of the class-action device to the MDL process is more complicated than it might appear. As we will see when we study class actions in detail in Chapter Four, class actions can be a powerful aggregation device; in many ways, class actions and MDL transfer compete as the two best methods of aggregation presently available in federal court. For reasons that we will also explore, however, the ability to obtain class treatment is limited, especially in the mass-tort context. For instance, in the *Vioxx* litigation, after transfer of the case to the Eastern District of Louisiana, certain plaintiffs filed a case on behalf of a class of Vioxx victims, but the transferee judge denied class certification. *See* In re Vioxx Prods. Liab. Litig., 239 F.R.D. 450 (E.D.La. 2006). In these cases, the only method to achieve widespread aggregation is the MDL process. The Panel is certainly not oblivious to this fact. Therefore, while overlapping class actions provide a reason to use the MDL process, the inability to use class actions also provides a reason to use the MDL process. *See* Edward F. Sherman, *The MDL Model for Resolving Complex Litigation If a Class Action Is Not Possible*, 82 TUL. L. REV. 2205 (2008).

7.   One factor that the MDL Panel claims not to be influenced by is the substantive law that the transferee court will apply. At one point, the Panel intimated that, with regard to issues of federal law, the law of the transferor circuit law applied in the transferee court after a §1407 transfer. In re Plumbing Fixtures Litig., 342 F. Supp. 756 (J.P.M.L. 1972). But the Panel subsequently backed away from that position, and now holds to the view that "[w]hen determining whether to transfer an action under Section 1407 . . . it is not the business of the Panel to consider what law the transferee court might apply. . . . Any suggestion to the contrary in dictum found in [*Plumbing Fixtures*] is withdrawn." In re Gen. Motors Class E Stock Buyout Sec. Litig., 696 F. Supp. 1546, 1547 & n.1 (J.P.M.L. 1988).

8.   According to Professor Marcus, in recent years the Panel has moved from a "minimalist" to a "maximalist" view of its function:

> Repeatedly and understandably, the Panel has gone well beyond a minimalist view of its authority, using its transfer power for far more than merely facilitating orderly development of discovery. Instead, it has repeatedly employed its transfer power to achieve what might be called substantive objectives and sometimes overtly encouraged consideration of settlement. And it has taken an interest in the posttransfer handling and fate of the cases it has transferred. Partly because of its attitude toward its role, the great majority of cases have been resolved in the transferee districts, and many have led to major settlements resolving widespread litigation.

Richard L. Marcus, *Cure-All for an Era of Dispersed Litigation? Toward a Maximalist Use of the Multidistrict Litigation Panel's Transfer Power*, 82 TUL. L. REV. 2245, 2295 (2008). Professor Marcus suggests that this tendency reflects other trends in modern American litigation. He admits that "[t]hose who emphasize maximum individual control of litigation may find this record unnerving," *id.*, and suggests that the maximalist tendency raises concerns for bias in the selection of the Panel members and in the members' attitudes toward the cases they choose for MDL treatment.

9.   Once the Panel decides that transfer is appropriate, it must select the transferee court and judge. A number of factors seem to influence the Panel's selection, including the experience of potential transferee judges with the particular litigation and with large-scale litigation more generally; the consent of the transferee judge; the convenience of possible forums for the parties and lawyers; the situs of the events giving rise to the cases; the desires of the parties; the dockets of potential transferee judges; and the number of cases pending in various forums. *See* Daniel A. Richards, Note. *An Analysis of the Judicial Panel on Multidistrict Litigation's Selection of Transferee District and Judge*, 78 FORDHAM L. REV. 311 (2009) (analyzing the factors that the Panel cites in selecting a transferee forum and judge). The transferee judge need not have any related cases pending on his or her docket. *See* In re Silicone Gel Breast Implants Prods. Liab. Litig., 793 F. Supp. 1098 (J.P.M.L. 1992).

Often the parties do not contest the multidistrict transfer, but they fight tooth-and-nail over the forum to which the case should be transferred. You see a few of those sharp elbows in *Asbestos Products (No. VI)* and *Vioxx. See also Silicone Gel*, 793 F. Supp. at 1100 ("We are troubled . . . by the volume and tone of the negative arguments with which opposing counsel have sought to denigrate each other's forum choices, litigation strategies and underlying motives.") The reason for the fighting is evident. Most MDL cases end in the transferee court — whether by way of dismissal, summary judgment, or settlement. (The authority of the transferee court to settle transferee cases or to decide dispositive motions is beyond cavil. *See* R.J.P.M.L. 7.6(a); In re "Agent Orange" Prod. Liab. Litig., 996 F.2d 1425 (2d Cir. 1993).) Moreover, although we defer examination of the case-management powers that judges can employ in aggregated litigation until Part Two of the casebook, it should not surprise you to learn that different methods of managing complex litigation can lead to markedly different outcomes. Judges have different approaches toward case management. In short, the transferee judge exercises great influence over the outcome of an MDL proceeding. Typically the lawyers are familiar with the transferee-judge candidates either from their handling of some of the cases being considered for MDL treatment or from other MDLs. Understandably, lawyers prefer judge(s) whose approach will help their side.

Is it appropriate to let so much ride on the Panel's choice of a transferee judge? Should the transferee judge's discretion to manage, settle, or dispose of MDL cases be constrained by specific rules or by stronger case-management guidance from the Panel? As *Asbestos (No. VI)* and *Vioxx* show, the Panel presently disclaims any interest in such endeavors. *See also* In re Data Gen. Corp. Antitrust Litig., 510 F. Supp. 1220, 1226-27 (J.P.M.L. 1979) ("The Panel has neither the statutory authority nor the inclination to review decisions of . . . transferee courts.").

10. In choosing the transferee court and judge, the Panel is not constrained by *Hoffman v. Blaski*, 363 U.S. 335 (1960), which held that § 1404 transfers can be made only to venues in which the case could have been brought originally. In re FMC Corp. Patent Litig., 422 F. Supp. 1163 (J.P.M.L. 1976). That fact, plus the centralized decision-making authority of the Panel, the ready capacity of the MDL process to deal with tag-along actions, and the capacity to consolidate large numbers of cases, makes § 1407 MDL transfer a better vehicle for aggregating cases than either Rule 42(a) consolidation or § 1404 transfer.

In other ways, however, § 1407 transfer is not the silver bullet of aggregation. It permits consolidation only of cases on the federal level; the Panel has no authority to transfer cases from state to federal court. Nor is there a comparable body that can transfer cases from one state court to another. Its capacity to handle problems of temporal dispersion is limited by the duration of the MDL proceeding, although (as the *Asbestos (No. VI)* MDL shows) the MDL proceeding can be held open for long periods of time to sweep in new cases. *See supra* p. 152, Note 3. A final important limitation on the MDL process is described in the following case, which is the only Supreme Court decision examining the breadth of § 1407's powers.

LEXECON INC. V. MILBERG WEISS BERSHAD HYNES & LERACH

523 U.S. 26 (1998)

■ JUSTICE SOUTER delivered the opinion of the Court.

28 U.S.C. § 1407(a) authorizes the Judicial Panel on Multidistrict Litigation to transfer civil actions with common issues of fact "to any district for coordinated or consolidated pretrial proceedings," but imposes a duty on the Panel to remand any such action to the original district "at or before the conclusion of such pretrial proceedings." The issue here is whether a district court conducting such "pretrial proceedings" may invoke § 1404(a) to assign a transferred case to itself for trial. We hold it has no such authority.

I

[Petitioners, a law and economics consulting firm and one of its principals (collectively, Lexecon), were defendants in a class action brought against Charles Keating and the American Continental Corporation in connection with the failure of Lincoln Savings and Loan. It and other actions arising out of that failure were transferred for pretrial proceedings to the District of Arizona under 28 U.S.C. § 1407(a). Before the pretrial proceedings ended, the plaintiffs and Lexecon reached a "resolution," and the claims against Lexecon were dismissed.

[Lexecon then brought this diversity action in the Northern District of Illinois against two law firms — Milberg Weiss Bershad Hynes & Lerach (Milberg) and Cotchett, Illston & Pitre (Cotchett). It alleged several torts, including malicious prosecution and defamation, arising from the firms' conduct as counsel for the class-action plaintiffs. The Panel ordered the case transferred under § 1407(a) to the District of Arizona. Due to certain comments he had made regarding Lexecon's suit, the original MDL judge recused himself from handling the case. After the other parties to the *Lincoln Savings* litigation settled, Lexecon moved the District Court of Arizona to refer the case to the Panel for remand to the Northern District of Illinois. Milberg and Cotchett filed a countermotion requesting the district court to use § 1404(a) to transfer the case to itself for trial.

[The court transferred the case to itself for trial and denied Lexecon's motion to remand. The defamation claim, which was the sole claim remaining after summary judgment, proceeded to trial. Milberg won, and Lexecon appealed the transfer order. In a split decision, the Ninth Circuit affirmed on the ground that permitting the transferee court to assign a case to itself upon completion of its pretrial work was not only consistent with the statutory language but conducive to efficiency.] Judge Kozinski . . . dissented, relying on the texts of §§ 1407(a) and 1404(a) and a presumption in favor of a plaintiff's choice of forum. We granted certiorari to decide whether § 1407(a) does permit a transferee court to entertain a § 1404(a) transfer motion to keep the case for trial.

II

A

In defending the Ninth Circuit majority, Milberg may claim ostensible support from two quarters. First, the Panel has itself sanctioned such assignments in a rule issued in reliance on its rulemaking authority under 28 U.S.C. § 1407(f). The Panel's Rule 14(b) provides that "[e]ach transferred action that has not been terminated in the transferee district court shall be remanded by the Panel to the transferor district for trial, unless ordered transferred by the transferee judge to the transferee or other district under 28 U.S.C. § 1404(a) or 28 U.S.C. § 1406."* Thus, out of the 39,228 cases transferred under § 1407 and terminated as of September 30, 1995, 279 of the 3,787 ultimately requiring trial were retained by the courts to which the Panel had transferred them. Although the Panel's rule and the practice of self-assignment have not gone without challenge, *see, e.g.,* [Roger H.] Trangsrud, *Joinder Alternatives in Mass Tort Litigation,* 70

---

* Rule 14(b) of the Rules of the Judicial Panel on Multidistrict Litigation, to which the Court refers, is now contained in Rule 7.6(b). After *Lexecon,* it was amended by deleting the "unless" clause from its text. — ED.

CORNELL L. REV. 779, 809 (1985), federal courts have treated such transfers with approval, beginning with the Second Circuit's decision in *Pfizer, Inc. v. Lord*, 447 F.2d 122, 124-125 (2d Cir. 1971) (per curiam) . . . .

The second source of ostensible authority for Milberg's espousal of the self-assignment power here is a portion of text of the multidistrict litigation statute itself:

> "When civil actions involving one or more common questions of fact are pending in different districts, such actions may be transferred to any district for coordinated or consolidated pretrial proceedings." 28 U.S.C. § 1407(a). . . .

. . . [A]t first blush, the statutory limitation to "pretrial" proceedings suggests no reason that a § 1407 transferor court could not entertain a § 1404(a) motion. . . . Such transfer requests are typically resolved prior to discovery, and thus are classic "pretrial" motions.

Beyond this point, however, the textual pointers reverse direction, for § 1407 not only authorizes the Panel to transfer for coordinated or consolidated pretrial proceedings, but obligates the Panel to remand any pending case to its originating court when, at the latest, those pretrial proceedings have run their course.

> "Each action so transferred shall be remanded by the panel at or before the conclusion of such pretrial proceedings to the district from which it was transferred unless it shall have been previously terminated." § 1407(a) (proviso without application here omitted).

The Panel's instruction comes in terms of the mandatory "shall," which normally creates an obligation impervious to judicial discretion. In the absence of any indication that there might be circumstances in which a transferred case would be neither "terminated" nor subject to the remand obligation, then, the statutory instruction stands flatly at odds with reading the phrase "coordinated or consolidated pretrial proceedings" so broadly as to reach its literal limits, allowing a transferee court's self-assignment to trump the provision imposing the Panel's remand duty. If we do our job of reading the statute whole, we have to give effect to this plain command, even if doing that will reverse the longstanding practice under the statute and the rule.

As the Ninth Circuit panel majority saw it, however, the . . . "focus" of § 1407 was said to be constituting the Panel and defining its authority, not circumscribing the powers of district courts under § 1404(a). Milberg presses this point in observing that § 1407(a) does not, indeed, even apply to transferee courts, being concerned solely with the Panel's duties, whereas § 1407(b), addressed to the transferee courts, says nothing about the Panel's obligation to remand. But this analysis fails to persuade, for the very reason that it rejects that central tenet of interpretation, that a statute is to be considered in all its parts when construing any one of them. To emphasize that § 1407(b) says nothing about the Panel's obligation when addressing a transferee court's powers is simply to ignore the necessary consequence of self-assignment by a transferee court: it conclusively thwarts the Panel's capacity to obey the unconditional command of § 1407(a). . . .

B

Milberg proffers two further arguments for overlooking the tension between a broad reading of a court's pretrial authority and the Panel's remand obligation. First, it relies on a subtle reading of the provision of § 1407(a) limiting the Panel's remand obligation to cases not "previously terminated" during the pretrial period. To be sure, this exception to the Panel's remand obligation indicates that the Panel is not meant to issue ceremonial remand orders in cases already concluded by summary judgment, say, or dismissal. But according to Milberg, the imperative to remand is also inapplicable to cases self-assigned under § 1404, because the self-assignment "terminates" the case insofar as its venue depends on § 1407. When the § 1407 character of the action disappears, Milberg argues, the strictures of § 1407 fall away as well, relieving the Panel of any further duty in the case. The trouble with this creative argument, though, is that the statute manifests no such subtlety. Section 1407(a) speaks not in terms of imbuing transferred actions with some new and distinctive venue character, but simply in terms of "civil actions" or "actions." It says that such an action, not its acquired personality, must be terminated before the Panel is excused from ordering remand. . . .

Second, Milberg tries to draw an inference in its favor from the one subsection of § 1407 that does authorize the Panel to transfer a case for trial as well as pretrial proceedings. Subsection (h) provides that,

> "[n]otwithstanding the provisions of section 1404 or subsection (f) of this section, the judicial panel on multidistrict litigation may consolidate and transfer with or without the consent of the parties, for both pretrial purposes and for trial, any action brought under section 4C of the Clayton Act." . . .

Subsection (h) is not merely valueless to Milberg, however; it is ammunition for Lexecon. For the one point that subsection (h) does demonstrate is that Congress knew how to distinguish between trial assignments and pretrial proceedings in cases subject to § 1407. Although the enactment of subsection (a) [in 1968] preceded the enactment of subsection (h) [in 1976], the fact that the later section distinguishes trial assignments from pretrial proceedings generally is certainly some confirmation for our conclusion, on independent grounds, that the subjects of pretrial proceedings in subsections (a) and (b) do not include self-assignment orders. . . .

D

In sum, none of the arguments raised can unsettle the straightforward language imposing the Panel's responsibility to remand, which bars recognizing any self-assignment power in a transferee court and consequently entails the invalidity of the Panel's Rule 14(b). *See* 28 U.S.C. § 1407(f). Milberg may or may not be correct that permitting transferee courts to make self-assignments would be more desirable than preserving a plaintiff's choice of venue (to the degree that § 1407(a) does so), but the proper venue for resolving that issue remains the floor of Congress. . . .

III

The remaining question goes to the remedy, which Milberg argues may be omitted under the harmless error doctrine. Milberg posits a distinction between a first category of cases erroneously litigated in a district in which (absent waiver) venue may never be laid under the governing statute, . . . and a second category, in which the plaintiff might originally have chosen to litigate in the trial forum to which it was unwillingly and erroneously carried, as by a transfer under § 1404. . . . Milberg argues, this case falls within the second category and should escape reversal because none of Lexecon's substantial rights was prejudicially affected, *see* 28 U.S.C. § 2111. Assuming the distinction may be drawn, however, we think this case bears closer analogy to those in the first category, in which reversal with new trial is required because venue is precluded by the governing statute.

Milberg's argument assumes the only kind of statute entitled to respect in accordance with its uncompromising terms is a statute that categorically limits a plaintiff's initial choice of forum. But there is no apparent reason why courts should not be equally bound by a venue statute that just as categorically limits the authority of courts (and special panels) to override a plaintiff's choice. . . . [The] strict remand requirement contained in § 1407 should suffice to establish the substantial significance of any denial of a plaintiff's right to a remand once the pretrial stage has been completed. . . .

Accordingly, the judgment of the Court of Appeals is reversed, and the case is remanded for further proceedings consistent with this opinion.

Notes

1. *Lexecon* was a unanimous decision (except with regard to one small portion of the opinion, which we edited out, that Justice Scalia declined to join). As the Court recites, the lower federal courts that considered the issue had gone unanimously in the other direction. On the specific issue of whether an MDL transferee court can use § 1404 to self-transfer, the decision is important. But it is hardly earth-shattering. As we have noted, transferee judges resolve most MDL proceedings before trial. *See supra* p. 161, Note 9. Indeed, the statistics cited in *Lexecon* suggest that the ruling affects less than one percent of all cases that are transferred under § 1407. Moreover, even in these cases, the parties can avoid *Lexecon* by consenting to trial in the MDL forum. In re Carbon Dioxide Indus. Antitrust Litig., 229 F.3d 1321 (11th Cir. 2000); *see* Armstrong v. LaSalle Bank Nat'l Ass'n, 552 F.3d 613 (7th Cir. 2009) (refusing to find consent or waiver on the specific facts of the case). And in some cases, a party has avoided *Lexecon* by

convincing a court in which a putative tag-along action is filed to order a § 1404 transfer — which, unlike a § 1407 transfer, includes a transfer for trial — to the MDL transferee forum. Schecher v. Purdue Pharma L.P., 317 F. Supp. 2d 1253 (D. Kan. 2004); *but see* In re Oxycontin Antitrust Litig., 314 F. Supp. 2d 1388 (J.P.M.L. 2004) (refusing to allow the pendency of some § 1404 motions to affect § 1407 transfer of cases).

2.   Rather, the true significance of *Lexecon* is the message that it sends about the Supreme Court's view of the role of the MDL process. Recall Professor Marcus's description of minimalist and maximalist views toward MDL transfer. *See supra* p. 160, Note 8. Is the Supreme Court taking a minimalist view of the MDL statute — one that places a higher priority on the value of individual litigation as opposed to aggregation?

Recall as well the way in which the *Asbestos (No. VI)* MDL proceeding has been kept open and continues to sweep new asbestos cases into its aggregation process, as well as the protests of some plaintiffs who have been unable to force the transferee court or the Panel to remand asbestos cases or punitive-damage claims for trial. *See supra* p. 152, Note 3. Is *Lexecon* consistent with the way in which the MDL process is being used to handle federal asbestos cases?

3.   It would be difficult to imagine a less compelling case for § 1404 self-transfer than *Lexecon*: The transferred case had little to do with the multidistrict proceedings; the multidistrict proceeding had already wound down; and the multidistrict transferee judge, who was familiar with the litigation, recused himself. Is there any room in *Lexecon*'s analysis to limit the holding to these facts?

4.   Aside from its mention of the plaintiff's venue privilege, *Lexecon* is devoid of discussion of the policy implications of § 1407 transfers. Does that silence mean that, policy implications such as reducing litigation costs, avoiding inconsistent judgments, and achieving uniformity are irrelevant in interpreting § 1407? What does this analysis portend for the proper interpretation of other statutory terms, such as "common questions of fact," "convenience of parties and witnesses," and "the just and efficient conduct of such actions"? The legacy of *Lexecon* may lie in the answers to these questions, rather than in its specific holding on self-transfer.

5.   *Lexecon* reminds us of a basic truth: MDL transfers constitute a significant inroad on plaintiffs' venue privilege. Self-transfer for trial made that inroad even more severe, expanded the power of the transferee judge, and treated cases that fell within § 1407 under a different set of rules than cases that did not. As we noted at the outset of this chapter, consolidation for trial may well affect the outcome at trial. We have also seen that the timing of the consolidation — especially consolidation when a case is still immature — may affect the outcome of the litigation. Was *Lexecon* therefore correct to end the practice of self-transfer, which was laden with these policy implications, and thus to force the legislative branch to weigh the appropriate degree of consolidation?

6. Congress has in fact weighed in on the *Lexecon* issue. Shortly after *Lexecon* was decided, bills were introduced to change its result and to give MDL transferee judges the power to self-transfer a case under § 1404 for trial, and they have continued to be introduced, in increasingly refined form, ever since. *See, e.g.*, Multidistrict Litigation Restoration Act of 2005, H.R. 1038, 109th Cong. (2005). Such legislation has passed the House on numerous occasions. At one point, the House passed such a bill as part of a larger set of judicial reforms it wanted. The Senate passed just the *Lexecon* overrule, but not the remainder of the bill. The legislative term ended before a joint committee could reconcile the differences. Thus, both houses of Congress are on record as opposing *Lexecon*, but the decision remains on the books. *Cf.* Eldon E. Fallon et al., *Bellwether Trials in Multidistrict Litigation*, 82 TUL. L. REV. 2323, 2354 n. 107 (2008) (suggesting that "the primary perceived benefit of legislatively overruling *Lexecon*, namely authorizing transferee courts to try cases transferred by the MDL Panel, may be outweighed by the unintended consequence of a diminished threat of remand").

7. The American Law Institute has proposed legislation that far exceeds the limited goal of overruling *Lexecon*. The ALI's proposal repeals the present § 1407 and replaces it with a "Complex Litigation Panel" that has the power to transfer cases to a single state or federal forum for both pretrial and trial purposes. The criteria for transfer are essentially the same as those found in § 1407, but reductions in duplicative litigation, cost, and inconsistent rulings are explicitly mentioned as factors in determining whether transfer "will promote the just, efficient, and fair conduct of the litigation." The legislation also gives the Complex Litigation Panel the power to order cases removed from state to federal court, and conversely permits the Panel to transfer the cases to state court. *See* AM. L. INST., COMPLEX LITIGATION app. A (1994). Thus far, Congress has shown no interest in this proposal.

8. The Panel rarely orders remand until the transferee judge suggests to the Panel that remand is appropriate. *See* R.J.P.M.L. 7.6(d) ("The Panel is reluctant to order remand absent a suggestion of remand from the transferee district court."); In re Data Gen. Corp. Antitrust Litig., 510 F. Supp. 1220, 1226 (J.P.M.L. 1979); *see* In re Patenaude, 210 F.3d 135 (3d Cir. 2000) (refusing to entertain petition for writ of mandamus requiring the Panel to order remand unless the petitioners first requested remand from the transferee judge); *but see* In re Baseball Bat Antitrust Litig., 112 F. Supp. 2d 1175 (J.P.M.L. 2000) (ordering remand of entire case despite suggestions of the transferee judge to remand only some claims). Next, the Panel's decision not to order remand is reviewable only through the extraordinary writ of mandamus. In re Wilson, 451 F.3d 161 (3d Cir. 2006); In re Collins, 233 F.3d 809, 812 (3rd Cir. 2000).

9. Once the Panel remands a case, the rulings of the transferee court travel with the case, and any appeals of the transferee court's rulings are taken to the transferor court's circuit. *See* In re Briscoe, 448 F.3d 201, 213 (3d Cir. 2006); *but see* In re Food Lion, Inc., Fair Labor Standards Act

"Effective Scheduling" Litig., 73 F.3d 528 (4th Cir. 1996) (ordering the Panel to transfer cases back to the MDL forum to permit appeals of the MDL court's rulings to occur in the transferee circuit); *cf.* In re Rhone-Poulenc Rorer Pharm., Inc., 138 F.3d 695 (7th Cir. 1998) (refusing to issue a writ of mandamus against a transferee judge's order limiting the number of expert witnesses that could testify in trials to be conducted in transferor forums). Transferor judges are reluctant to reconsider rulings made in the transferee forum, both because doing so upsets § 1407's goal of achieving uniformity and because reconsideration is inconsistent with the law-of-the-case doctrine. U.S. *ex rel.* Staley v. Columbia/HCA Healthcare Corp., 587 F. Supp. 2d 757 (W.D. Va. 2008); *but see* In re Ford Motor Co., 591 F.3d 406 (5th Cir. 2009) (granting a writ of mandamus when a transferor court refused to overturn an MDL court's decision not to dismiss a case on *forum non conveniens* grounds; noting that the MDL court's decision conflicted with the law of the transferor circuit). The Panel itself "is neither empowered nor inclined to direct, or to suggest to, a transferor judge how he or she should conduct further proceedings in actions after remand." In re A.H. Robins Co. "Dalkon Shield" IUD Prods. Liab. Litig., 453 F. Supp. 108, 110 (J.P.M.L. 1978).

4. An Interim Assessment

As we saw in the last section, the initial response to aggregation — the system of joinder — is insufficient. Joinder rules are capacious enough to accomplish a socially optimal level of aggregation in many cases. But the joinder rules typically place into the hands of litigants the decision about how much aggregation to accomplish; and the parties, driven by their adversarial desire to achieve litigative advantage, do not always attain the optimal level of aggregation. That fact led us to question how valuable the adversarial system's preference for litigant autonomy was, especially in complex cases that raise concerns for the costliness of individual litigation, inconsistency of judgments, and insufficient assets to satisfy similarly situated claimants. But departing from the model of litigative autonomy in joinder decisions carries its own difficulties. The decisions whether and when to aggregate are not outcome-neutral, so that departures from the model require justification if claimants in complex litigation experience different outcomes than those in routine litigation. Moreover, the joinder rules cannot handle all of the problems of geographical, jurisdictional, and temporal dispersion of claims that often infect complex litigation.

This section adds important information for evaluating the capacity of the modern American litigation system to aggregate cases. Consolidation and transfer, which start from the premise that individual litigants will use joinder rules to advance their private interests, act as a patch on this system, allowing more group treatment of related claims (and thus a level of aggregation closer to the socially optimal level). But the patch is only partial. As we saw throughout this section, respect for the forum choices of the parties and for the rights of litigants to individualized adjudication remains relevant in determining the scope of consolidation and transfer.

Moreover, consolidation and transfer doctrines are most useful as a response to the geographical dispersion of cases.   Neither Rule 42(a), 28 U.S.C. § 1404(a), nor 28 U.S.C. § 1407 is adept at responding to temporal dispersion; aside from the creative use of the MDL process in cases such as *Asbestos (No. VI)* — a use whose textual justification is thin — none of these devices can aggregate nonparties, especially "future plaintiffs" whose claims have not yet matured.   None of the devices permits consolidation of federal and state cases.   Nor do these devices work in the state-court-to-state-court context.

Therefore, our present quilt of joinder, consolidation, and transfer doctrines stops short of single-venue aggregation for complex litigation.   In the following two sections, we examine other devices — especially stays, injunctions, and preclusion — that can in limited situations fill in some of the remaining gaps in the present quilt.   As we examine these devices, we continue to ask whether the present approach to aggregating complex litigation has achieved the right balance of competing interests.

D. AGGREGATION THROUGH STAYS, DISMISSALS, AND ANTISUIT INJUNCTIONS

The traditional method by which aggregation of related cases could be accomplished was by means of stays or injunctions.   With a stay, a court essentially enjoins itself from proceeding in favor of a proceeding elsewhere. A stay does not directly result in aggregation; but in some situations, a stay induces a party to file suit or intervene in the related proceeding in whose favor the present case has been stayed.   Related to — but more radical than — the stay is a court's dismissal of a case due to the availability of another forum in which the case can be brought; the court's outright dismissal clearly forces the parties to commence litigation elsewhere.   In contrast to a stay and a dismissal, an antisuit injunction typically orders parties not to file or prosecute their claims or defenses in any court other than the court issuing the injunction.   Again, such an injunction does not directly aggregate related litigation.   But the injunction makes the present litigation the only game in town, so parties that wish to proceed with their cases during the pendency of the injunction have no alternative but to litigate in the court issuing the injunction.   The power to issue antisuit injunctions descends from the power of equity to entertain bills of peace that were brought by parties seeking sanctuary from multiple common-law actions; this equitable proceeding first enjoined the common-law actions and then resolved the litigation-provoking questions once and for all. *See* Zechariah Chafee, Jr., *Bills of Peace with Multiple Parties*, 45 HARV. L. REV. 1297 (1932).

Both plaintiffs and defendants can seek stays, dismissals, and injunctions; courts can also issue them sua sponte.   As a general rule, a party wishing aggregation prefers an antisuit injunction to a stay, at least in situations in which litigation is spread across multiple forums.   The reason is simple: An injunction issues from a single court, while stays or dismissals must issue from all the courts other than the one in which the party wishes to proceed.

Despite their pedigree, stays, dismissals, and injunctions are not today a favored approach to the problem of aggregation. Unless the court can make the stay or injunction permanent or else adjudicate the underlying dispute once and for all, a stay or injunction is relatively powerless against a party with the patience (and the time remaining on the statute of limitations) to outlast the case in whose favor the stay or injunction was entered. Moreover, the work that stays, dismissals, and injunctions have historically accomplished can often be done more directly and effectively by joinder, consolidation, and transfer doctrines of more recent origin.

Nonetheless, stays, dismissals, and antisuit injunctions have potential to plug some of the holes in the newer doctrines. As the last section showed, consolidation and transfer doctrines have little capacity to handle problems of temporal and jurisdictional dispersion. Stays, dismissals, and antisuit injunctions likewise have only a limited ability to handle the problem of temporal dispersion. With regard to jurisdictional dispersion between federal and state courts or among state courts, stays, dismissals, and antisuit injunctions often are the only means of reducing or eliminating repetitive litigation.

This section begins by exploring the capacity of stays, dismissals, and antisuit injunctions to avoid relitigation of issues in cases that are filed in courts of coordinate authority (in other words, federal-to-federal, state-to-state, or country-to-country stays and injunctions). It then turns to their use when some related cases are filed in state court and others are filed in federal court. In this last context, we encounter the concept of federalism, which poses new challenges for achieving optimal aggregation.

1. Stays, Dismissals, and Injunctions in Courts of Coordinate Authority

This subsection explores the ways in which stays, injunctions, and related doctrines have been used to reduce repetitive litigation among courts of coordinate authority. The analysis begins with the use of stays, injunctions, and dismissals among the federal courts, and then moves to the use of these doctrines among the state courts and in the context of litigation carried on among court systems in different countries.

a. Among the Federal Courts

There are circumstances in which federal courts have crafted stays, dismissals, or injunctions to deal with repetitive litigation: when a federal court has jurisdiction over a *res* and when a later *in personam* lawsuit is essentially duplicative of other *in personam* litigation.

i. *In Rem* Litigation

In American law, a longstanding "principle, applicable to both federal and state courts, is established that the court first assuming jurisdiction over the property may maintain and exercise that jurisdiction to the exclusion of the other." Penn Gen. Cas. Co. v. Pa. ex rel. Schnader, 294 U.S. 189, 195 (1935); *see* Mandeville v. Canterbury, 318 U.S. 47, 48-49 (1943) (holding that, when when two cases "are *in rem* or *quasi in rem*, so that the court or its officer must have possession or control of the property . . . to proceed with the cause and to grant the relief sought, the court first acquiring jurisdiction or assuming control of such property is entitled to maintain and exercise its jurisdiction to the exclusion of the other"). This exclusive-jurisdiction principle seems appropriate. If two federal courts assert jurisdiction over a *res*, the possibility exists that one court will decide that Claimant A owns the property, while the other court will find that Claimant B is the owner.

A corollary of the exclusive-jurisdiction rule is this: The court that obtains jurisdiction over a *res* has the power to enjoin other proceedings that seek to adjudicate interests in that property. Such a power exists, for instance, in a bankruptcy proceeding, in which a bankruptcy court administers a debtor's estate (which is a specific type of *res*). The automatic stay in bankruptcy suspends all proceedings in all courts against a debtor upon the filing of a bankruptcy petition. *See* 11 U.S.C. § 362. Likewise, the bankruptcy court can issue any injunction "that is necessary or appropriate to carry out the provisions of" the Bankruptcy Act. *Id.* § 105.

The powers to enjoin litigation affecting a *res* remains limited. The existence of a *res* is central to the legitimate exercise of this power. Some federal courts have relaxed the requirement of a *res* in the federal-court-to-state-court context (*see infra* pp. 183-88), arguably expanding the scope of injunctive power in the federal-court-to-federal-court context as well.

ii. *In Personam* Litigation

A federal court has no general power to stay or enjoin *in personam* litigation that is related to litigation pending in other federal courts. But there are a couple of exceptions to this rule. First, in Section B.2.b of this chapter, we saw that federal courts have an injunctive power, akin to the power in *in rem* proceedings, to enjoin related federal litigation in statutory interpleader. Under 28 U.S.C. § 2361, a court that obtains jurisdiction under 28 U.S.C. § 1335 "may . . . enter its order restraining [the interpleader defendants] from instituting or prosecuting any proceeding in any State or *United States court* affecting the property, instrument or obligation involved in the interpleader action." (Emphasis added.) *State Farm Fire & Cas. Co. v. Tashire*, 386 U.S. 523 (1967) (*supra* p. 84) held that this injunctive power has limits; a court can only enjoin litigation affecting the property that is subject to interpleader. Thus, in *Tashire*, the federal court had no license to issue an injunction preventing parties from pursuing in multiple forums their *in personam* claims against defendants whose liability was not limited by the insurance policy at stake in the interpleader proceeding.   On the comparable antisuit injunctive power for rule interpleader, see 7 CHARLES ALAN WRIGHT ET AL., FEDERAL PRACTICE AND PROCEDURE § 1717 (3d ed. 2001).

Second, a federal court has a limited power to deal with duplicative *in personam* litigation pending in another federal court when the cases involve essentially the same parties and claims. The starting point is *Kerotest Manufacturing Co. v. C-O-Two Fire Equipment Co.*, 342 U.S. 180 (1952). In *Kerotest*, the first lawsuit was brought by a patent owner against a company that bought component parts alleged to infringe the patent. The second lawsuit, brought by the company that made the allegedly infringing component part against the patent owner, sought both a declaration that the patent was invalid and an injunction against the prosecution of the first lawsuit. The first suit was brought in the United States District Court for the Northern District of Illinois; the second was brought in the United States District Court for the District of Delaware. After the manufacturer was joined in the Illinois proceeding, the district court in Delaware court temporarily stayed its own proceedings. But the Delaware court eventually reversed course, and issued an injunction that forbade the patent holder from suing the manufacturer in the Illinois case. The Supreme Court held that the Delaware court should have stayed its hand until the completion of the Illinois case. Noting that "[w]ise judicial administration, giving regard to conservation of judicial resources and comprehensive disposition of litigation, does not counsel rigid mechanical solution of such problems," *id.* at 183, the Court thought that the Third Circuit had not abused its discretion in ordering the stay.

In the patent-infringement area, a nice body of law, replete with a rule (the first-filed case wins) and exceptions to the rule, has sprung up around the *Kerotest* stay. *See, e.g.*, Kahn v. Gen. Motors Corp., 889 F.2d 1078 (Fed. Cir. 1989); William Gluckin & Co. v. Int'l Playtex Corp., 407 F.2d 177 (2d Cir. 1969). But the *Kerotest* stay has not enjoyed broad use in complex litigation.   Because *Kerotest* involved essentially the same parties and claims in both proceedings — in other words, truly duplicative litigation — courts have tended to confine the *Kerotest* stay to its facts:

> [A] court faced with a duplicative suit will commonly stay the second suit, dismiss it without prejudice, enjoin the parties from proceeding with it, or consolidate the two actions. Of course, simple dismissal of the second suit is another common disposition because plaintiffs have no right to maintain two actions on the same subject in the same court, against the same defendant at the same time.

Curtis v. Citibank, N.A., 226 F.3d 133, 138-39 (2d Cir. 2000).

Although courts have not been adventurous in building on the *Kerotest* doctrine to create a more general theory of staying, dismissing, or enjoining later-filed cases in related litigation, a tantalizing possible exception lurks in some opinions. In *Asset Allocation and Management Co. v. Western*

Employers Insurance Co., 892 F.2d 566, 572-73 (7th Cir. 1989), Judge Posner argued that:

> Despite the absence of a clear source of authority for enjoining a second, nonharassing lawsuit (albeit one identical to the first), there is overwhelming case authority that the first court has power, independently of the equitable doctrine that bars vexatious litigation, to enjoin the defendant from bringing a separate suit against the plaintiff in another court . . . .
>
> The real basis for the power, it seems to us, is practical. A court — some court — should have the power to prevent the duplication of litigation even though neither party is acting abusively . . . . It is not a traditional equitable power that the courts are exercising in these cases but a new power asserted in order to facilitate the economical management of complex litigation.
>
> But it is a power, not a duty. It is to be exercised with due regard for the balance of convenience in litigating the parties' disputes in one forum rather than another.

Likewise, in *Schauss v. Metals Depository Corp.*, 757 F.2d 649, 654 (5th Cir. 1985), the court of appeals suggested that an antisuit injunction "may be effective against non-parties." Both *Asset Allocation* and *Schauss*, however, involved the standard *Kerotest* problem of the same parties involved in duplicative litigation in two federal courts. Their statements are dicta, and they have not been pursued in later cases.

Therefore, as a general proposition, if Plaintiff A files suit for injuries arising from a defendant's conduct in one federal court, the action of Plaintiff B, who files a similar suit for his own injuries in a second federal court, would not be subject to a stay, dismissal, or injunction. Moreover, *Kerotest* recognized § 1404 transfers as an option that diminished the need to seek antisuit injunctions or stays against inconvenient litigation. 342 U.S. at 186. In light of the transfer provisions in §§ 1404 and 1407, the *Kerotest* stay has become an esoteric aspect of federal-court practice.

When the *Kerotest* doctrine applies, the first-filed suit gets priority in the absence of special circumstances or a strong showing of inconvenience. Adam v. Jacobs, 950 F.2d 89, 92 (2d Cir. 1991). The decision to stay or otherwise block proceedings in the second-filed suit "rests with a district judge's discretion," but "a district court can go beyond the allowable bounds of discretion when it refuses to stay or dismiss a duplicative suit." *Id.* (internal quotations omitted). *See also* I.A. Durbin, Inc. v. Jefferson Nat'l Bank, 793 F.2d 1541, 1551-52 (11th Cir. 1986) ("Trial courts are afforded broad discretion in determining whether to stay or dismiss litigation in order to avoid duplicating a proceeding already pending in another federal court."); In re Salomon Smith Barney Mut. Fund Fees Litig., 441 F. Supp. 2d 579, 609 (S.D.N.Y. 2006) ("Deference to the first filing embodies considerations of judicial administration and conservation of resources.") (internal quotations omitted).

b. Among the State Courts

For related litigation in state courts, the same basic division between *in rem* and *in personam* actions exists, with essentially the same rules that pertained in litigation among the federal courts. But the independence of state courts from each other raises a couple of novel twists.

i. *In Rem* Litigation

Many state courts adopt the principle of exclusive jurisdiction, so that the first court within a state to assume jurisdiction over a *res* obtains jurisdiction to the exclusion of other courts within the same state. In re Forfeiture of Certain Personal Property, 490 N.W.2d 322 (Mich. 1992). It is more difficult to find cases in which a state court that exercises jurisdiction over a *res* enjoins parties from litigating issues concerning the *res* in courts of other states. (One reason is a court's jurisdiction over a *res* depends on the physical presence of the *res* within the court's territorial boundaries; and most property, especially real property, cannot simultaneously be found within the physical boundaries of two states.) Nonetheless, in dicta or holdings, a few cases suggest that a court exercising *in rem* jurisdiction enjoys a power to enjoin proceedings in other state courts concerning the *res*. *See* Hall v. Michael Bello Ins. Agency, 880 A.2d 451 (N.J. Super. Ct. Ap. Div. 2005); Cloverleaf Enters., Inc. v. Centaur Rosecroft, LLC, 815 N.E.2d 513, 521 (Ind. App. 2004); Garamendi v. Executive Life Ins. Co., 21 Cal. Rptr. 2d 578, 588 (Cal. App. 1993); Doerr v. Warner, 76 N.W.2d 505, 514 (Minn. 1956).

ii. *In Personam* Litigation

Some states have rules, equivalent to the *Kerotest* doctrine, that permit a state court to issue an antisuit injunction against other courts within the same state, or to stay its hand in favor of another court within the same state. *See, e.g.,* Atkinson v. Arnold, 893 S.W.2d 294, 296 (Tex. App. 1995) (noting that antisuit injunctions may "issue to prevent a multiplicity of suits or to protect a party from vexatious or harassing litigation"); CAL. CIV. PRO. CODE § 526(a)(6) (permitting issuance of an injunction "[w]here the restraint is necessary to prevent a multiplicity of judicial proceedings"). In addition, some states have designated a particular court as a "complex litigation court" or have created a special "complex litigation docket" to coordinate related cases arising in the same county or state. *See, e.g.,* Cal. R. Los Angeles Super. Ct. 7.3(f), (k). Other states have created intrastate Judicial Panels on Multidistrict Litigation to coordinate or transfer litigation within their court systems. *See* OKLA. STAT. tit. 20, § 81; TEX. GOV'T CODE § 74.161.

More difficult issues arise with regard to related cases pending in the courts of two different states. Here, three distinct doctrines come into play. First, akin to a *Kerotest* stay, a number of state courts are willing to dismiss or stay their own proceedings when an identical case is proceeding in another forum. Most of these cases involve stays that run in favor of a first-filed federal proceeding involving the same parties and same issues, *see* Seabury v. Cheminova, 868 S.2d 625 (Fla. Dist. Ct. App. 2004), but there is no reason in principle why the same result should not hold with regard to comparable litigation in another state's court. Dura Pharms., Inc. v. Scandipharm, Inc., 713 A.2d 925 (Del. Ch. 1998) (staying Delaware action in favor of first-filed Alabama action); LA. CODE CIV. PROC. art. 532 (permitting Louisiana courts to stay proceedings when litigation "on the same transaction or occurrence, between the same parties in the same capacities" is "pending in a court of another state or of the United States"). As *Dura Pharmaceuticals* explained:

> [T]his Court's discretion should be exercised freely in favor of the stay when there is a prior action pending elsewhere, in a court capable of doing prompt and complete justice, involving the same parties and the same issues, and that as a general rule, litigation should be confined to the forum in which it is first commenced, and that a defendant should not be permitted to defeat the plaintiff's choice of forum in a pending suit by commencing litigation involving the same cause of action in another jurisdiction of its own choosing. These principles are impelled by considerations of comity and the necessities of an orderly and efficient administration of justice. [713 A.2d at 928 (internal quotation marks omitted).]

Second, and more broadly, courts in most states apply the doctrine of *forum non conveniens* to stay or dismiss litigation in favor of litigation that has been or could be filed elsewhere. In general terms, the doctrine permits a court to stay or dismiss an action that when it believes that another forum is more convenient. The factors that a court considers vary from state to state, but they usually are divided into public-interest factors (such as having local controversies determined in a court familiar with the relevant law) and private-interest factors (such as the convenience to the parties and witnesses, and respect for the plaintiff's choice of forum). *See* Gulf Oil Co. v. Gilbert, 330 U.S. 501, 508 (1947); TEX. CIV. PRAC. & REM. CODE § 71.051 (listing six statutory factors). At the federal level, 28 U.S.C. § 1404, which allows transfer between district courts on a similar showing of convenience, has all but replaced *forum non conveniens*.

As its name implies, the *forum non conveniens* doctrine is principally calibrated to deal with issues of convenience, not with issues of complex repetitive litigation. In *Sabino v. Ruffolo*, 562 A.2d 1134, 1138 (Conn. App. 1989), the court indicated in dicta that the presence of "multiple parties" and "complex litigation" were two circumstances in which the general reluctance to dismiss an action on *forum non conveniens* grounds might be overcome. *Cf.* Auerbach v. Frank, 685 A.2d 404 (D.C. 1996) (upholding an antisuit injunction issued against a proceeding in another state court and a refusal to stay the case under the *forum non conveniens* doctrine); Sartori v. Soc'y of Am. Military Eng'rs, 499 A.2d 883, 888 (D.C. 1985) (stating that "the mere pendency of litigation elsewhere does not bar suit in the District of Columbia"). Nonetheless, the doctrine's lack of tailoring to the needs of complex litigation and the reality that *forum non conveniens* requires a party desiring aggregation to file a motion in every case other than the court in which it wishes aggregation to occur make the doctrine only fitfully useful in dealing with repetitive complex litigation.

Third, and most controversially, some state courts issue antisuit injunctions against parties to prevent them from proceeding with cases in the courts of other states. Advanced Bionics Corp. v. Medtronic, Inc., 59 P.3d 231, 237 (Cal. 2002) (refusing to authorize an antisuit injunction against a later-filed action involving the same subject matter unless "an exceptional circumstance . . . outweighs the threat to judicial restraint and comity principles"); Golden Rule Ins. Co. v. Harper, 925 S.W.2d 649, 651 (Tex. 1996). *Golden Rule* stated the standard position:

> An anti-suit injunction is appropriate in four instances: 1) to address a threat to the court's jurisdiction; 2) to prevent the evasion of important public policy; 3) to prevent a multiplicity of suits; or 4) to protect a party from vexatious or harassing litigation. The party seeking the injunction must show that "a clear equity demands" the injunction. A single parallel proceeding in a foreign forum, however, does not constitute a multiplicity nor does it, in itself[,] create a clear equity justifying an anti-suit injunction. [*Id.* at 651 (internal quotations omitted).]

Accord Cloverleaf Enters., Inc. v. Centaur Rosecroft, LLC, 815 N.E.2d 513, 521 (Ind. App. 2004); Staton v. Russell, 565 S.E.2d 103, 109 (N.C. Ct. App. 2002); *see* Ackerman v. Ackerman, 631 N.Y.S.2d 657, 657 (1995) ("The rule of comity forbids our courts from enjoining an action in a sister State unless it is clearly shown that the suit sought to be enjoined was brought in bad faith, motivated by fraud or an intent to harass the party seeking an injunction, or if its purpose was to evade the law of the domicile of the parties.") (internal quotations omitted).

As might be expected, such injunctions are not always heeded in other forums. A common reason is that the enjoining court lacks jurisdiction over the persons enjoined. *See* Robbins v. Reliance Ins. Co., 102 S.W.3d 739 (Tex. App. 2001), *withdrawn*, 2003 WL 1847115 (Tex. App. Apr. 10, 2003); Mahan v. Gunther, 663 N.E.2d 1139 (Ill. App. Ct. 1996). Even if jurisdiction exists, a court is not required to give full faith and credit to the antisuit injunctions of other states, and will do so only when comity dictates. *Mahan*, 663 N.E.2d at 1144; *see* Baker v. Gen. Motors Corp., 522 U.S. 222, 236 (1998) (stating that, under the principle of full faith and credit, "antisuit injunctions regarding litigation elsewhere, even if compatible with due process as a direction constraining parties to the decree, in fact have not controlled the second court's actions regarding litigation in that court"). What happens when one state issues the injunction and the other state refuses to abide by it? *Cf.* James v. Grand Trunk W. R.R., 152 N.E.2d 858 (Ill. 1958) (after a Michigan court issued an antisuit injunction, holding that an Illinois court had the power to issue a "counterinjunction" — in effect, an anti-antisuit injunction — that prevented the party that obtained the Michigan injunction from seeking its enforcement in Michigan).

These doctrines address the problem of repetitive interstate litigation fitfully. The lack of a simple and effective device to aggregate or consolidate litigation spread across the state courts — something akin to the § 1404 and § 1407 transfers of the federal-court level — makes the state-court system less aggregation-friendly than the federal courts.

c. Among the Courts of Different Nations

The same issues and unsatisfying solutions that infect repetitive federal-court-to-federal-court and state-court-to-state-court litigation can arise when courts in another country are adjudicating cases that are related to litigation pending in American courts (whether federal or state).

i. *In Rem* Litigation

Duplicative international *in rem* proceedings are uncommon. When they arise, American courts tend to follow the rule that they use in domestic litigation: The first court to assert jurisdiction over a *res* has exclusive jurisdiction.   *See* Dailey v. Nat'l Hockey League, 987 F.2d 172, 175-78 (3d Cir. 1993) (stating that a federal court "must yield" to a Canadian court that was first to assert *quasi in rem* jurisdiction over a pension plan); Chesley v. Union Carbide Corp., 927 F.2d 60, 66 (2d Cir. 1991) (noting that "the rule [is] equally applicable to requested interference by American courts with a *res* under the jurisdiction of a foreign court"). *Cf.* SEC v. Banner Fund Int'l, 211 F.3d 602 (D.C. Cir. 2000) (affirming a refusal to stay American litigation that was filed before litigation in Belize that was arguably *in rem*). Once *in rem* or *quasi in rem* jurisdiction attaches, an American court can issue an antisuit injunction preventing a party from pursuing the case elsewhere. China Trade and Dev. Corp. v. M.V. Choong Yong, 837 F.2d 33, 36 (2d Cir. 1987) ("When a proceeding is *in rem*, and res judicata alone will not protect the jurisdiction of the first court, an anti-suit injunction may be appropriate.").

ii. *In Personam* Litigation

Although international comity and the distinctive procedural and substantive law of foreign countries make the application of these doctrines a delicate matter, the same techniques — stays or dismissals in favor of foreign litigation and antisuit injunctions against foreign litigation — all have possible application,. First, under *forum non conveniens*, a federal or state court can dismiss or stay a case in favor of litigation in a foreign forum when the standard *forum non conveniens* factors suggest that the foreign litigation is more convenient. For instance, *Piper Aircraft Co. v. Reyno*, 454 U.S. 235 (1981), upheld a federal court's *forum non conveniens* dismissal in favor of litigation in Scottish courts when an airplane carrying Scottish subjects crashed in Scotland, even though the defective plane was manufactured in the United States, Scottish law was less favorable, and the plaintiff had chosen an American forum. *See also* Chambers v. Merrell-Dow Pharms., Inc. 519 N.E.2d 370 (Ohio 1988) (recognizing the doctrine of *forum non conveniens* in Ohio and upholding dismissal of state-court litigation in favor of litigation in a British court).

Second, some American courts have developed a tailored approach, akin to the *Kerotest* stay, that stays or dismisses American litigation in favor of duplicative litigation that is first filed in a foreign court. *See* Philips Elecs., N.V. v. N.H. Ins. Co., 692 N.E.2d 1268 (Ill. App. Ct. 1998) (upholding a stay of two claims in favor of related British litigation and a denial of a stay with respect to two less related claims). In *Caspian Investments, Ltd. v. Vicom Holdings, Ltd.*, 770 F. Supp. 880, 884 (S.D.N.Y. 1991), the court explained:

> The relevant factors in determining whether to grant a stay or a dismissal because of litigation in an overseas forum include the similarity of parties and issues involved, promotion of judicial efficiency, adequacy of relief available in the alternative forum, considerations of fairness to all parties and possible prejudice to any of them, and the temporal sequence of filing for each action.

Third, American courts claim the power to issue antisuit injunctions that bar parties from pursuing litigation in foreign courts. The classic case is *Laker Airways Ltd. v. Sabena, Belgian World Airlines*, 731 F.2d 909 (D.C. Cir. 1984). Laker brought an antitrust suit in federal court against foreign airlines. The airlines then filed claims, which would have been counterclaims in the American suit, against Laker in a British court. The real purpose of the British suit was to obtain an injunction barring Laker from prosecuting its American suit. The British court issued the injunction. Laker then obtained an injunction from the federal court barring the defendants from prosecuting the British suit. The British injunction and American counterinjunction created an international dilemma that subsided when the House of Lords vacated the British injunction. British Airways Bd.v . Laker Airways Ltd., [1985] A.C. 58 (H.L.).

In *Laker*, the D.C. Circuit affirmed the district court's issuance of the counterinjunction, but indicated that such injunctions should be issued only (1) when the conduct by the parties against whom the injunction is sought amounted to harassment or a war of attrition, (2) to protect the court's ability to provide a full and fair adjudication, or (3) to protect an important policy of the forum. 731 F.2d at 928-33. Significantly, *Laker* thought that, due to concerns for international comity, "duplication of parties and issues alone is not sufficient to justify issuance of an antisuit injunction." *Id.* at 928. Nor was the possibility of a race to judgment. *Id.* at 928-29. *See also* Karaha Bodas Co., L.L.C. v. Perusahaan Pertambangan Minyak Dan Gas Bumi Negara, 500 F.3d 111 (2d Cir. 2007) (upholding an antisuit injunction against an action in the Cayman Islands designed to thwart the American enforcement of an arbitral award); Goss Int'l Corp. v. Man Roland Druckmaschinen Aktiengesellschaft, 491 F.3d 355 (8th Cir. 2007) (reversing an antisuit injunction issued against maintenance of a Japanese lawsuit that was designed to "claw back" the proceeds of an American judgment).

State courts too have become entangled with foreign litigation, and they express comparable reluctance to enjoin foreign proceedings. *See* Gannon v. Payne, 706 S.W.2d 304 (Tex. 1986); *but see* Owens-Corning Fiberglas Corp. v. Baker, 838 S.W.2d 838 (Tex. App. 1992) (affirming the issuance of an "anti-antisuit injunction" against defendants that had asked Canadian courts to enjoin Canadian plaintiffs from filing cases in Texas courts).

2. Stays and Injunctions Between Federal and State Courts

One of the principal challenges to the single-venue aggregation of related cases is jurisdictional dispersion — in other words, litigation spread among federal and state courts. To some extent, jurisdictional dispersion between state and federal courts presents the same aggregation issues as the problem of jurisdictional dispersion among courts of coordinate jurisdiction. But, because the problem also touches on the concerns for federalism that the American constitutional structure engenders, using techniques such as stays or injunctions (as well as forum-related dismissals) to aggregate cases dispersed between federal and state courts generates unique issues.

We defer consideration of one technique — removal of cases from state to federal court — until the next chapter, which examines more generally the jurisdictional constraints of federal courts to aggregate cases. *See infra* pp. 297-303. Here we examine the ways in which dismissals, stays, and antisuit injunctions achieve indirectly a degree of jurisdictional aggregation that joinder, consolidation, and transfer do not.

a. *In Rem* Litigation

The starting point for discussing the powers of federal and state courts to stay or enjoin proceedings is the basis of the courts' jurisdiction. When federal and state courts assert *in rem* or *quasi in rem* jurisdiction over a *res*, the standard rule is simple: The court that first secures jurisdiction over the *res* has exclusive jurisdiction to hear the case. A corollary of this rule is that the court first obtaining jurisdiction has the power to enjoin any other proceedings that seek to determine the interests in the *res*. Thus, a federal court that obtains *in rem* jurisdiction can enjoin state-court proceedings relating to the property. Kline v. Burke Constr. Co., 260 U.S. 226 (1922). Conversely, a state court that first obtains *in rem* jurisdiction can enjoin federal proceedings. Princess Lida of Thurn & Taxis v. Thompson, 305 U.S. 456 (1939).

The same jurisdictional rule and power to enjoin related cases has been extended to *quasi in rem* proceedings. *See* Donovan v. City of Dallas, 377 U.S. 408, 412 (1964); *see generally* Richard S. Arnold, *State Court Power to Enjoin Federal Court Proceedings*, 51 VA. L. REV. 59 (1965).

Although it is not technically an *in rem* or *quasi in rem* proceeding, *see* Metro. Prop. & Cas. Ins. Co. v. Shan Trac, Inc., 324 F.3d 20 (1st Cir. 2003), statutory interpleader also allows a federal court to enjoin state-court litigation regarding the property at stake in the interpleader proceeding. 28 U.S.C. § 2361. For a comparable rule authorizing a state court to issue an injunction against federal litigation in a "concursus proceeding," which is equivalent to interpleader, see LA. CODE CIV. PROC. art. 4660.

Other than bankruptcy or comparable receivership matters in state court, however, few complex cases are *in rem*, *quasi in rem*, or in the nature of interpleader. The simple and aggregation-friendly approach for *in rem* and *quasi in rem* proceedings has not carried over to *in personam* actions.

b. *In Personam* Litigation

With *in personam* actions, it is easiest to begin with the power of the state courts to enjoin federal proceedings, and then to examine the thornier question of federal-court injunctions against state-court proceedings. We then briefly analyze the use of stays and dismissals as a means of aggregating cases in state or federal courts.

i. State-Court Injunctions Against Federal Proceedings

Simply put, in an *in personam* action, a state court's power to enjoin a related federal case is non-existent. Although no statute precludes state injunctions of federal proceedings, the Supreme Court has long followed Justice Story's opinion, from his treatise on equity, that "the State Courts cannot injoin proceedings in the Courts of the United States." 2 JOSEPH STORY, COMMENTARIES ON EQUITY JURISPRUDENCE 186 (1836); *see* Farr v. Thomson, 78 U.S. (11 Wall.) 139 (1871). In spite of a passing post-*Erie* suggestion that states might have such power, *see* Baltimore & Ohio R. Co. v. Kepner, 314 U.S. 44, 51-52 (1941), the Supreme Court strongly reaffirmed the lack of state power to enjoin federal *in personam* proceedings in *Donovan v. City of Dallas*, 377 U.S. 408 (1964).

It would be difficult to imagine a more compelling case for an injunction than *Donovan*. Plaintiffs commenced a class action in state court and lost. More than one hundred plaintiffs, some of whom had been plaintiffs in the state action, then brought suit in federal court on the same claims. The state court issued an injunction requiring all the plaintiffs to dismiss the federal case. They refused. On certiorari from the state court's order of contempt, the Supreme Court held that the state injunction was invalid:

> While Congress has seen fit to authorize courts of the United States to restrain state-court proceedings in some special circumstances, it has in no way relaxed the old and well-established judicially declared rule that state courts are completely without power to restrain federal-court proceedings, in *in personam* actions . . . . [377 U.S. at 412-13.]

The *Donovan* rule was strengthened in *General Atomic Co. v. Felter*, 434 U.S. 12 (1977). *Felter* arose out of a contract dispute that had spawned litigation all around the country. A New Mexico state court enjoined one of the principal parties (GAC) "from filing or prosecuting any original, third-party, or arbitration actions relating to the subject matter of the Santa Fe lawsuit . . . ." GAC was about to implead the plaintiff in the New Mexico case in a federal case. Although the case was distinguishable from *Donovan* — in *Felter*, the federal court had not yet obtained jurisdiction over the enjoined claim — the Supreme Court held that the injunction was invalid:

> There is even less basis for the injunction in this case [than in *Donovan*]. Here there is no final state-court judgment . . . . In addition, GAC's opportunity to fairly litigate the various claims arising from this complex action would be substantially prejudiced if the injunction were allowed to stand. What the New Mexico Supreme Court has described as "harassment" is principally GAC's desire to defend itself by impleading [another party] in the federal lawsuits and federal arbitration proceedings brought against it . . . . Federal courts are fully capable of preventing their misuse for purposes of harassment. [434 U.S. at 17-18.]

Justice Rehnquist dissented, arguing that, because federal courts can enjoin state proceedings when necessary to protect their jurisdiction or judgments (we will see why shortly), "a state court must have a similar power to forbid the initiation of vexatious litigation in federal court." *Id.* at 20.

Because the *Donovan-Felter* rule does not appear to be of constitutional dimension, it could be legislatively overturned. *Cf.* AM. L. INST., STUDY OF THE DIVISION OF JURISDICTION BETWEEN STATE AND FEDERAL COURTS § 1373 (1969) (recommending that Congress allow state courts to enjoin *in personam* federal actions when "warranted" by equitable principles and "the injunction is necessary to protect against vexatious and harassing relitigation of matters determined by an existing judgment of the State court in a civil action"). Until Congress acts, however, *Donovan* and *Felter* make it difficult, if not impossible, to argue that state courts can enjoin federal proceedings merely to prevent inefficient relitigation of claims.

ii. Federal-Court Injunctions Against State Proceedings

In his *Commentaries*, Justice Story also opined that what was sauce for the goose was sauce for the gander: that federal courts could not enjoin state courts. STORY, *supra*, at 186. This half of Story's opinion, however, has not been followed with the rigor of the bar against state-court injunctions. In 1793 Congress passed a statute declaring: "[N]or shall a writ of injunction be granted to stay proceedings in any court of a state." Act of Mar. 2, 1793, c. 22, § 5, 1 Stat. 333, 335 (1848). But federal courts created exceptions to this prohibition over the years, often enjoining state-court proceedings. The Supreme Court swept away most of these exceptions in *Toucey v. New York Life Insurance Co.*, 314 U.S. 118 (1941). In 1948, however, Congress enacted the Anti-Injunction Act, 28 U.S.C. § 2283, which maintained a general prohibition on federal-court injunctions against state-court proceedings but also created three important exceptions. Section 2283 provides in full:

> A court of the United States may not grant an injunction to stay proceedings in a State court except as expressly authorized by Act of Congress, or where necessary in aid of its jurisdiction, or to protect or effectuate its judgments.

The Anti-Injunction Act does not vest any power in the federal courts to enjoin state-court proceedings. The Act assumes that such power exists elsewhere, and then constrains it. Therefore, the critical issues are whether federal courts have the power to enjoin the litigation of related complex cases in state court and, if so, whether any of the exceptions in the Anti-Injunction Act can be construed to permit such an injunction.

In re Baldwin-United Corp.

770 F.2d 328 (2d Cir. 1985)

■ MANSFIELD, Circuit Judge.

Thirty-one states appeal a preliminary injunction issued in the Southern District of New York by Judge Charles L. Brieant, Jr., in the course of a consolidated multi-district, class action against various broker-dealers who sold securities of the now-bankrupt Baldwin-United Corporation and its insurance subsidiaries. Appellants, with the exception of the State of Maine, were neither parties to nor intervenors in the district court proceedings below. . . . Because we find that the issuance of the injunction was within the scope of the district court's power and was not an abuse of its discretion, we affirm.

[More than 100 federal securities lawsuits were consolidated in a multidistrict proceeding. The plaintiffs were 100,000 holders of Baldwin single-premium deferred annuities (SPDAs). The defendants were 26 broker-dealers who sold the SPDAs by representing them to be safe and desirable investments. In addition to federal securities-law claims, many plaintiffs also raised related state-law claims, such as consumer-protection claims. The district court certified the case as a class action; less than 400 of the 100,000 plaintiffs chose to opt out of the action. Eventually 18 of the 26 broker-dealers agreed to settle the class's claims for approximately $140 million; in return, the plaintiffs agreed to release their federal and state-law claims. Only 50 plaintiffs objected to this settlement.]

On hearing of the proposed settlements the representatives of 40 states in the National Association of Attorneys General (NAAG), concluded that the proposal did not adequately compensate plaintiffs for their federal and state law claims. The states were also concerned about violations by the Baldwin companies of various state regulatory and criminal laws enforced by each state's attorney general. . . . [Nonetheless, shortly afterwards] the district court preliminarily approved the settlement and scheduled a hearing on its fairness.

Meanwhile, . . . some 10 states had issued subpoenas or other requests for information from various defendants. The states' objective . . . is to enforce state laws authorizing them in their representative capacities to seek restitution and monetary recovery from the defendants to be paid over to those of the states' citizens who are plaintiffs in the consolidated class actions before Judge Brieant. In addition, some states may wish to pursue other state remedies, including prospective injunctive relief and enforcement of state criminal and regulatory laws . . . .

. . . [Twenty-two states] submitted an amicus brief opposing the settlements as inadequate. No state intervened except Maine . . . . In mid-February, several defendants received from the State of New York notices of its intent to bring a suit seeking restitution for New York citizens who held Baldwin SPDAs. These defendants moved the district court to enjoin the imminent New York actions. . . .

[Relying on the All Writs Act, 28 U.S.C. § 1651, and on Federal Rule 23(d),] Judge Brieant issued the injunction on March 19, 1985. The order enjoins the New York Attorney General and "all other persons having actual knowledge of th[e] Order" from

> commencing any action or proceeding of any kind against any defendant . . . on behalf of or derivative of the rights of any plaintiff or purported class member . . . or which action or proceeding may in any way affect the rights of any plaintiff . . . or which action or proceeding seeks money damages arising out of the sale to any plaintiff . . . [of the Baldwin annuities] . . . or which action or proceeding seeks any declaratory relief with respect to any of the above. . . .

The injunction was to continue in effect until the entry of final judgment in all of the multidistrict proceedings.

The defendants served a copy of the injunction on every state attorney general. . . .

Thirty states then filed the present appeal and sought a stay from this court . . . . Meanwhile, on May 1, 1985, the district court approved the proposed settlements as fair, reasonable and adequate, and entered final judgments in 18 of the 26 consolidated class actions.

DISCUSSION

A preliminary injunction will be overturned only when the district court abuses its discretion. An abuse of discretion may be found when the district court relies on clearly erroneous findings of fact or on an error of law in issuing the injunction. . . .

Federal courts have authority under the All-Writs Act, 28 U.S.C. § 1651 (1982), to "issue all writs necessary or appropriate in aid of their respective jurisdictions and agreeable to the usages and principles of law." . . . While the parties agree that the Anti-Injunction Act is inapplicable here since the injunction below issued before any suits were commenced in state court, *see* Dombrowski v. Pfister, 380 U.S. 479, 484 n.2 (1965), cases interpreting this clause of the Anti-Injunction Act have been helpful in understanding the meaning of the All-Writs Act.

We do not find independent authority for the issuance of the injunction in the Fed. R. Civ. P. 23(d) provision empowering the district judge to issue orders appropriate ["to protect class members and fairly conduct the action"]; that rule is a rule of procedure and creates no substantive rights or remedies enforceable in federal court. . . .

When a federal court has jurisdiction over its case in chief, as did the district court here, the All-Writs Act grants it ancillary jurisdiction to issue writs "necessary or appropriate in aid of" that jurisdiction. This provision permits a district court to enjoin actions in state court where necessary to prevent relitigation of an existing federal judgment, *see* United States v. N.Y. Tel. Co., 434 U.S. 159, 172 (1977), notwithstanding the fact that the parties to the original action could invoke res judicata in state courts against any subsequent suit brought on the same matters. Even before a federal judgment is reached, however, the preservation of the federal court's jurisdiction or authority over an ongoing matter may justify an injunction against actions in state court. Such "federal injunctive relief may be necessary to prevent a state court from so interfering with a federal court's consideration or disposition of a case as to seriously impair the federal court's flexibility and authority to decide that case." Atl. Coast Line R.R. v. Bhd. of Locomotive Eng'rs, 398 U.S. 281, 295 (1970) (dicta) (Anti-Injunction Act).

On the other hand, the mere existence of a parallel lawsuit in state court that seeks to adjudicate the same *in personam* cause of action does not in itself provide sufficient grounds for an injunction against a state action in favor of a pending federal action. *See* Vendo Co. v. Lektro-Vend Corp., 433 U.S. 623, 642 (1977) . . . . This principle does not apply when federal courts have jurisdiction over a *res* in an *in rem* action; in such a case, because the "exercise by the state court of jurisdiction over the same *res* necessarily impairs, and may defect, the jurisdiction of the federal court already attached," the federal court is empowered to enjoin any state court proceeding affecting that *res*. Kline v. Burke Constr. Co., 260 U.S. [226, 229 (1922)].

Here the findings of the district court that the injunction was necessary to preserve its jurisdiction and protect its judgments, if sustainable, would be sufficient to justify the issuance of the injunction under the All-Writs Act. We must therefore examine whether the district court's finding that the maintenance of actions in state court would impair its jurisdiction and authority over the consolidated federal multidistrict actions was clearly erroneous.

At the time when the injunction issued the parties in 18 of the 26 class actions had reached stipulated settlements that had been provisionally approved by the court and were awaiting final court approval, and the parties in the remaining 8 suits were continuing settlement negotiations. Final judgments in the 18 settling actions were entered shortly after the injunction issued. As for the defendants participating in the stipulated settlements, we conclude that the injunction was "necessary or appropriate in aid of" the court's jurisdiction. There is no question that an injunction could have been appropriately ordered after the 18 final federal judgments were entered, since it would properly have forestalled relitigation of those judgments. Because, as a condition of the settlement, the plaintiffs agreed to release all claims arising under federal and state law on account of the purchase of the Baldwin SPDAs from the settling defendants, such as post-settlement injunctions would have barred the states from bringing state law claims derivative of the plaintiffs' rights. Were this not the case, the finality of virtually any class action involving pendent state claims could be defeated by subsequent suits brought by the states asserting rights derivative of those released by the class members. For instance, as a practical matter no defendant in the consolidated federal actions in the present case could reasonably be expected to consummate a settlement of those claims if their claims could be reasserted under state laws, whether by states on behalf of the plaintiffs or by anyone else, seeking recovery of money to be paid to the plaintiffs. . . . The effect would be to threaten to reopen the settlement unless and until it had been reduced to a judgment that would have res judicata consequences.

We recognize that under the line of cases typified by *Kline v. Burke Construction Co.*, until the issuance of a final federal judgment the pendency of duplicative *in personam* actions in state court — even those actions derivative of the rights of parties of the federal action — would not ordinarily justify enjoining the state court actions. Here, however, the potential for an onslaught of state actions posed more than a risk of inconvenience or duplicative litigation; rather, such a development threatened to "seriously impair the federal court's flexibility and authority" to approve settlements in the multi-district litigation. The circumstances faced by Judge Brieant threatened to frustrate proceedings in a federal action of substantial scope, which had already consumed vast amounts of judicial time and was nearing completion. . . . Settlement negotiations in the federal court had been under way for many months, agreement had been reached, and all that remained was approval of the settlement by the district court. . . .

The existence of multiple and harassing actions by the states could only serve to frustrate the district court's efforts to craft a settlement in the multidistrict litigation before it. The success of any federal settlement was dependent on the parties' ability to agree to the release of any and all related civil claims the plaintiffs had against the settling defendants based on the same facts. If states or others could derivatively assert the same claims on behalf of the same class or members of it, there could be no certainty about the finality of any federal settlement. Any substantial risk of this prospect would threaten all of the settlement efforts by the district court and destroy the utility of the multidistrict forum otherwise ideally suited to resolving such broad claims. To the extent that the impending state court suits were vexatious and harassing, our interest in preserving federalism and comity with the state courts is not significantly disturbed by the issuance of injunctive relief.

. . . In effect, unlike the situation in the *Kline v. Burke Construction Co.* line of cases, the district court had before it a class action proceeding so far advanced that it was the virtual equivalent of a *res* over which the district judge required full control. Similar authority for the injunction comes from the court's power to protect and effectuate its order provisionally approving the 18 settlements.

Under the circumstances we conclude that the injunction protecting the settling defendants was unquestionably "necessary or appropriate in aid of" the federal court's jurisdiction. Although the question is closer as to the application of the injunction to the 8 defendants who have not yet settled, we cannot find that the injunction was erroneous as to them. Given the extensive involvement of the district court in settlement negotiations to date and in the management of this substantial class action, we perceive a major threat to the federal court's ability to manage and resolve the actions against the remaining defendants should the states be free to harass the defendants through state court actions designed to influence the defendants' choices in the federal litigation. So long as there is a substantially significant prospect that these 8 defendants will settle in the reasonably near future, we conclude that the injunction entered by the district court is not improper. If, however, at some point in the continued progress of the actions against the remaining 8 defendants it should appear that prompt settlement was no longer likely, we anticipate that upon application the injunction against parallel actions by the states might be lifted; in that event the situation would fall within the [*Kline v. Burke*] *Construction Co.* rule that *in personam* proceedings in state court cannot be enjoined merely because they are duplicative of actions being heard in federal court. That situation, however, does not presently exist.

Having found the injunction necessary and appropriate in aid of the district court's jurisdiction we conclude that it is no less valid because it applies to states other than New York. An important feature of the All-Writs Act is its grant of authority to enjoin and bind non-parties to an action when needed to preserve the court's ability to reach or enforce its decision in a case over which it has proper jurisdiction. *See, e.g., United States v. N.Y. Tel. Co.*, 434 U.S. at 174 ("The power conferred by the Act, extends, under appropriate circumstances, to persons who, though not parties to the original action or engaged in wrongdoing, are in a position to frustrate the implementation of a court order or the proper administration of justice, [citations omitted], and encompasses even those who have not taken any affirmative action to hinder justice."). The power to bind non-parties distinguishes injunctions issued under the Act from injunctions issued in situations in which the activities of the third parties do not interfere with the very conduct of the proceeding before the court. . . .

As for notice the requirements of the All-Writs Act are satisfied if the parties whose conduct is enjoined have actual notice of the injunction and an opportunity to seek relief from it in the district court. These requirements were met here, since each state's attorney general was served with the injunction and since each had the opportunity to present arguments against it to the district court. . . . So long as the injunction is limited to those engaged in such conduct with actual notice of the terms of the injunction, as is the injunction here, we cannot say that it must fail for lack of notice, even though it appears that not all of the appellant states were aware in advance that an order of injunction was being entered that would limit their conduct as well as the conduct of the State of New York.

[The Second Circuit then rejected the argument that the injunction violated the Eleventh Amendment.]

Having rejected the state[s'] objections to the district court's injunction, we affirm.

RETIREMENT SYSTEMS OF ALABAMA V. J.P. MORGAN CHASE & CO.

386 F.3d 419 (2d Cir. 2004)

■ CABRANES, Circuit Judge.

At issue in this appeal is whether the United States District Court for the Southern District of New York (Denise Cote, Judge), the venue for multidistrict securities litigation arising from the collapse of WorldCom, was authorized to enter an injunction ordering an Alabama state court to postpone the trial of a related case until after the District Court had completed its own trial. On April 23, 2004, the District Court ordered the Alabama action to be rescheduled from October 18, 2004, to a date no earlier than sixty days following the completion of a class action trial that is scheduled to begin in the District Court on January 10, 2005. The plaintiffs in the Alabama Action, collectively known as the Retirement Systems of Alabama ("RSA"), who are not plaintiffs in the securities litigation in the District Court, appeal from the injunction. . . .

I. BACKGROUND

A. *The Securities Litigation in the District Court*

On June 25, 2002, WorldCom announced a massive restatement of its financial statements, precipitating the filing of numerous individual and class actions in state and federal courts across the country.

On August 15, 2002, numerous class actions that had been filed in the Southern District of New York were consolidated before Judge Cote under the caption *In re WorldCom, Inc. Securities Litigation.* The Consolidated Class Action Complaint named [former officers and directors of WorldCom, WorldCom's underwriters, auditor, and various other analysts]. The complaint asserted claims under Sections 11, 12(a)(2) and 15 of the

Securities Act of 1933 ("Securities Act") and Sections 10(b) and 20(a) of the Securities Exchange Act of 1934 ("Exchange Act").

WorldCom filed for bankruptcy in July 2002 — the largest bankruptcy filing in United States history. Thereafter, the defendants in various state court actions removed those actions to federal court on the ground that they were related to WorldCom's bankruptcy. The Judicial Panel on Multidistrict Litigation ("MDL Panel") ordered that actions pending in federal courts across the country, including actions that had been removed from state court, be centralized in the Southern District of New York before Judge Cote. Prior to the MDL Panel's order, however, a handful of actions removed to federal court had been remanded to state court. One of these state court actions, *Retirement Systems of Alabama v. J.P. Morgan Chase & Co.*, (the "Alabama Action"), is pending in the Alabama Circuit Court for Montgomery County, and is the subject of this appeal.

In December 2002, the consolidated class action and the actions transferred by the MDL Panel — collectively, the "Securities Litigation" — were consolidated for pretrial purposes. The District Court certified a class on October 24, 2003, and shortly thereafter set a date of January 10, 2005 for the trial of the consolidated class action, with the trials of the individual actions to follow.

[Eventually the parties, Judge Cote, and the state court judges in the remanded actions attempted to coordinate discovery in all the actions.] On January 30, 2004, Judge Cote issued a Discovery Coordination Order (the "Coordination Order"), and sent it to the state court judges in the three remanded actions (the Alabama Action, and actions in Illinois and Pennsylvania) that were approaching or were already in the discovery stage. The Coordination Order, which invited the state judges to sign it if they wished to adopt it, provided that "[d]iscovery and trial in the [remanded] [a]ctions shall not delay or interfere with discovery in and trial of the Class Action" in the Securities Litigation in the Southern District of New York, and that the first trial would be the class action trial in the Securities Litigation, scheduled for January 10, 2005.

The state court judges in each of the three remanded actions have generally coordinated discovery in those actions with discovery in the Securities Litigation. Additionally, the state court judges in two of the remanded actions, those in Illinois and Pennsylvania, scheduled their respective trials to follow the class action trial in the Securities Litigation. In contrast, Judge Charles Price, presiding over the Alabama Action, declined to adopt all the principles of the Coordination Order, and scheduled trial to begin on October 18, 2004 — three months in advance of the class action trial date in the Securities Litigation.

B. *The Alabama Action*

The Alabama Action was filed on July 15, 2002, two-and-one-half months after the first class action was filed in the Southern District of New York. The complaint alleges violations of federal and Alabama statutory and common law, including claims under Sections 11, 12, and 15 of the Securities Act that are also pleaded in the Securities Litigation. The defendants include [virtually the same defendants sued in the Securities Litigation. In addition, the district court found that the "Alabama Action arises from and pleads the same course of conduct on which the Securities Litigation is premised."] The plaintiffs in the Alabama Action are several retirement funds . . . Notably, RSA is not a party to any of the various federal actions consolidated in the Securities Litigation, and expressly opted out of the consolidated class action. . . .

On February 17, 2004, the defendants in the Alabama Action moved in that case for the adoption of Judge Cote's Coordination Order. On March 5, before Judge Price had ruled on the motion, defendants moved in the alternative to modify Judge Price's scheduling order by extending the trial date of October 18, 2004 by nine months. On March 18, Judge Price denied defendants' motions.

C. *The District Court's Injunction*

After Judge Price denied defendants' requests for a later trial date, defendants applied to Judge Cote, pursuant to the All Writs Act, 28 U.S.C. § 1651, for an order directing RSA to show cause why a writ should not issue that would stay trial of the Alabama Action until after the conclusion of the class action trial in the Securities Litigation. . . .

On April 23, 2004, the District Court ordered that "the Circuit Court of Alabama is enjoined from resolving any summary judgment motion or beginning the trial in [the Alabama Action] until at least sixty days following the entry of a verdict in the class action trial in the Securities Litigation." The District Court rejected plaintiffs' argument that the injunction was precluded by the Anti-Injunction Act, 28 U.S.C. § 2283 . . . . The Court held that the injunction was necessary in aid of its jurisdiction because it was "necessary to preserve the schedule in the Securities Litigation and to keep the federal MDL litigation on its own 'path to judgment.'"

The District Court determined that, "[i]f the Alabama Action proceeds to trial in October, or at any time before the class action trial, it will inevitably delay the beginning of the class action trial far beyond January 10." The District Court identified two causes for the delay. First, the Court found that "a decision on a summary judgment motion or any verdict in the Alabama Action will necessarily engender complicated and time-consuming motion practice in the [class action] in order to permit the ramifications, including any collateral estoppel effect, of that litigation to be determined before the class action trial begins." Second, the Court found that "[t]he energies of the defendants in the [class action] who are also defendants in the Alabama Action will necessarily be diverted by the need to prepare for and participate in the Alabama Action's October trial." The Court concluded that "[t]he date for the class action trial . . . will be held hostage to the Alabama Action, and this Court's ability to control the schedule of this complex, multi-district securities litigation will be hamstrung." . . .

II. DISCUSSION

RSA argues on appeal that the District Court's injunction (1) violated the Anti-Injunction Act, (2) violated the Eleventh Amendment, (3) was contrary to the *Rooker-Feldman* doctrine, and (4) was contrary to the abstention required by *Younger v. Harris*, 401 U.S. 37 (1971). Because we hold that the injunction violated the Anti-Injunction Act, we do not reach the other grounds.

A. *Standard of Review*

We review the District Court's issuance of an injunction for abuse of discretion. To the extent a district court's injunction involves questions of law, review is plenary; but a district court's findings of fact may be overturned only if clearly erroneous. . . .

B. *The All Writs Act and the Anti-Injunction Act*

1. *Statutory language*

The All Writs Act, 28 U.S.C. § 1651(a), provides federal courts with the power to "issue all writs necessary or appropriate in aid of their respective jurisdictions and agreeable to the usages and principles of law." This grant of authority is limited by the Anti-Injunction Act, 28 U.S.C. § 2283, which bars a federal court from enjoining a proceeding in state court unless that action is "expressly authorized by Act of Congress, or where necessary in aid of its jurisdiction, or to protect or effectuate its judgments." If the District Court's injunction was in fact necessary in aid of its jurisdiction, then the injunction was authorized by the All Writs Act, and was not barred by the Anti-Injunction Act. If, as RSA argues, the injunction was not necessary in aid of the District Court's jurisdiction, then it exceeded the District Court's authority under the All Writs Act and — in the absence of another applicable statutory exception — violated the Anti-Injunction Act.

In interpreting the Anti-Injunction Act, the Supreme Court has directed that "[a]ny doubts as to the propriety of a federal injunction against state court proceedings should be resolved in favor of permitting the state courts to proceed in an orderly fashion to finally determine the controversy." Atl. Coast Line R.R. v. Bhd. of Locomotive Eng'rs, 398 U.S. 281, 297 (1970).

2. *Injunctions in* in rem *and* in personam *actions*

The Supreme Court in *Kline v. Burke Construction Co.*, 260 U.S. 226 (1922), addressing the propriety of enjoining state-court actions under the All Writs Act, distinguished *in rem* from *in personam* actions. A federal court with jurisdiction over an *in rem* action may enjoin a later-filed state court action involving the same *res* . . . . , because the effect of filing the *in rem* action in federal court "is to draw to the federal court the possession or control, actual or potential, of the *res*," and a state court's exercise of jurisdiction "necessarily impairs, and may defeat," the federal court's jurisdiction. *Id.* at 229. In contrast, an *in personam* action involves a controversy over liability rather than over possession of a thing: "[A] controversy over a mere question of personal liability does not involve the possession or control of a thing, and an action brought to enforce such a liability does not tend to impair or defeat the jurisdiction of the court in which a prior action for the same cause is pending." *Id.* at 230. . . .

Since *Kline*, the Supreme Court has never held that a district court may enjoin, as necessary in aid of the district court's jurisdiction, a parallel in personam state action. *See* Vendo Co. v. Lektro-Vend Corp., 433 U.S. 623, 642 (1977) (plurality opinion) ("We have never viewed parallel *in personam* actions as interfering with the jurisdiction of either court . . . ."). There is no dispute that the Securities Litigation, although a complex, multidistrict litigation, is an *in personam* action against defendants. Defendants argue that, under our decision in *In re Baldwin-United Corp.*, 770 F.2d 328 [(2d Cir. 1985) (*supra* p. 183)], the Securities Litigation is the "virtual equivalent of a *res*," *id.* at 337, so that the District Court was authorized to enjoin a later-filed related action in the Alabama Circuit Court.

3. Baldwin-United *and its application*

We recognized in *Baldwin-United* that an injunction may be appropriate even in in personam actions under certain limited circumstances. . . .

Clearly, our decision in *Baldwin-United* did not create a blanket rule or presumption that a federal court in any multidistrict action may enjoin parallel state proceedings. We held that an injunction of related state court proceedings could be warranted even in an *in personam* action, but it was crucial to our analysis that most of the defendants had already settled, and that there was a "substantially significant prospect that [the other eight defendants] will settle in the reasonably near future." *Id.* [at 338]. . . .

Defendants argue that here, as in *Baldwin-United*, an injunction was necessary to prevent proceedings in the Alabama Action from thwarting settlement discussions in the Securities Litigation. They also argue that, even setting aside the prospects of settlement, the injunction was proper because a trial in the Alabama Action would interfere with the trial schedule in the Securities Litigation.

i. *Whether the injunction was justified as necessary to preserve the prospects of settlement*

Defendants' first argument — that the District Court's injunction was justified under *Baldwin-United* by the need to protect the possibility of settlement in the Securities Litigation — can be quickly rejected.

The District Court did not rely on the prospect of a prompt settlement in concluding that an injunction was proper. . . .

Defendants . . . note that (1) settlement discussions in fact occurred, and (2) on May 7, 2004, two weeks after the District Court's injunction, two appellees — Citigroup Inc. and Citigroup Global Markets Inc. — signed a Memorandum of Agreement with the plaintiff class in the Securities Litigation, settling the class action claims. Yet the fact that settlement discussions occurred in no way suggests that prompt settlement was likely. Nor can the District Court's injunction be retroactively justified by the bare fact that, two weeks later, two defendants settled the class action claims against them.

Even if defendants had demonstrated that, as in *Baldwin-United*, a prompt settlement in the Securities Litigation was likely, they have failed to explain how the District Court's injunction was necessary to protect that prospective settlement. Defendants therefore have not shown that the rationale of *Baldwin-United* — protecting an actual or impending settlement in a federal action from being undone or thwarted by state-court litigation — justifies the District Court's injunction of the Alabama Action.

> ii. *Whether the injunction was justified as necessary to preserve the District Court's trial date*

The District Court found that the injunction was necessary in aid of its jurisdiction because an October 2004 trial in the Alabama Action would "inevitably delay the beginning of the class action trial far beyond January 10[, 2005]." The Court relied on broad language in *Baldwin-United* that the "need to enjoin conflicting state proceedings arises because the jurisdiction of a multidistrict court is analogous to that of a court in an *in rem* action . . . where it is intolerable to have conflicting orders from different courts." As discussed above, *Baldwin-United* did not hold that multidistrict class actions are, in general, to be deemed virtual *in rem* proceedings; it involved circumstances where an injunction was necessary to preserve a settlement or the prospects of an imminent settlement. Defendants nonetheless argue that there are other circumstances, including the circumstances of this case, in which a district court may, as necessary in aid of its jurisdiction, enjoin a related state-court proceeding.

As an initial matter, we note that a federal district court, even assuming it has some interest in avoiding delay in its own proceedings, has no interest — no interest that can be vindicated by the exercise of the federal injunction power — in being the first court to hold a trial on the merits . . . and thereby avoid issues of collateral estoppel . . . . Accordingly, the District Court could only have sought to justify its injunction as necessary to preserve its trial date, rather than as necessary to allow it to hold the first trial. . . .

Defendants' position — that a district court, in multidistrict class action litigation that is nearing trial, may enjoin related state proceedings to avoid delay — is flawed because it does not admit of principled limits. Any time parallel state and federal actions are proceeding against the same defendant, it is conceivable that occurrences in the state action will cause delay in the federal action, by provoking motion practice in federal court regarding the effects of state-court rulings, or simply by diverting the attention of the defendant. Such a rule would in effect create an additional exception to the Anti-Injunction Act for circumstances where a federal court finds it convenient to enjoin related state proceedings — an approach contrary to the Supreme Court's direction that we construe doubts about the permissibility of an injunction "in favor of permitting the state courts to proceed in an orderly fashion to finally determine the controversy." *Atl. Coast Line R.R.*, 398 U.S. at 297.

Finally, it should be noted that the District Court's observations that "the Alabama Plaintiffs have not been able to articulate any valid reason why their action should be tried in 2004," and that the injunction will affect only the timing of the Alabama Action, are simply not relevant to whether its injunction was barred by the Anti-Injunction Act. In requiring that an injunction be "necessary in aid of" a district court's jurisdiction, the Anti-Injunction Act does not invite district courts to balance the interests of state courts against their own. Nor does the statutory language contain an exception for injunctions of limited duration.

[The court of appeals then held that it was unnecessary to consider RSA's remaining arguments regarding the impropriety of the injunction.]

CONCLUSION

We hold that a district court may not, consistent with the All Writs Act and the "necessary in aid of its jurisdiction" exception to the Anti-Injunction Act, enjoin a state-court trial in order to avoid delay in the district court's trial. The District Court's judgment is therefore reversed, and its injunction is vacated. We remand for further proceedings consistent with this opinion.

IN RE BRIDGESTONE/FIRESTONE, INC., TIRES PRODUCTS LIABILITY LITIGATION

333 F.3d 763 (7th Cir. 2003)

■ EASTERBROOK, Circuit Judge.

This appeal is successive to last year's decision that the district court abused its discretion by certifying nationwide classes covering multiple models of Ford vehicles and Firestone tires sold between 1990 and 2001. Classes comprising owners of more than 60 million tires and 3 million vehicles, including many different models, are unsuitable [for class-action treatment] for several reasons, we concluded . . . .

[L]awyers representing the plaintiffs decided to try again, in other courts. Class suits have been filed in many jurisdictions; in at least five suits, plaintiffs seek certification of the same nationwide classes that our opinion nixes. One state judge certified a nationwide class on the day complaint was filed, without awaiting a response from the defendants and without giving reasons. Ford and Firestone asked the district judge to enforce our decision by enjoining other class actions — not just other efforts to launch nationwide classes, but any class action, even one limited to a single product in a single state. The district court denied this motion, and the defendants immediately appealed on the authority of 28 U.S.C. § 1292(a)(1). . . .

The Anti-Injunction Act, 28 U.S.C. § 2283, forbids any federal injunction or stay of state litigation "except as expressly authorized by Act of Congress, or where necessary in aid of its jurisdiction, or to protect or effectuate its judgments." Defendants contend that an anti-class-action injunction is necessary to carry out our decision of last year. Yet the only classes that had been certified had national scope, and the only judgment that could be protected or effectuated is one concerning such classes. . . . The district court had not certified, and our opinion thus did not address, any statewide class. Although we suggested that even a single-state class covering multiple models of tire or SUV would be unmanageable and inferior to supervision by the National Highway Transportation Safety Administration, this assessment did not become part of our judgment. State courts are free to decide for themselves how much effort to invest in creating subclasses (so that each model of tire or SUV receives appropriate consideration); advice designed to ward off what a federal court deems an unproductive investment of judicial time does not create a "judgment" that forbids any state tribunal to make the effort. Indeed, our opinion contemplated that states would certify narrower classes . . . . So the district court properly denied Ford's request for an injunction that would preclude any class suit in any state court. . . .

What we did hold is that a class covering owners in every state may not be certified over the defendants' opposition. . . . The Anti-Injunction Act permits a federal court to protect and effectuate that judgment by equitable relief. Normally the second court determines the preclusive effect of a judgment, so the appropriate course is to deny a request for an anti-suit injunction even when § 2283 does not itself close the door. But when federal litigation is followed by many duplicative state suits, it is sensible to handle the preclusive issue once and for all in the original case, rather than put the parties and state judges through an unproductive exercise. That these suits are multiplying suggests that some lawyers have adopted a strategy of filing in as many courts as necessary until a nationwide class comes into being and persists. . . .

Relitigation can turn even an unlikely outcome into reality. Suppose that every state in the nation would as a matter of first principles deem inappropriate a nationwide class covering these claims and products. What this might mean in practice is something like "9 of 10 judges in every state would rule against certifying a nationwide class" . . . . Although the 10% that see things otherwise are a distinct minority, one is bound to turn up if plaintiffs file enough suits — and, if one nationwide class is certified, then all the no-certification decisions fade into insignificance. A single positive trumps all the negatives. Even if just one judge in ten believes that a nationwide class is lawful, then if the plaintiffs file in ten different states the probability that at least one will certify a nationwide class is 65% (0.9^{10} = 0.349). Filing in 20 states produces an 88% probability of national class certification (0.9^{20} = 0.122). This happens whenever plaintiffs can roll the dice as many times as they please — when nationwide class certification sticks (because it subsumes all other suits) while a no-certification decision has no enduring effect. Section 2283 permits a federal court to issue an injunction that will stop such a process in its tracks and hold both sides to a fully litigated outcome, rather than perpetuating an asymmetric system in which class counsel can win but never lose.

Nonetheless, class counsel tells us, the legal system entitles them to the benefit of this heads-I-win, tails-you-lose situation. This is so, class counsel contend, for three principal reasons: first, this federal action has not produced a final judgment; second, states may employ their own rules of preclusion; third, the federal court lacks personal jurisdiction over state-court plaintiffs who did not participate in the federal proceeding. None of these arguments is sound.

Although claim preclusion (res judicata) depends on a final judgment, issue preclusion (collateral estoppel) does not.

> The rules of res judicata are applicable only when a final judgment is rendered. However, for purposes of issue preclusion (as distinguished from merger and bar), "final judgment" includes any prior adjudication of an issue in another action that is determined to be sufficiently firm to be accorded conclusive effect.

RESTATEMENT (SECOND) OF JUDGMENTS § 13 (1980). Our decision that no nationwide class is tenable is "sufficiently firm" for this purpose. . . .

The preclusive effect of a judgment rendered by a federal court depends on national rather than state law. Semtek Int'l Inc. v. Lockheed Martin Corp., 531 U.S. 497 (2001). Although *Semtek* adds that federal law usually incorporates state law when the federal judgment stems from litigation under the diversity jurisdiction, this does not assist class counsel: the master complaint included two claims under federal law. What is more, the norm stated in *Semtek* has a proviso: state rules that undermine the finality of federal judgments are not incorporated. . . . Nothing in *Baker v. General Motors Corp.*, 522 U.S. 222 (1998), on which class counsel heavily rely, undermines this conclusion. *Baker* holds that one state court's decision about a procedural issue need not bind another state court. It does not discuss the effect of federal judgments under the federal law of preclusion. And the sort of procedural issue at stake in *Baker* — who may give evidence, and under what restrictions — is very different from a ruling on class certification, which determines the identity of the parties and stakes of the case. Determining the permissible scope of litigation is as much substantive as it is procedural. Our judgment was based not simply on a belief that managing national classes would consume too much of a federal court's limited supply of time; it also was based on a conclusion that certification of national classes would compromise the legitimate interests of defendants. *Baker* thus has no bearing on the preclusive effect (in state court) of rulings about class status made by a federal court.

Class counsel's jurisdictional argument starts from the premise that only named class representatives, and not members of putative classes, are treated as parties to litigation. Unnamed class members cannot be brought in involuntarily, class counsel insist, because federal courts lack the authority to issue process nationwide. As a result, class members other than the named representatives cannot be bound by an adverse decision and are free to file their own class actions elsewhere. The proposition that the federal court lacks the power to issue nationwide process must be qualified by the proviso "unless a federal statute authorizes this step"; and one of the claims in the master complaint rested on RICO, which does authorize nationwide service of process. *See* 18 U.S.C. § 1965(b). What is more, unnamed class members have the status of parties for many purposes and are bound by the decision whether or not the court otherwise would have had personal jurisdiction over them. *See Phillips Petroleum Co. v. Shutts*, 472 U.S. 797 (1985) [*infra* p. 276]. . . .

A decision with respect to the class is conclusive only if the absent members were adequately represented by the named litigants and class counsel. That requirement has been met. The district court found that both the named plaintiffs and their lawyers furnished adequate representation to the other members of the putative classes. . . .

True, the district court did not offer unnamed class members an opportunity to opt out of the certification decision. Plaintiffs now contend that this is fatal to any invocation of preclusion. Yet no statute or rule requires notice, and an opportunity to opt out, before the certification decision is made; it is a post-certification step. *See* Fed. R. Civ. P. 23(c)(2). No one is entitled to opt out of the certification, a decision necessarily made on a class-wide, all-or-none basis; one opts out of a certified class. And a person who opts out receives the right to go it alone, not to launch a competing class action. Preserving the right to litigate individually, as one's own champion, is the point of opting out. . . . Every person included in the district court's class definition still has the right to proceed on his own. What such a person now lacks is the right to represent a national class of others similarly situated . . . .

Our prior judgment is binding *in personam* with respect to the unnamed class members. The district judge must enforce that judgment by issuing an injunction that prevents all members of the putative national classes, and their lawyers, from again attempting to have nationwide classes certified over defendants' opposition with respect to the same claims. The case is remanded for the entry of such an injunction. To the extent defendants seek broader relief, however, the district court's decision is affirmed.

Notes

1.   Can you reconcile the decisions in *Baldwin-United, Retirement Systems*, and *Bridgestone/Firestone*?   *Retirement Systems* distinguishes *Baldwin-United* because the pending settlement in *Baldwin-United* made the class action the "virtual equivalent of a *res*" over which the district court properly asserted exclusive control; the same control did not exist over the trial date in *Retirement Systems*. *Bridgestone/Firestone* emphasized the need to protect the finality — and to prevent the circumvention — of the federal court's ruling.   That theory can also explain the outcome in *Baldwin-United* (at least after the district court finalized the settlement), but can it explain *Retirement Systems*? *Bridgestone/Firestone* indicated that the class-action ruling was at least as substantive as it was procedural. Is the trial date in *Retirement Systems* any more procedural, and less substantive, than the class-action ruling in *Bridgestone/Firestone*?

2.   *Bridgestone/Firestone* thwarted single-venue aggregation even in a state whose class-action rule would have allowed aggregation. Granting that Rule 23 did not allow a single nationwide class action, why prevent plaintiffs from making the case that one or more state class-action rules allowed such aggregation? Unless a state court construes its class-action rule in the exactly same way that federal courts construe Rule 23, no issue-preclusive effect attaches to the federal court's ruling, and class certification in state court poses no affront to the federal judgment.

On the other hand, even though it might serve the interests of some litigants, single-venue aggregation is not always the socially optimal level of aggregation. Consider *Bridgestone/Firestone*'s discussion of probability. Even an event that is unlikely to happen at any given instant has a significant probability of occurring if the condition that might lead to that event is repeated often enough. Assuming that 90% of judges believe that single-venue aggregation is bad, should we allow parties to file in state court after state court in order to achieve a level of aggregation that is, at least in the view of most judges, socially sub-optimal? On this theory, *Bridgestone/Firestone*'s antisuit injunction preserves optimal aggregation, rather than thwarts it. Therefore, whether *Bridgestone/Firestone*'s view of the broad scope of the antisuit injunctive power is "correct" depends on whether aggregation in a single nationwide class action is sub-optimal — a question that the court does not consider directly.

3.   Would it be better to recognize explicitly an antisuit injunctive power that can be exercised to achieve optimal aggregation? Some courts have come close to fashioning this principle. For instance, in *In re Diet Drugs*, 282 F.3d 220, 235 (3d Cir. 2002), the court held that, "[u]nder an appropriate set of facts, a federal court entertaining complex litigation, especially when it involves a substantial class of persons from multiple states, or represents a consolidation of cases from multiple districts, may appropriately enjoin state court proceedings in order to protect its jurisdiction."   Under this approach, the attempt to shoehorn antisuit injunctions into the traditional *in rem* category is more or less abandoned:

We have acknowledged [a scenario other than *in rem* cases] in which the enjoining of a state court proceeding might be necessary and thus permissible. Called the "complex multi-state litigation" exception, it enables a district court to enjoin a state court proceeding in aid of its jurisdiction when it has retained jurisdiction over complex, *in personam* lawsuits.

In re Bayshore Ford Trucks Sales, Inc., 471 F.3d 1233, 1251 (11th Cir. 2006). Does this principle explain *Baldwin-United, Retirement Systems,* and *Bridgestone/Firestone*? Or were some of the cases wrongly decided?

Is this expansive principle faithful to the language and purpose of the All Writs Act? Is it faithful to the language and purpose of the Anti-Injunction Act? Should Congress articulate this power clearly, rather than allowing courts to mold it from the vague "necessary in aid of jurisdiction" language in these statutes? *See* AM. L. INST., COMPLEX LITIGATION app. A (1994) (recommending passage of a federal statute that allows a court in which cases are consolidated to "enjoin transactionally related proceedings, or portions thereof, pending in any state or federal court" if such proceedings interfere with the consolidated actions and the injunction will "promote the just, efficient, and fair resolution of the actions").

4. Consider how this principle would resolve the following situation. Plaintiffs in a federal MDL proceeding and those in a related case in a Texas state court agreed to cooperate during discovery. When the defendant refused to produce requested documents, plaintiffs moved in both courts to compel production. The defendant moved the MDL court for an injunction preventing the Texas court from ruling on its motion to compel until the MDL court had ruled. The defendant's theory was that, if the Texas court ordered production, the cat would be out of the bag and the MDL court would be unable to protect its jurisdiction over discovery matters. Should the injunction issue? *See* In re Columbia/HCA Healthcare Corp., Billing Practices Litig., 93 F. Supp. 2d 876 (M.D. Tenn. 2000) (issuing the injunction); *see also* Winkler v. Eli Lilly & Co., 101 F.3d 1196, 1205 (7th Cir. 1996) (vacating an injunction that prevented a state court from ordering production of documents that a federal court had not ordered the defendants to produce; noting that, although "district courts in charge of complex multidistrict litigation have the authority to issue injunctions to protect the integrity of their pre-trial rulings," an injunction was not warranted on the facts). The pretrial injunctions in *Columbia/HCA* and *Winkler* do not directly aggregate the cases, but they effectively channel an entire litigation through a single court.

5. The scope of the antisuit injunctive power claimed in *Baldwin-United* is significant. Before *Baldwin-United* cases had issued antisuit injunctions against parties who were undermining the federal case by maintaining another action in state court. *See, e.g.,* In re Corrugated Container Antitrust Litig., 659 F.2d 1332 (5th Cir. 1981). *Baldwin-United* claimed not only the power to enjoin these parties but also the power to enjoin those who were not parties in any case. It justified the power to enjoin nonparties by citing to *United States v. New York Telephone Co.,* 434

U.S. 159 (1977), which held that courts can use the All Writs Act to reach nonparties who "are in a position to frustrate the implementation of a court order or the proper administration of justice." *Id.* at 174. *New York Telephone* upheld an order requiring a telephone company to provide FBI agents with the access necessary to conduct surveillance during a criminal investigation — quite a different circumstance than requiring nonparties with legitimate claims not to file them in state court.

Without the capacity to bind nonparties, the antisuit injunctive power is far less valuable. As we have seen, one of the challenges in aggregating related cases is temporal dispersion: Putative litigants file claims at different times. Joinder, consolidation, and transfer devices have a difficult time handling temporal dispersion of claims. An antisuit injunctive power that is broad enough to force nonparties to channel their claims through a federal court in which related cases are pending could constitute a very useful adjunct to these mechanisms. Indeed, if they can bind nonparties, antisuit injunctions can help address both jurisdictional dispersion and temporal dispersion. Thus, critical questions are whether a court should be able to enjoin nonparties from prosecuting their claims in the courts of their choice when these potential claims threaten to interfere with existing litigation, and if so, what the limits on this power are.

6. In *Baldwin-United* all of the nonparties had existing claims; but they had failed to file them, and their saber-rattling threats to do so justified, in the court of appeal's judgment, the injunction. In the nomenclature often used among lawyers in complex cases, the nonparties were "present futures" — people with existing claims who had not yet filed suit. "Present future" plaintiffs are distinct from "future future" plaintiffs, whose claims have not yet matured. (On the facts of *Baldwin-United* it is unlikely that many "future futures" existed; but such plaintiffs are common in tort cases in which injuries resulting from exposure to a dangerous substance can manifest themselves over many years.)

Is it appropriate to extend an antisuit injunction to "future futures"? One problem with such an injunction, to which *Baldwin-United* alludes, is identifying and giving "future futures" notice of the injunction. Another problem, to which *Bridgestone/Firestone* alludes, is the jurisdictional power of the court over persons who lack contact with the federal court issuing the injunction. Next, it is hard to see what the court can enjoin: By definition "future futures" have no claims to file, so that an injunction telling them not to file these claims in state court seems pointless. Finally, consider the "future futures" whose claims mature only after the case in federal court has ended. Does the injunction remain effective, so the federal court that issued the injunction becomes, once and for all, the only court in which litigation on this controversy can occur? What is the basis for an antisuit injunction once the federal case ends and the threat to the case fades away?

7. Assuming that federal courts enjoy a power to enjoin litigation that causes sub-optimal aggregation, we need some way to measure what is sub-optimal. Until now, we have thought of that question principally in terms of what would be best for the litigation itself: in other words, whether a

series of related cases is best handled in one proceeding or in smaller chunks. But the power of federal courts to issue antisuit injunctions against state courts brings into play other worthy values — in particular, the value of state courts in a federal system of government. The "basic purpose" of the Anti-Injunction Act "is to prevent needless friction between state and federal courts." Mitchum v. Foster, 407 U.S. 225, 233 (1972) (internal quotation marks omitted). Because the Act "in part rests on the fundamental constitutional independence of the States and their courts, the exceptions should not be enlarged by loose statutory construction," Atl. Coast Line R.R. v. Bhd. of Locomotive Eng'rs, 398 U.S. 281, 287 (1970); nor is the Act "to be whittled away by judicial improvisation," Amalgamated Clothing Workers v. Richman Bros., 348 U.S. 511, 514 (1955).

Because of the federalism overtones, the cases and literature discussing the scope of the All Writs Act and the Anti-Injunction Act are voluminous. For the most part, the cases and literature focus on the interpretation of the Acts in ordinary litigation. As you might expect, the interpretive problems are knotty enough even without the overlay of complex litigation. Particular difficulties arise in determining the breadth of the three textual exceptions to the Anti-Injunction Act and in explaining non-textual exceptions that survive. *See* Leiter Minerals, Inc. v. United States, 352 U.S. 220 (1957) (holding that the Anti-Injunction Act does not apply to injunctions sought by the United States); *cf.* Simon v. S. Ry., 236 U.S. 115 (1915) (permitting an antisuit injunction against state-court enforcement of a fraudulently obtained judgment). For discussions of these intricacies, see RICHARD H. FALLON, JR. ET AL., HART & WECHSLER'S THE FEDERAL COURTS & THE FEDERAL SYSTEM 1019-41 (6th ed. 2009); 17A CHARLES ALAN WRIGHT ET AL., FEDERAL PRACTICE AND PROCEDURE §§ 4221-26 (3d ed. 2007).

Although it lies beyond this casebook to consider these issues in more depth, you should not underestimate the strength of the judicial desire to preserve the integrity of the state courts. For many people, the occasional inconvenience of sub-optimal aggregation pales in comparison to the need to maintain a robust system of state courts. Others strike the balance in the opposite direction. As we consider the proper scope of federal courts' power to enjoin state-court litigation, we must remember to balance the goal of optimal aggregation against other goals that our litigation system is also bound to respect.

8.   Whatever the precise breadth of the federal courts' power to enjoin repetitive state-court litigation, the power is broader than the non-existent power of state courts to enjoin federal *in personam* lawsuits. Hence, in terms of their capacity to achieve optimal aggregation, federal courts enjoy one decided advantage over state courts.

iii.   Stays and Dismissals: Abstention and Related Doctrines

Stays and dismissals are the flip-side of antisuit injunctions. They accomplish the same objective of directing the parties toward a consolidated litigation. Because they require each court to stay its hand in favor of litigation in another court, however, they are cumbersome to obtain when related cases are dispersed across many courts; it is easier for a party to ask the court in which the party wishes the consolidation to occur to enter an antisuit injunction. Nonetheless, as we have also seen, antisuit injunctions are often not available. Thus, in theory stays and dismissals have a limited capacity to aid the aggregation project.

The reality is something less than the theory. In the federal-state context, stays or dismissals in favor of a litigation in the other court system fall under a doctrine known as "abstention." There are numerous situations in which the courts of one system will abstain in favor of litigation that is proceeding in courts of the other system. In some cases, statutes either require a court to abstain from hearing a case or gives judges the discretion to abstain in appropriate circumstances. *See* 28 U.S.C. §§ 1332(d)(4) (mandatory abstention), 1332(d)(3) (discretionary abstention), 1367(c) (discretionary abstention). Most abstention doctrines, however, are judge-made. Such judicial doctrines have tended to develop out of a tension between the general statutory command to exercise jurisdiction over cases of this type and the belief that the courts of the other system are better situated to handle this specific case. Typically in the mix of considerations regarding a decision to abstain is federalism's concern for respecting the constitutional integrity and independence of a dual system of courts.

Because they are principally attuned to aspects of federalism, abstention doctrines have not so far been tailored to meet the aggregation needs of complex litigation. Indeed, the fit between complex cases and abstention is poor, and the federalism concerns that motivate abstention are as likely to thwart as to assist socially optimal aggregation.

(a) Abstention by Federal Courts in Favor of State Courts. Abstention by the federal courts is one of the most discussed and controversial aspects of federal jurisdiction. The materials in this section sail quickly over deep waters, describing the basics of abstention and its relationship to complex and complicated litigation. For those interested in more detailed treatment and two distinct views of the issue, see RICHARD H. FALLON, JR. ET AL., HART & WECHSLER'S THE FEDERAL COURTS AND THE FEDERAL SYSTEM 1049-151 (6th ed. 2009); MARTIN H. REDISH, FEDERAL JURISDICTION 281-308 (2d ed. 1990). Bibliographies on the abstention literature can be found in 17A CHARLES ALAN WRIGHT ET AL., FEDERAL PRACTICE AND PROCEDURE § 4241 n.1 (3d ed. 2007), and 17B WRIGHT ET AL, *supra*, § 4252 n.1.

There are at least three (and, some say, six) forms of federal abstention. The three "card-carrying" forms of abstention are *Pullman* abstention, *Burford* abstention, and *Younger* abstention. In addition, there are several other doctrines that the Supreme Court has not called abstention doctrines, but nonetheless act, look, and sound just like the classic forms of abstention. These are *Colorado River* abstention, *Thibodaux* abstention, and certification of state-law issues to the highest court of a state.

Five of the six forms of abstention have little relevance in the aggregation of complex cases. To begin, *Thibodaux* abstention is moribund.

Later decisions have so cabined in *Burford* abstention that it too is on life support, although it occasionally pops up in the context of state receivership proceedings or other litigation that can be regarded as complex. *See* Gonzalez v. Media Elements, Inc., 946 F.2d 157 (1st Cir. 1991) (*Burford* abstention in favor of state insolvency proceeding proper); Berman Enters., Inc. v. Jorling, 3 F.3d 602 (2d Cir. 1993) (given local administrative scheme to deal with pollution, *Burford* abstention in favor of state regulatory process proper for a claim that state environmental regulators were motivated by malice); *cf.* In re Joint E. & S. Dist. Asbestos Litig., 78 F.3d 764 (2d Cir. 1996) (*Burford* abstention to permit state courts to calculate certain set-off rights under settlement involving the trust of an insolvent debtor improper). Next, the need to certify an unclear question of state law might arise in a complex federal case, but such certification practice does nothing to aggregate related cases in a single forum. *Pullman* abstention allows federal courts to abstain when a state court's ruling on an unclear question of state law might obviate the need for a federal court to decide a constitutional issue that might create friction with important state policies. *Younger* abstention requires a federal court to abstain from deciding a federal (often constitutional) issue when the same issue is being raised in an ongoing criminal or civil-enforcement proceeding in the state system. Neither is likely to come into play in complex federal litigation.

That leaves *Colorado River* abstention, which has occasionally been described as "abstention to avoid duplicative litigation in complex cases." Behavioral Healthcare Partners, Inc. v. Gonzalez-Rivera, 392 F. Supp. 2d 191, 199-200 (D.P.R. 2005); Fifth Column, LLC v. Village of Valley View, 221 F.3d 1334 (Table), 2000 WL 799785, at *4 n.1 (6th Cir. June 13, 2000). Although this statement is an overclaim, it suggests the doctrine's potential utility in aggregating related cases. The thrust of the *Colorado River* doctrine is that, as a matter of "wise judicial administration," a federal court should sometimes abstain in favor of a parallel state proceeding. Colo. River Water Conservation Dist. v. United States, 424 U.S. 800, 818 (1976); *see* Will v. Calvert Fire Ins. Co., 437 U.S. 655 (1978); Moses H. Cone Mem'l Hosp. v. Mercury Constr. Co., 460 U.S. 1 (1983).

The critical question is to determine the circumstances in which abstention in favor of parallel state proceedings is proper. Three principles shape the federal courts' answer to this question. First, courts have a strong presumption against *Colorado River* abstention:

> [Federal courts have] the virtually unflagging obligation . . . to exercise the jurisdiction given them. . . . Given this obligation, and the absence of weightier considerations of constitutional adjudication and state-federal relations, the circumstances permitting the dismissal of a federal suit due to the presence of a concurrent state proceeding for reasons of wise judicial administration are . . . limited . . . . Only the clearest of justifications will warrant dismissal. [424 U.S. at 817-19.]

Second, "exceptional" circumstances do allow abstention. Read together, *Colorado River* and *Moses H. Cone* identified six factors relevant to deciding whether these circumstances were present: (1) the court that first assumes jurisdiction over property may exercise that jurisdiction to the exclusion of other courts; (2) the inconvenience of the federal forum; (3) the desirability of avoiding piecemeal litigation; (4) the order in which jurisdiction was obtained by the concurrent forums; (5) the source of governing law, whether state or federal; and (6) the adequacy of the state-court proceeding to protect the litigants' rights. *See Moses H. Cone*, 460 U.S. at 15-16, 23, 26. That list is not exhaustive. *See* Caminiti & Iatarola v. Behnke Warehousing, Inc., 962 F.2d 698 (7th Cir. 1992) (adding the relative progress of state and federal proceedings, the presence or absence of concurrent jurisdiction, the availability of removal, and the strength of the federal claim). No single factor is determinative, but in examining the relevant factors, "the balance [is] heavily weighted in favor of the exercise of jurisdiction." *Moses H. Cone*, 460 U.S. at 16.

Third, two critical variables in deciding whether *Colorado River* abstention is appropriate may well be the existence of a congressional intent to avoid duplicative litigation and a state proceeding which is a superior mechanism for resolution of the dispute between the parties. For instance, in *Colorado River*, which involved a dispute among the United States and more than 1,000 persons regarding water rights, the Court's decision to require abstention was influenced by a statute that contained a "clear federal policy" to avoid piecemeal adjudication of water rights and by its belief that adjudication of water rights was "appropriate for comprehensive treatment in the forums having the greatest experience and expertise, assisted by state administrative officers acting under the state courts." *See Moses H. Cone*, 460 U.S. at 16. In contrast, the Supreme Court found abstention to be inappropriate in *Moses H. Cone*, a case in which no statutory policy of avoiding piecemeal litigation was present, the state court had no institutional superiority in deciding the contractual and statutory issues in the case, and serious doubts existed about whether the state court could provide relief equivalent to the relief available in federal court.

Two other restrictions limit the utility of the *Colorado River* doctrine as an aggregation mechanism. First, it is generally thought that a case involving claims lying exclusively within federal jurisdiction should not be stayed in favor of related state litigation. *See* 17A WRIGHT ET AL, *supra*, § 4247, at 461 & n.57. Second, *Colorado River* abstention is not generally thought to be available unless the parties and claims in the federal case are included among the parties and claims in the state case. *See* Great Am. Ins. Co. v. Gross, 468 F.3d 199, 208 (4th Cir. 2006) ("[W]e have strictly construed the requirement of parallel federal and state suits, requiring that the parties involved be almost identical."); Mountain Pure, LLC v. Turner Holdings, LLC, 439 F.3d 920 (8th Cir. 2006); *but see* In re Chicago Flood Litig., 819 F. Supp. 762, 764 (N.D. Ill. 1993) (stating in dicta that *Colorado River* abstention can be appropriate when the defendants in the state and federal courts are the same and the state and federal plaintiffs "share equivalent litigation interests"; abstention nonetheless denied because the federal actions could be expeditiously resolved and tort issues were neither novel nor complex). Thus, if Plaintiff A sues Defendant B in federal court, while Plaintiffs C through Z sue Defendant B in state court, *Colorado River* abstention is inappropriate.

Colorado River abstention has received some use in insurance-coverage litigation. *See, e.g.,* Lumbermens Mut. Cas. Co. v. Conn. Bank & Trust Co., 806 F.2d 411, 414-15 (2d Cir. 1986) ("The critical factor . . . is the desirability of avoiding piecemeal litigation and the possibility of two interpretations of the same policy language in different courts, leaving the insured possibly with insufficient coverage from the insurers . . . ."); Ins. Co. of Pa. v. Syntex Corp., 964 F.2d 829 (8th Cir. 1992) (dismissing federal declaratory-judgment action by insurer in favor of more comprehensive insurance-coverage litigation in state court). *Colorado River* has also been used to dismiss a case in favor of a state class action that was capable of resolving all the issues in the federal suit. Allison v. Sec. Benefit Life Ins. Co., 980 F.2d 1213 (8th Cir. 1992) (alternate holding). Are these outcomes consistent with *Colorado River?*

Because of the high degree of parallelism that must exist between the state and federal cases, *Colorado River* abstention is a limited aggregation tool in complex litigation. The "virtually unflagging obligation" of the federal courts to exercise their jurisdiction and the presumption of equal competence of state and federal courts to adjudicate complex controversies make it even more difficult to use *Colorado River* to consolidate cases in a single state forum. Finally, *Colorado River* can help to achieve significant aggregation only when one comprehensive action has been filed in one state court. In situations involving geographical and jurisdictional dispersion, no single state court hosts all the related litigation. *Colorado River* might shift the litigation from the federal courts to the state courts, but it can do nothing to aggregate cases spread among the state courts.

(b) Abstention by State Courts in Favor of Federal Courts. State-court stays or dismissals in favor of federal-court litigation — in effect, "reverse abstention" — constitute less traveled ground. In some cases, a state court's refusal to hear federal-question claims can run afoul of the Supremacy Clause, which implicitly contemplates that state courts will hear cases arising under federal law when Congress provides state courts with concurrent subject-matter jurisdiction. *See* Howlett v. Rose, 496 U.S. 356, 372 (1990) (requiring state courts to hear federal claims unless the state court declines jurisdiction on the basis of a "neutral state rule regarding the administration of the courts"); Testa v. Katt, 330 U.S. 386 (1947); *cf.* Haywood v. Drown, 556 U.S. —, 129 S. Ct. 2108 (2009) (states cannot refuse to entertain federal civil-rights claims against certain government officials when it held its courts open to similar lawsuits against other officials); *but see* Douglas v. N.Y., New Haven & Hartford R.R., 279 U.S. 377, 378 (1929) (allowing a state court to decline jurisdiction of a case arising under federal law when it had a "valid excuse" — in other words, a ground that did not discriminate against enforcement of federal rights); *see generally* RICHARD H. FALLON, JR. ET AL., HART & WECHSLER'S THE FEDERAL COURTS AND THE FEDERAL SYSTEM 408-17 (6th ed. 2009) (analyzing cases).

Prior to *Howlett*, some state courts adopted something akin to reverse-*Pullman* or reverse-*Burford* abstention when a decision on a federal issue might obviate the need to decide a difficult issue of state constitutional law or when state-court review of a difficult issue of federal law threatened federal policy. *See* Gnutti v. Heintz, 539 A.2d 118 (Conn. 1988) (requiring state courts to abstain from hearing Medicaid disability suits until federal administrative and judicial avenues are exhausted); Del. Tire Ctr., Inc. v. Del., 508 A.2d 470 (Table), 1986 WL 16794, at *1 (Del. 1986) (refusing an interlocutory appeal in an action alleging violations of federal regulations, when "principles of comity and abstention would seem to dictate that a federal court is the more appropriate forum to litigate such issues"). It is not clear whether *Howlett* nullifies these "reverse abstention" cases.

In addition, a number of states stay or dismiss cases under a rule of comity that operates like reverse-*Colorado River* abstention: The state court stays its hand when a similar case is already pending in federal court. *See, e.g.,* Farmland Irrigation Co. v. Dopplmaier, 308 P.2d 732 (Cal. 1957); Consumers Power Co. v. Pub. Utils. Comm'n, 258 N.W. 250 (Mich. 1935). In most states this power is judge-made; in North Carolina it is statutory. *See* N.C. GEN. STAT. § 1-75.12(a) ("If, in any action pending in any court of this State, the judge shall find that it would work substantial injustice for the action to be tried in a court of this State."); *cf.* 2009 CONN. PRACTICE BOOK § 23-14 ("The judge to whom complex litigation cases have been assigned may stay any or all further proceedings in the cases . . . ."). This rule of comity applies to *in personam* and *in rem* actions; thus, a state court may stay an action even when a federal court could not enjoin the action.

The power to stay has been applied to claims brought under both state and federal law. *See, e.g.,* Eways v. Governor's Island, 391 S.E.2d 182 (N.C. 1990) (affirming dismissal of a case based on state law when a federal court sitting in bankruptcy was the first court to acquire jurisdiction); Barnes v. Peat, Marwick, Mitchell & Co., 344 N.Y.S.2d 645 (N.Y. App. Div. 1973) (stay issued in case alleging violation of federal and state securities law); *Consumers Power*, 258 N.W. 250 (suspending suit on a state ratemaking claim while the issue is pending in federal court); *but see* Tonnemacher v. Touche Ross & Co., 920 P.2d 5, 9 n.3 (Ariz. Ct. App. 1996) (rejecting *Eways*). Is reverse-*Colorado River* abstention of a federal-question claim a "neutral state rule regarding the administration of the courts" under *Howlett*?

Before answering that question, you might want to know more about the contours of reverse-*Colorado River* abstention. The circumstances under which abstention in favor of an earlier-filed federal case should occur vary among the states. California considers six factors: whether multiple litigation is designed to harass an adverse party, the avoidance of unseemly conflicts with the federal court, whether the rights of the parties can best be determined by the state court or the federal court, the availability of witnesses, the stage to which the proceedings in federal court have already advanced, and whether the federal action is pending in a California federal court as opposed to another federal court. *Farmland Irrigation*, 308 P.2d 732; Thomson v. Cont'l Ins. Co., 427 P.2d 765 (Cal. 1967); Caiafa Prof'l Law

Corp. v. State Farm Fire & Cas. Co., 19 Cal. Rptr. 2d 138 (Cal. Ct. App. 1993). North Carolina courts have considered eight factors: the nature of the case; the convenience of the witnesses; the availability of compulsory process to produce witnesses; the relative ease of access to sources of proof; the applicable law; the burden of litigating matters not of local concern; the desirability of litigating matters of local concern in local courts; and convenience and access to another forum, *see* Home Indem. Co. v. Hoechst-Celanese Corp., 393 S.E.2d 118 (N.C. Ct. App. 1990); but in a recent case one North Carolina court affirmed a refusal to stay a state proceeding in favor of a federal bankruptcy proceeding solely on the ground that the issues overlapped but were not identical, *see* Park E. Sales, LLC v. Clark-Langley, Inc., 651 S.E.2d 235 (N.C. Ct. App. 2007). Similarly, despite a more generous standard in past years, *see Barnes*, 344 N.Y.S.2d 645; Grand Cent. Bldg., Inc. v. N.Y. & Harlem R.R., 398 N.Y.S.2d 888 (N.Y. App. Div. 1977), New York has recently adopted a stringent rule permitting abstention only when the parties, the causes of action, and the requested relief are identical, or when the first-filed federal action will necessarily determine the issues in the state case. Allied Props., LLC v. 236 Cannon Realty LLC, 769 N.Y.S.2d 880 (N.Y. App. Div. 2004); Guilden v. Baldwin Secs. Corp., 592 N.Y.S.2d 725 (N.Y. App. Div. 1993). Florida too seems to require an identity of parties and issues, and will further refuse a stay if the federal docket is too congested. City of Miami Beach v. Miami Beach Fraternal Order of Police, 619 So.2d 447 (Fla. Dist. Ct. App. 1993); Koehlke Components, Inc. v. S.E. Connectors, Inc., 456 So.2d 554 (Fla. Dist. Ct. App. 1984). Texas requires a stay in cases between the same parties unless there is fraud, sinister motive, inattention, or delay in the filing and prosecution of the federal suit. Alpine Gulf, Inc. v. Valentino, 563 S.W.2d 358 (Tex. App. 1978).

There are other doctrinal disagreements as well. State courts differ on:

- Whether issuance of a stay is a matter of discretion or duty. *Compare* Sumitomo Bank of Cal. v. Davis, 6 Cal. Rptr. 2d 381 (Cal. Ct. App. 1992) (discretion), *and* Greenhouse v. Hargrave, 509 P.2d 1360 (Okla. 1973) (discretion), *with Alpine Gulf*, 563 S.W.2d 358 (nearly unflagging duty), and *Koehlke Components*, 456 So.2d 554 (same).

- Whether a stay should be issued in favor of a case in a federal court of another state. *Compare Caiafa*, 19 Cal. Rptr. 2d 138 (no), *with* Reliance Ins. Co. v. Tiger Int'l, Inc., 457 N.Y.S.2d 813 (N.Y. App. Div. 1983) (staying New York action in favor of California suit), *and Alpine Gulf*, 563 S.W.2d 358 (staying Texas action in favor of District of Columbia suit).

- Whether the proper remedy is a stay or a dismissal. *Compare Koehlke Components*, 456 So.2d 554 (stay), *with* Terracom Dev. Group, Inc. v. Village of Westhaven, 568 N.E.2d 376 (Ill. App. Ct. 1991) (dismissal).

- Whether the source of the law underlying the case should influence a decision to stay. *Compare* Polaris Pub. Income Funds v. Einhorn,

625 So.2d 128 (Fla. Dist. Ct. App. 1993) (staying state case brought under Florida law in favor of federal action brought under federal and New York law), *with* CBS, Inc. v. Fitchelberg, 452 N.Y.S.2d 596 (N.Y. App. Div. 1982) (refusing a stay in favor of later-filed federal action in part because state-law issues were more properly interpreted by state rather than federal judiciary), *and Home Indemnity*, 393 S.E.2d 118 (stating that applicable law is a relevant consideration).

There is general agreement that the federal suit must be filed first for the state court to consider a stay. *See* Dep't of Game v. Puyallup Tribe, Inc., 548 P.2d 1058 (Wash. 1976), *vacated on other grounds*, 433 U.S. 165 (1977); Goldblum v. Boyd, 267 So.2d 610 (La. Ct. App. 1972) (no stay when state and federal cases filed on same day). In this respect, reverse-*Colorado River* abstention varies from *Colorado River* abstention, in which the order of filing is a relevant but not dispositive factor.

E. AGGREGATION THROUGH PRECLUSION

Joinder, consolidation, stays, and antisuit injunctions have varying capacities to address geographical, temporal, and jurisdictional dispersion, which together make the optimal aggregation of claims and parties so difficult. To take one step back, the reason that we sometimes believe that aggregation is socially optimal is the potential for unfairness or inefficiency that non-aggregated litigation creates: When the same issues are litigated across the country, over time, and among court systems, some litigants can be denied an effective remedy, and other litigants are put in the position of litigating, at great expense, the identical issues again and again.

In this section, we consider a final mechanism with significant potential to chop away at the root of repetitive litigation. Assume that a product has allegedly caused injuries to significant numbers of people around the country. Unless we can aggregate all the potential plaintiffs by means of joinder, consolidation, stays, or injunctions, the issue of the product's defectiveness will be litigated over and over. You might ask why it is necessary to do so — in other words, why the decision of the first court on the question of defectiveness doesn't determine the question for everyone. If the first court decided that the product was not defective, then the litigation would be over, and the need to aggregate would never arise. If the first court decided that the product was defective, then later cases could at least avoid the expense of trying and determining that issue.

We are describing, of course, a rule of preclusion — a rule that differs vastly from the traditional American rule that only parties in a case are bound (or precluded) by the outcome of that case. As described by Justice Brandeis, the traditional rule holds that, "[u]nless duly summoned to appear in a legal proceeding, a person not a privy may rest assured that a judgment recovered therein will not affect his legal rights." Chase Nat'l Bank v. Norwalk, 291 U.S. 431, 441 (1934). Chief Justice Rehnquist expressed the same principle more recently: "Joinder as a party . . . is the method by which potential parties are . . . bound by a judgment or decree." Martin v. Wilks, 490 U.S. 755, 765 (1989) (*infra* p. 222). Indeed, this chapter's focus on joinder, consolidation, stays, and injunctions is a direct consequence of this principle; if nonparties could be bound to the outcome of another lawsuit, there would be no need to worry about joining parties and claims, or about consolidating, staying, or enjoining related lawsuits. But if a court can bind nonparties to the outcome of a lawsuit, they will have a huge incentive to join or consolidate with that lawsuit. Indirectly, therefore, a rule precluding repetitive litigation of previously decided claims or issues could foment aggregation and eliminate parties' incentives to disperse claims across the country and among the state and federal courts. It could also deal with temporal dispersion by binding later-filing claimants to the outcome of earlier-filed cases.

As we have described it, the traditional preclusion rule sounds like an undesirable feature that we should reject in complex litigation. But the rule also has important benefits, including vindicating each individual's right to participate in lawsuits that affect his or her interests and its assurance that important decisions are not made hastily or without full information. (Recall Professor McGovern's discussion of the life cycle of complex litigation, in which early cases tend to be resolved in defendants' favor, in part because informational asymmetries favor defendants in early cases. *See supra* p. 56.)

This section examines traditional preclusion doctrine, the inroads that have already been made on the doctrine, the limitations that prevent the doctrine from being the "silver bullet" of optimal aggregation, and the arguments on both sides of the vigorous, ongoing debate about role that preclusion should play in complex litigation.

1. A Primer on Preclusion

Preclusion encompasses two distinct doctrines: claim preclusion (formerly called either res judicata or merger and bar) and issue preclusion (formerly composed of two related doctrines, direct estoppel and collateral estoppel). In its classic form, claim preclusion bars a claim asserted in a subsequent case when (1) the judgment in the prior case was valid, final, and on the merits, and (2) the claim asserted in the subsequent case either had been brought or should have been brought in the prior case. In most courts, the measure of when a claim "should have been brought" is the transactional approach familiar to us from the law of joinder: whether the claims in the prior and subsequent cases arise from facts that are related in time, place, and motivation. Thus, a claim that was not raised or decided in the prior case can be precluded. Claim preclusion bars litigation of the entire claim, not merely factual or legal issues within the claim. Claim preclusion is available only when both the party invoking the doctrine and the party against whom it was invoked were parties in the prior case. A limited exception to the "same parties" requirement exists when the prior case is brought by a person in privity with the party to the second case; a judgment obtained by a privy binds the party in the subsequent case.

Unlike claim preclusion, issue preclusion does not bar an entire claim; it bars relitigation of factual or legal issues within a claim. An issue is precluded when (1) the judgment in a prior case was valid, final, and on the merits, (2) the issue was actually litigated in the prior case, (3) the issue was determined in the prior case, and (4) the determination was necessary to support the judgment in the prior case. Like claim preclusion, issue preclusion traditionally had a "same parties" requirement. In the past half century, however, the strict requirement of mutuality has disappeared in nearly all American jurisdictions, and — subject to some important restrictions — issue preclusion is available as long as the party against whom preclusion is invoked was a party (or in privity with a party) to the prior case, even if the party seeking to invoke issue preclusion was not. A nonparty to the prior case who seeks to preclude a plaintiff's relitigation of a previously decided issue in the subsequent case does so under the doctrine of defensive collateral estoppel. A nonparty to a prior case who seeks to preclude a defendant's relitigation of a previously decided issue does so under the doctrine of offensive collateral estoppel.

These rules have been forged from the compromise of competing values. On the one side, favoring broad rules of preclusion, are the need for finality in litigation, the inefficiency of relitigating claims or issues, the attempt to avoid inconsistent rulings, and the generous opportunities for joining claims and parties that our modern litigation system provides. On the other side, favoring narrower rules of preclusion, are the desire to afford each litigant a day in court and the goal of deciding each issue as accurately as possible. Unsurprisingly, the rules and their application vary among cases and between jurisdictions as courts put emphasis on the different reasons for or against affording judgments broad preclusive effect.

This brief overview has papered over important interpretive issues, some of which we examine shortly. For now, focus on the status of the party sought to be bound in the subsequent case. When this party was a party in the prior case, then the judgment from that prior case precludes that party's relitigation in a subsequent case in two situations: (1) when the person seeking to invoke the preclusive effect of the judgment was a party in the prior case; and (2) when the party seeking to invoke the judgment can take advantage of the doctrines of defensive or offensive collateral estoppel. Notably, a third situation has no preclusive effect: Claim preclusion does not bar a party's relitigation of a claim in a later case against a person who was not a party in the prior case. On the other hand, when the party sought to be bound by a judgment from a prior case was not a party to that case, the doctrines of both claim and issue preclusion are clear: Unless the nonparty is in privity with a party in the prior case, the nonparty can never be bound by the judgment in that case.

We focus on the party status of the person seeking preclusion for a reason. The law of preclusion initially dealt with relitigation of claims or issues between the same parties. That scenario is unusual in complex repetitive litigation; typically some of the parties in subsequent cases are different, and the issue is whether the determinations made in a prior case can bear on the claims or issues raised in subsequent cases by nonparties to the prior case. As the last paragraph described, the answer at the present time depends significantly on whether the person sought to be bound was — or was not — a party in the prior case. As we examine these two situations, the important question is whether the demands of complex litigation to prevent needless relitigation of common issues require further expansion in the law of preclusion.

2. Precluding Parties that Participated in a Prior Case

For the most part, using claim preclusion to bar relitigation of claims by a party is an infrequent occurrence in complex litigation. The reason is that the plaintiff, who asserts the claim, usually does not file serial claims against the same defendant. There is one very important exception to this statement: class actions, in which members of the class might have their claims determined in a class proceeding, and then try to bring the same or related claims in a subsequent lawsuit. Under certain circumstances, class members are precluded by the class-action judgment from bringing the same or related claims in a later case. In other circumstances, they are not. Understanding the precise breadth of the preclusive effect of class actions is a difficult issue that lies at the heart of class-action practice. Therefore, we postpone detailed consideration of the issue until Chapter Four. *See infra* p. 525.

On the other hand, using issue preclusion against a party in a prior case is more common. The typical fact pattern involves a defendant whose conduct has injured multiple plaintiffs. In a prior case, one of the plaintiffs has won, and the plaintiff in a subsequent case wishes to preclude the defendant from relitigating common issues decided in the prior case. In other words, subsequent plaintiffs wish to invoke the doctrine of offensive collateral estoppel. If successfully employed, this doctrine holds out some promise as a vehicle for avoiding the relitigation of common issues. The following case shows some of the barriers to using the doctrine in this way.

HARDY V. JOHNS-MANVILLE SALES CORP.

681 F.2d 334 (5th Cir. 1982)

■ GEE, Circuit Judge.

This appeal arises out of a diversity action brought by various plaintiffs — insulators, pipefitters, carpenters, and other factory workers — against various manufacturers, sellers, and distributors of asbestos-containing products. The plaintiffs, alleging exposure to the products and consequent disease, assert various causes of action, including negligence, breach of implied warranty, and strict liability. The pleadings in each of the cases are substantially the same. . . .

Defendants' interlocutory appeal under 28 U.S.C. § 1292(b) is directed . . . at the district court's amended omnibus order dated March 13, 1981, which applies collateral estoppel to this mass tort. The omnibus order is, in effect, a partial summary judgment for plaintiffs based on nonmutual offensive collateral estoppel and judicial notice derived from this court's opinion in *Borel v. Fibreboard Paper Products Corp.*, 493 F.2d 1076 (5th Cir. 1973), *cert. denied*, 419 U.S. 869 (1974) (henceforth *Borel*). *Borel* was a diversity lawsuit in which manufacturers of insulation products containing asbestos were held strictly liable to an insulation worker who developed asbestosis and mesothelioma and ultimately died. The trial court construed *Borel* as establishing as a matter of law and/or of fact that: (1) insulation products containing asbestos as a generic ingredient are "unavoidably unsafe products," (2) asbestos is a competent producing cause of mesothelioma and asbestosis, (3) no warnings were issued by any asbestos insulation manufacturers prior to 1964, and (4) the "warning standard" was not met by the *Borel* defendants in the period from 1964 through 1969.[1] . . . The sole issue on appeal is the validity of the order on grounds of collateral estoppel or judicial notice.

In *Flatt v. Johns-Manville Sales Corp.*, 488 F. Supp. 836 (E.D. Tex. 1980), the same court outlined the elements of proof for plaintiffs in asbestos-related cases. [Among the elements that plaintiffs were required to prove were that "[p]roducts containing asbestos are unreasonably dangerous" and that "[a]sbestos dust is a competent producing cause of mesothelioma."] The parties agree that the effect of the trial court's collateral estoppel order in this case is to foreclose [these two elements]. Under the terms of the omnibus order, both parties are precluded from presenting evidence on the "state of the art" — evidence that, under Texas law of strict liability, is considered by a jury along with other evidence in order to determine whether as of a given time warning should have been given of the dangers knew or should have known of the dangerous propensities of their products and therefore should have warned consumers of these dangers, defendants being precluded from showing otherwise. On appeal, the defendants contend that the order violates their rights to due process and to trial by jury. Because we conclude that the trial court abused its discretion in applying collateral estoppel and judicial notice, we reverse.

---

1. The omnibus order states in relevant part:

1. . . . Issue preclusion may extend to the ultimate issue of marketing an unreasonably dangerous product or be limited to cluster issues depending upon the particular facts of the case.

2. In any event, no evidence shall be introduced on the issue of whether asbestos causes either asbestosis or mesothelioma.

3. Further, no evidence shall be introduced on the issue of knowledge as it may relate to a duty to warn due to the res judicata and/or collateral estoppel effect of [*Borel*]. In essence, no evidence shall be admitted with respect to a state of the art defense. . . .

[The court first found that federal, not Texas, law determined the scope of the preclusive effect of *Borel's* judgment. It then discussed *Parklane Hosiery Co. v. Shore*, 439 U.S. 322 (1979), which first adopted the doctrine of offensive collateral estoppel at the federal level. After holding that offensive collateral estoppel did not apply against the fourteen defendants that were not party to *Borel* (*see infra* p. 241), the court turned to six defendants that were parties to *Borel*.]

The party asserting the estoppel must show that: (1) the issue to be concluded is identical to that involved in the prior action; (2) in the prior action the issue was "actually litigated"; and (3) the determination made of the issue in the prior action must have been necessary and essential to the resulting judgment.

> If it appears that a judgment may have been based on more than one of several distinctive matters in litigation and there is no indication which issue it was based on or which issue was fully litigated, such judgment will not preclude, under the doctrine of collateral estoppel, relitigation of any of the issues.

FEDERAL PROCEDURE, LAWYERS ED. § 51.218 at 151 (1981).

Appellants argue that *Borel* did not necessarily decide that asbestos-containing insulation products were unreasonably dangerous because of failure to warn. According to appellants, the general *Borel* verdict, based on general instructions and special interrogatories, permitted the jury to ground strict liability on the bases of failures to test, of unsafeness for intended use, of failures to inspect, or of unsafeness of the product. Strict liability on the basis of failure to warn, although argued to the jury by trial counsel for the plaintiff in *Borel*, was, in the view of the appellants, never formally presented in the jury instructions and therefore was not essential to the *Borel* jury verdict.

Appellants' view has some plausibility. The special interrogatories answered by the *Borel* jury were general and not specifically directed to failure to warn. Indeed, . . . the jury was instructed in terms of "breach of warranty." Although the jury was accurately instructed as to "strict liability in tort" as defined in section 402A of the Restatement (Second) of Torts, that phrase was never specifically mentioned in the jury's interrogatories. It is also true that the general instructions to the *Borel* jury on the plaintiff's causes of action did not charge on failure to warn, except in connection with negligence. Yet appellants' argument in its broadest form must ultimately fail. We concluded in *Borel*:

> The jury found that the unreasonably dangerous condition of the defendants' product was the proximate cause of Borel's injury. This necessarily included a finding that, had adequate warnings been provided, Borel would have chosen to avoid the danger. . . .

. . . Our conclusion in *Borel* was grounded in that trial court's jury instructions concerning proximate cause and defective product . . . . Close reading of these instructions convinced our panel in *Borel* that a failure to warn was necessarily implicit in the jury's verdict. While the parties invite us to reconsider our holding in *Borel* that failure to warn grounded the jury's strict liability finding in that case, we cannot, even if we were so inclined, displace a prior decision of this court absent reconsideration en banc. Further, there is authority for the proposition that once an appellate court has disposed of a case on the basis of one of several alternative issues that may have grounded a trial court's judgment, the issue decided on appeal is conclusively established for purposes of issue preclusion. Nonetheless, we must ultimately conclude that the judgment in *Borel* cannot estop even the *Borel* defendants in this case for three interrelated reasons.

First, after review of the issues decided in *Borel*, we conclude that *Borel*, while conclusive as to the general matter of a duty to warn on the part of manufacturers of asbestos-containing insulation products, is ultimately ambiguous as to certain key issues. As the authors of the *Restatement (Second) — Judgments* § 29, comment g (1982), have noted, collateral estoppel is inappropriate where the prior judgment is ambivalent:

> The circumstances attending the determination of an issue in the first action may indicate that it could reasonably have been resolved otherwise if those circumstances were absent. Resolution of the issue in question may have entailed reference to such matters as the intention, knowledge, or comparative responsibility of the parties in relation to each other. . . . In these and similar situations, taking the prior determination at face value for purposes of the second action would extend the effects of imperfections in the adjudicative process beyond the limits of the first adjudication, within which they are accepted only because of the practical necessity of achieving finality.

The *Borel* jury decided that Borel, an industrial insulation worker who was exposed to fibers from his employer's insulation products over a 33-year period (from 1936 to 1969), was entitled to have been given fair warning that asbestos dust may lead to asbestosis, mesothelioma, and other cancers. The jury dismissed the argument that the danger was obvious and regarded as conclusive the fact that Borel testified that he did not know that inhaling asbestos dust could cause serious injuries until his doctor so advised him in 1969. The jury necessarily found "that, had adequate warnings been provided, Borel would have chosen to avoid the danger." In *Borel*, the evidence was that the industry as a whole issued no warnings at all concerning its insulation products prior to 1964, that Johns-Manville placed a warning[ ] label on packages of its products in 1964, and that Fibreboard and Rubberoid placed warnings on their products in 1966.

Given these facts, it is impossible to determine what the *Borel* jury decided about when a duty to warn attached. Did the jury find the defendants liable because their warnings after 1966, when they acknowledged that they knew the dangers of asbestosis, were insufficiently explicit as to the grave risks involved? If so, as appellants here point out, the jury may have accepted the state of the art arguments provided by the defendants in *Borel* — i.e., that the defendants were not aware of the danger of asbestosis until the 1960's. Even under this view, there is a second ambiguity: was strict liability grounded on the fact that the warnings issued, while otherwise sufficient, never reached the insulator in the field? If so, perhaps the warnings, while insufficient as to insulation workers like Borel, were sufficient to alert workers further down the production line who may have seen the warnings — such as the carpenters and pipefitters in this case. Alternatively, even if the *Borel* jury decided that failure to warn before 1966 grounded strict liability, did the duty attach in the 1930's when the "hazard of asbestosis as a pneumoconiotic dust was universally accepted," or in 1965, when documentary evidence was presented of the hazard of asbestos insulation products to the installers of these products?

As we noted in *Borel*, strict liability because of failure to warn is based on a determination of the manufacturer's reasonable knowledge . . . . [A] determination that a particular product is so unreasonably hazardous as to require a warning of its dangers is not an absolute. Such a determination is necessarily relative to the scientific knowledge generally known or available to the manufacturer at the time the product in question was sold or otherwise placed in the stream of commerce.

Not all the plaintiffs in this case were exposed to asbestos-containing insulation products over the same 30-year period as plaintiff Borel. Not all plaintiffs here are insulation workers isolated from the warnings issued by some of the defendants in 1964 and 1966. Some of the products may be different from those involved in *Borel*. Our opinion in *Borel*, "limited to determining whether there (was) a conflict in substantial evidence sufficient to create a jury question," did not resolve that as a matter of fact all manufacturers of asbestos-containing insulation products had a duty to warn as of 1936, and all failed to warn adequately after 1964. Although we determined that the jury must have found a violation of the manufacturers' duty to warn, we held only that the jury could have grounded strict liability on the absence of a warning prior to 1964 or "could have concluded that the (post-1964 and post-1966) 'cautions' were not warnings in the sense that they adequately communicated to Borel and other insulation workers knowledge of the dangers to which they were exposed so as to give them a choice of working or not working with a dangerous product." . . . [O]ur opinion in *Borel* merely approved of the various ways the jury could have come to a conclusion concerning strict liability for failure to warn. We did not say that any of the specific alternatives that the jury had before it were necessary or essential to its verdict. . . . Like stare decisis, collateral estoppel applies only to issues of fact or law necessarily decided by a prior court. Since we cannot say that *Borel* necessarily decided, as a matter of fact, that all manufacturers of asbestos-containing insulation products knew or should have known of the dangers of their particular products at all relevant times, we cannot justify the trial court's collaterally estopping the defendants from presenting evidence as to the state of the art.

Even if we are wrong as to the ambiguities of the *Borel* judgment, there is a second, equally important, reason to deny collateral estoppel effect to it: the presence of inconsistent verdicts. In *Parklane Hosiery v. Shore*, 439

U.S. at 330-31, the Court noted that collateral estoppel is improper and "unfair" to a defendant "if the judgment relied upon as a basis for the estoppel is itself inconsistent with one or more previous judgments in favor of the defendant." Not only does issue preclusion in such cases appear arbitrary to a defendant who has had favorable judgments on the same issue, it also undermines the premise that different juries reach equally valid verdicts. One jury's determination should not, merely because it comes later in time, bind another jury's determination of an issue over which there are equally reasonable resolutions of doubt.

. . . [T]he parties inform us that there have been approximately 70 similar asbestos cases thus far tried around the country. Approximately half of these seem to have been decided in favor of the defendants. . . . [T]he appellants inform us of several products liability cases in which the state of the art question was fully litigated, yet the asbestos manufacturers were found not liable. Although it is usually not possible to say with certainty what these juries based their verdicts on, in at least some of the cases the verdict for the defendant was not based on failure to prove exposure or failure to show an asbestos-related disease. . . . We conclude that the court erred in arbitrarily choosing one of these verdicts, that in *Borel*, as the bellwether.

Finally, we conclude that even if the *Borel* verdict had been unambiguous and the sole verdict issued on point, application of collateral estoppel would still be unfair with regard to the *Borel* defendants because it is very doubtful that these defendants could have foreseen that their $68,000 liability to plaintiff Borel would foreshadow multimillion dollar asbestos liability. As noted in *Parklane*, it would be unfair to apply collateral estoppel "if a defendant in the first action is sued for small or nominal damages (since) he may have little incentive to defend vigorously, particularly if future lawsuits are not foreseeable." While in absolute terms a judgment for $68,000 hardly appears nominal, the Supreme Court's citation of *Berner v. British Commonwealth Pacific Airlines*, 346 F.2d 532 (2d Cir. 1965) (application of collateral estoppel denied where defendant did not appeal an adverse judgment awarding damages of $35,000 and defendant was later sued for over $7 million), suggests that the matter is relative. The reason the district court here applied collateral estoppel is precisely because early cases like *Borel* have opened the floodgates to an enormous, unprecedented volume of asbestos litigation. According to a recent estimate, there are over 3,000 asbestos plaintiffs in the Eastern District of Texas alone and between 7,500 and 10,000 asbestos cases pending in United States District Courts around the country. The omnibus order here involves 58 pending cases, and the many plaintiffs involved in this case are each seeking $2.5 million in damages. Such a staggering potential liability could not have been foreseen by the *Borel* defendants.

The trial court's application of issue preclusion to the "fact" that asbestos is in all cases a competent producing cause of mesothelioma and asbestosis involves similar problems. *Borel* dealt with the disease-causing aspects of asbestos dust generated by insulation materials. That case did not determine as a matter of fact that because airborne asbestos dust and fibers from thermal insulation materials are hazardous, all products containing asbestos — in whatever quantity or however encapsulated — are hazardous. . . . [Appellant Garlock, Inc.] points out that its products, unlike the loosely woven thermal insulation materials in *Borel* that, when merely handled, emitted large quantities of airborne asbestos dust and fibers, are linoleum-type products in which the asbestos is encapsulated in a rubber-like coating. According to Garlock, its gasket products do not release significant amounts of dust or fibers into the air and have never been demonstrated to be dangerous in installation, use, or removal. Certainly, defendants ought to be free, even after *Borel*, to present evidence of the scientific knowledge *associated with their particular product* without being prejudiced by a conclusive presumption that asbestos in all forms causes cancer. The court regarded collateral estoppel in this context as precluding merely the "can it" question rather than the "did it" question. The problem is that the "can it" and "did it" questions cannot in this instance be so easily segregated, and a determination that asbestos generally is hazardous threatens to undermine a defendant's possibly legitimate defense that its product was not scientifically known to be hazardous, now or at relevant times in the past. If the trial court's application of issue preclusion on the generic danger of asbestos is not meant to burden a defendant's ability to present such evidence, then we fail to see the intended usefulness of the court's action.

For much the same reasons, the court's alternative justification for this aspect of its omnibus order — relying upon judicial notice of adjudicative fact under Fed. R. Evid. 201(b)(2) and (c) — is likewise improper. . . . [J]udicial notice applies to self-evident truths that no reasonable person could question, truisms that approach platitudes or banalities. The proposition that asbestos causes cancer, because it is inextricably linked to a host of disputed issues — e.g., can mesothelioma arise without exposure to asbestos, is the sale of asbestos insulation products definitely linked to carcinoma in the general population, was this manufacturer reasonably unaware of the asbestos hazards in 1964 — is not at present so self-evident a proposition as to be subject to judicial notice. . . . Surely where there is evidence on both sides of an issue the matter is subject to reasonable dispute. Judicial notice was therefore inappropriate here.

. . . [We] sympathize with the district court's efforts to streamline the enormous asbestos caseload it faces. None of what we say here is meant to cast doubt on any possible alternative ways to avoid reinventing the asbestos liability wheel. We . . . [invite] district courts to attempt innovative methods for trying these cases. We hold today only that courts cannot read *Borel* to stand for the proposition that, as matters of fact, asbestos products are unreasonably dangerous or that asbestos as a generic element is in all products a competent producing cause of cancer. To do otherwise would be to elevate judicial expedience over considerations of justice and fair play.

Reversed.

Notes

1. As a practical matter, the scope of offensive collateral estoppel is usually the critical preclusion issue in complex litigation. Although direct preclusion in a second case between parties that were both involved in a prior lawsuit and defensive collateral estoppel against a plaintiff in a prior lawsuit can arise, the fact that defendants often engage in a pattern of conduct that allegedly injures many persons makes offensive collateral estoppel the form of issue preclusion that is most useful in eliminating repetitive litigation. Indeed, without a strong doctrine of offensive collateral estoppel, preclusion law cannot solve the problems of relitigation, and we must resort to either joinder or another aggregation solution.

2. *Hardy* presents three reasons that offensive collateral estoppel is inapposite. Two reasons are straight-forward applications of two exceptions mentioned in *Parklane Hosiery* — inconsistent prior verdicts and insufficient incentive to contest the issue in the first case. *Hardy* also bases its holding on a third reason — the ambiguity in the jury's verdict in *Borel*. This ground applies generally to issue preclusion, not just to offensive collateral estoppel. *Hardy*'s holdings, if they are correct, seriously impede the use of offensive collateral estoppel in mass-tort or large-scale litigation. *See* Roger H. Trangsrud, *Joinder Alternatives in Mass Tort Litigation*, 70 CORNELL L. REV. 779, 815 (1985) ("[W]hile offensive collateral estoppel may contribute to the fair and efficient adjudication of some cases, its limited utility in most mass tort cases makes it unsuitable as a primary technique for the management of mass tort litigation").

3. The most debatable point in *Hardy* is whether the earlier *Borel* case provided adequate incentive for the *Borel* defendants to litigate the issue of dangerousness vigorously. If *Hardy* had come out differently, though, defendants facing the potential of future litigation will leave absolutely no stone unturned in the first lawsuit, even when future litigation is unlikely. It isn't obvious that this result is desirable.

4. With respect to *Borel*'s concern for the ambiguity of the jury's verdict, it would have been possible to avoid some of the ambiguity if a special verdict or general verdict accompanied by interrogatories had been used. We look more generally at these devices when we examine techniques to reduce trial complexity. *See infra* p. 1132. Sometimes the solution to one complexity-causing problem can also be a solution for a different manifestation of complexity.

5. *Hardy* does not discuss two other limitations on offensive collateral estoppel mentioned in *Parklane Hosiery*: procedural opportunities that the *Borel* defendants might not have enjoyed in the *Borel* litigation and Hardy's opportunity to join *Borel*. We consider each of these limitations in turn.

(a) Since both *Borel* and *Hardy* were tried in federal court, the "lack of procedural opportunity" exception did not come into play in *Borel*. The exception can arise, however, in certain circumstances. For instance, it might arise when the judge in the first case declined to admit evidence that was deemed to be important to the defense in the second case. *See* Snider

v. Consol. Coal Co., 973 F.2d 555 (7th Cir. 1992). A second scenario occurs when an issue is litigated and decided in a multiparty suit, a party is joined on claims that do not require the party to litigate that issue, and the issue is decided in a way adverse to the party's interests. *See* Ala. ex rel. Siegelman v. United States Envtl. Prot. Agency, 911 F.2d 499 (11th Cir. 1990). A third, related scenario occurs when the claims against a party in the first suit are severed, so the first party cannot participate in the trial at which findings adverse to the party's interests are made. *See* Lempel & Son Co. v. Boden, 1993 WL 256711 (S.D.N.Y. July 7, 1993); *but see* County of Cook v. Midcon Corp., 574 F. Supp. 902 (N.D. Ill. 1983) (finding that party that had remained in the first suit to contest an unrelated issue was subject to issue preclusion in second suit because it had had an opportunity to contest the issue). You should keep in mind severance's effect on issue preclusion when we examine the circumstances under which a court can split up claims for pretrial and trial purposes. *See infra* pp. 814, 1033.

(b) Now consider *Parklane Hosiery*'s other limitation — the opportunity to join the original litigation. Suppose that Hardy had been injured at the same time as Borel, and knew about Borel's suit. Should that knowledge, combined with the arguable ability of Hardy to intervene in *Borel*, prevent Hardy from using *Borel*'s findings? *Compare* In re Air Crash Disaster at Stapleton Int'l Airport, Denver, Colorado, on Nov. 15, 1987, 720 F. Supp. 1505, 1523 (D. Colo. 1989), *rev'd on other grounds*, 964 F.2d 1059 (10th Cir. 1992) ("We find that in cases not consolidated for trial, justice, fairness and equity weigh against permitting 'wait and see' plaintiffs to assert non-mutual offensive collateral estoppel."), *with* In re Air Crash at Detroit Metro. Airport, Detroit, Mich., on Aug. 16, 1987, 776 F. Supp. 316, 325-26 (E.D. Mich. 1991) (permitting issue preclusion in favor of "wait and see" plaintiffs when the plaintiffs would have been unable to participate in the trial even had they filed suit earlier).

Presumably, this limitation should not be enforced if Hardy (a) had not been injured at the time of *Borel*; (b) had no notice of *Borel*; or (c) was unable to join the suit. With respect to this last factor, would Hardy have been able to join the original suit? The only apparent basis for joinder would be intervention under Rule 24. Note that the scope of the law of joinder may be inversely proportional to the scope of offensive collateral estoppel: the easier that it is for the plaintiff to join the prior suit, the less successful the plaintiff's invocation of offensive collateral is likely to be; while the harder joinder is, the easier collateral estoppel is. Should this fact affect our attitude about liberalizing joinder rules?

In *Avila v. Van Ru Credit Corp.*, 1995 WL 41425 (N.D. Ill. Jan. 31, 1995), the court decided to certify a class action in part because it thought that a class action was more efficient than filing of thousands of individual suits in which the issue of offensive collateral estoppel would be raised. Is *Avila* correct that mandatory-joinder rules such as class actions are usually more efficient than preclusion rules? If so, do preclusion rules do less violence to litigant autonomy than mandatory-joinder rules, so they are a better accommodation of autonomy and efficiency concerns?

6. *Parklane Hosiery*'s four exceptions to offensive collateral estoppel are not exhaustive; other circumstances in which it is unfair to apply collateral estoppel against a defendant also exist. In *Schwab v. Philip Morris USA, Inc.*, 449 F. Supp. 2d 992 (E.D.N.Y. 2006), *rev'd on other grounds sub nom.* McLaughlin v. Am. Tobacco Co., 522 F.3d 215 (2d Cir. 2008), Judge Weinstein did not use adverse findings from a prior lawsuit against tobacco manufacturers because one manufacturer had prevailed in the prior case. He thought that applying preclusion to all but one defendant would make case administration more difficult; moreover, the plaintiffs needed to introduce much of the evidence to prove other issues in any event. As an additional reason, Judge Weinstein noted that the tobacco companies had prevailed on the same issue in other prior cases.

7. Although not raised on the facts of *Hardy*, another common problem with applying issue preclusion, including offensive collateral estoppel, is whether there exists an "identity of issues" in the first and second proceedings. In re Sonus Networks, Inc., Shareholder Derivative Litig., 499 F.3d 47 (1st Cir. 2007). The "identity of issues" requirement sometimes destroys the issue-preclusive effect of a prior judgment. For instance, courts generally hold that there is not an identity of issues when the legal significance of the relevant facts is different in the two cases. *See* Raytech Corp. v. White, 54 F.3d 187, 191 (3d Cir. 1995) (difference in legal standards must be "substantial"); *cf.* Engquist v. Ore. Dept. of Agric., 478 F.3d 985 (9th Cir. 2007) (noting that, under Oregon law, the "strict standard for the 'identity of issues' requirement . . . [requires] that 'the precise question was raised and determined in the former suit'"). Second, the issues are not deemed to be identical when the burdens of proof in the two cases differ. *See* United States v. One Assortment of 89 Firearms, 465 U.S. 354 (1984); CFTC v. Wellington Precious Metals, Inc., 950 F.2d 1525 (11th Cir. 1992).

A third situation arises when the issue in the first litigation is heavily fact-bound. In *Schneider v. Lockheed Aircraft Corp.*, 658 F.2d 835 (D.C. Cir. 1981), plaintiffs that had allegedly suffered injuries during the explosive decompression of an airplane cabin sought to use the favorable verdict in a case involving another passenger that suffered the same injuries to estop the defendant from contending that decompression had not caused their injuries. Although the prior case had established that decompression could cause the type of injury from which the plaintiffs suffered, the court of appeals held the finding should not be given preclusive effect:

> Delineating the proper scope of the estopped issue is often a difficult and delicate task. The court must weigh the burden of repetitious litigation against the risk of denying a party his day in court. Many of the criteria we look to in determining "substantial identity of issues" have been met here: evidence of the accident is the same for each case; the claims are closely related; the arguments and issues of law are virtually identical. But the cases are also different in one important respect: they involve different individuals, each with his own physical constitution and developmental history, and each alleging a particular set of symptoms caused by the accident. [*Id.* at 852.]

8. A few mass-tort cases have experimented with a controversial technique that raises "identity of issues" questions. Assume that a court has before it the cases of 5,000 plaintiffs. The court tries liability issues, and also tries the individual causation and damages issues for a selected sample of plaintiffs. The court then uses the judgments in the sample cases to determine the causation and damages issues for the remaining plaintiffs. For example, assume that the cases of 25 of the plaintiffs were tried, and that the average judgment was $50,000. The court then awards $50,000 to each of the 4,975 plaintiffs whose cases had not yet been tried. We examine this practice, known as "trial by statistics," in Chapter Ten. *See infra* p. 1058. Courts do not usually analyze this practice in terms of offensive collateral estoppel. But isn't that what court is going on?

9. In studied dicta, the Sixth Circuit forbade the use of offensive collateral estoppel in mass torts. In re Bendectin Prods. Liab. Litig., 749 F.2d 300, 305 n.11 (6th Cir. 1984) ("In *Parklane Hosiery*, the Supreme Court explicitly stated that offensive collateral estoppel could not be used in mass tort litigation."). *Bendectin* cited footnote 14 of *Parklane Hosiery*, which described a famous hypothetical in which fifty plaintiffs are injured in an accident, the defendant wins the first twenty-five cases, and a plaintiff finally wins the twenty-sixth case. *Parklane Hosiery* stated that the remaining twenty-three plaintiffs should not be able to use the findings from the twenty-sixth case. Did the Sixth Circuit correctly read *Parklane Hosiery* to bar all uses of offensive collateral estoppel in mass-tort litigation? *Cf.* In re Air Crash at Detroit Metro. Airport, Detroit, Mich., on August 16, 1987, 791 F. Supp. 1204, 1214, 1215 (E.D. Mich. 1992) (in a case involving defensive collateral estoppel, rejecting the "contention that collateral estoppel should not be applied in mass disaster litigation" and limiting *Bendectin* to situations in which collateral estoppel "would be unfair to the defendant"), *aff'd*, 86 F.3d 498 (6th Cir. 1996).

10. In *Cullen v. Margiotta*, 811 F.2d 698 (2d Cir. 1987), the defendants argued that the plaintiffs, who had unsuccessfully sought to certify a class action in state court, were collaterally estopped from arguing that they were entitled to maintain a class action in federal court. The court rejected the argument because of a lack of "identity of issues"; "the standards governing the propriety of the suit as a class action in the state court and the federal court differed significantly." *Id.* at 733. What should the result be if the state and federal standards are identical? *Cf.* J.R. Clearwater Inc. v. Ashland Chem. Co., 93 F.3d 176 (5th Cir. 1996) (federal court cannot enjoin plaintiffs that unsuccessfully sought federal certification from commencing a state-court action also seeking class certification; federal ruling was not sufficiently final to constitute an exception to the bar of the Anti-Injunction Act). *Cullen* and *Clearwater* cast a new light on the antisuit injunction authorized in *In re Bridgestone/Firestone, Inc., Tires Products Liability Litigation*, 333 F.3d 763 (7th Cir. 2003) (*supra* p. 194).

11. Offensive collateral estoppel is not the only "preclusion" doctrine that might apply in complex cases: Stare decisis does some of the same work. In an opinion decided shortly before *Hardy*, the Fifth Circuit refused

to hold that *Borel* was stare decisis on the issue of the dangerousness of asbestos. At most, *Borel* established that a reasonable jury could find dangerousness, not that every reasonable jury must so find. Migues v. Fibreboard Corp., 662 F.2d 1182 (5th Cir. 1981). *Migues* is nonetheless instructive. If a party can convince a judge that no reasonable jury could dispute an issue decided by a court whose decisions bind the judge, stare decisis might bind later parties (whether they were involved in the prior litigation or not) to the determination of the issue. For an analysis of stare decisis from within a preclusion framework, see Amy Coney Barrett, *Stare Decisis and Due Process*, 74 U. COLO. L. REV. 1011 (2003).

Stare decisis binds nonparties as well as parties. In the next subsection we turn to the idea of binding nonparties to the outcome or findings of a prior case. For now, recall that stare-decisis effects are often regarded as a ground for intervention of right under Rule 24. *See supra* p. 119, Note 4(c). If judges take a broad view of stare decisis, won't they also create the condition for sprawling multiparty cases? Does this possibility suggest that a broad construction of stare decisis is undesirable in complex cases?

3. Precluding Persons that Did Not Participate in a Prior Case

The last subsection examined the limits of using preclusion doctrines against persons that were involved in prior litigation. Even if preclusion doctrines were broadly construed in this context (and they are not), these doctrines would still be an incomplete response to the problems posed by repetitive litigation. The reason is that these preclusion doctrines ran only against *parties* to a prior case; they did not run against *nonparties*. This subsection examines whether nonparties can ever be precluded from litigating claims or issues decided in a prior case. If preclusion doctrines can work in this context, the subsequent litigation will be significantly pared down, or possibly avoided altogether. On the other hand, precluding nonparties means binding persons who did not participate in shaping the proofs and arguments to an outcome. That result flies in the face of the participatory right that is, according to Professor Fuller, the cornerstone of any adversarial system. Are there circumstances in which this adversarial right does, or should, yield to the concerns of structural complexity?

MARTIN V. WILKS

490 U.S. 755 (1989)

■ CHIEF JUSTICE REHNQUIST delivered the opinion of the Court.

A group of white firefighters sued the city of Birmingham, Alabama (City), and the Jefferson County Personnel Board (Board) alleging that they were being denied promotions in favor of less qualified black firefighters. They claimed that the City and the Board were making promotion decisions on the basis of race in reliance on certain consent decrees, and that these decisions constituted impermissible racial discrimination in violation of the Constitution and federal statute. The District Court held that the white firefighters were precluded from challenging employment decisions taken pursuant to the decrees, even though these firefighters had not been parties to the proceedings in which the decrees were entered. We think this holding contravenes the general rule that a person cannot be deprived of his legal rights in a proceeding to which he is not a party.

The litigation in which the consent decrees were entered began in 1974, when the Ensley Branch of the National Association for the Advancement of Colored People and seven black individuals filed separate class-action complaints against the City and the Board. They alleged that both had engaged in racially discriminatory hiring and promotion practices in various public service jobs in violation of Title VII of the Civil Rights Act of 1964, 42 U.S.C. § 2000e et seq., and other federal law. After a bench trial on some issues, but before judgment, the parties entered into two consent decrees, one between the black individuals and the City and the other between them and the Board. These proposed decrees set forth an extensive remedial scheme, including long-term and interim annual goals for the hiring of blacks as firefighters. The decrees also provided for goals for promotion of blacks within the fire department.

The District Court entered an order provisionally approving the decrees and directing publication of notice of the upcoming fairness hearings. Notice of the hearings, with a reference to the general nature of the decrees, was published in two local newspapers. At that hearing, the Birmingham Firefighters Association (BFA) appeared and filed objections as *amicus curiae*. After the hearing, but before final approval of the decrees, the BFA and two of its members also moved to intervene on the ground that the decrees would adversely affect their rights. The District Count denied the motions as untimely and approved the decrees. Seven white firefighters, all members of the BFA, then filed a complaint against the City and the Board seeking injunctive relief against enforcement of the decrees. The seven argued that the decrees would operate to illegally discriminate against them; the District Court denied relief.

Both the denial of intervention and the denial of injunctive relief were affirmed on appeal. The District Court had not abused its discretion in refusing to let the BFA intervene, thought the Eleventh Circuit, in part because the firefighters could "institut[e] an independent Title VII suit, asserting specific violations of their rights." And, for the same reason, petitioners had not adequately shown the potential for irreparable harm from the operation of the decrees necessary to obtain injunctive relief.

A new group of white firefighters, the *Wilks* respondents, then brought suit against the City and the Board in District Court. They too alleged that, because of their race, they were being denied promotion in favor of less qualified blacks in violation of federal law. The Board and the City admitted to making race conscious employment decisions, but argued that the decisions were unassailable because they were made pursuant to the consent decrees. A group of black individuals, the *Martin* petitioners, were allowed to intervene in their individual capacities to defend the decrees.

The defendants moved to dismiss the reverse discrimination cases as impermissible collateral attacks on the consent decrees. . . . After trial the District Court granted the motion to dismiss. . . .

On appeal, the Eleventh Circuit reversed. It held that, "because . . . [the *Wilks* respondents] were neither parties nor privies to the consent decrees, . . . their independent claims of unlawful discrimination are not precluded." The court explicitly rejected the doctrine of "impermissible collateral attack" espoused by other Courts of Appeals to immunize parties to a consent decree from charges of discrimination by nonparties for actions taken pursuant to the decree. . . . Although it recognized a "strong public policy in favor of voluntary affirmative action plans," the panel acknowledged that this interest "must yield to the policy against requiring third parties to submit to bargains in which their interests were either ignored or sacrificed." The court remanded the case for trial of the discrimination claims . . . .

We granted certiorari, . . . and now affirm the Eleventh Circuit's judgment. All agree that "it is a principle of general application in Anglo-American jurisprudence that one is not bound by a judgment *in personam* in a litigation in which he is not designated as a party or to which he has not been made a party by service of process." Hansberry v. Lee, 311 U.S. 32, 40 (1940). *See, e.g.,* Parklane Hosiery Co. v. Shore 439 U.S. 322, 327, n.7 (1979). This rule is part of our "deep-rooted historic tradition that everyone should have his own day in court." A judgment or decree among parties to a lawsuit resolves issues to those proceeding.[2]

Petitioners argue that, because respondents failed to timely intervene in the initial proceedings, their current challenge to actions taken under the consent decree constitutes an impermissible "collateral attack." They argue that respondents were aware that the underlying suit might affect them, and if they chose to pass up an opportunity to intervene, they should not be permitted to later litigate the issues in a new action. . . .

We begin with the words of Justice Brandeis in *Chase National Bank v. Norwalk*, 291 U.S. 431 (1934):

"The law does not impose upon any person absolutely entitled to a hearing the burden of voluntary intervention in a suit to which he is a stranger. . . . Unless duly summoned to appear in a legal proceeding, a

---

2. We have recognized an exception to the general rule when, in certain limited circumstances, a person, although not a party, has his interests adequately represented by someone with the same interests who is a party. *See* Hansberry v. Lee, 311 U.S. 32, 41-42 (1940) ("class" or "representative" suits); Fed. R. Civ. P. 23 (same); Montana v. United States, 440 U.S. 147, 154-155 (1979) (control of litigation on behalf of one of the parties in the litigation). Additionally, where a special remedial scheme exists expressly foreclosing successive litigation by nonlitigants, as for example in bankruptcy or probate, legal proceedings may terminate preexisting rights if the scheme is otherwise consistent with due process. Neither of these exceptions, however, applies in this case.

person not a privy may rest assured that a judgment recovered therein will not affect his legal rights."

While these words were written before the adoption of the Federal Rules of Civil Procedure, we think the Rules incorporate the same principle; a party seeking a judgment binding on another cannot obligate that person to intervene; he must be joined. Against the background of permissive intervention set forth in *Chase National Bank*, the drafters cast Rule 24, governing intervention, in permissive terms. *See* Fed. R. Civ. P. 24(a) (intervention as of right) ("Upon timely application anyone shall be permitted to intervene"); Fed. R. Civ. P. 24(b) (permissive intervention) ("Upon timely application anyone may be permitted to intervene").[*] They determined that the concern for finality and completeness of judgments would be "better [served] by mandatory joinder procedures." Accordingly, Rule 19(a) provides for mandatory joinder in circumstances where a judgment rendered in the absence of a person may "leave . . . persons already parties subject to a substantial risk of incurring . . . inconsistent obligations . . . ."[†] Rule 19(b) sets forth the factors to be considered by a court in deciding whether to allow an action to proceed in the absence of an interested party.

Joinder as a party, rather than knowledge of a lawsuit and an opportunity to intervene, is the method by which potential parties aresubjected to the jurisdiction of the court and bound by a judgment or decree. The parties to a lawsuit presumably know better than anyone else the nature and scope of relief sought in the action, and at whose expense such relief might be granted. It makes sense, therefore, to place on them a burden of bringing in additional parties where such a step is indicated, rather than placing on potential additional parties a duty to intervene when they acquire knowledge of the lawsuit. The linchpin of the "impermissible collateral attack" doctrine — the attribution of preclusive effect to a failure to intervene — is therefore quite inconsistent with Rule 19 and Rule 24.

Petitioners argue that our decision[ ] in *Penn-Central Merger and N & W Inclusion Cases*, 389 U.S. 486 (1968), . . . suggest[s] an opposite result. The *Penn-Central* litigation took place in a special statutory framework enacted by Congress to allow reorganization of a huge railway system. Primary jurisdiction was in the Interstate Commerce Commission, with very restricted review in a statutory three-judge District Court. Review proceedings were channeled to the District Court for the Southern District of New York, and proceedings in other District Courts were stayed. The District Court upheld the decision of the Interstate Commerce Commission in both the merger and the inclusion proceedings, and the parties to that proceeding appealed to this Court. Certain Pennsylvania litigants had sued in the District Court for the Middle District of Pennsylvania to set aside the Commission's order, and this action was stayed . . . . We held that the borough of Moosic, one of the Pennsylvania

---

[*]   In 2007 amendments to Rules 24(a) and (b), the quoted language, but not its meaning, was slightly altered. — ED.

[†]   In a 2007 amendment to Rule 19(a), the quoted language, but not its meaning, was slightly altered. — ED.

litigants, could not challenge the Commission's approval of the merger and inclusion in the Pennsylvania District Court, pointing out the unusual nationwide character of the action and saying "in these circumstances, it would be senseless to permit parties seeking to challenge the merger and the inclusion orders to bring numerous suits in many different district courts."

We do not think that this holding in *Penn Central*, based as it was upon the extraordinary nature of the proceedings challenging the merger of giant railroads and not even mentioning Rule 19 or Rule 24, affords a guide to the interpretation of the rules relating to joinder and intervention in ordinary civil actions in a district court. . . .

Petitioners contend that . . . the need to join affected parties will be burdensome and ultimately discouraging to civil rights litigation. Potential adverse claimants may be numerous and difficult to identify; if they are not joined, the possibility for inconsistent judgments exists. Judicial resources will be needlessly consumed in relitigation of the same question.

Even if we were wholly persuaded by these arguments as a matter of policy, acceptance of them would require a rewriting rather than an interpretation of the relevant Rules. But we are not persuaded that their acceptance would lead to a more satisfactory method of handling cases like this one. It must be remembered that the alternatives are a duty to intervene based on knowledge, on the one hand, and some form of joinder, as the Rules presently provide, on the other. No one can seriously contend that an employer might successfully defend against a Title VII claim by one group of employees on the ground that its actions were required by an earlier decree entered in a suit brought against it by another, if the later group did not have adequate notice or knowledge of the earlier suit.

The difficulties petitioners foresee in identifying those who could be adversely affected by a decree granting broad remedial relief are undoubtedly present, but they arise from the nature of the relief sought and not because of any choice between mandatory intervention and joinder. Rule 19's provisions for joining interested parties are designed to accommodate the sort of complexities that may arise from a decree affecting numerous people in various ways. We doubt that a mandatory intervention rule would be any less awkward. As mentioned, plaintiffs who seek the aid of the courts to alter existing employment policies, or the employer who might be subject to conflicting decrees, are best able to bear the burden of designating those who would be adversely affected if plaintiffs prevail; these parties will generally have a better understanding of the scope of likely relief than employees who are not named but might be affected. Petitioners' alternative does not eliminate the need for, or difficulty of, identifying persons who, because of their interests, should be included in a lawsuit. It merely shifts that responsibility to less able shoulders.

Nor do we think that the system of joinder called for by the Rules is likely to produce more relitigation of issues than the converse rule. The breadth of a lawsuit and concomitant relief may be at least partially shaped in advance through Rule 19 to avoid needless clashes with future litigation.

And even under a regime of mandatory intervention, parties who did not have adequate knowledge of the suit would relitigate issues. Additional questions about the adequacy and timeliness of knowledge would inevitably crop up. We think that the system of joinder presently contemplated by the Rules best serves the many interests involved in the run of litigated cases, including cases like the present one.

Petitioners also urge that the congressional policy favoring voluntary settlement of employment discrimination claims . . . also supports the "impermissible collateral attack" doctrine. But once again it is essential to note just what is meant by "voluntary settlement." A voluntary settlement in the form of a consent decree between one group of employees and their employer cannot possibly "settle," voluntarily or otherwise, the conflicting claims of another group of employees who do not join in the agreement. . . .

Insofar as the argument is bottomed on the idea that it may be easier to settle claims among a disparate group of affected persons if they are all before the court, joinder bids fair to accomplish that result as well as a regime of mandatory intervention.

For the foregoing reasons we affirm the decision of the Court of Appeals for the Eleventh Circuit. . . .

■ JUSTICE STEVENS, with whom JUSTICE BRENNAN, JUSTICE MARSHALL, and JUSTICE BLACKMUN join, dissenting.

As a matter of law there is a vast difference between persons who are actual parties to litigation and persons who merely have the kind of interest that may as a practical matter be impaired by the outcome of a case. Persons in the first category have a right to participate in a trial and to appeal from an adverse judgment; depending on whether they win or lose, their legal rights may be enhanced or impaired. Persons in the latter category have a right to intervene in the action in a timely fashion, or they may be joined as parties against their will. But if they remain on the sidelines, they may be harmed as a practical matter even though their legal rights are unaffected. One of the disadvantages of sideline-sitting is that the bystander has no right to appeal from a judgment no matter how harmful it may be.

In these cases the Court quite rightly concludes that the white firefighters who brought the second series of Title VII cases could not be deprived of their legal rights in the first series of cases because they had neither intervened nor been joined as parties. The consent decrees obviously could not deprive them of any contractual rights, such as seniority, or accrued vacation pay, or of any other legal rights, such as the right to have their employer comply with federal statutes like Title VII. There is no reason, however, why the consent decrees might not produce changes in conditions at the white firefighters' place of employment that, as a practical matter, may have a serious effect on their opportunities for employment or promotion even though they are not bound by the decrees in any legal sense. The fact that one of the effects of a decree is to curtail the job opportunities of nonparties does not mean that the nonparties have been deprived of legal rights or that they have standing to appeal from that decree without becoming parties.

Persons who have no right to appeal from a final judgment — either because the time to appeal has elapsed or because they never became parties to the case — may nevertheless collaterally attack a judgment on certain narrow grounds. If the court had no jurisdiction over the subject matter, or if the judgment is the product of corruption, duress, fraud, collusion, or mistake, under limited circumstances it may be set aside in an appropriate collateral proceeding. This rule not only applies to parties to the original action, but also allows interested third parties collaterally to attack judgments. In both civil and criminal cases, however, the grounds that may be invoked to support a collateral attack are much more limited than those that may be asserted as error on direct appeal. Thus, a person who can foresee that a lawsuit is likely to have a practical impact on his interests may pay a heavy price if he elects to sit on the sidelines instead of intervening and taking the risk that his legal rights will be impaired. . . .

Hence, there is no basis for collaterally attacking the judgment as collusive, fraudulent, or transparently invalid. Moreover, respondents do not claim — nor has there been any showing of — mistake, duress, or lack of jurisdiction. Instead, respondents are left to argue that somewhat different relief would have been more appropriate than the relief that was actually granted. Although this sort of issue may provide the basis for a direct appeal, it cannot, and should not, serve to open the door to relitigation of a settled judgment. . . .

. . . [I]n complex litigation this Court has squarely held that a sideline-sitter may be bound as firmly as an actual party if he had adequate notice and a fair opportunity to intervene and if the judicial interest in finality is sufficiently strong. *See* Penn-Central Merger and N & W Inclusion Cases, 389 U.S. 486, 505-506 (1968).

There is no need, however, to go that far in order to agree with the District Court's eminently sensible view that compliance with the terms of a valid decree remedying violations of Title VII cannot itself violate that statute or the Equal Protection Clause. The city of Birmingham, in entering into and complying with this decree, has made a substantial step toward the eradication of the long history of pervasive racial discrimination that has plagued its fire department. The District Court, after conducting a trial and carefully considering respondents' arguments, concluded that this effort is lawful and should go forward. Because respondents have thus already had their day in court and have failed to carry their burden, I would vacate the judgment of the Court of Appeals and remand for further proceedings consistent with this opinion.

Notes

1. *Martin v. Wilks* is one of the central cases in complex litigation because it makes joinder, rather than preclusion, the principal vehicle

through which aggregation must occur. But the case is ambiguous in one critical respect: whether its holding is based on an interpretation of the Federal Rules of Civil Procedure or on the Constitution. Most of the language in the opinion concerns the structure of the federal joinder rules, especially Rules 19 and 24. *Chase National Bank v. Norwalk*, 291 U.S. 431 (1934), on which the Court also relies, is ambiguous, but it seems grounded on either principles of equity or traditional principles of law. *Hansberry v. Lee*, 311 U.S. 32 (1941), was grounded in the Due Process Clause.

The issue matters. If *Martin v. Wilks* is based on the Federal Rules of Civil Procedure or on federal common law, then state courts, Congress, and federal or state rulemakers could devise a "nonparty preclusion after notice and opportunity to intervene" rule. On the other hand, if *Martin v. Wilks* is grounded in the Constitution, such efforts are futile.

2. In *Richards v. Jefferson County*, 517 U.S. 793 (1996), the Supreme Court seemed to put *Martin v. Wilks* on a constitutional plane. In *Richards* the plaintiffs contested the constitutionality of a county tax in state court. The plaintiffs lived in Jefferson County. A prior lawsuit, commenced by the acting director of finance for the city of Birmingham and by three taxpayers who lived in Jefferson County had asserted the same grounds for the tax's illegality. In this prior lawsuit (known as the *Bedingfield* litigation), the Alabama Supreme Court had upheld the tax. In the subsequent *Richards* litigation, the Alabama Supreme Court held that *Bedingfield* bound the plaintiffs. Because the *Richards* case arose in state court, the only ground on which the United States Supreme Court could overturn the decision was on a federal constitutional ground.

The United States Supreme Court unanimously held that the Alabama Supreme Court could not bind the *Richards* plaintiffs to the outcome in *Bedingfield*. The opening line of Justice Stevens' opinion set the tone:

> In *Hansberry v. Lee*, 311 U.S. 32 (1940), we held that it would violate the Due Process Clause of the Fourteenth Amendment to bind litigants to a judgment rendered in an earlier litigation to which they were not parties and in which they were not adequately represented. [517 U.S. at 794.]

Relying extensively on *Hansberry* and *Martin v. Wilks*, the Court stated that "[s]tate courts are generally free to develop their own rules for protecting against the relitigation of common issues or the piecemeal resolution of disputes," but that "extreme applications of the doctrine of res judicata may be inconsistent with a federal right that is fundamental in character." *Id.* at 797 (internal quotation marks omitted). Reiterating the exceptions (from *Martin v. Wilk*'s footnote 2 (*supra* p. 224)) that permit some nonparties to be bound, the Court found that none of these exceptions applied; the *Richards* plaintiffs were not in privity with the *Bedingfield* plaintiffs, nor were they adequately represented by the *Bedingfield* plaintiffs. The Court also rejected the county's invitation to create an exception for repetitive public-law litigation challenging a tax whose invalidation might have disastrous revenue consequences.

At the same time, *Richards* was careful to point out that the *Richards* plaintiffs had not received any notice that the *Bedingfield* lawsuit "would conclusively resolve their legal rights." *Id.* at 799. Nor, the Court observed, did they have "the opportunity to participate in[ ] the *Bedingfield* action." *Id.* at 802. The Court concluded:

> Because petitioners received neither notice of, nor sufficient representation in, the *Bedingfield* litigation, that adjudication, as a matter of federal due process, may not bind them and thus cannot bar them from challenging an allegedly unconstitutional deprivation of their property. [*Id.* at 805.]

Note that this conclusion leaves unresolved the constitutionality of a "nonparty preclusion after notice and opportunity to intervene" scheme. *Richards* says only that a "nonparty preclusion without notice and opportunity to intervene" scheme is unconstitutional — at least without a finding of privity or adequate representation. In trying to read *Richards'* tea leaves on this issue, a relevant passage is footnote 5, which observed that "mere notice may not suffice to preserve one's right to be heard in a case such as the one before us." The Court cited *Chase National Bank* for the proposition that the law does not generally require nonparties to join lawsuits, and distinguished *Penn-Central Merger and N & W Inclusion Cases*, 389 U.S. 486 (1968), with the observation that "absent parties were invited to intervene by the court." *Id.* at 800 n.5.

For comparable cases following *Richards*, see S. Cent. Bell Tel. Co. v. Ala., 526 U.S. 160 (1999); Nelson v. Adams USA, Inc., 529 U.S. 460 (2000).

3. You can test yourself on the constitutional question by considering two subsequent developments. First, shortly after the Court's decision, Congress legislatively overturned *Martin v. Wilks* for Title VII cases. Today 42 U.S.C. § 2000e-2(n)(1) prohibits collateral challenges to "litigated or consent judgments" in the employment-discrimination context:

> (i) by a person who, prior to the entry of the judgment or order described in subparagraph (A), had —

> > (I) actual notice of the proposed judgment or order sufficient to apprise such person that such judgment or order might adversely affect the interests and legal rights of such person and that an opportunity was available to present objections to such judgment or order by a future date certain; and

> > (II) a reasonable opportunity to present objections to such judgment or order; or

> (ii) by a person whose interests were adequately represented by another person who had previously challenged the judgment or order on the same legal grounds and with a similar factual situation, unless there has been an intervening change in law or fact.

The statute also states that it was not intended to "alter the standards for intervention under rule 24 of the Federal Rules of Civil Procedure" and that it does not apply when the prior judgment "was obtained through collusion or fraud, or is transparently invalid or was entered by a court lacking subject matter jurisdiction." 42 U.S.C. §§ 2000e-2(n)(2)(A), -(C).

This statute overturns *Martin v. Wilks* only in the specific context of employment discrimination, but leaves it operative in other areas. Of broader interest, therefore, is a second proposal in which the American Law Institute suggested that judges in certain aggregated cases be given the power to preclude nonparties when:

> "(1)   an existing claim or claims of nonparties involve one or more questions of fact in common with the actions pending before the transferee court and arise out of the same transaction, occurrence, or series of transactions or occurrences;
>
> "(2)   intervention will advance the efficient, consistent, and final resolution of both the parties' and nonparties' claims; and
>
> "(3)   intervention will not impose upon either the nonparties or parties undue prejudice, burden, or inconvenience."

Preclusion could occur only after the court had "informing the nonparties who are within the court's jurisdiction . . . that they may intervene in the action and in any event will be bound by the determinations made to the same extent as a party, unless otherwise provided by law." AM. L. INST., COMPLEX LITIGATION § 5.05(a) (1994). Unlike 42 U.S.C. § 2000e-2(n), the ALI proposal operates as a rule of issue preclusion rather than claim preclusion. According to the ALI:

> The impact of the procedure set out is not likely to be as harsh or broad-ranging as might appear at first glance. . . . [I]t is expected that the procedure will be used only infrequently or for a small number of litigants; most parties to complex litigation are likely to have filed suit
> . . . .
>
> . . . The mandatory joinder approach . . . is harsher on nonparties because it forces them either to participate or default, losing their entire claim; the procedure set out in this section allows them to join or be bound. If the result is favorable to their claim, they may benefit because the judgment precludes only issues, not claims. [§ 5.05 cmt. *a*.]

In light of *Martin v. Wilks* and *Richards*, are § 2000e-2(n) and the ALI's § 5.05(a) constitutional? *See generally* Robert G. Bone, *Rethinking the "Day in Court" Ideal and Nonparty Preclusion*, 67 N.Y.U. L. REV. 193, 288 (1992) (arguing that nonparties can be bound under certain theories); Samuel Issacharoff, *When Substance Mandates Procedure:* Martin v. Wilks *and the Rights of Vested Incumbents in Civil Rights Consent Decrees*, 77 CORNELL L. REV. 189 (1992) (defending the result in *Martin v. Wilks*).

4.   Footnote 2 in *Martin v. Wilks* mentions a few exceptions to the principle that a judgment can bind only those joined as parties. One is the class action, which we consider in Chapter Four. Another is bankruptcy, which we consider in Chapter Five. Indeed, the principal reason that class actions and bankruptcy have emerged as important devices in complex litigation is their promise in avoiding the horns of an undesirable dilemma:

either joining all potential parties in one case or suffering through repetitive litigation of related claims and issues in multiple cases.

An exception not mentioned in *Martin v. Wilks* is privity between a party in the prior case and a party in the latter case. Traditionally, the idea of privity was narrow, requiring a close legal relationship between the party and the privy; for instance, if a parent sued on behalf of a minor child, the child could not sue again after reaching the age of majority. Over time, some courts fused privity with adequate representation (borrowed from class actions) into a doctrine known as "virtual representation": If the interests of a party in a prior case were closely aligned with the interests of a party in a subsequent case and if the party in the prior case adequately represented those interests, the first party was the "virtual representative" of the second party, and the second party was bound to the outcome of the first case. A seminal case adopting this theory was *Aerojet-General Corp. v. Askew*, 511 F.2d 710 (5th Cir. 1975).

After *Richards*, such a theory might seemed doomed, but some courts kept it alive. The issue reached the Supreme Court in the following case.

TAYLOR V. STURGELL

553 U.S. 880 (2008)

■ JUSTICE GINSBURG delivered the opinion for a unanimous Court.

"It is a principle of general application in Anglo-American jurisprudence that one is not bound by a judgment *in personam* in a litigation in which he is not designated as a party or to which he has not been made a party by service of process." Hansberry v. Lee, 311 U.S. 32, 40 (1940). Several exceptions, recognized in this Court's decisions, temper this basic rule. In a class action, for example, a person not named as a party may be bound by a judgment on the merits of the action, if she was adequately represented by a party who actively participated in the litigation. In this case, we consider for the first time whether there is a "virtual representation" exception to the general rule against precluding nonparties. Adopted by a number of courts, including the courts below in the case now before us, the exception so styled is broader than any we have so far approved.

The virtual representation question we examine in this opinion arises in the following context. [Petitioner Brent Taylor was president of the Antique Aircraft Association, an organization to which Greg Herrick also belonged. Herrick was trying to restore an F-45 airplane. To do so, Herrick needed certain documents from the Federal Aviation Administration (FAA). When the FAA denied his Freedom of Information Act (FOIA) request, Herrick brought suit in the United States District Court for the District of Wyoming. He lost, and the Court of Appeals for the Tenth Circuit affirmed the dismissal. Less than a month after the Tenth Circuit's decision, Taylor filed a lawsuit under FOIA seeking the same documents from the FAA. Taylor filed a case in the United States District Court for the District of

Columbia. His lawsuit sought to litigate one issue that Herrick had litigated, as well as two issues Herrick had not litigated.] The two men have no legal relationship, and there is no evidence that Taylor controlled, financed, participated in, or even had notice of Herrick's earlier suit. Nevertheless, the D.C. Circuit held Taylor's suit precluded by the judgment against Herrick because, in that court's assessment, Herrick qualified as Taylor's "virtual representative."

We disapprove the doctrine of preclusion by "virtual representation," and hold, based on the record as it now stands, that the judgment against Herrick does not bar Taylor from maintaining this suit.

I

. . .

. . . [According to the record, Taylor and Herrick] are "close associate[s]"; Herrick asked Taylor to help restore Herrick's F-45, though they had no contract or agreement for Taylor's participation in the restoration; Taylor was represented by the lawyer who represented Herrick in the earlier litigation; and Herrick apparently gave Taylor documents that Herrick had obtained from the FAA during discovery in his suit.

Fairchild [Corporation, which had intervened as a defendant,] and the FAA conceded that Taylor had not participated in Herrick's suit. The D.C. District Court determined, however, that Herrick ranked as Taylor's virtual representative . . . . Accordingly, the District Court held Taylor's suit, seeking the same documents Herrick had requested, barred by the judgment against Herrick.

The D.C. Circuit affirmed. . . .

Rejecting [the] approaches [of other circuits], the D.C. Circuit announced its own five-factor test. The first two factors — "identity of interests" and "adequate representation" — are necessary but not sufficient for virtual representation. In addition, at least one of three other factors must be established: "a close relationship between the present party and his putative representative," "substantial participation by the present party in the first case," or "tactical maneuvering on the part of the present party to avoid preclusion by the prior judgment."

Applying this test to the record in Taylor's case, the D.C. Circuit found both of the necessary conditions for virtual representation well met. As to identity of interests, the court emphasized that Taylor and Herrick sought the same result — release of the F-45 documents. Moreover, the D.C. Circuit observed, Herrick owned an F-45 airplane, and therefore had "if anything, a stronger incentive to litigate" than Taylor, who had only a "general interest in public disclosure and the preservation of antique aircraft heritage."

Turning to adequacy of representation, the D.C. Circuit acknowledged that some other Circuits regard notice of a prior suit as essential to a determination that a nonparty was adequately represented in that suit. Disagreeing with these courts, the D.C. Circuit deemed notice an "important" but not an indispensable element in the adequacy inquiry. The court then concluded that Herrick had adequately represented Taylor even though Taylor had received no notice of Herrick's suit. For this conclusion, the appeals court relied on Herrick's "strong incentive to litigate" and Taylor's later engagement of the same attorney . . . .

The D.C. Circuit also found its "close relationship" criterion met, for Herrick had "asked Taylor to assist him in restoring his F-45" and "provided information to Taylor that Herrick had obtained through discovery"; furthermore, Taylor "did not oppose Fairchild's characterization of Herrick as his 'close associate.'" . . .

II

The preclusive effect of a federal-court judgment is determined by federal common law. . . . The federal common law of preclusion is, of course, subject to due process limitations. *See* Richards v. Jefferson County, 517 U.S. 793, 797 (1996).

Taylor's case presents an issue of first impression in this sense: Until now, we have never addressed the doctrine of "virtual representation" adopted (in varying forms) by several Circuits and relied upon by the courts below. Our inquiry, however, is guided by well-established precedent regarding the propriety of nonparty preclusion. We review that precedent before taking up directly the issue of virtual representation.

A

The preclusive effect of a judgment is defined by claim preclusion and issue preclusion, which are collectively referred to as "res judicata." Under the doctrine of claim preclusion, a final judgment forecloses "successive litigation of the very same claim, whether or not relitigation of the claim raises the same issues as the earlier suit." Issue preclusion, in contrast, bars "successive litigation of an issue of fact or law actually litigated and resolved in a valid court determination essential to the prior judgment," even if the issue recurs in the context of a different claim. By "preclud[ing] parties from contesting matters that they have had a full and fair opportunity to litigate," these two doctrines protect against "the expense and vexation attending multiple lawsuits, conserv[e] judicial resources, and foste[r] reliance on judicial action by minimizing the possibility of inconsistent decisions."

A person who was not a party to a suit generally has not had a "full and fair opportunity to litigate" the claims and issues settled in that suit. The application of claim and issue preclusion to nonparties thus runs up against the "deep-rooted historic tradition that everyone should have his own day in court." Indicating the strength of that tradition, we have often repeated the general rule that "one is not bound by a judgment *in personam* in a litigation in which he is not designated as a party or to which he has not been made a party by service of process." *Hansberry*, 311 U.S. at 40. *See also, e.g., Richards*, 517 U.S. at 798; Martin v. Wilks, 490 U.S. 755, 761 (1989) [*supra* p. 222].

B

Though hardly in doubt, the rule against nonparty preclusion is subject to exceptions. For present purposes, the recognized exceptions can be grouped into six categories.

First, "[a] person who agrees to be bound by the determination of issues in an action between others is bound in accordance with the terms of his agreement." 1 RESTATEMENT (SECOND) OF JUDGMENTS § 40, p. 390 (1980) (hereinafter RESTATEMENT). . . .

Second, nonparty preclusion may be justified based on a variety of pre-existing "substantive legal relationship[s]" between the person to be bound and a party to the judgment. Qualifying relationships include, but are not limited to, preceding and succeeding owners of property, bailee and bailor, and assignee and assignor. *See* 2 RESTATEMENT §§ 43-44, 52, 55. . . .[8]

Third, we have confirmed that, "in certain limited circumstances," a nonparty may be bound by a judgment because she was "adequately represented by someone with the same interests who [wa]s a party" to the suit. *Richards*, 517 U.S. at 798. Representative suits with preclusive effect on nonparties include properly conducted class actions, and suits brought by trustees, guardians, and other fiduciaries.

Fourth, a nonparty is bound by a judgment if she "assume[d] control" over the litigation in which that judgment was rendered. Because such a person has had "the opportunity to present proofs and argument," he has already "had his day in court" even though he was not a formal party to the litigation.

Fifth, a party bound by a judgment may not avoid its preclusive force by relitigating through a proxy. Preclusion is thus in order when a person who did not participate in a litigation later brings suit as the designated representative of a person who was a party to the prior adjudication. . . .

Sixth, in certain circumstances a special statutory scheme may "expressly foreclos[e] successive litigation by nonlitigants . . . if the scheme is otherwise consistent with due process." *Martin*, 490 U.S. at 762 n.2. Examples of such schemes include bankruptcy and probate proceedings . . . or other suits that "under [the governing] law, [may] be brought only on behalf of the public at large."

---

8. The substantive legal relationships justifying preclusion are sometimes collectively referred to as "privity." *See, e.g.*, Richards v. Jefferson County, 517 U.S. 793, 798 (1996); 2 RESTATEMENT § 62, Comment *a*. The term "privity," however, has also come to be used more broadly, as a way to express the conclusion that nonparty preclusion is appropriate on any ground. To ward off confusion, we avoid using the term "privity" in this opinion.

III

. . .

B

Fairchild and the FAA do not argue that the D.C. Circuit's virtual representation doctrine fits within any of the recognized grounds for nonparty preclusion. Rather, they ask us to abandon the attempt to delineate discrete grounds and clear rules altogether. Preclusion is in order, they contend, whenever "the relationship between a party and a non-party is 'close enough' to bring the second litigation within the judgment." Courts should make the "close enough" determination, they urge, through a "heavily fact-driven" and "equitable inquiry." Only this sort of diffuse balancing, Fairchild and the FAA argue, can account for all of the situations in which non-party preclusion is appropriate.

We reject this argument for three reasons. First, our decisions emphasize the fundamental nature of the general rule that a litigant is not bound by a judgment to which she was not a party. *See, e.g., Richards,* 517 U.S. at 798-99; *Martin,* 490 U.S. at 761-62. Accordingly, we have endeavored to delineate discrete exceptions that apply in "limited circumstances." Respondents' amorphous balancing test is at odds with the constrained approach to nonparty preclusion our decisions advance. . . .

Our second reason for rejecting a broad doctrine of virtual representation rests on the limitations attending nonparty preclusion based on adequate representation. A party's representation of a nonparty is "adequate" for preclusion purposes only if, at a minimum: (1) the interests of the nonparty and her representative are aligned, *see Hansberry,* 311 U.S. at 43; and (2) either the party understood herself to be acting in a representative capacity or the original court took care to protect the interests of the nonparty, *see Richards,* 517 U.S. at 801-02. In addition, adequate representation sometimes requires (3) notice of the original suit to the persons alleged to have been represented, *see Richards,* 517 U.S. at 801. In the class-action context, these limitations are implemented by the procedural safeguards contained in Federal Rule of Civil Procedure 23.

An expansive doctrine of virtual representation, however, would "recogniz[e], in effect, a common-law kind of class action." That is, virtual representation would authorize preclusion based on identity of interests and some kind of relationship between parties and nonparties, shorn of the procedural protections prescribed in *Hansberry, Richards,* and Rule 23. These protections, grounded in due process, could be circumvented were we to approve a virtual representation doctrine that allowed courts to "create *de facto* class actions at will."

Third, a diffuse balancing approach to nonparty preclusion would likely create more headaches than it relieves. Most obviously, it could significantly complicate the task of district courts faced in the first instance with preclusion questions. An all-things-considered balancing approach might spark wide-ranging, time-consuming, and expensive discovery tracking factors potentially relevant under seven- or five-prong tests. And after the relevant facts are established, district judges would be called upon to evaluate them under a standard that provides no firm guidance. Preclusion doctrine, it should be recalled, is intended to reduce the burden of litigation on courts and parties. "In this area of the law," we agree, "'crisp rules with sharp corners' are preferable to a round-about doctrine of opaque standards."

C

Finally, . . . the FAA maintains that nonparty preclusion should apply more broadly in "public-law" litigation than in "private-law" controversies. To support this position, the FAA offers two arguments. First, the FAA urges, our decision in *Richards* acknowledges that, in certain cases, the plaintiff has a reduced interest in controlling the litigation "because of the public nature of the right at issue." . . .

. . .[W]e said in *Richards* only that, for the type of public-law claims there envisioned, States are free to adopt procedures limiting repetitive litigation. In this regard, we referred to instances in which the first judgment foreclosed successive litigation by other plaintiffs because, "under state law, [the suit] could be brought only on behalf of the public at large."[12] *Richards* spoke of state legislation, but it appears equally evident that Congress, in providing for actions vindicating a public interest, may "limit the number of judicial proceedings that may be entertained." It hardly follows, however, that this Court should proscribe or confine successive FOIA suits by different requesters. Indeed, Congress' provision for FOIA suits with no statutory constraint on successive actions counsels against judicial imposition of constraints through extraordinary application of the common law of preclusion.

The FAA next argues that "the threat of vexatious litigation is heightened" in public-law cases because "the number of plaintiffs with standing is potentially limitless." . . . [I]t is theoretically possible that several persons could coordinate to mount a series of repetitive lawsuits.

But we are not convinced that this risk justifies departure from the usual rules governing nonparty preclusion. First, stare decisis will allow courts swiftly to dispose of repetitive suits brought in the same circuit. Second, even when stare decisis is not dispositive, "the human tendency not to waste money will deter the bringing of suits based on claims or issues that have already been adversely determined against others." . . .

IV

For the foregoing reasons, we disapprove the theory of virtual representation on which the decision below rested. The preclusive effects

---

12. Nonparty preclusion in such cases ranks under the sixth exception . . .: special statutory schemes that expressly limit subsequent suits.

of a judgment in a federal-question case decided by a federal court should instead be determined according to the established grounds for nonparty preclusion described in this opinion. . . .

We now turn back to Taylor's action to determine whether . . . the result reached by the courts below can be justified on one of the recognized grounds for nonparty preclusion. . . .

It is uncontested that four of the six grounds for nonparty preclusion have no application here: There is no indication that Taylor agreed to be bound by Herrick's litigation, that Taylor and Herrick have any legal relationship, that Taylor exercised any control over Herrick's suit, or that this suit implicates any special statutory scheme limiting relitigation. Neither the FAA nor Fairchild contends otherwise.

It is equally clear that preclusion cannot be justified on the theory that Taylor was adequately represented in Herrick's suit. Nothing in the record indicates that Herrick understood himself to be suing on Taylor's behalf, that Taylor even knew of Herrick's suit, or that the Wyoming District Court took special care to protect Taylor's interests. Under our pathmarking precedent, therefore, Herrick's representation was not "adequate."

That leaves only the fifth category: preclusion because a nonparty to an earlier litigation has brought suit as a representative or agent of a party who is bound by the prior adjudication. Taylor is not Herrick's legal representative and he has not purported to sue in a representative capacity. He concedes, however, that preclusion would be appropriate if respondents could demonstrate that he is acting as Herrick's "undisclosed agen[t]."

. . . We therefore remand to give the courts below an opportunity to determine whether Taylor, in pursuing the instant FOIA suit, is acting as Herrick's agent. Taylor concedes that such a remand is appropriate.

. . . We note, however, that courts should be cautious about finding preclusion on this basis. A mere whiff of "tactical maneuvering" will not suffice; instead, principles of agency law are suggestive. They indicate that preclusion is appropriate only if the putative agent's conduct of the suit is subject to the control of the party who is bound by the prior adjudication. . . .

[The Court then held that Taylor did not need to bear the burden of proving he is not acting as Herrick's agent.] Claim preclusion, like issue preclusion, is an affirmative defense. Ordinarily, it is incumbent on the defendant to plead and prove such a defense, and we have never recognized claim preclusion as an exception to that general rule. . . .

* * * * *

For the reasons stated, the judgment of the United States Court of Appeals for the District of Columbia Circuit is vacated, and the case is remanded for further proceedings consistent with this opinion.

It is so ordered.

Notes

1. Despite its protestation not to be doing so, *Taylor v. Sturgell* assays what appears to be a comprehensive list of the circumstances in which nonparty preclusion is possible in federal court. Included on the list are the circumstances mentioned in footnote 2 of *Martin v. Wilks* (class actions and special statutory schemes such as bankruptcy — *see supra* p. 224), as well as several other circumstances that had developed at common law and that might loosely be described as exceptions based on "privity." *Taylor v. Sturgell* itself eschews use of the term "privity" because of its malleability; we will see whether other courts follow suit.

2. The critical message from *Taylor v. Sturgell* is not to get creative with this list of exceptions: As a general proposition, nonparty preclusion is not permissible. In particular, the Court tamped down the "virtual representation" theory, which had emerged as the only exception with significant potential for use in complex litigation. For the most part, even the courts that had recognized the theory were hardly lavish in using it; the boundaries that they put on the theory made it only occasionally helpful in precluding relitigation in complex cases. *Cf.* Tice v. Am. Airlines, Inc., 162 F.3d 966 (7th Cir. 1998) (expressing doubt about the viability of "virtual representation," especially when a nonparty had no notice of the prior lawsuit). After *Taylor v. Sturgell*, the theory appears to be a dead letter. Of course, *Taylor v. Sturgell* was itself not a complex case, and so there is arguably room to distinguish it in widely dispersed complex cases in which the need for nonparty preclusion is far greater. But the Court's refusal to recognize the need for virtual representation in "public-law litigation" — a phrase that is sometimes used interchangeably with, or described as a species of, complex litigation — makes it unlikely that a "complexity exception" to the "no virtual representation" rule will emerge.

3. *Taylor v. Sturgell* was clear that its decision was based on federal common law, and governed the preclusive effect of a judgment entered in federal court in federal-question cases. To what extent are state courts free to fashion a "virtual representation" rule that might reduce repetitive litigation in complex cases? The answer depends on the extent to which the holding in *Taylor v. Sturgell* is not merely inspired by, but is actually controlled by, the Due Process Clause.

In *State ex rel. Schachter v. Ohio Public Employees Retirement Bd.*, 905 N.E.2d 1210 (Ohio 2009), the Ohio Supreme Court stated that its rules regarding privity were "amorphous," and seized on language from both *Taylor v. Sturgell* and *Richards v. Jefferson County*, 517 U.S. 793 (1996), to argue that it had freedom to create a more generous approach to nonparty preclusion than that permitted in *Taylor v. Sturgell*. *See* 905 N.E.2d at 1217-18. *Schachter* involved two public defenders who had worked in the same office and subsequently filed applications for benefits on the theory that they were public employees. An administrative board denied their claims. One of the lawyers appealed, and the other testified on his behalf. After he lost his administrative appeal, the other lawyer filed a suit in state court to overturn the decision in her case. The Ohio Supreme Court held that she was precluded by the administrative determination in the other lawyer's case because the two lawyers were in privity.

Like many states, in certain situations Ohio accords preclusive effect to the decisions of administrative tribunals; *Schachter* is not remarkable in that regard. Accepting that fact, do you agree with the Ohio Supreme Court that *Taylor v. Sturgell* does not bar the use of nonparty preclusion in this situation? If so, then state courts have a distinct advantage over federal courts whenever nonparty preclusion is a valuable technique for addressing dispersed complex litigation. This result is novel. With respect to other techniques such as multidistrict transfer and antisuit injunctions, we saw that federal courts have a distinct advantage over state courts.

4. The consistent message of the United States Supreme Court — from *Hansberry* through *Martin v. Wilks*, *Richards v. Jefferson County*, and *Taylor v. Sturgell* — is the fundamental importance of an individual's right to control his or her legal claims. This right of control is the cornerstone of the adversarial system. Throughout the chapter, we have stressed the ways in which this adversarial right comes at a price: the relitigation of common claims and issues whenever parties have an incentive to disperse their claims geographically, temporally, and among the federal and state courts. We have been searching for devices that can prevent the relitigation of claims or issues. By now, however, it should be obvious that all of these devices also come at a price: the loss of individual autonomy and control. To what extent is the Supreme Court telling us that this loss is too dear, and that the cost of repetitive litigation is one that we simply must bear as the price of a strong adversarial system in which everyone is entitled to his or her day in court?

One way to think about this question is to ask why we even care about trying to aggregate cases — why we have been on this quest for some technique or set of techniques that is the Holy Grail of aggregation. There are two distinct harms — one grounded in fairness and one in efficiency — that repetitive litigation can cause. The fairness concern is that repetitive litigation threatens the ability of other parties to have their day in court. For instance, if the early-filed cases in a mass-tort litigation exhaust all of the defendant's assets, then those whose claims do not mature until later (the "future plaintiffs," as we have called them) have no effective day in court. Likewise, if (as in *Martin v. Wilks*) later-filing plaintiffs can undo an injunction that early-filing plaintiffs obtained, then the early-filing plaintiffs' day in court is rather meaningless. The efficiency concern, of course, is that repetitive litigation of the same claims or issues is expensive; what can be done well once need not be done 1,000 times over.

Should the law of aggregation respond to these two harms in the same way? Arguably not. If preserving the "day in court" ideal is imperative (as the Supreme Court has said repeatedly), then shouldn't courts be more sympathetic to aggregating cases when non-aggregation raises fairness concerns than when it raises only efficiency concerns? The reason is that, if the only concern is efficiency, the Court has suggested that the value of litigant autonomy is greater. On the other hand, when the concern is also fairness, some litigants are going to lose the right to control their claims unless cases are aggregated. Of course, if cases are aggregated, others will lose their right of control. If aggregation leads, overall, to less loss of this right than non-aggregation, isn't aggregation justified? Or is such a cost-benefit analysis of a fundamental individual right impermissible?

5.   Note that, in discussing the three necessary conditions for adequate representation, *Taylor v. Sturgell* arguably leaves the window open for a "preclusion after notice and opportunity to intervene" rule. As we have seen, such a rule operates as a rule of issue preclusion, not claim preclusion. More generally, *Hansberry*, *Martin v. Wilks*, *Richards*, and *Taylor v. Sturgell* all involved claim preclusion in the nonparty context. Nothing in the cases suggests that the Court's general skepticism toward nonparty preclusion ought to be lifted in the context of issue preclusion. On the other hand, issue preclusion does not involve quite the same loss of control and litigant autonomy as claim preclusion. Is there more room for nonparty issue preclusion than for nonparty claim preclusion? Consider the following two cases.

HARDY V. JOHNS-MANVILLE SALES CORP.

681 F.2d 334 (5th Cir. 1982)

■   GEE, Circuit Judge.

[The facts in *Hardy* are described *supra* p. 211. Briefly, due to the adverse findings in prior litigation (the *Borel* case), the district court had ordered that the defendants in an asbestos product liability case were collaterally estopped from relitigating the unavoidably unsafe nature of asbestos, the absence or ineffectiveness of warnings on asbestos products, and the ability of asbestos to cause mesothelioma and asbestosis. The order estopped not only the six defendants that had been parties in *Borel*, but also fourteen defendants that had not been parties in *Borel*. In this portion of the opinion, the court considered whether such issue preclusion against the fourteen nonparty defendants was permissible.]

. . . [A] right, question, or fact distinctly put in issue and directly determined as a ground of recovery by a court of competent jurisdiction collaterally estops a party or his privy from relitigating the issue in a subsequent action. . . . The right to a full and fair opportunity to litigate an issue is, of course, protected by the due process clause of the United States Constitution. Hansberry v. Lee, 311 U.S. 32 (1940). While [*Parklane Hosiery Co. v. Shore*, 439 U.S. 322 (1979),] made the doctrine of mutuality effectively a dead letter under federal law, the case left undisturbed the requisite of privity, i.e., that collateral estoppel can only be applied against parties who have had a prior "'full and fair' opportunity to litigate their claims." The requirement that a person against whom the conclusive effect of a judgment is invoked must be a party or a privy to the prior judgment retains its full vigor after *Parklane* and has been repeatedly affirmed by our court. . . .

This is the first and, in our view, insurmountable problem with the trial court's application of collateral estoppel in the case sub judice. The omnibus order under review here does not distinguish between defendants who were parties to *Borel* and those who were not; it purports to estop all defendants because all purportedly share an "identity of interests" sufficient to constitute privity. The trial court's action stretches "privity" beyond meaningful limits. While we acknowledge the manipulability of the notion of "privity," this has not prevented courts from establishing guidelines on the permissibility of binding nonparties through res judicata or collateral estoppel. Without such guidelines, the due process guarantee of a full and fair opportunity to litigate disappears. Thus, we noted in *Southwest Airlines Co. v. Texas International Airlines*, 546 F.2d 84, 95 (5th Cir. 1977):

> Federal courts have deemed several types of relationships "sufficiently close" to justify preclusion. First, a nonparty who has succeeded to a party's interest in property is bound by any prior judgments against that party. . . . Second, a nonparty who controlled the original suit will be bound by the resulting judgment. . . . Third, federal courts will bind a nonparty whose interests were represented adequately by a party in the original suit.

The rationale for these exceptions — all derived from *Restatement (Second) of Judgments* §§ 30, 31, 34, 39-41 (1982) — is obviously that in these instances the nonparty has in effect had his day in court. In this case, the exceptions elaborated in *Southwest Airlines* and in the Restatement are inapplicable. First, the *Borel* litigation did not involve any property interests. Second, none of the non-*Borel* defendants have succeeded to any property interest held by the *Borel* defendants. Finally, the plaintiffs did not show that any non-*Borel* defendant had any control whatever over the *Borel* litigation. "To have control of litigation requires that a person have effective choice as to the legal theories and proofs to be advanced in behalf of the party to the action. He must also have control over the opportunity to obtain review." . . . Many of our circuit's cases evince a . . . concern with keeping the nonparties' exceptions to res judicata and collateral estoppel within strict confines.

The fact that all the non-*Borel* defendants, like the *Borel* defendants, are engaged in the manufacture of asbestos-containing products does not evince privity among the parties. The plaintiffs did not demonstrate that any of the non-*Borel* defendants participated in any capacity in the *Borel* litigation — whether directly or even through a trade representative — or were even part of a trustee-beneficiary relationship with any *Borel* defendant. On the contrary, several of the defendants indicate on appeal that they were not even aware of the *Borel* litigation until those proceedings were over and that they were not even members of industry or trade associations composed of asbestos product manufacturers. . . .

. . . The court's omnibus order here amounts to collateral estoppel based on similar legal positions . . . We agree with the Texas Supreme Court that "privity is not established by the mere fact that persons may happen to be interested in the same question or in proving the same state of facts," and hold that the trial court's actions here transgress the bounds of due process.

Our conclusion likewise pertains to those defendants who, while originally parties to the *Borel* litigation, settled before trial. The plaintiffs here did not show that any of these defendants settled out of the *Borel* litigation after the entire trial had run its course and only the judicial act of signing a final known adverse judgment remained. Such action would suggest settlement precisely to avoid offensive collateral estoppel and, in an appropriate case, might preclude relitigation. All the indications here are, however, that the defendants in question settled out of the case early because of, for example, lack of product identification. Like the non-*Borel* defendants, these defendants have likewise been deprived of their day in court by the trial court's omnibus order.

LYNCH V. MERRELL-NATIONAL LABORATORIES

646 F. Supp. 856 (D. Mass. 1986), *aff'd on other grounds*, 830 F.2d 1190 (1st Cir. 1987)

■ MAZZONE, District Judge.

This matter is before the Court on the defendant's motion for summary judgment. The case involves a claim for damages brought by the parents on behalf of a minor plaintiff, Margo Lynch, and individually as well, against the defendant Merrell-National Laboratories ("Merrell Dow"). The plaintiffs allege that Margo Lynch sustained injury in the form of the congenital absence of her right forearm as a result of the ingestion of the defendant's prescription pharmaceutical, Bendectin, by plaintiff's mother, Margaret Lynch, during her pregnancy. . . .

The two issues are: (1) whether the plaintiffs are collaterally estopped from relitigating the issue of Bendectin's role in the causation of birth defects; and (2) whether there is any factual dispute on the issue of causation. As to the first issue, the defendants claim the plaintiffs should be bound by the result of the multidistrict trial in which the jury concluded that Bendectin did not cause human birth defects. The plaintiffs say that because they did not participate in that trial, they are not bound by that result, and further, that the result is not conclusive because other cases have produced a different result favorable to them. . . .

[The Judicial Panel for Multidistrict Litigation transferred hundreds of Bendectin cases to Judge Rubin in the Southern District of Ohio. The cases were transferred for pretrial proceedings, not for trial. Among the cases transferred was *Lynch*, which had been filed in the District of Massachusetts.] Upon completion of multidistrict discovery, Judge Rubin consolidated for trial all cases originally filed in the Northern and Southern Districts of Ohio, and adopted an "opt-in" procedure, allowing plaintiffs in cases filed in other districts to participate in the proceedings upon application of plaintiffs' counsel. Approximately 1174 plaintiffs were represented at that trial. For reasons not clear in the record, the plaintiffs in the present case, although participating in the multidistrict discovery, elected not to participate in the trial. They chose instead to have their case returned to this court for a separate proceeding.

The large number of cases involved in the consolidated trial required unusual and innovative procedures. [Principal among these procedures was Judge Rubin's decision to "bifurcate" the case, so that the only issue decided at trial was whether Bendectin was capable of causing the types of birth defects from which the plaintiffs suffered. *See infra* p. 1034. Judge Rubin also designed a unique juror questionnaire, and he excluded all of the plaintiffs, many of whom had significant birth defects, from the courtroom, so that the jury did not see them. The consolidated trial lasted twenty-one days, and consisted largely of expert testimony (ten called by the plaintiffs and nine by Merrell Dow). The jury's verdict in favor of Merrell Dow was unanimous; Judge Rubin entered judgment against the plaintiffs in all 1,174 cases.]

The case is now before this Court for further proceedings. In a nutshell, the plaintiffs in the present case seek to relitigate the issue of whether Bendectin causes human birth defects. Plaintiffs here assert that they should not be precluded from relitigating this issue because they were not named parties in the consolidated trial, nor were they in "privity" with any parties to that proceeding. They claim that they had no financial or proprietary interest in the consolidated case, nor did they supply an attorney or in any manner exercise control over that litigation. Furthermore, plaintiffs claim that the exercise of their discretionary right not to intervene in the earlier, consolidated litigation, should not preclude the assertion of their claim here and that they would be denied their constitutional right to a trial if they were precluded. I turn, then, to the first question: whether the doctrine of collateral estoppel should be invoked under these facts to preclude plaintiffs from relitigating the issue of Bendectin's alleged responsibility for human birth defects. . . .

. . . Other circuits have invoked the doctrine of collateral estoppel when, as in this case, a plaintiff has elected as a matter of litigation strategy to forego an opportunity to intervene in an action. *In National Wildlife Fed'n v. Gorsuch*, 744 F.2d 963 (3rd Cir. 1983), the Third Circuit held that collateral estoppel was properly invoked against plaintiffs who, though not parties to an earlier action, bypassed an opportunity to intervene in the earlier action. Like the plaintiffs in *Gorsuch*, the plaintiffs here "were not outsiders unaware of litigation in progress that would ultimately affect their interests." In *Bronson v. Board of Educ.*, 525 F.2d 344 (6th Cir. 1975), the Court of Appeals for the Sixth Circuit refused to allow relitigation of racial discrimination claims by new plaintiffs following an earlier action on the same issues brought by different plaintiffs, noting that it would be inequitable to require the defendant school board to repeatedly battle the "same charge of improper conduct if it has been vindicated in an action brought by a person or group who validly and fairly represent those whose rights are alleged to have been infringed."

In *Gerrard v. Larsen*, 517 F.2d 1127, 1135 (8th Cir. 1975), the court stated that the determination of who should be bound by a prior adjudication ought to be conducted "on a case by case basis by an examination of underlying facts and circumstances rather than by reliance solely upon the formal status of persons against whom an estoppel is asserted." After examination of the underlying facts and circumstances of this case, I conclude that the plaintiffs here should be bound by the results of the consolidated trial.

The issue of causation with respect to Bendectin and birth defects was extensively litigated in the consolidated trial, and the outcome of that litigation should be accorded finality. The claims by plaintiffs in the consolidated trial were representative of all potential claims involving birth defects allegedly caused by the maternal ingestion of Bendectin, and all of the opinion witnesses designated by plaintiffs in this case testified at the consolidated trial. The plaintiffs here unconvincingly argue that their claim differs from those in the consolidated trial. They emphasize that a trial before this Court would focus on the *specific* incident of Margaret Lynch's ingestion of Bendectin. But the central issue in any proceeding involving Bendectin and its role in birth defects is that of causation, and that issue has already been fully litigated in the consolidated trial.

If this case were to be tried, there would be no reason to depart from the careful, thoughtful and fair procedure adopted by Judge Rubin in the earlier trial. Bifurcation would certainly be appropriate. The jury's attention should be focused quickly and without distraction if both sides are to receive a fair resolution. The issue is complex; approximately 19 experts would be expected to testify, and the 4 cases tried to date lasted an average of 38 trial days. The jury would be selected in the same manner, employing the same questionnaire and voir dire procedures, and receiving essentially the same instructions. Margo Lynch would not be present in the courtroom, although she could observe the proceedings from the adjoining lobby by electronic means. The jury would be instructed at the outset that while the immediate issue was a medical-legal one, the case involved real people and birth deformity. Therefore, this would not be a mere "academic debate between the medical and scientific experts for each side," as the plaintiffs describe the consolidated trial. The plaintiffs attribute the defendant's verdict in the consolidated trial to the fact that "no individual cases were discussed" or that "confronted with the causation issue in a vacuum, the jury returned a verdict for the defendant." Not only does this argument belittle the jury's role, but it demonstrates the plaintiffs' hope that the presence of Margo Lynch in the courtroom would produce a different and favorable result. This is a case in which there would be no new medical or scientific evidence, no new expert opinion, no new studies, no new data or theories. The plaintiffs point out that a plaintiff's verdict was returned in *Oxendine v. Merrell Dow Pharmaceuticals*, 506 A.2d 1100 (D.C.C.A. 1986), but that state court trial did not have the full record of the consolidated trial, nor was the case tried under the same procedures. It produced the very inconsistency which the doctrine of collateral estoppel was designed to prevent.

The plaintiffs' constitutional arguments are not persuasive. A significant commonality of interest, sufficient to overcome the plaintiffs' due process objections, existed between the Lynches and the more than 1100 plaintiffs participating in the consolidated trial. The "opt-in" procedure adopted by Judge Rubin was not a commitment that every out-of-state plaintiff would receive a separate jury trial. . . . As stated earlier, the record is silent as to the reasons plaintiffs elected not to participate in the consolidated trial. Were the record to reflect a worthy explanation, a lack of confidence in trial counsel, or a compelling distinction between the Lynches' claims and the others, I would have analyzed the doctrine in that light. But the plaintiffs have not provided a single sound reason for their decision. One permissible inference is that the plaintiffs elected not to participate because they felt they would not be bound by a defendants' verdict, but could take advantage of a plaintiffs' verdict by negotiating a favorable settlement or, ironically, by asserting issue preclusion or offensive collateral estoppel against the defendant. This would be the type of tactical or procedural maneuvering that should be discouraged and not rewarded. Imagine the consternation of the over 1100 plaintiffs involved in the prior litigation if the plaintiffs here were allowed to obtain an inconsistent adjudication by nothing more than a change in forum.

I am not unmindful of the harshness this ruling visits on the plaintiffs. But what it boils down to is that the plaintiffs want a second chance. Conclusiveness of adjudication is an important principle. Justice is achieved when a competent jury hears all the relevant and material evidence by competent witnesses on the issue, presented by able, competent counsel, and returns a unanimous verdict. That was achieved in the prior trial and I conclude the plaintiffs here are bound by that result.

[The court then held that, even if collateral estoppel were not appropriate, the available scientific evidence failed to demonstrate a sufficient causal link between Bendectin and human birth defects.]

The defendant's motion for summary judgment is granted and the complaint is to be dismissed.

Notes

1. Can you reconcile *Lynch* with *Hardy*, or with the Supreme Court's decisions in *Martin v. Wilks*, *Richards v. Jefferson County*, and *Taylor v. Sturgell*? All of the Court's decisions postdate *Lynch*. Given this fact, could a court today come out as *Lynch* did?

The First Circuit affirmed the judgment in *Lynch* on the ground that the plaintiffs had failed to prove causation. Lynch v. Merrell-National Labs., 830 F.2d 1190 (1st Cir. 1987). Although it thought that "[t]he question is close and the thoughtful analysis by the district court all but compelling," *id.* at 1192, the court of appeals expressed doubt about the trial court's ruling on issue preclusion:

> . . . [W]e do not believe that either federal or state law would warrant the application of collateral estoppel in the present context. . . . [T]he Sixth Circuit noted . . . that later plaintiffs could not invoke to their benefit a favorable result in mass tort litigation. In re Bendectin Products Liability Litigation, [749 F.2d 300, 305 (6th Cir. 1984)]. If later plaintiffs could not, why should the defendant? . . . [T]he plaintiffs were allowed to think that they could withdraw from [the MDL trial] and lose nothing. They did not have a fair opportunity when they understood that their withdrawal would not prejudice them. If they were now bound, the multi-district litigation would in effect have been a class action leaving the Lynches no true option. We believe that their freedom to withdraw and come back to Boston was not illusory. [830 F.2d at 1192-93.]

2. Is there an argument that, because *Lynch* was consolidated for some time and for some purposes with the cases of the 1,174 plaintiffs who lost, using issue preclusion was permissible? The argument would take the form that the Lynches were not true nonparties to the MDL *Bendectin* litigation. Or is that argument inconsistent with *Lexecon Inc. v. Milberg Weiss Bershad Hynes & Lerach,* 523 U.S. 26 (1998) (*supra* p. 162), in which the Court held that an MDL judge must remand multidistricted cases for trial? Even if there were an argument, *Lynch*'s nonparty issue preclusion would be useful only when some MDL cases are transferred back to the transferor court and others are tried in the transferee forum.

3. Is there an argument that the near-categorical ban on nonparty preclusion has less force with issue preclusion than with claim preclusion? Issue preclusion does not bar entire claims, only certain issues within claims; in this sense, it is less severe than claim preclusion. We know of no case that has ever adopted this distinction, although *Tyus v. Schoemehl,* 93 F.3d 449 (8th Cir. 1996), which adopted a broad "virtual representation" theory, went out of its way to point out that its ruling was based on issue rather than claim preclusion — even though it seemed to be a claim-preclusion decision. *Id.* at 453 n.5. In any event, *Tyus* was in many critical ways indistinguishable from *Taylor v. Sturgell,* and was one of the "virtual representation" cases that *Taylor v. Sturgell* singled out as adopting an impermissibly broad view of "virtual representation."

4. Sometimes a defendant wishes to settle, but is unwilling to do so because it fears that it will be subject to further claims (typically, claims for contribution or indemnity) from actual or potential co-defendants. In this situation, the defendant has no reason to settle the litigation with the plaintiffs only to continue the litigation in another form and with ongoing exposure to liability. To facilitate the settlement, some courts have entered "collateral bar" or "settlement bar" orders. These orders prevent others from pursuing third-party or other claims against the settling defendant. *See* In re HealthSouth Corp. Sec. Litig., 572 F.3d 854 (11th Cir. 2009); In re U.S. Oil & Gas Litig., 967 F.2d 489, 491 (11th Cir. 1992) (*infra* p. 1229).

We examine these orders in more detail in Chapter Twelve. *See infra* p. 1229. In essence, however, the collateral bar order precludes nonparties from bringing valid claims. Can they be justified in light of *Taylor v. Sturgell* and the other cases you have read in this subsection?

5. In *Tyus*, despite his deep disagreement with the court's use of a "virtual representation" theory, Judge Henley concurred in the result because he believed that the plaintiffs in the second case had notice of the first lawsuit and were sufficiently represented in the first lawsuit. 93 F.3d at 458. His concurrence brings back again the ALI proposal to adopt a rule of issue preclusion after notice and an opportunity to intervene. *See supra* p. 230, Note 3. When all is said and done, and assuming that such a rule is constitutional, do you now favor such an approach?

4. A Final Assessment

The material on preclusion brings us back full circle to the start of the chapter. As we have seen, preclusion is unlikely to be useful in many repetitive-litigation situations — almost never when the attempt is to bind a nonparty to a prior case, and less frequently than it might initially seem even when the attempt is to bind someone who was a party in the prior case. Rather, our legal system's strong orientation — one that does not give much even in the face of the demands of complex litigation to rein in the geographical, temporal, and jurisdictional dispersion of claims — is toward joinder as the means by which the aggregation of claims and parties occur. (In some instances consolidation, stays, and antisuit injunctions are also useful.) Joinder decisions are driven principally by the private outcome-maximizing behavior of the litigants, not by the desire to reduce unfair or inefficient relitigation of related claims and issues. Litigant autonomy, adversarial process, and each individual's right to a "day in court" remain highly valued ideals in American litigation, whatever their cost.

Our study of preclusion introduced a couple of important exceptions to this conclusion: in particular, class actions and bankruptcy, which we examine in Chapters Four and Five respectively. Of the two, the class action is the more useful device. Therefore, class actions enjoy a central place in any study of the methods by which to aggregate related cases.

Before we come to class actions, however, we stop to examine another set of rules that imposes significant barriers to the aggregation of related cases in a single forum: the rules of territorial jurisdiction and subject-matter jurisdiction. These rules, which reflect important decisions about the distribution of power within a federal system of government, were developed without the unique problems of repetitive litigation in mind. As a result, they can frustrate aggregation even when the initial barriers imposed by our hodgepodge of joinder, consolidation, injunction, and preclusion rules permit aggregation to occur.

CHAPTER THREE

AGGREGATION AND JURISDICTION IN A FEDERAL SYSTEM

In an adversarial system, the plaintiff is the "master of the complaint" — which means that the plaintiff has the first opportunity to select the parties to be sued, the claims to be asserted, and the court to hear the case. These issues are intimately connected to each other. The parties or claims that the plaintiff wishes to include may determine the court in which the plaintiff files; conversely, the court in which the plaintiff wishes to file the case may determine the parties and claims that the plaintiff includes. Rules of jurisdiction (both territorial and subject-matter) limit the power of courts to hear certain claims and to bind certain parties.

The last chapter essentially ignored the issue of jurisdiction. Rather, in examining the approaches by which plaintiffs could aggregate related cases, as well as the ways in which the defendant and the court could overcome aggregation-frustrating decisions of plaintiffs who did not or could not aggregate, we assumed that the forum in which related cases were (or should be) aggregated had the power to adjudicate all the claims asserted by and against all parties. This chapter demonstrates that courts do not always possess this jurisdictional power. In fact, jurisdictional rules impose additional barriers to aggregating related cases, and are also an additional cause of the unfairness and inefficiency that dispersed complex litigation can spawn.

Jurisdiction brings a new consideration into the aggregation mix. In the last chapter, we explored aggregation principally from the viewpoint of the tension between the benefits of aggregation and the benefits of giving litigants the autonomy to control legal claims, which can be one of their principal assets or liabilities. Because adjudicating claims is one of the principal powers that governments exercise over citizens, jurisdictional rules focus on the proper allocation of that power between federal and state courts and among the state courts. This distribution of power among courts is one aspect of "Our Federalism." Thus, this chapter principally considers the question of aggregation from the viewpoint of the tension between the benefits of aggregation and the benefits of federalism. As in the last chapter, we continue to explore whether the need to bring related litigation into a single forum is so pressing a concern that rules developed for simpler cases should be altered.

Remaining in the mix of considerations, however, is the value of litigant autonomy. In the first place, federalism is not valuable for its own sake; it is valuable because our system of government believes that a distribution of power among branches and levels of government best protects the well-being of individual citizens. Second, in our adversarial system, plaintiffs make the initial selection of the claims, the parties, and the court. Often they structure their cases to invoke the jurisdiction of the court in which they believe they stand the best chance of a favorable outcome. Defendants will often attempt to upset that jurisdictional choice because they believe that their best outcome lies in a different court. Thus, the battle over jurisdiction is often not a struggle over abstract principles of federalism but a critical tipping point that can determine the success of the litigation. The ability to invoke a court's jurisdiction and the autonomy of litigants to advance their own claims and defenses are intertwined.

This last paragraph suggests a potentially useful distinction: that we should be more respectful of jurisdictional rules that frustrate the aggregation of complex litigation when they vindicate the public values of federalism than when they are used by litigants as tactical weapons to achieve better outcomes in private litigation. Does this distinction make sense? Or are even the supposedly "public values of federalism" reducible to the private interests of individuals? Consider these questions as you read the following materials, which take up the issues of territorial jurisdiction and subject-matter jurisdiction. As you study the stumbling blocks that jurisdictional rules place in the way of single-forum aggregation, ask whether plaintiffs, defendants, or judges should ever be entitled to override the ordinary rules governing the chess match played out in the intersection of an adversarial system that allows parties to strive for private tactical advantage and a federal system that limits the powers of courts to adjudicate disputes.

A. LIMITATIONS ON AGGREGATION IMPOSED BY TERRITORIAL JURISDICTION

In a basic course on civil procedure, you were probably exposed to the concept of territorial jurisdiction. Most likely, you focused on whether a court in one jurisdiction can constitutionally exercise adjudicatory power over a defendant that the plaintiff wishes to join. This question goes to the heart of the meaning of a federal system of government, for the scope of a court's territorial jurisdiction over persons and property simultaneously acts to limit the power of any single government within the federal system, protects the sovereignty of other governments within the federal system, and defines an important freedom enjoyed by all citizens against the power of the government. But this question also has a practical dimension. As the last chapter discussed (*see supra* p. 208), a party is not bound by a judgment entered in a court that has not exercised jurisdiction over that party. Hence, in thinking about the joinder or aggregation of related cases, the rules of territorial jurisdiction are as foundational as the rules of party joinder or preclusion.

The rules of territorial jurisdiction are rife with distinctions, and thus can be studied in many ways. Perhaps the most common distinction made for analytical purposes is the difference between *in rem* and *in personam* jurisdiction. Traditionally, a court within whose borders a *res* was located had jurisdiction — to the exclusion of all other courts — over *in rem* cases involving that *res*. But few complex cases are *in rem* in nature. (The rules for *quasi in rem* proceedings are less simple. *See* Shaffer v. Heitner, 433 U.S. 186 (1977). Because few complex cases are *quasi in rem* in nature, we need not consider those further.) Most complex cases are *in personam*, and here the rules are more complicated.

Courts can exercise *in personam* (or personal) jurisdiction over the parties when (1) a statute or court rule authorizes the exercise and (2) this exercise is consistent with the United States Constitution (and, in state courts, the state's constitution). In particular, the Due Process Clauses of the Fifth Amendment (for federal-court exercises of personal jurisdiction) and the Fourteenth Amendment (for state-court exercises of personal jurisdiction) limit the power of courts to exercise jurisdiction over the parties. The Supreme Court and lower courts have developed a rich body of law specifying the scope of the statutory and constitutional limits. In brief, a court can exercise jurisdiction over a party in certain situations: when a party consents to jurisdiction, when the party is transitorily present within a state and is served with process while in the state, when a court has "general jurisdiction" over a party, and when a court has "specific jurisdiction" over a party. As a general rule in complex litigation, consent, transitory presence, and general jurisdiction will not give a court territorial jurisdiction over all the parties. For instance, a state can exercise general jurisdiction over a party who has continuous, significant, and ongoing contacts with that state. *See* Milliken v. Meyer, 311 U.S. 457 (1940). In most multiparty cases, however, no state has general jurisdiction over all the parties. Suppose that A, a citizen of Indiana, manufactures a part and sells it to B, a citizen of Virginia. B then assembles the part into a finished product, and sells it nationwide through retailers. Plaintiff C is a citizen of, and is injured in, New York. A and B have operations only in their home states. In this case, no state has general jurisdiction over all three parties; and, all the parties consent to jurisdiction in one state or can be served while transitorily there, these bases of jurisdiction are also inapplicable.

Hence, in most complex cases, specific *in personam* jurisdiction is the basis for a court's territorial jurisdiction over the parties. If the doctrine permits the broad exercise of jurisdiction over parties, territorial jurisdiction poses a lower barrier to single-forum aggregation. On the other hand, if it is narrow, territorial jurisdiction imposes a significant hurdle to the aggregation of related cases. Because specific jurisdiction is the critical issue in complex litigation, these materials focus almost exclusively on its breadth and limits.

Specific jurisdiction can be subdivided into two issues: jurisdiction over defendants and jurisdiction over plaintiffs. The question of jurisdiction over defendants is obvious: What limits does our federal system place on the power of a court to bind a defendant to its judgment when the defendant does not enjoy continuous, significant, and ongoing contacts with that forum? Jurisdiction over plaintiffs raises an issue that you may not have addressed in Civil Procedure. The reason is that, in a standard lawsuit, there is no issue of jurisdiction over plaintiffs; by filing suit in a particular court, plaintiffs are deemed to have consented to the jurisdiction of that court. As we saw in the last chapter, however, in certain circumstances courts can join plaintiffs on a mandatory basis or to preclude their later litigation of certain claims or issues. These plaintiffs have no more consented to the jurisdiction of the forum than the defendants. Should the same limits that are applied to defendants also apply to plaintiffs?

1. Personal Jurisdiction over Defendants

As mentioned above, a court's exercise of specific personal jurisdiction over a defendant requires both a statute or rule authorizing the exercise and fidelity to the Due Process Clause. On the latter question, the Supreme Court has been committed to a "minimum contacts" analysis since *International Shoe Co. v. Washington*, 326 U.S. 310 (1945). Perhaps the best hornbook summary of this approach can be found in *World-Wide Volkswagen Corp. v. Woodson*, 444 U.S. 286, 291-93 (1980):

> The Due Process Clause of the Fourteenth Amendment limits the power of a state court to render a valid personal judgment against a nonresident defendant. A judgment rendered in violation of due process is void in the rendering State and is not entitled to full faith and credit elsewhere. Due process requires that the defendant be given adequate notice of the suit, and be subject to the personal jurisdiction of the court, Int'l Shoe Co. v. Wash., 326 U.S. 310 (1945). . . .

> As has long been settled, and as we reaffirm today, a state court may exercise personal jurisdiction over a nonresident defendant only so long as there exist "minimum contacts" between the defendant and the forum State. The concept of minimum contacts, in turn, can be seen to perform two related, but distinguishable, functions. It protects the defendant against the burdens of litigating in a distant or inconvenient forum. And it acts to ensure that the States through their courts, do not reach out beyond the limits imposed on them by their status as coequal sovereigns in a federal system.

The protection against inconvenient litigation is typically described in terms of "reasonableness" or "fairness." We have said that the defendant's contacts with the forum State must be such that maintenance of the suit "does not offend 'traditional notions of fair play and substantial justice.'" . . . Implicit in this emphasis on reasonableness is the understanding that the burden on the defendant, while always a primary concern, will in an appropriate case be considered in light of other relevant factors, including the forum State's interest in adjudicating the dispute; the plaintiff's interest in obtaining convenient and effective relief, at least when that interest is not adequately protected by the plaintiff's power to choose the forum; the interstate judicial system's interest in obtaining the most efficient resolution of controversies; and the shared interest of the several States in furthering fundamental substantive social policies.

The limits imposed on state jurisdiction by the Due Process Clause, in its role as a guarantor against inconvenient litigation, have been substantially relaxed over the years. . . . [T]his trend is largely attributable to a fundamental transformation in the American economy
 . . . .

Nevertheless, we have never accepted the proposition that state lines are irrelevant for jurisdictional purposes, nor could we, and remain faithful to the principles of interstate federalism embodied in the Constitution. . . . The sovereignty of each State, in turn, implied a limitation on the sovereignty of all of its sister States — a limitation express or implicit in both the original scheme of the Constitution and the Fourteenth Amendment.

World-Wide Volkswagen suggested a two-step analysis for minimum contacts: first, ensure that no damage will be done to the federal structure as a result of the court's exercise of territorial jurisdiction; and second, ensure that the defendant will not be unfairly inconvenienced by the exercise of jurisdiction. The first step is sometimes referred to as the "sovereignty prong" or the "power prong"; the second step is referred to as the "convenience prong." *Cf.* Ins. Corp. of Ir. v. Compagnie des Bauxites de Guinée, 456 U.S. 694, 702 (1982) (recasting the sovereignty prong as an "individual liberty interest"). *World-Wide Volkswagen* indicated that the sovereignty prong has been fulfilled when the defendant "'purposefully avails itself of the privilege of conducting activities within the forum State.'" 444 U.S. at 297 (quoting Hanson v. Denckla, 357 U.S. 235, 253 (1958)). The convenience prong is determined by applying the five factors listed at the end of the third quoted paragraph above.

Neither *International Shoe, World-Wide Volkswagen*, nor any other Supreme Court cases involving specific jurisdiction arose in the context of burdensome repetitive litigation for which single-forum aggregation would be a fair and efficient response. In light of the values that it seeks to protect, ought the doctrine of specific personal jurisdiction be altered to accommodate the needs of complex litigation? Consider the following case.

SIMON V. PHILIP MORRIS, INC.

86 F. Supp. 2d 95 (E.D.N.Y. 2000)

■ WEINSTEIN, Senior District Judge. . . .

This case poses the question: can a foreign national holding company always shield itself against a mass tort suit in New York? In this instance it cannot. It may not hide behind narrow jurisdictional concepts created for another day when its own acts and those of its co-conspirators have allegedly caused great harm in this state.

Plaintiffs sue various tobacco companies and affiliated organizations in a nationwide smoker personal injury class action. They allege that for decades the tobacco industry, in the face of what it knew was overwhelming evidence of the addictiveness of nicotine and of the adverse health consequences of smoking, has conspired to deceive the American public, including the plaintiffs.

B.A.T. Industries, p.l.c. ("BAT"), the British holding company parent of United States defendant, Brown & Williamson Tobacco Corp. ("B & W"), has moved to dismiss for lack of personal jurisdiction. It claims that it is a passive stockholding parent corporation with no connection to the fraud and conspiracy alleged by the plaintiffs. . . .

[The district court first held that the plaintiffs bore the burden of proving the existence of personal jurisdiction.]

III. FACTS

A. *BAT's Organization*

BAT is a holding company based in London, England and incorporated under the laws of England and Wales. Its existence dates to 1976, when it became the controlling parent corporation of the British American Tobacco Company, Ltd. ("BATCo"). BAT currently has over five hundred subsidiaries in some forty countries primarily engaged in the tobacco and financial services businesses. The majority of its revenues derive from its tobacco-related activities.

BAT bills itself as "the world's most international cigarette manufacturer" owning the leading cigarette brand in over thirty different markets. In 1995, it sold 670 billion cigarettes, achieving a 12.4 percent share of the world market. A substantial percentage of these cigarettes were purchased by United States smokers.

In public filings and promotional documents, BAT sometimes refers to itself as the "BAT Group" . . . .

BATCo is a United Kingdom-based corporation that sells tobacco products and conducts tobacco-related scientific research. From 1902 until its 1976 acquisition by BAT, it was the controlling parent company of the BAT Group, which consisted of hundreds of tobacco subsidiaries. It acquired the stock of B & W in 1927. . . . BATCo produced over 300 cigarette brands worldwide and produced the leading cigarette in forty countries. Its most profitable area of operation was North America. . . .

B & W is a Delaware Corporation based in Louisville Kentucky. It is the third largest cigarette company in the United States market. Its domestic brands include Kool, Carlton, Pall Mall and Viceroy. B & W exports such leading international brands as Kent, Lucky Strike, Barclay and Capri. Since 1976, B & W has been an indirect wholly-owned subsidiary of BAT. . . .

C. *BAT's New York Contacts*

BAT has no New York office, mailing address, phone listing, or bank account and pays no New York taxes. It does not directly own, use or possess any New York real estate.

BAT neither manufactures nor sells cigarettes. These functions are carried out by its tobacco subsidiaries, one of which is B & W. B & W currently has a United States market share of eighteen percent. Since 1987 the BAT Group has earned billions in pre-tax dollar profits from its United States tobacco operations. While the percentage of these profits ultimately traceable to New York is unclear, B & W's strong market presence and the size of the New York population strongly support the inference of substantial New York cigarette sales roughly proportional to the percentage of New York residents in the total United States population — somewhere in the neighborhood of seven percent. Thus, for purposes of this jurisdiction motion, it can be inferred that BAT's earnings in New York through B & W in the last decade were many millions of dollars.

Some of BAT's major institutional investors have been based in New York. BAT Board Members and other representatives have visited New York frequently in connection with BAT's solicitation of investors.

D. *Tobacco Industry Conspiracy*

Plaintiffs allege that BAT participated in a conspiracy to manufacture hazardous products and deceive American consumers about the adverse health consequences of using them. The available evidence of such a conspiracy is substantial. . . .

. . . [I]t was not until the early to mid-1950's, when a series of important studies linking smoking to cancer in humans and animals was published, that the health consequences of smoking became a public issue in the United States. Reacting, the United States tobacco companies jointly formed the Tobacco Industry Research Committee ("TIRC"). A January 1954 newspaper advertisement published nationwide announced TIRC's formation. Entitled "A Frank Statement to Cigarette Smokers," the advertisement was signed by the heads of most of the major tobacco companies, including B & W. This original tobacco industry "position paper" [played] down the connection between cigarettes and disease . . . .

The documents reveal that TIRC was the product of the tobacco industry's public relations, legal and political needs rather than of any concern for public health. A 1973 memorandum by B & W's general counsel, Ernest Pepples, describes the multiple functions of TIRC, later renamed the Council for Tobacco Research ("CTR") . . . .

Four years after it created TIRC, the tobacco industry established the Tobacco Institute ("TI") as its lobbying and public relations arm. TI has served as the industry's "focal point for criticism of research that indicates a connection between smoking and health." . . .

Available documents indicate that the industry, acting as a whole and with the implicit cooperation of all its members, reacted to the rising tide of public concern resulting from the issuance of these reports by embarking on an advertising campaign designed, among other things, to discredit the evidence of a causal link between smoking and disease. . . .

Individual companies participated in the public relations effort to undermine the scientific evidence on causation. In 1969, for example, a series of advertisements was developed for B & W focusing on the lack of proof of causation and the individual's right to smoke. . . .

In addition to research grants awarded by its Scientific Advisory Board, the CTR funded "special projects" designed largely to generate research data and witnesses for use in defending lawsuits and opposing tobacco regulation. . . .

E. *New York as a Situs of the Tobacco Industry Conspiracy*

Multiple events and actors link the tobacco industry conspiracy alleged by the plaintiffs to New York. First, Philip Morris, Inc. and Lorillard Corp., co-defendants and alleged co-conspirators of BAT, have their principal places of business in New York City. . . .

The available evidence implicates Lorillard and Philip Morris in industry activities aimed at promoting the deceptive notion of a smoking and health scientific "controversy." Both companies have been members of CTR from its inception. . . .

CTR and TI, major vehicles for perpetuating the tobacco industry's stance on smoking and health, were both incorporated in New York. CTR's offices in New York City generated critical data with which to dispute and deflect attention from the evidence linking smoking to lung cancer, heart disease and other illnesses.

[Hill & Knowlton ("H & K"),] the public relations firm instrumental in the formation of both CTR and TI, was . . . deeply involved in the operation of both these organizations. H & K is a New York corporation with its principal place of business in New York.

[Jacob Medinger & Finnegan ("JM & F")], the law firm which . . . and played an important role in CTR "special projects" is located in New York City. Many "special projects" . . . funding recommendations were written

on JM & F's New York letterhead. Approvals of funds were transmitted to
the firm in New York.

F. *BAT's Tortious Conduct in Furtherance of the Conspiracy*

BAT contends that the conduct complained of in the instant case is that
of its subsidiaries and that the plaintiffs have produced no evidence of
independent wrongdoing on its part. The plaintiffs argue that BAT itself
participated in the tortious conduct that forms the basis of their suit.
Specifically, they allege that BAT instructed its subsidiaries to perpetuate
a fraudulent smoking and health position and prohibited them from
designing and manufacturing a less harmful product even though they had
the technical capability to do so.   Plaintiffs further allege that BAT
promoted the enhancement of the nicotine content of its subsidiaries'
products.

[The court discussed the evidence that BAT or BATCo asserted the
position that there was a "genuine scientific controversy" respecting the
adverse health effects of smoking, even though it had significant evidence
from BATCo research that this was not true. Likewise, evidence existed
that BAT's Chairman suppressed development of a safer cigarette being
developed by one of BAT's subsidiaries because "in attempting to develop
a 'safe' cigarette you are, by implication in danger of being interpreted as
accepting that the current product is 'unsafe' and this is not a position that
I think we should take." The court also found "ample evidence in the record
from which it can be inferred that tobacco with higher nicotine content and
tobacco treatment processes that enhanced nicotine delivery were
encouraged."   Finally, it noted that, due to " B & W's greater vulnerability
to product liability litigation," BAT and B & W "appear to have worked
together to prevent damaging smoking health information generated by
BAT Group research from reaching United States product liability plaintiffs
and the general American public."

[BAT argued that many of these actions were taken by employees of
their subsidiaries.] [I]n the absence of an agency relationship or a basis for
piercing the corporate veil, [the actions of BATCo scientists] may arguably
not be attributed to BAT. Nevertheless, the knowledge of BATCo and its
research and development staff is properly imputed to BAT. BATCo
conducted Group tobacco research for its hundreds of subsidiaries for
decades before its 1976 acquisition by BAT. The fact that during the first
few years of BAT's existence, its Board and the BATCo Board were
essentially identical, and that BAT's first two Chairmen were former
BATCo Chairmen, creates an especially strong basis for ascribing to BAT
BATCo's knowledge that smoking causes human disease. . . .

G. *BAT's Extensive Participation in the Marketing and in Research*
and Development of Cigarettes

The record contains evidence of BAT's involvement in numerous aspects
of the marketing, research and development of BAT Group cigarettes. . . .

IV. NEW YORK STATUTORY BASES FOR JURISDICTION

In a diversity suit, personal jurisdiction is determined in accordance with the law of the forum state. *But cf.* AMERICAN LAW INSTITUTE, COMPLEX LITIGATION: STATUTORY RECOMMENDATIONS AND ANALYSIS § 3.08 cmt. *b*, at 150 (1994) [("ALI, COMPLEX LITIGATION")] (given that complex litigation "is by definition a national phenomenon . . . it would be odd to allow the efficient resolution of complex diversity cases to depend on the reach of a particular state's long arm statute"). Plaintiffs assert . . . that BAT may be subjected to suit in New York on the basis of both systematic and continuous New York contacts, *see* N.Y. CPLR 301, and specific acts by BAT and by its agents and co-conspirators, *see* N.Y. CPLR 302(a)(1), (2), (3). . . .

A. *Conspiracy Theory of Jurisdiction*

1. *Law*

New York's CPLR 302(a)(2) confers jurisdiction over a nondomiciliary who "in person or through an agent . . . commits a tortious act within the state." To support the exercise of jurisdiction under this section, the act in question must be "purposeful," and there must be some "articulable nexus" between it and the claim asserted.

The term "agent" for purposes of CPLR 302(a)(2) has been read to include co-conspirators. . . .

To establish jurisdiction over a nonresident defendant on the basis of the New York acts of a co-conspirator, the plaintiff must: (1) establish a prima facie case of conspiracy; (2) allege specific facts warranting the inference that the defendant was a member of the conspiracy; and (3) demonstrate the commission of a tortious act in New York during, and pursuant to, the conspiracy. . . .

2. *Application of Law to Facts*

First, it should be noted that New York state and federal courts have recognized the applicability of the conspiracy theory of jurisdiction to BAT in other tobacco litigations.

[The court found that the evidence satisfied the prima facie elements of a civil conspiracy, and that some of the acts of BAT's co-conspirators occurred in New York.]

In sum, plaintiffs have met the requirements for the exercise of conspiracy-based personal jurisdiction over BAT.

. . . Nothing in [the language of CPLR 302(a)(2)] either expressly or impliedly excludes claims connected to injuries incurred outside the state. The focus of the section is on the locus of the act not that of the resulting injury. Its aim is to subject to the personal jurisdiction of the New York courts those non-resident defendants who engage in tortious conduct in the state. The claims of all proposed class members may be said, at least in part, to "arise from" tortious acts committed in New York. Thus, all of the plaintiffs-whether resident in or outside New York-may rely on CPLR 302(a)(2).

B. *Other Theories of Personal Jurisdiction*

Because the case for conspiracy jurisdiction is so strong, detailed consideration of plaintiffs' other theories supporting the exercise of personal jurisdiction is unnecessary. It bears noting, however, that jurisdiction may also be appropriate under CPLR 301 and 302(a)(3)(ii).

1. *CPLR 302(a)(3)(ii)*

CPLR 302(a)(3)(ii) provides for personal jurisdiction over a nondomiciliary who commits an out-of-state tortious act causing in-state injury in a case arising out of that act, provided that the nondomiciliary "expects or should reasonably expect the act to have consequences in the state and derives substantial revenue from interstate or international commerce . . . ." The exercise of jurisdiction under this section requires a showing that (1) the defendant committed a tortious act outside of New York, (2) this act caused injury in New York to a person or property, (3) defendant reasonably should have expected this act to have New York consequences, and (4) defendant earns substantial revenue from interstate or international commerce. Each of these elements has been established.

For purposes of the instant case, each plaintiff's injury may be deemed to have occurred in the state where his or her damages were felt. *See* In re DES Cases, 789 F. Supp. 552, 570 (E.D.N.Y. 1992).

Those plaintiffs who cannot independently meet the "injury in New York" requirement may rely on the factual and jurisdictional links of proposed class members who were injured here. The New York class members may be considered the jurisdictional representatives of the entire nationwide class in much the same way as the named plaintiffs are its citizenship representatives for purposes of determining diversity competence of the federal court.

2. *CPLR 301*

Jurisdiction theory and practice, like other areas of the law, evolve to meet political, economic, social, and technological changes. *See, e.g.,* Int'l Shoe Co. v. Wash., 326 U.S. 310 (1945).

The common law and equitable continuing development of traditional jurisdictional bases argue in support of the exercise of jurisdiction pursuant to CPLR 301. This provision permits the court to exercise "such jurisdiction . . . *as might have been exercised heretofore.*" ([E]mphasis added). In considering the meaning of the CPLR, "the drafters' stated 'objectives' are well worth consideration." Chief among these were "[t]o make it possible, with very limited exceptions, for a litigant in the New York courts to take full advantage of the state's constitutional power over persons." Limitations in CPLR 302 did not change that primary thrust. . . .

One relevant well accepted concept strongly favoring the exercise of jurisdiction under CPLR 301 is basic fairness of the forum choice as between plaintiff and defendant. Another recognizable relevant factor would be the interest of New York in reducing transaction costs to its residents in mass tort cases by bringing together in one case all related New York and non-New York plaintiffs and all defendants necessary to the fair disposition of the litigation.

V. DUE PROCESS

A. *Law*

The Due Process Clause of the Fourteenth Amendment has been interpreted as limiting state courts' power to exercise personal jurisdiction over nonresident defendants. *See, e.g.*, Burger King Corp. v. Rudzewicz, 471 U.S. 462, 471-72 (1985); Helicopteros Nacionales de Colombia, S.A. v. Hall, 466 U.S. 408, 412-14 (1984). One statement of the current due process test for personal jurisdiction requires considerations of two elements. The first prong of the inquiry — the "minimum contacts" prong — has been described as a "fair warning" requirement. It "focuses on 'the relationship among the defendant, the forum and the litigation.'" Keeton v. Hustler Magazine, Inc., 465 U.S. 770, 775 (1984) (quoting Shaffer v. Heitner, 433 U.S. 186, 204 (1977)). Where the "general" jurisdiction of the court is invoked, the plaintiff must establish the defendant's "continuous and systematic general business contacts with the forum." *Helicopteros*, 466 U.S. at 416. Where "specific" jurisdiction is asserted, the "minimum contacts" requirement is satisfied by a showing that the defendant "purposefully directed" his activities at forum residents and that the suit arises out of those activities. *See Burger King*, 471 U.S. at 472. . . .

The second phase of the due process inquiry assesses the reasonableness of exercising jurisdiction once "minimum contacts" have been established. *See id.* at 476-77.

The strengths of the showings required to satisfy the "minimum contacts" and "reasonableness" prongs are inversely related. The more reasonable the assertion of jurisdiction, the weaker the defendant-forum links necessary support it. *See id.* at 477. By the same token, where activities have been purposefully directed toward state residents, the defendant "must present a compelling case that the presence of some other considerations would render jurisdiction unreasonable." *Id.* at 477.

1. *Minimum Contacts*

a. *Membership in a Conspiracy*

Whether the forum contacts of an in-state actor may be attributed to an out-of-state co-conspirator for due process purposes or whether the latter must independently satisfy the "minimum contacts" requirement is open to question. While some New York courts have taken the latter approach, others have dispensed with the due process inquiry where conspiracy-based jurisdiction is asserted. The attributional view has been criticized by a number of commentators. Yet, as one court of appeals has noted, it is not clear why personal jurisdiction should be an exception to the general rule of attributing the acts of one conspirator within the scope of the conspiracy to the other conspirators. Which is the correct view need not be decided here since BAT's New York contacts far surpass any due process requirements.

"Minimum contacts" . . . are established by showing that the defendant "purposefully avail[ed] itself of the privilege of conducting activities within the forum State." Hanson v. Denckla, 357 U.S. 235, 253 (1958). The analysis of those New York courts that have addressed the constitutionality of conspiracy jurisdiction has centered on the defendant's awareness of the commission of acts pursuant to the conspiracy in New York. . . .

New York acts occurring prior to the defendant's having joined the conspiracy may also provide a sufficient link to the state.

b. *Intentional Tortious Acts Aimed at the Forum*

Jurisdiction based on the in-state effects of intentional out-of-state forum-directed conduct was held to be consistent with the requirements of the Due Process Clause in *Calder v. Jones*, 465 U.S. 783 (1984). In *Calder*, a professional performer who lived and worked in California brought suit in connection with a National Enquirer article alleging libel, invasion of privacy and intentional infliction of emotional distress. The National Enquirer is a Florida corporation with its principle place of business in Florida, where the article in question was written and edited. Petitioners, the writer and editor of the article, argued that its foreseeable circulation in California, a process in which they had no input and over which they had no control, was an insufficient basis for the exercise of personal jurisdiction. . . . The Court disagreed, distinguishing for purposes of the minimum contacts analysis, between "mere untargeted negligence" and "intentional, and allegedly tortious, actions . . . expressly aimed at California." . . .

Jurisdiction under *Calder*'s "effects" test is not limited to the libel context in which it originated. The doctrine has been applied in a variety of cases involving deliberate wrongdoing.

2. *Reasonableness*

Once it is determined that minimum contacts exist, the reasonableness of exercising jurisdiction must be assessed. Five factors enter into the analysis:

(1) the burden on the defendant;

(2) the interest of the forum state in adjudicating the controversy;

(3) the interest of the plaintiff in obtaining convenient and effective relief;

(4) the interest of the interstate judicial system in obtaining the most efficient resolution of the dispute; and

(5) the shared interest of the states in furthering fundamental social policies.

See Asahi [Metal Indus. Co. v. Superior Court, 480 U.S. 102, 113 (1987)]; *see also Burger King*, 471 U.S. at 477; World-Wide Volkswagen Corp. v. Woodson, 444 U.S. 286, 292 (1980).

Where personal jurisdiction is sought over an alien defendant, consideration of "the procedural and substantive policies of other nations whose interests are affected by the assertion of jurisdiction by the [state] court," substitutes for the final two factors, and "the Federal interest in Government's foreign relations polices" also may be a factor. *Asahi*, 480 U.S. at 115.

3. *Adaptation of Due Process to Mass Tort Context*

The New York Civil Practice Law and Rules and the Federal Rules of Civil Procedure require that both state and federal jurisdictional provisions be construed to promote fairness and litigation efficiencies. These goals are impeded in multistate mass tort litigation by continued reliance on a defendant-forum territorial nexus as a precondition for the exercise of personal jurisdiction. *See generally In re DES Cases*, 789 F. Supp. [at] 574-577; *see also* [ALI, COMPLEX LITIGATION,] § 3.08 cmt. *b*, at 151 (the "minimum contacts" requirement "act[s] as an impediment to achieving the most efficient consolidation of complex cases"). A more workable test is needed. *Cf.*, *e.g.*, Phillips Petroleum Co. v. Shutts, 472 U.S. 797, 811-12 (1985) [*infra* p. 276] ("minimum contacts" not required to bind absent members of plaintiff class so long as they were provided with "minimal procedural due process protections" consisting of "best practicable notice," a right to opt out and a showing of adequate representation by named plaintiffs).

Recognition of the unique jurisdictional challenges posed by mass litigations has led the American Law Institute to propose adoption of a national-contacts personal jurisdiction standard for complex litigation. *See* ALI, COMPLEX LITIGATION § 3.08; *see also id.* cmt. *e* (likely constitutionality of "a federal national-contacts long-arm statute for use in complex cases"). Adoption of the ALI's proposal would doubtless present a significant improvement since it would enlarge the size of the forum by reference to which "minimum contacts" are assessed. But the retention of a territorial nexus requirement — even where the relevant territory is the entire country — would still permit foreign defendants to organize their affairs in such a way as to avoid jurisdiction in the United States even where federal interest in a dispute is great, and subjecting the defendant to suit here would not be unduly burdensome. Adaptation of existing precedent is required if the jurisdictional obstacles preventing the effective adjudication of multistate or multination mass torts are to be overcome.

The idea of defendant-forum contacts as a jurisdictional prerequisite was developed in *Pennoyer v. Neff*, 95 U.S. 714 (1877), which held that state courts could exercise personal jurisdiction only over those defendants who either consented to jurisdiction or were present in the state. This restrictive view was justified as a necessary accommodation of, and check upon, the sovereignty interests of the several states. . . .

The doctrinal twists and turns necessitated by such a rigid conception of due process limits on personal jurisdiction culminated in the somewhat relaxed "minimum contacts" formulation of *International Shoe Co. v. Washington*, 326 U.S. 310, 316 (1945). The *International Shoe* Court grounded its due process test on considerations of both fairness and state sovereignty. This dual justification also finds expression in subsequent Supreme Court cases. *See, e.g., World-Wide Volkswagen*, 444 U.S. [at] 294.

More recent Supreme Court cases appear to reject sovereignty concerns as a justification for due process limits on personal jurisdiction, positing the protection of individual liberty interests as their primary rationale. In *Insurance Corp. of Ireland v. Compagnie des Bauxites de Guinée*, [456 U.S. 694, 703-03 (1982),] for example, the Court stated:

> The personal jurisdiction requirement recognizes and protects an individual liberty interest. It represents a restriction on judicial power not as a matter of sovereignty, but as a matter of individual liberty.

When jurisdictional due process is analyzed in terms of the liberty interests of absent defendants, retention of a defendant-forum territorial nexus as a jurisdictional prerequisite becomes difficult to justify. To the extent that individual liberty interests are protected by fair warning of possible assertions of jurisdiction, it is the forum state's jurisdictional law interpreted in light of the Due Process Clause, rather than defendant-forum contacts, which provides notice that a defendant should reasonably anticipate defending a suit in that state. *See In re DES Cases*, 789 F. Supp. at 571.

To the extent that the imposition of an undue burden on out-of-state defendants is a concern, it must be appreciated that defendant-forum contacts are a notoriously weak indicator of the inconvenience of being forced to litigate in a foreign forum. The inadequacy of purely geographically based protections of absent defendants is particularly apparent in the modern information age, in which technological developments have dramatically decreased the difficulties of long distance litigation. In mass cases, defendant-forum contacts are even less relevant to the question of a defendant's burden and inconvenience. Limitations on the scope of discovery required by Federal Rule of Civil Procedure 26(b)(2)(iii), the use of local counsel, and collaboration among defendants significantly reduce the cost of defending these litigations.

A modified due process standard for mass torts was explicated in *In re DES Cases*. It replaced territorial contacts with state interest as the constitutional touchstone of *in personam* jurisdiction and limited the second step of the inquiry to a hardship assessment:

I. The court must first determine if the forum state has an appreciable interest in the litigation, i.e., whether the litigation raises serious issues whose resolution would be affected by, or have a probable impact on the vindication of, policies expressed in the substantive, procedural or remedial laws of the forum. If there is an appreciable state interest, the assertion of jurisdiction is prima facie constitutional.

II. Once a prima facie case is made, the assertion of jurisdiction will be considered constitutional unless, given the actual circumstances of the case, the defendant is unable to mount a defense in the forum state without suffering relatively substantial hardship.

Evidence to be considered in determining the defendant's relative hardship includes, inter alia, (1) the defendant's available assets; (2) whether the defendant has or is engaged in substantial interstate commerce; (3) whether the defendant is being represented by an indemnitor or is sharing the cost of the defense with an indemnitor or co-defendant; (4) the comparative hardship defendant will incur in defending the suit in another forum; and (5) the comparative hardship to the plaintiff if the case were dismissed or transferred for lack of jurisdiction.

The constitutionality of exercising jurisdiction over BAT in this mass tobacco litigation may also be analyzed under this standard.

B. *Application of Law to Facts*

. . . [T]he facts all point to forum personal jurisdiction over BAT.

1. *Minimum Contacts*

The evidence of BAT's contacts with New York is more than sufficient to support the exercise of personal jurisdiction. When BAT joined the alleged tobacco industry conspiracy it either knew or should have known that substantial acts in furtherance had already occurred in New York and that more were likely to take place. Since a number of the large tobacco companies and the CTR were headquartered in the state, additional New York conspiratorial conduct was foreseeable. Jurisdiction may be asserted in connection with the claims of the entire proposed class since each plaintiff's claim in some sense "arises out of or relates to" the New York acts of BAT's co-conspirators.

The requirement of "minimum contacts" is also satisfied by the New York effects of what could be construed as intentional and purposeful acts by BAT in furtherance of the alleged conspiracy to mislead and addict the plaintiffs. That BAT trained its sights on a larger, more diffuse target — smokers and their families in all fifty states as opposed to only one — does not render the "effects" test inapplicable. *Calder*'s reasoning does not hinge on the fact that only one plaintiff living in only one state was involved. The main point of the case is its distinction between intentional and negligent wrongdoing for purposes of assessing minimum contacts.

BAT is alleged to have directed identical deliberate tortious conduct at the residents of every state in the union. In doing so, it participated in the creation of a general nationwide population of addicted smokers whose claims are, in that sense, all related to each other and to the conduct directed at each of them in their home states and all other states. Thus personal jurisdiction over BAT extends to cover all of the plaintiffs' claims since all may be said to "arise out of or relate to" BAT's contacts with New York. Even if this were not so, the jurisdictional links of those plaintiffs injured in New York are sufficient, as already pointed out, to support jurisdiction in connection with the claims of the remainder of the proposed class. Once jurisdiction over part of the case and the defendant is acquired by a state, it is up to that state, not the defendant, to decide how much of the total controversy affecting other states and residents of other states it will try in one litigation. From the point of view of prospective litigants and the world at large, the United States court system is an integrated and cooperative entity. That the reality often does not measure up to that perception cannot be used as an excuse for a defendant's utilization of jurisdiction theory to manipulate itself out of an effective litigation process in a state which appropriately entertains jurisdiction over the subject matter and the person.

Finally, it should be noted that BAT, through its substantial contribution to the marketing, research and development of its subsidiaries' products may be considered a de facto designer of cigarettes. As such, jurisdiction may be exercised over it on a stream of commerce theory. *See Asahi*, 480 U.S. at [112] (listing "designing a product for th[e] state's market" as an example of "additional conduct" beyond placement of products into the stream of commerce that could satisfy "minimum contacts").

2. *Reasonableness*

Those cases in which jurisdiction is so unreasonable as to defeat a showing of "minimum contacts" are rare. *See Burger King*, 471 U.S. at 477 (defendant must present a "compelling case" of unreasonableness in such cases). . . . Reasonableness considerations militate heavily in favor of the exercise of personal jurisdiction over BAT. First, no appreciable hardship would be suffered by BAT's defending in New York rather than in England. BAT is not some "mom and pop" tobacco shop in the suburbs of London, but a multibillion dollar multinational enterprise whose executives regularly travel to New York seeking capital and for other business reasons. It has all the resources and connections necessary for it to adequately defend this suit in New York with relative ease.

New York has a strong interest in providing relief for its injured citizens and in discouraging further harmful conduct from being directed at the state. Its interest in preventing the commission of tortious acts within its borders, whether the injured parties are New Yorkers or residents of other states, is equally pressing. . . .

Lastly, New York has a decided interest in a comprehensive resolution of related claims in a single litigation against this defendant and related defendants. It shares this interest with other states. Providing an efficient, unitary forum for the resolution of all smoker personal injury claims will benefit plaintiffs, the interstate judicial system and the defendants by eliminating the need for repetitious litigation around the country and abroad.

The interests of all the plaintiffs, whether New Yorkers or non-New Yorkers, in obtaining convenient and effective relief is obvious. New Yorkers and other Americans should not be forced to sue some defendants in the United States and then sue others in England, repeating the same evidence and theories at great expense and inconvenience. Plaintiffs' interest in litigating here is heightened by the fact that certain features of the English legal system, such as the lack of a right to a jury trial, could work to their disadvantage.

The last factor to be considered, the procedural and substantive policies of other nations whose interests are implicated by the exercise of jurisdiction, does not disfavor a finding of personal jurisdiction in New York. While it is hazardous for an American court to interpret the law of other countries, subjecting BAT, an English corporation, to suit in the United States does not appear to violate any substantive policies of English law. The law of England recognizes product liability causes of action.

Whether English procedural policies would be offended by the assertion of jurisdiction over BAT is unclear. For example, it may be that a money judgement in the instant case would be unenforceable in England. . . . [T]hose seeking to enforce judgments rendered by [United States] courts must bring a common law action in contract to collect a debt, claiming the United States judgment as the debt owed. Under the applicable common law rules, for a foreign judgment to be enforceable the court that rendered it would have to have had a satisfactory basis for exercising personal jurisdiction over the defendant from the point of view of the English court. This condition will apparently only be met if the defendant was present in the forum at the time the action was instituted, voluntarily appeared in the forum court, or contractually submitted to the forum court's jurisdiction. . . . It should be noted that regardless of the enforceability of an American judgment against BAT in an English court, such a judgment might well be enforceable in one of the myriad countries in which BAT owns assets.

England is not the only nation whose policies could be impinged upon by the exercise of personal jurisdiction over BAT in New York. The interests of the European Union are also affected, as are those of the numerous countries where BAT and its subsidiaries operate. Any assertion of jurisdiction over the person of a foreign entity has potential international implications.

These global concerns are usefully assessed by considering, to the extent practicable on this motion, how the question of jurisdiction over an American or other foreign corporation alleged to have inflicted large-scale tortious injury in a way similar to BAT might be resolved under international and regional jurisdictional treaties as well as under the jurisdictional law of individual nations. A preliminary survey of the law in this area suggests that, at least in this instance, jurisdiction would not be denied over an American version of BAT. . . .

With regard to the jurisdictional law of individual states, a . . . somewhat superficial view of the jurisdictional law of some of our major trading partners will suffice. England's civil procedure rules provide for jurisdiction in connection with tort claims if "the damage was sustained, or resulted from an act committed, within the jurisdiction." To the extent that this provision would subject an American company to suit in England on the basis of injuries suffered there, reciprocal jurisdiction over BAT would seem to be reasonable. [The court then found that "neither France nor Japan would deny jurisdiction over an American BAT analogue."]

. . . There is no persuasive argument of mutuality, of foreign policy, or of comity with other nations suggesting that jurisdiction should be denied in the instant case. Defendant has not met its burden of proving that the exercise of jurisdiction would be unreasonable.

3. Mass Torts Due Process Standard

Finally, jurisdiction can be asserted under the mass due process standard explicated in such cases as *In re DES Cases*. New York's interest in the dispute is intense, and the burden on BAT is minimal compared to the difficulty of the plaintiffs' litigating in England.

VI. CONCLUSION

The facts and law provide several bases for exercising personal jurisdiction over the defendant. Any other result would be contrary to developing jurisdictional doctrine in this country and the Federal Rules of Civil Procedure and New York's CPLR. It would substantially increase the burdens on all the other litigants as well as our courts. Considerations of fairness and due process further support denial of defendant BAT's motion to dismiss for lack of personal jurisdiction.

Notes

1. *Simon*, a long and rich opinion, was written by the Honorable Jack Weinstein, who is one of the great scholars and jurists in the field of complex litigation. (We read one of Judge Weinstein's briefer opinions in the last chapter (*see supra* p. 134), and we will encounter a number more in the rest of this book.) We edited *Simon* heavily, while trying to retain the main lines of the argument and some of the opinion's nuances.

Although BAT might beg to disagree, *Simon* is an intellectual *tour de force*. It tries to remain faithful to the law of personal jurisdiction handed down by the Supreme Court, while simultaneously achieving Judge Weinstein's goals of (1) aggregating tobacco litigation in one American courtroom and (2) advocating for a very different approach to personal jurisdiction in mass-tort litigation — an approach he first proposed in *In re DES Cases*, 789 F. Supp. 552, 570 (E.D.N.Y. 1992).

Before we come to the merits of Judge Weinstein's critique, let us examine some of the issues that the opinion raises.

2.   To begin, you might wonder why the personal-jurisdiction law of New York applied to the case, given that *Simon* was filed in federal court. The answer is Fed. R. Civ. P. 4(k)(1)(A), which requires that federal courts can exercise personal jurisdiction only over a defendant "who is subject to the jurisdiction of a court of general jurisdiction in the state where the district is located."

Rule 4(k) contains two important exceptions to this rule, although neither was implicated on the facts of *Simon*. First, broader service is available "when authorized by a federal statute." Fed. R. Civ. P. 4(k)(1)(C). A number of federal statutes permit "nationwide service of process," which means that a federal court in Maine could exercise personal jurisdiction over a defendant located in Hawai'i. Nationwide-service-of-process statutes that are regularly implicated in complex litigation include 15 U.S.C. § 22 (Clayton Act cases); 15 U.S.C. § 78aa (securities actions); 18 U.S.C. § 1965(b) (RICO actions); 28 U.S.C. § 2361 (statutory interpleader); and 29 U.S.C. § 1451(d) (ERISA actions).

Second, Rule 4(k)(2) permits nationwide service of process when (1) the plaintiff is asserting a federal-question claim, (2) the defendant is not subject to the personal jurisdiction of any state court, and (3) "exercising jurisdiction is consistent with the United States Constitution." Rule 4(k)(2) overrode *Omni Capital International v. Rudolf Wolff & Co.*, 484 U.S. 97 (1987), in which the Court refused to allow nationwide service of process to fill in the gap created when a defendant on a federal-question claim lacked sufficient contacts with any state. In recent years, Rule 4(k)(2) has received its most noteworthy use in mass-tort cases seeking to assert jurisdiction over foreign terrorists and their alleged supporters. *See* Mwani v. bin Laden, 417 F.3d 1 (D.C. Cir. 2005); In re Terrorist Attacks on September 11, 2001, 349 F. Supp. 2d 765 (S.D.N.Y. 2005).

Although the Supreme Court has never determined the scope of the due-process limits on nationwide service of process, it is often thought that such service is constitutional if a defendant has minimum contacts with the United States as a whole. *Mwani*, 417 F.3d at 11; Bd. of Trustees, Sheet Metal Workers' Nat'l Pension Fund v. Elite Erectors, Inc., 212 F.3d 1031, 1035-36 (7th Cir. 2000). But some courts have held that due process requires the defendant to have some connection with the forum court. NGS Am., Inc. v. Jefferson, 218 F.3d 519, 524 n.5 (6th Cir. 2000); Peay v. BellSouth Med. Assistance Plan, 205 F.3d 1206, 1211 (10th Cir. 2000).

3. Because their power is limited by their geographical boundaries, no state legislature or state court can create a rule of nationwide service of process. Moreover, many of the nationwide-service-of-process statutes provide for exclusive federal jurisdiction, so state courts cannot exercise such jurisdiction. Moreover, some statutes permit only federal courts to exercise nationwide service of process. *See* 28 U.S.C. § 2361 (giving authority only to "a district court"); Kelly v. McKesson HBOC, Inc., 2002 WL 88939, at *19 (Del. Super. Jan. 17, 2002) (holding that the nationwide service of process authorized by 15 U.S.C. § 77v "is not available to [plaintiffs] if they choose to pursue their securities act litigation in a state proceeding"). This fact is another reason that federal courts are often seen as a better forum for aggregating related litigation than state courts.

4. Assuming that nationwide service of process is unavailable, then a court can assert personal jurisdiction over a defendant only when the defendant has contacts with the state in which the court is located. As *Simon* says, these contacts can either be so pervasive and continuous that general jurisdiction exists, or they can be less systematic but nonetheless sufficiently related to the plaintiff's claim that specific jurisdiction is appropriate. Put differently, specific jurisdiction requires that the lawsuit have some connection to the defendant's contacts with the state.

In *Simon* this fact created a problem. *Simon* was a class action whose members came from all across the country. The usual rule is that a court must possess jurisdiction over the defendant with respect to each claim asserted by each plaintiff. *See* 4A CHARLES ALAN WRIGHT & ARTHUR R. MILLER, FEDERAL PRACTICE AND PROCEDURE § 1069.7 (3d ed. 2002) ("[A] plaintiff ... must secure personal jurisdiction over a defendant with respect to each claim she asserts."). Some of the *Simon* plaintiffs were not from New York, had never purchased cigarettes or smoked in New York, and had no connection to New York. In what sense, therefore, could their claims be related to BAT's contacts with New York?

One response to this problem would be to argue that BAT had such a pervasive presence in New York (either itself or through its agents) that New York had general jurisdiction over BAT. A principal Supreme Court case regarding general jurisdiction is *Helicopteros Nacionales de Colombia, S.A. v. Hall*, 466 U.S. 408 (1984). *Simon*'s citations to *Helicopteros* suggest that the court was trying to characterize BAT's contacts as sufficiently pervasive to justify general jurisdiction, but in the end *Simon* does not place much weight on this form of personal jurisdiction. Therefore, jurisdiction over BAT was specific in nature. That fact left *Simon* with a difficult question to answer: In what way were BAT's contacts with New York related to the injuries suffered by class members who were, for example, lifelong citizens of California?

This question exposes an unresolved ambiguity in specific jurisdiction: the breadth of the "related to" standard. Three principal approaches have developed: a "proximate cause" test that requires the defendant's contacts to be the legal cause of the plaintiff's injury, a more relaxed "but-for" test that asks whether the plaintiff's claim would not have arisen but for the defendant's contacts with the state, and an even looser "substantial connection" test that analyzes whether the connection between the plaintiff's claim and the defendant's contacts make the assertion of jurisdiction fair. *See* O'Connor v. Sandy Lane Hotel Co., 496 F.3d 312 (3d Cir. 2007) (declining to adopt any test). Arguably the third approach justifies the assertion of personal jurisdiction over BAT on behalf of the non-New York class members in *Simon*, but the other two would not.

Simon avoided the "related to" issue by contending that, once the court had specific jurisdiction over the claims of the New York class members whose claims are related to BAT's New York contacts, it then had discretion to adjudicate the cases of non-New York class members who could not have invoked the specific jurisdiction of a New York court had they filed separately. On *Simon*'s view, therefore, class actions expand an important limitation on a court's exercise of personal jurisdiction.

Do you agree with *Simon*'s approach to permit what might be described as "pendent-plaintiff personal jurisdiction"? Assuming that BAT must already defend itself in a New York court on New York-related claims, what harm occurs if it must defend the claims unrelated to New York? What if BAT could show that single-forum aggregation prejudiced its chance for victory, or that California courts had stingier juries on damages? What factors should a court consider in deciding whether to exercise its discretion to adjudicate the claims of such "pendent-plaintiff" class members?

5. The issue of "pendent-plaintiff personal jurisdiction" arises because our rules of personal jurisdiction were mostly developed in a time of (and for) one-claim, two-party suits, but our rules of party joinder now allow the aggregation of multiple claims and plaintiffs in one case. A comparable issue that arises from our generous joinder rules is "pendent personal jurisdiction": A plaintiff joins one claim over which nationwide service of process exists with other claims to which ordinary state-based rules of personal jurisdiction apply. If the plaintiff asserts both claims against a defendant in a court that can exercise personal jurisdiction over the defendant on the first claim, but that would not have had jurisdiction over the second claim had the plaintiff brought only that claim, does the court have the power to render a binding judgment on the second claim?

This issue has received more attention than the "pendent-party personal jurisdiction" question in *Simon*. Thus far, the courts of appeals to consider the issue have all accepted the theory, although they typically require the two claims to arise from "a common nucleus of operative fact." *See* SunCoke Energy Inc. v. MAN Ferrostaal Aktiengesellschaft, 563 F.3d 211, 221 (6th Cir. 2009); Action Embroidery Corp. v. Atl. Embroidery, Inc., 368 F.3d 1174 (9th Cir. 2004). The decision whether to exercise this jurisdiction lies within the discretion of the trial court. Because the typical scenario involves a federal claim over which nationwide service of process exists, using "pendent personal jurisdiction" in a diversity case with two state-law claims remains relatively uncharted water. *See SunCoke*, 563 F.3d at 221 (noting that "'pendent personal jurisdiction' has been sparingly permitted in federal diversity cases"); Rice v. Nova Biomedical Corp., 38

F.3d 909 (7th Cir. 1994) (permitting jurisdiction). *See generally* 4A WRIGHT & MILLER, *supra*, § 1069.7 (analyzing cases).

6.   The last two Notes have focused on the difficulty presented in ensuring that a court has jurisdiction to enter a binding judgment on each *claim* that a plaintiff asserts against a defendant — a problem exacerbated as the number of claims and the number of plaintiffs asserting them proliferate. In complex litigation, the number of defendants can proliferate, and as *Simon* shows, a court's power over one defendant does not automatically give the court power over other defendants. Put differently, there is no "pendent-defendant personal jurisdiction."

To overcome this difficulty, *Simon* took two tacks. First, it tried to show that BAT itself had significant contacts with New York. Second, it tried to show that BAT's alleged co-conspirators had significant contacts with New York. Because of the numerous New York contacts of BAT's alleged co-conspirators, much of *Simon* was directed toward the latter "conspiracy theory of personal jurisdiction."

As *Simon* intimates, the "conspiracy theory of personal jurisdiction" — that the contacts of a defendant's co-conspirators with a state gives a court within that state the power to exercise jurisdiction over the defendant — is controversial. It has also become increasingly popular among plaintiffs as a way to hale defendants with no direct forum contacts into the forum of their choosing. As with any theory of personal jurisdiction, the exercise of jurisdiction under this theory requires both that the relevant long-arm statute permit it and that due process be satisfied by the exercise of jurisdiction. *See* Stauffacher v. Bennett, 969 F.2d 455, 460 (7th Cir. 1992); Brown v. Kerkhoff, 504 F. Supp. 2d 464 (S.D. Iowa 2007).

Simon is one of a growing number of courts that have accepted the theory. *See* Jungquist v. Sheikh Sultan Bin Khalifa al Nahyan, 115 F.3d 1020 (D.C. Cir. 1997); Remmes v. Int'l Flavors & Fragrances, Inc., 389 F. Supp. 2d 1080 (N.D. Iowa 2005). But other courts have rejected it. *See* Delta Brands Inc. v. Danieli Corp., 99 Fed. App'x 1, 5 (5th Cir. 2004) (requiring a conspirator "individually, and not as part of the conspiracy, ha[ve] minimum contacts with" the state); In re New Motor Vehicles Canadian Export, 307 F. Supp. 2d 145, 158 (D. Me. 2004). *Cf.* In re W. States Wholesale Natural Gas Litig., 605 F. Supp. 2d 1118, 1138 (D. Nev. 2009) ("[T]to the extent a conspiracy theory of personal jurisdiction is viable, it must be limited to the context of specific jurisdiction and cannot support general jurisdiction."). *See generally Brown*, 504 F. Supp. 2d at 513 nn.33-34 (collecting cases on each side); Ann Althouse, *The Use of Conspiracy Theory to Establish In Personam Jurisdiction: A Due Process Analysis*, 52 FORDHAM L. REV. 234 (1983) (critiquing the theory); Stuart M. Riback, Note, *The Long Arm and Multiple Defendants: The Conspiracy Theory of In Personam Jurisdiction*, 84 COLUM. L. REV. 506 (1984) (same). The Supreme Court has never addressed the theory.

Even among the courts that accept the theory on principle, a plaintiff must make detailed allegations of the conspiracy; otherwise, the court will reject it. *See* Lolavar v. de Santibanes, 430 F.3d 221, 229-30 (4th Cir. 2005); *Jungquist*, 115 F.3d at 1031.

7.   Assuming that the conspiracy theory of jurisdiction is improper, did BAT have enough independent contacts with New York to justify *Simon*'s assertion of jurisdiction over it? Most of the evidence that *Simon* marshals proves, at most, that BAT knew about the activities of others, including its subsidiaries, that were directed at the New York forum. The district court also relied on BAT's intentional conduct to take advantage of its expansive reading of *Calder*'s "effects" test, but most of that conduct was conspiracy-related. Look again at *Simon*'s due-process analysis. Aside from the acts of co-conspirators in New York, aren't BAT's contacts with New York far too minimal to satisfy due process? Does *Simon* seriously argue otherwise?

Simon makes brief reference to the "stream of commerce" theory as an alternate basis to uphold the constitutionality of its assertion of personal jurisdiction. The theory holds that a manufacturer is subject to jurisdiction in the state in which its product causes injury, on the principle that a manufacturer who releases a defective product into the stream of commerce has reason to expect being sued in the state in which the product causes injury. *Simon* fails to indicate that the Supreme Court has given the theory a chilly reception. *See* Asahi Metal Indus. Co. v. Superior Court, 480 U.S. 102 (1987); World-Wide Volkswagen Corp. v. Woodson, 444 U.S. 286, 292 (1980). Here is the full quote from *Asahi* that *Simon* excerpts:

> The placement of a product into the stream of commerce, without more, is not an act of the defendant purposefully directed toward the forum State. Additional conduct of the defendant may indicate an intent or purpose to serve the market in the forum State, for example, designing the product for the market in the forum State, advertising in the forum State, establishing channels for providing regular advice to customers in the forum State, or marketing the product through a distributor who has agreed to serve as the sales agent in the forum State. But a defendant's awareness that the stream of commerce may or will sweep the product into the forum State does not convert the mere act of placing the product into the stream into an act purposefully directed toward the forum State. [480 U.S. at 112.]

This portion of *Asahi* commanded only a plurality of four votes. But accepting this quotation as a correct statement of the law, did BAT do anything that was sufficiently targeted toward New York to justify the invocation of the "stream of commerce" theory against it? In particular, did BAT do anything to design its cigarettes specifically for the New York market (perhaps by making them in the shape of the New York Yankees logo), as *Simon* claims?

8.   It is also possible to exercise personal jurisdiction over a parent corporation like BAT if it engages in active, day-to-day control of a subsidiary over which personal jurisdiction is proper. *See, e.g.*, LaSalle Nat'l Bank v. Vitro, S.A., 85 F. Supp. 2d 857 (N.D. Ill. 2000). In *Simon*, no one claimed that BAT exercised this degree of control.

9. By now, you should be able to appreciate the roadblock that the personal-jurisdiction requirement creates for aggregating related claims. Personal jurisdiction must exist with respect to *each* claim asserted by *each* plaintiff against *each* defendant; otherwise, the court's decision on that claim cannot bind the defendant. Assume that a plaintiff wants to sue A, B, and C. With respect to this plaintiff's claim, there is either general or specific jurisdiction over A in Alabama, Alaska, and Arizona; for B, New Jersey, Alaska, and Alabama; and for C, Wisconsin, Arizona, and Alabama. The only forum that overlaps all three defendants is Alabama. But suppose that the plaintiff doesn't want to sue in Alabama. Then the plaintiff will need to leave at least one of the defendants out, and sue in another forum.

If we add more plaintiffs and defendants into the mix, then it gets harder and harder to find any single forum that overlaps all of the claims (indeed, as the numbers grow, it is very likely that no forum will overlap for all of the cases). It also gets less and less likely that all plaintiffs will want to file in that forum.

You can see how the doctrine of personal jurisdiction can help to cause the geographical dispersion of cases across the country.

10. The one aggregation device that is impervious to this problem is MDL consolidation. The Judicial Panel on Multidistrict Litigation has held:

> Transfers under Section 1407 are simply not encumbered by considerations of *in personam* jurisdiction and venue. A transfer under Section 1407 is, in essence, a change of venue for pretrial purposes. Following a transfer, the transferee judge has all the jurisdiction and powers over pretrial proceedings in the actions transferred to him that the transferor judge would have had in the absence of transfer.

In re FMC Corp. Patent Litig., 422 F. Supp. 1163, 1165 (J.P.M.L. 1976). At the same time, nothing in § 1407 expands the jurisdiction of the transferee court or allows the exercise of *in personam* jurisdiction beyond the jurisdiction that the transferor courts enjoyed. In re Telectronics Pacing Sys., Inc., 953 F. Supp. 909, 914 (S.D. Ohio 1997). In terms of aggregation, the capacity to handle related cases in one forum without concern for the personal-jurisdiction limitations of that forum is one of the strongly positive features of the MDL process.

Suppose that an MDL transferee court in the District of Utah enters summary judgment against a defendant who was not subject to personal jurisdiction in Utah courts. Does the decision bind the defendant? Under the *FMC* analysis, the answer is yes, but, to our knowledge, no authority directly analyzes the point. In the analogous context of the binding effect of a transferee court's rulings on plaintiffs over whom the MDL court had no personal jurisdiction, courts have held that the MDL court's decisions bound the plaintiffs. *See* In re Bridgestone/Firestone, Inc., Tires Prods. Liab. Litig., 333 F.3d 763, 768 (7th Cir. 2003) (*supra* p. 194); In re Diet Drugs (Phentermine, Fenfluramine, Dexfenfluramine) Prods. Liab. Litig., 282 F.3d 220, 231 (3rd Cir. 2002). Is an MDL court's jurisdiction over the parties before it implicit in § 1407 — as a type of common-law nationwide service of process? The issue is important; most cases are resolved in the MDL court, so the binding effect of an MDL court's decisions is significant.

11. A defendant must carefully preserve a defense of lack of personal jurisdiction or it is waived. The way in which the defense is preserved varies among states. For the federal approach, see Fed. R. Civ. P. 12(b)(2), -(g), -(h)(2). In many states and the federal system, participation in the litigation also can amount to a waiver of the defense. *See* Cont'l Bank, N.A. v. Meyer, 10 F.3d 1293, 1296-97 (7th Cir. 1993). But neither plaintiffs nor the court can count on such a waiver occurring, so waiver does not act as a very large path through the personal-jurisdiction barrier.

12. Perhaps you can now appreciate the reasons that a number of commentators, including Judge Weinstein, believe that complex litigation requires another approach to personal jurisdiction. *Simon* mentions as one alternative the ALI's recommendation: to create a nationwide-service-of-process statute. AM. L. INST., COMPLEX LITIGATION § 3.08 (1994); *id.* app. A, at 448; *see also* AM. BAR ASS'N, COMM'N ON MASS TORTS, REPORT TO THE HOUSE OF DELEGATES 84 (1989) (recommending nationwide service of process in federal mass torts). The ALI's recommendation formed part of a comprehensive set of proposals (other parts of which we studied in Chapter Two) to aggregate litigation in one forum, either federal or state. The service-of-process statute that the ALI proposed was vague on a state court's capacity to exercise nationwide service of process. *See supra* p. 269, Note 3 (questioning whether state courts can exercise such jurisdiction). For that reason, such a statute, should it be passed, points to federal courts as the more natural forum for aggregation.

13. Believing that the nationwide-service-of-process approach is an insufficient response to the need for single-forum aggregation, Judge Weinstein proposed an even more radical alternative: to overthrow the defendant-centered approach to personal jurisdiction altogether. *DES Cases* developed the argument for this approach — as well as the reasons for believing that the approach was consistent with the evolution of the law of personal jurisdiction — in greater detail. *Simon* provides highlights of this argument. Some of *DES Cases*'s arguments for this approach were specific to the unique substantive products-liability law that New York had developed for DES litigation, which involved a nationwide market in a fungible drug. Those reasons would not have pertained in the *Simon* tobacco litigation. In this respect, *Simon* represents an expansion of Judge Weinstein's original proposal.

Courts have not tended to adopt this approach. Aside from *DES Cases* and *Simon*, Judge Weinstein applied the theory in a case against gun manufacturers. Hamilton v. Accu-Tek, 32 F. Supp. 2d 47 (E.D.N.Y. 1998). Other courts have rejected it. *Terrorist Attacks*, 349 F. Supp. 2d at 810; Waste Mgmt., Inc. v. Admiral Ins. Co., 649 A.2d 379 (N.J. 1994) (calling *DES Cases* an "unprecedented jurisdictional formulation"; distinguishing it due to the unique features of New York law). In *Boaz v. Boyle & Co.*, 46 Cal. Rptr. 2d 888, 900-01 (Cal. Ct. App. 1995), the court stated:

Whatever might be said of [the *DES Cases*] approach in philosophical terms, it runs counter to United States Supreme Court decisions about the assertion of personal jurisdiction over nonresidents. . . .

. . . We have no warrant to jettison these principles in favor of an approach which recognizes no defined limits to the assertion of jurisdiction against any defendant whose national marketing somehow affects commerce in the forum state.

14. In another tobacco case, Judge Weinstein proposed the creation of worldwide service of process for certain claims, but found jurisdiction under ordinary principles. Nat'l Asbestos Workers Med. Fund v. Philip Morris, Inc., 86 F. Supp. 2d 137 (E.D.N.Y. 2000). Having now studied the reasons to aggregate cases, the ways in which personal jurisdiction can frustrate aggregation, and the values that the personal jurisdiction serves, you can judge for yourself whether Judge Weinstein's alternatives are preferable.

15. One of the growth areas in the law of personal jurisdiction involves the internet. Any individual or company with a website is, at least in a virtual sense, present in every state in the country. For the past dozen years, courts have been delineating the circumstances in which internet contacts in a forum constitute sufficient contacts for purposes of long-arm statutes and due process. From the viewpoint of complex litigation, if internet presence equals jurisdictional contacts, then more forums open up as places in which related cases can be aggregated. (Of course, the flip side is that such contacts also expand the number of forums into which related cases can disperse, thus making aggregation more difficult.)

A complete treatment of the interrelationship between the internet and personal jurisdiction is beyond this book, but it is fair to say that, so far, internet presence has not caused a large breach in the jurisdictional ramparts. Courts tend to distinguish between passive websites that are informational and e-commerce websites that allow consumers to make online purchases; the former websites do not create jurisdiction, while the latter can if the amount of e-commerce is large enough. *See, e.g.,* Zippo Mfg. Co. v. Zippo Dot Com, Inc., 952 F. Supp. 1119 (W.D. Pa. 1997). One of the broadest decisions, which subjected a company to the state's general jurisdiction when six percent of its internet sales were made within the state, was subsequently withdrawn. Gator.com Corp. v. L.L. Bean, Inc., 341 F.3d 1072 (9th Cir. 2003), *vacated as moot,* 398 F.3d 1125 (9th Cir. 2005) (en banc). Whether this intersection between cyberlaw and personal jurisdiction will affect aggregation in complex litigation remains to be seen.

2. Personal Jurisdiction over Plaintiffs

As a general rule, a court has personal jurisdiction over the plaintiffs who file suit; by filing suit, they are deemed to consent to the court's jurisdiction. In some situations, however, plaintiffs are joined involuntarily to a suit or else are bound by the outcome of that suit. As Chapter Two showed, involuntary joinder and nonparty preclusion are rare, but they do happen. In some of these cases, the plaintiff that is joined or the potential plaintiff that is precluded has limited or no contacts with the forum. Thus, the involuntary joinder or nonparty preclusion of a potential plaintiff raises the same concern as the involuntary joinder or preclusion of a defendant: When is it fair for a court that lacks minimum contacts with a plaintiff or nonparty to adjudicate or preclude that person's claim? Should the personal-jurisdiction rules be the same as they are in the context of defendants? Or are there reasons that they should be more liberal? On the assumption that involuntary joinder or preclusion of potential plaintiffs is a greater affront to the adversarial system than the joinder or preclusion of defendants, perhaps the rules should be even stricter?

PHILLIPS PETROLEUM CO. V. SHUTTS

472 U.S. 797 (1985)

■   JUSTICE REHNQUIST delivered the opinion of the Court.

Petitioner is a Delaware corporation which has its principal place of business in Oklahoma. During the 1970's it produced or purchased natural gas from leased land located in 11 different States, and sold most of the gas in interstate commerce. Respondents are some 28,000 of the royalty owners possessing rights to the leases from which petitioner produced the gas; they reside in all 50 States, the District of Columbia, and several foreign countries. Respondents brought a class action against petitioner in the Kansas state court, seeking to recover interest on royalty payments which had been delayed by petitioner. They recovered judgment in the trial court, and the Supreme Court of Kansas affirmed the judgment over petitioner's contentions that the Due Process Clause of the Fourteenth Amendment prevented Kansas from adjudicating the claims of all the respondents . . . . We reject petitioner's jurisdictional claim . . . .

[Philips Petroleum, the petitioner, paid royalties to the owners of land from which it extracted natural gas. The royalty was based on the price Philips received for the gas. When Phillips wished to sell gas in excess of an established rate, it needed to obtain the approval of the Federal Power Commission. While the request for an increase was pending, Philips could sell the gas at the higher rate, subject to the proviso that it refund the excess charge if the Commission did not ultimately approve the increase. Even though it received a higher price for its gas, Philips in most cases paid royalties based only on the established rate until the Commission approved the increase; only after approval did it pay the owners the remainder of their royalties. Philips' reason for not paying the higher royalty amount immediately was the complications that could arise if the increase were ultimately disapproved: Philips would need to refund the difference to customers and then collect from the owners a portion of their royalties. But the effect of Philips' decision was also to give it the interest-free use of a portion of the owners' royalties while the request for a rate increase was pending.] In three written opinions the Commission approved all of petitioner's tentative price increases, so petitioner paid to its royalty owners the suspended royalties of $3.7 million in 1976, $4.7 million in 1977, and $2.9 million in 1978. Petitioner paid no interest to the royalty owners although it had the use of the suspended royalty money for a number of years.

Respondents Irl Shutts, Robert Anderson, and Betty Anderson filed suit against petitioner in Kansas state court, seeking interest payments on their suspended royalties which petitioner had possessed pending the Commission's approval of the price increases. Shutts is a resident of Kansas, and the Andersons live in Oklahoma. Shutts and the Andersons own gas leases in Oklahoma and Texas. Over petitioner's objection the Kansas trial court granted respondents' motion to certify the suit as a class action under Kansas law. KAN. STAT. ANN. § 60-223 *et seq.* (1983). The class as certified was comprised of 33,000 royalty owners who had royalties suspended by petitioner. The average claim of each royalty owner for interest on the suspended royalties was $100.

After the class was certified respondents provided each class member with notice through first-class mail. The notice described the action and informed each class member that he could appear in person or by counsel; otherwise each member would be represented by Shutts and the Andersons, the named plaintiffs. The notices also stated that class members would be included in the class and bound by the judgment unless they "opted out" of the lawsuit by executing and returning a "request for exclusion" that was included with the notice. The final class as certified contained 28,100 members; 3,400 had "opted out" of the class by returning the request for exclusion, and notice could not be delivered to another 1,500 members, who were also excluded. Less than 1,000 of the class members resided in Kansas. Only a minuscule amount, approximately one quarter of one percent, of the gas leases involved in the lawsuit were on Kansas land.

After petitioner's mandamus petition to decertify the class was denied, the case was tried to the court. The court found petitioner liable under Kansas law for interest on the suspended royalties to all class members....

Petitioner ... in its appeal to the Supreme Court of Kansas ... asserted that the Kansas trial court did not possess personal jurisdiction over absent plaintiff class members as required by *International Shoe Co. v. Washington*, 326 U.S. 310 (1945), and similar cases. Related to this ... claim was petitioner's contention that the "opt-out" notice to absent class members, which forced them to return the request for exclusion in order to avoid the suit, was insufficient to bind class members who were not residents of Kansas or who did not possess "minimum contacts" with Kansas. ...

The Supreme Court of Kansas held that the entire cause of action was maintainable under the Kansas class-action statute, and ... that the absent class members were plaintiffs, not defendants, and thus the traditional minimum contacts test of *International Shoe* did not apply. The court held that nonresident class-action plaintiffs were only entitled to adequate notice, an opportunity to be heard, an opportunity to opt out of the case, and adequate representation by the named plaintiffs. If these procedural due process minima were met, according to the court, Kansas could assert jurisdiction over the plaintiff class and bind each class member with a judgment on his claim. The court surveyed the course of the litigation and concluded that all of these minima had been met. . . .

I

As a threshold matter we must determine whether petitioner has standing to assert the claim that Kansas did not possess proper jurisdiction over the many plaintiffs in the class who were not Kansas residents and had no connection to Kansas. . . .

. . . Petitioner seeks to vindicate its own interests. As a class-action defendant petitioner is in a unique predicament. If Kansas does not possess jurisdiction over this plaintiff class, petitioner will be bound to 28,100 judgment holders scattered across the globe, but none of these will be bound by the Kansas decree. Petitioner could be subject to numerous later individual suits by these class members because a judgment issued without proper personal jurisdiction over an absent party is not entitled to full faith and credit elsewhere and thus has no res judicata effect as to that party. Whether it wins or loses on the merits, petitioner has a distinct and personal interest in seeing the entire plaintiff class bound by res judicata just as petitioner is bound. The only way a class action defendant like petitioner can assure itself of this binding effect of the judgment is to ascertain that the forum court has jurisdiction over every plaintiff whose claim it seeks to adjudicate, sufficient to support a defense of res judicata in a later suit for damages by class members.

. . . [P]etitioner has alleged that it would be obviously and immediately injured if this class-action judgment against it became final without binding the plaintiff class. We think that such an injury is sufficient to give petitioner standing on its own right to raise the jurisdiction claim in this Court.

II

Reduced to its essentials, petitioner's argument is that unless out-of-state plaintiffs affirmatively consent, the Kansas courts may not exert jurisdiction over their claims. Petitioner claims that failure to execute and return the "request for exclusion" provided with the class notice cannot constitute consent of the out-of-state plaintiffs; thus Kansas courts may exercise jurisdiction over these plaintiffs only if the plaintiffs possess the sufficient "minimum contacts" with Kansas as that term is used in cases involving personal jurisdiction over out-of-state defendants. *E.g.,* *International Shoe,* 326 U.S. 310 (1945); Shaffer v. Heitner, 433 U.S. 186 (1977); World-Wide Volkswagen Corp. v. Woodson, 444 U.S. 286 (1980). Since Kansas had no prelitigation contact with many of the plaintiffs and leases involved, petitioner claims that Kansas has exceeded its jurisdictional reach and thereby violated the due process rights of the absent plaintiffs.

In *International Shoe* we were faced with an out-of-state corporation which sought to avoid the exercise of personal jurisdiction over it as a defendant by a Washington state court. We held that the extent of the defendant's due process protection would depend "upon the quality and nature of the activity in relation to the fair and orderly administration of the laws . . . ." We noted that the Due Process Clause did not permit a State to make a binding judgment against a person with whom the State had no contacts, ties, or relations. If the defendant possessed certain minimum contacts with the State, so that it was "reasonable and just, according to our traditional conception of fair play and substantial justice" for a State to exercise personal jurisdiction, the State could force the defendant to defend himself in the forum, upon pain of default, and could bind him to a judgment.

The purpose of this test, of course, is to protect a defendant from the travail of defending in a distant forum, unless the defendant's contacts with the forum make it just to force him to defend there. As we explained in *Woodson, supra,* the defendant's contacts should be such that "he should reasonably anticipate being haled" into the forum. . . .

Although the cases like *Shaffer* and *Woodson* which petitioner relies on for a minimum contacts requirement all dealt with out-of-state defendants or parties in the procedural posture of a defendant, petitioner claims that the same analysis must apply to absent class-action plaintiffs. In this regard petitioner correctly points out that a chose in action is a constitutionally recognized property interest possessed by each of the plaintiffs. Mullane v. Central Hanover Bank & Trust Co., 339 U.S. 306 (1950). An adverse judgment by Kansas courts in this case may extinguish the chose in action forever through res judicata. Such an adverse judgment, petitioner claims, would be every bit as onerous to an absent plaintiff as an adverse judgment on the merits would be to a defendant. Thus, the same due process protections should apply to absent plaintiffs: Kansas should not be able to exert jurisdiction over the plaintiffs' claims unless the plaintiffs have sufficient minimum contacts with Kansas.

We think petitioner's premise is in error. The burdens placed by a State upon an absent class-action plaintiff are not of the same order or magnitude as those it places upon an absent defendant. An out-of-state defendant summoned by a plaintiff is faced with the full powers of the forum State to render judgment *against* it. The defendant must generally hire counsel and travel to the forum to defend itself from the plaintiff's claim, or suffer a default judgment. The defendant may be forced to participate in extended and often costly discovery, and will be forced to respond in damages or to comply with some other form of remedy imposed by the court should it lose the suit. The defendant may also face liability for court costs and attorney's fees. These burdens are substantial, and the minimum contacts requirement of the Due Process Clause prevents the forum State from unfairly imposing them upon the defendant.

A class-action plaintiff, however, is in quite a different posture. The Court noted this difference in *Hansberry v. Lee,* 311 U.S. 32, 40-41 (1940), which explained that a "class" or "representative" suit was an exception to the rule that one could not be bound by judgment *in personam* unless one was made fully a party in the traditional sense. As the Court pointed out in *Hansberry*, the class action was an invention of equity to enable it to proceed to a decree in suits where the number of those interested in the litigation was too great to permit joinder. The absent parties would be bound by the decree so long as the named parties adequately represented the absent class and the prosecution of the litigation was within the common interest.[1]

Modern plaintiff class actions follow the same goals, permitting litigation of a suit involving common questions when there are too many plaintiffs for proper joinder. Class actions also may permit the plaintiffs to pool claims which would be uneconomical to litigate individually. For example, this lawsuit involves claims averaging about $100 per plaintiff; most of the plaintiffs would have no realistic day in court if a class action were not available.

In sharp contrast to the predicament of a defendant haled into an out-of-state forum, the plaintiffs in this suit were not haled anywhere to defend themselves upon pain of a default judgment. . . .

A plaintiff class in Kansas and numerous other jurisdictions cannot first be certified unless the judge, with the aid of the named plaintiffs and defendant, conducts an inquiry into the common nature of the named plaintiffs' and the absent plaintiffs' claims, the adequacy of representation, the jurisdiction possessed over the class, and any other matters that will bear upon proper representation of the absent plaintiffs' interest. *See, e. g.*, KAN. STAT. ANN. § 60-223 (1983); Fed. R. Civ. P. 23. Unlike a defendant in a civil suit, a class-action plaintiff is not required to fend for himself. *See* KAN. STAT. ANN. § 60-223(d) (1983). The court and named plaintiffs protect his interests. Indeed, the class-action defendant itself has a great interest in ensuring that the absent plaintiffs' claims are properly before the forum. In this case, for example, the defendant sought to avoid class certification by alleging that the absent plaintiffs would not be adequately represented and were not amenable to jurisdiction.

The concern of the typical class-action rules for the absent plaintiffs is manifested in other ways. Most jurisdictions, including Kansas, require that a class action, once certified, may not be dismissed or compromised without the approval of the court. In many jurisdictions such as Kansas the court may amend the pleadings to ensure that all sections of the class are represented adequately. KAN. STAT. ANN. § 60-223(d) (1983); *see also, e.g.*, Fed. R. Civ. P. 23(d).

Besides this continuing solicitude for their rights, absent plaintiff class members are not subject to other burdens imposed upon defendants. They need not hire counsel or appear. They are almost never subject to

1.   . . . [I]n the present case there is no question that the named plaintiffs adequately represent the class, and that all members of the class have the same interest in enforcing their claims against the defendant.

counterclaims or cross-claims, or liability for fees or costs. Absent plaintiff class members are not subject to coercive or punitive remedies. Nor will an adverse judgment typically bind an absent plaintiff for any damages, although a valid adverse judgment may extinguish any of the plaintiff's claims which were litigated.

Unlike a defendant in a normal civil suit, an absent class-action plaintiff is not required to do anything. He may sit back and allow the litigation to run its course, content in knowing that there are safeguards provided for his protection. In most class actions an absent plaintiff is provided at least with an opportunity to "opt out" of the class, and if he takes advantage of that opportunity he is removed from the litigation entirely. This was true of the Kansas proceedings in this case. . . .

Petitioner contends, however, that the "opt out" procedure provided by Kansas is not good enough, and that an "opt in" procedure is required to satisfy the Due Process Clause of the Fourteenth Amendment. Insofar as plaintiffs who have no minimum contacts with the forum State are concerned, an "opt in" provision would require that each class member affirmatively consent to his inclusion within the class.

Because States place fewer burdens upon absent class plaintiffs than they do upon absent defendants in nonclass suits, the Due Process Clause need not and does not afford the former as much protection from state-court jurisdiction as it does the latter. The Fourteenth Amendment does protect "persons," not "defendants," however, so absent plaintiffs as well as absent defendants are entitled to some protection from the jurisdiction of a forum State which seeks to adjudicate their claims. In this case we hold that a forum State may exercise jurisdiction over the claim of an absent class-action plaintiff, even though that plaintiff may not possess the minimum contacts with the forum which would support personal jurisdiction over a defendant. If the forum State wishes to bind an absent plaintiff concerning a claim for money damages or similar relief at law,[3] it must provide minimal procedural due process protection. The plaintiff must receive notice plus an opportunity to be heard and participate in the litigation, whether in person or through counsel. The notice must be the best practicable, "reasonably calculated, under all the circumstances, to apprise interested parties of the pendency of the action and afford them an opportunity to present their objections." *Mullane*, 339 U.S. at 314-15. The notice should describe the action and the plaintiffs' rights in it. Additionally, we hold that due process requires at a minimum that an absent plaintiff be provided with an opportunity to remove himself from the class by executing and returning an "opt out" or "request for exclusion" form to the court. Finally, the Due Process Clause of course requires that the

---

3.   Our holding today is limited to those class actions which seek to bind known plaintiffs concerning claims wholly or predominately for money judgments. We intimate no view concerning other types of class actions, such as those seeking equitable relief. Nor, of course, does our discussion of personal jurisdiction address class actions where the jurisdiction is asserted against a *defendant* class.

named plaintiff at all times adequately represent the interests of the absent class members. *Hansberry*, 311 U.S. at 42-43, 45.

We reject petitioner's contention that the Due Process Clause of the Fourteenth Amendment requires that absent plaintiffs affirmatively "opt in" to the class, rather than be deemed members of the class if they do not "opt out." We think that such a contention is supported by little, if any precedent, and that it ignores the differences between class-action plaintiffs, on the one hand, and defendants in nonclass civil suits on the other. Any plaintiff may consent to jurisdiction. The essential question, then, is how stringent the requirement for a showing of consent will be.

We think that the procedure followed by Kansas, where a fully descriptive notice is sent first-class mail to each class member, with an explanation of the right to "opt out," satisfies due process. Requiring a plaintiff to affirmatively request inclusion would probably impede the prosecution of those class actions involving an aggregation of small individual claims, where a large number of claims are required to make it economical to bring suit. The plaintiff's claim may be so small, or the plaintiff so unfamiliar with the law, that he would not file suit individually, nor would he affirmatively request inclusion in the class if such a request were required by the Constitution. If, on the other hand, the plaintiff's claim is sufficiently large or important that he wishes to litigate it on his own, he will likely have retained an attorney or have thought about filing suit, and should be fully capable of exercising his right to "opt out."

In this case over 3,400 members of the potential class did "opt out," which belies the contention that "opt out" procedures result in guaranteed jurisdiction by inertia. Another 1,500 were excluded because the notice and "opt out" form was undeliverable. We think that such results show that the "opt out" procedure provided by Kansas is by no means *pro forma*, and that the Constitution does not require more to protect what must be the somewhat rare species of class member who is unwilling to execute an "opt out" form, but whose claim is nonetheless so important that he cannot be presumed to consent to being a member of the class by his failure to do so. Petitioner's "opt in" requirement would require the invalidation of scores of state statutes and of the class-action provision of the Federal Rules of Civil Procedure, and for the reasons stated we do not think that the Constitution requires the State to sacrifice the obvious advantages in judicial efficiency resulting from the "opt out" approach for the protection of the *rara avis* portrayed by petitioner.

We therefore hold that the protection afforded the plaintiff class members by the Kansas statute satisfies the Due Process Clause. The interests of the absent plaintiffs are sufficiently protected by the forum State when those plaintiffs are provided with a request for exclusion that can be returned within a reasonable time to the court. Both the Kansas trial court and the Supreme Court of Kansas held that the class received adequate representation, and no party disputes that conclusion here. We conclude that the Kansas court properly asserted personal jurisdiction over the absent plaintiffs and their claims against petitioner. . . .

[The remainder of *Shutts*, discussing whether a Kansas court could constitutionally apply its law to the claims of the plaintiffs with no connection to Kansas, is discussed *infra* p. 637.]

We therefore affirm the judgment of the Supreme Court of Kansas insofar as it upheld the jurisdiction of the Kansas courts over the plaintiff class members in this case . . . .

■   JUSTICE POWELL took no part in the decision of this case.

■   [The opinion of JUSTICE STEVENS, concurring in part and dissenting in part on the choice-of-law issue, is omitted.]

IN RE: GENERAL MOTORS CORP.
PICK-UP TRUCK FUEL TANK
PRODUCTS LIABILITY LITIGATION

134 F.3d 133 (3d Cir. 1998)

■   BECKER, Circuit Judge.

[Certain General Motors pick-up trucks had fuel systems that allegedly created a risk of explosion during a crash. Truck owners sued in state and federal courts. The Judicial Panel on Multidistrict Litigation consolidated 277 federal cases the Eastern District of Pennsylvania under 28 U.S.C. § 1407. General Motors agreed to settle the claims of pick-up truck owners, and, together with the federal plaintiffs, moved the MDL court to certify a nationwide opt-out class action of all 5.7 million pick-up truck owners. The court did so, and also approved the settlement as fair and reasonable. On appeal, the Third Circuit held that the district court erred in certifying the class. This ruling meant the district court again had before it only the claims of the 277 plaintiffs whose cases had been consolidated under § 1407, rather than the claims of all 5.7 million class members.

[Meanwhile, plaintiffs in a Louisiana state-court action negotiated a settlement similar to the one that had been negotiated in federal court. The Louisiana plaintiffs and General Motors moved to certify the case as an opt-out class action. The Louisiana state court conditionally certified a class action. At that point, some of the persons that had successfully objected to the proposed federal settlement moved the federal court in Pennsylvania to enjoin the proceedings in Louisiana. The district court refused, and the objectors appealed. While the federal case was on appeal, the Louisiana trial court approved the settlement.

[The Louisiana plaintiffs and General Motors raised a host of arguments in support of the district court's decision not to enjoin the Louisiana proceeding. The first was personal jurisdiction.]

At the threshold, we must examine our power over the parties. Appellees assert that the district court had no jurisdiction to enjoin the Louisiana court in the first instance (had it chosen to do so), and thus we can have no jurisdiction to enjoin that court on appeal. This contention is grounded upon appellees' submission that any injunction issued by this Court would affect the nationwide group of 5.7 million people who have already settled their claims with GM through the Louisiana proceedings, and therefore, that any injunction of the Louisiana Court would necessarily enjoin those 5.7 million individual settling class members and would require this Court to exercise personal jurisdiction over them. We agree.

The minimum standards of due process require that "in order to subject a defendant to a judgment *in personam*, if he not be present within the territory of the forum, he must have certain minimum contacts with it such that the maintenance of the suit does not offend 'traditional notions of fair play and substantial justice.'" International Shoe Co. v. Washington, 326 U.S. 310, 316 (1945) (citations omitted). In the Rule 23(b)(3) context, the Supreme Court has held that it is possible for a court to bind an absentee class member to a judgment without abrogating minimal due process protection, even if the party did not have minimum contacts with the forum. *See* Phillips Petroleum Co. v. Shutts, 472 U.S. 797, 812-13 (1985). But here . . . there is no class pending before the MDL court, and thus, virtually none of the 5.7 million class members in Louisiana are before this Court in any respect, and there is no basis upon which we can infer their consent.[2]

To be more precise, the Louisiana class members are not parties before us; they have not constructively or affirmatively consented to personal jurisdiction; and they do not, as far as has been demonstrated, have minimum contacts with Pennsylvania. Therefore, due process deprives us of personal jurisdiction and prevents us from issuing the injunction prayed for by appellants.

Notes

1.   Although Justice Stevens dissented on another issue in *Shutts*, the Court's decision on the personal-jurisdiction issue was unanimous. *Shutts* establishes that the law of personal jurisdiction, which had developed to protect defendants from distant and burdensome litigation, has salience with respect to plaintiffs who find themselves involuntarily aggregated in a class action. *GM Pick-Up* extends that insight to another method — the antisuit injunction — by which aggregation can also incur.

2.   We note that enjoining the few Louisiana class members that the MDL court does have personal jurisdiction over (the 200 named MDL plaintiffs who have successfully intervened in the Louisiana proceeding) would serve no purpose. . . . [I]t is conceivable that we could direct the district court to enjoin those 200 plaintiffs from pursuing their state damage remedies in Louisiana. As the district court properly pointed out, however, since the appellants' stated goal here is to prevent the Louisiana court from further consideration of the settlement *in toto*, little would be accomplished by enjoining only those 200 plaintiffs, and we have not been asked to do so. At all events, the limited injunction would not halt the Louisiana proceedings because the original Louisiana plaintiffs (over whom we have no jurisdiction) could simply continue with the settlement.

2. Did *GM Pick-Up* take an unduly broad reading of *Shutts*? Shouldn't a federal court be able to enjoin persons that have minimum contacts with the federal system as a whole from taking actions that would irreparably harm a case pending in federal court? Is the point in *GM Pick-Up* that the actions of class members in the Louisiana litigation did not threaten such harm to the federal MDL proceeding, and not that the federal court lacked personal jurisdiction over absent plaintiffs?

In many ways, *GM Pick-Up* is analogous to *In re Bridgestone/Firestone, Inc., Tires Products Liability Litigation*, 333 F.3d 763 (7th Cir. 2003), which we examined *supra* p. 194. In *Bridgestone/Firestone*, an MDL court enjoined persons from seeking class certification in state court after the federal court ruled that a federal class action could not be maintained. The enjoined parties unsuccessfully argued that the MDL court was powerless to enter the injunction because it had no jurisdiction over them:

> . . . Unnamed class members cannot be brought in involuntarily, class counsel insist, because federal courts lack the authority to issue process nationwide. As a result, class members other than the named representatives cannot be bound by an adverse decision and are free to file their own class actions elsewhere. The proposition that the federal court lacks the power to issue nationwide process must be qualified by the proviso "unless a federal statute authorizes this step"; and one of the claims in the master complaint rested on RICO, which does authorize nationwide service of process. What is more, unnamed class members have the status of parties for many purposes and are bound by the decision whether or not the court otherwise would have had personal jurisdiction over them. *See* Phillips Petroleum Co. v. Shutts, 472 U.S. 797 (1985). . . .
>
> A decision with respect to the class is conclusive only if the absent members were adequately represented by the named litigants and class counsel. That requirement has been met. The district court found that both the named plaintiffs and their lawyers furnished adequate representation to the other members of the putative classes. That decision was not challenged on the first appeal and is not contested now. [*Id.* at 768-69.]

Bridgestone/Firestone is distinguishable from *GM Pick-Up* in a few ways. First, neither of the two federal-law claims in *GM Pick-Up* provided for nationwide service of process. Second, the plaintiffs' lawyers seeking certification in state court were different from the ones who had lost the class-action argument in federal court (although this fact might not be especially salient because the defendant, General Motors, was complicit in both the federal and state cases). Third, *GM Pick-Up* had expressed doubts about the adequacy of the representation afforded by both the class representatives and the class counsel. In re Gen. Motors Corp. Pick-Up Truck Fuel Tank Prods. Liab. Litig., 55 F.3d 768, 800-04 (3d Cir. 1995).

Accepting those distinctions as sufficient justification to explain the different outcomes in the two cases, the rule in *GM Pick-Up* — if it is indeed a correct interpretation of *Shutts* — will still have application in the many circumstances in which a federal court seeks to issue an antisuit injunction or otherwise to preclude relitigation of issues when (1) none of the allegations in the federal case permit nationwide service of process, (2) the parties and lawyers pursuing state litigation are different from those in the federal litigation, or (3) the federal case does not involve class allegations in which the adequacy of representation is demonstrated.

3.   *Shutts* requires us to consider the constitutional concerns created by all attempts to aggregate plaintiffs involuntarily — whether by joinder, by transfer or consolidation, by antisuit injunction, or by preclusion. Aside from class actions, however, these aggregation devices do not involve a representative suing on a plaintiff's behalf, and thus impose no requirement of adequate representation. Without this protection, which was crucial in *Shutts*, must a court applying an aggregation device to a non-consenting plaintiff have traditional personal jurisdiction over that plaintiff?

Shutts itself does not answer this question. Sometimes the aggregation device itself makes the answer clear. For instance, Rule 19(a) states that a required party "who is subject to service of process . . . must be joined as a party." If the court lacks personal jurisdiction over the party, then it must consider whether to dismiss the case, *see* Fed. R. Civ. P. 19(b); Rule 19 denies a court power to join nonparties over whom it lacks jurisdiction.

Take another example: transfer under 28 U.S.C. § 1404(a). A § 1404(a) transfer can be made only to a transferee court that could have exercised personal jurisdiction over the *defendant* if the case had been filed in the transferee court originally. *See* Hoffman v. Blaski, 363 U.S. 335 (1960). A number of courts have held, however, that a § 1404(a) transfer can occur even though the transferee court lacks personal jurisdiction over the *plaintiff*. *See, e.g.*, Morrow v. Vertical Doors Inc., 2009 WL 1698560, at *2 (D. Ariz. June 17, 2009); Viron Int'l Corp. v. David Boland, Inc., 237 F. Supp. 2d 812, 819 (W.D. Mich. 2002). As one court explained:

> [P]ersonal jurisdiction over a plaintiff in the transferee forum is irrelevant on a motion to transfer venue under § 1404(a) because the consideration is whether the plaintiff could have brought suit in the transferee court, and a plaintiff, by bringing a suit[,] consents to the jurisdiction of the Court.

Rogan v. United States, 2008 WL 282351, at *7 n.5 (N.D. Ind. Jan. 31, 2008). Having read *Shutts*, do you agree with this analysis?

4.   Aside from the general pall that *Shutts* casts over efforts to join, consolidate, enjoin or preclude non-consenting persons over whom a court has no jurisdiction, *Shutts* has a very significant limiting effect on the use of class actions as an aggregation device. To explain this fact requires that you understand just a bit about one aspect of class actions. In general, class actions can be divided into two types: mandatory and opt-out. As its name implies, an opt-out class action allows class members to exit from the case; thereafter, they are no longer parties to the action and the class action's outcome cannot bind them. In contrast, a mandatory class action does not allow class members to leave the action; the action's outcome binds them.

Because the standard for an opt-out class action tends to be easier to meet, a majority of class actions are opt-out class actions. Speaking in general terms, opt-out class actions seek damages; for the most part, mandatory class actions do not seek monetary recovery, but equitable relief. But there are exceptions under which mandatory class actions can provide damages. From the viewpoint of single-forum aggregation (and from the viewpoint of obtaining larger monetary recovery), a mandatory class action is superior to an opt-out class action when the class seeks damages. Unsurprisingly, therefore, lawyers sometimes engage in creative efforts to turn class actions seeking damages into mandatory class actions.

One of the largest sticking points in these efforts is footnote 3 in *Shutts*, which has become vitally important in class-action practice. Indeed, trying to sort out the meaning of this footnote has been something of a cottage industry for courts and commentators. Read one way, footnote 3 suggests that no class action seeking damages can be certified as a mandatory class action; class members in such class actions must have the right to opt out (a possibility that reduces the appeal of the class action to the parties as well as the capacity of the class-action device to achieve single-forum resolution of an entire controversy seeking damages). Read another way, it requires that all class actions — even those not seeking damages — must provide an opt-out right. Read a third way, the footnote confirms the present status quo, because mandatory class actions generally do not "predominately" award damages. Reading footnote 3 yet another way, *Shutts* requires a state court to provide an opt-out right when the state lacks contacts with a class member; but it has no effect on the ability of federal courts to use mandatory class actions as long as class members have minimum contacts with the country as a whole (even when members have no contact with the state in which the federal class action is pending).

5. The Supreme Court twice granted certiorari to resolve the issue of whether the Due Process Clause requires an opt-out right in mandatory class actions, but each time has dismissed the writ as improvidently granted. Ticor Title Ins. Co. v. Brown, 511 U.S. 117 (1994) (*infra* p. 420); Adams v. Robertson, 520 U.S. 83 (1997). The issue was also presented in a third case that the Supreme Court decided on another ground.   Ortiz v. Fibreboard Corp., 527 U.S. 815 (1999) (*infra* p. 506). *Ortiz* held that the case did not meet the criteria for mandatory class treatment, but made a cryptic and perhaps telling reference to the *Shutts* issue:

> The inherent tension between representative suits and the day-in-court ideal is only magnified if applied to damage claims gathered in a mandatory class. Unlike [opt-out] class members, objectors to the collectivism of a mandatory [class] action have no inherent right to abstain. The legal rights of absent class members (which in a class like this one would include claimants who by definition may be unidentifiable when the class is certified) are resolved regardless either of their consent, or, in a class with objectors, their express wish to the contrary.   And in settlement-only class actions the procedural protections built into [Rule 23] to protect the rights of absent class

members during litigation are never invoked in an adversarial setting
. . . .

In related circumstances, we raised the flag on this issue of due
process more than a decade ago in *Phillips Petroleum Co. v. Shutts*, 472
U. S. 797 (1985). *Shutts* . . . held that out-of-state plaintiffs could not
invoke the same due process limits on personal jurisdiction that out-of-
state defendants had . . . . But we also saw that before an absent class
member's right of action was extinguishable due process required that
the member "receive notice plus an opportunity to be heard and
participate in the litigation," and we said that "at a minimum . . . an
absent plaintiff [must] be provided with an opportunity to remove
himself from the class." [*Id.* at 847-48.]

In a footnote, the Court added: "In *Shutts*, as an important caveat to our
holding, we made clear that we were only examining the procedural
protections attendant on binding out-of-state class members whose claims
were 'wholly or predominately for money damages.'" *Id.* at 848 n.24.

Ortiz was a federal case involving Federal Rule of Civil Procedure 23.
Its dicta suggest that the lesson of *Shutts* cannot be confined to state-court
class actions, but the opinion said nothing about whether the degree of
protection in federal and state class actions was different or whether a class
member's contact with the country as a whole was sufficient contact to deny
Shutts's opt-out right to absent class members.

6.   Courts have tried various methods to avoid the roadblock imposed
by *Shutts*'s footnote 3.   The most notable efforts occurred in antitrust
actions brought by football players against the National Football League.
The actions sought both injunctive and monetary remedies. After the NFL
agreed to settle the case on a class basis, the district court certified a non-
opt-out class and approved the settlement. It then sought to enjoin players
from commencing their own suits elsewhere. The problem was that the
court, sitting in Minnesota, had no minimum contacts with most of the
5,000 class members.

The district court first circumvented *Shutts* by holding that *Shutts* did
not apply to mandatory class actions in which claims for injunctive relief
predominated over claims for monetary relief. White v. Nat'l Football
League, 822 F. Supp. 1389, 1410 (D. Minn. 1993). It then held that "where
sufficient alternative procedural safeguards are employed, opt-out rights
are not constitutionally required." *Id.* at 1411. Those safeguards existed
when "the objectors have been: (1) adequately represented by the named
plaintiffs; (2) adequately represented by capable and experienced class
counsel; (3) provided with adequate notice of the proposed settlement; (4)
given an opportunity to object to the settlement; and (5) assured that the
settlement will not be approved unless the court, after analyzing the facts
and law of the case and considering all objections to the proposed
settlement, determines it to be fair, reasonable and adequate." *Id.* at 1412.

On appeal, the Eighth Circuit took a different tack, holding that, since
the objectors had appeared in the district court to contest the merits of the

settlement, and not just the court's jurisdiction, the district court had jurisdiction over them. White v. Nat'l Football League, 41 F.3d 402, 407-08 (8th Cir. 1994); *cf.* In re Real Estate Title & Settlement Servs. Antitrust Litig., 869 F.2d 760, 770-71 (3rd Cir. 1989) (court did not have jurisdiction over a class member whose appearance contested only jurisdiction). The court of appeals therefore did "not reach the issue . . . left undecided by *Shutts*, namely whether a trial court may certify a non-opt-out plaintiff class in an action brought primarily for injunctive relief." 41 F.3d at 408.

Another tack, used in a few opinions though never really a favorite, is to argue that *Shutts* is irrelevant in federal court; federal courts can exercise jurisdiction with respect to anyone who has minimum contacts with the nation as a whole. The district court in *Ortiz* used this argument as an alternative rationale. *See* Ahearn v. Fibreboard Corp., 1995 U.S. Dist. LEXIS 11523, at *36-37 (E.D. Tex. July 27, 1995); 7AA CHARLES A. WRIGHT ET AL., FEDERAL PRACTICE AND PROCEDURE § 1789.1 (3d ed. 2005) (raising issue); *but see* Arthur R. Miller & David Crump, *Jurisdiction and Choice of Law in Multistate Class Actions After* Phillips Petroleum v. Shutts, 96 YALE L.J. 1 (1986) (arguing that *Shutts* applies in federal court). Might there also be an argument that *Shutts* applies only to state-law claims, and not to claims based on federal law?

Still another tack, proposed by Professors Miller and Crump, is to use a four-factor test to determine whether *Shutts* should apply. The four factors are efficiency, equity, prevention of abusive use of a distant forum, and plaintiffs' interests in individual control. *Id.* at 55-57. The authors acknowledge that *Shutts* itself does not suggest such a test, and that "the theory is supported only by the broadest inferences from *Shutts*." *Id.* at 56.

For other decisions concerning the application of *Shutts*, see In re Joint E. & S. Dist. Asbestos Litig., 78 F.3d 764 (2d Cir. 1996); In re Joint E. & S. Dist. Asbestos Litig., 982 F.2d 721 (2d Cir. 1992), *modified*, 993 F.2d 7 (2d Cir. 1993); In re Drexel Burnham Lambert Group, Inc., 960 F.2d 285 (2d Cir. 1992); *cf.* In re Integra Realty Res., Inc., 354 F.3d 1246 (10th Cir. 2004) (not applying *Shutts* because an attempt to recover fraudulently transferred money in a defendant class action did not seek monetary relief); In re A.H. Robins Co., 880 F.2d 709, 745 (4th Cir. 1989) (not following *Shutts* when a *de facto* opt-out right was provided in a mandatory class action).

7. *Shutts* contains another ambiguity. The class members in *Shutts* for whom an opt-out right was constitutionally required had no minimum contacts with Kansas. Was *Shutts* holding only that an opt-out right must be extended to out-of-state residents without minimum contacts, or was it holding more broadly that an opt-out right needed to be extended to all claims involving money damages — even those with whom Kansas did have minimum contacts? Though the tenor of the opinion would seem to favor the former interpretation, *see* Grimes v. Vitalink Commc'ns Corp., 17 F.3d 1553, 1560 n.8 (3d Cir. 1994) (a court can "bind absent class members who had sufficient minimum contacts with the forum" even in the absence of an opt-out provision), there is enough loose language in *Shutts* to support the

latter view. *See* Patricia A. Solomon, Note, *Are Mandatory Class Actions Constitutional?* 72 NOTRE DAME L. REV. 1627 (1997).

8.   *Shutts* contains a final ambiguity.   In *Shutts*, all class members were known and received individual notice of their right to opt out. In some cases, individual notice to all class members is impossible.   Does *Shutts* preclude a court from exercising jurisdiction over plaintiffs that have no minimum contact and that did not receive actual notice of their right to opt out? *See* In re "Agent Orange" Prod. Liab. Litig. MDL No. 381, 818 F.2d 145 (2d Cir. 1987) (*Shutts* does not require individual notice); In re "Agent Orange" Prod. Liab. Litig., 996 F.2d 1425 (2d Cir. 1993) (same).

9.   It is a slight — but only a slight — exaggeration to say that the fate of class actions — and perhaps all of mandatory aggregation — hinges on the uncertain scope of *Shutts*. If *Shutts* affects only state courts, then federal courts enjoy a significant aggregation advantage. If it affects only state-law claims, then asserting federal-question claims is the key to aggregation. If *Shutts* applies to claims primarily for monetary relief, then a predominance of injunctive claims is the key to involuntary aggregation of plaintiffs. If *Shutts* is subject to a mutli-factor test, then the balance of the relevant interests determines the legitimate scope of aggregation. If *Shutts* requires an opt-out right be extended to all plaintiffs who are subject to some form of mandatory aggregation but who lack minimum contacts with the forum, then mandatory aggregation is impossible in most widely dispersed litigation.

One way to think about the scope of *Shutts* is to focus on its holding that an opt-out right is necessary for at least some cases involving involuntary joinder.   What exactly is the point of an opt-out right? Presumably, such a right is valuable because it allows an individual to exercise control over his or her personal rights — to act, in other words, in a manner consistent with basic adversarial notions. If that is so, then neither a "state court vs. federal court" nor a "state-law claim vs. federal claim" distinction is really relevant to the basic concern of *Shutts*. Nor is the four-factor balancing test.   In some cases, however, the exercise of individual control is incompatible with the equal exercise of this right of control by others — in other words, some plaintiffs' lawsuits threaten the ability of other plaintiffs to have their day in court. (For instance, early-filing plaintiffs will shape the injunctive relief in such a way as to make it difficult for later plaintiffs to obtain relief; or early-filing plaintiffs will obtain all of a defendant's assets, leaving none for later filers.) Should *Shutts* be read to require an opt-out right for absent class members unless that right infringes on the right of others to control their cases?

B. LIMITATIONS ON AGGREGATION IMPOSED BY SUBJECT-MATTER JURISDICTION

This section focuses on the rules of subject-matter jurisdiction in the federal courts.   Understanding these rules is vital for any student or practitioner of complex litigation. When we studied stays, dismissals, and antisuit injunctions in Chapter Two, we saw that the existence of two court systems allowed plaintiffs to disperse related litigation between the state and federal systems, thus making single-forum aggregation more difficult. Therefore, understanding the circumstances in which a case can be filed in different court systems — as well as the ways in which jurisdictional rules can be used to overcome aggregation-frustrating dispersion between state and federal courts — is critical.

We focus on federal subject-matter jurisdiction for two reasons. First, federal courts have certain advantages for resolving complex cases, such as a uniform and generous system of joinder, a greater reach of territorial jurisdiction, greater resources, greater antisuit-injunction powers, and a greater ability to transfer cases to a single courtroom. Most lawyers, judges, and scholars agree that, if cases are to be aggregated, the federal system is the logical system in which to aggregate. Studying the ways in which to invoke the jurisdiction of the federal system, and thus to gain access to these advantages, is critical.

Second, even when federal courts do not possess these advantages, federal subject-matter jurisdiction provides the backdrop against which to consider state-court subject-matter jurisdiction. Although the statement is somewhat misleading, it is often said that state courts are courts of "general jurisdiction," while federal courts are courts of "limited jurisdiction." The point of this distinction is that state courts can hear cases involving all types of subject matter, but federal courts can hear only those cases or controversies that fit within (1) one of the nine grants of jurisdiction listed in Article III, § 2 of the United States Constitution, and (2) an act of Congress authorizing federal jurisdiction. "General jurisdiction" does not mean that any state court can hear any possible legal claim. Many state-court systems have courts of limited or special jurisdiction (for instance, probate or family courts), and no state court can entertain claims that lie within the exclusive jurisdiction of the federal courts. Nonetheless, as a general proposition, if a case does not fit within federal subject-matter jurisdiction, the plaintiff must file it in state court. Thus, by studying federal subject-matter jurisdiction, we indirectly learn the contours of state-court subject-matter jurisdiction.

Subject-matter jurisdiction continues the inquiry begun in the last section. Like rules of territorial jurisdiction, rules of subject-matter jurisdiction allocate judicial power among courts. Territorial jurisdiction principally involves "horizontal" allocation among the various state courts, while subject-matter jurisdiction principally involves "vertical" allocation between state and federal courts. But subject-matter jurisdiction, like territorial jurisdiction, asks how we should allocate power to preserve the vitality of both state and federal institutions, and to preserve individual freedoms against excessive interference from either. In the context of complex litigation, the rules of subject-matter jurisdiction also force us to decide how much we value federalism when its cost is the unfairness and inefficiency of repetitive litigation.

1. Federal-Question, Diversity, Supplemental, and Removal Jurisdiction: The Basics

This subsection briefly reiterates the rules of federal subject-matter jurisdiction that you likely learned in Civil Procedure, and shows the ways in which they operate to make single-forum aggregation more difficult in complex litigation. In doing so, we travel quickly over some unclear issues of federal jurisdiction.

As mentioned, the Constitution provides federal courts with nine grants of jurisdiction. These grants are a ceiling on federal jurisdiction, not a floor; courts cannot add to them. *See* Marbury v. Madison, 5 U.S. (1 Cranch) 137 (1803). With the exception of two grants of original jurisdiction to the Supreme Court, it is not usually thought that the grants of jurisdiction are self-executing; Congress must also pass legislation creating lower federal courts and investing them with jurisdiction. When it grants subject-matter jurisdiction, Congress is not required to — and typically has not — given federal courts the full scope of the jurisdiction that the Constitution allows. In addition, Congress has the power to make federal jurisdiction exclusive of the state courts, but in practice it has done so infrequently. Indeed, the presumption is that the subject-matter jurisdiction of the federal courts is *concurrent* with that of the state courts; even when a case falls within federal jurisdiction, in most cases a plaintiff can file the case in state court rather than in federal court. Tafflin v. Levitt, 493 U.S. 455 (1990).

Among the constitutional grants of jurisdiction, the workhorses in the federal courts, including in complex litigation, are the federal-question grant and the diversity grants. (Other grants, such as admiralty and suits involving ambassadors or consuls, have little application in complex litigation. The grant of jurisdiction for cases in which the United States is a party is important, but most of these cases would arise under the federal-question grant in any event.) For that reason, we focus on federal-question and diversity jurisdiction.

With respect to federal-question jurisdiction, the breadth of the Constitution's grant of jurisdiction is open to significant debate among scholars. The leading case is *Osborn v. Bank of the United States*, 22 U.S. (9 Wheat.) 738 (1824). In *Osborn*, as well as in a companion case, Chief Justice Marshall stated that the Constitution authorized federal-question jurisdiction as long as an issue of federal law constituted an "original ingredient" of a case, even when the issue was not contested or disputed in the case itself. *Id.* at 824. Later cases have stretched this idea to mean that, as long as a party can dispute (by way of claim or defense) an issue arising under federal law, constitutional federal-question jurisdiction exists — even when none of the parties make such an allegation. *See* Am. Nat'l Red Cross v. S.G., 505 U.S. 247 (1992). Other, even broader theories of federal-question jurisdiction have been propounded and debated among scholars and some Supreme Court Justices over the years. But even on *Osborn*'s theory, as subsequently construed, federal-question jurisdiction is exceedingly broad, especially in the modern world in which federal law and regulation are pervasive. It is a poor legal imagination that cannot conceive of some federal issue that might possibly arise in a lawsuit.

What holds back a flood of cases from entering the federal courts under the federal-question grant is the statutory grant of jurisdiction. For the most part, the federal-question statutes that Congress has enacted have steered far clear — or at least the Supreme Court has interpreted them to steer far clear — of granting the full constitutional scope of jurisdiction. Many statutes provide federal-question jurisdiction in specific areas such as bankruptcy (28 U.S.C. § 1334), antitrust (28 U.S.C. § 1337), patents (28 U.S.C. § 1338), and civil rights (28 U.S.C. § 1343). But the principal grant of federal-question jurisdiction is 28 U.S.C. § 1331, which provides that "district courts shall have original jurisdiction of all civil actions arising under the Constitution, laws, or treaties of the United States."

The Supreme Court has interpreted § 1331 to contain two significant jurisdictional limitations not found in Article III. The first is the "well-pleaded-complaint" rule, which requires that the federal issue in the case must be part of the plaintiff's original complaint and cannot be contained in an answer, a counterclaim, or another pleading. *See* Louisville & Nashville R.R. v. Mottley, 211 U.S. 149 (1908). Second, for the most part, the federal issue that must appear on the face of the well-pleaded complaint is a federal claim — in other words, a claim in which both the right and the remedy are supplied by federal law. A very small exception exists when a federal issue forms a necessary component of a state-law claim. The size of this exception has ebbed and flowed with the years. *Compare* Merrell Dow Pharms. Inc. v. Thompson, 478 U.S. 804 (1986) (no jurisdiction under § 1331 when a complaint alleged a state-law negligence *per se* claim based on a violation of a federal statute that itself provided no private remedy), *with* Grable & Sons Metal Prods., Inc. v. Darue Eng'g & Mfg., 545 U.S. 308 (2005) (jurisdiction under § 1331 when a complaint alleged a violation of a tax statute in part of a state-law quiet title action). But the exception has never been a significant way by which federal jurisdiction can be established.

The diversity grants of jurisdiction tell a similar story — a capacious constitutional authority and stingier statutory authority. Four of the nine jurisdictional grants in Article III are diversity-based; put together, they grant federal courts the jurisdiction to hear disputes between citizens of different states, or between American citizens and citizens or subjects of foreign countries. These grants of jurisdiction contain no minimum amount that must be in controversy. Moreover, they require only "minimal diversity": Federal jurisdiction exists as long as one party on either side of the case is of diverse citizenship from at least one party on the other side of the case. Thus, a lawsuit in which ten plaintiffs from Virginia sue ten defendants from Virginia and one defendant from Indiana lies within Article III's diversity grant. *See* State Farm Fire & Cas. Co. v. Tashire, 386 U.S. 523 (1967) (*supra* p. 84).

The statutory grants of diversity jurisdiction sometimes exploit the minimal-diversity requirement. *See, e.g.,* 28 U.S.C. §§ 1332(d)(2) (class actions; in the aggregate, more than $5,000,000 in dispute also required), 1335(a) (statutory interpleader; $500 amount-in-controversy also required), 1369 (multiparty, multiforum jurisdiction). But the basic grant of diversity jurisdiction, 28 U.S.C. § 1332(a), has long been construed to require "complete diversity," which means that no plaintiff may have the same citizenship as any defendant. *See* Strawbridge v. Curtiss, 7 U.S. (3 Cranch) 267 (1806). Thus, if ten plaintiffs from Virginia sue ten defendants from Indiana and one defendant from Virginia, § 1332(a) denies jurisdiction, even though the bulk of the lawsuit involves diverse parties. Corporations carry the citizenship both of their state of incorporation and of the state of their principal place of business — a fact that can make complete diversity harder to achieve in some cases. *See* 28 U.S.C. § 1332(c)(1); Hertz Corp. v. Friend, 559 U.S. —, 130 S. Ct. 1181 (2010) (adopting the corporate-headquarters test for determining the principal place of business). An exception to the requirement of complete diversity exists for class actions brought under § 1332(a); here, the citizenship of the class is measured by the citizenship only of the class representative(s). Thus, if ten class representatives from Virginia sue ten defendants from Indiana, the diversity requirement has been met, even if some class members are from Indiana. Supreme Tribe of Ben-Hur v. Cauble, 255 U.S. 356 (1921).

A second requirement of § 1332(a) (as well as most other diversity-based grants of jurisdiction) is a minimum amount in controversy. At present, to invoke § 1332(a) jurisdiction, a plaintiff must have a claim whose value exceeds $75,000. The Supreme Court has held that, in a multi-plaintiff case, each plaintiff must meet the amount in controversy; it is not enough that some plaintiffs meet the requirement or that, when added together, the sum of all plaintiffs' claims exceeds the jurisdictional amount. Unlike the citizenship requirement, the amount-in-controversy requirement did not bend for class actions: Section 1332(a) requires the claim of each class member to independently meet the amount in controversy; it is not enough that the class representative(s) have the requisite amount in controversy, or that the class as a whole does. *See* Zahn v. Int'l Paper Co., 414 U.S. 291 (1973); Snyder v. Harris, 394 U.S. 332 (1969).

The fact that our rules of joinder permit multiple claims and parties to be joined in one case creates another jurisdictional issue: What if some claims, or the claims against some parties, lie within federal jurisdiction but other claims do not? For instance, suppose a plaintiff from Virginia wishes to assert a federal-question claim and a state-law claim against a defendant who is also from Virginia. Or suppose that a plaintiff from Virginia sues a defendant from Indiana for $76,000, and wants to join (a) a defendant from Virginia and (b) another plaintiff from Indiana whose claim is worth only $50,000. Moreover, what are the jurisdictional effects of the joinder of counterclaims under Rule 13, or the joinder of additional parties under Rules 14 (third parties), 19 (required parties), or 24 (intervenors) when these claims have no independent basis of federal jurisdiction?

The answers to these questions lie in the doctrine of supplemental jurisdiction. Descendent from older doctrines such as ancillary jurisdiction, pendent jurisdiction, and pendent-party jurisdiction, supplemental jurisdiction permits federal courts, in some circumstances, to hear these add-on claims that federal courts would have been powerless to hear had they been filed independently. Traditionally, courts exercised ancillary and pendent jurisdiction without specific statutory authorization. The Supreme Court described the scope of ancillary jurisdiction (encompassing such areas as impleader, intervention, and counterclaims) broadly: It arose when a "logical relationship" or a "close connection" existed between the claim within federal jurisdiction and the ancillary claim. Moore v. N.Y. Cotton Exch., 270 U.S. 593, 610 (1926). The scope of pendent jurisdiction (encompassing the joinder of a plaintiff's state-law claim to the plaintiff's federal-question claim) was also broad: It arose when the state and federal claims "derive[ ] from a common nucleus of operative fact." United Mine Workers v. Gibbs, 383 U.S. 715, 725 (1966). The Court never recognized the doctrine of pendent-party jurisdiction, under which a plaintiff or defendant whose claim lacked federal jurisdiction could be joined with the claims of other parties that did satisfy federal jurisdiction; but its holding was based on the relevant jurisdictional statutes rather than on the Constitution. *See* Finley v. United States, 490 U.S. 545 (1989). The combined effect of the doctrines was that federal courts had subject-matter jurisdiction over most related claims asserted in a case, but not over permissive counterclaims, claims involving required parties under Rule 19, claims of permissive intervenors, or claims that added Rule 20 plaintiffs or defendants but did not have an independent basis of federal jurisdiction.

In 1990, Congress finally knit these various threads of jurisdiction together under the term "supplemental jurisdiction." *See* 28 U.S.C. § 1367. For the most part, § 1367 left in place the extant rules of jurisdiction, but in one regard it significantly expanded jurisdiction — by providing jurisdiction over pendent-party claims attached to federal-question claims, *see* § 1367(a) — and other regards it constrained jurisdiction — by refusing to afford jurisdiction of claims of intervention of right when the claim was based on state law and § 1332(a) gave no jurisdiction over the claim, and by giving federal courts discretion to refuse jurisdiction under certain circumstances, *see* § 1367(c). Section 1367 contained interpretive ambiguities that festered until the Supreme Court clarified the statute in *Exxon Mobil Corp. v. Allapattah*, 545 U.S. 546 (2005). *Allapattah* held that, as long as at least one plaintiff in a diversity-based case alleged a claim exceeding § 1332(a)'s amount in controversy, § 1367 gave supplemental jurisdiction over the claims of other plaintiffs who failed to meet that amount when these plaintiffs were joined either under Rule 20(a) or as class members under Rule 23.

Taken together, §§ 1331 and 1332(a) provide federal subject-matter jurisdiction in a broad range of cases, and § 1367 further expands federal subject-matter jurisdiction to make federal courts more hospitable fora for the multi-claim, multi-party disputes that are common in complex litigation. But these statutes cannot invest federal courts with jurisdiction in all complex disputes; for instance, victims of a mass tort who are citizens of the same state as a major defendant must file in state court unless they can plead a legitimate federal claim, and victims of small-stakes fraud, in which no plaintiff has more than $75,000 at stake, likewise can get to federal court only if they can make a claim arising under federal law.

The rules that limit federal jurisdiction (for instance, the well-pleaded-complaint rule and the requirement of complete diversity) were, for the most part, fashioned in cases that were not complex. They were not created with the aggregation needs of complex litigation in mind. (A partial exception is *Merrell Dow*, which was one case in the Bendectin mass-tort litigation; but due to the operation of the doctrine of *forum non conveniens*, creating federal-question jurisdiction in *Merrell Dow* would have done nothing to achieve single-forum aggregation.) Some stray language in a few Supreme Court decisions suggests that the ordinary jurisdictional rules might be shaped differently in complex litigation. *See* Franchise Tax Bd. v. Constr. Laborers Vacation Trust, 463 U.S. 1, 8 (1983) (noting that § 1331's "arising under" phrase "masks a welter of issues regarding the interrelation of federal and state authority and the proper management of the federal judicial system"); *Merrell Dow*, 478 U.S. at 810 ("We have consistently emphasized that, in exploring the outer reaches of § 1331, determinations about federal jurisdiction require sensitive judgments about congressional intent, judicial power, and the federal system."). But the Court has never considered "complexity exceptions" that change the usual glosses it has placed on the jurisdictional statutes in order to open up the federal courts to handle more related litigation.

how π can stay in state court

Even if such exceptions were made, the present jurisdictional statutes provide ample opportunity for plaintiffs who wish to avoid a federal forum to do so. If a plaintiff pleads no claim that arises under federal law (thus avoiding § 1331), and then either adds a non-frivolous claim against a non-diverse defendant or keep the amount in controversy to $75,000 or less (thus avoiding § 1332(a)), the case must remain in state court. Although § 1367 expands federal jurisdiction, supplemental jurisdiction still requires the plaintiff to plead at least one claim lying within federal jurisdiction to which the additional claim is a supplement. Similarly, because §§ 1331, 1332(a), and 1367 do not provide for exclusive federal jurisdiction, a plaintiff can file a complaint containing a federal question, or a complaint seeking more than $75,000 from diverse defendants, in state court, taking advantage of state courts' concurrent jurisdiction over most disputes.

The upshot of these standard jurisdictional rules is that plaintiffs who want to invoke federal jurisdiction can usually do so by adding some federal claims or by trimming some non-diverse parties from their cases. (There are exceptions: Consider the situation of 10,000 Virginia, Maryland, and Pennsylvania consumers, each bilked out of $20 by a Massachusetts company's unscrupulous business practice, which is illegal under the respective states' laws, but not under federal law.) But the converse is also true: Plaintiffs who do not want to invoke federal jurisdiction can do so by trimming federal claims or adding non-diverse parties. Because we allow plaintiffs to be "masters of their complaints" (i.e., to choose which claims to assert and which parties to join), *see* The Fair v. Kohler Die & Specialty Co.,

228 U.S. 22 (1913), the present jurisdictional rules contribute to the dispersion of related cases across the federal and state systems. They are, in other words, a cause of repetitive litigation.

One possible solution to this problem is to take away from plaintiffs their "master of the complaint" status, and to provide either defendants or the court with the power to remove to federal court cases that plaintiffs filed in state court. To some extent, this "removal jurisdiction" already exists. Although there are other removal grants scattered across the United States Code, the principal statute authorizing removal jurisdiction is 28 U.S.C. § 1441(a). In cases in which diversity is the basis for federal jurisdiction, §§ 1441(b) and 1446(b) contain important exceptions to removal under § 1441(a); but as a general rule, § 1441(a) permits (but does not require) a defendant to remove a case over which a federal court would have had original jurisdiction if the plaintiff had filed it there. Plaintiffs who want to make their choice of state court bullet-proof to removal must ensure that their complaints state no grounds for federal jurisdiction.

Because a defendant typically must invoke removal jurisdiction, and because § 1441(a) creates no jurisdiction when a plaintiff assiduously avoids pleading any basis for federal jurisdiction in a state-court complaint, § 1441(a) is only a partial solution to plaintiffs' ability to disperse related cases across state and federal forums. The following case considers whether the power of removal should be expanded in a way that makes it a more useful tool for preventing jurisdictional dispersion.

SYNGENTA CROP PROTECTION, INC. V. HENSON

537 U.S. 28 (2002)

■   CHIEF JUSTICE REHNQUIST delivered the opinion for a unanimous Court.

Respondent Hurley Henson filed suit in state court in Iberville Parish, Louisiana, against petitioner Syngenta Crop Protection, Inc. (then known as Ciba-Geigy Corp.) asserting various tort claims related to petitioners' manufacture and sale of a chlordimeform-based insecticide. A similar action, *Price v. Ciba-Geigy Corp.*, was already underway in the United States District Court for the Southern District of Alabama. The Louisiana court stayed respondent's action when respondent successfully intervened in the *Price* suit and participated in the ensuing settlement.   That settlement included a stipulation that the *Henson* action, "including any and all claims . . . against [petitioners], shall be dismissed, with prejudice," as of the approval date.

Following the approval of the settlement, the Louisiana state court conducted a hearing to determine whether the *Henson* action should be dismissed. Counsel for respondent told the court that the *Price* settlement required dismissal of only some of the claims raised in *Henson*. Although this representation appeared to be contrary to the terms of the settlement agreement, the Louisiana court relied upon it and invited respondent to amend the complaint and proceed with the action.

Counsel for petitioners did not attend the hearing. Upon learning of the state court's action, however, petitioners promptly removed the action to the Middle District of Louisiana, relying on 28 U.S.C. § 1441(a). The notice of removal asserted federal jurisdiction under the All Writs Act, § 1651, and under the supplemental jurisdiction statute, § 1367. The Middle District of Louisiana granted a transfer to the Southern District of Alabama pursuant to § 1404(a), and the Alabama court then dismissed *Henson* as barred by the *Price* settlement and sanctioned respondent's counsel for his misrepresentation to the Louisiana state court.

The Court of Appeals for the Eleventh Circuit affirmed the sanctions but vacated the District Court's order dismissing the *Henson* action. The court reasoned that § 1441 by its terms authorizes removal only of actions over which the district courts have original jurisdiction. But the All Writs Act authorizes writs "in aid of [the courts'] respective jurisdictions" without providing any federal subject-matter jurisdiction in its own right. Therefore, the Court of Appeals concluded, the All Writs Act could not support removal of the *Henson* action from state to federal court.

In so holding, the Court of Appeals recognized that several Circuits have held that the All Writs Act gives a federal court the authority to remove a state-court case in order to prevent the frustration of orders the federal court has previously issued. . . . We granted certiorari to resolve this controversy, and now affirm.

The All Writs Act, 28 U.S.C. § 1651(a), provides that "[t]he Supreme Court and all courts established by Act of Congress may issue all writs necessary or appropriate in aid of their respective jurisdictions and agreeable to the usages and principles of law." Petitioners advance two arguments in support of their claim that removal of the *Henson* action was proper under the All Writs Act: (1) The All Writs Act authorized removal of the *Henson* action, and (2) the All Writs Act in conjunction with the doctrine of ancillary enforcement jurisdiction authorized the removal. We address these contentions in turn.

First, petitioners, like the courts that have endorsed "All Writs removal," rely upon our statement in *United States v. New York Telephone Co.*, 434 U.S. 159, 172 (1977), that the Act authorizes a federal court "to issue such commands . . . as may be necessary or appropriate to effectuate and prevent the frustration of orders it has previously issued in its exercise of jurisdiction otherwise obtained." Petitioners also cite *Pennsylvania Bureau of Correction v. United States Marshals Service*, 474 U.S. 34, 41 (1985), for the proposition that the All Writs Act "fill[s] the interstices of federal judicial power when those gaps threate[n] to thwart the otherwise proper exercise of federal courts' jurisdiction." They argue that the Act comes into play here because maintenance of the *Henson* action in state court in Louisiana frustrated the express terms of the *Price* settlement, which required that "any and all claims" in Henson be dismissed.

But *Pennsylvania Bureau* made clear that "[w]here a statute specifically addresses the particular issue at hand, it is that authority, and not the All Writs Act, that is controlling." The right of removal is entirely a creature of statute and a suit commenced in a state court must remain there until cause is shown for its transfer under some act of Congress. These statutory procedures for removal are to be strictly construed. Petitioners may not, by resorting to the All Writs Act, avoid complying with the statutory requirements for removal.

Petitioners' question presented to this Court suggests a variation on this first argument, asking whether the All Writs Act "vests federal district courts with authority to exercise removal jurisdiction under 28 U.S.C. § 1441." . . . Under the plain terms of § 1441(a), in order properly to remove the *Henson* action pursuant to that provision, petitioners must demonstrate that original subject-matter jurisdiction lies in the federal courts. They concede that the All Writs Act does not, by its specific terms, provide federal courts with an independent grant of jurisdiction. Because the All Writs Act does not confer jurisdiction on the federal courts, it cannot confer the original jurisdiction required to support removal pursuant to § 1441.

Second, petitioners contend that some combination of the All Writs Act and the doctrine of ancillary enforcement jurisdiction support the removal of the *Henson* action. As we explained in *Peacock v. Thomas*, 516 U.S. 349, 355 (1996), "[a]ncillary jurisdiction may extend to claims having a factual and logical dependence on 'the primary lawsuit.'" Petitioners emphasize that the Southern District of Alabama retained jurisdiction over the *Price* settlement . . . . They argue that respondent's maintenance of the *Henson* action undermined the *Price* settlement and that, in light of the Alabama court's retained jurisdiction, ancillary enforcement jurisdiction was necessary and appropriate.* But they fail to explain how the Alabama District Court's retention of jurisdiction over the *Price* settlement authorized removal of the *Henson* action. Removal is governed by statute, and invocation of ancillary jurisdiction, like invocation of the All Writs Act, does not dispense with the need for compliance with statutory requirements.

. . . [P]erhaps petitioners' argument is that ancillary jurisdiction authorizes removal under 28 U.S.C. § 1441. As we explained in *Peacock*, however, a "court must have jurisdiction over a case or controversy before it may assert jurisdiction over ancillary claims." Ancillary jurisdiction, therefore, cannot provide the original jurisdiction that petitioners must show in order to qualify for removal under § 1441.

Section 1441 requires that a federal court have original jurisdiction over an action in order for it to be removed from a state court. The All Writs Act, alone or in combination with the existence of ancillary jurisdiction in a

---

*   Petitioners' assertion that removal was "necessary" is unpersuasive on its own bottom. One in petitioners' position may apply to the court that approved a settlement for an injunction requiring dismissal of a rival action. Petitioners could also have sought a determination from the Louisiana state court that respondent's action was barred by the judgment of the Alabama District Court.

federal court; is not a substitute for that requirement. Accordingly, the judgment of the Court of Appeals is

Affirmed.

■   [The concurring opinion of JUSTICE STEVENS is omitted.]

Notes

1.   The defendant's actions in *Syngenta* show the two steps that must be often taken to achieve single-forum aggregation in a federal forum. First, the case must be removed from state to federal court. Removal occurs to the federal district encompassing the state court from which removal occurs. *See* 28 U.S.C. §§ 1441(a), 1446(a). Unless that district is also the district in which the aggregation of related cases is going to occur, the second step is to find a vehicle (most likely, either § 1404 or § 1407 transfer — *see supra* pp. 134-69) to relocate the case in the aggregating district. *Syngenta* cut off the attempt to aggregate the cases at the first step.

2.   *Syngenta* does not necessarily end the aggregation effort. In the last chapter, we saw that, in circumstances akin to *Syngenta*, federal courts sometimes entered antisuit injunctions against state-court cases that threatened a federal-court settlement. *See supra* pp. 183-88. The courts held that the power to issue these injunctions derived from the All Writs Act. Does *Syngenta* suggest that this use of the Act is illegitimate? Here is the argument: From the viewpoint of aggregating cases and preventing relitigation, it does not matter whether the state-court cases are removed or enjoined. In either situation, the state-court litigation stops. So if a court cannot use the All Writs Act to remove a state-court case when it threatens a federal judgment, then it cannot use the Act to enjoin that case.

If this argument is correct, then federal courts will have lost one of their important advantages — the antisuit injunction — that makes them a more attractive forum for aggregating related litigation. Of course, nothing in *Syngenta* suggests that this argument is right. Viewed from a different perspective, there is a great difference between a power to create jurisdiction and a power to issue an injunction. The All Writs Act could authorize the latter without authorizing the former.

3.   From the viewpoint of complex litigation, a straightforward removal power would in most instances be preferable to the more circuitous power to issue antisuit injunctions. But *Syngenta* was unwilling to use the All Writs Act creatively to carve out a "complexity exception" that could have made removal a more useful tool for aggregating related cases and preventing repetitive litigation. Thus, despite the unfairness or inefficiency that the choice might cause, a plaintiff who wants a state forum needs only to avoid pleading claims lying within federal jurisdiction. *Syngenta* refuses to upset the usual rule that the plaintiff is the "master of the complaint."

4.   In light of *Syngenta*, should Congress enact a removal statute designed specifically to prevent relitigation in state and federal court? As

part of its larger series of recommendations to give courts the power to stop needless relitigation of claims, the American Law Institute proposed a removal statute that allowed defendants or a federal judge to remove related cases pending in state court. Among the factors that the federal judge was to consider were the value of the removed claims, the number and size of the actions involved, the number of jurisdictions in which the state-court cases are filed, the interest in uniform determination of issues, the presence of any special local or state interests, changes in the governing law that might cause "undue unfairness" to a party, "the possibility of facilitating informal cooperation or coordination with the state courts," and, more generally, "whether removal will unduly disrupt or impinge upon state court or regulatory proceedings or impose an undue burden on the federal courts." AM. L. INST., COMPLEX LITIGATION § 5.01 (1994). *See also* AM. BAR ASS'N, COMM'N ON MASS TORTS, REPORT TO THE HOUSE OF DELEGATES 48 (1989) (recommending the creation of legislation to permit removal of mass torts to federal court).

Would such a grant of statutory jurisdiction be constitutional? The ALI argued that, because the state-court cases would be related transactionally to the federal-court cases, federal jurisdiction was "analogous to the court's supplemental jurisdiction powers." COMPLEX LITIGATION, *supra*, § 5.01 cmt. d. The ABA argued that, because of their effect on national commerce, mass torts could "be deemed to arise under the laws of the United States," thus suggesting a federal-question basis for such removal jurisdiction. REPORT TO THE HOUSE OF DELEGATES, *supra*, at 48.

For both the ALI and the ABA, removal jurisdiction was a linchpin of their proposals to end repetitive litigation. They also both recognized the damage that removal inflicted on the values of federalism, but believed that the cost was necessary to create single-forum aggregation.

5. Congress has never risen to the bait and created a special removal statute for complex litigation. In light of that fact and the holding in *Syngenta*, it is therefore necessary to attend closely to the present scope and limits of removal jurisdiction. Here are a few highlights that involve commonly recurring issues or that are relevant to later material:

- The Supreme Court has said repeatedly that, due to the friction they create with state courts, removal statutes are to be construed strictly; thus, federalism bars expansive interpretations of removal. *See, e.g.*, Shamrock Oil & Gas Co. v. Sheets, 313 U.S. 100 (1941).

- Under § 1441(a), all of the defendants must usually join in the removal notice. Unless all defendants consent, the case remains in state court. *See* 14C CHARLES ALAN WRIGHT ET AL., FEDERAL PRACTICE AND PROCEDURE § 3731 (3d ed. 1998) (discussing the rule and some exceptions).

- It is more difficult to remove a case based on diversity jurisdiction than on federal-question jurisdiction due to two important limitations. First, a case cannot be removed from state court when the case is filed in the court of a state of which at least one defendant is a citizen. 28 U.S.C. § 1441(b). This restriction does not apply to federal-question cases, which can be removed regardless of the citizenship of the parties. *Id.* Second, once a case has been pending in state court for more than one year, it cannot be removed even though it first becomes removable only after the year passes. 28 U.S.C. § 1446(b). This rule can lead to tactical jockeying. For instance, a plaintiff who wants a state forum can join a marginally involved non-diverse defendant, dismiss that defendant from the case a year and a day later, and retain the state forum. In contrast, if a plaintiff first asserts a federal question in a complaint two years into the state-court litigation, the case is removable.

• Generally, when a district court determines that the case was improperly removed due to a lack of subject-matter jurisdiction, the order of remand is not appealable. 28 U.S.C. § 1447(d). When the judge orders remand for a reason other than a lack of jurisdiction, the decision can often be challenged in the appellate courts. *See* Thermtron Products, Inc. v. Hermansdorfer, 423 U.S. 336 (1976); *but see* Carlsbad Tech., Inc. v. HIF Bio, Inc., 556 U.S. —, 129 S. Ct. 1862 (2009) (in three separate concurring opinions, four Justices expressing dissatisfaction with the *Thermtron* rule).

6.   Under § 1441(a), only "the defendant or the defendants" have the right to remove a case. The Supreme Court has held that this language precludes plaintiffs from removing a case even if they become defendants to a counterclaim that contains a basis for federal jurisdiction. *Shamrock*, 313 U.S. 100. Most courts have extended the *Shamrock* rule and denied third-party defendants and similar litigants the right to remove. *See* 14C WRIGHT ET AL., *supra*, § 3731. Congress has occasionally altered this rule, and in a tailored removal statute has given a party other than a defendant the right to remove. *See, e.g.,* 12 U.S.C. §§ 1441a(a)(11), 1441a(*l*)(3), 1819(b)(2)(B) (providing right of removal to, respectively, the Thrift Depository Oversight Board, the Resolution Trust Corporation, and the FDIC); 28 U.S.C. §§ 1442, 1442a (providing removal right to federal officers and members of the armed forces).

An interesting and open question is whether federal judges possess a sua sponte power to order removal when the defendants choose not to remove eligible state-court cases that are related to cases in federal court. Before *Syngenta*, some courts claimed this power; they often cited the All Writs Act as its source. *See* In re "Agent Orange" Prod. Liab. Litig., 996 F.2d 1425, 1431 (2d Cir. 1993); Ryan v. Dow Chem. Co., 781 F. Supp. 902, 918 (E.D.N.Y. 1991); *accord,* In the Matter of VMS Sec. Litig., 103 F.3d 1317 (7th Cir. 1996). *See also* In re Metlife Demutualization Litig., 2006 WL 2524196, at *3 n.3 (E.D.N.Y. Aug. 28, 2006) (leaving the issue open). For the most part, however, the defendants in these cases had filed removal notices themselves, so the issue of sua sponte power was not squarely presented, and the courts' statements were dicta.

Syngenta did not address, and therefore did not forbid, the practice of sua sponte removal, but its narrow view of the All Writs Act suggests caution — especially because removal statutes such as § 1441(a) give specific parties the power of removal, but never mention judges. Moreover, because it is often thought that federal courts do not have sua sponte power to remand a case to state court for procedural defects in the removal petition, *see* In re Allstate Ins. Co., 8 F.3d 219 (5th Cir. 1993), the case for a sua sponte power to remove cases from state court becomes weaker.

7.   Defendants in dispersed litigation sometimes look for ways to escape from the jurisdictional handcuffs imposed by § 1441. For instance, defendants frequently argue that certain plaintiffs or defendants in the state-court litigation were fraudulently joined to prevent removal; once the improperly joined parties are disregarded, then the remaining case falls within federal jurisdiction. We saw such an argument in *In re Prempro Products Liability Litigation*, 591 F.3d 613 (8th Cir. 2010) (*supra* p. 65), which discusses how courts have responded to a claim of fraudulent joinder. Fraudulent joinder is difficult to prove, but sometimes defendants are successful in doing so.

Similarly, when a case involves repetitive claims against a government contractor, the contractor sometimes claims that it can remove the case under 28 U.S.C. § 1442, the federal-officer removal provision. *See, e.g.,* Watson v. Philip Morris Cos., 551 U.S. 142 (2007) (rejecting a contractor's claim of federal-officer status). One of the advantages of federal-officer removal is that it allows removal on the basis of a federal defense (which is, usually, that the defendant's actions may have been prima facie wrongful under state law, but they were justified under a federal duty that the officer was performing). In this regard, § 1442 authorizes removal jurisdiction broader than the federal courts' original jurisdiction, which is constrained by the well-pleaded-complaint rule.

8.   Leaving aside limited-use statutes such as § 1442, the bottom line, which *Syngenta* reinforces, is this: Federal courts have no more jurisdiction on removal than they have as an original matter. Therefore, understanding the scope of the original-jurisdiction statutes (especially §§ 1331, 1332, and 1367) is essential to understanding § 1441 and removal more generally. If §§ 1331, 1332, and 1367 can stretch to accommodate the aggregation of complex cases, removal can be an effective tool for reducing repetitive state and federal litigation. Otherwise, it cannot. *Cf.* In re Sugar Antitrust Litig., 588 F.2d 1270, 1273-74 (9th Cir. 1978) (holding that defendants seeking to remove state-law antitrust claims in order to join them with federal antitrust claims could not use removal "as a bill of peace, designed simply to put together in one forum all claims based upon the same cause of action").

2. Additional Jurisdictional Barriers to Aggregation

Beyond the basic rules of federal jurisdiction, additional jurisdictional doctrines sometimes pose a barrier to aggregation in a federal forum. Three arise with some frequency in complex litigation: justiciability, abstention, and the Eleventh Amendment. The difficult issues that these doctrines pose for federal jurisdiction are discussed in much greater detail in classes such as Constitutional Law and Federal Courts. Here we attempt only to alert you to the ways in which they can arise in complex cases.

Justiciability doctrines — ripeness, mootness, political question, advisory opinion, and especially standing — derive from Article III's "case or controversy" requirement. Most complex cases present no justiciability issues, but some do so with regularity. Environmental controversies, for example, often raise questions of standing — a doctrine intended to ensure that the plaintiff has an actual, redressable injury due to the defendant's conduct. *See* Mass. v. EPA, 549 U.S. 497 (2007); Lujan v. Defenders of Wildlife, 504 U.S. 555 (1992). So can certain other public-law controversies against the government. *See* DaimlerChrysler Corp. v. Cuno, 547 U.S. 332 (2006).

An unresolved question of standing involves an important category of plaintiffs in some complex cases: "future plaintiffs." As we have seen, future plaintiffs — those who are at risk of injury because of a defendant's conduct but who have not yet suffered an actual injury — can pose difficult aggregation issues, especially in mass torts, because such claims disperse related litigation temporally. Rather than waiting for each injury to be suffered and each case to mature into litigation, some defendants have tried to handle the problem of future plaintiffs by creating a settlement fund to pay their claims. The basic problem of such an approach is one of preclusion: How can the defendant bind future plaintiffs to accept payment from the fund rather than to file lawsuits. The answer, whose limits we explore in the next chapter, has been a device known as a "settlement class action"; class representatives, who themselves are future plaintiffs, agree to accept the settlement on behalf of a class of future plaintiffs.

A critical question is whether the plaintiffs in such a settlement class action have standing to bring a case seeking approval of the settlement in federal court. By definition, the class representatives and class members have no existing claims, only the uncertain possibility of claims at an unknown future date. In both cases involving settlement class actions that the Supreme Court has considered, the Court has raised the standing issue. *See* Ortiz v. Fibreboard Corp., 527 U.S. 815, 830-31 (1999) (*infra* p. 506); Amchem Prods., Inc. v. Windsor, 521 U.S. 591, 612-13 (1997) (*infra* p. 493). Because it found logically antecedent defects in both settlement class actions, the Court did not address the standing question in either case, but its cautionary note in *Amchem* that "Rule 23's requirements must be interpreted in keeping with Article III constraints," 521 U.S. at 613, suggests that the matter is in some doubt. For the district court's thorough (albeit mooted) discussion of the justiciability issues raised in *Amchem*'s future-plaintiff settlement class action, see Carlough v. Amchem Prods., Inc., 834 F. Supp. 1437 (E.D. Pa. 1993).

Second, judicially created abstention doctrines can require a federal court to decline jurisdiction that Congress has authorized. We examined these doctrines briefly in Chapter Two. *See supra* pp. 201-08. As we saw, for the most part, these doctrines have little effect — either positive or negative — on the aggregation of complex cases. Because abstention doctrines have applicability across a range of cases, however, their potential applicability in a complex case can never be ignored.

Third, the Eleventh Amendment and its penumbra make the assertion of monetary claims against state defendants problematic in many cases. Since 1995, the Supreme Court has been very active establishing the modern boundaries of the Eleventh Amendment, which provides: "The Judicial power of the United States shall not be construed to extend to any suit in law or equity, commenced or prosecuted against one of the United States by Citizens of another State, or by Citizens or Subjects of any Foreign State." In a series of decisions whose 5-4 votes highlight the instability of the present understanding of the Amendment, the Court has, for the most part, denied federal courts the jurisdiction to hear monetary claims against the states when the claim arises under any federal law passed pursuant to Congress's Article I powers. *See* Seminole Tribe of Fla. v. Florida, 517 U.S. 44 (1996); *but see* Cent. Va. Cmty. Coll. v. Katz, 546 U.S. 356 (2006) (holding that a federal court could entertain a bankruptcy proceeding disgorging preferential transfers made to a state agency). The Court has also extended this jurisdictional immunity to similar cases brought in state court as a matter not of the Eleventh Amendment but of the Constitution's overarching structure. *See* Alden v. Maine, 527 U.S. 706 (1999).

The Eleventh Amendment still allows a wide array of claims to be asserted, including most injunctive claims against states or state officials, monetary claims against state officials that are to be paid by the officials, monetary or injunctive claims by the United States or other states against a state, and monetary claims arising under a federal law passed pursuant to Congress's Fourteenth Amendment powers. States can also consent to jurisdiction. Nonetheless, when a state is a potential defendant in a series of complex cases, the Eleventh Amendment and its penumbra make the aggregation of all related cases in federal court a tricky matter.

Justiciability doctrines, which keep the federal courts as an institution focused on legal as opposed to political disputes, developed principally from a concern for separation of powers. Abstention and Eleventh Amendment doctrines have developed principally from a concern for federalism. Thus far, courts have created no "complexity exceptions" designed to avert the potential anti-aggregative effect of these jurisdictional limitations.

3. Expanding Federal Jurisdiction in Complex Cases

Federal courts do not possess unlimited subject-matter jurisdiction. Nonetheless, because they possess more effective powers in areas such as transfer, consolidation, antisuit injunctions, and territorial reach, federal courts are usually perceived to be better positioned than state courts to avoid the geographical dispersion of claims, and thus to achieve the single-forum aggregation that complex litigation can require. If achieving such aggregation is important, then federal jurisdiction must be expanded beyond the boundaries of §§ 1331, 1332(a), and 1367. As we have seen, as a constitutional matter, both the federal-question grant of jurisdiction and the diversity grants of jurisdiction have unused jurisdictional capacity — the "original ingredient" route suggested in *Osborn* and the "minimal diversity" route used in *Tashire* — that give Congress plenty of room to create aggregation-friendly jurisdictional statutes.

The calls for Congress to create a statute expanding federal jurisdiction in complex cases is common. *See, e.g.*, REPORT OF THE FED. COURTS STUDY COMM. 38-48 (1990) (recommending that federal jurisdiction generally be contracted, but that jurisdiction in complex litigation be expanded). But such legislation creates concerns. One is defining "complex litigation" — in other words, the cases that require single-forum aggregation. Until now, we have operated with a rather loose definition of such litigation: that litigation is "complex" if related cases ought to be aggregated for reasons of fairness or efficiency. How do we translate that idea into jurisdictional language that neither excludes from federal jurisdiction cases we want federal courts to adjudicate nor includes cases with which we do not wish to bog down the federal system? A second concern is federalism. Does a jurisdictional approach that puts complex litigation in the federal courts turn the state courts into a minor-league farm system? Shouldn't state courts decide complex cases, especially when they involve issues of state, rather than federal, law? Other concerns include autonomy and uniformity: Why should we change the "master of the complaint" rule for this group of cases but not for others?

In this section, we address these questions by examining the situations in which Congress has expanded original jurisdiction to permit greater aggregation of related cases in federal court. In each case, Congress chose the minimal-diversity approach to create federal jurisdiction. The first statute, enacted in 1926, was 28 U.S.C. § 1335, which permits interpleader when two or more claimants are diverse and $500 or more is at stake. As we saw in Chapter Two (*supra* p. 84), however, statutory interpleader is not a general panacea for the problem of repetitive litigation.

In recent years, Congress has enacted two more statutes that expand federal jurisdiction and allow federal courts to hear related disputes. It passed the first — the Multiparty, Multiforum Trial Jurisdiction Act — in 2002. It passed the second — the Class Action Fairness Act — in 2005. These statutes expand federal jurisdiction in very specific ways and with very specific limits designed to respect the role of state courts. Neither statute solves all (or even most) of the problems created by the jurisdictional dispersion of related litigation. But together they suggest the possible shape of a general, and more widely useful, jurisdictional statute that can establish a single federal forum for complex cases. They also suggest some of the difficulties with such a statute.

a. Multiparty, Multiforum Jurisdiction

Read 28 U.S.C. §§ 1369 and 1441(e). The first subsection (§ 1369(a)) creates federal subject-matter jurisdiction; the second subsection (§ 1369(b)) requires federal courts to abstain from exercising this jurisdiction in certain circumstances. Section 1369 contains no minimal amount in controversy.

Because of the recency of § 1369 and the requirement that the case involve at least 75 deaths, courts have had few opportunities to interpret the statute and its ambiguities. The following case is the seminal effort.

PASSA V. DERDERIAN

308 F. Supp. 2d 43 (D.R.I. 2004)

■ LAGUEUX, Senior United States District Judge.

On February 20, 2003, a deadly fire destroyed a nightclub located in West Warwick, Rhode Island, known to its patrons as "The Station." The fire started during the first minutes of a performance by the rock band Great White, while the club itself was crowded with spectators, staff, and performers. When defendants, Jack Russell, Mark Kendall, David Filice, and Eric Powers, members of the band "Great White" (hereafter referred to as "Band Members")[,] took the stage that night, they and their tour manager, Daniel Bichele, ignited pyrotechnic devices as a part of their performance. These "pyrotechnics," also described as stage fireworks, or sparklers, caused flaming sparks to explode behind the stage area. According to witnesses, the sparks from these fireworks ignited foam insulation material previously installed in the club's ceiling and walls for soundproofing purposes. Once started, the fire quickly spread throughout The Station, creating a fiery inferno in its wake. In less than three minutes, the entire establishment was ablaze, and a reported 412 people inside the building that night were scrambling to escape the conflagration. According to this Court's best estimates, this tragic fire left 100 individuals dead and more than 200 injured. Only seventy-seven people are reported to have escaped the building without physical harm, yet, even for these lucky few who escaped bodily injury, the disaster continues to haunt their memories and affect their lives. The impact of this tragedy on the victims, the survivors, their families and friends, and the entire community cannot be overstated. . . .

In the wake of this tragedy, numerous lawsuits have been filed throughout southern New England in both state and federal courts. At present, this Court is concerned with five of these cases, two originally filed here in the United States District Court for the District of Rhode Island and three cases removed here from the Rhode Island Superior Court.

Three of these cases, *Passa*, *Guindon*, and *Kingsley*, are civil actions filed by fire victims, their estates, and surviving family members alleging a variety of different state law tort claims against a host of different named

Defendants. These named Defendants include the surviving Band Members (including their tour manager), their management company, and their record label; nightclub owners Jeffrey and Michael Derderian (the "Derderians"), a corporation owned by the Derderians, DERCO, Inc.; a real estate company, Triton Realty, Inc. ("Triton Realty"); insulation manufacturers American Foam Corporation ("American Foam") and Foamex International, Inc. (Foamex); pyrotechnic manufacturer Luna Tech, Inc. ("Luna Tech"); event sponsors such as Anheuser-Busch Companies, Inc. ("Anheuser-Busch"), McLaughlin & Moran, Inc. ("McLaughlin & Moran"), Shell Oil Company ("Shell"), Motiva Enterprises, LLC ("Motiva"), WHJY-FM radio, Clear Channel Communications, Inc. ("Clear Channel"); and representatives of government agencies establishing fire code regulations and enforcing compliance, including the West Warwick Town Fire Inspector, the Town of West Warwick, the Rhode Island State Fire Marshall, and the State itself. . . .

The other two cases, *Alves* and *O'Brien*, are miscellaneous petitions . . . removed to this Court by Anheuser-Busch. These two petitions were filed soon after the tragedy by victims and other supporting entities and potential defendants in an effort to preserve physical evidence . . . . Unlike the civil actions at issue, these miscellaneous petitions name only a handful of Defendants, termed therein as "Respondents" or "Interested Parties."

At issue before the Court is the question of jurisdiction. In each of the five cases described above, jurisdiction in federal court is alleged under a new statute, 28 U.S.C. § 1369, popularly known as the Multiparty, Multiforum, Trial Jurisdiction Act of 2002 ("MMTJA"). This is a new jurisdictional act greatly expanding the original and removal jurisdiction of the federal courts, and to date no court has had the occasion to apply or interpret it. As a result, this writer will be the first to construe § 1369, and thus, is forced to be the first to bite the proverbial bullet.

[In each of the five cases, the Derderians and American Foam moved to dismiss or to remand to state court because the district court lacked jurisdiction under § 1369(a) and because it was required to abstain under § 1369(b). Other defendants opposed the motions. Among the plaintiffs, some supported, and others opposed, the motions.]

DISCUSSION

. . .

Federal courts are courts of limited subject matter jurisdiction. . . . Prior to 2002, federal subject matter jurisdiction was limited to . . . cases where a question of federal law was presented, or where the parties had complete diversity of state citizenship and an amount in controversy greater than $75,000.00. In September of 2002, only months before the Station nightclub tragedy, Congress enacted a new jurisdictional statute, the MMTJA. . . .

This new jurisdictional statute, by its terms, expands the original jurisdiction of federal courts to include lawsuits arising from accidents where more than 75 natural persons die at a discrete location, provided that the other requirements of the statute are satisfied. The first part of the statute, § 1369(a), grants the federal district court original jurisdiction over any civil action stemming from such a tragedy with minimal diversity between the parties, provided that one of the following factors is also present: (1) a defendant resides in a different state from where a substantial part of the accident took place, regardless of whether a substantial portion of the accident also took place in his or her own state; (2) any two defendants reside in different states, regardless of whether these defendants happen to reside in the same state as another defendant; or (3) substantial parts of the accident took place in different states. Neither side of this jurisdictional controversy disputes the application of § 1369(a) to the facts of the Station nightclub tragedy . . . .

It is the second part of the MMTJA, § 1369(b), that has the different parties to these motions in disagreement . . . . Section 1369(b) . . . . mandates that a district court judge abstain from hearing any civil action meeting the requirements of § 1369(a) where two conditions are both satisfied: abstention is required when (1) "the substantial majority of plaintiffs are citizens of a single State of which the primary defendants are also citizens" and (2) "the claims asserted will be governed primarily by the laws of that State." Opponents of federal jurisdiction argue that § 1369(b)'s exception operates as a limitation on the statute's grant of original federal jurisdiction[,] . . . that the facts of the Station fire and the nature of the claims presented satisfy both § 1369(b)(1) and (2), and that therefore this Court . . . [is] required to dismiss and/or remand these cases. Proponents of federal jurisdiction disagree, arguing that the statutory text of § 1369(b) . . . is a mandatory abstention doctrine rather than a jurisdictional limitation provision, that the facts of the disaster fail to satisfy the tenets of § 1369(b)(1), and that, as a result, mandatory abstention by this Court is not required. . . .

Here, as the parties make clear in their submissions, the terminology used in § 1369(b) does not "point unerringly in a single direction." Specifically, § 1369(b) and (b)(1) present this writer with three different textual nuances whose meaning cannot be resolved without additional study: (1) the potentially dichotomous title and text "Limitation on jurisdiction of district courts. — The district court shall abstain from hearing any civil action described in subsection (a) in which—"; (2) the clause "substantial majority of all plaintiffs," and (3) the term "primary defendants," all three of which the statute itself fails to explain or define. The statutory language of this subsection is thus capable of more than one reasonable interpretation. As a result, this Court is obliged to look beyond the words of the statute and consider other sources to determine Congressional intent and purpose in creating this new statutory provision. . . .

. . . [I]t is clear that in enacting § 1369, Congress intended to create a mechanism whereby litigation stemming from one major disaster could easily be consolidated in one federal court for discovery and trial. It is also clear that Congress' motivation in passing this legislation was to promote judicial efficiency while avoiding multiple lawsuits concerning the same subject matter strewn throughout the country in various state and federal courts. . . .

. . . [I]t is [also] clear that Congress was concerned about a small subset of disaster cases finding their way into federal court — cases where the substantial majority of the plaintiffs and the "primary" defendants are all from the same state, and where the claims asserted will be governed primarily by the laws of that same state. By creating § 1369(b), Congress attempted to create a statutory exception, or "safeguard" whereby these local disaster cases could continue to be heard in state court . . . .

Now, in light of this history, the Court turns to the three statutory clauses from § 1369(b) at issue. . . .

While the outcome of this debate [about whether § 1396(b) was a mandatory abstention clause or a part of the jurisdictional grant] may seem academic, the parties in these cases argue intensively that its resolution has an impact on the instant motions to dismiss/remand. [In particular, the parties argued that the issue affected the burden of proof; the parties asserting federal jurisdiction bear the burden of proving jurisdiction, while the party requesting abstention bears the burden of proving that abstention is proper. In addition, a jurisdictional defect can be raised at any time, while a decision not to abstain cannot usually be revisited.]

. . . In developing § 1369(b), it was Congress' intention to provide an "exception" or "safeguard" limiting the exercise of federal jurisdiction under § 1369 in those cases arising from purely local disasters. Reading § 1369(b) as an abstention provision is most consistent with this intended result. . . . Here, as the text of § 1369(b) demonstrates, Congress identified certain exceptional circumstances in disaster litigation cases where the state court's interest in hearing the matter outweighs the federal interest in multidistrict, multiforum consolidation — namely, where the tragedy is sufficiently local in character as to satisfy the tenets of § 1369(b)(1)and (2). In these cases, although jurisdiction is otherwise proper under § 1369(a), the text of § 1369(b) instructs district courts to abstain from hearing them. Thus, viewing § 1369(b) as a mandatory abstention provision is consistent with the legislative history characterizing the subsection as an exception to the minimal diversity rule contained in § 1369(a).

In addition, interpreting § 1369(b) as a mandatory abstention provision is consistent with the language of the statute itself, which reads, "The district court shall abstain[.]" . . . .

. . . [T]he Court now considers whether or not this statutory subsection requires abstention in the five cases at issue. As stated above, there are three elements that must be satisfied before abstention under § 1369(b) is required. First, the Court must find that the "substantial majority of all plaintiffs" are all from the same state, here, Rhode Island. Second, the Court must find that the "primary defendants" are also from Rhode Island. Third, the Court must determine that the claims asserted will be governed primarily by the laws of Rhode Island. The last of these elements is not in contention, as it is clear that Rhode Island law will govern the tort claims asserted in the five cases at bar. Thus, this court must turn its attention to ascertaining whether the first two elements are satisfied.

A. *The Substantial Majority of All Plaintiffs*

The first prerequisite to abstention in § 1369(b) centers on this Court's interpretation of the phrase, "the substantial majority of all plaintiffs are citizens of a single State[.]" Opponents of federal jurisdiction argue that abstention is warranted in the five cases at issue because "the substantial majority of all plaintiffs" in litigation stemming from the Station nightclub fire are all citizens of Rhode Island. . . . In order to evaluate this issue, [the Court] must focus on two interpretative questions. First, to whom does the phrase "all plaintiffs" refer?   Second, what amount constitutes a "substantial majority" under the statute?

Several possible interpretations of the term "all plaintiffs" have been suggested to the Court. One suggestion is that as the statute uses the term "plaintiffs" rather than victims, this Court should consider only those parties who have filed suit to date in each case, and thus, are plaintiffs in litigation arising from the Station fire, in determining whether abstention is necessary under § 1369(b). However, in light of the legislative history documenting Congress' interest in broad consolidation of multiple lawsuits arising from a single accident in one judicial forum, this Court feels that reading the term "plaintiffs" in such a limited fashion is not warranted.

Although only a limited number of plaintiffs have filed suit to date, it is certain, based on the large number of fire victims, that many more suits will follow in the days to come. According to reports of the fire, 412 individuals were present in the Station nightclub on the night of the fire. Out of these persons present, 100 individuals died as a result of the fire. In addition to this number, more than 200 persons are reported to have suffered some form of injury as a result of the tragedy.[13] According to the Derderians, only 77 individuals are believed to have escaped the fire without injury. Splitting the difference, this Court estimates that there are at least a total of 335 potential plaintiffs who have or may litigate claims arising from the Station nightclub fire. This figure does not include potential derivative claimants (spouses, children, and other dependants of fire victims), as that number of potential plaintiffs is much larger, and indeed, at this point, incalculable.

A case-by-case reading of the term "all plaintiffs," considering only those plaintiffs who have filed, would frustrate Congress' desire for consolidation. Currently, this Court has been transferred three additional

---

13. According to data in the *Providence Journal*, 412 individuals were present at the Station the night of the fire. . . . [T]he *Journal* listed approximately 255 persons as from Rhode Island, making Rhode Islanders represent 61.89% of the people inside the club before the fire. This figure is less than two-thirds of the total, and it takes into account all those present, not merely those killed or injured.

cases arising from the Station nightclub fire from Connecticut and Massachusetts. The plaintiffs in these cases are not all from Rhode Island — indeed, in *Estate of Henault v. American Foam*, the filing plaintiffs are all from Connecticut, and have jurisdiction in this court based on the federal diversity statute, 28 U.S.C. § 1332. This Court has no power to transfer the *Henault* case to Rhode Island state court. As a result, even if this Court were to abstain from hearing the five cases at issue, it would still be required to hear cases arising from the Station fire. Since the defendants in these cases and the issues are likely to be identical, such an interpretation would foster the possibility for inconsistent discovery rulings and even verdicts on liability. Thus, . . . limiting the term "all plaintiffs" to those individuals who have filed suit in each case runs contrary to Congress' intent in enacting § 1369. A broader construction is necessary.

. . . [I]n light of the legislative history on § 1369, any interpretation of "all plaintiffs" under the statute must include all potential plaintiffs, meaning all those who have died or suffered injury as a result of the tragedy at issue. Such an interpretation is consistent with Congress' desire to consolidate all cases arising from one major disaster in one federal court, as it conditions abstention on the citizenship of all potential claimants rather than considering only those who are the first to file suit. At present, however, and indeed, for years into the future, as the statute of limitation on tort claims under Rhode Island law tolls for minors, *see* R.I. Gen. Laws § 9-1-19, an exact count of the number of derivative claimants is incalculable. Therefore, [the Court] will consider the statistics available on the tragedy in terms of percentages, and will assume that potential derivative claims will fall in line with these percentages.

As [the Court] stated previously, an estimated 335 individuals died or suffered injury in the Station nightclub fire. Out of these 335 people, the Derderians have submitted documentation to the court placing 148 as residents of Rhode Island, 57 from Massachusetts, 9 from Connecticut, 2 from California, 1 from Florida, 1 from Maine, 1 from Nevada, and 1 from Ohio. The residence of the remaining fire victims is currently unestablished before the Court. Placing this in terms of percentages, . . . 44.18% of those killed or injured in the Station nightclub fire are believed to be from Rhode Island, 17.01% from Massachusetts, 2.69% from Connecticut, 0.60% from California, and 0.30% from Florida, Maine, Nevada, and Ohio, respectively. According to this Court's estimates, the residency of a remaining 34.33% of those believed killed or injured in the nightclub fire is currently unestablished in the documentation . . . .

As Congress enacted § 1369 to promote consolidation, [the Court] believes that a "substantial majority of all plaintiffs" must be determined not by comparing the statistics of two particular states affected by a tragedy, but rather by determining whether the number of potential plaintiffs from a single state makes up a substantial majority of all potential plaintiffs with claims arising from the same disaster. Here, Rhode Island residents make up approximately 44.18% of the group . . . identified as representing potential plaintiffs. While it is true that Rhode Islanders make up the largest group of potential plaintiffs, it cannot be said that they constitute a "substantial majority of all plaintiffs." According to [the Court's] calculations, Rhode Island residents make up less than 50% of the total number of potential plaintiffs identified at this time, and thus, at this point they fail to constitute a simple majority, let alone a substantial majority. While this [Court] rejects Proponents' argument that the term "substantial majority" should be read to mean "virtually all," the Court does agree that a "majority" must make up more than 50% of the whole, and that a "substantial majority" must constitute a number somewhat in excess of that figure, such as two-thirds or three-fourths. Therefore, as Rhode Island residents fail to measure a "substantial majority of all plaintiffs," this [Court] finds abstention unwarranted under § 1369(b)(1).

B. *The Primary Defendants*

Although the Court could end its discussion with this conclusion, [it] feels compelled to complete [its] analysis of § 1369(b) by interpreting the last undefined term in the statute, namely, the term "primary defendants." For abstention to be required under the statute, both the substantial majority of all plaintiffs and the primary defendants must all reside in a single state. . . . To state this another way, § 1369 does not require this court to abstain if any one of the so-called "primary defendants" is from a state other than Rhode Island. As with the other terms at issue, "primary defendants" is not defined within the text of § 1369. Legislative history also fails to shed much light on which defendants Congress considered "primary."

Opponents of federal jurisdiction argue that the "primary defendants" in this case include only Rhode Island defendants, such as the Derderians, American Foam, Triton Realty, and McLaughlin & Moran. As the Opponents do not want federal jurisdiction to attach, they argue that the Band members and their tour manager, Daniel Bichele, are not primary defendants. The Band [M]embers and Bichele, who allegedly started the nightclub fire, are all residents of California. Proponents would expand the list of primary defendants to include, at a minimum, the Band Members and their tour manager, and, at a maximum, other parties sued on theories of joint and several liability, including Anheuser-Busch, Clear Channel, Shell Oil, and others, all of whom claim residence in other states. . . .

Several different definitions of "primary defendants" have been offered to the Court by the parties. First, some of the litigants have suggested to this Court that the "primary defendants" should be defined as those defendants with the "deepest pockets." [The Court] rejects that contention outright, as the measure of a particular defendant's ability to pay a judgment should have no bearing on this Court's evaluation of a Rule 12(b)(1) motion.

Second, it has been argued that this Court should consider those defendants that are most culpable for the nightclub fire as "primary defendants." However, at such an early stage in the court proceedings, before either discovery or a trial on the merits, it becomes difficult, if not impossible, . . . to assign either culpability or liability for the tragic events of February 20, 2003. To utilize this standard as a baseline, the Court would be forced to reserve ruling on abstention until the issues of liability were resolved. As a result, it is an unworkable standard . . . .

The last possible definition of the term "primary defendants" . . . interprets the term "primary defendants" as including all defendants facing direct liability, and excluding all defendants joined as secondary or third-party defendants for purposes of vicarious liability, indemnification or contribution. . . . [T]he Court concludes that this is not only the most workable definition of the term "primary defendants" as used in § 1369(b)(1), but also the interpretation most consistent with its use in existing tort case law. . . .

. . . [T]his definition of primary defendants is . . . the most workable under the statute, as it does not require the Court to make a pre-trial determination of liability or culpability, but rather requires only a review of the complaint to determine which defendants are sued directly. If all defendants facing direct liability are from a single state, then that portion of § 1369(b)(1) relating to primary defendants is satisfied. If all defendants facing direct liability are from more than one state, however, the requirement is not met, and abstention is not mandated.

Here, the Court need not engage in an in-depth analysis of how each of the defendants is sued, because it is clear that the Band [M]embers and their tour manager, alleged to have started the fire resulting in 100 deaths and over 200 injured persons, are sued directly in three of the five causes of action at issue, *Passa*, *Kingsley*, and *Guindon*. In these three causes of action, the primary defendants are not all from a single state, and therefore, abstention under § 1369(b) is not required.

C. *Removal under 28 U.S.C. § 1441(e)(1)(B)*

In addition, . . . Defendant Anheuser-Busch's removal of the two miscellaneous petitions and the *Kingsley* matter is proper under the new removal statute, 28 U.S.C. § 1441(e)(1)(B), also created by Congress as a part of the MMTJA . . . .

Here, Anheuser-Busch is a named defendant in each of the two cases originally filed in this Court alleging jurisdiction under § 1369, *Passa* and *Guindon*. As a result, § 1441(e)(1)(B) allows Anheuser-Busch to remove to federal court any civil action arising from the same accident in which it is named as a defendant, including the *Kingsley* case and the two miscellaneous petitions, *Alves* and *O'Brien*. . . .

CONCLUSION

For the aforementioned reasons, Opponents' motions to dismiss and/or remand for lack of subject matter jurisdiction are denied. . . .

It is the intention of the Court to consolidate all the Station fire cases filed in, removed, or transferred to this Court for discovery purposes so that discovery can proceed in an orderly and coordinated fashion.

Notes

1.   In addition to original and removal jurisdiction, the Multiparty, Multiforum Trial Jurisdiction Act (MMTJA) provides for service of process "at any place within the United States, or anywhere outside the United States if otherwise permitted by law." 28 U.S.C. § 1697; *see also* 28 U.S.C. § 1785 (permitting comparably broad service for subpoenas). Thus, the MMTJA helps to aggregate cases in a single forum not only by expanding subject-matter jurisdiction, but also by expanding territorial jurisdiction.

2.   The MMTJA requires as a jurisdictional predicate a single accident that causes seventy-five deaths. As *Passa* shows, jurisdiction is not limited just to the claims of those killed in the accident. The court can also hear the claims of injured plaintiffs. It is also not necessary that any of the parties in the case have been among those killed. In this sense, the MMTJA is a different animal from statutes such as §§1331, 1332(a), and 1367, which are predicated on the claims or party status of litigants in the case.

3.   Is the MMTJA constitutional? Suppose that an injured Rhode Island plaintiff sues only the Derderians, who are also Rhode Island citizens, alleging only state-law claims. If the plaintiff sues in federal court, it is not clear whether § 1369(a) creates jurisdiction; it depends on whether the word "defendants" in § 1369(a)(2) refers just to the persons sued or to all possible defendants (an interpretive question akin to the "all plaintiffs" ambiguity that *Passa* addressed) and whether "adverse parties" in § 1369(a) likewise refers just to the present litigants or to all possible litigants (a comparable interpretive question). If the plaintiff sues in state court, however, § 1441(e)(1)(B) clearly gives removal jurisdiction. On what basis can the federal court exercise this jurisdiction, either as an original matter or on removal? There is no diversity of citizenship between the parties. Is Article III's diversity requirement satisfied by the diversity of potential litigants? If not, can jurisdiction be premised on Article III's federal-question grant, on the theory that the plaintiff might have (but did not) plead a federal question, so that federal law is an "original ingredient" of the case? Or is it a kind of supplemental jurisdiction, in which jurisdiction exists because the plaintiff's claim arises from a common nucleus of operative fact with cases pending in federal court?

Is it possible that § 1369(a) is constitutional but § 1441(e)(1)(2) is not, at least as applied to factual patterns like the one in the last paragraph?

4.   As *Passa* shows, the MMTJA contains drafting ambiguities that leave its reach uncertain. If you read the Act closely, you also noted that the word "injury" is defined in § 1369(c)(3), even though the word is used nowhere in the statute. The definition was a relic of an earlier version of the MMTJA, in which federal jurisdiction was triggered by a discrete

accident in which at least twenty-five people were killed or else "incurred injury" in an amount greater than $150,000. Failing to remove the definition of "injury" was sloppy drafting.

5.   Despite *Passa*'s generous reading of the MMTJA, the jurisdictional trigger of seventy-five deaths and the fact that a large number of injuries does not trigger federal jurisdiction combine to limit the MMTJA's capacity to address the problem of dispersed litigation.

A similar limit is the MMTJA's requirement that the deaths arise from a "single accident" at a "discrete location." 28 U.S.C. § 1369(a); *see id.* § 1369(c)(4) (defining "accident" to require that the deaths occur at "a discrete location"). The import of the "single accident" limit is to render § 1369 unavailable for most mass torts; it is most useful for aggregating airplane crashes and catastrophic explosions or chemical spills.

Nor is the MMTJA useful for all large-scale catastrophes. The MMTJA was passed shortly the terrorist attacks on September 11th. Congress did not intend § 1369 as a jurisdictional response to those attacks; it had enacted other legislation specifically for that purpose. But if we consider a comparable tragedy, in which 100 people die in a terrorist incident, would § 1369(a) grant federal jurisdiction? Is a deliberate attack an "accident"?

6.   The MMTJA's abstention provision, § 1369(b), reduces the statute's potential to aggregate litigation. This provision evinces Congress's concern for federalism, and ensures that single-state controversies remain in that state's court system. The aggregation-friendly interpretations that *Passa* gives to § 1369(b) lessen the impact of the abstention requirement, and expand marginally § 1369's potential to bring related cases into a single federal forum.

In its desire to create a federal forum, did *Passa* cook the books on the "substantial majority" issue? *Passa* mentions the newspaper data finding that 61.89% of the people inside the Station (not all of whom were injured) were from Rhode island. Isn't that a substantial majority? When the court then used the available information on the citizenship of those who had been killed or injured — 148 from Rhode Island, 57 from Massachusetts, 9 from Connecticut, 2 from California, 1 from Florida, 1 from Maine, 1 from Nevada, 1 from Ohio, and 115 of undetermined citizenship — it assumed that all 115 of undetermined citizenship were not Rhode Islanders; on that assumption, the court calculated that only 44.18% of the plaintiffs were from Rhode Island. But if you compare the number of known Rhode Islanders (148) to the total number of those with known citizenship (220), you find that Rhode Islanders composed 67.27% of the plaintiffs with known citizenship. Isn't that a "substantial majority"? Should Congress have specified a percentage (say, 66.7% or 75%, as *Passa* suggests), rather than use the vague term "substantial majority"? Isn't clarity important in jurisdictional statutes?

Likewise, *Passa*'s interpretation of "primary defendants" seems plausible on first blush. But elsewhere § 1369 uses the word "defendant" or "defendants" — without the adjective "primary" — to mean those parties facing direct liability.   In using the modifier "primary" in § 1369(b), Congress must presumably have meant a subset of these defendants, not all defendants facing direct liability.   Can you think of a better interpretation of "primary" than the "deep pockets" or "most wrongful" interpretations rejected in *Passa*?

7.   Even on *Passa*'s broad reading, § 1369 makes only a small dent in the jurisdictional rules that foment the dispersion of mass claims. But the MMTJA is still important, for it serves as one possible roadmap for a statute that would create broad federal jurisdiction designed to avoid the unfairness and inefficiency of repetitive litigation. Indeed, as the following subsection shows, certain elements of the MMTJA reappear in a statute with much greater potential to aggregate related cases in a federal forum.

b. The Class Action Fairness Act

Read 28 U.S.C. §§ 1332(d) and 1453. Passed in 2005, the Class Action Fairness Act (CAFA) borrowed certain elements from the Multiparty, Multiforum Trial Jurisdiction Act, such as hinging federal jurisdiction on minimal diversity and providing for abstention in three situations in which a dispute is in essence a single-state controversy. Unlike the Multiparty, Multiforum Trial Jurisdiction Act, however, CAFA contains a minimum amount in controversy, and its jurisdictional trigger is not a certain number of deaths, but something quite different: filing a class-action complaint.

Prior to CAFA, federal courts had diversity jurisdiction over many state-law class actions under § 1332(a). In a modified complete-diversity rule that created more federal jurisdiction over class actions, only class representatives needed to be diverse from the parties opposing the class; the citizenship of the class members was irrelevant. *See* Supreme Tribe of Ben-Hur v. Cauble, 255 U.S. 356 (1921). After passage of § 1367 and the Supreme Court's interpretation of the statute in *Exxon Mobil Corp. v. Allapattah*, 545 U.S. 546 (2005), class members were not required to meet the   amount-in-controversy   requirement   as   long   as   the   class representative(s) did. By picking the right class representatives, counsel in a class action could fairly well structure the case to get a federal forum.

But the converse was also true: Counsel who wanted to keep class actions in state court had a fairly simple way of doing so: Name class representatives that were not diverse or failed to meet the amount-in-controversy requirement. Congress believed that state-court adjudication of interstate or nationwide class actions was inappropriate and that certain plaintiffs' lawyers were taking advantage of the jurisdictional rules to keep such cases out of federal court. But Congress also wanted to preserve state-court adjudication over class actions that really were single-state affairs. The result was CAFA, which contains the most complicated, fact-intensive jurisdictional provisions that Congress has ever created. Sorting out the meaning of these provisions — especially the discretionary and mandatory abstention clauses in §§ 1332(d)(3), -(4)(A), and -(4)(B) — will likely take years. The following three cases are early efforts.

IN RE HANNAFORD BROS. CO. CUSTOMER DATA SECURITY BREACH LITIGATION

564 F.3d 75 (1st Cir. 2009)

■ LYNCH, Chief Judge.

This appeal presents an issue of first impression for this circuit regarding the application of the home state exception to federal jurisdiction under the Class Action Fairness Act of 2005 ("CAFA"). Congress enacted CAFA in response to perceived abuses by plaintiffs' counsel in keeping class action cases of national importance out of the federal courts. Defendant's essential argument is that the plaintiff has drawn his complaint in terms limiting the class and the defendants in order to defeat federal jurisdiction in violation of congressional intent. . . .

Here, a class defined to consist entirely of Florida citizens sued a single corporation, also a Florida citizen, in Florida state court. After defendant removed to federal court under CAFA, plaintiff sought remand to the state court under CAFA's home state exception, which requires a federal court to decline to exercise jurisdiction if at least two-thirds of the members of all proposed plaintiff classes in the aggregate and the primary defendants are citizens of the state where the action was originally filed. *See* 28 U.S.C. § 1332(d)(4)(B).

The district court . . . granted the plaintiff's motion to remand. We agree and reject, on the facts here, the defendant's argument that the application of CAFA's home state exception depends on a broader assessment of the claims brought by others who do not fall within the complaint's class definition or of the claims available to the class against other possible defendants.

I.

Defendant Kash N' Karry Food Stores, Inc. operates a chain of grocery stores in Florida. A computer hacker stole the credit card information of customers who had shopped at Kash N' Karry's stores between December 2007 and March 2008. Plaintiff Thomas Grimsdale, III regularly shopped at Kash N' Karry's stores in Tampa, Florida during this period and paid for his purchases using his bank debit card.

On April 4, 2008, Grimsdale sued Kash N' Karry in Florida state court, alleging that Kash N' Karry had failed to adopt adequate security measures to protect its customers' credit card information. He sought to represent a class of approximately 1.6 million persons who had "used credit/debit cards at [Kash N' Karry's] stores between December 7, 2007 and March 10, 2008 and/or had their personal and sensitive Confidential Information stolen and/or compromised as a result of the [security] Breach." The class definition explicitly excluded "any persons and entities who are not citizens of the State of Florida."

Kash N' Karry removed the case to federal court in Florida under CAFA on April 17, 2008. On April 25, 2008, Grimsdale filed a motion to remand the case to state court, arguing that CAFA's home state exception applied.

On October 8, 2008, the Judicial Panel on Multidistrict Litigation transferred the case to the District of Maine, where twenty-four other suits had been consolidated against entities related to Kash N' Karry . . . . [T]he multidistrict litigation involved an estimated 4.2 million class members. On December 10, 2008, the district court granted Grimsdale's motion to remand . . . .

Kash N' Karry timely petitioned for leave to appeal the district court's remand order under 28 U.S.C. § 1453(c). . . .

II.

. . . Here, our focus is on the home state exception, which provides:

> A district court shall decline to exercise jurisdiction [where] . . . two-thirds or more of the members of all proposed plaintiff classes in the aggregate, and the primary defendants, are citizens of the State in which the action was originally filed.

28 U.S.C. § 1332(d)(4)(B).[2]

There is a threshold question of which party bears the burden of showing that CAFA's home state exception applies. We hold that the burden is on the plaintiff to show that an exception to jurisdiction under CAFA applies. . . .

At first blush, the requirements of CAFA's home state exception appear to be satisfied here. As Grimsdale has defined the class in his complaint, all class members are Florida citizens. Kash N' Karry, the only defendant in this case, is also a Florida citizen because its principal place of business is in Florida. And this case was originally filed in Florida state court.

Still, Kash N' Karry offers a different reading of CAFA's home state exception, turning on the interpretation of the sub-phrase "the members of all proposed plaintiff classes in the aggregate" within the home state exception. Specifically, Kash N' Karry argues that the plain meaning of "all proposed plaintiff classes in the aggregate" requires reference outside the four corners of the complaint in the particular case before the court to all previously filed class actions which arise from a core nucleus of operative facts such as to meet an "Article III case or controversy" requirement. It contends that the term "aggregate" means that Congress intended to refer beyond the plaintiff's complaint; otherwise, Congress would have simply

---

2. To remain in federal court, this case must both satisfy the minimal diversity requirement for federal jurisdiction under 28 U.S.C. § 1332(d)(2) and also not fall under CAFA's home state exception in § 1332(d)(4)(B). Kash N' Karry therefore argues that its dual citizenship as a Delaware corporation with its principal place of business in Florida creates the requisite minimal diversity for jurisdiction under § 1332(d)(2). We are skeptical of this argument . . . .

used the term "class members" as it did in § 1332(d)(1)(D).[4] Applying this principle here, Kash N' Karry says the previously filed national class actions involving Hannaford that were consolidated by the Judicial Panel on Multidistrict Litigation are the appropriate reference point to measure "the members of all proposed plaintiff classes in the aggregate."

We reject Kash N' Karry's reading as contrary to the plain language of § 1332(d)(4)(B). The most natural reading of the home state exception is that Congress meant § 1332(d)(4)(B) to be read in conjunction with the federal class action rule, Fed. R. Civ. P. 23, or similar state statutes and rules of judicial procedure. . . . Under Rule 23, "a class may be divided into subclasses that are each treated as a class under this rule." Fed. R. Civ. P. 23(c)(5). The home state exception's use of the plural "classes," therefore, does not indicate that Congress intended an inquiry into what Kash N' Karry has termed the broader "Article III case or controversy" because a single complaint may contain multiple classes.[6]

In rejecting Kash N' Karry's reading of § 1332(d)(4)(B), we do not mean to say that the four corners of the plaintiff's complaint necessarily control the question of whether CAFA's home state exception applies. We do not rely on the maxim that the plaintiff is the master of his own complaint . . . . We can imagine situations — for example, if the plaintiff has omitted an indispensable defendant — where looking beyond the four corners of the plaintiff's complaint may be necessary to determine whether the home state exception applies. But that situation is not before us here . . . .

Kash N' Karry argues that our reading, which here gives effect to the plaintiff's choice to define the scope of the suit narrowly, will ultimately cause the home state exception to defeat CAFA's broader purpose of expanding federal jurisdiction. . . .

It is common for removing defendants trying to remain in federal court under CAFA to make this generic argument . . . . For example, in *Freeman v. Blue Ridge Paper Products, Inc.*, 551 F.3d 405 (6th Cir. 2008), five separate state court class actions were filed by plaintiffs from the same state for the same injuries covering sequential time periods. Each suit sought damages of $4.9 million, just below CAFA's $5 million jurisdictional minimum. The Sixth Circuit held that this type of structuring is impermissible where "there is no colorable basis" for dividing the suit "other than to frustrate CAFA." Whether or not we would agree with *Freeman*,

---

4. Likewise, Kash N' Karry argues that CAFA's reference to "primary defendants" requires a court to look beyond the plaintiff's complaint to consider unnamed defendants against whom the class could pursue a claim arising from the same core set of facts. This claim is analytically similar to Kash N' Karry's argument as to class membership, and we reject it for the same reasons.

6. Moreover, Kash N' Karry's reading would present serious administrability problems, which Congress surely did not intend. It would be extremely difficult to define the scope of what Kash N' Karry calls the "Article III case or controversy." And Kash N' Karry's own definition is arbitrary: nothing in its theory supports its limitation to already-filed national actions. Indeed, Kash N' Karry uses the phrase "Article III case or controversy" in ways very different from the usual understanding of the phrase.

this case is very different. Grimsdale has not artificially split his class of Florida plaintiffs into multiple suits to avoid federal jurisdiction. . . .

There is no one-size-fits-all response to a claim of evasion of congressional intent. The analysis will turn on the precise language of that section of CAFA. Our job is to effectuate the intent expressed in the plain language Congress has chosen, not to effectuate purported policy choices regardless of language.

In any event, we are dubious about the policy arguments. Several factors make it unlikely that the exception will swallow the rule entirely. In particular, CAFA's home state exception is fairly narrow, encompassing only those suits where at least two-thirds of the class members and all of the primary defendants are citizens of the same state. Suits involving a primary defendant who is not a citizen of the forum state cannot qualify for the exception. Moreover, plaintiffs potentially sacrifice a great deal in terms of the parties they can sue and the claims they can bring by narrowing their pleadings to fit within the home state exception. And to the extent that the home state exception in practice creates an undesirable loophole, Congress may choose to amend the statute to address those problems as they arise.

Beyond that, many of the policy concerns that motivated Congress to enact CAFA are simply not implicated where the suit qualifies for the home state exception. . . . According to Congress, [plaintiffs' attorneys'] abusive practices included forum shopping to take advantage of potential state court biases against foreign defendants. But where, as here, the defendant is also a citizen of the forum state, the concern for bias simply does not arise. Likewise, Congress in enacting CAFA was concerned that state courts were "making judgments that impose their view of the law on other States and bind the rights of the residents of those States." But again, that potential problem is not implicated where the class members are largely citizens of the forum state. . . .

The district court's remand order is affirmed.

PRESTON V. TENET HEALTHSYSTEM MEMORIAL MEDICAL CENTER, INC.

485 F.3d 804 (5th Cir. 2007)

■ STEWART, Circuit Judge.

. . .

I. FACTUAL AND PROCEDURAL BACKGROUND

Preston represents a putative class of patients and the relatives of deceased and allegedly injured patients hospitalized at [Tenet Health Systems Memorial Medical Center ("Memorial")] when Hurricane Katrina made landfall in New Orleans, Louisiana. Memorial owned and operated the hospital, and [LifeCare Hospitals of New Orleans, L.L.C. (collectively "LifeCare")] leased the seventh floor of the facility for an acute care center. On October 6, 2005, Preston brought suit against Memorial in the Civil District Court for the Parish of Orleans. Preston asserted claims for negligence and intentional misconduct . . . and involuntary euthanization. Preston alleged that Memorial failed to design and maintain the premises in a manner that avoided loss of power in the building. Preston further alleged that Memorial and LifeCare failed to develop and implement an evacuation plan for the patients. According to the petition, Memorial's and LifeCare's failure to maintain the premises and timely evacuate the facility resulted in the deaths and injuries of hospitalized patients. . . .

. . . LifeCare filed a timely notice of removal. Memorial never consented to removal from the state court. . . . Preston filed a motion to remand under the local controversy exception of CAFA. [Memorial later renewed this motion.] On November 21, 2006, the district court remanded the lawsuit to state court under the local controversy exception, home state exception, and the discretionary jurisdiction provision. . . . LifeCare filed a timely petition for appeal pursuant to 28 U.S.C. § 1453. On February 5, 2007, this court granted permission to appeal. LifeCare only contests the district court's citizenship findings under CAFA's exceptions to federal jurisdiction.

II. STANDARD OF REVIEW

We review the district court's factual findings as to the citizenship of the parties for clear error. . . .

The standard of review for a district court's remand under the discretionary provision constitutes an issue of first impression. We review the district court's remand order for abuse of discretion. . . .

. . . LifeCare cogently argues that the local controversy and home state exceptions should be construed narrowly and resolved in favor of federal jurisdiction based on the "shall decline to exercise jurisdiction" language . . ., which represents the classic formulation for abstention. Under the discretionary jurisdiction provision, however, Congress permitted the district court greater latitude to remand class actions to state court. . . .

III. DISCUSSION

A. *Statutory Background*

Congress enacted CAFA to expand federal jurisdiction over interstate class action lawsuits of national interest. CAFA contains a basic jurisdictional test for removal, which requires the removing defendant to prove minimal diversity and an aggregated amount in controversy of $5,000,000 or more. § 1332(d). CAFA eliminates the standard requirements of unanimous consent among the defendants and the one-year removal deadline. § 1453(b). The district court can decline jurisdiction under three provisions: (1) the home state exception, § 1332(d)(4)(B); (2) the local controversy exception, § 1332(d)(4)(A); and (3) discretionary jurisdiction, § 1332(d)(3). . . .

[The court of appeals quoted the language of the three exceptions, setting out in full the six statutory factors in § 1332(d)(3)(A)-(F) that guide a district court's discretionary-jurisdiction decision.]

B. *Discretionary Jurisdiction Provision*

The district court remanded this class action lawsuit to state court under all three carve-outs to federal jurisdiction: the local controversy exception, the home state exception, and the discretionary jurisdiction provision. Each CAFA exception requires the court to make an objective factual finding regarding the percentage of class members that were citizens of Louisiana at the time of filing the class petition. The local controversy and home state exceptions to federal jurisdiction are separate and distinct statutory provisions with a common requirement — greater than "two-thirds of the members of all proposed plaintiff classes in the aggregate [must be] citizens of the State in which the action was originally filed." . . .

Under CAFA's discretionary jurisdiction provision, the citizenship requirement lowers to require that "greater than one-third but less than two-thirds of the members of all proposed plaintiff classes in the aggregate . . . are citizens of the State in which the action was originally filed . . . ." § 1332(d)(3). . . .

Congress crafted CAFA to exclude only a narrow category of truly localized controversies, and § 1332(d)(3) provides a discretionary vehicle for district courts to ferret out the "controversy that uniquely affects a particular locality to the exclusion of all others." After careful review of the record, the discretionary jurisdiction provision proves to be a particularly well-suited framework for considering the interconnections between the underlying facts giving rise to the alleged legal claims and the extenuating circumstances affecting this preliminary jurisdictional determination. The district court determined that a distinct nexus exists between the forum of Louisiana, the Defendants, and the proposed class. We observe, more specifically, that Preston alleges that LifeCare and Memorial, citizens of Louisiana, committed acts in Louisiana causing injuries and deaths to patients hospitalized in New Orleans, Louisiana, when Hurricane Katrina made landfall. The claims asserted in the petition involve issues of negligence governed by state law. Memorial does not contest that the instant lawsuit fulfills the threshold requirements for removal under CAFA, i.e. the requisite number of proposed class members, minimal diversity, and the necessary aggregate amount in controversy. *See* § 1332(d)(2). Accordingly, we limit our review to whether Memorial presented sufficient evidence to show that at least one-third of the putative class members were citizens of Louisiana at the time that the suit was filed.

1. *Burden of Proof*

. . . Under CAFA, the moving party on the remand motion, not the defendant seeking federal jurisdiction, bears the burden to establish the domicile of at least one-third of the class members at the time of filing the lawsuit. . . .

2. *Evidentiary Standard for Proving Citizenship*

. . . . Preston filed this class action lawsuit on October 6, 2005; therefore, Memorial must prove citizenship as of this date. . . . Pursuant to well-settled principles of law, we hold that the party moving for remand under the CAFA exceptions to federal jurisdiction must prove the citizenship requirement by a preponderance of the evidence. This holding means that Memorial, as the movant, must demonstrate by a preponderance of the evidence that at least one-third of the putative class members were citizens of Louisiana. . . .

3. *Evidence Adduced to Prove Citizenship Requirement*

. . .

a. *Residency: Medical Records and Current Addresses*

. . .

LifeCare retained a private investigator, Robert Mazur, to trace the current mailing addresses of potential class members located throughout the country. LifeCare maintained that forty-nine of 146 persons identified as potential class members, more than one-third, currently reside outside of Louisiana. LifeCare's citizenship numbers include patients and surviving beneficiaries. In assessing these documents, the district court noted that "this information presents a valuable indication of the citizenship of the proposed class" but admonished LifeCare's failure to prove "residence and intent, both at the date the suit was filed." . . .

We agree with the district court's treatment of LifeCare's rebuttal evidence. The pre-Katrina addresses in the medical records, however, only make a prima facie showing of domicile, and citizenship requires residency and the intent to return or remain in the state. A party's residence alone does not establish domicile. We now turn to the evidence establishing intent, the second element of citizenship.

b. *Intent: Statements from Potential Class Members*

. . . Preston submitted eight affidavits regarding the intent of potential class members to return to New Orleans, Louisiana, even though they currently resided in a different state. The named plaintiffs provided six of the eight affidavits. For example, the affidavit of Darlene Preston states her former address in New Orleans prior to Hurricane Katrina; her current address in Houston, Texas; and concludes by stating that "[s]he is planning on returning as soon as housing becomes available to her. She is a resident and domiciliary of and has always intended on returning to the City of New Orleans." . . .

. . . LifeCare points to no objective evidence in the record indicating that the affidavits misrepresented the plaintiffs' intent of returning to New Orleans. . . .

In addition to the medical records and affidavits, LifeCare suggests that Memorial should adduce evidence of citizenship in accordance with traditional diversity cases involving one defendant. . . . This suggestion not only affects the moving party but suggests that at this threshold stage of the case, the district court must engage in the arduous task of examining the domicile of every proposed class member before ruling on the citizenship requirement. We decline to adopt such a heightened burden of proof considering the far greater number of plaintiffs involved in a class action as compared to the traditional diversity case. From a practical standpoint, class action lawsuits may become "totally unworkable in a diversity case if the citizenship of all members of the class, many of them unknown, had to be considered." The requisite showing under CAFA prompts this court to reconcile congressional intent, our precedent for determining citizenship, and judicial economy. Thus, the evidentiary standard for establishing the domicile of more than one hundred plaintiffs must be based on practicality and reasonableness. . . .

. . . The uncontroverted affidavits of eight beneficiaries stating an intent to return to New Orleans, the emergency contact phone numbers of the deceased patients, and the uncontroverted data gathered from the medical records, however, permitted the district court to make a reasonable assumption that at least one-third of the class members were citizens of Louisiana during the relevant time period regardless of the rebuttal evidence placed in the record. Upon reviewing the medical records, [an expert for Memorial] averred that only seven of the 256 patients hospitalized at the time of Hurricane Katrina gave permanent addresses outside the state of Louisiana, which equates to 2.83% of the total number of hospitalized patients. . . .

. . . Therefore, based on the record as a whole, the district court made a reasonable assumption that at least one-third of the class were Louisiana citizens at the time of filing the lawsuit on October 6, 2005, less than two months after the storm hit New Orleans. We do not find the district court's findings of fact clearly erroneous. . . .

4. *Determination of Class Size*

LifeCare argues that Memorial fails to establish the number of people composing the proposed class. Arguably, without knowing the number of persons in the class, the court cannot determine whether one-third of the class members are citizens of Louisiana. . . .

Here, we conclude that the submitted evidence provides an adequate basis for the district court to make a credible estimate of the class members domiciled in Louisiana. CAFA requires the district court to make a threshold jurisdictional determination. Thus, the district court must balance the need for discovery while not unduly delaying the resolution of this preliminary question. . . .

. . . The record reflects that the plaintiffs defined a reasonably confined class and the district court, based on a preponderance of the evidence, made a credible estimate that at least one-third of the class were citizens of Louisiana at the time of filing suit.

5. *Statutory Factors for Determining the Interest of Justice*

a. *Whether Claims Involve National or Interstate Interest*

LifeCare argues that the evacuation of medical and other facilities during disasters such as Hurricane Katrina is an issue of national concern. This broad statement could swallow the rule, however, as many events isolated to one area at any particular time may reoccur in another geographic location in the future. Under CAFA, the terms local and national connote whether the interests of justice would be violated by a state court exercising jurisdiction over a large number of out-of-state citizens and applying the laws of other states. Just because the nation takes interest in Hurricane Katrina does not mean that the legal claims at issue in this class action lawsuit qualify as national or interstate interest. The factual scenario presented in this class action involves two Louisiana businesses operating a local hospital during a natural disaster destroying New Orleans and the compounded devastation of the local levee breach. The evacuation plans, building maintenance, and emergency care procedures are the work product and property of these local entities. . . . [A]lthough the nation may still be watching the ever-evolving after effects of Hurricane Katrina, this class action lawsuit does not affect national interest as contemplated under the statute.

b. *Whether Claims Are Governed by Louisiana Law and Whether the Class Action Was Pleaded to Avoid Federal Jurisdiction*

. . . The majority of the claims asserted in the class petition involve negligence issues governed under Louisiana law. . . .

c. *Whether a Distinct Nexus Exists between the Forum and the Class Members, Alleged Harm, and the Defendants*

The conduct alleged in the class action petition as causing the deaths and injuries of patients hospitalized at Memorial and LifeCare occurred at the defendants' medical facilities in New Orleans, Louisiana. Memorial owned and operated the hospital, and LifeCare leased one floor of the hospital for the operation of an acute care center. Both Memorial and LifeCare are Louisiana corporations organized under the laws of the state, and based on the medical records, nearly ninety-seven percent of the patients permanently resided in Louisiana at the time of admission to these health centers. In light of the localized events giving rise to the alleged negligent conduct and the undisputed residency and citizenship information of the patients and the healthcare providers, we conclude that a distinct nexus exists between the forum of Louisiana and the class members, alleged harm, and the defendants.

d. *State Citizenship of the Class Members*

. . . Based on the record, an overwhelming number of patients permanently resided in New Orleans, Louisiana . . . . After the hurricane, many New Orleans residents were forced to relocate to surrounding areas in Louisiana and other states. As evinced through the affidavits, however, citizens of Louisiana are hindered from immediately acting on their desires to move back home due to employment, housing, and other related issues. Undoubtedly, some evacuees hold no intention of returning to Louisiana but surely are dispersed throughout the nation as opposed to one other state. For these reasons, we determine that the proposed class meets this requirement.

e. *Whether Similar Class Actions Filed in Preceding Three-Year Period*

We find no evidence, and neither party raises the issue, of a class action being filed during the three-year period preceding the filing of this class action asserting the same or similar claims on behalf of the same or other persons.

IV. CONCLUSION

We recognize that Congress crafted CAFA to exclude only a narrow category of truly localized controversies . . . . This particular Hurricane Katrina case symbolizes a quintessential example of Congress' intent to carve-out exceptions to CAFA's expansive grant of federal jurisdiction when our courts confront a truly localized controversy. Based on the medical records, affidavits, and attending factual circumstances, we determine that the district court did not clearly err in finding that one-third of the class members were citizens of Louisiana at the time of filing suit. Accordingly, we affirm the district court's judgment.

Notes

1. In a class action akin to *Preston*, filed against another hospital and infirmary for their actions during Hurricane Katrina, the hospital removed

the case from state court. Holding that more than two-thirds of the class members were from Louisiana, the district court ordered remand to state court under the local-controversy exception to CAFA. § 1332(d)(4)(A). On appeal, the Fifth Circuit reversed the order. Preston v. Tenet Healthsystem Mem'l Med. Ctr., Inc., 485 F.3d 793 (5th Cir. 2007). (The two cases had the same title because they had been consolidated for appeal.) Although records reflected that 200 of the 242 patients at the hospital had provided a New Orleans address, the court of appeals stated that residence did not prove domicile — especially in 2006, when the case was filed. The plaintiffs had made no further efforts to prove the citizenship of the class members. The court concluded:

> The CAFA exceptions are "designed to draw a delicate balance between making a federal forum available to genuinely national litigation and allowing the state courts to retain cases when the controversy is strongly linked to that state." . . . [T]he evidence adduced by [the class representative] is insufficient to allow a credible estimate to be made that at least two-thirds of the proposed class members were domiciled in Louisiana at the time of filing the class action. [485 F.3d at 803-04.]

Does the difference in result in the two *Preston* cases make sense? Note that discretionary-jurisdiction provision under § 1332(d)(3) is available only when "greater than one-third but less than two-thirds" of the class members are citizens of the forum state. Granting that the defendant seeking remand failed to disprove that at least one-third of the class members were not citizens of Louisiana when the case was filed, wouldn't it have been easy to disprove that, even on the plaintiffs' own evidence, that more than two-thirds of the class members were Louisiana citizens? (Note that the court of appeals cites evidence that 97% of hospitalized patients appeared to be from Louisiana.) Should Memorial have tried to disprove the two-thirds upper limit, rather than the one-third lower limit? In this regard, the second *Preston* case, described above, might have proven a barrier.

2. *Preston* invoked the usual rule that citizenship is determined as of the date that the case is filed in federal court; earlier or later events do not affect the question. *Kaufmann* refused to use the date of filing as the determinative point for deciding which defendants were "significant" under the local-controversy exception. Can you reconcile the difference?

3. Note the importance of the burden of proof in these cases. In *Hannaford*, the burden of proof mattered less because the issues were essentially legal. In *Preston*, however, the issues — the size of the class and the citizenship of the class members — were intensely factual. In many circumstances it is cost-prohibitive to engage in individualized determinations of the size of the class and of class members' citizenship. (The plaintiffs in *Hannaford* avoided the problem by pleading class actions in which all class members were from one state.)

Because the party bearing the burden of proof is at a disadvantage, the issue of which party bears the burden of proving the court's jurisdiction or an entitlement to remand has been one of the most litigated issues since the passage of CAFA. To some extent the burden depends on whether the case was originally filed in federal court or was removed to federal court, and to some extent on whether the party is contesting jurisdiction under the minimal-diversity and amount-in-controversy requirements of § 1332(d)(2), or is contesting jurisdiction under the discretionary or mandatory declination-of-jurisdiction provisions of §§ 1332(d)(3) and (d)(4). For two cases discussing the possible approaches to these issues, see Lowdermilk v. United States Bank Nat'l Ass'n, 479 F.3d 994 (9th Cir. 2007); Serrano v. 180 Connect, Inc., 478 F.3d 1018 (9th Cir. 2007).

4. *Hannaford* and *Preston* deal with two of the three principal exceptions to CAFA jurisdiction — respectively, the home-state exception (§ 1332(d)(4)(B)) and the discretionary-jurisdiction exception (§ 1332(d)(3)). For a case discussing For a case interpreting the third exception, the local-controversy exception (§ 1332(d)(4)(A)) and especially its phrases "significant basis" and "principal injuries," see Kaufman v. Allstate N.J. Ins. Co., 561 F.3d 144 (3d Cir. 2009).

5. CAFA reworks the ordinary jurisdictional rules for diversity class actions. It replaces the modified complete-diversity requirement of § 1332(a) with a minimal-diversity rule. 28 U.S.C. § 1332(d)(2). It replaces the idea of measuring the amount in controversy from the viewpoint of each plaintiff with a $5,000,000 threshold measured from the viewpoint of the defendant. *Id.* Despite these changes, which open up federal courts to most state-law class actions, CAFA has important limitations:

- It does not affect jurisdiction over class actions that plead a federal question. *Id.*

- It does not apply to diversity-based class actions with fewer than 100 members. *Id.* § 1332(d)(5)(B).

- It does not apply to diversity-based class actions in which the court could probably not grant relief against government officials or entities in any event. *Id.* § 1332(d)(5)(A).

- It does not apply to diversity-based class actions involving shareholder claims against a corporation's management or certain state-law claims alleging securities fraud. *Id.* § 1332(d)(9). Federal jurisdiction over state-law securities-fraud class actions is already covered in other provisions of the United States Code.

6. As *Hannaford* and *Preston* show, CAFA also contains complex provisions, driven by concerns for federalism, that carve certain state-law class actions that are local in nature out of federal jurisdiction. Each of the three cases focuses on one of the three exceptions. It is easy to confuse them, but it is important to keep in mind their differences. Some differences are obvious. For instance, the first exception, § 1332(d)(3), is discretionary, while the latter two exceptions — the local-controversy exception of § 1332(d)(4)(A) and the home-state exception of § 1332(d)(4)(B) — are mandatory. But other differences are subtle. For instance, the local-controversy exception requires that "greater than two-thirds" of the class be from one state, while the home-state exception provides that "two-thirds or more" of the class must be from one state. Likewise, the former talks

about defendants whose "alleged conduct forms a significant basis" of the case, while the latter talks about the "primary defendants." The language of the statute is providing litigants with plenty of opportunity to argue for broader or narrower views of CAFA.

7. CAFA's mandatory home-state exception, § 1332(d)(4)(B), uses the phrase "primary defendants," which is the same phrase that Congress had previously used in the mandatory abstention provision of the Multiparty, Multiforum Trial Jurisdiction Act, §1369(b)(1). Should the phrases be interpreted the same way in both statutes? So far, the interpretation that *Passa v. Derderian*, 308 F. Supp. 2d 43 (D.R.I. 2004) (*supra* p. 307), gave to the phrase in the § 1369(b) context — that primary defendants are those parties that plaintiffs seek to hold directly liable — has influenced courts in interpreting CAFA. *See, e.g.*, Laws v. Priority Trustee Servs. of N.C., L.L.C., 2008 WL 3539512 (W.D.N.C. Aug. 11, 2008).

8. CAFA also significantly reworks the ordinary rules regarding removal jurisdiction. Under the usual rules, removal must occur within thirty days after the case first becomes removable, all defendants must join in the removal notice, diversity-based cases cannot be removed more than one year after they are filed, diversity-based class actions cannot be removed from a court in the defendant's home state, the decision of a federal court to remand a removed case is not ordinarily appealable, and the decision to deny remand is appealable only after the case is over. *See* 28 U.S.C. §§ 1441, 1446, 1447; *supra* pp.301-02, Notes 5-6. CAFA's removal rule does not change the thirty-day rule for seeking removal, but it does change the remaining requirements to make removal of class actions easier. *See* 28 U.S.C. § 1453(b)-(c). One important change is to gives courts of appeal the authority to hear appeals from orders granting or denying remand; the court of appeals must decide the appeal within sixty days. *See* Hertz Corp. v. Friend, 559 U.S. —, 130 S. Ct. 1181 (2010) (holding that the sixty-day limit does not preclude Supreme Court review of an appellate decision rendered within sixty days, even if the Supreme Court's decision is not rendered within sixty days of the order granting appeal).

9. In *Hannaford* and *Preston*, the courts of appeals ordered a remand to state court. From these cases, you might therefore get the false impression that CAFA hasn't expanded federal jurisdiction all that much. That impression would be wrong. Although it will take years to determine the full effect of CAFA, the early results suggest that federal courts have seen an increase in class-action activity of 72% compared to pre-CAFA federal filings. *See* EMERY G. LEE III & THOMAS E. WILLGING, FED. JUDICIAL CTR., THE IMPACT OF THE CLASS ACTION FAIRNESS ACT OF 2005 ON THE FEDERAL COURTS 1 (2008).

Nonetheless, the three cases show that CAFA is not a perfect statute from the viewpoint of single-system aggregation. That fact is shown most obviously in *Hannaford*, in which CAFA failed a defendant that had successfully aggregated its other cases in a federal MDL proceeding. If *Hannaford* is correct, a determined plaintiff's lawyer can still avoid single-forum class-action aggregation by limiting the case to a one-state class.

10. Before CAFA, federal jurisdiction over class actions was obtained under the traditional diversity grant of § 1332(a), as modified by § 1367. Does the comprehensiveness of § 1332(d) destroy the diversity jurisdiction formerly provided under § 1332(a)? In *Exxon Mobil Corp. v. Allapattah Services, Inc.*, 545 U.S. 546, 571-72 (2005), the Court noted that the passage of CAFA did not affect the question of how to interpret § 1367, nor did it moot the § 1367 question before the Court.

In any event, the generosity of the jurisdictional and removal provisions of §§ 1332(d) and 1453 effectively moots traditional class-action jurisdiction in all but a small set of class actions. This set includes class actions with fewer than 100 class members or less than $5 million in aggregate value; the traditional rules might also be relevant when either § 1332(d)(3) permits or §1332(d)(4) requires a federal court to decline jurisdiction.

11. One question that has divided the courts is what should happen when a class action is removed from state court, but the federal court fails to certify the case as a class action. Must the case now be remanded to state court? If so, can the plaintiffs again seek class certification in state court? If they do, can the can again be removed to federal court in some sort of vicious infinite regression? Consider the following case.

CUNNINGHAM CHARTER CORP. V. LEARJET, INC.

592 F.3d 805 (7th Cir. 2010)

■   POSNER, Circuit Judge.

Cunningham Charter Corporation sued Learjet, Inc. in an Illinois state court asserting claims for breach of warranty and products liability on behalf of itself and all other buyers of Learjets who had received the same warranty from the manufacturer that Cunningham had received. The defendant removed the case to federal district court under the Class Action Fairness Act of 2005, 28 U.S.C. § 1332(d), and the plaintiff then moved to certify two classes. The district judge denied the motion on the ground that neither proposed class satisfied the criteria for certification set forth in Rule 23 of the Federal Rules of Civil Procedure. The judge then ruled that the denial of class certification eliminated subject-matter jurisdiction under the Act, and so he remanded the case to the state court. Learjet petitioned for leave to appeal the order of remand. 28 U.S.C. § 1453(c). We granted the petition in order to resolve an issue under the Class Action Fairness Act that this court has not heretofore had to resolve.

The Act creates federal diversity jurisdiction over certain class actions in which at least one member of the class is a citizen of a different state from any defendant (that is, in which diversity may not be complete). 28 U.S.C. § 1332(d)(2). The Act defines class action as "any civil action filed under rule 23 of the Federal Rules of Civil Procedure or similar State statute or rule of judicial procedure authorizing an action to be brought by 1 or more representative persons as a class action." § 1332(d)(1)(B).

A later section says the Act applies "to any class action [within the Act's scope] before or after the entry of a class certification order." § 1332(d)(8). Probably all this means is that the defendant can wait until a class is certified before deciding whether to remove the case to federal court. If (d)(8) said "the" instead of "a" class certification order, it might be thought to imply that the Act was limited to cases in which such an order was eventually issued. But that would be inconsistent with (d)(1)(B), the section quoted above that defines class action as a suit filed under a statute or rule authorizing class actions, even though many such suits cannot be maintained as class actions because the judge refuses to certify a class. As actually worded, (d)(8), insofar as it relates to jurisdiction at all (it doesn't mention the word — the conferral of jurisdiction is limited to (d)(2)), implies at most an expectation that a class will or at least may be certified eventually. The absence of such an expectation could mean that the suit was not within the jurisdiction conferred by the Class Action Fairness Act — that it wasn't really a class action. Frivolous attempts to invoke federal jurisdiction fail, and compel dismissal. If a plaintiff sued in state court a seller of fish tanks on behalf of himself and 1,000 goldfish for $5,000,001 and the defendant removed the case to federal district court, that court would have to dismiss the case, as it would have been certain from the outset of the litigation that no class could be certified.

Another section of the Act defines "class certification order" as "an order issued by a court approving the treatment of some or all aspects of a civil action as a class action." § 1332(d)(1)(C). Read in isolation from the rest of the Act, this could mean that in the absence of such an order a suit is not a class action. But remember that jurisdiction attaches when a suit is filed as a class action, and that invariably precedes certification. All that section 1332(d)(1)(C) means is that a suit filed as a class action cannot be maintained as one without an order certifying the class. That needn't imply that unless the class is certified the court loses jurisdiction of the case.

We assumed in *Bullard v. Burlington Northern Santa Fe Ry.*, 535 F.3d 759, 762 (7th Cir. 2008), that federal jurisdiction under the Class Action Fairness Act does not depend on certification, and we now join *Vega v. T-Mobile USA, Inc.*, 564 F.3d 1256, 1268 n.12 (11th Cir. 2009), in so holding. That is the better interpretation — and not only as a matter of semantics. For if a state happened to have different criteria for certifying a class from those of Rule 23, the result of a remand because of the federal court's refusal to certify the class could be that the case would continue as a class action in state court. That result would be contrary to the Act's purpose of relaxing the requirement of complete diversity of citizenship so that class actions involving incomplete diversity can be litigated in federal court.

Our conclusion vindicates the general principle that jurisdiction once properly invoked is not lost by developments after a suit is filed, such as a change in the state of which a party is a citizen that destroys diversity. The general principle is applicable to this case because no one suggests that a class action must be certified before it can be removed to federal court under the Act; section 1332(d)(8) scotches any such inference.

There are, it is true, exceptions to the principle that once jurisdiction, always jurisdiction, notably where a case becomes moot in the course of the litigation. Or, if the plaintiff amends away jurisdiction in a subsequent pleading, the case must be dismissed. And likewise if after the case is filed it is discovered that there was no jurisdiction at the outset — not that this is really an exception to the principle that jurisdiction, once it attaches, sticks; it is a case in which there never was federal jurisdiction.

These points are applicable to the Class Action Fairness Act, but inapplicable to the present case. Although the district court found "a number of fatal flaws" in the plaintiff's motion for class certification, they are not so obviously fatal as to make the plaintiff's attempt to maintain the suit as a class action frivolous. Behind the principle that jurisdiction once obtained normally is secure is a desire to minimize expense and delay. If at all possible, therefore, a case should stay in the system that first acquired jurisdiction. It should not be shunted between court systems; litigation is not ping-pong. (This consideration cuts against the proposal that having declined to certify a class the federal court should abstain in favor of the state courts; that would be the equivalent of returning the case to the state court in which it had originated.) An even more important consideration is that the policy behind the Class Action Fairness Act would be thwarted if because of a remand a suit that was within the scope of the Act by virtue of having been filed as a class action ended up being litigated as a class action in state court.

The judgment of the district court is reversed and the case remanded to that court for further proceedings consistent with this opinion.

Notes

1. As Judge Posner says, the Eleventh Circuit had come to the same conclusion — that events occurring after removal do not deprive a federal court of jurisdiction — in *Vega v. T-Mobile USA, Inc.*, 564 F.3d 1256, 1268 n.12 (11th Cir. 2009). In *Vega*, the plaintiff filed a nationwide class action in Florida state court. Hedging his bets after removal of the case to federal court, the plaintiff also filed a Florida-only subclass. The district court refused to certify a nationwide class action, but certified the Florida-only class. The court of appeals reversed, finding that the Florida-only subclass, which likely contained fewer than 100 members, failed to meet the "numerosity" requirement of Rule 23(a)(1). The court noted that this fact did not deprive the district court of subject-matter jurisdiction, even though CAFA applies only to class actions containing 100 members or more. Its reasoning was not as detailed as that of *Cunningham Charter*.

2. Although Judge Posner did not mention this fact, the result in *Cunningham Charter* is also consistent with CAFA's legislative history. *See* S. Rep. No. 109-14, at 70-71 (2005), *reprinted in* 2005 U.S.C.C.A.N. 3, 66

("Current law (that [CAFA] does not alter) is also clear that, once a complaint is properly removed to federal court, the federal court's jurisdiction cannot be 'ousted' by later events."). Reluctance to rely on the Senate Report is understandable. Aside from all the usual difficulties of relying on legislative history to determine a statute's meaning — a debate that rages in both courts and academic circles — the Report presents unique problems. It is dated February 28, 2005 — eleven days after CAFA's passage and ten days after President Bush had signed CAFA into law. Some courts have therefore expressed skepticism about the probative value of the Report. Blockbuster, Inc. v. Galeno, 472 F.3d 53, 58 (2d Cir. 2006). On the other hand, according to the *Congressional Record*, the Report (or at least a draft of it) was submitted while the Senate was deliberating on CAFA. Lowery v. Ala. Power Co., 483 F.3d 1184, 1206 n.50 (11th Cir. 2007). *See also* Estate of Pew v. Cardarelli, 527 F.3d 25, 32-33 (2d Cir. 2008) (discussing both sides of the debate before deciding "it appropriate in this case to examine the legislative history of these particularly knotty provisions").

C. COORDINATION AND COOPERATION AS AN ALTERNATIVE TO AGGREGATION

Although rules of territorial jurisdiction and subject-matter jurisdiction have enough play to allow for a great deal of aggregation in a single (usually federal) forum, one of the clear messages of this chapter is that jurisdictional doctrines limit our ability to aggregate cases. In addition, litigant choice, particularly the "master of the complaint" rule, causes dispersion of claims even when jurisdictional rules permit aggregation; individuals seeking the forum that provides maximal private advantage will often pick a forum other than the one that is best from the viewpoint of socially optimal aggregation.

Even if optimal aggregation fails due to jurisdictional boundaries or litigant autonomy, all is not lost. It is possible to achieve some of the advantages of single-forum aggregation if judges coordinate their efforts. The following article studied eleven instances in which state and federal judges cooperated, and synthesized its observations into recommendations for making state-federal coordination more effective.

William W Schwarzer et al., JUDICIAL FEDERALISM IN ACTION: COORDINATION OF LITIGATION IN STATE AND FEDERAL COURTS

78 VA. L. REV. 1689, 1733-45, 1748-49 (1992)

This Section discusses a wide range of issues relevant to the achievement of effective intersystem coordination . . . .

A. *Initiation of Contact*

. . .

Coordination obviously cannot take place until a judge contacts his or her counterpart in the other judicial system. Some judges prefer not to initiate contact until they have systems in place and can offer tangible resources to the other court. . . . The majority of judges interviewed, however, preferred early contact so that the state and federal judges could coordinate their schedules, consider joint discovery, and begin thinking about greater cooperation. . . .

B. *Maintaining Contact*

The judges' initial conversations tend to focus on general perspectives of the litigation, case management strategies, and areas appropriate for state-federal cooperation. As the cases progress, the judges need to maintain contact on a range of matters including scheduling, simply keeping abreast of cases in the other system, preparing for joint hearings, making joint rulings, or consulting on matters of procedure or substantive law. . . .

C. *The Working Relationship*

Those who have engaged in intersystem coordination tend to agree that the strength of the personal and working relationship developed between the judges influences the success of the enterprise more than any other factor. As Judge Weinstein puts it: "Coordination has nothing to do with procedures; it has to do with personality." A number of important dimensions of this relationship can be highlighted. Successful coordination requires flexibility and willingness to compromise in order to develop arrangements acceptable to both courts. Judge Zampano explains that an "exchange of communication, discussion, and camaraderie is very important. . . . There can't be egos here." His collaborator Judge Meadow agrees, adding that coordination requires "two judges that are not going to in any way let their personalities get in the way of their objectives." Judge Bechtle suggests that state and federal judges trying to develop a supportive relationship need to take into account "[s]ome degree of informality" as well as "more diplomacy and more consideration and more public relations and courtesy." Judge Rubin also stresses the need for informality. A true partnership cannot emerge unless the judges feel comfortable with one another and let down barriers. . . .

D. *The Role of Attorneys*

Coordination obviously requires that each judge learn of related cases pending in the other court system. Attorneys can be helpful in that regard because they often have related cases pending in both court systems and generally favor intersystem coordination because it can spare them and their clients unnecessary costs and duplication of effort. . . .

The role of attorneys in state-federal coordination extends beyond getting it started. Their active participation is vital at every stage of coordination. Attorneys may be more knowledgeable than the court about numerous matters relevant to coordination, such as relationships among counsel, parties' different priorities and stages of preparation, or ongoing settlement talks. . . .

Coordination requires not only that attorneys communicate with the court, but also cooperate with one another. . . .

Yet, cooperation among attorneys has limits. In the Hyatt Skywalk litigation, the attorneys in federal court preferred a class action while the attorneys in the state cases wanted to handle their cases individually, and considerable tension resulted. In general, lawyers favor state-federal coordination of discovery and settlement, but are sometimes reluctant to proceed further because they have consciously chosen to proceed in one forum, and do not want to see the significance of that decision diminished. Courts should be sensitive to their interests and seek the lawyers' approval (not merely their grudging acceptance) of such intersystem coordination as seems desirable. This may involve assuring counsel that even when matters are jointly briefed, argued, and even decided, the judge in whose court the case is brought will not abdicate his or her responsibility to give the matter independent consideration.

E. *Situations Most Conducive to Effective Coordination*

Most coordination has occurred in litigation arising out of a single, discrete event. Although such cases are typically the best candidates for coordination, they are not the only ones. . . . There are, however, certain circumstances under which coordination has proven most feasible.

1. *Proximity*

Not surprisingly, judges have found that coordination works best when the state and federal courts are in close proximity. . . .

2. *Intrasystem Aggregation*

The possibility of intersystem coordination is enhanced when the cases within each system are aggregated. When one judge is in charge of all the cases in a system, that judge can structure the litigation and ensure uniform treatment of the cases. This, in turn, makes it possible to develop a coherent plan for coordinating related cases with another court. . . . Such things as coordinated scheduling, a common case management plan, and joint hearings require extensive effort and communication between two judges and become far more difficult as the number of judges increases. Moreover, when only a few judges manage all of the related cases, these judges have access to all of the parties and thus an opportunity to encourage a global settlement, which would be far less likely if the cases were scattered among many courts. In all of the cases studied, some form of aggregation was achieved within both the state and federal systems. . . .

3. *A Supportive Legal Community*

Although the actual state-federal coordination usually involves the work of a few individual judges, the appropriate judicial environment throughout a jurisdiction can facilitate coordination. For example, Judge Shortell describes the Alaska court systems as "more relaxed" than those in larger jurisdictions such that "[t]here is not so much formality" and certainly no "friction" between the state and federal courts. Because of this, he says, "there is no impediment . . . even to [judges] who don't know each other, getting together and talking [about their cases]." . . .

F. *Federalism Concerns*

The potential benefits of intersystem coordination should be clear. There are, however, potential drawbacks as well, mostly stemming from the fact that intersystem coordination invites tampering with the traditional jurisdictional boundaries of the state and federal court systems. The United States Constitution envisions two separate judiciaries. For the country at large, this division provides varied laboratories in which to test different approaches. For individual litigants dual judiciaries can offer a choice of where to pursue or defend against a claim. Judges must be sensitive to the possibility that state-federal coordination can undermine these interests.

1. *Shared Power Relationship*

Coordination requires judges to make joint decisions involving both case management and legal interpretation. Certain risks inhere in any joint decisionmaking situation. First, the necessary compromises will, in the perception of an individual judge, sometimes come at the expense of excellence. . . .

Another potential problem with any power-sharing arrangement is that one party may exert too much influence. As a result, the methods and interpretations of the subordinate partner are lost. . . . In addition, judges risk diminishing the integrity of their court's decisionmaking process if they become a rubber stamp for another court. In several of the cases under study, one judge essentially controlled the litigation in both systems. It was not uncommon for the federal court to play this role. In light of federal courts' greater resources, this tendency is understandable, but judges should take care that dominance be avoided if possible. In addition to the risks described, federal courts should be wary of overstepping their Article III function by making decisions affecting persons over whom they have no jurisdiction. . . .

2. *Litigant Choice*

Perhaps the greatest concern is that intersystem coordination can diminish the litigants' benefits of their choice of forum. They might have had good reason for selecting one court system over the other, and when judges work together and influence one another, or mold their rules to conform to those of another system, or decide matters jointly, litigants may lose the advantages of their chosen forum. . . .

3. *Deference on Substantive Issues*

. . .

[A] middle path offers a fruitful possibility to federal and state courts coordinating their companion cases: although the state court should not automatically follow the federal court's determinations on federal law, it may accord them great weight, perhaps even a rebuttable presumption of correctness. This policy of deference would seem especially justified in light of the value of producing consistent results in related cases. As long as the deference is not blind, the state court arguably fulfills its responsibility. . . .

. . . [I]t is settled doctrine that the decisions of lower state courts on matters of state law, although not binding on federal courts, carry significant weight. In the context of companion state-federal cases, the value of consistency arguably justifies the federal court giving the state court's interpretation of state law even more weight than it otherwise might — albeit still making sure that it regards the state court's interpretation as reasonable. This also ensures that the federal court does not excessively interfere with the development of state law.

Notes

1. In recent years, judicial coordination and cooperation have received significant attention. For instance, the *Manual for Complex Litigation*, published by the Federal Judicial Center, is the "bible" for judges handling pretrial and trial matters in complex litigation. Neither the 1960 precursor to the *Manual* nor the original 1970 edition contained any references to intersystem cooperation and coordination. The second edition, published in 1985, briefly described and weakly recommended cooperation and coordination. *See* MANUAL FOR COMPLEX LITIGATION (SECOND) § 31.31 (1985). The third edition of the *Manual*, published in 1995 under the leadership of Judge Schwarzer, took a more enthusiastic attitude toward cooperation and coordination. *See* MANUAL FOR COMPLEX LITIGATION, THIRD § 31.31 (1995). The present edition of the *Manual* expands significantly on this discussion. *See* MANUAL FOR COMPLEX LITIGATION, FOURTH §§ 20.31-.313 (2004). In addition, in 1997, the Federal Judicial Center, the National Center for State Courts, and the State Justice Institute jointly published a 248-page manual specifically on the subject. JAMES G. APPLE ET AL., FED.

JUD. CTR. & NAT'L CTR. FOR STATE COURTS, MANUAL FOR COOPERATION BETWEEN STATE AND FEDERAL COURTS (1997).

2.   Intersystem coordination and cooperation have certain advantages over mechanisms that aggregate cases in one (usually federal) forum. In addition to the benefits described by Judge Schwarzer and his co-authors, coordination and cooperation foster respect for both state and federal courts and avoid concentrating too much power in a single judge. Two judicial heads can also be better than one. On the other hand, coordination and cooperation possess the drawbacks identified by Judge Schwarzer and his co-authors. On balance, does coordination or lack of coordination seem the greater evil?

3.   The authors' recommendations for effective coordination raise certain concerns that we have previously explored. For instance, is it appropriate for a federal judge to defer to a lower state-court judge's view on unclear state law? Doesn't this deference create a form of "abstention" much broader than *Pullman*, *Burford*, and *Thibodaux* abstention, which among them have worked out the parameters of federal-court deference on matters of unclear state law? *See supra* pp. 202-03. In states with certification statutes, isn't certification the proper mechanism for a federal judge to use when confronted with uncertain state law? Conversely, in light of concurrent jurisdiction and the requirement that state courts hold themselves open to hear federal claims, *see, e.g.*, Howlett v. Rose, 496 U.S. 356 (1990) (discussed *supra* pp. 205-06), can a state judge legitimately defer to a federal judge's views on questions of federal law? As a policy matter, doesn't our federal system value the views of state judges on federal questions as much as it values the views of federal judges?

Moreover, suppose that the federal (or state) judge sincerely believes that his or her counterpart is making a mistake on a matter for which the other judge is taking lead substantive responsibility. Is it ethical to communicate this belief ex parte to the other judge?

4.   Whatever your views on the merits, intersystem coordination and cooperation are the order of the day if aggregation efforts fail. Coordination and cooperation occur not only among judges, but also among lawyers. In many types of complex litigation, lawyers handling related litigation create networks and share information. Moreover, because it is too costly for small firms to reinvent the wheel in each case, repetitive litigation is often controlled by a few plaintiffs' or defense firms that associate with other firms around the country, further aiding the coordination process. A classic article describing successful cooperation and coordination among plaintiffs' lawyers is Paul D. Rheingold, *The MER/29 Story — An Instance of Successful Mass Disaster Litigation*, 56 CAL. L. REV. 116 (1968).

5.   The possibility of coordination among lawyers also has an effect on at least one intrasystem aggregation device: multidistrict transfer. One of the factors that the Judicial Panel on Multidistrict Litigation sometimes cites when it decides not to consolidate cases is the ability of lawyers in the related cases to coordinate their efforts. *See, e.g.*, In re A. H. Robins Co., Inc., 505 F. Supp. 221 (J.P.M.L. 1981). On the other hand, good cooperation

is not always a decisive factor, and appears to have exercised less influence over the Panel in recent years. For instance, in *In re: Mentor Corp. ObTape Transobturator Sling Products Liability Litigation*, 588 F. Supp. 2d 1374 (J.P.M.L. 2008), the only defendant was represented by one national law firm and most of the plaintiffs were represented by one of two law firms. The Panel nonetheless consolidated the cases, observing:

> While we applaud voluntary efforts to cooperate and coordinate among the parties and their counsel, we observe that centralization under Section 1407 "has the benefit of placing all actions in this docket, as well as any additional related actions that may be forthcoming, before a single transferee judge who can structure pretrial proceedings to ensure that pretrial discovery and rulings will occur in a manner that minimizes the risk of duplication or inconsistency and that thereby leads to the just and expeditious resolution of all actions to the overall benefit of those involved." [*Id.* at 1375.]

CHAPTER FOUR

CLASS ACTIONS

Until now we have studied numerous devices — joinder, preclusion, antisuit injunctions, and consolidation — designed to resolve the claims of similarly situated persons in one forum. Each of these devices is useful in some circumstances, but none is a panacea for the problem of repetitive litigation of related claims. We now turn to the class action as a device that might overcome some of the hurdles that these other devices have been unable to overcome.

To locate the class action in the context of these other devices, it is an device that combines elements of joinder and preclusion. The class action permits a representative person (or group of persons) to bring a claim on behalf of all persons similarly situated. Once a judgment in a class action is entered, the members of the class receive the same benefits and suffer the same consequences of claim and issue preclusion as individually joined parties. In a sense, the class members are joined as parties. But that is really a legal fiction. In reality, class members are bound to the outcome of a case litigated by others.

The decision whether or not to certify a class action has enormous practical consequences. In many cases the certification decision is the decisive ruling in the case. It determines the settlement leverage of the parties, the size of the fees that may earned by both plaintiff and defense counsel, the likely costs of discovery and trial, and the publicity which will or will not attend the litigation. Moreover, the potential for class treatment exerts an influence on the very nature of the case; lawyers sometime choose to sue on certain substantive grounds, and forgo others, in an effort to qualify for or to avoid class certification.

No other federal rule of civil procedure has generated as much debate, or as much division, as the modern class action rule — Rule 23. The class action has alternately been viewed as the cure-all for or the cause of complex civil litigation. *See* Arthur R. Miller, *Of Frankenstein Monsters and Shining Knights: Myth, Reality, and the "Class Action Problem,"* 92 HARV. L. REV. 664 (1979).

Historically, class actions were unknown in civil-law and other procedural systems. They began as a creature of Anglo-American equity practice. With roots that can be traced back to Federal Equity Rule 38, the original version of Rule 23 promulgated in 1938 created three categories of class actions — true, hybrid, and spurious. The original Rule 23 proved to be little used and of little importance. The practicing bar found its meaning obscure and its reach uncertain. Consequently, very few class actions were brought under the rule between 1938 and 1966. *See* Roger H. Trangsrud, *James F. Humphreys Lecture: The Adversary System and Modern Class Action Practice,* 76 GEO. WASH. L. REV. 181, 183-184 (2008).

In 1966 the class action rule was completely rewritten as part of a larger set of amendments to the federal joinder rules. The new class action was a revolutionary attempt to define when and in what circumstances group litigation should be allowed in the federal courts. Although the 1966 class-action rule has been amended in important ways twice — in 1998 and in 2003 — the stated criteria for the certification of federal class actions has not changed since 1966.

The influence of Rule 23 is also felt at the state level; many states in the years since 1966 have adopted state class-action rules that are identical or similar to the federal rule. This chapter therefore begins by exploring the requirements for certifying class actions in federal court, and then goes on to examine various federal statutes and constitutional provisions that affect class-action practice. As you read these materials, you should ask why we maintain a rule that is in such evident tension with traditional norms of adversarial practice.

Before you go on, however, you should read Rule 23 now. Basic familiarity with the rule is presumed in the following sections. In particular, be sure you understand the difference between mandatory (i.e., (b)(1) and (b)(2)) class actions and opt-out (i.e., (b)(3)) class actions.

A. THE REQUIREMENTS OF CLASS ACTIONS

In this section we consider the requirements for two types of class actions — litigation class actions (class actions in which the class representative proposes to litigate the controversy with the defendant) and settlement class actions (class actions in which the class representative brings the case to effectuate a class-wide settlement on which the class representative and the defendant have agreed). For reasons that we will see, it is useful to distinguish between these two types of class actions, but it is not important to get hung up on the difference now. Most class actions — even those that start as litigation class actions — end up settling; indeed, if a litigation class action is certified, the enormous risks that a loss poses for the defendant makes settlement the likeliest outcome — a reality that often drives defendants' opposition to class certification.

Both types of class action have common features. First, both must meet the requirements of Rules 23(a), (b), and (g). Second, the person(s) seeking class treatment (usually the class representative(s)) has the burden of proving that the elements of Rules 23(a) and 23(b) are met. Third, the class can be composed of plaintiffs or defendants. (Because defendant class actions are rare, however, we focus on plaintiff class actions.) Finally, when the certification criteria are met, the outcome of the class action (whether a judgment or a settlement) is binding on the members of the class.

It is this last feature — the binding effect of a class action on absent class members — that is so critical to understanding the value of a class action as an aggregation mechanism. Individual joinder or consolidation becomes unnecessary; a single lawsuit sweeps all related claims together. At the same time, this preclusive effect is one of the greatest sources of worry about class actions. What prevents the class representatives and class counsel from selling out the interests of the class members in return for large payoffs for themselves? This risk seems less of an issue with injunctive relief when all the class members are identically situated, but what if the interests of class members in obtaining injunctive relief are not identical? What if the plaintiffs seek damages? When the interests of class members are not identical (and they rarely are), how do we justify the class members' loss of autonomy to control their own cases?

In the "granddaddy" of modern class actions, the Supreme Court offered a way to think about some of these questions. *See* Hansberry v. Lee, 311 U.S. 32 (1940). *Hansberry* famously held that, for a class action to have a binding effect on the claims of class members, the Due Process Clause requires that the class representatives adequately represent the interests of the class. But *Hansberry* was less clear about exactly what constituted adequate representation, about why the swap of autonomy for adequacy was a constitutionally fair deal, or about which circumstances justified this swap and which did not. In a sense, the law of class actions has ever since been working out the answers to the issues that *Hansberry* left open.

The following material on litigation and settlement class actions represents how far we have come in our thinking on these issues. As you read it, consider the extent to which class actions solve problems that other methods of aggregation could not, the problems that class actions do not solve, and the new difficulties that class actions interject.

1. Litigation Class Actions

To be certified as a class action, each of the elements of Rule 23(a) and Rule 23(g), plus at least one of the elements of Rule 23(b), must be met. Once the hurdles of Rule 23(a) are cleared, Rule 23(b) requires that the class meet one of four additional requirements for class treatment. The first three of the Rule 23(b) class actions (the (b)(1)(A), (b)(1)(B), and (b)(2) class actions) are usually referred to as "mandatory class actions," because class members cannot ordinarily remove themselves from the class. The final class action (the (b)(3) class action) is called the "opt-out class action," because class members must be given notice of the pendency of the class action and an opportunity to exclude themselves (i.e., opt out).

The Rule 23(a) and -(g) elements exist principally to protect absent class members — they provide the framework to ensure that each class action meets *Hansberry*'s constitutional command of adequate representation. Likewise, for the most part, the Rule 23(b) elements provide the reasons that justify class treatment — the circumstances in which our society believes that sacrificing individual autonomy and binding class members to the outcome achieved by an adequate representative is appropriate.

a. The Rule 23(a) and Rule 23(g) Requirements

Rule 23(a) enumerates four requirements that every class action must meet. These requirements are referred to as numerosity, commonality, typicality and adequacy. Federal courts have long held that two additional requirements inhere in Rule 23(a): The class must be adequately defined, and the class representative must be a member of the class. *See* Roman v. ESB, Inc., 550 F.2d 1343, 1348 (4th Cir. 1976) (adequately defining the class is an essential prerequisite to maintaining a class action); Long v. D.C., 469 F.2d 927, 930 (D.C. Cir. 1972) ("A person simply cannot represent a class of which he is not a member."). We examine all six requirements, plus the Rule 23(g) requirement that class counsel be adequate.

i. The Existence and Definition of a Class

The requirement that the class be adequately defined and identified derives from the language of Rule 23, which speaks of "members of a *class*" suing or being sued. Properly defining a class is critical for many reasons. First, it is impossible to know whether the Rule 23 criteria have been met until the class is defined; for instance, how can a court determine if the class representatives adequately represent the class when it is not clear who is in the class? A proper class definition can also be important for determining the notice that might need to be given to class members, the scope of discovery, the applicable law, the scope of the remedy, and the binding effect of any judgment or settlement.

RICE V. CITY OF PHILADELPHIA

66 F.R.D. 17 (E.D. Pa. 1974)

■ FULLAM, District Judge.

[The plaintiffs alleged the existence of a pattern or practice that resulted in the illegal detention of persons charged with crime due to delays in holding preliminary arraignments. They sought declaratory, injunctive, and compensatory relief against the City of Philadelphia, its Police Commissioner, its District Attorney, and its Municipal Court judges. The plaintiffs sought to certify the case as a class action on behalf of "all persons who are, who have been, or who will be illegally detained by the Police Department of the City of Philadelphia between arrest and preliminary arraignment, and who are denied a prompt preliminary arraignment by defendants." The plaintiffs also proposed to certify a defendant class consisting of the 22 judges of the Philadelphia Municipal Court, to be represented by the President Judge of that Court.

[The court declined to certify the defendant class. It also addressed the request for certification of a Rule 23(b)(2) plaintiff class with respect to the injunctive and declaratory claims and a Rule 23(b)(3) plaintiff class with respect to the claims for monetary relief.]

This case brings into sharp focus the relationship between class actions under Rule 23(b)(2), and class actions under Rule 23(b)(3). The provisions of Rule 23(b)(2) are designed to cover cases in which the primary concern is the grant of injunctive or declaratory relief. In such cases, there is no requirement that notice be given to all of the class members, and there is no opportunity for putative class members to "opt out." Moreover, the precise definition of the class is relatively unimportant. If relief is granted to the plaintiff class, the defendants are legally obligated to comply, and it is usually unnecessary to define with precision the persons entitled to enforce compliance, since presumably at least the representative plaintiffs would be available to seek, and interested in obtaining, follow-up relief if necessary.

In a (b)(3) action, on the other hand, because of the notice and "opt out" features, greater precision in class definition is required. Moreover, most such actions involve claims for damages, and it is usually necessary, at some point, to identify individual members of the class.

In the present case, plaintiffs argue that the primary thrust of their action is for injunctive and declaratory relief, and that the case should therefore be permitted to proceed as a (b)(2) class action. Plaintiffs appear to concede that their proposed definition of the class would be unsatisfactory for a (b)(3) action. However, plaintiffs also are seeking damages, contending that this is merely incidental to the basic purpose of the action; and it is this feature which causes difficulties.

Defining a class as consisting of all persons who have been or will be affected by the conduct charged to the defendants is entirely appropriate where only injunctive or declaratory relief is sought. Indeed, the principal beneficiaries of an injunctive decree would seem likely to be those class members whose rights have not yet been violated. But the proposed class definition is clearly unsatisfactory where damage claims are asserted. Persons whose rights have not yet been violated cannot very well obtain damages. Moreover, the definition is too broad, since it purports to include all persons whose rights have ever been violated in the past, in the respects complained of. If for no other reason than the statute of limitations, this definition would be unacceptable. . . .

In the present case, not only would the calculation of the amount of damages depend upon the individual facts of each claimant's case, but virtually all of the issues would have to be litigated individually in order to determine whether a particular alleged class member was entitled to any damages at all. Each claimant, in order to obtain the benefits of the class suit, would have to establish his membership in the class (i.e., that his rights were violated).

Of perhaps greater significance, the issues involved in determining whether the plaintiff class is entitled to injunctive or declaratory relief are simply not the same issues involved in determining whether individual members of the class may be entitled to damages. There could be many reasons for denying injunctive or declaratory relief which ought not to have the effect of precluding particular class members from obtaining damages.
. . .

Plaintiffs appear to concede the impracticability of giving notice to the proposed class. And, as mentioned above, there is no right to opt out in a (b)(2) action. I find particularly troublesome the notion that individuals who may never learn of the pendency of this case might encounter difficulty in pursuing meritorious individual litigation in the future, on the basis of lis pendens, res judicata, or collateral estoppel. In short, I believe this is the kind of case in which notice should be required before permitting a class action for damages, even incidentally. Since notice is not feasible, class action treatment on issues of liability for damages should not be permitted.

In conformity with the views expressed above, this action will be permitted to proceed as a class action under Rule 23(b)(2), but only as to issues relating to injunctive and declaratory relief. The plaintiff class will be defined as

> ". . . all persons who, within two years last past, have been, or who are being, or who will in the future be illegally detained by the Police Department of the City of Philadelphia by reason of unreasonable or otherwise unlawful delay of their preliminary arraignment."

Notes

1.   If a court finds that a proposed class action has been inadequately defined, it can either dismiss the class action or redefine the class in a manner that satisfies Rule 23. *See* 7A CHARLES A. WRIGHT ET AL., FEDERAL PRACTICE AND PROCEDURE § 1760 (3d ed. 2005). Courts sometimes express an unwillingness to dismiss a case when a change in class definition can fix the problem. *See* In re Monumental Life Ins. Co., 365 F.3d 408, 414 (5th Cir. 2004) ("[C]ourts are permitted to limit or modify class definitions to provide the necessary precision."); *but see* Heaven v. Trust Co. Bank, 118 F.3d 735 (11th Cir. 1997) ("The district court has no sua sponte obligation to subclassify; it is the plaintiff's burden to designate an appropriate class."); *see also* Chiang v. Veneman, 385 F.3d 256, 269 (3d Cir. 2004) (sua sponte "reform[ing] the class definition based on our understanding of the main thrust of [the class representative's] claims").

2.   *Monumental Life* observed that "[a] precise class definition is necessary to identify properly 'those entitled to relief, those bound by the judgment, and those entitled to notice.'" 365 F.3d at 413. Given the

multiple purposes that a proper class definition is designed to serve, was *Rice* correct to focus solely on the nature of the remedy the class is pursuing? *See id.* ("Some courts have stated that a precise class definition is not as critical where certification of a class for injunctive or declaratory relief is sought under rule 23(b)(2). Where notice and opt-out rights are requested, however, a precise class definition becomes just as important as in the rule 23(b)(3) context.").

3. Did *Rice* hold that the class was inadequately defined, that the representatives' claims for damages were not typical of the claims of other class members (*see* Fed. R. Civ. P. 23(a)(3)), that the class representatives did not adequately represent the damages claims of class members (*see* Fed. R. Civ. P. 23(a)(4)), or that the individual damages issues of class members predominated over common issues (*see* Fed. R. Civ. P. 23(b)(3))? *Rice* shows that the class-definition issue spills over into the other requirements of class certification. Should these other requirements influence the issue of class definition? *Cf.* Carpenter v. Davis, 424 F.2d 257, 260 (5th Cir. 1970) (finding that "[i]t is not necessary that the members of the class be so clearly identified that any member can be presently ascertained" when the other elements of Rule 23(a) and (b) are established); Rink v. Cheminova, Inc., 203 F.R.D. 648, 660 (M.D. Fla. 2001) ("A vague class definition portends significant manageability problems for the court.").

Perhaps proving the interplay of the class-definition issue with the other issues of class certification, some courts hold that the class-definition issue is part of Rule 23(a)(1)'s inquiry into numerosity. *See* O'Neill v. The Home Depot U.S.A., Inc., 243 F.R.D. 469, 477 (S.D. Fla. 2006). Likewise, in *Rahman v. Chertoff*, 530 F.3d 622, 625 (7th Cir. 2008), the court cited a host of problems with the class definition: "the classes grow or shrink with the plaintiffs' contentions as the case progresses"; "[e]ven in retrospect the court will not know who is in the class and who is not"; and "it is impossible to tell whether all of the named plaintiffs are (or will be at the end of the case) members of the classes they purport to represent." Rather than finding the class definition too imprecise, however, *Rahman* found that the class failed to meet Rule 23(a)(3)'s typicality requirement.

4. The usual rule is to deny class certification when the class definition is "overly broad, amorphous, and vague, or where the number of individualized determinations required to determine class membership becomes too administratively difficult." Perez v. Metabolife Int'l, Inc., 218 F.R.D. 262, 269 (S.D. Fla. 2003); *see* White v. Williams, 208 F.R.D. 123 (D.N.J. 2002) ("The proposed class may not be 'amorphous, vague, or indeterminate' and it must be 'administratively feasible to determine whether a given individual is a member of the class.'"). Thus, courts have traditionally been reluctant to certify classes whose membership depends upon the "state of mind" of the class member or other subjective criteria. *See* Simer v. Rios, 661 F.2d 655 (7th Cir. 1981); DeBremaecker v. Short, 433 F.2d 733 (5th Cir. 1970). At the same time, courts do not usually insist that every class member be identified at the beginning of the litigation, although they may require that the general size of the class be known and that the

identity of particular class members be ascertainable in the future with reasonable effort. *See* 7A WRIGHT ET AL., *supra*, § 1760.

For the most part, courts have also accepted *Rice*'s view that class definitions can be less precise in (b)(2) injunctive actions than in (b)(3) damages actions. *See* MANUAL FOR COMPLEX LITIGATION, FOURTH § 21.222 (2004). But *Rahman*, which sought injunctive relief, proves that precision is important even in (b)(2) class actions.

5.   As *Rice* says, one reason that it is important for the identity of the class members be known with some precision is the need to provide notice to class members if the class representatives propose to dismiss or settle the case. Granting the force of this concern, is it ever possible to define a class action that includes persons that have not yet suffered an identifiable injury? *Rice* casts doubt on the possibility. If *Rice* is correct, the utility of the class action as a device either to litigate or settle the claims of future victims under Rule 23(b)(3) or to settle claims on a truly global basis under any provision of Rule 23(b) is in jeopardy. *See infra* p. 492 (discussing the use of settlement class actions to resolve future claims).

Another reason to require a well-defined class in Rule 23(b)(3) class actions is that the damages must be distributed to an identifiable group. Could a class be more loosely defined if some other method for distributing damages were found? *See infra* p. 1205 (discussing the use of fluid-recovery and cy-pres remedies in some class actions).

ii.   Membership in a Class

A second implied requirement of Rule 23(a) is that the class representative be a member of the class. This requirement has its roots in the opening language of Rule 23 ("[o]ne or more members of a class may sue or be sued"), in the Article III requirement of standing, and in the real-party-in-interest requirement of Rule 17(a). The most difficult situation created by the class-membership prerequisite arises when a class action brought by or against a union or other cooperative association seeking to represent its members. A number of courts have held that, even though an association may seem to be an appropriate representative for the class, its inability to obtain a remedy for itself prevents it from being a member or representative of the class. *See, e.g.,* Farmers Co-op. Oil Co. v. Socony-Vacuum Oil Co., 133 F.2d 101 (8th Cir. 1942) (co-op cannot represent individual farmers in an antitrust suit); Wilhite v. S. Cent. Bell Tel. & Tel. Co., 426 F. Supp. 61 (E.D. La. 1976) (union can represent its members when seeking injunctive relief for discrimination in employment, but not for monetary relief). Rule 23.2 ameliorates some of the problems that the class-membership requirement creates in suits by or against unincorporated associations.

iii.   Numerosity

Rule 23(a)(1) provides that a class action may be certified only if "the class is so numerous that joinder of all members is impracticable." What is the purpose of this requirement? How many potential parties is too many to make individual joinder impracticable? Is it a set number (say 100)? Is it the number that makes class resolution is more efficient than individual litigation? Should it matter whether individual litigation is unlikely because of the small stakes involved?

ROBIDOUX v. CELANI

987 F.2d 931 (2d Cir. 1993)

■ PECKHAM, Senior District Judge.

This is an action by three recipients of public assistance in Vermont seeking to represent a class of persons whose applications for public assistance have been delayed unlawfully by the Vermont Department of Social Welfare (Department). . . . Appellants challenge the district court's refusal to certify their suit as a class action and the district court's subsequent dismissal of the suit as moot. For the reasons stated below, we vacate the judgment of the district court and remand for further proceedings consistent with this opinion.

I. BACKGROUND AND PROCEEDINGS BELOW

The Vermont Department of Social Welfare administers several public assistance programs, including the Food Stamp Program [and] the Aid to Needy Families with Children Program (ANFC) . . . . [Federal and state regulations required that state social-welfare agencies determine applicants' eligibility within thirty days of the date of application.]

. . . In spring 1991, finding their resources inadequate to support their families, Robidoux, Rock, and Bevins applied for Food Stamp and/or ANFC benefits to supplement their incomes. The Department did not process any of these applications within the 30-day deadlines. . . .

The plaintiff[s] . . . moved, pursuant to Fed. R. Civ. P. 23(b)(2), to certify as a class "[a]ll current and future Vermont applicants for assistance from the Food Stamp [and] ANFC . . . Programs." In support of their motion for class certification, Appellants submitted two documents. One was a letter from the Department's Commissioner to the U.S. Department of Agriculture which indicated that from July to September 1990, 8 percent of the approximately 800 monthly Vermont Food Stamp applications, or about 65 applications per month, had taken more than 30 days to process. The second document was a monitoring record by the U.S. Department of Health and Human Services, which indicated that 71 of 4017, or nearly 2 percent, of quarterly ANFC applications had taken the Department more than 45 days to process during that same period.

The district court denied the motion for class certification. The district court concluded that Appellants had not shown sufficient evidence of numerosity, because

class definition

[p]laintiff has the burden to show that the class is so large that joinder is impossible. Plaintiff has only shown three people who may be affected, and speculatively an undetermined number of future class members. . . .

In support of their motion for reconsideration of the denial of class certification, Appellants submitted a Department report showing overdue applications for May 1990, December 1990, and February 1991. This document indicated that decisions in ANFC were overdue in 22 cases (6% of 365 cases) in May 1990, 74 cases (14% of 528) in December 1990, and 68 cases (13% of 522) in February 1991. Overdue Food Stamp decisions totalled 52 cases (10% of 518) in May 1990, 133 cases (15% of 884) in December 1990, and 113 cases (13% of 867) in February 1991. The study indicated that an increase in applications caused the increase in overdue cases. . . .

[The district court denied the motion for reconsideration, and then granted summary judgment for the defendant.]

II. DISCUSSION

. . .

If the district court has applied the proper legal standards in deciding whether to certify a class, its decision may be overturned only if it has abused its discretion. At the same time, however, abuse of discretion can be found more readily on appeals from the denial of class status than in other areas, for the courts have built a body of case law with respect to class action status. . . .

Appellants first argue that the district court applied an incorrect legal standard in requiring plaintiffs to show the existence of a class so numerous that "joinder is impossible," while Rule 23(a) requires a finding that the numerosity makes joinder of all class members "impracticable."

Impracticable does not mean impossible. Thus, the district court . . . applied the wrong standard.

Appellants further contend that, under the proper standard, they met the burden of showing numerosity. We agree. Courts have not required evidence of exact class size or identity of class members to satisfy the numerosity requirement.

Appellants presented documentary evidence of delays in 22 to 133 cases per month, depending on the month and whether the assistance sought was Food Stamps or ANFC. Other government benefits cases have held that class representatives who presented similar numbers of potential class members satisfied the numerosity requirement. *See, e.g.,* Grant v. Sullivan, 131 F.R.D. 436, 446 (M.D. Pa. 1990) (a court "may certify a class even if it is composed of as few as 14 members"). A leading treatise concludes, based on prevailing precedent, that the difficulty in joining as few as 40 class members should raise a presumption that joinder is impracticable. . . .

The district court also failed to address other factors relevant to the practicability of joinder. Determination of practicability depends on all the circumstances surrounding a case, not on mere numbers. Relevant considerations include judicial economy arising from the avoidance of a multiplicity of actions, geographic dispersion of class members, financial resources of class members, the ability of claimants to institute individual suits, and requests for prospective injunctive relief which would involve future class members.

Many of these additional factors are present in this case. Consolidating in a class action what could be over 100 individual suits serves judicial economy. Moreover, the potential class members are distributed over the entire area of Vermont. They are also economically disadvantaged, making individual suits difficult to pursue. An injunction requiring the Department to comply with the statutory deadlines would affect all potential class members, and individual suits could lead to potentially inconsistent results.

Thus, the district court abused its discretion in determining that the class was not so numerous that joinder of all members would be impracticable. . . .

[The court of appeals then held that the class met the Rule 23(a)(3) typicality requirement and that the claims were not moot.]

CONCLUSION

The district court's judgment dismissing the complaint is vacated, and the case is remanded for further proceedings not inconsistent with the foregoing, including . . . certification of a class comprising at least "all current and future Vermont applicants for assistance from the Food Stamp and ANFC programs" . . . .

Notes

1.   The district court in *Robidoux* was not entirely off base. In common parlance, "impracticable" means "Not practicable; that cannot be carried out, effected, accomplished, or done; practically impossible." VII OXFORD ENGLISH DICTIONARY 736 (2d ed. 1989). "Impracticable" has become a term of art in class-action practice. If a class action could be used only when it was "practically impossible" to join all plaintiffs under other aggregation rules, class actions would be far less useful for aggregating related claims. Rather than engaging in a literalist interpretation of "impracticable," most courts engage in a multi-factor inquiry like the one used in *Robidoux*. *See* 7A CHARLES A. WRIGHT ET AL., FEDERAL PRACTICE & PROCEDURE § 1762 (3d ed. 2005). Some courts use presumptions regarding the numerosity requirement. *See* In re Amerifirst Sec. Litig., 139 F.R.D. 423, 427 (S.D. Fla. 1991) ("[T]he numerosity requirement . . . is generally assumed to have been met in class action suits . . . involving nationally traded securities"); Taylor v. Hous. Auth. of New Haven, 257 F.R.D. 23, 29 (D. Conn. 2009)

(noting that "numerosity is presumed at a level of 40 members"). Other cases suggest that, when the number of class members reaches a certain threshold, "the impracticability requirement is usually satisfied by the numbers alone." In re Am. Med. Sys., Inc., 75 F.3d 1069, 1079 (6th Cir. 1996) (*infra* p. 367). Still others explicitly compare the manageability issues of traditional joinder and class certification to find the most practical way of organizing the litigation. *See* Boggs v. Divested Atomic Corp., 141 F.R.D. 58, 63 (S.D. Ohio 1991) ("Satisfaction of the numerosity requirement does not require that joinder is impossible, but only that plaintiff will suffer a strong litigational hardship or inconvenience if joinder is required.").

One things is clear: There is no magic number above which Rule 23(a)(1) is automatically satisfied and below which it is automatically not. *See* Gen. Tel. Co. of Nw. v. EEOC, 446 U.S. 318, 330 (1980) (noting that the "numerosity requirement requires examination of the specific facts of each case and imposes no absolute limitations," but suggesting that 15 putative plaintiffs would be too few). Some courts have certified a class of as few as 13 members, while others have denied certification of classes with over 300 members. *See* Hum v. Dericks, 162 F.R.D. 628, 634 (D. Haw. 1995) (citing cases; denying certification of a class containing 200 individuals, 39 of whom were "likely class members"); *compare* Boyd v. Interstate Brands Corp., 256 F.R.D. 340 (E.D.N.Y. 2009) (finding Rule 23(a)(1) satisfied with a class of at least 59 and perhaps 140 members), *with* Clark v. State Farm Mut. Auto. Ins. Co., 245 F.R.D. 478 (D. Colo. 2007) (rejecting a class of 115 members, half of whom had settled with the defendant).

2. What should happen when the size of the class is unknowable? In *Doe v. Charleston Area Medical Center, Inc.*, 529 F.2d 638 (4th Cir. 1975) the court certified a Rule 23(b)(2) class action filed to prevent enforcement of an anti-abortion policy in a government hospital even though the number of local women who would be obliged to go outside the state for abortions was impossible to assess accurately. But, in *Golden v. City of Columbus*, 404 F.3d 950, 966 (6th Cir. 2005), the court held that a class of tenants whose water was turned off due to their landlords' indebtedness failed to prove numerosity when they showed only that there were 150,000 renters in the city; the number of class members remained "bare speculation." *Accord* Vega v. T-Mobile USA, Inc., 564 F.3d 1256 (11th Cir. 2009).

3. Should the amount of the claims affect the numerosity analysis? *Compare* Esler v. Northrop Corp., 86 F.R.D. 20, 34 (W.D. Mo. 1979) (holding that numerosity is satisfied more easily "when the individual claims are for small amounts of damages"), *with* Strykers Bay Neighborhood Council, Inc. v. City of N.Y., 695 F. Supp. 1531, 1538 (S.D.N.Y. 1988) (holding that a class of 32 families was insufficient to satisfy the numerosity test because they could combine their resources and find a lawyer or could seek pro bono representation). *See also* Cuzco v. Orion Builders, Inc., 262 F.R.D. 325 (S.D.N.Y. 2009) (finding Rule 23(a)(1) satisfied with a class of 67 workers, in part because of "the low probability of any other individual suits").

4. Should the geographical dispersion of class members matter? *Andrews v. Bechtel Power Corp.*, 780 F.2d 124 (1st Cir. 1985), denied class

certification in part because the 49 plaintiffs all lived near each other and thus could join together. *Cf.* Trevizo v. Adams, 455 F.3d 1155 (10th Cir. 2006) (noting that 84 individuals was not too numerous to join individually when "all the names and addresses of potential plaintiffs had been provided during discovery"). But won't dispersed class members make the class action less manageable? Is the inquiry into geographical dispersion distinct from the inquiry into the efficiency of a class action? *See* Attenborough v. Constr. & Gen. Bldg. Laborers' Local 79, 238 F.R.D. 82, 93 (S.D.N.Y. 2006) ("The purpose of the numerosity requirement is to promote judicial economy by avoiding a multiplicity of actions.").

5. Some courts have said that numerosity is more easily satisfied when injunctive relief, as opposed to damages, is sought. *See, e.g.,* Holland v. Steele, 92 F.R.D. 58 (N.D. Ga. 1981). What justifies this distinction?

6.   Like the issue of class definition, the issue of numerosity turns more on policy issues — especially whether class treatment yields efficiency gains — than on pure historical fact. Granting that policy issues dominate any class-certification decision, should they permeate every element? Would an objective standard for numerosity make sense? *Cf.* 28 U.S.C. § 1332(d)(5)(B) (excepting from federal jurisdiction certain class actions with fewer than 100 members).

iv.   Commonality, Typicality, and Adequacy of Representation

Rule 23(a)(2) requires that there must be "questions of law or fact common to the class"; Rule 23(a)(3) requires that "the claims or defenses of the representative parties are typical of the claims or defenses of the class"; and Rule 23 (a)(4) requires that "the representative parties will fairly and adequately protect the interests of the class." In addition, Rule 23(g) sets out the criteria for class counsel. In combination, these criteria seek to assure that a class has proper representation, is free of substantial internal antagonisms, and is manageable. They establish, in other words, the irreducible minimum on which our legal system insists in return for class members' sacrifice of their autonomy to control their own litigation.

These criteria interlock and easily spill from one into another. Hence, we study all three criteria together.

GENERAL TELEPHONE CO. OF THE SOUTHWEST V. FALCON

457 U.S. 147 (1982)

■ JUSTICE STEVENS delivered the opinion of the Court.

The question presented is whether respondent Falcon, who complained that petitioner did not promote him because he is a Mexican-American, was properly permitted to maintain a class action on behalf of Mexican-American applicants for employment whom petitioner did not hire.

I

In 1969 petitioner initiated a special recruitment and training program for minorities. Through that program, respondent Falcon was hired in July 1969 as a groundman, and within a year he was twice promoted, first to lineman and then to lineman-in-charge. He subsequently refused a promotion to installer-repairman. In October 1972 he applied for the job of field inspector; his application was denied even though the promotion was granted several white employees with less seniority.

Falcon thereupon filed a charge with the Equal Employment Opportunity Commission stating his belief that he had been passed over for promotion because of his national origin and that petitioner's promotion policy operated against Mexican-Americans as a class. In due course he received a right-to-sue letter from the Commission and, in April 1975, he commenced this action under Title VII, 42 U.S.C § 2000e et seq., in the United States District Court for the Northern District of Texas. His complaint alleged that petitioner maintained "a policy, practice, custom, or usage of: (a) discriminating against [Mexican-Americans] because of national origin and with respect to compensation, terms, conditions, and privileges of employment, and (b) . . . subjecting [Mexican-Americans] to continuous employment discrimination." Respondent claimed that as a result of this policy whites with less qualification and experience and lower evaluation scores than respondent had been promoted more rapidly. The complaint contained no factual allegations concerning petitioner's hiring practices.

Respondent brought the action "on his own behalf and on behalf of other persons similarly situated, pursuant to Rule 23(b)(2) of the Federal Rules of Civil Procedure." . . .

After responding to petitioner's written interrogatories, respondent filed a memorandum in favor of certification of "the class of all hourly Mexican American employees who have been employed, are employed, or may in the future be employed and all those Mexican Americans who have applied or would have applied for employment had the Defendant not practiced racial discrimination in its employment practices." His position was supported by the ruling . . . in *Johnson v. Georgia Highway Express*, Inc., 417 F.2d 1122 (5th Cir. 1969), that any victim of racial discrimination in employment may maintain an "across the board" attack on all unequal employment practices alleged to have been committed by the employer pursuant to a policy of racial discrimination. Without conducting an evidentiary hearing, the District Court certified a class including Mexican-American employees and Mexican-American applicants for employment who had not been hired.

Following trial of the liability issues, the District Court entered separate findings of fact and conclusions of law with respect first to respondent and then to the class. The District Court found that petitioner had not discriminated against respondent in hiring, but that it did discriminate against him in its promotion practices. The court reached converse conclusions about the class, finding no discrimination in promotion practices, but concluding that petitioner had discriminated against Mexican-Americans at its Irving facility in its hiring practices.

After various post-trial proceedings, the District Court ordered petitioner to furnish respondent with a list of all Mexican-Americans who had applied for employment at the Irving facility during the period between January 1, 1973, and October 18, 1976. Respondent was then ordered to give notice to those persons advising them that they might be entitled to some form of recovery. Evidence was taken concerning the applicants who responded to the notice, and backpay was ultimately awarded to 13 persons, in addition to respondent Falcon. The total recovery by respondent and the entire class amounted to $67,925.49, plus costs and interest.[7]

. . . The Court of Appeals rejected . . . rejected petitioner's argument that the class had been defined too broadly. For, under the Fifth Circuit's across-the-board rule, it is permissible for "an employee complaining of one employment practice to represent another complaining of another practice, if the plaintiff and the members of the class suffer from essentially the same injury. In this case, all of the claims are based on discrimination because of national origin." . . .

On the merits, the Court of Appeals [remanded to the district court for further consideration of both the disparate-treatment-in-promotion claims and the disparate-impact-in-hiring claims.] With the merits of both respondent's promotion claim and the class hiring claims remaining open for reconsideration in the District Court on remand, we granted certiorari to decide whether the class action was properly maintained on behalf of both employees who were denied promotion and applicants who were denied employment.

II

The class-action device was designed as "an exception to the usual rule that litigation is conducted by and on behalf of the individual named parties only." Class relief is "peculiarly appropriate" when the "issues involved are common to the class as a whole" and when they "turn on questions of law applicable in the same manner to each member of the class." For in such cases, "the class-action device saves the resources of both the courts and the parties by permitting an issue potentially affecting every [class member] to be litigated in an economical fashion under Rule 23."

Title VII . . . contains no special authorization for class suits maintained by private parties. An individual litigant seeking to maintain a class action under Title VII must meet "the prerequisites of numerosity, commonality, typicality, and adequacy of representation" specified in Rule 23(a). These

---

7.   Respondent's individual recovery amounted to $1,040.33. A large share of the class award, $28,827.50, represented attorney's fees. . . .

requirements effectively "limit the class claims to those fairly encompassed by the named plaintiff's claims."

We have repeatedly held that "a class representative must be part of the class and 'possess the same interest and suffer the same injury' as the class members." East Texas Motor Freight System, Inc. v. Rodriguez, 431 U.S. 395, 403 (1977). . . .

. . . [In *East Texas Motor Freight*, we] recognized the theory behind the Fifth Circuit's across-the-board rule, noting our awareness "that suits alleging racial or ethnic discrimination and often by their very nature class suits, involving classwide wrongs," and that "[c]ommon questions of law or fact are typically present." In the same breath, however, we reiterated that "careful attention to the requirements of Fed. R. Civ. P. 23 remains nonetheless indispensable" and that the "mere fact that a complaint alleges racial or ethnic discrimination does not in itself ensure that the party who has brought the lawsuit will be an adequate representative of those who many have been the real victims of that discrimination."

We cannot disagree with the proposition underlying the across-the-board rule — that racial discrimination is by definition class discrimination. But the allegation that such discrimination has occurred neither determines whether a class action may be maintained in accordance with Rule 23 nor defines the class that may be certified. Conceptually, there is a wide gap between (a) an individual's claim that he has been denied a promotion on discriminatory grounds, and his otherwise unsupported allegation that the company has a policy of discrimination, and (b) the existence of a class of persons who have suffered the same injury as that individual, such that the individual's claim and the class claims will share common questions of law or fact and that the individual's claim will be typical of the class claims.[13] For respondent to bridge that gap, he must prove much more than the validity of his own claim. Even though evidence that he was passed over for promotion when several less deserving whites were advanced may support the conclusion that respondent was denied the promotion because of his national origin, such evidence would not necessarily justify the additional inferences (1) that this discriminatory

---

13. The commonality and typicality requirements of Rule 23(a) tend to merge. Both serve as guideposts for determining whether under the particular circumstances maintenance of a class action is economical and whether the named plaintiff's claim and the class claims are so interrelated that the interests of the class members will be fairly and adequately protected in their absence. Those requirements therefore also tend to merge with the adequacy-of-representation requirement, although the latter requirement also raises concerns about the competency of class counsel and conflicts of interest. In this case, we need not address petitioner's argument that there is a conflict of interest between respondent and the class of rejected applicants because an enlargement of the pool of Mexican-American employees will decrease respondent's chances for promotion. *See* Gen. Tel Co. of Nw. v. EEOC, 446 U.S. 318, 331 (1980) ("In employment discrimination litigation, conflicts might arise, for example, between employees and applicants who were denied employment and who will, if granted relief, compete with employees for fringe benefits or seniority. Under Rule 23, the same plaintiff could not represent these classes").

treatment is typical of petitioner's promotion practices, (2) that petitioner's promotion practices are motivated by a policy of ethnic discrimination that pervades petitioner's Irving division, or (3) that this policy of ethnic discrimination is reflected in petitioner's other employment practices, such as hiring, in the same way it is manifested in the promotion practices. There additional inferences demonstrate the tenuous character of any presumption that the class claims are "fairly encompassed" within respondent's claim.

Respondent's complaint provided an insufficient basis for concluding that the adjudication of his claim of discrimination in promotion would require the decision of any common question concerning the failure of petitioner to hire more Mexican-Americans. Without any specific presentation identifying the questions of law or fact that were common to the claims of respondent and of the members of the class he sought to represent, it was error for the District Court to presume that respondent's claim was typical of other claims against petitioner by Mexican-American employees and applicants. If one allegation of specific discriminatory treatment were sufficient to support an across-the-board attack, every Title VII case would be a potential companywide class action. We find nothing in the statute to indicate that Congress intended to authorize such a wholesale expansion of class-action litigation.[15]

The trial of this class action followed a predictable course. Instead of raising common questions of law or fact, respondent's evidentiary approaches to the individual and class claims were entirely different. He attempted to sustain his individual claim by proving intentional discrimination. He tried to prove the class claims through statistical evidence of disparate impact. Ironically, the District Court rejected the class claim of promotion discrimination, which conceptually might have borne a closer typicality and commonality relationship with respondent's individual claim, but sustained the class claim of hiring discrimination. As the District Court's bifurcated findings on liability demonstrate, the individual and class claims might as well have been tried separately. It is clear that the maintenance of respondent's action as a class action did not advance "the efficiency and economy of litigation which is a principal purpose of the procedure." Am. Pipe & Constr. Co. v. Utah, 414 U.S. 538, 553 (1974).

---

15. If petitioner used a biased testing procedure to evaluate both applicants for employment and incumbent employees, a class action on behalf of every applicant or employee who might have been prejudiced by the test clearly would satisfy the commonality and typicality requirements of Rule 23(a). Significant proof that an employer operated under a general policy of discrimination conceivably could justify a class of both applicants and employees if the discrimination manifested itself in hiring and promotion practices in the same general fashion, such as through entirely subjective decisionmaking processes. In this regard it is noteworthy that Title VII prohibits discriminatory employment practices, not an abstract policy of discrimination. The mere fact that an aggrieved private plaintiff is a member of an identifiable class of persons of the same race or national origin is insufficient to establish his standing to litigate on their behalf all possible claims of discrimination against a common employer.

We do not, of course, judge the propriety of a class certification by hindsight. The District Court's error in this case, and the error inherent in the across-the-board rule, is the failure to evaluate carefully the legitimacy of the named plaintiff's plea that he is a proper class representative under Rule 23(a). As we noted in *Coopers & Lybrand v. Livesay*, 437 U.S. 463 (1978), "the class determination generally involves considerations that are 'enmeshed in the factual and legal issues comprising the plaintiff's cause of action.'" Sometimes the issues are plain enough from the pleadings to determine whether the interests of the absent parties are fairly encompassed within the named plaintiff's claim, and sometimes it may be necessary for the court to probe behind the pleadings before coming to rest on the certification question. Even after a certification order is entered, the judge remains free to modify it in the light of subsequent developments in the litigation. For such an order, particularly during the period before any notice is sent to members of the class, "is inherently tentative." This flexibility enhances the usefulness of the class-action device; actual, not presumed, conformance with Rule 23(a) remains, however, indispensable.

III

The need to carefully apply the requirements of Rule 23(a) to Title VII class actions was noticed by a member of the Fifth Circuit panel that announced the across-the-board rule. In a specially concurring opinion in *Johnson v. Georgia Highway Express, Inc.*, 417 F.2d at 1125-27, Judge Godbold emphasized the need for "more precise pleadings," for "without reasonable specificity the court cannot define the class, cannot determine whether the representation is adequate, and the employer does not know how to defend." He termed as "most significant" the potential unfairness to the class members bound by the judgment if the framing of the class is overbroad. And he pointed out the error of the "tacit assumption" underlying the across-the-board rule that "all will be well for surely the plaintiff will win and manna will fall on all members of the class." With the same concerns in mind, we reiterate today that a Title VII class action, like any other class action, may only by certified if the trial court is satisfied, after a rigorous analysis, that the prerequisites of Rule 23(a) have been satisfied.

The judgment of the Court of Appeals affirming the certification order is reversed, and the case is remanded for further proceedings consistent with this opinion.

■ CHIEF JUSTICE BURGER, concurring in part and dissenting in part.

I agree with the Court's decision insofar as it states the general principles which apply in determining whether a class should be certified in this case under Rule 23. However, in my view it is not necessary to remand for further proceedings since it is entirely clear on this record that no class should have been certified in this case. . . .

As the Court notes, the purpose of Rule 23 is to promote judicial economy by allowing for litigation of common questions of law and fact at one time. We have stressed that strict attention to the requirements of Rule 23 is indispensable in employment discrimination cases. This means that class claims are limited to those "fairly encompassed by the named plaintiff's claims."

The record in this case clearly shows that there are no common questions of law or fact between respondent's claim and the class claim; the only commonality is that respondent is a Mexican-American and he seeks to represent a class of Mexican-Americans. . . .

Like so many Title VII cases, this case has already gone on for years, draining judicial resources as well as resources of the litigants. Rather than promoting judicial economy, the "across-the-board" class action has promoted multiplication of claims and endless litigation. Since it is clear that the class claim brought on behalf of unsuccessful applicants for jobs with petitioner cannot succeed, I would simply reverse and remand with instructions to dismiss the class claim.

Notes

1.   To demonstrate the interwoven nature of the Rule 23(a) inquiry, ask yourself whether *Falcon* is a commonality decision, a typicality decision, or an adequacy decision. Does it matter?

Here is one way to think about what is going on. Taken as a group, the requirements of Rule 23(a) and (g) are trying to do two kinds of work. First, they are trying to ensure that the class members will be adequately represented by the class representative and class counsel. Second, they are trying to ensure that a class action, which presents manageability issues and can be costly to sustain, is an efficient vehicle for resolving related claims. The three requirements of commonality, typicality, adequacy of the class representative, and adequacy of class counsel are four filters, each of a progressively finer gauge. Commonality removes the cases that obviously do not deserve class treatment; if the class representative has no issues of law or fact in common with class members, then it is hard to see how a class action is efficient and there is reason to doubt that the class representative will vigorously represent the interests of others. Typicality then refines the analysis; it insists that the claim of the class representative be typical. If it is typical, then it is likely that the class representative will pursue pretty much the same litigation strategies as class members would have done if they sued separately, and it also ensures that economies of scale can be achieved by bundling the class representative's claim with those of others. Finally, adequacy of the class representative and class counsel take a final pass, making sure that the class representative and class counsel have no peculiar deficiencies that will lead them to abandon the interests of class members in favor of their own.

On this explanation, the ultimate goal is achieving adequacy and efficiency; the tools that we use to assure ourselves that these goals are met are commonality, typicality, and adequacy. The reason that the three requirements seem to tie together is that they all work to serve the same goals, each in its own way. Is *Falcon* consistent with this explanation?

2. Despite *Falcon*'s gestalt approach to Rule 23(a) (and our attempt to justify it), courts typically analyze the requirements of (a)(2), (a)(3), and (a)(4) separately; and plenty of law has grown up around what each of these terms means. Far and away the *least* important of these three constraints is the (a)(2) requirement of a common question of law or fact. A single shared question is often viewed as sufficient to satisfy this test; rarely will a proposed class action falter on the commonality ground alone. For instance, in *Dukes v. Wal-Mart, Inc.*, 509 F.3d 1168, 1177 (9th Cir. 2007), *reh'g en banc granted*, 556 F.3d 919 (9th Cir. 2009), the court observed that "[t]he commonality test is qualitative rather than quantitative — one significant issue common to the class may be sufficient to warrant certification." *Accord* Staton v. Boeing Co., 327 F.3d 938, 953 (9th Cir. 2003) ("Rule 23(a)(2) has been construed permissively."); In re Veeco Instruments, Inc. Sec. Litig., 235 F.R.D. 220, 238 (S.D.N.Y. 2006) ("The commonality requirement has been applied permissively in the context of securities fraud litigation."). This liberality has led some courts to conclude that the (a)(2) commonality test is, for all practical purposes, superfluous. *See, e.g.*, Edgington v. R.G. Dickinson & Co., 139 F.R.D. 183, 189 (D. Kan. 1991); Smith v. MCI Telecomms. Corp., 124 F.R.D. 665, 675 (D. Kan. 1989).

3. But perhaps not entirely superfluous. One court of appeals has held that "[t]he common questions must be dispositive and over-shadow other issues." Lienhart v. Dryvit Sys., Inc., 255 F.3d 138 (4th Cir. 2001). That standard lies outside of the norm, but in other cases the Rule 23(a)(2) requirement still retains some salience. For instance, *Mulligan v. South Carolina Department of Transportation*, 446 F. Supp. 2d 446 (D.S.C. 2006), held that the plaintiffs, who stated a meritorious disparate-impact claim on their own behalf, failed to show that the members of the class that they purported to represent shared the claim. Likewise, in *Fotta v. Trustees of the United Mine Workers of America*, 319 F.3d 612, 619 (3d Cir. 2003), the court held that a class of 116,000 miners lacked a common issue when each class member's claim depended on an individual determination of whether the defendant had acted wrongfully toward that member and "the remedy for each class member [was] an individual determination. . . . Because both liability and the appropriate remedy must be determined for each plaintiff, no common issues of law or fact exist." Taken literally, does *Fotta* make certification of any mass-tort class action impossible?

4. *Falcon* has been distinguished — and a finding of commonality made — when plaintiffs offer direct evidence of a defendant's pattern of conduct and allege a common injury arising out of such conduct, Hinman v. M & M Rental Ctr., Inc., 545 F. Supp. 2d 802, 805 (N.D. Ill. 2008); when plaintiffs create individual classes for each form of discrimination, Smith v. Nike Retail Servs., Inc., 234 F.R.D. 648, 661 n. 12 (N.D. Ill. 2006); where the differences among the class members' job descriptions is minimal, Whiteway v. FedEx Kinko's Office & Print Servs., Inc. 2006 WL 2642528 (N.D. Cal. Sept. 14, 2006); and where plaintiffs allege a claim of systemic

discrimination, Disability Rights Council of Greater Wash. v. Wash. Metro. Area Transit Auth., 239 F.R.D. 9, 26 (D.D.C. 2006).

5. In *In re Initial Public Offering Securities Litigation*, 471 F.3d 24, 32-33 (2d Cir. 2006), *clarified on reh'g*, 483 F.3d 70 (2d Cir. 2007) (*"IPO"*), the Second Circuit grabbed *Falcon*'s "rigorous analysis" language and insisted that courts ensure that the requirements of Rule 23(a) are in fact met — not just presumed or weakly shown. *See id.* at 40 ("[W]e can no longer continue to advise district courts that 'some showing' of meeting Rule 23 requirements will suffice."). This "rigorous analysis" standard has also ignited a debate about how carefully courts should examine the merits of the plaintiffs' substantive claims when the substantive merits intertwine with a requirement in Rule 23. *See id.* at 41 (holding that "the obligation to make . . . determinations [that Rule 23's requirements are met] is not lessened by overlap between a Rule 23 requirement and a merits issue, even a merits issue that is identical with a Rule 23 requirement"). *See also* In re Hydrogen Peroxide Antitrust Litig., 552 F.3d 305 (3d Cir. 2008) (adopting the *IPO* approach) (*infra* p. 455); *infra* pp. 463-64, Notes 1-2 (discussing the fate of the *IPO* approach in other federal courts).

6. Although the district court has great discretion in determining whether Rule 23(a)'s elements have been met, *see, e.g., IPO*, 471 F.3d at 41, one factor channeling this discretion was the addition in 1998 of Rule 23(f), under which courts of appeal "may permit" an appeal of an order granting or denying certification if a party petitions for permission to appeal within fourteen days of the order. As a result, in recent years the courts of appeal have been more active in developing the law of Rule 23(a). The seminal case describing the factors that a court should consider in allowing an appeal is *Blair v. Equifax Check Servs., Inc.*, 181 F.3d 832 (7th Cir. 1999).

7. Although commonality stymies few class certifications, cases that raise commonality concerns, like *Falcon*, tend to fail the typicality analysis. The reason is simple: If commonality within the class is weak, the chance that the representative's claim will be typical of the claims of class members is small. *See, e.g.*, Attenborough v. Const. & Gen. Bldg. Laborers' Local 79, 238 F.R.D. 82 (S.D.N.Y. 2006). As a practical matter, lawyers do not want to limp across the commonality line; they want to soar across because the more difficult issues of typicality and adequacy loom. The following cases continue our exploration of the Rule 23(a)(2)-(4) issues, with an emphasis on typicality and adequacy concerns.

IN RE HEALTHSOUTH CORP. SECURITIES LITIGATION

213 F.R.D. 447 (N.D. Ala. 2003)

■ BOWDRE, District Judge.

. . . Plaintiffs seek to have certified as a class "all persons who purchased or otherwise acquired the securities of HealthSouth Corporation

('HealthSouth' or the 'Company') between April 24, 1997 and September 30, 1998 (the 'Class Period'), including those persons who acquired HealthSouth securities in exchange for the securities of Horizon/CMS Healthcare Corporation ('Horizon') in a merger consummated on or about October 29, 1997, and those persons who acquired HealthSouth securities in exchange for the securities of National Surgery Centers, Inc. ('NSC') in a merger consummated on or about July 22, 1998, and were injured thereby." . . .

I. BACKGROUND

. . .

The plaintiffs basically allege that during the class period, April 24, 1997 to September 30, 1998, HealthSouth and its top officers and directors engaged in a fraud on HealthSouth's investors that artificially inflated the price of HealthSouth stock by making false statements about the true financial state of HealthSouth and concealing the allegedly devastating effects the Balanced Budget Act of 1997 ("BBA") would have on HealthSouth. [The plaintiffs alleged that 60% of HealthSouth's patient mix involved Medicare, and that the defendants knew that the BBA would result in dramatically lower Medicare payments, tremendous pricing pressures on companies like HealthSouth, and lower reimbursement payments for companies acquired by HealthSouth.]

Plaintiffs allege that despite the adverse impact that defendants knew the BBA was having on HealthSouth's business, defendants falsely represented throughout the Class Period that HealthSouth was maintaining its historical performance, and that the BBA would be of little or no consequence. . . . [D]efendants were determined to maintain HealthSouth's stock price to facilitate the Horizon acquisition; continue the illusion that it could keep pace with its historical rate of 15%-20% growth in revenues . . .; and hide some of its operating deficiencies via the use of acquisition-related writeoffs. . . .

Plaintiffs further purport that the false statements made by defendants throughout the Class Period had the intended effect. HealthSouth's stock was artificially inflated from $18¾ at the start of the Class period in April 1997, to almost $28 by early November 1997, reaching an all time high of $30.81 on April 20, 1998. This artificial inflation enabled HealthSouth to acquire Horizon on October 29, 1997 for approximately $960 million in HealthSouth stock and the assumption of approximately $700 million in debt; to acquire NSC . . . on July 22, 1998, in another stock swap of some $590 million of HealthSouth stock; and to let the individual defendants sell over 6 million shares of their own HealthSouth stock, reaping proceeds in excess of $163 million, within weeks of the BBA's enactment. . . .

[In September, 1998, the defendants admitted the difficulties that the company was having. HealthSouth's stock price lost 43% of its value as earnings plummeted, and the company was obliged to close many facilities.]

The first of these seven consolidated lawsuits reached the court on October 16, 1998 . . . The plaintiffs assert violations of §§ 11 and 15 of the Securities Act; § 10(b) of the Exchange Act and Rule 10(b)-5; and § 20(a) of the Exchange Act. The plaintiffs rely on the fraud-on-the-market theory to establish a presumption of reliance. That theory rests on the assumption that the market price of a security traded in an efficient market will be based on the material information available and that the market will respond to that information with buyers and sellers relying indirectly on material omissions or misrepresentations concerning the security. *See* Basic Inc. v. Levinson, 485 U.S. 224, 247 (1988). The fraud-on-the-market theory creates a *rebuttable* presumption of reliance.

II. DISCUSSION

. . . [T]he class proposed by the plaintiffs include three separate but distinct groups: (1) purported class members who obtained their shares of HealthSouth stock on the open market; (2) former owners of Horizon stock or options whose interests were converted to HealthSouth stock or options; and (3) former owners of NSC stock or options whose interests were converted to HealthSouth stock or options. . . .

Granted, class actions in securities fraud cases have received favorable treatment in the Eleventh Circuit. Securities class actions benefit both the public interest in maintaining the integrity of the market and the private interest of investors whose redress of grievances is not limited to a multitude of small individual claims. However, class certification is not automatic; the court must perform a "rigorous analysis" of the propriety of class certification. *See* Gen. Tel. Co. of Sw. v. Falcon, 457 U.S. 147, 161 (1982) [*supra* p. 353]. The court must conduct a searching inquiry, including a possible "probe behind the pleadings before coming to rest on the certification question."

[After concluding that the numerosity requirement of Rule 23(a)(1) and the commonality requirement of Rule 23(a)(2) were satisfied, the court turned to the typicality requirement of Rule 23(a)(3).]

3. *Typicality*

To meet the typicality requirement, plaintiffs must show that the claims and defenses of the representative plaintiffs are typical of the claims and defenses of the class as a whole. In other words, both representative plaintiffs and the other class members must be able to travel to court on the same claims. The requirement of typicality precludes certification of a class "where the legal theories of the named plaintiffs potentially conflict with those of the absentees." . . .

The defendants argue that the claims of class representatives Orman and Smith — and those of other class members who acquired shares as a result of the Horizon or NSC acquisitions — are atypical of the claims of the remainder of the class who purchased their shares on the open market under very different circumstances. Both Horizon and NSC operated within the healthcare industry and many of those shareholders were company employees. As such, the former employee/shareholders of these companies, like Orman and Smith, who ultimately received HealthSouth shares or options were experienced in the healthcare industry. These employee/shareholders had knowledge and information not available to the open market purchasers. This knowledge and information of these shareholder/employees may provide distinct defenses to their claims. For example, Orman admitted during her deposition that she had first hand knowledge of the Balanced Budget Act's impact on reimbursements for hospitals and rehabilitation facilities, and of the resulting pricing pressures exerted by managed care payors. Plaintiffs Orman and Smith were aware of the very facts the plaintiffs claim were withheld by the defendants or that caused certain statements by defendants to be misleading. Other former employee/shareholders of NSC and Horizon also presumably would have such insider knowledge because of their experience in the healthcare industry.

Plaintiffs' knowledge of material facts that defendants allegedly failed to disclose provides a defense to a cause of action under 10(b)-5. Also, plaintiffs Orman and Smith became employees of HealthSouth after the acquisition of NSC, as did other NSC and Horizon employee/shareholders. These employee/shareholders had — or had opportunities to have — conversations with some of the individual defendants during the proposed class period. For example, plaintiff Smith testified that he relied on oral representations made to him by some of the individual defendants during July, August, and September of 1998. Plaintiffs Orman and Smith, like other former employee/shareholders of NSC and Horizon, thus, have unique claims of reliance apart from the fraud-on-the-market theory and would be subject to unique defenses so that their claims cannot be typical of the proposed class. . . .

The claims of Orman and Smith, and other former employee/shareholders of NSC and Horizon, are not typical of the class for another reason. Orman and Smith, like other former employees of NSC and Horizon, had no choice but to acquire HealthSouth stock through HealthSouth's acquisition of their employer. The alleged misrepresentations or omissions by the defendants then did not influence their decisions to acquire HealthSouth stock. Their claims, thus, do not rest on the fraud-in-the-market theory that underlies the claims of the purported class. . . .

The court recognizes that the mere presence of factual differences and different defenses does not automatically defeat typicality. However, concerns over whether the claims of Orman and Smith are typical of the claims of the class as a whole pose only one of the problems the court sees with certifying a class in this case. These concerns, coupled with the other problems with plaintiffs' proof, make certifying a class in this case improper.

As the court wrestled with the intraclass conflicts discussed *infra,* the court also recognized another way in which the claims of certain class representatives are atypical of the claims of some class members. Representatives Pittman, Weaver, and McQueen all purchased their stock on the open market. These open market representatives lack standing to assert at least some of the claims resting in those class members who acquired their HealthSouth shares through the mergers with NSC and Horizon. The NSC/Horizon class members in essence complain that HealthSouth acquired their companies with inflated stock dollars and that if information about the true effect of the BBA had been disclosed, those mergers could not have been consummated because HealthSouth stock value would have fallen. These NSC/Horizon class members claim to have been damaged by the exchange of their valuable shares for less valuable HealthSouth stock. However, Pittman, Weaver, McQueen and the class members who held HealthSouth stock at the time of those acquisitions benefitted from those transactions brought about by the allegedly inflated HealthSouth share price. Plaintiffs' own expert acknowledged the benefit obtained by existing HealthSouth shareholders by virtue of obtaining NSC and Horizon with inflated stock dollars. Thus, because the open market representatives were not injured by use of inflated stock to acquire NSC and Horizon, they do not have standing to assert that component of the NSC/Horizon class members claim.

For these reasons, the court finds that the claims of the representatives Orman and Smith are not typical of the class, and that the open market representatives (Pittman, Weaver, and McQueen) do not have standing to assert the claims of the former NSC/Horizon shareholders/employees. . . .

4. *Adequate Representation*

Under Fed. R. Civ. P. 23(a)(4), the plaintiffs must show that, as class representatives, they will fairly and adequately protect the interests of the class. The adequacy evaluation encompasses two inquiries: (1) whether any substantial conflicts of interest exist between the representatives and the class; and (2) whether the representatives will adequately prosecute the action. *See* Sosna v. Iowa, 419 U.S. 393, 403 (1975).

The defendants challenge the adequacy of the representatives under both prongs of the *Sosna* test. They point to the deposition testimony of various individual lead plaintiffs for evidence that the individual representatives lack knowledge about the factual and legal theories of the case. While the court finds some of the testimony by the representatives troubling, the court is not persuaded that these representatives would not adequately pursue prosecution of the action.

Until the Supreme Court or the Eleventh Circuit announces a new standard, this court will continue to follow the well-established standard for testing the adequacy of representatives' ability to prosecute a case. That inquiry focuses on whether plaintiffs' counsel are qualified, experienced, and able to conduct the litigation. Kirkpatrick [v. J.C. Bradford & Co., 827 F.2d 718, 726 (11th Cir. 1987) (*infra* p. 448)]. The fact that defendants do not challenge the abilities of plaintiffs' counsel does not surprise the court.

Merely finding . . . that plaintiffs' counsel are capable and that plaintiffs will adequately pursue prosecution of the lawsuit does not end the inquiry into the adequacy of the class representatives. The court must also examine whether any antagonistic interests exist between the proposed representatives and the rest of the class.

For purposes of that analysis:

[a]ntagonistic interests are not only those which directly oppose one another, but also are those which may be hostile to one another or unharmonious such that one party's interest may be sacrificed for another's . . . . In challenging the representatives' adequacy, the defendant "does not have to show *actual* antagonistic interests; the potentiality is enough."

Due process requires that no potential conflicts exist between class representatives and class members that would interfere with the representation of the class.

The defendants vigorously argue two intra-class conflicts: the "seller/purchaser conflict" and the "equity conflicts." The seller/purchaser conflict, according to defendants, exists between class members who sold stock during the class period, thereby benefitting from the alleged price inflation, as compared to other class members who bought stock and were damaged by the inflated price. The defendants argue the equity conflict exists between class members who retained their stock and whose stock could be adversely affected by this litigation against HealthSouth and those class members who sold their stock prior to judgment and stand to gain by the litigation.

The defendants rely primarily upon *In re Seagate Technology II Securities Litigation* ("*Seagate II*"), 843 F. Supp. 1341 (N.D. Cal. 1994) . . . . The Eleventh Circuit has yet to wrestle with this issue. This court need not tackle the thorny issues of seller/purchaser and equity conflicts as espoused in *Seagate II* because other more significant conflicts, along with other problems, work against class certification in this case.

. . . [T]he court cannot ignore the conflicts that exist between the class members who purchased their stock on the open market and the class members who acquired their stock via the Horizon and NSC mergers. The class members who held stock at the time of the Horizon merger on October 29, 1997, and/or at the time of the NSC merger on July 22, 1998, actually benefitted from the alleged inflated share price. The owners of HealthSouth — by definition the shareholders — acquired assets with inflated stock dollars, thereby acquiring more value for the price paid. Thus open market class representatives Pittman, Weaver, and McQueen cannot represent the interest of the NSC/Horizon former shareholders because the open market representatives benefitted from the conduct that harmed the NSC/Horizon former shareholders.

In fact, plaintiffs' own expert acknowledged this conflict. . . .

This matter presents "the occasional extreme case where a conflict of this type is too great and simply dominates the landscape too completely to ignore." This court cannot certify a class "when its members have opposing interest *or when it consists of members who benefit from the same acts alleged to be harmful to other members of the class*." Pickett v. Iowa Beef Processors, 209 F.3d 1276, 1280 (11th Cir. 2000) (emphasis added). Therefore, the court concludes that the conflicts among the representatives, among subclasses, and between the representatives and the class as a whole are too great to ignore and negate the adequacy of representation. Because of these conflicts, the plaintiffs have failed to satisfy the requirements of Rule 23(a). Accordingly, the court cannot certify the proposed class. Other reasons also support denial of class certification.

[The court went on to find that Rule 23(b)(3) was also not satisfied because common questions of fact did not predominate over individual questions and a class action was not superior to other methods for adjudicating this dispute.]

Therefore, . . . the court denies the plaintiffs' motion for class certification.

IN RE AMERICAN MEDICAL SYSTEMS, INC.

75 F.3d 1069 (6th Cir. 1996)

■ SUHRHEINRICH, Circuit Judge.

Petitioners American Medical Systems ("AMS") and Pfizer, Inc., defendants below, both seek a writ of mandamus directing the district court to vacate orders conditionally certifying a class in a products liability suit involving penile prostheses. . . . [O]n the extraordinary facts of this case we find that the district judge's disregard of class action procedures was of such severity and frequency so as to warrant its issuance here.

I.

Since 1973, AMS, a wholly-owned subsidiary of Pfizer, has manufactured and marketed penile prostheses, which are used to treat impotence. The plaintiffs, respondents in this proceeding, all use or have used AMS' products.

Plaintiff Paul Vorhis was implanted with an AMS penile prosthesis on April 25, 1989. It failed to function in January of 1993, and Vorhis had the prosthesis replaced with an AMS 700 Ultrex prosthesis in May 1993. This second prosthesis caused him pain and discomfort, and plaintiff had it removed in August of 1993 and replaced with a third AMS prosthesis, with which he is presently satisfied. Vorhis filed this action against defendant AMS in the Southern District of Ohio on December 5, 1994, individually and on behalf of others similarly situated who suffered damages as a result of the implantation of penile prostheses manufactured by AMS. The complaint alleges strict product liability, negligence, breach of implied and express warranties, fraud and punitive damages, and seeks a declaratory judgment for medical monitoring. . . .

. . . AMS challenged Vorhis' suitability as a class representative on several grounds. First, AMS pointed out that Vorhis had a history of psychiatric problems, for which he received total and permanent disability benefits from the State of Ohio. AMS introduced reports prepared by Vorhis' psychiatrist and psychologist showing that Vorhis suffered from memory loss, impaired concentration, and a lack of common sense, all factors which AMS maintained would interfere with plaintiff's ability to make rational decisions on behalf of other members of the purported class. AMS also contended that Vorhis was an unsuitable representative because his need for the prosthesis stemmed from a unique condition, Peyronie's disease, or curvature of the penis. Third, AMS argued that because Vorhis had a problem with only one of the ten types of prostheses AMS manufactured, he could not represent those who had problems with the other kinds of devices.

[Vorhis subsequently added three more class representatives, and, without any further discovery, the district court certified the class.]

III.

. . .

We begin our analysis by considering whether the lower court committed patent error . . . .

The Supreme Court has required district courts to conduct a "rigorous analysis" into whether the prerequisites of Rule 23 are met before certifying a class. The trial court has broad discretion in deciding whether to certify a class, but that discretion must be exercised within the framework of Rule 23. . . .

1.

[After finding that 15,000 to 120,000 class members existed, the court of appeals held the numerosity requirement was satisfied.]

2.

Rule 23(a)(2) requires that for certification there must be "questions of law or fact common to the class." . . .

Plaintiffs' complaint and class certification motion simply allege in general terms that there are common issues without identifying any particular defect common to all plaintiffs. Yet AMS introduced uncontradicted evidence that since 1973 AMS has produced at least ten different models, and that these models have been modified over the years. Plaintiffs' claims of strict liability, fraudulent misrepresentation to both the FDA and the medical community, negligent testing, design and manufacture, and failure to warn will differ depending upon the model and the year it was issued.

Proofs as to strict liability, negligence, failure to warn, breach of express and implied warranties will also vary from plaintiff to plaintiff because complications with an AMS device may be due to a variety of factors, including surgical error, improper use of the device, anatomical incompatibility, infection, device malfunction, or psychological problems. Furthermore, each plaintiff's urologist would also be required to testify to determine what oral and written statements were made to the physician, and what he in turn told the patient, as well as to issues of reliance, causation and damages.

The amended complaint reflects that the plaintiffs received different models and have different complaints regarding each of those models. In the absence of more specific allegations and/or proof of commonality of any factual or legal claims, plaintiffs have failed to meet their burden of proof on Rule 23(a)(2).

This failure of proof highlights the error of the district judge. Despite evidence in the record presented by the nonmoving party that at least ten different models existed, testimony from a urologist that there is no "common cause" of prostheses malfunction, and conclusory allegations by the party with the burden of proof on certification, we find not even the hint of any serious consideration by the judge of commonality. Moreover, although not dispositive, it is noteworthy that a Judicial Panel on Multidistrict Litigation denied consolidation of all federal AMS penile prostheses case pursuant to 28 U.S.C. § 1407, concluding that "the degree of factual commonality among the actions in this litigation [does not] rise[ ] to a level that warrants Section 1407 transfer." In re Penile Implants Prod. Liab. Litig., MDL No. 1020 (J.P.M.L. Sept. 30, 1994). The district judge was made aware of this ruling, and still did not give the question of commonality any discernible degree of scrutiny.

3.

Rule 23(a)(3) requires that "claims or defenses of the representative parties [be] typical of the claims or defenses of the class."

> Typicality determines whether a sufficient relationship exists between the injury to the named plaintiff and the conduct affecting the class, so that the court may properly attribute a collective nature to the challenged conduct. In other words, when such a relationship is shown, a plaintiff's injury arises from or is directly related to a wrong to a class, and that wrong includes the wrong to the plaintiff. Thus, a plaintiff's claim is typical if it arises from the same event or practice or course of conduct that gives rise to the claims of other class members, and if his or her claims are based on the same legal theory.

[1 HERBERT B. NEWBERG & ALBA CONTE, NEWBERG ON CLASS ACTIONS, § 3-13 (3d ed. 1992).] See also Gen. Tel. Co. of Nw. v. EEOC, 446 U.S. [318, 330 (1980)] ("typicality requirement is said to limit the class claims to those fairly encompassed by the named plaintiffs' claims"); Senter [v. Gen. Motors Corp., 532 F.2d 511, 525 n.31 [(6th Cir. 1976)] ("[t]o be typical, a representative's claim need not always involve the same facts or law, provided there is a common element of fact or law"). A necessary consequence of the typicality requirement is that the representative's interests will be aligned with those of the represented group, and in pursuing his own claims, the named plaintiff will also advance the interests of the class members.

Vorhis' claim relates to a previous AMS penile prosthesis . . . . Based on what little we have to go on, it is hard to imagine that Vorhis' claim is typical of the class certified in this case.

Because the district judge issued its amended order of certification before discovery of the plaintiffs other than Vorhis, we have less information about them. However, we know from the amended complaint that each plaintiff used a different model, and each experienced a distinct difficulty. . . . These allegations fail to establish a claim typical to each other, let alone a class.

Once again, it should have been obvious to the district judge that it needed to "probe behind the pleadings" before concluding that the typicality requirement was met. *See Falcon*, 457 U.S. at 160. Instead, the district judge gave no serious consideration to this factor, but simply mimicked the language of the rule. This was error.

4.

Rule 23(a)(4) allows certification only if "the representative parties will fairly and adequately protect the interests of the class." This prerequisite is essential to due process, because a final judgment in a class action is binding on all class members. Hansberry v. Lee, 311 U.S. 32 (1940).

In *Senter*, we articulated two criteria for determining adequacy of representation: "1) the representative must have common interests with unnamed members of the class, and 2) it must appear that the representatives will vigorously prosecute the interests of the class through qualified counsel." The adequate representation requirement overlaps with the typicality requirement because in the absence of typical claims, the class representative has no incentives to pursue the claims of the other class members.

Although the district judge considered the qualifications of plaintiff's counsel, he made no finding on the first *Senter* criterion, and did not consider whether Vorhis or the other plaintiffs would "vigorously prosecute the interests of the class." AMS raised a serious question as to Vorhis' suitability to serve as a class representative given his history of psychological problems. . . . At the hearing, the judge made no finding regarding plaintiff, but remarked that:

> I don't think he is going to control anything. I don't think a client in a class action ever controls anything. And if you want my feeling on it, he is a name. He's a symbol. I just want to make sure there aren't

defenses against that symbol that would then be transmitted against the class.

This statement is clearly contrary to our holding in *Senter*. . . .

As amply illustrated, plaintiffs' complaint and class certification motion simply allege the elements of Rule 23(a) in conclusory terms without submitting any persuasive evidence to show that these factors are met. Because the plaintiffs did not create a factual record, and petitioners have demonstrated that the products at issue are very different and that each plaintiff's claim is unique, class certification was inappropriate.

[The court then held that the requirements of Rule 23(b)(3) had also not been established, and that the other factors necessary to obtain mandamus relief were present.]

IV.

For all the foregoing reasons, the petitions for writ of mandamus are granted, and the district judge is directed to decertify the plaintiff class.

Notes

1. Along with *Falcon*, the most important Supreme Court decision interpreting the requirements of Rule 23(a) is *Amchem Products, Inc. v. Windsor*, 521 U.S. 591 (1997), which we study *infra* p. 493. *Amchem* dealt with the adequacy-of-representation requirement of Rule 23(a)(4). Because it involved a settlement class action and also raises other issues, it is best to defer consideration of *Amchem* for the time being. But it is important not to neglect *Amchem* as you consider the meaning of Rule 23(a).

2. *American Medical Systems* granted a writ of mandamus against a judge who had certified a class. Mandamus is an extraordinary remedy, but a number of appellate courts used mandamus as the vehicle to examine the propriety of class-certification orders, which otherwise were not appealable until after the conclusion of the litigation. Because class certification was often the ball game — after such an order, the case was very likely to settle, so the propriety of the order might never be tested on appeal — this somewhat questionable use of mandamus (of which *American Medical Systems* was one example) grew steadily through the 1990s. It was the need for immediate appellate review of such outcome-influencing rulings that led to the promulgation of Rule 23(f), which we discussed *supra* p. 361, Note 6.

3. After denying class certification in *HealthSouth*, the trial court used Rule 42(a) to consolidate the litigation. First, the court consolidated the claims of shareholders who acquired HealthSouth stock via merger into "the Merger Cases." The trial court then consolidated the open-market purchaser cases into "the Stockholder Litigation." Next, it consolidated the Merger Cases with the Stockholder Litigation for all purposes. Finally, the court consolidated the bondholder actions into the "Bondholder Litigation"

and consolidated the Bondholder Litigation with the Stockholder Litigation, but only for discovery and pretrial purposes. In re HealthSouth Corp. Sec. Litig., No. CV-98-BE-2634-S, 6-8 (N.D. Ala. June 24, 2003).

If the court believed the claims worthy of consolidation, why didn't it provide for a class action for each separate group? *See* In re HealthSouth Corp. Sec. Litig., 261 F.R.D. 616 (N.D. Ala. 2009) (certifying a class in the Bondholder Litigation); In re HealthSouth Corp. Sec. Litig., 257 F.R.D. 260 (N.D. Ala. 2009) (certifying a class in the Stockholder Litigation).

4.   What is the precise purpose of the typicality requirement? What is the precise purpose of the adequacy requirement? Don't both the (a)(3) typicality and the (a)(4) adequacy requirements focus on whether the proposed representative is suitable to act as a fiduciary for the interests of the class? Should the two inquiries be collapsed into one? Some courts and commentators have suggested that the typicality requirement serves no independent purpose. *See, e.g.,* Rosado v. Wyman, 322 F. Supp. 1173 (E.D.N.Y. 1970), *aff'd on other grounds,* 437 F.2d 619 (2d Cir. 1970). But the Supreme Court and most federal courts view the two requirements as being complementary, even if they do not always explain exactly how.

American Medical Systems suggests one way to distinguish the two. The typicality inquiry looks at the claim that the class representative possesses and compares it to the claims that class members possess. The class representative's claim must be "typical" — it must involve the same basic evidence and legal theory, so the court can be confident that, in pressing his or her own claim, the class representative is equally pressing the interests of the class members. The adequacy inquiry looks at (1) whether the class representative, while possessing a typical claim, has unique deficiencies (like Vorhis's diminished mental capacity) that make the court worry about the representative's ability to carry out the requisite tasks, and (2) whether class counsel is competent. Since 2003, this latter inquiry has been moved from Rule 23(a)(4) to Rule 23(g). Therefore, Rule 23(a)(4) should focus only on any peculiar limitations that keep the class representative from advancing the interests of the class members — mental or physical infirmities, evidence showing a lack of conscientiousness or trustworthiness (perhaps a conviction for breach of a fiduciary duty), or evident conflicts of interests (such as being the CEO of the defendant).

5.   Although this analysis is tidy, it is not evident that courts view the distinction between typicality and adequacy in this way. One of the most common issues regarding typicality and adequacy is the potential for conflicting or antagonistic interests within a class. The concern for conflicting interests grew out of the Supreme Court's seminal class-action decision, *Hansberry v. Lee,* 311 U.S. 32 (1940). Briefly, *Hansberry* involved a racially restrictive covenant that prevented the sale of covenanting properties to African-Americans. The covenant took effective after owners of 95% of the frontage signed, and it ran with the land (so that it was binding on successor owners). A prior case to enforce the covenant against an owner who sold his property to an African-American was brought as a class action on behalf of all the signers. In that case, the parties stipulated

that the covenant had been signed by the requisite 95% of the frontage and was therefore valid; and the court entered judgment enforcing the covenant on the basis of this stipulation. In the *Hansberry* case, an African-American family bought a house from a successor in interest to one of the class members in the prior case. The Hansberrys tried to challenge the covenant by arguing that it had never been signed by the requisite 95%, but the Illinois Supreme Court held that they were barred from doing so because they were bound by the prior case's finding that the covenant was valid. The United States Supreme Court held, that as a matter of due process, the Hansberrys could not be bound by the judgment in the prior class action:

> It is one thing to say that some members of a class may represent other members in a litigation where the sole and common interest of the class in the litigation, is either to assert a common right or to challenge an asserted obligation. It is quite another to hold that all those who are free alternatively either to assert rights or to challenge them are of a single class, so that any group merely because it is of the class so constituted, may be deemed adequately to represent any others of the class in litigating their interests in either alternative. Such a selection of representatives for purposes of litigation, whose substantial interests are not necessarily or even probably the same as those whom they are deemed to represent, does not afford that protection to absent parties which due process requires. The doctrine of representation of absent parties in a class suit has not hitherto been thought to go so far. Apart from the opportunities it would afford for the fraudulent and collusive sacrifice of the rights of absent parties, we think that the representation in this case no more satisfies the requirements of due process than a trial by a judicial officer who is in such situation that he may have an interest in the outcome of the litigation in conflict with that of the litigants. [*Id.* at 44-45.]

Hansberry's concern for conflicting interests among class members — which, in its most malignant form, can manifest itself in collusion between the defendant and the class representative or class counsel — has colored how courts and commentators have thought about adequacy ever since. For instance, notice how *HealthSouth* looked for antagonism within the class; on finding it, the court used this divergence in interest as part of both its Rule 23(a)(3) analysis and its Rule 23(a)(4) analysis.

Hansberry itself was decided under an Illinois equitable class-action practice that did not have separate typicality and adequacy prongs. So, in modern parlance, is *Hansberry* a "typicality" case or an "adequacy" case? Does either word accurately capture what *Hansberry*'s concern was? Conversely, once a court determines that there are no conflicts of interest among class members, are the inquiries into typicality and adequacy over?

6.   These questions become harder once you realize that, because of the way that Rule 23(b) operates, conflicting interests among class members and between class members and class counsel are almost inevitable. We will see why that is so in the next subsection. In the meantime, for a proof of the point, see Jay Tidmarsh, *Rethinking Adequacy of Representation*, 87

TEX. L. REV. 1137, 1158-75 (2009). *See also* Charles Silver & Lynn Baker, *I Cut, You Choose: The Role of Plaintiffs' Counsel in Allocating Settlement Proceeds*, 84 VA. L. REV. 1465, 1468-69 (1998). ("Conflicts of interest and associated tradeoffs among plaintiffs are an unavoidable part of all group lawsuits and all group settlements."); *cf.* Patrick Woolley, *Rethinking the Adequacy of Adequate Representation*, 75 TEX. L. REV. 571, 574 (1997) (arguing that adequacy of representation is a necessary but not a sufficient condition to satisfy due process).

7.   The Eleventh Circuit has said the "the existence of minor conflicts alone will not defeat a party's claim to class certification: the conflict must be a 'fundamental' one going to the specific issues in controversy. A fundamental conflict exists where some party members claim to have been harmed by the same conduct that benefitted other members of the class." Valley Drug Co. v. Geneva Pharms., Inc., 350 F.3d 1181, 1189 (11th Cir. 2003). Granting that "fundamental" conflicts defeat certification, does *Hansberry* allow a court to close its eyes to "minor" conflicts? Or does it exhibit a zero-tolerance policy toward all conflicts? Read literally, *Valley Drug* says that all conflicts (other than the "fundamental" conflict that it identifies) are minor. That can't be right, can it? If not, what distinguishes minor from fundamental? *HealthSouth* is one of a growing number of cases holding that a defendant can prove a conflict of interest within the meaning of Rule 23(a)(4) by showing harm to some class members and benefit to others from the defendant's course of conduct. *See also* Pickett v. Iowa Beef Processors, 209 F.3d 1276, 1280-81 (11th Cir. 2000).

8.   In speaking of adequacy of representation in the larger *Hansberry* sense rather than in the narrower Rule 23(a)(4) sense, Professor Nagareda has observed that "[f]or all the agreement on the centrality of adequate representation to the modern class action . . . there remains remarkably little agreement on the content of that concept or how to enforce it." Richard A. Nagareda, *Administering Adequacy in Class Representation*, 82 TEX. L. REV. 287, 288 (2003).

9.   To see what Professor Nagareda means, try your hand at a few recurring scenarios:

(a) Suppose that a class representative is subject to unique defenses, as in *HealthSouth*. Is this a typicality problem or an adequacy problem? *HealthSouth* sees it as a typicality problem. *But see* Beck v. Maximus, 457 F.3d 291, 296 (3d Cir. 2006) (stating that "unique defenses bear on both the typicality and adequacy of a class representative"; citing cases).

(b) Suppose that a plaintiff has been injured by one defendant, and he seeks to represent a class that has been injured not only by that defendant but also by other defendants that have independently engaged in precisely the same conduct. Is his claim typical? Is he an adequate representative? *See* Easter v. Am. W. Fin., 381 F.3d 948 (9th Cir. 2004) (representative lacks standing to assert any claims against other defendants); La Mar v. H & B Novelty & Loan Co., 489 F.2d 461 (9th Cir. 1973) (representative fails Rule 23(a)(3)'s typicality test). What if the plaintiffs allege that the defendants conspired to engage in the same conduct?

(c) Suppose that the defendant polluted a neighborhood over the course of many years, but the extent of each neighbor's injury is related to the length of exposure to the defendant's chemicals. Is the claim of a class representative who has lived in the neighborhood for a number of years typical of those who have lived there for longer or shorter periods? Is that individual an adequate representative? *See* Ball v. Union Carbide Corp., 385 F.3d 713 (6th Cir. 2004) (no typicality; also finding a lack of commonality). What if the defendants produced a dangerous chemical that polluted different neighborhoods around the country and then conspired to conceal its dangerous effects? *See* In re Methyl Tertiary Butyl Ether ("MTBE") Prods. Liab. Litig., 209 F.R.D. 323, 337 (S.D.N.Y. 2006) (no typicality because "the contamination of each named plaintiff's well comes about through a factually unique set of circumstances").

(d) What if a class representative claiming only injunctive relief seeks to represent class members who have damage claims? Typical? Adequate? *See MBTE*, 209 F.R.D. at 338-39 (no). What if every plaintiff has suffered damage, but the amount of damage is different for each plaintiff? Does any plaintiff have a typical claim? Can anyone adequately represent a class of people who have suffered varying levels of damage? *See* Broussard v. Meineke Disc. Muffler Shops, 155 F.3d 331, 342 (4th Cir. 1998) (holding that no typicality exists when "each putative class member's claim for lost profits damages was inherently individualized and thus not easily amenable to class treatment"). On *Broussard*'s theory, should *HealthSouth* have denied class certification at the very outset?

(e) Suppose that no plaintiff has suffered a very large injury, but the defendant's conduct has in total caused a great deal of harm. Can any single plaintiff be regarded as a typical or adequate representative when the size of one claim is dwarfed by the totality of the injury and the number of claims? *See* Dolgow v. Anderson, 43 F.R.D. 472 (E.D.N.Y. 1968) (Weinstein, J.) (finding that the requirements of Rule 23(a) are met). On the other hand, is a class representative with a much larger stake than the average class member atypical? *See* In re Integra Realty Res., Inc., 354 F.3d 1246, 1259-60 (10th Cir. 2004) (no).

(f) What if the class representative holding the claim is an assignee of the original victim? Typical? Adequate? *See* Cordes & Co. Fin. Servs., Inc. v. A.G. Edwards & Sons, Inc., 502 F.3d 91 (2d Cir. 2007) (holding that assignees who obtained antitrust claims in the assignor's bankruptcy were not automatically inadequate, but remanding for further examination of the issue).

10. Look again at *Falcon*. Why is Falcon suitable to represent the class of Mexican-American employees seeking promotion, but unsuitable to represent the class of Mexican-American applicants? The Court says that, in applying the typicality requirement, it is imperative to consider carefully the kind of evidence to be proffered by the class representative on behalf of the class. If Falcon and his counsel are competent to present statistical evidence of discrimination on behalf of Falcon's co-employees, why can't they do the same on behalf of the applicants? What genuine differences

divide the applicant class from the promotion class, so that it is not appropriate for Falcon to represent both? *Cf.* Dukes v. Wal-Mart, Inc., 509 F.3d 1168, 1177 (9th Cir. 2007), *reh'g en banc granted*, 556 F.3d 919 (9th Cir. 2009) (holding that, in an employment-discrimination case, six class representatives presented typical claims and were adequate representatives of a class of 1.5 million members who worked in every occupation from part-time clerk to store manager).

In footnote 15, *Falcon* observes that an actual or potential conflict of interest may exist between the applicant and employee classes because enlargement of the pool of Mexican-American employees will decrease an individual employee's chances for promotion. The Court noted, however, that its decision did not rest on this ground. Isn't this potential antagonism more troubling than the differences in proof relied on by the Court?

11. Can you distill a single principle about when commonality, typicality, and adequacy are met from *Falcon, HealthSouth, American Medical Systems*, and the cases in Note 9? Perhaps there is no single answer; rather, the analysis is something of a sliding scale that tips against certification as more individual issues emerge. If so, what else belongs on this scale? The need to deter wrongful behavior that would otherwise evade liability? The need for deterrence more generally? The efficiency of class treatment compared to other aggregation methods? The substantive law (and if so, which types of cases most deserve class treatment: mass torts, securities-fraud cases, antitrust cases, or employment-discrimination cases)? The remedy sought? The size of the remedy sought?

12. Notice another sliding scale at work. As some courts interpret commonality, typicality, and adequacy to require great cohesion within a class, the size of the permissible class shrinks. In some cases, the numbers might shrink enough that the numerosity requirement can no longer be met. In other cases, multiple classes will need to be certified — a result that might not be as efficient as one large class.

13. Should we even worry about typicality or adequacy? As long as class counsel is competent and does not represent conflicting interests, isn't the incentive to obtain a fee a sufficient guarantee of vigorous representation? This argument, which the district court in *American Medical Systems* advanced, is sometimes known as the "figurehead" argument, on the view that the class representative is just a symbol with little control over class counsel. Thus, the real focus should be on the quality of class counsel. *See* Jean W. Burns, *Decorative Figureheads: Eliminating Class Representatives in Class Actions*, 42 HASTINGS L. J. 165, 167-86 (1990) (contending that named class plaintiffs have no legal authority and serve no useful purpose); *cf.* Jonathan R. Macey & Geoffrey P. Miller, *The Plaintiffs' Attorney's Role in Class Action and Derivative Litigation: Economic Analysis and Recommendation for Reform*, 58 U. CHI. L. REV. 1, 93-94 (1991) (arguing that discovery into the characteristics of the named plaintiffs should be prohibited since they are mere figureheads).

On the other hand, if it is true that conflicts among class members inhere in every case, *see supra* p. 373, Note 6, these conflicts do not go away by putting a pit bull of a lawyer in charge of the class. This strategy merely shifts the problem of dealing with the conflicts onto the lawyer's shoulders. Although we will explore some limits on this principle in Chapter Seven, *see infra* pp. 733-52, the usual rule is that class counsel must also be free of conflicting loyalties to be regarded as adequate.

14. Are there other ways out of the conundrum? The Private Securities Litigation Reform Act of 1995 (PSLRA) requires that a plaintiff who brings a securities-fraud case as a class action must place a notice of the suit in a widely circulating business-oriented newspaper or news service, and invite others to seek the position of lead plaintiff. From among the persons that apply for the position, the court is then to choose the "most adequate plaintiff." The Act establishes a presumption that the "most adequate plaintiff" will be the person that "has the largest financial interest in the relief sought by the class" and that has "otherwise satisfied the requirements of Rule 23." The presumption can be rebutted only by showing either that the presumptive lead plaintiff "will not fairly and adequately protect the interests of the class" or "is subject to unique defenses that render such plaintiff incapable of adequately representing the class." *See* 15 U.S.C. § 78u-4. Once the "most adequate plaintiff" is selected, then that plaintiff chooses the counsel for the class. *Id.*; *see* In re Cendant Corp. Litig., 264 F.3d 201 (3d Cir. 2001) (*infra* p. 724). The Act also places a prohibition on so-called "professional plaintiffs" who own small numbers of shares in many corporations and who are often affiliated with certain plaintiffs' firms; a person may be "a lead plaintiff, or an officer, director, or fiduciary of a lead plaintiff, in no more than 5 securities class actions brought as plaintiff class actions pursuant to the Federal Rules of Civil Procedure during any 3-year period." 15 U.S.C. § 78u-4.

It is difficult to argue with the intent of the PSLRA to ensure vigorous representation by the class representative and class counsel. On the other hand, some have argued that the PLSRA was intended to have, and has had, a chilling effect on securities litigation. Should rules similar to those in the PSLRA be adopted for all class actions under Rule 23?

15. Claims that the class counsel is flatly incompetent or inadequate under Rule 23(g) are infrequently successful. *See* Robert H. Klonoff, *The Judiciary's Flawed Application of Rule 23's "Adequacy of Representation" Requirement*, 2004 MICH. ST. L. REV. 671, 689 (2004) (noting that out of 687 cases during the ten year sample period only 31 found class counsel inadequate); *but see, e.g.*, LeBeau v. United States, 222 F.R.D. 613, 618-19 (D.S.D. 2004) (questioning whether the proposed class counsel was adequate and appointing a more experienced attorney to serve as lead counsel and the original applicant as "co-counsel").

16. If a trial court finds the named plaintiffs to be inadequate representatives of the class, but the class action to be otherwise permissible, should the trial court attempt to identify class members who would be adequate representatives of the class? In *Birmingham Steel Corp. v. Tennessee Valley Authority*, 353 F.3d 1331 (11th Cir. 2003) the Eleventh Circuit held that a district court had abused its discretion in decertifying

a class action after discovery was complete without affording an opportunity for a new class representative to be substituted.

17. By now, you should be getting the sense (correctly) that the words "commonality," "typicality," and "adequacy" are freighted with meaning. But go back to first principles: What does any of this have to do with the reasons that these doctrines exist? If the doctrines are ultimately designed to ensure that (1) the risk of collusive or inequitable mishandling of the class members' claims is very low, and (2) the economy of class treatment is very high, then can't we scrape off the barnacles that have accumulated on Rules 23(a)(2), -(a)(3), and -(a)(4) and determine the class-certification question by seeing if a class action advances these two policies?

b. The Rule 23(b) Requirement

If a court determines that any elements of Rules 23(a) or -(g) is not met, it cannot certify a class action. On the other hand, if it determines that all of the elements are met, it moves on to determine if *one* of the elements of Rule 23(b) is also met. Rule 23(b) authorizes four distinct class actions; a class needs to fit into only one of these types to be certified. It is possible (and sometimes advantageous) for the class representative to seek certification under more than one theory, but it is not required.

Of the four types of class action, three are mandatory: the (b)(1)(A), (b)(1)(B), and (b)(2) class actions. In a mandatory class action, class members generally have no opt-out right; once the class is certified, they are powerless to remove themselves. Nor, at least until settlement, are they generally entitled to receive notice of the fact that they are members of the class. Indeed, it is possible that you have been a member of a mandatory class action and never known about it at the time.

On the other hand, the fourth type of class action — the Rule 23(b)(3) class action — affords an opt-out right. To make this right meaningful, class members in a (b)(3) class action must be given notice of the pendency of the class action and of their right to opt out of it. This notice must be in plain English, and it must be sent individually (usually by first-class mail) to all class members who can be identified with reasonable effort. *See* Fed. R. Civ. P. 23(c)(2); Eisen v. Carlisle & Jacquelin, 417 U.S. 156, 177 (1974). For less easily identified members, various forms of substituted notice (traditionally, newspapers and TV, but now also web sites, e-mail, Facebook pages, and even Twitter accounts) might also be necessary.

Because notice can be costly and because opt-outs can diminish the bargaining leverage of class counsel, plaintiffs' lawyers typically prefer to certify a mandatory class action whenever possible. For the opposite reasons, defendants tend to vigorously resist certification of mandatory classes, but sometimes a defendant that seeks finality is more amenable to the idea. From the court's viewpoint, a mandatory class action can conserve judicial resources by preventing the relitigation of common issues that might occur if no class action is certified or if some class members opt out of the class.

Conversely, in terms of respecting the autonomy of class members to control their own litigation, an opt-out class action, while not as good as an opt-in class action (or no class action at all), is far better than a mandatory class action. Likewise, although opt-out class actions raise these issues to some degree, the compulsion inherent in mandatory class actions creates significant questions about the limits of judicial power, the proper balance between federal and state courts, the functional coercion on defendants to settle, and, relatedly, the influence of procedure in determining outcomes.

For the most part (as we will see, this generalization is overbroad), mandatory class actions involve injunctive relief and (b)(3) class actions involve damages. Therefore, as you might expect, much of the controversy concerning class actions surrounds Rule 23(b)(3), the rule under which the majority of class actions are certified. THOMAS E. WILLGING ET AL., FED. JUD. CTR., EMPIRICAL STUDY OF CLASS ACTIONS IN FOUR FEDERAL DISTRICT COURTS (1996) (reporting that 61% are (b)(3) class actions).

As you examine the four different types of class actions, pay attention to an important dynamic. For the most part (another generalization!), Rule 23(a) says "*If* a class action is to be certified, then the class action must meet the following conditions." But Rule 23(a) doesn't explain *why* we might want to certify a class action. This is the task of Rule 23(b); each of its four provisions describes a factual circumstance in which trading individual control for adequate representation is thought necessary.

i. Mandatory Class Actions

(A)   (b)(1)(A) and (b)(1)(B) Class Actions

Unlike the (b)(2) and (b)(3) class actions, which are of modern vintage, (b)(1)(A) and (b)(1)(B) class actions descend directly from equity practice. The Rule 23(b)(1)(A) class action attempts to avoid the risk of "inconsistent or varying adjudications . . . that would establish incompatible standards of conduct for the party opposing the class" if class members filed individual suits. The original cases certifying what we now call (b)(1)(A) class actions involved large groups of taxpayers, bondholders, insureds, alleged patent infringers, or land owners who sought or required equitable or declaratory relief against a defendant. *See* 7AA CHARLES A. WRIGHT ET AL., FEDERAL PRACTICE AND PROCEDURE § 1773 (3d ed. 2005). Absent a unitary adjudication of the rights of the class members against the defendant, there was a risk that the defendant would be subject to conflicting judgments that dictated its future behavior toward individual members of the class. Because dictating future behavior is usually the job of injunctions, Rule 23(b)(1)(A) class actions have almost always involved injunctive relief.

Class actions under (b)(1)(A) bear a strong family relationship to the required joinder under Rule 19(a)(1)(B)(ii) (*see supra* p. 91) and to interpleader under either Rule 22(1) or 28 U.S.C. § 1335 (*see supra* p. 84). These devices protect a defendant from multiple monetary judgments and orders of inconsistent injunctive relief. By drawing everyone into one case (and not letting them opt out), they can also prevent the possibility that later-filing plaintiffs who seek injunctive relief will destroy the injunctive relief that early-filing plaintiffs obtained.

Rule 23(b)(1)(B) class actions avoid the risk associated with individual lawsuits that "would be dispositive of the interests of other [class] members . . . or would substantially impair or impede their ability to protect their interests." Because stare-decisis effects were not regarded as sufficient impairments, the number of cases that classically fell within this rule were few. *See* 7AA WRIGHT ET AL., *supra*, § 1774. One example was a dispute about the beneficial ownership or operation of a trust in which many persons claimed an interest; a successful individual suit by one beneficiary might effectively bar relief in favor of other beneficiaries of the trust. Another commonly cited — but rarely invoked — example was a situation in which the plaintiffs could assert claims against a fund that was clearly insufficient to satisfy all the claims; early individual lawsuits might exhaust the fund's assets and leave nothing for later-filing claimants. A (b)(1)(B) class action thus might involve either injunctive or monetary relief, but awards of monetary relief occurred only in a narrow range of cases.

Class actions under (b)(1)(B) bear a strong family relationship to required joinder under Rule 19(a)(1)(B)(i) (*see supra* p. 91), to interpleader (*see supra* p. 84), and to intervention under Rule 24(a)(2) (*see supra* p. 104), each of which also attempts to protect nonparties from the consequences of litigation that practically limits their right to a remedy. It is necessary to draw everyone into the case, affording no one the right to opt out, in order to achieve equity within the entire class.

In recent years, lawyers have pushed to expand the boundaries of (b)(1)(A) and (b)(1)(B) class actions to make them available in a larger range of cases, especially cases involving monetary relief. Before we consider their efforts, however, we examine one case that sets out the traditional understanding of the scope of (b)(1)(A) and (b)(1)(B) class actions.

IN RE DENNIS GREENMAN SECURITIES LITIGATION

829 F.2d 1539 (11th Cir. 1987)

■ HENLEY, Senior Circuit Judge.

This is an appeal from a final district court judgment certifying a class action and approving a settlement in a complex securities fraud case. The plaintiffs are victims of a fraud perpetrated by Dennis Greenman, a securities seller. The defendants are brokerage firms that employed Greenman while he was conducting the fraud as well as others who might be liable for Greenman's actions. Appellants, some alleged victims of Greenman, contend that the district court erred in certifying the class for settlement purposes pursuant to Fed. R. Civ. P. 23(b)(1). For reasons to be stated, we reverse.

Greenman conducted the fraud over a period of almost four years beginning in mid-1977 as a broker for or associate of three different brokerage firms . . . . [In essence, Greenman ran a Ponzi scheme. His clients invested $86 million, of which they lost $50 million after the bubble burst. The Securities and Exchange Commission obtained an order appointing a receiver, who recaptured $17,280,681.76 and distributed it to investors. Individual plaintiffs also sued the firms for which Greenman had worked, alleging violations of federal securities laws, the Racketeer Influenced and Corrupt Organizations (RICO) Act, and state statutory and common-law doctrines. They sought monetary relief: the value of their lost investments, treble damages under RICO, and punitive damages.]

After receiving advice from counsel and conducting hearings, the district court consolidated and stayed the individual suits and certified a class action pursuant to Fed. R. Civ. P. 23(b)(1). . . .

After a year and a half of discovery, the parties . . . reached an agreement. Adherence to the agreement was conditioned upon the district court certifying a class action pursuant to Rule 23(b)(1). The district court certified a class for settlement purposes pursuant to Rule 23(b)(1) and approved the settlement. . . .

In certifying the class, the district court again emphasized the special circumstances of the case. The court reasoned that the cohesion among the plaintiffs' claims caused each plaintiff's ability to recover to be intertwined with that of other plaintiffs. Specifically, the court expressed concern that plaintiffs, who brought their actions first, might bankrupt potential sources of recovery and, thereby, preclude recovery for those plaintiffs who brought later actions. In addition, the district court feared that individual actions would cause the defendants to face incompatible standards of conduct or create for them inconsistent adjudications. The court also noted that Rule 23(b)(1) certification would aid in equitably distributing the receivership fund. The court further recited several negative consequences that would result if the class was not certified pursuant to Rule 23(b)(1). Individual defendants would lose the ability to set off, against their investors' claims, the money they paid through the receivership fund to those who invested at other brokerage firms. Individual actions would also create both burdens for the court and the prospect of enormous attorneys' fees. The court also expressed concern that by not certifying the class pursuant to Rule 23(b)(1), most plaintiffs would be deprived of the settlement they desire.

A group of plaintiffs, named the *Baer* plaintiffs, brought this appeal challenging the district court's class certification under Rule 23(b)(1). Appellants contend that the class should have been certified pursuant to Rule 23(b)(3) to allow class members to opt out. . . .

Determination of the question whether a lawsuit may proceed as a class action is committed to the sound discretion of the district court, and its determination will not be overturned absent a showing that it has abused its discretion. . . . Nonetheless, the district court erred by certifying the class pursuant to Rule 23(b)(1).

A class must satisfy the requirements of one of the subsections to Rule 23(b). We note that the propriety of certification under the various subsections is quite controversial and not well defined. At stake are the nature of the notice to be given to class members and their right to opt out from or refuse to be part of the class. . . . These practical differences affect the ability of plaintiffs to bring class actions as well as their attractiveness to defendants. Applying the various subsections of Rule 23(b) requires a balance between an individual's due process rights and the judiciary's need to expedite the orderly resolution of conflict. . . .

The district court certified the class both under subpart (A) and (B) of Rule 23(b)(1). . . .

As a threshold consideration to certification under sub-part A, it must be ascertained that separate actions would result if the class was not certified pursuant to Rule 23(b)(1). It is clear in this case that separate actions would be filed if the class was not certified pursuant to Rule 23(b)(1). At the time the district court first certified the class, twenty-five separate actions were pending. Indeed, the appellants bring this appeal for the purpose of prosecuting or being able to prosecute their own actions. Consequently, this threshold concern is satisfied.

The identity of judicial action that creates "inconsistent or varying adjudications" is not clear. Many courts confronting the issue have held that Rule 23(b)(1)(A) does not apply to actions seeking compensatory damages. These courts reason that inconsistent standards for future conduct are not created because a defendant might be found liable to some plaintiffs and not to others. Implicit in these decisions is the view that only actions seeking declaratory or injunctive relief can be certified under this section. Underlying is the concern that if compensatory damage actions can be certified under Rule 23(b)(1)(A), then all actions could be certified under the section, thereby making the other sub-sections of Rule 23 meaningless, particularly Rule 23(b)(3).

Albeit reluctantly, we must agree. Although sound criticism exists for this interpretation, the Advisory Committee Notes support the proposition that (b)(1)(A) certification is for cases seeking injunctive and declaratory relief. The relevant Note states that the section is proper in suits to invalidate a bond issue, to declare the rights and duties of riparian owners or landowners, or to abate a common nuisance. Since the plaintiffs sought compensatory damages, the district court erred by certifying the class pursuant to (b)(1)(A).

The district court [also] found that if separate cases were litigated "determination in the prior action would as a practical matter create a predisposition to a similar determination in a subsequent action."

It is settled that the possibility that an action will have either precedential or stare decisis effect on later cases is not sufficient to satisfy Rule 23(b)(1)(B). A contrary rule would enable any action, with the possibility that it might be one of multiple actions, to be certified pursuant to Rule 23(b)(1)(B). Consequently, the district court's finding that earlier

(b)(1)(A) only proper for declaratory/injunctive relief

decisions would create a "predisposition" for the determination of later actions standing alone is clearly not a sufficient basis for certification.

The district court also certified the settlement class pursuant to Rule 23(b)(1)(B) because a limited fund existed. Limited fund cases exist where a fund is insufficient to satisfy all of the claims against it. The district court found two bases for certification based on this theory. First, the district court relied on the existence of the receivership fund. The court indicated that the fund has been and would be protected throughout the litigation and "that certification under Rule 23(b)(1) will aid in protecting, managing and equitably distributing this fund." We do not find this to be an adequate basis for certification. The district court doubtless stated correctly that the fund would be protected but that protection does not depend upon Rule 23(b)(1) certification. In addition, the district court did not indicate that the receivership fund initially was intended to be the sole source of recovery for plaintiffs. It is of no consequence that the receivership fund now contains settlement contributions. Consequently, the receivership fund is not a limited fund for purposes of Rule 23(b)(1).

The district court also found a limited fund on the basis that some investors may bankrupt potential sources of recovery. The court made no specific findings of the defendants' financial status. Absent such findings the district court could not properly rely on this ground for certification. . . .

Accordingly, we reverse the district court's judgment now under attack and remand for further proceedings consistent with this opinion.

Notes

1. *La Mar v. H & B Novelty & Loan Co.*, 489 F.2d 461, 467 (9th Cir. 1973) explained the relationship between Rules 23(b)(1)(A) and -(b)(1)(B) as follows:

> In essence, (b)(1)(A) and (b)(1)(B) of Rule 23 are opposite sides of the same coin — a coin which determines suitability for class action by reference to either the awkwardness, irrationality, or the probability of severe prejudice of separate actions.

Does this understanding suggest that the motivation behind (b)(1)(A) and (b)(1)(B) is preventing inequity among actual or potential plaintiffs — (b)(1)(A) to deal with the problems that suits by later-filing plaintiffs might pose for the remedy obtained by the present plaintiffs, and (b)(1)(B) to deal with the problems that the present suit might pose to later-filing plaintiffs trying to obtain a meaningful remedy? If so, some class members are advantaged either by filing early or by filing late.

If joining all class members in one case is necessary to achieve some measure of intra-class equity, won't there be inevitable conflicts among class members? This is most evident in the (b)(1)(B) limited-fund situation, in which the early-filing class members would have received the lion's share of the fund, but must now share and share alike with others. Even in the (b)(1)(A) context, the reason that the defendant might be subject to inconsistent obligations is that different class members have interests that lead them to want the defendant to act in different ways. Can you imagine any (b)(1)(A) or (b)(1)(B) situation in which these conflicting interests do not exist? Should *Greenman* therefore have denied class certification on inadequate-representation grounds? More generally, are all (b)(1)(A) and (b)(1)(B) class actions unconstitutional because they deny class members the adequate representation that the Due Process Clause guarantees?

2. *Greenman* sets out the classic understanding of the limits of (b)(1)(A) and (b)(1)(B) class actions. First, damages are not available in (b)(1)(A) cases; Rule 23(b)(1)(A) is reserved for injunctive claims. Second, damages might be available in (b)(1)(B) class actions, but only on a strong showing that the fund against which claims are made is insufficient to satisfy all claims. (On this issue, we examine the Supreme Court's subsequent and authoritative decision on limited-fund class actions later. *See* Ortiz v. Fibreboard Corp., 527 U.S. 815 (1999) (*infra* p. 506).) Third, although the comparable language of Rule 24(a)(2) is often read to permit stare decisis or other precedential effects to justify intervention (*see supra* p. 119, Note 4(c)), these effects are not sufficient to trigger class treatment under (b)(1)(B). *Accord* Tilley v. TJX Cos., 345 F.3d 34, 42 (1st Cir. 2003).

We now turn to some creative efforts to expand these mandatory class actions in order to achieve greater aggregation of related cases.

IN RE MERCK & CO., INC. SECURITIES, DERIVATIVE & "ERISA" LITIGATION

2009 WL 331426 (D.N.J. Feb. 10, 2009)

■ CHESLER, District Judge.

This matter comes before the Court upon the motion for class certification, pursuant to Fed. R. Civ. P. 23 . . . . Merck & Co., Inc. ("Merck"), various individual Merck defendants, and Merck-Medco Managed Care, LLC ("Merck-Medco") (collectively, "Defendants") oppose this motion . . . . For the reasons that follow, Plaintiffs' motion will be granted in part and denied in part.

BACKGROUND

The Plaintiffs in these consolidated cases are participants in various retirement benefit plans, seeking to represent a class of all others similarly situated, during the period between October 1, 1998 through September 30, 2004 (the "Class Period"). The plans at issue are the Merck & Co., Inc. Employee Savings and Security Plan, Merck & Co., Inc. Employee Stock Purchase and Savings Plan, and the Merck-Medco Managed Care LLC 401(k) Savings Plan (collectively, the "Plans"). The Plans are defined contribution benefit plans.

In brief, this dispute concerns claims that Plan participants incurred losses in their individual accounts due to artificial inflation of the value of Merck stock, and that such losses were caused by Defendants' breach of fiduciary duties owed to Plaintiffs under the Employment Retirement Income Security Act ("ERISA"). Plaintiffs allege inflation of the value of Merck stock in connection with Merck's sale of the drug Vioxx.

Plaintiffs' Consolidated Amended Class Action Complaint (the "Amended Complaint") alleges four causes of action, all asserting liability to restore losses to the Plans, pursuant to ERISA §§ 409, 502(a)(2) and (a)(3): 1) failure to prudently and loyally manage the Plans (the "prudence claim"); 2) failure to provide complete and accurate information (the "communications claim"); 3) failure to monitor fiduciaries; and 4) co-fiduciary liability. . . .

Plaintiffs now ask this Court to certify a class, pursuant to Fed. R. Civ. P. 23, defined as follows:

All persons, other than Defendants, who were participants in, or beneficiaries of, the Merck & Co., Inc. Employee Savings & Security Plan [ ], the Merck & Co., Inc. Employee Stock Purchase & Savings Plan [ ], the Merck Puerto Rico Employee Savings & Security Plan [ ] and the Merck-Medco Managed Care, LLC 401(k) Savings Plan [ ] (collectively the "Plans") at any time between October 1, 1998 and September 30, 2004 and whose Plan accounts invested in the Merck Common Stock Fund and/or Merck common stock.

ANALYSIS

. . .

The parties' briefs regarding Plaintiffs' motion for class certification focus on two claims: the prudence claim and the communications claim. Defendants argue that class certification should not be granted for the communications claim because adjudication of that claim requires individualized determinations, precluding finding sufficient typicality under Rule 23(a)(3). This Court agrees.

The gist of the communications claim is that Defendants failed to disclose complete and accurate information to Plan participants regarding Vioxx and the prudence of investing in Merck stock and the Merck Common Stock Fund ("MCSF"), which caused Plan participants to acquire the stock at inflated prices and, subsequently, to incur losses when the stock price dropped. Plaintiffs assert causes of action pursuant to ERISA §§ 502(a)(2) and 502(a)(3). Defendants contend that detrimental reliance on the misrepresentations or omissions is a necessary element of this claim. . . .

This Court finds that the communications to participants, and the individual participants' consequent investment choices, are central elements of the communications claim. These claims are not conducive to efficient litigation on a class-wide basis. Investment choices are highly individualized, and thus the individual circumstances of the plaintiffs markedly differ. Furthermore, individual plaintiffs will have to prove individual losses.

. . . [T]he example most relevant to this case given in the Advisory Committee Note to Rule 23 states that certification under 23(b)(1)(b) is appropriate when there is a breach of fiduciary duty "similarly affecting the members of a large class . . . ." The individual character of the communications claims prevents concluding that the alleged breach has similarly affected the potential class members. As to the communications claim, the proposed class fails to satisfy the requirements for certification under Rule 23. . . .

As to the prudence claim, Defendants do not dispute that the proposed class meets the numerosity and commonality requirements, but contend that the proposed class representatives fail to meet the typicality and adequacy requirements.

[The court found the claims of the class representatives were "typical" of the class because those claims did not depend on whether and how individual plaintiffs were affected by the choice of Merck stock as an investment, but rather turned on whether the defendants breached a fiduciary duty of prudence to the Plans by choosing to invest in Merck stock. Although the court found one class representative inadequate, it found the other two representatives were adequate under Rule 23(a)(4). The court then modified the class definition in minor respects and turned to whether the proposed class satisfied Rule 23(b)(1).]

Plaintiffs assert that the proposed class meets the requirements of either subsection (A) or (B). Defendants contend that class certification is not appropriate under either subsection.

a. *Class certification under Rule 23(b)(1)(B)*

Plaintiffs content that class certification is most appropriate under Rule 23(b)(1)(B). In opposition, Defendants argue, vaguely, that the drafters of the provision did not intend the Rule to extend to a case like this one. Defendants refer to the Advisory Committee Notes for the 1966 Amendments, but, as Plaintiffs contend, the instant case appears similar to one kind of case that the notes describe: "an action which charges a breach of trust by an indenture trustee or other fiduciary similarly affecting the members of a large class of security holders or other beneficiaries, and which requires an accounting or like measures to restore the subject of the trust." Plaintiffs charge a breach of trust by a fiduciary, affecting a large class of beneficiaries, which requires an accounting to restore the subject of the trust. Defendants do not persuade to the contrary. . . .

Rule 23(b)(1)(B) requires that individual adjudications of the prudence claim be dispositive of the interests of the other members or substantially impair or impede the ability of other members to protect their interests. This is true for this case. ERISA § 409(a) expressly empowers this Court to provide relief by removing a fiduciary. If the prudence claims proceeded individually, and one court removed a Plan fiduciary, this would be, as a practical matter, dispositive of the interests of the other Plan members in that particular regard. Certification is appropriate under Rule 23(b)(1)(B).

b. *Class certification under Rule 23(b)(1)(A)*

Plaintiffs contend that class certification is also appropriate pursuant to Rule 23(b)(1)(A). Defendants offer two arguments against class certification under subsection (A): 1) certification under this subsection is not appropriate when the primary relief sought is money damages; and 2) Defendants have assumed the risk of inconsistent adjudications. . . .

[Defendant's first argument] inserts a requirement into [Rule] 23(b)(1) (A) that is not present. The subsection requires that the varying adjudications "would establish incompatible standards of conduct for the party opposing the class." This language does not require that the varying adjudications would establish incompatible standards as the exclusive or even primary remedy. It only requires that varying adjudications would establish incompatible standards, and Plaintiffs have persuaded this Court that this requirement is met.[7] Defendants fail to persuade that a class action case principally seeking money damages, but also seeking to establish a standard of conduct for Defendants, cannot qualify under [Rule] 23(b)(1)(A).

As to the second argument, the position that defendants may defeat a motion for class certification by declaring that they are willing to assume the risk of inconsistent adjudications is absurd. It costs defendants nothing to make such an offer and, if defendants could defeat class certification by it, it would be a costless and automatic strategy that would effectively render 23(b) (1)(A) useless. The Federal Rules of Civil Procedure do not give Defendants the option of waiving any requirements of Rule 23.

Defendants do not address the fact that . . . many courts have certified classes under 23(b)(1)(A) in ERISA stock drop cases. . . .

Plaintiffs argue that, were class members to prosecute the prudence claims individually, it would create a risk of inconsistent adjudications that would establish incompatible standards of conduct for the fiduciaries. This Court agrees. Pursuing separate actions would raise a substantial risk that different courts would reach inconsistent conclusions about the standards of conduct for the fiduciaries, and that different courts might order conflicting injunctive or other remedies.[9]

---

7. As discussed above, § 409(a) authorizes courts to order "such other equitable or remedial relief as the court may deem appropriate, including removal of [the] fiduciary." If one court ordered the removal of a fiduciary, and another court enjoined that fiduciary in a particular way, incompatible standards of conduct would be established.

9. Furthermore, Defendants argue that participants have an interest in advocating diverse dates on which Merck stock became an imprudent investment. If this is so, pursuing separate actions would raise a substantial risk that courts would reach inconsistent conclusions on this key question.

The risk of establishing inconsistent standards under ERISA is particularly strong where, as here, a central element of the prudence claims is not an individual matter: the fiduciary duties are owed to the plan. Plaintiffs do not claim that Defendants owed fiduciary duties to individual participants in the plan, but to the plan itself. A Court adjudicating a suit by an individual plaintiff would determine the issues of the existence of the fiduciary duty and its breach not in relation to the individual plaintiff, but in relation to the entire plan. The language of 29 U.S.C. §1109 makes clear that the liability of the fiduciary is to the plan, and that a fiduciary found liable for damages due to a breach must reimburse the plan. Thus the Supreme Court stated: "Section 502(a)(2) provides for suits to enforce the liability-creating provisions of § 409, concerning breaches of fiduciary duties that harm *plans*." Larue [v. DeWolff, Boberg & Assocs., 552 U.S. 248, 251 (2008)] (italics added). This produces a significant risk that separate actions would establish differing standards for the duty under ERISA owed by a fiduciary to the plan. Plaintiffs have shown that, as to the prudence claim, class certification under Rule 23(b)(1)(A) is proper. . . .

. . . [T]he motion for class certification as to Count III and Count IV will be granted only to the extent that these claims are predicated on the prudence claim, that is, only insofar as Plaintiffs seek to impose liability deriving from breaches of the fiduciary duty of prudence. . . .

The class issues are: 1) whether Defendants breached fiduciary duties of prudence under ERISA owed to class Plaintiffs as participants in the Plans by: a) permitting the Plans to offer MCSF as a Plan investment option; b) permitting the Plans to invest Plan assets in the MCSF; and c) investing MCSF assets in Merck stock; 2) if such a breach occurred, the date on which Merck stock became an imprudent investment; 3) if such a breach occurred, whether it caused a loss to the Plans; 4) whether Defendants breached a duty to monitor the performance of imprudent fiduciaries, resulting in a loss to the Plans; and 5) whether any Defendant is liable for a breach of fiduciary responsibility of another fiduciary, pursuant to 29 U.S.C. § 1105(a). . . .

For the reasons stated above, Plaintiffs' motion for class certification will be granted in part and denied in part.

IN RE TELECTRONICS PACING SYSTEMS, INC., ACCUFIX ATRIAL "J" LEADS PRODUCTS LIABILITY LITIGATION

172 F.R.D. 271 (S.D. Ohio 1997)

■ SPIEGEL, Senior District Judge.

. . . There has been much discussion regarding the need to reform or improve how federal courts deal with mass tort litigation. While we agree changes might be appropriate, the district courts are left to fight the battles and resolve the Parties disputes' with the tools provided by Congress and our appellate courts. Thus, we must grant or deny certification on the basis of the federal rules as written today and interpreted by the Sixth Circuit and the Supreme Court.

In deciding this question, the Court is mindful of the applicable law and rules, the procedural and substantive legal rights of the Parties and the ethical concerns raised by adjudication of mass tort claims. Recently, several Circuit Court[s] have been highly critical of the use of class actions in mass tort and product liability cases. While we recognize the difficulties inherent in [diversity-based] class actions as outlined by the Circuit Courts, we continue to believe that [the] class action provides the fairest, most efficient and economical means of dealing with these types of cases. We believe courts must play an important role in the efficient resolution of mass tort action[s]. This is especially so where, as here, there is a danger that the expense of litigation and potential for large damage awards threaten to bankrupt the defendant and leave some class members without a remedy. . . .

We also strongly disagree with those Circuit Courts which have allowed their apparent economic biases to influence their interpretation of the requirements of Rule 23. For example, in *Castano v. American Tobacco Co.*, 84 F.3d 734 (5th Cir. 1996) [*infra* p. 471], the Fifth [C]ircuit found that class certification of all nicotine dependent individuals was not superior under Rule 23(b)(3) because of the strategic effect class certification has upon the defendants' chances.

> In the context of mass tort class actions, certification dramatically affects the stakes for defendants. Class certification magnifies and strengthens the number of unmeritorious claims. Aggregation of claims also makes it more likely that a defendant will be found liable and results in significantly higher damage awards.

See also In re Rhone-Poulenc Rorer, Inc., 51 F.3d 1293 (7th Cir. 1995). To credit the Fifth Circuit's statement is to also state that its converse — denying class certification makes it less likely defendants will be found liable or responsible for lower damage awards — is true. Plaintiffs in individual actions will have to bear a greater share of the cost and risk for maintaining their action as compared to plaintiffs in a class action. Often an individual action pits a single plaintiff relying on his or her own resources to fund the litigation against the vast resources of a large manufacturer and the large law firms which represent[ ] it.

Obviously, the procedural rules affect the outcome of litigation. These Circuit Courts seemed to ignore the essence of Rule 23 because of their philosophical disagreement with the effects of Rule 23.

[The case involved pacemakers that had an allegedly defective J-shaped retention wire that fractured and caused serious injury to the heart or surrounding blood vessels. The pacemakers were made by TPLC, Inc., a wholly owned subsidiary of TPSI, Inc. Both companies were in turn owned by an Australian holding company, Nucleus, which was later purchased by another Australian company, Pacific Dunlop Limited (PDL). PDL had more than 225 corporate affiliates, and annual sales of $5.5 billion.

[Approximately 25,000 of the defective pacemakers were implanted in American citizens prior to 1994, when seven fracture-related injuries were reported. In response to the fracture problem, TPLC created an institute to manage the recall of the defective wires. It also formed a Physicians' Advisory Committee to provide advice to physicians concerning the clinical management of patients. It further agreed to pick up reasonable, unreimbursed expenses for screening patients and for extracting pacemakers.

[The Judicial Panel on Multidistrict Litigation consolidated the federal cases in the Southern District of Ohio. Seeking compensatory and punitive damages, the MDL complaint alleged negligence, strict liability, breach of warranty, misrepresentation, fear of product failure, and infliction of emotional distress. Also included was a claim for medical monitoring. The MDL court then certified a nationwide class action.

[After *In re American Medical Systems, Inc.*, 75 F.3d 1069 (6th Cir. 1996) (*supra* p. 367), the MDL court decertified the class. Among its concerns was that a single nationwide class would involve the application of numerous state laws, and would therefore run afoul of the requirements of Rule 23(a). The plaintiffs responded by seeking certification of ten subclasses: a single nationwide subclass on the medical-monitoring claim, two subclasses to account for state-law variations on negligence, four subclasses to account for state-law variations on strict liability, and three subclasses to account for state-law variations on punitive damages. The court found that the Rule 23(a) requirements were satisfied for all ten subclasses. It then certified the medical-monitoring subclass under Rules 23(b)(1)(A), -(b)(1)(B), and -(b)(3). It also certified the negligence and strict liability class actions under Rule 23(b)(3). Finally it held that the punitive-damages subclasses could not be certified under any provision of Rule 23(b). The following excerpt is from the court's ruling on the medical-monitoring subclass.]

. . . "Certification under Rule 23(b)(1) is appropriate when a unitary decision is essential." "Rule 23(b)(1) classes are designed to avoid prejudice to the defendant or absent class members if individual actions were prosecuted in contrast to a class suit yielding a unitary adjudication." However, the possibility that some plaintiffs might recover and others might not does not justify class certification under Rule 23(b)(1)(A).

A. *Class Certification of Medical Monitoring pursuant to Rule 23(b)(1)(A).*

Rule 23(b)(1)(A) states that class certification is proper if separate actions "would create a risk of inconsistent or varying adjudications with respect to individual members of the class which would establish incompatible standards of conduct for the party opposing the class. . . ." Fed.R.Civ.P. 23(b)(1)(A). "The phrase 'incompatible standards of conduct' is thought to refer to the situation where different results in separate actions would impair the opposing party's ability to pursue a uniform continuing course of conduct." "[S]ubdivision (b)(1)(A) is applicable when practical necessity forces the opposing party to act in the same manner toward the individual class members and thereby makes inconsistent adjudications in separate actions unworkable or intolerable."

The medical monitoring claim here is an ideal candidate for class certification pursuant to Rule 23(b)(1)(A) because separate adjudications would impair TPLC's ability to pursue a single uniform medical monitoring program. . . . TPLC asserts that medical monitoring beyond that recommended by TPLC's Physicians' Advisory Committee is not warranted. TPLC's research program is a uniform benefit to the class of "J" lead implantees as a whole. Any judicially-imposed modification of this program would then, by necessity, affect all of the "J" lead implantees. Furthermore, separate judicial orders pertaining to medical monitoring could require TPLC to institute differing types of monitoring programs which TPLC would have to reconcile.

TPLC argues that the recommendations of the Physicians' Advisory Committee are subject to approval by the FDA. TPLC insists that "the Court [will] have to reconcile its involvement in a medical monitoring program with FDA's statutorily mandated oversight function. . . . The potential for unnecessary conflict and expense with no patient benefit is readily apparent, with TPLC caught in an impossible position between the judicial and executive branches of government." Whether FDA regulations preempt or otherwise limit state law tort claims for medical monitoring goes to the merits of the class claims and must be determined at a later date.

However, individual adjudication of implantees claims for medical monitoring would not alleviate TPLC's fear of conflicting standards of medical monitoring imposed by the judicial branch and executive branch. In fact, the danger of courts imposing conflicting duties upon Telectronics would only be compounded if the question of medical monitoring is not certified as a class action pursuant to Rule 23(b)(1)(A). Presently, there are over 400 individual actions consolidated before this Court by the Judicial Panel for Multidistrict Litigation. Certainly, a large number of similar cases are pending in state courts across the country. Thus, TPLC could still face multiple and conflicting orders rendered from different courts regarding the scope and necessity of a medical monitoring program which may also conflict with FDA imposed requirements. Accordingly, the Court certifies the medical monitoring subclass under Rule 23(b)(1)(A).

. . . [T]here are also significant policy reasons for requiring one medical monitoring class. Any research component should be coordinated in order to maximize resources and avoid duplication. To promote consistency in treatment, doctors should also be given one set of advice in terms of treatment options for their "J" lead patients.

B. *Class Certification of Medical Monitoring pursuant to Rule 23(b)(1)(B).*

The argument for certification of a medical monitoring subclass is bolstered by the fact that separate adjudications may adversely affect other implantees' ability to recover anything. . . . The most common use of subsection (b)(1)(B) is in limited fund cases. "A limited fund exists when a fixed asset or piece of property exists in which all class members have a preexisting interest, and an apportionment or determination of the interests of one class member cannot be made without affecting the proportionate interests of other class members similarly situated." In the same limited circumstances, the potential or probable insolvency of the defendant due to a large number of pending tort actions can create a limited fund appropriate for adjudication under Rule 23(b)(1)(B).

According to previous pleadings and the representations of counsel for both sides, TPLC has recently sold all of its assets to another corporation. Thus, TPLC is no longer an operating corporation. TPLC received approximately $105 million for all of its assets. TPLC also has a $25 million liability policy. This policy is a diminishing policy; that is defense costs are deducted from the total coverage. TPLC has depleted approximately $9 million of their insurance coverage to cover legal fees and medical monitoring expenses. Thus, TPLC currently has approximately $120 million in assets and insurance to cover its liabilities related to the "J" lead litigation.[10]

In the United States, an estimated 25,000 individuals have had the "J" Lead implanted. Dividing $120 million by the number of implantees, TPLC has about $4800 to spend on each of the implantees for medical monitoring and any potential damage awards. TPLC has spent over $2.5 million on medical monitoring since it agreed to pay for the reasonable unreimbursed expenses of fluoroscopy and explantation. Because the Parties did not submit evidence regarding the potential cost of the medical monitoring program, the Court cannot determine whether TPLC faces insolvency as a result its expenses arising out of the "J" lead controversy. The possibility of the existence of a limited fund, however, lends further support to a conclusion that medical monitoring class should be certified under Rule 23(b)(1).

Notes

1. *Merck* and *Telectronics* demonstrate that it is possible to certify a class under different provisions of Rule 23(b). When the same class is eligible for certification under both Rule 23(b)(3) and one of the mandatory provisions, some courts state a "preference" for certifying class under the mandatory rule. *See* Bing v. Roadway Express, Inc., 485 F.2d 441, 447 (5th Cir. 1973). This preference dispenses with the requirement of an opt-out notice, and assures that all class members will be bound. Is this the right presumption, or should the presumption favor giving absent class members the right to opt out and proceed with individual litigation?

---

10. Plaintiffs have also sued TPLC's parent companies, Pacific Dunlop Limited and Nucleus Limited. Plaintiffs have not moved to certify a class action against these defendants. Furthermore, there is a substantial question whether Pacific Dunlop or Nucleus can be held liable for the activities of their subsidiary, TPLC.

2. What is really at stake in cases like *Merck* and *Telectronics* is how broadly Rules 23(b)(1)(A) and -(b)(1)(B) can be construed. Start from this fact. Rule 23(b)(2) provides clear authority to certify classes when the primary form of relief that is sought is injunctive or declaratory in nature. Therefore, unless Rules 23(b)(1)(A) and -(b)(1)(B) are entirely redundant of Rule 23(b)(2), they must encompass some class actions seeking non-injunctive or non-declaratory relief. In *Merck*, the plaintiffs want monetary relief. In *Telectronics*, the plaintiffs want a medical-monitoring program, which might or might not involve monetary relief — depending on whether the program creates special facilities for monitoring the plaintiffs' health or instead compensates plaintiffs for expenses that they incur in seeking medical assistance from their regular physicians.

The question is how many class actions seeking damages fall within (b)(1)(A) and (b)(1)(B). The traditional answer has been very, very few.

3. *Merck* is one of a small but expanding number of cases finding that ERISA cases fall within the narrow windows opened by Rules 23(b)(1)(A) and -(b)(1)(B) for class actions seeking damages. *See also* Taylor v. United Techs. Corp., 2008 WL 2333120, at *6 (D. Conn. June 3, 2008) ("ERISA actions alleging breach of fiduciary duty affecting a large class of beneficiaries 'presents a paradigmatic example' for application of Rule 23(b)(1)."). Is *Merck*'s argument for mandatory treatment persuasive? Granting that a past breach of a fiduciary relationship might serve as grounds for removal of a fiduciary, that injunctive remedy was not the one the plaintiffs in *Merck* necessarily sought; they wanted damages for the past breach, not a curative remedy to prevent future breaches. *Merck* also argued that individual cases seeking damages might result in the fiduciaries owing different duties to the ERISA plan, but is that any more true in the ERISA context than it is in any other context (say, individual mass-tort cases, some of which might find a defendant breached duties to the victims and some of which might not)? As we saw in *Greenman, supra* p. 380, the "differing duties" argument does not usually allow mandatory Rule 23(b)(1) treatment of damages claims.

George v. Kraft Foods Global, Inc., 251 F.R.D. 338, 344 (N.D. Ill. 2008), developed a different argument: "In the event plaintiffs prove excessive fees, and that leads to injunctive relief that affects how the Plan pays out fees in the future, that will redound to the benefit of future participants." Is this argument a more persuasive basis for the mandatory treatment of monetary ERISA class actions? How widely can it be used? Can't you craft a similar argument for the mandatory treatment of securities-fraud, antitrust, and mass-tort cases that seek damages?

Finally, *In re Syncor ERISA Litigation*, 227 F.R.D. 338, 346 (C.D. Cal. 2005), offered this rationale under Rule 23(b)(1)(B):

If the primary relief is to the Plan as a whole, then adjudications with respect to individual members of the class would "as a practical matter" alter the interests of other members of the class — if one plaintiff forces the Defendants to pay damages to the Plan, the benefit would affect everyone who has a right to disbursements from the Plan.

Is this argument persuasive? Doesn't Rule 23(b)(1)(B) require that individual litigation impair the interests of class members? How does a lawsuit that brings money into the ERISA plan impair anyone's interests?

4. Another context in which a court has recently upheld class certification of a class seeking damages under Rule 23(b)(1) is *In re Integra Realty Res., Inc.*, 354 F.3d 1246 (10th Cir. 2004), an unusual situation in which a bankruptcy trustee sought to recover the proceeds of an allegedly fraudulent transfer that the debtor had already distributed to its innocent shareholders. The court upheld the certification of a defendant class of shareholders (a rare event in itself!) on the theory that, if the trustee sued any shareholder individually, the issue of the fraudulent transfer "would almost inevitably prove dispositive" in future cases against shareholders. *Id.* at 1264.

5. Another circumstance in which (b)(1)(A) and (b)(1)(B) class actions have been invoked is the medical-monitoring context that *Telectronics* presents. As the opening part of *Telectronics* describes, a number of courts during the 1990s turned strongly against the use of class actions for mass torts. But mass-tort lawyers can be clever and resourceful people, and the medical-monitoring theory became all the rage as the way to certify mass-tort class actions. A bonus was that class actions using the medical-monitoring theory were mandatory in nature, which kept maximal settlement pressure on the defendants.

Indeed, two years after *Telectronics*, the defendants entered into a limited-fund settlement with the plaintiff class. The district court approved the settlement, but the Sixth Circuit reversed, finding the limited-fund settlement barred by *Ortiz v. Fibreboard Corp.*, 527 U.S. 815 (1999) (*infra* p. 506). *See* In re Telectronics Pacing Sys., Inc., Accufix Atrial "J" Leads Prods. Liab. Litig., 221 F.3d 870, 873 (6th Cir. 2000). Does this fact affect the district court's (b)(1)(B) certification of the medical-monitoring class?

6. The medical-monitoring theory has had a checkered history since *Telectronics*, which a number of courts have distinguished or rejected. Most notably, in *Zinser v. Accufix Research Institute, Inc.*, 253 F.3d 1180 (9th Cir. 2001), a plaintiff proposed to certify essentially the same class of atrial-lead plaintiffs as *Telectronics* had. *Zinser* upheld a district court's refusal to certify the class. On the medical-monitoring theory, it distinguished *Telectronics* because the plaintiff in *Zinser* wanted to create a medical-monitoring fund, as opposed to the medical monitoring program that *Zinser* read *Telectronics* as approving. Ordering establishment of a program was injunctive relief, while establishing a reserve fund for past and future medical expenses was monetary relief. *Zinser* also thought that the plaintiffs' request for an order requiring the defendants to engage in medical research did not change the fact that "Zinser primarily seeks money damages," *id.* at 1194, and that Zinser has failed to show, beyond a conclusory assertion, how differing monitoring programs the defendants might be asked to develop for different plaintiffs would lead to inconsistent standards of conduct that the defendants could not simultaneously meet. For an argument that a class action seeking to create a medical-monitoring

program could be classified as mandatory, but a class action seeking a medical-monitoring fund should go forward only on an opt-out basis, see AM. L. INST., PRINCIPLES OF THE LAW OF AGGREGATE LITIGATION § 2.04 cmt. *b*, illus. 3-4 (2009).

7.   *Telectronics* noted the substantial variance in state laws concerning medical monitoring justified certification under Rule 23(b)(1)(A). *See also* In re Welding Fume Prod. Liab. Litig., 245 F.R.D. 279, 291-92 (N.D. Ohio 2007) (discussing variations in medical-monitoring theories). Do the many variations in state law argue for or against certification of a nationwide class action? If the reason to certify a class in *Telectronics* is the difference in state law — and thus difference in remedy — how can any class representative be regarded as an adequate class representative of an entire class? Won't persons in states with generous rights of medical monitoring have conflicts with those in states with less generous rights, and won't both sets have conflicts with those who live in states that recognize no right of monitoring? We have asked this question before, but aren't there inevitable conflicts of interest among class members whenever the defendant might be subject to "incompatible standards of conduct"? So is Rule 23(b)(1)(A) a cruel hoax, on the theory that any class that might be certified under its provisions is automatically disqualified under Rules 23(a)(3) and -(a)(4)? If not, how is the court to manage the conflicts within the class? By picking representatives from the jurisdiction with the most stringent law? By using subclasses for different states' laws (as *Telectronics* did with respect to damages actions)? By re-conceiving the individual interests as a single group interest? By becoming a super-guardian of the interests of all?

8.   One of the clear motivations behind the outcome in *Telectronics* was Judge Spiegel's strong view that class actions were a necessary tool for efficiently handling mass torts and for leveling the playing field between the little guy and powerful corporations. He also recites policy arguments on the opposite side — especially the fear that class treatment will put undue burden on defendants to settle meritless claims and will affect substantive outcomes. How much should such policy concerns affect the interpretation of the text of Rules 23(b)(1)(A) and -(b)(1)(B), which never mention any of these concerns?

On the other hand, what concerns do you discern in the language of these two class actions? Put differently, why is a class action necessary — so necessary that we sacrifice the autonomy of class members to pursue their claims on their own — when defendants face the risk of incompatible standards of conduct or when individual litigation substantially impairs some class members' interests? Is the concern efficiency-based? Is it justice- or fairness-based? On what theory of justice or fairness?

9.   In answering these questions, you should consider another situation in which mandatory classes have sometimes been used to handle monetary claims: the limited-fund concept of Rule 23(b)(1)(B) that *Telectronics* uses. The basic idea behind the limited-fund theory is that the claims of the class members exceed the defendant's assets, so that early-filing claimants would exhaust the defendant's resources and leave the later-filing claimants with

nothing. This theory has certain difficulties, and we defer full examination of it until we study *Ortiz*, 527 U.S. 815 (*infra* p. 506), which was a settlement class action based on the limited-fund rationale. Here we note two things. First, *Zinser*, which was decided after *Ortiz*, rejected the limited-fund theory of *Telectronics*, which had been decided before *Ortiz*. Like the Sixth Circuit's decision denying class certification of the *Telectronics* settlement class action, *Zinser* doubted that such a class action could be formed when several of the defendants remained solvent enough to satisfy all of the plaintiffs' claims. Second, in part because of the constraints that *Ortiz* imposed on the limited-fund theory, plaintiffs' lawyers went back to the drawing board and spawned a related but distinct theory — the limited-punishment theory — to justify mandatory class treatment of monetary claims. The following case explores this theory.

IN RE SIMON II LITIGATION

407 F.3d 125 (2d Cir. 2005)

■ OAKES, Senior Circuit Judge.

Defendant-appellant tobacco companies appeal from the . . . order of the United States District Court for the Eastern District of New York, Jack B. Weinstein, Judge, which certified a nationwide non-opt-out class of smokers seeking only punitive damages under state law for defendants' alleged fraudulent denial and concealment of the health risks posed by cigarettes. Having granted permission to appeal pursuant to Federal Rule of Civil Procedure 23(f), we must decide whether the district court properly certified this class under Rule 23(b)(1)(B).

Defendant-appellants challenge the propriety of certifying this action as a limited fund class action pursuant to a "limited punishment" theory. The theory postulates that a constitutional limit on the total punitive damages that may be imposed for a course of fraudulent conduct effectively limits the total fund available for punitive awards.

We hold that the order certifying this punitive damages class must be vacated because there is no evidence by which the district court could ascertain the limits of either the fund or the aggregate value of punitive claims against it, such that the postulated fund could be deemed inadequate to pay all legitimate claims, and thus plaintiffs have failed to satisfy one of the presumptively necessary conditions for limited fund treatment under *Ortiz v. Fibreboard Corp.*, 527 U.S. 815 (1999) [*infra* p. 506]. . . .

I. FACTS AND PROCEDURAL HISTORY

. . .

The industry conspiracy prompting this litigation is described briefly in the allegations of the Third Amended Complaint and in considerable detail in the Certification Order. We will simply excerpt a relevant portion of the district court's description of the allegations:

> Plaintiffs allege, and can provide supporting evidence, that, beginning with a clandestine meeting in December 1953 at the Plaza Hotel in New York City among the presidents of Philip Morris, R.J. Reynolds, American Tobacco, Brown & Williamson, Lorillard and U.S. Tobacco, tobacco companies embarked on a systematic, half-century long scheme to . . .: (a) stop competing with each other in making or developing less harmful cigarettes; (b) continue knowingly and willfully to engage in misrepresentations and deceptive acts by, among other things, denying knowledge that cigarettes caused disease and death and agreeing not to disseminate harmful information showing the destructive effects of nicotine and tobacco consumption; (c) shut down research efforts and suppress medical information that appeared to be adverse to the Tobacco Companies' position that tobacco was not harmful; (d) not compete with respect to making any claims relating to the relative health-superiority of specific tobacco products; and (e) to confuse the public about, and otherwise distort, whatever accurate information about the harmful effects of their products became known despite their "[efforts to conceal such information.]" . . .

. . . [T]he district court certified a punitive damages non-opt-out class pursuant to Rule 23(b)(1)(B). The class definition included current and former smokers of defendants' cigarettes who are U.S. residents, or who resided in the U.S. at time of death, and were first diagnosed between April 9, 1993, and the date of dissemination of class notice, with one or more of the following diseases: lung cancer, laryngeal cancer, lip cancer, tongue cancer, mouth cancer, esophageal cancer, kidney cancer, pancreatic cancer, bladder cancer, ischemic heart disease, cerebrovascular heart disease, aortic aneurysm, peripheral vascular disease, emphysema, chronic bronchitis, or chronic obstructive pulmonary disease. . . .

The district court determined that the class action would proceed in three stages. In the first stage, a jury would make a class-wide determination of liability and estimated total value of national undifferentiated compensatory harm to all members of the class. The sum of compensatory harm would not be awarded but will serve as a predicate in determining non-opt-out class punitive damages. The same jury would determine compensatory awards, if any, for individual class representatives, although the class itself did not seek compensatory damages. In the second stage, the same jury would determine whether defendants engaged in conduct that warrants punitive damages. In the third stage, the same jury would determine the amount of punitive damages for the class and decide how to allocate damages on a disease-by-disease basis. The court would then distribute sums to the class on a pro-rata basis by disease to class members who submit appropriate proof. Any portion not distributed to class members would be allocated by the court on a cy pres basis to treatment and research organizations working in the field of each disease on advice of experts in the fields. The order specified that the jury would apply New

York law according to conflicts of laws principles, and reiterated that the court was not presented with and did not rule upon a compensatory class. The district court noted that although plaintiffs chose the more limited course in pursuing a punitive class only, certification "for determination of compensatory damages to be distributed using an appropriate matrix would be possible and might be desirable in coordination with the class now certified."

II. DISCUSSION

. . .

We review the district court's order granting class certification for abuse of discretion . . .

We note that this case raises issues of first impression insofar as this Circuit has never squarely passed on the validity of certifying a mandatory, stand-alone punitive damages class on the proposed "limited punishment" theory. . . .

The district court found that the proposed class satisfied the Rule 23(a) requirements of numerosity, commonality, typicality, and adequacy of representation. Appellants do not contest these particular findings. Rather, they direct their arguments to the district court's conclusion that this class action could be maintained under Rule 23(b)(1)(B). . . .

The district court, in certifying the punitive damages class under Rule 23(b)(1)(B), cited recent scholarship and court decisions that have concluded that the theory of limited punishment supports a punitive damages class action. "Under this theory," the district court stated, "the limited fund involved would be the constitutional cap on punitive damages, set forth in BMW v. Gore[, 517 U.S. 559 (1996),] and related cases."

The premise for this theory is that there is a constitutional due process limitation on the total amount of punitive damages that may be assessed against a defendant for the same offending conduct. . . .

Despite the long-recognized possibility that defendants may be subjected to large aggregate sums of punitive damages if large numbers of victims succeed in their individual punitive damages claims, the United States Supreme Court has not addressed whether successive individual or class action punitive awards, each passing constitutional muster under the relevant precedents, could reach a level beyond which punitive damages may no longer be awarded. . . .

This brings us to appellants' chief argument — that class certification under Rule 23(b)(1)(B) is precluded by the Supreme Court's decision in *Ortiz v. Fibreboard Corp.*, 527 U.S. 815 (1999), because the proposed class plaintiffs have failed to demonstrate what the Supreme Court identified as the "presumptively necessary" conditions for certification in limited fund cases. [One of those conditions a fund "with a definitely ascertained limit." *Id.* at 838.] . . .

The proposed fund in this case, the constitutional "cap" on punitive damages for the given class's claims, is a theoretical one, unlike any of those in the cases cited in *Ortiz*, where the fund was either an existing res or the total of defendants' assets available to satisfy claims. The fund here is — in essence — postulated, and for that reason it is not easily susceptible to proof, definition, or even estimation, by any precise figure. It is therefore fundamentally unlike the classic limited funds of the historical antecedents of Rule 23.

Not only is the upper limit of the proposed fund difficult to ascertain, but the record in this case does not evince a likelihood that any given number of punitive awards to individual claimants would be constitutionally excessive, either individually or in the aggregate, and thus overwhelm the available fund.

Without evidence indicating either the upper limit or the insufficiency of the posited fund, class plaintiffs cannot demonstrate that individual plaintiffs would be prejudiced if left to pursue separate actions without having their interests represented in this suit, as Rule 23(b)(1)(B) would require. . . .

The proposed class having failed to satisfy the threshold requirements for certification set forth in *Ortiz* and Rule 23(b)(1)(B), we must vacate the district court's certification order and remand for further proceedings.

Notes

1.   Other courts have followed *Simon II* in holding that class-wide punitive damage awards are improper if the plaintiff class has not proved all of the elements needed to establish its entitlement to compensatory damages. *See, e.g.,* Engle v. Liggett Group, Inc., 945 So. 2d 1246 (Fla. 2006) (*infra* p. 483).

2.   The "limited generosity" theory as a justification for a mandatory class action of punitive damage claims may have suffered a fatal blow in *Philip Morris USA v. Williams*, 549 U.S. 346 (2007). *Philip Morris* held that the Due Process Clause requires that the defendant not be punished for harm caused to anyone other than the plaintiff before the court. While the Court did not directly address the effect of this requirement on class actions, the logic of its holding strikes at the heart of the "limited generosity" theory. *See* Laura J. Hines, *Due Process Limitations on Punitive Damages: Why* State Farm *Won't Be the Last Word*, 37 AKRON L. REV. 779, 811 (2004) ("If every mass tort punitive damage award is properly and constitutionally calculated to punish only the harm to a particular plaintiff, then it would seem every mass tort plaintiff could recover punitive damage awards for the same conduct — because prior plaintiffs would only have been awarded punitive damages based on their own harm."). Professor Stier argues that *Philip Morris* strengthens the "due process argument against certification of mass tort punitive damage class actions where injuries or liability issues are not uniform throughout the class."

Byron G. Stier, *Now It's Personal: Punishment and Mass Tort Litigation After* Philip Morris v. Williams, 2 CHARLESTON L. REV. 433, 434-35 (2008). He adds that after *Philip Morris* there is no longer a risk that individual trials will result in multiple punishment of the defendant for the same harm. *Id.* at 457-58. *Compare* Aileen L. Nagy, Note, *Certifying Mandatory Punitive Damage Classes in a Post-*Ortiz *and* State Farm *World*, 58 VAND. L. REV. 599, 624 (2005) ("While the certification of mandatory punitive damage classes may not be reconcilable with current legal precedent, utility and fairness suggest a need for the availability of such certification.").

3. Although his proposal turned out to have been unneeded in light of the court of appeals' decision, you might have noticed Judge Weinstein's creative method to determine the size of the punitive-damage fund. We examine this approach in detail in Chapter Eight. *See infra* p. 971.

4. Assuming that the limited-punishment theory or the limited-fund theory for punitive damages retains any viability, note that the class action is certified only on one issue — that of punitive damages. Insofar as the plaintiffs' compensatory claims are concerned, they must be asserted on an individual basis, or a court must find some other vehicle for aggregating them. (For instance, recall that, in *Telectronics* (*supra* p. 388), the court certified Rule 23(b)(3) classes for the compensatory theories of recovery.) It is possible to certify a class action "with respect to particular issues." Fed. R. Civ. P. 23(c)(4). Certifying a class just on certain issues raises interesting questions. An important legal question is whether the class members face claim-preclusive consequences when they assert only the punitive-damages theory, given that their compensatory-damage theory arises from the same transaction or occurrence and that plaintiffs cannot usually split claims under the rules of claim preclusion. Moreover, if claim preclusion occurs, can the class representatives in *Simon* be regarded as adequate when they abandon important and valuable individual claims of class members? We examine these issues *infra* p. 525.

If no preclusive consequences attach, a second, more practical question is what aggregative benefits come from deciding just one theory, given that separate lawsuits will still be needed to decide remaining issues. One part of the answer is that these later suits no longer need to deal with the punitive-damage claims in case afer case. But the real answer, which is not found in Rule 23 but which everyone knew, is that, after an appropriate period of discovery and after much saber-rattling on both sides, a class action of *Simon*'s size would almost inevitably have settled for some large figure. As part of the settlement, the defendants would have undoubtedly insisted on a release of all claims by class members, including claims for compensatory damages. To get the case to the point at which such a global settlement can be worked out, though, some vehicle — in *Simon*, the punitive-damages theory — is needed to hold everyone together.

Does this reality — the promise of ending all tobacco litigation in the United States in one fell swoop — make you think better or worse of the result in *Simon*?

5.   To beat this drum one last time, how could any class representative or group of representatives adequately represent the entire class in *Simon* if the amount of punitive damages was indeed limited (either by law or by the amount of the defendants' assets)?   Under *Simon's* theory, the class members who filed their cases early and who would therefore get the lion's share of any punitive-damage awards would be required to share a part of their awards with late-filing claimants, who would have received nothing in individual litigation but who now received a pro rata share of the recovery.   Isn't there a conflict of interest within the meaning of *Hansberry v. Lee* and Rules 23(a)(3) and -(a)(4)?   How can one person or group of people represent the conflicting interests?   Why did the defendants in *Simon* concede typicality and adequacy?   Do *Hansberry* and Rule 23(a) mean that an impermissible conflict exists only when the class members' interests diverge with regard to the legal theory, as opposed to the outcome that class members can derive from that common theory?   If so, what is the point of Rule 23(a)(4)?

(B)   (b)(2) Class Actions

Rule 23, the modern class-action rule was promulgated in 1966, just two years after passage of the landmark Civil Rights Act of 1964.   Although it seems redundant of Rule 23(b)(1)(A), Rule 23(b)(2) was drafted to ensure that class actions would be available to remedy the effects of race and other forms of discrimination.   Often called the "equitable class action rule," Rule 23(b)(2) requires that the party opposing the class have acted in a way that justifies injunctive or declaratory relief for the class as a whole.   While the Advisory Committee Notes make clear that Rule 23(b)(2) was not limited to civil-rights cases, many of the class actions certified under this section were of a civil-rights or public-law stripe.   The Advisory Committee Notes also included a curious sentence that has formed much of the subsequent debate about Rule 23(b)(2): "The subdivision does not extend to cases in which the appropriate final relief relates exclusively or predominantly to money damages."   Did the Advisory Committee therefore contemplate that (b)(2) class actions could be used to award some (i.e., non-predominant) monetary relief on a non-opt-out basis?

ROBINSON V. METRO-NORTH COMMUTER RAILROAD CO.

267 F. 3d 147 (2d Cir. 2001)

■ WALKER, Chief Judge.

Plaintiffs-appellants (the "Class Plaintiffs") appeal from a September 29, 2000 judgment of the United States District Court for the Southern District of New York . . . that denied Class Plaintiffs' motions for class certification and bifurcation, and that directed entry of judgment in favor of defendant-appellee Metro-North Commuter Railroad ("Metro-North").

The district court's judgment dismissing the action is vacated. On remand, the district court is instructed to certify the Class Plaintiffs' disparate impact claim for Rule 23(b)(2) class treatment, and consider whether the pattern-or-practice disparate treatment claim is appropriate for (b)(2) certification in light of the standard we set forth herein. If the court determines that (b)(2) certification of the pattern-or-practice claim is inappropriate, it shall bifurcate the claim, *see* Fed. Civ. P. 42(b), and certify the liability stage of the claim for (b)(2) class treatment, *see* Fed. R. Civ. P. 23(c)(4)(A).

BACKGROUND

. . .

The Class Plaintiffs are present and former Metro-North employees who are African American. They bring this putative class action against defendant Metro-North on behalf of all African-American employees of Metro-North for the period from 1985 through 1996 — an estimated 1,300 persons. Metro-North is a public benefit corporation responsible for providing commuter rail transportation between New York City and its northern suburbs. It has approximately 5,700 employees in 220 different occupations spread over 37 departments.

The Class Plaintiffs assert both pattern-or-practice disparate treatment and disparate impact claims pursuant to Title VII of the Civil Rights Act of 1964, as amended, 42 U.S.C. § 2000e et seq. Specifically, they challenge Metro-North's company-wide policy of delegating to department supervisors discretionary authority to make employment decisions related to discipline and promotion. Relying on statistical and anecdotal evidence, the Class Plaintiffs argue that this delegated authority has been exercised in a racially discriminatory manner and has a disparate impact on African-American employees. In their prayer for relief, the Class Plaintiffs seek injunctive and equitable relief for the class as a whole, including back and front pay, and also compensatory damages for individual members of the class who were allegedly the victims of individual acts of intentional discrimination. No request for punitive damages was made. . . .

. . . [T]he Class Plaintiffs moved in the district court for (b)(2) class certifications of both the pattern-or-practice disparate treatment claim and the disparate impact claim. As an alternative to class certification of the pattern-or-practice claim in its entirety, Class Plaintiffs sought bifurcation of the claim between the liability and remedial stages, and (b)(2) class certification of just the liability stage. *See* Fed. R. Civ. P. 23(c)(4)(A) [now Fed. R. Civ. P. 23(c)(4) — ED.] (permitting class certification of "particular issues").

The district court denied the motions. Relying on the Fifth Circuit's recent decision in *Allison v. Citgo Petroleum Corp.*, 151 F.3d 402, 415 (5th Cir. 1998), the district court reasoned that (b)(2) certification of the entire pattern-or-practice disparate treatment claim was inappropriate because the individualized compensatory damage issues would predominate over the class-wide equitable relief question. Central to the district court's conclusion was its belief that

> determination of the damages suffered by individual members of the class would require individualized proof and proceedings to determine whether each such member suffered intentional discrimination on the part of his or her department manager, what injuries each such member thereby suffered, what individualized damages were appropriate to redress such injuries, etc. . . . [The] multiple individual determinations of damages for the numerous members of the class, the district court concluded, would overwhelm class[-]wide injunctive issues, from both the standpoint of the individual plaintiffs and the standpoint of the Court.

With respect to the Class Plaintiffs' alternative request that the pattern-or-practice claim be bifurcated and the liability stage certified for class treatment as a (b)(2) class, the district court reasoned that the individual determinations will overwhelm the liability phase of any trial nearly as much as they would overwhelm any damages phase, once again rendering class action treatment inappropriate under Rule 23(b)(2). The district court based this conclusion on its belief that the liability phase would require an individualized determination of each of the allegedly discriminatory acts of particular department managers in particular individual situations.

The district court did not set forth a basis for denying (b)(2) certification of the disparate impact claim. . . .

DISCUSSION

At the outset, we observe that this appeal does not involve consideration of the merits of the case. Rather, it concerns whether the district court abused its discretion in denying class certification. And, in particular, it requires us to consider how the passage of the Civil Rights Act of 1991 ("the 1991 Act"), affected the class certification analysis in employee discrimination cases. As we discuss below, contrary to both Metro-North's arguments on appeal and the Fifth Circuit's recent decision in *Allison*, we find that the changes made by the 1991 Act are not fatal to class treatment of employment discrimination claims.

To understand why, it is first necessary to consider the changes brought about by the 1991 Act. . . .

I.   THE 1991 ACT AND TITLE VII CLAIMS GENERALLY

A.   *The 1991 Act*

Prior to the passage of the 1991 Act, a plaintiff seeking a monetary award for disparate treatment and disparate impact claims under Title VII could recover only back pay and front pay. Because back pay and front pay have historically been recognized as equitable relief under Title VII, neither party was entitled to a jury trial; both disparate treatment and disparate impact claims were tried to the bench.

The 1991 Act enhanced Title VII's remedial scheme for disparate treatment claims. In addition to back pay and front pay, it authorized the recovery of compensatory and punitive damages in disparate treatment disputes, and afforded a jury trial where these additional remedies are sought. The 1991 Act did not alter the remedial structure for disparate impact claims.

B. *Proving Title VII Claims*

1. *Pattern-or-Practice Disparate Treatment Claims*

Pattern-or-practice disparate treatment claims focus on allegations of widespread acts of intentional discrimination against individuals. To succeed on a pattern-or-practice claim, plaintiffs must prove more than sporadic acts of discrimination; rather, they must establish that intentional discrimination was the defendant's standard operating procedure.

Generally, a pattern-or-practice suit is divided into two phases: liability and remedial. At the liability stage, the plaintiffs must produce sufficient evidence to establish a prima facie case of a policy, pattern, or practice of intentional discrimination against the protected group. Plaintiffs have typically depended upon two kinds of circumstantial evidence to establish the existence of a policy, pattern, or practice of intentional discrimination: (1) statistical evidence aimed at establishing the defendant's past treatment of the protected group, and (2) testimony from protected class members detailing specific instances of discrimination.

Statistics alone can make out a prima facie case of discrimination if the statistics reveal "a gross disparity in [the] treatment of workers based on race." . . .

If individual relief such as back pay, front pay, or compensatory recovery is sought in addition to class-wide injunctive relief, the court must conduct the "remedial" phase. Class members enter this second phase with a presumption in their favor that any particular employment decision, during the period in which the discriminatory policy was in force, was made in pursuit of that policy.

The effect of the presumption from the liability stage is to substantially lessen each class member's evidentiary burden relative to that which would be required if the employee were proceeding separately with an individual disparate treatment claim . . . . Rather than having to make out a prima facie case of discrimination and prove that the employer's asserted business justification is merely a pretext for discrimination, a class member at the remedial stage of a pattern-or-practice claim need only show that he or she suffered an adverse employment decision "and therefore was a potential victim of the proved [class-wide] discrimination." The burden of persuasion then shifts to "the employer to demonstrate that the individual [was subjected to the adverse employment decision] for lawful reasons."

If the employer is unable to establish a lawful reason for an adverse employment action, the employee is entitled to individualized equitable relief, which may include back pay and front pay. Class members who seek compensatory damages in addition to individualized equitable relief must then prove that the discrimination caused them "emotional pain, suffering, inconvenience, mental anguish, loss of enjoyment of life, [or] other nonpecuniary losses." 42 U.S.C. § 1981a(b)(3).

2. *Disparate Impact Claims*

Like pattern-or-practice disparate treatment claims, disparate impact claims "are attacks on the systemic results of employment practices." However, where the inquiry in a pattern-or-practice disparate treatment claim is focused on determining the existence of discriminatory intent, disparate impact claims are concerned with whether employment policies or practices that are neutral on their face and were not intended to discriminate have nevertheless had a disparate effect on the protected group. "The doctrine seeks the removal of employment obstacles, not required by business necessity, which create built-in headwinds and freeze out protected groups from job opportunities and advancement." . . .

As with the liability phase of a pattern-or-practice disparate treatment claim, statistical proof almost always occupies center stage in a prima facie showing of a disparate impact claim. . . .

Should the plaintiffs succeed in establishing a Title VII disparate impact violation, the court may order prospective class-wide injunctive relief. Still, in order for an employee to obtain individual relief (e.g., back or front pay), an inquiry similar to the remedial stage of a pattern-or-practice disparate treatment claim is generally required.[6] Each class member must show that he or she was among those adversely affected by the challenged policy or practice. If this showing is made, the class member is entitled to individual relief unless the employer in turn can establish by a preponderance of the evidence that a legitimate non-discriminatory reason existed for the particular adverse action. . . .

III. CERTIFICATION OF THE PATTERN-OR-PRACTICE CLAIM

With respect to the district court's denial of class certification of the pattern-or-practice disparate treatment claim, the Class Plaintiffs argue that the court abused its discretion (1) by applying an erroneous standard to decide whether to certify the claim under Rule 23(b)(2) or, alternatively,

---

6.   Both parties correctly note that some cases may require class-wide, rather than individualized, assessments of monetary relief. However, as Metro-North argues, this is the exception, not the rule: Where possible, "there should be . . . a determination on an individual basis as to which class members are entitled to [recovery] and the amount of such recovery."

(2) in failing to sever and certify under Rule 23(b)(2) at least the liability phase of the claim.[7]

A. *Claim Certification*

The Class Plaintiffs contend that the district court utilized an unduly stringent standard in refusing (b)(2) certification of the pattern-or-practice claim. We agree.

1. *Standards for Assessing Predominance: A Bright-line or Ad Hoc Approach?*

The (b)(2) class action is intended for cases where broad, class-wide injunctive or declaratory relief is necessary to redress a group-wide injury. The text of Rule 23(b)(2) is silent as to what extent — if at all — monetary relief may also be sought. The advisory committee's note to Rule 23 contemplates (b)(2) class certification of at least some claims for monetary recovery:

> . . . The subdivision does not extend to cases in which the appropriate final relief relates exclusively or *predominantly* to money damages. (Emphasis added)

To date, our circuit precedent has provided no guidance to lower courts faced with assessing whether "final relief relates . . . predominantly to money damages" to preclude (b)(2) class treatment. Without a clear standard discernible from either the text of Rule 23(b)(2) or our circuit precedent, the district court applied a standard recently set forth by the Fifth Circuit in *Allison*, 151 F.3d at 410. This standard, the incidental damages approach, provides that:

> In any such action in which both injunctive and monetary relief [are] sought, the inherently individualized nature of the determination of damages . . . render[s] it predominant, and thereby makes class action status under Rule 23(b)(2) inappropriate, except in those rare incidences in which the request for monetary relief [is] wholly "incidental" to the requested injunctive relief. : . .

Robinson [v. Metro-N. Commuter R.R., 197 F.R.D. 85, 87 (S.D.N.Y. 2000)]. The district court went on to state that incidental damages

> should at least be capable of computation by means of objective standards and not dependent in any significant way on the intangible,

---

7. *See generally* 1 Herbert B. Newberg & Alba Conte, Newberg on Class Actions § 4.14, at 4-51 to 4-52 (3d ed. 1992) (noting four alternatives utilized by courts in Rule 23(b)(2) class actions seeking injunctive relief coupled with individual damage claims: (1) limit certification to certain issues; (2) certify the claims for injunctive relief under Rule 23(b)(2) and the damages claims under Rule 23(b)(3); certify the entire class under Rule 23(b)(2) and reconsider the certification category if the class is successful at the liability stage; and (4) certify certain issues and treat other issues as incidental ones to be determined separately after liability to the class has been resolved).

subjective differences of each class member's circumstances. Liability for incidental damages should not require additional hearings to resolve the disparate merits of each individual's case; it should neither introduce new and substantial legal or factual issues, nor entail complex individualized determinations.

Id. at 88 (quoting *Allison*, 151 F.3d at 415).

By limiting (b)(2) certification to claims involving no more than incidental damages, the standard utilized by the district court forecloses (b)(2) class certification of all claims that include compensatory damages (or punitive damages) even if the class-wide injunctive relief is the "form of relief in which the plaintiffs are primarily interested." This bright-line prohibition follows from the fact that "the very nature of [compensatory] damages, compensating plaintiffs for emotional and other intangible injuries, necessarily implicates the subjective differences of each plaintiff's circumstances . . . ." *Allison*, 151 F.3d at 417. By definition, however, incidental damages must be susceptible to "computation by means of objective standards and not dependent in any significant way on the [class members'] intangible, subjective differences," which compensatory damages clearly are.

Thus, the question we must decide is whether this bright-line bar to (b)(2) class treatment of all claims for compensatory damages and other non-incidental damages (e.g., punitive damages) is appropriate. For the reasons we discuss below, we believe that it is not and therefore decline to adopt the incidental damages approach set out by the Fifth Circuit in *Allison* and followed by the district court below. Rather, we hold that when presented with a motion for (b)(2) class certification of a claim seeking both injunctive relief and non-incidental monetary damages, a district court must "consider[ ] the evidence presented at a class certification hearing and the arguments of counsel," and then assess whether (b)(2) certification is appropriate in light of "the relative importance of the remedies sought, given all of the facts and circumstances of the case." The district court may allow (b)(2) certification if it finds in its "informed, sound judicial discretion" that (1) "the positive weight or value [to the plaintiffs] of the injunctive or declaratory relief sought is predominant even though compensatory or punitive damages are also claimed," and (2) class treatment would be efficient and manageable, thereby achieving an appreciable measure of judicial economy.

Although the assessment of whether injunctive or declaratory relief predominates will require an ad hoc balancing that will vary from case to case, before allowing (b)(2) certification a district court should, at a minimum, satisfy itself of the following: (1) even in the absence of a possible monetary recovery, reasonable plaintiffs would bring the suit to obtain the injunctive or declaratory relief sought; and (2) the injunctive or declaratory relief sought would be both reasonably necessary and appropriate were the plaintiffs to succeed on the merits. Insignificant or sham requests for injunctive relief should not provide cover for (b)(2) certification of claims that are brought essentially for monetary recovery.

2.   *Considerations Supporting the Ad Hoc Approach*

Several considerations inform our decision to adopt this ad hoc approach over the incidental damages standard with its absolute bar to claims seeking compensatory and punitive damages.

Foremost among these is the fact that Rule 23 has historically been understood to vest district courts with the authority to determine whether, in their informed discretion, based on the particulars of the case, the certification prerequisites have been satisfied. We see no basis for the imposition of a bright-line rule such as the incidental damages standard that would plainly nullify the district court's legislatively granted . . . discretion in making certification determinations.

Additionally, we find that an ad hoc approach satisfies the very concerns that have led other courts to adopt the incidental damages standard — specifically, (1) achieving judicial efficiency, and (2) ensuring due process for absent class members. With respect to the former concern, permitting district courts to assess issues of judicial economy and class manageability on a case-by-case basis is superior to the one-size-fits-all approach of the incidental damages standard. As for the latter concern, as we discuss below, options other than the adoption of the incidental damages approach exist to eradicate the due process risks posed by (b)(2) class certification of claims for damages.

Where class-wide injunctive or declaratory relief is sought in a (b)(2) class action for an alleged group harm, there is a presumption of cohesion and unity between absent class members and the class representatives such that adequate representation will generally safeguard absent class members' interests and thereby satisfy the strictures of due process. This presumption of cohesion and unity continues where incidental damages are also sought because entitlement to such damages does not vary based on the subjective considerations of each class member's claim, but "flow[s] directly from a finding of liability on the . . . claims for class-wide injunctive and declaratory relief."

In contrast, where non-incidental monetary relief such as compensatory damages are involved, due process may require the enhanced procedural protections of notice and opt out for absent class members. This is because entitlement to non-incidental damages may vary among class members depending on the circumstances and merits of each claim. The presumption of class homogeneity and cohesion falters, and thus, adequate representation alone may prove insufficient to protect absent class members interests. Absent class members may therefore need notice that their claims are being pursued in the class action and the opportunity either to opt out and pursue their claims separately or to intervene, should they conclude such active participation would better protect their individual interests.

However, certification of a claim for non-incidental damages under Rule 23(b)(2) poses a due process risk because this provision does not expressly afford the procedural protections of notice and opt out. The bright-line prohibition of (b)(2) class treatment for claims seeking nonincidental damages eliminates this risk. It ensures that claims presenting individual specific damage issues that might require heightened due process protections are not certified under (b)(2). But, any due process risk posed by (b)(2) class certification of a claim for non-incidental damages can be eliminated by the district court simply affording notice and opt out rights to absent class members for those portions of the proceedings where the presumption of class cohesion falters — i.e., the damages phase of the proceedings. . . .

To recap, we hold that the district court erred in applying the incidental damages standard to deny the Class Plaintiffs' request for (b)(2) certification of the pattern-or-practice disparate treatment claim. . . . However, because we recognize that, even under the discretionary standard we endorse, the district court may still conclude that (b)(2) certification of the entire pattern-or-practice disparate treatment claim is inappropriate, we turn to consider the Class Plaintiffs' alternate contention that the district court erred in denying partial certification of the claim.

B. *Partial Certification*

The Class Plaintiffs argue that the district court erred in refusing to bifurcate the pattern-or-practice claim and certify the liability stage of the claim for (b)(2) class treatment. *See* Fed. R. Civ. P. 23(c)(4). We agree.

Rule 23(c)(4)(A) [now Fed. R. Civ. P. 23(c)(4) — ED.] provides that "an action may be brought or maintained as a class action with respect to particular issues." District courts should "'take full advantage of this provision' to certify separate issues in order . . . 'to reduce the range of disputed issues' in complex litigation" and achieve judicial efficiencies.

Here, litigating the pattern-or-practice liability phase for the class as a whole would both reduce the range of issues in dispute and promote judicial economy. For example, if the class should succeed and, even assuming that the remedial stage is ultimately resolved on a non-class basis, the issues and evidence relevant to these individual adjudications would be substantially narrowed. . . . If, on the other hand, Metro-North succeeds at the liability stage, the question of whether it engaged in a pattern or practice of intentional discrimination that injured its African-American employees would be completely and finally determined, thereby eliminating entirely the need for a remedial stage inquiry on behalf of each class member. . . .

. . . [T]he liability phase is largely preoccupied with class-wide statistical evidence directed at establishing an overall pattern or practice of intentional discrimination. To the extent that evidence regarding specific instances of alleged discrimination is relevant during the liability stage, it simply provides "texture" to the statistics. Such anecdotal evidence is not introduced to establish that the particular instances of discrimination actually occurred nor that the particular employees were in fact victims of discrimination. Indeed, to ensure that the liability phase remains manageable, the district court may limit the anecdotal evidence as it deems appropriate.

Accordingly, we hold that the district court abused its discretion in not certifying the liability stage of the pattern-or-practice disparate treatment claim for (b)(2) class treatment.

IV. CERTIFICATION OF THE DISPARATE IMPACT CLAIM

The Class Plaintiffs contend that the district court abused its discretion in declining to certify the disparate impact claim for (b)(2) class treatment. Here again, we agree.

In considering the propriety of the district court's decision to deny (b)(2) certification, we are mindful that, prior to the enactment of the Civil Rights Act of 1991, Title VII discrimination claims seeking both injunctive and equitable monetary relief, like the disparate impact claim here, were routinely certified as (b)(2) classes.

Given that the 1991 Act did not alter the general remedial structure of disparate impact claims, we think it plain that (b)(2) certification of disparate impact claims seeking both injunctive and equitable monetary relief remains appropriate. . . .

[The Second Circuit then rejected Metro-North's argument that the proposed certification of a disparate-impact class would violate the Seventh Amendment jury-trial guarantee. On this issue, see *infra* p. 480, Note 8.]

CONCLUSION

We vacate the district court's judgment dismissing the Class Plaintiffs' suit. The district court is instructed to certify the disparate impact claim under Rule 23(b)(2). The district court is also instructed to reconsider the propriety of certifying the entire pattern-or-practice disparate treatment claim in light of the standard set out herein. If the court determines in its discretion that (b)(2) certification of the entire claim is still inappropriate, then the district court shall bifurcate the pattern-or-practice claim and certify the liability stage under Rule 23(b)(2).

Notes

1.   The lower federal courts remain divided on whether to follow the *Robinson* or the *Allison* approach in Title VII litigation and in other kinds of cases in which plaintiffs are seeking compensatory damages under Rule 23(b)(2) in addition to injunction relief. Several circuits have directly or indirectly adopted the *Robinson* approach. For instance, in *Molski v. Gleich*, 318 F.3d 937, 950 (9th Cir. 2003), the Ninth Circuit refused to adopt the *Allison* approach, asserting it would "have troubling implications for the viability of future civil rights actions" and urging courts to consider "the intent of the plaintiffs in bringing the suit." Ultimately, however, *Molski*

found that the actual and treble damage sought by the plaintiffs were not incidental and held the district court erred in not affording class members notice and opt-out rights. *Accord* Dukes v. Wal-Mart, Inc., 509 F.3d 1168, 1186-88 (9th Cir. 2007), *reh'g en banc granted*, 556 F.3d 919 (9th Cir. 2009) (approving certification under Rule 23(b)(2) of a large class alleging sex discrimination and seeking an injunction, compensatory damages, and punitive damages; court looked to whether the plaintiffs' "primary goal in bringing this action is to obtain injunctive relief").

Other circuits have followed *Allison*. In *Coleman v. General Motors Acceptance Corp.*, 296 F. 3d 443, 447-50 (6th Cir. 2002), the Sixth Circuit held that Equal Credit Opportunity Act plaintiffs seeking compensatory damages cannot seek class certification under 23(b)(2) because the request for damages necessarily predominates over any requested injunctive or declaratory relief. In a later Title VII action, the Sixth Circuit went beyond *Allison* by adopting a per se rule that individual compensatory damages are never recoverable by a (b)(2) class. Reeb v. Ohio Dep't of Rehab. & Corr., 435 F.3d 639, 651 (6th Cir. 2006). *Accord* Lemon v. Int'l Union of Operating Eng'rs, 216 F.3d 577, 580-81 (7th Cir. 2000) (holding that requested monetary damages were not incidental to equitable relief although also recognizing partial certification as an available option). The Eleventh Circuit has also embraced the *Allison* approach. Murray v. Auslander, 244 F.3d 807, 812 (11th Cir. 2001) (holding that, due to the individual nature of compensatory or punitive damage awards, cases seeking such awards are not appropriate for (b)(2) certification); Cooper v. S. Co., 390 F.3d 695, 720-21 (11th Cir. 2004) (noting the *Murray* decision conclusively established the *Allison* incidental-damage standard as the law of the circuit).

2.   The Fifth Circuit itself, however, seems to have backed off from the bright-line approach of *Allison* in cases in which the calculation of damages is merely a "mechanical task." In re Monumental Life Ins. Co., 365 F.3d 408, 419 (5th Cir. 2004) (class alleged discrimination in amounts blacks and whites paid for the same policy). The plaintiffs in *Monumental* proposed using "standardized formulas or restitution grids" to calculate each class member's damages; the Fifth Circuit reversed the district court's denial of class certification, finding the "damage calculation should neither introduce new and substantial legal or factual issues, nor entail complex individualized determinations." *Id.* at 415.

3.   Commentators remain divided on the issue of *Robinson* and *Allison*. *Compare* W. Lyle Stamps, *Getting Title VII Back on Track: Leaving* Allison *Behind for the* Robinson *Line*, 17 BYU J. PUB. L. 411 (2003) (arguing that *Robinson* best meets the goals of Title VII and *Allison* would cripple private enforcement of the statute), *with* Jeffrey H. Dasteel & Ronda McKaig, *What's Money Got to Do With It? How Subjective, Ad Hoc Standards for Permitting Money Damages in Rule 23(b)(2) Injunctive Relief Classes Undermine Rule 23's Analytical Framework*, 80 TUL. L. REV. 1881 (2006) (advocating use of Rule 23(b)(3) for treatment of non-incidental damages).

4.   As *Metro-North* shows, the failure to obtain class certification under (b)(2) is not necessarily the end of the line; a hybrid (b)(2)-(b)(3) class action

might still be possible. Although *Allison* refused to certify a (b)(3) class for the claims of individual damages, other Title VII suits have used (b)(3) to deal with monetary claims. *See* Diaz v. Hillsborough County Hosp. Auth., 165 F.R.D. 689 (M.D. Fla. 1996) (certifying a (b)(2) class for injunctive relief sought on behalf of pregnant women allegedly subjected to non-consensual medical experimentation and a (b)(3) class for related damage claims). Should resort to (b)(3) be automatic in these cases? *See* George Rutherglen, *Notice, Scope, and Preclusion in Title VII Class Actions,* 69 VA. L. REV. 11, 27-28 (1983) (arguing that civil rights actions should be bifurcated into (b)(2) and (b)(3) class actions). *Cf.* Air Line Stewards & Stewardesses Ass'n, Local 550 v. Am. Airlines, Inc., 490 F.2d 636 (7th Cir. 1973) (affording employees in a Title VII sex discrimination case the right to opt out if they disagreed with the type of relief granted).

5.   *Metro-North* skirts the issue whether the Due Process Clause requires notice and an opportunity to opt out before the monetary claims of absent class members are adjudicated in a preclusive fashion. We discuss this issue more fully in the following subsection.

6.   Civil-rights actions seeking only injunctive relief are routinely filed by individuals on behalf of proposed classes. What advantage is there in suing as a class? For instance, if an individual plaintiff obtains an injunction forbidding sex discrimination in hiring, won't others be able to rely on this injunction? Why would an individual go through all the hassles and delays of class certification? Indeed, on occasion courts have held that it is not necessary to certify a (b)(2) class action because the injunction sought by the individual plaintiff will inure to the benefit of the entire putative class anyway. *See, e.g.,* Galvan v. Levine, 490 F.2d 1255 (2d Cir. 1973). The majority of courts, however, have held that, unless a class action is certified, an injunction only protects the individual plaintiffs; thus a class action is appropriate and useful. *See* Zepeda v. INS, 753 F.2d 719 (9th Cir. 1985); McKinnon v. Patterson, 568 F.2d 930 (2d Cir. 1977). Moreover, certification as a (b)(2) class can avoid dismissal of the case when the named plaintiff's claim becomes moot or the named plaintiff is found to be an unsatisfactory class representative. *See* E. Tex. Motor Freight Sys., Inc. v. Rodriguez, 431 U.S. 395 (1977); Pasadena City Bd. of Educ. v. Spangler, 427 U.S. 424 (1976). Granting these facts to be true, why is it in the interest of the individual plaintiff to seek class certification? Is it because a class action will increase the likelihood of a favorable settlement? Is it because many civil-rights class actions are brought by advocacy organizations whose interests extend beyond the individual plaintiff? If you are a lawyer employed or retained by such an organization, who is your client: the class representative or the cause for which the organization advocates?

Conversely, why is it in the interest of the class members to be represented? Aren't they better off by sitting on the sidelines, hoping for a good injunction that they can use to their advantage, and not being bound by a bad result? What if, as in Rule 23(b)(1)(A) cases, different class members want injunctions that would require the defendant to engage in different (and incompatible) standards of conduct? If it is in the practical best interests of some or all class members not to be part of a class action, how can the class representative and class counsel adequately represent their interests? Put differently, aren't there inherent conflicts of interest — of the type that the Due Process Clause and Rule 23(a) care about — looming in every (b)(2) class action?

7. Assuming that *Allison* is correct, plaintiffs and their counsel are faced with difficult tactical decisions. Do they forgo the monetary remedies and jury-trial rights available under the 1991 Civil Rights Act and seek only an injunction and equitable remedies like backpay to maximize their chances for certification of a class under Rule 23(b)(2)? Or do they seek these remedies and demand a jury trial, even those this tack may be fatal to their request for class certification? *Cf.* Phyllis T. Baumann, et al., *Substance in the Shadow of Procedure: The Integration of Substantive and Procedural Law in Title VII Cases,* 33 B.C. L. REV. 211, 257 (1992) (asserting that certain Supreme Court decisions have crippled class actions as a workable device for seeking collective relief in Title VII cases). Does a plaintiff who decides to abandon monetary remedies in order to obtain class certification risk being regarded as an inadequate representative? The answer to this question depends on the claim-preclusive consequences that attach to the abandonment of the monetary claims — a subject we consider *infra* p. 525.

8. As we have noted, there are strong connections between Rule 23(b)(1)(A) and Rule 23(b)(2). The latter was essentially an outgrowth of the former; because it is worded more simply and because it seems to allow (albeit unclearly to what extent) some non-predominant monetary relief, certification under Rule 23(b)(2) has tended to dominate over certification under Rule 23(b)(1)(A) when parties seek injunctive or declaratory relief. But any claim seeking such relief can be considered under either provision. For instance, we saw in *Telectronics* (*supra* p. 388) that claims or theories seeking to create medical-monitoring programs are sometimes cognizable under Rules 23(b)(1)(A) and -(b)(1)(B). Are the issues or results different if a class representative seeks to establish a medical-monitoring program under Rule 23(b)(2)? Consider the next two cases, the first of which was authored by the same judge who certified the medical-monitoring class in *Telectronics.*

DAY V. NLO, INC.

144 F.R.D. 330 (S.D. Ohio 1992)

■ SPIEGEL, District Judge.

[The defendants operated the Feed Materials Production Center ("FMPC"). The plaintiffs, who were former FMPC employees and others who worked at the FMPC, claimed that the defendants operated the FMPC in a way that negligently or intentionally exposed them to dangerous levels of radioactive and hazardous materials. As a result of this exposure, the plaintiffs contended that their personal property has been damaged and that they suffered severe emotional distress due to increased fear of contracting cancer. After holding that the class met the requirements of Rule 23(a) and that class counsel was also adequate, the court analyzed whether the class satisfied the requirements of Rule 23(b)(2).]

The plaintiffs in this action primarily seek relief in the form of a court-supervised medical monitoring program. The defendants contend that such relief does not constitute injunctive relief because the defendants will simply be required to pay money to finance the program. Therefore, the defendants claim, this is simply an action for damages, and rule 23(b)(2) is inapplicable.

Relief in the form of medical monitoring may be by a number of means. First, a court may simply order a defendant to pay a plaintiff a certain sum of money. The plaintiff may or may not choose to use that money to have his medical condition monitored. Second, a court may order the defendants to pay the plaintiffs' medical expenses directly so that a plaintiff may be monitored by the physician of his choice. Neither of these forms of relief constitute injunctive relief as required by rule 23(b)(2).

However, a court may also establish an elaborate medical monitoring program of its own, managed by court-appointed court-supervised trustees, pursuant to which a plaintiff is monitored by particular physicians and the medical data produced utilized for group studies. In this situation, a defendant, of course, would finance the program as well as being required by the court to address issues as they develop during program administration. Under these circumstances, the relief constitutes injunctive relief as required by rule 23(b)(2).

. . . If the plaintiffs in this case ultimately prove their allegations, the class members will be entitled to injunctive relief in the form of an extensive court-supervised medical monitoring program. Therefore, we conclude that the party opposing class certification (the defendants) allegedly acted or refused to act on grounds generally applicable to the class for which final injunctive relief with respect to the class as a whole may be appropriate. . . .

For the reasons set forth above, the plaintiffs in this case have satisfied the requirements of rule 23(a) and rule 23(b)(2) . . . .

IN RE ST. JUDE MEDICAL, INC., SILZONE HEART VALVE PRODUCTS LIABILITY LITIGATION

425 F. 3d 1116 (8th Cir. 2005)

■ RILEY, Circuit Judge.

St. Jude Medical, Inc. (SJM) produced the Silzone prosthetic heart valve. A test conducted by SJM showed a slightly higher risk of paravalvular leaks at the site where the valves were implanted. SJM thereafter recalled all unimplanted Silzone valves. Numerous suits were then filed across the nation, and the cases were later consolidated in Minnesota. On motions by the plaintiffs, the district court issued three orders that collectively had the result of certifying two subclasses — one seeking damages based on Minnesota's consumer protection statutes, and another seeking primarily injunctive relief. SJM appeals these two class certifications. We reverse and remand.

I. BACKGROUND

. . .

[In the federal multidistrict proceeding] five plaintiffs filed a consolidated amended class action complaint, claiming to represent over 11,000 Silzone valve recipients. The plaintiffs alleged common law strict liability, breach of implied and express warranties, negligence and medical monitoring, and claims under various Minnesota consumer statutes-the False Advertising Act, the Consumer Fraud Act, the Unlawful Trade Practices Act, and the Uniform Deceptive Trade Practices Act. The plaintiffs moved for class certification of an injunctive class, called the "medical monitoring class," and a personal injury class seeking money damages, although both classes made many of the same claims under the same legal theories noted above. [The district court conditionally certified a class raising the common-law claims under Rule 23(b)(3), unconditionally certified a class raising consumer-protection and deceptive-trade-practices claims under Rule 23(b)(3), and conditionally certified a medical-monitoring class under Rule 23(b)(2). It subsequently decertified the common-law class.]

II. DISCUSSION

[The court of appeals reversed and remanded the order certifying the consumer-protection class, finding the district court insufficiently analyzed the conflict-of-law issues presented by such a class action. It then turned to the order certifying a medical monitoring class.]

. . . SJM argues this class defies *Erie*'s command that federal courts refrain from altering or creating new state law. SJM further argues certification of this class as one seeking injunctive relief under Rule 23(b)(2) violates the Due Process Clause. Finally, SJM argues certification of this class is improper due to diverse legal and factual issues that would make a classwide trial inefficient and unmanageable. We conclude the diverse legal and factual issues preclude class certification, and we reverse on this ground. As this ground again is dispositive, we do not address the *Erie* and due process arguments.

Class certification under Rule 23(b)(2) is proper only when the primary relief sought is declaratory or injunctive. Although Rule 23(b)(2) contains no predominance or superiority requirements, class claims thereunder still must be cohesive.   Barnes v. Am. Tobacco Co., 161 F.3d 127, 143 (3d Cir. 1998).   Because unnamed members are bound by the action without the opportunity to opt out of a Rule 23(b)(2) class, even greater cohesiveness generally is required than in a Rule 23(b)(3) class. A "suit could become unmanageable and little value would be gained in proceeding as a class action . . . if significant individual issues were to arise consistently." "At base, the (b)(2) class is distinguished from the (b)(3) class by class cohesiveness . . . . Injuries remedied through (b)(2) actions are really group, as opposed to individual injuries.   The members of a (b)(2) class are generally bound together through 'preexisting or continuing legal relationships' or by some significant common trait such as race or gender."

Proposed medical monitoring classes suffer from cohesion difficulties, and numerous courts across the country have denied certification of such classes. . . . [*Amchem Products, Inc. v. Windsor*, 521 U.S. 591, 624 (1997) (*infra* p. 493),] listed some of the individual variations precluding class certification: "[Exposure-only plaintiffs] will also incur different medical expenses because their monitoring and treatment will depend on singular circumstances and individual medical histories." Differences in state laws on medical monitoring further compound these disparities.

In this case, like in *Windsor*, each plaintiff's need (or lack of need) for medical monitoring is highly individualized. Every patient in the 17-state class who has ever been implanted with a mechanical heart valve already requires future medical monitoring as an ordinary part of his or her follow-up care. A patient who has been implanted with the Silzone valve may or may not require additional monitoring, and whether he or she does is an individualized inquiry depending on that patient's medical history, the condition of the patient's heart valves at the time of implantation, the patient's risk factors for heart valve complications, the patient's general health, the patient's personal choice, and other factors. The plaintiffs concede the states recognizing medical monitoring claims as a separate cause of action have different elements triggering culpability. Simply put, the medical monitoring class presents a myriad of individual issues making class certification improper. . . .

Bolstering our conclusion is the fact the plaintiffs never demonstrated to the district court they "would sue for the medical monitoring program sought here even in the absence of a claim for damages." In re Rezulin Prods. Liab. Litig., 210 F.R.D. 61, 73 (S.D.N.Y. 2002). As the Southern District of New York ruled, a district court certifying a medical monitoring class must be satisfied

> that a reasonable plaintiff, based on a medical and economic calculus, would have sued solely for a medical monitoring program, not merely that a lawyer could have been found who would have located a plaintiff and brought a class action in the hope of a fee, else the test would be meaningless. . . .

While every mechanical heart valve patient will require follow-up care in connection with the implant, the question of additional monitoring above that required for normal mechanical heart valve implantation is not clear.

For the above reasons, we conclude class certification of the medical monitoring class was an abuse of discretion. We reverse the district court's certification of this class.

Notes

1.   After remand, the district court again certified the class asserting violations of Minnesota's consumer-protection statutes. In re St. Jude Med., Inc., Silzone Heart Valves Prod. Liab. Litig., 2006 WL 2943154 (D. Minn. Oct. 13, 2006). That certification was then reversed. In re St. Jude Med., Inc., Silzone Heart Valve Prod. Liab. Litig., 522 F.3d 836 (8th Cir. 2008). The Eighth Circuit concluded that, even if Minnesota law applied to all of the class members' claims, common issues would not predominate over noncommon issues, as required by Rule 23(b)(3).

2.   Whether Rule 23(b)(2) should be construed to require a finding that the class is sufficiently "cohesive," as *St. Jude Medical* asserts, is not settled. *See, e.g.,* In re Welding Fume Prod. Liab. Litig., 245 F.R.D. 279, 315 n.189 (N.D. Ohio 2007) (citing cases; noting that "whether there is an implicit cohesiveness requirement within Rule 23(b)(2) is not settled in this Circuit"). The Third Circuit requires cohesiveness. Barnes v. Am. Tobacco Co., 161 F.3d 127, 142-43 (3d Cir. 1998). The Ninth Circuit does not, at least in civil-rights cases. Walters v. Reno, 145 F.3d 1032, 1047 (9th Cir. 1998) ("Although common issues must predominate for class certification under Rule 23(b)(3), no such requirement exists under [Rule] 23(b)(2)."). *See also* In re Propulsid Prods. Liab. Litig., 208 F.R.D. 133, 147 (E.D. La. 2007) (denying class certification of a medical-monitoring and personal-injury class because of "variations involving proof of causation, the effect of warnings, the significance of the defendant's direct marketing to consumers, and other similar issues may swamp any common issues and defeat cohesiveness"); In re New Motor Vehicles Canadian Exp., 2006 WL 623591 (D. Me. 2006) (requiring and finding class cohesiveness for antitrust claims seeking a class-wide injunction).

3.   Should courts impose a factor like cohesiveness when the language of Rule 23(b)(2) says nothing of the kind? Has this factor become necessary because Rule 23(b)(2) is now being used in ways that its drafters never contemplated? Is cohesiveness a distinct requirement from the typicality requirement of Rule 23(a)(3)? If so, how and why should it differ?

In *In re Welding Fume Products Liability Litigation*, 245 F.R.D. 279 (N.D. Ohio 2007), welders brought products liability and other claims against various manufacturers, suppliers, and distributors of welding rod products, alleging that they were exposed to fumes from welding rods that could cause permanent neurological injury. They also sought injunctive relief in the form of medical monitoring. The plaintiffs asked the court to certify eight state-wide classes, with two subclasses each — one sub-class of current welders and one sub-class of former welders. The trial court indicated that the request appeared to satisfy the requirements of Rule

23(b)(2) because the relief being sought was equitable in nature, *id.* at 290; and found that the proposed state-wide classes largely addressed the problems of variations in state law on medical-monitoring claims, *id.* at 294. Nonetheless, it rejected certification of the medical-monitoring classes because the Rule 23(a)(3) typicality requirement was not satisfied: "Given the large size of the class, the differences in defendants' conduct, and the variable working environments in which all of the welder plaintiffs performed, each class member's claims involve so many distinct factual questions that class certification becomes inappropriate." *Id.* at 303. Why was typicality satisfied in *Day*, but not in *Welding Fume*?

4. Related to cohesiveness is a requirement imposed in *Heffner v. Blue Cross & Blue Shield of Alabama, Inc.*, 443 F.3d 1330 (11th Cir. 2006). *Heffner* emphasized the requirement in Rule 23(b)(2) that injunctive or declaratory relief be "appropriate respecting the class as a whole" to argue that, when class members needed to prove individualized reliance to obtain an injunction, Rule 23(b)(2) was not available. It reasoned that injunctive relief "will not automatically flow to the class 'as a whole' even if [the class representative] succeeds in proving reliance." *Id.* at 1345.

5. Also related to cohesiveness is another requirement that some courts have imposed on Rule 23(b)(2) class actions: that the class action must be manageable. Shook v. El Paso County, 386 F.3d 963 (10th Cir. 2004) ("Elements of manageability and efficiency are not categorically precluded in determining whether to certify a [Rule] 23(b)(2) class."); Lowery v. Circuit City Stores, Inc., 158 F.3d 742, 757 (4th Cir. 1998). Other courts disagree. Forbush v. J.C. Penney Co., 994 F.2d 1101, 1105 (5th Cir. 1993), ("[Q]uestions of manageability and judicial economy are . . . irrelevant to [Rule] 23(b)(2) class actions."). *See also* Dukes v. Wal-Mart, Inc., 509 F.3d 1168, 1190 (9th Cir. 2007), *reh'g en banc granted*, 556 F.3d 919 (9th Cir. 2009) (finding a massive Rule 23(b)(2) class manageable, but not stating whether manageability is an element of such class actions).

Proponents of building a manageability inquiry into Rule 23(b)(2) face two hurdles. First, manageability is specifically listed as a relevant concern in Rule 23(b)(3)(D); the failure to include the same language in the contemporaneously written Rule 23(b)(2) is problematic. Second, the argument might be foreclosed by *Califano v. Yamasaki*, 442 U.S. 682, 701 (1979), in which the Court strongly endorsed the use of a Rule 23(b)(2) class action, noting that "class relief is consistent with the need for case-by-case adjudication."

6. The propriety of certifying medical-monitoring claims under Rule 23(b)(2) divides the courts. For a summary of the cases, see *Welding Fume*, 245 F.R.D. 279. The commentators on this issue are also divided. *Compare* Pankaj Venugopal, Note, *The Class Certification of Medical Monitoring Claims*, 102 COLUM. L. REV. 1659, 1659 (2002) (asserting that, because "a medical monitoring fund is an equitable remedy, nonpreclusive of future damage claims, and groupwide in nature, the (b)(2) class category adequately protects the due process rights of class plaintiffs"), *with* John C.P. Goldberg & Benjamin C. Zipursky, *Unrealized Torts*, 88 VA. L. REV.

1625, 1704-05 (2002) (asserting that too many substantive and procedural questions haunt medical-monitoring claims to certify them under (b)(2)). The *Manual for Complex Litigation* also took note of the division, stating that "Rule 23(b)(2) generally applies when the relief sought is a court-supervised program for periodic medical examination and research to detect diseases attributable to the product in question." MANUAL FOR COMPLEX LITIGATION, FOURTH § 22.74 (2004). If, instead, "money damages are the relief primarily sought in a medical monitoring class, as in programs that pay class members but leave it to the members to arrange for and obtain tests, certification must generally meet the Rule 23(b)(3) standards." *Id.* Is this a sensible distinction or a triumph of form over substance?

Should courts be sponsoring medical research and the delivery of medical care? How far afield from the traditional adjudicatory role should judges go in order to achieve mandatory aggregation? Can a judge choose to certify a class seeking a medical-monitoring program over a competing class seeking a medical-monitoring fund that better meets the needs of class members to gain the leverage that forces the parties to come to a settlement on all issues?

7. As we end our examination of the (b)(2) class action, you should ask why a class action predominantly (but not necessarily exclusively) seeking injunctive relief demands class-action treatment. Is it efficiency? Is it fairness? Can you articulate a theory of efficiency or sense of fairness with enough particularly to explain why injunctive class actions with a bit of monetary relief are proper but class actions with a large monetary component are not? *Cf.* AM. L. INST., PRINCIPLES OF THE LAW OF AGGREGATE LITIGATION §§ 2.04, 2.07 (2009) (suggesting that mandatory class aggregation is appropriate whenever remedies are "indivisible").

(C)   Opting Out of a Mandatory Class Action

The great advantage of Rules 23(b)(1)(A), -(b)(1)(B), and -(b)(2) over Rule 23(b)(3) (and over virtually all other forms of aggregation) is their mandatory nature. In cases fitting within their terms, all the claims of all the plaintiffs can be swept into a single forum and resolved once and for all. Not all litigants and courts view this mandatory aggregation as an unadulterated good, especially in cases seeking monetary relief. Until now, in laying out the issues on both sides of this debate, we have assumed that mandatory class actions are in fact mandatory — that class members have no ability to exit from a (b)(1) or (b)(2) class action. If they could opt out, the debate over these class actions would certainly shift.

So are (b)(1) and (b)(2) class actions mandatory? Rule 23 is not explicit on the point. According to Rule 23(c)(2)(B), class members must receive notice of the right to opt out in (b)(3) class actions; and according to Rule 23(e)(4), the judge can give class members in (b)(3) actions a second right to opt out at the time a settlement is announced. Both rules are quite clear that the opt-out right involves (b)(3) class actions. The obvious implication is that Rule 23 does not permit class members to opt out of (b)(1) and (b)(2) class actions.

At the same time, Rules 23(d)(1)(A) and -(E), which describe some of the judge's powers to manage a class action, have enough wiggle room possibly to give a judge the authority to permit class members in (b)(1) and (b)(2) cases to opt out. A handful of cases have recognized that district courts have the discretion, on unique facts, to allow class members to opt out of mandatory class actions. *See* Eubanks v. Billington, 110 F.3d 87 (D.C. Cir. 1997); County of Suffolk v. Long Island Lighting Co., 907 F.2d 1295 (2d Cir. 1990); Holmes v. Cont'l Can Co., 706 F.2d 1144, 1160 (11th Cir. 1983); *but see* Thomas v. Albright, 139 F.3d 227 (D.C. Cir. 1998) (district court abused its discretion in permitting plaintiffs to opt out). *Eubanks* noted that opt-outs should not be permitted "when doing so would undermine the policies behind (b)(1) or (b)(2) certification." 110 F.3d at 94-95.

That is as far as the analysis of Rule 23 takes us. But the Federal Rules of Civil Procedure cannot trump the Constitution. So does the Due Process Clause require an opt-out right? The absolutely critical case is *Phillips Petroleum Co. v. Shutts*, 472 U.S. 797 (1985), which we examined in Chapter Three (*supra* p. 276). Recall that *Shutts* involved a Kansas state-court lawsuit brought under a class-action rule identical to Rule 23(b)(3). The defendant argued that, for class members who lacked minimum contacts with Kansas, the Due Process Clause required the class members to affirmatively opt into the class. The Supreme Court disagreed, holding that the Due Process Clause required only an opt-out right. Because the Kansas class-action rule provided an opt-out right, the Court found the Due Process Clause satisfied. In dicta that has bedeviled the world of class-action practice ever since, the Court then said: "Our holding today is limited to those class actions which seek to bind known plaintiffs concerning claims wholly or predominately for money judgments. We intimate no view concerning other types of class actions, such as those seeking equitable relief." 472 U.S. at 811 n.3.

Is *Shutts*'s recognition of a constitutionally grounded opt-out right applicable only to state-court class actions? Is it applicable only to state-law claims? Is it applicable only to (b)(3) actions? Is it applicable to any class action in which monetary relief is sought, including (b)(1) and (b)(2) actions? Is it applicable only to the monetary claims asserted in hybrid injunctive-monetary class actions? Or is it applicable to all class actions, even those seeking only injunctive relief?

TICOR TITLE INSURANCE CO. V. BROWN

511 U.S. 117 (1994)

■ PER CURIAM.

[Following on the heels of an FTC enforcement proceeding against the defendants, plaintiffs filed a series of antitrust class actions seeking treble damages and injunctive relief. After the Judicial Panel on Multidistrict Litigation consolidated the cases in the Eastern District of Pennsylvania (MDL No. 633), the parties reached a settlement. The settlement awarded equitable relief, but provided class members with no monetary relief — even though the settlement specifically extinguished monetary claims. The MDL court provisionally certified the class under Rules 23(b)(1) and -(b)(2). Objecting class members challenged the fairness of the settlement and argued that due process required that class members with damage claims be afforded the opportunity to opt out of the class. After a hearing, the trial court rejected these objections, certified the class, and approved the settlement. The Third Circuit affirmed and the Supreme Court denied certiorari.

[Certain class members later filed antitrust damage claims against the defendants in federal court in the District of Arizona. The district court granted summary judgment on the claims on the ground, among others, that the plaintiffs were bound by the terms of the earlier Pennsylvania settlement. The Ninth Circuit reversed, finding that, while the plaintiffs had been adequately represented in the Pennsylvania class action, the Due Process Clause denied preclusive effect to the settlement because the plaintiffs had not been afforded an opportunity to opt out.]

. . . [I]n this Court, petitioners present only a single question — viz., "[w]hether a federal court may refuse to enforce a prior federal class action judgment, properly certified under Rule 23 on grounds that absent class members have a constitutional due process right to opt out of any class action which asserts monetary claims on their behalf." . . .

That certified question is of no general consequence if, whether or not absent class members have a constitutional right to opt out of such actions, they have a right to do so under the Federal Rules of Civil Procedure. Such a right would exist if, in actions seeking monetary damages, classes can be certified only under Rule 23(b)(3), which permits opt-out, and not under Rules 23(b)(1) and (b)(2), which do not. That is at least a substantial possibility — and we would normally resolve that preliminary nonconstitutional question before proceeding to the constitutional claim. The law of res judicata, however, prevents that question from being litigated here. It was conclusively determined in the MDL No. 633 litigation that respondents' class fit within Rules 23(b)(1)(A) and (b)(2); even though that determination may have been wrong, it is conclusive upon these parties, and the alternative of using the Federal Rules instead of the Constitution as the means of imposing an opt-out requirement for this settlement is no longer available.

The most obvious consequence of this unavailability is, as we have suggested, that our resolution of the posited constitutional question may be quite unnecessary in law, and of virtually no practical consequence in fact, except with respect to these particular litigants. Another consequence, less apparent, is that resolving the constitutional question on the assumption of proper certification under the Rules may lead us to the wrong result. If the Federal Rules, which generally are not affirmatively enacted into law by Congress are not entitled to that great deference as to constitutionality which we accord federal statutes, they at least come with the *imprimatur* of the rulemaking authority of this Court. In deciding the present case, we must assume either that the lack of opt-out opportunity in these circumstances was decreed by the Rules or that it was not (though the parties are bound by an erroneous holding that it was). If we make the former assumption we may approve, in the mistaken deference to prior Supreme Court action and congressional acquiescence, action that neither we nor Congress would independently think constitutional. If we make the latter assumption, we may announce a constitutional rule that is good for no other federal class action. Neither option is attractive.

The one reason to proceed is to achieve justice in this particular case. Even if the constitutional question presented is hypothetical as to everyone else, it would seem to be of great practical importance to these litigants. But that is ordinarily not sufficient reason for our granting certiorari — even when unnecessary constitutional pronouncements are not in the picture. Moreover, as matters have developed it is not clear that our resolution of the constitutional question will make any difference even to these litigants. On the day we granted certiorari we were informed that the parties had reached a settlement designed to moot the petition, which now awaits the approval of the District Court.

In these circumstances, we think it best to dismiss the writ as improvidently granted.

■ JUSTICE O'CONNOR, with whom THE CHIEF JUSTICE and JUSTICE KENNEDY join, dissenting. . . .

The Court's assertion that "our resolution of the posited constitutional question may be . . . of virtually no practical consequence in fact," is unsound. The lower courts have consistently held that the presence of monetary damages claims does not preclude class certification under Rules 23(b)(1)(A) and (b)(2). Whether or not those decisions are correct (a question we need not, and indeed should not, decide today), they at least indicate that there are a substantial number of class members in exactly the same position as respondents. Under the Ninth Circuit's rationale in this case, every one of them has the right to go into federal court and relitigate their claims against the defendants in the original action. The individuals, corporations, and governments that have successfully defended against class actions or reached appropriate settlements, but are now subject to relitigation of the same claims with individual class members, will rightly dispute the Court's characterization of the constitutional rule in this case as inconsequential.

The Court is likewise incorrect in suggesting that a decision in this case "may be quite unnecessary in law." Unless and until a contrary rule is adopted, courts will continue to certify classes under Rules 23(b)(1) and (b)(2) notwithstanding the presence of damages claims; the constitutional opt-out right announced by the court below will be implicated in every such action, at least in the Ninth Circuit. Moreover, because the decision below is based on the Due Process Clause, presumably it applies to the States;

although we held in *Phillips Petroleum Co. v. Shutts*, 472 U.S. 797 (1985) [*supra* p. 276], that there is a constitutional right to opt out of class actions brought in state court, that holding was expressly "limited to those class actions which seek to bind known plaintiffs concerning claims wholly or predominately for money judgments." The Ninth Circuit's rule, by contrast, applies whenever "substantial damage claims" are asserted. The resolution of a constitutional issue with such broad-ranging consequences is both necessary and appropriate.

Notes

1.   The same issue again came before the Supreme Court in *Adams v. Robertson*, 520 U.S. 83 (1997), but the court again dismissed the writ as improvidently granted — this time finding that the issue had not been properly preserved in the lower-court proceedings. The issue was preserved and squarely presented in *Ortiz v. Fibreboard Corp.*, 527 U.S. 815 (1999) (*infra* p. 506), a limited-fund class action that was brought under Rule 23(b)(1)(B), provided monetary remedies to class members, and contained no opt-out right. The Court resolved *Ortiz* on other grounds. It did, however, flag the *Shutts* issue in studied dicta that we quoted *supra* p. 287, Note 5. Although the Court intimated some willingness to apply *Shutts* to a (b)(1)(B) class action, the question whether substantial monetary damage claims may be adjudicated or settled in (b)(1) or (b)(2) class actions without affording class members an opportunity to opt out remains open and unsettled.

2.   The question is enormously important for class-action practice. As we have noted, mandatory class actions are more desirable as vehicles for aggregating related litigation: They are less costly due to the absence of notice to the class, they place additional settlement pressure that can achieve a global resolution, and they aid finality. Whether these features of mandatory class actions are benefits or curses is a question whose answer lies in the eye of the beholder.   For good or for ill, fate of mandatory (b)(1) and (b)(2) class actions (especially those seeking monetary relief, with which *Shutts* was especially concerned) depends entirely on the reading given to *Shutts*, in particular its footnote 3. For further discussion of this issue, including the various ways in which courts have sought to limit the effect of *Shutts* in mandatory class actions, see *supra* pp. 286-90, Notes 3-9.

3.   In *Johnson v. General Motors Corp.*, 598 F.2d 432 (5th Cir. 1979), a (b)(2) class action alleging race discrimination resulted in an injunction and monetary relief for the class representatives, but no monetary recovery for class members. When one class member later brought an action for damages, the court of appeals permitted the suit to go forward: "Before an absent class member may be forever barred from pursuing an individual damage claim . . . due process requires that he receive some form of notice that the class action is pending and that his damage claims may be adjudicated as part of it." *Id.* at 438. The Ninth Circuit had reached the

same conclusion in *Ticor* itself. Brown v. Ticor Title Ins. Co., 982 F.2d 386 (9th Cir. 1992). Some state courts have come to an opposite conclusion. *See, e.g.,* Nottingham Partners v. Dana, 564 A.2d 1089 (Del. Super. 1989) (holding that the certification of a mandatory class action and a resulting settlement precluded class members from later asserting either equitable or monetary claims).

4. Assuming that an opt-out right must in some circumstances be afforded to some absent members in mandatory class actions, exactly which class members get the right? All class members? Or just those who lack sufficient contacts with the forum state? If the latter (which seems likely), what test do we use to sort those with sufficient contacts from those without? Do we use a simple presence test — domicile or property within the state that is related to the dispute? Or do we develop a minimum-contacts approach? For instance, suppose a class member in *Shutts* lived in Oklahoma and the land from which the oil was extracted was in Oklahoma, but she used a Kansas lawyer to negotiate her royalties agreement and she regularly used her royalty money to shop in Kansas stores. Does she enjoy an opt-out right under *Shutts*? Applying an individualized minimum-contacts test to determine who gets *Shutts*'s opt-out right could be very time-consuming and expensive.

5. Assume that *Shutts* requires an opt-out right for absent class members in all class actions "predominately" seeking monetary recovery, as footnote 3 implies. What is the reasoning behind such a distinction? Is it a hostility to using class actions to resolve monetary claims? Is it a tip of the hat to the historical division between law and equity? (Recall that the common law, which awarded monetary relief, had no class actions; while equity, which awarded injunctive relief, did.) Should the dead hand of the forms of English law dictate the tools available to resolve modern complex litigation? If historical practice explains footnote 3, what about the fact that equity also handled limited-fund cases, in which monetary recovery occurred?

ii. Opt-Out (b)(3) Class Actions

Rule 23(b)(3) authorizes class actions when "common questions of law or fact predominate over questions affecting only individual members" and "a class action is superior to other available methods for fairly and efficiently adjudicating the controversy." To aid in the determination of "predominance" and "superiority," as these two elements are usually known, Rule 23(b)(3) provides four factors, most of which go toward the issue of a class action's superiority. The most significant of these is the manageability factor of Rule 23(b)(3)(D).

The evident rationale for (b)(3) class actions is efficient and fair adjudication. In most situations, Rule 23(b)(3) is the only class action that is available to plaintiffs seeking damages for widespread harms. Rule 23(b)(3) promises to resolve many related cases in one forum. But the Rule's impulse for efficient and fair adjudication of related claims has its limits: Class members may opt out of a (b)(3) class action, and they must receive notice of this right.

Despite the opt-out right, Rule 23(b)(3) represents a potentially powerful tool for aggregating many types of claims seeking damages: tort, environmental, antitrust, securities fraud, consumer protection, and the like. Not surprisingly, it has also been the most controversial form of class action since its creation in 1966. After some skirmishes in the early years, the principle that opt-out class actions can be certified for damages claims arising under various federal statutes regulating commercial activity (e.g., the Sherman Act, the Clayton Act, the Securities Act of 1933, the Securities Exchange Act of 1934, and some federal consumer-protection statutes) has won fairly broad acceptance. Many of these class actions are "negative-value" cases — in other words, cases in which few, if any, class members suffer losses that are sufficient to justify individual litigation. In these cases, it is a class action or nothing. Recognizing the value of class actions in this context, courts frequently certify (b)(3) class actions in negative-value commercial contexts — although of late new questions have been raised about the utility of (b)(3) in some of these cases.

For many years — especially from 1980 through the late 1990s — the real battleground was the use of (b)(3) class actions in mass torts. Before 1980, the federal courts were decidedly opposed to certification of any mass tort, even when all of the plaintiffs' injuries arose out a single event and the only individual issues in the case concerned the amount of damages. *See, e.g.*, Hobbs v. Ne. Airlines, 50 F.R.D. 76 (E.D. Pa. 1970). Beginning in the early 1980s, however, the attitude began to change toward one of openness to (b)(3) mass-tort class actions. The pendulum swung again in the other direction in the mid-1990s, and certifications of (b)(3) litigation class actions in mass-tort cases are rare today.

The following materials consider the use and limits of (b)(3) class actions in a variety of commercial and mass-tort contexts.

(A)   Commercial Class Actions

This subsection examines (b)(3) class actions in a range of situations that can loosely be described as commercial in nature. Typically the cases involve a large corporate defendant whose conduct has caused economic losses to many "little guys" — consumers and customers, shareholders, insureds, and the like. Often the relationships between the parties are defined by contract. As we will see, the application of Rule 23(b)(3) in these cases often requires an interplay between the procedural "predominance" and "superiority" requirements and the substantive law. It is not precisely true that there is one set of (b)(3) rules for RICO class actions, another for securities-fraud class actions, and so on. But the common concerns that animate predominance and superiority play out differently in each substantive context.

The first case concerns consumer-protection claims.

SMILOW V. SOUTHWESTERN BELL MOBILE SYSTEMS, INC.

323 F.3d 32 (1st Cir. 2003)

■ LYNCH, Circuit Judge.

This is an appeal from a decision decertifying a class action brought by and on behalf of wireless phone customers of Cellular One, the doing-business name of Southwestern Bell Mobile Systems, Inc. The putative class members are Massachusetts and New Hampshire residents who were charged for incoming calls despite having signed a standard form contract, used mainly between August 1994 and February 1996, purportedly guaranteeing free incoming call service.

Class representative Jill Ann Smilow brought suit in 1997 for breach of contract and violations of Massachusetts General Laws chapter §§ 93A, 2(a), 9, 11, and the Telecommunications Act (TCA) of 1996, 47 U.S.C. § 201(b). The district court first certified and then decertified the contract, ch. 93A, and TCA classes. This court vacated the decertification order and remanded; the district court subsequently reinstated its decertification order. We reverse.

I.

Smilow and proposed class representative Margaret L. Bibeau each signed a standard form contract for cellular telephone services with Cellular One in 1995. The form contract says, "Chargeable time for calls originated by a Mobile Subscriber Unit starts when the Mobile Subscriber Unit signals call initiation to C1's facilities and ends when the Mobile Subscriber Unit signals call disconnect to C1's facilities and the call disconnect signal has been confirmed." The parties contest the meaning of "originated." Smilow alleges that this language precludes Cellular One from charging for incoming calls. It is undisputed that a large group of Cellular One customers signed the same contract and were subject to charges for incoming calls. The contract contains an integration clause providing that changes must be in writing and signed by both parties.

Smilow and Bibeau purport to represent a class of Massachusetts and New Hampshire residents who subscribed for Cellular One services under this contract. The potential class members all signed the standard form contract, which was in broad use from August 1994 to February 1996. They did have a variety of rate plans and usage patterns. Some Cellular One customers paid a flat fee for a fixed number of minutes each month and an additional per-minute charge if they exceeded this fixed amount of air time (for example, $40/month for the first 300 minutes/month and 10 cents/minute thereafter). Many Cellular One customers paid different rates for day- and night-time calls.

Cellular One charged Smilow, Bibeau and the potential class members for incoming as well as outgoing calls. Smilow received just one incoming call; Bibeau received many incoming calls. Cellular One invoices clearly indicate that customers are charged for incoming calls. The user guide mailed to new Cellular One customers also states that the company charges for both incoming and outgoing calls. Bibeau paid her invoices knowing she was being charged for incoming calls.

II.

On February 11, 1997, Smilow, as a purported class representative, filed suit in federal district court against Cellular One for breach of contract and violations of ch. 93A and the TCA. The district court had jurisdiction over the federal claims under 28 U.S.C. § 1331 and over the state law claims under 28 U.S.C. § 1367. The district court originally certified the ch. 93A, breach of contract, and TCA classes on October 9, 1998. . . .

On March 22, 2001, the district court granted defendants' pending motion to decertify the "incoming call" class, on the grounds that common issues of fact do not predominate. . . .

. . . On July 12, 2001, this court vacated the entire March 22, 2001 decertification order, noting that the district court had not addressed the ch. 93A claim.

After remand . . ., the district court decertified the class for the contract, ch. 93A, and TCA claims. . . .

Plaintiffs again appealed. This court granted plaintiffs permission to appeal pursuant to Fed. R. Civ. P. 23(f).

III.

A. *Standard of Review*

Orders certifying or decertifying a class are reviewed for abuse of discretion. . . . Here the district court abused its discretion in decertifying the contract class and the ch. 93A class.

B. *Class Certification*

1. *General Standards*

A district court must conduct a rigorous analysis of the prerequisites established by Rule 23 . . . . From its earlier certification order the district court necessarily concluded that the Rule 23(a) elements had been met.

The district court decertified on the basis of its analysis of Rule 23(b)(3) . . . . The district court examined the predominance, but not the superiority, requirement of Rule 23(b)(3).

2. *The Predominance Requirement*

The district court's decertification of the classes for the contract, ch. 93A, and TCA claims . . . rested on fundamental errors of law and fact.

Once these errors are corrected, it becomes clear that common issues as to both liability and damages predominate on the elements of the breach of contract and ch. 93A claims. We first consider the contract claim.

a. *Breach of Contract Claim*

The first error was initially contained in the following statement from the district court's March 22, 2001 opinion decertifying the class:

> Proof of charges and payments is not evidence of harm or an amount of harm on the basis of which damages could be awarded in the face of (i) a strong likelihood that services were received in return for billed payments and (ii) lack of admissible evidence to rebut that strong likelihood. . . .

From this statement we understand the district court to have believed that the defendant would be entitled to payment for incoming calls on a theory of quantum meruit even if plaintiffs were to prevail on their breach of contract claim. Under the doctrine of quantum meruit, one who renders goods or services in the absence of an enforceable contract may be entitled to payment for those services to the extent the recipient benefitted from them. . . . Though we do not decide the question here, it would . . . seem that where a defendant is clearly not due payment under the terms of an enforceable contract, such defendant cannot claim a right to payment under quantum meruit.

The district court's reliance on the doctrine of quantum meruit led it to overlook questions of law and fact common to all class members. As plaintiffs' brief says, "The plaintiffs' claims are based entirely on a standard form contract which the defendant used with every member of the class." The common factual basis is found in the terms of the contract, which are identical for all class members. The common question of law is whether those terms precluded defendant from charging for incoming calls.

Cellular One's waiver defense is also common to the class. Affirmative defenses should be considered in making class certification decisions. Again, both the factual basis for and the legal defense of waiver present common issues for all class members. . . .

Even in the unlikely event that individual waiver determinations prove necessary, the proposed class may still satisfy the predominance requirement. Courts traditionally have been reluctant to deny class action status under Rule 23(b)(3) simply because affirmative defenses may be available against individual members. . . .

Cellular One argues that even if there are common questions of law and fact, the district court did not abuse its discretion by decertifying the class because individual issues predominate on damages. This is largely an issue of whether plaintiffs could use a computer program to extract from Cellular One's computer records information about individual damages. The district court viewed this question as mostly beside the point and its decertification orders rested mainly on other grounds.

The individuation of damages in consumer class actions is rarely determinative under Rule 23(b)(3). Where, as here, common questions predominate regarding liability, then courts generally find the predominance requirement to be satisfied even if individual damages issues remain.

There is even less reason to decertify a class where the possible existence of individual damages issues is a matter of conjecture. Common issues predominate where individual factual determinations can be accomplished using computer records, clerical assistance, and objective criteria — thus rendering unnecessary an evidentiary hearing on each claim.

Still, the parties here dispute whether it will be possible to establish breach, causation, and damages using a mechanical process. Cellular One argues that Smilow has not shown that she could use defendant's computer records either to distinguish the subset of incoming call recipients who exceeded their monthly allotment of "free" minutes or to calculate how much extra each class member was charged as a result of receiving incoming calls.

The plaintiffs' expert, Erik Buchakian, says he could fashion a computer program that would extract from Cellular One's records (1) a list of customers who received incoming calls during the class period; (2) a list of customers who paid extra during the class period because they were billed for incoming calls; and (3) actual damages for each class member during the class period. Buchakian had access to more than adequate materials — including a sample computer tape and the deposition of defendant's expert — and has more than adequate expertise — degrees in business and computer science and thirteen years of relevant work experience. The affidavits of defendant's expert, Susan Quintiliani, are consistent with Buchakian's conclusions.

If later evidence disproves Buchakian's proposition, the district court can at that stage modify or decertify the class, or use a variety of management devices. Indeed, even if individualized determinations were necessary to calculate damages, Rule 23(c)(4)(A) would still allow the court to maintain the class action with respect to other issues.

Consideration of the policy goals underlying Rule 23(b)(3) also supports class certification. The class certification prerequisites should be construed in light of the underlying objectives of class actions. Rule 23(b)(3) is intended to be a less stringent requirement than Rule 23(b)(1) or (b)(2). The core purpose of Rule 23(b)(3) is to vindicate the claims of consumers and other groups of people whose individual claims would be too small to warrant litigation. . . .

In this case, the claims of most if not all class members are too small to vindicate individually. Smilow, for example, received just a single incoming call and so can obtain only minimal contract damages.

Overall, we find that common issues of law and fact predominate here. The case turns on interpretation of the form contract, executed by all class members and defendant.

b. *The Ch. 93A Class*

The decertification of the ch. 93A class is similarly flawed: it also rests on the premise that individual inquiries would be required because "services were received" for the charges on incoming calls. . . .

Our prior discussion is adequate to dispose of any argument that decertification would be required because of a need for individual damages determinations. Since Smilow can compute actual damages using a computer program, we need not address plaintiffs' argument that common issues would predominate only on a claim for statutory damages, and not on a claim for individual damages. As to statutory damages, the Supreme Judicial Court has held that plaintiffs who cannot show actual damages under ch. 93A may nonetheless obtain statutory damages if liability is established.

We are left with the district court's concern that any ch. 93A class would be composed of two groups: a statutory damages group and an actual damages group. But plaintiffs' position is that should any conflict develop between the two groups, the action would seek only statutory damages, class members would be given notice to that effect, and those who wish to pursue individual claims for actual damages could opt-out. We agree this is an option and, in this context, the hypothetical conflict provides no basis for decertification.

[The court then held that Smilow had waived her argument concerning certification of the TCA claim by failing to brief it.]

IV.

We reverse the orders decertifying the class under the contract and ch. 93A theories.

Notes

1. The class representative in *Smilow* had been billed for exactly one incoming call. Clearly she was not going to make a federal case out of that. Indeed, it was unlikely that any customer had received enough calls to make an individual suit worthwhile. *Smilow* is a classic negative-value case. Looked at from one perspective, it is the type of case for which class actions are essential; otherwise, in our mass society, defendants can cheat many people out of small amounts of money and amass great profits from their wrongdoing. Viewed from the opposite perspective, there would have been no case at all but for Rule 23, which enriches class counsel far more than it benefits any member of the class.

2. The seminal article objecting to the use of class actions in small-stakes or negative-value cases is Milton Handler, *The Shift from Substantive to Procedural Innovation in Antitrust Suits — The Twenty-Third Annual Antitrust Review*, 71 COLUM. L. REV. 1 (1971). Professor

Handler coined the term "legalized blackmail" to describe small-stakes antitrust class actions. *Id.* at 9. Professor Handler's attitude toward small-stakes class actions held sway for a while, but by 1997, the Supreme Court was describing these negative-value suits as the quintessential fodder for (b)(3) class treatment. *See* Amchem Prods., Inc. v. Windsor, 521 U.S. 591, 617 (1997) (*infra* p. 493).

Whether right or wrong, the modern view is that, for negative-value cases, a (b)(3) class action is superior to other methods of adjudicating the dispute. (Indeed, in such cases, no other method is likely to adjudicate the dispute.) Therefore, in cases like *Smilow*, the argument is over predominance, not superiority.

3.   Courts have treated *Smilow* favorably.   As a general rule, if common liability issues exist, then individualized damages issues do not defeat predominance. *See* Tardiff v. Knox County, 365 F.3d 1, 6-7 (1st Cir. 2004) ("[T]he court could enter a judgment of liability, leaving class members to pursue damages claims in separate law suits."); *see also* S. States Police Benevolent Ass'n Inc. v. First Choice Armor & Equip., Inc., 241 F.R.D. 85, 89 (D. Mass. 2007) ("[T]he possibility of differing damages calculations is insufficient to deny certification."); Zeno v. Ford Motor Co., Inc., 238 F.R.D. 173, 190 n.18 (W.D. Pa. 2006) (certifying state-wide class of customers for determination of liability but reserving right to decertify class if liability was determined in favor of plaintiff); In re Pharm. Indus. Average Wholesale Price Litig., 230 F.R.D. 61, 90-91 (D. Mass. 2005) (expressing concern that bifurcated trial will prove unmanageable when determination of damages will require individualized proceedings, but certifying the class under Rule 23(b)(3) given rule 23(c)(4)(A)).

4.   Courts have also agreed that the existence of individual affirmative defenses should not preclude certification. *See* Salvas v. Wal-Mart Stores, Inc., 893 N.E.2d 1187, 1211-12 (Mass. 2008).

5.   The First Circuit, however, declined to allow certification of state-law automobile consumer class actions when the plaintiffs could not show that they all had been injured. It distinguished *Smilow* by noting that the fact of injury, as opposed to its extent, was a liability rather than a damages issue, and therefore questioned whether predominance was met. In re New Motor Vehicles Canadian Exp. Antitrust Litig., 522 F.3d 6, 28-30 (1st Cir. 2008) (vacating certification and remanding for further consideration).

6.   Is the reasoning in *Smilow* circular? *See* Allan Erbsen, *From "Predominance" to "Resolvability": A New Approach to Regulating Class Actions*, 58 VAND. L. REV. 995, 1073 (2005) (arguing that courts should pay closer attention to whether liability questions or damages questions predominate instead of assuming that liability questions are more important than damages questions in the predominance analysis).

7.   If the *Smilow* class had not been certified, it would have been, to use a phrase common in class-action practice, the "death knell" for the case. Before Rule 23(f), failing to certify a class (or decertifying a previously certified class) was not immediately appealable; Smilow would have needed

to litigate the case to conclusion and then appeal the denial of class certification. As a practical matter, Smilow could not have afforded to do that, so the case would have been over. Rule 23(f) gives both plaintiffs and defendants the chance to appeal from an adverse ruling regarding class certification; while most appeals are filed by defendants, *Smilow* is the rare case in which the "death knwll" idea worked in the plaintiffs' favor. For a discussion of *Smilow*, Rule 23(f), and the "death knell" doctrine, see Charles R. Flores, *Appealing Class Action Certification Decisions Under Federal Rule of Civil Procedure 23(f)*, 4 SETON HALL CIR. REV. 27, 45-46 (2007).

8. Other types of consumer (b)(3) class actions remain popular. For example, antitrust price-fixing claims are frequently certifed under (b)(3) as class actions. *See, e.g.,* In re Indus. Diamonds Antitrust Litig., 167 F.R.D. 374 (S.D.N.Y. 1996) (finding a class action superior to consolidation as a device for managing price-fixing claims against industrial diamond producers). Consumer class actions have not, however, always been received warmly. *See, e.g.,* Heaven v. Trust Co. Bank, 118 F.3d 735 (11th Cir. 1997) (failing to certify a class under the Consumer Leasing Act not an abuse of discretion); Ratner v. Chem. Bank N.Y. Trust Co., 54 F.R.D. 412 (S.D.N.Y. 1972) (refusing to certify a class under the Truth in Lending Act).

Ratner is especially well-known; its class of 130,000 customers claimed that the defendant's violation entitled each of them to $100 (the statute's minimum fine) for "what is at most a technical and debatable violation of the Truth in Lending Act" that the defendant had since corrected. *Id.* at 416. Judge Frankel thought that $13,000,000 in damages was a bit too stiff and beyond Congress's intention in enacting TILA. In the course of ruling, he noted that no other class members had evinced any interest in bringing suit and that TILA provided reasonable attorneys' fees. If a statute provides for attorneys' fees in individual actions, does Congress not wish (b)(3) class actions to be filed for violations of that statute? Why? Is it because a (b)(3) class action is no longer superior to individual litigation?

9. The following case examines predominance and superiority in the context of RICO claims. It also adds a wrinkle, not present in *Smilow*, that becomes a recurring theme in the rest of this chapter and in Chapter Six: variations in state law.

KLAY v. HUMANA, INC.

382 F.3d 1241 (11th Cir. 2004)

■ TJOFLAT, Circuit Judge.

This is a case of almost all doctors versus almost all major health maintenance organizations (HMOs), coming before us for the third time in as many years; there have been twenty-one published orders and opinions in this case from various federal courts. The plaintiffs are a putative class of all doctors who submitted at least one claim to any of the defendant HMOs between 1990 and 2002. They allege that the defendants conspired with each other to program their computer systems to systematically underpay physicians for their services. We affirm the district court's certification of the plaintiffs' federal claims, though we strongly urge the district court to revisit the definition of these classes, and reverse the district court's certification of the plaintiffs' state claims. . . .

I.

The plaintiffs are physicians who were reimbursed by one or more of the defendant HMOs for treating patients covered by those HMOs. The plaintiffs allege that the backbone of their relationship with the HMOs is that they "will be paid, in a timely manner, for the covered, medically necessary services they render." In a phrase that will undoubtedly play well with a jury, the doctors alliteratively claim that the defendants systematically "deny, delay and diminish the payments due to [them]," and fail to tell doctors that they are being underpaid. . . .

If an agreement between a physician and an HMO exists, its terms govern the physician's reimbursement. The HMOs also "represent to the medical profession at large" that when a physician treats a patient who belongs to an HMO with which the physician does not have a contract, the HMO will still reimburse him. . . .

The complaint alleges that physicians under contract with HMOs are compensated through one of two different methods — fee-for-service or capitation. Physicians who do not have a contractual relationship with an HMO are reimbursed only under a fee-for-service regime. Although the plaintiffs allege that they are being systematically underpaid under both payment methods, the exact ways in which this is purportedly accomplished differ; we will consider each reimbursement scheme in turn.

A.

Under a fee-for-service plan, an HMO agrees to reimburse doctors for any medically necessary services they perform on covered individuals, whether or not those doctors are under contract with the HMO. This gives doctors an incentive to perform as many tests and procedures as they can convince the HMO are medically necessary; HMOs, in contrast, have an incentive to approve as few procedures as possible. Both parties claim they are acting in their patients' best medical interests.

To claim reimbursement, physicians are required to fill out an HCFA-1500 form, developed by the federal government and the American Medical Association. These forms employ a "current procedural terminology" coding procedure ("CPT coding") whereby medical procedures are identified by standardized designators. . . . Each HCFA-1500 form is processed by the defendants' computer systems, which specify the amount that the physician should be paid.

The plaintiffs allege that these computer systems are programmed to systematically underpay the plaintiffs through a variety of methods. . . .

[T]he plaintiffs allege that the forms the HMOs send to physicians explaining the amounts of their reimbursements, called "explanation of benefits" forms ("EOBs"), "misrepresent or conceal the actual manner in which Plaintiffs' . . . payment requests were processed so as to induce them to accept reduced payments in reliance thereon."

B.

Even plaintiffs whose contracts establish a capitation payment plan are not free from the defendants' alleged manipulation. Under a capitation agreement, each patient specifies a physician as his "primary care provider." The HMO is obligated to pay each physician a small monthly fee, called a capitation payment, for each patient registered to him. The physician, in turn, is obligated to provide whatever medical services each registered patient requires. Thus, a capitation system is a flat-rate scheme in which a physician's payments are "based on the number of patients they agree to treat rather than on the services they actually render." A capitation method gives a physician an incentive to provide as few services as possible to each patient, whether or not medically necessary, because his payments are not tied to the quality or extent of services he provides. The HMOs, in turn, have an incentive to register as few patients as possible with each physician, so as to reduce their monthly per-patient outlays.

The plaintiffs contend that the HMOs are underpaying physicians by failing to pay capitation fees for many patients who have registered with a physician but never visited him. Consequently, plaintiffs allege, they are receiving capitation payments based on a much smaller pool of patients than that to which they are entitled.

This is not the only way in which the defendants have allegedly cheated doctors reimbursed under a capitation scheme. Before sending physicians their capitation payments, HMOs withhold a small amount of money to establish a "pharmacy risk pool," which is used to pay for their insured patients' medication. The plaintiffs contend that the defendants are withholding too much from their capitation reimbursements . . . .

The defendants are also contractually obligated to pay the plaintiffs an extra bonus if there is money left in the pharmaceutical risk fund at the end of the year . . . The plaintiffs allege, however, that defendants somehow "adjust" the year-end statements for the risk fund so as to avoid making these payments. Finally, not all services are covered by the capitation plan; for certain non-covered services, physicians are required to submit HCFA-1500 forms. The plaintiffs allege that when capitation-plan doctors submit these forms, they are subjected to the same types of fraudulent behavior as the fee-for-service doctors, discussed in the previous Section.

C.

The plaintiffs sued a variety of large HMOs because they claim that these practices are not occurring in isolation, but are instead the end-product of a decades-long nefarious conspiracy to undermine the American health care system. . . . To support this allegation, the plaintiffs point to the fact that most of the HMOs run their reimbursement processes in substantially the same way, and participate in various industry groups, trade associations, and standards-promulgation projects.

D.

This case originated when lawsuits were filed in four federal judicial districts against Humana, Inc. . . . These suits were consolidated by the Judicial Panel on Multidistrict Litigation (the "Panel") in the Southern District of Florida. Later, the Panel decided to combine the suits against Humana with several other similar federal suits from across the country filed against other major HMOs. . . .

Once the cases were consolidated, the plaintiffs filed an amended complaint against all of the defendants. It requested that the district court certify three classes. First, the plaintiffs requested certification of a Global Class, including "all medical doctors who provided services to any person insured by any defendant from August 14, 1990 to [the date of certification]," to pursue their claims that the defendants conspired to violate the Racketeer Influenced and Corrupt Organizations Act (RICO), and aided and abetted each other in doing so. Second, the plaintiffs sought recognition of a National Subclass, comprised of all "medical doctors who provided services to any person insured by a Defendant, when the doctor has a claim against such Defendant and is not bound to arbitrate the claim," to pursue various state-law claims against the defendants, as well as claims based on "direct" (substantive, as opposed to inchoate) RICO violations. Finally, the plaintiffs requested certification of a California Subclass, comprised of "medical doctors who provided services to any person insured in California by any defendant, when the doctor was not bound to arbitrate the claim being asserted," to pursue alleged violations of Cal. Bus. & Prof. Code § 17200. The district court certified all three classes, and the HMOs now appeal. . . .

In this appeal, the defendants do not challenge the standing of the named plaintiffs or any of the district court's findings concerning Rule 23(a); they contend only that certification under Rule 23(b)(3) was improper. They raise three separate arguments. . . .

II.

The defendants' first claim is that the district court erred in certifying a Global Class to pursue federal RICO claims based on conspiracy and aiding-and-abetting, and a National Class to pursue federal claims based on "direct" RICO violations, because the common issues of fact and law these claims involve do not predominate over individualized issues. . . . [A]lthough we conclude that the district court acted within the proper scope of its power, Section D offers an observation that we strongly urge the court to consider in potentially redefining the scope of these classes.

A.

. . . To violate RICO, a defendant must engage in a pattern of racketeering activities. RICO designates the violation of certain federal criminal laws as "racketeering activities," *see* 18 U.S.C. § 1961(1). The plaintiffs contend that the defendants committed racketeering activities by engaging in mail and wire fraud, in violation of 18 U.S.C. §§ 1341 and 1343; extortion, in violation of 18 U.S.C. §§ 1951(a) and (b)(2); and violations of the Travel Act, 18 U.S.C. § 1952(a)(3).

The defendants allegedly committed mail and wire fraud by withholding from the plaintiffs information concerning the various practices described above. . . . For example, the plaintiffs allege that the "Defendants misrepresented to Plaintiffs and class members that Defendants would pay Plaintiffs and class members for medically necessary services and procedures according to the CPT codes for the services and procedures they provided." . . .

The defendants allegedly engaged in extortion by

forcing Plaintiffs and members of the class to accept capitation contracts, accept the loss of compensation for treating Defendants' insureds which results from their misrepresentation and manipulation of the workings of the capitation payment system, and accept the denial, reduction and delay of payments for covered, medically necessary services . . . through fear of economic loss. Defendants create this fear through threats, both veiled and explicit, that doctors will lose the patient base Defendants control, be blacklisted, and in the case of noncontract doctors, not be paid at all.

The final racketeering activity in which the defendants allegedly engaged was violating the Travel Act, which makes it a crime to "travel[ ] in interstate or foreign commerce or use[ ] the mail or any facility in interstate or foreign commerce, with intent to . . . promote, manage, establish, carry on or facilitate the promotion, management, establishment, or carrying on, of any unlawful activity." 18 U.S.C. § 1952(a)(3). The defendants purportedly used "the mail or other facilities of interstate commerce . . . to carry on their extortion" as described above. . . .

B.

The defendants' main contention is that the district court erred in certifying classes to litigate the RICO claims discussed above because the common issues of fact and law these claims involve do not predominate over the individualized issues involved that are specific to each plaintiff. Under Rule 23(b)(3), "[i]t is not necessary that all questions of fact or law be common, but only that some questions are common and that they predominate over individual questions." In determining whether class or individual issues predominate in a putative class action suit, we must take into account "the claims, defenses, relevant facts, and applicable substantive law," Castano [v. Am. Tobacco Co., 84 F.3d 734, 744 (5th Cir.

1996) (*infra* p. 471)], to assess the degree to which resolution of the classwide issues will further each individual class member's claim against the defendant.

"Whether an issue predominates can only be determined after considering what value the resolution of the class-wide issue will have in each class member's underlying cause of action." Common issues of fact and law predominate if they "have a direct impact on every class member's effort to establish liability and on every class member's entitlement to injunctive and monetary relief." Where, after adjudication of the classwide issues, plaintiffs must still introduce a great deal of individualized proof or argue a number of individualized legal points to establish most or all of the elements of their individual claims, such claims are not suitable for class certification under Rule 23(b)(3). . . .

. . . Put simply, if the addition of more plaintiffs to a class requires the presentation of significant amounts of new evidence, that strongly suggests that individual issues (made relevant only through the inclusion of these new class members) are important. . . .

C.

In certifying the plaintiffs' RICO claims, the district court found that common questions of fact and law predominate because this case "involves a conspiracy and joint efforts to monopolize and restrain trade." The common factual issues that predominated over individualized ones included

> Defendants' medical necessity requirements, Defendants' use of actuarial guidelines, Defendants' use of automated claims system and comparable software capable of adjusting CPT codes and reimbursement rates and automatically delaying and denying claims as well as other uniform activities designed to deny, delay or decrease reimbursement or payments to physicians.

The existence of a conspiracy, and whether the defendants aided and abetted each other, were also issues common to all of the plaintiffs that tended to predominate. We agree with this analysis. . . .

1.

. . . In this case, . . . all of the defendants operate nationwide and allegedly conspired to underpay doctors across the nation, so the numerous factual issues relating to the conspiracy are common to all plaintiffs. . . .

2.

The defendants contend that class certification is inappropriate because the RICO claims are based, in large part, on allegations of mail and wire fraud. . . . [R]eliance may not be presumed in fraud-based RICO actions; instead, the evidence must demonstrate that each individual plaintiff actually relied upon the misrepresentations at issue. . . . The defendants contend that, because each individual plaintiff must specifically show that he, personally, relied on the misstatements at issue, this individualized issue necessarily predominates. . . .

Under well-established Eleventh Circuit precedent, the simple fact that reliance is an element in a cause of action is not an absolute bar to class certification. . . . First, the common issues of fact . . . concerning the existence of a national conspiracy, a pattern of racketeering activity, and a Managed Care Enterprise, are quite substantial. They would tend to predominate over all but the most complex individualized issues.

Second, while each plaintiff must prove his own reliance in this case, we believe that, based on the nature of the misrepresentations at issue, the circumstantial evidence that can be used to show reliance is common to the whole class. That is, the same considerations could lead a reasonable factfinder to conclude beyond a preponderance of the evidence that each individual plaintiff relied on the defendants' representations.

The alleged misrepresentations in the instant case are simply that the defendants repeatedly claimed they would reimburse the plaintiffs for medically necessary services they provide to the defendants' insureds, and sent the plaintiffs various EOB forms claiming that they had actually paid the plaintiffs the proper amounts. While the EOB forms may raise substantial individualized issues of reliance, the antecedent representations about the defendants' reimbursement practices do not. It does not strain credulity to conclude that each plaintiff, in entering into contracts with the defendants, relied upon the defendants' representations and assumed they would be paid the amounts they were due. . . . Consequently, while each plaintiff must prove reliance, he or she may do so through common evidence (that is, through legitimate inferences based on the nature of the alleged misrepresentations at issue). For this reason, this is not a case in which individualized issues of reliance predominate over common questions.

3.

The defendants point out that individualized determinations are necessary to determine the extent of damages allegedly suffered by each plaintiff. While this is undoubtedly true, it is insufficient to defeat class certification under Rule 23(b)(3). . . .

It is primarily when there are significant individualized questions going to liability exist that the need for individualized assessments of damages is enough to preclude 23(b)(3) certification. Of course, there are also extreme cases in which computation of each individual's damages will be so complex, fact-specific, and difficult that the burden on the court system would be simply intolerable, but we emphasize that such cases rarely, if ever, come along.

In this case, even though individualized damage inquiries are necessary, many of them can be accomplished simply through reference to the HCFA-1500 forms or the HMO's records of which patients registered with doctors who are reimbursed through a capitation system. In addition, even if many plaintiffs' claims require corroboration and individualized consideration, such inquiries are outweighed by the predominating fact that the defendants allegedly conspired to commit, and proceeded to engage in, a pattern of racketeering activities to further their Managed Care Enterprise. It is ridiculous to expect 600,000 doctors across the nation to repeatedly prove these complicated and overwhelming facts.

D.

Because we are reviewing the district court's certifications under an abuse of discretion standard, we affirm. Nevertheless, it seems that the plaintiffs could comfortably be split into two Subclasses based on their reimbursement scheme: those operating on a fee-for-service basis and those with capitation contracts. While the existence of the conspiracy is equally relevant to both groups of plaintiffs, it seems that the capitation providers' claims revolve around some additional common issues that are not relevant to the fee-for-service providers. Moreover, because the capitation providers' primary allegation is that the HMOs did not pay them for all the patients actually registered to them, their individualized damage inquiries seem to be limited to an examination of the HMOs' records, and do not require as much potentially in-depth analysis as the fee-for-service providers' claims. Because this issue was not raised on appeal, however, we leave it to the district court to consider in the first instance whether the creation of these Subclasses might be a superior way of proceeding.

III.

[The court turned to the four state-law claims in the case: breach-of-contract claims, unjust enrichment, alleged violations of state prompt-pay statutes, and alleged violations of California law.]

A.

The plaintiffs' breach of contract claims are not amenable to class certification under Rule 23(b)(3) because, although they are based on questions of contract law that are common to the whole class, the individualized issues of fact they entail will probably predominate.

"In a multi-state class action, variations in state law may swamp any common issues and defeat predominance." *Castano,* 84 F.3d at 741. . . . [C]lass certification is impossible where the fifty states truly establish a large number of different legal standards governing a particular claim. . . .

On the other hand, if a claim is based on a principle of law that is uniform among the states, class certification is a realistic possibility. . . .

Similarly, if the applicable state laws can be sorted into a small number of groups, each containing materially identical legal standards, then certification of subclasses embracing each of the dominant legal standards can be appropriate. . . .

[handwritten margin note: effect of variations in state law]

. . . [W]e accept the proposition that the applicable state laws governing contract interpretation and breach are sufficiently identical to constitute common legal issues in this case.

While this relatively simple issue of law is common to all the breach of contract claims, it is far outweighed by the individualized issues of fact pertinent to these claims. The plaintiffs contend that all of the agreements at issue require that doctors be reimbursed at a "reasonable rate" for the "medically necessary" services they provide. We nevertheless recognize that this case involves the actions of many defendants over a significant period of time and that each defendant throughout this period utilized many different form contracts. Indeed, each defendant contracted with different types of care-providing entities, including individual physicians, partnerships, medical practice groups, and the like, each of which necessitated a different type of contract. The sheer number of contracts involved is one factor that makes us hesitant to conclude that common issues of fact predominate; this is not a situation in which all plaintiffs signed the same form contract. . . .

The facts that the defendants conspired to underpay doctors, and that they programmed their computer systems to frequently do so in a variety of ways, do nothing to establish that any individual doctor was underpaid on any particular occasion. The evidence that each doctor must introduce to make out each breach claim is essentially the same whether or not a general conspiracy or policy of breaching existed. For example, regardless of whether facts about the conspiracy or computer programs are proven, each doctor, for each alleged breach of contract (that is, each alleged underpayment), must prove the services he provided, the request for reimbursement he submitted, the amount to which he was entitled, the amount he actually received, and the insufficiency of the HMO's reasons for denying full payment. There are no common issues of fact that relieve each plaintiff of a substantial portion of this individual evidentiary burden. . . .

Another crucial reason why the plaintiffs cannot establish predominance of classwide facts on their breach of contract claims is that, although each of the defendants allegedly breached their contracts in the same general ways, they did so through a variety of specific means that are not subject to generalized proof for a large number of physicians. . . .

. . . The algorithms by which the computer programs allegedly groups procedures appear to be . . . varied and complicated . . . . Instead of applying one specific universal rule to cheat all doctors (e.g. automatically deducting $100 from everyone's claim), the reimbursement programs are instead alleged to apply a variety of more individually tailored rules, each of which applies to only a subset of the plaintiff class. For example, if the doctors proved that the programs automatically grouped together all lung transplants with all heart transplants, reimbursing all doctors who submitted a claim for both only for heart transplants, this fact would be irrelevant to the breach of contract claims of most members of the plaintiff class. . . .

This case stands in stark contrast to *Allapattah* [*Servs. v. Exxon Corp.*, 333 F.3d 1248 (11th Cir. 2003), *aff'd on other grounds*, 545 U.S. 546 (2005)], in which we affirmed certification of a class of approximately 10,000 Exxon dealers who sued Exxon Corp. for breaching their dealer agreements by overcharging them for wholesale fuel purchases. The dealers alleged that Exxon had promised them that it would reduce the price of gasoline by 1.7 cents per gallon, but secretly eliminated that price reduction after a few months.

In *Allapattah*, Exxon cheated all of the plaintiffs in exactly the same way — by secretly eliminating its 1.7 cent-per-gallon price reduction. Once the plaintiffs proved that Exxon engaged in this behavior, each individual plaintiff's breach of contract claim was substantially advanced. . . . Here, in contrast, classwide proof that the computer systems were programmed to sometimes cheat doctors in a variety of ways, through a variety of algorithms, does not tend to demonstrate that any particular doctor was cheated on any particular occasion, or by how much. . .

For these reasons, we conclude that, even though the plaintiffs' breach of contract claims involve some relatively simple common issues of law and possibly some common issues of fact, individualized issues of fact predominate. . . .

B.

The plaintiffs' unjust enrichment claims . . . require the same extensive determinations of individualized fact as the breach of contract claims discussed above because the facts necessary to support the two types of claims are almost identical. . . .

C.

The most immediate problem with certifying a nationwide class for [the prompt-payment claims] is that only thirty-two states have prompt-pay statutes at all, and of those only five states expressly provide a cause of action, with courts in another six states having recognized an implied cause of action under their respective statutes. Even assuming these claims were otherwise certifiable, the district court abused its discretion by certifying them as to a nationwide class of physicians, rather than a subclass confined to a subset of only certain states.

Even a properly restricted subclass, however, would be unable to meet Rule 23(b)(3)'s predominance requirement. There are few common issues of law because, as the defendant HMOs point out, "[s]tates define differently what constitutes a 'clean' claim for payment. States have also adopted different deadlines for making 'prompt' payment."

Compounding the problem of disparate laws is the need for individualized findings of fact. . . .

In conclusion, the district court abused its discretion in certifying the plaintiffs' breach of contract, unjust enrichment, and prompt-pay claims because individualized issues of law or fact predominate over common, classwide issues. We do not reach whether the court should have certified a California Subclass alleging violations of the California Business and Professions Code.

IV.

The preceding Parts focused exclusively on whether common issues of fact and law stemming from the plaintiffs' federal and state claims predominate over individualized issues. We held that while the plaintiffs' federal claims satisfy this requirement, their state claims do not. We now turn to whether the plaintiffs' federal claims satisfy the second prong of the Rule 23(b)(3) test — that "a class action is superior to other available methods for the fair and efficient adjudication of the [claims]." Our focus is not on the convenience or burden of a class action suit per se, but on the relative advantages of a class action suit over whatever other forms of litigation might be realistically available to the plaintiffs.

In many respects, the predominance analysis of Part II has a tremendous impact on the superiority analysis of this Part for the simple reason that, the more common issues predominate over individual issues, the more desirable a class action lawsuit will be as a vehicle for adjudicating the plaintiffs' claims. Rule 23(b)(3) contains a "non[-]exhaustive" list of four factors courts should take into account in making this determination. There is no reason to believe that the putative class members in this case have any particular interest in controlling their own litigation, so the first factor does not counsel against class certification. Similarly, there are no class members separately pursuing other cases involving the same claims and parties, so the second specified factor does not aid the defendants, either. The parties focus most of their discussion on the remaining two factors — the desirability of litigating these claims in a single forum, and the manageability of such a large case. We address each of these concerns in turn. We then turn to two additional arguments against class certification raised by the defendants.

A.

The first factor the parties seriously contest is whether it is desirable to concentrate this litigation in a single forum. Once the plaintiffs establish that common issues of fact and law predominate over individualized issues, there are typically three main reasons why it is desirable to litigate multiple parties' claims in a single forum. First, class actions "offer[ ] substantial economies of time, effort, and expense for the litigants . . . as well as for the court." Holding separate trials for claims that could be tried together "would be costly, inefficient, and would burden the court system" by forcing individual plaintiffs to repeatedly prove the same facts and make the same legal arguments before different courts. Where predominance is established, this consideration will almost always mitigate in favor of certifying a class.

Second, as the Supreme Court has recognized in a related context, class actions often involve "an aggregation of small individual claims, where a large number of claims are required to make it economical to bring suit. The plaintiff's claim may be so small, or the plaintiff so unfamiliar with the law, that he would not file suit individually . . . ." Phillips Petroleum Co. v. Shutts, 472 U.S. 797, 813 (1985) [*supra* p. 276]; *see also* Amchem Prods., Inc. v. Windsor, 521 U.S. 591, 617 (1997) (noting that, in enacting Rule 23(b)(3), "the Advisory Committee had dominantly in mind vindication of 'the rights of groups of people who individually would be without effective strength to bring their opponents into court at all'") [*infra* p. 493]. This consideration supports class certification in cases where the total amount sought by each individual plaintiff is small in absolute terms. It also applies in situations where, as here, the amounts in controversy would make it unlikely that most of the plaintiffs, or attorneys working on a contingency fee basis, would be willing to pursue the claims individually. This is especially true when the defendants are corporate behemoths with a demonstrated willingness and proclivity for drawing out legal proceedings for as long as humanly possible and burying their opponents in paperwork and filings.

Third, it is desirable to concentrate claims in a particular forum when that forum has already handled several preliminary matters. In this case, various individual claims were consolidated before the district court by the Panel on Multidistrict Litigation, and the court has done a fine job in addressing a wide range of pretrial motions. . . .

There are also several reasons courts commonly cite as to why it is particularly undesirable to litigate a class's claims in a single judicial forum. Perhaps most importantly, we assess whether the potential damages available in a class action are grossly disproportionate to the conduct at issue. Where the defendant's alleged behavior is deliberate or intentional, we have had no problem allowing class actions to proceed. Where defendants are being sued for statutory damages for unintentional acts under a strict liability standard, however, courts take a harder look at whether a defendant deserves to be subject to potentially immense liability. *See* Ratner v. Chem. Bank N.Y. Trust Co., 54 F.R.D. 412, 416 (S.D.N.Y. 1972). . . .

. . . Furthermore, since RICO violations must be intentional, there is no danger that the defendants will be subject to an unjustly harsh verdict for accidental behavior. . . .

Without delving into whether the plaintiffs' claims in this case are sufficiently new or innovative to count as an "immature" tort . . ., we reject this as a legitimate consideration in making a "superiority" determination. There is no reason why, even with so-called "immature torts," district and circuit courts cannot make the necessary determinations under Rule 23 based on the pleadings and whatever evidence has been gathered through discovery. Moreover, there is no basis in Rule 23 for arbitrarily foreclosing plaintiffs from pursuing innovative theories through the vehicle of a class action lawsuit. Particularly when the considerations discussed at the beginning of this Section would preclude most plaintiffs from individually litigating their personal claims, a class action may be the only way that most people can have their rights — even "innovative" or "immature" rights — enforced. Furthermore, if an "immature tort" truly raises a variety of new or complicated legal questions, then those questions constitute significant common issues of law. Their resolution in a single class-action forum would greatly foster judicial efficiency and avoid unnecessary, repetitious litigation. For these reasons, it is desirable to litigate the plaintiffs' federal claims in a single forum.

B.

Manageability Problems?

The final factor expressly specified in Rule 23(b)(3) that courts must weigh in deciding to certify a class action is whether certification will cause manageability problems. This concern will rarely, if ever, be in itself sufficient to prevent certification of a class.

In this case, the district court concluded that there were no "unsurmountable difficulties" with managing the case. While recognizing that "reliance, causation and damages may create complications during the course of this litigation," the court found that "the potential difficulties are nowhere near the magnitude of problems that could arise from 600,000 separate actions."

In reviewing this determination, we recall two points generally applicable throughout this "superiority" analysis. First, we are not assessing whether this class action will create significant management problems, but instead determining whether it will create relatively more management problems than any of the alternatives (including, most notably, 600,000 separate lawsuits by the class members). Second, where a court has already made a finding that common issues predominate over individualized issues, we would be hard pressed to conclude that a class action is less manageable than individual actions.

While each plaintiff must prove some individualized factual issues to support his RICO claim,

> there are a number of management tools available to a district court to address any individualized damages issues that might arise in a class action, including: (1) bifurcating liability and damage trials with the same or different juries; (2) appointing a magistrate judge or special master to preside over individual damages proceedings; (3) decertifying the class after the liability trial and providing notice to class members concerning how they may proceed to prove damages; (4) creating subclasses; or (5) altering or amending the class.

In light of these considerations, we hold that the district court acted well within its discretion in concluding that it would be better to handle this case as a class action instead of clogging the federal courts with innumerable individual suits litigating the same issues repeatedly. The defendants have failed to point to any specific management problems —

aside from the obvious ones that are intrinsic in large class actions — that would render a class action impracticable in this case.

C.

Moving beyond the factors enumerated in Rule 23(b)(3), the defendants offer two additional reasons why a class action is inferior to a host of individual suits in resolving these disputes. First, they maintain that "a single jury, in a single trial, should not decide the fate of the managed care industry."

We find such reasoning unpersuasive and contrary to the ends of justice. This trial is not about the managed care industry; it is about whether several large HMOs conspired to systematically underpay doctors. The issue is not whether managed care is wrong, but whether particular managed care companies failed to live up to their agreements. . . .

D.

Second, the defendants contend that a class action creates "unfair and coercive pressures on [them]" to settle that are unrelated to the merits of the plaintiffs' claims. . . .

Mere pressure to settle is not a sufficient reason for a court to avoid certifying an otherwise meritorious class action suit. . . .

Moreover, while affirming certification may induce some defendants to settle, overturning certification may create similar "hydraulic" pressures on the plaintiffs, causing them to either settle or — more likely — abandon their claims altogether. . . . Because one of the parties will generally be disadvantaged regardless of how a court rules on certification, this factor should not be weighed.

V.

For the reasons articulated above, we affirm the district court's grants of class certification as to all RICO-related claims, though we urge it to reconsider the precise scope of the classes, and reverse the district court's grant of class certification as to all state-law claims other than the claim based on California law.

Notes

1. *Klay* is a rich case at many levels. At a doctrinal level, it shows the impact of the source of law — whether federal or state — in determining whether the issue of predominance has been met. It also shows the effect that reliance as an element of a claim can have on the predominance issue as well. At a policy level, it addresses a number of standard arguments that have been made both for and against (b)(3) treatment: whether class

treatment is more efficient, whether the negative-value nature of the lawsuits should affect class certification, whether the cases are "mature or immature," whether class-wide relief is out of proportion to the wrong done, whether a class action is a "bet the industry" proposition that is unsuitable for judicial resolution, and whether class actions impose undue pressure to settle meritless cases. Courts and commentators have raised and debated many of these points; and while they have differed in their views and therefore not all come to the same resolution of each issue as *Klay*, *Klay* is remarkable for the degree to which one case synthesizes many of the most common doctrinal and policy arguments in (b)(3) litigation.

2. At the level of policy, *Klay* uses some policy arguments — notably, the efficiency garnered from class treatment — to bolster its result, while it rejects other policy arguments — such as the effect on the industry and the pressure to settle. What are "good" policy arguments and what are "bad" arguments? Should courts pay attention to no policy arguments, and just enforce the letter of Rule 23 as written? Can *Klay*'s concern for efficiency be justified because efficiency is mentioned in the text of Rule 23(b)(3)? On the other hand, the text of Rule 23(b)(3) also mentions justice. Can't arguments concerning negative social effects to an important industry and the effects of undue settlement pressure on defendants both be seen as arguments about justice?

In a sense, these questions again return to the fundamental issue posed by all four of the Rule 23(b) class actions: Assuming that representation is adequate, when is class treatment appropriate? How much efficiency and what form of justice must be achieved in a (b)(3) action, given that this action aggregates claimants in a way that sacrifices their right to control their own cases?

3. At the level of doctrine, we will again see the role that variations in state law plays in (b)(3) certification decisions when we examine the issue of mass torts. *Klay* shows the reluctance of many federal courts to certify nationwide class actions that involve significantly varying state laws. You might wonder why the same is not true of federal law, which can vary from circuit to circuit. We examine these issues in more detail in Chapter Six; for now, let us observe that federal courts have for the most part solved the problem of inter-circuit variations in federal law in a way that results in the application of a single version of federal law (hence avoiding predominance issues). Although we will examine some choice-of-law techniques by which courts can also avoid the application of varying state laws in nationwide class actions, for the most part courts have been less successful in accomplishing this goal (hence not avoiding the predominance issue). As long as *Klay*'s view on the detrimental effect that significantly varying state laws have on the predominance inquiry remains dominant, plaintiffs seeking to certify class actions must either certify state-by-state (or at least variation-by-variation) classes or forgo state-law claims.

What if the best claims are state-law claims? For instance, in *Klay*, the breach-of-contract claims seem far simpler to prove than the RICO claims. If the class representative and class counsel do not assert these claims in order to achieve class certification on the RICO claims, does the doctrine of claim preclusion bar class members from asserting them later? If so, can the class representative and class counsel possibly be regarded as adequate when they abandon valuable claims? We examine this issue in Section B. *See infra* p. 525.

4.   Because reliance is an element of many consumer-protection, RICO, and fraud cases, the way in which courts treat the intersection of reliance and predominance is one of the central questions in (b)(3) practice. A soft "rule" has emerged that, when plaintiffs need to prove individual reliance on the defendant's statements or conduct as an element of recovery, then individual issues predominate and (b)(3) treatment is not appropriate. *See, e.g.*, Sikes v. Teleline, Inc., 281 F.3d 1350 (11th Cir. 2002). *Klay* evinces a more generous approach to the issue of reliance than some cases, showing that the rule against certifying (b)(3) class actions when individual reliance must be proven is not ironclad. But a case in which individual reliance on the defendant's words or conduct is a central disputed question is swimming upstream in terms of (b)(3) certification.

There is a close relationship between substantive and procedural law in this context. When plaintiffs in RICO, securities-fraud, and consumer-protection cases argue that individual reliance is not an essential element of the claim, often their reason for doing so is not to make the proof of the substantive claim easier (although it does that); the point is to avoid a stumbling block that might destroy class certification. Thus, *Bridge v. Phoenix Bond & Indemnity Co.*, 553 U.S. 639 (2008) — a case holding that plaintiffs need not prove individual reliance to recover in RICO claims — is likely to have an expansive effect on (b)(3) class actions in RICO cases. *Bridge* would not have changed the result in *Klay*; but it would have changed the reasoning. *Bridge* is likely to undermine the precedential value of other RICO cases, such as *Sikes*, that had refused to certify a (b)(3) RICO class because the need to prove individual reliance defeated predominance. *Cf.* In re Zyprexa Prods. Liab. Litig., 253 F.R.D. 69, 188-91 (E.D.N.Y. 2008) (distinguishing a pre-*Bridge* Second Circuit case that had denied class certification of RICO claims).

5.   The following case continues to investigate the role of reliance in certifying (b)(3) class actions. It involves securities fraud, which is one of the common battlegrounds for (b)(3) class certification.

Before we begin, a bit of background. Starting in the 1960s, and continuing apace thereafter, large numbers of (b)(3) class actions asserted securities-fraud claims against corporations, their officers and directors, and others for misrepresentations or omissions of material fact in public statements related to their securities. Many were brought under Rule 10b-5 of the Securities Exchange Act of 1934. *See* 15 U.S.C. § 78j(b); 17 C.F.R. § 240.10(b)-5. A plaintiff needs to prove six elements to establish a Rule 10b-5 claim: a misstatement or omission, materiality, scienter, reliance, proximate causation, and damages. The first three elements are readily provable on a class-wide basis. The remaining three elements (actual reliance, proximate causation, and damages) raise factual questions that seemingly require individual proof peculiar to each plaintiff. Despite this vexing problem, many federal courts certified 10b-5 class actions after the promulgation of Rule 23(b)(3) in 1966 — largely based on the conviction that not to do so would cripple the private enforcement of federal securities laws and deny individual investors a day in court. *See, e.g.*, Green v. Wolf, 406 F.2d 291, 301 (2d Cir. 1968). They dismissed objections to certification with vague references to using subclasses and bifurcated trials.

In 1972 the Supreme Court interpreted substantive securities law in a way that reduced these procedural difficulties. It held that a plaintiff bringing a 10b-5 "omissions" case (as opposed to a misrepresentation case) did not need to prove that any class member relied on the omission; reliance was presumed if the omission was material. Affiliated Ute Citizens of Utah v. United States, 406 U.S. 128 (1972). This theory did not apply to "misrepresentation" cases, and plaintiffs continued to struggle with the task of how to prove the non-common questions in such class actions.

KIRKPATRICK V. J.C. BRADFORD & CO.

827 F.2d 718 (11th Cir. 1987)

■ KRAVITCH, Circuit Judge.

. . .

I. BACKGROUND

These are a few of the many cases arising out of the virtual collapse in 1984 of the Petro-Lewis oil and natural gas investment funds. From 1970 to 1984, about 180,000 people purchased more than $3 billion worth of Petro-Lewis securities and limited partnerships. When the price of oil and gas declined in 1981 and 1982, Petro-Lewis began borrowing funds to pay partnership distributions, to service its debt, and to promote the sale of additional programs. In February 1984, revealing for the first time that it was in dire financial straits, Petro-Lewis announced that it would implement a series of drastic economy measures, including cutting partnership distributions by as much as 50 per cent and selling between one quarter and one third of its reserves. Numerous lawsuits followed.

[A federal court in Colorado approved a $23.5 million settlement of eleven securities-fraud class actions brought against the directors and certain corporate entities of the Petro-Lewis organization. Subsequently, the plaintiffs in this litigation filed suit against broker-dealers that sold Petro-Lewis securities and limited partnerships.]

. . . [P]laintiffs allege that the actions of the defendant brokerage firms and individuals in selling and promoting interests in Petro-Lewis violated sections 11 and 12(2) of the Securities Act of 1933, section 10 of the Securities Exchange Act of 1934, Rule 10b-5 promulgated thereunder, and various common law and statutory obligations under state law. Claiming to represent classes of plaintiffs who, between January 1, 1981 to February 6, 1984, purchased, reinvested in, or otherwise acquired Petro-Lewis limited partnership interests from the defendant firms, the plaintiffs alleged that the defendants knowingly or recklessly participated with Petro-Lewis in disseminating materially misleading information regarding Petro-Lewis' financial condition and failed to provide other information that would have made the statements not misleading.

After discovery and hearings, the district court issued an order and an amended order denying certification of the classes under Rule 23 . . . . [T]he court certified its order for an interlocutory appeal pursuant to 28 U.S.C. § 1292(b). We accepted jurisdiction.

II. RULE 23(b)(3): PREDOMINANCE OF COMMON OR INDIVIDUAL QUESTIONS

. . .

In holding that certification was improper under Rule 23(b)(3), the court concluded that common questions of law and fact in the 10(b) and 10b-5 claims were dominated by individual questions of reliance on the part of the particular purchasers, statutes of limitations in each state in which there may be class members, and arbitration agreements in many of the purchase contracts. The court viewed the state law claims to be inappropriate for class action treatment because liability would depend upon the substantive law of the different states. Finally, the court refused to consider certifying classes limited to the section 11 and 12(2) claims after concluding that the 10(b) and state law claims were the dominant claims asserted in the complaints.

A. *Section 10(b) and Rule 10b-5*

. . . [T]he plaintiffs assert three theories of liability under which common issues of law and fact necessarily would outweigh individual issues. They first contend that their claims concern primarily acts of omission and thus that reliance on the part of individual purchasers should be presumed under the rule of *Affiliated Ute Citizens v. United States*, 406 U.S. 128 (1975). Second, they argue that the claims fall under the fraud-on-the-market theory adopted by our predecessor court in *Shores v. Sklar*, 647 F.2d 462 (5th Cir. 1981) (en banc). Finally, they argue that the allegations involve a common course of conduct toward all defendants, and thus that any issues of individual reliance could not predominate over common questions of facts. Kennedy v. Tallant, 710 F.2d 711 (11th Cir. 1983). . . .

We agree with the district court that under the precedent of this circuit the plaintiffs' complaints cannot be properly characterized as omissions cases under the standards of *Affiliated Ute*. . . .

We cannot agree, however, with the court's rejection of the fraud-on-the-market theory as a basis for class action treatment. In *Shores v. Sklar*, *supra*, the former Fifth Circuit sitting en banc held that, in fraud claims asserted under Rules 10b-5(1) and (3), the reliance element of Rule 10b-5 may be satisfied by proof that the plaintiff relied on the integrity of the market rather than on specific misrepresentations by the defendants. Under *Shores*, reliance may be established by proof that securities not traded on the open market could not have been issued but for a fraudulent scheme by the defendants. Here, consistent with *Shores*, plaintiffs alleged that the Petro-Lewis shares, which were not traded on the open market, could not have been marketed but for the defendants' fraud.

In rejecting this claim as improper for class treatment, the court relied solely on its conclusion that the plaintiffs' allegations lacked evidentiary support. Despite the court's assertions to the contrary, this determination was an inappropriate inquiry into the merits of the plaintiffs' claims. Certainly, as the court noted in its order, a court may look beyond the allegations of the complaint in determining whether a motion for class certification should be granted. Gen. Tel. Co. of Sw. v. Falcon, 457 U.S. 147, 160 (1982) [*supra* p. 353]. . . . Here, however, the court's rejection of the fraud-on-the-market theory was based upon nothing other than the court's assessment of the plaintiffs' likelihood of success on the claims. This is an improper basis for deciding the propriety of a class action. *E.g.*, Eisen v. Carlisle & Jacquelin, 417 U.S. 156, 177-78 (1974).

Nor can the court's rejection of the fraud-on-the-market theory be upheld under the rationale that fraud-on-the-market claims are improper for class treatment where, as here, the evidence indicates that the named plaintiffs relied on the advice of their brokers rather than solely on the integrity of the market. As the defendants note, several district courts have denied class certification for fraud-on-the-market claims where evidence indicates that the named plaintiffs may in fact have relied on factors other than the market's integrity. These cases, however, generally have concerned fraud-on-the-market claims involving securities traded in an open market. That version of the fraud-on-the-market theory focuses on the plaintiffs' reliance on the integrity of an open and developed market to set a price accurately reflecting the security's value. . . .

Because the Petro-Lewis shares were not traded on the open market, we need not now consider the appropriateness of class certification of traditional fraud-on-the-market claims involving securities that are openly traded. We conclude, however, that where as here, a complaint alleges that a security not traded on the open market could not have been issued but for the fraud of the defendants, class action treatment is not precluded by the possibility that some purchasers, including the named plaintiffs, might have relied on factors other than the integrity of the market. . . .

We conclude for similar reasons that the district court also improperly found that the plaintiffs' 10b-5(2) misrepresentation claims were not suited for class treatment. The basis for the court's denial of class certification of the misrepresentation claims was the court's conclusion that the claims involved primarily oral representations and thus would present individual issues of reliance. To arrive at this conclusion, the court focused on deposition evidence indicating that the named plaintiffs relied not so much on prospectuses and other written materials as on the recommendations of their individual brokers. The court further found that the plaintiffs had uncovered no evidence to show that their particular brokers had attended the Petro-Lewis sales sessions or explicitly followed the standardized sales pitch.

Contrary to the court's construction of the claims, however, the complaints alleged that the defendant brokerage firms and individual officers engaged in a common course of conduct to misrepresent, by affirmative acts and by omission, the financial condition of Petro-Lewis. Neither the complaints nor the deposition testimony relied upon by the district court indicate that any oral representations to the named plaintiffs varied materially from the misleading information alleged to have been disseminated generally as a result of the defendants' common schemes. Consequently, the possibility that the named plaintiffs or other potential class members may have obtained the allegedly misleading information via their individual brokers rather than through widely distributed written information cannot transform the allegations of the complaints into claims concerning primarily questions of individual reliance. The claims essentially involve allegations that the defendants "committed the same unlawful acts in the same method against the entire class."

As in any 10b-5(2) misrepresentation claim, each potential class member must prove reliance on some form of the allegedly misleading information in order to recover. In view of the overwhelming number of common factual and legal issues presented by plaintiffs' misrepresentation claims, however, the mere presence of the factual issue of individual reliance could not render the claims unsuitable for class treatment. Here, . . . each of the complaints alleges "a single conspiracy and fraudulent scheme against a large number of individuals" and thus is "particularly appropriate for class action." Moreover, given the numerous and substantial common issues presented by both the fraud-on-the-market and the misrepresentation claims, the common questions in these cases cannot legitimately be considered subordinate to the individual questions presented by the different state statutes of limitations that may be applicable or by the arbitration agreements contained in some of the purchasers' contracts. "Rule 23 does not require that all the questions of law and fact raised by the dispute be common."

. . . "Separate actions by each of the class members would be repetitive, wasteful, and an extraordinary burden on the courts." The district court thus abused its discretion in ruling that the requirements of Rule 23(b)(3) were not satisfied in this case. . . .

B. *State Law Claims*

In concluding that the state law claims failed to satisfy the requirements of Rule 23(b)(3), the district court reasoned that the differing standards of liability required by the laws of the various states would render class action treatment unmanageable. We agree with the district court that the state law claims would require application of the standards of liability of the state in which each purchase was transacted. The district court thus did not abuse its discretion in denying class certification on these claims.

C. *Section 11 and 12(2) Claims*

In explaining its denial of class certification of the section 11 and 12(2) claims, the district court stated that it "did not address" these claims individually because to separate these claims from the Rule 10b-5 and state law claims would be "unduly burdensome" on the court. The court consequently denied class certification of the Rule 11 and 12(2) claims based upon its conclusion that the 10b-5 and the state law claims did not meet the requirements of Rule 23(b)(3). In view of our determination that the court erroneously ruled that the 10b-5 claims did not meet the requirements of Rule 23(b)(3), the court must of course reconsider its decision regarding the section 11 and 12(2) claims. . . .

IV. CONCLUSION

For the foregoing reasons, the order of the district court is reversed in part, affirmed in part, and remanded with instructions.

Notes

1. The essence of the fraud-on-the-market theory is that a section 10b-5 plaintiff alleging material misrepresentations by a corporation or its officers does not need to prove his own personal reliance on the particular misrepresentation; instead, reliance will be presumed because the plaintiff is deemed to have relied on the market price, which was distorted by the misrepresentation. The fraud-on-the-market theory in section 10b-5 cases was first articulated in *Blackie v. Barrack*, 524 F.2d 891 (9th Cir. 1975). Other circuits followed *Blackie*. Shortly after *Kirkpatrick*, a plurality of the Supreme Court at last embraced this theory. Basic, Inc. v. Levinson, 485 U.S. 224 (1988). *Basic* creates a presumption of individual reliance by class members in 10b-5 actions when material misrepresentations and omissions are made public concerning a publicly traded security in an efficient market. As a practical matter, defendants find the presumption of reliance virtually irrebuttable. *See Basic*, 485 U.S. at 256 n.7 (White, J., dissenting). In *In re Salomon Analyst Metromedia Litigation*, 544 F.3d 474 (2d Cir. 2008), the Second Circuit held that the fraud-on-the-market presumption created by *Basic* is also available in suits against "secondary actors" like research analysts, as well as primary actors like the issuers of securities. But *Salomon* remanded the case to allow the analyst to rebut the presumption of reliance. *Accord* Oscar Private Equity Invs. v. Allegiance Telecom, Inc., 487 F.3d 261, 270 (5th Cir. 2007).

2. By contrast the Second Circuit has held that the fraud-on-the-market presumption is not applicable in markets for consumer goods that are "anything but efficient." McLaughlin v. Am. Tobacco Co., 522 F.3d 215 (2d Cir. 2008) (reversing certification of a class of cigarette smokers who were allegedly deceived into believing that "light" cigarettes were healthier than "full-flavored" cigarettes) (*infra* p. 1076).

3. Some courts have questioned whether section 10b-5 class actions that rely on the fraud-on-the-market approach should be routinely certified. One argument is that in many fraud-on-the-market cases, class plaintiffs that purchased securities at different points during the allegedly fraudulent course of behavior have inherent conflicts of interest on matters of proof and damages. This fact is especially true when the corporation makes a series of partially curative disclosures before the misrepresentation is fully disclosed. For an important explication of this theory, finding that the conflicting interests of various shareholders who bought and sold during the period rendered the class representatives inadequate under Rule 23(a)(4), see In re Seagate Tech. II Sec. Litig., 843 F. Supp. 1341 (N.D. Cal. 1994). In response to this opinion, the plaintiffs modified the definition of the class so that it consisted only of one subclass of purchasers that retained their stock throughout the entire class period. The district court then certified the class. *See* In re Seagate Tech. II Sec. Litig., 156 F.R.D. 229 (N.D. Cal. 1994).

Some courts followed *Seagate II* and declined to certify Rule 10b-5 class actions due to conflicts. *See, e.g.,* Ballan v. Upjohn Co., 159 F.R.D. 473 (W.D. Mich. 1994). Other courts deemed *Seagate* aberrational and continued to certify Rule 10b-5 class actions. *See, e.g.,* Welling v. Alexy, 155 F.R.D. 654 (N.D. Cal. 1994); Picard Chem. Inc. Profit Sharing Plan v. Perrigo Co., 1996 WL 739170 (W.D. Mich. Sept. 27, 1996) (collecting cases).

4. A different argument against the fraud-on-the-market theory is to attack the theory's basic assumption: that markets are indeed perfectly efficient (in the sense that the value of the stock exactly reflects all the available information). Thus, some courts require proof that the stock was bought and sold in an efficient market. For instance, *Unger v. Amedisys Inc.*, 401 F.3d 316 (5th Cir. 2005), held that the evidence did not establish that an efficient market existed for a small-cap stock traded in low volume on the NASDAQ exchange; therefore, it refused to apply the fraud-on-the-market theory to the case and vacated an order certifying a (b)(3) class action. *See also* In re PolyMedica Corp. Sec. Litig., 432 F.3d 1, 19 (1st Cir. 2005) (requiring only proof of "basic facts" to invoke the fraud-on-the-market presumption for class-certification, rather than trial, purposes).

5. *Blackie* acknowledged the conflicts of interest that partial curative disclosures created within a section 10b-5 class, but asserted that, if the conflicts proved too troublesome under the out-of-pocket loss measure of damages in such cases, the court could adopt a different measure of damages, such as rescission or compensatory damages. 524 F.2d at 908-11. Can it ever be proper to skirt a problem with a proposed aggregation device (i.e., the class action) by changing the proper remedy due the plaintiffs?

6. The Supreme Court itself has recently made it more difficult for plaintiffs to bring securities-fraud class actions by holding that investors who allege securities fraud must provide specific allegations that the purported fraud actually caused the loss at issue. It is not sufficient to simply allege that the misrepresentations or omissions led the stock price to be inflated. Dura Pharms., Inc. v. Broudo, 544 U.S. 336 (2005).

7. In 1995 Congress passed, over the President's veto, the Private Securities Litigation Reform Act ("PSLRA"). Pub. L. No. 104-67, 109 Stat. 737. The PSLRA was intended to curb the number of securities-fraud class actions and the behavior of the entrepreneurial lawyers who had often initiated such suits.

While the PSLRA does not alter the criteria to be applied in deciding whether to certify a (b)(3) securities-fraud class, it contains many provisions which may indirectly influence this decision. For example, it requires:

- that the plaintiff must plead the fraud with particularity, including each statement alleged to be misleading and why;

- that discovery should be automatically stayed while a defendant's motion to dismiss is pending; and

- that plaintiff attorneys fees should be no more than a reasonable percentage of the funds recovered by the class;

The PSLRA also established new procedures for selecting the class representative by creating a special notice and selection procedure with a presumption that the class member with the largest claimed loss is the "most adequate" class representative. This court-appointed representative is then empowered to select counsel for the class. The goal of the class-action provisions was to eliminate "professional class representatives" who owned one share of many corporations and filed many lawsuits each year.

8. Surprisingly, perhaps, the PSLRA seems not to have slowed the filing of securities-fraud law suits. See, e.g., Warren R. Stern & Sarah E. McCallum, *The Private Securities Litigation Reform Act: Ten Years After*, 38 REV. SEC. & COMMODITIES REG. 789 (2005) (finding an unexpected increase in filings, settlements, and disposition times for cases brought under the new act); C. Evan Stewart, *Securities Class Action: Beginning of the End, or End of the Beginning*, 35 SEC. REG. & L. RPT. 2143 (2003) (finding an increase in securities class actions and a decrease in dismissals since passage of the PSLRA).

9. More generally, the common theme running through these notes is the interplay between substance and procedure. The push toward the fraud-on-the-market theory or toward a looser theory of loss causation was fueled by the need to overcome the predominance requirement of Rule 23(b)(3); in many securities-fraud cases, the lack of other good aggregation mechanisms, especially for small claims that are not worthwhile to assert individually, makes a class action the only option for recovery; when proof of individual reliance and loss was making it difficult to certify securities-fraud cases as class actions, the substantive law changed. Conversely, the push back against the fraud-on-the-market theory and toward stronger

proof of loss causation is clearly fueled by the recognition that securities-fraud cases will be harder to certify, and fewer will therefore be brought.

Given this interplay between substance and procedure, is Rule 23 merely a procedural rule, rather than a rule that "abridge[s], enlarge[s], or modif[ies] any substantive right," in contravention of 28 U.S.C. § 2072(b)? For an article arguing that the desire for class certification is driving plaintiffs toward aggregate proof of claims that can in turn inappropriately change the substantive law, see Richard A. Nagareda, *Class Certification in the Age of Aggregate Proof*, 84 N.Y.U. L. REV. 97 (2009).

10. *Kirkpatrick* noted that the district court's skepticism about the merits of the plaintiffs' substantive theory should not influence its decision whether common questions justified (b)(3) treatment. In *In re Initial Public Offering Securities Litigation*, 471 F.3d 24 (2d Cir. 2006), *clarified on reh'g*, 483 F.3d 70 (2d Cir. 2007), the court took the opposite position, holding that, to the extent relevant to deciding a class-certification motion, district courts should evaluate the merits of the plaintiffs' assertions. *See supra* p. 361, Note 5. The following case takes up this issue in the context of antitrust claims, which are often the subject of (b)(3) certification disputes.

IN RE HYDROGEN PEROXIDE ANTITRUST LITIGATION

552 F. 3d 305 (3rd Cir. 2008)

■ SCIRICA, Chief Judge.

At issue in this antitrust action are the standards a district court applies when deciding whether to certify a class. We will vacate the order certifying the class in this case and remand for proceedings consistent with this opinion.

In deciding whether to certify a class under Fed. R. Civ. P. 23, the district court must make whatever factual and legal inquiries are necessary and must consider all relevant evidence and arguments presented by the parties. In this appeal, we clarify three key aspects of class certification procedure. First, the decision to certify a class calls for findings by the court, not merely a "threshold showing" by a party, that each requirement of Rule 23 is met. Factual determinations supporting Rule 23 findings must be made by a preponderance of the evidence. Second, the court must resolve all factual or legal disputes relevant to class certification, even if they overlap with the merits — including disputes touching on elements of the cause of action. Third, the court's obligation to consider all relevant evidence and arguments extends to expert testimony, whether offered by a party seeking class certification or by a party opposing it.

I.

Purchasers of hydrogen peroxide and related chemical products brought this antitrust conspiracy action against chemical manufacturers. [Hydrogen peroxide is used principally as a bleach for pulp and paper. In addition, two other products, sodium percarbonate and sodium perborate (together known as persalts), contained hydrogen peroxide and were used as detergents. Only Solvay produced and sold sodium percarbonate in the United States during the class period. Solvay Chemicals, Degussa Corp., and FMC sold sodium perborate in the United States during the class period. Other defendants — Akzo, Arkema, and Kemira — did not sell or produce sodium perborate in the United States during the class period.

[American and European Commission investigators began examining possible violations of the antitrust laws in the hydrogen-peroxide industry. In 2005, EC regulators charged eighteen manufacturers with price fixing, and Solvay and Azko pleaded guilty in American courts to price fixing. After several plaintiffs filed class actions against producers of hydrogen peroxide and persalts alleging a conspiracy in restraint of trade under § 1 of the Sherman Act, the Judicial Panel on Multidistrict Litigation transferred all federal actions to the United States District Court for the Eastern District of Pennsylvania, which consolidated the cases.] The consolidated amended complaint alleged that during an eleven-year class period (January 1, 1994–January 5, 2005) defendants (1) communicated about prices they would charge, (2) agreed to charge prices at certain levels, (3) exchanged information on prices and sales volume, (4) allocated markets and customers, (5) agreed to reduce production capacity, (6) monitored each other, and (7) sold hydrogen peroxide at agreed prices.

The District Court denied defendants' motion to dismiss the complaint for failure to state a claim. Following extensive discovery, plaintiffs moved to certify a class of direct purchasers of hydrogen peroxide, sodium perborate, and sodium percarbonate, over an eleven-year class period. In support of class certification, plaintiffs offered the opinion of an economist. Defendants, opposing class certification, offered the opinion of a different economist. Defendants separately moved to exclude the opinion of plaintiffs' economist as unreliable under *Daubert v. Merrell Dow Pharmaceuticals, Inc.*, 509 U.S. 579 (1993). Concluding plaintiffs' expert's opinion was admissible and supported plaintiffs' motion for class certification, the District Court certified a class of direct purchasers of hydrogen peroxide, sodium perborate, and sodium percarbonate under Fed.R.Civ.P. 23(b)(3). The District Court identified seven issues to be tried on a class-wide basis: (1) whether defendants and others engaged in a combination and conspiracy to fix, raise, maintain, or stabilize prices; allocate customers and markets; or control and restrict output of hydrogen peroxide, sodium perborate, and sodium percarbonate sold in the United States; (2) the identity of the participants in the alleged conspiracy; (3) the duration of the alleged conspiracy and the nature and character of defendants' acts performed in furtherance of it; (4) the effect of the alleged conspiracy on the prices of hydrogen peroxide and persalts during the class period; (5) whether the alleged conspiracy violated the Sherman Act; (6) whether the activities alleged in furtherance of the conspiracy or their effect on the prices of hydrogen peroxide and persalts during the class period injured named plaintiffs and the other members of the class; and (7) the proper means of calculating and distributing damages. The class was defined as:

> All persons or entities, including state, local and municipal government entities (but excluding defendants, their parents, predecessors, successors, subsidiaries, and affiliates as well as federal government entities) who purchased hydrogen peroxide, sodium perborate, or sodium percarbonate in the United States, its territories, or possessions, or from a facility located in the United States, its territories, or possessions, directly from any of the defendants, or from any of their parents, predecessors, successors, subsidiaries, or affiliates, at any time during the period from September 14, 1994 to January 5, 2005.

We granted defendants' petition for an interlocutory appeal under Fed. R. Civ. P. 23(f).

II.

Class certification is proper only "if the trial court is satisfied, after a rigorous analysis, that the prerequisites" of Rule 23 are met. Gen. Tel. Co. of Sw. v. Falcon, 457 U.S. 147, 161 (1982) [*supra* p. 353]; *see also* Amchem Prods., Inc. v. Windsor, 521 U.S. 591, 615 (1997) (Rule 23(b)(3) requirements demand a "close look") [*infra* p. 493].

The trial court, well-positioned to decide which facts and legal arguments are most important to each Rule 23 requirement, possesses broad discretion to control proceedings and frame issues for consideration under Rule 23. But proper discretion does not soften the rule: a class may not be certified without a finding that each Rule 23 requirement is met. Careful application of Rule 23 accords with the pivotal status of class certification in large-scale litigation, because

> denying or granting class certification is often the defining moment in class actions (for it may sound the "death knell" of the litigation on the part of plaintiffs, or create unwarranted pressure to settle non-meritorious claims on the part of defendants). . . .

Newton v. Merrill Lynch, Pierce, Fenner & Smith, Inc., 259 F.3d 154, 162 (3d Cir. 2001). In some cases, class certification "may force a defendant to settle rather than incur the costs of defending a class action and run the risk of potentially ruinous liability." Accordingly, the potential for unwarranted settlement pressure "is a factor we weigh in our certification calculus." The Supreme Court recently cautioned that certain antitrust class actions may present prime opportunities for plaintiffs to exert pressure upon defendants to settle weak claims. *See* Bell Atl. Corp. v. Twombly, 550 U.S. 544 (2007) [*infra* p. 785].

III.

Here, the District Court found the Rule 23(a) requirements were met, a determination defendants do not now challenge. Plaintiffs sought certification under Rule 23(b)(3) . . . . The twin requirements of Rule 23(b)(3) are known as predominance and superiority.

Only the predominance requirement is disputed in this appeal. Predominance "tests whether proposed classes are sufficiently cohesive to warrant adjudication by representation," *Amchem,* 521 U.S. at 623, a standard "far more demanding" than the commonality requirement of Rule 23(a), *id.* at 623-24 . . . . Because "the nature of the evidence that will suffice to resolve a question determines whether the question is common or individual," "a district court must formulate some prediction as to how specific issues will play out in order to determine whether common or individual issues predominate in a given case." "If proof of the essential elements of the cause of action requires individual treatment, then class certification is unsuitable." Accordingly, we examine the elements of plaintiffs' claim "through the prism" of Rule 23 to determine whether the District Court properly certified the class.

A.

The elements of plaintiffs' claim are (1) a violation of the antitrust laws — here, § 1 of the Sherman Act, (2) individual injury resulting from that violation, and (3) measurable damages. Importantly, individual injury (also known as antitrust impact) is an element of the cause of action; to prevail on the merits, every class member must prove at least some antitrust impact resulting from the alleged violation.

In antitrust cases, impact often is critically important for the purpose of evaluating Rule 23(b)(3)'s predominance requirement because it is an element of the claim that may call for individual, as opposed to common, proof.

Plaintiffs' burden at the class certification stage is not to prove the element of antitrust impact, although in order to prevail on the merits each class member must do so. Instead, the task for plaintiffs at class certification is to demonstrate that the element of antitrust impact is capable of proof at trial through evidence that is common to the class rather than individual to its members. Deciding this issue calls for the district court's rigorous assessment of the available evidence and the method or methods by which plaintiffs propose to use the evidence to prove impact at trial.

Here, the District Court found the predominance requirement was met because plaintiffs would be able to use common, as opposed to individualized, evidence to prove antitrust impact at trial. On appeal, defendants contend the District Court erred in three principal respects in finding plaintiffs satisfied the predominance requirement: (1) by applying too lenient a standard of proof for class certification, (2) by failing meaningfully to consider the views of defendants' expert while crediting plaintiffs' expert, and (3) by erroneously applying presumption of antitrust impact . . . .

We review a class certification order for abuse of discretion, which occurs if the district court's decision "rests upon a clearly erroneous finding of fact, an errant conclusion of law or an improper application of law to fact." . . .

B.

. . . As noted, both plaintiffs and defendants presented the opinions of expert economists. Importantly, the experts disagreed on the key disputed predominance issue — whether antitrust impact was capable of proof at trial through evidence common to the class, as opposed to individualized evidence.

Plaintiffs' expert, John C. Beyer, Ph.D., offered an opinion purporting to show that "there is common proof that can be used to demonstrate that the alleged conspiracy to raise prices, restrict output and allocate customers would have impacted all purchasers of hydrogen peroxide, sodium perborate, and sodium percarbonate." Beyer's "market analysis" suggested that conditions in the hydrogen peroxide industry favored a conspiracy that would have impacted the entire class. First, hydrogen peroxide and persalts are fungible, undifferentiated commodity products, which means producers compete on price, not quality or other features. Second, production is heavily concentrated in a small group of manufacturers. Third, there are high barriers to entry in the industry and no close economic substitutes, preventing any competitors from entering the market and undercutting prices. Fourth, defendants' geographic markets overlapped, so that purchasers would have benefitted from price competition if not for the alleged conspiracy. . . .

Beyer identified two "potential approaches" to estimating damages on a class-wide basis: (1) benchmark analysis, which would compare actual prices during the alleged conspiracy with prices that existed before the class period; and (2) regression analysis, through which it "may be possible . . to estimate the relationship between price of hydrogen peroxide, sodium perborate, and sodium percarbonate and the various market forces that influence prices, including demand and supply variables." These methods, according to Beyer, could be used to estimate the prices plaintiffs would have faced but for the conspiracy. Beyer stated that "sufficient reliable data" exist to allow him to employ one or both of the potential approaches.

Defendants offered the opinion of their own expert economist, Janusz A. Ordover, Ph.D. . . . . Ordover set out to address "whether, assuming a conspiracy of the kind described in the Complaint, the Plaintiffs will be able to show, through common proof, that all or virtually all of the members of the proposed class suffered economic injury caused by the alleged conspiracy." Ordover also "opine[d] on whether a formulaic approach exists by which impact could be demonstrated and damages to the class could be reasonably calculated." Ordover responded to and disputed many of Beyer's opinions. . . .

. . . Ordover opined that the statistical methods by which Beyer proposed to demonstrate common impact and damages were not feasible. Given the record of prices and output in the industry and the apparent influence of individualized factors on pricing, "class-wide assessment of impact based on aggregate price information [was] impossible," and any formulaic approach to determine a set of "but-for prices" would have to incorporate a multitude of different "variables," defeating any reasonable notion of proof common to the class. . . .

In addition to presenting Ordover's testimony, defendants moved to exclude Beyer's testimony as unreliable, citing *Daubert* . . . .

C.

The District Court concluded the predominance requirement was met. . . .

The District Court held that it was sufficient that Beyer proposed reliable methods for proving impact and damages; it did not matter that Beyer had not completed any benchmark or regression analyses, and the court would not require plaintiffs to show at the certification stage that either method would work.

IV.

A.

Defendants contend the District Court applied too lenient a standard of proof with respect to the Rule 23 requirements by (1) accepting only a "threshold showing" by plaintiffs rather than making its own determination, (2) requiring only that plaintiffs demonstrate their "intention" to prove impact on a class-wide basis, and (3) singling out antitrust actions as appropriate for class treatment even when compliance with Rule 23 is "in doubt." . . .

1.

The following principles guide a district court's class certification analysis. First, the requirements set out in Rule 23 are not mere pleading rules. The court may "delve beyond the pleadings to determine whether the requirements for class certification are satisfied."

An overlap between a class certification requirement and the merits of a claim is no reason to decline to resolve relevant disputes when necessary to determine whether a class certification requirement is met. Some uncertainty ensued when the Supreme Court declared in *Eisen v. Carlisle & Jacquelin*, 417 U.S. 156, 177 (1974), that there is "nothing in either the language or history of Rule 23 that gives a court any authority to conduct a preliminary inquiry into the merits of a suit in order to determine whether it may be maintained as a class action." . . . *Eisen* is best understood to preclude only a merits inquiry that is not necessary to determine a Rule 23 requirement. Other courts of appeals have agreed. Because the decision whether to certify a class "requires a thorough examination of the factual and legal allegations," the court's rigorous analysis may include a "preliminary inquiry into the merits," and the court may "consider the substantive elements of the plaintiffs' case in order to envision the form that a trial on those issues would take." A contested requirement is not forfeited in favor of the party seeking certification merely because it is similar or even identical to one normally decided by a trier of fact. Although the district court's findings for the purpose of class certification are conclusive on that topic, they do not bind the fact-finder on the merits.

The evidence and arguments a district court considers in the class certification decision call for rigorous analysis. A party's assurance to the court that it intends or plans to meet the requirements is insufficient. . . .

[The court then examined amendments to Rule 23 in 2003, which it asserted supported its view.] To summarize: because each requirement of Rule 23 must be met, a district court errs as a matter of law when it fails to resolve a genuine legal or factual dispute relevant to determining the requirements.

2.

. . .

. . . [A] district court exercising proper discretion in deciding whether to certify a class will resolve factual disputes by a preponderance of the evidence and make findings that each Rule 23 requirement is met or is not met, having considered all relevant evidence and arguments presented by the parties. . . .

B.

Although the District Court properly described the class certification decision as requiring "rigorous analysis," some statements in its opinion depart from the standards we have articulated. The District Court stated, "So long as plaintiffs demonstrate their intention to prove a significant portion of their case through factual evidence and legal arguments common to all class members, that will now suffice. It will not do here to make judgments about whether plaintiffs have adduced enough evidence or whether their evidence is more or less credible than defendants'." With respect to predominance, the District Court stated that "[p]laintiffs need only make a threshold showing that the element of impact will predominantly involve generalized issues of proof, rather than questions which are particular to each member of the plaintiff class." . . . It is incorrect to state that a plaintiff need only demonstrate an "intention" to try the case in a manner that satisfies the predominance requirement. Similarly, invoking the phrase "threshold showing" risks misapplying Rule 23. . . .

. . . [In addition,] the District Court reasoned, "[i]t is well recognized that private enforcement of [antitrust] laws is a necessary supplement to government action. With that in mind, in an alleged horizontal price-fixing conspiracy case when a court is in doubt as to whether or not to certify a class action, the court should err in favor of allowing the class." . . . These statements invite error. Although the trial court has discretion to grant or deny class certification, the court should not suppress "doubt" as to whether a Rule 23 requirement is met — no matter the area of substantive law. . . .

To the extent that the District Court's analysis reflects application of incorrect standards, remand is appropriate.

C.

Defendants contend the District Court erred as a matter of law in failing to consider the expert testimony of defendants' expert, Ordover, instead deferring to the opinion of plaintiffs' expert, Beyer. Plaintiffs do not dispute that a district court may properly consider expert opinion with respect to Rule 23 requirements at the class certification stage, but maintain that in this case the District Court considered and rejected Ordover's opinion and defendants' arguments based on it.

. . . [I]n addressing the Rule 23 requirements, the court did not confront Ordover's analysis or his substantive rebuttal of Beyer's points. . . . The court appears to have assumed it was barred from weighing Ordover's opinion against Beyer's for the purpose of deciding whether the requirements of Rule 23 had been met. This was erroneous. . . .

Expert opinion with respect to class certification, like any matter relevant to a Rule 23 requirement, calls for rigorous analysis. It follows that opinion testimony should not be uncritically accepted as establishing a Rule 23 requirement merely because the court holds the testimony should not be excluded, under *Daubert* or for any other reason. . . .

. . . Rigorous analysis need not be hampered by a concern for avoiding credibility issues; as noted, findings with respect to class certification do not bind the ultimate fact-finder on the merits. A court's determination that an expert's opinion is persuasive or unpersuasive on a Rule 23 requirement does not preclude a different view at the merits stage of the case. . . .

D.

Defendants contend the District Court, by relying on *Bogosian v. Gulf Oil Corp.*, 561 F.2d 434 (3d Cir. 1977), erroneously presumed the predominance requirement was met. In *Bogosian*, . . . we reasoned that "when an antitrust violation impacts upon a class of persons who do have standing, there is no reason in doctrine why proof of the impact cannot be made on a common basis so long as the common proof adequately demonstrates some damage to each individual. Whether or not fact of damage can be proven on a common basis therefore depends upon the circumstances of each case."

The District Court, upon review of all the evidence consistent with this opinion, may again consider whether the reasoning in *Bogosian* is compatible with the record of this case. *See* In re Salomon Analyst Metromedia Litig., 544 F.3d 474, 485-86 (2d Cir. 2008) (remanding for opportunity for party opposing class certification to present evidence rebutting the fraud-on-the-market presumption, because Rule 23 requires a "definitive assessment" as to the predominance requirement).

V.

For the foregoing reasons, we will vacate the class certification order and remand for proceedings consistent with this opinion.

Notes

1.   Along with *In re Initial Public Offering Securities Litigation*, 471 F.3d 24, 32-33 (2d Cir. 2006), *clarified on reh'g*, 483 F.3d 70 (2d Cir. 2007) ("*IPO*"), *Hydrogen Peroxide* has been described (at least by defense lawyers) as the most significant class-action decision of its decade. The reason is not their specific holdings on the certification of the class actions before them; rather, their importance lies in their insistence that courts rigorously enforce the requirements of Rule 23, even when those requirements overlap with issues going to the merits. As *Hydrogen Peroxide* says, for a long time courts read *Eisen v. Carlisle & Jacquelin*, 417 U.S. 156, 177 (1974), as denying them authority to conduct "a preliminary inquiry into the merits." *Hydrogen Peroxide* shows, however, that sometimes the two sets of issues are inextricably intertwined.

In view of *IPO* and *Hydrogen Peroxide*, how much discovery should be allowed the parties prior to the certification decision? In many cases trial courts bifurcate discovery into "class" discovery versus "merits" discovery. *See, e.g.*, Blair v. Source One Mortgage Serv. Corp., 1997 WL 79289 (E.D. La. Feb. 24, 1997). The most recent edition of the *Manual for Complex Litigation* recognizes that this may be necessary and discusses how best it might be managed. MANUAL FOR COMPLEX LITIGATION, FOURTH § 21.14 (2004). If the certification decision requires detailed findings overlapping with the merits of the plaintiffs claims, must the certification decision be postponed until the end of discovery? Won't this delay disserve everyone's interests? *See* Blades v. Monsanto Co., 400 F.3d 562, 567 (8th Cir. 2005) ("When the decision on class certification comes before full merits discovery has been completed, the court must necessarily conduct this preliminary inquiry prospectively. A decision to certify or not to certify a class may therefore require revisiting upon completion of full discovery.").

2.   In terms of class-action practice, the Second and Third Circuits are routinely two of the three largest circuits in the nation. Therefore, their insistence on a more rigorous analysis into the requirements of Rule 23 has a significant impact on the certification of many class actions. But the hard-look concept has also caught on in other circuits; the Fourth, Fifth, and Seventh Circuits have adopted similar approaches. *See* Unger v. Amedisys Inc., 401 F.3d 316, 321-22 (5th Cir. 2005) (requiring courts to find

facts favoring class certification through the use of "rigorous, though preliminary, standards of proof"); Gariety v. Grant Thornton, LLP, 368 F.3d 356, 366 (4th Cir. 2004) (requiring that "the factors spelled out in Rule 23 . . . be addressed through findings"); Szabo v. Bridgeport Machs., Inc., 249 F.3d 672, 675-76 (7th Cir. 2001) (requiring "whatever factual and legal inquiries are necessary under Rule 23" to "resolve the disputes before deciding whether to certify the class"). The Eighth Circuit, on the other hand, has stayed closer to *Eisen*'s language. *See Blades*, 400 F.3d at 567 ("The closer any dispute at the class certification stage comes to the heart of the claim, the more cautious the court should be in ensuring that it must be resolved in order to determine the nature of the evidence the plaintiff would require."). The First Circuit has also shown reluctance to engage in a hard look at the class-certification stage, *see* In re PolyMedica Corp. Sec. Litig., 432 F.3d 1, 19 (1st Cir. 2005), but it recently struck a compromise:

> We do not need to resolve now whether "findings" regarding the class certification criteria are ever necessary, but we do hold that when a Rule 23 requirement relies on a novel or complex theory as to injury, as the predominance inquiry does in this case, the district court must engage in a searching inquiry into the viability of that theory and the existence of the facts necessary for the theory to succeed.

In re New Motor Vehicles Canadian Exp. Antitrust Litig., 522 F.3d 6, 26 (1st Cir. 2008). *See also* AM. L. INST., PRINCIPLES OF THE LAW OF AGGREGATE LITIGATION §§ 2.06 (2009) (adopting the *IPO* approach).

3.   At least some of the players in the hydrogen-peroxide industry were engaged in antitrust violations of criminal proportions. Is it troubling that they might escape civil liability for their conduct if no class action can be certified? Should a court consider that fact in deciding the rigor with which the plaintiffs must establish predominance and the other Rule 23 elements? *Cf.* Robinson v. Tex. Auto. Dealers Ass'n, 387 F.3d 416, 421 (5th Cir. 2004) (stating that "the strength of a plaintiff's claim should not affect the certification decision").

4.   Critical to *Hydrogen Peroxide* was the issue whether the plaintiffs' proof of antitrust impact and damage could be proven on a class-wide basis. In Chapters Eight and Ten, we examine more closely the idea of attempting to prove through statistical sampling or modeling the fact and amount of damage suffered by a class. *See infra* pp. 971, 1058. To the extent that this idea (sometimes known as "trial by statistics") works, it makes both proof of the substantive claim simpler and class certification more likely. Again, substance and procedure work hand in hand.

5.   When an individualized inquiry is necessary to determine if class members suffered an antitrust injury, some courts have argued that (b)(3) treatment is inappropriate due to a lack of predominance. *See Robinson*, 387 F.3d 416 (also reversing district court's certification because the court failed to discuss how it would administer a trial, thus running afoul of the superiority requirement). *See also* Cordes & Co. Fin. Servs., Inc. v. A.G. Edwards & Sons, Inc., 502 F.3d 91, 107 (2d Cir. 2007) (remanding to determine "whether injury-in-fact can be proved by common evidence").

6.   Antitrust cases can also fail to meet the predominance requirement when the class members operate in geographically dispersed markets and pay (or are paid) different prices. *See Blades*, 400 F.3d 562.

7.   On the other hand, following the idea that we first encountered in *Smilow v. Southwestern Bell Mobile Systems, Inc.*, 323 F.3d 32 (1st Cir. 2003) (*supra* p. 426), courts recognize that predominance can be met "even where there are individual variations in damages." *See* In re Scrap Metal Antitrust Litig., 527 F.3d 517, 535 (6th Cir. 2008).

(B)   Mass-Tort Class Actions

Two of the primary differences between most commercial class actions and most mass-tort class actions are that commercial class actions typically arise under federal law and involve small individual stakes. In contrast, mass torts often arise under state law and involves significant claims of injury. Thus, it is often worthwhile for individuals to litigate these cases. Given the preference for party autonomy that underlies the adversarial system, what reason is there to aggregate these cases in a single forum? Is it desirable to certify a class action for a mass tort when the claims are immature, and their viability is uncertain? Given the amount of money involved in most mass torts, won't the certification of a mass tort put defendants in the position of betting their companies on a single jury verdict? Won't it create incentives to settle meritless claims?

There are three standard replies to these arguments from those who favor certification. First, class-action aggregation of mass-tort victims leads to a higher, and therefore better, level of deterrence. Second, the efficiency that the class action generates outweighs concerns for autonomy. Third, those who wish to pursue their own cases are always free to opt out.

The history for mass-tort (b)(3) class actions divides into three phases. First, the drafters of Rule 23(b)(3) did not expect the (b)(3) class action to be generally suitable for mass torts. *See* Advisory Comm. Note to the 1966 Amendment to Rule 23, 39 F.R.D. 98, 103 (1966). Following the drafters' concern that such cases would devolve into multiple lawsuits whose non-common issues of liability and damages would need to be tried separately, federal courts in the 1960s and in the 1970s generally refused to certify mass-tort class actions. Second, during the 1980s the perception began to shift, and courts began to certify more mass-tort class actions. Third, as a result of a series of appellate and Supreme Court decisions during the latter half of the 1990s, courts again became deeply skeptical of certifying (b)(3) mass-tort class actions. Today, we remain in this period of skepticism, and few mass torts are certified as class actions, at least at the federal level. (And, as a result of the subject-matter jurisdiction provided by the Class Action Fairness Act, 28 U.S.C. §§ 1332(d) and 1453, virtually all mass-tort class actions land in federal court.)

These are the issues that swirl around the Rule 23(b)(3) mass-tort class action, which forces us to focus squarely on how much we value efficient aggregation in relation to other values.

Roger H. Trangsrud, JOINDER ALTERNATIVES IN MASS TORT LITIGATION

70 CORNELL L. REV. 779, 820-822 (1985)

The Federal Rules of Civil Procedure recognize an individual litigant's interest in controlling the prosecution of his own tort claim as an important consideration limiting the desirability of the common question class action. The individual's interest in personal control directly relates to the nature and size of his tort claim. Recently courts have certified class actions where the plaintiffs have suffered only property damage or relatively minor personal injuries. They have been extremely reluctant, however, to do so in serious personal injury or wrongful death cases because the nature of the claim indicates a strong interest in personal control over its management. As the severity of the plaintiff's injury increases, the psychological and emotional importance of individually vindicating his rights against the responsible parties also increases. . . .

In a mass tort case several factors affect the plaintiff's interest in individual control over his personal injury or wrongful death claim. First, the individual plaintiff may perceive a number of tactical advantages in proceeding alone. Because significant differences in likely jury awards for particular injuries are perceived to exist between judicial districts, an individual plaintiff will probably file his case in the most convenient, high-award district that the applicable venue and jurisdictional rules permit. Defendants have a very heavy burden to overcome when trying to disturb the plaintiff's choice of forum in individual cases. In a mass tort case, however, if a class action is requested, or the transfer of the related claims to a single forum proposed, the deciding court is much less likely to defer to the forum preferences of individual litigants. . . . The individual plaintiff may thus find himself before an unfamiliar jury in a district where jury awards tend to be less generous than those generally granted in the original forum. . . .

Second, if a class action is certified, the individual plaintiff may find that the state law applied by the forum court is not as favorable as the law which would have been applied had he been able to choose his own forum. The individual plaintiff also runs the risk that the representative plaintiffs in a class action will elect to proceed on liability theories better suited for class treatment at the expense of theories especially favorable to the individual plaintiff. These important considerations may not be highlighted during the certification process because named representatives and attorneys for the putative class have strong personal or financial interests in securing certification and will down-play possible conflicts of interest within the class.

Third, class members lack the direct control that an individual tort litigant can exercise over his own personal lawyer. . . . Class counsel proceeds based upon his estimation of what the interests of the class as a whole are, rather than those of individual plaintiffs, because no internal

procedures exist by which a class can make decisions. Class counsel can thus easily ignore or poorly serve the interests of individual class members.
. . .

In summary, given the traditional respect afforded an individual tort litigant's right to control the prosecution of a substantial personal injury or wrongful death claim, and that the plaintiff loses much of this individual control when the court certifies a class action, courts should avoid using this joinder device to try these cases.

JENKINS V. RAYMARK INDUSTRIES, INC.

782 F.2d 468 (5th Cir. 1986)

■ REAVLEY, Circuit Judge.

In this interlocutory appeal, the thirteen defendants challenge the decision of District Judge Robert M. Parker to certify a class of plaintiffs with asbestos-related claims. We affirm.

I. BACKGROUND TO JUDGE PARKER'S PLAN

Experts estimate that at least 21 million American workers have been exposed to "significant" amounts of asbestos at the workplace since 1940; other millions have been exposed through environmental contact or contact with relatives who have worked with the products. Because of its injurious propensities, such exposure, in human terms, has meant that literally tens of thousands of people fall ill or die from asbestos-related diseases every year. In legal terms, it has translated into thousands of lawsuits, over 20,000 as of 1983 . . . .

Courts, including those in our own circuit, have been ill-equipped to handle this "avalanche of litigation." Our numerous opinions in asbestos-related cases have repeatedly recognized the dilemma confronting our trial courts, and expressed concern about the mounting backlog of cases and inevitable, lengthy trial delays.

About 5,000 asbestos-related cases are pending in this circuit. Much, though by no means all, of the litigation has centered in the Eastern District of Texas. Nearly nine hundred asbestos-related personal injury cases, involving over one thousand plaintiffs, were pending there in December of 1984. Despite innovative streamlined pretrial procedures and large-scale consolidated trials of multiple plaintiffs, the dockets of that district's courts remained alarmingly backlogged. Plaintiffs had waited years for trial, some since 1979 — and new cases were (and still are) being filed every day. It is predicted that, because asbestos-related diseases will continue to manifest themselves for the next 15 years, filings will continue at a steady rate until the year 2000.

In early 1985, ten of these plaintiffs responded by moving to certify a class of all plaintiffs with asbestos-related personal injury actions pending in the Eastern District on December 31, 1984. These plaintiffs hoped to determine in the class action one overarching issue — the viability of the "state of the art" defense. Because the trial of that issue consistently consumed substantial resources in every asbestos trial, and the evidence in each case was either identical or virtually so, they argued, a class determination would accelerate their cases.

II. THE PLAN

[The district court declined to certify the class on a limited-fund theory under Rule 23(b)(1)(B), but certified a class under Rule 23(b)(3).] Drawing on his past experience, the judge concluded that evidence concerning the "state of the art" defense would vary little as to individual plaintiffs while consuming a major part of the time required for their trials. Considerable savings, both for the litigants and for the court, could thus be gained by resolving this and other defense and defense-related questions, including product identification, product defectiveness, gross negligence and punitive damages, in one class trial. . . . Accordingly, it certified the class as to the common questions, ordering them resolved for the class by a class action jury. The class jury would also decide all the individual issues of the unnamed members which would be resolved later in "mini-trials" of seven to ten plaintiffs. Although the class action jury would evaluate the culpability of defendants' conduct for a possible punitive damage award, any such damages would be awarded only after class members had won or settled their individual cases. . . .

[The defendants were allowed to take an interlocutory appeal.] On appeal, defendants challenge the court's decision on three grounds: (1) the class fails to meet the requirements of Rule 23; (2) Texas law proscribes a bifurcated determination of punitive damages and actual damages; and (3) the contemplated class format is unconstitutional.

III. DISCUSSION

The purpose of class actions is to conserve "the resources of both the courts and the parties by permitting an issue potentially affecting every [class member] to be litigated in an economical fashion." Gen. Tel. Co. of Sw. v. Falcon, 457 U.S. 147, 155 (1982) [*supra* p. 353]. . . . Assuming the court considers the Rule 23 criteria, we may reverse its decision only for abuse of discretion. . . .

In addition, Rule 23(c)(4)(A) [now Rule 23(c)(4) — ED.] allows certification as to only certain issues, where appropriate.

IV. RULE 23

Defendants argue that this class meets none of the Rule 23 requirements, except "numerosity." There is no merit to this argument.

The threshold of "commonality" is not high. Aimed in part at "determining whether there is a need for combined treatment and a benefit to be derived therefrom," the rule requires only that resolution of the common questions affect all or a substantial number of the class members. Defendants do not claim that they intend to raise a "state of the art" defense in only a few cases; the related issues are common to all class members.

The "typicality" requirement focuses less on the relative strengths of the named and unnamed plaintiffs' cases than on the similarity of the legal and remedial theories behind their claims. Defendants do not contend that the named plaintiffs' claims rest on theories different from those of the other class members.

The "adequacy" requirement looks at both the class representatives and their counsel. Defendants have not shown that the representatives are "inadequate" due to an insufficient stake in the outcome or interests antagonistic to the unnamed members. Neither do they give us reason to question the district court's finding that class counsel is "adequate" in light of counsel's past experience in asbestos cases, including trials involving multiple plaintiffs.

We similarly find no abuse in the court's determination that the certified questions "predominate," under Rule 23(b)(3). In order to "predominate," common issues must constitute a significant part of the individual cases. It is difficult to imagine that class jury findings on the class questions will not significantly advance the resolution of the underlying hundreds of cases.

Defendants also argue that a class action is not "superior"; they say that better mechanisms, such as the Wellington Facility[7] and "reverse bifurcation,"[8] exist for resolving these claims. Again, however, they have failed to show that the district court abused its discretion by reaching the contrary conclusion. We cannot find that the Wellington Facility, whose merits we do not question, is so superior that it must be used to the exclusion of other forums. Similarly, even if we were prepared to weigh the merits of other procedural mechanisms, we see no basis to conclude that this class action plan is an abuse of discretion.

Courts have usually avoided class actions in the mass accident or tort setting. Because of differences between individual plaintiffs on issues of liability and defenses of liability, as well as damages, it has been feared that separate trials would overshadow the common disposition for the class. The courts are now being forced to rethink the alternatives and priorities by the current volume of litigation and more frequent mass disasters. If Congress leaves us to our own devices, we may be forced to abandon

---

7.   The Wellington Facility, funded by major asbestos producers, is a newly-operational center designed to resolve asbestos-related claims. . . .

8.   "Reverse bifurcation" originated in the Third Circuit as a means of processing that circuit's backlog of asbestos-

related cases. As its name suggests, it is a modified bifurcated trial format whereby plaintiffs in a first trial prove only that exposure to some asbestos product has caused their damages. Thereafter, either the cases are settled or remaining issues are resolved in second or third trials.

repetitive hearings and arguments for each claimant's attorney to the extent enjoyed by the profession in the past. Be that as time will tell, the decision at hand is driven in one direction by all the circumstances. Judge Parker's plan is clearly superior to the alternative of repeating, hundreds of times over, the litigation of the state of the art issues with, as that experienced judge says, "days of the same witnesses, exhibits and issues from trial to trial."

This assumes plaintiffs win on the critical issues of the class trial. To the extent defendants win, the elimination of issues and docket will mean a far greater saving of judicial resources. Furthermore, attorneys' fees for all parties will be greatly reduced under this plan, not only because of the elimination of so much trial time but also because the fees collected from all members of the plaintiff class will be controlled by the judge. From our view it seems that the defendants enjoy all of the advantages, and the plaintiffs incur the disadvantages, of the class action — with one exception: the cases are brought to trial. That counsel for plaintiffs would urge the class action under these circumstances is significant support for the district judge's decision.

Necessity moves us to change and invent. . . . We approve of the district court's decision in finding that this "mass tort" class could be certified.

V. OTHER CONTENTIONS

Defendants' remaining arguments challenge the bifurcated trials under Texas law and the United States Constitution. Defendants contend that, under Texas law, punitive damages cannot be determined separately from actual damages because the culpability of their conduct must be evaluated relative to each plaintiff. We disagree. . . .

The format in this case allows for the district court's review of the reasonableness of each plaintiff's punitive damage award and for our review of the standards which the court has applied. Texas law does not require more.

Defendants' constitutional challenges to bifurcation are equally unavailing. Like their other claims, these arguments only recast in constitutional terms their concern that, because the representatives' cases are "better" than the unnamed plaintiffs', the jury's view of the class claims will be skewed.

Although it fails to raise an issue of constitutional magnitude, this concern is nevertheless legitimate. Care must, of course, be taken to ensure fairness. . . . The jury must not assume that all class members have equivalent claims: whatever injuries the unnamed plaintiffs have suffered may differ from the class representatives' as well as from one another's. Should the jury be allowed to award in the aggregate any punitive damages it finds appropriate, it must be instructed to factor in the possibility that none of the unnamed plaintiffs may have suffered any damages. Alternatively, the jury could be allowed to award an amount of money that each class member should receive for each dollar of actual damages awarded. Either way, the jury should understand that it must differentiate between proven and still-unproved claims, and that all class members, who recover actual damages from a defendant held liable for punitive damages, will share in the punitive award.

Furthermore, fairness as well as necessity dictates that both the parties and the court ensure that all of the necessary findings can be and are made in the class action trial. Sufficient evidence must be adduced for every one of each defendant's products to which a class member claims exposure so that the class jury can make the requisite findings as to each product and each defendant for such questions as periods of manufacture; areas and dates of distribution; "state of the art" knowledge for each relevant kind of product, use and user; when, if ever, conduct was grossly negligent; and dates and types of warnings if marketing defect is alleged.

The task will not be easy. Nevertheless, particularly in light of the magnitude of the problem and the need for innovative approaches, we find no abuse of discretion in this court's decision to try these cases by means of a Rule 23(b)(3) class suit.

Affirmed.

CASTANO V. AMERICAN TOBACCO CO.

84 F.3d 734 (5th Cir. 1996)

■ SMITH, Circuit Judge.

In what may be the largest class action ever attempted in federal court, the district court in this case embarked "on a road certainly less traveled, if ever taken at all," and entered a class certification order. The court defined the class as ["all nicotine-dependent persons in the United States . . . who have purchased and smoked cigarettes manufactured by the defendants," as well as the estates, spouses, children, relatives and "significant others" of nicotine-dependent cigarette smokers]. The plaintiffs limit the claims to years since 1943.

This matter comes before us on interlocutory appeal, under 28 U.S.C. § 1292(b), of the class certification order. Concluding that the district court abused its discretion in certifying the class, we reverse.

I.

A. *The Class Complaint*

The plaintiffs filed this class complaint against the defendant tobacco companies and the Tobacco Institute, Inc., seeking compensation solely for the injury of nicotine addiction. The gravamen of their complaint is the novel and wholly untested theory that the defendants fraudulently failed to inform consumers that nicotine is addictive and manipulated the level of nicotine in cigarettes to sustain their addictive nature. The class complaint alleges nine causes of action: fraud and deceit, negligent misrepresentation, intentional infliction of emotional distress, negligence and negligent infliction of emotional distress, violation of state consumer protection statutes, breach of express warranty, breach of implied warranty, strict product liability, and redhibition pursuant to the Louisiana Civil Code.

The plaintiffs seek compensatory and punitive damages and attorneys' fees. In addition, the plaintiffs seek equitable relief . . . . The equitable remedies include a declaration that defendants are financially responsible for notifying all class members of nicotine's addictive nature, a declaration that the defendants manipulated nicotine levels with the intent to sustain the addiction of plaintiffs and the class members, an order that the defendants disgorge any profits made from the sale of cigarettes, restitution for sums paid for cigarettes, and the establishment of a medical monitoring fund.

. . . Plaintiffs conceded that addiction would have to be proven by each class member; the defendants argued that proving class membership will require individual mini-trials to determine whether addiction actually exists.

In response to the district court's inquiry, the plaintiffs proposed a four-phase trial plan. In phase 1, a jury would determine common issues of "core liability." Phase 1 issues would include (1) issues of law and fact relating to defendants' course of conduct, fraud, and negligence liability (including duty, standard of care, misrepresentation and concealment, knowledge, intent); (2) issues of law and fact relating to defendants' alleged conspiracy and concert of action; (3) issues of fact relating to the addictive nature/dependency creating characteristics and properties of nicotine; (4) issues of fact relating to nicotine cigarettes as defective products; (5) issues of fact relating to whether defendants' wrongful conduct was intentional, reckless or negligent; (6) identifying which defendants specifically targeted their advertising and promotional efforts to particular groups (e.g. youths, minorities, etc.); (7) availability of a presumption of reliance; (8) whether defendants' misrepresentations/suppression of fact and/or of addictive properties of nicotine preclude availability of a "personal choice" defense; (9) defendants' liability for actual damages, and the categories of such damages; (10) defendants' liability for emotional distress damages; and (11) defendants' liability for punitive damages.

Phase 1 would be followed by notice of the trial verdict and claim forms to class members. In phase 2, the jury would determine compensatory damages in sample plaintiff cases. The jury then would establish a ratio of punitive damages to compensatory damages, which ratio thereafter would apply to each class member. Phase 3 would entail a complicated procedure to determine compensatory damages for individual class members. The trial plan envisions determination of absent class members' compensatory economic and emotional distress damages on the basis of claim forms, "subject to verification techniques and assertion of defendants' affirmative defenses under grouping, sampling, or representative procedures to be determined by the Court."

The trial plan left open how jury trials on class members' personal injury/wrongful death claims would be handled, but the trial plan discussed the possibility of bifurcation. In phase 4, the court would apply the punitive damage ratio based on individual damage awards and would conduct a review of the reasonableness of the award.

B. *The Class Certification Order*

Following extensive briefing, the district court granted, in part, plaintiffs' motion for class certification, concluding that the prerequisites of Fed. R. Civ. P. 23(a) had been met. The court rejected certification, under Fed. R. Civ. P. 23(b)(2), of the plaintiffs' claim for equitable relief, including the claim for medical monitoring. . . .

The court did grant the plaintiffs' motion to certify the class under Fed. R. Civ. P. 23(b)(3), organizing the class action issues into four categories: (1) core liability; (2) injury-in-fact, proximate cause, reliance and affirmative defenses; (3) compensatory damages; and (4) punitive damages. It then analyzed each category to determine whether it met the predominance and superiority requirements of rule 23(b)(3). [The district court found that a class action was appropriate for "core liability" issues such as fraud, breach of warranty, and strict liability, as well as for punitive damages. It did not certify a class on the issues of injury-in-fact, proximate cause, reliance, affirmative defenses, and compensatory damages.] Using its power to sever issues for certification under Fed. R. Civ. P. 23(c)(4), the court certified the class on core liability and punitive damages, and certified the class conditionally pursuant to Fed. R. Civ. P. 23(c)(1). . . .

II.

A district court must conduct a rigorous analysis of the rule 23 prerequisites before certifying a class. . . .

The district court erred in its analysis in two distinct ways. First, it failed to consider how variations in state law affect predominance and superiority. Second, its predominance inquiry did not include consideration of how a trial on the merits would be conducted.

Each of these defects mandates reversal. Moreover, at this time, while the tort is immature, the class complaint must be dismissed, as class certification cannot be found to be a superior method of adjudication.

A. *Variations in State Law*

. . .

In a multi-state class action, variations in state law may swamp any common issues and defeat predominance. . . .

A district court's duty to determine whether the plaintiff has borne its burden on class certification requires that a court consider variations in state law when a class action involves multiple jurisdictions. "In order to make the findings required to certify a class action under Rule 23(b)(3) . . . one must initially identify the substantive law issues which will control the outcome of the litigation." Ala. v. Blue Bird Body Co., 573 F.2d 309, 316 (5th Cir. 1978).

A requirement that a court know which law will apply before making a predominance determination is especially important when there may be differences in state law. . . .

In response to the defendants' extensive analysis of how state law varied on fraud, products liability, affirmative defenses, negligent infliction of emotional distress, consumer protection statutes, and punitive damages,[15] the court examined a sample phase 1 jury interrogatory and verdict form, a survey of medical monitoring decisions, a survey of consumer fraud class actions, and a survey of punitive damages law in the defendants' home states. The court also relied on two district court opinions granting certification in multi-state class actions.

The district court's consideration of state law variations was inadequate. . . .

The court also failed to perform its duty to determine whether the class action would be manageable in light of state law variations. The court's only discussion of manageability is a citation to [*Jenkins v. Raymark Industries, Inc.*, 782 F.2d 468 (5th Cir. 1986)] and the claim that "while manageability of the liability issues in this case may well prove to be difficult, the Court finds that any such difficulties pale in comparison to the specter of thousands, if not millions, of similar trials of liability proceeding in thousands of courtrooms around the nation."

---

15. We find it difficult to fathom how common issues could predominate in this case when variations in state law are thoroughly considered. . . The class members were exposed to nicotine through different products, for different amounts of time, and over different time periods. Each class member's knowledge about the effects of smoking differs, and each plaintiff began smoking for different reasons. Each of these factual differences impacts the application of legal rules such as causation, reliance, comparative fault, and other affirmative defenses.

Variations in state law magnify the differences. In a fraud claim, some states require justifiable reliance on a misrepresentation, while others require reasonable reliance. States impose varying standards to determine when there is a duty to disclose facts.

Products liability law also differs among states. Some states do not recog-

nize strict liability. . . . Among the states that have adopted the *Restatement*, there are variations.

Differences in affirmative defenses also exist. Assumption of risk is a complete defense to a products claim in some states. In others, it is a part of comparative fault analysis. Some states utilize "pure" comparative fault; others follow a "greater fault bar"; and still others use an "equal fault bar."

Negligent infliction of emotional distress also involves wide variations. Some states do not recognize the cause of action at all. Some require a physical impact.

Despite these overwhelming individual issues, common issues might predominate. We are, however, left to speculate. The point of detailing the alleged differences is to demonstrate the inquiry the district court failed to make.

The problem with this approach is that it substitutes case-specific analysis with a generalized reference to *Jenkins*. The *Jenkins* court, however, was not faced with managing a novel claim involving eight causes of action, multiple jurisdictions, millions of plaintiffs, eight defendants, and over fifty years of alleged wrongful conduct. Instead, *Jenkins* involved only 893 personal injury asbestos cases, the law of only one state, and the prospect of trial occurring in only one district. Accordingly, for purposes of the instant case, *Jenkins* is largely inapposite.

In summary, whether the specter of millions of cases outweighs any manageability problems in this class is uncertain when the scope of any manageability problems is unknown. Absent considered judgment on the manageability of the class, a comparison to millions of individual trials is meaningless.

B. *Predominance*

The district court's second error was that it failed to consider how the plaintiffs' addiction claims would be tried, individually or on a class basis. The district court, based on *Eisen v. Carlisle & Jacquelin*, 417 U.S. 156, 177-78 (1974), believed that it could not go past the pleadings for the certification decision. The result was an incomplete and inadequate predominance inquiry. . . .

A district court certainly may look past the pleadings to determine whether the requirements of rule 23 have been met. Going beyond the pleadings is necessary, as a court must understand the claims, defenses, relevant facts, and applicable substantive law in order to make a meaningful determination of the certification issues.

. . . Absent knowledge of how addiction-as-injury cases would actually be tried, . . . it was impossible for the court to know whether the common issues would be a "significant" portion of the individual trials. The court just assumed that because the common issues would play a part in every trial, they must be significant. The court's synthesis of *Jenkins* and *Eisen* would write the predominance requirement out of the rule, and any common issue would predominate if it were common to all the individual trials. . . .

[The court then applied its analysis to the fraud claim.] The problem with the district court's approach is that after the class trial, it might have decided that reliance must be proven in individual trials. The court then would have been faced with the difficult choice of decertifying the class after phase 1 and wasting judicial resources, or continuing with a class action that would have failed the predominance requirement of rule 23(b)(3).[21]

---

21. Severing the defendants' conduct from reliance under rule 23(c)(4) does not save the class action. A district court cannot manufacture predominance through the nimble use of subdivision (c)(4). The proper interpretation of the interaction between subdivisions (b)(3) and (c)(4) is that a cause of action, as a whole, must satisfy the predominance requirement of (b)(3) and that (c)(4) is a housekeeping

III.

In addition to the reasons given above, regarding the district court's procedural errors, this class must be decertified because it independently fails the superiority requirement of rule 23(b)(3). In the context of mass tort class actions, certification dramatically affects the stakes for defendants. Class certification magnifies and strengthens the number of unmeritorious claims. Aggregation of claims also makes it more likely that a defendant will be found liable and results in significantly higher damage awards.

In addition to skewing trial outcomes, class certification creates insurmountable pressure on defendants to settle, whereas individual trials would not. The risk of facing an all-or-nothing verdict presents too high a risk, even when the probability of an adverse judgment is low. These settlements have been referred to as judicial blackmail.

It is no surprise then, that historically, certification of mass tort litigation classes has been disfavored. The traditional concern over the rights of defendants in mass tort class actions is magnified in the instant case. Our specific concern is that a mass tort cannot be properly certified without a prior track record of trials from which the district court can draw the information necessary to make the predominance and superiority requirements required by rule 23. This is because certification of an immature tort results in a higher than normal risk that the class action may not be superior to individual adjudication.

We first address the district court's superiority analysis. The court acknowledged the extensive manageability problems with this class. Such problems include difficult choice of law determinations, subclassing of eight claims with variations in state law, *Erie* guesses, notice to millions of class members, further subclassing to take account of transient plaintiffs, and the difficult procedure for determining who is nicotine-dependent. . . .

The district court's rationale for certification in spite of such problems — i.e., that a class trial would preserve judicial resources in the millions of inevitable individual trials — is based on pure speculation. Not every mass tort is asbestos, and not every mass tort will result in the same judicial crises. . . .

Severe manageability problems and the lack of a judicial crisis are not the only reasons why superiority is lacking. The most compelling rationale for finding superiority in a class action — the existence of a negative value suit — is missing in this case.

. . . [I]ndividual damage claims are high, and punitive damages are available in most states. The expense of litigation does not necessarily turn

---

rule that allows courts to sever the common issues for a class trial. Reading rule 23(c)(4) as allowing a court to sever issues until the remaining common issue predominates over the remaining individual issues would eviscerate the predominance requirement of rule 23(b)(3); the result would be automatic certification in every case where there is a common issue, a result that could not have been intended.

this case into a negative value suit, in part because the prevailing party may recover attorneys' fees under many consumer protection statutes.

. . . [W]e cannot say that it would be a waste to allow individual trials to proceed, before a district court engages in the complicated predominance and superiority analysis necessary to certify a class.

The remaining rationale for superiority — judicial efficiency — also lacking. In the context of an immature tort, any savings in judicial resources is speculative, and any imagined savings would be overwhelmed by the procedural problems that certification of a *sui generis* cause of action brings with it. . . .

The district court's predominance inquiry, or lack of it, squarely presents the problems associated with certification of immature torts. Determining whether the common issues are a "significant" part of each individual case has an abstract quality to it when no court in this country has ever tried an injury-as-addiction claim. . . .

Yet, an accurate finding on predominance is necessary before the court can certify a class. It may turn out that the defendant's conduct, while common, is a minor part of each trial. Premature certification deprives the defendant of the opportunity to present that argument to any court and risks decertification after considerable resources have been expended. . . .

Through individual adjudication, the plaintiffs can winnow their claims to the strongest causes of action. The result will be an easier choice of law inquiry and a less complicated predominance inquiry. State courts can address the more novel of the plaintiffs' claims, making the federal court's *Erie* guesses less complicated. It is far more desirable to allow state courts to apply and develop their own law than to have a federal court apply "a kind of Esperanto [jury] instruction." [In re Rhone-Poulenc Rorer, Inc., 51 F.3d 1293, 1300 (7th Cir. 1995).] . . .

Another factor weighing heavily in favor of individual trials is the risk that in order to make this class action manageable, the court will be forced to bifurcate issues in violation of the Seventh Amendment. This class action is permeated with individual issues, such as proximate causation, comparative negligence, reliance, and compensatory damages. In order to manage so many individual issues, the district court proposed to empanel a class jury to adjudicate common issues. A second jury, or a number of "second" juries, will pass on the individual issues, either on a case-by-case basis or through group trials of individual plaintiffs.

The Seventh Amendment entitles parties to have fact issues decided by one jury, and prohibits a second jury from reexamining those facts and issues. Thus, [the] Constitution allows bifurcation of issues that are so separable that the second jury will not be called upon to reconsider findings of fact by the first. . . .

The Seventh Circuit recently addressed Seventh Amendment limitations to bifurcation. In *Rhone-Poulenc*, 51 F.3d at 1302-03, Chief Judge Posner described the constitutional limitation as one requiring a court to "carve at the joint" in such a way so that the same issue is not reexamined by different juries. "The right to a jury trial . . . is a right to have juriable issues determined by the first jury impaneled to hear them (provided there are no errors warranting a new trial), and not reexamined by another finder of fact."

Severing a defendant's conduct from comparative negligence results in the type of risk that our court forbade in *Blue Bird*. Comparative negligence, by definition, requires a comparison between the defendant's and the plaintiff's conduct. At a bare minimum, a second jury will rehear evidence of the defendant's conduct. There is a risk that in apportioning fault, the second jury could reevaluate the defendant's fault, determine that the defendant was not at fault, and apportion 100% of the fault to the plaintiff. In such a situation, the second jury would be impermissibly reconsidering the findings of a first jury. The risk of such reevaluation is so great that class treatment can hardly be said to be superior to individual adjudication. . . .

IV.

The district court abused its discretion by ignoring variations in state law and how a trial on the alleged causes of action would be tried. Those errors cannot be corrected on remand because of the novelty of the plaintiffs' claims. Accordingly, class treatment is not superior to individual adjudication.

We have once before stated that "traditional ways of proceeding reflect far more than habit. They reflect the very culture of the jury trial. . . ." In re Fibreboard Corp., 893 F.2d 706, 711 (5th Cir. 1990). The collective wisdom of individual juries is necessary before this court commits the fate of an entire industry or, indeed, the fate of a class of millions, to a single jury. For the forgoing reasons, we reverse and remand with instructions that the district court dismiss the class complaint.

Notes

1. The trial process in *Jenkins* turned out to be far more cumbersome and difficult than *Jenkins* envisioned. For the end of the story, see *infra* p. 1066.

2. What do *Jenkins* and *Castano* tell us about when common questions "predominate"? If it is intended to be a quantitative test, then aren't there more non-common than common questions in *Jenkins*? If it is not a quantitative test and instead a test of desirability or efficiency of aggregate treatment, then how is it distinct from the superiority test?

3. How should the superiority test be applied? Must the court consider all available aggregation devices — such as Rule 19 and 20 joinder, Rule 24 intervention, §1404 transfer, MDL consolidation, antisuit injunctions, and perhaps even bankruptcy (which Chapter Five considers) — as well as the alternative of individualized adjudication of the claims?

Must it consider the jurisdictional limits on the use of these devices? Must the court analyze superiority in relation to an ideal world or in relation to the aggregation efforts that are being employed at the time that class certification is being considered? You can see that nearly everything that we have discussed in Chapters Two and Three, as well as what we discuss in Chapter Five, bears on the question of (b)(3) superiority.

4.   One of the critical factors in *Castano* was the variability of state law. We saw exactly the same issue with (b)(3) commercial class actions; for instance, *Klay v. Humana, Inc.*, 382 F.3d 1241 (11th Cir. 2004) (*supra* p. 432), refused to certify a class for state-law consumer-protection claims because there was considerable variability in the relevant statutes. If the court can reduce the number of applicable state laws, the predominance prong becomes easier to satisfy. Whether courts can reduce the number of state laws is often tied up in the choice-of-law issue, which Chapter Six addresses.

5.   As *Castano* also says, lawyers who file (b)(3) litigation class actions need to demonstrate that they have a plan for getting the case through the pretrial and trial processes. The point might be obvious, but it bears emphasis: If a court cannot see a way to bring a litigation class action to conclusion, the class action cannot be regarded as superior. The techniques that class counsel might employ to move a (b)(3) class action, or any aggregated case, through pretrial and trial are discussed in Chapters Seven through Ten.

6.   Indeed, it is no exaggeration to say that most of this book is directly relevant to the questions of either predominance or superiority. Virtually every issue concerning structural, pretrial, trial, and remedial complexity can arise in analyzing these two questions, especially in the mass-tort context.

7.   Rule 23(b)(3) lists four factors "pertinent" to the issues of predominance and superiority. All four factors seem obviously relevant to the superiority test, but do factors bear at all on whether common questions predominate over non-common questions? *Cf.* Haley v. Medtronic, Inc., 169 F.R.D. 643 (C.D. Cal. 1996) (finding that common questions predominated, but that a class action was not superior; applying the four factors only to the superiority inquiry).

Rule 23(b)(3) offers no explanation of how the four factors are to be weighed against one another. Factor (A) reflects the preference for traditional litigation. But how is this normative preference to be balanced against the efficiency gains of class litigation? Why is Factor (B) relevant, and which way does the existence of pending litigation cut? How much has Factor (C) been undercut by the subsequent enactment of 28 U.S.C. § 1407? Since most class actions pose substantial management difficulties compared to any single one-on-one lawsuit, does Factor (D) require a comparison between the total management issues presented in all the cases handled through other means? What if the cases have such small value that they would never be filed individually? By definition, isn't a (b)(3) class action less manageable than no litigation?

Note that neither *Jenkins* nor *Castano* directly addresses the four factors, focusing instead on the questions of predominance and superiority. The same is true of a number of appellate mass-tort decisions. *See, e.g.*, In re Rhone-Poulenc Rorer, Inc., 51 F.3d 1293 (7th Cir. 1995); In re Am. Med. Sys., Inc., 75 F.3d 1069 (6th Cir. 1996) (*supra* p. 367); Valentino v. Carter-Wallace, Inc., 97 F.3d 1227 (9th Cir. 1996). Use of the four factors tends to be more common in district-court opinions.

8. In Chapter Ten, we evaluate more closely the Seventh Amendment argument that *Castano* raises as a barrier to class certification. *See infra* pp. 1046-47, Notes 4-5. The basic idea is that a second jury is, as a general matter, constitutionally prohibited from re-examining the facts found by a prior jury; thus, if the plan to try a (b)(3) class action splits the trial into separate parts, care must be taken that a second jury not revisit the factual findings of the first jury. Avoiding this problem is harder than it might seem in mass-tort class actions, because the common issues on which the first trial is likely to focus (such as the degree of the defendant's negligence) are often integrally related to individual issues of causation, damages, and contributory negligence that a second or later trial would determine.

In another opinion by Judge Smith, the Fifth Circuit raised a second Seventh Amendment problem with (b)(3) class actions. *Allison v. Citgo Petroleum Corp.*, 151 F.3d 402 (5th Cir. 1998), involved a class of 1,000 African-American workers in an employment-discrimination case. Because the workers sought injunctive relief, back pay (often regarded as equitable relief), and compensatory and punitive damages, the plaintiffs moved for certification on both (b)(2) and (b)(3) grounds. In a holding that we examined in connection with *Robinson v. Metro-North Commuter Railroad Co.*, 267 F. 3d 147 (2d. Cir. 2001) (*supra* p. 401), *Allison* first held that the claims for damages were not incidental to injunctive and back pay relief, and could not be asserted as part of a (b)(2) claim. That ruling left the fallback of (b)(3) certification for the damage claims. Relying on *Castano*, *Allison* then held that (b)(3) was unavailable, on the now-familiar reasoning that the claims' focus on "facts and issues specific to individuals rather than the class as a whole," *id.* at 419, defeated predominance and superiority.

Allison bootstrapped that finding into an argument to deny certification of the (b)(2) class. The plaintiffs argued that the judge could sever the equitable claims for class treatment under Rule 23(b)(2), reserving until after trial the decision to certify the damage claims under Rule 23(b)(3). *Allison* rejected the idea because the Seventh Amendment requires a jury, which decides legal claims, to first determine any factual issues relevant to both the legal claims and the equitable claims that a judge decides. Because a severed (b)(2) class action would result in a judge deciding factual issues that overlapped with the class members' non-certified (but potentially certifiable) damage claims, *Allison* held that the Seventh Amendment barred a (b)(2) class action. *Allison*'s conclusion has been strongly criticized. *See* Allen v. Int'l Truck & Engine Corp., 358 F.3d 469 (7th Cir. 2004) (holding that Seventh Amendment problems can be avoided by allowing class representatives' damage claims to be tried at the same time as the (b)(2) claims, with the jury's findings on overlapping issues binding the judge on the equitable claims); *see also* Carnegie v. Household Int'l, Inc., 376 F.3d 656, 661 (7th Cir. 2004) (Posner, J.) (allowing district courts "to devise imaginative solutions" to the Seventh Amendment problem); Tobias Barrington Wolff, *Preclusion in Class Action Litigation,* 105 COLUM. L. REV. 717, 777-80 (2005) (arguing that the Re-Examination Clause should be interpreted "dynamically" to "allow for procedural innovation" because its purpose is to "guard against the possibility that federal judges might usurp the role of the jury in a given proceeding").

Allison and *Allen* were employment-discrimination cases; *Carnegie* was a RICO case. None was a mass tort. To the extent that *Allison*'s reading of the Seventh Amendment is correct, however, plaintiffs in a mass-tort case that combines equitable relief (perhaps a medical-monitoring claim) with requests for damages will find a constitutional roadblock.

9.   *Castano* was the last of three appellate decisions that emerged in a very short period in 1995 and 1996. The first was *Rhone-Poulenc*, 51 F.3d 1293, from which *Castano* cribs. Because of its impact on the certification of (b)(3) mass-tort class actions, the heart of Judge Posner's reasoning in *Rhone-Poulenc* is worth examining. The case involved 5,000 persons with hemophilia who had died from or contracted AIDS as a result of the defendants' alleged negligence. The district court certified a (b)(3) class for litigation purposes. In twelve of the thirteen individual suits that had been tried to that point, the defendants had won. Granting a writ of mandamus, Judge Posner ordered that the class be decertified:

> [The defendant] could not be confident that the defenses would prevail. They might, therefore, easily be facing $25 billion in potential liability (conceivably more), and with it bankruptcy. They may not wish to roll these dice. That is putting it mildly. They will be under intense pressure to settle. . . .

> [There] is a concern with forcing these defendants to stake their companies on the outcome of a single jury trial, or be forced by fear of the risk of bankruptcy to settle even if they have no legal liability, when it is entirely feasible to allow a final, authoritative determination of their liability . . . to emerge from a decentralized process of multiple trials, involving different juries, and different standards of liability, in different jurisdictions; and when, in addition, the preliminary indications are that the defendants are not liable for the grievous harm that has befallen the members of the class. These qualifications are important. In most class actions — and those the ones in which the rationale for the procedure is most compelling — individual suits are infeasible because the claim of each class member is tiny relative to the expense of litigation. That plainly is not the situation here. A notable feature of this case, and one that has not been remarked upon or encountered, so far as we are aware, in previous cases, is the demonstrated great likelihood that the plaintiffs' claims, despite their human appeal, lack legal merit. . . . But whether they do or not, the result will be robust if these further trials are permitted to go forward,

because the pattern that results will reflect a consensus, or at least a pooling of judgment, of many different tribunals.

For this consensus or maturing of judgment the district judge proposes to substitute a single trial before a single jury instructed in accordance with no actual law of any jurisdiction — a jury that will receive a kind of Esperanto instruction, merging the negligence standards of the 50 states and the District of Columbia. One jury, consisting of six persons (the standard federal civil jury nowadays consists of six regular jurors and two alternates), will hold the fate of an industry in the palm of its hand. This jury, jury number fourteen, may disagree with twelve of the previous thirteen juries — and hurl the industry into bankruptcy. . . .

. . . If one instruction on negligence will serve to instruct the jury on the legal standard of every state of the United States applicable to a novel claim, implying that the claim . . . would be decided identically in all 50 states and the District of Columbia, one wonders what the Supreme Court thought it was doing in the *Erie* case when it held that it was *unconstitutional* for federal courts in diversity cases to apply general common law rather than the common law of the state whose law would apply if the case were being tried in state rather than federal court. Erie R.R. v. Tompkins, 304 U.S. 64, 78-80 (1938). [*Id.* at 1299-1300].

The second case rejecting certification of a (b)(3) mass-tort class was *In re American Medical Systems*, 75 F.3d 1069 (6th Cir. 1996) (*supra* p. 367), which we have studied for its Rule 23(a) holdings. In a portion of the decision that we did not examine, the Sixth Circuit held that the class failed to meet the Rule 23(b)(3) requirements of predominance and superiority due to the number of individual issues presented by the range of product defects and the variations in state law. *Id.* at 1084-86. *Castano* followed quickly on the heels of *American Medical Systems*. Then, in 1997, in a case involving a (b)(3) settlement class action, the Supreme Court further expressed doubts about the ability of large-scale mass torts to meet the (b)(3) standards. *See* Amchem Prods., Inc. v. Windsor, 521 U.S. 591 (1997) (*infra* p. 493). Taken together, these cases knocked the wind out of the sails of efforts to use Rule 23(b)(3) to aggregate mass torts for litigation purposes.

10. Plaintiffs' lawyers initially regrouped, and began to bring single-state (b)(3) class actions to avoid the variations-in-state-law argument. Courts tended to rebuff this effort, finding that even a single state's law was insufficient to tip the predominance scale against the individual issues tort cases present. *See* Barnes v. Am. Tobacco Co., 161 F.3d 127 (3d Cir. 1998) (rejecting the certification of medical-monitoring claims brought by a Pennsylvania-only class of smokers under Rules 23(b)(2) and -(b)(3)); Arch v. Am. Tobacco Co., 175 F.R.D. 469 (E.D. Pa. 1997) (same). Likewise, cases in which plaintiffs created subclasses under Rule 23(c)(5), with one subclass representing class members subject to the same variation in state law, have tended to fail. Not only does each subclass still involve significant individual issues, but the presence of subclasses creates other manageabil-

ity issues. *See* In re Paxil Litig., 218 F.R.D. 242 (C.D. Cal. 2003) (holding that a (b)(3) class action with twelve subclasses was unmanageable).

11. As a result, certifying a federal mass-tort class action is like passing the proverbial camel through the eye of the needle. *Compare* Mejdrech v. Met-Coil Sys. Corp., 319 F.3d 910 (7th Cir. 2003) (Posner, J.) (affirming certification of a (b)(3) class of residents near a chemical plant that had polluted the groundwater and diminished property values; certification was limited to common issues of the existence and extent of contamination), *and* Olden v. Lafarge Corp., 383 F.3d 495 (6th Cir. 2004) (upholding certification of a (b)(3) class of residents for personal injuries and property damage due to pollution emitted from the defendant's plant), *with* Ball v. Union Carbide Corp., 385 F.3d 713 (6th Cir. 2004) (upholding denial of certification of a (b)(3) class of residents injured due to emissions from a manufacturing facility when levels of exposure varied), *and* In re Methyl Tertiary Butyl Ether ("MTBE") Prods. Liab. Litig., 209 F.R.D. 323 (S.D.N.Y. 2002) (denying (b)(2) and (b)(3) certification of a nationwide class of property owners whose wells and groundwater were polluted by chemicals added to gasoline when the circumstances of leakage varied for each gasoline station and pipeline. As a rule, it seems easier to obtain certification when environmental or property claims are involved, rather than personal injuries. *See, e.g.,* In re Sch. Asbestos Litig., 921 F.2d 1338 (3d Cir. 1990) (refusing to issue a writ of mandamus requiring decertification of a class seeking recovery of costs for asbestos removal); Sterling v. Velsicol Chem. Corp., 855 F.2d 1188 (6th Cir. 1988) (chemical waste burial site).

12. The difficulty of certifying a mass tort in federal court since the 1990s has had two effects. The first is to put greater pressure on other aggregation devices, such as multidistrict proceedings, as "next best" substitutes for class aggregation. Indeed, the greater responsiveness of the Judicial Panel on Multidistrict Litigation to mass torts, *see supra* pp. 144-62, can be seen as a necessary reaction to the limits of Rule 23(b)(3) as an aggregation mechanism for mass torts. The second was to drive plaintiffs who sought class certification for mass torts into state courts, which often interpreted rules equivalent the Rule 23(b)(3) in a way more hospitable to class aggregation. This latter move has essentially stopped as a result of the Class Action Fairness Act of 2005 (CAFA), which now gives federal courts jurisdiction over nearly all mass-tort class actions. *See supra* p. 317. The following case, which arose before CAFA, shows similarities to — but also important contrasts with — the federal approach.

ENGLE V. LIGGETT GROUP, INC.

945 So. 2d 1246 (Fla. 2006)

■ PER CURIAM.

This case arises from the Third District Court of Appeal's reversal of a final judgment entered in a smokers' class action lawsuit that sought damages against cigarette companies and industry organizations for alleged smoking-related injuries. The final judgment awarded $12.7 million in compensatory damages to three individual plaintiffs and $145 billion in punitive damages to the entire class. . . .

. . . [A]lthough we approve the Third District's reversal of the $145 billion class action punitive damages award, we quash the remainder of the Third District's decision. A majority of the Court (Anstead, Pariente, Lewis and Quince) holds that the compensatory damages award in favor of Mary Farnan in the amount of $2,850,000 and Angie Della Vecchia in the amount of $4,023,000 should be reinstated. However, the court unanimously agrees that the compensatory damages award in favor of Frank Amodeo must be vacated based on the statute of limitations.

Further, a majority of the Court (Anstead, Pariente, Lewis and Quince) concludes that . . . the certification of the class action and the Phase I trial process were not abuses of the trial court's discretion; and that certain common liability findings can stand. However, we also conclude that the remaining issues, including individual causation and apportionment of fault among the defendants, are highly individualized and do not lend themselves to class action treatment. Thus, we remand with directions that the class should be decertified without prejudice to the class members filing individual claims within one year of the issuance of our mandate in this case with res judicata effect given to certain Phase I findings. . . .

FACTS AND PROCEDURAL HISTORY

On October 31, 1994, the trial court certified as a nationwide class action a group of smokers and their survivors under Florida Rule of Civil Procedure 1.220(b)(3). The class representatives on behalf of themselves, and all others similarly situated, filed an amended class action complaint seeking compensatory and punitive damages against major domestic cigarette companies and two industry organizations (hereinafter collectively referred to as "Tobacco") for injuries allegedly caused by smoking.

The trial court defined the class as: "All United States citizens and residents, and their survivors, who have suffered, presently suffer or who have died from diseases and medical conditions caused by their addiction to cigarettes that contain nicotine." . . . On January 31, 1996, the Third District affirmed the trial court's order certifying the class but reduced the class to include only Florida smokers. . . .

On February 4, 1998, the trial court issued a trial plan, dividing the trial proceedings into three phases. Phase I consisted of a year-long trial to consider the issues of liability and entitlement to punitive damages for the class as a whole. The jury considered common issues relating exclusively to the defendants' conduct and the general health effects of smoking. On July 7, 1999, at the conclusion of Phase I, the jury rendered a verdict for the *Engle* Class and against Tobacco on all counts.

[Among the jury's Phase I findings for the class were: (1) smoking cigarettes causes aortic aneurysm, bladder cancer, cerebrovascular disease, cervical cancer, chronic obstructive pulmonary disease, coronary heart disease, esophageal cancer, kidney cancer, laryngeal cancer, lung cancer, complications in pregnancy, oral cavity/tongue cancer, pancreatic cancer, peripheral vascular disease, pharyngeal cancer, and stomach cancer; (2) nicotine in cigarettes is addictive; (3) the defendants placed cigarettes on the market that were defective and unreasonably dangerous; (4) the defendants concealed or omitted material information or failed to disclose material facts concerning the health effects or addictive nature of smoking cigarettes; (5) the defendants agreed to conceal or omit information regarding the health effects of cigarettes or their addictive nature with the intention that smokers and the public would rely on this information to their detriment; (6) all of the defendants sold or supplied cigarettes that, at the time of sale or supply, did not conform to representations of fact made by said defendants; and (7) all of the defendants were negligent. The jury also found that "all of the defendants' conduct rose to a level that would permit an award of punitive damages."]

Phase II was divided into two subparts — Phase II-A and Phase II-B. Phase II-A was intended to resolve the issues of entitlement and amount of compensatory damages, if any, that the three individual class representatives — Frank Amodeo, Mary Farnan, and Angie Della Vecchia — should receive. Phase II-B was designed to result in a jury determination of a total lump sum punitive damage award, if any, that should be assessed in favor of the class as a whole.

At the conclusion of Phase II-A, the jury determined that the three individual class representatives were entitled to compensatory damages in varying amounts, which were offset by their comparative fault. The total award was $12.7 million. The jury subsequently determined in Phase II-B the lump-sum amount of punitive damages for the entire class to be $145 billion, without allocation of that amount to any class member. . . .

According to the trial plan, in Phase III, new juries are to decide the individual liability and compensatory damages claims for each class member (estimated to number approximately 700,000). Thereafter, the plan contemplated that the trial court would divide the punitive damages previously determined equally among any successful class members. Pursuant to the omnibus order, interest on the punitive award began accruing immediately.

Tobacco filed an appeal and the Third District reversed the final judgment with instructions that the class be decertified.

ANALYSIS

. . .

2. *Punitive Damages Award*

. . . [W]e must vacate the classwide punitive damages award because we unanimously agree with the Third District that the trial court erred in allowing the jury to determine a lump sum amount before it determined the amount of total compensatory damages for the class. As a matter of law, the punitive damages award violates due process because there is no way to evaluate the reasonableness of the punitive damages award without the amount of compensatory damages having been fixed. The amount awarded is also clearly excessive because it would bankrupt some of the defendants. A majority of the Court further concludes that the trial court erred in allowing the jury to consider entitlement to punitive damages during the Phase I trial. We address these issues separately.

A. *Phase I Finding on Entitlement to Punitive Damages*

The last question on the Phase I verdict form asked the jury to determine whether "[u]nder the circumstances of this case, . . . the conduct of any Defendant rose to a level that would permit a potential award or entitlement to punitive damages." The jury answered "yes" with respect to each of the defendants. In Phase II-B, the jury awarded a total of $ 145 billion in punitive damages to the class.

. . . A majority of the Court (Anstead, Pariente, Lewis, and Quince) concludes that an award of compensatory damages is not a prerequisite to a finding of entitlement to punitive damages. . . .

Because a finding of entitlement to punitive damages is not dependent on a finding that a plaintiff suffered a specific injury, an award of compensatory damages need not precede a determination of entitlement to punitive damages. Therefore, we conclude that the order of these determinations is not critical. *See* Jenkins v. Raymark Indus., Inc., 782 F.2d 468, 474 (5th Cir. 1986) [*supra* p. 467].

A different majority of the Court (Wells, Anstead, Pariente, and Bell) concludes that under our decision in *Ault v. Lohr*, 538 So. 2d 454, 456 (Fla. 1989), a finding of liability is required before entitlement to punitive damages can be determined, and that liability is more than a breach of duty. A finding of liability necessarily precedes a determination of damages, but does not compel a compensatory award. . . .

In this case, the Phase I verdict did not constitute a "finding of liability" under *Ault*. This is evidenced by the fact that had the jury found for Tobacco on the legal cause and reliance issues during Phase II, there would have been no opportunity for the jury to award the named plaintiffs damages of any type. In other words, Phase II findings for Tobacco on legal causation and reliance would have precluded the jury from awarding compensatory or punitive damages. It was error for the trial court to allow the jury to consider entitlement to punitive damages before the jury found that the plaintiffs had established causation and reliance.

In Phase I, the jury decided issues related to Tobacco's conduct but did not consider whether any class members relied on Tobacco's misrepresentations or were injured by Tobacco's conduct. As the Third District noted, the Phase I jury "did not determine whether the defendants were liable to anyone." It was therefore error for the Phase I jury to consider whether Tobacco was liable for punitive damages.

B. *Excessiveness*

[After reviewing United States Supreme Court and Florida precedents, the Florida Supreme Court concluded that] courts must ensure that the measure of punishment is both reasonable and proportionate to the amount of harm to the plaintiff and to the general damages recovered. Thus, the amount of compensatory damages must be determined in advance of a determination of the amount of punitive damages awardable, if any, so that the relationship between the two may be reviewed for reasonableness.

. . . The trial plan allowed a lump sum determination of punitive damages for the entire class when compensatory damages had been determined only for the three individual class representatives. This approach does not provide a reviewing court with an adequate starting point to compare the lump sum punitive damages amount to compensatory damages to ensure there is some reasonable relationship. Accordingly, even if there was no error in allowing the Phase I jury to find entitlement to punitive damages, the classwide punitive damages award must be reversed.
. . .

4. *Three-Phase Trial Plan — Decertification*

We agree with the Third District that problems with the three-phase trial plan negate the continued viability of this class action. We conclude that continued class action treatment for Phase III of the trial plan is not feasible because individualized issues such as legal causation, comparative fault, and damages predominate. . . .

Florida Rule of Civil Procedure 1.220(d)(4)(A) provides that "[w]hen appropriate . . . a claim or defense may be brought or maintained on behalf of a class concerning particular issues." Although no Florida cases address whether it is appropriate under rule 1.220(d)(4)(A) to certify class treatment for only limited liability issues, several decisions by federal appellate courts applying a similar provision in the Federal Rules of Civil Procedure provide persuasive authority for this approach.

Federal Rule of Civil Procedure 23(c)(4)(A) [now Rule 23(c)(4) — ED.] provides that "[w]hen appropriate . . . an action may be brought or maintained as a class action with respect to particular issues." In determining whether the predominance requirement of Federal Rule of Civil Procedure 23(b)(3) has been met, several United States Courts of Appeals have concluded that under federal rule 23(c)(4)(A) a trial court can properly separate liability and damages issues, certifying class treatment of liability while leaving damages to be determined on an individual basis.
. . .

In this case, the Phase I trial has been completed. The pragmatic solution is to now decertify the class, retaining the jury's Phase I findings other than those on the fraud and intentional infliction of emotion distress claims, which involved highly individualized determinations, and the finding on entitlement to punitive damages questions, which was premature. Class members can choose to initiate individual damages actions and the Phase I common core findings we approved above will have res judicata effect in those trials. . . .

CONCLUSION

. . .

We approve the Phase I findings for the class [that were listed above in the opinion, except for the finding that the defendants' conduct rose to the level justifying an award of punitive damages]. Therefore, these findings in favor of the *Engle* Class can stand.

. . . However, we conclude for the reasons explained in this opinion that continued class action treatment is not feasible and that upon remand the class must be decertified. Individual plaintiffs within the class will be permitted to proceed individually with the findings set forth above given res judicata effect in any subsequent trial between individual class members and the defendants, provided such action is filed within one year of the mandate in this case. We remand this case to the Third District for further proceedings consistent with this opinion.

■   [The opinion of LEWIS, C.J., concurring in part and dissenting in part, in which QUINCE, J., concurred, is omitted.]

■   [The opinion of WELLS, J., concurring in part and dissenting in part, in which BELL, J., concurred, is omitted.]

■   CANTERO, J., recused.

Notes

1.   As of July, 2007, twenty-five "*Engle* progeny" cases had already been filed by seventy-six plaintiffs. Bonenfant v. R.J. Reynolds Tobacco Co., 2007 WL 2409980 (S.D. Fla. July 31, 2007). Later that year, the Judicial Panel on Multidistrict Litigation denied a request to consolidate twenty-seven cases in the Southern District of Florida. *See* In re Engle Progeny Tobacco Prods. Liab. Litig., 2007 WL 4480080 (J.P.M.L. Dec. 12, 2007). The Panel reasoned:

Discovery on common factual issues occurred in the underlying state court action, which gave rise to the factual findings relied upon by the plaintiffs in the present actions. The proponents of centralization have failed to convince us that any remaining and unresolved common questions of fact among these actions are sufficiently complex and/or numerous to justify Section 1407 transfer at this time. Alternatives to transfer exist that may minimize whatever possibilities there might be of duplicative discovery and/or inconsistent pretrial rulings. [*Id.* at *1.]

2. *Engle* had yielded, by far, the largest verdict in American history. As a result, it is easy to focus attention on the Florida Supreme Court's invalidation of the $145 billion punitive-damages award. The Florida Supreme Court's insistence that the amount of punitive damages can be established only after determining the amount of compensatory damages derives from the United States Supreme Court's determination that the Due Process Clause requires an investigation into the proportionality of punitive to compensatory damages. Unavoidably, this requirement also diminishes the utility of the class-action device to aggregate punitive-damage aspects of mass torts. If the amount of punitive damages cannot be assessed until the amount of each class member's compensatory damages is assessed, then the individual issues and individual trials associated with compensatory damages are likely to defeat — on both predominance and superiority grounds — the attempt to certify a (b)(3) punitive-damages class that sets the amount of punitive damages. In this regard, *Engle* should be read together with the cases that we examined in the material on Rule 23(b)(1)(B), in which we saw the difficulties of using that rule to certify punitive-damage classes. *See supra* pp. 396-401.

Is there any way out of this conundrum? In Chapter Ten, we examine the idea that damages might be awardable based on a sample of the class that yields, to a reasonable degree of statistical certainty, the total amount of punitive damages that should be awarded. *See infra* pp. 1058-88. The theory is controversial. If it is unsuccessful, then *Engle* and the other cases we have examined make (b)(3) class actions designed to determine the amount of punitive damages in a mass tort highly problematic.

3. It is also important to focus on what *Engle* upholds. Most important, it validates all the factual findings from the Phase I trial — including the finding that the defendants had acted in a manner deserving of punitive damages — and allows them to be used in subsequent individual litigation. As a result, the *Engle* progeny cases are much streamlined; the basic issues of the defendants's liability and the egregiousness of their conduct need not be litigated time and again. Resolving the common issues once and for all is a huge savings in future trials, as well as a strong inducement to the defendants to look toward settling these cases.

Although the case did not start this way (it was designed to dispose of all claims and issues over the course of its phases), *Engle* ended up becoming what is known as an "issue class action" — in other words, a class action that resolves only discrete legal or factual issues on a class-wide basis. The idea of an issue class is that class members and defendants are bound by issue preclusion to the findings in the class proceeding, and can use them (either offensively if the findings favor the plaintiffs or defensively if they favor the defendants) in future individual litigation. As *Engle* notes, Federal Rule 23(c)(4) authorizes issue class actions; it then adopts the same rule for Florida class actions.

Are issue class actions a way to certify mass torts? The idea is to certify only the common issues — negligence, strict liability, nature of the warranty, "general" causation (i.e., the types of injuries that the defendant's product can cause, as opposed to whether the product caused any given plaintiff's injury), and so on. By definition, these common issues would predominate, because only the common issues are litigated on a class-wide basis. Likewise, litigating these common issues once and for all seems far superior to litigating them repetitively in court after court.

Indeed, *Jenkins* initially proposed just such a class action, seeking to certify a class on the single dispositive issue of the state-of-the-art defense (although its trial plan also suggested somewhat more ambitious goals to resolve the entire controversy). It is less obvious from the decision, but the trial judge in *Castano* had similarly certified the class only on the common issues of nicotine dependence and other common issues; it never contemplated that the class action would resolve individual issues such as contributory negligence and damages.

With regard to issue classes, however, *Castano* took a strongly negative view that seems to be in direct opposition to the view taken in *Engle*. You might wish to re-read *Castano*'s footnote 21, *supra* p. 475. It argues that a court cannot certify a class just for certain issues if it could not have certified the class for all purposes. On the other hand, *Engle* allows a class to be certified for common issues, even though it holds that the case could not be certified for all purposes because of predominant individual issues.

4.   So which case is right — *Castano* or *Engle*? The problem of using issue classes has divided the federal courts. Perhaps the best illustration is to look at the Second Circuit. In *In re Nassau County Strip Search Cases*, 461 F.3d 219, 225-27 (2d Cir. 2006), the court rejected *Castano*'s view, and held that a (b)(3) issue class could be certified even if a (b)(3) class could not have been certified on the class's entire claims:

> . . . We first conclude that, contrary to the District Court's reservations, a court may employ Rule 23(c)(4)[ ] to certify a class on a particular issue even if the action as a whole does not satisfy Rule 23(b)(3)'s predominance requirement. . . .

> Whether a court may employ Rule 23(c)(4)[ ] to certify a class as to a specific issue where the entire claim does not satisfy Rule 23(b)(3)'s predominance requirement is a matter of first impression in this Circuit. It also is a matter as to which the Circuits have split. [The Court then discussed the "strict application" view of *Castano* and the contrary view of the Ninth Circuit.]

> We agree with the Ninth Circuit's view of the matter. First, the plain language and structure of Rule 23 support the Ninth Circuit's view. . . . As the rule's plain language and structure establish, a court must first identify the issues potentially appropriate for certification "and . . . then" apply the other provisions of the rule, i.e., subsection (b)(3) and its predominance analysis. . . .

> Second, the Advisory Committee Notes confirm this understanding. With respect to subsection (c)(4), the notes set forth that, "[f]or example, in a fraud or similar case the action may retain its 'class' character only through the adjudication of liability to the class; the members of the

class may thereafter be required to come in individually and prove the amounts of their respective claims." . . .

In addition, . . . the Fifth Circuit's view renders subsection (c)(4) virtually null, which contravenes the "well-settled" principle "that courts should avoid statutory interpretations that render provisions superfluous." Pursuant to the Fifth Circuit's view, "a court considering the manageability of a class action — a requirement for predominance under Rule 23(b)(3)(D) — [would have] to pretend that subsection (c)(4) — a provision specifically included to make a class action more manageable — does not exist until after the manageability determination [has been] made." Accordingly, "a court could only use subsection (c)(4) to manage cases that the court had already determined would be manageable without consideration of subsection (c)(4)."

Subsequently, however, the Second Circuit seems to have retreated somewhat. *McLaughlin v. American Tobacco Co.*, 522 F.3d 215 (2d Cir. 2008) (*infra* p. 1076), decertified a (b)(3) class of smokers that claimed RICO and other violations resulting from the tobacco companies' untruthful advertising regarding the health benefits of light cigarettes. It then cursorily rejected the argument that an issue class on common issues was still maintainable:

> . . . We recognize that a court may employ Rule 23(c)(4) to certify a class as to common issues that do exist, "regardless of whether the claim as a whole satisfies Rule 23(b)(3)'s predominance requirement." *In re Nassau County Strip Search Cases*, 461 F.3d at 227. Nevertheless, in this case, given the number of questions that would remain for individual adjudication, issue certification would not "reduce the range of issues in dispute and promote judicial economy." Certifying, for example, the issue of defendants' scheme to defraud, would not materially advance the litigation because it would not dispose of larger issues such as reliance, injury, and damages. We therefore decline plaintiffs' request for issue certification. [522 F.3d at 234.]

State courts are not, of course, bound to apply the federal courts' interpretation of Rule 23 when they interpret their own class-action rules. Do you think that *Engle* would have interpreted its rule as it did had the trial court not (as it turned out) erroneously certified an all-issues class and a jury had not already returned a verdict on the common issues?

5.   Many articles explore the advantages and disadvantages of class aggregation in mass-tort cases. *See, e.g.,* David Rosenberg, *Mandatory-Litigation Class Actions: The Only Option for Mass Tort Cases*, 115 HARV. L. REV. 831 (2002); Richard A. Nagareda, *Autonomy, Peace, and Put Options in the Mass Tort Class Action*, 115 HARV. L. REV. 747 (2002); David Rosenberg, *Class Actions for Mass Torts: Doing Individual Justice by Collective Means*, 62 IND. L.J. 561 (1987); Francis E. McGovern, *An Analysis of Mass Torts for Judges*, 73 TEX. L. REV. 1821 (1995); Linda S. Mullenix, *Beyond Consolidation: Post-Aggregative Procedure in Asbestos Mass Tort Litigation*, 32 WM. & MARY L. REV. 475 (1991). For a strong criticism of the American class action, see MARTIN REDISH, WHOLESALE JUSTICE (2009).

2. Settlement Class Actions

Class actions, like most lawsuits, are settled far more often than they are tried. Given the enormous consequences to both sides should they lose, this fact is hardly surprising. In recent years, however, the parties have found a new, and rather different, use for class actions — the settlement class action. Unlike the litigation class action that settles, the settlement class action is designed at the outset to settle the contested issues between class members and the defendants. The negotiations over the terms of the settlement occur before the class is certified, and the defendants agree to settle the case only if the case is settled on a class-wide basis. Therefore, rather than fighting class certification, the defendants actively support it. The class action promises to bring defendants "global peace" from further litigation; they substitute a fixed cost for the uncertainties of litigation.

Because of this difference, the standard policy arguments regarding class actions have different weight. For instance, the concern that class actions excessively deter defendants' behavior disappears; defendants have agreed to the settlement's terms. Likewise, the court's manageability concerns are downplayed; the case will never be litigated. On the other hand, concerns for adequacy of representation and collusion dramatically rise; the defendants might have shopped for lawyers who gave them the best deal, and who sold out the class in return for a hefty fee and little work. As a result, the trade-off between individual control and adequate representation that *Hansberry v. Lee* and Rule 23(a) have struck takes on a new mien. Concerns that parties are using courts as relief-distribution agencies are also significant. Finally, without the benefit of adversarial presentation (since both the class representative and the defendants are favoring settlement), the court's role might need to shift toward protection of the rights of absent class members, but that role seems inconsistent with the adjudicatory neutrality that courts ordinarily maintain.

One of the great advantages of the settlement class action — at least to those who wish to resolve all cases in a single forum — is that it can be used to settle not only the claims of those with present injuries, but also the claims of those whose injuries will not manifest themselves until some point in the future. We encountered the issue of these "future plaintiffs" very briefly in Chapter Three. (*See supra* p. 304.) In many types of class-action litigation, there are no future plaintiffs; for instance, in a typical securities-fraud case, a past misrepresentation has already caused all the legally cognizable financial harm that it can before the lawsuit commences. On the other hand, in a race-discrimination class action seeking injunctive relief, every class member might be a "future plaintiff," in the sense that the threatened conduct, and thus the threatened harm, has not yet occurred. The type of "future plaintiffs" that we describe here, however, are a hybrid; they are victims of wrongful conduct that occurred in the past, but injunctive relief cannot prevent their harms from maturing in the future. The classic "future plaintiffs" are those that have been exposed to a toxic substance in the past (thus, the wrongful conduct has occurred), but due to the latency period before injury develops have no present injury (thus the harm has not yet occurred).

Because these future plaintiffs do not, by definition, have present injuries, it is difficult to bring them within the confines of a litigation class action. But a settlement class action is not necessarily so constrained. Defendants have always been able to settle — on an individual basis — the claims of plaintiffs who cannot yet litigate their claims. The issue is whether they can use class action to conduct negotiations with the class representative and avoid the costs of settling with everyone individually.

Simply put, the settlement class action portends to be the most powerful aggregation device we have seen, at least once defendants decide that they want to settle. But the language of Rule 23 does not mention settlement class actions. Are settlement class actions permissible? Can they resolve the claims of future plaintiffs? In the two cases that follow, the Supreme Court explored these questions, and at the same time added significantly to our understanding of Rules 23(a)(4), -(b)(1)(B), and -(b)(3).

AMCHEM PRODUCTS, INC. V. WINDSOR

521 U.S. 591 (1997)

■ JUSTICE GINSBURG delivered the opinion of the Court.

This case concerns the legitimacy under Rule 23 of the Federal Rules of Civil Procedure of a class-action certification sought to achieve global settlement of current and future asbestos-related claims. The class proposed for certification potentially encompasses hundreds of thousands, perhaps millions, of individuals tied together by this commonality: each was, or some day may be, adversely affected by past exposure to asbestos products manufactured by one or more of 20 companies. Those companies, defendants in the lower courts, are petitioners here.

The United States District Court for the Eastern District of Pennsylvania certified the class for settlement only, finding that the proposed settlement was fair and that representation and notice had been adequate. That court enjoined class members from separately pursuing asbestos-related personal-injury suits in any court, federal or state, pending the issuance of a final order. The Court of Appeals for the Third Circuit vacated the District Court's orders, holding that the class certification failed to satisfy Rule 23's requirements in several critical respects. We affirm the Court of Appeals' judgment.

I

A

The settlement-class certification we confront evolved in response to an asbestos-litigation crisis. A United States Judicial Conference Ad Hoc

Committee on Asbestos Litigation, appointed by the Chief Justice in September 1990, described facets of the problem in a 1991 report:

> . . . The most objectionable aspects of asbestos litigation can be briefly summarized: dockets in both federal and state courts continue to grow; long delays are routine; trials are too long; the same issues are litigated over and over; transaction costs exceed the victims' recovery by nearly two to one; exhaustion of assets threatens and distorts the process; and future claimants may lose altogether. . . .

Real reform, the report concluded, required federal legislation creating a national asbestos dispute-resolution scheme. . . . To this date, no congressional response has emerged.

In the face of legislative inaction, the federal courts — lacking authority to replace state tort systems with a national toxic tort compensation regime — endeavored to work with the procedural tools available to improve management of federal asbestos litigation. . . . [T]he Judicial Panel on Multidistrict Litigation (MDL Panel) . . . transferred all asbestos cases then filed, but not yet on trial in federal courts to a single district, the United States District Court for the Eastern District of Pennsylvania . . . . *See* In re Asbestos Prods. Liab. Litig. (No. VI), 771 F. Supp. 415, 422-24 (J.P.M.L. 1991) [*supra* p. 144].   The order aggregated pending cases only; no authority resides in the MDL Panel to license for consolidated proceedings claims not yet filed.

B

After the consolidation, attorneys for plaintiffs and defendants formed separate steering committees and began settlement negotiations. Ronald L. Motley and Gene Locks — later appointed, along with Motley's law partner Joseph F. Rice, to represent the plaintiff class in this action — co-chaired the Plaintiffs' Steering Committee. Counsel for the Center for Claims Resolution (CCR), the consortium of 20 former asbestos manufacturers now before us as petitioners, participated in the Defendants' Steering Committee. Although the MDL order collected, transferred, and consolidated only cases already commenced in federal courts, settlement negotiations included efforts to find a "means of resolving . . . future cases."
. . .

. . . [Negotiations] yielded the mass settlement agreement now in controversy. At the time, the former heads of the Plaintiffs' Steering Committee represented thousands of plaintiffs with then-pending asbestos-related claims — claimants the parties to this suit call "inventory" plaintiffs. CCR indicated in these discussions that it would resist settlement of inventory cases absent "some kind of protection for the future."

Settlement talks thus concentrated on devising an administrative scheme for disposition of asbestos claims not yet in litigation. In these negotiations, counsel for masses of inventory plaintiffs endeavored to represent the interests of the anticipated future claimants, although those lawyers then had no attorney-client relationship with such claimants.

Once negotiations seemed likely to produce an agreement purporting to bind potential plaintiffs, CCR agreed to settle, through separate agreements, the claims of plaintiffs who had already filed asbestos-related lawsuits. In one such agreement, CCR defendants promised to pay more than $200 million to gain release of the claims of numerous inventory plaintiffs. After settling the inventory claims, CCR, together with the plaintiffs' lawyers CCR had approached, launched this case, exclusively involving persons outside the MDL Panel's province — plaintiffs without already pending lawsuits.

C

The class action thus instituted was not intended to be litigated. Rather, within the space of a single day, January 15, 1993, the settling parties — CCR defendants and the representatives of the plaintiff class described below — presented to the District Court a complaint, an answer, a proposed settlement agreement, and a joint motion for conditional class certification.

The complaint identified nine lead plaintiffs, designating them and members of their families as representatives of a class comprising all persons who had not filed an asbestos-related lawsuit against a CCR defendant as of the date the class action commenced, but who (1) had been exposed — occupationally or through the occupational exposure of a spouse or household member — to asbestos or products containing asbestos attributable to a CCR defendant, or (2) whose spouse or family member had been so exposed. Untold numbers of individuals may fall within this description. All named plaintiffs alleged that they or a member of their family had been exposed to asbestos-containing products of CCR defendants. More than half of the named plaintiffs alleged that they or their family members had already suffered various physical injuries as a result of the exposure. The others alleged that they had not yet manifested any asbestos-related condition. The complaint delineated no subclasses; all named plaintiffs were designated as representatives of the class as a whole.
. . .

A stipulation of settlement accompanied the pleadings; it proposed to settle, and to preclude nearly all class members from litigating against CCR companies, all claims not filed before January 15, 1993, involving compensation for present and future asbestos-related personal injury or death. An exhaustive document exceeding 100 pages, the stipulation presents in detail an administrative mechanism and a schedule of payments to compensate class members who meet defined asbestos-exposure and medical requirements. The stipulation describes four categories of compensable disease: mesothelioma; lung cancer; certain "other cancers" (colon-rectal, laryngeal, esophageal, and stomach cancer); and "non-malignant conditions" (asbestosis and bilateral pleural thickening). Persons with "exceptional" medical claims — claims that do not fall within the four described diagnostic categories — may in some instances qualify for compensation, but the settlement caps the number of "exceptional" claims CCR must cover.

For each qualifying disease category, the stipulation specifies the range of damages CCR will pay to qualifying claimants. Payments under the settlement are not adjustable for inflation. Mesothelioma claimants — the most highly compensated category — are scheduled to receive between $20,000 and $200,000. The stipulation provides that CCR is to propose the level of compensation within the prescribed ranges; it also establishes procedures to resolve disputes over medical diagnoses and levels of compensation.

Compensation above the fixed ranges may be obtained for "extraordinary" claims. But the settlement places both numerical caps and dollar limits on such claims. The settlement also imposes "case flow maximums," which cap the number of claims payable for each disease in a given year.

Class members are to receive no compensation for certain kinds of claims, even if otherwise applicable state law recognizes such claims. Claims that garner no compensation under the settlement include claims by family members of asbestos-exposed individuals for loss of consortium, and claims by so-called "exposure-only" plaintiffs for increased risk of cancer, fear of future asbestos-related injury, and medical monitoring. "Pleural" claims, which might be asserted by persons with asbestos-related plaques on their lungs but no accompanying physical impairment, are also excluded. Although not entitled to present compensation, exposure-only claimants and pleural claimants may qualify for benefits when and if they develop a compensable disease and meet the relevant exposure and medical criteria. Defendants forgo defenses to liability, including statute of limitations pleas.

Class members, in the main, are bound by the settlement in perpetuity, while CCR defendants may choose to withdraw from the settlement after ten years. A small number of class members — only a few per year — may reject the settlement and pursue their claims in court. Those permitted to exercise this option, however, may not assert any punitive damages claim or any claim for increased risk of cancer. Aspects of the administration of the settlement are to be monitored by the AFL-CIO and class counsel. Class counsel are to receive attorneys' fees in an amount to be approved by the District Court.

D

On January 29, 1993, as requested by the settling parties, the District Court conditionally certified, under Federal Rule of Civil Procedure 23(b)(3), an encompassing opt-out class. . . . Judge Weiner appointed Locks, Motley, and Rice as class counsel, noting that "[t]he Court may in the future appoint additional counsel if it is deemed necessary and advisable." At no stage of the proceedings, however, were additional counsel in fact appointed. Nor was the class ever divided into subclasses. In a separate order, Judge Weiner assigned to Judge Reed, also of the Eastern District of Pennsylvania, "the task of conducting fairness proceedings and of determining whether the proposed settlement is fair to the class." Various class members raised objections to the settlement stipulation, and Judge Weiner granted the objectors full rights to participate in the subsequent proceedings.

In preliminary rulings, Judge Reed held that the District Court had subject-matter jurisdiction, and he approved the settling parties' elaborate plan for giving notice to the class. The court-approved notice informed recipients that they could exclude themselves from the class, if they so chose, within a three-month opt-out period.

Objectors raised numerous challenges to the settlement. They urged that the settlement unfairly disadvantaged those without currently compensable conditions in that it failed to adjust for inflation or to account for changes, over time, in medical understanding. They maintained that compensation levels were intolerably low in comparison to awards available in tort litigation or payments received by the inventory plaintiffs. And they objected to the absence of any compensation for certain claims, for example, medical monitoring, compensable under the tort law of several States. Rejecting these and all other objections, Judge Reed concluded that the settlement terms were fair and had been negotiated without collusion. He also found that adequate notice had been given to class members, and that final class certification under Rule 23(b)(3) was appropriate. . . .

Strenuous objections had been asserted regarding the adequacy of representation, a Rule 23(a)(4) requirement. Objectors maintained that class counsel and class representatives had disqualifying conflicts of interests. In particular, objectors urged, claimants whose injuries had become manifest and claimants without manifest injuries should not have common counsel and should not be aggregated in a single class. Furthermore, objectors argued, lawyers representing inventory plaintiffs should not represent the newly formed class.

Satisfied that class counsel had ably negotiated the settlement in the best interests of all concerned, and that the named parties served as adequate representatives, the District Court rejected these objections. Subclasses were unnecessary, the District Court held, bearing in mind the added cost and confusion they would entail and the ability of class members to exclude themselves from the class during the three-month opt-out period. . . . Declaring class certification appropriate and the settlement fair, the District Court preliminarily enjoined all class members from commencing any asbestos-related suit against the CCR defendants in any state or federal court. . . .

E

The Court of Appeals, in a long, heavily detailed opinion by Judge Becker, first noted several challenges by objectors to justiciability, subject-matter jurisdiction, and adequacy of notice. These challenges, the court said, raised "serious concerns." However, the court observed, "the jurisdictional issues in this case would not exist but for the [class action] certification." Turning to the class-certification issues and finding them dispositive, the Third Circuit declined to decide other questions.

On class-action prerequisites, the Court of Appeals referred to an earlier Third Circuit decision, *In re General Motors Corp. Pick-Up Truck Fuel Tank Products Liability Litigation*, 55 F.3d 768 (3d Cir. 1995) (hereinafter *GM Trucks*), which held that although a class action may be certified for settlement purposes only, Rule 23(a)'s requirements must be satisfied as if the case were going to be litigated. The same rule should apply, the Third Circuit said, to class certification under Rule 23(b)(3). While stating that the requirements of Rule 23(a) and (b)(3) must be met "without taking into account the settlement," the Court of Appeals in fact closely considered the terms of the settlement as it examined aspects of the case under Rule 23 criteria. . . .

II

Objectors assert in this Court, as they did in the District Court and Court of Appeals, an array of jurisdictional barriers. Most fundamentally, they maintain that the settlement proceeding instituted by class counsel and CCR is not a justiciable case or controversy within the confines of Article III of the Federal Constitution. In the main, they say, the proceeding is a nonadversarial endeavor to impose on countless individuals without currently ripe claims an administrative compensation regime binding on those individuals if and when they manifest injuries.

Furthermore, objectors urge that exposure-only claimants lack standing to sue . . . . Objectors also argue that exposure-only claimants did not meet the then-current amount-in-controversy requirement (in excess of $50,000) specified for federal-court jurisdiction based upon diversity of citizenship. See 28 U.S.C. § 1332(a).

As earlier recounted, the Third Circuit declined to reach these issues because they "would not exist but for the [class action] certification." We agree that "[t]he class certification issues are dispositive"; because their resolution here is logically antecedent to the existence of any Article III issues, it is appropriate to reach them first . . . . We therefore follow the path taken by the Court of Appeals, mindful that Rule 23's requirements must be interpreted in keeping with Article III constraints, and with the Rules Enabling Act, which instructs that rules of procedure "shall not abridge, enlarge or modify any substantive right," 28 U.S.C. § 2072(b). *See also* Fed. R. Civ. P. 82 ("rules shall not be construed to extend . . . the [subject matter] jurisdiction of the United States district courts").

III

To place this controversy in context, we briefly describe the characteristics of class actions for which the Federal Rules provide. . . .

In addition to satisfying Rule 23(a)'s prerequisites, parties seeking class certification must show that the action is maintainable under Rule 23(b)(1), (2), or (3). . . . Rule 23(b)(1)(A) "takes in cases where the party is obliged by law to treat the members of the class alike (a utility acting toward customers; a government imposing a tax), or where the party must treat all alike as a matter of practical necessity (a riparian owner using water as against downriver owners)." Rule 23(b)(1)(B) includes, for example, "limited fund" cases, instances in which numerous persons make claims against a fund insufficient to satisfy all claims. *See* Advisory Committee's Notes on Fed. R. Civ. P. 23 (hereinafter *Adv. Comm. Notes*).

Rule 23(b)(2) permits class actions for declaratory or injunctive relief where "the party opposing the class has acted or refused to act on grounds generally applicable to the class." Civil rights cases against parties charged with unlawful, class-based discrimination are prime examples.

In the 1966 class-action amendments, Rule 23(b)(3), the category at issue here, was "the most adventuresome" innovation. *See* Kaplan, *A Prefatory Note,* 10 B.C. IND. & COM. L. REV. 497, 497 (1969) (hereinafter Kaplan, *Prefatory Note*). Rule 23(b)(3) added to the complex-litigation arsenal class actions for damages designed to secure judgments binding all class members save those who affirmatively elected to be excluded. . . .

Framed for situations in which "class-action treatment is not as clearly called for" as it is in Rule 23(b)(1) and (b)(2) situations, Rule 23(b)(3) permits certification where class suit "may nevertheless be convenient and desirable." *Adv. Comm. Notes.* . . . In adding "predominance" and "superiority" to the qualification-for-certification list, the Advisory Committee sought to cover cases "in which a class action would achieve economies of time, effort, and expense, and promote . . . uniformity of decision as to persons similarly situated, without sacrificing procedural fairness or bringing about other undesirable results." *Id.* Sensitive to the competing tugs of individual autonomy for those who might prefer to go it alone or in a smaller unit, on the one hand, and systemic efficiency on the other, the Reporter for the 1966 amendments cautioned: "The new provision invites a close look at the case before it is accepted as a class action. . . ."

Rule 23(b)(3) includes a nonexhaustive list of factors pertinent to a court's "close look" at the predominance and superiority criteria . . . . [The Court quoted Rule 23(b)(3)(A)-(D).] In setting out these factors, the Advisory Committee for the 1966 reform anticipated that in each case, courts would "consider the interests of individual members of the class in controlling their own litigations and carrying them on as they see fit." *Adv. Comm. Notes.* They elaborated:

> The interests of individuals in conducting separate lawsuits may be so strong as to call for denial of a class action. On the other hand, these interests may be theoretic rather than practical; the class may have a high degree of cohesion and prosecution of the action through representatives would be quite unobjectionable, or the amounts at stake for individuals may be so small that separate suits would be impracticable. . . .

As the Third Circuit observed in the instant case: "Each plaintiff [in an action involving claims for personal injury and death] has a significant interest in individually controlling the prosecution of [his case]"; each "ha[s] a substantial stake in making individual decisions on whether and when to settle."

While the text of Rule 23(b)(3) does not exclude from certification cases in which individual damages run high, the Advisory Committee had dominantly in mind vindication of "the rights of groups of people who individually would be without effective strength to bring their opponents into court at all." Kaplan, *Prefatory Note*[, at] 497. As concisely recalled in a recent Seventh Circuit opinion:

> "The policy at the very core of the class action mechanism is to overcome the problem that small recoveries do not provide the incentive for any individual to bring a solo action prosecuting his or her rights. A class action solves this problem by aggregating the relatively paltry potential recoveries into something worth someone's (usually an attorney's) labor." Mace v. Van Ru Credit Corp., 109 F.3d 338, 344 (1997).

To alert class members to their right to "opt out" of a (b)(3) class, Rule 23 instructs the court to "direct to the members of the class the best notice practicable under the circumstances, including individual notice to all members who can be identified through reasonable effort." Fed. R. Civ. P. 23(c)(2).[*]

No class action may be "dismissed or compromised without [court] approval," preceded by notice to class members. Fed. R. Civ. P. 23(e).[†] . . .

In the decades since the 1966 revision of Rule 23, class action practice has become ever more "adventuresome" as a means of coping with claims too numerous to secure their "just, speedy, and inexpensive determination" one by one. *See* Fed. R. Civ. P. 1. The development reflects concerns about the efficient use of court resources and the conservation of funds to compensate claimants who do not line up early in a litigation queue. . . .

Among current applications of Rule 23(b)(3), the "settlement only" class has become a stock device. Although all Federal Circuits recognize the utility of Rule 23(b)(3) settlement classes, courts have divided on the extent to which a proffered settlement affects court surveillance under Rule 23's certification criteria.

In *GM Trucks*, 55 F.3d, at 799-800, and in the instant case, the Third Circuit held that a class cannot be certified for settlement when certification for trial would be unwarranted. Other courts have held that settlement obviates or reduces the need to measure a proposed class against the enumerated Rule 23 requirements. . . .

---

[*] The 2003 amendments to Rule 23 slightly altered this language and moved it to Rule 23(c)(2)(B). No substantive change was intended. — ED.

[†] The 2003 amendments to Rule 23 slightly altered this language. Again, no substantive change was intended by the amendment. — ED.

IV

We granted review to decide the role settlement may play, under existing Rule 23, in determining the propriety of class certification. The Third Circuit's opinion stated that each of the requirements of Rule 23(a) and (b)(3) "must be satisfied without taking into account the settlement." That statement, petitioners urge, is incorrect.

We agree with petitioners to this limited extent: settlement is relevant to a class certification. The Third Circuit's opinion bears modification in that respect. But, as we earlier observed, the Court of Appeals in fact did not ignore the settlement; instead, that court homed in on settlement terms in explaining why it found the absentees' interests inadequately represented. The Third Circuit's close inspection of the settlement in that regard was altogether proper.

Confronted with a request for settlement-only class certification, a district court need not inquire whether the case, if tried, would present intractable management problems, *see* Fed. R. Civ. P. 23(b)(3)(D), for the proposal is that there be no trial. But other specifications of the rule — those designed to protect absentees by blocking unwarranted or overbroad class definitions — demand undiluted, even heightened, attention in the settlement context. Such attention is of vital importance, for a court asked to certify a settlement class will lack the opportunity, present when a case is litigated, to adjust the class, informed by the proceedings as they unfold. *See* Fed. R. Civ. P. 23(c), (d).

And, of overriding importance, courts must be mindful that the rule as now composed sets the requirements they are bound to enforce. Federal Rules take effect after an extensive deliberative process involving many reviewers: a Rules Advisory Committee, public commenters, the Judicial Conference, this Court, the Congress. *See* 28 U.S.C. §§ 2073, 2074. The text of a rule thus proposed and reviewed limits judicial inventiveness. Courts are not free to amend a rule outside the process Congress ordered, a process properly tuned to the instruction that rules of procedure "shall not abridge . . . any substantive right." § 2072(b).

Rule 23(e) . . . was designed to function as an additional requirement, not a superseding direction, for the "class action" to which Rule 23(e) refers is one qualified for certification under Rule 23(a) and (b). Subdivisions (a) and (b) focus court attention on whether a proposed class has sufficient unity so that absent members can fairly be bound by decisions of class representatives. That dominant concern persists when settlement, rather than trial, is proposed.

The safeguards provided by the Rule 23(a) and (b) class-qualifying criteria, we emphasize, are not impractical impediments — checks shorn of utility — in the settlement class context. First, the standards set for the protection of absent class members serve to inhibit appraisals of the chancellor's foot kind — class certifications dependent upon the court's gestalt judgment or overarching impression of the settlement's fairness.

Second, if a fairness inquiry under Rule 23(e) controlled certification, eclipsing Rule 23(a) and (b), and permitting class designation despite the impossibility of litigation, both class counsel and court would be disarmed. Class counsel confined to settlement negotiations could not use the threat of litigation to press for a better offer, and the court would face a bargain proffered for its approval without benefit of adversarial investigation.

Federal courts, in any case, lack authority to substitute for Rule 23's certification criteria a standard never adopted — that if a settlement is "fair," then certification is proper. Applying to this case criteria the rulemakers set, we conclude that the Third Circuit's appraisal is essentially correct. Although that court should have acknowledged that settlement is a factor in the calculus, a remand is not warranted on that account. The Court of Appeals' opinion amply demonstrates why — with or without a settlement on the table — the sprawling class the District Court certified does not satisfy Rule 23's requirements.

A

We address first the requirement of Rule 23(b)(3) that "[common] questions of law or fact . . . predominate over any questions affecting only individual members." The District Court concluded that predominance was satisfied based on two factors: class members' shared experience of asbestos exposure and their common "interest in receiving prompt and fair compensation for their claims, while minimizing the risks and transaction costs inherent in the asbestos litigation process as it occurs presently in the tort system." The settling parties also contend that the settlement's fairness is a common question, predominating over disparate legal issues that might be pivotal in litigation but become irrelevant under the settlement.

The predominance requirement stated in Rule 23(b)(3), we hold, is not met by the factors on which the District Court relied. The benefits asbestos-exposed persons might gain from the establishment of a grand-scale compensation scheme is a matter fit for legislative consideration, but it is not pertinent to the predominance inquiry. That inquiry trains on the legal or factual questions that qualify each class member's case as a genuine controversy, questions that preexist any settlement.[18]

The Rule 23(b)(3) predominance inquiry tests whether proposed classes are sufficiently cohesive to warrant adjudication by representation.[19] The

18. In this respect, the predominance requirement of Rule 23(b)(3) is similar to the requirement of Rule 23(a)(3) that "claims or defenses" of the named representatives must be "typical of the claims or defenses of the class." The words "claims or defenses" in this context — just as in the context of Rule 24(b)(2) governing permissive intervention — "manifestly refer to the kinds of claims or defenses that can be raised in courts of law as part of an actual or impending law suit."

19. This case, we note, involves no "limited fund" capable of supporting class treatment under Rule 23(b)(1)(B), which does not have a predominance requirement. The settling parties sought to proceed exclusively under Rule 23(b)(3).

inquiry appropriate under Rule 23(e), on the other hand, protects unnamed class members "from unjust or unfair settlements affecting their rights when the representatives become fainthearted before the action is adjudicated or are able to secure satisfaction of their individual claims by a compromise." But it is not the mission of Rule 23(e) to assure the class cohesion that legitimizes representative action in the first place. If a common interest in a fair compromise could satisfy the predominance requirement of Rule 23(b)(3), that vital prescription would be stripped of any meaning in the settlement context.

The District Court also relied upon this commonality: "The members of the class have all been exposed to asbestos products supplied by the defendants. . . ." Even if Rule 23(a)'s commonality requirement may be satisfied by that shared experience, the predominance criterion is far more demanding. Given the greater number of questions peculiar to the several categories of class members, and to individuals within each category, and the significance of those uncommon questions, any overarching dispute about the health consequences of asbestos exposure cannot satisfy the Rule 23(b)(3) predominance standard.

The Third Circuit highlighted the disparate questions undermining class cohesion in this case:

> "Class members were exposed to different asbestos-containing products, for different amounts of time, in different ways, and over different periods. Some class members suffer no physical injury or have only asymptomatic pleural changes, while others suffer from lung cancer, disabling asbestosis, or from mesothelioma. . . . Each has a different history of cigarette smoking, a factor that complicates the causation inquiry.
>
> "The [exposure-only] plaintiffs especially share little in common, either with each other or with the presently injured class members. It is unclear whether they will contract asbestos-related disease and, if so, what disease each will suffer. They will also incur different medical expenses because their monitoring and treatment will depend on singular circumstances and individual medical histories." [83 F.2d] at 626.

Differences in state law, the Court of Appeals observed, compound these disparities. *See id.* at 627 (citing Phillips Petroleum Co. v. Shutts, 472 U.S. 797, 823 (1985) [*supra* p. 276]).

No settlement class called to our attention is as sprawling as this one. Predominance is a test readily met in certain cases alleging consumer or securities fraud or violations of the antitrust laws. *See Adv. Comm. Notes.* Even mass tort cases arising from a common cause or disaster may, depending upon the circumstances, satisfy the predominance requirement. The Advisory Committee for the 1966 revision of Rule 23, it is true, noted that "mass accident" cases are likely to present "significant questions, not only of damages but of liability and defenses of liability, . . . affecting the individuals in different ways." And the Committee advised that such cases are "ordinarily not appropriate" for class treatment. But the text of the rule does not categorically exclude mass tort cases from class certification, and district courts, since the late 1970s, have been certifying such cases in increasing number. The Committee's warning, however, continues to call for caution when individual stakes are high and disparities among class members great. As the Third Circuit's opinion makes plain, the certification in this case does not follow the counsel of caution. That certification cannot be upheld, for it rests on a conception of Rule 23(b)(3)'s predominance requirement irreconcilable with the rule's design.

B

Nor can the class approved by the District Court satisfy Rule 23(a)(4)'s requirement that the named parties "will fairly and adequately protect the interests of the class." The adequacy inquiry under Rule 23(a)(4) serves to uncover conflicts of interest between named parties and the class they seek to represent. *See* Gen. Tel. Co. of Sw. v. Falcon, 457 U.S. 147, 157-58, n.13 (1982). "[A] class representative must be part of the class and 'possess the same interest and suffer the same injury' as the class members." E. Tex. Motor Freight Sys., Inc. v. Rodriguez, 431 U.S. 395, 403 (1977).[20]

As the Third Circuit pointed out, named parties with diverse medical conditions sought to act on behalf of a single giant class rather than on behalf of discrete subclasses. In significant respects, the interests of those within the single class are not aligned. Most saliently, for the currently injured, the critical goal is generous immediate payments. That goal tugs against the interest of exposure-only plaintiffs in ensuring an ample, inflation-protected fund for the future. . . .

The disparity between the currently injured and exposure-only categories of plaintiffs, and the diversity within each category are not made insignificant by the District Court's finding that petitioners' assets suffice to pay claims under the settlement. Although this is not a "limited fund" case certified under Rule 23(b)(1)(B), the terms of the settlement reflect essential allocation decisions designed to confine compensation and to limit defendants' liability. For example, as earlier described, the settlement includes no adjustment for inflation; only a few claimants per year can opt out at the back end; and loss-of-consortium claims are extinguished with no compensation.

The settling parties, in sum, achieved a global compromise with no structural assurance of fair and adequate representation for the diverse groups and individuals affected. Although the named parties alleged a

---

20. The adequacy-of-representation requirement "tend[s] to merge" with the commonality and typicality criteria of Rule 23(a) . . . . Gen. Tel. Co. of Sw. v. Falcon, 457 U.S. 147, 157, n.13 (1982). The adequacy heading also factors in competency and conflicts of class counsel. *See id.* at 157-58, n.13. Like the Third Circuit, we decline to address adequacy-of-counsel issues discretely in light of our conclusions that common questions of law or fact do not predominate and that the named plaintiffs cannot adequately represent the interests of this enormous class.

range of complaints, each served generally as representative for the whole, not for a separate constituency.   In another asbestos class action, the Second Circuit spoke precisely to this point:

> "[W]here differences among members of a class are such that subclasses must be established, we know of no authority that permits a court to approve a settlement without creating subclasses on the basis of consents by members of a unitary class, some of whom happen to be members of the distinct subgroups.   The class representatives may well have thought that the Settlement serves the aggregate interests of the entire class.   But the adversity among subgroups requires that the members of each subgroup cannot be bound to a settlement except by consents given by those who understand that their role is to represent solely the members of their respective subgroups." In re Joint E. & S. Dist. Asbestos Litig., 982 F.2d 721, 742-743 (2d Cir. 1992), *modified on reh'g* sub nom. In re Findley, 993 F.2d 7 (2d Cir. 1993).

The Third Circuit found no assurance here — either in the terms of the settlement or in the structure of the negotiations — that the named plaintiffs operated under a proper understanding of their representational responsibilities.   That assessment, we conclude, is on the mark.

C

Impediments to the provision of adequate notice, the Third Circuit emphasized, rendered highly problematic any endeavor to tie to a settlement class persons with no perceptible asbestos-related disease at the time of the settlement.   Many persons in the exposure-only category . . . may not even know of their exposure, or realize the extent of the harm they may incur.   Even if they fully appreciate the significance of class notice, those without current afflictions may not have the information or foresight needed to decide, intelligently, whether to stay in or opt out.

Family members of asbestos-exposed individuals may themselves fall prey to disease or may ultimately have ripe claims for loss of consortium. Yet large numbers of people in this category — future spouses and children of asbestos victims — could not be alerted to their class membership.   And current spouses and children of the occupationally exposed may know nothing of that exposure.

Because we have concluded that the class in this case cannot satisfy the requirements of common issue predominance and adequacy of representation, we need not rule, definitively, on the notice given here.   In accord with the Third Circuit, however, we recognize the gravity of the question whether class action notice sufficient under the Constitution and Rule 23 could ever be given to legions so unselfconscious and amorphous.

V

The argument is sensibly made that a nationwide administrative claims processing regime would provide the most secure, fair, and efficient means of compensating victims of asbestos exposure. Congress, however, has not adopted such a solution. And Rule 23, which must be interpreted with fidelity to the Rules Enabling Act and applied with the interests of absent class members in close view, cannot carry the large load CCR, class counsel, and the District Court heaped upon it. As this case exemplifies, the rule-makers' prescriptions for class actions may be endangered by "those who embrace [Rule 23] too enthusiastically just as [they are by] those who approach [the rule] with distaste."

For the reasons stated, the judgment of the Court of Appeals for the Third Circuit is affirmed.

■ JUSTICE O'CONNOR took no part in the consideration or decision of this case.

■ JUSTICE BREYER, with whom JUSTICE STEVENS joins, concurring in part and dissenting in part.

Although I agree with the Court's basic holding that "settlement is relevant to a class certification," I find several problems in its approach that lead me to a different conclusion. First, I believe that the need for settlement in this mass tort case, with hundreds of thousands of lawsuits, is greater than the Court's opinion suggests. Second, I would give more weight than would the majority to settlement-related issues for purposes of determining whether common issues predominate. Third, I am uncertain about the Court's determination of adequacy of representation, and do not believe it appropriate for this Court to second-guess the District Court on the matter without first having the Court of Appeals consider it. Fourth, I am uncertain about the tenor of an opinion that seems to suggest the settlement is unfair. And fifth, in the absence of further review by the Court of Appeals, I cannot accept the majority's suggestions that "notice" is inadequate. . . .

The issues in this case are complicated and difficult. The District Court might have been correct. Or not. Subclasses might be appropriate. Or not. I cannot tell. . . . But there is no reason in this case to believe that the Court of Appeals conducted its prior review with an understanding that the settlement could have constituted a reasonably strong factor in favor of class certification. For this reason, I would provide the courts below with an opportunity to analyze the factual questions involved in certification by vacating the judgment, and remanding the case for further proceedings.

ORTIZ V. FIBREBOARD CORP.

527 U.S. 815 (1999)

■ JUSTICE SOUTER delivered the opinion of the Court.

This case turns on the conditions for certifying a mandatory settlement class on a limited fund theory under Federal Rule of Civil Procedure 23(b)(1)(B). We hold that applicants for contested certification on this rationale must show that the fund is limited by more than the agreement of the parties, and has been allocated to claimants belonging within the class by a process addressing any conflicting interests of class members.

I

Like *Amchem Products, Inc. v. Windsor*, 521 U.S. 591 (1997), this case is a class action prompted by the elephantine mass of asbestos cases, and our discussion in *Amchem* will suffice to show how this litigation defies customary judicial administration and calls for national legislation. In 1967, one of the first actions for personal asbestos injury was filed in the United States District Court for the Eastern District of Texas against a group of asbestos manufacturers. In the 1970's and 1980's, plaintiffs' lawyers throughout the country, particularly in East Texas, honed the litigation of asbestos claims to the point of almost mechanical regularity, improving the forensic identification of diseases caused by asbestos, refining theories of liability, and often settling large inventories of cases.

Respondent Fibreboard Corporation was a defendant in the 1967 action. . . . As the tide of asbestos litigation rose, Fibreboard found itself litigating on two fronts. On one, plaintiffs were filing a stream of personal injury claims against it, swelling throughout the 1980's and 1990's to thousands of new claims for compensatory damages each year. On the second front, Fibreboard was battling for funds to pay its tort claimants. From May, 1957, through March, 1959, respondent Continental Casualty Company had provided Fibreboard with a comprehensive general liability policy with limits of $1 million per occurrence, $500,000 per claim, and no aggregate limit. Fibreboard also claimed that respondent Pacific Indemnity Company had insured it from 1956 to 1957 under a similar policy. Beginning in 1979, Fibreboard was locked in coverage litigation with Continental and Pacific in a California state trial court, which in 1990 held Continental and Pacific responsible for indemnification as to any claim by a claimant exposed to Fibreboard asbestos products prior to their policies' respective expiration dates. . . . The insurance companies appealed.

With asbestos case filings continuing unabated, and its secure insurance assets almost depleted, Fibreboard in 1988 began a practice of "structured settlement," paying plaintiffs 40 percent of the settlement figure up front with the balance contingent upon a successful resolution of the coverage dispute. By 1991, however, the pace of filings forced Fibreboard to start settling cases entirely with the assignments of its rights against Continental, with no initial payment. To reflect the risk that Continental might prevail in the coverage dispute, these assignment agreements generally carried a figure about twice the nominal amount of earlier settlements. Continental challenged Fibreboard's right to make unilateral assignments, but in 1992 a California state court ruled for Fibreboard in that dispute.

Meanwhile, in the aftermath of a 1990 Federal Judicial Center conference on the asbestos litigation crisis, Fibreboard approached a group of leading asbestos plaintiffs' lawyers, offering to discuss a "global settlement" of its asbestos personal-injury liability. Early negotiations bore relatively little fruit, save for the December 1992 settlement by assignment of a significant inventory of pending claims. This settlement brought Fibreboard's deferred settlement obligations to more than $1.2 billion, all contingent upon victory over Continental on the scope of coverage and the validity of the settlement assignments.

In February 1993, after Continental had lost on both issues at the trial level, and thus faced the possibility of practically unbounded liability, it too joined the global settlement negotiations. Because Continental conditioned its part in any settlement on a guarantee of "total peace," ensuring no unknown future liabilities, talks focused on the feasibility of a mandatory class action, one binding all potential plaintiffs and giving none of them any choice to opt out of the certified class. Negotiations continued throughout the spring and summer of 1993, but the difficulty of settling both actually pending and potential future claims simultaneously led to an agreement in early August to segregate and settle an inventory of some 45,000 pending claims, being substantially all those filed by one of the plaintiffs' firms negotiating the global settlement. The settlement amounts per claim were higher than average, with one-half due on closing and the remainder contingent upon either a global settlement or Fibreboard's success in the coverage litigation. This agreement provided the model for settling inventory claims of other firms.

With the insurance companies' appeal of the consolidated coverage case set to be heard on August 27, the negotiating parties faced a motivating deadline, and about midnight before the argument, in a coffee shop in Tyler, Texas, the negotiators finally agreed upon $1.535 billion as the key term of a "Global Settlement Agreement." $1.525 billion of this sum would come from Continental and Pacific, in the proportion established by the California trial court in the coverage case, while Fibreboard would contribute $10 million, all but $500,000 of it from other insurance proceeds. The negotiators also agreed to identify unsettled present claims against Fibreboard and set aside an as-then unspecified fund to resolve them, anticipating that the bulk of any excess left in that fund would be transferred to class claimants. The next day, as a hedge against the possibility that the Global Settlement Agreement might fail, plaintiffs' counsel insisted as a condition of that agreement that Fibreboard and its two insurers settle the coverage dispute by what came to be known as the "Trilateral Settlement Agreement." The two insurers agreed to provide Fibreboard with funds eventually set at $2 billion to defend against asbestos claimants and pay the winners, should the Global Settlement Agreement fail to win approval.

On September 9, 1993, as agreed, a group of named plaintiffs filed an action in the United States District Court for the Eastern District of Texas, seeking certification for settlement purposes of a mandatory class comprising three groups: all persons with personal injury claims against Fibreboard for asbestos exposure who had not yet brought suit or settled their claims before the previous August 27; those who had dismissed such a claim but retained the right to bring a future action against Fibreboard; and "past, present and future spouses, parents, children, and other relatives" of class members exposed to Fibreboard asbestos. The class did not include claimants with actions presently pending against Fibreboard or claimants "who filed and, for cash payment or some other negotiated value, dismissed claims against Fibreboard, and whose only retained right is to sue Fibreboard upon development of an asbestos-related malignancy." . . .

As finally negotiated, the Global Settlement Agreement provided that in exchange for full releases from class members, Fibreboard, Continental, and Pacific would establish a trust to process and pay class members' asbestos personal injury and death claims.   Claimants seeking compensation would be required to try to settle with the trust. If initial settlement attempts failed, claimants would have to proceed to mediation, arbitration, and a mandatory settlement conference. Only after exhausting that process could claimants go to court against the trust, subject to a limit of $500,000 per claim, with punitive damages and prejudgment interest barred. Claims resolved without litigation would be discharged over three years, while judgments would be paid out over a 5- to 10-year period. The Global Settlement Agreement also contained spendthrift provisions to conserve the trust, and provided for paying more serious claims first in the event of a shortfall in any given year.

After an extensive campaign to give notice of the pending settlement to potential class members, the District Court allowed groups of objectors, including petitioners here, to intervene. After an 8-day fairness hearing, the District Court certified the class and approved the settlement as "fair, adequate, and reasonable," under Rule 23(e). Satisfied that the requirements of Rule 23(a) were met, the District Court certified the class under Rule 23(b)(1)(B), citing the risk that Fibreboard might lose or fare poorly on appeal of the coverage case or lose the assignment-settlement dispute, leaving it without funds to pay all claims. . . .

On appeal, the Fifth Circuit affirmed both as to class certification and adequacy of settlement. . . .

Shortly thereafter, this Court decided *Amchem* and proceeded to vacate the Fifth Circuit's judgment and remand for further consideration in light of that decision. On remand, the Fifth Circuit again affirmed, in a brief per curiam opinion, distinguishing *Amchem* on the grounds that the instant action proceeded under Rule 23(b)(1)(B) rather than (b)(3), and did not allocate awards according to the nature of the claimant's injury. . . .

We granted certiorari, and now reverse.

II

The nub of this case is the certification of the class under Rule 23(b)(1)(B) on a limited fund rationale, but before we reach that issue, there are two threshold matters. First, [the Court declined to address the standing issue].

Petitioners also argue that the Fifth Circuit on remand disregarded *Amchem* in passing on the Rule 23(a) issues of commonality, typicality, and adequacy of representation. We agree that in reinstating its affirmance of the District Court's certification decision, the Fifth Circuit fell short in its attention to *Amchem*'s explanation of the governing legal standards. Two aspects in particular of the District Court's certification should have received more detailed treatment by the Court of Appeals. First, the District Court's enquiry into both commonality and typicality focused almost entirely on the terms of the settlement. Second, and more significantly, the District Court took no steps at the outset to ensure that the potentially conflicting interests of easily identifiable categories of claimants be protected by provisional certification of subclasses under Rule 23(c)(4), relying instead on its post-hoc findings at the fairness hearing that these subclasses in fact had been adequately represented. As will be seen, however, these points will reappear when we review the certification on the Court of Appeals's "limited fund" theory under Rule 23(b)(1)(B). We accordingly turn directly to that.

III

A

Although representative suits have been recognized in various forms since the earliest days of English law, class actions as we recognize them today developed as an exception to the formal rigidity of the necessary parties rule in equity, as well as from the bill of peace, an equitable device for combining multiple suits. . . . From these roots, modern class action practice emerged in the 1966 revision of Rule 23. In drafting Rule 23(b), the Advisory Committee sought to catalogue in "functional" terms "those recurrent life patterns which call for mass litigation through representative parties." . . .

Among the traditional varieties of representative suit encompassed by Rule 23(b)(1)(B) were those involving "the presence of property which call[ed] for distribution or management." . . . One recurring type of such suits was the limited fund class action, aggregating "claims . . . made by numerous persons against a fund insufficient to satisfy all claims." . . . As the Advisory Committee recognized . . ., equity required absent parties to be represented, joinder being impractical, where individual claims to be satisfied from the one asset would, as a practical matter, prejudice the rights of absent claimants against a fund inadequate to pay them all.

Equity, of course, recognized the same necessity to bind absent claimants to a limited fund when no formal imposition of a constructive trust was entailed. . . .

B

The cases forming this pedigree of the limited fund class action as understood by the drafters of Rule 23 have a number of common characteristics, despite the variety of circumstances from which they arose. The points of resemblance are not necessarily the points of contention resolved in the particular cases, but they show what the Advisory Committee must have assumed would be at least a sufficient set of conditions to justify binding absent members of a class under Rule 23(b)(1)(B), from which no one has the right to secede.

The first and most distinctive characteristic is that the totals of the aggregated liquidated claims and the fund available for satisfying them, set definitely at their maximums, demonstrate the inadequacy of the fund to pay all the claims. The concept driving this type of suit was insufficiency, which alone justified the limit on an early feast to avoid a later famine. The equity of the limitation is its necessity.

Second, the whole of the inadequate fund was to be devoted to the overwhelming claims. It went without saying that the defendant or estate or constructive trustee with the inadequate assets had no opportunity to benefit himself or claimants of lower priority by holding back on the amount distributed to the class. The limited fund cases thus ensured that the class as a whole was given the best deal; they did not give a defendant a better deal than seriatim litigation would have produced.

Third, the claimants identified by a common theory of recovery were treated equitably among themselves. The cases assume that the class will comprise everyone who might state a claim on a single or repeated set of facts, invoking a common theory of recovery, to be satisfied from the limited fund as the source of payment. . . .

In sum, mandatory class treatment through representative actions on a limited fund theory was justified with reference to a "fund" with a definitely ascertained limit, all of which would be distributed to satisfy all those with liquidated claims based on a common theory of liability, by an equitable, pro rata distribution.

C

The Advisory Committee, and presumably the Congress in approving subdivision (b)(1)(B), must have assumed that an action with these characteristics would satisfy the limited fund rationale cognizable under that subdivision. The question remains how far the same characteristics are necessary for limited fund treatment. While we cannot settle all the details of a subdivision (b)(1)(B) limited fund here (and so cannot decide the ultimate question whether settlements of multitudes of related tort actions are amenable to mandatory class treatment), there are good reasons to treat these characteristics as presumptively necessary, and not merely sufficient, to satisfy the limited fund rationale for a mandatory action. At the least, the burden of justification rests on the proponent of any departure from the traditional norm.

It is true, of course, that the text of Rule 23(b)(1)(B) is on its face open to a more lenient limited fund concept, just as it covers more historical antecedents than the limited fund. But the greater the leniency in departing from the historical limited fund model, the greater the likelihood of abuse in ways that will be apparent when we apply the limited fund criteria to the case before us. The prudent course, therefore, is to presume that when subdivision (b)(1)(B) was devised to cover limited fund actions, the object was to stay close to the historical model. As will be seen, this limiting construction finds support in the Advisory Committee's expressions of understanding, minimizes potential conflict with the Rules Enabling Act, and avoids serious constitutional concerns raised by the mandatory class resolution of individual legal claims, especially where a case seeks to resolve future liability in a settlement-only action.

To begin with, the Advisory Committee looked cautiously at the potential for creativity under Rule 23(b)(1)(B), at least in comparison with Rule 23(b)(3). Although the committee crafted all three subdivision of the Rule in general, practical terms, without the formalism that had bedeviled the original Rule 23, the Committee was consciously retrospective with intent to codify pre-Rule categories under Rule 23(b)(1), not forward-looking as it was in anticipating innovations under Rule 23(b)(3). Thus, the Committee intended subdivision (b)(1) to capture the "standard" class actions recognized in pre-Rule practice.

Consistent with its backward look under subdivision (b)(1), as commentators have pointed out, it is clear that the Advisory Committee did not contemplate that the mandatory class action codified in subdivision (b)(1)(B) would be used to aggregate unliquidated tort claims on a limited fund rationale. None of the examples cited in the Advisory Committee Notes or by Professor Kaplan in explaining Rule 23(b)(1)(B) remotely approach what was then described as a "mass accident" case. While the Advisory Committee focused much attention on the amenability of Rule 23(b)(3) to such cases, the Committee's debates are silent about resolving tort claims under a mandatory limited fund rationale under Rule 23(b)(1)(B). It is simply implausible that the Advisory Committee, so concerned about the potential difficulties posed by dealing with mass tort cases under Rule 23(b)(3), with its provisions for notice and the right to opt out, *see* Rule 23(c)(2), would have uncritically assumed that mandatory versions of such class actions, lacking such protections, could be certified under Rule 23(b)(1)(B). We do not, it is true, decide the ultimate question whether Rule 23(b)(1)(B) may ever be used to aggregate individual tort claims, *cf.* Ticor Title Ins. Co. v. Brown, 511 U. S. 117, 121 (1994) (per curiam) [*supra* p. 420]. But we do recognize that the Committee would have thought such an application of the Rule surprising, and take this as a good reason to limit any surprise by presuming that the Rule's historical antecedents identify requirements.

The Rules Enabling Act underscores the need for caution. As we said in *Amchem*, no reading of the Rule can ignore the Act's mandate that "rules of procedure 'shall not abridge, enlarge or modify any substantive right.'" Petitioners argue that the Act has been violated here, asserting that the Global Settlement Agreement's priorities of claims and compromise of full recovery abrogated the state law that must govern this diversity action under 28 U.S.C. § 1652. Although we need not grapple with the difficult choice-of-law and substantive state-law questions raised by petitioners' assertion, we do need to recognize the tension between the limited fund class action's pro rata distribution in equity and the rights of individual tort victims at law. Even if we assume that some such tension is acceptable under the Rules Enabling Act, it is best kept within tolerable limits by keeping limited fund practice under Rule 23(b)(1)(B) close to the practice preceding its adoption.

Finally, if we needed further counsel against adventurous application of Rule 23(b)(1)(B), the Rules Enabling Act and the general doctrine of constitutional avoidance would jointly sound a warning of the serious constitutional concerns that come with any attempt to aggregate individual tort claims on a limited fund rationale. First, the certification of a mandatory class followed by settlement of its action for money damages obviously implicates the Seventh Amendment jury trial rights of absent class members. We noted in *Ross v. Bernhard*, 396 U. S. 531, 541 (1970), that since the merger of law and equity in 1938, it has become settled among the lower courts that "class action plaintiffs may obtain a jury trial on any legal issues they present." By its nature, however, a mandatory settlement-only class action with legal issues and future claimants compromises their Seventh Amendment rights without their consent.

Second, and no less important, mandatory class actions aggregating damage claims implicate the due process "principle of general application in Anglo-American jurisprudence that one is not bound by a judgment in personam in a litigation in which he is not designated as a party or to which he has not been made a party by service of process," Hansberry v. Lee, 311 U.S. 32, 40 (1940), it being "our 'deep-rooted historic tradition that everyone should have his own day in court,'" Martin v. Wilks, 490 U. S. 755, 762 (1989) [*supra* p. 222]; *see* Richards v. Jefferson County, 517 U. S. 793, 798-99 (1996). . . .

The inherent tension between representative suits and the day-in-court ideal is only magnified if applied to damage claims gathered in a mandatory class. Unlike Rule 23(b)(3) class members, objectors to the collectivism of a mandatory subdivision (b)(1)(B) action have no inherent right to abstain. The legal rights of absent class members (which in a class like this one would include claimants who by definition may be unidentifiable when the class is certified) are resolved regardless either of their consent, or, in a class with objectors, their express wish to the contrary.[23] And in settlement-only class actions the procedural protections built into the Rule

---

23. It is no answer in this case that the settlement agreement provided for a limited, back-end "opt out" in the form of a right on the part of class members eventually to take their case to court if dissatisfied with the amount provided by the trust. The "opt out" in this case requires claimants to exhaust a variety of alternative dispute mechanisms, to bring suit against the trust, and not against Fibreboard, and it limits damages to $500,000, to be paid out in installments over 5 to 10 years, despite multimillion-dollar jury verdicts sometimes reached in asbestos suits. Indeed, on approximately a dozen occasions, Fibreboard had settled for more than $500,000.

to protect the rights of absent class members during litigation are never invoked in an adversarial setting, *see Amchem*, 521 U.S. at 620.

In related circumstances, we raised the flag on this issue of due process more than a decade ago in *Phillips Petroleum Co. v. Shutts*, 472 U. S. 797 (1985) [*supra* p. 276]. . . . After losing at trial, the defendant, Phillips Petroleum, argued that the state court had no jurisdiction over claims of out-of-state plaintiffs without their affirmative consent. We said no and held that out-of-state plaintiffs could not invoke the same due process limits on personal jurisdiction that out-of-state defendants had under *International Shoe Co. v. Washington*, 326 U.S. 310 (1945), and its progeny. But we also saw that before an absent class member's right of action was extinguishable due process required that the member "receive notice plus an opportunity to be heard and participate in the litigation," and we said that "at a minimum . . . an absent plaintiff [must] be provided with an opportunity to remove himself from the class."

IV

The record on which the District Court rested its certification of the class for the purpose of the global settlement did not support the essential premises of mandatory limited fund actions. It failed to demonstrate that the fund was limited except by the agreement of the parties, and it showed exclusions from the class and allocations of assets at odds with the concept of limited fund treatment and the structural protections of Rule 23(a) explained in *Amchem*.

A

The defect of certification going to the most characteristic feature of a limited fund action was the uncritical adoption by both the District Court and the Court of Appeals of figures agreed upon by the parties in defining the limits of the fund and demonstrating its inadequacy. When a district court, as here, certifies for class action settlement only, the moment of certification requires "heightene[d] attention," *Amchem*, 521 U.S. at 620, to the justifications for binding the class members. This is so because certification of a mandatory settlement class, however provisional technically, effectively concludes the proceeding save for the final fairness hearing. And, as we held in *Amchem*, a fairness hearing under Rule 23(e) is no substitute for rigorous adherence to those provisions of the Rule "designed to protect absentees," *id.*, among them subdivision (b)(1)(B). Thus, in an action such as this the settling parties must present not only their agreement, but evidence on which the district court may ascertain the limit and the insufficiency of the fund, with support in findings of fact following a proceeding in which the evidence is subject to challenge . . . .

We have already alluded to the difficulties facing limited fund treatment of huge numbers of actions for unliquidated damages arising from mass torts, the first such hurdle being a computation of the total claims. It is simply not a matter of adding up the liquidated amounts, as in the models of limited fund actions. Although we might assume *arguendo* that prior judicial experience with asbestos claims would allow a court to make a sufficiently reliable determination of the probable total, the District Court here apparently thought otherwise, concluding that "there is no way to predict Fibreboard's future asbestos liability with any certainty." Nothing turns on this conclusion, however, since there was no adequate demonstration of the second element required for limited fund treatment, the upper limit of the fund itself, without which no showing of insufficiency is possible.

The "fund" in this case comprised both the general assets of Fibreboard and the insurance assets provided by the two policies. As to Fibreboard's assets exclusive of the contested insurance, the District Court and the Fifth Circuit concluded that Fibreboard had a then-current sale value of $235 million that could be devoted to the limited fund. While that estimate may have been conservative, at least the District Court heard evidence and made an independent finding at some point in the proceedings. The same, however, cannot be said for the value of the disputed insurance.

The insurance assets would obviously be "limited" in the traditional sense if the total of demonstrable claims would render the insurers insolvent, or if the policies provided aggregate limits falling short of that total; calculation might be difficult, but the way to demonstrate the limit would be clear. Neither possibility is presented in this case, however. Instead, any limit of the insurance asset here had to be a product of potentially unlimited policy coverage discounted by the risk that Fibreboard would ultimately lose the coverage dispute litigation. This sense of limit as a value discounted by risk is of course a step removed from the historical model, but even on the assumption that it would suffice for limited fund treatment, there was no adequate finding of fact to support its application here. Instead of undertaking an independent evaluation of potential insurance funds, the District Court (and, later, the Court of Appeals), simply accepted the $2 billion Trilateral Settlement Agreement figure as representing the maximum amount the insurance companies could be required to pay tort victims . . . .

Settlement value is not always acceptable, however. One may take a settlement amount as good evidence of the maximum available if one can assume that parties of equal knowledge and negotiating skill agreed upon the figure through arms-length bargaining, unhindered by any consider-ations tugging against the interests of the parties ostensibly represented in the negotiation. But no such assumption may be indulged in this case, or probably in any class action settlement with the potential for gigantic fees. In this case, certainly, any assumption that plaintiffs' counsel could be of a mind to do their simple best in bargaining for the benefit of the settle-ment class is patently at odds with the fact that at least some of the same lawyers representing plaintiffs and the class had also negotiated the separate settlement of 45,000 pending claims, the full payment of which was contingent on a successful global settlement agreement or the successful resolution of the insurance coverage dispute (either by litigation or by agreement, as eventually occurred in the Trilateral Settlement Agreement). Class counsel thus had great incentive to reach any agreement in the global settlement negotiations that they thought might survive a Rule 23(e) fairness hearing, rather than the best possible arrangement for the substantially unidentified global settlement class. The resulting incentive to favor the known plaintiffs in the earlier settlement was, indeed, an egregious example of the conflict noted in *Amchem* resulting from divergent interests of the presently injured and future claimants. *See* 521 U. S at 626-27 (discussing adequacy of named representatives under Rule 23(a)(4)).

We do not, of course, know exactly what an independent valuation of the limit of the insurance assets would have shown. . . . But objecting and unidentified class members alike are entitled to have the issue settled by specific evidentiary findings independent of the agreement of defendants and conflicted class counsel.

B

The explanation of need for independent determination of the fund has necessarily anticipated our application of the requirement of equity among members of the class. There are two issues, the inclusiveness of the class and the fairness of distributions to those within it. On each, this certification for settlement fell short.

The definition of the class excludes myriad claimants with causes of action, or foreseeable causes of action, arising from exposure to Fibreboard asbestos. While the class includes those with present claims never filed, present claims withdrawn without prejudice, and future claimants, it fails to include those who had previously settled with Fibreboard while retaining the right to sue again "upon development of an asbestos related malignancy," plaintiffs with claims pending against Fibreboard at the time of the initial announcement of the Global Settlement Agreement, and the plaintiffs in the "inventory" claims settled as a supposedly necessary step in reaching the global settlement. . . . It is a fair question how far a natural class may be depleted by prior dispositions of claims and still qualify as a mandatory limited fund class, but there can be no question that such a mandatory settlement class will not qualify when in the very negotiations aimed at a class settlement, class counsel agree to exclude what could turn out to be as much as a third of the claimants that negotiators thought might eventually be involved, a substantial number of whom class counsel represent.

Might such class exclusions be forgiven if it were shown that the class members with present claims and the outsiders ended up with comparable benefits? The question is academic here. On the record before us, we cannot speculate on how the unsettled claims would fare if the Global Settlement were approved, or under the Trilateral Settlement. As for the settled inventory claims, their plaintiffs appeared to have obtained better terms than the class members. They received an immediate payment of 50 percent of a settlement higher than the historical average, and would get the remainder if the global settlement were sustained (or the coverage litigation resolved, as it turned out to be by the Trilateral Settlement Agreement); the class members, by contrast, would be assured of a 3-year payout for claims settled, whereas the unsettled faced a prospect of mediation followed by arbitration as prior conditions of instituting suit, which would even then be subject to a recovery limit, a slower payout and the limitations of the trust's spendthrift protection. Finally, as discussed below, even ostensible parity between settling nonclass plaintiffs and class members would be insufficient to overcome the failure to provide the structural protection of independent representation as for subclasses with conflicting interests.

On the second element of equity within the class, the fairness of the distribution of the fund among class members, the settlement certification is likewise deficient. Fair treatment in the older cases was characteristically assured by straightforward pro rata distribution of the limited fund. While equity in such a simple sense is unattainable in a settlement covering present claims not specifically proven and claims not even due to arise, if at all, until some future time, at the least such a settlement must seek equity by providing for procedures to resolve the difficult issues of treating such differently situated claimants with fairness as among themselves.

First, it is obvious after *Amchem* that a class divided between holders of present and future claims (some of the latter involving no physical injury and to claimants not yet born) requires division into homogeneous subclasses under Rule 23(c)(4)(B) [now Rule 23(c)(5) — ED.], with separate representation to eliminate conflicting interests of counsel.[31] . . . No such procedure was employed here, and the conflict was as contrary to the equitable obligation entailed by the limited fund rationale as it was to the requirements of structural protection applicable to all class actions under Rule 23(a)(4).

Second, the class included those exposed to Fibreboard's asbestos products both before and after 1959. The date is significant, for that year saw the expiration of Fibreboard's insurance policy with Continental, the one which provided the bulk of the insurance funds for the settlement. Pre-1959 claimants accordingly had more valuable claims than post-1959 claimants, the consequence being a second instance of disparate interests within the certified class. While at some point there must be an end to reclassification with separate counsel, these two instances of conflict are well within the requirement of structural protection recognized in *Amchem*.

It is no answer to say, as the Fifth Circuit said on remand, that these conflicts may be ignored because the settlement makes no disparate allocation of resources as between the conflicting classes. The settlement decides that the claims of the immediately injured deserve no provisions

---

31. This adequacy of representation concern parallels the enquiry required at the threshold under Rule 23(a)(4), but as we indicated in *Amchem*, the same con-cerns that drive the threshold findings under Rule 23(a) may also influence the propriety of the certification decision under the subdivisions of Rule 23(b).

more favorable than the more speculative claims of those projected to have future injuries, and that liability subject to indemnification is no different from liability with no indemnification. The very decision to treat them all the same is itself an allocation decision with results almost certainly different from the results that those with immediate injuries or claims of indemnified liability would have chosen.

Nor does it answer the settlement's failures to provide structural protections in the service of equity to argue that the certified class members' common interest in securing contested insurance funds for the payment of claims was so weighty as to diminish the deficiencies beneath recognition here. This argument is simply a variation of the position put forward by the proponents of the settlement in *Amchem*, who tried to discount the comparable failure in that case to provide separate representatives for subclasses with conflicting interests. . . . Here, just as in the earlier case, the proponents of the settlement are trying to rewrite Rule 23; each ignores the fact that Rule 23 requires protections under subdivisions (a) and (b) against inequity and potential inequity at the precertification stage, quite independently of the required determination at postcertification fairness review under subdivision (e) that any settlement is fair in an overriding sense. A fairness hearing under subdivision (e) can no more swallow the preceding protective requirements of Rule 23 in a subdivision (b)(1)(B) action than in one under subdivision (b)(3).

C

A third contested feature of this settlement certification that departs markedly from the limited fund antecedents is the ultimate provision for a fund smaller than the assets understood by the Court of Appeals to be available for payment of the mandatory class members' claims; most notably, Fibreboard was allowed to retain virtually its entire net worth. Given our treatment of the two preceding deficiencies of the certification, there is of course no need to decide whether this feature of the agreement would alone be fatal to the Global Settlement Agreement. To ignore it entirely, however, would be so misleading that we have decided simply to identify the issue it raises, without purporting to resolve it at this time.

Fibreboard listed its supposed entire net worth as a component of the total (and allegedly inadequate) assets available for claimants, but subsequently retained all but $500,000 of that equity for itself. On the face of it, the arrangement seems irreconcilable with the justification of necessity in denying any opportunity for withdrawal of class members whose jury trial rights will be compromised, whose damages will be capped, and whose payments will be delayed. With Fibreboard retaining nearly all its net worth, it hardly appears that such a regime is the best that can be provided for class members. . . .

The District Court in this case seems to have had a further point in mind, however. One great advantage of class action treatment of mass tort cases is the opportunity to save the enormous transaction costs of piecemeal litigation, an advantage to which the settlement's proponents have referred in this case. Although the District Court made no specific finding about the transaction cost saving likely from this class settlement, estimating the amount in the "hundreds of millions," it did conclude that the amount would exceed Fibreboard's net worth as the Court valued it (Fibreboard's net worth of $235 million "is considerably less than the likely savings in defense costs under the Global Settlement"). If a settlement thus saves transaction costs that would never have gone into a class member's pocket in the absence of settlement, may a credit for some of the savings be recognized in a mandatory class action as an incentive to settlement? It is at least a legitimate question, which we leave for another day.

VI

In sum, the applicability of Rule 23(b)(1)(B) to a fund and plan purporting to liquidate actual and potential tort claims is subject to question, and its purported application in this case was in any event improper. The Advisory Committee did not envision mandatory class actions in cases like this one, and both the Rules Enabling Act and the policy of avoiding serious constitutional issues counsel against leniency in recognizing mandatory limited fund actions in circumstances markedly different from the traditional paradigm. Assuming *arguendo* that a mandatory, limited fund rationale could under some circumstances be applied to a settlement class of tort claimants, it would be essential that the fund be shown to be limited independently of the agreement of the parties to the action, and equally essential under Rule 23(a) and (b)(1)(B) that the class include all those with claims unsatisfied at the time of the settlement negotiations, with intraclass conflicts addressed by recognizing independently represented subclasses. In this case, the limit of the fund was determined by treating the settlement agreement as dispositive, an error magnified by the representation of class members by counsel also representing excluded plaintiffs, whose settlements would be funded fully upon settlement of the class action on any terms that could survive final fairness review. Those separate settlements, together with other exclusions from the claimant class, precluded adequate structural protection by subclass treatment, which was not even afforded to the conflicting elements within the class as certified.

The judgment of the Court of Appeals, accordingly, is reversed, and the case is remanded for further proceedings consistent with this opinion.

■ [The concurrence of CHIEF JUSTICE REHNQUIST, with whom JUSTICE SCALIA and JUSTICE KENNEDY joined, is omitted.]

■ JUSTICE BREYER, with whom JUSTICE STEVENS joins, dissenting. . . .

Four special background circumstances underlie this settlement and help to explain the reasonableness and consequent lawfulness of the relevant District Court determinations. First, as the majority points out, the settlement comprises part of an "elephantine mass of asbestos cases," which "defies customary judicial administration." . . .

Second, an individual asbestos case is a tort case, of a kind that courts, not legislatures, ordinarily will resolve. It is the number of these cases, not their nature, that creates the special judicial problem. The judiciary cannot treat the problem as entirely one of legislative failure, as if it were caused, say, by a poorly drafted statute. Thus, when "calls for national legislation" go unanswered, judges can and should search aggressively for ways, within the framework of existing law, to avoid delay and expense so great as to bring about a massive denial of justice.

Third, in that search the district courts may take advantage of experience that appellate courts do not have. . . .

Fourth, the alternative to class-action settlement is not a fair opportunity for each potential plaintiff to have his or her own day in court. Unusually high litigation costs, unusually long delays, and limitations upon the total amount of resources available for payment, together mean that most potential plaintiffs may not have a realistic alternative. And Federal Rule of Civil Procedure 23 was designed to address situations in which the historical model of individual actions would not, for practical reasons, work.

For these reasons, I cannot easily find a legal answer to the problems this case raises by referring, as does the majority, to "our 'deep-rooted historic tradition that everyone should have his own day in court.'" Instead, in these circumstances, I believe our Court should allow a district court full authority to exercise every bit of discretionary power that the law provides. And, in doing so, the Court should prove extremely reluctant to overturn a fact-specific or circumstance-specific exercise of that discretion, where a court of appeals has found it lawful. . . .

The case falls within the Rule's language as long as there was a significant "risk" that the total assets available to satisfy the claims of the class members would fall well below the likely total value of those claims, for in such circumstances the money would go to those claimants who brought their actions first, thereby "substantially impair[ing]" the "ability" of later claimants "to protect their interests." And the District Court found there was indeed such a "risk." . . .

. . . [T]he majority apparently concedes the conceptual point that a fund's limit may equal its "value discounted by risk." But the majority sets forth three additional conditions, which it says are "sufficient . . . to justify binding absent members of a class under Rule 23(b)(1)(B), from which no one has the right to secede." [The dissent then argued that each condition had been satisfied.]

Notes

1. *Amchem* and *Ortiz* are as interesting for their dicta as for their holdings. First, they contain the Court's most extended discussions of the relationship among all of the Rule 23(a) and Rule 23(b) provisions. Next, *Amchem* goes out of its way to state that class actions can be used in mass-tort cases and to disown any contrary implications in the 1966 Advisory

Committee Notes. Indeed, *Amchem* seems to bless mass-tort litigation class actions in appropriate "circumstances," although the Court refused to describe exactly what those "circumstances" might be. Of course, te Court's blessing arose in the context of its discussion of the predominance requirement of Rule 23(b)(3), and did not indicate whether a similar attitude should carry over to other Rule 23 requirements.

Third, the Court recognizes in both cases that settlement class actions are sometimes appropriate, and that these class actions do not necessarily need to meet all of the requirements that a litigation class action would need to meet. The Court also admits that the existence of a settlement is relevant in determining whether the requirements of a class action have been established, but that the settlement context of the class certification requires heightened attention to the Rule 23(a)(4) requirement of adequacy of representation. Finally, the Court holds that the substantive fairness of the settlement cannot act as a surrogate for these requirements, nor can the common interests in the settlement be used to satisfy the common interest requirements of Rule 23(a) and (b)(3).

2. Aside from these statements, and the Court's observation that *Amchem* was too "sprawling," do you have a sense about when a settlement class action is appropriate and when it is not? How much influence should *Amchem* and *Ortiz* exercise over cases involving smaller stakes, in which individual suits are not economically viable? What if the same conflicts of interest are not present? Do the cases signal that settlements in less mature litigation are automatically in trouble, or is maturity not a relevant factor in certifying settlement classes? Do *Amchem* and *Ortiz* mean that the efficient resolution of widespread controversies is irrelevant to the certification decision in a settlement class action? Do they mean that no future claims can be settled through the class action device? Do they affect the ability to use settlement class actions in non-tort cases?

More generally, is it fair to say that *Amchem* and *Ortiz* play class actions close to the vest, tamping down their more adventuresome uses in both litigation and settlement? How should that attitude affect some of the more ambitious uses of class actions to aggregate litigation that we have seen elsewhere in this chapter? Without a strong class-action rule, can courts achieve optimal aggregation of related claims?

3. The returns on the effect of *Amchem* and *Ortiz* are mixed. Courts have continued to approve some mass-tort settlement class actions. *See* In re Silicone Gel Breast Implant Litig., Nos. CV 92-P-10000-S and CV 97-P-11441-S (N.D. Ala. Jul. 7, 1999) ((b)(1)(B) settlement pre-*Ortiz*); In re Orthopedic Bone Screw Prods. Liab. Litig., 176 F.R.D. 158 (E.D. Pa. 1997) ((b)(1)(B) settlement pre-*Ortiz*). Settlement class actions in non-tort areas have also been approved. See In re Mego Fin. Corp. Sec. Litig., 213 F.3d 454 (9th Cir. 2000) ((b)(3) securities-fraud settlement); Hanlon v. Chrysler Corp., 150 F.3d 1011 (9th Cir. 1998) ((b)(3) settlement of consumer claims arising from defective minivans); Shaw v. Toshiba Am. Info. Sys., Inc., 91 F. Supp. 2d 942 (E.D. Tex. 2000) ((b)(3) computer defect); In re Austrian & German Bank Holocaust Litig., 80 F. Supp. 2d 164 (S.D.N.Y. 1999)

(settlement of claims of Holocaust survivors); Collier v. Montgomery County Hous. Auth., 192 F.R.D. 176 (E.D. Pa. 2000) ((b)(2) settlement of lead paint injunctive claims); In re Toys "R" Us Antitrust Litig., 191 F.R.D. 347 (E.D.N.Y. 2000) ((b)(2) and (b)(3) settlement of antitrust cases); In re Tex. Prison Litig., 191 F.R.D. 164 (W.D. Mo. 2000) ((b)(2) settlement of prisoners' claims) In re Found. for New Era Philanthropy Litig., 175 F.R.D. 202, 205 (E.D. Pa. 1997) ((b)(1)(B) securities-fraud class action against insolvent debtor; distinguishing *Amchem* in part because claims were "exclusively for economic injury" and in part because *Amchem* indicated approval of class actions in securities cases).

On the other hand, numerous courts have refused to certify settlement class actions, in both the mass-tort area and elsewhere. *See* In re Telectronics Pacing Sys., Inc., Accufix Atrial "J" Leads Prods. Liab. Litig., 221 F.3d 870 (6th Cir. 2000) (reversing certification under Rule 23(b)(1)(B) of a mass-tort settlement class action); Levell v. Monsanto Res. Corp., 191 F.R.D. 543 (S.D. Ohio 2000) (settlement not fair); In re: Diet Drugs (Phentermine, Fenfluramine, Dexfenfluramine) Prods. Liab. Litig., 1999 WL 782560 (E.D. Pa. Sept. 27, 1999) (terms of Rule 23(b)(1)(B) not met in a mass-tort settlement class action); In re Synthroid Marketing Litig., 1998 WL 526566 (N.D. Ill. Aug. 17, 1998) (denying approval of $98 million deceptive-practices class settlement); Walker v. Liggett Group, Inc., 175 F.R.D. 226 (S.D. W.Va. 1997) (terms of Rule 23(a) not met in a limited-fund tobacco settlement).

4. *Amchem* makes clear that the conflicts of interest within a class cannot be smoothed over by the common interests of a class in a settlement. Do *Amchem* and *Ortiz* suggest that class actions must be viewed as the aggregation of individual persons with individual interests, rather than as a collective entity with group interests? *Cf.* David L. Shapiro, *Class Actions: The Class as Party and Client*, 73 NOTRE DAME L. REV. 913, 917-18 (1998) (arguing that "the notion of the class as entity should prevail over more individually oriented notions of aggregate litigation"). If so, does any conflict between two individual class members mean that a single class cannot be certified? If not, how much variation in interests is permissible before we say that a single class can no longer be used?

Note *Amchem*'s suggestion (again mentioned in *Ortiz*) that some of the conflicts of interest can be avoided by subclassing members with different interests, presumably into groups with similar litigation interests. How would such a system work? Would separate counsel need to be appointed for each subclass? Would the subclasses need to be changed every time there was a change in the terms of the settlement? Isn't there a risk that one subclass will engage in strategic behavior to obtain a disproportionate share of the settlement? Whether strategic or not, what happens when one subclass declines to go along with the settlement, and jeopardizes the interests of all class members in the settlement?

5. In *Amchem* and *Ortiz*, the Court did not examine the issues of the potential conflicts of interest between class counsel and the class or of the alleged collusion between class counsel and the defendants. Both of these

claims had been main lines of attack that objectors had launched against the settlement in the trial court. *See* Georgine v. Amchem Prods., Inc., 157 F.R.D. 246, 294-311 (E.D. Pa. 1994) (finding as a matter of fact that neither conflicts of interest nor collusion existed) (*infra* p. 739). For a passionate argument that such conflicts existed, written by a professor that was an expert witness on legal ethics for the objectors, see Susan P. Koniak, *Feasting While the Widow Weeps:* Georgine v. Amchem Products, Inc., 80 CORNELL L. REV. 1045 (1995). Professor Koniak argued that the future class members in *Amchem* were treated worse than class counsel's "inventory" plaintiffs, with whom the CCR defendants settled in a separate deal, and that class counsel sold out the interests of future claimants in order to obtain higher fees on their inventory cases.

The potential for conflicts of the type seen in *Amchem* and *Ortiz*, either within the class or between class counsel and class members, lurk in virtually any settlement of class-action claims for money. The reason is that, unless the class action can be certified on a mandatory basis (an unlikely proposition after *Ortiz*), defendants interested in a truly global settlement must work with the lawyers handling most of the present claims; otherwise, these counsel will simply opt their clients out of the settlement, and the defendants won't be much better off than they were before. Unless counsel settles present claims on exactly the same terms (adjusted for inflation, as *Amchem* says) as future claims, any favorable treatment of the counsel's non-class plaintiffs raises a concern for conflict of interest and collusion. Should the problem be dealt with by insisting that, in order to meet the Rule 23(a)(4) adequacy requirement, class counsel define the class in a way that all of counsel's clients fit within the class? Should it be dealt with by requiring that counsel representing future claimants not represent any present claimants? Will this latter alternative lead to the appointment of class counsel that is less able and experienced than individual counsel are?

More generally, cases such as *Amchem* and *Ortiz* force us to consider the ethical responsibilities of lawyers in class actions. We examine the ethical concerns of representing groups in Chapter Seven (*infra* p. 733). As a general proposition, however, our ethical rules are premised on traditional, adversarial, bipolar adjudication. Class actions, and especially settlement class actions, lie far afield from this model. Should the standard rules of ethical conflicts control in the world of settlement class actions?

6. In *Ortiz*, should the outcome have been different if Fibreboard had paid in all of its assets before making the limited-fund argument? What incentive would there be for Fibreboard to settle the case if it had to give away the entire company to obtain class certification? Isn't Fibreboard entitled to some discount for the possibility that it might prevail in some cases, that its assets might not be consumed in litigation, and that it is saving plaintiffs the transaction costs of litigation? How big a discount? To what extent should the fairness of the insurance settlement that created the fund influence the question whether (b)(1)(B) treatment is appropriate? How is a court to determine the fairness of the insurance settlement?

7.   As a practical matter, if we assume that *Amchem* and *Ortiz* signal a cutback in the ability to use settlement class actions in mass-tort cases, plaintiffs, defendants, and courts will need to find other ways to aggregate and resolve these cases. Will the likely ultimate effect of *Amchem* be the use of more inventory settlements like the Trilateral Settlement? Because these settlements often occur without court approval (*see infra* pp. 1166-78), don't these agreements provide less protection to individual plaintiffs than a class settlement? *See* Howard M. Erichson, *A Typology of Aggregate Settlements*, 80 NOTRE DAME L. REV. 1769 (2005). Isn't that a bad idea? Will the likely effect be the greater use of bankruptcy by defendants like Fibreboard and the CCR companies? If so, will class members and other creditors of asbestos defendants fare better or worse in bankruptcy? *See* S. ELIZABETH GIBSON, FED. JUD. CTR., CASE STUDIES OF MASS TORT LIMITED FUND CLASS ACTION SETTLEMENTS AND BANKRUPTCY (2000). Should the Court have considered these questions in deciding *Amchem* and *Ortiz*, or are such consequences irrelevant to a proper understanding of Rule 23 in the settlement context?

8.   Are any of *Amchem*'s holdings of constitutional stature, and thus binding on state courts? Given the Class Action Fairness Act, fewer litigation class actions are remaining in state courts, so the question has less salience. But with settlement class actions, the class counsel and the defense counsel can agree on a state forum they believe will be hospitable to settling the case. Of course, their choice is subject to the right of objectors to remove to federal court, *see* 28 U.S.C. § 1453, but often there are few objectors to settlements. *See* THOMAS E. WILLGING, FED. JUD. CTR., EMPIRICAL STUDY OF CLASS ACTIONS IN FOUR FEDERAL DISTRICT COURTS 57 (1996) (reporting objectors in 42% to 64% of all class settlements). Will an unintended consequence of *Ortiz* be that class counsel and defense counsel will conspire to seek judges who will not scrutinize settlement agreements? *See* David A. Dana, *Adequacy of Representation After Stephenson: A Rawlsian/Behavioral Economics Approach to Class Action Settlements*, 55 EMORY L.J. 279, 337-38 (2006) (yes).

9.   *Amchem* and *Ortiz* have raised grave doubts about whether multistate mass-tort settlements involving numerous state laws are still possible. *See* Stephen B. Burbank, *The Class Action Fairness Act of 2005 in Historical Context: A Preliminary View*, 156 U. PA. L. REV. 1439, 1498 (2008). Neither case directly addresses the constitutional question, left open by *Shutts*, whether mandatory class actions for damages interfere with a litigant's "autonomous ability to control the nature and course of his own suit." Martin H. Redish & Nathan D. Larsen, *Class Actions, Litigant Autonomy, and the Foundations of Procedural Due Process*, 95 CALIF. L. REV. 1573, 1601 (2007). *Ortiz* dropped some large hints on the question, and they do not look good for non-opt-out class actions that fail to hue closely to a type of claim that equity would traditionally have handled. If so, the ancient forms of English law are not without influence, even in the modern world of complex litigation.

10. As we leave our initial exploration of the requirements for class certification, you should already be forming the view that class certification is hardly a given, that federal courts have shown reluctance to treat class actions as expansively as they could be treated, and that class actions are not the silver bullet for achieving optimal aggregation. Class actions are a tool in the aggregation toolbox, and while there is still much confusion about exactly when lawyers and courts can reach for this particular tool, the answer, rather clearly, is "Not all the time."

B. THE SCOPE OF PRECLUSION AND COLLATERAL ATTACKS ON CLASS JUDGMENTS AND SETTLEMENTS

We can now assume that a class action has resulted in a judgment or settlement. *Hansberry v. Lee*, 311 U.S. 32 (1940), established the single most fundamental principle of class actions: The result of a class action binds the members of the class when the class representative adequately represents the interests of the members. This rule of preclusion, which is what makes class actions so powerful as an aggregation device, means that the class members are now bound to the outcome of the class action. Or are they? Recognizing that class actions have a preclusive effect does not answer the question about the scope of that preclusive effect. To take one example, we saw that courts sometimes certify certain claims for class treatment but not others. What happens to the claims that are not asserted on a class basis? Can class members still assert them in individual or other group litigation? Or, under the usual rule that litigants cannot split claims, are they barred?

Whatever its precise scope, this preclusive power also means that class members are bound to a judgment even though they never appeared in the case, never chose to sue anyone, and never retained or probably even met their lawyer. To assuage these concerns, *Hansberry* substituted for the idea of individual control the idea of adequate representation; a vigorous representative and faithful counsel recompense the loss in autonomy. But risks remain. In its worst form, there might be collusion between the class representative or class counsel and the defendant. Even in cases in which collusion does not exist, however, only the hopelessly optimistic can believe that class representatives and class counsel represent the interests of each and every class member just as well as a lawyer dedicated just to that class member would have. To recur to the same example, a lawyer dedicated to one class member would have asserted all available claims, not just the claims that could be certified on a class basis. What should happen when class members get a poor result from the class judgment or settlement, and believe that the reason for the result was the inadequacy of the class representative or class counsel? Can they file individual lawsuits, prove in those cases that the representation was defective, and escape the binding effect of the judgment or settlement? Such lawsuits are usually described as "collateral attacks" — should we tolerate them?

This section examines the scope of the preclusive power of a class action and the ability of class members to collaterally attack class judgments or settlements. These two issues are closely related. As a class judgment or settlement loses preclusive effect — either because the scope of preclusion is interpreted narrowly or because disgruntled class members can avoid the judgment or settlement in later proceedings by showing inadequate representation — the class action loses utility as an aggregation device: If the class action cannot preclude certain claims or issues, then it has little value in preventing the repetitive litigation of claims and issues. On the other hand, as the preclusive effect of a class judgment or settlement expands, the concern for inadequate representation grows.

The precise scope of the preclusive effect of a class judgment or settlement and the ability of class members to collaterally attack a judgment or settlement are issues that are absolutely critical to understanding the effectiveness of class actions as aggregation devices. They are also among the most contentious.

COOPER V. FEDERAL RESERVE BANK OF RICHMOND

467 U.S. 867 (1984)

■ JUSTICE STEVENS delivered the opinion of the Court.

The question to be decided is whether a judgment in a class action determining that an employer did not engage in a general pattern or practice of racial discrimination against the certified class of employees precludes a class member from maintaining a subsequent civil action alleging an individual claim of racial discrimination against the employer.

I

On March 22, 1977, the Equal Employment Opportunity Commission commenced a civil action against respondent, the Federal Reserve Bank of Richmond. Respondent operates a branch in Charlotte, N.C. (the Bank), where during the years 1974-1978 it employed about 350-450 employees in several departments. The EEOC complaint alleged that the Bank was violating § 703(a) of Title VII of the Civil Rights Act of 1964 by engaging in "policies and practices" that included "failing and refusing to promote blacks because of race."

Six months after the EEOC filed its complaint, four individual employees[2] were allowed to intervene as plaintiffs. In their "complaint in intervention," these plaintiffs alleged that the Bank's employment practices violated 42 U.S.C. § 1981, as well as Title VII; that each of them was the victim of employment discrimination based on race; and that they could

---

2. Sylvia Cooper, Constance Russell, Helen Moore, and Elmore Hannah, Jr., sometimes referred to by the District Court as the "intervening plaintiffs" and by the parties as the "Cooper petitioners." . . .

adequately represent a class of black employees against whom the Bank had discriminated because of their race. In due course, the District Court entered an order conditionally certifying the following class pursuant to Federal Rules of Civil Procedure 23(b)(2) and (3):

> "All black persons who have been employed by the defendant at its Charlotte Branch Office at any time since January 3, 1974 [6 months prior to the first charge filed by the intervenors with EEOC], who have been discriminated against in promotion, wages, job assignments and terms and conditions of employment because of their race."

After certifying the class, the District Court ordered that notice be published in the Charlotte newspapers and mailed to each individual member of the class. The notice described the status of the litigation, and plainly stated that members of the class "will be bound by the judgment or other determination" if they did not exclude themselves by sending a written notice to the Clerk. Among the recipients of the notice were Phyllis Baxter and five other individuals employed by the Bank. It is undisputed that these individuals — the Baxter petitioners — are members of the class represented by the intervening plaintiffs and that they made no attempt to exclude themselves from the class.

At the trial the intervening plaintiffs, as well as the Baxter petitioners, testified. The District Court found that the Bank had engaged in a pattern and practice of discrimination from 1974 through 1978 by failing to afford black employees opportunities for advancement and assignment equal to opportunities afforded white employees in pay grades 4 and 5. Except as so specified, however, the District Court found that "there does not appear to be a pattern and practice of discrimination pervasive enough for the court to order relief." With respect to the claims of the four intervening plaintiffs, the court found that the Bank had discriminated against Cooper and Russell, but not against Moore and Hannah. Finally, the court somewhat cryptically stated that although it had an opinion about "the entitlement to relief of some of the class members who testified at trial," it would defer decision of such matters to a further proceeding.

Thereafter, on March 24, 1981, the Baxter petitioners moved to intervene, alleging that each had been denied a promotion for discriminatory reasons. With respect to [one of the Baxter petitioners], the court denied the motion because she was a member of the class for which relief had been ordered and therefore her rights would be protected in the Stage II proceedings to be held on the question of relief. With respect to the other five Baxter petitioners, the court also denied the motion, but for a different reason. It held that because all of them were employed in jobs above the grade 5 category, they were not entitled to any benefit from the court's ruling with respect to discrimination in grades 4 and 5. The District Court stated: "The court has found no proof of any classwide discrimination above grade 5 and, therefore, they are not entitled to participate in any Stage II proceedings in this case." The court added that it could "see no reason why, if any of the would be intervenors are actively interested in pursuing their claims, they cannot file a Section 1981 suit next week. . . ."

A few days later the Baxter petitioners filed a separate action against the Bank alleging that each of them had been denied a promotion because of their race in violation of 42 U.S.C. § 1981. The Bank moved to dismiss the complaint on the ground that each of them was a member of the class that had been certified in the Cooper litigation, that each was employed in a grade other than 4 or 5, and that they were bound by the determination that there was no proof of any classwide discrimination above grade 5. The District Court denied the motion to dismiss, but certified its order for interlocutory appeal under 28 U.S.C. § 1292(b). The Bank's interlocutory appeal from the order was then consolidated with the Bank's pending appeal in the Cooper litigation.

The United States Court of Appeals for the Fourth Circuit reversed the District Court's judgment on the merits in the Cooper litigation, concluding that (1) there was insufficient evidence to establish a pattern or practice of racial discrimination in grades 4 and 5, and (2) two of the intervening plaintiffs had not been discriminated against on account of race. The court further held that under the doctrine of res judicata, the judgment in the Cooper class action precluded the Baxter petitioners from maintaining their individual race discrimination claims against the Bank. The court thus reversed the order denying the Bank's motion to dismiss in the Baxter action, and remanded for dismissal of the Baxter complaint. We granted certiorari to review that judgment, and we now reverse.

II

Claims of two types were adjudicated in the Cooper litigation. First, the individual claims of each of the four intervening plaintiffs have been finally decided in the Bank's favor. Those individual decisions do not, of course, foreclose any other individual claims. Second, the class claim that the Bank followed "policies and practices" of discriminating against its employees has also been decided. It is that decision on which the Court of Appeals based its res judicata analysis.

There is of course no dispute that under elementary principles of prior adjudication a judgment in a properly entertained class action is binding on class members in any subsequent litigation. *See, e.g.,* Supreme Tribe of Ben-Hur v. Cauble, 255 U.S. 356 (1921). Basic principles of res judicata (merger and bar or claim preclusion) and collateral estoppel (issue preclusion) apply. A judgment in favor of the plaintiff class extinguishes their claim, which merges into the judgment granting relief. A judgment in favor of the defendant extinguishes the claim, barring a subsequent action on that claim. A judgment in favor of either side is conclusive in a subsequent action between them on any issue actually litigated and determined, if its determination was essential to that judgment.

III

A plaintiff bringing a civil action for a violation of § 703(a) of Title VII of the Civil Rights Act of 1964, 42 U.S.C. § 2000e-2(a), has the initial burden of establishing a prima facie case that his employer discriminated against him on account of his race, color, religion, sex, or national origin. A plaintiff meets this initial burden by offering evidence adequate to create an inference that he was denied an employment opportunity on the basis of a discriminatory criterion enumerated in Title VII.

A plaintiff alleging one instance of discrimination establishes a prima facie case justifying an inference of individual racial discrimination by showing that he (1) belongs to a racial minority, (2) applied and was qualified for a vacant position the employer was attempting to fill, (3) was rejected for the position, and (4) after his rejection, the position remained open and the employer continued to seek applicants of the plaintiff's qualifications. Once these facts are established, the employer must produce "evidence that the plaintiff was rejected, or someone else was preferred, for a legitimate, nondiscriminatory reason." At that point, the presumption of discrimination "drops from the case," and the district court is in a position to decide the ultimate question in such a suit: whether the particular employment decision at issue was made on the basis of race. The ultimate burden of persuading the trier of fact that the defendant intentionally discriminated against the plaintiff regarding the particular employment decision "remains at all times with the plaintiff," and in the final analysis the trier of fact "must decide which party's explanation of the employer's motivation it believes."

In *Franks v. Bowman Transportation Co*[.], 424 U.S. 747 (1976), . . . we held that demonstrating the existence of a discriminatory pattern or practice established a presumption that the individual class members had been discriminated against on account of race. Proving isolated or sporadic discriminatory acts by the employer is insufficient to establish a prima facie case of a pattern or practice of discrimination; rather it must be established by a preponderance, of the evidence that "racial discrimination was the company's standard operating procedure — the regular rather than the unusual practice." While a finding of a pattern or practice of discrimination itself justifies an award of prospective relief to the class, additional proceedings are ordinarily required to determine the scope of individual relief for the members of the class.

The crucial difference between an individual's claim of discrimination and a class action alleging a general pattern or practice of discrimination is manifest. The inquiry regarding an individual's claim is the reason for a particular employment decision, while "at the liability stage of a pattern-or-practice trial the focus often will not be on individual hiring decisions, but on a pattern of discriminatory decisionmaking."

. . . [A] class plaintiff's attempt to prove the existence of a companywide policy, or even a consistent practice within a given department, may fail even though discrimination against one or two individuals has been proved. The facts of this case illustrate the point.

The District Court found that two of the intervening plaintiffs, Cooper and Russell, had both established that they were the victims of racial discrimination but, as the Court of Appeals noted, they were employed in grades higher than grade 5 and therefore their testimony provided no support for the conclusion that there was a practice of discrimination in grades 4 and 5. Given the burden of establishing a prima facie case of a pattern or practice of discrimination, it was entirely consistent for the District Court simultaneously to conclude that Cooper and Russell had valid individual claims even though it had expressly found no proof of any classwide discrimination above grade 5. It could not be more plain that the rejection of a claim of classwide discrimination does not warrant the conclusion that no member of the class could have a valid individual claim. "A racially balanced work force cannot immunize an employer from liability for specific acts of discrimination."

The analysis of the merits of the Cooper litigation by the Court of Appeals is entirely consistent with this conclusion. In essence, the Court of Appeals held that the statistical evidence, buttressed by expert testimony and anecdotal evidence by three individual employees in grades 4 and 5, was not sufficient to support the finding of a pattern of bankwide discrimination within those grades. . . .

The Court of Appeals was correct in generally concluding that the Baxter petitioners, as members of the class represented by the intervening plaintiffs in the Cooper litigation, are bound by the adverse judgment in that case. The court erred, however, in the preclusive effect it attached to that prior adjudication. That judgment (1) bars the class members from bringing another class action against the Bank alleging a pattern or practice of discrimination for the relevant time period and (2) precludes the class members in any other litigation with the Bank from relitigating the question whether the Bank engaged in a pattern and practice of discrimination against black employees during the relevant time period. The judgment is not, however, dispositive of the individual claims the Baxter petitioners have alleged in their separate action. Assuming they establish a prima facie case of discrimination . . ., the Bank will be required to articulate a legitimate reason for each of the challenged decisions, and if it meets that burden, the ultimate questions regarding motivation in their individual cases will be resolved by the District Court. Moreover, the prior adjudication may well prove beneficial to the Bank in the Baxter action: the determination in the Cooper action that the Bank had not engaged in a general pattern or practice of discrimination would be relevant on the issue of pretext.

The Bank argues that permitting the Baxter petitioners to bring separate actions would frustrate the purposes of Rule 23. We think the converse is true. The class-action device was intended to establish a procedure for the adjudication of common questions of law or fact. If the Bank's theory were adopted, it would be tantamount to requiring that every member of the class be permitted to intervene to litigate the merits of his individual claim.

It is also suggested that the District Court had a duty to decide the merits of the individual claims of class members, at least insofar as the individual claimants became witnesses in the joint proceeding and subjected their individual employment histories to scrutiny at trial. Unless these claims are decided in the main proceeding, the Bank argues that the duplicative litigation that Rule 23 was designed to avoid will be encouraged, and that defendants will be subjected to the risks of liability without the offsetting benefit of a favorable termination of exposure through a final judgment.

This argument fails to differentiate between what the District Court might have done and what it actually did. The District Court did actually adjudicate the individual claims of Cooper and the other intervening plaintiffs, as well as the class claims, but it pointedly refused to decide the individual claims of the Baxter petitioners. Whether the issues framed by the named parties before the court should be expanded to encompass the individual claims of additional class members is a matter of judicial administration that should be decided in the first instance by the District Court. Nothing in Rule 23 requires as a matter of law that the District Court make a finding with respect to each and every matter on which there is testimony in the class action. Indeed, Rule 23 is carefully drafted to provide a mechanism for the expeditious decision of common questions. Its purposes might well be defeated by an attempt to decide a host of individual claims before any common question relating to liability has been resolved adversely to the defendant. We do not find the District Court's denial of the Baxter petitioners' motion for leave to intervene in the Cooper litigation, or its decision not to make findings regarding the Baxter petitioners' testimony in the Cooper litigation, to be inconsistent with Rule 23.

The judgment of the Court of Appeals is reversed, and the case is remanded for further proceedings consistent with this opinion.

■ JUSTICE MARSHALL concurs in the judgment.

■ JUSTICE POWELL took no part in the decision of this case.

Notes

1.   What is the scope of claim preclusion in class actions after *Cooper*? *Cooper* holds that, unlike ordinary litigation, the preclusive effect of a class action judgment extends only to those claims that the plaintiffs did or could have pursued on a class basis, not to all transactionally related claims the plaintiffs could have asserted. Individual claims for relief that are based on grounds not generally applicable to the class survive the judgment, and can still be asserted in separate lawsuits. Are you persuaded by *Cooper*'s rationale for creating an exception to the usual rule that a judgment bars not only the claims that were litigated but all transactionally related claims that could have been litigated? Is allowing the Baxter plaintiffs to engage in theory-splitting necessary to preserve the efficiency of class actions? Doesn't allowing theory-splitting reduce the efficacy of class actions as aggregation devices? Should *Cooper* have balanced the costs of additional complexity if individual claims become part of the class action against the costs of repetitive litigation of these claims in other forums?

In thinking through this question, we must assume that the class members' individual claims are worth asserting; otherwise, whether the class judgment operates preclusively is as a practical matter irrelevant, because no one will assert the claims in later proceedings anyway. If the individual claims are worth bringing, then is it worse for them all to be consolidated in one forum along side the class action, or to be dispersed across forums in individual cases? If they are dispersed, won't federal courts attempt to consolidate them (through multidistricting, § 1404 transfers, or Rule 42(a) consolidation) in any event? Won't they be incompletely successful in doing so because some cases will land in state courts? So isn't it simpler to use the class action as the device by which complete aggregation occurs? If so, then the only way to enforce this aggregation is to adopt a rule of broad claim preclusion opposite to *Cooper*'s rule, and to preclude the non-certified claims of class members.

But is that approach fair to class members? Is it consistent with due process? Should it matter whether class members have the right to opt out as a means of avoiding the preclusive effect of a judgment? *See* Samuel Issacharoff, *Preclusion, Due Process, and the Right to Opt Out*, 77 NOTRE DAME L. REV. 1077 (2002); *cf.* Ticor Title Ins. Co. v. Brown, 511 U.S. 117 (1994) (per curiam) (raising without deciding whether an opt-out right is necessary before class members can be precluded in cases seeking damages) (*supra* p. 420).

2. Is *Cooper* limited to employment class actions? Is it limited to claims arising under federal law? Or does it apply to all class judgments rendered by a federal court? In the last section, for example, we saw that federal courts are often willing to certify a class action on a theory of federal law, but not to certify factually related claims based on state law, due to the variations in states' laws. Assuming that a judgment is rendered for the class on the federal theory and that the statute of limitations has not yet run on the state-law claims, may individual class members now sue the defendant for the state-law violations if they lose their federal claims?

In answering this question, note that the Supreme Court has held that the preclusive effect of a federal judgment is a question of federal common law, even in cases in which state law provides the rule of decision. *See* Semtek Int'l Inc. v. Lockheed Martin Corp., 531 U.S. 497 (2001). *Semtek* also held that, with respect to state-law claims, federal courts should ordinarily choose as the federal rule the law of preclusion used in the state in which the federal court is sitting. *Semtek* did not involve a class action, nor did it indicate whether federal common law or the forum state's preclusion law should govern the preclusive effect of a judgment decided on federal grounds, when the unasserted and uncertifiable claims were based on state law.

3. It does not appear that *Cooper* is a case of constitutional stature, so states should be free to adopt a different rule of preclusion for class actions filed in state court. Indeed, some states have done so. For instance, Texas follows the view that class members are precluded "from asserting claims in subsequent individual litigation which arose from the same transaction

or subject matter and either could have been or were litigated in the prior suit." Bowden v. Phillips Petroleum Co., 247 S.W.3d 690, 697 (Tex. 2008); *see also* Thompson v. Am. Tobacco Co., 189 F.R.D. 544, 550 (D. Minn. 1999) (suggesting that the same rule might apply in Minnesota); Pearl v. Allied Corp., 102 F.R.D. 921, 923 (E.D. Pa. 1984) (raising the same concern in a case asserting claims under state law).

4.   The breadth of the preclusive effect of a class judgment matters for another reason. If class counsel abandons the individual claims to obtain class certification on the common claims (for instance, by not pleading monetary claims but only injunctive claims), and if class members are then precluded from asserting the individual claims in later litigation, a question about the adequacy of representation arises. Some courts have deemed inadequate a class representative who abandons the claims of class members that would be precluded. For instance, in *McClain v. Lufkin Industries, Inc.*, 519 F.3d 264 (5th Cir. 2008), the class representatives in an employment-discrimination case chose not to plead the class members' claims for compensatory and punitive damages, and to plead only claims for injunctive relief, to obtain class certification under the Rule 23(b)(2). The district court held that, in doing so, the class representatives proved themselves inadequate, and denied certification. *McClain* agreed: "[I]f the price of a Rule 23(b)(2) disparate treatment class both limits individual opt outs and sacrifices class members' rights to avail themselves of significant legal remedies, it is too high a price to impose." *Id.* at 283. *Accord* Zachery v. Texaco Exploration & Prod., Inc., 185 F.R.D. 230 (W.D. Tex. 1999).

Other courts have recognized that the abandonment of claims is a relevant consideration in determining whether the class representative and class counsel are adequate, but reject the idea that "class representatives who split the claims of the class are per se inadequate." *Bowden*, 247 S.W.3d at 697. In *In re Universal Service Fund Telephone Billing Practices Litigation*, 219 F.R.D. 661, 669 (D. Kan. 2004), the class representative chose not to assert common-law fraud claims "that [were] probably not certifiable" and to focus only on the federal antitrust claims and state-law breach-of-contract claims that could be certified. The court rejected the notion that this strategy made the class representatives inadequate:

> . . . While the court can certainly appreciate the fact that a named plaintiff's failure to assert certain claims of the absent class members might give rise to a conflict of interest when the named plaintiff is advancing his or her own interests at the expense of the class, the mere fact that a named plaintiff elects not to pursue one particular claim does not necessarily create such a conflict. Here, the named plaintiffs' decision to abandon the fraud claim appears to have been a choice that advances the named plaintiffs' interests as well as the interests of the absent class members, and therefore the court is unpersuaded that any impermissible conflict of interest exists.

> The court further wishes to observe that if defendants' argument were taken to its logical extreme, class action defendants could routinely defeat class certification by simply injecting the argument

that a conflict of interest exists between the named plaintiffs and the absent class members because the named plaintiffs are not pursuing potential fraud claims. [*Id.* at 670.]

Accord Sullivan v. Chase Inv. Servs. of Boston, Inc., 79 F.R.D. 246 (N.D. Cal. 1978).

Notice the whipsaw effect in *McClain*'s holding. On the one hand, if a class representative abandons some claims in order to certify the rest, the representative is inadequate. On the other hand, if the representative includes all the claims, certification might falter on commonality and typicality grounds — and on predominance grounds as well in a (b)(3) class. Given the fact that a single course of conduct often invokes multiple legal theories, some of which are more amenable to class treatment than others, is there any way to avoid the horns of this dilemma? The question has become an extremely important one in class-action practice.

The evident answer is to keep the scope of the preclusive effect of a judgment within narrow boundaries. If a class judgment does not preclude the claims that cannot be certified (which is one reading of *Cooper*), then the decision to abandon these claims cannot constitute inadequacy, can it? Is *McClain* wrong because it fails to read *Cooper* in an appropriately narrow light? Does the *McClain* problem provide a reason to read *Cooper* narrowly rather than broadly, as Note 1 discusses?

5.   To be clear, the *McClain* problem is an issue of the adequacy of representation under Rule 23(a)(4) in the first case. *Cooper* is an issue of the preclusive effect of the class judgment in a subsequent case. They are distinct issues. But the latter issue informs the former.

6.   Can a court do anything to shape the scope of the preclusive effect of a class judgment, perhaps by issuing an order along with the judgment specifying the parallel cases or substantive claims to which the preclusive effect of the judgment should not attach? *See* Tobias Barrington Wolff, *Preclusion in Class Action Litigation,* 105 COLUM. L. REV. 717, 768-76 (2005) (discussing ways to limit the preclusive effect of a class judgment; acknowledging that some of these tools require the court in a later case to accept the limits imposed by the court in the class suit).

7.   You might wonder whether, in light of statutes of limitation, it matters if the class members' individual claims are precluded; by the time that the class action concludes, the statute is likely to have run on individual claims in any event. The answer is that the issue matters in a number of situations. First, some class members might have asserted their individual claims in separate litigation before the statutes of limitation ran; if the class action comes to judgment first, its preclusive effect matters in the class members' individual cases. Second, the Supreme Court has created a tolling rule, so that the statutes of limitation for the claims of class members are suspended during the pendency of the class action. Am. Pipe & Constr. Co. v. Utah, 414 U.S. 538 (1974); *see also* Crown Cork & Seal Co. v. Parker, 462 U.S. 345 (1983) (holding that the statute of limitation is tolled even if the district court does not ultimately certify the class);

compare Wade v. Danek Med., Inc., 182 F.3d 281 (4th Cir. 1999) (holding that state tolling law, not the *American Pipe* rule, applies with respect to diversity cases), *with* Adams Pub. Sch. Dist. v. Asbestos Corp., 7 F.3d 717, 719 (8th Cir. 1993) (intimating that *American Pipe* applies in diversity cases in the absence of a state tolling provision). Finally, with regard to monetary claims that have not yet matured for filing, the statute of limitations will not have begun to run.

8. Until now, we have not focused on the nationality of the class members or the possibility of a transnational class action. If a class action includes members from foreign countries, a critical issue is whether the foreign country will give any preclusive effect to a class judgment. Many countries are deeply skeptical of American-style class actions, and while many countries (numbering around thirty at the time of this writing) have adopted some form of class action in recent years, a great number of countries are unlikely to enforce an American class-action judgment. Should that fact affect the membership of the class action? *See* In re Vivendi Universal, S.A. Sec. Litig., 242 F.R.D. 76 (S.D.N.Y. 2007) (analyzing the preclusive effect that various European countries would give to an American class action; excluding members from Germany and Austria due to the lack of preclusive effect in those countries).

More generally, with the rise of foreign class actions, the relationship between American class actions and foreign class actions, and the binding effect that each will give to each other's judgments, is a subject that bears close watching in upcoming years. For one examination of the issue, see Richard A. Nagareda, *Aggregate Litigation and the Future of American Exceptionalism*, 62 VAND. L. REV. 1 (2009).

9. Most class actions settle. Somewhat different considerations apply with respect to settlement. Most evidently, although class settlements require judicial approval, no judgment exists unless the parties settle by means of a consent decree. Nonetheless, the terms of the settlement and the releases that the class representatives sign spell out the consequences of the settlement on other claims that class members might bring, and thus provide a contractual equivalent to preclusion. *See* Wolff, *supra*, at 765-67 (noting the formal and practical similarities, as well as differences, between judgments and settlements).

10. Assume that a class judgment or settlement has a binding effect on class members' claims. Assume as well that the outcome of the settlement or judgment is highly unfavorable to some class members. In a settlement, class members have the right to object to the terms of the settlement, *see* Fed. R. Civ. P. 23(e)(5), and a court can sometimes afford disgruntled class members a right to opt out of the settlement, *see* Fed. R. Civ. P. 23(e)(4). But the disadvantageous features of some settlements do not reveal themselves to class members until the opt-out period is over and the settlement has been approved. Class members have no opportunity to opt out of, or object to, an unfavorable judgment once it has been announced. So do disadvantaged class members have any recourse? In particular, can they escape from the preclusive effect of the judgment or settlement by

filing a new lawsuit and claiming, as in *Hansberry v. Lee*, that they were inadequately represented and therefore cannot constitutionally be bound? This approach, known as "collateral attack," is the subject of the next case.

STEPHENSON V. DOW CHEMICAL CO.

273 F.3d 249 (2d Cir. 2001), *aff'd in part by an equally divided Court and vacated in part*, 539 U.S. 111 (2003)

■   PARKER, Circuit Judge.

. . . Daniel Stephenson and Joe Isaacson are two Vietnam War veterans who allege that they were injured by exposure to Agent Orange while serving in the military in Vietnam. In the late 1990s, Stephenson and Isaacson (along with their families) filed separate lawsuits against manufacturers of Agent Orange. . . .

In 1984, however, some twelve years before these suits, virtually identical claims against these defendants, brought by a class of military personnel who were exposed to Agent Orange while in Vietnam between 1961 and 1972, were globally settled. . . . Judge Weinstein, who presided over the 1984 settlement, dismissed the claims of Stephenson and Isaacson, concluding that the prior settlement barred their suits. On appeal, plaintiffs chiefly contend . . . that they were inadequately represented and, therefore, due process considerations prevent the earlier class action settlement from precluding their claims. . . . [W]e vacate the district court's dismissal and remand for further proceedings.

I. BACKGROUND

. . .

In 1983, the district court certified the following class under Federal Rule of Civil Procedure 23(b)(3):

> those persons who were in the United States, New Zealand or Australian Armed Forces at any time from 1961 to 1972 who were injured while in or near Vietnam by exposure to Agent Orange or other phenoxy herbicides, including those composed in whole or in part of 2, 4, 5-trichlorophenoxyacetic acid or containing some amount of 2, 3, 7, 8-tetrachlorodibenzo-p-dioxin. The class also includes spouses, parents, and children of the veterans born before January 1, 1984, directly or derivatively injured as a result of the exposure.

The court also ordered notice by mail, print media, radio and television to be provided to class members, providing in part that persons who wished to opt out must do so by May 1, 1984.

[On the eve of trial, the parties settled. The defendants paid $180 million into a settlement fund. The settlement provided that "[t]he Class specifically includes persons who have not yet manifested injury."]

The district court held fairness hearings throughout the country, and approved the settlement as fair, reasonable and adequate. . . .

Seventy-five percent of the $180 million was to be distributed directly "'to exposed veterans who suffer from long-term total disabilities and to the surviving spouses or children of exposed veterans who have died.'" . . . Payments were to be made for ten years, beginning January 1, 1985 and ending December 31, 1994:

> No payment will be made for death or disability occurring after December 31, 1994. Payment will be made for compensable deaths occurring both before and after January 1, 1985. Payments will be made for compensable disability to the extent that the period of disability falls within the ten years of the program's operation. . . .

[On appeal, this court] affirmed class certification, settlement approval and much of the distribution plan. . . . We specifically rejected an attack based on adequacy of representation . . . . We additionally concluded that the notice scheme devised by Judge Weinstein was the "best notice practicable" under Federal Rule of Civil Procedure 23(c)(2). Finally, we affirmed the settlement as fair, reasonable and adequate, given the serious weaknesses of the plaintiffs' claims.

[In 1989 and 1990, two class actions, known as the *Ivy/Hartman* litigation, were filed on behalf of veterans exposed to Agent Orange. The plaintiffs alleged that their injuries and the injuries of fellow class members manifested themselves only after the May 7, 1984 settlement. The district court held that the veterans were bound by the settlement, and dismissed the cases. The court of appeals affirmed the judgment. Ivy v. Diamond Shamrock Chems. Co., 996 F.2d 1425 (2d Cir. 1993).]

II. DISCUSSION

. . .

B. *Collateral Attack*

The parties devote much energy to debating the permissibility of a collateral attack in this case. Plaintiffs assert that, since the Supreme Court's decision in *Hansberry v. Lee*, 311 U.S. 32 (1940), courts have allowed collateral attacks on class action judgments based upon due process concerns. Defendants strenuously disagree and contend that to allow plaintiffs' suit to go forward, in the face of the 1984 global settlement, would "violate defendants' right to due process of law." . . .

Defendants contend that Supreme Court precedent permits a collateral attack on a class action judgment "only where there has been no prior determination of absent class members' due process rights." According to defendants, because the "due process rights of absent class members have been extensively litigated in the *Agent Orange* litigation," these plaintiffs cannot now attack those prior determinations. We reject defendants' arguments and conclude that plaintiffs' collateral attack, which seeks only to prevent the prior settlement from operating as res judicata to their claims, is permissible.

First, even if, as defendants contend, collateral attack is only permitted where there has been no prior determination of the absent class members' rights, plaintiffs' collateral attack is allowed. It is true that, on direct appeal and in the *Ivy/Hartman* litigation, we previously concluded that there was adequate representation of all class members in the original Agent Orange settlement. However, neither this Court nor the district court has addressed specifically the adequacy of representation for those members of the class whose injuries manifested after depletion of the settlement[ ] funds. Therefore, even accepting defendants' argument, plaintiffs' suit can go forward because there has been no prior adequacy of representation determination with respect to individuals whose claims arise after the depletion of the settlement fund.

Second, the propriety of a collateral attack such as this is amply supported by precedent. In *Hansberry v. Lee*, 311 U.S. 32 (1940), the Supreme Court entertained a collateral attack on an Illinois state court class action judgment that purported to bind the plaintiffs. The Court held that class action judgments can only bind absent class members where "the interests of those not joined are of the same class as the interests of those who are, and where it is considered that the latter fairly represent the former in the prosecution of the litigation." Additionally, we have previously stated that a "[j]udgment in a class action is not secure from collateral attack unless the absentees were adequately and vigorously represented." . . .

. . . Plaintiffs do not attack the merits or finality of the settlement itself, but instead argue that they were not proper parties to that judgment. If plaintiffs were not proper parties to that judgment, as we conclude below, res judicata cannot defeat their claims. Further, such collateral review would not, as defendants maintain, violate defendants' due process rights by exposing them to double liability. Exposure to liability here is not duplicative if plaintiffs were never proper parties to the prior judgment in the first place.

We therefore hold that a collateral attack to contest the application of res judicata is available. We turn next to the merits of this attack.

C. *Due Process Considerations and Res Judicata*

The doctrine of res judicata dictates that "a final judgment on the merits of an action precludes the parties or their privies from relitigating issues that were or could have been raised in that action." Res judicata ordinarily applies "if the earlier decision was (1) a final judgment on the merits, (2) by a court of competent jurisdiction, (3) in a case involving the same parties or their privies, and (4) involving the same cause of action." . . . .

Plaintiffs' argument focuses on element number three in the res judicata analysis: whether they are parties bound by the settlement.

Plaintiffs rely primarily on the United States Supreme Court's decisions in *Amchem Products, Inc. v. Windsor*, 521 U.S. 591 (1997) [*supra* p. 493], and *Ortiz v. Fibreboard Corp.*, 527 U.S. 815 (1999) [*supra* p. 506].

In *Amchem*, the Supreme Court confronted, on direct appeal, a challenge to class certification for settlement purposes in an asbestos litigation. The class defined in the complaint included both individuals who were presently injured as well as individuals who had only been exposed to asbestos. The Supreme Court held that this "sprawling" class was improperly certified under Federal Rules of Civil Procedure 23(a) and (b). Specifically, the Court held that Rule 23(a)(4)'s requirement that the named parties "'will fairly and adequately protect the interests of the class'" had not been satisfied. The Court reasoned that

> named parties with diverse medical conditions sought to act on behalf of a single giant class rather than on behalf of discrete subclasses. In significant respects, the interests of those within the single class are not aligned. Most saliently, for the currently injured, the critical goal is generous immediate payments. That goal tugs against the interest of exposure-only plaintiffs in ensuring an ample, inflation-protected fund for the future. . . .

In *Ortiz*, the Supreme Court again addressed a settlement-only class action in the asbestos litigation context. *Ortiz,* however, involved a settlement-only limited fund class under Rule 23(b)(1)(B). The Supreme Court ultimately held that the class could not be maintained under Rule 23(b)(1)(B), because "the limit of the fund was determined by treating the settlement agreement as dispositive, an error magnified" by conflicted counsel. In so holding, *Ortiz* noted that "it is obvious after *Amchem* that a class divided between holders of present and future claims (some of the latter involving no physical injury and attributable to claimants not yet born) requires division into homogeneous subclasses under Rule 23(c)(4)(B), with separate representation to eliminate conflicting interests of counsel."

Res judicata generally applies to bind absent class members except where to do so would violate due process. Due process requires adequate representation "at all times" throughout the litigation, notice "reasonably calculated . . . to apprise interested parties of the pendency of the action," and an opportunity to opt out. Phillips Petroleum Co. v. Shutts, 472 U.S. 797, 811-12 (1985) [*supra* p. 276].

Both Stephenson and Isaacson fall within the class definition of the prior litigation: they served in the United States military, stationed in Vietnam, between 1961 and 1972, and were allegedly injured by exposure to Agent Orange. However, they both learned of their allegedly Agent Orange-related injuries only after the 1984 settlement fund had expired in 1994. Because the prior litigation purported to settle all future claims, but only provided for recovery for those whose death or disability was discovered prior to 1994, the conflict between Stephenson and Isaacson and the class representatives becomes apparent. No provision was made for post-1994 claimants, and the settlement fund was permitted to terminate in 1994. *Amchem* and *Ortiz* suggest that Stephenson and Isaacson were not adequately represented in the prior Agent Orange litigation.[8] Those cases indicate that a class which purports to represent both present and future claimants may encounter internal conflicts.

Defendants contend that there was, in fact, no conflict because all class members' claims were equally meritless and would have been defeated by the "military contractor" defense. This argument misses the mark. At this stage, we are only addressing whether plaintiffs' claims should be barred by res judicata. We are therefore concerned only with whether they were afforded due process in the earlier litigation. Part of the due process inquiry (and part of the Rule 23(a) class certification requirements) involves assessing adequacy of representation and intra-class conflicts. The ultimate merits of the claims have no bearing on whether the class previously certified adequately represented these plaintiffs.

Because these plaintiffs were inadequately represented in the prior litigation, they were not proper parties and cannot be bound by the settlement. We therefore must vacate the district court's dismissal and remand for further proceedings. We, of course, express no opinion as to the ultimate merits of plaintiffs' claims. . . .

Notes

1. *Stephenson* squarely conflicted with a legally and factually complex case from the Ninth Circuit, *Epstein v. MCA, Inc.*, 179 F.3d 641 (9th Cir. 1999). Briefly, *Epstein* involved alleged securities violations. Some plaintiffs commenced a class action in federal court, which had exclusive jurisdiction over some of the federal securities claims. Other plaintiffs filed a class action in Delaware state court, asserting claims under Delaware state law. The state claims appeared to be considerably weaker than the federal claims. The defendant struck a deal with class counsel in the state-court action on what appeared to be very favorable terms for the defendant. (Indeed, what seemed to have been going on was a reverse auction, in which the defendant played the two sets of class counsel against each other to get the lowest settlement.) The Delaware state court found the settlement fair (even though it could not have awarded damages for the federal violations at trial), and also found the representation by the class representative and class counsel in the state proceeding adequate. The *Epstein* plaintiffs then pressed their case in federal court, claiming that they had not been adequately represented. *Epstein* held that, as long as the state court found that the representation was adequate, the class members who did not opt out were bound to accept that finding and were barred from maintaining their federal suit.

---

8.   We also note that plaintiffs likely received inadequate notice. *Shutts* provides that adequate notice is necessary to bind absent class members. As described earlier, *Amchem* indicates that effective notice could likely not ever be given to exposure-only class members. Because we have already concluded that these plaintiffs were inadequately represented, and thus were not proper parties to the prior litigation, we need not definitively decide whether notice was adequate.

The ability of absent class members to disavow a negative result and to continue to litigate is an important issue, touching on the effectiveness of the class action as an aggregation device. The broader the ability of class members to attack judgments or settlements collaterally, the less effective class actions are in preventing repetitive litigation. The Supreme Court granted certiorari to resolve the conflict between *Epstein* and *Stephenson*. After vacating a part of the case regarding removal, the Court affirmed *Stephenson* in a 4-4 decision, with Justice Stevens not participating. The affirmance has no precedential value, and the issue remains open today.

2.   After remand in *Stephenson*, fourteen sets of plaintiffs alleging injuries discovered after 1994 joined the *Stephenson* litigation. In re Agent Orange Prod. Liab. Litig., 517 F.3d 76, 85 (2d Cir. 2008). The Second Circuit affirmed both the grant of summary judgment on the plaintiffs' defective-design claim and the denial of their requests for additional discovery. At the same time the Second Circuit affirmed the dismissal of a product-liability suit by Vietnamese nationals and a Vietnamese non-profit group. Vietnam Ass'n for Victims of Agent Orange v. Dow Chem. Co., 517 F.3d 104, 114 (2d Cir. 2008).

3.   *Stephenson*'s collateral attack involves an issue-preclusion question wrapped up within a claim-preclusion question. The claim-preclusion question is obvious: If the *Stephenson* plaintiffs are proper members of the prior class action, they are bound by its settlement and judgment, and are precluded from asserting the claim again. As *Hansberry v. Lee* holds, however, claim preclusion applies only if they are adequately represented in the first class action. The district court in the first action found that the class members, including the *Stephenson* plaintiffs, had been adequately represented. Hence, the question is whether, in their new cases, the *Stephenson* plaintiffs are precluded from contesting the finding of adequate representation made in the first litigation — a classic question of issue preclusion. If they are precluded, then *Hansberry* avails them not, and claim preclusion ends their cases. If issue preclusion does not bind them to the adequacy finding, then they can contest adequacy; and if they are successful in proving inadequacy (as *Stephenson* held they were), then *Hansberry* destroys the claim-preclusive effect of the first litigation.

Although *Hansberry v. Lee* is the starting point for thinking about collateral attacks, the case itself provides little direct guidance. In the prior class action that was under attack in *Hansberry*, the trial court had never made any findings about whether the representation was adequate.

4.   Strong arguments can be made on both sides of the collateral-attack question. At stake, from one perspective, is the finality of judgments, and of class judgments in particular; having spent enormous resources to litigate a case to conclusion, and having spent perhaps an enormous sum to settle the case, the defendant does not want the case reopened fifteen or twenty years down the line. If the class action cannot promise perpetual peace from litigation, then its utility as a device to decide all related claims has been curtailed. *See* David A. Dana, *Adequacy of Representation After* Stephenson: *A Rawlsian/Behavioral Economics Approach to Class Action*

Settlements, 55 EMORY L. J. 279 (2006). From the opposite perspective, however, if class members are unable to disavow later a deal that turns out to be collusive or otherwise disastrous to their interests because of the inadequacy of their representatives or counsel, then the loss of their autonomy in class proceedings is dear indeed. *See* Tobias Barrington Wolff, *Federal Jurisdiction and Due Process in the Era of the Nationwide Class Action*, 156 U. PA. L. REV. 2035 (2008) (arguing that concerns over the impact of collateral attacks on settlements may be overstated).

Both sides in this debate have valid points, don't they? The issue cuts to the very heart of what class actions are and should be. Perhaps you can see why the Supreme Court was as closely divided as it was, and why the issue creates strong feelings among those who work with class actions. Can you think of any reasonable middle ground between the poles of "no collateral attacks" and "always collateral attacks"?

5. The *Epstein-Stephenson* question has generated significant judicial and academic debate. In an early case, *Gonzales v. Cassidy*, 474 F.2d 67 (5th Cir. 1973), the trial court granted retroactive relief to the class representative, but only prospective relief to all other class members. No appeal was taken. In a later lawsuit, the Fifth Circuit held that the failure of the class representative to appeal the denial of retroactive relief to the class rendered the representative inadequate. Several courts have followed *Gonzales* and *Stephenson* in holding that class members who were not adequately represented may collaterally attack a judgment. *See, e.g.*, Janik v. Rudy, Exelrod & Zieff, 119 Cal. App. 4th 930, 944 n.3 (2004); Wilkes v. Phoenix Home Life Mut. Ins. Co., 902 A.2d 366 (Pa. 2006).

It is fair to say, however, that the cases are strongly trending toward the *Epstein* approach, and away from *Stephenson*. Indeed, a different panel of the Second Circuit has limited *Stephenson* to its facts:

> *Stephenson* is not directly on point, however, because that case involved future claimants, whereas this case does not. Here, injured parties may obtain remuneration from the settlement fund . . . . [T]he essential question in determining whether the Settlement complies with the adequate representation doctrine is whether the interests that were served by the Settlement were compatible with those of [the class members] when plaintiffs negotiated a release of the . . . claims [that the class members were pursuing in separate litigation].

Wal-Mart Stores, Inc. v. Visa U.S.A., Inc., 396 F.3d 96, 110 (2d Cir. 2005) (*infra* pp. 1152, 1178). For other cases rejecting *Stephenson*, see In re Diet Drugs (Phentermine/Fenfluramine/Dexfenfluramine) Prods. Liab. Litig., 431 F.3d 141 (3d Cir. 2005); Lamarque v. Fairbanks Capital Corp., 927 A.2d 753 (R.I. 2007); Hospitality Mgmt. Assocs., Inc. v. Shell Oil Co., 591 S.E.2d 611 (S.C. 2004). *But see* Hesse v. Sprint Corp., — F.3d —, 2010 WL 790340 (9th Cir. Mar. 10, 2010) (allowing collateral attack when the state court made no finding of adequate representation regarding the claims asserted in the subsequent litigation).

For a slice of the academic commentary, see Samuel Isaacharoff & Richard A. Nagareda, *Class Settlements Under Attack*, 156 U. PA. L. REV.

1649 (2008) (arguing for a broad ban on collateral attacks); William B. Rubenstein, *Finality in Class Action Litigation: Lessons from Habeas*, 82 N.Y.U. L. REV. 790 (2007); Patrick Woolley, *The Availability of Collateral Attack for Inadequate Representation in Class Suits*, 79 TEX. L. REV. 383, 388 (2000) ("The argument for limiting collateral attack contradicts two fundamental principles: first, a court has no jurisdiction over absent class members who have not been adequately represented; second, a judgment entered without jurisdiction may be collaterally attacked if the party bound by the judgment did not appear and had no obligation to do so."); Henry P. Monaghan, *Antisuit Injunctions and Preclusion Against Absent Nonresident Class Members*, 98 COLUM. L. REV. 1148 (1998); Geoffrey C. Hazard, Jr. et al., *An Historical Analysis of the Binding Effect of Class Suits*, 146 U. PA. L. REV. 1849 (1998). The American Law Institute has weighed in on the side of severely restricting the right of class members to attack a class judgment or settlement collaterally. AM. L. INST., PRINCIPLES OF THE LAW OF AGGREGATE LITIGATION § 2.07(a) (2009).

C. CLASS ACTIONS AND FEDERALISM

Class actions in federal court raise interesting problems of federalism. The problems are most acute with respect to state-law claims. A single federal class action can sweep up thousands of claimants and deprive state courts of the opportunity to determine for themselves the content of their law and to enforce that law in their own courts according to their own procedures. To the extent that state courts should be seen as collaborative partners in the development of federal law, the same problems exist with respect to class adjudication or settlement of claims based on federal law.

We have already examined some of the federalism issues posed by class actions. For instance, *Phillips Petroleum Co. v. Shutts*, 472 U.S. 797 (1985) (*supra* p. 276), as well as the issues that spin out from it (such as the availability of mandatory class actions for monetary claims and the ability of class members to collaterally attack a judgment), implicate the proper division of authority among the states and between the states and the federal government. The Class Action Fairness Act of 2005, some of whose nuances Chapter Three explored, manifests a very different attitude — one considerably less deferential to state authority — by granting federal courts the subject-matter jurisdiction to hear virtually every class action of national or interstate significance. We also saw the reluctance that federal courts have shown toward certifying class actions that implicate the laws of multiple states; but conversely, if *Cunningham Charter Corp. v. Learjet, Inc.*, 592 F.3d 805 (7th Cir. 2010) (*supra* p. 331), is correct, the federal courts' unwillingness to certify state-law claims does not necessarily translate into an unwillingness to adjudicate those claims.

In this section, we examine two other points of contact between class actions and issues of federalism. The first is the scope of the Anti-Injunction Act in federal class actions. The second is the effect of *Erie* on the applicability of Rule 23 to claims based on the law of a state whose class-action rule differs substantially from Rule 23.

IN RE FEDERAL SKYWALK CASES

680 F.2d 1175 (8th Cir. 1982)

■ McMILLIAN, Circuit Judge.

[The collapse of two skywalks at the Hyatt Regency Hotel in Kansas City, Missouri in July, 1981 gave rise to numerous lawsuits in state and federal court. The federal district judge, invoking Rules 23(b)(1)(A) and 23(b)(1)(B), certified a class on the issues of liability for compensatory and punitive damages and on the amount of punitive damages.

[The Eighth Circuit first determined that the certification order was appealable under 28 U.S.C. § 1292(a)(1). To invoke § 1292, however, the court of appeals needed to demonstrate that the certification order was an injunction.]

In the present case, contrary to the class's assertion, the district court expressly prohibited class members from settling their punitive damage claims . . . . In addition, the substantial effect of the order also enjoined the state plaintiffs from pursuing their pending state court actions on the issues of liability for compensatory and punitive damages and the amount of punitive damages. . . .

It is true that parties to a mandatory class are not free to initiate actions in other courts to litigate class certified issues. However, in the present case the objectors had commenced their state court actions before the motion for class certification had been filed in district court. The state court cases had been filed, consolidated, and discovery had begun. It is this injunction against pending state court actions that gives us jurisdiction under 28 U.S.C. § 1292(a). . . .

Our conclusion that the order enjoins pending state proceedings necessitates an inquiry as to the propriety of that order under the Anti-Injunction Act, 28 U.S.C. § 2283. The Act provides that "[a] court of the United States may not grant an injunction to stay proceedings in a state court except as expressly authorized by Act of Congress, or where necessary in aid of its jurisdiction, or to protect or effectuate its judgment."

In *Atlantic Coast Line R.R. v. Locomotive Engineers*, 398 U.S. 281, 286-87 (1970), the Supreme Court recognized that the Act imposes a flat and positive prohibition:

On its face the present Act is an absolute prohibition against enjoining state court proceedings, unless the injunction falls within one of three specifically defined exceptions. The respondents here have intimated that the Act only establishes a "principle of comity," not a binding rule on the power of the federal courts. The argument implies that in certain circumstances a federal court may enjoin state court proceedings even if that action cannot be justified by any of the three exceptions. We cannot accept any such contention. . . .

Therefore, if the injunction is to be upheld, it must be on the basis that the district court's authority derives from one of the three exceptions. On appeal the class relies on the "necessary in aid of its jurisdiction" exception. In support it first draws an analogy between the order and a Rule 22 interpleader under which a federal court can enjoin claimants from prosecuting claims in state court. The class reasons that here, as in the interpleader situation, there is a limited fund and that the class action is necessary to protect all claimants. We disagree.

The analogy is based on the premise that the possibility of defendants being required to pay only one punitive damage award is comparable to the limited fund concept underlying federal interpleader. That premise is erroneous. "Federal interpleader jurisdiction depends on identifiable property or a limited fund or pecuniary obligation, and it is not proper to predicate jurisdiction on the mere potential to recover damages for pecuniary injury."

In the present case the class has an uncertain claim for punitive damages against defendants who have not conceded liability. The claim does not qualify as a limited fund which is a jurisdictional prerequisite for federal interpleader. Without the limited fund there is no analogy to an interpleader and no reason to treat the class action as an interpleader for purposes of the Anti-Injunction Act. . . .

Next the class argues that allowing individual actions in state court will nullify the purpose of the class. The Supreme Court has narrowly interpreted the "necessary in aid of jurisdiction" exception, and a pending state suit must truly interfere with the federal court's jurisdiction. As the objectors correctly point out, a plurality of the Supreme Court reaffirmed in [*Vendo Co. v. Lektro-Vend Corp.*, 433 U.S. 623 (1977),] its earlier holdings that a simultaneous *in personam* state action does not interfere with the jurisdiction of a federal court in a suit involving the same subject matter. . . .

In the present case the federal and state actions are *in personam* claims for compensatory and punitive damages. Therefore, based on the foregoing principles, we are compelled to hold that despite Judge Wright's legitimate concern for the efficient management of mass tort litigation, the class certification order must be vacated. . . .

■   HEANEY, Circuit Judge, dissenting. . . .

Admittedly, the relationship between mandatory class actions and the Anti-Injunction Act appears to present an open question. The approach adopted by the majority, however, broadly forecloses mandatory class actions whenever a class member has commenced state court proceedings. I would agree that class actions should not become a vehicle for circumventing the ordinary relations between state and federal courts. The requirements for a mandatory class action, however, are quite rigorous and, by their nature, will prevent any such trend from developing. Moreover, there are unusually strong reasons for certifying the mandatory class here, a procedure which the district court found was essential to fair adjudication of all claims. Such circumstances will not often arise; yet in face of them, the majority has adopted a rule which broadly defeats the purpose of mandatory class action jurisdiction. I do not agree that such a rule is required by the Anti-Injunction Act, nor by any sensible view of the relations between state and federal courts.

Notes

1. The Anti-Injunction Act applies only to injunctions aimed at cases pending in state court at the time that the federal injunction issues. The question, therefore, is whether the Act bars mandatory class actions when some class members have filed actions in state court. On this point, several courts have agreed with the majority in *Federal Skywalk* that the Anti-Injunction Act precludes certification of federal limited-fund class actions. *See, e.g.*, Waldron v. Raymark Indus., Inc., 124 F.R.D. 235 (N.D. Ga. 1989); In re Glenn W. Turner Enters. Litig., 521 F.2d 775 (3d Cir. 1975); *cf.* In re Sch. Asbestos Litig., 789 F.2d 996 (3rd Cir. 1986) (Anti-Injunction Act concern gave appellate jurisdiction over Rule 23(b)(1)(B) certification order; court did not state whether the order was an injunction). In addition, the Eleventh Circuit has intimated, without deciding, that the Anti-Injunction Act forbids a mandatory class action that has the effect of enjoining pending state actions. In re Temple, 851 F.2d 1269 (11th Cir. 1988); In re Dennis Greenman Sec. Litig., 829 F.2d 1539 (11th Cir. 1987) (*supra* p. 380).

2. On the other hand, federal judges are thought to have the power to enjoin pending state litigation while a class-action settlement in federal court is under consideration. *See* In re Baldwin-United Corp., 770 F.2d 328 (2d. Cir. 1985) (*supra* p. 183); In re Corrugated Container Antitrust Litig., 659 F.2d 1332 (5th Cir. 1981); In re Joint E. & S. Dist. Asbestos Litig., 134 F.R.D. 32 (E. & S.D.N.Y. 1990). An injunction against filing state cases has also been granted to facilitate a federal settlement class action. *See* Carlough v. Amchem Prods., Inc., 10 F.3d 189, 203 (3d Cir. 1993).

3. Two developments since *Federal Skywalk* have tempered the arguable conflict between mandatory class actions and the Anti-Injunction Act. One is the Class Action Fairness Act, which moves many state-court class actions into federal court. The other is the more dubious attitude toward the use of mandatory class actions, especially of the limited-fund variety, that federal courts have exhibited in the mass-tort area. *Federal Skywalk* was one of the early cases using Rule 23 to handle a mass tort, but as we have seen, the pendulum has swung rather far in the other direction.

4. Once you grant the premise that certification of a mandatory class action implicitly enjoins class members from maintaining a previously filed state case, or that a judge who certifies a mandatory class action has the power to enjoin class members from proceeding elsewhere, the outcome in *Skywalk* seems required under the Anti-Injunction Act. But is the premise

flawed? Plaintiffs have always been able to file contemporaneous lawsuits in both state and federal court, and in complex and complicated litigation they often do. The fact that the plaintiff is an involuntary class member in the federal suit shouldn't change the practice of dual filings, should it?

SHADY GROVE ORTHOPEDIC ASSOCIATES, P.A. v. ALLSTATE INSURANCE CO.

559 U.S. —, 2010 WL 1222272 (2010)

■ JUSTICE SCALIA announced the judgment of the Court and delivered the opinion of the Court with respect to Parts I and II-A, an opinion with respect to Parts II-B and II-D, in which THE CHIEF JUSTICE, JUSTICE THOMAS, and JUSTICE SOTOMAYOR join, and an opinion with respect to Part II-C, in which THE CHIEF JUSTICE and JUSTICE THOMAS join.

New York law prohibits class actions in suits seeking penalties or statutory minimum damages.[1] We consider whether this precludes a federal district court sitting in diversity from entertaining a class action under Federal Rule of Civil Procedure 23.

I

The petitioner's complaint alleged the following: Shady Grove Orthopedic Associates, P. A., provided medical care to Sonia E. Galvez for injuries she suffered in an automobile accident. As partial payment for that care, Galvez assigned to Shady Grove her rights to insurance benefits under a policy issued in New York by Allstate Insurance Co. Shady Grove tendered a claim for the assigned benefits to Allstate, which under New York law had 30 days to pay the claim or deny it. Allstate apparently paid, but not on time, and it refused to pay the statutory interest that accrued on the overdue benefits (at two percent per month).

1. N.Y. CIV. PRAC. LAW ANN. § 901 (West 2006) provides:

"(a) One or more members of a class may sue or be sued as representative parties on behalf of all if:

"1. the class is so numerous that joinder of all members, whether otherwise required or permitted, is impracticable;

"2. there are questions of law or fact common to the class which predominate over any questions affecting only individual members;

"3. the claims or defenses of the representative parties are typical of the claims or defenses of the class;

"4. the representative parties will fairly and adequately protect the interests of the class; and

"5. a class action is superior to other available methods for the fair and efficient adjudication of the controversy.

"(b) Unless a statute creating or imposing a penalty, or a minimum measure of recovery specifically authorizes the recovery thereof in a class action, an action to recover a penalty, or minimum measure of recovery created or imposed by statute may not be maintained as a class action."

Shady Grove filed this diversity suit in the Eastern District of New York to recover the unpaid statutory interest. Alleging that Allstate routinely refuses to pay interest on overdue benefits, Shady Grove sought relief on behalf of itself and a class of all others to whom Allstate owes interest. The District Court dismissed the suit for lack of jurisdiction. It reasoned that N.Y. CIV. PRAC. LAW ANN. § 901(b), which precludes a suit to recover a "penalty" from proceeding as a class action, applies in diversity suits in federal court, despite Federal Rule of Civil Procedure 23. Concluding that statutory interest is a "penalty" under New York law, it held that § 901(b) prohibited the proposed class action. And, since Shady Grove conceded that its individual claim (worth roughly $500) fell far short of the amount-in-controversy requirement for individual suits under 28 U.S.C. § 1332(a), the suit did not belong in federal court.

The Second Circuit affirmed. The court did not dispute that a federal rule adopted in compliance with the Rules Enabling Act, 28 U.S.C. § 2072, would control if it conflicted with § 901(b). But there was no conflict because . . . the Second Circuit concluded that Rule 23 and § 901(b) address different issues. Finding no federal rule on point, the Court of Appeals held that § 901(b) is "substantive" within the meaning of *Erie R. Co. v. Tompkins*, 304 U.S. 64 (1938), and thus must be applied by federal courts sitting in diversity. . . .

II

The framework for our decision is familiar. We must first determine whether Rule 23 answers the question in dispute. If it does, it governs — New York's law notwithstanding — unless it exceeds statutory authorization or Congress's rulemaking power. *See* Hanna v. Plumer, 380 U.S. 460 (1965). We do not wade into *Erie*'s murky waters unless the federal rule is inapplicable or invalid. *See* 380 U.S. at 469-71.

A —  mayority

The question in dispute is whether Shady Grove's suit may proceed as a class action. Rule 23 provides an answer. It states that "[a] class action may be maintained" if two conditions are met: The suit must satisfy the criteria set forth in subdivision (a) (i.e., numerosity, commonality, typicality, and adequacy of representation), and it also must fit into one of the three categories described in subdivision (b). By its terms this creates a categorical rule entitling a plaintiff whose suit meets the specified criteria to pursue his claim as a class action. (The Federal Rules regularly use "may" to confer categorical permission . . . .) Thus, Rule 23 provides a one-size-fits-all formula for deciding the class-action question. Because § 901(b) attempts to answer the same question — i.e., it states that Shady Grove's suit "may *not* be maintained as a class action" (emphasis added) because of the relief it seeks — it cannot apply in diversity suits unless Rule 23 is ultra vires.

The Second Circuit believed that § 901(b) and Rule 23 do not conflict because they address different issues. Rule 23, it said, concerns only the criteria for determining whether a given class can and should be certified; section 901(b), on the other hand, addresses an antecedent question: whether the particular type of claim is eligible for class treatment in the first place — a question on which Rule 23 is silent. . . .

We disagree. To begin with, the line between eligibility and certifiability is entirely artificial. Both are preconditions for maintaining a class action. . . .

There is no reason, in any event, to read Rule 23 as addressing only whether claims made eligible for class treatment by some *other* law should be certified as class actions. Allstate asserts that Rule 23 neither explicitly nor implicitly empowers a federal court "to certify a class in each and every case" where the Rule's criteria are met. But that is exactly what Rule 23 does: It says that if the prescribed preconditions are satisfied "[a] class action *may be maintained* " (emphasis added) — not "*a class action may be permitted*." Courts do not maintain actions; litigants do. The discretion suggested by Rule 23's "may" is discretion residing in the plaintiff: He may bring his claim in a class action if he wishes. And like the rest of the Federal Rules of Civil Procedure, Rule 23 *automatically* applies "in all civil actions and proceedings in the United States district courts," Fed. R. Civ. P. 1. *See* Califano v. Yamasaki, 442 U.S. 682, 699-700 (1979). . . .

Allstate next suggests that the structure of § 901 shows that Rule 23 addresses only certifiability. Section 901*(a)*, it notes, establishes class-certification criteria roughly analogous to those in Rule 23 . . . . But § 901(b)'s rule barring class actions for certain claims is set off as its own subsection, and where it applies § 901(a) does not. . . . Both of § 901's subsections undeniably answer the same question as Rule 23: whether a class action may proceed for a given suit.

The dissent argues that § 901(b) has nothing to do with whether Shady Grove may maintain its suit as a class action, but affects only the *remedy* it may obtain if it wins. . . .

We need not decide whether a state law that limits the remedies available in an existing class action would conflict with Rule 23; that is not what § 901(b) does. By its terms, the provision precludes a plaintiff from "maintain[ing]" a class action seeking statutory penalties. Unlike a law that sets a ceiling on damages (or puts other remedies out of reach) in properly filed class actions, § 901(b) says nothing about what remedies a court may award; it prevents the class actions it covers from coming into existence at all.[4] . . .

4.   Contrary to the dissent's implication, we express no view as to whether state laws that set a ceiling on damages recoverable in a single suit . . . are preempted. Whether or not those laws conflict with Rule 23, § 901(b) does conflict because it addresses not the remedy, but the procedural right to maintain a class action. . . . [S]everal federal statutes also limit the recovery available in class actions. *See, e.g.,* 12 U.S.C. § 2605(f)(2)(B); 15 U.S.C. § 1640(a)(2)(B); 29 U.S.C. § 1854(c)(1). But Congress has plenary power to override the Federal Rules, so its enactments, unlike those of the States, prevail even in case of a conflict.

. . . The dissent all but admits that the literal terms of § 901(b) address the same subject as Rule 23 — i.e., whether a class action may be maintained — but insists the provision's *purpose* is to restrict only remedies. . . .

This evidence of the New York Legislature's purpose is pretty sparse. But even accepting the dissent's account of the Legislature's objective at face value, it cannot override the statute's clear text. Even if its aim is to restrict the remedy a plaintiff can obtain, § 901(b) achieves that end by limiting a plaintiff's power to maintain a class action. . . .

The dissent's approach of determining whether state and federal rules conflict based on the subjective intentions of the state legislature is an enterprise destined to produce "confusion worse confounded," Sibbach v. Wilson & Co., 312 U.S. 1, 14 (1941). It would mean, to begin with, that one State's statute could survive pre-emption (and accordingly affect the procedures in federal court) while another State's identical law would not, merely because its authors had different aspirations. It would also mean that district courts would have to discern, in every diversity case, the purpose behind any putatively pre-empted state procedural rule, even if its text squarely conflicts with federal law. That task will often prove arduous. Many laws further more than one aim, and the aim of others may be impossible to discern. Moreover, to the extent the dissent's purpose-driven approach depends on its characterization of § 901(b)'s aims as substantive, it would apply to many state rules ostensibly addressed to procedure. Pleading standards, for example, often embody policy preferences about the types of claims that should succeed — as do rules governing summary judgment, pretrial discovery, and the admissibility of certain evidence. . . .

But . . . that is not the central difficulty of the dissent's position. The central difficulty is that even artificial narrowing cannot render § 901(b) compatible with Rule 23. *Whatever* the policies they pursue, they flatly contradict each other. Allstate asserts (and the dissent implies) that we can (and must) *interpret* Rule 23 in a manner that avoids overstepping its authorizing statute. If the Rule were susceptible of two meanings — one that would violate § 2072(b) and another that would not — we would agree. *See* Ortiz v. Fibreboard Corp., 527 U.S. 815, 842 (1999) [*supra* p. 506]. But it is not. Rule 23 unambiguously authorizes *any* plaintiff, in *any* federal civil proceeding, to maintain a class action if the Rule's prerequisites are met. . . . We must therefore confront head-on whether Rule 23 falls within the statutory authorization.

B

Erie involved the constitutional power of federal courts to supplant state law with judge-made rules. In that context, it made no difference whether the rule was technically one of substance or procedure; the touchstone was whether it "significantly affect[s] the result of a litigation." Guaranty Trust Co. v. York, 326 U.S. 99, 109 (1945). That is not the test for either the constitutionality or the statutory validity of a Federal Rule of Procedure. Congress has undoubted power to supplant state law, and undoubted power to prescribe rules for the courts it has created, so long as those rules regulate matters "rationally capable of classification" as procedure. *Hanna*, 380 U.S. at 472. In the Rules Enabling Act, Congress authorized this Court to promulgate rules of procedure subject to its review, 28 U.S.C. § 2072(a), but with the limitation that those rules "shall not abridge, enlarge or modify any substantive right," § 2072(b).

We have long held that this limitation means that the Rule must "really regulat[e] procedure, — the judicial process for enforcing rights and duties recognized by substantive law and for justly administering remedy and redress for disregard or infraction of them," *Sibbach*, 312 U.S. at 14; *see Hanna*, 380 U.S. at 464. The test is not whether the rule affects a litigant's substantive rights; most procedural rules do. What matters is what the rule itself regulates: If it governs only "the manner and the means" by which the litigants' rights are "enforced," it is valid; if it alters "the rules of decision by which [the] court will adjudicate [those] rights," it is not.

Applying that test, we have rejected every statutory challenge to a Federal Rule that has come before us. We have found to be in compliance with § 2072(b) rules prescribing methods for serving process, and requiring litigants whose mental or physical condition is in dispute to submit to examinations. Likewise, we have upheld rules authorizing imposition of sanctions upon those who file frivolous appeals, or who sign court papers without a reasonable inquiry into the facts asserted. Each of these rules had some practical effect on the parties' rights, but each undeniably regulated only the process for enforcing those rights; none altered the rights themselves, the available remedies, or the rules of decision by which the court adjudicated either.

Applying that criterion, we think it obvious that rules allowing multiple claims (and claims by or against multiple parties) to be litigated together are also valid. *See, e.g.*, Fed. R. Civ. P. 18 (joinder of claims), 20 (joinder of parties), 42(a) (consolidation of actions). Such rules neither change plaintiffs' separate entitlements to relief nor abridge defendants' rights; they alter only how the claims are processed. For the same reason, Rule 23 — at least insofar as it allows willing plaintiffs to join their separate claims against the same defendants in a class action — falls within § 2072(b)'s authorization. A class action, no less than traditional joinder (of which it is a species), merely enables a federal court to adjudicate claims of multiple parties at once, instead of in separate suits. And like traditional joinder, it leaves the parties' legal rights and duties intact and the rules of decision unchanged.

Allstate contends that the authorization of class actions is not substantively neutral: Allowing Shady Grove to sue on behalf of a class "transform[s] [the] dispute over a five *hundred* dollar penalty into a dispute over a five *million* dollar penalty." Allstate's aggregate liability, however, does not depend on whether the suit proceeds as a class action. Each of the 1,000-plus members of the putative class could (as Allstate acknowledges) bring a freestanding suit asserting his individual claim. It is undoubtedly true that some plaintiffs who would not bring individual suits for the relatively small sums involved will choose to join a class action. That has no bearing, however, on Allstate's or the plaintiffs' legal rights. The likelihood that some (even many) plaintiffs will be induced to sue by the availability of a class action is just the sort of "incidental effec[t]" we have long held does not violate § 2072(b).

Allstate argues that Rule 23 violates § 2072(b) because the state law it displaces, § 901(b), creates a right that the Federal Rule abridges — namely, a "substantive right . . . not to be subjected to aggregated class-action liability" in a single suit. To begin with, we doubt that that is so. Nothing in the text of § 901(b) (which is to be found in New York's procedural code) confines it to claims under New York law; and of course New York has no power to alter substantive rights and duties created by other sovereigns. As we have said, the *consequence* of excluding certain class actions may be to cap the damages a defendant can face in a single suit, but the law itself alters only procedure. In that respect, § 901(b) is no different from a state law forbidding simple joinder. As a fallback argument, Allstate argues that even if § 901(b) is a procedural provision, it was enacted "for *substantive reasons*" (emphasis added). Its end was not to improve "the conduct of the litigation process itself" but to alter "the outcome of that process."

The fundamental difficulty with both these arguments is that the substantive nature of New York's law, or its substantive purpose, *makes no difference*. A Federal Rule of Procedure is not valid in some jurisdictions and invalid in others — or valid in some cases and invalid in others — depending upon whether its effect is to frustrate a state substantive law (or a state procedural law enacted for substantive purposes). That could not be clearer in *Sibbach*:

> The petitioner says the phrase ["substantive rights" in the Rules Enabling Act] connotes more; that by its use Congress intended that in regulating procedure this Court should not deal with important and substantial rights theretofore recognized. Recognized where and by whom? . .
>
> The asserted right, moreover, is no more important than many others enjoyed by litigants in District Courts sitting in the several states before the Federal Rules of Civil Procedure altered and abolished old rights or privileges and created new ones in connection with the conduct of litigation. . . . If we were to adopt the suggested criterion of the importance of the alleged right we should invite endless litigation and confusion worse confounded. The test must be whether a rule really regulates procedure.

Hanna unmistakably expressed the same understanding that compliance of a Federal Rule with the Enabling Act is to be assessed by consulting the Rule itself, and not its effects in individual applications:

> [T]he court has been instructed to apply the Federal Rule, and can refuse to do so only if the Advisory Committee, this Court, and Congress erred in their prima facie judgment that the Rule in question

transgresses neither the terms of the Enabling Act nor constitutional restrictions.

In sum, it is not the substantive or procedural nature or purpose of the affected state law that matters, but the substantive or procedural nature of the Federal Rule. We have held since *Sibbach*, and reaffirmed repeatedly, that the validity of a Federal Rule depends entirely upon whether it regulates procedure. If it does, it is authorized by § 2072 and is valid in all jurisdictions, with respect to all claims, regardless of its incidental effect upon state-created rights.

C

A few words in response to the concurrence. We understand it to accept the framework we apply — which requires first, determining whether the federal and state rules can be reconciled (because they answer different questions), and second, if they cannot, determining whether the Federal Rule runs afoul of § 2072(b). The concurrence agrees with us that Rule 23 and § 901(b) conflict, and departs from us only with respect to the second part of the test, i.e., whether application of the Federal Rule violates § 2072(b). Like us, it answers no, but for a reason different from ours.

The concurrence would decide this case on the basis, not that Rule 23 is procedural, but that the state law it displaces is procedural, in the sense that it does not "function as a part of the State's definition of substantive rights and remedies." A state procedural rule is not preempted, according to the concurrence, so long as it is "so bound up with," or "sufficiently intertwined with," a substantive state-law right or remedy "that it defines the scope of that substantive right or remedy."

This analysis squarely conflicts with *Sibbach*, which established the rule we apply. The concurrence contends that *Sibbach* did not rule out its approach, but that is not so. Recognizing the impracticability of a test that turns on the idiosyncrasies of state law, *Sibbach* adopted and applied a rule with a single criterion: whether the Federal Rule "really regulates procedure." That the concurrence's approach would have yielded the same result in *Sibbach* proves nothing; what matters is the rule we did apply, and that rule leaves no room for special exemptions based on the function or purpose of a particular state rule. We have rejected an attempt to read into *Sibbach* an exception with no basis in the opinion, and we see no reason to find such an implied limitation today. . . .

The concurrence also contends that applying *Sibbach* and assessing whether a Federal Rule regulates substance or procedure is not always easy. Undoubtedly some hard cases will arise (though we have managed to muddle through well enough in the 69 years since *Sibbach* was decided). But as the concurrence acknowledges, the basic difficulty is unavoidable: The statute itself refers to "substantive right[s]," § 2072(b), so there is no escaping the substance-procedure distinction. What is more, the concurrence's approach does nothing to diminish the difficulty, but rather magnifies it many times over. Instead of a single hard question of whether a Federal Rule regulates substance or procedure, that approach will present hundreds of hard questions, forcing federal courts to assess the substantive or procedural character of countless state rules that may conflict with a single Federal Rule. And it still does not sidestep the problem it seeks to avoid. At the end of the day, one must come face to face with the decision whether or not the state policy (with which a putatively procedural state rule may be "bound up") pertains to a "substantive right or remedy," that is, whether it is substance or procedure. The more one explores the alternatives to *Sibbach*'s rule, the more its wisdom becomes apparent.

D

We must acknowledge the reality that keeping the federal-court door open to class actions that cannot proceed in state court will produce forum shopping. That is unacceptable when it comes as the consequence of judge-made rules created to fill supposed "gaps" in positive federal law. For where neither the Constitution, a treaty, nor a statute provides the rule of decision or authorizes a federal court to supply one, "state law must govern because there can be no other law." But divergence from state law, with the attendant consequence of forum shopping, is the inevitable (indeed, one might say the intended) result of a uniform system of federal procedure. Congress itself has created the possibility that the same case may follow a different course if filed in federal instead of state court. The short of the matter is that a Federal Rule governing procedure is valid whether or not it alters the outcome of the case in a way that induces forum shopping. To hold otherwise would be to "disembowel either the Constitution's grant of power over federal procedure" or Congress's exercise of it.

* * *

The judgment of the Court of Appeals is reversed, and the case is remanded for further proceedings.

■ JUSTICE STEVENS, concurring in part and concurring in the judgment.

The New York law at issue, N.Y. CIV. PRAC. LAW ANN. (CPLR) § 901(b), is a procedural rule that is not part of New York's substantive law. Accordingly, I agree with JUSTICE SCALIA that Federal Rule of Civil Procedure 23 must apply in this case and join Parts I and II-A of the Court's opinion. But I also agree with JUSTICE GINSBURG that there are some state procedural rules that federal courts must apply in diversity cases because they function as a part of the State's definition of substantive rights and remedies.

I

. . .

Although the Enabling Act and the Rules of Decision Act "say, roughly, that federal courts are to apply state 'substantive' law and federal 'procedural' law," the inquiries are not the same. The Enabling Act does not invite federal courts to engage in the "relatively unguided *Erie* choice," but instead instructs only that federal rules cannot "abridge, enlarge or modify any substantive right," § 2072(b). The Enabling Act's limitation does not mean that federal rules cannot displace state policy judgments; it means only that federal rules cannot displace a State's definition of its own rights or remedies. . . .

In our federalist system, Congress has not mandated that federal courts dictate to state legislatures the form that their substantive law must take. . . . When a State chooses to use a traditionally procedural vehicle as a means of defining the scope of substantive rights or remedies, federal courts must recognize and respect that choice. . . .

II

. . .

The court must first determine whether the scope of the federal rule is "sufficiently broad" to "control the issue" before the court, "thereby leaving no room for the operation" of seemingly conflicting state law. If the federal rule does not apply or can operate alongside the state rule, then there is no "Ac[t] of Congress" governing that particular question, 28 U.S.C. § 1652, and the court must engage in the traditional Rules of Decision Act inquiry under *Erie* and its progeny. In some instances, the "plain meaning" of a federal rule will not come into " 'direct collision' " with the state law, and both can operate. In other instances, the rule "when fairly construed," with "sensitivity to important state interests and regulatory policies," will not collide with the state law.[5]

If, on the other hand, the federal rule is "sufficiently broad to control the issue before the Court," such that there is a "direct collision," the court must decide whether application of the federal rule "represents a valid exercise" of the "rulemaking authority . . . bestowed on this Court by the Rules Enabling Act."

Thus, the second step of the inquiry may well bleed back into the first. When a federal rule appears to abridge, enlarge, or modify a substantive right, federal courts must consider whether the rule can reasonably be interpreted to avoid that impermissible result. . . .

JUSTICE SCALIA believes that the sole Enabling Act question is whether the federal rule "really regulates procedure," (plurality opinion), which means, apparently, whether it regulates "the manner and the means by which the litigants' rights are enforced." I respectfully disagree. This

---

5. I thus agree with JUSTICE GINSBURG that a federal rule, like any federal law, must be interpreted in light of many different considerations, including "sensitivity to important state interests" and "regulatory policies." I disagree with JUSTICE GINSBURG, however, about the degree to which the meaning of federal rules may be contorted, absent congressional authorization to do so, to accommodate state policy goals.

interpretation of the Enabling Act is consonant with the Act's first limitation to "general rules of practice and procedure," § 2072(a). But it ignores the second limitation that such rules also "not abridge, enlarge or modify *any* substantive right," § 2072(b) (emphasis added), and in so doing ignores the balance that Congress struck between uniform rules of federal procedure and respect for a State's construction of its own rights and remedies. It also ignores the separation-of-powers presumption that counsel against judicially created rules displacing state substantive law.

. . . JUSTICE SCALIA worries that if federal courts inquire into the effect of federal rules on state law, it will enmesh federal courts in difficult determinations about whether application of a given rule would displace a state determination about substantive rights. I do not see why an Enabling Act inquiry that looks to state law necessarily is more taxing than JUSTICE SCALIA's. But in any event, that inquiry is what the Enabling Act requires: While it may not be easy to decide what is actually a "substantive right," "the designations substantive and procedural become important, for the Enabling Act has made them so." The question, therefore, is not what rule we think would be easiest on federal courts. The question is what rule Congress established. Although[ ] JUSTICE SCALIA may generally prefer easily administrable, bright-line rules, his preference does not give us license to adopt a second-best interpretation of the Rules Enabling Act. Courts cannot ignore text and context in the service of simplicity. . . .

III

JUSTICE GINSBURG views the basic issue in this case as whether and how to apply a federal rule that dictates an answer to a traditionally procedural question (whether to join plaintiffs together as a class), when a state law that "defines the dimensions" of a state-created claim dictates the opposite answer. As explained above, I readily acknowledge that if a federal rule displaces a state rule that is "'procedural' in the ordinary sense of the term," but sufficiently interwoven with the scope of a substantive right or remedy, there would be an Enabling Act problem, and the federal rule would have to give way. In my view, however, this is not such a case.

Rule 23 Controls Class Certification

When the District Court in the case before us was asked to certify a class action, Federal Rule of Civil Procedure 23 squarely governed the determination whether the court should do so. That is the explicit function of Rule 23. Rule 23, therefore, must apply unless its application would abridge, enlarge, or modify New York rights or remedies. . . .

At bottom, the dissent's interpretation of Rule 23 seems to be that Rule 23 covers only those cases in which its application would create no *Erie* problem. The dissent would apply the Rules of Decision Act inquiry under *Erie* even to cases in which there is a governing federal rule, and thus the Act, by its own terms, does not apply. But "[w]hen a situation is covered by one of the Federal Rules, the question facing the court is a far cry from the typical, relatively unguided *Erie* choice." *Hanna*, 380 U.S. at 471. The question is only whether the Enabling Act is satisfied. Although it reflects a laudable concern to protect "state regulatory policies," JUSTICE GINSBURG's approach would, in my view, work an end run around Congress' system of uniform federal rules, *see* 28 U.S.C. § 2072, and our decision in *Hanna*.

Applying Rule 23 Does Not Violate the Enabling Act

As I have explained, in considering whether to certify a class action such as this one, a federal court must inquire whether doing so would abridge, enlarge, or modify New York's rights or remedies, and thereby violate the Enabling Act. This inquiry is not always a simple one because "[i]t is difficult to conceive of any rule of procedure that cannot have a significant effect on the outcome of a case," and almost "any rule can be said to have . . . 'substantive effects,' affecting society's distribution of risks and rewards." Faced with a federal rule that dictates an answer to a traditionally procedural question and that displaces a state rule, one can often argue that the state rule was really some part of the State's definition of its rights or remedies.

In my view, however, the bar for finding an Enabling Act problem is a high one. The mere fact that a state law is designed as a procedural rule suggests it reflects a judgment about how state courts ought to operate and not a judgment about the scope of state-created rights and remedies. And for the purposes of operating a federal court system, there are costs involved in attempting to discover the true nature of a state procedural rule and allowing such a rule to operate alongside a federal rule that appears to govern the same question. The mere possibility that a federal rule would alter a state-created right is not sufficient. There must be little doubt.

The text of CPLR § 901(b) expressly and unambiguously applies not only to claims based on New York law but also to claims based on federal law or the law of any other State. And there is no interpretation from New York courts to the contrary. It is therefore hard to see how § 901(b) could be understood as a rule that, though procedural in form, serves the function of defining New York's rights or remedies. This is all the more apparent because lawsuits under New York law could be joined in federal class actions well before New York passed § 901(b) in 1975, and New York had done nothing to prevent that. . . .

The legislative history of § 901 . . . reveals a classically procedural calibration of making it easier to litigate claims in New York courts (under any source of law) only when it is necessary to do so, and not making it *too* easy when the class tool is not required. This is the same sort of calculation that might go into setting filing fees or deadlines for briefs. There is of course a difference of degree between those examples and class certification, but not a difference of kind . . . .[18]

---

18. JUSTICE GINSBURG asserts that class certification in this matter would   "transform a $500 case into a $5,000,000 award." But in fact, class certification

The difference of degree is relevant to the forum shopping considerations that are part of the Rules of Decision Act or *Erie* inquiry. If the applicable federal rule did not govern the particular question at issue (or could be fairly read not to do so), then those considerations would matter, for precisely the reasons given by the dissent. But that is not *this* case. . . .

Because Rule 23 governs class certification, the only decision is whether certifying a class in this diversity case would "abridge, enlarge or modify" New York's substantive rights or remedies. § 2072(b). Although one can argue that class certification would enlarge New York's "limited" damages remedy, such arguments rest on extensive speculation about what the New York Legislature had in mind when it created § 901(b). But given that there are two plausible competing narratives, it seems obvious to me that we should respect the plain textual reading of § 901(b), a rule in New York's procedural code about when to certify class actions brought under any source of law, and respect Congress' decision that Rule 23 governs class certification in federal courts. In order to displace a federal rule, there must be more than just a possibility that the state rule is different than it appears.

Accordingly, I concur in part and concur in the judgment.

■   JUSTICE GINSBURG, with whom JUSTICE KENNEDY, JUSTICE BREYER, and JUSTICE ALITO join, dissenting.

The Court today approves Shady Grove's attempt to transform a $500 case into a $5,000,000 award, although the State creating the right to recover has proscribed this alchemy. If Shady Grove had filed suit in New York state court, the 2% interest payment authorized by NEW YORK INS. LAW ANN. § 5106(a) as a penalty for overdue benefits would, by Shady Grove's own measure, amount to no more than $500. By instead filing in federal court based on the parties' diverse citizenship and requesting class certification, Shady Grove hopes to recover, for the class, statutory damages of more than $5,000,000. The New York Legislature has barred this remedy . . . . The Court nevertheless holds that Federal Rule of Civil Procedure 23, which prescribes procedures for the conduct of class actions in federal courts, preempts the application of § 901(b) in diversity suits.

The Court reads Rule 23 relentlessly to override New York's restriction on the availability of statutory damages. Our decisions, however, caution us to ask, before undermining state legislation: Is this conflict really necessary? Had the Court engaged in that inquiry, it would not have read Rule 23 to collide with New York's legitimate interest in keeping certain monetary awards reasonably bounded. I would continue to interpret Federal Rules with awareness of, and sensitivity to, important state

would transform 10,000 $500 cases into one $5,000,000 case. It may be that without class certification, not all of the potential plaintiffs would bring their cases. But that is true of any procedural vehicle; without a lower filing fee, a conveniently located courthouse, easy-to-use federal procedural rules, or many other features of the federal courts, many plaintiffs would not sue.

regulatory policies. Because today's judgment radically departs from that course, I dissent.

I

. . .

In pre-*Hanna* decisions, the Court vigilantly read the Federal Rules to avoid conflict with state laws. . . .

In all of these cases, the Court stated in *Hanna*, "the scope of the Federal Rule was not as broad as the losing party urged, and therefore, there being no Federal Rule which covered the point in dispute, *Erie* commanded the enforcement of state law." In *Hanna* itself, the Court found the clash "unavoidable" . . . . Even as it rejected the Massachusetts prescription in favor of the federal procedure, however, "[t]he majority in *Hanna* recognized . . . that federal rules . . . must be interpreted by the courts applying them, and that the process of interpretation can and should reflect an awareness of legitimate state interests."

Following *Hanna*, we continued to "interpre[t] the federal rules to avoid conflict with important state regulatory policies." . . .

In sum, both before and after *Hanna*, . . . federal courts have been cautioned by this Court to "interpre[t] the Federal Rules . . . with sensitivity to important state interests," and a will "to avoid conflict with important state regulatory policies." The Court veers away from that approach . . . in favor of a mechanical reading of Federal Rules, insensitive to state interests and productive of discord. . . .

The Court, I am convinced, finds conflict where none is necessary. Mindful of the history behind § 901(b)'s enactment, the thrust of our precedent, and the substantive-rights limitation in the Rules Enabling Act, I conclude, as did the Second Circuit and every District Court to have considered the question in any detail, that Rule 23 does not collide with § 901(b). . . . Rule 23 prescribes the considerations relevant to class certification and postcertification proceedings — but it does not command that a particular remedy be available when a party sues in a representative capacity. Section 901(b), in contrast, trains on that latter issue. Sensibly read, Rule 23 governs procedural aspects of class litigation, but allows state law to control the size of a monetary award a class plaintiff may pursue.

In other words, Rule 23 describes a method of enforcing a claim for relief, while § 901(b) defines the dimensions of the claim itself. In this regard, it is immaterial that § 901(b) bars statutory penalties in wholesale, rather than retail, fashion. The New York Legislature could have embedded the limitation in every provision creating a cause of action for which a penalty is authorized; § 901(b) operates as shorthand to the same effect. . . .

The Court single-mindedly focuses on whether a suit "may" or "may not" be maintained as a class action. Putting the question that way, the

Court does not home in on the reason *why*. Rule 23 authorizes class treatment for suits satisfying its prerequisites because the class mechanism generally affords a fair and efficient way to aggregate claims for adjudication. Section 901(b) responds to an entirely different concern; it does not allow class members to recover statutory damages because the New York Legislature considered the result of adjudicating such claims en masse to be exorbitant. The fair and efficient *conduct* of class litigation is the legitimate concern of Rule 23; the *remedy* for an infraction of state law, however, is the legitimate concern of the State's lawmakers and not of the federal rulemakers.

Suppose, for example, that a State, wishing to cap damages in class actions at $1,000,000, enacted a statute providing that "a suit to recover more than $1,000,000 may not be maintained as a class action." Under the Court's reasoning — which attributes dispositive significance to the words "may not be maintained" — Rule 23 would preempt this provision, nevermind that Congress, by authorizing the promulgation of rules of procedure for federal courts, surely did not intend to displace state-created ceilings on damages. . . .

The absence of an inevitable collision between Rule 23 and § 901(b) becomes evident once it is comprehended that a federal court sitting in diversity can accord due respect to both state and federal prescriptions. Plaintiffs seeking to vindicate claims for which the State has provided a statutory penalty may pursue relief through a class action if they forgo statutory damages and instead seek actual damages or injunctive or declaratory relief; any putative class member who objects can opt out and pursue actual damages, if available, and the statutory penalty in an individual action. . . . In sum, while phrased as responsive to the question whether certain class actions may begin, § 901(b) is unmistakably aimed at controlling how those actions must end. On that remedial issue, Rule 23 is silent.

By finding a conflict without considering whether Rule 23 rationally should be read to avoid any collision, the Court unwisely and unnecessarily retreats from the federalism principles undergirding *Erie*. Had the Court reflected on the respect for state regulatory interests endorsed in our decisions, it would have found no cause to interpret Rule 23 so woodenly — and every reason not to do so.

II

Because I perceive no unavoidable conflict between Rule 23 and § 901(b), I would decide this case by inquiring "whether application of the [state] rule would have so important an effect upon the fortunes of one or both of the litigants that failure to [apply] it would be likely to cause a plaintiff to choose the federal court." . . .

In short, Shady Grove's effort to characterize § 901(b) as simply "procedural" cannot successfully elide this fundamental norm: When no federal law or rule is dispositive of an issue, and a state statute is outcome affective in the sense our cases on *Erie* (pre- and post-*Hanna*) develop, the Rules of Decision Act commands application of the State's law in diversity suits. As this case starkly demonstrates, if federal courts exercising diversity jurisdiction are compelled by Rule 23 to award statutory penalties in class actions while New York courts are bound by § 901(b)'s proscription, "substantial variations between state and federal [money judgments] may be expected." The "variation" here is indeed "substantial." Shady Grove seeks class relief that is *ten thousand times* greater than the individual remedy available to it in state court. As the plurality acknowledges, forum shopping will undoubtedly result if a plaintiff need only file in federal instead of state court to seek a massive monetary award explicitly barred by state law. The "accident of diversity of citizenship" should not subject a defendant to such augmented liability.

It is beyond debate that "a statutory cap on damages would supply substantive law for *Erie* purposes." . . .

. . . By barring the recovery of statutory damages in a class action, § 901(b) controls a defendant's maximum liability in a suit seeking such a remedy. The remedial provision could have been written as an explicit cap: "In any class action seeking statutory damages, relief is limited to the amount the named plaintiff would have recovered in an individual suit." That New York's Legislature used other words to express the very same meaning should be inconsequential. . . .

III

The Court's erosion of *Erie*'s federalism grounding impels me to point out the large irony in today's judgment. Shady Grove is able to pursue its claim in federal court only by virtue of the recent enactment of the Class Action Fairness Act of 2005 (CAFA), 28 U.S.C. § 1332(d). In CAFA, Congress opened federal-court doors to state-law-based class actions so long as there is minimal diversity, at least 100 class members, and at least $5,000,000 in controversy. By providing a federal forum, Congress sought to check what it considered to be the overreadiness of some state courts to certify class actions. In other words, Congress envisioned fewer — not more — class actions overall. Congress surely never anticipated that CAFA would make federal courts a mecca for suits of the kind Shady Grove has launched: class actions seeking state-created penalties for claims arising under state law-claims that would be barred from class treatment in the State's own courts.

* * *

I would continue to approach *Erie* questions in a manner mindful of the purposes underlying the Rules of Decision Act and the Rules Enabling Act, faithful to precedent, and respectful of important state interests. I would therefore hold that the New York Legislature's limitation on the recovery of statutory damages applies in this case, and would affirm the Second Circuit's judgment.

Notes

1.   What could the New York legislature now do if it did not want class actions to be used to enforce its law in federal court? If the legislature wrote the language of § 901(b) into the text of each statute permitting an award of a statutory penalty, would that be a sufficient response?

2.   For reasons that are better explored in other classes, *Shady Grove* seems yet another zig-zag in the Court's ever tortuous path toward reconciling the goals of *Erie* with the interests of federal courts in applying their own procedural rules in cases they adjudicate. For our purposes, however, you should consider the vision of class actions that *Shady Grove* evinces. Throughout this chapter we have seen courts express concern for the potential of class actions to put excessive pressure on defendants to settle and to overdeter wrongful behavior. Are these concerns any longer relevant if Rule 23 is, as Justice Scalia says in the plurality part of the decision, just a "traditional joinder" device that aggregates related claims? Note that Justice Stevens seems to take this same view in footnote 18 of his concurrence. So are the concerns about the adventuresome use of Rule 23 expressed in *Amchem Prods., Inc. v. Windsor*, 521 U.S. 591 (1997) (*supra* p. 493), and *Ortiz v. Fibreboard Corp.*, 527 U.S. 815 (1999) (*supra* p. 506), no longer operative after *Shady Grove*? Is there no longer any Rules Enabling Act concern with Rule 23?

3.   How might the results in some of the cases in this chapter that refused to certify class actions change under *Shady Grove*'s vision for Rule 23?

4.   In the Class Action Fairness Act, Congress quite consciously turned federal courts into the adjudicatory forum for most large class actions because it believed that the federal courts' interpretation of Rule 23 avoided some of the ills that looser state class-certification standards had created. As Justice Ginsburg points out, there is an irony in *Shady Grove*, because the federal forum that CAFA created actually opened up the possibility of a class certification for Shady Grove that it did not have before. On the other hand, had *Shady Grove* come out the other way, how effective would CAFA have been? Could state legislatures have written laws that mandated class-action treatment for some claims? Would the federal courts have been required to respect that judgment under Justice Ginsburg's view? Would that approach be consistent with CAFA? Neither CAFA nor *Shady Grove* gives great deference to the federalism concerns that animated some cases.

D. THE DEATH OF CLASS ACTIONS?

In recent years, some commentators have suggested that, either in particular types of cases or even more generally, class actions are nearing death. *See, e.g.*, Myriam Gilles, *Opting Out of Liability: The Forthcoming, Near-Total Demise of the Modern Class Action*, 104 MICH. L. REV. 373,

391-412 (2005); Melissa Hart, *Will Employment Discrimination Class Actions Survive?*, 37 AKRON L. REV. 813 (2004). Like Mark Twain, class actions might find the reports of their death greatly exaggerated. But the point that these commentators make is a valid one.

To begin, the rules for certifying class actions in federal court have tended to become more restrictive in recent years. Certifying mass torts is nigh-impossible; certifying employment-discrimination claims that seek injunctive relief, back pay, and damages is very tricky; and certifying any claim involving the application of multiple state laws or proof of individual reliance is hard to do. By the time that all the doctrinal filters do their work, few cases emerge as certified class actions. As long as state courts provided a more hospitable set of rules for certification, class actions could still be maintained in state forums. But with the advent of the Class Action Fairness Act, major class actions now find themselves in federal court.

Another reason that class actions have become less central as a solution to the problem of aggregation is the rise of class-action waivers in consumer contracts. If you look at the fine print of almost any consumer-credit contract into which you have recently entered, you are likely to find that you waived the right to file a class action to enforce any rights you have. You are likely to have waived your right to file any lawsuit at all, and to have agreed to arbitrate your dispute. And it is likely that you waived the right even to arbitrate on a class-wide basis. In cases based on contract (which are the bulk of disputes eligible for class-action treatment after the demise of the mass-tort class action), the negative-value nature of most disputes combine with the contractual waivers that consumers sign to leave fewer and fewer disputes for Rule 23 to operate on.

Right now courts around the country are wrestling with whether class-action waivers are unconscionable. A valuable treatment of agreements with class-arbitration waivers and other restrictions is *Kristian v. Comcast Corp.*, 446 F.3d 25 (1st Cir. 2006) (striking down prohibitions against treble damages, attorney fees, and class processing in consumer arbitration agreement for antitrust claims); *see also, e.g.*, Discover Bank v. Superior Court, 113 P. 3d 1100, 1103 (Cal. 2005) ("[W]e conclude that, at least under some circumstances, the law in California is that class action waivers in consumer contracts of adhesion are unenforceable, whether the consumer is being asked to waive the right to class action litigation or the right to classwide arbitration. We further conclude that the [Federal Arbitration Act does not preempt] California law in this respect."). Several recent federal decisions have struck down class-arbitration waiver provisions under both federal and state law. *See, e.g.*, Chalk v. T-Mobile USA, Inc., 560 F.3d 1087 (9th Cir. 2009) (provision substantively unconscionable under Oregon law; inseparability makes entire arbitration clause unenforceable); Homa v. Am. Express Co., 558 F.3d 225 (3d Cir. 2009) (provision unconscionable under New Jersey law because of lack of opportunity to negotiate and because it made individual consumer-fraud claims not viable; no preemption of state law by Federal Arbitration Act); In re Am. Express Merchants' Litig., 554 F.3d 300 (2d Cir. 2009) (provision unenforceable because it would make credit-card issuer effectively immune to federal antitrust liability). As of this writing, the Supreme Court seems likely to decide a case that might clarify some issues about the scope of class-action waivers in arbitration. *See* Stolt-Nielsen SA v. AnimalFeeds Int'l Corp., 548 F.3d 85 (2d Cir. 2008), *cert. granted*, No. 08-1198 (June 15, 2009).

Despite these restrictions, class actions are still filed, and classes are still certified. Even if the reports of the death of class actions have been exaggerated, the continued evolution of this most powerful, and most controversial, aggregation tool bears watching.

CHAPTER FIVE

AGGREGATION THROUGH BANKRUPTCY

Our search for the Holy Grail — the procedural tool that permits the aggregation of all the claims of all the parties as a means of preventing inefficient or unjust repetitive litigation — has foundered. In many cases the traditional aggregation tools — joinder, consolidation and transfer, stays and injunctions, and preclusion — are not up to the task of bringing together claimants who are separated by geography, court system, and time from others with related claims. Part of the reason for this failure is the barrier imposed by principles of jurisdiction in a federal system. Another part is the litigant autonomy that our adversarial system respects and fosters. We allow litigants to decide whether, when, where, with whom, and against whom to file suit according to their private interests; unsurprisingly, those interests do not always correspond with the social interest in optimal aggregation. As a general rule, our society does require bystanders who cannot or do not wish to join a case to do so.

Class actions can overcome some of these problems (although at the cost of the autonomy of class members). As we have seen, however, class actions do not plug all the gaps left by our patchwork of aggregation doctrines. The requirements for obtaining a class action are rigorous; concerns for the adequacy of the class members' representation and for manageability derail many class actions at the start. Moreover, in many circumstances in which class actions are certified, class members can opt out and proceed with individual litigation — either because the class-action rule allows it or the Due Process Clause requires it (in the case of class members without sufficient contacts with the forum). Third, at least until a settlement appears imminent, a federal judge has no power to prevent class members from proceeding in state or federal court with individual suits identical to the class action; a state-court judge usually has even less injunctive power than this. Finally, class actions have not proven to be an especially effective tool for dealing with the problem of future claimants.

This chapter considers a final option: bankruptcy. Although the field of bankruptcy is centuries old, using bankruptcy as a tool to aggregate related litigation is a relative recent development. In 1982, Johns-Manville, then the world's largest manufacturer of asbestos, filed for Chapter 11 bankruptcy. The filing sent shock waves through the legal community. Part of the shock resulted from the fact that Johns-Manville was still solvent. The other part resulted from the way in which Johns-Manville proposed to use bankruptcy: to consolidate both present and future claims in one forum, to create a mechanism to pay all present and future claims, and to emerge from the Chapter 11 reorganization intact, healthy, and litigation-free.

In this chapter we examine whether bankruptcy can accomplish what Johns-Manville set out to do. In Section A, we examine briefly bankruptcy's basic substantive, jurisdictional, and procedural principles. In Section B, we examine the use and limits of bankruptcy as a way to aggregate related cases in one forum. We focus on three aggregation issues: the scope of the bankruptcy court's power to aggregate claims involving the party (usually a defendant) seeking bankruptcy; the court's power to aggregate claims involving parties other than the party filing for bankruptcy; and the power of the bankruptcy court to handle the claims of future plaintiffs.

A. THE BASICS OF BANKRUPTCY

Our modest goal in this section is to provide enough information for you to appreciate the benefits and drawbacks of bankruptcy as an aggregation device in complex cases. We begin with a cursory explanation of the substance of bankruptcy law. We then examine bankruptcy's jurisdictional and procedural provisions. Without question, these provisions make bankruptcy the most powerful and comprehensive aggregation device we have studied. The one problem with using this set of tools, of course, is that a party (usually a defendant) must go into bankruptcy to take advantage of them.

1. Substance

Bankruptcy provides a means by which a person (called the debtor) can get out from under his or her debts. The terms under which the debtor can obtain this relief are specified in the Bankruptcy Code, which is presently found in Title 11 of the United States Code. Under the Code, a bankruptcy court collects a debtor's assets (called the bankruptcy estate), and then distributes them to those of debtor's creditors that file a claim against the estate. The distribution occurs according to the payment priorities contained in the Code; depending on the size of the estate, some creditors might receive full payment, and others receive partial or no payment. After the assets are distributed, the debtor receives a "discharge," which wipes away the debts and allows the debtor a "fresh start" free of legal obligations that the debtor had incurred up to the time of the bankruptcy. The Bankruptcy Code allows the debtor to exclude certain assets from the estate, and it does not discharge certain types of debt. It also provides a power by which the bankruptcy court can void certain preferential transfers that the debtor made in the months leading up to the bankruptcy.

The process of collecting the debtor's assets, voiding preferential transfers, and distributing the assets can be complex, and in many cases the court appoints a bankruptcy trustee to accomplish these tasks. In some cases, the court allows a debtor corporation to continue to operate the business; the debtor is known as a "debtor in possession." In other cases, the court appoints the trustee or another person to run the business. In either event, once the debtor enters bankruptcy, the corporation is run to maximize its value for the creditors. The bankruptcy estate is seen in the law as a separate legal entity — a *res* over which the bankruptcy court can exercise jurisdiction.

Contrary to popular wisdom, a debtor does not need to be insolvent before entering bankruptcy. Sometimes bankruptcy is necessary to deal with severe cash-flow problems in a solvent corporation, especially when some creditors refuse to re-negotiate debts on reasonable terms. Because bankruptcy discharges legal claims against the debtor, a defendant facing thousands of lawsuits can also find bankruptcy useful. On the other hand, a debtor risks losing control of the business once the bankruptcy petition is filed; for this reason, bankruptcy is often seen as a last resort.

Any person or entity can use bankruptcy. For our purposes, however, we focus on corporate bankruptcies. One reason is that we are considering bankruptcy as a tool for aggregating related litigation in one forum. As a rule, the debtors most likely to have enough assets and to face the number of lawsuits that make bankruptcy a legitimate option are corporations.

The second reason to focus on corporate bankruptcy is the availability of a form of bankruptcy unique to corporations. The various chapters of the Bankruptcy Code provides for a number of different forms of bankruptcy. For our purposes, the two most important are Chapter 7 liquidations and Chapter 11 corporate reorganizations. As its name suggests, a Chapter 7 liquidation sells off all of the assets in the bankruptcy estate and gives the proceeds to the creditors. If the debtor is a corporation, Chapter 7 does not offer a discharge. But after distribution of the assets, the corporation has no remaining value and it is effectively dead. A Chapter 11 reorganization, however, allows the corporation to pay its debts and to emerge after discharge as a going concern. The latter option is obviously more attractive to corporate managers.

Reorganization is also more important from the standpoint of complex litigation. If a corporation liquidates under Chapter 7, then it is really rather indifferent about how the claims asserted against it are paid. Assume that the corporation has $500 million in assets, is facing judgments in 500 cases for $1 million (i.e., $500 million), is facing 50,000 additional claims for $1 million apiece (i.e., $50 billion in claims), and knows that 100,000 more people are likely to have $1 million claims in the future (i.e.,

$100 billion). In this situation, it doesn't matter to the corporation if its assets go to pay the claims already reduced to judgment, or if those with present or future claims also receive some of the assets. In particular, it seems likely that the 100,000 future claimants will be out of luck. Because they do not yet have legal claims to assert, they do not meet the ordinary definition of a creditor. Their claims will therefore not be discharged, and by the time that they have claims, the corporation will have liquidated and they will be without an effective remedy against it. Thus, Chapter 7 liquidations do nothing to avoid the unfairness caused by the temporal dispersion of claims — an unfairness that has been a primary motivation in our search for better aggregation tools. If the corporation reorganizes, however, the situation is different. It has little incentive to go through bankruptcy if it still faces the prospect of 100,000 new suits after discharge. If the reorganization process can figure out a way to handle not only the present claims but also the future claims, then Chapter 11 holds out significant promise as a way to aggregate — and resolve — related claims against a defendant in a large-scale case.

For these reasons, the cases on which this chapter focuses are Chapter 11 reorganizations. The basic goal of a Chapter 11 reorganization is to construct a reorganization plan that simultaneously satisfies the needs of creditors and the goal of the corporation to remain a financially viable concern after bankruptcy. The Bankruptcy Code allows a debtor to submit a plan for accomplishing these aims; creditors and other interested parties can submit competing plans. A distinction exists between impaired and unimpaired creditors; unimpaired creditors are fully paid under the plan, while impaired creditors receive less than full value.

The Code requires the bankruptcy court to organize the creditors and other interested parties into classes of claims and classes of interests. As a general rule, each class of impaired creditors must vote to accept a reorganization plan before it becomes effective. (Unimpaired creditors are not entitled to vote.) A class of claims accepts the plan when a majority in number as two-thirds in dollar amount vote in favor of the plan. In addition, the plan must also receive approval from all classes of interests (most typically shareholders in the corporation), but here approval requires a favorable vote of those holding two-thirds in dollar amount. 11 U.S.C. § 1126. The classes' consent is not along sufficient to result in the plan's approval; the classes' approval is just one of sixteen statutory findings that a bankruptcy court must make before approving the plan. *See* 11 U.S.C. § 1129(a). For the most part, however, a plan that meets all classes' approval is likely to satisfy the remaining statutory factors. The likeliest hiccup is that the bankruptcy court can deny approval to a plan if it determines that the plan was not proposed in good faith.

In limited circumstances, a bankruptcy court can also accept a plan when one or more classes of claims or interests reject it. To do so, the court invokes Chapter 11's "cramdown" provision — so named because the court crams the plan down the throats of unwilling classes. The plan must still meet all of statutory factors other than approval of all classes. At that point, the court can approve the plan if it determines that the plan is "fair and equitable." 11 U.S.C. § 1129(b)(2). The phrase has a particular meaning in this context. Essentially, a plan is "fair and equitable" when each person in each class of secured claims that did not approve the plan receives full value, and each person in each class of unsecured claims or interests that did not approve the plan either (1) receives the full allowed value of their claims or (2) receives less than the full amount but no class of claims or interests that are "junior" (in terms of payment priority) to the disapproving class receives anything of value. This last provision is known as the "absolute-priority rule." As a general matter, secured claims take priority over unsecured claims, which in turn take priority over shareholder and other interests. Therefore, it is impossible to cram down a plan that gives secured creditors less than full value or that give shareholders any value if unsecured claims are less than fully compensated.

It is common in Chapter 11 bankruptcy for various creditors to organize a committee that works to hammer out a plan with the debtor and, if applicable, trustee. Such a committee often tries to include representatives from each class of creditors and interests. Negotiations occur against the backdrop of the debtor's plan and the limit on the court's cramdown power that the absolute-priority rule imposes.

It should be evident that a critical variable in the success or failure of a reorganization plan is the composition of the classes of claims and interests. In theory, a bankruptcy court can stack the deck in favor of or against a plan by putting into the same class various combinations of persons that support or oppose the plan. The Bankruptcy Code imposes some limits on a bankruptcy court's power to classify claims; a plan cannot place "a claim or interest in a particular class unless such claim or interest is substantially similar to the other claims or interests of such class." 11 U.S.C. § 1122(a). Nonetheless, classification of claims "can be a creative process (and an important one too if the debtor needs an affirmative vote of a non-insider-impaired creditor class to set up a cram-down of an objecting creditor class under section 1129(b))." STAN BERNSTEIN, AM. BAR ASS'N, BUSINESS BANKRUPTCY ESSENTIALS 94 (2009). Debtors' plans often try to gerrymander classes to secure the most favorable voting treatment. "At present, the issue of how far a debtor can go in creatively classifying claims under a chapter 11 plan of reorganization is unresolved." *Id.* at 95.

Another critical variable is the allowance and estimation of claims that have not yet been reduced to judgment. Assume that, in our hypothetical, the only unsecured creditors are the plaintiffs and potential plaintiffs (in other words, the 500 holding $1 million judgments against the debtor, the 50,000 with present but unresolved claims, and the 100,000 with future claims). It is easy to know the value of the claims of the first 500. But what about the remainder? Must the bankruptcy court determine whether each of the 150,000 present and future claimants has a viable claim, and how much it is worth? The answer is critical, because a court cannot approve a plan without determining that half in number and two-thirds in value of those with legitimate claims have voted in favor of the plan. Obviously, the court cannot wait for each case to come to judgment before holding the vote; and from the debtor's viewpoint, the point of bankruptcy is to get out from under the weight of such claims, not to endure them in a new forum.

Collecting assets, voiding preferences, allowing and estimating claims, establishing classes of claims and interests, fostering negotiations with creditors' committees, conducting balloting, approving or cramming down plans — these are just some of the large legal issues that bankruptcy courts face. Beneath these issues lie doctrinal details and business practicalities that make bankruptcy one of the most challenging and specialized fields in American law. Bankruptcy litigation can be complex, time-consuming, and very expensive. Our short overview stops here, now that you have the basic information to appreciate the cases that follow. Before we turn to these cases, we examine the procedural powers of a bankruptcy court. These powers make bankruptcy, whatever its complexities and limitations, an attractive aggregation tool in certain circumstances.

2. Jurisdiction and Procedure

As we have seen, an ideal aggregation mechanism must possess certain features: (1) a single court system with subject-matter jurisdiction over all claims asserted by and against the relevant parties and or potential parties; (2) if jurisdiction is not exclusive, a mechanism for removal of claims from parallel courts; (3) once related cases are aggregated in a court system, a transfer mechanism to allow all of the cases to be consolidated in one venue for pretrial and trial purposes; (4) the aggregating court's ability to assert territorial jurisdiction over all parties and potential parties; (5) the aggregating court's power to stay proceedings in other courts; and (6) a mechanism for joining (or precluding) the claims of potential parties who cannot or do not wish to assert their claims at the present time. Let's examine how bankruptcy fares on these metrics.

Subject-Matter Jurisdiction. 28 U.S.C. § 1334(a) grants to the federal district courts "original and exclusive jurisdiction of all cases under title 11." (Title 11 is the Bankruptcy Code, and should not be confused with Chapter 11, which contains the reorganization provisions within the Bankruptcy Code.) In addition, 28 U.S.C. § 1334(b) grants "original but not exclusive jurisdiction of all civil proceedings arising under title 11, or arising in or related to cases under title 11." This language makes a distinction among (1) a "case," which is the process triggered when the debtor files a bankruptcy petition that seeking a discharge from debt, (2) a "civil proceeding," which is a controversy that is resolved in the context of settling the debtor's affairs, and (3) a "related to" case, which (in general terms) is a case that might affect the debtor's estate. *See* DOUGLAS G. BAIRD, THE ELEMENTS OF BANKRUPTCY 22 (rev. ed. 1993); In re Resorts Int'l, Inc., 372 F.3d 154, 162 (3d Cir. 2004). Although the court has exclusive jurisdiction only with respect to the "case" itself, the concurrent jurisdiction over "civil proceedings" and "related to" cases provides one court that can in theory hear the claims by or against all the parties. *But see* RICHARD H.

FALLON, JR. ET AL., HART & WECHSLER'S THE FEDERAL COURTS AND THE FEDERAL SYSTEM 765-68 (6th ed. 2009) (describing constitutional issues with "related to" jurisdiction).

There is, however, a fly in the jurisdictional ointment. Under 28 U.S.C. § 1334(c)(1), a district court generally *may*, "in the interest of justice, or in the interest of comity with State courts or respect for State law, . . . abstain[ ] from hearing a particular proceeding arising under title 11 or arising in or related to a case under title 11." *See* In re Legates, 381 B.R. 111 (Bankr. D. Del. 2008) (listing 12 factors to consider when invoking discretionary abstention). Moreover, under § 1334(c)(2), a district court *must* abstain, upon timely motion, in "a proceeding based upon a State law claim or State law cause of action, related to a case under title 11 but not arising under title 11, with respect to which an action could not have been commenced in a court of the United States absent jurisdiction under [§ 1334]" if the "action is commenced, and can be timely adjudicated, in a State forum of appropriate jurisdiction." Mandatory abstention has one important limitation: The liquidation or estimation of personal-injury and wrongful-death claims "shall not be subject to the mandatory abstention provisions of section 1334(c)(2)." 28 U.S.C. § 157(b)(4).

Removal. Because federal jurisdiction is not exclusive for civil proceedings and "related to" cases, some mechanism for removal of these cases is necessary if global aggregation is to occur. In most circumstances, 28 U.S.C. § 1452(a) gives a "party" the right to remove "any claim or cause of action in a civil action . . . to the district court for the district where such civil action is pending, if such district court has jurisdiction of such claim or cause of action under section 1334 of [Title 28]." Bankruptcy courts are not, however, required to hear all removed claims. Under § 1452(b), the district court "may remand such [removed] claim or cause of action on any equitable ground."

Another hitch in removal jurisdiction is that removal occurs to the federal district encompassing the state court from which the case was removed; a venue-transfer mechanism for aggregating related proceedings in one federal forum is still required. *Cf.* In re Trafficwatch, 138 B.R. 841 (Bankr. E.D. Tex. 1992) (holding that removal to district in which bankruptcy case was filed is a non-jurisdictional defect that can be waived).

Venue and Transfer. 28 U.S.C. § 1408, bankruptcy's venue provision, locates the bankruptcy case either in the district of the debtor's domicile, residence, principal place of business, or principal location of assets, or in the district in which certain related bankruptcy proceedings are pending. With minor exceptions, proceedings and "related to" cases also "may be commenced" in the district court in which the bankruptcy case has been filed. 28 U.S.C. § 1409(a). So far, so good: The bankruptcy case, as well as civil proceedings and "related to" cases, can be venued in a single forum.

There are, however, two problems. First, we need a mechanism to transfer removed cases from the district to which they have been removed to the district in which the bankruptcy case is pending. Second, § 1409 says "may," not "shall." Some cases hold that, despite the use of the word "may,"

§ 1409(a) requires that proceedings and "related to" cases be filed in the district in which the bankruptcy case is pending. *See* Jeffrey T. Ferriell, *The Perils of Nationwide Service of Process in a Bankruptcy Context*, 48 WASH. & LEE L. REV. 1199, 1207 n.43 (1991). The better reading of § 1409 and related provisions, however, is that proceedings and "related to" cases can be commenced in any federal district in which venue exists. *See* Brock v. Am. Messenger Serv., Inc., 65 B.R. 670 (D.N.H. 1986).

To solve these problems, the bankruptcy statutes have two distinct transfer provisions. First, 28 U.S.C. § 1412 provides that "[a] district court may transfer a case or proceeding under title 11 to a district court for another district, in the interest of justice or for the convenience of the parties." A split in authority exists over whether § 1412 or § 1404 governs the transfer of "related to" cases. *See* Dunlap v. Friedman's, Inc., 331 B.R. 674 (S.D. W. Va. 2005). The issue matters because § 1412 transfers are not encumbered by § 1404's requirement that transfer can occur only to a district in which venue was initially proper. *See* Hoffman v. Blaski, 363 U.S. 335 (1960); *supra* p. 137, Note 5.

The second venue-transfer provision is 28 U.S.C. § 157(b)(5), which requires "personal injury tort and wrongful death claims" to be tried either "in the district court in which the bankruptcy case is pending, or in the district court in the district in which the claim arose, as determined by the district court in which the bankruptcy case is pending." While judges typically use § 157(b)(5) to transfer tort cases to forums other than the forum in which the bankruptcy case is pending, it also can be used as a means to consolidate tort cases in the bankruptcy forum. As with § 1412, § 157(b)(5) does not limit transfer just to those federal districts in which the case might initially have been brought.

Both § 1412 and § 157(b)(5) allow the transfer of a case for all purposes, including trial. Nonetheless, proceedings and "related to" cases can often be brought in multiple venues. Except for tort claims, no mechanism, akin to § 1407, provides for transfer of all cases and proceedings to a single forum. To achieve global aggregation, reliance on other venue transfer mechanisms is required. Venue-transfer provisions are therefore a weak link in bankruptcy's potential use as an aggregation tool.

Territorial Jurisdiction. Bankruptcy courts have their own rules of procedure, which often mimic the Federal Rules of Civil Procedure. One rule that is significantly different, however, is Bankruptcy Rule 7004(d), which states in full: "The summons and complaint and all other process except a subpoena may be served anywhere in the United States." Thus, district courts sitting in bankruptcy enjoy nationwide service of process. *But see* Ferriell, *supra* (suggesting use of minimum-contacts standard to avoid constitutional difficulties, unfairness, and forum shopping). *Cf.* Edward S. Adams & Rachel E. Iverson, *Personal Jurisdiction in the Bankruptcy Context: A Need for Reform*, 44 CATH. U. L. REV. 1081 (1995) (suggesting need for broader personal jurisdiction over foreign defendants).

Staying Related Litigation. Some of the deficiencies in subject-matter jurisdiction, removal, and venue can be cured if the bankruptcy court has the power to stay cases in other forums. The primary source for a stay in bankruptcy is 11 U.S.C. § 362. Section 362 is long and intricate; here we highlight only basic principles. The fundamental point of § 362 is that the filing of a petition automatically "operates as a stay, applicable to all entities, of . . . the commencement or continuation . . . of a judicial, administrative, or other action or proceeding against the debtor that was or could have been commenced before the commencement of the case under this title." Section 362 also stays various actions that are designed to jump a particular creditor ahead of the queue and disadvantage other creditors and the bankruptcy estate. Note that the stay does not make distinctions among the bankruptcy case, civil proceedings, and "related to" cases; *any* actions and proceedings that might affect the debtor's estate must halt.

The automatic stay of § 362 has significant limits. A large number of claims, few of which are likely to arise in complex litigation, are not stayed. § 362(b). Moreover, under § 362(d), a party can petition the bankruptcy court for relief from the automatic stay. The standard ground for requesting, and for granting, such relief is that a party in interest in the bankruptcy case lacks "adequate protection," *see* § 362(d)(1), which means in essence that the party's interest in specific property is likely to become less valuable during the pendency of the bankruptcy case. Most litigants, who typically have unsecured claims, cannot take advantage of § 362(d).

Another way in which the stay is limited is that it stays only those proceedings that affect the debtor's estate. Thus, actions against third parties do not typically come within the stay. Even should a stay run to third parties, the stay is not permanent; it expires, at the latest, at the end of the bankruptcy case. *See* § 362(c). The case against the debtor having ended, the cases against third parties can now proceed — unless a global settlement of all claims is achieved in the bankruptcy proceeding.

The stay is usually operative only against those claims that were or could have been brought on the date of the filing of the bankruptcy petition. It does not affect proceedings or cases that first arise after the petition was filed. With post-petition cases, the stay is important only in the sense that it prevents any effort to enforce a judgment against the debtor. Bellini Imports, Ltd. v. Mason & Dixon Lines, Inc., 944 F.2d 199 (4th Cir. 1991).

A second source of power to enter a stay is § 105, which authorizes a court to "issue any order, process, or judgment that is necessary or appropriate to carry out the provisions of this title." This grant suggests a quasi-All Writs Act power that can smooth over the limitations of § 362, but it is not quite as broad as it sounds: A § 105 stay is available only when "a policy embraced in some other part of the Bankruptcy Code justifies it." *See* BAIRD, *supra*, at 9; In re Joint E. & S. Dist. Asbestos Litig., 982 F.2d 721, 751 (2d Cir. 1992) ("equitable considerations . . . [are] not a license to courts to invent remedies that overstep statutory limitations").

Joining or Precluding Nonparties. The automatic stay prevents prosecution of claims not only of present litigants, but also of those who could have brought claims prior to the filing of the petition. Thus, the stay solves a part of the bystander problem. But other parts of the problem still remain. The stay cannot affect those nonparties who do not yet have a claim. Furthermore, a stay is a very small stick to force nonparties into the bankruptcy proceeding; barring statute-of-limitations issues, nonparties can wait out the bankruptcy case and file after the stay has dissolved. What is really needed is a way either to mandate joinder of nonparties or to preclude their claims if they fail to join.

The Bankruptcy Code adopts the preclusive method. The end result of a successful bankruptcy is a discharge of the debtor's debts. (There are important types of debts that cannot be discharged in bankruptcy, but we do not explore them here. *See* 11 U.S.C. § 523.) The discharge "voids any judgment at any time obtained, to the extent that such judgment is a determination of the personal liability of the debtor with respect to any debt discharged," and it also "operates as an injunction against the commencement or continuation of an action, the employment of process, or an act, to collect, recover, or offset any such act as a personal liability of the debtor." *Id.* §§ 524(a)(1), -(a)(2). Therefore, a person who, as of the date of the filing of the petition for bankruptcy, has a claim against the debtor must assert the claim within the bankruptcy proceeding — or else the claim is forever barred. *See* Martin v. Wilks, 490 U.S. 755, 762 n.2 (1989) (*supra* p. 222) (noting that bankruptcy was an exception to the usual rule that a court can preclude only parties' claims).

This preclusion method has one qualification and two important limitations. The qualification is simply that a particular debt cannot be discharged (and thus the claimant precluded from further suit) unless the debt was listed or placed on a schedule of liabilities in such a way that the creditor had an opportunity to file a timely proof of claim. *Id.* § 523(a)(3).

The first limitation of the bankruptcy discharge is that the court can discharge only debts accrued up to a specified time during the bankruptcy proceedings. (For some of the provisions establishing cut-off dates, see §§ 502(f), 727(b), 1141(d).) Because later-accruing claims are typically unrelated to discharged claims, this limitation usually poses no problem for the aggregation of related cases. When long latency periods create a mass of future plaintiffs, however, problems can arise; a defendant has little reason to go through bankruptcy and receive a discharge of present claims, only to face a new onslaught of claims thereafter.

Second, the bankruptcy discharge is effective only against the debtor, not against other defendants (unless they too file for bankruptcy). The discharge cannot resolve all aspects of a multi-defendant controversy.

Other Provisions. Two other provisions merit mention. First, most activity in bankruptcy cases occurs before bankruptcy judges, who are Article I appointees. The requirement that cases be adjudicated by Article III judges limits the powers of bankruptcy judges, and has led to a curious division of responsibility in which district judges are authorized to (and almost always do) refer to bankruptcy judges most "core proceedings," but cannot refer to bankruptcy judges "non-core proceedings" and tort actions that are core proceedings. *See* 28 U.S.C. § 157. We will not wade into the swampy distinctions between "core" and "non-core" proceedings or address the constitutional issues engendered by this division of responsibility — except to note that important issues remain unresolved. Our point is that bankruptcy acts as an imperfect aggregator. Some proceedings are likely to be conducted by the district judge and some by the bankruptcy judge, with the district judge acting in effect as an appellate court over the bankruptcy judge's decisions. *See* 28 U.S.C. §§ 157, 158. A district judge can avoid this split by declining to refer a case to the bankruptcy court or by withdrawing an order of reference. *See* §§ 157(a), (d). Given the intricacies of bankruptcy law, however, district judges are loathe to exercise this power even in complex cases.

Second, the Seventh Amendment, which guarantees the right to jury trial in certain civil actions, casts a large shadow over bankruptcy law. Bankruptcy itself was equitable in nature, so jury trials did not obtain. Therefore, the essential functions of the bankruptcy court — collecting the debtor's assets, allowing claims against the estate, and distributing the assets — do not involve jury trial. But many of the civil proceedings and "related to" cases over which the district court has jurisdiction carry a right to jury trial. There is considerable debate about how far the jury-trial right carries into bankruptcy proceedings and whether Article I bankruptcy judges can conduct jury trials. *See* Granfinanciera, S.A. v. Nordberg, 492 U.S. 33 (1989); BAIRD, *supra*, at 20-22.

Conclusion. Bankruptcy has more aggregation tools than any device in American law. Even though it is the most comprehensive device for the aggregation of related cases in a single forum, it has important limits. The following section examines how courts have tried to adapt the bankruptcy mechanism to the needs of complex litigation.

B. STRETCHING BANKRUPTCY TO MEET THE AGGREGATION NEEDS OF COMPLEX LITIGATION

The enemy of optimal aggregation is the geographical, temporal, and jurisdictional dispersion of claims. The prior section showed bankruptcy's potential for overcoming certain types of dispersion, but also pointed out some of the limits of present bankruptcy law as a means of aggregating related cases. In general terms, the limits fall into three categories. First, in mass-injury litigation in which the debtor is the only defendant, a court sitting in bankruptcy is limited in its ability to aggregate all present claims against the debtor in the bankruptcy forum. Second, the bankruptcy court is limited in its ability to aggregate all present claims brought against defendants other than the debtor in the bankruptcy forum. Third, the bankruptcy court is limited in its ability to handle claims that mature only after the bankruptcy proceeding. The first two limits involve problems of geographical and jurisdictional dispersion. The third involves temporal dispersion.

The success of bankruptcy as an aggregation method hinges its ability to solve these problems. In this section we examine how bankruptcy has attempted to respond to each problem. As you read the progression from the first problem to the third, ask whether, at some point, the usefulness of bankruptcy as an aggregation mechanism breaks down.

1. Using the Bankruptcy Forum to Resolve Present Cases and Claims Against a Debtor

Despite bankruptcy's breadth as an aggregation device, our discussion of the substance, jurisdiction, and procedures of bankruptcy uncovered certain challenges that the law places in the way of aggregating existing claims or cases in the bankruptcy forum. The following cases reflect some of the issues involved when seeking to overcome these limits. The first two cases involve procedural roadblocks; the last a substantive roadblock.

SHARED NETWORK USERS GROUP, INC. v. WORLDCOM TECHNOLOGIES, INC.

309 B.R. 446 (E.D. Pa. 2004)

■ BARTLE, District Judge.

In March, 2000, plaintiff Shared Network Users Group, Inc. ("Shared Network") instituted this action in the Court of Common Pleas of Montgomery County, Pennsylvania for breach of contract and for violation of the Communications Act of 1934, 47 U.S.C. §§ 201-02. Shared Network sought to enjoin defendants WorldCom Technologies, Inc. and MCI WorldCom, Inc. (collectively, "WorldCom") from carrying out their threat to disconnect the telecommunication services they were providing to Shared Network. Shared Network also requested damages. WorldCom counterclaimed for amounts due under their contract, quantum meruit, and unjust enrichment.

Almost four years later, on January 16, 2004, WorldCom removed the action to this court pursuant to . . . 28 U.S.C. §§ 1334, 1441(b), and 1452(a). WorldCom has moved to transfer venue to the United States District Court for the Southern District of New York under 28 U.S.C. § 1412. Shared Network has moved to remand to the state court on the ground that removal was untimely or alternatively that the court should exercise its equitable authority to remand and/or abstain under § 1452(b) or § 1334(c)(1).

In 2002, WorldCom and certain of its subsidiaries commenced proceedings under Chapter 11 of the Bankruptcy Code, 11 U.S.C. §§ 101 et seq., in the Southern District of New York where they have been consolidated and are being jointly administered. On January 22, 2003, Shared Network filed a proof of claim in the amount of $507,671.20 in the bankruptcy court in that district. This is essentially the same claim that is the subject of the complaint originally filed in the state court. On January 13, 2004, WorldCom filed an objection to the proof of claim and asserted virtually the same counterclaim in the bankruptcy court which it had filed against Shared Network in the Montgomery County action. WorldCom seeks $884,512.08. Three days later, WorldCom removed the state court action to this court.

I.

[The court first held that WorldCom's removal of the state-court action was timely.]

II.

Having determined that removal of the entire action was timely, we must now decide whether we should refuse to exercise subject matter jurisdiction over this action. Shared Network appears to move for remand under § 1452(b) and/or permissive abstention under § 1334(c)(1). Section 1452(b) provides that "the court to which [a] claim or cause of action is removed may remand such claim or cause of action on any equitable ground." Similarly, § 1334(c)(1) reads:

> Nothing in this section prevents a district court in the interest of justice, or in the interest of comity with State courts or respect for State law, from abstaining from hearing a particular proceeding arising under title 11 or arising in or related to a case under title 11.

In assessing whether to abstain or to remand, a court considers the following non-inclusive factors:

> the effect on the efficient administration of the bankruptcy estate; the extent to which issues of state law predominate; the difficulty or unsettled nature of applicable state law; comity; the degree of relatedness or remoteness of the proceeding to the main bankruptcy case; the existence of a right to a jury trial; and[ ] prejudice to the involuntarily removed defendants.

Shared Network argues that comity, the right to a jury trial, and the predominance of state law issues all militate in favor of remand. WorldCom contends that the effect on the efficient administration of the estate, the degree of relatedness of the bankruptcy and state court proceedings, and the waiver by Shared Network of its right to a jury trial by subjecting itself to the equitable administration of the bankruptcy court all support denying Shared Network's remand motion and transferring the entire action to the Southern District of New York.

. . . [T]he parties agree that the claims and originally filed counterclaim in the state court action constitute "core proceedings." *See* 28 U.S.C. § 157. "Thus, it is clear that [the claims and counterclaims are] . . . quite related to the bankruptcy and also that remand would impede the efficient administration of the bankrupt estate." Because the state court action was voluntarily and temporarily stayed, Shared Network's proof of claim and WorldCom's objection thereto in the bankruptcy court are just as far along in the litigation process as the state court action. The remand and subsequent delay would negatively affect the efficient administration of WorldCom's bankruptcy estate.

In addition, the lack of complexity of the applicable state law for breach of contract, quantum meruit, and unjust enrichment, together with "the absence of any special state interest . . . weigh[ ] strongly against abstention."

Shared Network argues that its right to a jury trial will be unfairly lost if it is forced to litigate in bankruptcy court. We are not convinced. Shared Network has voluntarily subjected itself to the equitable jurisdiction of the bankruptcy court by filing its proof of claim there. It could have moved to terminate the automatic stay on the state court action if it had been interested in expeditiously resolving the dispute in state court before a jury. It did not do so.

In light of the above analysis, we find that neither permissive abstention nor equitable remand is appropriate. Accordingly, we will deny Shared Network's motion to remand this action to the Court of Common Pleas of Montgomery County.

III.

Finally, we turn to WorldCom's motion to transfer venue to the Southern District of New York. Under 28 U.S.C. § 1412, "a district court may transfer a case or proceeding under Title 11 to a district court for another district, in the interest of justice or for the convenience of the parties." Our Court of Appeals has outlined the factors to consider under 28 U.S.C. § 1404(a) in *Jumara v. State Farm Ins. Co.*, 55 F.3d 873 (3d Cir. 1995). Since much of the essential wording of § 1412 is similar to § 1404(a), we view the reasoning of Jumara to be applicable here, taking into consideration the particular circumstances arising out of a bankruptcy.

While there is no exclusive list of factors, there are a variety of private and public interests to be considered in deciding a motion to transfer venue. The private interests include not only the debtor's choice of forum but also the convenience of the parties as indicated by the physical and financial condition and the location of books and records. The public interests, on the other hand, include such matters as the enforcement of any judgment, "practical considerations that could make the trial easy, expeditious, or inexpensive," court congestion, and local interests.

Here, we find the overwhelmingly significant factor, outweighing all others, is the judicial economy to be achieved in having the entire controversy decided in one forum, in this case the bankruptcy court which is already administering the WorldCom bankruptcy. If we ruled otherwise, it is inevitable that proceedings will be delayed and to some extent duplicated for a tremendous waste of time and money for all concerned. Having the Southern District of New York as the venue is particularly compelling since Shared Network has filed a proof of claim against WorldCom in the bankruptcy court in that district, WorldCom has filed a counterclaim against Shared Network there, and all agree that the claims and counterclaim are core proceedings so that they may be adjudicated before the presiding bankruptcy judge.

We will grant the motion to transfer.

A.H. ROBINS CO. V. PICCININ

788 F.2d 994 (4th Cir. 1986)

■ RUSSELL, Circuit Judge.

Confronted, if not overwhelmed, with an avalanche of actions filed in various state and federal courts throughout the United States by citizens of this country as well as of foreign countries seeking damages for injuries allegedly sustained by the use of an intrauterine contraceptive device known as a Dalkon Shield, the manufacturer of the device, A.H. Robins Company, Incorporated (Robins) filed its petition under Chapter 11 of the Bankruptcy Code in August, 1985.

Background

. . . By the middle of 1985, when the Chapter 11 petition was filed the number of such suits arising out of the continued sale and use of the Dalkon Shield device earlier put into the stream of commerce by Robins had grown to 5,000. More than half of these pending cases named Robins as the sole defendant; a codefendant or codefendants were named in the others. Prior to the filing, a number of suits had been tried and, while Robins had prevailed in some of the actions, judgments in large and burdensome amounts had been recovered in others. Many more had been settled.[4] Moreover, the costs of defending these suits both to Robins and to its insurance carrier had risen into the millions. A large amount of the time and energies of Robins' officers and executives was also being absorbed in preparing material for trial and in attending and testifying at depositions and trials. The problems arising out of this mounting tide of claims and suits precipitated this Chapter 11 proceeding. . . .

The . . . appeal questions the validity of the district court's order of November 9, 1985, fixing the venue for the trial of all Dalkon Shield cases and providing for the transfer of such cases to the District Court of the Eastern District of Virginia at Richmond. . . .

[The court first held that the order was immediately appealable.]

Turning to the merits of the appeal . . ., we address first the power of the district court, sitting in bankruptcy, to enter an order fixing the venue for the trial of tort personal injury claims against the debtor and for transferring all such cases to the bankruptcy court for trial and disposition.

---

4. . . . A recent article . . . states that by mid 1985, Robins, along with its insurer, Aetna Casualty & Surety Company, "had paid roughly $517 million for 25 trial judgments and 9,300 settlements since the first verdict in 1975."

. . . We do not understand the appellants to contend that under [28 U.S.C.§ 157(b)(5)] the district court did not have authority . . . to issue an order fixing the venue for trial of cases against a Chapter 11 debtor. They do argue, however, that the sense of the section, if not its precise language, was to decentralize the trial of these tort claims and to permit their continuance for trial in the court in which the complaints were filed and that the ruling of the district judge in this case fixing venue in the district court in which the bankruptcy petition was filed flies in the face of this congressional purpose. . . . [T]o accept the view of the appellants on the construction of the statute would be completely at variance with the House version of the bill, which was in effect accepted by the Conference Committee, and would be to adopt the Senate version, which, according to Congressman Kastenmeier's statement as a House Conference member, was "largely reject[ed]" by the Conference Committee and "would have dissipated the assets of the estate by creating a multiplicity of forums for the adjudication of parts of a bankruptcy case." . . .

The primary point of difference between the parties, however, relates not so much to the power of the district court in this case to fix venue for all the pending Dalkon Shield tort cases — that power is stated in unmistakable terms in section 157(b)(5) — but to the manner in which that power may be exercised. Concededly, section 157(b)(5) does not prescribe any procedure. The appellants suggest that the procedure to be followed is laid out in 28 U.S.C. § 1412, which provides that "[a] district court may transfer a case or proceeding under title 11 to a district court for another district, in the interest of justice or for the convenience of the parties." As the appellants correctly construe section 1412, the authority to transfer a suit under that statute rests solely with the court in which the suit is pending and it provides no authority whatsoever to a district court sitting in bankruptcy in one district and having jurisdiction of the bankruptcy to transfer the venue of a case against the bankrupt to another district. Section 157(b)(5), however, expressly confers on the district court sitting in bankruptcy and having jurisdiction of the bankruptcy proceedings the power to fix the venue of any tort case against the debtor pending in other districts. The purpose of this latter statute was . . . to centralize the administration of the estate and to eliminate the "multiplicity of forums for the adjudication of parts of a bankruptcy case." That purpose would be thwarted and the plain language of section 157(b)(5) nullified if the power of the district court sitting in bankruptcy to fix the venue for tort claims against a debtor was to be preempted by the provisions of section 1412. We do not believe this to have been the intention of Congress in enacting the two statutes. Section 157(b)(5) was drafted to cover the procedure in connection with a special group of cases, to wit, personal injury tort claims against a debtor in Chapter 11 proceedings wherever pending and in that connection the section is supreme. In all other cases related to the bankruptcy proceedings, however, the general statute (i.e., section 1412) would govern. . . . We, therefore, have no difficulty in finding that the district judge's authority to fix venue of personal injury tort actions against the debtor exists under § 157(b)(5), irrespective of the district in which such controversy is pending.

And there are very real considerations that support a centralization of all the Dalkon Shield claims, *at least at first*, in the district court having jurisdiction of the bankruptcy. The "single focal point" of this proceeding is the development of a reasonable plan of reorganization for the debtor, one which will work a rehabilitation of the debtor and at the same time assure fair and non-preferential resolution of the Dalkon Shield claims. These Dalkon Shield claims, asserted by thousands of individuals in courts throughout the United States on behalf of both citizens of this country and citizens or residents of other countries, represent what are characterized in the Act as "contingent or unliquidated claims." 11 U.S.C. § 502. Ordinarily such claims would be "estimated" by the bankruptcy court as a "core proceeding," 28 U.S.C. § 157(b)(2), for purpose of allowance if failure to do so "would unduly delay the administration of the case." 11 U.S.C. § 502(c). That duty of estimation in a proper case under section 502(c) is not a permissive one; it is a mandatory obligation of the bankruptcy court. This customary process of estimation of contingent claims is, however, different where the unliquidated, contingent claims are personal injury tort claims.

Section 157(b)(2)(B) excepts from the definition of "core proceedings" personal tort claims against the debtor. The bankruptcy court thus is without authority under the Act over "the liquidation or estimation of contingent or unliquidated personal injury or wrongful death claims against the estate for purposes of *distribution* under Title 11[.]" 28 U.S.C. § 157(b)(2)(B). (Italics added[.]) It will be observed, however, that the statute denies authority to the bankruptcy court to "estimate" contingent claims only if the purpose is to make a "distribution" of the assets of the debtor; the statute does not in express terms deny to the bankruptcy court the authority, or relieve it of the duty, to "estimate" the contingent "personal injury" claims for purposes of determining the feasibility of a reorganization. . . .

This is not to say the personal injury claimants in this proceeding will not be ultimately entitled, if they elect to do so, to have a jury trial of their claim in the district court. Section 157(b)(5) gives them that right. But, even though the tort claimants may be entitled to their jury trials, the bankruptcy court is not relieved of its duty in a Chapter 11 proceeding to estimate those contingent claims. The real question thus arises as to which proceedings take precedence, whether the estimation by the bankruptcy court of the claims or the jury trials in the district court of the claims. The authorities which have considered this question in connection with a complicated products liability situation such as this are all unanimous. The estimations of the potential and pending claims by the bankruptcy courts should precede any trials of the claims. . . . After all, the first and primary purpose of the proceedings . . . is to ascertain whether a fair reorganization of the debtor can be achieved. This purpose may well be thwarted if the energies of the debtor's executives and officers are initially diverted by, and the resources of the debtor dissipated in the expenses of litigating, the trial of thousands of personal injury suits in courts throughout the land spread over an interminable period of time. . . .

There are 5,000 suits pending against the debtors in this proceeding. There are perhaps an equal number not filed. If all these claims were to be tried, the expense of discovery proceedings and trial would likely consume all the assets of the debtor and exhaust all the resources of its executives and employees. . . . Since the Dalkon Shield litigation began, forty claims have actually been tried but over $517,000,000 have been expended in defending or settling Dalkon Shield suits or claims. It is impossible to anticipate the stupendous costs that would be involved if all the claims here had to be tried. If the claimants as a whole are to realize reasonable compensation for their claims, it is obviously in the interest of the class of claimants as a whole to obviate the tremendous expense of trying these cases separately. If the bankruptcy court could arrive at a fair estimation of the value of all the claims and submit a fair plan of reorganization based on such estimation, with some mechanism for dispute resolution and acceptable to all interested parties, great benefit to all the claimants could be achieved and the excessive expense of innumerable trials, stretching over an interminable time, could be avoided. In addition, the real purpose of the proceeding (i.e., a reorganization of the debtor and its continuance as a going business) could be attained.

It is manifest, of course, that the process of estimation will involve some examination of the claims. But this examination will be conducted by the court, will likely not involve duplicative discovery, and can be accomplished expeditiously. . . .

No progress along estimating these contingent claims, however, can be made until all Dalkon Shield claims and suits are centralized before a single forum where all interests can be heard and in which the interests of all claimants with one another may be harmonized. . . . We approve of the idea and find it conducive of the interests of all concerned.

[The court then held that the Due Process Clause required "notice and opportunity for a hearing before there can be a change of venue and before trial of a personal injury tort cause of action against a debtor may be transferred *finally* from the court in which the cause was initially filed to the district where the bankruptcy proceedings are pending." Because no notice was given to the individual Dalkon Shield claimants, but was instead given only to a Committee of Representatives of Dalkon Shield Claimants created in the bankruptcy proceeding, the court of appeals concluded that the district court's transfer order needed to be modified to give Dalkon Shield claimants individual notice, an opportunity to object, and an opportunity to be heard "before the order became final in any case where the plaintiff has filed an objection."]

We do not presume to suggest rigid guidelines for the district judge to follow when considering objections to the transfer. We believe it important, however, to observe that although there may be distinct advantages of the tort claims being transferred to Richmond, those advantages should be balanced against the disadvantages that may be advanced at the hearing.

In that regard, some cases may be fully prepared and ready for state trial. Some cases may require substantial numbers of local witnesses. Claimants may be receiving critical medical, physical or psychological care in a local area which would have to be halted or transferred to Richmond. All of these factors are relevant. Moreover, there are issues of state law that may substantially affect the results in individual cases.

In summary, we . . . remand with directions the order fixing venue for all pending suits against the debtor and transferring the suits to the district court before which the bankruptcy proceedings were pending.

Notes

1.   *WorldCom*, which was a small skirmish in the largest bankruptcy up to that point in history, and *Piccinin*, which involved one of the largest bankruptcies of its day, show how it is possible to aggregate related cases, at least temporarily, in a single forum. But the limits of their holdings also show how aggregation is far from automatic.

2.   To some extent, the jurisdictional and venue issues discussed in *WorldCom* and *Piccinin* are less critical because of the automatic stay and the discharge in bankruptcy. Between them, they stop dispersed litigation against a debtor and effectively force claimants with existing claims against the debtor to file claims in the bankruptcy forum. Therefore, jurisdictional and venue issues often have greater bite in the context of cases against co-defendants of the debtor, a subject we study in the following subsection. Nonetheless, because the stay can be lifted (and, even if it is not, is ends after the bankruptcy has concluded), and because the discharge does not cover all debts, aggregating related claims against the debtor in the bankruptcy forum is still a desirable goal, as *WorldCom* shows.

3.   *WorldCom* shows that a debtor can overcome the jurisdictional dispersion of claims through removal under 28 U.S.C. § 1452. Under the broad power of this section, core proceedings, as well as civil proceedings and "related to" cases, can be removed without the restrictions that we saw in some other removal statutes. *See* In re WorldCom, Inc. Sec. Litig., 293 B.R. 308 (S.D.N.Y. 2003) (holding that, unlike § 1441(a), § 1452(a) does not require unanimous consent of the defendants to removal, and that parties other than the defendant are allowed to remove).

Nonetheless, before the federal court can claim jurisdiction, the case must run a gauntlet. First as *WorldCom* shows, the removed case must navigate the abstention provisions in §§ 1334(c) and 1452(b). In some courts this task is made easier: Because the removal provisions of § 1452 are separate from the original jurisdiction granted in § 1334, a minority of courts have held that the mandatory-abstention provisions of § 1334(c)(2) do not apply to removed actions. *See* In re Adelphia Comm'ns Corp., 285 B.R. 127 (Bankr. S.D.N.Y. 2002) (collecting cases on both sides; holding that mandatory abstention is inapplicable in a removed case). This holding is not especially significant in cases by or against the debtor — the cases that are the focus of this subsection. The reason is that cases by or against a debtor will almost always be core proceedings, and § 1334(c)(2) requires abstention only in non-core "related to" proceedings — and even then, only when the case can be "timely adjudicated" in a state court.

WorldCom addresses the more nettlesome discretionary-abstention and equitable-remand provisions found, respectively, in §§ 1334(c)(1) and 1452(b). *WorldCom* treats these provisions as fungible, suggesting that the same considerations apply to both statutes. Other courts also conflate the two statutes, arguing that a case meeting the terms for remand under § 1334(c)(1) presents "an 'equitable ground' justifying remand under § 1452(b)." Stoe v. Flaherty, 436 F.3d 209, 215 (3d Cir. 2006); In re Nat'l Century Fin. Enters., Inc., Inv. Litig., 323 F. Supp. 2d 861, 885 (S.D. Ohio 2004). The seven factors that *WorldCom* lists as being relevant to the abstention/remand inquiry are often cited in other cases. *See* In re Ameribuild Constr. Mgmt., Inc., 399 B.R. 129, 134 (Bankr. S.D.N.Y. 2009); *see also* In re Coleman, 200 B.R. 403, 406 (Bankr. S.D. Ala. 1996) (also mentioning as factors "[w]hether judicial resources will be duplicated"; "[w]hat is the most economical use of judicial resources"; "[w]hether the possibility of an inconsistent result is lessened by remand"; and "[t]he expertise of the court where action originated"); *National Century*, 323 F. Supp. 2d at 885 (listing thirteen factors).

4. Certain securities cases present unique removal issues. *See* Cal. Pub. Employees' Ret. Sys. v. WorldCom, Inc., 368 F.3d 86 (2d Cir. 2004) (holding that § 1452(a) prevailed over Section 22(a) of the Securities Act of 1933, which prevents removal of certain securities cases; recognizing split in authority).

5. Can a bankruptcy court order removal, using the broad injunctive power contained in 11 U.S.C. § 105(a)? *Cf.* Celotex Corp. v. Edwards, 514 U.S. 300, 329 (1995) (Stevens, J., dissenting) (arguing that § 105 could not be used to enjoin other courts); In re Cont'l Airlines, 203 F.3d 203, 211 (3d Cir. 2000) (*infra* p. 604) (holding that bankruptcy court could not transfer a case to a state court in which the case had not commenced; noting that "section 105(a) . . . does not create substantive rights that would otherwise be unavailable under the Bankruptcy Code") (quotation marks omitted); Fraidin v. Stutz, 515 A.2d 775 (Md. Ct. Spec. App. 1987) (holding that a state-court judge could not order transfer of case to bankruptcy court).

6. Once the jurisdictional issues are settled, venue issues arise. In *WorldCom* the district court used § 1412 to transfer the case to the court in which bankruptcy proceedings were pending against the debtor. When many cases are pending against the debtor around the country, this transfer process can be onerous because the party seeking aggregation in the bankruptcy forum must move for transfer in each other court. Due to the equitable nature of the § 1412 transfer decision, complete success of the motion in every court is hardly guaranteed. *See* Unico Holdings, Inc. v. Nutramax Prods., Inc., 264 B.R. 779 (Bankr. S.D. Fla. 2001) (denying transfer to bankruptcy forum and ordering remand to state court when the case was nearing conclusion in state court and most of the evidence was

located in that state). Moreover, § 1412 transfer is a two-edged sword, and can be used to transfer cases out of the bankruptcy forum. *Cf.* In re Enron Corp., 317 B.R. 629 (Bankr. S.D.N.Y. 2004) (declining to order transfer).

7. As *Piccinin* shows, courts have a special venue provision for tort cases: 28 U.S.C. § 157(b)(5). Notwithstanding the plaintiffs' arguments in *Piccinin*, § 157(b)(5) clearly gives district judges the power to consolidate tort cases against the debtor in the bankruptcy forum. *See also* In re Dow Corning Corp., 86 F.3d 482 (6th Cir. 1996) (adopting *Piccinin*'s analysis). Can *Piccinin*'s use of § 157(b)(5) nonetheless be criticized because it in effect gives a bankruptcy court the ability to create a "quasi-class-action" only for mass-tort bankruptcies? *Cf.* RICHARD B. SOBOL, BENDING THE LAW: THE STORY OF THE DALKON SHIELD BANKRUPTCY 326 (1991) (criticizing the use of bankruptcy as a substitute for mandatory class actions).

Should district judges have this power only for tort cases? Why must parties rely on § 1412, under which the judge in the transferor forum decides on transfer, except in tort cases, for which § 157(b)(5) provides the transferee judge with the transfer power? The lack of a bankruptcy court's general transfer power is to some extent alleviated by the MDL process: The Judicial Panel on Multidistrict Litigation can transfer cases meeting § 1407's standards to the district handling the bankruptcy proceeding. *See* In re WorldCom, Inc., Sec. Litig., 308 F. Supp. 2d 236, 241 (S.D.N.Y. 2004) (mentioning the MDL transfer of ten cases against the debtor); *cf.* In re Asbestos Bankruptcy Litig., 1992 WL 423943 (J.P.M.L. Dec. 9, 1992) (declining to order the transfer of bankruptcy proceedings against eight asbestos defendants into the asbestos MDL). Does the injunctive power in 11 U.S.C. § 105(a) provide a vehicle through which the bankruptcy court can transfer non-tort cases to the bankruptcy forum? *See* In re Interlink Home Health Care, Inc., 283 B.R. 429 (Bkrtcy. N.D. Tex. 2002) (holding that § 105(a) gave a bankruptcy court no power to order another court to transfer related bankruptcy proceedings pending in the other court). *Cf.* In re BWP Gas, LLC, 354 B.R. 701 (E.D. Pa. 2006) (holding that § 105(a) created no power to transfer a case to a state court in which the case had not commenced).

8. *Piccinin* shows that a § 157(b)(5) transfer is fragile. Although the related cases can be preliminarily consolidated for purposes of trying to work out a reorganization plan, the decision implies that the cases should ordinarily be returned to the original forum for trial.

9. *Piccinin* argues that one reason for consolidating cases is to assist the court in the process of estimating the plaintiffs' claims. The estimation process is critical in a Chapter 11 reorganization. Until the parties and the court have a sense of the number and value of unliquidated, contingent claims like tort claims, it is impossible to prepare an adequate disclosure to voting classes, to determine whether a class of creditors has voted to accept the reorganization plan, to see if the plan is fair and adequate, or to distribute assets. In a standard bankruptcy, the court does not estimate claims. Rather, the appropriate courts try the claim, thereby reducing them to a value certain. But in a mass-tort bankruptcy, a trial of each claim

against the debtor would take incredibly long and would be tremendously costly. The following case, which also involves the *Dalkon Shield* bankruptcy, considers whether it is possible to overcome this problem and to approve a reorganization plan that proposes to resolve mass numbers of claims without individual litigation. The successful use of bankruptcy as an aggregation mechanism hinges on the answer.

IN RE A.H. ROBINS CO.

880 F.2d 694 (4th Cir. 1989)

■ WIDENER, Circuit Judge.

On July 26, 1988, the bankruptcy court and the district court jointly confirmed the "Sixth Amended and Restated Plan of Reorganization" (the Plan) submitted by A.H. Robins Company, Inc. (Robins). Rosemary Menard-Sanford and certain other personal injury claimants, who voted against the Plan, appeal. They challenge the district court's approval of the disclosure statement, the district court's use of a one claimant one vote voting procedure, [and] the district court's feasibility finding . . . . We affirm. . . .

On April 1, 1988, the district court approved the "Sixth Amended and Restated Disclosure Statement". The appellants argue that the disclosure statement does not contain adequate information. 11 U.S.C. § 1125(b) requires that before solicitation of approval or disagreement of a plan of reorganization the disclosure statement must contain "adequate information" and be approved by the court. 11 U.S.C. § 1125(a)(1) defines "adequate information" as "information of a kind, and in sufficient detail, as far as is reasonably practicable in light of the nature and history of the debtor and the condition of the debtor's books and records, that would enable a hypothetical reasonable investor typical of holders of claims or interests of the relevant class to make an informed judgment about the plan." The determination of whether the disclosure statement has adequate information is made on a case by case basis and is largely within the discretion of the bankruptcy court. The challenged disclosure statement began its 261 pages of information with a thorough summary of the complex plan in terms that almost anyone could understand. It explained, among much more, the amount to be put into trust and made available for the payment of claims, the various estimates of how much money was required, a warning that the funds furnished to pay the estimates might not be enough to pay all claims in full, the sources of funding, an explanation of the various funding provisions which depended on the outcome of various appeals, how claims would be handled, the four options for processing claims and the background of the case. . . .

The appellants' principal challenge to the disclosure statement . . . is that it is inadequate because it does not contain ranges of recovery for claimants with specified injuries. . . . There is no requirement in case law or statute that a disclosure statement estimate the value of specific unliquidated tort claims. In fact, with so many various unliquidated personal injury claims which vary so much in the extent and nature of injury, medical evidence and causation factors, any specific estimates may well have been more confusing than helpful and certainly would be more calculated to mislead. Given the quantity and quality of the information in the disclosure statement we can not say that the district court abused its discretion in finding that it contained "adequate information."

The appellants next challenge the legality of the voting procedure used to confirm the Plan. The difficulty surrounding the voting procedure resulted from the 195,000 unliquidated claims for personal injuries (Dalkon Shield Claims). The controlling legal provisions for the reorganization include 11 U.S.C. § 1126(a) which provides that a "holder of a claim or interest allowed under section 502 of this title" is entitled to vote on the acceptance of a plan. 11 U.S.C. § 502(a) provides that a claim filed "is deemed allowed unless a party in interest" objects. Robins objected to all the Dalkon Shield Claims. [Bankruptcy Rule] 3018(a) provides that "[n]otwithstanding objection to a claim or interest, the court after notice and hearing may temporarily allow the claim or interest in an amount which the court deems proper for the purpose of accepting or rejecting a plan." The district court, after notice and a hearing, ordered that, for purposes of voting, each Dalkon Shield Claim was estimated and allowed to be equal. It found, fully supported by the record, that any attempt to evaluate each of the 195,000 individual claims for voting purposes would cause intolerable delay. The challenge to the voting procedure relies on 11 U.S.C. § 1126(c) which requires that for a plan to be approved by a class the creditors "that hold at least two-thirds in amount and more than one-half in number" accept the plan. The argument is that § 1126(c) requires use of a weighted voting method which estimates the value of the claims and gives larger claims more votes.

We do not decide whether the district court's voting procedure violated § 1126(c) because, in view of the outcome of the vote, the challenged procedure was at most harmless error. 139,605 claimants voted. Of that 131,761 (94.38%) voted in favor of the Plan. . . . Given that 94.38% of the Dalkon Shield Claimants voted for the Plan, we hold that, at most, harmless error was committed.[3]

Appellants' next point on appeal is that the district court erred in finding that the Plan complied with 11 U.S.C. § 1129(a)(7)(A)(ii) which requires that an impaired class of claims such as the Dalkon Shield

---

3. We are not persuaded by the argument that the 5.62% NO votes were from the claimants with the largest claims, that being necessary of course to make up more than one-third of the claims in amount. The argument goes that such claimants have the most to gain from a rejection of the Plan, but that proposition, we think, is not only supported by no evidence, it is not supported by logic, and is no more likely than the fact that the largest claimants have the most to lose by a rejection of the Plan. . . . [W]ith a rejection of the Plan which resulted in liquidation, the largest claimants would be the biggest losers. . . .

claimants must "receive . . . under the Plan . . . property of a value . . . that is not less than the amount that . . . [they would] receive . . . if the debtor were liquidated under Chapter 7" and § 1129(a)(11) which requires that confirmation is not likely to be followed by liquidation or the need for further reorganization. This latter is called the feasibility requirement.

Both such complaints are based on the "same source: the failure of the district court to break out the components of the $2.475 billion figure."[*] The argument is that since the figure was not broken down, if it turned out to be too low, then the Plan would not be feasible because it could not pay all the claimants in full, which, as the appellants note, is an assumption of the Plan and the disclosure statement. . . . [W]e think there is no merit to the claim, but that the care the district court took in arriving at its estimate deserves mention.

. . . To assist in the estimation process, the district court appointed Professor Francis E. McGovern, who was familiar with such matters, as the court's expert to develop a data base regarding Dalkon Shield Claims. The Dalkon Shield Claimant's Committee, the Unsecured Creditor's Committee, the Future Claimant's Representative, the Equity Security Holder's Committee, Robins and Aetna all had experts to assist Professor McGovern. The data base included the results of a two page "Dalkon Shield Questionnaire and Claim Form" from more than 195,000 claimants. It also contained roughly 6,000 responses to a fifty page, "McGovern Survey Questionnaire" and medical records from a random sample of 7,500 claimants. The data collection process lasted more than a year and a half. Each of the experts hired by the various parties used the basic data in various ways to arrive at an estimation.

The district court conducted an estimation hearing from November 5, 1987 to November 11, 1987. At the hearing the parties' various experts testified. The district court considered that the testimony of the various experts estimated the claims as follows: Robins' — .8 to 1.3 billion, Equity Security Holders' — 1.03 billion, Unsecured Creditors' — 1.54 billion, Aetna's' — 2.2 to 2.5 billion, and the Dalkon Shield Claimants' — 4.2 to 7 billion. The district court decided that the proper estimate was 2.475 billion. . . .

. . . [T]he district court entered a bar date on claims and prescribed a very informal method of advising the court that a claim was being filed. The bar date of course limited the potential claimants. From these potential claimants, there were eliminated, by standard statistical and analytical methods, about one-third of the initial claims which had been filed. A detailed analysis of those claims not eliminated was performed by sending the detailed questionnaire previously mentioned to a randomly selected sample of several thousand of the claims remaining. The questionnaire asked for information, which, in the most general sense, was received back, concerning the insertion of the Dalkon Shield in the claimant

---

[*] The $2.475 billion figure was the district court's estimate of the total value of all the Dalkon Shield claims that could be asserted against Robins. — ED.

and the nature of the claimant's injuries, including verification by way of medical records where possible.

A detailed analysis of all of the responses was then performed by the expert witnesses who testified in the case. A good example of competent testimony was that of Dr. Francine F. Rabinovitz, who testified on behalf of Aetna. [Dr. Rabinovitz' methods led her to conclude that the proper range lay between $2.0 and $2.5 billion with a $2.2 billion to $2.3 billion range as most likely.]

From our brief recital of a small part of the evidence before the district court, we see that its finding of 2.475 billion dollars as the estimate to include all Dalkon Shield claims is not clearly erroneous . . . . Indeed, we think the district court would have been quite justified in accepting Dr. Rabinovitz' testimony, so appellants may not complain about the district court's arrival at a somewhat higher figure. . . .

The orders of the district court appealed from are accordingly affirmed.

Notes

1.   The estimation method outlined in *Robins* is described more fully in Francis E. McGovern, *Resolving Mature Mass Torts*, 69 B.U. L. REV. 659 (1989). After collecting information from present claimants in bankruptcy, Professor McGovern correlating the data with data for past Dalkon Shield users, and then extrapolated the results to the universe of Dalkon Shield claimants. The experts for each party were then able to estimate a value for the tort claims as a whole. This approach to estimation required, to use McGovern's phrase, a "mature mass tort," in which good data on a large number of past judgments and settlements exist. What happens when the absolute numbers are inadequate or the quality of the data is too poor to make the necessary statistical inferences?

2.   In *Robins*, the Fourth Circuit applauded the McGovern approach to estimation. Let us, however, raise some problems. First, note that the range of estimates (from Robins' estimates to that of the claimants) varied by a factor of ten, which suggests that the process is imprecise and leaves considerable latitude for the judge sitting in bankruptcy to impose his or her own view of a fair figure. Second, the estimation process was hardly free of flaws. Of 6,340 claimants surveyed, 2,000 were not eligible to participate in the fund, and the survey garnered only a 65% response rate — facts that gave the statisticians room to maneuver. *See* RICHARD B. SOBOL, BENDING THE LAW: THE STORY OF THE DALKON SHIELD BANKRUPTCY 176, 184 (1991). Similarly, the McGovern method did not address the actual number of Dalkon Shield claimants that could prevail against Robins, and the experts varied widely in their opinions about this number. *See id.* at 183; RONALD J. BACIGAL, THE LIMITS OF LITIGATION 99-102 (1990). Third, the statistical experts did not always inspire confidence. For instance, one expert stated that a particular hypothetical claimant with certain characteristics should receive $5,000 based on the proposed

settlement formula. The actual plaintiff after whom the hypothetical claimant was modeled had received $710,000. BACIGAL, *supra*, at 102. Fourth, Judge Merhige, who presided over the estimation hearing, adamantly refused to allow Dalkon Shield victims to testify. In fact, he did not even want them in the courtroom. SOBOL, *supra*, at 179-80.

3. The Robins' reorganization plan created a claims-resolution facility that provided scheduled benefits to claimants. The level of benefit depended on the amount of evidence that the claimant submitted and the degree of the claimant's injury. One option for claimants willing to run a gauntlet of efforts designed to settle the dispute and to risk a loss of any benefits was a trial. As it turned out, few claimants went all the way to trial; effectively, therefore, the plan's claims-resolution methods resolved virtually all of the tort claims outside of the judicial system.

When we come to the issue of trial complexity, we will see that, with some exceptions, most courts have been unreceptive to using a comparable "trial by statistics" method — in which all individual claimants receive an average value calculated from a statistical sampling of comparable claims — to resolve mass-tort controversies that are not in bankruptcy. *See infra* p. 1058. Among the courts' reasons for not adopting this method are the hostility of the relevant substantive law to this approach, the loss of the right to jury trial, and the damage that this method causes to the adversarial right to present individualized proofs and arguments. Should we permit in bankruptcy a dispute-resolution method that has been largely rejected in non-bankruptcy contexts? If we do, bankruptcy becomes an even more important avenue for the aggregation and resolution of complex cases. On the other hand, is the reorganization of a debtor an adequate reason for creating differential procedural treatment?

4. One response to these concerns is to say that bankruptcy claimants are free to give up their rights to individualized adversarial procedure if they desire. If Dalkon Shield claimants wanted individual trials, they could have voted the plan down. But this response is somewhat disingenuous. The claimants had no choice about their collectivization for purposes of estimation. Once the estimation had occurred, and a reorganization plan had been proposed, all the momentum shifted toward accepting the plan.

Moreover, this response is only as valid as the legitimacy and accuracy of the voting procedures. The basic problem with voting is the requirement of 11 U.S.C. § 1126(c): that creditors who hold "at least two-thirds in amount" of the allowed claims for a particular class must accept the plan in order for the class as a whole to accept the plan. How could the judge know whether "two-thirds in amount" of the Dalkon Shield claimants had accepted the plan without trials through which the value of each claimant's claim would be established? The Fourth Circuit had two replies, neither entirely adequate. First, the court suggested that the district court could set any "proper" amount as the value of their claims because Robins had objected to them. *See* FED. R. BANKR. P. 3018(a). But this argument begs the question about what is a "proper" amount. When there is an objection, 11 U.S.C. § 502(b) says that the court, "after notice and a hearing, shall determine the amount of such claim . . . and shall allow such claim in such amount except to the extent . . . such claim is unenforceable against the debtor and property of the debtor." The only alternative to § 502(b) is § 502(c), which allows a court sitting in bankruptcy to "estimate[ ] for purpose of allowance" contingent claims (such as tort claims) whose precise allowance "would unduly delay administration of the case." Nothing in Rule 3018(a), § 502(b), or § 502(c) allows the court to make up a value for a claim out of thin air; the $1 value must have some reasonable basis. Hence, we are back to square one: How do we establish a proper value?

Second, the Fourth Circuit upheld the district court's decision to treat each claim as having an equal value; since 94% of the votes favored reorganization, this assumption meant that the court could say that 94% of the value of the class also supported the reorganization. Doesn't this assumption, which equates voting right with value, fly in the face of Congress' decision to distinguish these two facts by requiring half of the votes and two-thirds of the value to approve a plan? As a practical matter, this solution also had problems:

> The vast majority of the women eligible to vote within the class of Dalkon Shield claimants — some 94 percent according to a study performed for Robins — had not and would not have made a claim against the company outside of bankruptcy. Many had only minor or insupportable claims, and would be glad to accept a plan that offered them a quick, albeit small, payment without proof of Dalkon Shield use or injury. An estimated 35,000 of the eligible voters — potential future claimants who responded to the notice — did not even claim to have suffered an injury. [SOBOL, *supra*, at 228.]

There is an amazing correspondence between the 94% of claimants unlikely to sue and the 94% of claimants who voted to accept the plan. Was it the same 94%? Should the court have checked? At a minimum, should the court have tried to get a rough sense of the value of the claims that were voting for and against the plan? *See* SOBOL, *supra*, at 329 ("If it is too difficult or too burdensome to conduct a vote that accords claimants a voice in that decision in proportion to the size of their claims, as required by the Bankruptcy Code, the appropriate conclusion is that there can be no effective waiver of the right to absolute priority, not that it can be waived under some lesser standard."). *Cf.* In re Quigley, 346 B.R. 647 (Bankr. S.D.N.Y. 2006) (using equal-value and weighted-value methods to calculate vote totals; finding that, under either method, the plan was approved).

The "equal-value" approach does make it easier to dispose of related cases in a single forum, and is consistent in spirit, if not in precise language, with the Bankruptcy Code's "strong preference for facilitating reorganizations." *See* Kane v. Johns-Manville Corp., 843 F.2d 636, 647 (2d Cir. 1988) (finding that use of "vote equals value" rule was "harmless error" when 95.8% of class claimants voted to approve reorganization plan).

5.   A judge can establish as many or as few classes of creditors and interests as the judge deems expedient, as long as a single class contains claims that are "substantially similar" to each other. 11 U.S.C. § 1122(a).

The way in which these classes are established can have a significant effect on the chances for a plan's confirmation. In *Robins* Judge Merhige put all the Dalkon Shield claimants into one class. Had he broken them into two classes — dividing the more seriously injured women from the less seriously injured — it is possible that the former class would have voted down the reorganization plan. This created a problem, because two key elements of Robins' bankruptcy plan — a limited fund from which Dalkon Shield claimants would seek compensation, and providing Robins' stockholders with $900 million in excess value, *see* SOBOL, *supra,* at 327-28 — violated the absolute-priority rule of Chapter 11, making it impossible for Judge Merhige to cram down the reorganization plan if any impaired class of creditors or interests opposed it. In a very real sense, the organization of voting classes determined the outcome of the *Robins* reorganization.

Should Judge Merhige have put all the Dalkon Shield victims in a single class? If this had been a class action which requires adequacy of representation, the two types of claimants might have needed separate representation. *Cf.* In re Joint E. & S. Dists. Asbestos Litig., 982 F.2d 721 (2d Cir. 1992), *modified,* 993 F.2d 7 (2d Cir. 1993) (requiring separate subclass for asbestos victims unlikely to be paid under a settlement). Because adequacy of representation is grounded in due process, might due process constrain a judge's ability to organize classes of claims and interests for purposes of voting? Does it concern you that judges in bankruptcy have discretion to organize interests to facilitate or hinder reorganization plans?

6. With its low administrative expenses, the Dalkon Shield Trust, which the plan established to compensate tort victims, ended up with a $1 billion excess. The district court ordered this money distributed on a pro rata basis to claimants who had submitted a certain level of proof, resulting in additional payments of about 75% of the original payments. *See* In re A.H. Robins Co., 86 F.3d 364 (4th Cir. 1996). Does the ultimate outcome of *Dalkon Shield* convince you that the bankruptcy solution was a good one?

7. Judge Merhige did not refer most aspects of Robins' reorganization to the bankruptcy court, a decision that guaranteed a single forum for resolution of the issues. Many of the tactics Judge Merhige used to ensure that the plan was approved are described, not entirely favorably, in SOBOL, *supra,* and BACIGAL, *supra.* This was Professor Bacigal's final assessment:

> While eschewing the activist label, Judge Merhige concedes that he "actively" adjusted the exercise of his judicial power to meet the conflicting demands of the litigants. At various stages of the proceedings the judge played the part of coercive mediator, courtroom tyrant, guardian of the victims, social conscience of corporate America, and practical businessman. The judge's role in the litigation is far removed from the classic image of trial judges as umpires or arbiters who merely react to the issues as framed by the litigants. Nonetheless, Judge Merhige insists that the propriety of his role in the case must be measured by the ultimate success or failure of the settlement trust fund in bringing the maximum equitable compensation to the maximum number of victims. [BACIGAL, *supra,* at 126.]

2. Using the Bankruptcy Forum to Aggregate Cases and Claims Against Other Defendants

Most complex litigation involves more than one defendant. If bankruptcy is able to aggregate only the claims against the debtor, it is an inadequate tool. Indeed, it creates the likelihood of disparate treatment among defendants, and it means that plaintiffs need to bear the cost of two sets of proceedings for the same injury.

This section examines whether it is ever possible to use bankruptcy to aggregate cases against a debtor with related cases against non-debtor defendants. From the standpoint of aggregation, using bankruptcy in this fashion presents an opportunity to achieve optimal joinder of related claims. From the standpoint of bankruptcy, this use threatens to create a Janus-faced proceeding in which the debtor's rehabilitation is a sideshow. Is bankruptcy doctrine flexible enough to achieve aggregation when (and only when) it is socially optimal to do so? Does such aggregation come at too high a price for bankruptcy policy? These are the central questions of this subsection, which examines whether a judge sitting in bankruptcy has jurisdiction over cases against co-defendants, whether the judge can transfer these related cases to the bankruptcy forum, and whether the judge can stay other courts from proceeding with related cases.

IN RE FEDERAL-MOGUL GLOBAL, INC.

300 F.3d 368 (3d Cir. 2002)

■ SLOVITER, Circuit Judge.

Before us is an appeal of the District Court's decision denying the motion to transfer tens of thousands of asbestos-related tort claims and remanding these claims to the state courts where they were originally filed, primarily on the ground that the District Court had no subject[-]matter jurisdiction. The appellants, who moved for the transfer in the District Court, argue that the District Court has subject-matter jurisdiction over these claims because they are "related to" the ongoing bankruptcy proceeding of Federal-Mogul Global . . . . The central issue before us is whether this court has jurisdiction to review the District Court's decision to deny the transfer and to remand.

I. BACKGROUND

A. *Procedural Posture*

Tens of thousands of individuals (Friction Product Plaintiffs or Plaintiffs) have brought personal injury and wrongful death claims in state courts across the country seeking damages for injuries allegedly caused by asbestos used in so-called friction products, such as brake pads (Friction

Product Claims). The Friction Product Plaintiffs allege that they were exposed to asbestos fibers through, *inter alia*, the manufacture, installation, repair, and/or use of friction products and that this exposure caused them or their decedents to develop severe respiratory diseases, such as asbestos-related mesothelioma, asbestos-related lung, laryngeal or esophageal cancer, or asbestosis. They have brought their tort claims against various manufacturers and distributors of friction products (including Federal-Mogul Global, Inc., which had acquired Apex and Wagner, makers of friction products) as well as against companies that made and sold products that incorporated friction products (in particular, automobile manufacturers that used brake pads containing asbestos).

On October 1, 2001, Federal-Mogul and its 156 affiliates and subsidiaries (Debtors) filed Chapter 11 petitions in the United States Bankruptcy Court for the District of Delaware. At that time, Debtors were co-defendants in many (though not all) of the thousands of Friction Product Claims now before us. The filing of the Debtors' Chapter 11 petitions stayed the state court proceedings as to them.

Thereafter, the Friction Product Plaintiffs began severing or dismissing their claims against Debtors. Other defendants named in the Friction Product suits (Friction Product Defendants or Defendants) began removing the claims against them from state courts to the appropriate federal district courts pursuant to 28 U.S.C. § 1452(a) (bankruptcy removal), arguing that the Friction Product Claims were "related to" the Debtors' bankruptcy proceeding and thus subject to the bankruptcy jurisdiction of the federal courts under 28 U.S.C. § 1334(b). The primary theory in support of "related to" jurisdiction is that the Friction Product Defendants would be able to seek indemnification or contribution from Debtors because some of the friction products used by Defendants were purchased from Debtors. . . .

[Among these defendants were the Big Three American automakers (Ford, DaimlerChrysler, and General Motors). Pursuant to 28 U.S.C. § 157(b)(5), the American automakers asked the Delaware district court to transfer provisionally to Delaware all of the removed Friction Product Claims pending against them. Other defendants followed suit.]

The primary reason offered by the Friction Product Defendants for the transfer was to consolidate the Friction Product Claims "for purposes of a threshold common issues trial devoted to the core issue of whether brakes and other automotive parts cause the diseases claimed." Specifically, Defendants wanted the District Court to conduct a "global *Daubert* hearing" in which the court would perform its "gatekeeper" function as outlined in *Daubert v. Merrell Dow Pharmaceuticals, Inc.*, 509 U.S. 579, 589 (1993) ("[U]nder the Rules [of Evidence] the trial judge must ensure that any and all scientific testimony or evidence admitted is not only relevant, but reliable.") . . . . [T]he Big Three Automakers maintained that there is "no reliable scientific evidence to support any claim based on exposure to [the Friction P]roducts." Accordingly, the Friction Product Defendants argued that the promise of the "global *Daubert* hearing" is to "excise[ ] [the Friction

Product Claims] from the American judicial system in one fell swoop and [lift] a substantial cloud . . . from over Federal Mogul."

The District Court granted the provisional transfer pursuant to § 157(b)[3] in order to consider the appropriateness of actual transfer as well as to examine its subject matter jurisdiction and the appropriateness of abstention and remand. . . .

B.   *District Court's Ruling*

After hearing oral arguments on the pending motions to transfer and remand, the District Court issued the following order, which [held that it lacked subject-matter jurisdiction because the claims against the Friction Product Defendants were not "related to" the Federal-Mogul bankruptcy proceedings. The court therefore denied the motions to transfer the Friction Products Claims to the Delaware district court and ordered those cases removed from state court remanded to the courts from which they had been removed. In making this ruling, the district court noted that there was "no evidence whatsoever of even a bare agreement to indemnify running between the debtors and the solvent co-defendants."]

Alternatively, . . . the District Court announced that, even if it did have jurisdiction, it would abstain from hearing the Friction Product Claims pursuant to 28 U.S.C. § 1334(c)(1) (bankruptcy abstention) in light of considerations of fairness, comity, and the integrity of the bankruptcy process. . . .

Having found that it lacked jurisdiction (or, in the alternative that abstention was appropriate), the District Court remanded the Friction Product Claims directly to the state courts from which they were removed pursuant to 28 U.S.C. § 1452(b). While the court acknowledged that it was "rare for a District Court in one state to remand a matter to the state courts of another state," the District Court concluded that such action was permitted by § 1452 and justified by principles of efficiency and fairness.

C.   *The Appeal*

. . .

The Friction Product Defendants argue that the District Court erred in (1) finding that it lacked "related to" jurisdiction, (2) deciding to remand the claims directly to the state courts from which they were removed, and (3) determining, in the alternative, that it would abstain. . . .

---

3.   Although § 157(b) does not explicitly allow for such provisional transfers, they have been permitted by some courts. *See, e.g.*, A.H. Robins Co. v. Piccinin (In re A.H. Robins Co.), 788 F.2d 994, 1015-16 (4th Cir. 1986) (approving district court's transfer order interpreting that order as "conditional" pending objections of the parties and requests for abstention) [*supra* p. 579]. The parties before us do not question the legitimacy of a provisional transfer and therefore we do not address that issue.

II. JURISDICTION

. . . To make an assessment of our jurisdiction we must first consider whether to construe the decision of the District Court as a denial of a transfer or as a remand order.

Because there are arguments to support construing the order as one denying the requested transfer and equally good arguments to construe the order as one remanding the cases, we will follow the prudent course and consider in turn our jurisdiction under each construction. Each presents substantial obstacles to our exercise of appellate jurisdiction. We will discuss the District Court's alternative holding abstaining from hearing the Friction Product Claims only if we need to reach that issue.

A. *Denial of Transfer*

1. *Reviewability*

It is a well-established rule in this circuit (and generally) that "orders transferring venue are not immediately appealable." However, we, like other courts, have held that "[m]andamus is . . . the appropriate mechanism for reviewing an allegedly improper transfer order." . . .

In reviewing a transfer order by mandamus, we recently observed, "While 28 U.S.C. § 1651(a) grants federal courts the general power to issue writs, it is widely accepted that mandamus is extraordinary relief that is rarely invoked." . . .

2. *District Court's Rationale for Denial of Transfer*

The District Court denied the Defendants' motion to transfer after holding that it lacked subject-matter jurisdiction over the Friction Product Claims because they were not "related to" Federal-Mogul's bankruptcy proceeding. That holding, in turn, was based on its understanding of this court's decision in *Pacor Inc. v. Higgins (In re Pacor)*, 743 F.2d 984 (3d Cir. 1984), where we interpreted the scope of the statutory "related to" jurisdiction of bankruptcy courts.

In *Pacor*, John and Louise Higgins sued Pacor in Pennsylvania state court for work-related injuries to John Higgins caused by exposure to asbestos supplied by Pacor. Pacor filed a third-party complaint impleading Johns-Manville, the manufacturer of the asbestos. Thereafter, Manville filed for Chapter 11 bankruptcy in the Southern District of New York. Pacor filed a petition for removal in the Bankruptcy Court for the Eastern District of Pennsylvania seeking to remove the Higgins' case from state court to federal bankruptcy court and simultaneously to transfer it from that court to the New York district court where it would be joined with the rest of the Johns-Manville bankruptcy proceedings. The theory of Pacor's petition was that the Higgins suit was "related to" the Manville bankruptcy proceeding. The bankruptcy court denied the petition and remanded the case. We affirmed. Analyzing the "related to" provision, we concluded:

> [T]he primary action between Higgins and Pacor would have no effect on the Manville bankruptcy estate, and therefore is not "related to" [the Manville] bankruptcy [proceeding]. At best, it is a mere precursor to the potential third party claim for indemnification by Pacor against Manville. Yet the outcome of the Higgins-Pacor action would in no way bind Manville, in that it could not determine any rights, liabilities, or course of action of the debtor. Since Manville is not a party to the Higgins-Pacor action, it could not be bound by res judicata or collateral estoppel. Even if the Higgins-Pacor dispute is resolved in favor of Higgins (thereby keeping open the possibility of a third party claim), Manville would still be able to relitigate any issue, or adopt any position, in response to a subsequent claim by Pacor. Thus, the bankruptcy estate could not be affected in any way until the Pacor-Manville third party action is actually brought and tried.

The arguments made by Pacor were not dissimilar to those made by Defendants here, but we rejected them . . . .

Pacor clearly remains good law in this circuit. Under our operating procedures, we cannot revisit *Pacor* unless we are sitting en banc. Moreover, the Supreme Court has endorsed the core of this court's opinion in *Pacor* . . . . Celotex Corp. v. Edwards, 514 U.S. 300, 308 (1995). . . .

Notwithstanding the widespread acceptance of *Pacor*, Defendants argue that the Friction Product Claims are "related to" the Federal-Mogul bankruptcy proceeding because the various claims against them could lead to substantial indemnification or contribution claims against Federal-Mogul, which would in turn significantly affect the administration of the bankruptcy estate and the development of an appropriate plan of reorganization. They focus on our articulation of the *Pacor* test for "related to" jurisdiction as "whether *the outcome of that proceeding could conceivably have any effect on the estate being administered in bankruptcy.*" *Pacor*, 743 F.2d at 994 (emphasis in original). . . . They argue that the outcome of the Friction Product Claims could conceivably have an effect on Debtors' estate, because it is "conceivable" that if the Friction Product Plaintiffs succeed in their claims against them, the Friction Product Defendants would seek indemnification and/or contribution from Federal-Mogul.

Their reading of the word "conceivable" ignores the precise holding of *Pacor* where, despite the seemingly broad language of the opinion, we found no "related to" jurisdiction for the Higgins lawsuit against Pacor because the outcome of that lawsuit could not result "in even a contingent claim" against the debtor (Manville); rather, "an entirely separate proceeding to receive indemnification" would have been required. The test articulated in *Pacor* for whether a lawsuit could "conceivably" have an effect on the bankruptcy proceeding inquires whether the allegedly related lawsuit would affect the bankruptcy proceeding without the intervention of yet another lawsuit. . . . We therefore conclude that the District Court's decision does not justify issuance of a writ of mandamus.

The arguments by the Friction Product Defendants for the existence of "related to" bankruptcy jurisdiction draw heavily on the decision of the Sixth Circuit in [*In re Dow Corning Corp.*], 86 F.3d 482 (6th Cir. 1996). Dow Corning, the largest producer of silicone-gel breast implants, also sold silicone materials to other manufacturers of such implants. It and other manufacturers and suppliers of silicone implants were sued by thousands of recipients of the implants for personal injuries related to the silicone implants. Dow Corning filed for Chapter 11 bankruptcy. The bankruptcy filing automatically stayed all of the silicone implant cases against it, but not the claims against Dow Chemical and Corning, Inc. (its co-defendants as well as its shareholders) or the claims against the other three co-defendants. As in this case, the various co-defendants removed many of these personal injury claims from state court to federal court. Dow Corning then moved to transfer the removed cases to the district court that had jurisdiction over its Chapter 11 proceedings, and the co-defendants joined in its motions, relying on the "related to" provision of the Bankruptcy Code. The district court held that it did not have "related to" jurisdiction over the claims against the co-defendants but the court of appeals, citing *Pacor*, reversed.

After noting that Dow Corning's co-defendants may have thousands of claims of indemnification and contribution against Dow Corning and that Dow Corning may have similar claims against them, the court concluded that the district court had "related to" jurisdiction over the silicone implant claims of Dow Corning's non-shareholder co-defendants based on the following reasoning:

> ... *The potential for Dow Corning's being held liable to the nondebtors in claims for contribution and indemnification, or vice versa, suffices to establish a conceivable impact on the estate in bankruptcy.* Claims for indemnification and contribution, whether asserted against or by Dow Corning, obviously would affect the size of the estate and the length of time the bankruptcy proceedings will be pending, as well as Dow Corning's ability to resolve its liabilities and proceed with reorganization. [*Id.* at 494 (emphasis added).] ...

The *Dow Corning* court distinguished *Pacor* as follows:

> In addition, we believe there is a qualitative difference between the single suit involved in *Pacor* and the overwhelming number of cases asserted against Dow Corning and the nondebtor defendants in this case. A single possible claim for indemnification or contribution simply does not represent the same kind of threat to a debtor's reorganization plan as that posed by the thousands of potential indemnification claims at issue here.

The Friction Product Defendants extrapolate from *Dow Corning* a rule that "related to" jurisdiction exists over claims against non-debtors when these non-debtors have potential contribution and indemnification claims. However, they cannot persuasively argue that *Dow Corning* rather than *Pacor* should have provided the rule of law the District Court should have followed. . . .

The Friction Product Defendants have not met this rigorous standard for the issuance of the extraordinary writ of mandamus as to the District Court's denial of the motion to transfer. We will deny the request to issue a writ of mandamus to compel the District Court to transfer the Friction Product Claims under § 1334(b).

B. *Remand Order*

1. *Appellate Jurisdiction*

We next consider whether we have jurisdiction to review the decision of the District Court if we construe that decision as a remand order.

. . . Giving effect to both § 1447(d) and § 1452(b) and applying them to a remand order involving claims allegedly "related to" a bankruptcy proceeding, it is apparent that such a remand is expressly "not reviewable by appeal or otherwise." 28 U.S.C. § 1452(b). *See also* 28 U.S.C. § 1447(d) (remand orders "not reviewable on appeal or otherwise[ ]").

Defendants argue that this court has jurisdiction to review the remand order because neither § 1447(c) nor § 1452(a) authorized the District Court to remand the Friction Product Claims to the state courts from which they were removed. Specifically, the Friction Product Defendants argue that the remand order was not authorized because § 1447(c) only authorizes remand by the district court to which the claims were removed and only authorizes remand to a court from which the removed claims most recently came. Relatedly, they note that the language of § 1452(b) is even more specific as it only authorizes remand by "[t]he court to which such claim or cause of action is removed." Therefore, they contend that once the District Court decided the jurisdictional issue against them, it only had the options of (i) vacating the provisional transfer order, (ii) denying the final transfer order, or (iii) transferring the claims back to the district courts from which they were provisionally transferred. In any event, as they view the situation, the District Court had no authority to remand the claims directly to the state courts. . . .

The case before us is in some ways similar to the recent decision of *Republic of Venezuela v. Philip Morris Inc.*, 287 F.3d 192 (D.C. Cir. 2002), in which foreign countries brought various actions in a Florida state court to recover damages from certain tobacco companies. The cases were removed to federal district court in Florida and then transferred to the federal district court in the District of Columbia. That court held that it lacked subject-matter jurisdiction under § 1447, and remanded four of the cases to the Florida state court. . . . The Court of Appeals for the District of Columbia held that, under § 1447, it lacked jurisdiction to review the district court's remand order. That holding is consistent with the statute and accords with our view of the appellate jurisdiction issue here. Accordingly, we hold that pursuant to § 1447(d), we do not have jurisdiction over the appeal of the District Court's order remanding the Friction Product Claims to the various state courts.

2. *Mandamus*

The Friction Product Defendants argue, as they did with respect to the denial of their motion to transfer, that we should construe their appeal as a petition for mandamus. They recognize that § 1447(d) states that "[a]n order remanding a case to the State court from which it was removed is not reviewable on appeal *or otherwise*." 28 U.S.C. § 1447(d) (emphasis added). . . . "[S]ection 1447(d) prohibits review of remand orders 'whether erroneous or not and whether review is sought by appeal or by extraordinary writ.'"

However, it is not as obvious that § 1452(b) prohibits review by mandamus. The language of that section provides that "[a]n order entered under this subsection remanding a claim or cause of action . . . is not reviewable by appeal or *otherwise* by the court of appeals *under* section 158(d), 1291, or 1292 of this title." 28 U.S.C. § 1452(b) (emphasis added).

On the one hand, the Friction Product Plaintiffs plausibly argue that the "or otherwise" language must refer to mandamus review. To read § 1452(b) as allowing for mandamus review renders the "or otherwise" language meaningless, in violation of the canon against surplusage. On the other hand, as the Friction Product Defendants argue, the statute enumerates the statutory sections that cannot be used to review remands and fails to mention 28 U.S.C. § 1651(a) (the All Writs Act). They construe this omission as permitting writs of mandamus. This is a plausible application of the *expressio unius est exclusio alterius* (inclusion of one thing indicates exclusion of the other) canon of statutory interpretation. . . .

[The Court then examined other cases and the legislative history of § 1452(b).] Both the statutory language itself and the intent of Congress as evidenced by the legislative history lead us to [conclude] . . . that § 1452(b), particularly when read together with § 1447(d), bars both appeal and mandamus review of orders remanding to state courts pursuant to § 1452(b) and/or § 1447(c). It follows that we must deny the requested petition for mandamus as to the District Court's order remanding to the state courts.[14]

C. *Coda*

We are neither unaware of nor unsympathetic to the argument of the Friction Product Defendants that the crisis created by the current asbestos litigation would be ameliorated were there a single proceeding . . . . The arguments of appellants are based on their optimistic view that a *Daubert* hearing would lead to the rejection of the causation claims of all Plaintiffs. However, the evidence creates an issue that could well go either way as to whether Plaintiffs satisfy the *Daubert* gatekeeping standard. . . .

---

14. In light of our decision that we have no jurisdiction to review the District Court's order denying transfer and remanding, we need not consider its alternate order abstaining. Moreover, a straightforward reading of 28 U.S.C. § 1334(d) supports the view that we do not have appellate jurisdiction to review a district court's decision to abstain pursuant to § 1334(c)(1) . . . .

Throughout Defendants' briefs and in their oral arguments they repeatedly contended that we are faced with the question "whether the American judicial system is capable of dealing with the recent explosion of automotive 'friction product' asbestos claims in a fair and rational manner." This is not dissimilar to the arguments made by the parties who sought approval of a settlement class of asbestos victims. The effort was rejected both by this court in *Georgine v. Amchem Products, Inc.*, 83 F.3d 610 (3d Cir. 1996), where we stated that "against the need for effective resolution of the asbestos crisis, we must balance the integrity of the judicial system," and by the Supreme Court, which affirmed that decision. Amchem Prods., Inc. v. Windsor, 521 U.S. 591 (1997) [*supra* p. 493]. Just as both courts declined to permit an end run around the requirements for class actions imposed by Federal Rule of Civil Procedure 23, so also are we unwilling to disregard the statutory impediments to our review of orders of the district courts transferring and remanding cases. Arguably, a procedure authorizing the aggregation of state court cases, such as the Friction Product Claims, into a nationwide class action would provide a mechanism for a *Daubert* hearing like the one Defendants seek, but such proposals, frequently made, have not passed both houses of Congress.

Notes

1. *Federal-Mogul*'s interpretation of "related to" jurisdiction was filtered through the lens of the proper appellate-review standards. In this regard, the case is a good reminder of the ways in which the jurisdiction provided in bankruptcy intersect with other jurisdictional principles to create a uniquely complex body of law.

2. The most direct way to aggregate related lawsuits is to create subject-matter jurisdiction in one court system, and then to provide removal and transfer mechanisms that allow the court in which some of the related cases are filed to bring together the cases dispersed elsewhere. The non-debtor defendants in *Federal-Mogul* were arguing that, taken together, 28 U.S.C. §§ 157(b)(5), 1334(b), and 1452(a) created such a mechanism.

Sometimes, however, aggregation becomes a mantra; it is not clear exactly how the cases, once aggregated, will be resolved, or whether that resolution will be more just or more efficient than individual resolutions. But the tangible benefit of aggregation was apparent in *Federal-Mogul*: The defendants had a specific plan for resolving all the related cases in the bankruptcy proceeding. As *Federal-Mogul* says, it is not clear that the plan would have worked, but *Federal-Mogul* denied the best opportunity for a single resolution that existed. In *Amchem*, which *Federal-Mogul* cited as a reason not to use bankruptcy creatively, the basis for the Court's refusal to permit aggregation was the harm that aggregation caused to individuals with valid claims, many of whom received nothing from *Amchem*'s proposed settlement. What harm would have befallen the Friction Products Plaintiffs or society at large if all related cases had been aggregated in the Delaware bankruptcy proceeding?

3.   The universally accepted view, which *Federal-Mogul* reflects, is that the only jurisdictional basis for a court sitting in bankruptcy to hear the claims or cases against non-debtors is § 1334(b)'s "related to" jurisdiction. The basic holding of *Pacor, Inc. v. Higgins*, 743 F.2d 984 (3d Cir. 1984) — that "related to" jurisdiction exists only when the claims or cases might conceivably affect the debtor's estate — has also been universally adopted. *See, e.g.,* Arnold v. Garlock, Inc., 278 F.3d 426 (5th Cir. 2001); In re Toledo, 170 F.3d 1340 (11th Cir. 1999); In re G.S.F. Corp., 938 F.2d 1467 (1st Cir. 1991).   The point of disagreement has occurred in applying *Pacor's* "conceivable effect" test to a given set of facts. *Federal-Mogul* represents the narrower and more common view: that the mere possibility of indemnity and contribution claims by non-debtor defendants against the debtor (or vice versa) does not justify federal jurisdiction. A greater connection is required. *See Toledo*, 170 F.3d 1340 ("related to" jurisdiction exists over the invalidation a mortgage owned in part by a non-debtor when the invalidation might affect the priority status of the mortgage holder); In re Philadelphia Newspapers, LLC, 407 B.R. 606, 612 (E.D. Pa. 2009) ("related to" jurisdiction exists over claims against a non-debtor when the debtor signed an indemnity agreement with the non-debtor). The Third Circuit continues to adhere to this approach. *See* In re W.R. Grace & Co., 591 F.3d 164 (3d Cir. 2009).

4.   A minority of courts have adopted a broader view. The most notable, which *Federal-Mogul* mentions, is *In re Dow Corning Corp.*, 86 F.3d 482 (6th Cir. 1996). *Dow Corning* was unusual because the debtor, a major American corporation, was a joint venture set up by the principal non-debtor defendants, which were two other major American corporations. All were being sued for the same course of conduct. *See Arnold*, 278 F.3d at 440 (distinguishing *Dow Corning* because "each of the co-defendants was closely involved in using the same material, originating with the debtor, to make the same, singular product, sold to the same market and incurring substantially similar injuries," thus creating "a unity of identity").

A recent, and potentially significant, case adopting the broad view is *In re WorldCom, Inc. Securities Litigation*, 293 B.R. 308 (S.D.N.Y. 2003). In *WorldCom*, a debtor accused of federal securities fraud sought Chapter 11 protection. Litigation against other defendants — including officers and directors of the debtor as well as the debtor's underwriters, accountants, and analysts — was consolidated in an MDL proceeding in the same district as the bankruptcy case. A plaintiff then filed a case in state court, raising federal and state claims, against essentially the same non-debtor defendants. The defendants removed the case under 28 U.S.C. § 1452. *WorldCom* held that "related to" jurisdiction existed over the case. The district court identified four ways in which claims against the directors might affect the bankruptcy estate: "(1) the ongoing, court-ordered payment of the [directors'] legal fees; (2) the indemnification rights stated in Article X of WorldCom's by-laws; (3) the WorldCom insurance policies that provide Director and Officer ("D & O") coverage for the [directors]; and (4) the statutory right to contribution." *Id.* at 320. It also identified three ways in which claims against the underwriters might affect the estate, including statutory and "common law theories for WorldCom's joint and several liability." *Id.* Finding that there was "a reasonable basis for at least the contribution claims," the court stated that "the effect of contribution claims on the bankruptcy estate is at the very least 'conceivable.'" *Id.* at 321.

The Second Circuit subsequently declined to rule on the propriety of the district court's "related to" ruling. Cal. Pub. Employees' Ret. Sys. v. WorldCom, Inc., 368 F.3d 86 (2d Cir. 2004). *Cf.* Steel Workers Pension Trust v. Citigroup, Inc., 295 B.R. 747 (E.D. Pa. 2003) (declining to follow *WorldCom*). Which approach — the narrow, complexity-insensitive approach of *Federal-Mogul* or the broad, complexity-sensitive approach of *WorldCom* — seems better? Which seems more in keeping with the purpose and language of the bankruptcy statutes?

5.   If a court finds "related to" subject-matter jurisdiction over claims against a non-debtor, aggregation is not yet assured. The court must next consider whether to abstain under §§ 1334(c)(1) and -(c)(2), or (in a removed case) to remand under the equitable-remand provision of § 1452(b). The mandatory-abstention provision of § 1334(c)(2) is especially significant, because it applies specifically to "related to" actions. In *WorldCom*, the district court refused to abstain under § 1334(c)(2) because it believed that state-court litigation did not meet the statute's "timely adjudication" requirement for abstention:

> The size of the WorldCom bankruptcy, the close connections between the defendants in this action and the debtor, and the complexity of this litigation suggest the contrary: remanding to state court could slow the pace of litigation dramatically. If each of the actions removed from state court were remanded, it would lead to duplicative motion practice and repetitious discovery, as well as requiring common issues to be resolved separately by courts across the country. [*Id.* at 331.]

Noting that "[t]he MDL panel has consolidated scores of WorldCom cases before this Court," *WorldCom* also declined to exercise its discretionary-abstention powers under § 1334(c)(1): "With the consolidation of the litigation in one court, the motion practice and discovery process can be managed to protect the rights of all parties and to preserve, to the extent possible, the maximum amount of assets for recovery by plaintiffs with meritorious claims." *Id.* at 333.

6.   Even when a court decides that it can assert "related to" jurisdiction over non-debtor cases, venue issues can block single-forum aggregation. In *Federal-Mogul* the district court conditionally transferred the cases to himself under the authority of § 157(b)(5). Given his ultimate decision not to exercise jurisdiction over the "related to" claims, *Federal-Mogul* had no occasion to pass on the propriety of such a transfer. Even if they are legitimate, however, § 157(b)(5) transfers are limited to tort claims. A court sitting in bankruptcy has no general power to transfer "related to" cases to itself. It must rely on the good offices of other courts — whether the Judicial Panel exercising its § 1407 power or individual transferor courts exercising their § 1412 powers — to accomplish aggregation. It is unlikely that all such courts will cooperate. *See* Spitfaden v. Dow Corning Corp.,

1995 WL 662663 (E.D. La. Nov. 8, 1995) (remanding claims against non-debtor defendants in the Dow Corning litigation on abstention and equitable-remand grounds).

7.   The jurisdiction-and-transfer route is not the only way in which cases can be aggregated. In Chapter Two, we learned that another way is to use stays and antisuit injunctions to prevent litigation elsewhere and effectively channel all litigation into a single forum. The following case examines the use of two distinct antisuit injunctive powers as a means of bringing debtor and non-debtor cases into one proceeding.

IN RE: CONTINENTAL AIRLINES

203 F.3d 203 (3d Cir. 2000)

■   RENDELL, Circuit Judge.

In this bankruptcy-related appeal, we consider the validity of a provision in Continental Airlines' plan of reorganization that released and permanently enjoined shareholder lawsuits against certain of Continental Airlines' present and former directors and officers who were not themselves in bankruptcy. . . . We will reverse the District Court's order approving the validity of this provision, which is legally and factually insupportable.

I.

Appellants are plaintiffs in several securities fraud class action lawsuits brought against directors and officers of Continental Airlines Holdings, Inc. Plaintiffs' class actions allege that the D&O defendants caused Continental Airlines Holdings to issue false and misleading statements of material facts in violation of, *inter alia*, section 10(b) of the Securities Exchange Act of 1934, Rule 10b-5, and common law. On December 3, 1990, Continental Holdings and affiliated entities ("Continental Debtors") filed petitions for relief under chapter 11 of the Bankruptcy Code in the District of Delaware.

. . . The Continental Debtors brought an adversary proceeding on January 17, 1991 to prevent Plaintiffs' class actions against the non-debtor D&O defendants from interfering with the Continental Debtors' reorganization process. The Bankruptcy Court temporarily enjoined Plaintiffs' pursuit of their class actions on February 2, 1991. That order was affirmed on appeal on June 28, 1993. . . . Plaintiffs' class actions remained pending, but inactive, during the reorganization proceedings.

On December 1, 1992, the Bankruptcy Court approved a settlement between the Continental Debtors, their D&Os, and D&O liability insurers. Under this Tripartite Settlement, "The Debtors, Insureds and the Insurers will provide releases to each other." The Continental Debtors released "any and all claims, demands, and causes of action of any kind . . . against the present or former officers or directors of the Continental Debtors . . . which arose prior to the date of this settlement and release." The D&O liability insurers were released from "any and all demands, claims, and causes of action . . . that they or any of them had, now have, or may have against the Insurers" in exchange for providing $5 million to the Continental Debtors to settle the Continental Debtors' claims and potential claims against their D&Os. In turn, the D&Os released their claims against the Continental Debtors. . . . This Tripartite Settlement makes no reference to Plaintiffs' class actions . . . .

The Continental Debtors later filed a plan of reorganization, amended several times, which contained a provision[, section 12.4,]releasing and permanently enjoining a broader range of claims, including Plaintiffs' class actions against the non-debtor D&O defendants . . . .

. . . The Bankruptcy Court approved Continental Debtors' plan of reorganization on April 16, 1993. Plaintiffs filed an appeal on June 28, 1993 . . . .

More than five years later, on September 30, 1998, the District Court issued a memorandum opinion and order affirming the Bankruptcy Court's confirmation order. . . .

Although the District Court acknowledged that involuntary releases of non-debtor parties are regarded with disfavor in general, the District Court also stated that a confirmed and implemented plan of reorganization should be disturbed for only "compelling reasons" and found no compelling reason to modify the Continental Debtors' plan based on the Plaintiffs' objections. The District Court . . . considered the release and permanent injunction of Plaintiffs' lawsuits to be a "key element" of the Continental Debtors' reorganization because the Continental Debtors were obliged to indemnify the D&Os, and thus Plaintiffs' lawsuits ultimately would diminish the funds available for the Continental Debtors' creditors and would burden the reorganized Continental Debtors with litigation. The District Court did not refer to any factual evidence in the record to support its conclusion that the release and permanent injunction were key to the Continental Debtors' reorganization or that the Continental Debtors would be unduly burdened. Rather, the District Court presumed that the reorganized Continental Debtors and their management would be distracted post-confirmation by discovery and litigation. The District Court also based its affirmance on its view that Plaintiffs' lawsuits would implicate the Continental Debtors' D&O liability insurance policy, and thus affected property of the Continental Debtors' bankruptcy estate. On October 30, 1998, Plaintiffs filed the instant appeal from the District Court's order. . . .

II.

. . .

Validity of non-debtor release and permanent injunction

At issue in this appeal is a provision releasing and permanently enjoining Plaintiffs' actions against the Continental Debtors' D&Os who have not formally availed themselves of the benefits and burdens of the bankruptcy process.   Plaintiffs argue that section 12.4(b)(ii) of the Continental Debtors' plan impermissibly releases and permanently enjoins their class actions against non-debtors without notice to individual class members and without consent or consideration, violating 11 U.S.C. § 524(e) by relieving non-debtor parties of liabilities.   Although Plaintiffs acknowledge that 11 U.S.C. § 105(a) has been used by some courts to enjoin actions against non-debtors when necessary or appropriate to enforce or implement court orders, Plaintiffs question the legal and factual basis for the District Court's finding of need and propriety in this particular instance.

Section 524(e) of the Bankruptcy Code makes clear that the bankruptcy discharge of a debtor, by itself, does not operate to relieve non-debtors of their liabilities.   The Bankruptcy Code does not explicitly authorize the release and permanent injunction of claims against non-debtors, except in one instance not applicable here.[6]   Section 105(a) of the Bankruptcy Code supplements courts' specifically enumerated bankruptcy powers by authorizing orders necessary or appropriate to carry out provisions of the Bankruptcy Code.   However, section 105(a) has a limited scope. It does not "create substantive rights that would otherwise be unavailable under the Bankruptcy Code."

We have not ruled previously on the validity of provisions in chapter 11 plans of reorganization releasing and permanently enjoining third party actions against non-debtors.   We will review briefly the relevant decisions from other circuits, leading us to the inescapable conclusion that, in this appeal, the release and permanent injunction of Plaintiffs' lawsuits are legally and factually insupportable.

The Courts of Appeals for the Ninth and Tenth Circuits have held that non-debtor releases and permanent injunctions are impermissible. "The bankruptcy court has no power to discharge the liabilities of a nondebtor pursuant to the consent of creditors as part of a reorganization plan." Underhill v. Royal, 769 F.2d 1426, 1432 (9th Cir. 1985). "Section 524(e) precludes discharging the liabilities of nondebtors."   Resorts Int'l v. Lowenschuss (In re Lowenschuss), 67 F.3d 1394, 1402 (9th Cir. 1995) (affirming district court's decision vacating global release provision). These courts find a release and permanent injunction to be indistinguishable from a bankruptcy discharge. See American Hardwoods, Inc. v. Deutsche Credit Corp., 885 F.2d 621, 626 (9th Cir. 1989).[8]

Other circuits have adopted a more flexible approach, albeit in the context of extraordinary cases.   In *Drexel* and *Manville*, the Court of Appeals for the Second Circuit upheld plans of reorganization containing releases and permanent injunctions of widespread claims against co-liable parties, but those plans also provided consideration to parties who would be enjoined from suing non-debtors. See SEC v. Drexel Burnham Lambert

---

6.   *See* 11 U.S.C. § 524(g) (establishing procedure for resolving asbestos claims).

8.   Quite a few courts have followed the lead of the Ninth and Tenth Circuits.   . . .

Group, Inc. (In re Drexel Burnham Lambert Group, Inc.), 960 F.2d 285, 293 (2d Cir. 1992); Kane v. Johns-Manville Corp. (In re Johns-Manville Corp.), 843 F.2d 636, 640, 649 (2d Cir. 1988). In *Robins*, the Court of Appeals for the Fourth Circuit likewise upheld non-debtor releases that were necessary to reorganization and were accompanied by consideration for mass tort claimants, provided in part by the non-debtors. *See* Menard-Sanford v. Mabey (In re A.H. Robins Co.), 880 F.2d 694, 702 (4th Cir. 1989) [*supra* p. 586]. A central focus of these three reorganizations was the global settlement of massive liabilities against the debtors and co-liable parties. Substantial debtor co-liable parties provided compensation to claimants in exchange for the release of their liabilities and made these reorganizations feasible.

In *AOV*, the Court of Appeals for the D.C. Circuit found that a plan provision releasing the liabilities of non-debtors was unfair because the plan did not provide additional compensation to a creditor whose claim against non-debtor was being released, *see* In re AOV Indus., Inc., 792 F.2d 1140, 1154 (D.C. Cir. 1986), thus indicating that it is necessary to provide adequate consideration to a claimholder being forced to release claims against non-debtors.

. . . In *Munford*, the Eleventh Circuit affirmed a district court's ruling that 11 U.S.C. § 105 and Fed. R. Civ. P. 16 authorized a bankruptcy court to permanently enjoin nonsettling defendants from asserting contribution and indemnification claims against a defendant consulting firm when the permanent injunction was integral to the debtor's settlement with the consulting firm and the bar order was fair and equitable. *See* Matter of Munford, Inc., 97 F.3d 449, 455 (11th Cir. 1996).

Plaintiffs do not ask us to establish a blanket rule prohibiting all non-consensual releases and permanent injunctions of non-debtor obligations. Given the manner in which the issue has been presented to us, we need not establish our own rule regarding the conditions under which non-debtor releases and permanent injunctions are appropriate or permissible. Establishing a rule would provide guidance prospectively, but would be ill-advised when we can rule on Plaintiffs' appeal without doing so. Considering the instant appeal in the context of the case law we have reviewed, we conclude that the provision in the Continental Debtors' plan releasing and permanently enjoining Plaintiffs' lawsuits against the non-debtor D&O defendants does not pass muster under even the most flexible tests for the validity of non-debtor releases. The hallmarks of permissible non-consensual releases — fairness, necessity to the reorganization, and specific factual findings to support these conclusions — are all absent here.

Bankruptcy Court

The Bankruptcy Court never specifically addressed the release and permanent injunction of Plaintiffs' claims. Thus, the order confirming the Continental Debtors' plan of reorganization and releasing and permanently enjoining Plaintiffs' claims was not accompanied by any findings that the release was fair to the Plaintiffs and necessary to the Continental Debtors' reorganization.[12]   Without such findings, a release and permanent injunction cannot stand on their merits under any of the standards set forth in the case law of other circuits.

District Court

In attempting to salvage the release and permanent injunction of Plaintiffs' claims, the District Court did not discuss the lack of findings of the Bankruptcy Court, but instead made its own findings. As previously mentioned, the District Court cited section 105(a) as a basis for upholding the validity of non-consensual releases and permanent injunctions that are essential to plan confirmation. The District Court required, but could not find, "compelling reasons" to disturb the Continental Debtors' plan based on the Plaintiffs' objections, particularly because the Plaintiffs did not object to or appeal the Tripartite Settlement. The District Court also considered the release and permanent injunction of Plaintiffs' claims to be a "key element" of the Continental Debtors' reorganization because the Continental Debtors were obliged to indemnify the D&Os and thus would ultimately bear the burden of Plaintiffs' lawsuits. The District Court concluded that the Plaintiffs' actions against the non-debtor D&O defendants implicated the Continental Debtors' D&O liability insurance policy, and thus affected property of the Continental Debtors' bankruptcy estate.

In making these findings, the District Court assumed facts not of record and drew superficial analogies based on inapposite case law. Contrary to the conclusion of the District Court and the arguments of the Continental Debtors, *Manville, Robins,* and *Drexel* do not support the validity of the release and permanent injunction of Plaintiffs' claims based on the record before us. First, unlike the courts in these cases, the District Court did not discuss whether the release and permanent injunction were fair to Plaintiffs and were given in exchange for reasonable consideration. Indeed, the Continental Debtors have not disputed Plaintiffs' contention that Plaintiffs received no consideration in exchange for having their lawsuits permanently enjoined. On this basis alone, *Manville, Drexel,* and *Robins* are inapplicable.

With respect to the District Court's view of the necessity of the release and permanent injunction, we find nothing in the record to even imply that

---

12. We also note, with some concern, that the Bankruptcy Court apparently never examined its jurisdiction to release and permanently enjoin Plaintiffs' claims against non-debtors. Although bankruptcy subject matter jurisdiction can extend to matters between non-debtor third parties affecting the debtor or the bankruptcy case, *see* 28 U.S.C. § 1334, a court cannot simply presume it has jurisdiction in a bankruptcy case to permanently enjoin third-party class actions against non-debtors. . . . We do not treat this very significant issue more fully, however, because the record does not permit us to resolve this issue and the parties have not raised and discussed it in their appellate briefs.

the success of the Continental Debtors' reorganization bore any relationship to the release and permanent injunction of Plaintiffs' class actions. Unlike in cases such as *Manville*, *Drexel*, and *Robins*, we have found no evidence that the non-debtor D&Os provided a critical financial contribution to the Continental Debtors' plan that was necessary to make the plan feasible in exchange for receiving a release of liability for Plaintiffs' claims. Nor did Plaintiffs' lawsuits themselves propel the Continental Debtors into bankruptcy; far from being the tail wagging the dog, we find it difficult to conceive that Plaintiffs' lawsuits were anything more than a flea.

We also take issue with the District Court's unsupported conclusion that the Continental Debtors' obligation to indemnify its D&Os transforms the release and permanent injunction of Plaintiffs' claims against non-debtor D&O defendants into a "key element" of the Continental Debtors' reorganization. . . . [F]ederal courts disfavor indemnity for federal securities law violations, calling into question the enforceability of these obligations. . . .

We find no evidence in the record before us supporting the possibility or probability of D&O indemnification as a factual or legal matter. Even if the D&O defendants' obligations culminating from Plaintiffs' class actions were indemnifiable, the fact that the reorganized Continental Airlines might face an indemnity claim sometime in the future, in some unspecified amount, does not make the release and permanent injunction of Plaintiffs' claims "necessary" to ensure the success of the Continental Debtors' reorganization.

Similarly unsupported is the District Court's conclusion that the non-debtor release and permanent injunction were warranted because Plaintiffs' lawsuits ultimately might implicate the D&O liability insurance policy, which was property of the Continental Debtors' bankruptcy estate under 11 U.S.C. § 541(a). One cannot assume too quickly that the proceeds of this policy are property of the estate when the non-debtor D&Os, not the Continental Debtors, are the direct beneficiaries of the policy. . . . Even assuming that the proceeds are property of the estate, this by itself does not justify a permanent injunction of Plaintiffs' actions against the insured non-debtor D&O defendants as necessary for the reorganization of the Continental Debtors.

We do not dispute that, some day in the future, the reorganized Continental Debtors may face litigation or experience some financial ramification based on liabilities of the D&Os as a result of the indemnity obligation or the D&O liability insurance policy. However, we cannot accept the District Court's conclusion that a purported "identity of interest" between the Continental Debtors and the non-debtor D&O defendants, forged by the indemnity obligation or the D&O liability insurance policy, established the necessity of releasing and permanently enjoining Plaintiffs' claims, nor does this identity of interest speak to the fairness of the release and permanent injunction that we construe cases such as *Manville*, *Drexel*, or *Robins* to require. We conclude that granting permanent injunctions to protect non-debtor parties on the basis of theoretical identity of interest alone would turn bankruptcy principles on their head. Nothing in the Bankruptcy Code can be construed to establish such extraordinary protection for non-debtor parties.

III.

For the foregoing reasons, we reverse the District Court's order.

Notes

1. *Continental Airlines* mentions two distinct stays entered in the bankruptcy court. The first stay froze litigation against non-debtors during the pendency of the bankruptcy proceeding. Such a stay is an offshoot of the automatic stay, 11 U.S.C. § 362, which immediately stops litigation against the debtor upon the filing of the bankruptcy petition. Section 362 does not in words extend the stay to litigation against non-debtors, but some courts have held that they have the power to enjoin litigation against non-debtors in "unusual circumstances." A.H. Robins Co. v. Piccinin, 788 F.2d 994, 999 (4th Cir. 1986) (*supra* p. 579). *Piccinin*, which is the leading case on the issue, identified four sources for this power: two provisions of the automatic-stay statute (§§ 362(a)(1) and -(a)(3)), the general injunctive power of 11 U.S.C. § 105, and the bankruptcy court's inherent power. Other courts have questioned this power. *See* In re Chugach Forest Prods., Inc., 23 F.3d 241 (9th Cir. 1994). But even in those courts adopting it, the "unusual circumstances" requirement has been tightly construed. *See Piccinin*, 788 F.2d at 999 (requiring "such identity between the debtor and the third-party defendant that the debtor may be said to be the real party defendant"); In re Philadelphia Newspapers, LLC, 407 B.R. 606, 616 (E.D. Pa. 2009) (requiring either "(i) the non-debtor and debtor enjoy such an identity of interests that the suit of the non-debtor is essentially a suit against the debtor; or (ii) the third-party action will have an adverse impact on the debtor's ability to accomplish reorganization"). The stay might also expire before the bankruptcy proceeding concludes. *See Philadelphia Newspapers*, 407 B.R. at 618 (affirming a sixty-day stay).

2. A stay that runs during the pendency of the litigation is important, because it channels attention to the bankruptcy process and gives all parties a forum in which to come to a global resolution of the dispute. But in the end, such a stay is temporary. Hence, the second stay mentioned in *Continental Airlines* — a permanent stay preventing subsequent litigation against non-debtors — is in the long run more significant. In effect, a permanent injunction acts as a form of claim preclusion, channeling all litigation through the reorganization process. In almost all cases, the enjoined plaintiffs also have claims against the debtor, and therefore are (or should be) parties to the bankruptcy process. Therefore, the principle that courts cannot preclude nonparties — a foundation of American law that we examined in detail in Chapter Two — is generally not relevant; to the extent that it is, *Martin v. Wilks*, 490 U.S. 755, 762 n.2 (1989) (*supra* p.

222), recognized bankruptcy as an exception to the usual rule that a court can preclude only parties' claims (albeit not in the context of an antisuit injunction running against non-debtors).

Continental Airlines provides an excellent survey of the main positions and cases on the issue. As the Third Circuit says, the Manville and Robins reorganizations led the way, as they did on many issues that pushed the envelope of bankruptcy. Some courts have reacted with caution to the use of antisuit injunctions against non-debtors, confining *Manville* and *Robins* to their facts. The principle that *Continental Airlines* reads the cases to stand for — that antisuit injunctions protecting non-debtors are permissible only when the non-debtors provide additional consideration to the plaintiffs through the bankruptcy proceeding — is not suggested in the cases. For instance, *Robins* argued that the non-debtor injunction was appropriate

> where the Plan was overwhelmingly approved, where the Plan in conjunction with insurance policies provided as a part of a plan of reorganization gives a second chance for even late claimants to recover[,] where, nevertheless, some have chosen not to take part in the settlement in order to retain rights to sue certain other parties, and where the entire reorganization hinges on the debtor being free from indirect claims such as suits against parties who would have indemnity or contribution claims against the debtor.

In re A.H. Robins, 880 F.2d 694, 702 (4th Cir. 1989) [*supra* p. 586]. *Drexel Burnham* described the power in this way: "In bankruptcy cases, a court may enjoin a creditor from suing a third party, provided the injunction plays an important part in the debtor's reorganization plan." In re Drexel Burnham Lambert Group, Inc., 960 F.2d 285, 293 (2d Cir. 1992). *See also* In re Dow Corning Corp., 280 F.3d 648, 658 (6th Cir. 2002) (listing seven factors that determine whether the "unusual circumstances" that allow an injunction against a non-debtor have been shown).

3. Even the broad reading of the bankruptcy power to enjoin suits against non-debtors has significant limits. All of the cases enjoin suits against non-debtors closely associated with the debtor — directors and officers, insurers, and the like. To be a truly effective power, the injunction needs to run against unrelated co-defendants, such as other manufacturers of a defective product. If such co-defendants could be brought within the bankruptcy proceeding and given the protection of an antisuit injunction when they contribute a reasonable amount to a victim-compensation fund established under the aegis of the reorganization plan, then bankruptcy could serve a critical role in resolving widely dispersed litigation.

It is not clear that such a use of bankruptcy is permissible; the point of Chapter 11 is to rehabilitate the debtor, not to use the debtor's distress as the vehicle to resolve disputes in which they are only tangentially related. Thus far, no court has stretched bankruptcy this much. In *Wedgeworth v. Fibreboard Corp.,* 706 F.2d 541 (5th Cir. 1983), co-defendants of Manville and another asbestos defendant that had entered bankruptcy asked judges in three district courts to extend the automatic stay of 11 U.S.C. § 362 to their cases until the bankruptcy proceedings concluded. One judge denied the stay; two granted it. The court of appeals held that § 362 did not authorize such a stay; it further held that the courts could not stay the cases under their "general discretionary power . . . to stay proceedings as a matter of their discretion to stay litigation in the interest of justice and in control of their dockets." *Id.* at 545. *Wedgeworth* effectively negates an earlier district-court decision from the Fifth Circuit that had applied the automatic stay to co-defendants of a debtor when "the allegations . . . arise from the same factual and legal basis." Fed. Life Ins. Co. (Mut.) v. First Fin. Group of Tex., Inc., 3 B.R. 375 (S.D. Tex. 1980). *See also* Stanford v. Foamex L.P., 2009 WL 1033607, at *3 n.10 (E.D. Pa. Apr. 15, 2009) (refusing to extend a stay when a "case involves alleged breaches of duties owed by the non-debtor defendants directly to plaintiff"); Williford v. Armstrong World Indus., Inc., 715 F.2d 124 (4th Cir. 1983) (holding that neither the automatic stay in bankruptcy nor discretionary-stay principles allowed a district court to stay proceedings against co-defendants of asbestos debtors).

In any event, the stay in cases like *Wedgeworth* would run only during the pendency of the debtor's bankruptcy action. Unless that action also resolves the non-debtors' claims, the stay merely postpones, rather than averts, the problems created by dispersed litigation.

4. Footnote 6 of *Continental Airlines* mentions 11 U.S.C. § 524(g) as the one exception to the rule that bankruptcy injunctions do not run against non-debtors. Section 524(g) is designed specifically to deal with asbestos bankruptcies. Providing that the reorganization plan meets certain criteria for the payment of asbestos-related claims, § 524(g)(4) extends the umbrella of the bankruptcy discharge over certain "third part[ies]," such as directors, officers, insurers, and financiers of the asbestos debtor. The most notable feature of § 524(g), however, is that it also bars claims by future plaintiffs against the reorganized asbestos debtor. The more general capacity of bankruptcy to handle future claims is the issue to which we now turn.

3. Using the Bankruptcy Forum to Aggregate the Claims of Future Plaintiffs

To be a completely effective aggregation device, bankruptcy must be able to aggregate the claims of all potential plaintiffs. When the debtor's conduct has already caused harm to potential plaintiffs, bankruptcy accomplishes this task very well. With only a few exceptions, the discharge that a bankruptcy court provides bars the prosecution of any claim that could have been allowed in the bankruptcy case. 11 U.S.C. § 524. Thus, the bankruptcy discharge forces claimants either to file a claim against the estate or to forfeit any chance for recovery.

In latent-injury cases, however, some persons may not have been injured until after the bankruptcy proceeding is over. The bankruptcy statute was not originally drafted with these "future plaintiffs" in mind, and the usual rule was that the bankruptcy court could not discharge legal obligations that first accrued after the case ended. Unless a debtor receives a discharge from the claims of future plaintiffs, however, it has little reason to enter bankruptcy, for it faces the prospect of a new onslaught of claims as soon as the bankruptcy case terminates. Being unable to discharge or enjoin such future litigation also threatens to undermine the future financial health of the debtor and thus to frustrate the purpose of the debtor's reorganization. Therefore, from the viewpoint of bankruptcy, finding a means of dealing with future claimants is vital. As we have also seen, other aggregation methods have also struggled with handling future claimants. If bankruptcy can find a way to handle future claims, it becomes a very powerful and important aggregation tool in latent-injury litigation.

GRADY V. A.H. ROBINS CO.

839 F.2d 198 (4th Cir. 1988)

■   WIDENER, Circuit Judge.

Rebecca Grady and the Legal Representative of the Future Claimants appeal an order of the district court deciding that Mrs. Grady's claim against A.H. Robins Co., Inc. (Robins) arose prior to the date Robins sought protection under the Bankruptcy Code and therefore was subject to the automatic stay provision of 11 U.S.C. § 362(a)(1). We affirm....

Mrs. Grady had had inserted a Dalkon Shield some years before [Robins' bankruptcy petition was filed on August 21, 1985] but thought that the device had fallen out. On August 21, 1985, she was admitted to Salinas Valley Memorial Hospital, Salinas, California, complaining of abdominal pain, fever and chills. X-rays and sonograms revealed the presence of the Dalkon Shield. On August 28, 1985, the Dalkon Shield was surgically removed.... She was again admitted to the hospital on November 14, 1985, on which admission she was diagnosed as having pelvic inflammatory disease, and underwent a hysterectomy. She blames the Dalkon Shield for those injuries.

On October 15, 1985 (almost two months after Robins filed its petition for reorganization), Mrs. Grady filed a civil action against Robins in the United States District Court for the Northern District of California. The case was subsequently transferred to the Eastern District of Virginia.

Mrs. Grady then filed a motion in the bankruptcy court, seeking a decision that her claim did not arise before the filing of the petition so that it would not be stayed by the automatic stay provision of the Code. If the claim arose when the Dalkon Shield was inserted into her, the district court reasoned, then it would be considered a claim under the Bankruptcy Code and its prosecution would be stayed by the provisions of 11 U.S.C. § 362(a)(1). If, however, the claim was found to arise when the injuries became apparent, then it might not be a claim for bankruptcy purposes and the automatic stay provision would be inapplicable.

The bankruptcy court determined that Mrs. Grady's claim against Robins arose when the acts giving rise to Robins' liability were performed, not when the harm caused by those acts was manifested. . . . It held that the right to payment under 11 U.S.C. § 101(4)(A) [now § 101(5)(A) — ED.] of Mrs. Grady's claim arose when the acts giving rise to the liability were performed and thus the claim was pre-petition under 11 U.S.C. § 362(a)(1).

We emphasize the narrowness of the district court's holding. It held only that the automatic stay provision of 11 U.S.C. § 362 applied . . . . It did not decide whether or not Mrs. Grady's claim would constitute an administrative expense under 11 U.S.C. § 503(b)(1)(A), and it also did not decide whether or not the Future Tort Claimants would have a dischargeable claim within the reorganization case. . . .

The district court correctly noted that the automatic stay is particularly critical to a debtor seeking to reorganize under Chapter 11 because he needs breathing room to restructure his affairs. While the importance of § 362 cannot be over-emphasized, its coverage extends only to claims against the debtor that arose prior to the filing of its petition. . . .

Mrs. Grady argues that her cause of action against Robins did not accrue until after Robins had filed its reorganization petition and therefore the stay provision is inapplicable. Under California law, she argues that she could not have sued Robins until she knew the nature of her injuries. The argument goes that because she had no right to payment from Robins under state law until she was injured, and since that injury occurred after the reorganization petition was filed, the stay provision of § 362 should not bar her case from its prosecution. . . .

We commence with the proposition that ". . . except where federal law, fully apart from bankruptcy, has created obligations by the exercise of power granted to the federal government, a claim implies the existence of an obligation created by State law." Vanston Committee v. Green, 329 U.S. 156, 167, 170 (1946) (Justice Frankfurter concurring), and further, from that concurring opinion, that "[b]ankruptcy legislation is superimposed upon rights and obligations created by the laws of the States." 329 U.S. at 171. The opinion of the court in *Vanston* further stands for the proposition that "In determining what claims are allowable and how a debtor's assets are to be distributed, a bankruptcy court does not apply the law of the State where it sits." 329 U.S. at 162. . . . The Code contemplates the broadest possible relief in the bankruptcy court. . . .

With those thoughts in mind, we turn to the pertinent parts of the statutes at hand. Section 362(a)(1) provides for an automatic stay of, among other things, judicial action against the debtor ". . . to recover a claim against the debtor that arose before the commencement of the case under this title." Section 101(4)(A) [now § 101(5)(A) — ED.] defines a claim to be a "right to payment[,] whether or not such right is reduced to judgment, liquidated, unliquidated, fixed, contingent, matured, unmatured, disputed, undisputed, legal, equitable, secured or unsecured." . . .

Mrs. Grady's claim, as well as whatever rights the other Future Tort Claimants have, is undoubtedly "contingent." It depends upon a future uncertain event, that event being the manifestation of injury from use of the Dalkon Shield. We do not believe that there must be a right to the immediate payment of money in the case of a tort or allied breach of warranty or like claim, as present here, when the acts constituting the tort or breach of warranty have occurred prior to the filing of the petition, to constitute a claim under § 362(a)(1). . . .

Not only do we think that a literal reading of the statute requires the result we have reached, our reading is fortified by other considerations. The broad reading of the word "claim" required by the legislative history . . . is considerable support. That the legislative history contemplates "the broadest possible relief in the bankruptcy court" also enters our reasoning. If Mrs. Grady and the Future Tort Claimants, who had no right to the immediate payment of money at the time of the filing of the petition, were participants in a Chapter 7 proceeding, the chances are that they would receive nothing, for no compensable result had manifested itself prior to the filing of the petition.

We also find persuasive the fact that the district court probably had authority to achieve the same result by staying Mrs. Grady's suit under 11 U.S.C. § 105(a) in the use of its equitable powers to assure the orderly conduct of reorganization proceedings.

We emphasize, as did the district court, that we do not decide whether or not Mrs. Grady's claim or those of the Future Tort Claimants are dischargeable in this case. Neither do we decide whether or not post-petition claims constitute an administrative expense. We hold only that the Dalkon Shield claim in the case before us, when the Dalkon Shield was inserted in the claimant prior to the time of filing of the petition, constitutes a "claim" "that arose before the commencement of the case" within the meaning of 11 U.S.C. § 362(a)(1).

EPSTEIN V. OFFICIAL COMMITTEE OF UNSECURED CREDITORS, OF THE ESTATE OF PIPER AIRCRAFT CORP.

58 F.3d 1573 (11th Cir. 1995)

■ BLACK, Circuit Judge.

This is an appeal by David G. Epstein, as the Legal Representative for the Piper future claimants (Future Claimants), from the district court's order of June 6, 1994, affirming the order of the bankruptcy court entered on December 6, 1993. The sole issue on appeal is whether the class of Future Claimants, as defined by the bankruptcy court, holds claims against the estate of Piper Aircraft Corporation (Piper), within the meaning of § 101(5) of the Bankruptcy Code. After review of the relevant provisions, policies and goals of the Bankruptcy Code and the applicable case law, we hold that the Future Claimants do not have claims as defined by § 101(5) and thus affirm the opinion of the district court.

I. FACTUAL AND PROCEDURAL BACKGROUND . . .

Piper has been manufacturing and distributing general aviation aircraft and spare parts throughout the United States and abroad since 1937. Approximately 50,000 to 60,000 Piper aircraft still are operational in the United States. . . . Piper has been a named defendant in several lawsuits based on its manufacture, design, sale, distribution and support of its aircraft and parts . . . .

On July 1, 1991, Piper filed a voluntary petition under Chapter 11 of Bankruptcy Code in the United States Bankruptcy Court for the Southern District of Florida. Piper's plan of reorganization contemplated finding a purchaser of substantially all of its assets or obtaining investments from outside sources, with the proceeds of such transactions serving to fund distributions to creditors. On April 8, 1993, Piper and Pilatus Aircraft Limited signed a letter of intent pursuant to which Pilatus would purchase Piper's assets. The letter of intent required Piper to seek the appointment of a legal representative to represent the interests of future claimants by arranging a set-aside of monies generated by the sale to pay off future product liability claims.

On May 19, 1993, the bankruptcy court appointed Appellant Epstein as the legal representative for the Future Claimants. The Court defined the class of Future Claimants to include:

> All persons, whether known or unknown, born or unborn, who may, after the date of confirmation of Piper's Chapter 11 plan of reorganization, assert a claim or claims for personal injury, property damages, wrongful death, damages, contribution and/or indemnification, based in whole or in part upon events occurring or arising after the Confirmation Date, including claims based on the law of product liability, against Piper or its successor arising out of or relating to aircraft or parts manufactured and sold, designed, distributed or supported by Piper prior to the Confirmation Date.

This Order expressly stated that the court was making no finding on whether the Future Claimants could hold claims against Piper under § 101(5) of the Code.

On July 12, 1993, Epstein filed a proof of claim on behalf of the Future Claimants in the approximate amount of $100,000,000. The claim was based on statistical assumptions regarding the number of persons likely to suffer, after the confirmation of a reorganization plan, personal injury or property damage caused by Piper's pre-confirmation manufacture, sale, design, distribution or support of aircraft and spare parts. The Official Committee of Unsecured Creditors (Official Committee), and later Piper, objected to the claim on the ground that the Future Claimants do not hold § 101(5) claims against Piper. After a hearing on the objection, the bankruptcy court agreed that the Future Claimants did not hold § 101(5) claims . . . . On June 6, 1994, the district court affirmed and accepted the decision of the bankruptcy court. . . .

II. DISCUSSION

The sole issue on appeal, whether any of the Future Claimants hold claims against Piper as defined in § 101(5) of the Bankruptcy Code, is one of first impression in this Circuit. Interpretation and application of the Bankruptcy Code is a question of law, to which this Court will apply a de novo standard of review.

A. *Statute*

Under the Bankruptcy Code, only parties that hold preconfirmation claims have a legal right to participate in a Chapter 11 bankruptcy case and share in payments pursuant to a Chapter 11 plan. 11 U.S.C. §§ 101(10), 501, 502. In order to determine if the Future Claimants have such a right to participate, we first must address the statutory definition of the term "claim." The Bankruptcy Code defines claim as:

> (A) right to payment, whether or not such right is reduced to judgment, liquidated, unliquidated, fixed, contingent, matured, unmatured, disputed, undisputed, legal, equitable, secured, or unsecured; or

> (B) right to an equitable remedy for breach of performance if such breach gives rise to a right to payment, whether or not such right to an equitable remedy is reduced to judgment, fixed, contingent, matured, unmatured, disputed, undisputed, secured, or unsecured.

11 U.S.C.A. § 101(5). The legislative history of the Code suggests that Congress intended to define the term claim very broadly under § 101(5), so that "all legal obligations of the debtor, no matter how remote or contingent, will be able to be dealt with in the bankruptcy case."

B. *Case Law*

Since the enactment of § 101(5), courts have developed several tests to determine whether certain parties hold claims pursuant to that section: the accrued state law claim test,[2] the conduct test, and the prepetition relationship test. The bankruptcy court and district court adopted the prepetition relationship test in determining that the Future Claimants did not hold claims pursuant to § 101(5).

Epstein primarily challenges the district court's application of the prepetition relationship test. He argues that the conduct test, which some

---

2.   The accrued state law claim theory states that there is no claim for bankruptcy purposes until a claim has accrued under state law.   The most notable case adopting this approach is the Third Circuit's decision in *In re: M. Frenville Co.*, 744 F.2d 332 (3d Cir. 1984). This test since has been rejected by a majority of courts as imposing too narrow an interpretation on the term claim. *See, e.g.*, Grady v. A.H. Robins Co., 839 F.2d 198, 201 (4th Cir. 1988). We agree with these courts and decline to employ the state law claim theory.

courts have adopted in mass tort cases,[3] is more consistent with the text, history, and policies of the Code. Under the conduct test, a right to payment arises when the conduct giving rise to the alleged liability occurred. *See A.H. Robins*, 839 F.2d at 199. Epstein's position is that any right to payment arising out of the prepetition conduct of Piper, no matter how remote, should be deemed a claim and provided for, pursuant to § 101(5), in this case. He argues that the relevant conduct giving rise to the alleged liability was Piper's prepetition manufacture, design, sale and distribution of allegedly defective aircraft. Specifically, he contends that, because Piper performed these acts prepetition, the potential victims, although not yet identifiable, hold claims under § 101(5) of the Code.

The Official Committee and Piper dispute the breadth of the definition of claim asserted by Epstein, arguing that the scope of claim cannot extend so far as to include unidentified, and presently unidentifiable, individuals with no discernible prepetition relationship to Piper. Recognizing, as Appellees do, that the conduct test may define claim too broadly in certain circumstances, several courts have recognized "claims" only for those individuals with some type of prepetition relationship with the debtor. In re: Jensen, 995 F.2d 925, 929-31 (9th Cir. 1993); In re: Chateaugay Corp., 944 F.2d 997, 1003-04 (2d Cir. 1991). The prepetition relationship test, as adopted by the bankruptcy court and district court, requires "some prepetition relationship, such as contact, exposure, impact, or privity, between the debtor's prepetition conduct and the claimant" in order for the claimant to hold a § 101(5) claim.

Upon examination of the various theories, we agree with Appellees that the district court utilized the proper test in deciding that the Future Claimants did not hold a claim under § 101(5). Epstein's interpretation of "claim" and application of the conduct test would enable anyone to hold a claim against Piper by virtue of their potential future exposure to any aircraft in the existing fleet. Even the conduct test cases, on which Epstein relies, do not compel the result he seeks. In fact, the conduct test cases recognize that focusing solely on prepetition conduct, as Epstein espouses, would stretch the scope of § 101(5). Accordingly, the courts applying the conduct test also presume some prepetition relationship between the debtor's conduct and the claimant. *See A.H. Robins*, 839 F.2d at 203; *Waterman*, 141 B.R. at 556.

While acknowledging that the district court's test is more consistent with the purposes of the Bankruptcy Code than is the conduct test supported by Epstein, we find that the test as set forth by the district court unnecessarily restricts the class of claimants to those who could be identified prior to the filing of the petition. Those claimants having contact with the debtor's product post-petition but prior to confirmation also could

---

3.   *See, e.g., A.H. Robins Co.*, 839 F.2d at 203 (Dalkon Shield); In re: Waterman S.S. Corp., 141 B.R. 552, 556 (Bankr. S.D.N.Y. 1992) (asbestos), *vacated on other grounds*, 157 B.R. 220 (Bankr. S.D.N.Y. 1993); In re: Johns-Manville Corp., 36 B.R. 743, 750 (Bankr. S.D.N.Y. 1984) (asbestos).

be identified, during the course of the bankruptcy proceeding, as potential victims, who might have claims arising out of debtor's prepetition conduct.

We therefore modify the test used by the district court and adopt what we will call the "Piper test" in determining the scope of the term claim under § 101(5): an individual has a § 101(5) claim against a debtor manufacturer if (i) events occurring before confirmation create a relationship, such as contact, exposure, impact, or privity, between the claimant and the debtor's product; and (ii) the basis for liability is the debtor's prepetition conduct in designing, manufacturing and selling the allegedly defective or dangerous product. The debtor's prepetition conduct gives rise to a claim to be administered in a case only if there is a relationship established before confirmation between an identifiable claimant or group of claimants and that prepetition conduct.

In the instant case, it is clear that the Future Claimants fail the minimum requirements of the Piper test. There is no preconfirmation exposure to a specific identifiable defective product or any other preconfirmation relationship between Piper and the broadly defined class of Future Claimants. As there is no preconfirmation connection established between Piper and the Future Claimants, the Future Claimants do not hold a § 101(5) claim arising out of Piper's prepetition design, manufacture, sale, and distribution of allegedly defective aircraft.

JONES V. CHEMETRON CORP.

212 F.3d 199 (3d Cir. 2000)

■ ROSENN, Circuit Judge.

[The defendant, Chemetron Corp., deposited radioactive and toxic waste at a dump in the plaintiffs' neighborhood. Chemetron filed for Chapter 11 reorganization in 1988, and its reorganization plan was confirmed in 1990. In 1992, fourteen plaintiffs filed suit in state court for injuries sustained as a result of exposure to Chemetron's materials. The number of plaintiffs eventually expanded to twenty-one. Chemetron removed the case, arguing that its discharge in bankruptcy barred the suits. The plaintiffs argued that their claims were not discharged both because they were unaware of their illnesses at the time of the discharge, and because they had received inadequate notice of the bankruptcy proceeding. The district court held that the plaintiffs had received adequate notice and, after a remand from an earlier appeal, also held that the plaintiffs had failed to show excusable neglect in not filing claims in the bankruptcy case.

[The court of appeals began by reciting its rule from *In re M. Frenville Co., Inc.*, 744 F.2d 332 (3d Cir. 1984), that "in most circumstances a 'claim' arises for bankruptcy purposes at the same time the underlying state law cause of action accrues." Acknowledging "the criticism the *Frenville* decision has engendered" in other circuits because of its restrictive view of the circumstances in which a bankruptcy court can discharge a later-developing claim, the court nonetheless held that, on the facts of the case, the claims of twenty of the plaintiffs had accrued before the date set in the bankruptcy proceeding for filing claims, and were therefore discharged in bankruptcy. The court also held that the district court had not erred in concluding that none of these plaintiffs had proven excusable neglect.]

We note, however, that one of the plaintiffs, Ivan Schaffer, was not born until August 27, 1992, more than two years after the bankruptcy court confirmed Chemetron's plan of reorganization. We believe his situation merits separate discussion.

Under Chapter 11 of the Bankruptcy Code, "the confirmation of a plan . . . discharges the debtor from any debt that arose before the date of such confirmation." 11 U.S.C. § 1141(d)(1)(A). Thus, in most circumstances, "confirmation of the debtor's reorganization plan discharges all prior claims against the debtor." Chemetron [Corp. v. Jones, 72 F.2d 341, 346 (3d Cir. 1995).][13] However, if a potential claimant lacks sufficient notice of a bankruptcy proceeding, due process considerations dictate that his or her claim cannot be discharged by a confirmation order.

Such due process considerations are often addressed by the appointment of a representative to receive notice for and represent the interests of a group of unknown creditors. In *In re Amatex*, 755 F.2d 1034 (3d Cir. 1985), this court held that a representative could be appointed to represent the interests of future unknown asbestos claimants in bankruptcy reorganization proceedings because such claimants are "sufficiently affected by the reorganization proceedings" as to require some voice in them and therefore qualify as "parties in interest" under 11 U.S.C. § 1109(b). *Accord* In re Forty-Eight Insulations, Inc., 58 B.R. 476, 477 (Bankr. N.D. Ill. 1986); In re UNR Indus., Inc., 46 B.R. 671, 675 (Bankr. N.D. Ill. 1985); In re Johns-Manville Corp., 36 B.R. 743, 747-49 (Bankr. S.D.N.Y. 1984). The *Amatex* court did not decide whether future claimants are "creditors" who possess "claims" that may be discharged by a bankruptcy confirmation order. We need not reach this issue, however, because in the instant case there exists a more fundamental problem. Ivan Schaffer cannot be deemed to have received adequate notice of Chemetron's Chapter 11 bankruptcy proceeding, because no effort was made to address his potential claims in that proceeding.

Where no action is taken to address the interests of unborn future claimants in a Chapter 11 bankruptcy reorganization proceeding, the reorganized former debtor cannot later avoid liability to such claimants by arguing that their claims were discharged in bankruptcy. Under fundamental notions of procedural due process, a claimant who has no appropriate notice of a bankruptcy reorganization cannot have his claim extinguished in a settlement pursuant thereto. *See, e.g.,* Mullane v. Cent. Hanover Bank & Trust Co., 339 U.S. 306, 314-19 (1950). Here, Ivan

---

13. *See also* Epstein v. Official Comm. of Unsecured Creditors of Estate of Piper Aircraft Corp., 58 F.3d 1573, 1576, 1577 (11th Cir. 1995); In re Waterman S.S. Corp., 157 B.R. 220, 221 (S.D.N.Y. 1993).

Schaffer had no notice of or participation in the Chemetron reorganization plan. No effort was made during the course of the bankruptcy proceeding to have a representative appointed to receive notice for and represent the interests of future claimants. Therefore, whatever claim Ivan Schaffer may now have was not subject to the bankruptcy court's bar date order, and was not discharged by that court's confirmation order.

Chemetron contends that as a future claimant, Ivan Schaffer had sufficient notice of the bankruptcy proceeding because his mother, also a plaintiff to this action, had notice of the proceeding and was qualified to act as guardian for her unborn children. Although we do not dispute that a parent can represent the interests of her minor children, because of the imponderables involved, we do not believe the law imposes a duty upon a parent to take action to protect a potential claim of a child not yet conceived or born. Nor do we believe that in a Chapter 11 reorganization, a bankruptcy court is obligated sua sponte to appoint a representative to deal with future interests if no request is made. *See* Locks v. United States Trustee, 157 B.R. 89, 95-99 (W.D. Pa. 1993).[15] Such a duty would impose an enormous and unreasonable responsibility of prescience on the courts. Accordingly, we hold that the potential claim of an unborn child not represented in bankruptcy reorganization proceedings is not discharged by a confirmation order. . . .

For the foregoing reasons, the judgment of the district court will be affirmed except as to plaintiff Ivan Schaffer. As to Ivan Schaffer, the May 18, 1999 order of the district court will be reversed and the case remanded with instructions to direct the bankruptcy court to issue a declaration that his potential claim was not discharged by the July 12, 1990 confirmation order.

Notes

1.   The standard rule is that bankruptcy discharges only those claims that arise before the confirmation of the reorganization plan. Therefore, people whose claims first arise after confirmation of the plan are free to sue the debtor without worrying about the discharge. For the most part, this rule is entirely appropriate; most post-confirmation claims deal with the debtor's post-confirmation behavior. But in the context of injuries with long latency periods, the post-confirmation claim concerns pre-confirmation behavior. A principal reason that debtors facing large numbers of claims use bankruptcy is to shed its exposure to these claims. If the debtor continues to face these claims after emerging from bankruptcy, it had little reason to enter bankruptcy. Nor, from the viewpoint of bankruptcy, does the persistence of these claims help to rehabilitate the debtor. Finally, from

---

15. We do not address whether such appointment is mandatory in bankruptcy liquidation proceedings. *Compare Forty-Eight Insulations*, 58 B.R. at 477 (appointing futures representative in liquidation proceeding because after debtor-entity dissolves, future claimants will have no recourse)[,] *with Locks*, 157 B.R. at 96 (appointment of futures representative in liquidation proceeding unnecessary).

society's viewpoint, resolving related claims in one proceeding can be beneficial, and treating claims discharged in bankruptcy differently from those that fortuitously arise afterwards is problematic. *See* Thomas A. Smith, *A Capital Markets Approach to Mass Tort Bankruptcy*, 104 YALE L.J. 367, 382 (1994) (Rawlsian "[h]ypothetical contract analysis indicates that, for mass tort bankruptcies that involve serious injury to at least some claimants, fairness requires equal treatment of claimants regardless of the timing of their claims. This result, I believe, is consistent with the moral intuitions of most people who have reflected on the issue.") Therefore, good reasons exists for a debtor and the bankruptcy court want to discharge these claims.

Of course, strong arguments exist on the other side as well. Claims that were adjudicated or settled before the bankruptcy proceeding received full value, so it is not necessarily fair to deny full value to claims that arose afterwards just because the claims in bankruptcy received pennies on the dollar. This is especially true if the debtor emerges from bankruptcy into a profitable concern. Which set of concerns seems more compelling?

2.   One of the major roadblocks for those who wish to use bankruptcy to resolve future claims is the language of the bankruptcy statute itself. Among them, *Grady*, *Epstein*, and *Jones* show the two critical bankruptcy doctrines that intersect with future claims: the automatic stay and the bankruptcy discharge. *Grady* is the leading case in the issue of extending the automatic stay to claims that are based on pre-petition conduct but that fully mature only after the petition is filed. The Fourth Circuit was clear that its decision to extend the automatic stay to a future claimant like Ms. Grady did not determine whether the court could discharge her claim in bankruptcy — which is the far more critical question. Nonetheless, because the court based its decision on an interpretation of the word "claim," and because the bankruptcy discharge under Chapter 11 covers the "claim" of any creditor, *see* 11 U.S.C. § 1141(a), *Grady*'s "conduct test" has inevitably had a significant influence on the more important question of a court's ability to discharge future claims.

Unlike *Grady*, *Epstein* says that some claimants without injuries that had manifested themselves before the petition was filed hold "claims" dischargeable in bankruptcy. *See also* In re UNR Indus., Inc., 20 F.3d 766, 770 (7th Cir. 1994) (strongly implying that future asbestos lawsuits were "claims" under 11 U.S.C. § 101(5)(A)). *Epstein* describes the various positions of the courts on the issue, and remains an influential decision in the area. *Epstein* describes four basic approaches: *Frenville*'s "accrual test," *Grady*'s "conduct test," *Chateaugay*'s "prepetition relationship test," and its own hybrid, the "*Piper* test." *See also* In re Oneida, Ltd., 383 B.R. 29 (Bankr. S.D.N.Y. 2008) (using a "relationship and contemplation" test, under which the future plaintiff must have a pre-petition relationship with the debtor and the contingent claim must have been in the contemplation of both parties at that time). Given the relevant policy considerations on both sides of the question, which of the tests seems best to you? Which fits most closely with the language of the Bankruptcy Code?

3. If we accept the idea that a court sitting in bankruptcy has the power to discharge — in other words, preclude — claims that cannot be asserted at the time that the petition is filed or the reorganization plan is confirmed, other concerns arise. The fundamental issue is due process. As we saw in Chapter Two, as a general matter, only parties to an action can be precluded by a judgment. Although the Supreme Court has recognized bankruptcy as an exception to that rule, it is not at all clear that this exception extends as far as precluding future plaintiffs, who did not even have claims to present during the bankruptcy process. The most basic requirements of due process are notice and an opportunity to be heard, and how a court can provide either notice or an opportunity to participate to people who don't have assertable claims is problematic.

As *Piper* shows, courts have tended to solve this problem by appointing a legal representative for future claimants. The seminal case finding the authority within the Bankruptcy Code to appoint such representatives is *In re Johns-Manville Corp.*, 52 B.R. 940 (S.D.N.Y. 1985). *Johns-Manville* did not determine that future plaintiffs possessed "claims" dischargeable in bankruptcy; it justified the appointment by holding that future plaintiffs were "parties in interest" under 11 U.S.C. § 1109.

According to *Jones*, without appointment of such a representative, it is almost certain that a court will find a lack of due process in the discharge of future claims. But does the appointment of a legal representative satisfy due process? Does the constitutional question depend on whether the claimants are "near-term" future claimants whose claims mature during the bankruptcy process, as opposed to "long-term" future claimants whose claims will not mature until after (perhaps years after) confirmation of the reorganization plan? Does it depend instead on whether the nature of the future claims and the extent of the claimants' injuries are foreseeable at the time of the reorganization process? Does it depend on whether the legal representative is himself or herself a future claimant? Or does the use of a legal representative always comport with due process? One way to test you answer to these questions is to consider Ivan Schaffer's situation. Suppose that the court in *Jones* had appointed a legal representative for "long-term futures," including the later-born. Would that appointment satisfy due process? Would the later-born need a separate representative dedicated to their interests? How can someone represent the interests of a person about whom, by definition, they know nothing?

The obvious analogy to a legal representative is the class representative appointed under Rule 23. Can a legal representative in bankruptcy satisfy due process if he or she does not meet the same typicality, adequacy, and other requirements that a class representative must meet? In *Epstein*, the legal representative was David Epstein, a noted bankruptcy lawyer and scholar. He did not apparently own a Piper airplane, nor did he have any intention of buying one. In *Johns-Manville*, the appointed representative was Leon Silverman, also a noted lawyer. There was no indication that he had been exposed to asbestos or might develop a compensable claim in the future. Were Epstein and Silverman adequate representatives? Can any legal representative be constitutionally adequate? *See UNR Industries*, 20 F.3d at 770 (dismissing constitutional concerns); Ralph R. Mabey & Jamie A. Gavrin, *Constitutional Limitations on the Discharge of Future Claims in Bankruptcy*, 44 S.C. L. REV. 745 (1993) (same); *but see* John C. Coffee, Jr., *Class Wars: The Dilemma of the Mass Tort Class Action*, 95 COLUM. L. REV. 1343, 1422-33 (1995) (questioning whether standing exists with regard to future claimants for bankruptcy purposes).

4. In thinking through these questions, two matters might be relevant. The first is the nature of the job that the legal representatives is expected to perform. As a rule, one goal of the reorganization is to find a way to fold the claims of future claimants into the reorganization plan, thus letting the debtor walk away from the bankruptcy without the future claims looming over them. As a quid pro quo, the plan must make provisions for handling future claims. Thus, the legal representative usually acts as the advocate for future claimants during negotiations over the plan.

Second, and relatedly, is the effectiveness of legal representatives as negotiators. One study of legal representatives was highly critical of legal representatives, in large part because they did not represent an identifiable group of existing claimants. Because future claims and claimants were abstract, they succumbed to the "vividness effect," and were often underestimated in number and size:

> Essentially, present claimants and equity holders can agree to split among themselves the share that belongs to future claimants under the equal-treatment norms. All that stands in the way of this split is the future claims representative, who is accountable not to the anonymous future claimants, but to the court, an institution with incentives that incline it less to fair allocation than to final agreement on a plan.

See Smith, *supra*, at 389; *id.* at 372 (arguing that "[s]trong forces militate against equal treatment of present and future claimants, causing what I call the 'fair distribution problem'"). For instance, in the *Manville* bankruptcy, Professor Smith concluded that the legal representative abetted the strategic behavior of equity holders and present claimants to divide most of the residual value of the reorganized Manville between them, leaving future claimants with no effective remedy: "He apparently saw his role not as the intransigent defender of future claimants, but as the honest broker among constituencies. That the [he] adopted the role of broker was not an accident, as [he] was the only claimant representative whose constituency was entirely unable to monitor his performance." *Id.* at 391. *Cf.* In re Combustion Eng'g, Inc., 391 F.3d 190, 241 (3d Cir. 2004) (finding that a reorganization plan violated "the fundamental bankruptcy policy of 'equality of distribution among creditors'" by using two distinct trusts to compensate present and future claimants, when the future-plaintiff trust paid out lower awards).

5. The usual way in which reorganization plans address future claims is to establish a separate trust from which future claimants must seek compensation. The bankruptcy court enters a "channeling injunction" that requires future claimants to seek compensation from the trust rather than

from the reorganized debtor. *See* Kane v. Johns-Manville Corp., 843 F.2d 636 (2d Cir. 1988).

A critical issue is the bankruptcy court's power to enter a channeling injunction. In asbestos cases, the power derives from 11 U.S.C. §§ 524(g)-(h). Congress adopted these provisions in 1994, after a number of courts had pioneered the trust-and-channeling-injunction approach for handling asbestos bankruptcies. The provisions were an after-the-fact attempt to ratify the approach, for which the bankruptcy courts' power was unclear. Basically, an asbestos-related trust must meet certain criteria — principally, that the trust assumes the liabilities of the debtor, is funded at least in part by the debtor's securities, and owns a majority of the debtor's shares. If it does, then the court can issue a channeling injunction as long as (1) there appears to be a large but indeterminate number of future claims that are "likely to threaten the plan's purpose to deal equitably with claims and future demands" and that "the trust will value, and be in a financial position to pay, present claims and future demands that involve similar claims in substantially the same manner," the court has the power to issue a channeling injunction, *see id.* § 524(g)(2)(B)(i)-(ii); (2) the class(es) covered by the trust also approve, by a 75% majority, the reorganization plan, *see id.* § 524(g)(2)(B)(ii)(IV)(bb); and (3) the court "appoints a legal representative for the purpose of protecting the rights of persons that might subsequently assert demands of such kind," *see id.* § 524(g)(4)(B)(i); and (4) the court determines that the plan is "fair and equitable with respect to the persons that might subsequently assert such demands," *see id.* § 524(g)(4)(B)(ii). (This is a quick summary of complex provisions; the statute imposes other requirements that we gloss over here.)

The injunction can run in favor not only of the debtor, but also any "third party" that (1) is "directly or indirectly liable for the conduct of, claims against, or demands on the debtor," and (2) is a director, officer, owner, insurer, or financier of the debtor. *Id.* § 524(g)(4)(A)(ii). If an asbestos non-debtor does not meet this description, the legal authority for an injunction that channels plaintiffs with claims against the non-debtors into the § 524(g) trust must lie elsewhere — or perhaps is non-existent. For instance, *Combustion Engineering* held that "[b]ecause § 524(g) expressly contemplates the inclusion of third parties' liability within the scope of a channeling injunction — and sets out the specific requirements that must be met in order to permit inclusion — the general powers of § 105(a) cannot be used to achieve a result not contemplated by the more specific provisions of § 524(g)." 391 F.3d at 236-37.

Before §§ 524(g)-(h), courts in asbestos bankruptcies had located the power to issue channeling injunctions in the general equitable power of 11 U.S.C. § 105(a). Many courts were uneasy about whether this power allowed channeling injunctions. *See Kane*, 843 F.2d at 641-46 (holding that present creditors lacked standing to assert the rights of future claimants to challenge the injunction). That unease remains relevant, because §§ 524(g)-(h) apply only to certain asbestos trusts. In the non-asbestos context, no comparably explicit legislative authority exists. Therefore, the authority to issue channeling injunctions in non-asbestos cases continues to rely on the uncertain foundation of § 105(a). *See* In re Metromedia Fiber Network, Inc., 416 F.3d 136, 142 (2d Cir. 2005).

Aside from the uncertainty about whether § 105(a) can be read so broadly, the power to issue channeling injunctions is complicated by §§ 524(g)-(h). Some courts have held that the explicit limitation of §§ 524(g)-(h) to asbestos case prohibits the use of channeling injunctions in non-asbestos cases. *See* Resorts Int'l, Inc. v. Lowenschuss, 67 F.3d 1394, 1401-02 & 1402 n.6 (9th Cir. 1995); *cf. Metromedia Network*, 416 F.3d at 142 (noting the "reluctance" to use channeling injunctions due to the language of §§ 524(g)(-(h)).

6.   The channeling injunction is an example of the ways in which the issues in the last two subsections — extending the protection of a discharge to non-debtors and extending its preclusive effect to future claims — intersect. For a reorganization plan to work, the channeling injunction must solve both issues, because non-debtors such as insurers often supply much of the capital to fund future-claim trusts, and they will not agree to fund such mechanisms if they remain exposed to future lawsuits.

In *Travelers Indemnity Co. v. Bailey*, 557 U.S. —, 129 S. Ct. 2195 (2009), the Supreme Court addressed obliquely a channeling injunction that blended issues of a court's power to resolve claims against non-debtors and to resolve future claims. *Travelers* arose out of the Manville bankruptcy. As part of the confirmation plan, the bankruptcy court in 1986 enjoined suits against Travelers, which had insured Manville. In 2002, Travelers asked the bankruptcy court to enjoin twenty-six cases in which the plaintiffs, all of whom were claiming injuries from exposure to Manville's asbestos products, claimed that Travelers had engaged in independent wrongdoing by hiding the dangers of asbestos from the public. The 1986 channeling injunction was somewhat ambiguous about whether such direct claims, as opposed to derivative claims for Manville's wrongdoing, were barred. Travelers agreed to settle the claims for $400 million in return for a "clarifying order" from the bankruptcy court that direct claims fell within the 1986 injunction. On appeal from an order approving the settlement, the Second Circuit held that the clarifying order exceeded the bankruptcy court's subject-matter jurisdiction and its statutory authority because the bankruptcy court had no jurisdiction to issue the original 1986 injunction in favor of Travelers. The Supreme Court reversed, holding that the clarifying order correctly interpreted the scope of 1986 injunction and that the plaintiffs could not collaterally attack the subject-matter jurisdiction of the court that issued the 1986 order in a proceeding many years later.

The Court was careful to limit its holding, declining to "resolve whether a bankruptcy court, in 1986 or today, could properly enjoin claims against nondebtor insurers that are not derivative of the debtor's wrongdoing" or to decide whether the plaintiffs had been "given constitutionally sufficient notice of the 1986 Orders." *Id.* at 2195.

7.   The last caveat mentioned in *Travelers* brings up again the question of the constitutionality of a process that bars future claimants. Note that

the Court had raised the same constitutional concern regarding future claimants in *Amchem Products, Inc. v. Windsor*, 521 U.S. 591, 628 (1997) (*supra* p. 493), in which the Court recognized "the gravity of the question whether class action notice sufficient under the Constitution and Rule 23 could ever be given to legions so unselfconscious and amorphous." Certainly, as *Jones* says, the Constitution is not satisfied when future plaintiffs receive no notice of the settlement of their clams. But is notice given to a legal representative constitutionally sufficient? *See* Mabey & Gavrin, *supra*, at 779-84 (rejecting notice concerns when a legal representative is given notice); *cf.* John C. Coffee, Jr., *Class Wars: The Dilemma of the Mass Tort Class Action*, 95 COLUM. L. REV. 1343, 1422-33 (1995) (questioning whether standing exists for future claimants in bankruptcy).

Indeed, "the grave representation and notice problems" played out on remand in *Travelers*. In re Johns-Manville Corp., — F.3d —, 2010 WL 1007832, at *18 (2d Cir. Mar. 22, 2010). The Second Circuit held that one of the insurers in the *Travelers* case, Chubb, failed to receive constitutionally adequate representation and constitutionally adequate notice in the 1986 order, and permitted Chubb to attack the orders collaterally. The court of appeals relied on *Amchem* and on its prior decision in *Stephenson v. Dow Chemical Co.*, 273 F.3d 249 (2d Cir. 2001), *aff'd in part by an equally divided Court and vacated in part*, 539 U.S. 111 (2003) (*supra* p. 536), to hold that Chubb's future interests and those of asbestos claimants diverged so much that Chubb could not be bound to the order.

8.   Another problem with future claimants is voting. Recall that every class of allowed claims and every class of interests must vote to accept the reorganization plan; if a class rejects the plan, the plan can be implemented only under the cramdown rules of 11 U.S.C. § 1129(b). If future claimants hold either allowed "claims" or "interests," they must be given a chance to vote. Moreover, in the asbestos context, 75% of a trust's beneficiaries must also vote to approve the plan. How can such a vote be taken, when by definition no one can know who the actual claimants entitled to vote are?

According to the voting process in bankruptcy, a creditor obtains the right to vote by filing a proof of claim; if no one objects to the claim, then the claimant has a right to vote. If an objection is made, the claimant must ask the court to allow the claim (and thus to vote). Giving notice to future claimants advising them of their right to vote might not yield many filings. Moreover, if the debtor or other creditors object to a filing, future claimants must go through the trouble of asking the court to allow the claim. As a result, many mass-tort bankruptcies dispense with the requirement of filing claims, and allow claimants to vote unfiled claims or allow attorneys to vote their clients' claims in a master ballot. *See* In re Quigley Co., 346 B.R. 647 (Bankr. S.D.N.Y. 2006). *See also Combustion Engineering*, 391 F.3d at 242-47 (discussing "stub claim" voting process and issues that it raises). But this process still requires claimants to step forward; and it is likely that only those that have contacted lawyers (i.e., those with near-future claims) are likely to do so in significant numbers. Does such a voting process result in a distorted representation of the true preferences of future claimants?

9.   One of the central concerns with using bankruptcy to handle future claims is the fear that the dynamics of the bankruptcy process will undervalue such claims, which lack the vividness of existing claims and the lack of vigorous representation that might result. It might be possible to assuage the concern by making it easy to modify the trust in the event that it proves inadequate to meet the needs of future plaintiffs. The most famous example of such a situation is the Manville trust, which ran out of money within a few years of opening its doors. Future plaintiffs then filed a lawsuit seeking significant modifications in the trust and additional contributions from the reorganized Manville. In a massive and erudite opinion, Judge Weinstein pushed the modifications through. In re Joint E. & S. Dist. Asbestos Litig., 129 B.R. 710 (E. & S.D.N.Y. 1991). The Second Circuit reluctantly reversed.   982 F.2d 721 (2d Cir. 1992), *modified*, 993 F.2d 7 (2d Cir. 1993). Judge Weinstein met the Second Circuit's concerns in subsequent proceedings. 878 F. Supp. 473 (E. & S.D.N.Y 1995). This time the Second Circuit substantially affirmed, but vacated a small portion of the opinion. 78 F.3d 764 (2d Cir. 1996). On remand Judge Weinstein fixed the problem. 929 F. Supp. 1 (E. & S.D.N.Y 1996).

Whether the story of the Manville trust shows that the system works, or is a cautionary tale about why bankruptcy courts should never address future claims, is a question whose answer lies in the eye of the beholder.

10. Class actions and bankruptcy overlap in important ways. Both can be used to draw together related claims that are asserted against multiple defendants, including claims asserted by future claimants. Should courts be reluctant to use Rule 23 expansively in contexts that might implicate bankruptcy? In *Ortiz v. Fibreboard Corp.*, 527 U.S. 815, 860 n.34 (1999) (*supra* p. 506), the Court's refusal to permit a limited-fund class action for future asbestos claimants was premised in part on the way in which such a class action might impinge on the bankruptcy process:

. . . While there is no inherent conflict between a limited fund class action under Rule 23(b)(1)(B) and the Bankruptcy Code, it is worth noting that if limited fund certification is allowed in a situation where a company provides only a *de minimis* contribution to the ultimate settlement fund, the incentives such a resolution would provide to companies facing tort liability to engineer settlements similar to the one negotiated in this case would, in all likelihood, significantly undermine the protections for creditors built into the Bankruptcy Code. We note further that Congress . . . amended the Bankruptcy Code to enable a debtor in a Chapter 11 reorganization in certain circumstances to establish a trust toward which the debtor may channel future asbestos-related liability, *see* 11 U.S.C. §§ 524(g), (h).

Likewise, in *In re Joint Eastern & Southern District Asbestos Litigation*, 14 F.3d 726 (2d Cir. 1993), an asbestos manufacturer filed a case seeking a stay of all litigation against it and approval of a mandatory limited-fund class action for settling all claims. After finding that the defendant had insufficient assets to compensate all asbestos victims, Judge Weinstein certified a class and ordered settlement discussions to begin. The court of appeals reversed. It noted the parallels between the finding of a limited fund and the finding of insolvency, between the antisuit injunction and the automatic stay, and between a class settlement and the cramdown and discharge provisions in bankruptcy. Using a class action to accomplish these results was "a self-evident evasion of the exclusive legal system established by Congress for debtors to seek relief." *Id.* at 732. Responding to the argument that the bankruptcy process would be more costly and would thus result in lower awards for claimants, the Second Circuit responded that "the function of federal courts is not to conduct trials over whether a statutory scheme should be ignored because a more efficient mechanism can be fashioned by judges." *Id.* at 733.

For a study comparing the costs and benefits of mandatory class actions and bankruptcy in several well-known mass torts, see S. ELIZABETH GIBSON, FED. JUDICIAL CTR., CASE STUDIES OF MASS TORT LIMITED FUND CLASS ACTION SETTLEMENTS & BANKRUPTCY REORGANIZATIONS (2000).

C. CONCLUDING THOUGHTS

Bankruptcy law, rightfully perhaps, focuses primarily on the situation of the debtor, not on the larger controversy of which the debtor is a part. The consequence of this focus is that the most useful aggregation tool in existence still falls short of being an adequate solution for the problem of structural complexity. Nonetheless, bankruptcy is important to the study of complex litigation for two reasons.

First, however inadequate bankruptcy is, it is the best that we have. In some cases, a patchwork of other doctrines can achieve comparable results. But in many cases nothing else will do. In terms of our present situation, bankruptcy is an essential piece of the puzzle.

Second, bankruptcy may limit on our ability to effect joinder through other devices. As some courts have suggested, mandatory class actions are inappropriate when a debtor's insolvency creates the "limited fund." The same argument might be made in other contexts as well: We should not use this or that aggregation method because to do so would override the specific protections of bankruptcy. This argument is likely to be important in a significant number of complex cases, because the insufficiency of a defendant's assets is a major cause of structural complexity. The explicit jurisdictional and procedural powers in bankruptcy might also make a judge wary of implying such powers in non-bankruptcy settings.

As we now leave our study of aggregation devices, we still lack the Holy Grail of aggregation. The bankruptcy system has the features that we want in a Holy Grail, but they are put to use only to advance the interests of the debtor and its creditors, not the social interest in optimal aggregation. So is structural complexity an inveterate feature of the litigation landscape, or can we some day look forward to its end?

CHAPTER SIX

AGGREGATION
AND CHOICE OF LAW

Part of the law of every court — whether federal, state, or foreign — is a set of choice-of-law rules. Such rules are needed because substantive and procedural laws vary among jurisdictions. This variance is obvious for claims founded on state law. It is less obvious, but equally true, for claims based on federal law: Often different districts or circuits have varying interpretations of federal law. In many cases, more than one jurisdiction has a legitimate claim to have its law applied to determine a legal controversy; as a matter of fairness, expectation, or comity, the forum state might wish not to apply its own law. The task of choice-of-law rules is to determine which jurisdiction's laws should decide a controversy.

Choice-of-law rules affect structural complexity in two distinct ways. First, choice-of-law rules can lead plaintiffs to file cases in different forums, thus creating the geographical and intersystem dispersion that frustrate single-forum aggregation. Ideally, all of the cases arising from a plane crash in Texas would be filed in Texas. When choice-of-law rules make it desirable for some plaintiffs to file in New York and others in Texas or Alaska, and when plaintiffs get to choose the forum in which to file their cases, choice-of-law rules scatter related cases across the country. While other factors may counteract this effect, choice-of-law rules are a cause of multiforum, complexity-inducing litigation.

Second, choice of law rules can make it impractical or impossible to aggregate cases in a single forum. Assume that a mass tort has injured persons in every state, that each state's law differs in some regards, and that each state's choice-of-law rule would lead to the application of its own law. If cases are filed in each state, and if the law of each transferor court must be applied, the court in which aggregation occurs must apply the laws of fifty different jurisdictions. In turn, different laws potentially require the court to tailor as many as fifty approaches to discovery and pretrial, jury instructions, and remedies. Indeed, as we saw in Chapter Four, because different laws can create such pretrial, trial, or remedial complexity that an aggregated case becomes unmanageable, a court might choose not to allow class certification.

It is fair to say that, until we solve the choice-of-law problem, we cannot solve the aggregation problem. Indeed, forum manipulation to secure advantageous choice-of-law rules is common among skillful lawyers. Professor Lowenfeld tells the story of a couple killed in an airplane crash in Texas. The couple had three daughters. The husband had recently moved from Florida to Connecticut to take a job in New York. Connecticut law was the most favorable to the daughters on the issue of damages. Had the lawyer filed the case in Connecticut, however, the state's choice-of-law rule would have required the use of Texas damage law. Hence, the lawyer filed the case in New York, whose choice-of-law rule required that damages be determined under the law of the decedent's domicile. A New York jury awarded nearly $8 million. Andreas F. Lowenfeld, *Mass Torts and the Conflict of Laws: The Airline Disaster*, 1989 U. ILL. L. REV. 157, 158 n.12.

We can avoid complexity-causing choice-of-law problems in one of three ways: (1) by dictating the substantive and procedural law that every court must use to resolve related cases; (2) by dictating a choice-of-law rule that makes every court choose the same substantive and procedural law; or (3) by allowing the court in which aggregation occurs to apply the same law to all claims. The following materials explore the viability and the drawbacks of each of these approaches. Section A begins by laying out the common-law and constitutional principles that constrain courts in their choice-of-law options. Section B examines the impact of federal courts on choice-of-law issues. Section C considers novel solutions designed to prevent nettlesome choice-of-law issues from derailing efforts to aggregate complex cases.

A. THE BASICS OF CHOICE OF LAW

Choice-of-law issues usually arise because, in a federal system such as ours, multiple governments promulgate law and some disputes affect the interests of more than one of those governments. For now, we assume that the only law-making jurisdictions are the federal government and each state government. In addition, we assume that the law of each of these jurisdictions is clear and undisputed. Finally, in this section, we assume that a state court is making the choice-of-law decision; the following section examines the choice-of-law issues in the federal courts.

When federal law applies, the Supremacy Clause requires state courts to give the law its proper effect. A more difficult choice-of-law issue for state courts is the "horizontal" question, in which state law provides the source of law but two or more states claim an interest in applying their law. One of the unassailable principles in choice-of-law analysis is the forum court's right to use the forum's choice-of-law rules to determine which state's law to choose. Should those rules ever require a state court to adopt non-forum law to decide the dispute? Under what circumstances? When related cases are aggregated in a single state forum, may a state court choose one law to govern the entire dispute? Does the Constitution constrain the state court's choice in any way?

The two excerpts that follow describe the main approaches used by state courts to decide which law should apply. We begin with the rules for choosing procedural law, and then turn to the more complicated picture for choosing substantive law.

RESTATEMENT (SECOND) OF CONFLICT OF LAWS

350 (1971)

§ 122. Issues Relating to Judicial Administration

A court usually applies its own local law rules prescribing how litigation shall be conducted even when it applies the local law of another state to resolve other issues in the case.

Friedrich K. Juenger, MASS DISASTERS AND THE CONFLICT OF LAWS

1989 U. ILL. L. REV. 105, 109-17

. . . Choice-of-law approaches that subject the victims' claims to different substantive laws are not merely unfair: by necessitating separate trials they further complicate complex litigation. How, then, do the various approaches proffered for application to mass disasters meet the twin goals of fairness and efficiency?

III. POSSIBLE APPROACHES

A. The Lex Loci Delicti

In air crash cases, some federal courts have applied, on differing rationales, the law of the place of the accident. . . . At first blush, the old rule has much to commend itself. Courts are currently "saddled with a cumbersome and unwieldy body of conflicts law that creates confusion, uncertainty and inconsistency . . . ." Judicial opinions that purport to apply that law to mass disasters are, in Willis Reese's words, "opaque" and "make for dreary reading." After plowing through some of these judicial efforts . . ., one begins to wonder whether reverting to a hard and fast rule would not be preferable. Clearly, the courts' quixotic attempts to divine interests or weigh contacts inspire little confidence in contemporary choice-of-law techniques. Apart from ease of application, the *lex loci delicti* rule also assures equal treatment of victims who perish in a common disaster.

Yet, simple and evenhanded as it may be, . . . *lex loci delicti* has become altogether unpalatable. . . . [T]he rule works well only in the limited group of mass disasters that, like plane crashes, happen in one particular place. Applying the law of the tortious impact does not produce uniformity in cases such as *Agent Orange*, where the injuries occurred in several different Indochinese locations. It would be patently absurd to relegate American service personnel to whatever remedies Vietnamese or Cambodian law may provide. Even where the injuries are suffered in one particular state, exclusive reliance on the *lex loci delicti* rule can be problematic. A plane, for instance, may crash in a state where it was not destined to go . . . .

Moreover, the place-of-the-wrong rule's seeming simplicity is deceptive. The traditional choice-of-law approach engendered a number of conceptual problems for which no solution has ever been found. . . . Should the plaintiffs, in addition to their tort claims, be able to sue in contract against the airline and to assert warranty cause of action against the aircraft's manufacturer? Can ceilings on wrongful death recovery be characterized as "procedural"? To what extent may the forum's public policy justify the disregard of the accident state's unreasonable rules? As this brief list shows, far from operating predictably and evenhandedly, the traditional rule poses more questions than it answers.

B. *The Most Significant Relationship*

The Second Restatement's "most-significant-relationship" formula is equally unhelpful. By now it should be apparent that this impressionistic phrase "means nothing except, perhaps, that the answer is not ready at hand." Such a nonrule approach does not work well even in fairly simple situations; much less can it resolve the choice-of-law problems posed by complex litigation such as the Dalkon Shield or asbestos cases, which, being truly multistate in nature, of necessity lack a center of gravity. As the *Second Restatement*'s reporter acknowledges, ". . . Formulations of this sort are hard for the courts to apply and afford little predictability of result. . . ."

C. *Interest Analysis*

. . . As applied to truly multistate situations, Currie's approach, quite apart from its questionable assumption that private litigation serves the purpose of vindicating governmental interests, is fundamentally unsatisfactory.

In practice, interest analysis amounts to little more than a long-winded pretext for the refusal to apply foreign law. An action will rarely be brought in a "disinterested" forum, because such a forum usually lacks the minimum contacts required for jurisdiction. An "interested forum," however, will usually apply its own law, even though judges may hesitate to endorse Currie's prescription to cut the Gordian knot of a "true conflict" in this parodical manner. The approach's forum bias produces desirable results only because it allows those plaintiffs who know how to forum shop to select the most favorable law. By permitting the parties to evade whatever interests other states may have, interest analysis enhances the protection of interstate accident victims.

In mass disaster cases, however, applying the law of the state where each action is brought makes little sense, especially if suits initially filed in various jurisdictions are later consolidated by the Panel on Multidistrict Litigation. In such cases, a court following the governmental interest approach would have to try the same set of facts under several different laws. It seems inconsistent on the one hand to offer a procedure that facilitates consolidation and, on the other, to countenance the kind of fragmentation that interest analysis inevitably entails.

D. *"Comparative Impairment"*

Twenty-five years ago, Baxter wrote an article that . . . urged the adoption of a "comparative-impairment" principle to resolve the "true conflicts" that governmental interest analysis creates. That principle was designed to allocate to the states spheres of law-making control by sacrificing, "in the particular case, the external objective of the state whose internal objective will be least impaired in general scope and impact by subordination in cases like the one at hand."

Baxter's proposal assumes that it is possible to measure the impairment of policies, a proposition that would be open to doubt even if governmental interests had more substance than they do have. In any event, Baxter's examples, which are simple two-state hypotheticals, shed no light on how his principle could be made to work in cases implicating the interests of numerous states. . . . [B]ecause the comparative impairment only applies to true conflicts, Baxter's approach has the effect of grouping victims into two categories: those who share the defendant's domicile and all others. Accordingly, it subjects victims of a common disaster to unequal treatment and, at the same time, complicates the disposition of mass disaster cases.

E. *"Comparative Impairment" California-Style*

Seidelson . . . also propounds the adoption of a comparative impairment principle, but one quite different from that which Baxter advocated. . . . Seidelson introduces a teleological component by according a higher rank to state interests in safeguarding health and human life than to interests in the defendants' economic integrity. This California variant of "comparative impairment" is, of course, at odds with Baxter's principle. Baxter . . . explicitly rejected "super-value judgments" about the quality of conflicting rules of decision.

Thus Seidelson, although ostensibly committed to interest analysis, in effect proposes a result-oriented approach premised on assumed differences in the intensity of various kinds of policies. . . . Seidelson's emphasis on teleology is commendable, for teleology indeed ought to play a role in the resolution of choice-of-law problems posed by mass disaster cases. His article, however, does not deal with such cases. . . . He therefore fails to come to grips with an aspect of complex litigation that ought to attract the interest analysts' attention: whenever there are multiple plaintiffs and defendants, the emphasis on the parties' domiciliary nexus is bound to generate a large number of "true conflicts." . . .

How courts should deal with such a proliferation of "true conflicts" is not apparent from Seidelson's article. Presumably, however, he, like Baxter, would single out for separate treatment those plaintiffs who share the defendant's residence . . . . Such differential treatment seems inequitable and would complicate the disposition of mass disaster cases. Even in simple two-state situations, Seidelson's methodology requires complex analyses, and his belief in counsel's ability to unravel these complexities is probably unfounded.

Notes

1. The *Restatement (Second)*'s approach on *procedural* law — in most cases the forum court applies its own procedures to a dispute — has some exceptions. *See* RESTATEMENT (SECOND) OF CONFLICT OF LAWS §§ 125, 133-34 (stating that a court should use non-forum procedural law if the substantive rights of the parties might be affected by the choice or if a procedural rule is designed to affect the outcome rather than the trial process). Professor Juenger describes varying approaches that courts use to decide which *substantive* law applies. As a result, courts often apply non-forum substantive law, while they rarely apply non-forum procedural law. Does the difference make sense? Don't procedural rules influence outcomes as much as substantive rules? Aren't substantive rules often promulgated against a particular procedural backdrop, so that their use in conjunction with another set of procedural rules might distort their intent?

Choice-of-law scholars rarely discuss the favored treatment for a forum's procedural rules, taking as a given that a forum usually has an overriding interest in applying its own procedural rules. They focus instead on the second-tier "characterization" problem of whether a particular rule is procedural or substantive. *See, e.g., Restatement (Second)*, § 7; EUGENE F. SCOLES ET AL., CONFLICT OF LAWS §§ 3.8-.12 (4th ed. 2004).

2. The fact that a court might apply its own law to procedural matters but another jurisdiction's law to substantive matters recognizes that choice-of-law principles must be applied issue-by-issue. You might have wondered whether the same is true of issues of substantive law, so that one state's law might apply on issues of liability and another state's law on issues of damage. This approach makes sure that the most relevant law is applied to each aspect of a case, but it also takes time, creates uncertainty, increases the incentives to forum shop, and makes the management of aggregated cases more difficult. Most of the modern approaches to choice of law accept the idea that different laws might apply to different aspects of a case or claim. *See, e.g.,* RESTATEMENT (SECOND), *supra*, §§ 145(2), 188(2). This concept travels under the name *dépeçage*.

3.   Another term of some importance to choice of law analysis is *renvoi*. Typically the forum court applies the forum's own choice-of-law rules to determine whose law applies. When the choice-of-law principles of State A require a court in State A to choose the law of State B, the issue arises whether the court should choose the substantive law of State B or the "whole law" of State B, including State B's choice-of-law principles. If the whole law of State B is adopted, then it might well be that the substantive law of State A (or even State C) will apply. Accepting the whole law, which is known as *renvoi*, is rare, but there are important exceptions. *See, e.g., Restatement (Second)*, § 8; SCOLES ET AL., *supra*, §§ 3.13-.14.

4.   Traditionally, American choice-of-law rules were *lex loci*, which means that the substantive law of the place of a specified event (in torts the place of the wrong, in contracts the place of the contract's signing) governed the case. *See* RESTATEMENT OF CONFLICT OF LAWS (1934). According to a recent survey, 10 states still adhere to the old *lex loci delicti* rule in tort cases, 23 follow the *Restatement (Second)*'s approach, 3 use a different "most significant relationship" approach, 2 (plus the District of Columbia) use interest analysis (with California using comparative impairment), 2 use a home-favoring *lex fori* approach, 5 use an approach pioneered by Professor Leflar to apply the "better law," and the rest adopt eclectic approaches. The numbers are roughly comparable for contract claims. *See* Symeon C. Symeonides, *Choice of Law in the American Courts in 2006: Twentieth Annual Survey*, 54 AM. J. COMP. LAW 697, 712 (2007).

The beauty of the old *lex loci* approach was that, for mass torts that cause injury in a single state (such as airplane crashes), one state's law applies regardless of the forum in which the case is filed. Plaintiffs have less incentive to sue in separate forums just to obtain favorable substantive law. Moreover, if cases from multiple forums are consolidated, a court need not worry about managing a case with multiple substantive laws. The *lex loci* approach therefore helps to avoid both ways in which choice-of-law rules can disperse cases and cause complexity. No modern approach performs these tasks as well.

These observations are not an unadulterated endorsement of *lex loci*. There were reasons, largely grounded in fairness and policy, that most courts abandoned lex loci rules in the latter half of the twentieth century. *See generally* SCOLES ET AL., *supra*, § 2.7 (tracing history). *Lex loci* principles can be inadequate or unfair. For instance, what happens when a dispersed mass tort causes injuries in many jurisdictions? Likewise, doesn't a *lex loci* rule ignore the interests of the victims' states in ensuring the safety and compensation of its citizens?

5.   The nature of choice-of-law analysis is to create one winner (the state whose law is adopted) and one or more losers (the state(s) whose law is not adopted). But choice-of-law issues arise because the controversy is larger than the law of any particular jurisdiction. Does it make sense to pick one law to the exclusion of others? Isn't that approach particularly senseless in complex litigation? Does it make more sense to create a synthesis or compromise among the laws of the interested states? Or does

that idea give too much power to judges to override the policy choices of legislatures and other states' courts? *See generally* FRIEDRICH K. JUENGER, CHOICE OF LAW AND MULTISTATE JUSTICE (1993) (arguing that judges should be able to create law that transcends state boundaries).

6.   Legislatures sometimes create choice of law rules. *See* RESTATE- MENT (SECOND), *supra*, § 6(1) (requiring courts to follow choice-of-law legislation). But choice-of-law rules are almost entirely judge-made. Thus, judges have the ability to create different choice of law rules to deal with complex cases. Unlike prior chapters of this book, in which judges needed to work around exogenously established jurisdictional or procedural rules to overcome complexity, judges control their destiny in this arena. Should they create special choice-of-law rules for complex cases? Should Congress or state legislatures? Exactly what should the content of these rules be?

7.   We return to these questions later in the chapter. The answers, however, are not grounded only in common law, statute, and policy. The following case explores important constitutional limits on a court's ability to apply a particular state's substantive law.

PHILLIPS PETROLEUM CO. V. SHUTTS

472 U.S. 797 (1985)

■   JUSTICE REHNQUIST delivered the opinion of the Court.

[The facts of the case are fully set out *supra* p. 276. In brief, a Kansas state court certified a class action that, after subtracting for opt outs, contained 28,100 class members. These class members resided in many states. The lawsuit involved the defendant's failure to pay interest on suspended royalties on gas leases in Kansas, Louisiana, Oklahoma, and Texas. Only .25% of the leases covered Kansas land, and fewer than 1,000 class members were from Kansas. In addition to the issue of whether Kansas had personal jurisdiction over class members who had no minimum contacts with the state, *Shutts* also considered whether a Kansas court could apply Kansas law to calculate the interest due to class members.]

. . . The [Kansas trial] court found petitioner liable under Kansas law for interest on the suspended royalties to all class members. The trial court relied heavily on an earlier, unrelated class action involving the same nominal plaintiff and the same defendant, Shutts, Executor v. Phillips Petroleum Co., 222 Kan. 527, 567 P. 2d 1292 (1977), *cert. denied*, 434 U.S. 1068 (1978). The Kansas Supreme Court had held in *Shutts, Executor* that a gas company owed interest to royalty owners for royalties suspended pending final [Federal Power] Commission approval of a price increase. . . . *Shutts, Executor* held as a matter of Kansas equity law that the applicable interest rates for computation of interest on suspended royalties were the interest rates at which the gas company would have had to reimburse its customers had its interim price increase been rejected by the Commission. The court in *Shutts, Executor* viewed these as the fairest interest rates because they were also the rates that petitioner required the royalty owners to meet in their indemnity agreements in order to avoid suspended royalties.

The trial court in the present case applied the rule from *Shutts, Executor*, and held petitioner liable for prejudgment and postjudgment interest on the suspended royalties, computed at the Commission rates governing petitioner's three price increases. The applicable interest rates were: 7% for royalties retained until October 1974; 9% for royalties retained between October 1974 and September 1979; and thereafter at the average prime rate. The trial court did not determine whether any difference existed between the laws of Kansas and other States, or whether another State's laws should be applied to non-Kansas plaintiffs or to royalties from leases in States other than Kansas. . . .

[The Supreme Court of Kansas affirmed. It] stated that generally the law of the forum controlled all claims unless "compelling reasons" existed to apply a different law. The court found no compelling reasons, and noted that "[the] plaintiff class members have indicated their desire to have this action determined under the laws of Kansas." The court affirmed as a matter of Kansas equity law the award of interest on the suspended royalties, at the rates imposed by the trial court. The court set the postjudgment interest rate on all claims at the Kansas statutory rate of 15%. . . .

III

The Kansas courts applied Kansas contract and Kansas equity law to every claim in this case, notwithstanding that over 99% of the gas leases and some 97% of the plaintiffs in the case had no apparent connection to the State of Kansas except for this lawsuit. Petitioner protested that the Kansas courts should apply the laws of the States where the leases were located, or at least apply Texas and Oklahoma law because so many of the leases came from those States. . . .

Petitioner contends that total application of Kansas substantive law violated the constitutional limitations on choice of law mandated by the Due Process Clause of the Fourteenth Amendment and the Full Faith and Credit Clause of Article IV, § 1. We must first determine whether Kansas law conflicts in any material way with any other law which could apply. There can be no injury in applying Kansas law if it is not in conflict with that of any other jurisdiction connected to this suit.

Petitioner claims that Kansas law conflicts with that of a number of States connected to this litigation, especially Texas and Oklahoma. [The Supreme Court stated that "there is no recorded Oklahoma decision dealing with interest liability for suspended royalties" and that "[e]ven if Oklahoma found such liability, petitioner shows that Oklahoma would most likely apply its constitutional and statutory 6% interest rate rather than the much higher Kansas rates applied in this litigation." With regard to Texas law, the Court observed that "[a]lthough Texas recognizes interest liability for suspended royalties," one Texas court had refused to award royalties on facts comparable to *Shutts*. Moreover, "Texas has never awarded any such interest at a rate greater than 6%, which corresponds with the Texas constitutional and statutory rate." Finally, the Court noted that the rate of interest in Louisiana was 7%.]

The conflicts on the applicable interest rates, alone — which we do not think can be labeled "false conflicts" without a more thoroughgoing treatment than was accorded them by the Supreme Court of Kansas — certainly amounted to millions of dollars in liability. We think that the Supreme Court of Kansas erred in deciding on the basis that it did that the application of its laws to all claims would be constitutional.

Four Terms ago we addressed a similar situation in *Allstate Ins. Co. v. Hague,* 449 U.S. 302 (1981). . . .

The plurality in *Allstate* noted that a particular set of facts giving rise to litigation could justify, constitutionally, the application of more than one jurisdiction's laws. The plurality recognized, however, that the Due Process Clause and the Full Faith and Credit Clause provided modest restrictions on the application of forum law. These restrictions required "that for a State's substantive law to be selected in a constitutionally permissible manner, that State must have a significant contact or significant aggregation of contacts, creating state interests, such that choice of its law is neither arbitrary nor fundamentally unfair." . . .

Petitioner owns property and conducts substantial business in the State, so Kansas certainly has an interest in regulating petitioner's conduct in Kansas. Moreover, oil and gas extraction is an important business to Kansas, and although only a few leases in issue are located in Kansas, hundreds of Kansas plaintiffs were affected by petitioner's suspension of royalties; thus the [Kansas Supreme Court] held that the State has a real interest in protecting "the rights of these royalty owners both as individual residents of [Kansas] and as members of this particular class of plaintiffs." The Kansas Supreme Court pointed out that Kansas courts are quite familiar with this type of lawsuit, and "[the] plaintiff class members have indicated their desire to have this action determined under the laws of Kansas." Finally, the Kansas court buttressed its use of Kansas law by stating that this lawsuit was analogous to a suit against a "common fund" located in Kansas.

We do not lightly discount this description of Kansas' contacts with this litigation and its interest in applying its law. There is, however, no "common fund" located in Kansas that would require or support the application of only Kansas law to all these claims. As the Kansas court noted, petitioner commingled the suspended royalties with its general corporate accounts. There is no specific identifiable *res* in Kansas, nor is there any limited amount which may be depleted before every plaintiff is compensated. Only by somehow aggregating all the separate claims in this case could a "common fund" in any sense be created, and the term becomes all but meaningless when used in such an expansive sense.

We also give little credence to the idea that Kansas law should apply to all claims because the plaintiffs, by failing to opt out, evinced their desire to be bound by Kansas law. Even if one could say that the plaintiffs "consented" to the application of Kansas law by not opting out, plaintiff's desire for forum law is rarely, if ever controlling. In most cases the plaintiff shows his obvious wish for forum law by filing there. "If a plaintiff could choose the substantive rules to be applied to an action . . . the invitation to forum shopping would be irresistible." *Allstate*, 449 U.S. at 337 (opinion of POWELL, J.). Even if a plaintiff evidences his desire for forum law by moving to the forum, we have generally accorded such a move little or no significance. . . . Thus the plaintiffs' desire for Kansas law, manifested by their participation in this Kansas lawsuit, bears little relevance.

The Supreme Court of Kansas in its opinion in this case expressed the view that by reason of the fact that it was adjudicating a nationwide class action, it had much greater latitude in applying its own law to the transactions in question than might otherwise be the case . . . .

We think that this is something of a "bootstrap" argument. The Kansas class-action statute, like those of most other jurisdictions, requires that there be "common issues of law or fact." But while a State may, for the reasons we have previously stated, assume jurisdiction over the claims of plaintiffs whose principal contacts are with other States, it may not use this assumption of jurisdiction as an added weight in the scale when considering the permissible constitutional limits on choice of substantive law. It may not take a transaction with little or no relationship to the forum and apply the law of the forum in order to satisfy the procedural requirement that there be a "common question of law." The issue of personal jurisdiction over plaintiffs in a class action is entirely distinct from the question of the constitutional limitations on choice of law; the latter calculus is not altered by the fact that it may be more difficult or more burdensome to comply with the constitutional limitations because of the large number of transactions which the State proposes to adjudicate and which have little connection with the forum.

Kansas must have a "significant contact or significant aggregation of contacts" to the claims asserted by each member of the plaintiff class, contacts "creating state interests," in order to ensure that the choice of Kansas law is not arbitrary or unfair. Given Kansas' lack of "interest" in claims unrelated to that State, and the substantive conflict with jurisdictions such as Texas, we conclude that application of Kansas law to every claim in this case is sufficiently arbitrary and unfair as to exceed constitutional limits.

When considering fairness in this context, an important element is the expectation of the parties. There is no indication that when the leases involving land and royalty owners outside of Kansas were executed, the parties had any idea that Kansas law would control. . . . Kansas "may not abrogate the rights of parties beyond its borders having no relation to anything done or to be done within them." Home Ins. Co. v. Dick, [281 U.S. 397, 410 (1930)].

Here the Supreme Court of Kansas took the view that in a nationwide class action where procedural due process guarantees of notice and adequate representation were met, "the law of the forum should be applied unless compelling reasons exist for applying a different law." Whatever practical reasons may have commended this rule to the Supreme Court of Kansas, for the reasons already stated we do not believe that it is consistent with the decisions of this Court. We make no effort to determine for ourselves which law must apply to the various transactions involved in this lawsuit, and we reaffirm our observation in *Allstate* that in many situations a state court may be free to apply one of several choices of law. But the constitutional limitations laid down in cases such as *Allstate* and *Home Insurance Co. v. Dick* must be respected even in a nationwide class action.

We therefore . . . reverse [the judgment of the Supreme Court of Kansas] insofar as it held that Kansas law was applicable to all of the transactions which it sought to adjudicate. We remand the case to that court for further proceedings not inconsistent with this opinion.

■ JUSTICE STEVENS . . . dissenting in part. . . .

. . . A fair reading of the Kansas Supreme Court's opinion in light of its earlier opinion [in *Shutts, Executor*] reveals that the Kansas court has examined the laws of connected jurisdictions and has correctly concluded that there is no "direct" or "substantive" conflict between the law applied by Kansas and the laws of those other States. Kansas has merely developed general common-law principles to accommodate the novel facts of this litigation — other state courts either agree with Kansas or have not yet addressed precisely similar claims. Consequently, I conclude that the Full Faith and Credit Clause of the Constitution did not require Kansas to apply the law of any other State, and the Fourteenth Amendment's Due Process Clause did not prevent Kansas from applying its own law in this case. . . .

. . . [I]t has long been settled that "a mere misconstruction by the forum of the laws of a sister State is not a violation of the Full Faith and Credit Clause." That Clause requires only that States accord "full faith and credit" to other States' laws — that is, acknowledge the validity and finality of such laws and attempt in good faith to apply them when necessary as they would be applied by home state courts. . . .

Merely to state these general principles is to refute any argument that Kansas' decision below violated the Full Faith and Credit Clause. . . .

In final analysis, the Court today may merely be expressing its disagreement with the Kansas Supreme Court's statement that in a "nationwide class action . . . the law of the forum should be applied unless compelling reasons exist for applying a different law."

Notes

1. On remand, the Kansas Supreme Court held that, even though there was no explicit agreement to this effect, the parties had implicitly

agreed to use the interest rate established by Federal Power Commission regulations, rather than the lower interest rates generally applied in Louisiana, Oklahoma, and Texas. Although no court in these states had ever used such an "implicit agreement" test, no court had squarely rejected the approach either. *See* Shutts v. Phillips Petroleum Co., 732 P.2d 1286 (Kan. 1987), *cert. denied*, 487 U.S. 1223 (1988). The Kansas Supreme Court also applied this ruling in a similar class action against a different oil company. Wortman v. Sun Oil Co., 755 P.2d 488 (Kan. 1987).

The United States Supreme Court granted certiorari in *Wortman*, and upheld the Kansas Supreme Court's interpretation of Louisiana, Oklahoma, and Texas law against full-faith-and-credit and due-process challenges:

> To constitute a violation of the Full Faith and Credit Clause or the Due Process Clause, it is not enough that a state court misconstrue the law of another State. Rather, our cases make plain that the misconstruction must contradict law of the other State that is clearly established and that has been brought to the court's attention. We cannot conclude that any of the interpretations at issue here runs afoul of this standard.

Sun Oil Co. v. Wortman, 486 U.S. 717, 730-31 (1988). The decision evoked a strong partial dissent by Justice O'Connor, which Chief Justice Rehnquist joined:

> ... Faced with the constitutional obligation to apply the substantive law of another State, a court that does not like that law apparently need take only two steps in order to avoid applying it. First, invent a legal theory so novel or strange that the other State has never had an opportunity to reject it; then, on the basis of nothing but unsupported speculation, "predict" that the other State would adopt that theory if it had the chance. To call this giving full faith and credit to the law of another State ignores the language of the Constitution and leaves it without the capacity to fulfill its purpose. [*Id.* at 749.]

2. If Justice O'Connor is correct, how serious an impediment are the Full Faith and Credit Clause and Due Process Clause in complex cases? Many complex cases are *sui generis*, so wouldn't it be easy for a court to create uniform law by adopting a unique legal theory that no state had squarely rejected and then claiming that every state would adopt that theory? (Note that *Shutts* began by saying that, unless the laws of the relevant states differed, the decision to apply one state's law was a false conflict and therefore constitutionally harmless error.) Do you worry that judges operating under a loose constitutional standard will have too much power to affect the outcome of complex litigation? Because aggregation will often occur in federal court, do you worry that a loose constitutional standard shifts too much power over state-law claims to a single federal judge? Or should the constitutional standard remain loose to give judges room to maneuver around complexity-causing choice-of-law problems?

3. At least on issues of substantive law, *Shutts* rules out a *lex fori* approach for claims that have no connection to the forum. *Cf.* Allstate Ins.

Co. v. Hague, 449 U.S. 302 (1981) (plurality decision) (stating that a state court can adopt the "better law" approach on issues of substantive law when the claims that have minimal connection to the forum). One of the beauties of the *lex fori* approach in complex litigation was that it could have led to the application of a single law for all cases filed in one forum. Assuming that one state's law was superior for plaintiffs, a *lex fori* approach would likely have reduced drastically, if not eliminated, the multistate forum shopping that the present plethora of choice-of-law rules engenders, and thus might have facilitated the aggregation of related cases in one forum.

Neither *Shutts* nor *Wortman* were complex cases, at least in the sense that different choice-of-law regimes (and different substantive laws) were likely to disperse related cases among numerous states. Nor would the use of four interest rates, as opposed to one rate, have been likely to create pretrial, trial, or remedial complexity. Do *Shutts* and *Wortman* leave open the constitutional possibility of using *lex fori* in cases in which the use of multiple laws would create some form of complexity? Here is the argument: *Lex fori* is permissible when a single law is needed to preserve the rational adjudication that lies at the heart of due process, and when the threat to rational adjudication outweighs the countervailing full-faith-and-credit and due-process considerations that animated *Shutts*. Does such an argument unfairly stack the deck against defendants, because plaintiffs in complex cases will choose the forum with the worst law for defendants?

4.   *Wortman* was also significant for a second holding. The Kansas Supreme Court applied a 5-year Kansas statute of limitations to the classes' claims. The statutes of limitations in Oklahoma, Texas, and Louisiana were shorter, and, if applicable, would have required the dismissal of most of the claims of class members from those states. The Court upheld the application of the Kansas statute of limitations to the out-of-state claims against a full-faith-and-credit challenge:

> The Full Faith and Credit Clause does not compel "a state to substitute the statutes of other states for its own statutes dealing with a subject matter concerning which it is competent to legislate." Since the procedural rules of its courts are surely matters on which a State is competent to legislate, it follows that a State may apply its own procedural rules to actions litigated in its courts. The issue here, then, can be characterized as whether a statute of limitations may be considered as a procedural matter for purposes of the Full Faith and Credit Clause. [*Id.* at 722-23.]

The Court then held that, even though a statute of limitation might be regarded as substantive for other purposes such as *Erie*, it was procedural for full-faith-and-credit purposes. It also rejected the idea that modern choice of law scholarship, which tended to characterize statutes of limitation as substantive, should affect this analysis:

> . . . [L]ong established and still subsisting choice-of-law practices that come to be thought, by modern scholars, unwise, do not thereby become unconstitutional. If current conditions render it desirable that forum States no longer treat a particular issue as procedural for conflict

of laws purposes, those States can themselves adopt a rule to that effect, or it can be proposed that Congress legislate to that effect under the second sentence of the Full Faith and Credit Clause. [*Id.* at 728-29].

Wortman similarly dismissed the defendant's due-process argument:

A State's interest in regulating the workload of its courts and determining when a claim is too stale to be adjudicated certainly suffices to give it legislative jurisdiction to control the remedies available in its courts by imposing statutes of limitations. Moreover, petitioner could in no way have been unfairly surprised by the application to it of a rule that is as old as the Republic. There is, in short, nothing in Kansas' action here that is "arbitrary or unfair," and the due process challenge is entirely without substance. [*Id.* at 730.]

5.   *Wortman* accepted, without significant discussion, the proposition that a state can constitutionally choose its own procedural rules, even when another state's substantive law applies. The Court spent its time on the "characterization" issue of whether a statute of limitations is procedural or substantive in the full-faith-and-credit context. You might wonder why state courts don't characterize all their laws as "procedural," thus allowing them to choose their laws all the time. The reason is that the Constitution erects an admittedly ill-defined barrier to such evasion. *See* John Hancock Life Mut. Ins. Co. v. Yates, 299 U.S. 178 (1936); Home Ins. Co. v. Dick, 281 U.S. 397 (1930); *cf.* RESTATEMENT (SECOND) OF CONFLICT OF LAWS § 122 cmt. *c* ("The Constitution of the United States places some limitations upon the power of a State which has no significant relationship to the transaction to characterize an issue as procedural in order to determine the issue in accordance with its own local law.").

B. CHOICE OF LAW IN THE FEDERAL COURTS

The last section examined the options and limits on state courts faced with choosing the substantive and procedural law to govern claims whose source lies in state law. The injection of federal law and federal courts complicates the choice-of-law picture. One part is easy: State and federal courts have no choice but to apply federal law to claims to which such law is relevant. Beyond that obvious proposition, however, things get trickier. First, consider a federal court (usually in a diversity case) that must decide claims based on state law. Do federal courts have the authority to create their own choice-of-law rules, or must they adopt the choice-of-law rules used in state court? If the latter, which state court? Do federal courts operate under the same constitutional constraints in choosing law that state courts do? When a case containing state-law claims is transferred from one court to another, is the transferee court bound to apply the choice-of-law principles used in the transferor court?

Second, in theory federal law is uniform, but in practice circuits and districts adopt different interpretations of federal law. Under the doctrine of stare decisis, courts within a circuit must choose the law of their own circuit. But what happens when the case is transferred to another circuit that adopts a different view of federal law? Is the transferee court bound to adopt the transferor court's interpretation of federal law?

The following materials examine these questions, first by looking at the choice-of-law approach that applies when federal courts hear state-law claims and then contrasting that approach with the approach used for claims based on federal law.

1. State-Law Issues

If a federal court must use the same choice-of-law rule that a state court in the same jurisdiction would use, then a federal forum provides no solution to the complexity-causing problems engendered by choice-of-law analysis. But if the federal court can independently choose the choice-of-law rule to apply, and then can adopt a choice-of-law rule that results in the choice of a single or limited number of state laws, the federal forum has advantages (in terms of of reducing complexity) that no state forum enjoys. The following case describes the conventional answer about the choice-of-law approach that federal courts employ take for issues based on state law.

IN RE VIOXX PRODUCTS LIABILITY LITIGATION

239 F.R.D. 450 (E.D.La. 2006)

■   FALLON, District Judge.

Before the Court is the Plaintiffs' Steering Committee's ("PSC") Motion for Certification of a Nation-Wide Class Action for Personal Injury and Wrongful Death. . . . For the following reasons, the PSC's motion is denied.

I. BACKGROUND

This multidistrict products liability litigation involves the prescription drug Vioxx . . . . Merck & Co., Inc. ("Merck"), a New Jersey corporation, researched, designed, manufactured, marketed, and distributed Vioxx to relieve pain and inflammation resulting from osteoarthritis, rheumatoid arthritis, menstrual pain, and migraine headaches. On May 20, 1999, the Food and Drug Administration ("FDA") approved Vioxx for sale in the United States. Vioxx remained on the market until September 30, 2004, at which time Merck withdrew it from the market when data from a clinical trial known as APPROVe indicated that the use of Vioxx increased the risk of cardiovascular thrombotic events such as myocardial infarctions (heart attacks) and ischemic strokes. Thereafter, thousands of individual suits and numerous class actions were filed against Merck in state and federal courts throughout the country alleging various tort and products liability claims. It is estimated that 105 million prescriptions for Vioxx were written in the United States between May 20, 1999 and September 30, 2004. Based on this estimate, it is thought that approximately 20 million patients have taken Vioxx in the United States.

On February 16, 2005, the Judicial Panel on Multidistrict Litigation ("JPML") conferred multidistrict litigation status on Vioxx lawsuits filed in federal court and transferred all such cases to this Court to coordinate discovery and to consolidate pretrial matters pursuant to 28 U.S.C. § 1407. . . . [More than 7,000 cases were filed in the Eastern District of Louisiana or transferred into the MDL. Merck had already produced 22 million pages of documents and a terabyte of data to the PSC. Depositions had been taken for more than 145 days, and 310 depositions had been noticed. The MDL court had ruled on more than 270 substantive motions, dealt with more than 1,000 procedural motions, and conducted 4 bellwether trials in individual cases.]

In addition to thousands of individual claims, this MDL currently includes over 160 class actions emanating from nearly every state. These class actions allege three types of claims: (1) personal injury and wrongful death claims; (2) medical monitoring claims; and (3) purchase claims. On June 2, 2005, the Court issued Pretrial Order No. 16 which directed the PSC to file master complaints in this Court with respect to each type of class action. Accordingly, on August 2, 2005, the PSC filed a Master Class Action Complaint for Cases Involving Personal Injury and Wrongful Death. The PSC also filed a Medical Monitoring Master Class Action Complaint and a Purchase Claims Master Class Action Complaint . . . . [T]his opinion deals only with the personal injury and wrongful death class actions.

. . . In the Master Class Action Complaint for Cases Involving Personal Injury and Wrongful Death ("Master Complaint"), the PSC alleges that Vioxx was a defective product; that Merck misrepresented the safety of Vioxx and negligently manufactured, marketed, advertised, and sold Vioxx as a safe prescription medication, when in fact Merck knew or should have known that Vioxx was not safe for its intended purpose; and that Vioxx caused serious medical problems, and in certain patients, catastrophic injuries, and death.

On December 8, 2005, the PSC filed the instant motion to certify a nationwide class action under Rule 23(b)(3) of the Federal Rules of Civil Procedure consisting of [all Vioxx users "who claim personal injuries or assert wrongful death claims arising from ingestion of Vioxx."] . . .

The PSC contends that New Jersey substantive law can and should be applied to all personal injury and wrongful death claims made by United States residents. The basic thrust of the PSC's argument in favor of applying New Jersey products liability law is that (1) Merck is headquartered in New Jersey and, thus, all of its decisions regarding the manufacturing, testing, labeling, marketing, and advertising of Vioxx originated in and emanated from New Jersey and (2) New Jersey has a unique and strong interest in regulating the conduct of its corporate citizens and specifically in deterring wrongful conduct by New Jersey pharmaceutical companies.

Merck opposes certification of a nationwide class action on two grounds. First, Merck argues that the proposed class members' claims must be adjudicated under the substantive laws of the states in which they resided, ingested, and were allegedly injured by Vioxx and, thus, there is no commonality of law.   Second, Merck contends that certification is inappropriate because each plaintiff's claim involves separate and distinct factual issues.

II. LAW & ANALYSIS

Before determining whether a nationwide class action may be certified under Rule 23 of the Federal Rules of Civil Procedure , the Court must first determine which state's or states' substantive law will govern the class. To make this determination, the Court must conduct a choice-of-law analysis. Each state has its own choice-of-law rules that its courts use to select the applicable law.   Therefore, the Court must first decide which state's choice-of-law rules to apply. . . .

A. *Choice of Law*

i.   *Selecting the Applicable Choice-of-Law Rules*

Federal courts sitting in diversity must apply the choice-of-law rules of the forum state. Klaxon Co. v. Stentor Elec. Mfg. Co., 313 U.S. 487, 496 (1941). In MDL cases, the forum state is typically the state in which the action was initially filed before being transferred to the MDL court. In the present case, the proposed class representatives originally filed their class action complaint in the United States District Court for the District of New Jersey; however, the PSC also subsequently filed a Master Complaint in this Court. Therefore, the Court could conceivably apply the choice-of-law rules of either New Jersey or Louisiana.

In *In re Propulsid Products Liability Litigation*, 208 F.R.D. 133, 140-41 (E.D. La. 2002), this Court was faced with the similar decision of whether to apply Indiana or Louisiana choice-of-law rules in an MDL class certification proceeding. In *Propulsid*, the Court determined that a master complaint is only an administrative device used to aid efficiency and economy and, thus, should not be given the status of an ordinary complaint. Accordingly, the Court looked to the underlying Indiana complaint and applied Indiana's choice-of-law rules.[6]

---

6. In *In re Bridgestone/Firestone, Inc. Tires Prods. Liab. Litig.*, 155 F. Supp. 2d 1069, 1078 (S.D. Ind. 2001), an MDL court reached the contrary conclusion and applied the choice-of-law rules of the forum in which it sat and in which the master complaint had been filed. The court did not examine the issue in detail, however, because the parties before it agreed on this course of action.

The Court finds no reason to depart from its prior holding, especially given that the parties in this case have not urged the Court to reconsider its view and apparently agree that New Jersey choice-of-law rules should be applied. Therefore, the Court will once again look to the specific action brought before it for class certification — the New Jersey complaint — and will apply New Jersey's choice-of-law rules to determine which state's or states' substantive law would govern the proposed nationwide class.

ii.   *Selecting the Applicable Substantive Law*

New Jersey applies a flexible "governmental interests" choice-of-law test to determine which state has the greatest interest in governing the specific issue in the underlying litigation. *See* Erny v. Estate of Merola, 792 A.2d 1208, 1216 (N.J. 2002); Fu v. Fu, 733 A.2d 1133, 1138 (N.J. 1999); Veazey v. Doremus, 510 A.2d 1187, 1189 (N.J. 1986). New Jersey's governmental interests test is a two-step inquiry. The first step is to determine whether an actual conflict exists between the laws of New Jersey and any other state with an interest in the litigation. In the present case, both the PSC and Merck acknowledge that there are conflicts between the law of New Jersey and the laws of the other fifty jurisdictions in regard to negligence, strict liability, failure to warn, learned intermediary, and defective design. The Court agrees, and therefore will advance to the second step.

The second step of New Jersey's governmental interests test is to determine which state has the most significant relationship to the occurrence and to the parties. In reaching this decision, the Court must identify the governmental policies of each state and how those policies are affected by the states' contacts to the litigation and to the parties. There are five factors that the Court must use to guide its decision: (1) the interests of interstate comity; (2) the interests underlying the field of tort law; (3) the interests of the parties; (4) the interests of judicial administration; and (5) the competing interests of the states. [*Fu*, 733 A.2d] at 1140-41. The third and fourth factors are the least significant. *Erny*, 792 A.2d at 1217. The fifth factor is the most important factor. *Fu*, 733 A.2d at 1142. The Court will now consider these five factors to determine which state has the most significant relationship to the occurrence and to the parties and, therefore, which state's or states' substantive law will govern the class.

a.   *Interests of Interstate Comity and Tort Law*

In this case, the interests of interstate comity and tort law, the first two factors, merge and will be considered together. The interests of interstate comity, the first factor, require the Court to consider whether the application of one state's law will frustrate the policies of other interested states. In the present case, the issue before the Court is not whether a specific aspect of a state's law, such as the learned intermediary doctrine or punitive damages, should be applied, but whether the entire scope of one state's products liability law, and all aspects arising thereunder, should be applied to the class. Thus, this situation requires the Court to consider the purpose of products liability laws in general, rather than just the purpose behind a specific state law.

The interests underlying the field of tort law, the second factor, require the Court to consider the degree to which deterrence and compensation, the two fundamental goals of tort law, would be furthered by the application of one state's law versus the application of every state's law. Not surprisingly, products liability laws are motivated by the same underlying purposes as the field of tort law in general, and therefore the interests of interstate comity and the interests underlying the field of tort law align in this case.

With regard to these two factors, the Court finds that each plaintiff's home jurisdiction has a stronger interest in deterring foreign corporations from personally injuring its citizens and ensuring that its citizens are compensated than New Jersey does in deterring its corporate citizens' wrongdoing. These interests arise by virtue of each state being the place where the plaintiffs reside and, therefore, the states in which the plaintiffs were prescribed Vioxx, where the plaintiffs ingested Vioxx, and where the alleged injuries occurred. Therefore, the Court finds that the first and second factors weigh in favor of applying the law of each plaintiff's home jurisdiction to his or her respective claims.

b. *Interests of the Parties*

The interests of the parties, the third factor, require the Court to consider each party's justified expectations and the need for predictability of result. This factor often plays a small role in the field of tort law because a party who causes an unintentional injury is generally not cognizant of the law that may be applied. Nevertheless, the Court finds that this factor supports Merck's argument.

The PSC contends that Merck's choice to operate in New Jersey means that it should reasonably expect to abide by New Jersey's laws. While this is true, it is just as true that Merck, an international corporation providing its drugs to every state in the nation, should expect to abide by every jurisdiction's laws. To the extent that problems developed with respect to Vioxx, Merck could have reasonably expected to be sued in every jurisdiction and be subject to every jurisdiction's laws. As to the individual plaintiffs, it is highly unlikely that a plaintiff residing outside of New Jersey could have reasonably expected that his or her personal injury claims would be governed by New Jersey law. As such, the Court finds that the third factor weighs in favor of applying the laws of each plaintiff's home jurisdiction to his or her respective claims.

c. *Interests of Judicial Administration*

The interests of judicial administration, the fourth factor, require the Court to consider the practicality of applying one jurisdiction's law in a specific instance. This factor weighs heavily in favor of applying New Jersey law. From the Court's perspective, the application of a single jurisdiction's law is more practical than the application of fifty-one different jurisdictions' laws. Therefore, the Court finds that the fourth factor weighs in favor of applying New Jersey law to the entire class. Ease of administration, however, is of minimal importance and must give way to the other factors. *See Erny*, 792 A.2d at 1217.

d.   *Competing Interests of the States*

The competing interests of the states, the fifth factor, is the most important factor under New Jersey's choice-of-law scheme. In deciding the competing interests factor, the Court must consider four separate sub-elements: (1) the place where the injury occurred; (2) the place where the conduct causing the injury occurred; (3) the domicile, residence, nationality, place of incorporation, and place of business of the parties; and (4) the place where the relationship between the parties is centered. *Fu*, 733 A.2d at 1142. Furthermore, in personal injury litigation, the place of injury is especially important, and when the conduct and injury occur in the same state, that jurisdiction's laws will generally apply except when another jurisdiction has a demonstrably dominant interest and no policy of the situs state would be frustrated. Throughout this analysis, the Court must focus on what a given legislature intended to protect by enacting the law at issue and how that legislature's concerns will be furthered by applying its law to the multistate situation.

Regarding the place of injury, the Court finds that the jurisdiction where each plaintiff resides qualifies as the place of injury. There is no evidence indicating otherwise and such a conclusion is based on common sense. Each plaintiff most likely was prescribed Vioxx, ingested Vioxx, and allegedly suffered personal injury in his or her state of residence. As such, in the present case, the injuries occurred in fifty-one jurisdictions, fifty of which are not New Jersey.

Regarding the conduct causing the injury, the Court finds that the jurisdiction where each plaintiff resided also qualifies as the place where the injury-causing conduct occurred. The PSC, however, would have the Court conclude that New Jersey was the place where the injury-causing conduct occurred because New Jersey is where the majority, if not all, of the relevant corporate decisions occurred. However, Vioxx was advertised in, marketed in, shipped into, prescribed in, sold in, ingested in, and allegedly caused harm in fifty-one jurisdictions. Merck's conduct may have originated in New Jersey, but it was effectuated and felt by every plaintiff in their own home jurisdiction. Accordingly, the conduct causing the plaintiffs' injuries occurred, and the plaintiffs' claims arose, in fifty-one jurisdictions, fifty of which are not New Jersey.

Regarding the residence, domicile, nationality, place of incorporation, and place of business of the parties, Merck is a New Jersey corporation that predominantly operates its business in New Jersey. On the other hand, the plaintiffs reside in fifty-one jurisdictions, fifty of which are not New Jersey.

Regarding the place where the relationship is centered, the Court finds that the relationship between each plaintiff and Merck is centered in the state where each plaintiff resides. This is where each plaintiff most likely was prescribed, purchased, ingested, and allegedly harmed by Vioxx. Moreover, it is difficult to fathom how the relationship could have been centered only in New Jersey. To the extent that any of the plaintiffs knew that Merck was the manufacturer of Vioxx, which in most cases is unlikely, it is even more doubtful that any of the plaintiffs knew that Merck was incorporated in and operated out of New Jersey. Furthermore, to the extent that any non-New Jersey resident knew both of these facts, it still would not change the center of the relationship unless he or she actively choose to travel to New Jersey, saw a doctor in New Jersey, was prescribed Vioxx in New Jersey, purchased Vioxx in New Jersey, and consumed Vioxx in New Jersey. Conversely, Merck consciously choose to advertise and market Vioxx throughout the United States, which ultimately led to the writing of Vioxx prescriptions, the sale of Vioxx, and the ingestion of Vioxx across the country. As such, the parties' relationships are centered in fifty-one jurisdictions, fifty of which are not New Jersey.-

Accordingly, the Court finds that the competing interests of the states, the fifth and most important factor, weighs in favor of applying the law of each plaintiff's home jurisdiction to his or her respective claims.

iii. *Choice-of-Law Conclusion*

The Court has applied New Jersey's choice-of-law rules in this case and therefore has considered the interests of interstate comity, the policies of deterrence and compensation, the interests of the parties, the interest of practicality, and the competing interests of the states to determine which state's or states' substantive law would be applied to the class. The relevant choice-of-law factors confirm that New Jersey substantive law should not be applied to the entire class, but instead, that the substantive law of each plaintiff's home jurisdiction must be applied to his or her respective claims. With this in mind, the Court now turns to Rule 23 of the Federal Rules of Civil Procedure to determine whether the putative class should be certified.

[The court then declined to certify a nationwide class action because of a lack of typicality and because common questions did not predominate over questions affecting only individual class members.]

Notes

1. *Vioxx* applies two standard choice-of-law principles for a federal court hearing state-law claims. First, a federal court must apply the choice-of-law rule that a court of the forum state would have applied. Second, a

federal court to which a case is transferred applies the choice-of-law principle that the transferor court would have adopted, rather than applying the choice-of-law rule of the transferee court; thus, even though the *Vioxx* case had been transferred to the Eastern District of Louisiana, the court applied the choice-of-law rule that the transferor court (the District of New Jersey) would have applied — which, due to the first principle mentioned above, meant New Jersey's choice-of-law rule.

2.   As *Vioxx* says, the first rule derives from *Klaxon Co. v. Stentor Electric Manufacturing Co.*, 313 U.S. 487 (1941). *See* Day & Zimmermann v. Challoner, 423 U.S. 3 (1975) (per curiam) (re-affirming *Klaxon*). *Klaxon* based its holding on *Erie Railroad Co. v. Tompkins*, 304 U.S. 64 (1938), which held that a federal court cannot create "federal general common law" when a state court in the same jurisdiction would apply state law to the claim; the federal court must also apply state law. *Klaxon*'s result might seem dictated by *Erie*: If a federal court applies a different choice-of-law rule than the state court across the street, different substantive law might apply. Thus, the evils of forum shopping and inequitable administration of law that *Erie* sought to eradicate, *see* 304 U.S. at 74-78, would be fomented if federal courts adopted their own choice-of-law rules.

In fact, the case for *Klaxon* is not nearly as strong as the case for *Erie*. Unlike *Erie*, in which the constitutional authority of federal courts to ignore state substantive law was uncertain, the constitutional authority of federal courts to create their own choice-of-law rules is clear. By definition, in the choice-of-law context, more than one state has an interest in the application of its law, and "the choice of *which* state's law applies in a federal court is surely a matter of federal concern." RICHARD H. FALLON, JR. ET AL., HART & WECHSLER'S THE FEDERAL COURTS & THE FEDERAL SYSTEM 565 (6th ed. 2009). Congress seems to possess the authority to enact choice-of-law rules under a number of constitutional grants: the Commerce Clause (Art. I, § 8), the Full Faith and Credit Clause (Art. IV, § 1), and the Judicial Power Clause (Art. III, § 2). *See* AM. L. INST., COMPLEX LITIGATION 310-13 (1994). To say that Congress can create choice of law rules is not, however, to say that federal courts can do so without congressional direction. Are *Erie*'s separation-of-powers and federalism concerns, when joined with the evils that *Erie* sought to prevent, adequate justification for *Klaxon*? Do federal courts have inherent authority to create choice-of-law rules?

3.   The particular reason to ask that question is to consider whether federal courts must apply *Klaxon* in complex cases. *Klaxon* was not a complex case, in the sense that differing state laws and differing choice-of-law regimes combined to disperse related litigation across forums. Indeed, *Klaxon* had no reason to consider the effect of its decision on repetitive litigation. Its holding was designed to prevent plaintiffs from engaging in vertical forum between state and federal courts. But *Klaxon*'s rule induces plaintiffs to engage in horizontal forum shopping to find the state court (or federal court, which must act exactly like the state court) with the choice-of-law rule that picks the best substantive and procedural law. As long as only one lawsuit is going to be filed, as in ordinary cases like *Klaxon*, the

system can be indifferent to the problem of horizontal forum shopping. In complex cases, however, the effect of horizontal forum shopping is the filing of lawsuits in different federal and state forums — and the effect of this filing is to create unfairness to litigants or social inefficiency.

Are unfairness and inefficiency sufficient bases on which to distinguish *Klaxon* and not apply the choice-of-law rule of the forum state? Start with inefficiency. Abandoning *Klaxon* might eliminate part of the expense of multiforum relitigation — but only if the choice-of-law rule that a federal court adopts in lieu of *Klaxon's* forum rule either reduces incentives to disperse litigation or makes aggregated litigation more manageable. What rule would that be? *Lex loci* works only if all the injuries arise in one state. "Most significant contacts" works only if all the claims have a clear center of gravity in one state; the same is true of interest analysis. *Lex fori* might work, but only if one state's law is so clearly better for plaintiffs that all plaintiffs would want to use that law; otherwise, a federal court's use of *lex fori* might actually induce plaintiffs, each seeking the best law for his or her own case, to disperse their cases among different courts. (And then there is the tricky problem whether a court can apply *lex fori* in light of *Phillips Petroleum Co. v. Shutts*, 472 U.S. 797 (1985), which threw considerable constitutional doubt on the method. *See supra* p. 637.) Even if the practical problem of finding an efficiency-enhancing choice-of-law principle could be solved, does the efficiency gained from this choice outweigh the separation-of-powers, federalism, and fairness concerns that underpin *Erie* (and by extension *Klaxon*)? Is added efficiency an adequate justification for the breach of trans-substantivism that occurs when *Klaxon's* rule results in choosing one set of substantive rules in routine cases and a non-*Klaxon* rule results in choosing different substantive law for complex cases?

Now consider unfairness. How would you answer the questions in the last paragraph when the dispersal of cases caused by *Klaxon* results in the use of varying state laws that either whipsaw defendants or prevent present and putative plaintiffs from obtaining an effective remedy? How many cases fall within these categories? Even in such cases, abandoning *Klaxon* is useful only if the court can adopt a choice-of-law rule that gives the parties no incentive to disperse litigation geographically.

In analyzing New Jersey's choice-of-law approach, *Vioxx* specifically mentioned the aggregation benefits that a single substantive law entailed. Granting that this consideration was not dispositive under New Jersey's choice-of-law regime, could the court have used these benefits to distinguish *Klaxon* and adopt am aggregation-friendly choice-of-law rule?

4. In addition, won't any departure from *Klaxon* likely drive some litigants — those who will not fare as well under the substantive law chosen by the federal court as they would have fared under the forum state's choice-of-law approach — into state court? Does the case for departing from *Klaxon* therefore depend on whether geographical dispersion or intersystem dispersion is the bigger problem?

5. *Klaxon* requires federal courts to apply the forum state's choice-of-law rule to determine which state's *substantive* law to apply. We have seen

that states also have adopted choice-of-law rules to determine which state's *procedural* law should apply; for the most part those rules result in the use of the forum state's procedural law. Must a federal court also choose the procedural law that a court in the forum state would choose to decide a state-law issue, or (as the forum court) can it choose its own procedural law? The answer is far more complicated than the comparable horizontal choice-of-law answer. In Civil Procedure, you likely studied the ways in which the *Erie* doctrine intersected with the Rules Enabling Act, 28 U.S.C. §§ 2071-77, and with federal courts' common-law rulemaking power, to determine whether a state or a federal procedural rule governed. *See, e.g.,* Shady Grove Orthopedic Assocs., P.A. v. Allstate Ins. Co., 559 U.S. —, 2010 WL 1222272 (2010) (*supra* p. 547); Gasperini v. Ctr. for Humanities, Inc., 518 U.S. 415 (1996); Hanna v. Plumer, 380 U.S. 460 (1965); Guaranty Trust Co. of N.Y. v. York, 326 U.S. 99 (1945). Sometimes federal courts choose their own procedures, but other times they must adopt the procedures that a state court in the forum state would adopt. For an overview, see SUZANNA SHERRY & JAY TIDMARSH, CIVIL PROCEDURE: ESSENTIALS 243-54 (2007).

6. *Vioxx*'s second important choice-of-law move is to adopt the same choice-of-law rule (New Jersey's rule) as the federal court from which the case had been transferred would have applied. As we have seen, federal courts enjoy some ability to transfer cases among districts, especially through all-purpose § 1404 and pretrial § 1407 transfers. Transfer creates a new choice-of-law question: Must the transferee court still apply the state choice-of-law rules law of the transferor forum? Must it use the choice-of-law rules of the transferee court's state? Or can it devise a unique body of federal choice-of-law principles to deal with the situation? The answer matters a great deal in complex litigation. Consider the three possibilities:

- If the transferee court must accept the choice-of-law rules of the transferor court, *Klaxon*'s requirement means that transferee courts must apply different choice-of-law rules to the related cases — which means that, except in the unlikely event that the varying choice-of-law rules all point to the use of a single substantive law, the management of transferred cases becomes harder and courts have less reason to transfer cases to a single forum.

- If the transferee court can apply its state's choice-of-law rules, it is hardly out of the woods; the state's choice-of-law rules might point toward different substantive law for the transferred cases. But at least the preliminary complexity of analyzing each case under the choice-of-law approach of the transferor court's state is avoided.

- If the transferee court can develop its own choice-of-law principles, unfettered by the approaches used in the transferor or transferee courts, it can in theory craft a choice-of-law rule that leads to the use of a single substantive law or a manageable number of substantive laws. But such power is not without problems. As we have discussed, no single choice-of-law approach perfectly fits every complex case. If a transferee court chooses (let's say) a *lex loci* approach because the injuries of all plaintiffs arose in Alaska, must future transferee courts also adopt the *lex loci* rule even when that rule doesn't lead to use of a single state's law? Should transferee courts have the power to pick and choose whatever choice-of-law approach results in the use of the fewest number of varying state laws, even if it means using different choice-of-law rules in different cases? Is that approach unprincipled?

7.   The Supreme Court has decided two cases addressing the transfer issue: *Van Dusen v. Barrack*, 376 U.S. 612 (1964), and *Ferens v. John Deere Co.*, 494 U.S. 516 (1990). *Van Dusen* held that, with § 1404 transfers, *Erie's* policies of preventing forum shopping and inequity in the administration of the laws required the transferee court to apply the choice-of-law rule of the transferor court — in other words, the first option described in the prior Note. *Ferens* extended the *Van Dusen* approach to include cases in which the plaintiff, rather than the defendant, sought transfer.

8.   *Ferens's* facts were striking. The plaintiffs' claim had arisen from a product-liability injury suffered in Pennsylvania, where they resided. They gamed the system. Even though Mississippi had no connection to the injury, they filed their tort claim in federal court in Mississippi. The reason was Mississippi's longer statute of limitations for tort claims; under the law of Pennsylvania, the tort claim had already expired. (Recall *Sun Oil Co. v. Wortman*, 486 U.S. 717 (1988), which held that a court can choose its own statute of limitations. *See supra* p. 643, Note 4.) The plaintiffs also filed a breach-of-warranty claim in federal court in Pennsylvania because the Pennsylvania limitations period had not run for that claim. Exercising a certain amount of *chutzpah*, the plaintiffs moved under 28 U.S.C. § 1404(a) to transfer the Mississippi case to the district in Pennsylvania in which the warranty claim was pending because it was more convenient to litigate both claims there. After the federal court in Mississippi transferred the case, the federal court in Pennsylvania distinguished *Van Dusen* and held that the plaintiffs could not carry the Mississippi statute of limitations forward.

Noting that "the desire to take a punitive view of the plaintiff's actions should not obscure the systemic costs of litigating in an inconvenient place," 494 U.S. at 530, the Supreme Court held that the *Van Dusen* rule applied:

> Applying the transferee law . . . would undermine the *Erie* rule in a serious way. It would mean that initiating a transfer under § 1404(a) changes the state law applicable to a diversity case. In general, however, we have seen § 1404(a) as a housekeeping measure that should not alter the state law governing a case under *Erie*. . . . [494 U.S. at 526.]

Justice Scalia, joined by Justices Brennan, Marshall, and Blackmun, wrote a dissent that concluded: "To ask, as in effect the Court does, whether *Erie* gets in the way of § 1404(a), rather than whether § 1404(a) requires adjustment of *Erie*, seems to me the expression of a mistaken sense of priorities." 494 U.S. at 539-40.

9.   *Van Dusen* and *Ferens* involved transfers under § 1404. Does the same rule apply to transfers under § 1407, which has important

applications in complex litigation? *Vioxx* assumes that the answer is "Yes." So do other MDL transferee courts. Indeed, given that § 1407 transfers are for pretrial purposes only (*see supra* p. 162) and that choice-of-law considerations are not relevant in making a § 1407 transfer decision (*see supra* p. 160, Note 7; In re Gen. Motors Class E Stock Buyout Sec. Litig., 696 F. Supp. 1546 (J.P.M.L. 1988)), it might seem difficult to argue that the MDL judge can ignore the transferor state's choice-of-law rules during the pendency of the case in the MDL forum. *See* In re Guidant Corp. Implantable Defibrillators Prods. Liab. Litig., 489 F. Supp. 2d 932, 936 (D. Minn. 2007) (holding that in a case multidistricted under § 1407, as "in a non-MDL setting, a transferor court's choice-of-law rules continue to apply even if the complaint is later amended in the transferee court").

But this result limits the utility of the MDL process as an aggregation device. Because the MDL judge felt constrained to apply New Jersey law after transfer, and because this law pointed to the use of the varying laws of fifty-one jurisdictions, he was unable to certify a class action — even though he admitted the management benefits that would flow from applying a single law to all the claims. Similarly, in *In re Conagra Peanut Butter Products Liability Litigation*, 251 F.R.D. 689, 695 (N.D. Ga. 2008), the MDL transferee court denied class certification because "applying the choice of law principles of each transferor court . . . would automatically make a class unmanageable."

10. In complex litigation, the *Van Dusen-Ferens* rule means that, when related cases are aggregated in a federal forum, the transferee court needs to determine the choice-of-law rules that apply to each transferred case. Depending on the content of those rules and the results they dictate, the transferee court might end up applying many laws to the aggregated cases. And that possibility might lead some courts not to transfer the cases in the first instance. *See Van Dusen*, 376 U.S. at 645 (suggesting that it is sometimes best not to transfer cases away from the district whose state's law will apply); Schleier v. Kaiser Found. Health Plan of the Mid-Atlantic States, Inc., 876 F.2d 174 (D.C. Cir. 1989) (holding that § 1404(a)'s "interest of justice" requirement was not satisfied when a case was transferred away from the forum whose state law governed the dispute).

Should a specific exception to *Van Dusen* and *Ferens* therefore be created when (1) not using the transferor forums' choice-of-law rules will reduce the number of substantive laws that apply to the transferred cases, and (2) as a result, aggregation is fairer or simpler? In order to figure out whether the first part of the exception applies, won't a court need to analyze the choice-of-law outcomes both under *Van Dusen* and *Ferens* and under the exception to *Van Dusen* and *Ferens*? In order to figure out whether the second part of the exception applies, won't the judge have to make an initial determinations about the "best" outcome of the case?

Even though the plaintiffs' gerrymandering in *Ferens* seems outrageous from one perspective, it is just good lawyering from another perspective. Do we want to set up a dynamic that discourages plaintiffs from seeking the transfer and consolidation of related cases? Do we want to create an exception that induces plaintiffs in large-scale litigation to file more cases in state court, from which single-forum aggregation is far more difficult?

11. Thus, despite the intuitively appealing idea of creating an exception to *Van Dusen* and *Ferens* in complex litigation, it is not necessarily true that such an exception will reduce unfairness or inefficiency. There is no *a priori* way to know whether the *Van Dusen-Ferens* rule or a different approach will lead to a "better" outcome from the viewpoint of optimal aggregation. Indeed, how much aggregation is "optimal" is itself a function, in part, of the substantive and procedural law that applies to claims. Therefore, even when the use of a single set of substantive and procedural rules makes aggregation more desirable, we must be careful not to let the tail wag the dog. As *Shutts* (*supra* p. 637) reminds us, the goal of simplifying litigation is an insufficient reason to visit arbitrary or unfair substantive and procedural rules on litigants.

The *Van Dusen-Ferens* problem is, frankly, more a symptom of other difficulties — especially varying state laws and varying state choice-of-law rules — than a primary disease to be treated and cured on its own. A complete cure should focus on reducing variations in state laws and/or state choice-of-law rules. In Section C, we examine possible solutions. Before we do, however, we stop to examine the comparable choice-of-law issues in cases arising under federal law — both because complex litigation often involves federal claims law and because the federal-law approach provides a useful comparison to the approach in the state-law context.

2. Federal-Law Issues

Varying state laws and varying state choice-of-law rules help to cause the dispersal of litigation and make aggregation difficult when state law is the source of a legal claim or defense. In theory, neither of these variations exists when federal law is the source of a claim or defense. Every court, state or federal, must choose federal law when it is the relevant source, and federal law is uniform. Because every state and federal court is choosing and applying exactly the same substantive law, *Klaxon*, *Van Dusen*, and *Ferens* have no salience. In theory, federal law does not cause the dispersal of claims, nor does it create manageability issues on aggregation.

Theory and practice are two different things. Federal law is not, in fact, uniform; different circuits and districts develop different interpretations. Likewise, although they sometimes defer to the interpretation of the federal circuit that encompasses them, state courts are free to develop their own interpretation of federal law. *See, e.g.*, Dewey v. R.J. Reynolds Tobacco Co., 577 A.2d 1239 (N.J. 1990). Although all courts must follow the decisions of the United States Supreme Court on federal law, the Supreme Court resolves only a tiny fraction of the interpretive differences presented in federal law, and its holdings often touch off further rounds of interpretive disagreements among state and lower federal courts.

In reality, differences in interpretation of federal law can cause plaintiffs to disperse cases among state and federal courts. As we saw in

Chapters Two and Three, however, the combination of removal jurisdiction and transfer devices at the federal level makes the aggregation of cases based on federal law fairly easy — at least if the federal transferee forum can apply a single version of federal law to the case. On the other hand, if it must choose the transferor courts's interpretation of federal law (*à la Van Dusen*), the aggregated case becomes less manageable, and the case for aggregation becomes less strong.

IN RE KOREAN AIR LINES DISASTER OF SEPTEMBER 1, 1983

829 F.2d 1171 (D.C. Cir. 1987), *aff'd on other grounds*
sub nom. Chan v. Korean Air Lines, 490 U.S. 122 (1989)

■ RUTH BADER GINSBURG, Circuit Judge.

This case arises out of an air disaster and raises turbulent federal questions. On September 1, 1983, Korean Air Lines (KAL) Flight 007, a commercial craft departing from Kennedy Airport in New York and bound for Seoul, South Korea, was destroyed over the Sea of Japan by Soviet Union military aircraft. Wrongful death actions were filed against KAL in several federal district courts; the Judicial Panel on Multidistrict Litigation transferred these actions to the District Court for the District of Columbia for pretrial proceedings pursuant to 28 U.S.C. § 1407.

The nub of the controversy relates to the per passenger damage limitation of the Warsaw Convention, raised to $75,000 by an accord among airlines known as the Montreal Agreement. By motion for partial summary judgment, plaintiffs sought a declaration "that [KAL] is liable without fault for compensatory damages without any limitation of $75,000." Plaintiffs grounded this motion on the inadequate type size of the liability limitation notice printed on KAL passenger tickets. The notice appeared in 8 point type; the Montreal Agreement specifies 10 point type. Denying plaintiffs' motion, the district court, on July 25, 1985, held that KAL could avail itself of the $75,000 per passenger limitation. In so ruling, the district court considered and rejected contrary Second Circuit precedent. . . .

[The MDL proceeding involved cases from the Eastern District of Michigan, the District of Massachusetts, the District of Columbia, and most significantly, the Southern and Eastern Districts of New York. The district court held in a subsequent order that its decision denying plaintiffs' motion applied to the cases transferred from all the districts.

[On appeal from this decision, the court of appeals began by adopting the district court's view that the $75,000 limitation applied despite the inadequate type size. That decision meant that the D.C. Circuit and the Second Circuit had opposing views on an issue of federal law. The views of the First and Sixth Circuits, from which the other MDL cases were transferred, were unknown. The court of appeals therefore turned to the question whether the district court properly applied its interpretation of the

Warsaw Convention/Montreal Agreement to the transferred actions, especially those transferred from district courts within the Second Circuit.]

The Supreme Court, in *Van Dusen v. Barrack*, 376 U.S. 612 (1964), addressed and resolved this question: when a defendant in a diversity action moves for a venue transfer under 28 U.S.C. § 1404(a), which state's law applies post-transfer? The state law that would have applied in the transferor court adheres to the case, the Supreme Court held; in the Court's words, "with respect to state law," the venue change will accomplish "but a change of courtrooms."

The *Van Dusen* interpretation of 28 U.S.C. § 1404(a), as the latter applies in diversity actions, rests on principles advanced in *Erie R.R. v. Tompkins*, 304 U.S. 64 (1938), and cases in the *Erie* line. *Van Dusen*, 376 U.S. at 637-40; *see particularly* Klaxon Co. v. Stentor Elec. Mfg. Co., 313 U.S. 387 (1941). . . .

The question before us is whether the *Van Dusen* rule — that the law applicable in the transferor forum attends the transfer — should apply to transferred federal claims. It is a question meriting attention from Higher Authority. Congress, it appears, has not focused on the issue, nor has the Supreme Court addressed it. The Judicial Panel on Multidistrict Litigation assumed, on at least one occasion, that the *Van Dusen* rule would apply to transferred federal claims, *see* In re Plumbing Fixtures Litig., 342 F. Supp. 756, 758 (J.P.M.L. 1972), but the Panel, from what we can glean, has given the matter only fleeting consideration. Recognizing that the question is perplexing, particularly in the context of 28 U.S.C. § 1407, a statute authorizing transfers only for pretrial purposes, we are persuaded by thoughtful commentary that "the transferee court [should] be free to decide a federal claim in the manner it views as correct without deferring to the interpretation of the transferor circuit." Richard L. Marcus, *Conflict Among Circuits and Transfers Within the Federal Judicial System*, 93 YALE L.J. 677, 721 (1984).

. . . [T]he *Erie* policies served by the *Van Dusen* decision do not figure in the calculus when the law to be applied is federal, not state. Given the reality of conflict among the circuits on the proper interpretation of federal law, however, why deny to a plaintiff with a federal claim the "venue privilege" a diversity claimant enjoys? Plaintiffs in the *Van Dusen* situation could effectively pick Pennsylvania rather than Massachusetts law and retain the benefit of that choice after transfer. Why deny a similar right of selection and retention to plaintiffs who would fare better under the Second Circuit's interpretation of federal law than under the D.C. Circuit's interpretation?

The point has been cogently made that venue provisions are designed with geographical convenience in mind, and not to "guarantee that the plaintiff will be able to select the law that will govern the case." Piper Aircraft Co. v. Reyno, 454 U.S. 235, 257 n.24 (1981). In diversity cases, however, federal courts are governed by *Klaxon* and therefore may not compose federal choice-of-law principles; instead, they must look to state prescriptions in determining which state's law applies. With "no federal choice-of-law principles that favor the application of the law of one state over the law of another," the diversity plaintiff's opening move or "venue privilege" ordinarily fills the gap — it "prevails by default." Marcus, *supra*, 93 YALE L.J. at 700-01. For the adjudication of federal claims, on the other hand, "the federal courts comprise a single system [in which each tribunal endeavors to apply] a single body of law," H.L. Green Co. v. MacMahon, 312 F.2d 650, 652 (2d Cir. 1962); there is no compelling reason to allow plaintiff to capture the most favorable interpretation of that law simply and solely by virtue of his or her right to choose the place to open the fray. . . .

Application of *Van Dusen* in the matter before us, we emphasize, would not produce uniformity. There would be one interpretation of federal law for the cases initially filed in districts within the Second Circuit, and an opposing interpretation for cases filed elsewhere. Applying divergent interpretations of the governing federal law to plaintiffs, depending solely upon where they initially filed suit, would surely reduce the efficiencies achievable through consolidated preparatory proceedings. Indeed, because there is ultimately a single proper interpretation of federal law, the attempt to ascertain and apply diverse circuit interpretations simultaneously is inherently self-contradictory. Our system contemplates differences between different states' laws; thus a multidistrict judge asked to apply divergent state positions on a point of law would face a coherent, if sometimes difficult, task. But it is logically inconsistent to require one judge to apply simultaneously different and conflicting interpretations of what is supposed to be a unitary federal law.

The district judge in the instant case observed that

> [i]f . . . more than one interpretation of federal law exists, the Supreme Court of the United States can finally determine the issue and restore uniformity in the federal system. The uniformity achieved in this [way] is an "informed uniformity" unlike the "blind uniformity" which would result from one court applying the interpretation of another by rote. . . .

We agree. The federal courts spread across the country owe respect to each other's efforts and should strive to avoid conflicts, but each has an obligation to engage independently in reasoned analysis. Binding precedent for all is set only by the Supreme Court, and for the district courts within a circuit, only by the court of appeals for that circuit.

We return, finally, to the most anomalous feature of this case. As earlier observed, we deal here not with an "all-purpose" transfer under 28 U.S.C. § 1404(a), but with a transfer under 28 U.S.C. § 1407 "for coordinated or consolidated pretrial proceedings." We have held, in accord with the district court, that the law of a transferor forum — here, the law of the Second Circuit — merits close consideration, but does not have stare decisis effect in a transferee forum situated in another circuit. Should the several cases consolidated for pretrial preparation in the instant proceeding eventually return to transferor courts outside this circuit, would our district court's Warsaw Convention/Montreal Agreement ruling, which we have affirmed, have binding force? We believe it should, as "law of the case," for if it did not, transfers under 28 U.S.C. § 1407 could be counterproductive, i.e., capable of generating rather than reducing the duplication and protraction Congress sought to check. On this issue in the case at hand, however, our circuit is not positioned to speak the last word.

We affirm the order of the district court that KAL is entitled to avail itself of the limitation on damages provided by the Warsaw Convention and raised to $75,000 by the Montreal Agreement; and we note again that the proper interpretation of the Convention and Agreement, as well as the scope of the transferee court's interpretive authority in a cause such as this one, are matters in need of definitive resolution for our national court system.

■ D. H. GINSBURG, Circuit Judge, concurring, in which WILLIAMS, Circuit Judge, joins. . . .

The conduct of multidistrict litigation, which is invariably time consuming as it is, will grind to a standstill while transferee judges read separate briefs, each based on the case law of a transferor circuit, on a single issue of federal law. Much of the advantage that transfer was intended to produce, and particularly the desiderata of furthering efficiency and preventing inconsistent rulings, will be lost by requiring transferee judges a wear a number of judicial hats. It is the prospect of this kind of quagmire that is likely to yield the result feared by the Court in *Van Dusen* — that courts would be "reluctant to grant transfers" and thereby "frustrate the remedial purposes of [section 1407]." It may well be preferable to have multidistrict litigation remain dispersed in the courts of origin than to have transferee judges burdened with the hopelessly complex task of sitting as several federal judges at once. Consequently, even though having transferee judges exercise independent judgment may in isolated instances result in an unraveling of a transferred case, I believe that this approach, although not a perfect solution, is by far the less problematic and the more consistent with the intent of Congress in enacting section 1407.

IN RE METHYL TERTIARY BUTYL ETHER (MTBE) PRODUCTS LIABILITY LITIGATION

241 F.R.D. 435 (S.D.N.Y. 2007)

■ SCHEINDLIN, District Judge.

[Because of leaking tanks in gasoline stations or breaks in pipelines, millions of gallons of gasoline have leached into groundwater around the country. Some gasoline additives, including MTBE, are toxic, and are likely carcinogens. Cases alleging that MTBE had caused losses in property values, personal injuries, and fear of cancer popped up in state and federal courts. The Judicial Panel on Multidistrict Litigation consolidated the federal cases in the Southern District of New York.

[One of the MDL cases was originally filed in Illinois state court. The complaint alleged that, in 1988, a pipeline break had dumped thousands of gallons of gasoline onto a farm, from which the gasoline leached into groundwater and affected residents of a nearby township. The defendants were companies involved with operating the pipeline. They removed the case to federal court; the Panel then transferred it to the MDL proceedings.

[After transfer, two plaintiffs moved to represent a class composed of the residents of the Illinois township. The plaintiffs proposed three subclasses: those who had suffered loss in property values, those who had abandoned their wells and incurred expenses hooking up to public water supplies, and those who suffered personal injuries or fear of cancer.]

A threshold question that must be addressed is whether the law of the transferor circuit should control when applying Rule 23 (i.e., Seventh Circuit) or, in the alternative, the law of the transferee circuit (i.e., Second Circuit). As explained below, the law of the transferor circuit applies to this motion for class certification under Rule 23.

This case was transferred to this Court pursuant to 28 U.S.C. § 1407 . . . . "The plain language of the statute does not explicitly resolve the issue of which circuit's law is binding, but it is important that section 1407 only allows cases to be transferred on the condition that such coordination 'will promote the just and efficient conduct of such actions.'" [In re MTBE Prods. Liab. Litig., 2005 WL 106936, at *5 (S.D.N.Y. Jan. 18, 2005) (quoting 28 U.S.C. § 1407).]

In the context of pre-trial issues such as motions to dismiss or discovery disputes, section 1407 requires the application of the law of the transferee circuit where the motions are being considered. For example, courts have held that the law of the transferee circuit controls pretrial issues such as whether the court has subject matter or personal jurisdiction over the action, or whether the cases should be remanded to state court because the cases were not properly removed. Likewise, the law of the transferee circuit controls discovery issues such as whether to compel a deposition or documents pursuant to a subpoena.

The law of the transferee circuit applies in each of these situations because the "objective of transfer is to eliminate duplication in discovery, avoid conflicting rulings and schedules, reduce litigation costs, and save the time and effort of the parties, the attorneys, the witnesses, and the courts." [MANUAL FOR COMPLEX LITIGATION, FOURTH § 20.131, at 220 (2004).] Section 1407 is aimed at eliminating "delay, confusion, conflict, inordinate expense and inefficiency" during the pretrial period. In other words, it promotes "just and efficient" resolution of the proceedings to apply the law of the transferee circuit to pretrial issues.

However, whether to certify an action on behalf of a class under Rule 23 is not merely a pretrial issue. In *Coopers & Lybrand v. Livesay*, [437 U.S. 463, 469 (1978),] the Supreme Court first observed that "the class determination generally involves considerations that are enmeshed in the factual and legal issues comprising the plaintiff's cause of action." . . .

More importantly, in *Amchem Products, Inc. v. Windsor*, [521 U.S. 501 (1997) (*supra* p. 493),] the Supreme Court held that when certifying a class action under Rule 23, the requirements of Rule 23(b)(3) must always be satisfied *for purposes of the trial* regardless of whether a jury will consider the case because the parties have settled. . . .

At the same time, the Supreme Court emphasized that "other specifications of the Rule — those designed to protect absentees by blocking unwarranted or overbroad class definitions — demand undiluted, even heightened, attention in the settlement context." Thus, courts must determine whether Rule 23 is satisfied for purposes of trial before granting certification.

Not only are class certification requirements inherently enmeshed with considerations of the trial, but under *Lexecon Inc. v. Milberg Weiss Bershad Hynes & Lerach*, [523 U.S. 26 (1998) (*supra* p. 162),] the authority of the transferee court in multi-district proceedings ends once the pretrial proceedings are completed. *Lexecon* requires this Court to return each case to its original district for trial after the pretrial phase has been completed. It would be neither just nor efficient to apply the law of this Circuit in considering class certification, and then force the transferor court to try a class action that it might never have certified.

Finally, Plaintiffs originally filed their state tort claims in Illinois state court. Defendants removed the action to federal court . . . under the federal officer removal statute and the case was then transferred to this Court by the Judicial Panel on Multidistrict Litigation. In a similar context, the *Manual for Complex Litigation* explains:

> Complexities may arise where the rulings turn on questions of substantive law. In diversity cases, the law of the transferor district follows the case to the transferee district. Where the claim or defense arises under federal law, however, the transferee judge should consider whether to apply the law of the transferee circuit or that of the transferor court's circuit, keeping in mind that statutes of limitations may present unique problems. [MANUAL FOR COMPLEX LITIGATION, *supra*, § 20.132, at 245.]

The case cited by the *Manual* for the statutes of limitations problem is *Berry Petroleum Co. v. Adams & Peck*, [518 F.2d 402, 412 (2d Cir. 1975),] in which the Second Circuit applied the law of the Fifth Circuit to determine if a suit has been timely brought. . . . Just as the statute of limitations encompassed questions of state substantive law, whether to certify a class involves issues pertaining to state substantive law. Neither party should be prejudiced in preparing for trial because the case was removed and transferred to another district in a different circuit.

Thus, in considering a motion for class certification of state claims under Rule 23, the law of the transferor circuit controls because that is the law that will bind the trial court and class certification is an issue on which the Supreme Court has directed courts to ensure that the requirements of Rule 23 are satisfied for purposes of trial. For pretrial motions, it is appropriate to apply the law of the transferee court in order to avoid duplication, conflicting rulings and schedules, and increased litigation costs. But, in the context of class certification and other issues inherently enmeshed with the trial, applying the law of the transferor court "promote[s] the just and efficient conduct of such actions."

[The court then held that, under the law of the Seventh Circuit, the requirements of Rule 23 had been satisfied with respect to two of the three subclasses, but that Seventh Circuit law did not permit certification of the personal-injury subclass. It also held that a class action was improper with respect to one set of defendants.]

Notes

1. Given the Second Circuit's favorable ruling on the inapplicability of the Warsaw Convention's damage limit, you might wonder why any plaintiffs filed their cases anywhere other than the Second Circuit. One answer is that many of the cases lacked sufficient connection with any district in the Second Circuit to support venue.

2. Despite then-Judge Ginsburg's appeal for clarification from "Higher Authority," neither Congress nor the Supreme Court has risen to the bait. In *Korean Air Lines* itself, the Supreme Court granted review, but, as might be expected, it resolved the underlying circuit split over the scope of the Warsaw Convention rather than deciding which law(s) an MDL court should choose in the face of a circuit split. It found that the D.C. Circuit's reading of the treaty was correct. Chan v. Korean Air Lines, 490 U.S. 122 (1989). Given that the Supreme Court is likely to behave in this way, will it ever determine whether the *Korean Air Lines* approach is correct?

3. Other federal courts have generally agreed with *Korean Air Lines*' holding that, with regard to issues of federal law, the law of the transferee circuit applies after a §1407 transfer. The same rule has also been applied to § 1404 transfers. *See, e.g.,* In re Gen. Am. Life Ins. Co. Sales Practices Litig., 391 F.3d 907, 911 (8th Cir. 2004) (dicta; § 1407 transfer); Murphy v. FDIC, 208 F.3d 959, 964-65 (11th Cir. 2000) (§ 1404 transfer); Menowitz v. Brown, 991 F.2d 36 (2d Cir. 1993) (§ 1407 transfer). *Cf.* In re Dow Co. "Sarabond" Prods. Liab. Litig., 666 F. Supp. 1466 (D. Colo. 1987) (in a case decided two months before *Korean Air Lines*, holding that the transferor circuit's law). Commentators have also accepted the rule. *See, e.g.,* AM. L. INST., COMPLEX LITIGATION § 6.08 (1994) ("[T]he transferee court shall not be bound by the federal law as interpreted in the circuits in which the actions were filed, but may determine for itself the federal law to be applied to the federal claims and defenses in the litigation.").

4. A narrow exception to *Korean Air Lines* has developed in some courts when federal law incorporates state law as the rule of decision. In this circumstance, "[w]hen the law of the United States is geographically non-uniform, a transferee court should use the rule of the transferor forum in order to implement the central conclusion of *Van Dusen* and *Ferens*: that a transfer under § 1404(a) accomplishes 'but a change of courtrooms.'" Eckstein v. Balcor Film Investors, 8 F.3d 1121, 1127 (7th Cir. 1993) (§1404 transfer); *accord* Olcott v. Del. Flood Co., 76 F.3d 1538 (10th Cir. 1996)

(§ 1404 transfer); In re United Mine Workers of Am. Employee Benefit Plans Litig., 854 F. Supp. 914 (D.D.C. 1994) (§1407 transfer). *Menowitz* has rejected this exception. 991 F.2d at 39-41.

5. *MTBE Products* creates yet another exception to the *Korean Air Lines* rule. Its decision is based on the language of § 1407(a), in particular the statute's requirement that the MDL process foster the "just and efficient conduct" of the litigation. Is its approach superior to the flat rule of *Korean Air Lines*? Is this approach better grounded in the text of § 1407? Does the approach better mesh with the Court's opinion in *Lexecon*, which was decided after *Korean Air Lines* (and which Justice Ginsburg joined).

MTBE Products can be read in two ways: either the law of the transferor circuit must apply to issues that are likely to affect the eventual trial in the transferor forum or the law of the transferor circuit must apply whenever the "just and efficient" conduct of an MDL proceeding requires it. Which reading is better?

6. *Korean Air Lines* involved an issue of substantive or remedial law, while *MTBE Products* involved an issue of procedure. But doesn't this distinction cut in the wrong direction? Presumably a transferee court has a greater interest in applying its circuit's procedural rules than in applying its substantive rules.

7. The *Korean Air Lines* approach to the choice of federal law is the mirror image of the approach that federal courts use for transferred state-law claims. For claims based on state law, *Van Dusen* and *Ferens* require that a transferee federal forum is required to adopt the choice-of-law rules that the transferor federal forum would adopt. For claims based on federal law, *Korean Air Lines* requires the transferee forum to adopt its own choice-of-law principle (in essence, *lex fori* of the transferee forum). Is a difference in the source of applicable law a sufficient reason for the dramatic difference in choice-of-law approach? Aside from federalism concerns, aren't the reasons that support *Van Dusen* and *Ferens* a point-by-point refutation of *Korean Air Lines*' approach? Conversely, aren't the reasons supporting *Korean Air Lines* a refutation of the *Van Dusen-Ferens* approach? Is *MTBE Products*' approach, which chooses the law that most justly and efficiently advances the litigation, superior to either *Van Dusen-Ferens* or *Korean Air Lines*?

How would a principle like "choose the law that advances the just and efficient conduct of the litigation" play out in complex litigation? In deciding what choice-of-law rule was just and efficient, would a court be able to consider what incentives using transferor or transferee law might have on the parties' willingness to aggregate?

8. Before *Korean Air Lines*, the Judicial Panel on Multidistrict Litigation had intimated that a MDL court should apply a transferor circuit's interpretation of federal law after a §1407 transfer. *See* In re Plumbing Fixtures Litig., 342 F. Supp. 756 (J.P.M.L. 1972). After *Korean Air Lines*, the Panel stated that "[w]hen determining whether to transfer an action under Section 1407 . . . it is not the business of the Panel to

consider what law the transferee court might apply" and "[a]ny suggestion to the contrary in [*Plumbing Fixtures*] is withdrawn." In re Gen. Motors Class E Stock Buyout Sec. Litig., 696 F. Supp. 1546, 1547 & n.1 (J.P.M.L. 1988). The Panel stated that *Van Dusen* was irrelevant to the issue of which circuit's interpretation of federal law should apply because *Van Dusen* was a diversity case. *Id.* at 1547 n.1.

At a theoretical level, the Panel's agnosticism about choice of law can be justified when the Panel is deciding *whether* to multidistrict. On the assumption that a change in law will advantage one side and disadvantage the other, this consideration is a wash. But can the Panel's agnosticism be justified when the Panel is deciding *where* to multidistrict a case?

At a practical level, isn't the Panel burying its head in the sand, and refusing to acknowledge one of the primary reasons that parties that are located in forums with unfavorable federal law seek an MDL transfer and one of the primary factors that motivates both sides to argue for transfer to a particular forum?

9. The *Korean Air Lines* approach raises some interesting questions of practical administration. Suppose that, like *Korean Air Lines*, applying the transferee circuit's law did not end the litigation. Unless the cases settled during the MDL process, *Lexecon* now requires that the cases be remanded to their original forums for trial. After remand, is the transferor court to apply the law of the transferor district or the law of the transferee district?

Korean Air Lines assumed that, under the "law of the case" doctrine, the law of the transferee circuit would continue to control after remand to the transferor court. This book does not explore in detail the "law of the case" doctrine, which can be important in complex litigation. Let us observe here that *Korean Air Lines*' assumption is not necessarily accurate. The "law of the case" doctrine holds that, "in the absence of extraordinary circumstances such as where a prior decision was 'clearly erroneous and would work a manifest injustice,'" a matter previously determined in a case cannot be challenged or re-litigated during later stages of the same case. *See* Christianson v. Colt Indus. Operating Co., 486 U.S. 800, 817 (1988); Joan Steinman, *Law of the Case: A Judicial Puzzle in Consolidated and Transferred Cases and in Multidistrict Litigation*, 135 U. PA. L. REV. 595 (1987). *Christianson* held that "the doctrine applies as much to the decisions of a coordinate court in the same case as to a court's own decisions." 486 U.S. at 816.

The first problem with *Korean Air Lines*' assumption is deciding which circuit's view of the "law of the case" doctrine applies: the doctrine of the transferor circuit or that of the transferee circuit, *See* Steinman, *supra*, at 683 (noting that the "law of the case" doctrine of transferee forum is usually applied, but arguing for the opposite result). Second, if one basis for *Korean Air Lines*' holding is the need for each court to use its independent judgment to determine federal law, using the "law of the case" doctrine, which denies the transferor court that right of independent determination after remand, is problematic; there is an inequity in allowing the MDL transferee court to discard the law of the tranferor circuit, but not permitting the transferor court to discard the law of the transferee circuit. Third, the same inefficiency that occurs when a transferee court must determine the law of a transferor court — an inefficiency that was one of the arguments used in *Korean Air Lines* — exists when the transferor court is forced to apply the law of the transferee court on remand.

10. In contrast to *Korean Air Lines'* dicta, some courts have assumed that a transferor court will apply its own law on remand — a possibility that creates its own problems. For instance, in *In re Food Lion, Inc., Fair Labor Standards Act "Effective Scheduling" Litigation*, 73 F.3d 528 (4th Cir. 1996), the MDL court issued orders dismissingd some claims of some plaintiffs. Because the orders dismissed fewer than all of the claims of the plaintiffs, however, plaintiffs could not immediately appeal. After the Panel remanded the remainder of the cases to their original forums, some of the plaintiffs sought to appeal from the MDL court's dismissal orders by asking transferor courts to enter judgment on the dismissed claims under Federal Rule of Civil Procedure 54(b), which allows a final judgment to be entered on a separate claim in a case. The Fourth Circuit, which was the circuit that encompassed the MDL transferee court, ordered the Panel Litigation to re-transfer the dismissed claims to the MDL transferee court, and then ordered the transferee court to enter Rule 54(b) judgments in the cases to allow aggrieved plaintiffs to appeal the dismissals to the Fourth Circuit. *Food Lion* reasoned that "[a] consolidated appeal, heard by the appellate court having jurisdiction over the transferee district court that entered the orders, is the best means of achieving the goals of efficient and uniform adjudication of numerous actions." 73 F.3d at 533.

Food Lion also suggested that the "better practice" would have been for the transferee court to have entered a Rule 54(b) judgment before remand of the cases occurred. *See* In re Am. Honda Motor Co. Dealerships Relations Litig., 958 F. Supp. 1045 (D. Md. 1997) (entering order permitting interlocutory appeal from order refusing to dismiss certain claims in MDL case). The Panel has expressed its disagreement with this aspect of *Food Lion*, at least when the MDL court's partial-dismissal order leaves only one action to be remanded. In re Baseball Bat Antitrust Litig., 112 F. Supp. 2d 1175 (J.P.M.L. 2000).

Both the *Food Lion* approach and the "law of the case" approach ensure that the law of the transferee circuit applies to claims dismissed in the MDL. The "law of the case" approach is broader, because it also requires the use of the MDL court's law even when MDL court issued no dispositive ruling. Which of the two approaches seems superior? Is either superior to an approach that allows the transferor court to apply the transferor circuit's law? The answers to these questions affect the efficacy of the MDL transfer process as an aggregation device. If the transferor court gives no deference to the law of the transferee circuit or the decisions of the MDL transferee court, won't aggrieved parties have an incentive not to resolve the case in the MDL forum but to hold out for remand whenever possible?

11. Suppose that the cases in an MDL proceeding raise both state law and federal law issues (as *Korean Air Lines* did). The *Van Dusen-Ferens* approach means that the law of the transferor forum applies for some issues, while the *Korean Air Lines* approach means that the law of the transferee forum applies for other issues. Can we justify this procedural disparity? If not should we reject *Korean Air Lines* and apply the law of the transferor forum to federal claims? Or should we reject *Van Dusen* and *Ferens* and apply the law of the transferee forum to state-law claims?

C. POSSIBLE SOLUTIONS TO THE CHOICE-OF-LAW CONUNDRUM

The last sections showed that varying substantive and procedural law, varying choice-of-law rules, and a dual system of courts all contribute to the dispersal of cases and difficulties in managing aggregated litigation, which are the problems that choice-of-law doctrines pose for complex litigation. In this section, we examine possible solutions (legislative and judicial) that might reduce or eliminate these problems. The six "solutions" in this section come with significant costs and push the choice-of-law envelope — perhaps too far, you might think. As we explore these options, do not be misled. Few complex cases have opted for any of the judicial approaches, and Congress shows no signs of acting. Most cases continue to labor within the traditional choice-of-law framework. Should they?

1. Manipulating Traditional Choice-of-Law Rules

With regard to state-law claims, common choice-of-law approaches — such as the "most significant contacts" approach and interest analysis — are easily manipulable. For instance, examine the multi-factor approach used in *Vioxx* (*supra* p. 645), which combined a dash of "most significant contacts" analysis with a dose of interest analysis. As *Vioxx* noted, the approach was "flexible." Had the court weighed the factors somewhat differently, it could have found that a single law applied to all of the class members' claims — a finding that would likely have allowed the court to certify the case as a class action and achieve a single-forum resolution of the dispute. *Vioxx* chose not to exploit this flexibility to choose a single law. But it could have done so. Consider the following case.

YSBRAND V. DAIMLERCHRYSLER CORP.

81 P.3d 618 (Okla. 2003)

[The defendant sold more than one million minivans with allegedly defective airbags. The plaintiffs sued in Oklahoma state court, seeking to certify a nationwide class action of minivan purchasers. The case alleged breach of express and implied warranties under the Uniform Commercial Code (UCC), as well as fraud and deceit. The trial court certified the class, which did not include any plaintiffs who had suffered personal injuries from the deployment of an airbag. The defendant appealed.]

DaimlerChrysler argues that common issues of law or fact do not predominate because varying state laws will apply to the asserted claims and defenses. . . .

1. *Choice of Law — UCC Claims*

The "most significant relationship" test applies to an action for breach of warranty in a sale of goods under Article 2 of the UCC. *See* Collins Radio Co. v. Bell, 623 P.2d 1039, 1046-47 (Okla. Civ. App. 1980). This test is guided by principles and contacts from the *Restatement (Second) of Conflicts*. It determines which state's law is most directly connected to the parties and the transaction.

Under section 6 of the Restatement, the factors relevant to any choice of law decision include:

(a) the needs of the interstate and international systems,

(b) the relevant policies of the forum,

(c) the relevant policies of other interested states and the relative interests of those states in the determination of the particular issue,

(d) the protection of justified expectations,

(e) the basic policies underlying the particular field of law,

(f) certainty, predictability and uniformity of result, and

(g) ease in the determination and application of the law to be applied.

The contacts to be considered in applying these principles to an issue in contract include:

(a) the place of contracting,

(b) the place of negotiation of the contract,

(c) the place of performance,

(d) the location of the subject matter of the contract, and

(e) the domicile, residence, nationality, place of incorporation and place of business of the parties.

The contacts are to be evaluated according to their relative importance with respect to the particular issue.

Id. § 188(2) (emphasis added). However, a third provision, section 191, applies to a sale of interests in chattel. "So in a contract for the sale of goods the most significant contact is the place of delivery unless another state has a more significant relationship." *Collins Radio*, 623 P.2d at 1047. As comment *f* to section 191 explains: "On occasion, a state which is not the place of delivery will nevertheless, with respect to the particular issue, be the state of most significant relationship to the transaction, the parties and the chattel and hence the state of the applicable law." The particular dispute in this matter presents such an occasion in which "the local law of some state other than that of delivery should be applied in any event because of the intensity of the interest of that state in the determination of the particular issue." *Id.*

All 50 states and the District of Columbia bear some relationship to the parties and transactions in this dispute by virtue of the nationwide sales of the minivans. The question becomes whether the relationship of each state where the vehicles were purchased is more significant to the parties and this litigation than that of Michigan, the principal place of business of DaimlerChrysler.

The *Restatement*'s section 188(2) contacts of the place of contracting, the place of negotiation and performance, and the location of the subject matter are of diminished significance to the sales of the minivans. The UCC warranties are not something which is negotiated in the purchase of a new car. Thus, the relative interest of each buyer's home state in applying its version of the UCC is more or less equal. By contrast, Michigan's interest in having its regulatory scheme applied to the conduct of a Michigan manufacturer is most significant.. Michigan is where the decisions concerning the design, manufacture, and distribution of the minivans were made. Michigan is the only state where conduct relevant to all class members occurred. The principal place of DaimlerChrysler's business is the most important contact with respect to the UCC warranty claims.

The selection of Michigan law furthers the relevant factors stated in section 6 of the Restatement. The needs of the interstate system and the basic policies of predictability and uniformity of result require that the issue of product defect be determined in one forum with one result rather than in 51 jurisdictions with the very real possibility of conflicting decisions. While the interest of each home state in applying its local law is significant, Michigan's interest in the conduct of its manufacturer, and thus its connection to the warranty issues, is greater. Michigan law applies. It should be noted that this conclusion is consistent with the constitutional imperative that "for a state's substantive law to be selected in a constitutionally permissible manner, that state must have a significant aggregation of contacts, creating state interests, such that choice of its law is neither arbitrary nor fundamentally unfair." Phillips Petroleum Co. v. Shutts, 472 U.S. 797, 818 (1985) [*supra* p. 637].

2.   *Choice of Law — Fraud and Misrepresentation*

Section 148 of the *Restatement* applies to actions to recover pecuniary damages for false representations whether fraudulent, negligent, or innocent. Subsection (2) applies to this dispute because the nationwide representations in DaimlerChrysler's advertising were made in states outside each class member's home state. The home state is where each class member acted in reliance on those representations by purchasing a minivan. Thus, this Court is directed to consider:

(a) the place, or places, where the plaintiff acted in reliance upon the defendant's representations,

(b) the place where the plaintiff received the representations,

(c) the place where the defendant made the representations,

(d) the domicil, residence, nationality, place of incorporation and place of business of the parties,

(e) the place where a tangible thing which is the subject of the transaction between the parties was situated at the time, and

(f) the place where the plaintiff is to render performance under a contract which he has been induced to enter by the false representations of the defendant.

The comments to subsection (2) describe (a), (b), (c), and (d) as the "more important of these contacts." . . . .

In this matter, each class member presumably received the representation in their home state, their place of domicile. Therefore, the contacts point to each class member's home state for the applicable law. Applying the law of 51 jurisdictions to the fraud claim presents an overwhelming burden which would make the class unmanageable and a class action determination of that claim inappropriate. The class action certified by the trial court will go forward only on the warranty claims asserted.

Notes

1. The most famous example of manipulating traditional rules to achieve a single substantive law is *In re Air Crash Disaster Near Chicago, Ill. on May 25, 1979*, 644 F.2d 594 (7th Cir. 1981). A crash of a DC-10 killed 273 people. The Judicial Panel on Multidistrict Litigation transferred 118 cases to the Northern District of Illinois, in which the crash had occurred. These cases had been filed in federal courts in Illinois, California, New York, Michigan, Hawaii, and Puerto Rico. The decedents were residents of California, Connecticut, Hawaii, Illinois, Indiana, Massachusetts, Michigan, New Jersey, New York, Vermont, Puerto Rico, Japan, the Netherlands, and Saudi Arabia. The defendants were the manufacturer of the airplane, which was incorporated in Maryland with its principal place of business in Missouri, and the airline, which was incorporated in Delaware with its principal place of business in New York (or possibly Texas — the issue was in dispute). The airplane was designed and built (negligently, according to the complaint) in California. It was maintained (also negligently, according to the complaint) in Oklahoma.

A critical issue in the case was whether punitive damages were available. As the court described the situation, "[t]he law of the place of the disaster, the law of the place of manufacture of the airplane, and the law of the primary place of business of the airline do not allow punitive damages; but, the law of the primary place of business of the manufacturer of the airplane and the law of the place of maintenance of the airline do allow punitive damages." *Id.* at 604. The MDL court dutifully analyzed the transferor choice-of-law rules for each case, and concluded that the transferor courts would choose substantive law as follows: Except for the actions arising from Puerto Rico, the transferor forums would choose the substantive law of a state that permitted punitive damages against the manufacturer; but no transferor forum would choose the law of a state that permitted punitive damages against the airline. In re Air Crash Disaster Near Chicago, Ill. on May 25, 1979, 500 F. Supp. 1044 (N.D. Ill. 1980).

Conducting exactly the same choice-of-law analysis, the court of appeals determined that the MDL court had correctly determined that the airline was not subject to punitive damages, but had erred with respect to the application of the choice-of-law principles to the airplane's manufacturer. The court of appeals re-analyzed the state choice-of-law approaches of each of the six transferor forums — two of which used a "most significant contacts" approach, one of which used interest analysis, one of which used *lex loci delicti*, one of which had used *lex loci delicti* but was in a state of flux, and one of which had chosen no choice-of-law approach. The court concluded that each transferor forum would have chosen the law of a state that did not permit punitive damages against the manufacturer. As a result, neither the airline nor the manufacturer was subject to punitive damages. At two points in the opinion, Judge Sprecher noted that "[o]ur result also comports with the *Restatement (Second)*'s principle that choice-of-law rules should be relatively simple and easy to apply," 644 F.2d at 616, and emphasized that

> this result in no way signifies a return to the mechanical, wooden law of *lex loci delicti*. Rather, it emphasizes the fact that there must be some principled method of decision when the standard "interest analysis" of conflicts law cannot settle the question. [*Id.* at 621.]

Judge Cudahy concurred, commending the "insight and creativity of Judge Sprecher's probing analysis" and noting that "the questions raised about state policy toward extraterritorial torts underline the need for a federal law to govern tort liability for these unthinkable air disasters." *Id.* at 633.

2. *Air Crash Disaster* is a lengthy and famous opinion, best known for the "miracle" by which the different choice-of-law rules all pointed to the same substantive result for both defendants. Indeed, despite Judge Sprecher's protestations to the contrary, isn't the result in *Air Crash Disaster* in essence a return to *lex loci delicti* in a situation — a mass disaster whose injuries all occur in one state — in which that approach is the simplest method for achieving the use of a single substantive law?

Some commentators have thought that this happy congruence resulted only from the court's unfair treatment of the interests of some of the relevant jurisdictions and its desire to reach a result that made the MDL litigation manageable. The ALI cited *Air Crash Disaster* as an example of what is wrong with the traditional choice-of-law approach in complex litigation, noting that the Seventh Circuit's result "underscores the lack of predictability in the choice of law regime as it is applied today." AM. L. INST., COMPLEX LITIGATION 307 (1994). Other academic commentary has been less restrained. Professor Lowenfeld said that "the airplane cases in the 1970s and 1980s seem to have made a parody not only of the conflict of laws but of the law of torts in general"; he analyzed *Air Crash Disaster* in detail to point out the problems of modern choice-of-law analysis. Andreas Lowenfeld, *Mass Torts and the Conflict of Laws: The Airline Disaster*, 1989 U. ILL. L. REV. 157, 158-63. Dean Kramer called the opinion "a virtual 'how-to' manual of ways to manipulate choice-of-law analysis." Larry Kramer, *Choice of Law in Complex Litigation*, 71 N.Y.U. L. REV. 547, 555 (1996). Kramer was especially unimpressed by the "fancy footwork" that the Seventh Circuit performed to say that domiciliary states had no interest in the application of their punitive-damage rules and by its decision to break the tie between two interested states "by choosing the law of an avowedly less interested third state" — a result that impaired the interests of both states. *Id.* at 556-57. Kramer also criticized the Seventh Circuit's misreading of New York's choice-of-law rules and its "grotesque distortion" of Michigan's choice-of-law rules. *Id.* at 557-59.

3. *Air Crash Disaster* is somewhat unusual; it involved an issue on which there were only two possible positions (punitive damages or no punitive damages) and there were enough jurisdictions that had lined up on each side of the question that it was easy to manipulate the choice-of-law rules to choose the law of a state that adopted the latter position. But *Air Crash Disaster* is hardly unique. Other mass torts that were transferred to a single federal court undertook similar analyses, with similar outcomes: the application of one or of a limited number of laws. *See* In re Air Crash Near Cali, Colom. on Dec. 20, 1995, 24 F. Supp. 2d 1340 (S.D. Fla. 1998) (applying Florida law); In re Air Crash Disaster at Sioux City, Iowa, on July 19, 1989, 734 F. Supp. 1425 (N.D. Ill. 1990) (applying Illinois law to all claims against the airline, California law to all claims against the plane manufacturer, and Ohio law to all claims against the engine manufacturer); In re Union Carbide Corp. Gas Plant Disaster, 634 F. Supp. 842 (S.D.N.Y.), *aff'd*, 809 F.2d 195 (2d Cir. 1986) (applying the law of India under all approaches). Professor Nafziger conducted a study of sixty-two air-crash cases (thirty-nine federal and twenty-three state) decided between 1960 and 1993, and found that courts often applied a single law to the controversy. James A.R. Nafziger, *Choice of Law in Air Disasters: Complex Litigation Rules and the Common Law*, 54 LA. L. REV. 1001 (1994).

4. The same tendency to manipulate choice-of-law rules in order to select one or a limited number of laws can be seen in large-scale business litigation. *See* Harmsen v. Smith, 693 F.2d 932 (9th Cir. 1982) (applying California's presumption of using forum law and requiring a defendant to prove that the laws of other states are different and the interests of other states would be impaired by applying California law); In re Seagate Techs. Sec. Litig., 115 F.R.D. 264 (N.D. Cal. 1987).

5. Of course, as *Ysbrand* acknowledges, the Full Faith and Credit Clause and the Due Process Clause impose limits on blatant manipulation. As long as the court chooses the law of a state with some connection to the dispute, however, these limits are easy to overcome.

6. In recent years, efforts to manipulate choice-of-law rules in order to apply a single rule have sometimes taken the form of arguing that a court should choose the law of the state in which the defendant (usually a corporation) is headquartered. Applying a "most significant contacts" approach, *Ysbrand* uses this approach for the warranty, but not the fraud, claims in the case. The idea behind this argument is that the state of the defendant's headquarters has an interest in all the claims asserted against the defendant. Hence, there are not likely to be full-faith-and-credit or due process issues with this choice. Indeed, under most of the standard choice-of-law approaches, the law of the defendant's headquarters is a reasonable and defensible choice: That state has significant contacts with the litigation, and an interest in having its law applied. Choosing this law can even fit under a *lex loci delicti* perspective *if* "the place of the wrong" is construed to mean the place in which the defendant made the decision causing harm rather than the place in which the injury arose.

7. Although *Ysbrand* did not, courts have sometimes applied the law of the defendant's headquarters even to fraud claims. *See* Int'l Union of Operating Eng'rs Local #68 Welfare Fund v. Merck & Co., 894 A.2d 1136 (N.J. Super. Ct. App. Div. 2006), *rev'd on other grounds*, 929 A.2d 1076 (N.J. 2007). In general, however, courts have not been receptive to this idea. For instance, in *In re Bridgestone/Firestone, Inc.*, 288 F.3d 1012 (7th Cir. 2002), cases involving SUVs sold with defective tires had been consolidated in an MDL proceeding in the Southern District of Indiana. Plaintiffs then filed a separate class action in the district, seeking to certify two classes: one against the car manufacturer that had sold SUVs and one against the tire manufacturer. Both classes contained plaintiffs who had either suffered physical injuries (a tort claim) or loss in value of their SUVs (a consumer-fraud claim). The car manufacturer's headquarters was in Michigan, and the tire manufacturer's headquarters was in Tennessee. Conveniently for the plaintiffs, both Michigan and Tennessee recognized the loss-in-value theory, even though many states did not. The district court found that, under Indiana's choice-of-law rule, the laws of the defendants' headquarters would apply; and because the laws of both states were identical, the class action was manageable. The Seventh Circuit reversed:

> Indiana is a *lex loci delicti* state: in all but exceptional cases it applies the law of the place where harm occurred.... [The physical and financial] injuries occurred in all 50 states, the District of Columbia, Puerto Rico, and U.S. territories such as Guam. The *lex loci delicti* principle points to the places of these injuries, not the defendants' corporate headquarters, as the source of law.
>
> ... Neither Indiana nor any other state has applied a uniform place-of-the-defendant's-headquarters rule to products-liability cases. It is not hard to devise an argument that such a uniform rule would be

good on many dimensions, but that argument has not carried the day with state judges, and it is state law rather than a quest for efficiency in litigation (or in product design decisions) that controls.

. . . If recovery for breach of warranty or consumer fraud is possible, the injury is decidedly where the consumer is located, rather than where the seller maintains its headquarters. . . . Indiana's choice-of-law rule selects the 50 states and multiple territories where the buyers live, and not the place of the sellers' headquarters, for these suits.

Because these claims must be adjudicated under the law of so many jurisdictions, a single nationwide class is not manageable. [*Id.* at 1016-18.]

In a products-liability case, the Eighth Circuit rejected a similar argument that "applying Minnesota law was proper because the parties, particularly [the defendant], had significant contacts with Minnesota, including [the defendant] being headquartered in Minnesota, and the fact that 'much of the conduct relevant' to the claims 'occurred or emanated from Minnesota.'" In re St. Jude Med., Inc., 425 F.3d 1116, 1119 (8th Cir. 2005). (For excerpts of other parts of the *St. Jude* decision, see *supra* p. 414). *St. Jude* suggested that the selection of Minnesota law might have been unconstitutional because the district court had not "conduct[ed the] thorough conflicts-of-law analysis with respect to each plaintiff class member" required by *Phillips Petroleum Co. v. Shutts*, 472 U.S. 797 (1985) (*supra* p. 276). *See* 425 F.3d at 1120. But it ultimately remanded the case for the district court to conduct a more thorough choice-of-law analysis under Minnesota law. On remand, the district court held that Minnesota law still applied; on appeal, the Eighth Circuit reversed on other grounds. *See* In re St. Jude Med., Inc., 522 F.3d 836 (8th Cir. 2008).

7.   For further discussion about the technique of using the law of a defendant's headquarters to "bootstrap" a case into a class action, see Samuel Issacharoff, *Getting Beyond Kansas*, 74 UMKC L. REV. 613 (2006); Richard A. Nagareda, *Bootstrapping in Choice of Law After the Class Action Fairness Act*, 74 UMKC L. REV. 661 (2006); Allison M. Gruenwald, Note, *Rethinking Place of Business as Choice of Law in Class Action Lawsuits*, 58 VAND. L. REV. 1925 (2005).

8.   One of the most original and thoughtful choice-of-law analyses occurred in a massive fraud case in which the plaintiffs alleged that the major players in the tobacco industry had conspired over decades to deceive consumers and the public about the safety of their cigarettes. A critical question in determining whether a nationwide class of smokers could be certified was the variation among state laws on fraud and punitive-damage issues. In the case, the major defendants had their corporate headquarters in New York. Applying New York's choice-of-law principles, as required by *Klaxon*, Judge Weinstein held that the law of New York determined all liability and punitive-damages issues in the case. New York's choice-of-law rule was based on a form of interest analysis, and Judge Weinstein was candid about the way in which the needs of complex litigation required that he exploit the flexibility in this approach to select a single law:

The history of choices of laws shows that notions of individual justice have trumped sovereign interests in affairs that by their nature have a supranational or suprastate scope. The unique nature of some cases demand flexibility and comparison of alternative results achieved by applying different laws. The changing forms of personal injury in the twentieth century, due to increased mobility of goods, people, and information, imposes strong pressures to account for the interests of all harmed parties and their states.

. . . Most modern scholarship concludes that choice of law rules can, and should, lead to the application of either a few state laws, a single state law, federal common law, national consensus law, or abandoning *Klaxon* analysis altogether in complex litigation. . . .

. . . Dispersal difficulties in the mass tort tobacco cases underscore the conclusion that conflict rules generally applicable to single tort situations do not control a case as complex as the present one . . . . As the place of incorporation and business of the major actors in the conspiracy New York also has an interest in seeing that they, as its wards, are not unduly punished by excessive punitive damages imposed in other states. . . .

Application of New York law in this case satisfies Due Process and Full Faith and Credit under *Shutts*. It is worth noting that *Shutts* itself was not a complex case. The potential application of four different state interest rates in *Shutts* was not likely to create the kind of joinder, pretrial, trial, or remedial complexity as does the case at bar. . . .

Shutts left open the possibility that the choice of a single law (or multiple state laws) is constitutionally permissible if the mechanical application of multiple laws threatens the rational adjudication that lies at the heart of due process, and "this threat outweighs the countervailing Due Process and Full Faith and Credit Clause considerations that animated *Shutts*." . . .

There are many nuances, both substantively and procedurally, in law from state to state. Courts, however, cannot ignore two fundamentals: 1) they deal with human institutions that, unlike the exquisite machinery of atomic physicists with tolerances approaching zero, must interpret the law reasonably, with some play in its joints, if it is to effectively serve its protective role, and 2) they respond here to a complex nationwide fraud allegedly created by defendants; the contention of the defendants that the plaintiff's claims are too widespread to be dealt with effectively by the courts must be considered in light of the allegations that it is defendants' pervasive fraud that has led to the need for nationally applicable effective remedies. The basic premise of law in this country remains that for every wrong there is a remedy, an effective and realistic remedy.

In re Simon II Litig., 211 F.R.D. 86, 171-72, 174, 176, 178 (E.D.N.Y. 2002) (*infra* p. 971). Anticipating that the Second Circuit might disagree with his analysis, Judge Weinstein proposed as a back-up plan to create subclasses based on variants in state law. The force of *Simon*'s analysis was much blunted, however, when the Second Circuit held that the class could not be certified for other reasons. In re Simon II Litig., 407 F.3d 125 (2d Cir. 2005) (*supra* p. 396).

9.   It is a mistake to believe that state and federal courts routinely manipulate choice-of-law rules to make a single or a limited number of laws apply. As *Vioxx* (*supra* p. 645) and *Bridgestone/Firestone* show, many cases find that the applicable choice-of-law rules require the use of different states' laws even when aggregation and management benefits would flow from using a single law. *See also* COMPLEX LITIGATION, *supra*, § 6.01, at 347-48 (collecting cases); *but see* In re Prudential Ins. Co. of Am. Sales Practices Litig., 962 F. Supp. 450 (D.N.J. 1997) (finding that differences in state law did not make a settlement class action unmanageable).

10. Manipulating choice-of-law rules to achieve the use of a single state's law effectively puts courts handling state-law claims in the same position as a transferee court that adopts *Korean Air Lines*' approach for issues of federal law. One argument for *Korean Air Lines*' approach is the equitable treatment of all those injured by a course of conduct. However compelling that desire for equality might have been in *Korean Air Lines*, which involved theoretically uniform federal law, isn't an inevitable consequence of a federal system, in which states can choose non-uniform laws, the unequal treatment of similarly situated victims? With state-law claims, manipulating choice-of-law rules puts into tension our need to resolve repetitive litigation equitably and our federalist *quid pro quo* that allows each state to establish and enforce rules of behavior affecting its interests as long as it respects the rights of other states to do the same.

10. What is wrong with admitting candidly that, when necessary to avoid unfairness or inefficiency, courts can "bend" the ordinary choice-of-law principles of the forum state to obtain a manageable number of state laws? Is this approach any different than creating special choice-of-law rules for complex cases (a subject that we consider *infra* p. 701)? Because a change in choice-of-law principles can be outcome-determinative, is the difference in treatment of routine and complex cases justified?

2. Choosing Federal (Common) Law

Federal law possesses important advantages from an aggregation standpoint: It creates federal jurisdiction, which brings cases into the federal courts with their powerful aggregation tools; and, to the extent that *Korean Air Lines*' approach holds, it allows a transferee court to apply uniform federal law to all parties. Thus, if federal law can be made to govern a dispute, the choice-of-law problem in complex litigation can be cut down at its root: A single law, rather than varying laws, will apply.

A principal difficulty with this approach is that "[f]ederal law is generally interstitial in its nature." RICHARD H. FALLON, JR. ET AL., HART & WECHSLER'S THE FEDERAL COURTS & THE FEDERAL SYSTEM 459 (6th ed. 2009). This incompleteness of federal law derives partly from constitutional limits on congressional power, and partly from political determinations not to regulate behavior that the national government has the constitutional authority to regulate. Should these important constraints bend in light of the needs of complex cases?

This subsection explores this question. Two sources for creating uniform federal law exist: statutes and regulations created in the political process, or federal common law created by judges. With regard to the first source, Congress is unlikely to pass legislation providing a uniform rule of decision for complex cases. Rather, parties are more likely to use federal statutes and regulations to contend that these federal laws preempt state-law claims, thus creating uniformity by suffocating state laws that impose varying burdens. In recent years, the Supreme Court has been active in the preemption area. In a series of close decisions, it has generally found that state-law remedies in the mass-tort area survive. *See* Wyeth v. Levine, 555 U.S. —, 129 S. Ct. 1187 (2009) (holding that the Food and Drug Administration's approval of a drug and its warning label did not bar state-law failure-to-warn claims); Altria Group, Inc. v. Good, 555 U.S. —, 129 S. Ct. 538 (2008) (holding that neither the Federal Cigarette Labeling and Advertising Act nor the Federal Trade Commission's regulatory decisions expressly or impliedly preempted state-law misrepresentation claims brought by smokers of light cigarettes). *But see* Riegel v. Medtronic, Inc., 552 U.S. 312 (2008) (holding that the Medical Devices Amendments of 1976 preempted state-law tort claims regarding an alleged defect in a medical device).

Preemption — especially some aspects of implied preemption — is a judicial construct, and thus spills over into the second source for creating uniform federal law: federal common law. *Erie Railroad Co. v. Tompkins*, 304 U.S. 64, 78 (1938), famously observed that federal courts have no constitutional authority to create "federal general common law." In light of *Erie*'s statement, is there room for a court to create such law when it might reduce the dispersal or increase the manageability of complex litigation? Consider the following cases.

KOHR V. ALLEGHENY AIRLINES, INC.

504 F.2d 400 (7th Cir. 1974)

■ SWYGERT, Chief Judge.

Defendants-appellants Allegheny Airlines, Inc. and the United States, appeal from the dismissal of their cross-claims and third-party complaints for indemnity and contribution against defendants-appellees Brookside Corporation (Brookside), Forth Corporation (Forth is a wholly-owned subsidiary of Brookside), and the estate of Robert W. Carey. The instant actions arise out of a mid-air collision on September 9, 1969, in the airspace over Fairland, Indiana between an Allegheny Airlines DC-9-31 jet aircraft and a Piper Cherokee aircraft piloted by Robert W. Carey and owned by Forth. . . .

. . . As a result of the mid-air collision both aircraft were totally destroyed and all eighty-three occupants were killed.

[Wrongful-death actions and suits for damage to the planes were filed in various federal courts. Claims against defendants Allegheny, Brookside, Forth, and the estate of Carey were based on diversity of citizenship. Claims against the United States were based on a federal statute, the Federal Tort Claims Act. The Judicial Panel on Multidistrict Litigation transferred all cases to the Southern District of Indiana. The United States and Allegheny then filed crossclaims and third-party claims against Brookside, Forth, and the estate of Carey for indemnity and contribution.

[The United States and Allegheny agreed to a pro-rata formula for compensating the plaintiffs. Under the agreement, the United States and Allegheny retained their rights to seek indemnity and contribution. The United States and Allegheny subsequently settled the plaintiffs' claims. The district court then granted the motions of Forth, Brookside, and the estate of Carey to dismiss these claims because Indiana law did not permit indemnity and contribution claims.]

II

. . . Allegheny urges that a federal rule of contribution and indemnity should govern in the instant action. Failing the application of a federal law of contribution Allegheny contends that in view of the multiplicity of state jurisdictions involved, with the various plaintiffs instituting actions in numerous states other than Indiana, the trial judge should have conducted an evidentiary hearing to facilitate a proper choice of law analysis. Had the district judge done so, it is claimed that jurisdictions other than Indiana would be found to have a more substantial interest in having their laws on contribution and indemnity applied. In addition, Allegheny contends that even assuming Indiana law controls, the district court misapplied the rules on contribution and indemnity.

Were it necessary, we would be inclined to agree with Allegheny that the district judge failed to engage in an adequate conflict of laws analysis and that he erred on the application of Indiana law on contribution and indemnity. We need not reach these issues, however, for we agree with Allegheny that there should be a federal law of contribution and indemnity governing mid-air collisions such as the one here.

III

The basis for imposing a federal law of contribution and indemnity is what we perceive to be the predominant, indeed almost exclusive, interest of the federal government in regulating the affairs of the nation's airways. Moreover, the imposition of a federal rule of contribution and indemnity serves a second purpose of eliminating inconsistency of result in similar collision occurrences as well as within the same occurrence due to the application of differing state laws on contribution and indemnity. Given the prevailing federal interest in uniform air law regulation, we deem it desirable that a federal rule of contribution and indemnity be applied. . . .

Congress has recognized the national responsibility for regulating air commerce. Federal control is intensive and exclusive. Planes . . . move only by federal permission, subject to federal inspection, in the hands of federally certified personnel and under an intricate system of federal commands. The moment a ship taxis onto a runway it is caught up in an elaborate and detailed system of controls. . . .

With the passage of the Federal Aviation Act of 1958, 49 U.S.C. §§ 1301, et seq., Congress expressed the view that the control of aviation should rest exclusively in the hands of the federal government. In section 1108 of the Act, 49 U.S.C. § 1508(a), it is clearly provided that:

> (a) The United States of America is declared to possess and exercise complete and exclusive national sovereignty in the airspace of the United States . . . .

The explicit objective of the Act is to foster the development of air commerce. To that end, it has been recognized that the principal purpose of the Act is to create one unified system of flight rules and to centralize in the Administrator of the Federal Aviation Administration the power to promulgate rules for the safe and efficient use of the country's airspace. When the notion of federal preemption over aviation is viewed in combination with the fact that this litigation ensues from a mid-air collision occurring in national airspace, that the Government is a party to the action pursuant to the Federal Tort Claims Act, and that this litigation has since its inception been subject to the supervision of the Judicial Panel created by the Multidistrict Litigation Act, there is no perceptible reason why federal law should not be applied to determine the rights and liabilities of the parties involved. The interest of the state wherein the fortuitous event of the collision occurred is slight as compared to the dominant federal interest. Accordingly, the rights and liabilities of Allegheny and the United States are peculiarly federal in nature and are to be governed by a federal rule of contribution and indemnity. . . .

[The court then held that, under federal common law, the "better rule" of contribution and indemnity was a rule "of contribution and indemnity on a comparative negligence basis."]

IN RE "AGENT ORANGE" PRODUCT LIABILITY LITIGATION

635 F.2d 987 (2d Cir. 1980)

■ KEARSE, Circuit Judge.

This appeal presents the question whether claims asserted by veterans of the United States armed forces against companies which supplied the United States government with chemicals that are alleged to have been contaminated and to have injured the veterans and their families, are governed by federal common law. Defendants-appellants Diamond Shamrock Corporation, Monsanto Company, Thompson-Hayward Chemical Company, Hercules Incorporated and the Dow Chemical Company were the manufacturers of various herbicides including "Agent Orange" (hereinafter collectively referred to as "Agent Orange") for use by the military as defoliants in the Vietnam War. The plaintiffs, veterans of that war and their families, allege that they have sustained various physical injuries by reason of the veterans' exposure to Agent Orange. Plaintiffs seek redress of those injuries under federal common law, and have invoked the "federal question" jurisdiction of the district court. 28 U.S.C. § 1331(a) (1976). Defendants contest the existence of a federal common law cause of action, and moved below to dismiss for want of jurisdiction. The United States District Court for the Eastern District of New York, George C. Pratt, Judge, denied their motion. Defendants obtained certification of the jurisdiction issue and took this appeal pursuant to 28 U.S.C. § 1292(b).

We agree with defendants that there is no federal common law right of action under the circumstances of this litigation. Accordingly, we reverse.

I

The present litigation began in late 1978 and early 1979, when several individual veterans and their families commenced actions in the Northern District of Illinois and the Southern and Eastern Districts of New York . . . . By order of the Judicial Panel on Multidistrict Litigation, thirteen such actions, involving thirty named plaintiffs, were transferred to the Eastern District of New York and assigned to Judge Pratt for coordinated or consolidated pretrial proceedings . . . . It appears that there are presently more than 800 named plaintiffs in these proceedings. . . .

What marks these proceedings as somewhat extraordinary are the size of the plaintiff class and the scope of the relief that is sought. Plaintiffs purport to represent the 2.4 million veterans who served as combat soldiers in Southeast Asia from 1962 through 1971, as well as most of the families or survivors of those veterans. Fifteen plaintiff subclasses are identified; many of these subclasses consist of persons who are "at risk" of, but have yet to sustain, various physical injuries. Plaintiffs have alleged that "the combined liquid assets of the 'corporate defendants' will be insufficient to fully compensate the entire class of plaintiffs." . . .

Plaintiffs argue that federal common law should be applied to their claims principally because of the unique federal nature of the relationship between the soldier and his government, relying chiefly on *United States v. Standard Oil Co.*, 332 U.S. 301, 305 (1947) ("Perhaps no relation between the Government and a citizen is more distinctively federal in character than that between it and members of its armed forces."). They contend that this interest brings the case within the doctrine of *Clearfield Trust Co. v. United States*, 318 U.S. 363, 366 (1943), which held that, in order to ensure uniformity and certainty," [the] rights and duties of the United States on commercial paper which it issues are governed by federal rather than local law." Plaintiffs argue that the government similarly has an interest in having all of its veterans compensated by government contractors who manufactured or marketed Agent Orange, and that application of the respective state laws would impede recovery on a uniform basis.

The district court rejected the contention that *Clearfield Trust* stated the controlling principle, recognizing that the United States, a party to *Clearfield Trust*, is not party to the plaintiffs' claims here.[6] Rather, the court recognized that since the present action involves only private parties, the federal common law issue is controlled by the principles set forth in *Miree v. DeKalb County*, 433 U.S. 25 (1977), and *Wallis v. Pan American Petroleum Corp.*, 384 U.S. 63 (1966). After reviewing the latter decisions, the district court applied a three-factor test to determine whether federal common law governs plaintiffs' claims:

> (1) the existence of a substantial federal interest in the outcome of a litigation; (2) the effect on this federal interest should state law be applied; and (3) the effect on state interests should state law be displaced by federal common law. . . .

. . . [T]he district court ruled that plaintiffs had stated valid causes of action under the federal common law. The court therefore held that it had subject matter jurisdiction over the case . . . .

II

Both plaintiffs and defendants accept the three-part test that the district court applied to the federal common law issue, and for purposes of discussion we accept that framework. But, focusing our consideration chiefly on the first factor of the test, i.e., "the existence of a substantial federal interest in the outcome of the litigation," we disagree with the district court's analysis and conclude that the court gave insufficient weight to the Supreme Court's repeated admonition that

> [in] deciding whether rules of federal common law should be fashioned, normally the guiding principle is that a *significant conflict between some federal policy or interest and the use of state law in the premises must first be specifically shown.* . . .

Wallis v. Pan American Petroleum Corp., 384 U.S. at 68, *quoted with emphasis in Miree v. DeKalb County*, 433 U.S. at 31. Principally we reject the district court's conclusion that there is an identifiable federal policy at stake in this litigation that warrants the creation of federal common law rules.

In considering plaintiffs' contentions, it is essential to delineate precisely the relation of the United States to the claims here at issue.

---

6. We note that the defendants have impleaded the United States in the present action. It is clear, however, that the jurisdiction of the district court over the claims of the plaintiffs is not enhanced by third party complaints. *Cf.* Louisville & Nashville RR. v. Mottley, 211 U.S. 149 (1908).

These claims are brought by former servicemen and their families against private manufacturers; they are not asserted by or against the United States, and they do not directly implicate the rights and duties of the United States. They are thus unlike the claims in *United States v. Standard Oil Co.*, in which the government brought suit to recover for its payments to a soldier injured as a result of the defendant's negligence, and *Clearfield Trust Co. v. United States*, in which the government brought suit to enforce its rights in commercial paper issued by it. In each of those cases the government was a party seeking to enforce its own asserted rights, and analysis reveals two federal concerns which are inherent in such cases. First, the government has an interest in having uniform rules govern its rights and obligations. Second, the government has a substantive interest in the contents of those uniform rules. The first interest prizes uniformity for its own sake and is content-neutral; it does not dictate the substance of the federal common law rule to be applied. Thus, in *United States v. Standard Oil Co.*, the Court applied federal common law, recognizing the government's interest in uniformity, but refused to impose the liability argued for by the United States as the substance of that law.

The present litigation is fundamentally different from *Standard Oil* and *Clearfield Trust* with respect to both uniformity interest and substantive interest in the content of the rules to be applied. Since this litigation is between private parties and no substantial rights or duties of the government hinge on its outcome, there is no federal interest in uniformity for its own sake. The fact that application of state law may produce a variety of results is of no moment. It is in the nature of a federal system that different states will apply different rules of law, based on their individual perceptions of what is in the best interests of their citizens. That alone is not grounds in private litigation for judicially creating an overriding federal law. . . .

The second fundamental difference between the present litigation and the *Clearfield Trust* type of case is that in the latter, the government's substantive interest in the litigation is essentially monothetic, in that it is concerned only with preserving the federal fisc, whereas here the government has two interests; and here the two interests have been placed in sharp contrast with one another. Thus, the government has an interest in the welfare of its veterans; they have given of themselves in the most fundamental way possible in the national interest. But the government also has an interest in the suppliers of its material; imposition, for example, of strict liability as contended for by plaintiffs would affect the government's ability to procure materiel without the exaction of significantly higher prices, or the attachment of onerous conditions, or the demand of indemnification or the like. . . . [U]nlike a simple uniformity interest, neither the government's interest in its veterans nor its interest in its suppliers is content-neutral. Each interest will be furthered only if the federal rule of law to be applied favors that particular group.

The extent to which either group *should* be favored, and its welfare deemed "paramount" is preeminently a policy determination of the sort reserved in the first instance for Congress. The welfare of veterans and that of military suppliers are clearly federal concerns which Congress should appropriately consider in setting policy for the governance of the nation, and it is properly left to Congress in the first instance to strike the balance between the conflicting interests of the veterans and the contractors, and thereby identify federal policy. Although Congress has turned its attention to the Agent Orange problem, it has not determined what the federal policy is with respect to the reconciliation of these two competing interests. . . .

We conclude that in the present case, while the federal government has obvious interests in the welfare of the parties to the litigation, its interest in the *outcome* of the litigation, i.e., in how the parties' welfares should be balanced, is as yet undetermined. The teaching of *Wallis* and *Miree* is that before federal common law rules should be fashioned, the use of state law must pose a threat to an "identifiable" federal policy. In the present litigation the federal policy is not yet identifiable. We conclude, therefore, that the district court erred in ruling that plaintiffs' claims were governed by federal common law. The order denying defendants' motion to dismiss for lack of subject matter jurisdiction is accordingly

Reversed.

■ FEINBERG, Chief Judge, dissenting. . . .

That the present case is *sui generis*, and national in proportions, is evident . . . .

. . . [T]hat the plaintiff veterans and the defendant contractors have opposing interests in this litigation hardly means that the paramount federal interest is somehow divided or self-contradictory. . . . [T]he United States' interest in the "welfare" of defendants cannot approach, either in magnitude or in quality, its interest in the welfare of the Agent Orange plaintiffs. In short, in the case before us the paramount interests of the United States are in the welfare of its veterans and in their fair and uniform treatment.

Having discerned a significant federal interest, we are next required to determine whether or not a "significant conflict" exists between that interest and the application of state law. . . . The application of state law to the present case would severely frustrate this federal interest: If . . . the laws of 30 or 40 state jurisdictions are separately applied, veterans' recoveries will vary widely — despite the fact that these soldiers fought shoulder to shoulder, without regard to state citizenship, in a national endeavor abroad. In sum, the federal interest here in uniformity would be defeated by the application of discrete and differing state laws.

The third and last factor involves the extent to which state interests would be affected, if state law were to be "displaced" by federal common law in the present case. . . . [T]he claims made by plaintiffs in this unique and unprecedented litigation do not fall within the developed area of state tort law. . . . [T]he states' product liability law is in flux; with respect to a case as novel as the one before us, a consistent and established body of state law is less discernible. Accordingly, I think Judge Pratt was correct in holding that the application of federal common law would not "displace" state law, because there is no substantial body of state law on this issue to be displaced. I thus conclude that all three factors, accepted by the majority as the proper analytical framework, point to the use of a federal common law rule in the present case, giving rise to federal question jurisdiction.

Notes

1.   A claim arising under federal common law creates federal-question jurisdiction under § 1331. *See* Textile Workers Union of Am. v. Lincoln Mills of Ala., 353 U.S. 448 (1957). Moreover, although state law may govern related claims or issues, federal common law displaces state law with respect to the precise claim or issue at stake. Thus, federal common law has dual advantages: It creates jurisdiction in federal court, in which aggregation is easier; and it displaces fifty (or more) potentially different laws with one law, thus reducing the incentive to disperse litigation and making aggregated more manageable during the pretrial and trial phases.

2.   Despite these evident advantages in complex litigation, federal common law has drawbacks. Among them are two constitutional concerns: a separation-of-powers problem (by what authority can a court make law in a constitutional democracy?) and a federalism problem (should federal law displace the lawmaking authority of the states?). These concerns have made courts leery about using federal common law expansively. The Supreme Court has never offered a comprehensive theory of the circumstances under which state and federal courts can make federal common law. Instead, it has tended to treat the issue on a case-by-case basis. The Supreme Court has suggested that federal common law should ordinarily be used in only two situations. First "Congress has given the courts the power to develop substantive law." Tex. Indus., Inc. v. Radcliff Materials, Inc., 451 U.S. 630, 640 (1981). Second, "a federal rule of decision is 'necessary to protect uniquely federal interests,'" *id.*, and "a 'significant conflict' exists between an identifiable 'federal policy or interest and the [operation] of state law,' or the application of state law would 'frustrate specific objectives' of federal legislation," Boyle v. United Techs. Corp., 487 U.S. 500, 507 (1988).

At present, there are six "enclaves" in which federal common law exists: cases involving the United States as a party, cases between two or more states, admiralty cases, certain cases touching international relations, admiralty, the government-contractor defense, and the preclusive effect of federal judgments. The list of enclaves has expanded slightly over the years (the fifth enclave was added in 1988, and the sixth in 2001). But the Supreme Court has shown great reluctance to add to the areas covered by federal common law. *See* Atherton v. FDIC, 519 U.S. 213 (1997) (declining to create federal common law for the standard of care owed by officers of federally chartered institutions); O'Melveny & Myers v. FDIC, 512 U.S. 79 (1994) (refusing to create federal common law to address the FDIC's liability when the FDIC was liable only as the receiver of a failed bank).

But see Musick, Peeler & Garrett v. Employers Ins. of Wausau, 508 U.S. 286, 292 (1993) (creating a federal common law of contribution for Rule 10b-5 securities actions; because Rule 10b-5 actions had been judicially created, courts could create "ancillary" common-law rules for those actions). *See generally* Jay Tidmarsh & Brian J. Murray, *A Theory of Federal Common Law*, 100 Nw. U. L. Rev. 585 (2006) (discussing the six enclaves and suggesting a unifying theory).

3. Consider *Kohr* and *Agent Orange*. Can they both be right? Or are they both wrong? Are there sufficient federal interests to create a law of indemnity and contribution for airplane crashes, but insufficient interests to create a law of product liability for harms done to our nation's soldiers in a foreign war? *See* Overseas Nat'l Airways, Inc. v. United States, 766 F.2d 97 (2d Cir. 1985) (refusing to create a federal common law of contribution for the United States in aviation litigation); In re Air Crash Near Cali, Colom. on Dec. 20, 1995, 24 F. Supp. 2d 1340 (S.D. Fla. 1998) (rejecting *Kohr* and applying Florida's contribution rule in air-crash litigation).

Kohr was decided two years after *Illinois v. City of Milwaukee*, 406 U.S. 91 (1972), in which the Court held that federal common law governed a claim of interstate pollution. *Illinois v. Milwaukee* is the modern high water mark of the courts' power to create federal common law. After *Miree v. DeKalb County*, 433 U.S. 25 (1977), which was decided after *Kohr* but before *Agent Orange*, the power began to recede. The common-law power recognized in *Illinois v. Milwaukee* was taken away in *City of Milwaukee v. Illinois*, 451 U.S. 304 (1981), on the theory that Congress's water-pollution legislation during the 1970s left no room for judicial lawmaking. *Cf.* Conn. v. Am. Elec. Power Co., 582 F.3d 309 (2d Cir. 2009) (using a federal common law of nuisance in a climate-change lawsuit brought by eight states against major utilities; citing *Illinois v. Milwaukee*); Hood ex rel. Miss. v. City of Memphis, 570 F.3d 625, 627 n.1 (5th Cir. 2009) (holding that federal common law governed an interstate dispute over water rights; citing *Illinois v. Milwaukee*).

But the power to create federal common law seemed to return with *Boyle*, which was decided in 1988, eight years after *Agent Orange*. *Boyle* held that a contractor for the federal government was entitled to a defense, created under federal common law, that it was not liable when its products met the government's specifications. That defense was a critical issue in the *Agent Orange* litigation; indeed, a number of contractors eventually prevailed on the defense. *See, e.g.*, In re Agent Orange Prod. Liab. Litig., 517 F.3d 76 (2d Cir. 2008). Recall, however, that federal defenses do not create § 1331 "arising under" jurisdiction; only federal claims do. Thus, *Boyle* does not cast doubt on the specific issue decided in *Agent Orange*: whether federal common law was the source of the veterans' claims. After *Boyle*, though, could a case be made that *Agent Orange* was wrong? Or is there a good reason to use federal common law to create a defense that a contractor can assert against a state-law claim but not use federal common law to create the claim that can be asserted against the contractor?

4. Even though complex litigation might by happenstance involve a claim or defense falling within one of the enclaves, there is not at present a "complex litigation" enclave that generally allows courts to displace varying state laws with uniform federal law when optimal aggregation so requires. *Kohr* was not a complex case; *Agent Orange* was (in part because the claims exceeded the defendants' assets, thus creating the potential for disparate treatment of similar claimants). Is the lesson of these two cases that the complexity of litigation is irrelevant to the question of whether federal courts have the power to create federal common law?

Although addressing a different point, the Supreme Court has resisted the argument that the need for uniform treatment in a particular type of litigation justifies the creation of federal common law. In *O'Melveny & Myers*, the Court found an insufficient conflict between state and federal law to warrant the creation of federal common law; instead, state law determined whether an employee's knowledge could be imputed to a corporation whose liabilities the FDIC had assumed. The Court observed:

> There is not even at stake that most generic (and lightly invoked) of alleged federal interests, the interest in uniformity. The rules of decision at issue here do not govern the primary conduct of the United States or any of its agents or contractors, but affect only the FDIC's rights and liabilities, as receiver, with respect to primary conduct on the part of private actors that has already occurred. Uniformity of law might facilitate the FDIC's nationwide litigation of these suits, eliminating state-by-state research and reducing uncertainty — but if the avoidance of those ordinary consequences qualified as an identifiable federal interest, we would be awash in "federal common-law" rules. [512 U.S. at 88.]

Does *O'Melveny & Myer* sound the death knell for using federal common law to overcome the problems of dispersal and unmanageability in complex litigation? Is the prevention of the unfairness and inefficiency that complex cases present a "uniquely federal interest"? If so, what is the "significant conflict" between this interest and the operation of state law?

5. The power of a federal court to create federal common law is only the first step in the analysis. Even when the *power* to create federal common law exists, courts still need to discern the *content* of the federal rule. In a number of situations, courts have, as a matter of discretion, chosen to adopt the relevant state-law rule as the federal rule. *See* Semtek Int'l Inc. v. Lockheed Martin Corp., 531 U.S. 497 (2001); United States v. Kimbell Foods, Inc., 440 U.S. 715 (1979). *Kimbell Foods* explained:

> Undoubtedly, federal programs that "by their nature are and must be uniform in character throughout the Nation" necessitate formulation of controlling federal rules. Conversely, when there is little need for a nationally uniform body of law, state law may be incorporated as the federal rule of decision. Apart from considerations of uniformity, we must also determine whether application of state law would frustrate specific objectives of the federal programs. If so, we must fashion special rules solicitous of those federal interests. Finally, our

choice-of-law inquiry must consider the extent to which application of a federal rule would disrupt commercial relationships predicated on state law. [440 U.S. at 728-29.]

For a defense of this approach, see Henry J. Friendly, *In Praise of Erie — And of the New Federal Common Law*, 39 N.Y.U. L. REV. 383 (1964). For trenchant criticism, see Martha A. Field, *Sources of Law: The Scope of Federal Common Law*, 99 HARV. L. REV. 881 (1986).

6. Congress can authorize courts to create federal common law. Should Congress legislate such authority for complex litigation? Can Congress define the cases to which this power extends with enough clarity that the power will be neither underinclusive nor overinclusive? For a legislative proposal to allow courts to make common law for "mass torts," see Linda S. Mullenix, *Class Resolution of the Mass-Tort Case: A Proposed Federal Procedure Act*, 64 TEX. L. REV. 1039, 1091, 1095 (1986). For an argument that this approach would lead to uncertainty and lack of uniformity, see AM. L. INST., COMPLEX LITIGATION 313-14 (1994).

7. Assuming that a power to create federal common law in complex litigation existed, what should this law look like? Will judge-made federal law favor plaintiffs or corporate defendants? Is it good to apply one set of (state-law) rules to routine disputes and another set of (federal common-law) rules to complex disputes? Will federal courts become the repository of "big" cases and state courts become a backwater of minor-league slip-and-falls lawsuits? Because "big" cases are often the ones that spur substantive and procedural innovation, will state law stagnate and atrophy? These questions highlight some of the issues surrounding the use of federal common law, which on first blush seems like a great way to avoid the complexities created by state choice-of-law rules. You might still think that it is the best approach, but you need to be aware of its costs.

3. Creating National-Consensus Law

If it is neither doctrinally possible nor theoretically desirable for courts to create federal common law, the affected states might achieve some of the advantages of federal common law by agreeing to sacrifice their parochial interests in using their own law and compromising on a single consensus law to govern a complex dispute. How likely is this scenario?

IN RE "AGENT ORANGE" PRODUCT LIABILITY LITIGATION

580 F. Supp. 690 (E.D.N.Y. 1984)

■ WEINSTEIN, Chief Judge.

A considerable number of Vietnam war veterans resident in all or almost all states, Puerto Rico and the District of Columbia and a number of foreign countries, and members of their families, claim to have suffered injury as a result of the veterans' exposure to herbicides in Vietnam. Defendants produced those herbicides. Individual claims, originally filed in all parts of the country, were transferred for pretrial purposes to this court. Subject to some powers to opt out, common issues presented by plaintiffs' claims will now be tried together since a class has been certified pursuant to Rule 23. . . .

As required by *Klaxon Co. v. Stentor Elec. Mfg. Co.*, 313 U.S. 487 (1941), this court has examined the conflict of law rules of the states in which the transferor courts sit. Van Dusen v. Barrack, 367 U.S. 612 (1964). For the reasons set forth below, it is concluded that under the special circumstances of this litigation, all the transferor states would look to the same substantive law for the rule of decision on the critical substantive issues.

I. *Introduction*

. . .

Essentially, there are five different conflicts of laws methodologies widely used in this country. [Here the court described the traditional *lex leci* approach of the *Restatement (First)*; the "most significant contacts" approach of the *Restatement (Second)*; governmental-interest analysis; Professor Leflar's approach of using the "better law"; and using forum law.] There is a sixth proposed approach that has some of the aura of Leflar, but which we treat separately as the von Mehren approach. Some states use a combination or variation of these techniques. . . . For purposes of this opinion, we have eschewed specific discussion of the effects of modern doctrine leading to renvoi, or the increased likelihood of dépeçage, though, as will be seen, both doctrines are implicated in the present case. Finally, it is unnecessary to consider whether any state's conflict of law rule would deprive a litigant of due process, equal protection, or other constitutional right since each of the states whose conflict rule might apply has sufficient nexus with the matter through residence or the like. . . .

[After examining the roles that the federal law played in the lawsuit with respect to jurisdictional, procedural, and evidentiary issues, and the role that state law played with respect to substantive issues, the court then turned to an idea that it called "national-consensus law."] While those close to the American law scene tend to emphasize the diversity of substantive law among the states and between the states and the federal government, to outside observers much of the differences must appear as significant as that among the Lilliputians to Swift's hero. Faced with a unique problem, American lawmakers and judges tend to react in much the same way, arriving at much the same result.

There are, of course, centrifugal forces in the law leading to different substantive and procedural results even in a single nation like the United States. With thousands of municipalities, 50 states, the District of Columbia and the Federal jurisdiction having many law-creating legislative bodies, executive departments, administrative bodies, and courts, this is to be expected. Yet, powerful centripetal tendencies often encourage the formulation of national consensus law. First, is the essential homogeneity of our unified technological-social structure increasingly tied together by national transportation, communication and educational-cultural networks. Second, is an Anglo-American legal system with common roots and a strongly integrated law school educational system relying upon national scholars, treatises and cases. National casebooks and fungibility of teaching materials, for example, create a strong unifying influence making it possible for lawyers to be trained in one section of the country and to transfer to other areas for practice. . . . The result is that law-making and law-applying authorities tend to utilize national standards and approaches.

Institutions such as the American Law Institute with its Restatements, the National Commissioners on Uniform State Laws with many widely-adopted uniform statutes . . . aid these unifying national tendencies. . . .

When presented with a new problem, we tend to proceed by analogy and by precedent. . . . Even though one state is not bound by the precedents of another, when a new problem arises courts tend to follow the decisions of courts of other American jurisdictions since the reasoning and pool of factual and legal data will tend to be the same.

The concept of a national law already exists in federal common law since federal law, by definition, is created to deal with problems that are national in scope. . . .

II. Claims of Defendants and
Misunderstanding of the Posture of Case

. . . [The defendants] argue in summary that (1) federal common law may only be applied where there is a substantial federal interest at stake, (2) the Second Circuit's decision [in *In re "Agent Orange" Product Liability Litigation*, 635 F.2d 987 (2d Cir. 1980) (*supra* p. 680),] constitutes a determination binding on this court that there is no such federal interest in this litigation, and (3) therefore, although they do not suggest any rational way by which a state may choose one state's law to apply, they conclude that this court may not apply federal or national consensus common law to any issue. . . .

The difference between federal law applying of its own force under the Supremacy Clause, which the Second Circuit's decision forbids in part, and applying a form of national consensus law or of federal law itself because a state court chooses to look to it as the rule of decision is well accepted. For example, state courts, in interpreting their state's constitution and statutes, will often follow the federal constitution and statutory authority although they may not be required to do so. States will often look to federal tax laws and federal rules of procedure in formulating and interpreting their own. In all of the above examples, states are looking to the federal government for the rule of decision despite the fact that no one would contend that the federal rule must be applied. . . .

III. *Conflict of Laws Rules*

While there are a number of analogous approaches and decisions, none is directly on point in connection with the special conflicts of law issue now posed. . . .

[The court examined how the *lex loci,* "most significant contacts," governmental-interest analysis, LeFlar's better law, and forum-law approaches would handle liability and damages issues in the case. After finding that they generally supported using national-consensus law in the unique circumstances of the case, the court turned to von Mehren's idea.]

F.   *von Merhen — Reconciling Conflicts*

The increasing incidence of conflicts of law problems result in large measure from the fact that the social, economic and technical worlds we live in far exceed in geographic scope the legal jurisdictions which establish and enforce controlling law.

One method of solving the conflict is for the forum state to create appropriate substantive law recognizing the policies of the various jurisdictions having an interest in the dispute. . . . As von Mehren put it:

> The clash of values or policies that has arisen within the *ad hoc* community of concerned states is to be resolved not by considering what value or policy of the forum can be advanced but rather by determining how the forum would, in general, resolve the clash in question. . . . Multistate situations involving true conflicts would thus present, just as do analogous domestic situations, the problem of deciding which among conflicting policies are, in general, to be preferred.

Arthur Taylor von Mehren, *Choice of Law and the Problem of Justice,* 41 LAW & CONTEMP. PROBS. [27,] 34 (Spring 1977) . . . .

In most cases the choice of one jurisdiction's domestic law would suffice. But in some instances a molding of the conflicting substantive laws to achieve a viable alternative compromise acceptable to the larger overarching community would be sensible and just. One approach is that of compromise. . . . And when the legislature does not act to make the necessary compromises, the courts must act. *Id.* at 39.

Most of the examples given by von Mehren involve two party cases that recur over and over again as a result of the use of our multistate road systems. How much more apt is the approach he posits where tens of thousands are involved in what is alleged to be a single and unique national disaster with repercussions in scores of jurisdictions.

There is much logical merit and conceptual appeal in von Mehren's suggestion of individually crafted compromise statements of substantive law to meet the choice of law problems where the domestic substantive law of none of the states having contacts with the parties and their disputes should control. In run-of-the-mill conflicts situations this approach would lead to excessive lack of predictability and cost. The burden on the system would be greater than the benefits in most cases since lawyers and judges would spend too much time on customizing the law in individual cases and there would undoubtedly be increased appeals and reversals when trial and appellate court judgments on what was sound in the particular case diverged. Nevertheless there are special cases with unique circumstances not likely to recur in the future where von Mehren's approach suggests the only sound method. Such a situation is now presented.

The overwhelming need for a uniform approach and a single substantive standard is obvious. . . . Although it could do so under its commerce or war powers, Congress has not enacted such a statute.

Given a failure of the legislature and the executive, the federal courts could be expected to step in by creating federal common law to cover a national problem. But the Second Circuit has blocked that route by denying that federal substantive law controls of its own force. Thus, under *Klaxon*, we look to the states to accomplish the sound result. As a federal court we sit as a surrogate for the state courts, attempting to predict how pragmatic and wise state judges would address the problem.

It is entirely reasonable to assume that the state courts would recognize the strong national interest in a uniform national rule. A considerable number of states have already recognized the unique nature of the *Agent Orange* litigation problem [by creating special statutes of limitation for *Agent Orange* cases or setting up commissions and outreach programs for *Agent Orange* veterans]. Given the strong state-federal interest in uniformity, the lack of a federal statute or of a uniform state statute, and the Second Circuit opinion denying that federal common law controls of its own force all substantive issues in *Agent Orange*, what would state courts do? Would they not look to the first court that dealt with the issue or to a neutral body to formulate the uniform rules they could all accept for this unique litigation? And is not a federal court charged with adjudicating all or nearly all the *Agent Orange* cases such a body? Professor von Mehren's analysis suggests that the answer to each of these questions is yes.

Once it is conceded, as we think it must be, that each of the jurisdictions involved would appreciate the overwhelming need for uniformity, to what single state's law could any state look to as controlling? Given the plethora of states and nations with contacts and the impossibility without a full trial of even knowing where the allegedly [toxic component in Agent Orange] was produced, it becomes apparent that no acceptable test can point to any single state. Thus, the law is driven in this most unusual case to either federal or national consensus substantive law as the only workable approach.

G. *National Consensus Restated*

At most, a state's contacts in an "Agent Orange" suit would consist of the individual plaintiff veteran's residence in that state — a factor readily subject to change in our transient society — and the fact that one of the seven defendant companies is either incorporated, has its principal place of business or manufactured its Agent Orange in that state. At the risk of restating the obvious, those contacts are dwarfed by the national contacts in the case. The only jurisdiction with which all elements in the litigation undoubtedly have significant contacts, and the only unifying factor, is the nation. . . .

In the litigation most clearly analogous to Agent Orange for present purposes, the federal court for the District of Columbia, sitting in a diversity case as a local District of Columbia court, had to decide the law applicable to claims arising out of the crash near Saigon of an Air Force C-5A carrying United States military and civilian personnel and 226 Vietnamese orphans. In re Air Crash Disaster Near Saigon, S. Vietnam on April 4, 1975, 476 F. Supp. 521 (D.D.C. 1979). . . . It noted that the District of Columbia follows the "interest analysis" methods in choice-of-law. It analyzed the relevant interests as follows:

> The United States government (as distinguished from any state of the United States) carried on [the Vietnam] war and ended it for national foreign policy and military purposes. . . . It is a "paramount" interest and concern of the United States federal government that its courts provide a just and reasonable resolution of claims such as those on behalf of the estates of the deceased orphans.

It applied District of Columbia law of survival to all parties despite the fact that plaintiffs resided all over the United States, and that Lockheed Aircraft Corp., a defendant with the United States, had its chief place of business and place of incorporation outside the District. District of Columbia law was really only a euphemism for a national substantive law of liability. Rejecting traditional conflicts of law, the court relied upon the *sui generis* nature of the case. . . .

Because of the *sui generis* nature of this litigation, it is not surprising that there are no cases directly on point. It is, however, common to find state courts and federal courts sitting as state courts under *Erie* applying federal law, because of the predominant federal interest in the litigation. Thus, state courts will often look to federal law if they feel it is appropriate.

That neither New York nor, as far as we have ascertained, any state has had a case such as this one before us does not permit our throwing up our hands and refusing to decide the question. Perhaps it would have been better if certification rules permitted posing the conflicts question to the more than half-a-hundred jurisdictions involved. But no such procedure is presently in place. In the meantime, this court must ascertain the living state law as best it can. The "evolutionary growth" of the law of conflicts means that each "litigant, whether in the federal or the state courts, has a right that his case shall be a part of this evolution — a live cell in the tree of justice." . . .

V. *Conclusion*

For the reasons noted, it is likely that each of the states would look to a federal or a national consensus law of manufacturer's liability, government contract defense and punitive damages. What is the nature of the national consensus or federal law is a subject for another memorandum.

We emphasize that this memorandum is a first general guide to the parties of the court's present thinking. It is subject to refinement and change as the legal issues, facts, and applicable law become clearer during the course of the pretrial and trial proceedings.

Notes

1. A national-consensus approach has important procedural consequences, one of which is its creation of common questions of law and fact. As we have seen, common questions are necessary for numerous aggregation devices, including joinder under Rule 20, class certification under Rule 23 and consolidation under Rule 42 and § 1407. Because a national-consensus claim is based on state law, federal jurisdiction still depends on diversity among the parties — unless the claim's incorporation of a federal common-law standard is a sufficient federal question for purposes of § 1331 "arising under" jurisdiction. *See* Grable & Sons Metal Prods., Inc. v. Darue Eng'g & Mfg., 545 U.S. 308 (2005); *supra* p. 293.

2. Does *Agent Orange* put you in mind of Justice O'Connor's dissent in *Sun Oil Co. v. Wortman*, 486 U.S. 717, 740 (1988) (*see supra* p. 641, Note 1), in which she opined that any choice-of-law rule can pass constitutional muster as long as a court can "invent a legal theory so novel or strange that the other State has never had an opportunity to reject it; [and] then, on the basis of nothing but unsupported speculation, 'predict' that the other State would adopt that theory if it had the chance"? Would *Agent Orange* pass constitutional muster under *Shutts* and *Wortman*?

3. Without identifying it as the "national consensus" approach, Judge Posner rejected a district court's effort to meld a national standard of negligence into a jury instruction in a products-liability mass tort. The district court had proposed such an instruction as a way to make a (b)(3) class action manageable. In re Rhone-Poulenc Rorer Inc., 51 F.3d 1293 (7th Cir. 1995). In a famous line, Judge Posner stated that, "[f]or this consensus or maturing of judgment the district judge proposes to substitute a single trial before a single jury instructed in accordance with no actual law of any jurisdiction — a jury that will receive a kind of Esperanto instruction, merging the negligence standards of the 50 states and the District of Columbia." *Id.* at 1300. He continued:

> ... One is put in mind of the concept of "general" common law that prevailed in the era of *Swift v. Tyson*. The assumption is that the common law of the 50 states and the District of Columbia, at least so far as bears on a claim of negligence against drug companies, is basically uniform and can be abstracted in a single instruction. ...
>
> We doubt that it is true in general, and we greatly doubt that it is true in a case such as this in which one of the theories pressed by the plaintiffs . . . is novel. If one instruction on negligence will serve to

instruct the jury on the legal standard of every state of the United States applicable to a novel claim, implying that the claim despite its controversiality would be decided identically in all 50 states and the District of Columbia, one wonders what the Supreme Court thought it was doing in the *Erie* case when it held that it was *unconstitutional* for federal courts in diversity cases to apply general common law rather than the common law of the state whose law would apply if the case were being tried in state rather than federal court. [*Id.*]

4. Is Judge Posner right that national-consensus law essentially creates a kind of federal common law that run afoul of *Erie* (and *Klaxon*)? Judge Weinstein might respond by suggesting that this approach is faithful to *Erie* and *Klaxon*, for it asks what law each state would adopt. But isn't it unlikely in the extreme that all fifty states would have agreed on this approach? According to Dean Kramer, Judge Weinstein's approach was flawed:

> One problem with Chief Judge Weinsten's argument that every state would choose "national consensus law" . . . is that not a single court had ever suggested such a thing . . ., a fact Weinstein failed to note. . . .
>
> There is an even more fundamental flaw . . . . Who said that a single law had to be chosen? More importantly, where did Chief Judge Weinstein get the idea that the question was what a state court would do if faced with the class action? The appropriate question was, what would the various courts of origin have done if the actions remained dispersed? And there is absolutely no reason to think they would have made up some novel "national consensus law" in that circumstance.

Larry Kramer, *Choice of Law in Complex Litigation*, 71 N.Y.U. L. REV. 547, 562-63 (1996).

4. The Second Circuit too has cast doubt on the national-consensus approach. Judge Weinstein had tentatively suggested the idea several months before he adopted it formally. *See* In re "Agent Orange" Prod. Liab. Litig., 100 F.R.D. 718, 724 (E.D.N.Y. 1983). In the meantime, the Second Circuit heard a petition for a writ of mandamus on Judge Weinstein's decision to certify a class, Judge Weinstein's suggestion to use national-consensus law made an appearance as a reason to uphold the decision to certify the class. The Second Circuit stated that "we will not disclaim considerable skepticism as to the existence of a 'national substantive rule,'" but nonetheless denied the writ because it thought that Judge Weinstein would employ subclasses for class members whose claims arose under the laws of different states. In re Diamond Shamrock Chems. Co., 725 F.2d 858, 861 (2d Cir. 1984). After the *Agent Orange* case settled, the Second Circuit took note of Judge Weinstein's "bold and imaginative," but noted in dicta:

> . . . [I]n light of our prior holding that federal common law does not govern plaintiffs' claims, every jurisdiction would be free to render its own choice of law decision, and common experience suggests that the

intellectual power of Chief Judge Weinstein's analysis alone would not be enough to prevent widespread disagreement.

In re "Agent Orange" Prod. Liab. Litig., 818 F.2d 145, 165 (2d Cir. 1987).

5.   Whatever its constitutional or legal merit, isn't there some wisdom in the *Agent Orange* approach? By definition, the controversy was larger than any single jurisdiction, yet standard choice-of-law analysis requires that one state's law "win" and the other states' law "lose." Isn't it more sensible to try to compromise the interests of the relevant states? *See* Stanley E. Cox, *Substantive, Multilateral, and Unilateral Choice of Law Approaches*, 37 WILLAMETTE L. REV. 171, 174, 179 (2000) (arguing that a choice-of-law approach in which the forum court sits as an "interstate court" giving no no special weight to the forum's interests works best in "mass disaster and consolidated or class litigation situations"). But even if this is true, what would such a compromise look like? Are courts in the best position to make the necessary compromise?

6.   Do the limits that Judge Weinstein imposes on national-consensus law make it useful only in extraordinary cases? What criteria determine if a case is extraordinary? For instance, would it be possible to use a national-consensus approach in domestic product-liability cases involving asbestos or tobacco? Would it apply to state-law fraud claims related to federal securities-law violations? Would the national-consensus approach apply whenever the case was larger than the interests of any given state? But isn't that every case that raises choice-of-law questions?

When asked to apply national-consensus law in other mass torts, Judge Weinstein has refused. For instance, Judge Weinstein declined to follow *Agent Orange* in a complex case involving the restructuring of the Manville asbestos trust fund. One of the issues in the restructuring involved the rights of certain persons to set offs or contribution from the fund. The laws of various states disagreed about the rights of such persons. Although he noted the "large interstate and national interests . . . being sacrificed by the now endemic problems of asbestos" and "the multitude of federal interests intertwined in this litigation," Judge Weinstein rejected the argument that national-consensus law should apply:

> This situation differs markedly from that presented by *Agent Orange*. . . . State tort law addressing questions of injuries caused by toxic exposure while serving in the armed services in Vietnam did not vary significantly from state to state leading the court to conclude that states faced with claims against government military contractors would refer to national consensus law. Here, the states have recently adopted statutes focusing on the precise issue [of set-off and contribution rights]. The law in the several jurisdictions is in flux and ought to be defined in the first instance by the state courts.

In re Joint E. and S. Dists. Asbestos Litig., 129 B.R. 710, 878 (E. & S.D.N.Y. 1991), *vacated on other grounds*, 982 F.2d 721 (2d Cir. 1992), *modified*, 993 F.2d 7 (2d Cir. 1993). *Cf.* In re Simon II Litig., 211 F.R.D. 86 (E.D.N.Y. 2002) (Weinstein, J.) (applying New York choice-of-law rules and New York substantive law to a mass tort against the tobacco industry) (*infra* p. 971), *vacated and remanded on other grounds*, In re Simon II Litig., 407 F.3d 125 (2d Cir. 2005) (*supra* p. 396). If the judicial architect of the national-consensus theory has declined to adopt it in the context of other mass torts, how viable is the theory?

4. Using the Law of the Most Restrictive State

The last two subsections have suggested two possible ways to select a single body of substantive law that applies to all cases. In this subsection, we consider a third method.

IN RE SCHOOL ASBESTOS LITIGATION

977 F.2d 764 (3d Cir. 1992)

■ BECKER, Circuit Judge.

[School systems that had spent money to remove asbestos from their buildings brought a nationwide class action seeking recovery on behalf of similarly situated schools and school systems. More than fifty companies were named as defendants. The district judge certified a compensatory-damage class under Rule 23(b)(3) and a punitive-damage class under Rule 23(b)(1). On the eve of trial, numerous defendants filed writs of mandamus seeking removal of the district judge and rejection of his trial plan. In the first portion of the opinion, the court of appeals ordered the district judge removed from the case. It then turned to the issue of managing the class action on remand.]

Throughout this litigation, an overriding concern of both the district court and this court has been the manageability of the class action. The defendants originally opposed class certification on the ground that because so many different state laws would have to be applied common issues could never predominate and the class action would be unmanageable. Counsel for the class plaintiffs repeatedly responded that the differences in state laws were not that great and that the plaintiffs were willing to prove their case according to the law of the "strictest" jurisdiction. Relying in part on those two representations, and on the possibility of certifying subclasses under Rule 23(c)(4) [now Rule 23(c)(5) — ED.], the district court certified the class. We affirmed that certification, albeit with explicit doubts about manageability and with the caveat that the district court could revoke the certification if that seemed appropriate. . . .

[The district court then asked the plaintiffs to submit the law that was most restrictive on each element of their claims, and indicated that the plaintiffs' burden of proof on each element would be "clear and convincing evidence." Although the court never formally implemented the approach, one of the defendants, Kaiser Cement, argued that the district court's apparent plan] to try the case according to the law of the strictest state, rather than according to the law of each individual jurisdiction, . . . runs afoul of the Supreme Court's ruling in *Phillips Petroleum Co. v. Shutts*, 472 U.S. 797 (1985) [*supra* p. 637].

Shutts held that due process requires that in a class action based on the laws of separate jurisdictions the adjudicating court must apply to any particular claim the substantive law of a jurisdiction having a significant interest in that claim. Courts may not simply apply the law of the forum state or, presumably, a hybrid or composite of state laws. Thus, *Shutts* suggests that each plaintiff in this case has the right to have its claims judged according to the law of its jurisdiction, not according to that of a putative or imaginary strictest state.

At first blush, one might question why Kaiser Cement, a defendant, has standing to raise this objection. After all, the strictest-state standard appears to make the plaintiffs' case more difficult to prove, and, thus, to advantage the defendants. Kaiser Cement's concern, however, is that even if it wins against the class plaintiffs, and even if the *class plaintiffs* have waived their *Shutts* claim, its victory will be hollow because *absent class members* from more "lenient" jurisdictions will be able to challenge the judgment collaterally. Kaiser Cement notes that the opt-out notice did not inform the class members that they were waiving their right to have their claims adjudicated according to their own states' (possibly more lenient) laws, and that they therefore could claim inadequate representation by the class plaintiffs. According to the petition, the current trial plan binds Kaiser Cement if it loses, but does not bind absent plaintiffs if it wins. Kaiser Cement thus views trial as unwinnable from a practical standpoint and, hence, fundamentally unfair, in violation of both Rule 23 and the Due Process Clause.

We agree that Kaiser Cement has standing to raise this claim, but we do not believe that the issue is ripe for our adjudication. First, it is far from clear how the district court intended to resolve issues other than the standard of proof. Second, even if the district court had taken a clear position on what law to apply, a new district judge will now be presiding over the case. If the newly assigned district judge insists on holding the class plaintiffs strictly to their earlier representations, then they or the defendants may seek review from this court at that time.

We expect that that will not prove necessary, however. Despite the barbs that have been traded and the parties' penchant for painting each other with black hats, it appears that both the class plaintiffs and the defendants agree, for different reasons, that *Shutts* requires the district court to apply the law of the individual jurisdictions. The plaintiffs believe that the case will be manageable if issues are put to the jury according to special interrogatories with the district court later molding the verdict according to the law of each state. The defendants continue to believe that such an approach will be unmanageable, and they therefore desire to have the class action decertified. As we stated in our earlier opinion, however, we believe that the district court will be in a much better position to evaluate and handle such manageability concerns initially, and at this stage we again prefer to defer to its judgment. For now, we simply urge the incoming district judge to examine *Shutts* carefully before submitting the case to the jury according to the law of a hypothetical strictest state, even if the class plaintiffs once agreed to that approach.

Notes

1. The most-restrictive-jurisdiction approach succeeds in using a single law — thus accomplishing the dual goals of making a class action manageable and avoiding the widespread dispersal of related cases. The Third Circuit rejected the approach because it feared a one-way-ratchet effect that bound defendants if they lost but allowed absent class members to escape an adverse judgment against them. Is the Third Circuit's fear correct? Contrary to the Third Circuit's claim, *Shutts* did not hold that "each plaintiff in this case has the right to have its claims judged according to the law of its jurisdiction." Rather, *Shutts* held that a court cannot constitutionally resolve an absent class member's claim under the law of a state that has no significant contacts with the class member. Therefore, the *School Asbestos* class members that had no significant contacts with the state that had the most restrictive law on an element would not be bound by a finding on that element. It is impossible to know how many plaintiffs would be affected (and on what elements) until the court determined which state's law was most restrictive on an element and how many plaintiffs had no significant contacts with that state. Whatever the number, it is probably fewer than all of the absent class members, as the Third Circuit implied.

Was the Third Circuit's real point that, if the class representatives acceded to a trial plan using the law of the most restrictive jurisdiction, absent plaintiffs could collaterally attack an adverse judgment by arguing inadequate representation? But is that point necessarily true? Couldn't class representatives, at least in some states of the world, rationally conclude that the efficiencies of a class trial outweighed the risks to absent class members of using the law of the most restrictive jurisdiction? If they make a reasonable calculation to this effect, is their representation inadequate? Recall the difficulty that class members encounter when they try to attack a finding of adequate representation in collateral proceedings. *See supra* p. 536.

Maybe the Third Circuit's point was that, at least insofar as the choice affected absent class members, using the law of the most restrictive state violated *Klaxon*'s command to use the choice-of-law method of the forum state. But can't class representatives, rationally and without being deemed inadequate representatives, waive the class's right to insist on *Klaxon*?

2. The Third Circuit's concerns are directed toward the adequacy of the representation that is due to absent class members. Can the most-restrictive-jurisdiction approach be used in litigation that is not aggregated on a class-action basis, and that does not have a comparable adequacy-of-representation requirement?

3.   The most-restrictive-jurisdiction method exudes a certain *machismo* ("I can beat you even under your best playing conditions"). But *School Asbestos* involved an extremely mature mass tort, in which the evidence against asbestos manufacturers was widely known and class counsel could make an informed judgment about the likelihood of success at trial even under the laws of the most restrictive jurisdiction. How likely is it that, in less mature torts, plaintiffs or their counsel will concede so readily to defendants the choice of legal standard?

4.   The most-restrictive-jurisdiction approach has not been popular. In one consumer-fraud class action, the plaintiffs proposed to use a "broad 'intent to deceive' jury instruction" derived from the *Restatement*. They argued that a finding of fraud under this instruction would satisfy the consumer-fraud states of most states. Nonetheless, the court found that "the use of amalgamated 'Esperanto'-type instructions would violate the due process rights of absent class members who reside in states where they can recover under state [consumer-fraud statutes] that have less stringent requirements." In re Pharm. Indus. Average Wholesale Price Litig., 252 F.R.D. 83, 93 (D. Mass. 2008) (citing In re Rhone-Poulenc Rorer Inc., 51 F.3d 1293, 1300 (7th Cir. 1995)). The court thought that the problem was "not an academic one" because it had already conducted one trial that had revealed how differences in the evidence could affect individual claims. It observed that "'Esperanto' instructions will not provide the silver bullet for the Tower-of-Babel problem here." *Id.* at 93.

5.   Could the concerns that *School Asbestos* and *Pharmaceutical Industry* expressed be avoided by any of three simple techniques: (1) appointing an adequate class representative from each state and securing the agreement of each representative to a trial plan using the most-restrictive-jurisdiction approach; (2) creating subclasses for each state and securing the consent of an adequate subclass representative to the plan; or (3) providing class members with a second notice describing the trial plan and providing a second opportunity to opt out of the class action at that point? None of these three options guarantees that the same law will be applied to all; a class or subclass representative may refuse to consent, or there may be a significant number of opt-outs. But at least the choice-of-law concerns would be reduced. Should the Third Circuit have remanded with instructions to consider these alternatives?

In a mandatory class action, presumably only the first two options would be available. Should the most-restrictive-jurisdiction approach be unavailable in mandatory class actions?

5.   Choosing a Single Law with a Right to Opt Out or Opt In

Another possibility — to which *School Asbestos* vaguely alluded — for reducing the complexity associated with multiple state laws is to choose one law that will be applied to a number of the aggregated cases, and then to give parties to whom that law would not have applied under traditional choice-of-law analysis the right to opt out of the litigation. The obvious defect of this possibility is that it fails to establish a single law under which everyone's case will be tried; those who are entitled to have different, more favorable law applied are likely to opt out unless they decide that the efficiencies from single-forum aggregation outweigh the benefits of the more favorable law to which they are entitled. Moreover, because an opt-out right must presumably exist for defendants as well as for plaintiffs, the utility of the opt-out method as a means for securing a single law applicable to an entire controversy is doubtful.

A related approach is to allow parties to opt into a trial that uses a particular state's law. The most famous case adopting the opt-in approach was the Bendectin litigation in the 1980s. More than 900 Bendectin cases were either filed in, removed to, or transferred by the Judicial Panel on Multidistrict Litigation to the Southern District of Ohio, where the manufacturer of Bendectin, was headquartered. Judge Rubin decided to conduct an initial trial only on the issue of causation. With respect to the cases filed in or removed to his court Judge Rubin determined that the law of Ohio applied to the issue of causation. The judge then gave the plaintiffs whose cases had been multidistricted to his court the opportunity to opt into the trial. Although Ohio law was less favorable on certain points than the laws of other jurisdictions, a surprising number of MDL plaintiffs (261 out of about 850) opted into the trial.

The trial turned out badly for the plaintiffs: The jury found that Bendectin did not cause their injuries. On appeal the Sixth Circuit rejected the argument of some of the multidistrict plaintiffs that this trial method was inappropriate. *See* In re Bendectin Litig., 857 F.2d 290, 302-03 (6th Cir. 1988) (*infra* p. 1034). As a practical matter, *Bendectin*'s well-known outcome — which on its facts was a variant of the most-restrictive-jurisdiction approach — has soured plaintiffs on the opt-in approach.

The Sixth Circuit noted, but did not base its holding on, the argument that the plaintiffs' consent waived any claim that using Ohio law was unfair. Even if the plaintiffs consented, do *Shutts* and *Klaxon*, which address federalism concerns larger than the interests of individual litigants, impose limits on this approach? (On the facts of *Bendectin*, *Shutts* seems inapposite because Ohio, as the defendant's headquarters, had a significant relationship to every claim. In other cases choosing a different opt-in law, however, it might be relevant.) In *Bendectin*, the individual plaintiffs consented to opt into the trial. Could a class representative consent to the opt-in approach on behalf of class members who lacked contact with the state whose law was chosen? After *Lexecon Inc. v. Milberg Weiss Bershad Hynes & Lerach*, 523 U.S. 26 (1998) (*supra* p. 162), can MDL plaintiffs give effective consent to opt into a trial in the MDL transferee forum?

6. Adopting a Single Choice-of-Law Principle

The fundamental problem that this chapter has addressed is variation in law — especially substantive state law. Variation in law gives incentives to plaintiffs to disperse litigation and makes it difficult to manage cases that are aggregated. An occasional cause of variation in substantive law is variation in choice-of-law rules: Applying different choice-of-law rules to aggregated cases can result in the use of varying substantive laws. But there is not a necessary correlation between varying choice-of-law rules and varying substantive law. It is possible that varying choice-of-law rules will all point to a single jurisdiction's law, just as it is possible that a single choice-of-law rule will point to many states' laws.

The last four subsections have examined techniques designed to attack the problem of varying state laws directly — by substituting a single law to govern multiple disputes. Each technique has limits that frustrate its general use. Therefore, this subsection pursues a different path, and examines whether courts in a complex cases can develop special choice-of-law principles for selecting the appropriate substantive law(s). Although this approach simplifies a court's choice-of-law analysis, which can itself be complicated, it does not necessarily result in the application of a single law that governs an issue or claim. Will it nonetheless reduce the problems of complexity created by choice-of-law doctrine?

ABA COMMISSION ON MASS TORTS, REPORT TO THE HOUSE OF DELEGATES

4d (1989)

Sec[.] 106. Choice of Law.

In consolidated mass tort litigation instituted, transferred, removed or maintained under this act, the district court shall determine the source or sources of applicable substantive law. Whenever State law supplies the rule of decision, the court may make its own determination in light of reason and experience as to which State(s) rule(s) shall apply to some or all of the actions, parties or issues.

AMERICAN LAW INSTITUTE, COMPLEX LITIGATION

321-23 (1994)

§ 6.01. Mass Torts

(a) Except as provided in §6.04 through §6.06, in actions consolidated under §3.01 or removed under §5.02 in which the parties assert the application of laws that are in material conflict, the transferee court shall choose the law governing the rights, liabilities, and defenses of the parties with respect to a tort claim by applying the criteria set forth in the following subsections with the objective of applying, to the extent feasible, a single state's law to all similar tort claims being asserted against a defendant.

(b) In determining the governing law under subsection (a), the court shall consider the following factors for purposes of identifying each state having a policy that would be furthered by the application of its laws:

(1) the place or places of injury;

(2) the place or places of the conduct causing the injury; and

(3) the primary places of business or habitual residences of the plaintiffs and defendants.

(c) If, in analyzing the factors set forth in sub-section (b), the court finds that only one state has a policy that would be furthered by the application of its law, that state's law shall govern. If more than one state has a policy that would be furthered by the application of its law, the court shall choose the applicable law from among the laws of the interested states under the following rules:

(1) If the place of injury and the place of the conduct causing the injury are in the same state, that state's law governs.

(2) If subsection (c)(1) does not apply but all of the plaintiffs habitually reside or have their primary places of business in the same state, and a defendant has its primary place of business or habitually resides in that state, that state's law governs the claims with respect to that defendant. Plaintiffs shall be considered as sharing a common habitual residence or primary place of business if they are located in states whose laws are not in material conflict.

(3) If neither subsection (c)(1) nor (c)(2) applies, but all of the plaintiffs habitually reside or have their primary places of business in the same state, and that state also is the place of injury, then that state's law governs. Plaintiffs shall be considered as sharing a common habitual residence or primary place of business if they are located in states whose laws are not in material conflict.

(4) In all other cases, the law of the state where the conduct causing the injury occurred governs. When conduct occurred in more than one state, the court shall choose the law of the conduct state that has the most significant relationship to the occurrence. . . .

(e) If the court determines that the application of a single state's law to all elements of the claims pending against a defendant would be inappropriate, it may divide the actions into subgroups of claims, issues, or parties to foster consolidated treatment under §3.01, and allow more than one state's law to be applied.

Notes

1. Although they have differences, the ABA and the ALI approaches agree on a basic premise: selecting a single choice-of-law rule, rather than selecting a single substantive law, is the best way to tackle state variations in tort law. (In other sections not quoted here, the ALI also developed

choice-of-law rules for contract claims, for statutes of limitation, and for compensatory and punitive damages. *See* COMPLEX LITIGATION, *supra*, §§ 6.02-.06.) The ALI argued that its approach was superior to approaches that led to the choice of a single substantive law, such as federal common law. First, a uniform choice-of-law rule required the use of extant state law, a result that limited the "unbridled discretion" that courts would enjoy if they chose the content of the applicable substantive law. Second, "federal choice of law rules should not be designed with the objective of promoting substantive preferences for one party rather than the other." Third, the choice-of-law standards proposed by the ALI were both "sufficiently flexible to protect against arbitrary results and to accommodate varying state interests by authorizing the court to sever issues to be treated under differing state laws when appropriate." *See id.* at 314-15, 318.

Granting these advantages, doesn't any solution that leaves untouched the variations in state law come up short as a means of reducing dispersion and enhancing manageability?

2.   The ALI attempted to overcome this problem, at least to some degree, by designing tiered choice-of-law rules that forced the choice of a single state's law in many circumstances. In essence, aren't the tiers created in § 6.01(c) a nuanced *lex loci* approach intended to avoid some of the injustices of the traditional *lex loci* rules? Recall that the ALI had strongly criticized the result-oriented manipulation of choice-of-law rules in *Air Crash Disaster* because the approach lacked predictability. *See supra* p. 672, Note 2. Isn't the ALI's proposal, which uses squishy terms such as "interests" and then tries to force the choice of a single law whenever possible, subject to precisely the same criticism? *Cf.* David E. Seidelson, *Section 6.01 of the ALI's Complex Litigation Project: Function Follows Form,* 54 LA. L. REV. 1111, 1111, 1137 (1994) (calling § 6.01 "jerry-built" and arguing that its subsections "don't work any better than they look").

3.   The ALI approach permits a court to make a choice-of-law determination on an issue-by-issue basis. Will this use of *dépeçage* make the court's task of finding a single law more difficult?

4.   The ALI's approach is more detailed and structured than the ABA's open-ended approach. Which approach is better? Does the answer depend on what the goal is — limiting the number of applicable state laws in order to avoid complexity, or enhancing predictability in the application of choice-of-law rules?

5.   If a detailed multi-factor approach is better, has the ALI identified the right factors? For a different list, see H.R. 1857, 105th Cong., 1st Sess. (1997) (including factors such as "place of injury," "place of the conduct causing the injury," "principal place of business or domiciles of the parties," "danger of creating unnecessary incentives for forum shopping," and "whether the choice of law would be reasonably foreseeable to the parties").

6.   Does the ALI's proposal pass constitutional muster under *Shutts*? Does the ABA's proposal?

7.   Now beginning from "the premise that choice of law is a dimension of the larger inquiry into the constraints imposed by substantive law on aggregation, not a matter of procedural choice akin to the decision to aggregate itself," the ALI seems to have given up on the idea of creating special choice-of-law rules for complex cases. *See* AM. L. INST., PRINCIPLES OF THE LAW OF AGGREGATE LITIGATION § 2.05 Reporters' Notes (2009). The ALI's present position is that, if the choice-of-law principles of the forum court dictate the use of a single substantive law (or "a limited number of patterns" of different laws), a court "may authorize aggregate treatment of multiple claims, or of a common issue therein." *Id.* § 2.05(b); *cf.* Ryan Patrick Phair, Note, *Resolving the "Choice-of-Law Problem" in Rule 23(b)(3) Nationwide Class Actions*, 67 U. CHI. L. REV. 835 (2000) (suggesting the use of subclasses and issue classes that group class members based on comparable state laws). But the ALI "contemplates no change in the body of choice-of-law principles that govern the court's selection of applicable substantive law." PRINCIPLES, *supra*, § 2.05 cmt. *a.*

Why the change of heart between the ALI's *Complex Litigation* in 1994 and its *Principles* in 2009?

8.   Both the ABA Report and the ALI proposal were written in the belief that Congress would need to legislate the choice-of-law principles that they espoused. Despite the introduction of numerous bills, Congress has never acted. Could a court adopt a new choice-of-law approach without waiting for congressional action? In *Gruber v. Price Waterhouse*, 117 F.R.D. 75 (E.D. Pa. 1987), the court faced a securities case containing pendent state claims. The defendant argued that the class action would be unmanageable because different state laws applied. Noting that "[s]everal courts have concluded that the law of the forum governs the common law claims of the entire class in securities cases," the court stated that it intended to apply Pennsylvania law to the claims of all class members. *Id.* at 81. The court avoided *Shutts* by stating that Pennsylvania, in which many of the wrongful acts occurred, had significant contacts with the case.

In part because it misread the case on which it had primarily relied — *In re Pizza Time Theatre Securities Litigation*, 112 F.R.D. 15 (N.D. Cal. 1986) — the precedential authority of *Gruber* is weak. Nonetheless, it raises an interesting question: Would a simple *lex fori* rule be the best choice-of-law principle, at least in cases in which the forum has significant contacts with the dispute? Or would this rule give plaintiffs too much leeway to secure the law they desire?

9.   As we conclude this section, consider the words of Professor Silberman:

> Aggregate litigation presents the question as to whether this type of litigation justifies a specialized choice of law rule designed to facilitate the aggregation. The answer will depend on (1) how one perceives the role of choice of law in the legal system; and (2) how one understands the function of the class action in its relationship to individual litigation. . . . When one posits that the claims of individuals in a class action would, in the absence of the class context, be decided

under different laws, it is not clear why aggregation should alter that result. . . . . To use the class action as the justification for altering choice of law rules would be to put the cart before the horse and to misunderstand the role of both class actions and choice of law. . . .

A more difficult question is whether legislatures (for federal courts it would be Congress; for state courts it would be the respective state legislatures) should readjust the substance of choice of law rules for class actions and other types of aggregate litigation.

Linda Silberman, *The Role of Choice of Law in National Class Actions*, 156 U. PA. L. REV. 2001, 2022, 2024 (2008). In a sense, this analysis captures the central question of this chapter and of the entire first part of this casebook: whether complex litigation must conform itself to the limits of pre-existing substantive and procedural law, or whether the ordinary rules of substantive and procedural law must yield to avoid the unfairness and inefficiency that dispersed, repetitive litigation can engender.

PART TWO

Pretrial Complexity

The prior chapters examined the difficulties of structuring a case that involves numerous dispersed parties. Structuring the case, however, is only the first step in deciding it. In our procedural system, we must now shepherd the case through a pretrial phase in which relevant facts and issues are exposed; a trial phase in which the legal claims associated with those facts and issues are adjudicated; and a remedial phase in which the judgment is implemented or enforced. In the next two chapters, we examine the pretrial phase. Chapter Seven explores an issue that is, in its way, also structural: determining the counsel and the judicial officers who will guide the case through the pretrial phase. Chapter Eight turns to the difficulties presented in expeditiously narrowing the issues and developing the factual issues in complex litigation.

On the surface, no necessary connection seems to exist between a case that is structurally complex and one that is complex in the pretrial phase. For instance, arguably the most complex pretrial proceeding of all time arose in a case that involved only two parties: the United States and AT&T. Nevertheless, a case that is structurally complex is likely to create pretrial difficulties as well. Great numbers of parties often generate great numbers of issues, as well as requests for a great deal of disclosure or discovery. Conversely, the manageability of the pretrial, trial, and remedial phases of the case can influence the court's decision about the best way to structure litigation. Therefore, structural and pretrial difficulties often go hand in hand, and they must be considered together.

Moreover, beneath the surface common themes emerge in structuring a case and ushering it through the pretrial process. Structuring a complex case often involves the need to override the one-on-one adversarial model of American litigation. In the pretrial phase as well, the traditional model, in which lawyers have the principal responsibility for defining the issues and obtaining the evidence, breaks down. The most typical response of our system has been to provide judges with greater powers in the pretrial phase in order to push, prod, and mold the litigation into a form that is ready for settlement or trial.

The central question of these two chapters is whether the additional powers that judges have asserted in the pretrial phase of large cases is justifiable. One way to think about answering that question is to use a distinction that we sometimes used in the previous chapters: Should we confine the use of greater judicial authority to those situations in which it is absolutely essential to preserve the power of a court to adjudicate fairly the claims of related parties, or can it be exercised whenever it is useful to make the case run more smoothly and efficiently? Time and again in these next two chapters, you will see judges claiming power that the traditional model of adversarial adjudication would not give them. You need to ask yourself whether you are comfortable with this more powerful judge, and why.

One final observation. Few cases in the American legal system, whether complex or routine, emerge from the pretrial process. The vast majority end without a trial. Hence, the issues considered in the next two chapters are, for the most part, the ball game. Certainly lawyers and judges act with an eye toward the possibility that the case will be tried, but they also act with an eye toward the much greater probability that the shape of the party structure and the pretrial process will determine the case's outcome.

CHAPTER SEVEN

DEFINING THE ROLES OF LAWYER AND JUDGE

The adversarial model expects that lawyers will accomplish the pretrial tasks of selecting the legal theories, gathering the facts, and narrowing the issues for trial. The judge is a passive umpire who becomes involved only when a dispute about a legal issue or an entitlement to obtain information arises. But this adversarial approach does not work well for many large cases, which can involve mountains of paper, blizzards of motions, torrents of depositions, and cornucopias of legal claims and defenses. Almost invariably, dozens of claims and parties produce large quantities of information. In a spiral that lawyers who are left to their own devices find difficult to break, this information often spins out new claims and implicates new parties — a fact that leads to new rounds of discovery. Discovering large quantities of information is also expensive. The ability to impose significant expense means that a better-financed party can oppress other parties. Expense also can warp the relationship between a plaintiff's lawyer, who often fronts the litigation expenses, and the plaintiff, who usually has far less at stake in the case than the lawyer.

One apparent solution is for the judge to become more actively involved in the pretrial process. This involvement, which is usually known as *case management*, is now a common feature in American litigation — in cases both complex and routine. The origins of case management lie in the post-World War II period, as judges struggled to deal with a spate of large and messy antitrust lawsuits. Because greater judicial involvement was viewed as having been a successful innovation in these complex cases, the idea of case management migrated into routine litigation in the 1970s and 1980s as a response to perceived excesses in cost and delay.

Today the central authority for case management in the federal system is Federal Rule of Civil Procedure 16. Rule 16 provides a wealth of case-management powers that federal judges can use. Case-management authority is committed to the trial court's discretion, and different judges faced with identical cases might manage them in very different ways. Whether case management has been successful in reducing cost and delay, and whether its arguable success is worth the sacrifice of litigant autonomy and uniformity in the treatment of similar cases, remain debated points.

What is not debated — at least not very much — is the importance of case management in complex litigation. The case-management techniques that judges employ in complex litigation are often different in both quantity and quality from those used in ordinary litigation. Most of the specific techniques are considered in Chapter Eight. There we will see that case management shifts significant control away from the parties and the lawyers and toward the judge. This chapter examines the basic terms of the case-management debate and the extent to which the needs of complex litigation justify a redefinition of the roles of lawyers and judges. It also addresses what is arguably the most important case-management power of the judge: the power to establish the counsel and judicial structure in the case. Only because of the exercise of this power, which fundamentally redefines the relationships among clients, lawyers, and judges, do many of the case-management powers that we study in the next chapter work.

A. THE CONCEPT OF CASE MANAGEMENT

This section lays out the goals of case management, the mindsets that case management inculcates in the judge and the lawyers, and the merits of this approach in relation to the traditionally passive role of the judge in an adversarial system.

HANDBOOK OF RECOMMENDED PROCEDURES FOR THE TRIAL OF PROTRACTED CASES

(1960), *reprinted in* 25 F.R.D. 351, 383-85 (1960)

Recommendation: When a protracted case is identified, the assigned judge should, at the earliest moment, take actual control of the case. The judge should make himself available at all reasonable times, holding frequent pre-trial conferences, offering constructive suggestions and maintaining a firm but understanding attitude towards the parties, with the objective of organizing and simplifying the issues and of obtaining the stipulation of all possible facts and an accurate statement of the material issues concerning which there is a genuine disagreement.
. . .

There can exist no question as to the power of the court to control the case from the time of its filing through all its procedural aspects to the conclusion of the trial itself. The nature of the long or protracted case is such that strong control must be exercised from the time of filing to its disposition. The "remedy is for the trial judge to take the case in hand at the outset, study it, and act as his best judgment dictates." Judge Prettyman coined the expression "Iron hearted Judges" . . . . The phrases repeatedly found in the literature suggesting that the judge "take the case in hand at the outset," "gain control of the case in an early stage," take "full control of a case from the time of filing," and exercise "rigid control" all suggest that firmness and resolved required of the trial judge in undertaking the pre-trial of the protracted case. "A judge must be willing to assume his role as the governor of a lawsuit. He can't just be the umpire." . . .

. . . Most of the actual work will be done by counsel, but it is the task of the trial judge to see that the work is done, the case organized and made ready for trial.

MANUAL FOR COMPLEX LITIGATION, FOURTH

12-13 (2004)

§ 10.13   Effective Management

Effective judicial management generally has the following characteristics:

- *It is active.* The judge anticipates problems before they arise rather than waiting passively for counsel to present them. Because the attorneys may become immersed in the details of the case, innovation and creativity in formulating a litigation plan frequently will depend on the judge.

- *It is substantive.* The judge becomes familiar at an early stage with the substantive issues in order to make informed rulings on issue definition and narrowing, and on related matters, such as scheduling, bifurcation and consolidation, and discovery control.

- *It is timely.* The judge decides disputes promptly, particularly those that may substantially affect the course or scope of further proceedings. Delayed rulings may be costly and burdensome for litigants and will often delay other litigation events. The parties may prefer that a ruling be timely rather than perfect.

- *It is continuing.* The judge periodically monitors the progress of the litigation to see that schedules are being followed and to consider necessary modifications of the litigation plan. Interim reports may be ordered between scheduled conferences.

- *It is firm, but fair.* Time limits and other controls and requirements are not imposed arbitrarily or without considering the views of counsel, and they revised when warranted. Once established, however, schedules are met, and, when necessary, appropriate sanctions are imposed . . . for derelictions and dilatory tactics.

- *It is careful.* An early display of careful preparation sets the proper tone and can enhance the judge's credibility and effectiveness with counsel. . . .

The attorneys — who will be more familiar than the judge with the facts and issues in the case — should play a significant part in developing the litigation plan and should have primary responsibility for its execution.

Judith Resnik, MANAGERIAL JUDGES

96 HARV. L. REV. 374, 376, 378, 408, 413, 417, 423-24, 427, 430-31 (1982)

Until recently, the American legal establishment embraced a classical view of the judicial role. Under this view, judges are not supposed to have an involvement or interest in the controversies they adjudicate. Disengagement and dispassion supposedly enable judges to decide cases fairly and impartially. . . .

. . . [T]he role of judges before adjudication is undergoing a change . . . . Judges have described their new tasks as "case management" — hence my term "managerial judges." As managers, judges learn more about cases much earlier than they did in the past. They negotiate with parties about the course, timing, and scope of both pretrial and posttrial litigation. These managerial responsibilities give judges greater power. Yet the restraints that formerly circumscribed judicial authority are conspicuously absent. Managerial judges frequently work beyond the public view, off the record, with no obligation to provide written, reasoned opinions, and out of reach of appellate review. . . .

. . . Informal judge-litigant contact provides judges with information beyond that traditionally within their ken. . . . The supposedly rigid structure of evidentiary rules, designed to insulate decision-makers from extraneous and impermissible information, is irrelevant in case management. . . . Instead, judges remove their blindfolds and become part of the sagas themselves. . . .

. . . During pretrial supervision, . . . appellate review is virtually unavailable. The judge has vast influence over the course and eventual outcome of the litigation. As a result, litigants have good reason to capitulate to judicial pressure rather than risk the hostility of a judge . . . . During pretrial management, judges are restrained only by personal beliefs about the proper role of judge-managers. . . .

Proponents of managerial judging typically assume that . . . case management decreases delay, produces more dispositions, and reduces litigation costs. But close examination of the currently available information reveals little support for the conclusion that management is responsible for efficiency gains (if any) at the district court level . . . .

Moreover, judicial management itself imposes costs. The judge's time is the most expensive resource in the courthouse. Rather than concentrate all of their energy deciding motions, charging juries, and drafting opinions, managerial judges must meet with parties, develop litigation plans, and compel obedience to their new management rules. . . .

. . . Moreover, judges are in close contact with attorneys during the course of management. Such interactions may become occasions for the development of intense feelings — admiration, friendship, or antipathy. Therefore, management becomes a fertile field for the growth of personal bias.

Further, judges with supervisory obligations may gain stakes in the cases they manage. Their prestige may ride on "efficient" management, as calculated by the speed and number of dispositions. Competition and peer pressure may tempt judges to rush litigants because of reasons unrelated to the merits of disputes. . . .

Unreviewable power, casual contact, and interest in outcome (or in aggregate outcomes) have not traditionally been associated with the "due process" decisionmaking model. These features do not evoke images of reasoned adjudication, images that form the very basis of both our faith in the judicial process and our enormous grant of power to federal judges. The literature of managerial judging refers only occasionally to the values of due process: the accuracy of decisionmaking, the adequacy of reasoning, and the quality of adjudication. Instead, commentators and the training sessions for district judges emphasize speed, control, and quantity. . . . Case processing is no longer viewed as a means to an end; instead, it appears to have become the desired goal.

E. Donald Elliott, MANAGERIAL JUDGING AND THE EVOLUTION OF PROCEDURE

53 U. CHI. L. REV. 306, 315-17, 319, 321-26, 328, 334-35 (1986)

. . .Some opponents of managerial judging, led by Professor Resnik, contend that managerial judging is ineffective — or at least that the effectiveness of managerial judging has not been demonstrated. Here I must respectfully part company with the loyal opposition. Both my personal experience as a litigator and the available published data convince me that at least some managerial techniques are effective in reducing the amount of time and effort invested in processing a given case. . . .

. . . Focusing on the effectiveness, rather than the fairness, of managerial judging diverts the debate from the more interesting and ultimately more important issue of the ad hoc and potentially arbitrary nature of managerial judging. There is an undeniable potential for arbitrariness in any procedure that forecloses issues in litigation without adequate consideration of their merit.

The potential for arbitrariness inherent in managerial judging was clearly demonstrated in a unique controlled experiment at the conference upon which this symposium is based. The participating judges were divided into separate workshop sessions, each of which was asked to propose approaches for managing the same hypothetical case. The reports from the workshops disclosed dramatic differences in the ways that individual judges would have handled the case. Based on her intuition that the case had little merit, one trial judge would have required thousands of plaintiffs to file individual, verified complaints — a move that would have made it all but impossible for the plaintiffs' lawyer to pursue the cases. On the other hand, another trial judge confronting exactly the same hypothetical case would have ordered the defendants to create a multi-million dollar settlement fund. . . .

It seems beyond serious debate, then, that discretionary managerial decisions may influence the outcome of litigation in ways that are arbitrary because judges act without the procedural safeguards that accompany decisions on the merits. . . .

. . . [T]he problem that managerial judging aims to solve is, at base, structural: it results from a fundamental imbalance in the Rules between the techniques available for developing and expanding issues and those for narrowing or resolving them prior to trial. . . .

To improve the issue-narrowing capacity of our present procedural system, we need to fill the gaping hole that now exists between the overly scrupulous standard for summary judgment and the essentially standardless procedures of managerial judging. If judges were permitted to find, from a preliminary assessment of the merits, that further development was unlikely to be worth its cost, narrowing of issues might be less arbitrary. . . .

To say that managerial judging arose originally as a way of narrowing issues is not to say, however, that issue-narrowing is either its permanent or only function. On the contrary, once a legal idea or practice wins acceptance, it takes on a life of its own. . . .

Only shortly after it achieved undisputed legitimacy, the institution of managerial judging has begun to undergo such a transformation. Managerial judging is evolving rapidly from a set of techniques for narrowing issues to a set of techniques for settling cases. . . .

The evolution toward greater use of managerial judging techniques to encourage settlement was predictable, if not inevitable. At base, the powers of managerial judging are the powers to impose costs, and thereby to increase the price of exercising the powers delegated to attorneys by the Federal Rules of Civil Procedure. There is good reason to believe, however, that the cost of litigation is one of the critical factors that affect decisions to settle. Thus, to the extent that managerial judging increases costs — and perhaps alters their timing and distribution as well — managerial judging can cause some cases to settle that would otherwise go to trial. . . .

. . . [T]he admission that there are costs to managerial judging in terms of real or perceived procedural unfairness should not by itself be dispositive. The proper issue is whether the benefits of managerial judging in enhancing substantive justice exceed its costs. At least in certain categories of cases, I believe that the benefits of managerial judging in enhancing substantive justice can exceed the costs in terms of procedural justice, and therefore I favor the judicious use of managerial judging despite the potential for arbitrariness which it admittedly entails.

John H. Langbein, THE GERMAN ADVANTAGE IN CIVIL PROCEDURE

52 U. CHI. L. REV. 823, 824, 858-62, 866 (1985)

My theme is that, by assigning judges rather than lawyers to investigate the facts, the Germans avoid the most troublesome aspects of [American] practice. . . .

Apart from fact-gathering, . . . the lawyers for the parties play major and broadly comparable roles in both the German and American systems. Both are adversary systems of civil procedure. There as here, the lawyers advance partisan positions from first pleadings to final arguments. German litigators suggest legal theories and lines of factual inquiry, they superintend and supplement judicial examination of witnesses, they urge inferences from fact, they discuss and distinguish precedent, they interpret statutes, and they formulate views of the law that further the interests of their clients. . . .

Important changes have occurred in recent years that [further] diminish the contrast between German and American civil procedure. Under the rubric of case management, American trial judges are exercising increasing control of the conduct of fact-gathering. . . .

What makes [the case-management approach] look "proto-Germanic" in the eyes of the comparative lawyer is the informal feel of "the conference method;" and the active judicial role in defining issues, promoting settlement, and fixing the sequence for fact-gathering. . . .

On the other hand, the haphazard growth of managerial judging has not been accompanied by Continental-style attention to safeguarding litigants against the dangers inherent in the greatly augmented judicial role. The career incentives for our judiciary are primitive, and the standards of appellate review barely touch the pretrial process.

The trend toward managerial judging is irreversible, because the trend toward complexity in civil litigation that gave rise to managerial judging is irreversible. If we were to learn from the success of the long established German tradition of managerial judging, we would not only improve our safeguards, we would encourage more complete judicial responsibility for the conduct of fact-gathering. For example, we might have the judge (or a surrogate such as a master or a magistrate) depose witnesses and assemble the rest of the proofs, working in response to adversary nomination and under adversary oversight as in German procedure. We might then be able to forbid the adversaries from contact with witnesses — in other words, we could abolish the coaching that disgraces our civil justice. . . .

Regardless of where managerial judging is headed for the future, it has already routed adversary theory. I take that as further support for the view . . . that adversary theory was misapplied to fact-gathering in the first place. Nothing but inertia and vested interests justify the waste and distortion of adversary fact-gathering. The success of German civil procedure stands as an enduring reproach to those who say that we must continue to suffer adversary tricksters in the proof of fact.

Notes

1. What are the most important qualities of a good case manager? What are the most important qualities of a judge? Do the two sets of qualities mesh with each other?

2. The modern history of case management can be traced to the *Report on Procedure in Anti-Trust and Other Protracted Cases* (1951), *reprinted in* 13 F.R.D. 62 (1953). This report is commonly known as the Prettyman Report after its principal author, Chief Judge E. Barrett Prettyman, who also coined the phrase "Iron hearted Judges" to describe the judge's role. The report responded to a series of post-World War II antitrust cases that, although modest by present standards, were larger and more unwieldy than any cases previously encountered in federal litigation. The Prettyman Report was short on the specifics of how the judge was to act. A series of seminars during the 1950s put more flesh on the case manager's skeleton. *See, e.g., Seminar on Procedures Prior to Trial*, 20 F.R.D. 485 (1957); *Proceedings of the Seminar on Protracted Cases*, 21 F.R.D. 395 (1957); *Proceedings of the Seminar on Protracted Cases for the United States Judges*, 23 F.R.D. 319 (1958). The culmination of these seminars was the *Handbook of Recommended Procedures*. The *Handbook* made concrete recommendations about the characteristics a case manager should have and the actions a case manager should take.

The *Handbook* was replaced in 1970 by the *Manual for Complex and Multidistrict Litigation*. This *Manual* went through five interim editions, two supplements, and a re-titling before being replaced by the *Manual for Complex Litigation (Second)* in1985. The *Manual (Second)* further developed the characteristics and actions of a successful case manager. The *Manual for Complex Litigation, Third* replaced the *Manual (Second)* in 1995, but added little to the description of the judge's role. The present *Manual for Complex Litigation, Fourth*, published in 2004, describes the case manager's characteristics in language nearly identical to that of the *Manual, Third*.

Over the course of its numerous editions, the *Manual for Complex Litigation* has become the Bible of case management. Having been written by the Federal Judicial Center, an arm of the Administrative Office for United States Courts, the *Manual* does not have the force of either statute or Federal Rule of Civil Procedure. Nonetheless, its influence is vast. Its principles are taught to federal and state judges alike, and it is often cited in judicial opinions. We will frequently refer to its recommendations on specific case-management techniques.

3.   Professors Resnik, Elliott, and Langbein provide varying opinions on the value of case management and its relationship to adversarial process. Professor Resnik's stance toward case management is critical, Professor Langbein's reaction is enthusiastic (at least as a first step on the road toward greater judicial authority over fact-gathering), and Professor Elliott's appraisal is measured. Each author wrote just as the case-management movement was taking wing in the federal courts.

Since that time, we have developed better data on the effectiveness of case-management techniques in reducing expense and delay. For the most part, the data are neutral to slightly favorable. Generally, case management does not significantly reduce expense or delay; but neither does it increase them. Case management has little effect on attorney or litigant satisfaction. With some case-management techniques, modest reductions in delay are offset by modest increases in cost.

Two case-management techniques have clear benefits. First, the technique of setting early, firm deadlines during pretrial reduces the time to dispose of a case with no increase in cost. Second, early management reduces the time to disposition without an increase in attorney hours when it is accompanied by discovery planning and case-management planning. *See* JAMES S. KAKALIK, AN EVALUATION OF JUDICIAL CASE MANAGEMENT UNDER THE CIVIL JUSTICE REFORM ACT (1996); James S. Kakalik et al., *Discovery Management: Further Analysis of the Civil Justice Reform Act Evaluation Data*, 39 B.C. L. REV. 613 (1998). For what it is worth, other data suggest that, except in a small subset of cases, lawyers do not believe that the present costs of discovery are excessive. *Id.*; Thomas E. Willging et al., *An Empirical Study of Discovery and Disclosure Practices under the 1993 Federal Rule Amendments*, 39 B.C. L. REV. 525 (1998).

4.   As Professor Resnik points out, focusing on the reduction of expense and delay excludes consideration of important procedural values. Echoing and amplifying some of these concerns, Professor Molot has engaged in a thorough critique of the trend toward case-management activism, especially as manifested in pretrial conferences and class-action settlements. He argues that the traditional adjudicatory role described by Professor Fuller (*supra* p. 36) should continue to act as the limit on judicial involvement. In particular, he contends that constitutional considerations and concerns for institutional competence undergird the traditional, non-managerial role that judges followed for centuries. Jonathan T. Molot, *An Old Judicial Role for a New Litigation Era*, 113 YALE L.J. 27 (2003).

5.   Professor Elliott suggests that focusing only on procedural values improperly excludes consideration of the substantive values that case management can advance. As Professors Silver and Baker out it, "[c]lass members would often rather have less procedural justice and more substantive justice than the reverse." Charles Silver & Lynn Baker, *I Cut,*

You Choose: The Role of Plaintiffs' Counsel in Allocating Settlement Proceeds, 84 Va. L. Rev. 1465, 1540 (1998).

6. Everyone agrees that case management places new powers in the judge's hands. As Professor Elliott points out, different judges can use the powers of case management to achieve different outcomes for complex litigation. Thus, case management increases the importance to the parties of finding a "hospitable" judge. It affects plaintiffs when they consider the size of their lawsuits and they select the initial forum; it affects defendants when they consider venue transfers or removal; and it affects both parties when they litigate over jurisdictional or aggregation doctrines.

Would aggregating related cases be less problematic if judges adhered to the traditional adjudicatory role? On the other hand, can judges who adhere to that role resolve aggregated proceedings? Whether our modern impulse toward aggregation has created the need for case management, or whether the availability of case management has created the modern impulse toward aggregation, is a wonderful "chicken and egg" question. If anything is clear from Part I of this casebook, however, it is the principle that aggregating litigation and managing litigation successfully are deeply interwoven concepts.

7. Are the arguments for case management in complex cases and routine cases the same? Note how important the definition of "complex litigation" is. If you define complex cases to be those cases in which lawyers are unable to accomplish the tasks the adversarial system has assigned them, then the judge must step into the vacuum in order to preserve rational adjudication. On this account, the preservation and promotion of rational adjudication provides both the reason for and the limit on case management in complex cases. On the other hand, if you define "complex litigation" to be those cases in which repetitive litigation is inefficient, efficiency determines the scope and limits of case management.

Neither definition says anything about whether judges should engage in case management in routine cases. Here the exercise of judicial power needs to be justified by different reasons that might suggest different limitations on judicial power.

Doesn't this question, and the concept of case management generally, acknowledge the impossibility of treating like cases procedurally alike?

8. The materials and questions in this section have an inevitably abstract quality until you see the case-management techniques that judges can employ in practice. You might want to revisit them after completing the next two chapters.

B. Selecting a Counsel Structure

In an adversarial system, each party chooses a lawyer to represent him or her. The lawyer has a duty to represent zealously the interests of the party, and to avoid any conflicts of interest that might divide the lawyer's loyalty. To safeguard clients and ensure zealous representation, our system has developed ethical rules by which lawyers must abide. As we have seen, however, complex cases often involve dozens or even thousands of parties on each side of a case. Individual representation seems an extravagance that would make timely resolution of large cases impossible. An obvious solution is to have a single lawyer represent a group of similarly situated clients. But who should pick this lawyer? And how can the lawyer deal with the almost inevitable conflicts of interest that arise when the interests of some clients in the group diverge from those of others? The following two subsections explore these questions.

1. The Selection of Counsel

RICHARDSON-MERRELL, INC. V. KOLLER

472 U.S. 424 (1985)

■ JUSTICE BRENNAN, concurring. . . .

A fundamental premise of the adversary system is that individuals have the right to retain the attorney of their choice to represent their interests in judicial proceedings. . . . [I]f an attorney is adequately qualified and has not otherwise acted so as to justify disqualification, the client need not obtain the permission of the court or of his adversary to retain the attorney of his choice. . . .

■ JUSTICE STEVENS, dissenting. . . .

Everyone must agree that the litigant's freedom to choose his own lawyer in a civil case is a fundamental right.

MANUAL FOR COMPLEX LITIGATION, FOURTH

24-25 (2004)

10.22. Coordination in Multiparty Litigation — Lead/Liaison Counsel and Committees

Complex litigation often involves numerous parties with common or similar interests but separate counsel. Traditional procedures in which all papers and documents are served on all attorneys, and each attorney files motions, presents arguments, and examines witnesses, may waste time and money, confuse and misdirect the litigation, and burden the court unnecessarily. Instituting special procedures for coordination of counsel early in the litigation will help avoid these problems.

In some cases the attorneys coordinate their activities without the court's assistance, and such efforts should be encouraged. More often, however, the court will need to institute procedures under which one or more attorneys are selected and authorized to act on behalf of other counsel and their clients with respect to specified aspects of the litigation. To do so, invite submissions and suggestions from all counsel and conduct an independent review . . . to ensure that counsel appointed to leading roles are qualified and responsible, that they will fairly and adequately represent all of the parties on their side, and that their charges will be reasonable. . . .

10.221 Organizational Structures

Attorneys designated by the court to act on behalf of other counsel and parties in addition to their own clients (referred to collectively as "designated counsel") generally fall into one of the following categories:

- *Liaison counsel.* Charged with essentially administrative matters, such as communications between the court and other counsel (including receiving and distributing notices, orders, motions, and briefs on behalf of the group), convening meetings of counsel, advising parties of developments, and otherwise assisting in the coordination of activities and positions. . . . Liaison counsel will usually have offices in the same locality as the court. The court may appoint (or the parties may select) a liaison for each side . . . .

- *Lead counsel.* Charged with formulating (in consultation with other counsel) and presenting positions on substantive and procedural issues during the litigation. Typically they act for the group — either personally or by coordinating the efforts of others — in presenting written and oral arguments and suggestions to the court, working with opposing counsel in developing and implementing a litigation plan, initiating and organizing discovery requests and responses, conducting the principal examination of deponents, employing experts, arranging for support services, and seeing that schedules are met.

- *Trial counsel.* Serves as principal attorney at trial for the group and organize and coordinate the work of the other attorneys on the trial team.

- *Committees of counsel.* Often called steering committees, coordinating committees, management committees, executive committees, discovery committees, or trial teams. Committees are most commonly needed when group members' interests and positions are sufficiently dissimilar to justify giving them representation in decision making. The court or lead counsel may task committees with preparing briefs or conducting portions of the discovery program if one lawyer cannot do so adequately. Committees of counsel can sometimes lead to substantially increased costs, and they should try to avoid unnecessary duplication of efforts and control fees and expenses. . . .

The types of appointments and assignments of responsibilities will depend on many factors. The most important is achieving efficiency and economy without jeopardizing fairness to parties. . . .

10.224 Court's Responsibilities

Few decisions by the court in complex litigation are as difficult and sensitive as the appointment of designated counsel. There is often intense competition for appointment by the court as designated counsel, an appointment that may implicitly promise large fees and a prominent role in the litigation. Side agreements among attorneys also may have a significant effect on positions taken in the proceedings. At the same time, because appointments of designated counsel will alter the usual dynamics of client representation in important ways, attorneys will have legitimate concerns that their clients' interests be adequately represented.

For these reasons, the judge is advised to take an active part in the decision on the appointment of counsel. Deferring to proposals by counsel without independent examination, even those that seem to have the concurrence of a majority of those affected, invites problems down the road . . . .

The court's responsibilities are heightened in class action litigation, where the judge must approve counsel for the class . . . .

VINCENT V. HUGHES AIR WEST, INC.

557 F.2d 759 (9th Cir. 1977)

■ WALLACE, Circuit Judge.

In consolidated cases arising out of a 1971 air crash disaster, the district court awarded attorneys' fees to four law firms that had comprised a plaintiffs' "committee of lead counsel" for discovery and other purposes. The award was to be paid out of the various settlements negotiated between the defendants, Hughes Air West, Inc. (Hughes) and the United States, and the next-of-kin of the crash victims. Some of the next-of-kin and their attorneys appeal, contending either that the district court had no authority to make the award or that the court erred in computing the award and designating the recipients. . . .

I

[The Judicial Panel on Multidistrict Litigation consolidated 11 cases arising out of the crash. On August 30, 1972, the MDL judge] appointed John D. Miller of the Miller firm "liaison counsel between plaintiffs' counsel" and directed Miller to call a meeting of plaintiffs' counsel

> for the purpose of agreeing upon lead counsel or a committee of lead counsel . . . to conduct all further discovery on liability and to try the case on liability, if that becomes necessary, and to voluntarily agree upon the contribution by non-members of such committee to a fund to be deposited with the Clerk from moneys paid by defendants resulting from the above-numbered lawsuits, to reimburse said committee

members for such additional work as may result from the activities of said committee, and for compensation of fees to the members of said committee for work performed for the benefit of all plaintiffs. . . .

At the ordered meeting of plaintiffs' counsel, a majority of those present selected four law firms to serve as a committee of lead counsel: the Miller firm [and three other firms]. . . . A majority of those present also agreed to let the district court determine the method and amount of payment to lead counsel for their work. Some objected to this plan.

The proceedings of this meeting were presented to the district judge and on December 11, 1972, he confirmed the appointment of the committee of lead counsel. . . . The court then outlined both the responsibilities of lead counsel — "to conduct all further pre-trial proceedings, to bring or oppose all motions, and to prepare and conduct the trial on the issue of liability" — and the concurrent restrictions on plaintiffs' counsel not so designated (nonlead counsel), constituting generally a prohibition against initiating either further discovery proceedings or pretrial motions without first securing approval of lead counsel. The court did not grant lead counsel an absolute veto, however. Nonlead counsel disappointed with a decision of lead counsel could "apply to the Court for an order authorizing him to file [his proposed] motion or initiate [his proposed] discovery proceeding."

[Subsequently, the court approved lead counsel's plan for attorneys' fees. The plan required each class member to deposit five percent of any judgment or settlement with the clerk of the court. That five percent, known as the Special Class Fund, was for the most part to be deducted from the contingent fee of the claimant's original attorney.]

As settlements were finalized and approved by the court and five percent of the recoveries deposited, the amount in the depository, generally referred to as the Special Class Fund, grew to over $450,000. . . .

[After a hearing, the district judge] found that the work of lead counsel was competent and benefitted all claimants by removing the liability issue, that any services of nonlead counsel were not "for and on behalf of the entire Class," and that the value of lead counsel's services was between five and ten percent of the gross recoveries. Accordingly, the district judge awarded the entire Special Class Fund, minus the costs incurred by individual attorneys on the liability issue, to the committee of lead counsel. . . .

Most attorneys not on the committee acquiesced in the orders. Five groups of claimants and attorneys, however, have appealed . . . .

IV

[The court held the district court's order was justified under the "common fund" doctrine, which requires the beneficiaries of a lawyer's efforts to create, increase, or preserve a common fund to compensate counsel for those efforts. It then turned to nonlead counsel's objection to the use of this doctrine.]

. . . [T]he disparity in the efforts of lead and nonlead counsel was effectively compelled by provisions in the district court's order confirming the appointment of lead counsel. On this appeal, nonlead counsel make a frontal attack on the power of the district court to promulgate such an order, specifically to appoint lead counsel in multiparty litigation and to restrict the activities of nonlead counsel. We believe that the district court has such power and that the district court properly exercised it in these consolidated cases.

In recent decades, complex multiparty litigation has become an increasingly frequent occurrence in the federal district courts. The causes are many and include, in addition to the substantive laws underlying much of this litigation, the liberal joinder and intervention rules of the Federal Rules of Civil Procedure, Rules 19-20, 24, the provisions of Rule 42(a) permitting consolidation of actions, the provisions of 28 U.S.C. § 1404 permitting transfer by a single district judge, and the significant transfer authority granted to the Judicial Panel on Multidistrict Litigation by 28 U.S.C. § 1407. With this advent of complex multiparty litigation have come serious administrative problems, and the federal courts have found it necessary to develop innovative procedures to meet the problems. One of the earlier-devised procedures was the appointment of a "liaison counsel." The liaison counsel serves all parties on one side of the dispute. He is selected either by his colleagues or by the court, and his duties are generally ministerial. For example, he may receive and distribute to the parties on his side notices and other documents from the court or adverse parties, or he may call meetings where joint action is considered. The concept of liaison counsel was incorporated in an early edition of the *Manual for Complex Litigation*.

The limited scope of both liaison counsel's authority and his duties, however, sometimes created new problems, especially for plaintiffs in multidistrict aircrash cases. Accordingly, proposals were advanced calling for creation of the role of "lead counsel," an attorney or group of attorneys with significant authority and a concomitant responsibility to conduct pretrial discovery and, if necessary, to litigate the liability issue. In 1972, the editors of the *Manual for Complex Litigation* incorporated many of these proposals in section 1.92 of the *Manual*.

Although some courts at an earlier time apparently doubted their power to create the role of lead counsel and oversee its filling, by the time section 1.92 was added to the *Manual for Complex Litigation* the authority of the district courts regarding lead counsel was well-established. *MacAlister v. Guterma*, 263 F.2d 65 (2d Cir. 1958), represented "the first time that the power of the courts to order consolidation for the pre-trial stages and the appointment of general [lead] counsel to supervise and coordinate the prosecution of plaintiffs' case [was] presented to a federal appellate court." Defendants in a stockholders' derivative suit moved the district court for an order consolidating various related actions and appointing lead counsel for the consolidated plaintiffs. The district court refused. On appeal, the Second Circuit held that the district court had the "inherent powers" to consolidate and appoint lead counsel but that in that case, the district judge had not abused his discretion in refusing to do so. In support of its decision regarding the district court's authority to appoint lead counsel, the Second Circuit noted:

> The benefits achieved by consolidation and the appointment of general counsel, i.e. elimination of duplication and repetition and in effect the creation of a coordinator of diffuse plaintiffs through whom motions and discovery proceedings will be channeled, will most certainly redound to the benefit of all parties to the litigation. The advantages of this procedure should not be denied litigants in the federal courts because of misapplied notions concerning interference with a party's right to his own counsel. . . .

The authority recognized in *MacAlister* has never been seriously disputed. . . .

We likewise hold that the district court had the authority to direct the appointment of a committee of lead counsel. Further, we do not disapprove of the manner in which the district judge exercised that power in this case. The procedures leading to creation of the committee of lead counsel followed closely the guidelines set forth in the *Manual for Complex Litigation* § 1.92. Indeed, the purpose of that section — to insure the orderly disposition of the actions with economy of time, money and effort for the court, counsel and the parties — was largely fulfilled in this case.

[The court then affirmed the award of fees except as to two groups of plaintiffs, one of whom paid a lawyer on an hourly basis to negotiate a settlement and the other of whom settled their cases before appointment of lead counsel.]

IN RE CENDANT CORP. LITIGATION

264 F.3d 201 (3d Cir. 2001)

■ BECKER, Chief Judge.

These are consolidated appeals from the District Court's approval of a $3.2 billion settlement of a securities fraud class action brought against Cendant Corporation and its auditors, . . . and the Court's award of $262 million in fees to counsel for the plaintiff class. Both the settlement and the fee award are challenged in these appeals. The enormous size of both the settlement and the fee award presages a new generation of "mega cases" that will test our previously developed jurisprudence.

This case is governed by the Private Securities Litigation Reform Act of 1995 (PSLRA or Reform Act). Under the Reform Act, one of a district court's first tasks is to select a lead plaintiff. Once the lead plaintiff has been appointed, the statute provides that the lead plaintiff "shall, subject to the approval of the court, select and retain counsel to represent the class." . . .

[Applying the criteria specified in the PLSRA, the district court selected as lead plaintiff a consortium composed of the California Public Employees' Retirement System (CalPERS) and two other retirement funds, collectively known as "the CalPERS Group."] The court then turned to selection of lead counsel. The CalPERS Group had filed a motion seeking to have Barrack, Rodos & Bacine (BRB) and Bernstein Litowitz Berger & Grossman LLP (BLBG) appointed lead counsel pursuant to a Retainer Agreement that it had negotiated with them, which dictated not only the formula for determining attorneys fees but also included a Plan for Monitoring Litigation, a section outlining a Theory of Recovery, and a part captioned Consultation Regarding Settlement Negotiations.[4] The District Court, however, decided to select lead counsel via auction. The court ... reasoned that "the Court's approval is subject to its discretionary judgment that lead plaintiff's choice of representative best suits the needs of the class," and concluded that "mechanisms" other than the lead plaintiff's choice were available to assist the court in making that determination. The court pointed to the "emerging trend" of using auctions "to simulate the free market in the selection of class counsel," and stated that it would hold an auction to select lead counsel and to determine its fee. Recognizing that the Reform Act confers upon the Lead Plaintiff the "opportunity" to "select and retain" lead counsel, the District Court ruled that counsel chosen by the CalPERS Group would have the chance to match what the court determined to be the lowest qualified bid. . . .

The District Court . . . received nine bids to serve as lead counsel in the main Cendant action. The District Court rejected the bid by counsel for appellant Aboff, which would have generated fees of 1-2% of the total settlement depending on the size of the settlement and the timing of the recovery, characterizing it as unrealistic and "quasi-philanthropic," and stating that "[u]nless the eventual monetary recovery in this case is in the billions, such an apparently 'cheap' fee does not make professional sense."[7] In contrast, the court expressly found that counsel proposed by the Lead Plaintiff was qualified and that its proposed fee scale was "realistic," but also concluded that another qualified bidder had submitted a lower "realistic" bid. Counsel chosen by the Lead Plaintiff exercised its power to meet this lower bid, and was thus appointed lead counsel.

---

4.   [The fee agreement provided for attorneys' fees to be calculated based on a combination of the point in the litigation at which the case settled and the amount of recovery. If the case settled after discovery commenced but before it ended, for instance, the firms would be entitled to 17.5% of any recovery up to $100 million, 10% of any recovery between $100 and $300 million, 7.5% of any recovery between $300 and $500 million, and 5% of any recovery above $500 million. Given the actual settlement of $3.2 billion, the attorneys would have been entitled to fees of $187 million, or $75 million less than they ultimately received. — ED.]

7.   The case did, of course, settle for an amount well into the billions, reflecting the perspicacity of Mr. Sirota, Aboff's counsel. We need not decide whether Mr. Sirota could have negotiated such a large settlement because we are satisfied that, from the perspective of the District Court at the time, its decision in selecting counsel was not an abuse of discretion.

[After the settlement was approved, one member of the CalPERS consortium appealed the district court's decision to conduct the auction for lead counsel — a decision that had cost the consortium $75 million. After holding that this member had standing to challenge the auction decision, the court of appeals turned to the merits of the challenge.]

The statutory section [of the PSLRA] most directly on point provides that "[t]he most adequate plaintiff shall, subject to the approval of the court, select and retain counsel to represent the class." This language makes two things clear. First, the lead plaintiff's right to select and retain counsel is not absolute — the court retains the power and the duty to supervise counsel selection and counsel retention. But second, and just as importantly, the power to "select and retain" lead counsel belongs, at least in the first instance, to the lead plaintiff, and the court's role is confined to deciding whether to "approv[e]" that choice. Because a court-ordered auction involves the court rather than the lead plaintiff choosing lead counsel and determining the financial terms of its retention, this latter determination strongly implies that an auction is not generally permissible in a Reform Act case, at least as a matter of first resort.

This conclusion gains support when we examine the overall structure of the PSLRA's lead plaintiff section. The Reform Act contains detailed procedures for choosing the lead plaintiff, indicating that Congress attached great importance to ensuring that the right person or group is selected. The only powers expressly given to the lead plaintiff, however, are to "select and retain" counsel. If those powers are seriously limited, it would seem odd for Congress to have established such a specific means for choosing the lead plaintiff. . . .

We respect the arguments advanced by Judge Shadur — a jurist of extraordinary distinction, who is one of the primary judicial advocates in favor of the auction method — as to why auctions are not inconsistent with the Reform Act, but we ultimately find them unpersuasive. Judge Shadur notes that the PSLRA provides that a movant's status as presumptive lead plaintiff may be overcome if it can be shown that the movant will not fairly and adequately represent the class, and observes that the statute makes the lead plaintiff's right to select and retain counsel "subject to the approval of the court." . . .

. . . Judge Shadur's view appears to be that any movant who is unwilling to be represented by the firm or firms that a court determines to be the lowest qualified bidder in a court-conducted auction has necessarily shown that it will not fairly and adequately represent the interests of the class. We disagree for two reasons. First, this approach is in considerable tension with the text of the PSLRA. As we explained above, the Reform Act makes clear that it is the lead plaintiff's job to "select and retain" lead counsel and it is the court's duty to decide whether to "approve" that choice. But under Judge Shadur's approach, a presumptive lead plaintiff's only option is to assent to the counsel and the fee terms that were chosen by the court via a court-ordered auction (because otherwise the movant will be disqualified from serving as lead plaintiff on the grounds that it will not fairly and adequately represent the interests of the class). Judge Shadur's reading of the statute in effect confers upon *the court* the right to "select and retain" counsel and limits the lead plaintiff to deciding whether to acquiesce in those choices, thus eliminating any discretion on the part of the lead plaintiff. We simply do not think that such a result is consistent with the statutory text.

Moreover, we do not agree that the fact that a presumptive lead plaintiff refuses to accede to the counsel or fee terms set via an auction demonstrates that it will not fairly and adequately represent the interests of the absent class members. . . . [I]f institutional investors are as good or better than courts at balancing quality and cost in selecting class counsel, then it follows that the fact that those investors may choose different lawyers and negotiate different fee arrangements than the court does not demonstrate that those investors will not fairly and adequately represent the interests of the class. We therefore respectfully disagree with Judge Shadur that the use of court-ordered auctions can be squared with the PSLRA in the ordinary case.

Instead, we think that the Reform Act evidences a strong presumption in favor of approving a properly-selected lead plaintiff's decisions as to counsel selection and counsel retention. When a properly-appointed lead plaintiff asks the court to approve its choice of lead counsel and of a retainer agreement, the question is not whether the court believes that the lead plaintiff could have made a better choice or gotten a better deal. Such a standard would eviscerate the Reform Act's underlying assumption that, at least in the typical case, a properly-selected lead plaintiff is likely to do as good or better job than the court at these tasks. Because of this, we think that the court's inquiry is appropriately limited to whether the lead plaintiff's selection and agreement with counsel are reasonable on their own terms.

In making this determination, courts should consider: (1) the quantum of legal experience and sophistication possessed by the lead plaintiff; (2) the manner in which the lead plaintiff chose what law firms to consider; (3) the process by which the lead plaintiff selected its final choice; (4) the qualifications and experience of counsel selected by the lead plaintiff; and (5) the evidence that the retainer agreement negotiated by the lead plaintiff was (or was not) the product of serious negotiations between the lead plaintiff and the prospective lead counsel.

We do not mean for this list to be exhaustive, or to intimate that district courts are required to give each of these factors equal weight in a particular case; at bottom, the ultimate inquiry is always whether the lead plaintiff's choices were the result of a good faith selection and negotiation process and were arrived at via meaningful arms-length bargaining. Whenever it is shown that they were not, it is the court's obligation to disapprove the lead plaintiff's choices.

Although we think, for reasons explained above, that an auction is impermissible in most Reform Act cases, we do not rule out the possibility that it could be validly used. If the court determines that the lead plaintiff's initial choice of counsel or negotiation of a retainer agreement is inadequate, it should clearly state why (for both the benefit of the lead plaintiff and for the record) and should direct the lead plaintiff to undertake an acceptable selection process.   If the lead plaintiff's response demonstrates that it is unwilling or unable to do so, then the court will, of necessity, be required to take a more active role.

At that point, a court will have several options. If a litigant were to have repeatedly undertaken a flawed process of selecting and retaining lead counsel, that may be enough to show that it will not fairly and adequately protect the interests of the class. In such a situation, the court would be justified in disqualifying that litigant from serving as lead plaintiff, selecting a new lead plaintiff, and directing that newly-appointed lead plaintiff to undertake an acceptable search.

On the other hand, it is possible that the court could conclude that, perhaps due to the nature of the case at hand, none of the possible lead plaintiffs is capable of fulfilling the model contemplated by the Reform Act, i.e., a sophisticated investor who has suffered sizeable losses and can be counted on to serve the interests of the class in an aggressive manner. In such a situation, it would be permissible for a court to conclude that its obligation to protect the interests of the plaintiff class makes it necessary for the court to assume direct control over counsel selection and counsel retention, and, were the court to so conclude, an auction would be one permissible means by which the court could select and retain counsel on behalf of the class. . . .

We now analyze whether, under these precepts, the District Court's decision to conduct an auction was justified. . . .

In its written opinion, the District Court gave several reasons for holding an auction. First, it . . . concluded that holding an auction would aid it in making this determination and in protecting the class's interests because it would simulate the market, thus providing a "benchmark of reasonableness." Second, the District Court stated that holding an auction would have the "salutary" effect of "remov[ing] any speculative doubt" about [Aboff's] pay-to-play allegations.

These reasons are not sufficient justification for holding an auction. The first (i.e., a generalized desire to hold down costs by "simulating" the market) would apply in every case, and thus cannot be enough to justify a procedure that we have concluded may only be used rarely. Further, there is no need to "simulate" the market in cases where a properly-selected lead plaintiff conducts a good-faith counsel selection process because in such cases — at least under the theory supporting the PSLRA — the fee agreed to by the lead plaintiff is the market fee. . . .

. . . [T]he District Court suggested that institutional investors may not do a good job of selecting lead counsel because "at times familiarity or a long time association between a client and a lawyer . . . may limit arms length bargaining." These "concerns" cannot justify the court's decision to hold an auction because there was simply no evidence of "familiarity or a long time association" between any member of the CalPERS Group and either of the firms that the Group proposed retaining, nor was there any evidence of or finding by the District Court that arms-length bargaining had not, in fact, taken place.

We are similarly unable to conclude that the auction was justified based on the District Court's statement . . . that "one can make the argument . . . that because of [their] economic power that at times [large investors] get a little complacent economically and therefore . . . they are not as cost effective as they should be." First, as a generic supposition, this intuition is directly at odds with the principles that animated the Reform Act. Second, the court never made findings that the CalPERS Group had been "complacent economically" or had demonstrated that it would not be "as cost effective as [it] should be." . . .

For the foregoing reasons, we hold that the District Court abused its discretion by conducting an auction because its decision to do so was founded upon an erroneous understanding of the legal standards undergirding the propriety of conducting an auction under the PSLRA. With regard to counsel selection, however, this error was harmless because the counsel selected via the auction process were the same as those whom the Lead Plaintiff sought to have appointed in the first place.

[The court of appeals remanded the case for further consideration of the award of attorneys' fees.]

Notes

1.   In *Richardson-Merrell*, the issue was whether a district's decision to disqualify a plaintiff's lawyer due to alleged improprieties was immediately appealable. The Supreme Court held that it was not. The excerpts from the concurrence by Justice Brennan and the dissent by Justice Stevens were made in the course of their opinions on that issue.

2.   The Supreme Court has never decided whether lower courts have the power to appoint lead counsel, liaison counsel, committees of counsel, or the like. As *Vincent* says, the earliest case suggesting such power was *MacAlister v. Guterma*, 263 F.2d 65 (2d Cir. 1958). In *MacAlister*, however, the court approved only the appointment of the weakest form of appointed counsel — a liaison counsel — and stressed that each party's lawyer was still free to present that party's case. The 1972 version of the *Manual* recommended that a court *not* appoint lead counsel, but allow the parties to do so; it also "encourage[d] the use of steering committees in appropriate cases." *See* MANUAL FOR COMPLEX LITIGATION § 1.92 (1972). *Vincent* was one of the first cases in which a court held that it had the power to appoint counsel over the objections of some affected parties. But *Vincent* was cautious in its way, tying the power to the existence of a common fund. Since *Vincent*, there has been a landslide victory for a more general power to appoint counsel. We are aware of no lower court that presently holds the contrary view. The *Manual, Fourth* reflects this consensus.

3. Claiming the power does not justify it. In a simple two-party car accident, a court probably could not reject the lawyer of the plaintiff's choosing and order a lawyer that the plaintiff has never met or heard of to represent him or her. What justifies a court's interference with a litigant's adversarial right to choose his or her own counsel in bigger cases?

In some cases, the power derives from a controlling text. For instance, Federal Rule 23(g)(2) requires the court to appoint class counsel according to certain criteria, and even gives the court power to choose the counsel that is "best able to represent the interests of the class" if more than one lawyer seeks appointment. As *Cendant* shows, some courts have read the Private Securities Litigation Reform Act to provide a comparable authority in securities class actions. Neither of these sources provides authority to override the parties' choice of counsel in non-class actions. *MacAlister* suggested that Rule 42(a), which authorizes federal courts in consolidated proceedings "to make such orders . . . as may tend to avoid unnecessary cost or delay," provides a source of authority. But few complex cases are consolidated for trial under Rule 42(a), and the generality of the quoted language is far from explicit textual authority.

In appointing a counsel structure for a group of litigants, courts have typically appealed to another of *MacAlister*'s suggested sources of power: a court's "inherent power" to control a case. The Fifth Circuit described the power to appoint counsel in these terms:

> A trial court has managerial power that has been described as "the power inherent in every court to control the disposition of the causes on its docket with economy of time and effort for itself, for counsel, and for litigants." Landis v. N. Am. Co., 299 U.S. 248, 254 (1936). . . . Managerial power is not merely desirable. It is a critical necessity. The demands upon the federal courts are at least heavy, at most crushing. Actions are ever more complex, the number of cases greater, and in the federal system we are legislatively given new areas of responsibility almost annually. . . . But court resources and capacities are finite. We face the hard necessity that, within proper limits, judges must be permitted to bring management power to bear upon massive and complex litigation to prevent it from monopolizing the services of the court to the exclusion of other litigants.

In re Air Crash Disaster at Fla. Everglades on Dec. 29, 1972, 549 F.2d 1006, 1012 (5th Cir. 1977).

Over the next several chapters, we will see courts resorting to their "inherent powers" to justify particular case-management practices. For now, are you persuaded that the inherent power to appoint counsel exists? In an adversarial system, isn't an appointment power the most drastic power that a court can wield, dwarfing all others? How can an individual meaningfully present his or her unique proofs and arguments when his case is only one among the hundreds for which the lawyer is responsible?

4. Whatever the answer to these questions, make no mistake that courts routinely appoint counsel for plaintiffs. As the *Manual, Fourth*

suggests, no magical formula determines which type of arrangement will work best in a given case. Often judges mix and match. For instance, a judge may appoint lead counsel for trial, but a committee of counsel for pretrial. She may divide the job of lead counsel among two or more "co-lead" counsel, and even appoint a non-lawyer with good organizational skills as liaison. Committee of counsel may be organized along procedural lines (e.g., a discovery team, a trial team, a settlement team), along substantive lines (e.g., one team working on causation, another on damages, another on liability), or along interest group lines (e.g., subclasses).

5. Although the appointment of lead counsel for plaintiffs is common, a judge rarely does more than appoint a liaison counsel to coordinate matters among defendants. *But see* Active Prod. Corp. v. A.H. Choitz & Co., 163 F.R.D. 274 (N.D. Ind. 1995) (appointing defense steering committee). Why the different treatment?

6. Most challenges to the appointment of lead counsel arise during arguments among law firms about which firm would make the best lead counsel, or, as in *Vincent*, during fee disputes in which the interested parties are lawyers, not clients. Only rarely is an appointment challenged because counsel is allegedly ignoring individual clients' interests, and even more rarely is such a challenge successful. *See, e.g.*, Koehler v. Brody, 483 F.3d 590 (8th Cir. 2007) (affirming dismissal of claims by a class representative against class counsel who supported an allegedly inadequate settlement); In re Ivan Boesky Sec. Litig., 948 F.2d 1358 (2d Cir. 1991) (rejecting class members' arguments that lead counsel improperly agreed to settle their claims and that the settlement was unfair); Farber v. Riker-Maxson Corp., 442 F.2d 457 (2d Cir. 1971) (rejecting argument that an order appointing lead counsel "den[ied] appellants an appropriate opportunity to participate in the litigation").

7. One of the problems associated with the appointment of counsel is the set of incentives that the appointment creates. As *Cendant* shows, successful lead counsel can expect significant compensation. This fee often exceeds the value of any individual's claims, and makes appointed counsel the largest stakeholder in the case. Is it realistic to believe that, under these circumstances, counsel will act only in the interests of their clients?

Courts have assayed different solutions to this problem, which is sometimes referred to as an "agency cost" (i.e., a cost of using agents whose own agendas result in imperfect protection of the principal's interests). One solution, which *Vincent* ignored but the *Manual, Fourth* demands, is to subject to critical evaluation any counsel structure on which the lawyers themselves have agreed. *See* John C. Coffee, Jr., *The Regulation of Entrepreneurial Litigation: Balancing Fairness and Efficiency in the Large Class Action*, 54 U. CHI. L. REV. 877, 907-08 (1987) (likening consensual counsel arrangements to political conventions in which access to work is traded for votes); In re Fine Paper Antitrust Litig., 98 F.R.D. 48, 71, 75 (E.D. Pa. 1983), *aff'd in part, rev'd in part, and remanded*, 751 F.2d 562 (3d Cir. 1984) (finding that the initial group of plaintiffs' lawyers had planned "the distribution of patronage," and that the committee structure "generate[d] wasted hours on useless tasks, propogate[d] duplication, and mask[ed] outright padding").

8. Auctioning the lead-counsel position is another way to control (albeit not eliminate) agency costs, and it had gained popularity before *Cendant*. As *Cendant* describes, some courts had been enthusiastic promoters of the auction process. The seminal case is *In re Oracle Securities Litigation*, 132 F.R.D. 538 (N.D. Cal. 1990).

Auctions raise numerous difficulties. For instance, they force parties to accept as their counsel lawyers with whom they had no prior contact. They can dramatically affect the market in legal services as firms jockey for plum appointments. Furthermore, as *Cendant* reflects, different bids often propose different fee structures, in which different litigation outcomes minimize or maximize attorneys' fees. When picking a bid, doesn't a judge inevitably have an incentive to make the case come out in a way that shows that the selected bid was best (although, as *Cendant* shows, this does not always happen)? Doesn't the auction process also provide winning counsel with a set of incentives that can shape the outcome of the case? Moreover, there are practical issues surrounding bidding. Keeping the bids sealed, so the other side cannot see them, condones ex parte communication with the judge, a clear adversarial no-no; disclosing bids provides the other side with a sense of their opponents' litigation strategy. *See* In re Cendant Corp., 260 F.2d 183 (3d Cir. 2001) (prohibiting sealed bids). *See generally* Jill E. Fisch, *Lawyers on the Auction Block: Evaluating the Selection of Class Counsel by Auction*, 102 COLUM. L. REV. 650 (2002) (discussing the difficulties with auctions and proposing an "empowered plaintiff" alternative).

Even though *Cendant* relied heavily on the language of the PSLRA to dismiss the routine use of class-counsel auctions, and therefore does not directly affect the use of auctions in non-PSLRA cases, *Cendant* has cooled off the trend toward auctions. Note the unusual dynamic in *Cendant*. The lead counsel is arguing in favor of an auction that, at the time of bidding, it had opposed. Opposing the auction is one of the entities composing the consortium that was the lead counsel's client, and on whose behalf counsel had opposed the auction. The reason for the lead counsel's about-face is that the lowest bidder's fee structure, which counsel had reluctantly agreed to match, actually yielded $75 million more in fees. On these facts, isn't the outcome in *Cendant* foreordained? *Cendant* seems to be a poster child for the problem of having courts rather than clients negotiate fee structures.

On the other hand, as a result of the remand and subsequent negotiations between CalPERS and its lead counsel, counsel agreed to limit its fee request to $55 million, right in line with Aboff's supposedly unrealistic 1-2% fee. The district court approved this award. In re Cendant Corp. Litig., 243 F. Supp. 2d 166 (D.N.J. 2003). Had the auction not taken place and the issue not been appealed, lead counsel would have walked off with $187 million in fees — $132 million more than it ultimately received.

9. The idea of auctioning the lead-counsel position is not half as radical as the auction proposal of Professors Macey and Miller. Their argument is that, in large-scale, small-claim litigation, no plaintiff has

much incentive to monitor the attorney's work. They propose auctioning off large-scale, small-claim cases to the highest bidder. The proceeds from the auction would be distributed among the claimants, who assign their claims to the winning bidder. The bidder can then press the case against the defendant. Any amounts by the winning bidder recovered in excess of the bid belong to the bidder as a profit; if the amount recovered is less than the bid, the bidder suffers a loss. (The defendant can also bid on the claims; if its bid is highest, then no litigation ensues.) The authors ague that this proposal places the litigation in the hands of someone with a significant interest in monitoring the work of the attorneys, ensures that plaintiffs will recover the market value of their claims, and increases the enforcement of small-claim cases. Although the authors do not mention it, this approach would remove the judge from the process of appointing counsel; the winning bidder can choose counsel for himself or herself. Jonathon R. Macey & Geoffrey P. Miller, *The Plaintiffs' Attorney's Role in Class Action and Derivative Litigation: Economic Analysis and Recommendations for Change*, 58 U. CHI. L. REV. 1 (1991).

10. To a large extent, the problem of agency costs is a consequence of the broad rules of aggregation that we studied in the first part of the book. Issues of aggregating a case and litigating it are connected, and to some degree are inversely proportional. Solving one problem can cause others.

11. Professor Chayes believed the defining features of public-law litigation to be an amorphous party structure and the broad participation of various interests. *See supra* p. 39. Lead counsel and committee arrangements reduce the amorphousness of that structure and aggregate interests in a way that inevitably reduces the ability of individual litigants to participate fully. Professor Fuller predicted this result when polycentric disputes are "shoe-horned" into the form of adjudication: Courts will be forced to ignore interests in an attempt to create a limited controversy capable of adjudication. *See supra* pp. 38-39. Does the reality of lead counsel and committees of counsel vindicate Professor Fuller? Is the use of lead counsel consistent with a truly public-law vision of litigation?

2. Ethical Responsibilities of Selected Counsel

Appointing a lawyer to represent a group of litigants creates ethical issues. In the adversarial model, the lawyer represents the client zealously within the bounds of the law. A corollary of this expectation is that the lawyer must have no conflicts of interest that might impinge on this loyalty to the client's interests. At the same time, as an officer of the court, the lawyer is expected to have an equal duty to ensure that justice is done.

For two reasons, meeting these dual expectations are especially difficult in large-scale litigation. The first involves representing multiple clients. Adversarial theory generally prefers that lawyers represent only one client. Multiple representations threaten to divide the attorney's loyalty, and raise the danger that the lawyer will disclose information obtained from one client to advance the interests of the second client. Moreover, aggregated groups of clients often have a welter of interests — a fact that makes it difficult for the lawyer to represent each client in the group with zeal.

Second, lead counsel in large cases often have a financial stake that far exceeds that of any individual client. The dichotomy between the client's and the lawyer's financial interests inheres even in ordinary litigation, but the size of the lawyer's stake (both in absolute dollars and in relation to that of any client's stake) creates peculiar temptations for the lawyers in large aggregated proceedings.

The following cases and notes explore some of these ethical concerns.

IN RE "AGENT ORANGE" PRODUCT LIABILITY LITIGATION

800 F.2d 14 (2d Cir. 1986)

■ KEARSE, Circuit Judge.

Stephen J. Schlegel, Esq., a member of the Plaintiffs' Management Committee ("PMC") in the "Agent Orange" product liability litigation, moved in this Court for an order disqualifying the law firm of Ashcraft & Gerel ("Ashcraft") and the Law Offices of Benton Musslewhite ("Musslewhite"), Inc., from representing in the captioned appeals certain class members and other plaintiffs who challenge the settlement of the litigation approved by the district court. Schlegel contends principally that Ashcraft and Musslewhite, as a result of their prior representation of parties supporting the settlement, have conflicts of interest requiring their disqualification as appellate counsel. . . .

I. BACKGROUND

[The *Agent Orange* lawsuits began in 1978, when veterans of the Vietnam War and their families brought personal-injury suits against chemical companies that had manufactured Agent Orange and other herbicides used by the military in the Vietnam War. The Judicial Panel on Multidistrict Litigation transferred the cases to the Eastern District of New York. The district court certified a Rule 23(b)(3) class consisting of members of the armed forces of United States, New Zealand, and Australia, and their spouses, parents, and children who were directly or derivatively injured. The class contained approximately 2.4 million members.]

A. *Representation of Class Plaintiffs*

. . .

Schlegel became counsel to various plaintiffs in the litigation as early as November 1978. He has been designated as one of plaintiffs' counsel of record throughout the Agent Orange litigation. Musslewhite became involved as plaintiffs' counsel in Agent Orange litigation as early as January 1979. He represents some 1,500 Vietnam veterans as individual clients. Ashcraft has represented plaintiffs in Agent Orange litigation on an active basis since early 1980. It represents more than 2,000 plaintiff class members, as well as 386 individuals who originally opted out of the class; 60 of those opt-outs later rejoined the class.

In 1980, after tentatively granting the class certification, the district court appointed Yannacone & Associates ("Yannacone") . . . as lead counsel to the class. Thereafter, Ashcraft acted as class action counsel under an agreement with Yannacone. At the request of or by agreement with Yannacone in early 1983, Schlegel, Musslewhite, and Ashcraft became members of the PMC. All functioned for a time thereafter as class counsel. In addition, Schlegel and Musslewhite were designated by the court as lead counsel.

Ashcraft was never appointed lead counsel, but as a member of the PMC and as class action counsel, it undertook a number of tasks on behalf of the class, including attending depositions, reviewing documents obtained through discovery, and writing, filing, and opposing motions in the district court. During Musslewhite's tenure as a member of the PMC, he was listed as counsel of record in numerous filings with the district court and joined in motions concerning class certification, proposed forms of notice to class members, and other substantive issues in the litigation.

[In September 1983, Yannacone withdrew as lead counsel. Ashcraft withdrew from the PMC at the same time. The district court ordered that the PMC, which consisted of Schlegel, Musslewhite, and another law firm, would serve as lead counsel for the class.]

B. *The Settlement Agreement, the Pending Appeals, and the Present Disqualification Motion*

Prior to May 7, 1984, with the class actions scheduled to go to trial on May 7, the parties negotiated a settlement of the class actions. The agreement called for the defendant chemical companies to pay a total of $180 million in settlement to the members of the plaintiff classes.

As a member of the PMC, Musslewhite had participated in the negotiations that led to the settlement agreement; he voted in favor of that agreement and spoke in support of it in the fairness hearings conducted by the district court in August 1984. Thereafter, however, Musslewhite became disenchanted with the proposed settlement agreement, and in January 1985, he withdrew from the PMC.

In January, 1985, the district court found the settlement to be fair, reasonable, and adequate under the circumstances. . . .

Following the entry of final judgments approving the settlement, Ashcraft and Musslewhite, on behalf of the thousands of plaintiffs they represent, filed appeals contending that the settlement should be set aside. Ashcraft, on behalf of its clients and on behalf of 21 law firms around the country claiming to represent some 3,000 additional class members, filed a brief challenging the fairness, reasonableness, and adequacy of the settlement and contending, in addition, that the district court lacked subject matter jurisdiction of the litigation and had denied individual claimants due process in certifying the class. . . .

Schlegel, on behalf of the PMC as it is presently constituted, moved to disqualify Ashcraft and Musslewhite from representing parties on the pending appeals, principally on the grounds that the combination of (1) Ashcraft's representation of both class members and individuals who chose to opt out of the class, (2) Musslewhite's participation in the negotiation of the proposed settlement on behalf of the class, and (3) the prior roles of Ashcraft and Musslewhite as members of the PMC and class counsel, have given them "such a direct conflict of interest as to create a clear impropriety in violation of controlling standards of professional conduct." For the reasons below, we have concluded that the motion should be denied.

II. DISCUSSION

As a matter of professional responsibility, an attorney owes a duty of loyalty to his client. This duty encompasses an obligation to defer to the client's wishes on major litigation decisions, not to divulge confidential communications from the client, and not to accept representation of a person whose interests are opposed to those of the client. E.g., A.B.A. Code of Prof'l Responsibility EC 7-1, 4-1, and 5-2.

These obligations do not necessarily end when the attorney-client relationship ends. Thus, we have ordered disqualification of a party's attorney where, as a result of his prior representation of another client, "the attorney is at least potentially in a position to use privileged information concerning the other side . . . thus giving his present client an unfair advantage." Bd. of Educ. v. Nyquist, 590 F.2d 1241, 1246 (2d Cir. 1979); see, e.g., In re Corn Derivatives Antitrust Litig., 748 F.2d 157, 161 (3d Cir. 1984) ("Corn Derivatives") ("In litigation, an attorney may not abandon his client and take an adverse position in the same case. This is not merely a matter of revealing or using the client's confidences and secrets, but of a duty of continuing loyalty to the client.").

Applying these traditional principles in non-class-action litigation, we have held that, in order to support a motion for disqualification, "the former client [need] show no more than that the matters embraced within the pending suit wherein his former attorney appears . . . are substantially related to the matters or cause of action where the attorney previously represented him, the former client." Although disqualification has the immediate adverse effect on the present client of depriving him of the attorney of his choice, removal of the attorney in such circumstances may be "necessary to preserve the integrity of the adversary process." Board of Education v. Nyquist, 590 F.2d at 1246.

Class action litigation presents additional problems that must be considered in determining whether or not to disqualify an attorney who has represented the class and who seeks to represent thereafter only a portion of the class. These problems are created by, *inter alia*, the facts that there are, by definition, numerous class members and that there is often no clear allocation of the decision-making responsibility between the attorney and his clients. Further, though there will be common questions affecting the claims of the class members, it is not unusual for their interests, especially at the relief stage, to diverge. Such a divergence presents special problems because the class attorney's duty does not run just to the plaintiffs named in the caption of the case; it runs to all of the members of the class. . . .

Automatic application of the traditional principles governing disqualification of attorneys on grounds of conflict of interest would seemingly dictate that whenever a rift arises in the class, with one branch favoring a settlement or a course of action that another branch resists, the attorney who has represented the class should withdraw entirely and take no position. Were he to take a position, either favoring or opposing the proposed course of action, he would be opposing the interests of some of his former clients in the very matter in which he has represented them.

Nonetheless, as Judge Adams noted in his concurring opinion in *Corn Derivatives*, although automatic disqualification might "promote the salutary ends of confidentiality and loyalty, it would have a serious adverse effect on class actions." When many individuals have modest claims against a single entity or group of entities, the class action may be the only practical means of vindicating their rights, since otherwise the expenses of litigation could exceed the value of the claim. . . . And when an action has continued over the course of many years, the prospect of having those most familiar with its course and status be automatically disqualified whenever class members have conflicting interests would substantially diminish the efficacy of class actions as a method of dispute resolution. This is so both because the quality of the information available to the court would likely be impaired and because even if a class member were familiar with all the prior proceedings, the amount of his stake in the litigation might well make it unattractive for him to participate actively, either on his own or through new counsel.

Our system of justice demands that the interests of all concerned be accommodated as fairly as possible, and this accommodation must include the preservation of the class action form of litigation without a wasteful multiplication of its cost. In order to proceed efficiently and fairly and to protect the interests of all members of the class, the court needs, insofar as is practicable, the benefit of the participation of attorneys who are familiar with the litigation. This need has been accommodated in many cases in which a technical conflict may exist, for the attorney for the class is normally allowed to oppose the contentions of class members who have appeared in court in opposition to a proposed settlement of the class action, although technically the Code of Professional Responsibility would seem to prohibit his doing so. In this case, for example, Schlegel, though moving to disqualify Ashcraft and Musselwhite for representing objectors in opposition to class members they formerly represented, himself represented as class counsel many of the objectors he now opposes.

Thus, we conclude that the traditional rules that have been developed in the course of attorneys' representation of the interests of clients outside of the class action context should not be mechanically applied to the problems that arise in the settlement of class action litigation. A motion to disqualify an attorney who has represented the entire class and who has thereafter been retained by a faction of the class to represent its interests in opposition to a proposed settlement of the action cannot be automatically granted. Rather, there must be a balancing of the interests of the various groups of class members and of the interest of the public and the court in achieving a just and expeditious resolution of the dispute.

Relevant considerations in determining whether the moving party has shown sufficient ground for disqualification of prior class counsel include "the amount and nature of the information that has been proffered to the attorney, its availability elsewhere, its importance to the question at issue, such as settlement, as well as actual prejudice that may flow from that information." The court must consider as well the costs to the class members of requiring that they obtain new counsel, taking into account such factors as the nature and value of the claim they are presenting, the ease with which they could obtain new counsel, the factual and legal complexity of the litigation, and the time that would be needed for new counsel to familiarize himself with all that has gone before.

In the present litigation, we conclude that the weighing of the various interests requires that the motion to disqualify Ashcraft and Musslewhite be denied. First, we note that Schlegel in his moving papers has failed to allege any actual prejudice that would result if Ashcraft and Musslewhite were not disqualified. He has not indicated that client confidences were received by Ashcraft or Musslewhite from pro-settlement members of the class. Nor, if such confidences be assumed, has he indicated how or even whether such confidences would be violated by these firms' continued participation in the appeals. Schlegel's general allegations of conflict of interest are insufficient to warrant a finding of prejudice.

Several factors weigh against disqualification here.... If the thousands of objectors were now deprived of the services of Ashcraft and Musslewhite, all of the choices confronting the court would be unattractive. . . . In the context of the present motion, which was made to this Court in December 1985 in connection with appeals to be argued in April 1986, we doubt that new counsel could have been found who would have been willing and able to assimilate these documents in such a short period. Alternatively the court could allow the objectors time for their new attorneys to familiarize themselves with the proceedings and the documents. This, of course, would delay for the other thousands of class members who favor the settlement the receipt of compensation they deem adequate, or at least acceptable, for their injuries.

Finally, we note that the size of the proposed settlement in light of the large number of class members could itself constrain the ability or incentive of objecting class members to obtain new counsel who would fully familiarize themselves with the pertinent facts of the litigation. The settlement distribution plan approved by the district court provided for a maximum payment of $12,800 to any one class member, with an average payment of approximately $4,200. Musslewhite's estimate as to individual recovery amounts is even lower, for he contends that there are some 243,000 claimants. If he is correct, the arithmetical mean share of the $180 million settlement fund, plus interest, would amount to approximately $850.

In all the circumstances, we conclude that disqualification of Ashcraft and Musslewhite is not "necessary to preserve the integrity of the adversary process." *Board of Education v. Nyquist*, 590 F.2d at 1246.

CONCLUSION

The motion for disqualification of counsel is denied.

GEORGINE V. AMCHEM PRODUCTS, INC.

157 F.R.D. 246 (E.D. Pa. 1994), *rev'd on other grounds*, 83 F.3d 610 (3d Cir. 1996), *aff'd* sub nom. Amchem Prods., Inc. v. Windsor, 521 U.S. 591 (1997) [*supra* p. 493]

■   REED, District Judge.

[After the Judicial Panel on Multidistrict Litigation consolidated the federal asbestos litigation (*see supra* p. 144), a group of twenty asbestos defendants, known as the "CCR," entered into settlement discussions with three plaintiffs' lawyers, Messrs. Locks, Motley, and Rice. All three lawyers were on the steering committee for the federal MDL, and Mr. Rice was a partner of Mr. Motley. Among them, these lawyers represented about 14,000 asbestos claimants that had filed cases against the CCR. The CCR had adopted a policy of refusing to settle any cases unless it achieved a global settlement of present *and* future cases.

[The discussions between the CCR and the three lawyers resulted in a two-prong settlement. First, the CCR agreed to settle the plaintiffs' lawyers' already filed cases, known as the "inventory cases." Next, it agreed to settle on a classwide basis the claims of asbestos victims who had not yet filed suit. A settlement class action was then filed by Messers. Locks, Motley, and Rice, who sought to be appointed as class counsel. This class settlement of "future plaintiffs" was ultimately overturned in *Amchem Products, Inc. v. Windsor*, 521 U.S. 591 (1997) (*supra* p. 493).

[The settlements contained two features of present significance. First, the cases of the inventory plaintiffs were settled on different terms than those of the future plaintiffs. The 14,000 inventory claimants received $215 million, or an average of $15,350 in compensation. On these claims, the attorneys received the contingency fee (presumably one-third) that they negotiated with their clients. On the class claims, the settlement provided an estimated $1.3 billion in benefits over its first ten years; the class was estimated to contain somewhere between 100,000 and 2,000,000 members. At the lower range of expected claims, the benefits per class member averaged $13,000; and this amount did not increase over time to account for inflation.   One exhibit at trial suggested that the inventory plaintiffs received between 54% and 72% more in compensation than class members were scheduled to receive.   Moreover, some of the inventory claimants received payments for injuries for which class members could not receive compensation.   The CCR also settled some of the plaintiffs' lawyers' own unfiled cases on the same terms as the inventory cases, even though those claimants would have received a lower payment or no payment had they been members of the class.   Although no attorneys' fees were ultimately awarded, the plaintiffs' lawyers would almost certainly have received less than a one-third contingency fee for their work in representing the class.

[Second, the settlement contained a provision that, "in the future, [Mr. Locks] will not handle or process claims against the CCR defendants unless they meet certain mutually agreeable disease criteria." A comparable condition bound Messrs. Motley and Rice.   The disease criteria essentially mirrored the criteria that the class settlement used to determine eligibility for settlement.   The lawyers later testified, and the Court found as true, that this provision meant only that the lawyers would not *recommend* to future clients that the clients sue the CCR if they did not met the disease criteria, but that the lawyers were free to sue the CCR if the client disregarded this advice.

[Against this backdrop the district court considered whether to approve the class settlement.   Among the issues it needed to address was whether the terms of Rule 23 had been met, which in turn required it to inquire into the adequacy of class counsel.]

III. ADEQUACY OF COUNSEL

A. *Legal Standard*

. . .

As many courts have recognized in a variety of different contexts, however, "courts cannot mechanically transpose to class actions the rules developed in the traditional lawyer-client setting context . . . [.]" In re Corn Derivatives Antitrust Litig., 748 F.2d 157, 163 (3d Cir. 1984) (Adams, J. concurring) . . . ; In re Agent Orange Prod. Liab. Litig., 800 F.2d 14, 18 (2d Cir. 1986).

Thus, it is appropriate for this Court to consider the Model Rules in determining the adequacy of representation, but ultimately it is this Court's task to determine whether, in the context of this litigation, Class Counsel were vigorous and diligent in negotiating the *Georgine* Stipulation, unburdened by any conflicts of interest or collusion.

B. *Conflict of Interest*

In this case, Objectors contend that Class Counsel had an impermissible conflict of interest, in violation of Model Rule 1.7(b), which adversely affected the *Georgine* settlement. Model Rule 1.7(b) provides:

> A lawyer shall not represent a client if the representation of that client may be materially limited by the lawyer's responsibilities to another client or to a third person, or by the lawyer's own interests, unless:
>
> (1) the lawyer reasonably believes the representation will not be adversely affected; and
>
> (2) the client consents after consultation. When representation of multiple clients in a single matter is undertaken, the consultation shall include explanation of the implications of the common representation and the advantages and risks involved.

Model Rule 1.7(b) proscribes any concurrent representation where that representation "may be materially limited by an" ongoing representation. As set forth in the comments to the Model Rule:

> A possible conflict does not itself preclude the representation. The critical questions are the likelihood that a conflict will eventuate and, if it does, whether it will materially interfere with the lawyer's independent professional judgment in considering alternatives or foreclose courses of action that reasonably should be pursued on behalf of the client. Consideration should be given to whether the client wishes to accommodate the other interest involved. . . .

At the time that Class Counsel negotiated what became the *Georgine* settlement, there was no attorney-client relationship between Class Counsel and the unformed *Georgine* class. Class Counsel nevertheless had a fiduciary responsibility to this putative class, that is, a duty of loyalty and a duty of due care. Thus, whether or not Model Rule 1.7(b) technically applies to this Court's determination, this Court concludes that the general principles of loyalty and due care are applicable here.

. . . Class Counsel's representation of the *Georgine* class was not materially limited by their representation of present clients with pending claims against the CCR defendants. Thus, the concurrent representation of present claimants, while negotiating the *Georgine* settlement, ultimately resulting in settlement terms for present clients that differed from the terms of *Georgine*, did not create an impermissible conflict of interest under Model Rule 1.7(b), or otherwise, and Class Counsel were not burdened with any such conflict throughout the negotiation of the *Georgine* settlement. . . .

. . . Class Counsel did not have an inherent conflict of interest in seeking to negotiate a futures settlement while concurrently settling their present inventory of cases with CCR provided they, as experienced asbestos litigators, reasonably believed the settlements were fair, reasonable and in the best interests of both the putative class and their present clients. This Court concludes that Class Counsel did indeed make these reasoned judgments and reasonably decided in favor of settling.

Class Counsel were not required to withdraw from the representation of their current clients in order to undertake the *Georgine* negotiations, as suggested by [one expert]. Such a step was not only not feasible, but would have prejudiced the representation of the present clients. Moreover, it was the very fact that Class Counsel represented such a substantial number of present clients, as leaders of the asbestos bar, that made them credible and appropriate counsel to negotiate on behalf of an inchoate futures class.

The negotiations of the *Georgine* settlement and the present inventory settlements were both the product of arm's length, good faith bargaining. In hindsight, those not participating in the negotiation process can always criticize specific settlement terms or assert that other terms should have been included in the settlement. The fact, however, that a settlement did not achieve all that others may have hoped for does not support the conclusion that the lawyers were burdened by an impermissible conflict of interest in negotiating that settlement. . . .

The fact that the inventory settlements included terms that differed from the terms of the *Georgine* settlement also does not reveal an impermissible conflict of interest. Present clients in the tort system are not identically situated to future claimants. They already have engaged a lawyer, they already have made or committed to expenditures, have a place in the trial queue and have expectations of a certain course of proceedings. The relevant question is not whether the terms of the *Georgine* settlement are identical to the terms of settlements in the past, but whether, given all the circumstances, the terms of *Georgine* are fair and reasonable. . . .

. . . Given the history of the asbestos litigation and the prior settlement efforts, there was nothing . . . that created a conflict of interest here. Mr. Motley and Mr. Locks were the Co-chairs of the Plaintiffs' Steering Committee in the MDL. All three Class Counsel were unquestionably experienced, highly respected leaders of the plaintiffs' asbestos bar. . . . If CCR wanted to succeed in reaching a global settlement that a Court would approve, they had no choice but to hope to negotiate with such counsel. . . .

C. *The Futures Provisions in the Inventory Settlements*

Model Rule 5.6(b) provides:

A lawyer shall not participate in offering or making:

. . .

   (b) an agreement in which a restriction on the lawyer's right to practice is part of the settlement of a controversy between private parties.

Objectors contend that the futures provisions in the inventory settlement agreements violate this Model Rule and that this violation is evidence that Class Counsel had an impermissible conflict of interest.

. . . [C]ounsel intended to act ethically and that these agreements do not violate Model Rule 5.6(b) in that they do not factually create a binding obligation on the part of Class Counsel not to represent clients who may wish to sue CCR but who did not yet meet the *Georgine* medical criteria. Rather, the provisions represent a good faith commitment on the part of Class Counsel to recommend the *Georgine* medical criteria to their clients while retaining their independence to conclude otherwise in an appropriate case.

This Court need not decide, however, whether or not a state bar disciplinary board would conclude that these provisions technically violated Rule 5.6, since that issue is not before this Court in determining the adequacy of counsel.

What is significant for this proceeding is that the futures provisions did not have any adverse or improper impact on the *Georgine* class. . . . [T]his Court concludes that the futures provisions did not restrict Class Counsel's negotiation of the *Georgine* Stipulation, they were superseded by subsequent provisions which did not restrict Class Counsel in their practice of law in any way, and they did not create an impermissible conflict of interest for Class Counsel.

D. *Collusion*

Objectors here contend . . . that the *Georgine* settlement was the product of collusion. [The plaintiffs' experts] testified to the contrary.

Collusion is defined as follows:

An agreement between two or more persons to defraud a person of his rights by the forms of law, or to obtain an object forbidden by law. It implies the existence of fraud of some kind, the employment of fraudulent means, or of lawful means for the accomplishment of an unlawful purpose. A secret combination, conspiracy or concert of action between two or more persons for fraudulent or deceitful purpose.

Thus, in order for this Court to conclude that the *Georgine* settlement was the product of collusion, it would have to find that Class Counsel and the CCR defendants "sought to accomplish an improper purpose, perpetrated a fraud," and acted "secretively." . . .

. . . [T]his Court concludes that the *Georgine* settlement was not the product of collusion. Class Counsel did not receive a premium in settling their inventory cases, nor did they "sell out" the *Georgine* class. Also, there is no evidence that Class Counsel or CCR attempted to keep the fact of their negotiations secret. The terms of the *Georgine* settlement, including the definition of the class, compensation ranges, medical criteria, case flow provisions, and eligibility criteria reflect neither "improper" nor "fraudulent" conduct on behalf of Class Counsel or CCR.

Further, the Court concludes that the fact that the lawsuit and settlement were filed simultaneously, or the fact that defendant CCR members were searching for a global solution to the asbestos litigation, including the settlement of present cases if a solution could be found for the future, does not support the conclusion that the *Georgine* settlement was the product of collusion. . . .

[The Court also found that the remaining criteria for class certification were satisfied, and that the settlement was fair, reasonable, and adequate.]

JACK B. WEINSTEIN, INDIVIDUAL JUSTICE IN MASS TORT LITIGATION

44, 46-47, 87-88 (1995)

. . . "[M]uch of the intellectual effort in the field of legal ethics during the past quarter century has been an attempt to reevaluate the rules that emerged during the 'golden age' of the solo practitioner and the small firm." Yet, the current American Law Institute project on Restatement of the Law Governing Lawyers ignores mass torts and largely restates the old models of the one-lawyer, one-client relationship and the two-litigant case.

My own experiences on the bench have led me to conclude that we need to . . . provide more realistic guidance to today's lawyers and judges. . . .

Because of the political, sociological, economic, and technological implications of many mass tort cases, we must consider not only the individual litigant and lawyer, but entire communities. We assume, properly I believe, that dignity is enhanced by individual control of litigation for each person's benefit. . . . But just as individualism run riot can be damaging in social matters, so too may it need checking in mass litigations. . . .

Once we recognize that large-scale representation in mass tort cases is both inevitable and desirable and accept the view that this form of representation makes the traditional one-on-one relationship between lawyer and client impracticable, we cannot avoid the need for a new formulation of the lawyer's ethical duty. Without such a new ethic, the lawyer will be too likely to be guided by his or her own interests where it becomes difficult to discern or follow the interests of the many clients.

. . . If the lawyer in the mass tort case understands his or her duty as running in part to the community to which clients belong, or the communities which may be affected by the result, individual needs may be better served. Such a communitarian ethic requires the lawyer to consider more than the optimal dollar recovery for the group. The lawyer must consider the impact of the benefit and harm on the community as a whole, in both the short and the long run. The lawyer should attempt to communicate with the communities as a whole to learn their needs and desires. The lawyer should understand that the significance of the case to a community will remain long after the lawyer has left the scene. . . .

These suggestions are tentative at best. Many questions are raised. Is it possible to regulate such a communitarian ethic or would be have to rely on lawyers to listen to the better angels of their nature? Is such an understanding of the lawyer's role incompatible with an adversarial system of dispute resolution? Would we be better off with a system that relies on lawyers — somewhat moderated by judges — to represent the needs of the community? Or are we better off with a system constructed primarily on lawyer's and client's self-interest?

Notes

1. In state courts, the code of ethics promulgated by the state's Supreme Court or bar association applies. *See, e.g.*, In re Complex Asbestos Litig., 283 Cal.Rptr. 732 (1991). In federal court, the ethical standards are a matter of federal law. *See, e.g.*, In re Am. Airlines, Inc., 972 F.2d 605 (5th Cir. 1992); MANUAL FOR COMPLEX LITIGATION, FOURTH § 10.23 n.70 (2004). Federal courts usually adopt the code of ethics used in state court, *see, e.g.*, In re Congoleum Corp., 426 F.3d 675 (3d Cir. 2005), although some courts promulgate their own standards, *see, e.g.*, Dondi Props. Corp. v. Commerce Sav. & Loan Ass'n, 121 F.R.D. 284 (N.D. Tex. 1988). *See also* In re Zyprexa Prods. Liab. Litig., 424 F. Supp. 2d 488, 492 (E.D.N.Y. 2006) ("The judiciary has well-established authority to exercise ethical supervision of the bar in both individual and mass actions," including the authority to review contingency-fee agreements).

2. In *Georgine*, the Third Circuit and the Supreme Court ultimately sidestepped the issue of counsel's ethical obligations by holding that the conflicts of interest among members of the class barred certification under Rule 23(a)(4) and that the class did not meet the terms of Rule 23(b)(3).

3. Many conflict-of-interest issues arise because of the structure of modern law firms. For instance, a partner in one office of a multi-branch firm might represent one client, and a partner in another branch might represent another client whose interests conflict with those of the first client. The risk of conflicts increases when firms merge, or when a partner, associate, paralegal, or secretary moves firms. Traditional rules of ethics view the entire firm, and all of the lawyers and staff within it, as a monolithic entity — one big "lawyer" that must never represent conflicting interests. *See* Fund of Funds, Ltd. v. Arthur Andersen & Co., 567 F.2d 225 (2d Cir. 1977) (conflict-of-interest analysis applied to local counsel associated with conflicted law firm); Lamb v. Pralex Corp., 333 F. Supp. 2d 361 (D. V.I. 2004) (conflict-of-interest rules apply when another firm hired a paralegal exposed to confidential information); Kapco Mfg. Co. v. C & D Enters., Inc., 637 F. Supp. 1231 (N.D. Ill. 1985) (same for office manager).

4. Between them, *Agent Orange* and *Georgine* present three of the most common fact patterns in cases concerning the ethical responsibilities of appointed counsel. Most claims of ethical impropriety involve either: (1) the simultaneous representation of inconsistent interests (as in *Georgine*), (2) a prior representation that compromises the lawyer's ability to be a vigorous advocate for present clients (as in *Agent Orange*), or (3) a conflict of interest between the represented group and the lawyer (as in *Georgine*).

Throughout this Note, the word "lawyer" refers to the entire firm — partners, associates, paralegals, and support staff.

(a) *Conflicts involving ongoing simultaneous representations.* The first, and usually simplest, conflict-of-interest scenario involves a lawyer who is presently representing two clients with interests that are possibly inconsistent. This situation raises two concerns. One is the fear that a lawyer will use information gained in the course of one (or both) of the representations to the disadvantage of the disclosing client, thus destroying a client's trust in the confidentiality of the communications with the lawyer. The other concern is the division of the lawyer's loyalty between two clients. The adversarial system, of course, is premised on both strict preservation of confidentiality and undivided loyalty.

One ethical rule is easy: A lawyer cannot represent two clients in a single lawsuit if the clients have adverse positions. A more difficult situation occurs when, on behalf of one client, a lawyer sues a second client whom the lawyer is representing on an unrelated matter. In this situation, simultaneous representation is "prima facie improper." *See* Cinema 5, Ltd. v. Cinerama, Inc., 528 F.2d 1384, 1387 (2d Cir. 1976); Int'l Bus. Machs., Inc. v. Levin, 579 F.2d 271 (3d Cir. 1978); Universal City Studios, Inc. v. Reimerdes, 98 F. Supp. 2d 449 (S.D.N.Y 2000). The lawyer can rebut the prima facie case by showing that the parties consented to or waived the conflict, or by showing the lack of "a significant risk of trial taint." Glueck v. Johnathan Logan, Inc., 653 F.2d 746, 748 (2d Cir. 1981).

A third type of conflict occurs when, on behalf of one client, a lawyer sues a party that belongs to a group or an association that is the lawyer's client. *See, e.g.,* Westinghouse Elec. Corp. v. Kerr-McGee Corp., 580 F.2d 1311 (7th Cir. 1978). Here a "substantial relationship" test has been employed: The court must disqualify the lawyer if "the subject matter of a suit is sufficiently related to the scope of the matters on which a firm represents an association as to create a realistic risk either that the plaintiff will not be represented with vigor or that unfair advantage will be taken of the defendant" that is a member of the association. *Glueck*, 653 F.2d at 749.

A fourth type of conflict arises when one lawyer represents a group of clients. Perfect alliance of interests within a group is the exception, not the rule. One client might prefer to settle, another to litigate; one might prefer more cash, another an injunction with less cash. In these situations, a lawyer cannot fully represent each client's interest. How much divergence from the adversarial ideal of fidelity to each client should we tolerate? One alternative is to say that the lawyer owes the usual duties of loyalty and confidentiality to the "client," but to redefine the "client" to be the group rather than any individual in the group. *See* David L. Shapiro, *Class Actions: The Class as Party and Client* 73 NOTRE DAME L. REV. 913 (1998) (advocating a model of "class as client"). Judge Weinstein's alternative is to make the "common good of all" the "client." Don't these alternatives allow the lawyer to do whatever he or she pleases? Perhaps not, if the judge also has responsibility for monitoring the lawyer's work. But doesn't that solution place the judge in the untenable position of being both a fiduciary for the group and the neutral adjudicator of its claims?

(b) *Conflicts between past and present representations.* A second conflict of interest occurs when a present representation is inconsistent with a prior representation. In this situation, the concern for disclosure of the former client's confidences remains alive; the concern for undivided loyalty, however, is less prominent. Because the policy concerns are less acute, courts have sometimes taken a more flexible approach to the question of sequential representation of conflicting interests.

As *Agent Orange* holds, the usual approach is to use the "substantial relationship" test. The meaning of "substantial relationship," however, varies somewhat from its meaning in *Glueck.* Because the primary concern is that the lawyer will betray confidences obtained from the previous client, some courts have held that the relationship is "substantial" only when the information developed in the prior representation might be useful in the present case. *See* Bennett Silvershein Assocs. v. Furman, 776 F. Supp. 800, 804 (S.D.N.Y. 1991) (collecting cases); *but see* Gov't of India v. Cook Indus., Inc., 569 F.2d 737, 740 (2d Cir. 1978) (substantial relationship exists only if relationship between two representations is "patently clear," or actions are "identical" or "essentially the same"). *Cf.* In re Fine Paper Antitrust Litig., 617 F.2d 22 (3d Cir. 1980) (counsel can sue former client who was an unnamed member of a class action with whom counsel had no contact).

Once the relationship is deemed substantial, the issue becomes whether the lawyer can nonetheless avoid disqualification by showing that no confidential information was or could be used in the present representation. Courts have developed two distinct presumptions for this inquiry. The first is that confidential information was shared by the prior client with the lawyer(s) who performed legal services. The second is that the attorney(s) who received this information shared it with the attorneys in the firm who represent the present client. *See* Novo Terapeutisk Laboratorium A/S v. Baxter Travenol Labs., Inc., 607 F.2d 186 (7th Cir. 1979); In re Corrugated Container Antitrust Litig., 659 F.2d 1341 (5th Cir. 1981). The combination of these presumptions makes it difficult for a lawyer with a substantial relationship to a former client to disprove a conflict of interest.

Whether the presumptions are rebuttable has been frequently litigated. The present consensus is that the first presumption — that confidential information was disclosed — is irrebuttable. *Corrugated Container*, 659 F.2d at 1347 (collecting cases); *but see* United States Football League v. Nat'l Football League, 605 F. Supp. 1448, 1461-62 (S.D.N.Y. 1985) (leaving issue open). Whether the second presumption can be rebutted is a more difficult question. A critical issues is whether the prior client has a long-standing relationship with the lawyer. *Compare Corrugated Container*, 659 F.2d at 1346 (with a long-standing client, suggesting that presumption may be irrebuttable), *and* Analytica, Inc. v. NPD Research, Inc., 708 F.2d 1263 (7th Cir. 1983) (holding that the presumption is irrebuttable even for an occasional client), *with* Duncan v. Merrill Lynch Pierce Fenner & Smith, Inc., 646 F.2d 1020, 1029 (5th Cir. 1981) (refusing to apply a mechanical rule of disqualification even with a long-standing prior client), *and* Hempstead Video, Inc. v. Inc. Village of Valley Stream, 409 F.3d 127 (2d

Cir. 2005) (allowing a lawyer to prove that a confidence entrusted by an occasional client to one attorney in the firm did not make its way to the attorney representing the second client). Courts often apply a different rule when an attorney whose old firm or government agency represented a client switches jobs to a new firm that is representing a client with adverse interests. Most courts are willing to permit the new firm to prove that the laterally hired attorney either has no access to confidential information from the prior client or has not disclosed the confidential information that he or she possesses. *See, e.g.,* Cheng v. GAF Corp., 631 F.2d 1052 (2d Cir. 1980), *vacated on other grounds,* 450 U.S. 903 (1981).

The strongest showing that a lawyer can make to overcome the two presumptions is that the lawyer took decisive measures to shield the attorney with information obtained in a prior representation from the present case and from substantive contacts with the lawyers representing the present client. These arrangements are usually called "Chinese walls." Courts often find Chinese walls ineffective to ward off disqualification, but some arrangements pass muster. Among the factors considered are whether the laterally hired attorney works in the same field; whether the lateral attorney was a partner involved in firm strategy or just an associate; whether the lawyer had a counseling or a litigation relationship with the prior client (the assumption being that, because litigation involves representation of discrete interests, disqualification is less likely); whether the lateral attorney had actual (not presumed) access to confidential information from the prior client; whether the lawyer came from government practice (a lower Chinese wall may be required for former government lawyers); whether a different office of the firm is handling the present representation; whether the firm is large or small (the assumption being that a Chinese wall is more difficult to erect in a small firm); whether the wall was immediately instituted; whether the attorney receives any money derived from the present representation; and whether the case of the second client is so complex that no other firm would be willing or able to handle the case. *See, e.g., Cheng,* 631 F.2d 1052; Nemours Found. v. Gilbane, Aetna, Fed. Ins. Co., 632 F. Supp. 418 (D. Del. 1986); *United States Football League,* 605 F. Supp. at 1459, 1466-68; INA Underwriters Ins. Co. v. Nalibotsky, 594 F. Supp. 1199, 1210 n.8 (E.D. Pa. 1984) (citing cases on Chinese wall); MANUAL, FOURTH § 10.23 n.73.

(c) *Conflicts between lawyer and client.* Conflicts between lawyers and their clients are inevitable. A lawyer working on a contingency fee doesn't have an incentive to squeeze out the best settlement or judgment if the marginal gain due to the additional recovery falls below the fee that the lawyer could earn on other cases. Conversely, the lawyer paid by the hour has an incentive to wring every dime out of a case before concluding it. These incentives increase as the size of a case, and its potential recovery, increases. Generally, however, something more needs to be shown to create a disqualifying conflict of interest between the lawyer and the client.

Some conflicts are self-evident. When a lawyer for a plaintiff owns stock in a defendant or has close relatives employed by a defendant, a conflict of interest arises. But those situations are rare. A trickier situation occurs when a settlement handsomely compensates the plaintiffs' lawyer but provides limited value to the plaintiffs. Is such a settlement a reflection of the weakness of the plaintiffs' claims, or an attempt by the lawyer to sacrifice the clients and bail out with a healthy fee? At some point, this question shades into collusion. Collusion, which is the strongest conflict of interest, involves an agreement between the lawyer and the opponent to undermine the clients' legal position, usually in return for payment from the opponent to the lawyer.

Lawyers who principally look to their own financial interests, as well as lawyers who collude with an adversary to sell out their clients, are acting unethically. In practice, however, figuring out whether an attorneys' fee is appropriate compensation or a bribe to make the lawyer sell out the client is a vexing problem. Lead counsel often garner very large sums of money for their work, so the charge of "sell-out" can be, and usually is, leveled against any lawyer who settles a large case.

Georgine is perhaps the most famous case testing the limits of this attorney-client conflict. To some extent, *Georgine* involved a conflict among the lawyers' ongoing representations, which subsection (a) of this Note discussed. The claimed conflict came up in an odd way, because it involved the simultaneous representation of two groups of plaintiffs, rather than the representation of the plaintiff in one case and the defendant in another. The conflict and collusion claims are also different from usual; the alleged sell-out was not to give the lawyers a sweetheart deal on the *Georgine* fees, but rather to give them a sweetheart deal on the inventory cases (and fees). Was there an ethical conflict — and even collusion? The case has ignited an academic debate, which includes contributions from two experts whose opinions Judge Reed rejected. *See* Susan P. Koniak, *Feasting While the Widow Weeps:* Georgine v. Amchem Products, Inc., 80 CORNELL L. REV. 1045 (1995); John C. Coffee, Jr., *Class Wars: The Dilemma of the Mass Tort Class Action*, 95 COLUM. L. REV. 1343 (1995). For an appraisal from a person not affiliated with the case, see Carrie Menkel-Meadow, *Ethics and the Settlement of Mass Torts: When the Rules Meet the Road*, 80 CORNELL L. REV. 1159 (1995).

Although impermissible conflicts and collusion are frequently asserted, it is unusual for a court to find either of them. *Cf.* Saylor v. Lindsley, 456 F.2d 896 (2d Cir. 1972) (remanding case for further discovery in light of such concerns). The fear of such conflicts and collusion, however, exercises an important influence. Courts often describe such fears as the reason that they examine class settlements closely, especially in the context of settlement class actions. *See, e.g.,* Staton v. Boeing Co., 327 F.3d 938 (9th Cir. 2003). Some cases with borderline conflicts of interest or collusion are decided on other grounds, such as the inadequacy of the class representative or the unfairness of the underlying settlement. *See, e.g.,* Amchem Prods., Inc. v Windsor, 521 U.S. 591 (1997) (reversing *Georgine* in part due to the inadequacy of the class representatives) (*supra* p. 493); In re Gen. Motors Corp. Pick-Up Truck Fuel Tank Prods. Liab. Litig., 55 F.3d 768 (3d

Cir. 1995) (overturning a settlement with a great disparity between plaintiffs' modest recovery and the attorneys' large fees). The lawyers' dubious behavior might influence courts' decisions on these other issues.

5. Sometimes a defendant engages in a practice known as a reverse auction, in which it negotiates with several groups of counsel who have filed competing or overlapping actions against the defendant. The defendant's implicit message to each counsel is "Give us a better deal, or we'll take the settlement, and all of the attorneys' fees, to someone else." How does the lawyer reconcile his or her ethical obligations with this practice?

6. Disqualification can occur for reasons other than conflict of interest. Thus, disqualification may occur when an attorney is a material witness, *see* Kalmanovitz v. G. Heileman Brewing Co., 610 F. Supp. 1319 (D. Del. 1985), unless disqualification imposes an undue hardship on the client, *see* Gen. Mill Supply Co. v. SCA Servs, Inc., 505 F. Supp. 1093 (E.D. Mich. 1981), *aff'd*, 697 F.2d 704 (6th Cir. 1982). Disqualification will occur when a spouse or a law partner is a named class representative, or when counsel is a member of the class. *See* Zylstra v. Safeway Stores, Inc., 578 F.2d 102 (5th Cir. 1978). Disqualification is possible when an attorney engages in misconduct, such as subornation of perjury, *see* Addamax Corp. v. Open Software Found., Inc., 151 F.R.D. 504 (D. Mass. 1993); making misrepresentations to a court, *see* In re Wirebound Boxes Antitrust Litig., 724 F. Supp. 648 (D. Minn. 1989); and ex parte communication with the judge, *see id.*

7. The appearance of impropriety can also lead to disqualification. This claim does not involve an ethical violation; rather, even though no ethical violation exists, the lawyer's conduct nonetheless appears improper. When the only apparent impropriety is an alleged violation of an ethical obligation, and the court has already refused to disqualify counsel because the violation does not exist, the court is unlikely to disqualify because of the mere appearance. *See, e.g., Bennett Silvershein*, 776 F. Supp. at 806 (the "appearance of impropriety" standard "does not confer a roving moral commission to disqualify attorneys based on conduct specifically treated in other" ethical obligations); Woods v. Covington County Bank, 537 F.2d 804, 813 (5th Cir. 1976) (while there does not need to be "proof of actual wrongdoing," there must be "a reasonable possibility that some specifically identifiable impropriety did in fact occur").

8. An attorney can overcome a disqualification motion by showing that all clients consented to the multiple representations, or by showing that the first client waived any conflict. Consent must be actual, not constructive. *See International Business Machines*, 579 F.2d 271. When it seems that no confidences of the first client will be disclosed, many courts are willing to enforce the first client's consent. *See, e.g.*, Interstate Props. v. Pyramid Co., 547 F. Supp. 178 (S.D.N.Y. 1982). When the risk of disclosure exists, courts insist that, at a minimum, the first client expressly consent to the use of its confidences against it; even then, some courts invalidate the consent. *See* Westinghouse Elec. Corp. v. Gulf Oil Corp., 588 F.2d 221 (7th Cir. 1978).

If the first client waits to object to a conflict of interest (often until the second case starts to go badly), courts are often unwilling to let tactical gamesmanship carry the day. *See, e.g.*, Jackson v. J.C. Penney Co., 521 F. Supp. 1032 (N.D. Ga. 1981) (fifteen months constitutes waiver).

9.   Even when a conflict exists, disqualification is not automatic. Some courts balance the ethical conflict against the harm that disqualification would cause. One formulation of the balance asks whether "the likelihood of public suspicion or obloquy outweighs the social interests which will be served by a lawyer's continued participation in a particular case." *Woods*, 537 F.2d at 813 n.12. A comparable formulation asks whether the violation "gives rise to a significant risk of trial taint. . . . [D]isqualification for an alleged conflict of interest is appropriate only if there is a significant risk that the conflict will affect the attorney's ability to represent his or her client with vigor or if the attorney is in a position to use privileged information acquired in the representation of a client against that client in another matter." *Reimerdes*, 98 F. Supp. 2d at 455. *See also* Gould v. Mitsui Mining & Smelting Co., 738 F. Supp. 1121 (N.D. Ohio 1990); SWS Fin. Fund v. Salomon Bros., Inc., 790 F. Supp. 1392 (N.D. Ill. 1992).

One factor that sometimes influences a court's disqualification decision is the potential for tactical abuse. An adversary will often make the motion to obtain a tactical advantage (whether replacing a well-qualified firm with a less qualified firm, delaying the litigation, or distracting the firm). This use (and abuse) has been noted by judges, As Justice Brennan observed:

> [T]he tactical use of attorney-misconduct disqualification motions is a deeply disturbing phenomenon in modern civil litigation. When a trial court mistakenly disqualifies a party's counsel as the result of an abusive disqualification motion, the court in essence permits the party's opponent to dictate his choice of counsel. . . . [T]his result is in serious tension with the premises of our adversary system . . . .

Richardson-Merrell, Inc. v. Koller, 472 U.S. 424, 441 (1985) (Brennan, J., concurring).

Other remedies also influence the court. For instance, the court can limit the scope of the lawyer's second representation. (The second client must, of course, consent to such a limitation.) *See Westinghouse*, 580 F.2d 1311. A rarely invoked remedy is to allow the law firm to choose the client it wishes to continue to represent. *See Gould*, 738 F. Supp. 1121. Malpractice actions and complaints with the disciplinary board are also possible. *See SWS*, 790 F. Supp. 1392; *Reimerdes*, 98 F. Supp. 2d 449.

10. Ethical issues surround not only the lawyer's representation of clients, but also the lawyer's decision to withdraw from that representation. Rules of professional conduct specify the circumstances in which counsel can withdraw. Courts are reluctant to permit counsel in a complex case to withdraw. For a case refusing to allow withdrawal, despite the ruinous financial obligations that the litigation tactics of the opposing party had forced counsel to incur, see Haines v. Liggett Group, Inc., 814 F. Supp. 414 (D.N.J. 1993). For a case permitting withdrawal and expressing more sympathy for overburdened counsel, see In re "Agent Orange" Prod. Liab. Litig., 571 F. Supp. 481 (E.D.N.Y. 1983).

11. *Agent Orange* and *Georgine*, as well as the excerpt from Judge Weinstein, make the point that the ethical rules for ordinary litigation ill fit the needs of complex litigation. *See also* Lazy Oil Co. v. Witco Corp., 166 F.3d 581 (3rd Cir. 1999). The court's power to appoint counsel has a large role to play in creating the ethical issues that lead counsel faces. This information might be relevant in deciding the proper limits of a court's power to appoint counsel.

12. If complex cases cannot be adjudicated within the framework of the adversarial system, we cannot expect the lawyers in these cases to operate under an adversarial system of ethics, can we? On the other hand, are you comfortable with ethical standards that vary with circumstance, and are defined ad hoc by courts? Can we justify two sets of ethical norms — one for routine cases and one for complex cases? Most basically, how do we want lawyers in complex cases to behave? Ethical questions lie at the very heart of complex litigation, and no proposed solution for complex litigation is adequate unless the solution works out its ethical implications.

C. SELECTING A JUDICIAL STRUCTURE

Not only must judges establish a counsel structure for a case, but they must also create a judicial structure that allows them to meet the demands of case management. Some of the judge's organizational infrastructure — law clerks and courtroom clerks — will already be in place. But the judge will often feel the need of additional assistance to help plan, supervise, and adjudicate the myriad pretrial matters that arise. In this section, we examine the judge's options to obtain additional assistance.

1. Using Multiple Judges During Pretrial

MANUAL FOR COMPLEX LITIGATION, FOURTH

11 (2004)

Although one judge should supervise the litigation, other judges may be requested to perform special duties, such as conducting settlement discussions . . . . Moreover, in the course of consolidated or coordinated pretrial proceedings, severable claims or cases may appear that could be assigned to other judges.

Notes

1. The reasons for having a single judge handle all aspects of a complex case include consistency, efficiency, appreciation of the big picture, scarcity of judicial resources, and finality. These goals could be undercut

by giving portions of the case to another judge. What "special duties" are compelling enough to overcome this concern?

2.   One commonly cited reason to use another judge is to preserve the first judge's neutrality. For instance, the *Manual*'s suggestion that other judges be used for settlement purposes reflects a long-standing practice of many judges. The rationale for this practice is that information learned during settlement negotiations makes it difficult for the judge to remain neutral during trial. But in complex litigation managerial judges have already taken off the blindfold and stepped into the pretrial fray. Is this rationale an implicit indictment of case management?

3.   Another reason to use a second judge is to allow the principal judge to concentrate on managing the case, while delegating discrete tasks that only a "full-fledged" judge (i.e., a judge appointed under Article III or its state-law counterpart) can perform. For instance, in *Georgine v. Amchem Prods., Inc.*, 157 F.R.D. 246 (E.D. Pa. 1994) (*supra* p. 739), *rev'd on other grounds*, 83 F.3d 610 (3d Cir. 1996), *aff'd sub nom.* Amchem Prods., Inc. v. Windsor, 521 U.S. 591 (1997) (*supra* p. 493), Judge Weiner took charge of the asbestos MDL litigation, which involved more than 30,000 cases. When twenty of the defendants proposed to settle on a classwide basis, the decisions on class certification and approval of the settlement required an Article III judge. Judge Weiner asked Judge Reed to handle the proceeding, which involved broad discovery and a five-week fairness hearing.

4.   In a sense, creating a hierarchy of judges with a "lead judge" at the top mirrors the use of lead counsel, committees of counsel, and the like. Because such an arrangement pulls another judge away from that judge's own caseload, however, using another judge waste scarce judicial resources. But there are other judicial officers who can play the requisite subservient role: magistrate judges and special masters. We turn to the use of these judicial officers in the following subsections.

2.   Using Magistrate Judges During Pretrial

Predecessors to the magistrate judge have existed since 1789, but modern magistrate judges trace their history to 1968, when Congress created the office. *See* 28 U.S.C. §§ 631-39. Magistrate judges are not Article III judges; they serve a term of eight years, and are eligible for reappointment. *Id.* §§ 631(e)-(f).

MANUAL FOR COMPLEX LITIGATION, FOURTH

13-14 (2004)

The judge should decide early in the litigation whether to refer all or any part of pretrial supervision and control to a magistrate judge. The judge should consider a number of factors:

·   the law of the circuit;

- the experience and qualifications of the available magistrate judges;
- the relationship among and attitude of the attorneys;
- the extent to which a district judge's authority may be required;
- the time the judge has to devote to the litigation;
- the novelty of the issues and the need for innovation;
- and the judge's personal preferences.

Some judges prefer to supervise complex litigation personally, even in courts routinely refer discovery or other pretrial procedures to magistrate judges. Referrals in complex cases may cause additional costs and delays when the parties seek judicial review, diminish supervisory consistency and coherence as the case proceeds to trial, create greater reluctance to try innovative procedures that might aid in resolution of the case, and cause the judge to be unfamiliar with the case at the time of trial. Other judges have believe that such referrals provide effective case management during the pretrial stage, enabling the judge to devote time to more urgent matters.

Even without general referral to a magistrate judge, referral of particular matters may be helpful. Such matters include supervision of all discovery matters, or supervision of particular discovery issues or disputes, particularly those that may be time consuming or require an immediate ruling (including resolving deposition disputes by telephone; ruling on claims of privilege and motions for protective orders; and conducting hearings on procedural matters, such as personal jurisdiction). Magistrate judges may also help counsel formulate stipulations and statements of contentions, and may facilitate settlement discussions.

Notes

1. With some exceptions, 28 U.S.C. § 636(b)(1)(A) permits a district judge to designate a magistrate judge to "hear and determine any pretrial matter pending before the court." Among the exceptions are dispositive motions (such as motions to dismiss and motions for summary judgment) and motions to certify a class. For these motions, a district judge can designate the magistrate judge "to conduct hearings, including evidentiary hearings, and to submit to a judge of the court proposed findings of fact and recommendations for the disposition." *Id.* § 636(b)(1)(B). A magistrate judge can also enter a binding decision on dispositive matters when the parties consent to the magistrate judge's jurisdiction. Appeals must be taken from a magistrate judge's ruling or report within ten days. The appeal of a non-dispositive ruling is made to the district judge, while the appeal of a dispositive ruling in a consented-to case is made to the court of appeals. *Id.* §§ 636(b)-(c).

The constitutional concerns surrounding the use of magistrate judges have for the most part been resolved. *See* Mathews v. Weber, 423 U.S. 261 (1976) (delegation of Social Security cases upheld); United States v.

Raddatz, 447 U.S. 667 (1980) (delegation of a hearing on suppression of evidence upheld); Peretz v. United States, 501 U.S. 923 (1991) (consensual use of magistrate to supervise felony jury selection upheld). In *Williams v. General Electric Capital Auto Lease, Inc.*, 159 F.3d 266 (7th Cir. 1998), the class representative consented to trial before a magistrate judge. After the case settled, members of the class filed a case in state court, contending that the class representative did not have the authority to consent on their behalf to adjudication before a non-Article III judicial officer. Affirming an antisuit injunction, the court of appeals rejected the argument.

2.   A study of case-management practices found that references to magistrate judges significantly increased attorney satisfaction, but did not significantly affect time to disposition, lawyers' work hours, or lawyers' views of fairness. *See* JAMES S. KAKALIK ET AL., AN EVALUATION OF JUDICIAL CASE MANAGEMENT UNDER THE CIVIL JUSTICE REFORM ACT 77-80 (1996). The study did not distinguish between complex and routine cases.

3.   The critical issue regarding pretrial references in complex cases is pragmatic: Because the magistrate judge, like the district judge, is likely a generalist, what is the advantage of using a magistrate judge to manage the pretrial aspects of a complex case? Can a magistrate judge do anything to promote the rational adjudication of a complex dispute that a district judge cannot? When time is of the essence (i.e., rational decision-making is threatened if the case is not adjudicated within a short time frame), and when no judge could perform all of the pretrial tasks within that time frame, the need for another judicial officer exists. But this circumstance is rare. Are you persuaded that the circumstances mentioned in the *Manual, Fourth* should lead a judge to use a magistrate judge in complex litigation?

4.   The *Manual* also mentions a number of arguments against using magistrate judges in complex cases. Professor Silberman sounds another cautionary note, arguing that "an uncensored, almost reflexive response to refer all pre-trial discovery to magistrates" may have "a hydraulic effect on discovery, now that there is an 'institutional setting' in which discovery disputes may flourish." Linda Silberman, *Judicial Adjuncts Revisited: The Proliferation of Ad Hoc Procedure*, 137 U. Pa. L. Rev. 2131, 2141 (1989). *Cf.* Richard A. Posner, *Coping with the Caseload: A Comment on Magistrates and Masters*, 137 U. PA. L. REV. 2215 (1989) (noting that reliance on magistrate judges leads to bureaucratization of the federal judiciary).

Another institutional concern is that magistrate judges typically fill one of three roles: as an additional judge, handling a consensual caseload; as a specialist, handling a particular type of case and building an expertise in that field; or as a team player, helping the district judge on pretrial matters in cases on the district judge's docket. *See* CARROLL SERON, THE ROLES OF MAGISTRATES (1985). Magistrate judges often work for more than one district judge. *See* CHRISTOPHER E. SMITH, UNITED STATES MAGISTRATES IN THE FEDERAL COURTS (1990). It is difficult for a magistrate judge to be a "team player" dedicated just to one judge's complex cases.

5.   Although the *Manual, Fourth* takes a dim view of referring all pretrial matters to a magistrate judge, some district judges do not share

these reservations. *See* In re MGM Grand Hotel Fire Litig., 570 F. Supp. 913, 917 (D. Nev. 1983) (assigning nearly all pretrial tasks, including management of discovery, to a magistrate judge). Other judges have delegated discrete pretrial tasks, including: (1) appointing the members of a plaintiffs' committee of counsel, and establishing the committee's responsibilities and fee structure, *see* Smiley v. Sincoff, 958 F.2d 498, 499 (2d Cir. 1992); (2) helping parties prepare a discovery plan and entering a case-management order, *see* Castano v. Am. Tobacco Co., 160 F.R.D. 544, 559 (E.D. La. 1995), *rev'd on other grounds*, 84 F.3d 734 (5th Cir. 1996) (*supra* p. 471); (3) determining relevance or privilege claims, *see* Harcourt Brace Jovanovich, Inc. Sec. Litig., 838 F. Supp. 109 (S.D.N.Y. 1993), and In re Combustion, Inc., 161 F.R.D. 51 (W.D. La. 1995), *aff'd*, 161 F.R.D. 54 (W.D. La. 1995); and (4) issuing a report and recommendation on class certification, *see* Leider v. Ralfe, 387 F. Supp. 2d 283 (S.D.N.Y. 2005). In these cases, the reference is reported in a matter-of-fact way; none of the cases entertains any doubt about the power to assign these tasks to a magistrate judge or discusses the wisdom of doing so.

6. In *Haines v. Liggett Group, Inc.*, 975 F.2d 81 (3rd Cir. 1992), a district judge delegated part of a non-dispositive discovery matter to a magistrate judge. The magistrate judge resolved the issue in a way generally favorable to the defendants. The plaintiff sought review from the district judge, who resolved the issue in a way more favorable to the plaintiffs. The district judge relied on evidence that had not been presented to the magistrate judge, but that he was aware of from related litigation he was handling. On mandamus, the court of appeals held that, because the delegated matter was non-dispositive, the district judge acted improperly. In large-scale litigation involving supervision by both a district judge and a magistrate judge, isn't it inevitable that the district judge will have information that the magistrate judge does not? After *Haines*, should judges be less inclined to use magistrate judges in complex cases?

7. 28 U.S.C. § 636(b)(2) and Fed. R. Civ. P. 53(h) allow a magistrate judge to be appointed as a special master. We turn to the use of special masters in the following subsection.

3. Using Special Masters During Pretrial

Special masters have a long (and not always glorious) history. In medieval times, the Chancellor in the English equity system called on masters to perform functions for which the Chancellor had no time. A principal function of masters was to conduct hearings and report to the Chancellor; those tasks later expanded to consider motions, investigate factual claims, and account for funds. Masters were compensated by charging the litigants for copies of their reports and by having the use of the funds during the suit. Hence, masters had little incentive to process disputes quickly. As early as 1382 one writer complained that masters were "over fatt both in bodie and purse and over well furred in their benefices, and put the king to verry great cost more than needed," *see* 1

WILLIAM HOLDSWORTH, A HISTORY OF ENGLISH LAW 426 (A.L. Goodhart & H.G. Hanbury eds., 7th rev. ed. 1956). In a less corrupt and corpulent form, masters survive in modern English Chancery practice, where they have significant responsibilities for pretrial matters. *See* R.E. Ball, *The Chancery Master*, 77 L.Q. 331 (1961).

Masters have also been used in America since colonial times, most often in equity. Masters were usually were drawn from the ranks of lawyers and private citizens. *See* Linda J. Silberman, *Masters and Magistrates Part II: The American Analogue*, 50 N.Y.U. L. REV. 1297 (1975); Irving R. Kaufman, *Masters in the Federal Courts: Rule 53*, 58 COLUM. L. REV. 452 (1958). They typically conducted trial hearings and assisted in post-trial proceedings such as accountings and calculating complex damage awards.

Today Rule 53 of the Federal Rules of Civil Procedure provides a federal court with the power to appoint a special master. Before extensive revisions of Rule 53 in 2003, a court's power to appoint a master to handle *pretrial* matters was ambiguous at best; former Rule 53 mentioned masters performing only trial and post-trial work, and in any event admonished that "[a] reference to a master shall be the exception and not the rule." Today Rule 53(a)(1)(C) permits references to special masters for "pretrial . . . matters that cannot be effectively and timely addressed by an available district judge or magistrate judge."

IN RE WELDING ROD
PRODUCTS LIABILITY LITIGATION

2004 WL 3711622 (N.D. Ohio Nov. 10, 2004)

■ O'MALLEY, District Judge.

On July 27, 2004, the parties in this matter filed a joint motion for appointment of a Special Master. . . . [T]hat motion is granted and, at the specific request of the parties, the Court now appoints as Special Master David R. Cohen, Esq. . . . .

This appointment is made pursuant to Fed. R. Civ. P. 53 and the inherent authority of the Court.[1] . . . .

This Court first discussed with the parties the advisability of appointing a Special Master during a case management conference on July 1, 2004.

---

1. "Beyond the provisions of [Rule 53] for appointing and making references to Masters, a Federal District Court has 'the inherent power to supply itself with this instrument for the administration of justice when deemed by it essential.'" Schwimmer v. United States, 232 F.2d 855, 865 (8th Cir. 1956) (quoting In re: Peterson, 253 U.S. 300, 311 (1920)). The Court's inherent power to appoint a Special Master, however, is not without limits. *See* Cobell v. Norton, 334 F.3d 1128, 1142 (D.C. Cir. 2003) (in the absence of consent by the parties, the inherent authority of the court does not extend to allow appointment of Special Master to exercise "wide-ranging extrajudicial duties" such as "investigative, quasi-inquisitorial, quasi-prosecutorial role[s]").

See Fed. R. Civ. P. 16(c)(8, 12) ("At any conference under this rule consideration may be given, and the court may take appropriate action, with respect to . . . (8) the advisability of referring matters to a magistrate judge or master; [or] . . . (12) the need for adopting special procedures for managing potentially difficult or protracted actions that may involve complex issues, multiple parties, difficult legal questions, or unusual proof problems"). The parties then filed their joint motion for appointment and, later, jointly requested the appointment of Mr. Cohen.

I. BACKGROUND

Beginning in early 2003, a number of plaintiffs around the country began filing lawsuits against various manufacturers, suppliers, and distributors of welding rod products, as well as related trade associations. The common theme of these lawsuits was that exposure to manganese contained in the fumes given off by welding rods caused physical harm to the plaintiffs, and the defendants knew or should have known that use of the welding rods caused these injuries.

. . . On June 23, 2003, the [Judicial Panel on Multidistrict Litigation consolidated and transferred] three related pending federal cases to the Northern District of Ohio . . . . Since that time, the MDL Panel has entered 16 different conditional transfer orders . . . .

In many of the cases that have been transferred to this MDL, a great number of unrelated plaintiffs joined to bring a single case. . . . The Court's best estimate is that there now exceed 5,700 individual plaintiffs from 20 different states pursuing cases in this MDL, not including the 3,000 or so plaintiffs whose cases this Court has already remanded to state court. . . . [M]any more plaintiffs are expected to file related cases in federal courts around the country "in the indefinite future." Of course, similar cases are also being filed in state courts across the country, and counsel for the parties in this MDL are working to coordinate their efforts with these state-court cases. About 70 different defendants have been named in the MDL lawsuits. In sum, the organizational challenge and the mass of litigants involved in this MDL is huge; discovery, case management, and other matters will require intensive oversight.

Furthermore, the issues that have already arisen in this relatively-young MDL are sophisticated and complex. For example, this Court has ruled on a series of motions to remand which raised complicated issues of federal jurisdiction hinging on the timeliness of defendants' notices of removal, the timeliness of plaintiffs' motions to remand, fraudulent joinder, and the military contractor defense. Currently pending are 26 "global" motions to dismiss, brought . . . by certain categories of defendants, which address variations in state law and also raise intricate issues of federal preemption. . . . Beyond these procedural aspects, this MDL presents advanced medical and scientific issues.

Put simply, it is clear that this MDL presents many difficult issues and will require substantial attention and oversight from the Court. Other

MDL courts, facing similar challenges, have easily concluded that appointment of a Special Master was appropriate to help the Court with various pretrial, trial, and post-trial tasks. Indeed, the appointment of a Special Master in cases such as this is common. The 2003 amendments to Rule 53 specifically recognize the pretrial, trial, and post-trial functions of masters in contemporary litigation. Thus, the Court agrees with the parties that appointment of a Special Master to "assist the Court in both effectively and expeditiously resolving their disputes" is appropriate.

II. RULE 53(b)(2)

Rule 53 was amended on December 1, 2003, and now requires an order of appointment to include certain contents. *See* Fed. R. Civ. P. 53(b)(2)....

A. *Master's Duties*

Rule 53(a)(1)(A) states that the Court may appoint a master to "perform duties consented to by the parties." The parties in this case consented to

> having a Special Master: 1) assist the Court with legal analysis of the parties' submissions; and 2) perform any and all other duties assigned to him by the Court (as well as any ancillary acts required to fully carry out those duties) as permitted by both the Federal Rules of Civil Procedure and Article III of the Constitution. The parties [further] request, however, that the Court retain sole authority to issue final rulings on matters formally submitted for adjudication.

The Court has reviewed recent legal authority addressing the duties of a Special Master that are permitted under the "Federal Rules of Civil Procedure and Article III of the Constitution." Consonant with this legal authority, the currently-anticipated needs of the court, and the parties' broad consent, the Court states that the Special Master in these proceedings shall have the authority to:

- assist with preparation for attorney conferences (including formulating agendas), court scheduling, and negotiating changes to the case management order;

- establish discovery and other schedules, review and attempt to resolve informally any discovery conflicts (including issues such as privilege, confidentiality, and access to medical and other records), and supervise discovery;

- oversee management of docketing, including the identification and processing of matters requiring court rulings;

- compile data and assist with, or make informal recommendations with regard to, interpretation of scientific and technical evidence;

- assist with legal analysis of the parties' motions or other submissions, whether made before, during, or after trials, and informally recommend findings of fact and conclusions of law;

- help to coordinate federal, state and international litigation;

- direct, supervise, monitor, and report upon implementation and compliance with the Court's Orders, and make findings and recommendations on remedial action if required;

- interpret any agreements reached by the parties;

- propose structures and strategies for settlement negotiations on the merits, and on any subsidiary issues, and evaluate parties' class and individual claims, as may become necessary;

- propose structures and strategies for attorneys fee issues and fee settlement negotiations, review fee applications, and evaluate parties' individual claims for fees, as may become necessary;

- administer, allocate, and distribute funds and other relief, as may become necessary;

- adjudicate eligibility and entitlement to funds and other relief, as may become necessary;

- monitor compliance with structural injunctions, as may become necessary;

- make formal or informal recommendations and reports to the parties, and make informal recommendations and reports to the Court, regarding any matter pertinent to these proceedings; and

- communicate with parties and attorneys as needs may arise in order to permit the full and efficient performance of these duties.

B. *Communications with the Parties and the Court*

Rule 53(b)(2)(B) directs the Court to set forth "the circumstances — if any — in which the master may communicate ex parte with the court or a party." The Special Master may communicate ex parte with the Court at the Special Master's discretion, without providing notice to the parties, in order to "assist the Court with legal analysis of the parties' submissions" (e.g., the parties' motions). The Special Master may also communicate ex parte with the Court, without providing notice to the parties, regarding logistics, the nature of his activities, management of the litigation, and other appropriate procedural matters. The Court may later limit the Special Master's ex parte communications with the Court with respect to certain functions, if the role of the Special Master changes.

The Special Master may communicate ex parte with any party or his attorney, as the Special Master deems appropriate, for the purposes of ensuring the efficient administration and management of this MDL, including the making of informal suggestions to the parties to facilitate compliance with Orders of the Court; such ex parte communications may, for example, address discovery or other procedural issues. Such ex parte communications shall not, however, address the merits of any substantive issue, except that, if the parties seek assistance from the Special Master in resolving a dispute regarding a substantive issue, the Special Master may engage in ex parte communications with a party or his attorney regarding the merits of the particular dispute, for the purpose of mediating or negotiating a resolution of that dispute, only with the prior permission of those opposing counsel who are pertinent to the particular dispute. . . .

E. *Compensation*

Rule 53(b)(2)(E) states that the Court must set forth "the basis, terms, and procedure for fixing the master's compensation." As agreed to between the parties and requested in their initial Motion for Appointment, the Special Master shall be compensated at the rate of $300 per hour, with the parties bearing this cost equally (50% by the plaintiffs and 50% by the defendants). After the Special Master has performed for 1,000 hours, the Court shall "assess the need for his ongoing involvement and will extend the terms of his compensation accordingly." . . . The Court has "consider[ed] the fairness of imposing the likely expenses on the parties and [has taken steps to] protect against unreasonable expense or delay." Rule 53(a)(3).

From time to time, on approximately a monthly basis, the Special Master shall submit to the Court an Itemized Statement of fees and expenses (not to include overhead), which the Court will inspect carefully for regularity and reasonableness.

Notes

1. Using masters for pretrial matters raises four distinct issues. The first is whether a court has the constitutional power to refer pretrial issues. The second is the source of the court's power to make references. The third is the legal standard that determines when a reference is permissible. The final issue involves the prudential considerations that govern the decision to make a reference.

(a) *Constitutional Constraints*. Two constitutional constraints place limits on using masters in complex litigation. The first is the concern, reflected in the parties' stipulation in *Welding Rod*, that the use of masters entrusts essential judicial functions to a non-Article III judicial officer. This constraint is a variant of the arguments that you have seen in other courses regarding the power of Congress to delegate adjudicatory responsibility to Article I courts, administrative agencies, and magistrate judges. *See* ERWIN CHEMERINSKY, FEDERAL JURISDICTION §§4.1-.5 (5th ed. 2007). The present (and confused) state of the law suggests that non-Article III officials can exercise "inherently judicial power" as long as they act as an adjunct to an Article III court or have significant expertise, and effective appellate review of their decisions exists. *See id.* § 4.5.4; United States v. Raddatz, 447 U.S. 667, 683 n.11 (1980) (analogizing magistrates to masters, and implying that using masters to take evidence at trial is constitutional); Crowell v. Benson, 285 U.S. 22, 51-52 (1932) (observing in dicta that the use of masters to aid juries was constitutional); Ex Parte Peterson, 253 U.S. 300, 312-14 (1920) (finding inherent power to appoint a common-law auditor). On the other hand, on mandamus review, the Supreme Court struck down as a clear "abdication of the judicial function" the reference of a trial to a master when the stated reasons for the reference were the case's complexity and the district court's crowded docket. La Buy v. Howes Leather Co., 352 U.S. 249, 256 (1957) (*infra* p. 1016).

Although the Supreme Court has never ruled on the constitutionality of the use of masters during pretrial, these cases suggest that a pretrial reference is improper if it amounts to an abdication of an Article III court's power to make findings of jurisdictional and constitutional fact and to decide questions of law. *Cf.* In re Bituminous Coal Operators' Ass'n, 949 F.2d 1165, 1168 (D.C. Cir. 1991) (stating that the limits on a reference are "impelled by the character of federal courts functioning under Article III"); Jack Walters & Sons Corp. v. Morton Bldg., Inc., 737 F.2d 698 (7th Cir. 1984) (describing constitutional limits in dicta); United States v. Conservation Chem. Co., 106 F.R.D. 210 (W.D. Mo.) (analyzing Article III concerns), *rev'd*, 770 F.2d 103 (8th Cir. 1985).

A second obstacle is the Seventh Amendment, which preserves the right of jury trial in civil cases. Unless a pretrial reference effectively eliminates the jury's right to make factual findings, however, the Seventh Amendment is unlikely to bar a reference. *See Peterson*, 253 U.S. at 309-12.

(b) *Sources of Authority. Welding Rod* identifies two sources of power to appoint masters: Rule 53 and the court's inherent power. Until its amendment in 2003, Rule 53 contained no explicit authority for a pretrial reference. Some commentators who examined the history of American masters and of Rule 53's drafting concluded that Rule 53 did not authorize the use of masters for pretrial tasks. *See* Linda Silberman, *Judicial Adjuncts Revisited: The Proliferation of Ad Hoc Procedure*, 137 U. Pa. L. Rev. 2131, 2135 (1989) (Rule 53 "does not quite fit the circumstances in which special masters are used today"); Wayne D. Brazil, *Authority to Refer Discovery Tasks to Special Masters: Limitations on Existing Sources and the Need for a New Federal Rule*, in Managing Complex Litigation 305 (Wayne D. Brazil et al. ed., 1983); Irving R. Kaufman, *Masters in the Federal Courts: Rule 53*, 58 Colum. L. Rev. 452, 462 (1958) ("[T]he operation of [Rule 53] in this area is doubtful.").

For Brazil and Kaufman, however, all was not lost; they contended that courts had an inherent power to appoint masters for pretrial tasks. Their bulwark of support was *Peterson*, a pre-Rule 53 case in which the Supreme Court upheld the appointment of an auditor to examine accounts before a trial. The Court held that federal courts

> have (at least in the absence of legislation to the contrary) inherent power to provide themselves with appropriate instruments for the performance of their duties. This power includes authority to appoint persons unconnected with the court to aid judges in the performance of specific judicial duties, as they may arise in the progress of a cause. [253 U.S. at 312.]

One purpose of the 2003 amendment was to create an explicit power for pretrial references, which is now contained in Rule 53(a)(1)(C). In addition to this provision, *Welding Rod* also identified Rule 53(a)(1)(A), which permits references by consent, as a source of authority for the reference. In light of these provisions, *Welding Rod*'s invocation of the court's inherent power is surprising. Do courts still enjoy inherent power to use masters?

(c) *The Legal Standard.* The legal standard that governs a reference varies with the source of authority. For references under Rule 53(a)(1)(C), the court must find that no district or magistrate judge can "timely and effectively" address the delegated pretrial matters. For consensual references under Rule 53(a)(1)(A), the rule provides no standard other than the consent of the parties. In *Kimberly v. Arms*, 129 U.S. 512 (1889), which involved a consensual reference to determine the facts and law at trial, the Supreme Court limited the district court's power to review a master's work because the parties had consented to a broad delegation of authority. On the other hand, in *Wilver v. Fisher*, 387 F.2d 66 (10th Cir. 1967), the defendants had refused to answer certain interrogatories. The parties consented to give a master the power to restate the interrogatories and to recommend the answers. On appeal, the Tenth Circuit held that "[t]he parties, not a Master, ask the questions and give the answers. . . . The order of reference here borders on an abdication of the judicial function and is not justified by the record." 387 F.2d at 69. *See also* Kaufman, *supra*, at 459 (arguing that "the permissive scope of the reference is broadened" when the parties consent, but cautioning that even a consensual reference might be inappropriate "where the public interest demands retention of the initial inquiry by the court").

Finally, to the extent that a court's inherent power remains a relevant source of authority, the standard is murkier. Before the 2003 amendment, Rule 53 contained language stating that references to masters were the "exception rather than the rule." Some commentators, like Judge Kaufman, believed that this "exception and not the rule" standard acted as the limit of the inherent power. Others, like Magistrate Judge Brazil, thought that judges could use a master in complex disputes whenever a reference "would contribute substantially to the expedition or orderliness of case preparation." Brazil, *supra*, at 385. Language in *Peterson* supports both the more restrictive view of Judge Kaufman and the broader view of Magistrate Judge Brazil. *See* 253 U.S. at 312-14.

(d) *Pragmatic Factors.* Even when a judge possesses the power to order a pretrial reference, the judge is not required to exercise that power. In *Welding Rod*, Judge O'Malley discusses some of the pragmatic factors that convinced her to appoint a master. Courts that have made references generally cite one or more of the following reasons: the greater amount of time that a master can devote to case management; the quicker response that a master can provide; the expertise that a master can bring to specialized pretrial tasks; the need for the judge to concentrate on major pretrial and trial tasks, both in the present case and in others; the informality and flexibility that a master provides; the master's accessibility; and preserving the trial judge's impartiality. *See also* Shira Scheindlin, *We Need Help: The Increasing Use of Special Masters in Federal Court*, 58

DEPAUL L. REV. 479 (2008) (listing as factors the scarcity of judicial time, the knowledge and expertise of a master, the need for an interdisciplinary team to resolve a case, and protecting the judge's neutrality). *Cf. La Buy*, 352 U.S. at 259(rejecting the complexity of the case and the crowdedness of the court's docket as reasons for a trial reference to a master).

Masters also have certain drawbacks, including the cost of a master (note the hourly rate of the master in *Welding Rod*); the delay and duplication of effort that ensue when the master's decisions are appealed to the district judge; the district judge's inability to control the details of the litigation; the master's lack of expertise in managing pretrial matters; the different quality of justice associated with informality; the possibility that the master will be tempted to shape the outcome to favor his private clients' interests; the master's lack of accountability; and the lack of acceptance that parties may feel toward adjudication by a non-judicial officer.

Professor Silberman raises another concern: "[T]he use of judicial adjuncts has pushed formalized procedure into retreat. . . . [D]evices such as special masters . . . have made trans-substantive rules a concept in name only." Silberman, *supra*, at 2177.

2. Judge O'Malley correctly notes that judges in MDL and other complex cases often appoint special masters to assist with pretrial tasks. A recent study showed that, in federal court, the incidence of requests to appoint special masters was low (about 2.7 cases per 1,000), but some types of cases often associated with complex litigation (airplane crashes, RICO claims, and environmental claims) showed an incidence of ten times the norm. Overall, courts granted the request to appoint a master about 60% of the time. A majority of the appointments were for pretrial purposes. FED. JUD. CTR., SPECIAL MASTERS' INCIDENCE AND ACTIVITY (2000).

On the other hand, in a number of complex cases in the 1980s and 1990s, district courts appointed masters to perform various pretrial tasks, only to have their decisions overturned on mandamus review. *See* Prudential Ins. Co. of Am. v. U.S. Gypsum Co., 991 F.2d 1080 (3d Cir. 1993) (asbestos-related property claims); *Bituminous Coal*, 949 F.2d 1165 (pension litigation); In re United States, 816 F.2d 1083 (6th Cir. 1987) (environmental dispute); In re Armco, Inc., 770 F.2d 103 (8th Cir. 1985) (environmental dispute). Each of the appellate courts recognized the district courts' power to delegate some pretrial tasks to masters, although they disagreed on the permissible scope of such references. *Compare Prudential*, 991 F.2d at 1085 (no pretrial references unless there exist "exceptional circumstances with which a magistrate judge could not deal effectively"), *with Armco*, 770 F.2d at 105 (forbidding a reference for trial but upholding that part of the reference that granted "the master broad authority to supervise and conduct pretrial matters, including discovery activity, the production and arrangement of exhibits and stipulations of fact, the power to hear motions for summary judgment or dismissal and to make recommendations with respect thereto"), *and United States*, 816 F.2d at 1091 (issuing a writ to prevent a the master from deciding dispositive matters, but permitting the master manage discovery). *See also* Stauble v.

Warrob, Inc., 977 F.2d 690, 695 n.6 (1st Cir. 1992) (stating in dicta that judges should not refer dispositive pretrial matters to masters).

3.   *Welding Rod* shows that broad references for pretrial matters still occur. Some district courts, however, are wary of such broad references. *See* United States v. Hooker Chem. & Plastics Corp., 123 F.R.D. 62 (W.D.N.Y. 1988); *see also* MANUAL FOR COMPLEX LITIGATION, FOURTH § 10.14, at 14 (2004) (stating that referral of pretrial management to a master is "not advisable," but suggesting that a referral "for limited purposes requiring special expertise may sometimes be appropriate").

References for discrete pretrial tasks are common. Among the tasks for which courts have appointed masters are: (1) organizing the litigation, *see* In re Wirebound Boxes Antitrust Litig., 128 F.R.D. 250 (D. Minn. 1989); (2) proposing case-management orders, *see* In re Shell Oil Refinery, 136 F.R.D. 588, 592 (E.D. La. 1991); (3) helping define issues, *see* Geoffrey C. Hazard, Jr. & Paul R. Rice, *Judicial Management of the Pretrial Process in Massive Litigation, in* MANAGING COMPLEX LITIGATION, *supra*, at 77, and Belfiore v. N.Y. Times Co., 654 F. Supp. 842 (D. Conn. 1986); (4) overseeing depositions and reviewing them to see if claims are established, *see* In re Estate of Ferdinand E. Marcos Human Rights Litig., 1994 WL 874222 (D. Haw. Jan. 3 1995); (5) presiding at scheduling and discovery conferences, *see* Roberts v. Heim, 1990 WL 306009 (N.D. Cal. decided Aug. 27, 1990); (6) ruling on privilege claims, *see* In re Sunrise Sec. Litig., 124 F.R.D. 99 (E.D. Pa. 1989); (7) handling discovery disputes, *see* Baxter v. Coca-Cola Co., 47 F.R.D. 345 (S.D.N.Y. 1969); and (8) ruling on class-certification motions, *see* In re K-Dur Antitrust Litig., 2008 WL 2699390 (D.N.J. Apr. 14, 2008).

Has case management in complex litigation become so essential that Rule 53's power to use masters for pretrial amounts to an unconstitutional "abrogation of the judicial function" within the meaning of *La Buy*?

4.   One of the arguments sometimes made for using masters in complex cases is that they can do certain things — such as holding ex parte conversations with parties or coordinating related state and federal proceedings — that judges acting in a traditional role cannot. *See* Wayne D. Brazil, *Special Masters in Complex Cases: Extending the Judiciary or Reshaping Adjudication*, 53 U. CHI. L. REV. 394, 420-22 (1986). The 2003 amendments to Rule 53 specifically require is a clear statement from the judge about the ability of a master to engage in ex parte communications. In *Welding Rod*, Judge O'Malley gave the master only limited ex parte power. *Cf.* Malletier v. Dooney & Bourke, Inc., 525 F. Supp. 2d 558 (S.D.N.Y. 2007) (refusing to find that ex parte contact between a master and an attorney for one party required the master's disqualification). Does an ex parte power impinge too drastically on an adversarial approach to litigation? Brazil, *Special Masters in Big Cases*, *supra*, at 71, 74. *Cf.* Amalia D. Kessler, *Our Inquisitorial Tradition: Equity Procedure, Due Process, and the Search for an Alternative to the Adversarial*, 90 CORNELL L. REV. 1181 (2005) (describing the inquisitorial origins of special masters).

5.   A judge can use a combination of masters and magistrate judges. In the massive *AT&T* antitrust litigation brought to break up AT&T —

arguably the most complex two-party lawsuit ever — Judge Greene initially assigned general responsibility for managing discovery to a magistrate judge with only a limited role for the masters. *See* United States v. Am. Tel. & Tel. Co., 461 F. Supp. 1314, 1348 (D.D.C. 1978). He subsequently reversed course and let the masters handle most of the significant pretrial matters. In a post-mortem analysis, the special masters concluded that the original division of responsibility was wrong and the latter division correct:

> [I]t is a mistake to have a horizontal division of responsibility between judge and magistrate or magistrate and special master. By horizontal division, we mean a coordinate division of responsibility over subject matter. In *United States v. AT&T* the division had discovery go to the magistrate, privilege claims to the special master, and everything else to the judge. . . . [T]he swirl of pretrial does not categorize so easily, and coordination by these means is slow and rigid. As things evolved, there emerged a vertical division of responsibility. We as special masters became responsible for almost all of the pretrial under the judicial authority and administrative superintendence of the judge. This allowed a division of labor between the judge and subordinate judicial officers but put the judge and us in a position to see and guide the case as [a] whole. The result was much closer coordination of the court responses to various parts of the case.

Hazard & Rice, *supra*, at 84. Professor Hazard and Mr. Rice make a case for not slicing pretrial responsibility into too many pieces, but do they make a case for giving masters the largest slice?

6. In Chapters Nine and Ten, we examine the judge's power to appoint experts and technical advisors to assist at trial. *See infra* p. 1026, Note 6; p. 1111. It is also possible to appoint experts or advisors to handle aspects of pretrial. *See* TechSearch, L.L.C. v. Intel Corp., 286 F.3d 1360, 1376-81 (Fed. Cir. 2002); THOMAS E. WILLGING, COURT-APPOINTED EXPERTS 18-20 (1986); MANUAL, FOURTH, *supra*, § 11.51. Unlike masters, experts and advisors have no formal decision-making power; they provide information to the judge for use in making a decision. The authority for appointing experts is Fed. R. Evid. 706. The authority for the appointing advisors is the inherent power of the court. *TechSearch* suggested the following guidelines "for minimally safeguarding the judicial process and the district court from undue influence by the technical advisor and to ensure that the technical advisor's role is properly limited to a tutoring function":

> [T]he district court in appointing a technical advisor must: use a "fair and open procedure for appointing a neutral technical advisor . . . addressing any allegations of bias, partiality or lack of qualifications" in the candidates; clearly define and limit the technical advisor's duties, presumably in a writing disclosed to all parties; guard against extra-record information; and make explicit, perhaps through a report or record, the nature and content of the technical advisor's tutelage concerning the technology. [286 F.3d at 1379.]

Is the use of experts or advisors a way to take the best of the special-master approach while avoiding the worst?

4. Ethical Responsibilities of Judicial Officers

Ideal qualities for a judge in an adversarial model are neutrality, objectivity, and passivity. Like the ethical rules applicable to counsel, the ethical rules applicable to judges were formed with this ideal judge in mind. But passivity is not an ideal quality in the judge who actively manages litigation; greater activity lessens a judge's ability to remain neutral and dispassionate. Therefore, just as representing multiple clients in complex litigation tests the ethical boundaries for lawyers, the case-management approach in complex litigation tests the ethical boundaries for judges.

The limits of a judge's departure from traditional ethical norms in complex litigation are usually explored through a party's motion to recuse a judge. Recusal is the judicial equivalent of a lawyer's disqualification: A judge is removed ("recused") from a case because of some actual or apparent impropriety. The extent to which the needs of complex litigation require an adjustment of judicial ethical norms is a critical question, for ultimately no judge can be a more creative case manager than ethical norms allow.

IN RE: KENSINGTON INTERNATIONAL LTD.

368 F.3d 289 (3d Cir. 2004)

■ GARTH, Circuit Judge.

[Senior Judge Alfred M. Wolin was assigned to handle coordinated case management for five asbestos-related bankruptcies (the "Five Asbestos Cases"), including the cases of USG Corp., Owens Corning, and W.R. Grace & Co. Creditors of the latter two debtors, as well as USG, sought writs of mandamus, alleging] that Judge Wolin had, through his association with certain consulting Advisors which he had appointed, created a perception that his impartiality "might reasonably be questioned" under 28 U.S.C. § 455(a). The Petitions asserted that disqualification was also warranted under 28 U.S.C. § 455(b)(1) as a result of ex parte communications among Judge Wolin and his advisors, the parties, and the attorneys.

[After a remand for factual development, Judge Wolin found that he did not need to recuse himself. The creditors then sought review.]

II. BACKGROUND

. . .

B. *Ex parte Communications and the Advisors*

On December 20, 2001, Judge Wolin held a case management conference for the Five Asbestos Cases. Although there is no official record of what was said at that conference, Judge Wolin produced a script ("talking points") which reflects what he said to the parties. According to the script,

Judge Wolin announced that "[i]n order to effectively case manage complex litigation, it is necessary for the judge to speak and/or meet with attorneys on an ex parte basis, without permission of adversary attorneys." Judge Wolin further announced that "[a]ny objection to such ex parte communications is deemed waived," but he assured the parties and attorneys that he would use his power to meet ex parte "sparingly." None of the parties objected at that time.

A week later, Judge Wolin named five "Court Appointed Consultants" (the "Advisors") to assist him in the Five Asbestos Cases. The five individuals he named were David Gross, Judson Hamlin, William Dreier, John Keefe, and Francis McGovern, all of whom had prior experience with asbestos or mass tort litigation either as state court judges, private practitioners, or academics. Pursuant to Judge Wolin's order, the Advisors were to "advise the Court and to undertake such responsibilities, including . . . mediation of disputes, holding case management conferences, and consultation with counsel, as the Court may delegate to them individually." The Advisors could also be delegated "certain authority to hear matters and to advise the Court on issues that may arise in these five large Chapter 11 cases." Judge Wolin's order provided that he could, "without further notice, appoint any of the Court-Appointed Consultants to act as a Special Master to hear any disputed matter and to make a report and recommendation to the Court on the disposition of such matter."

Over the next two years, Judge Wolin met repeatedly, on an ex parte basis, with the parties and their attorneys. Despite his prior assurance that he would do so "sparingly," he acknowledged more recently that he met ex parte with interested parties "on innumerable occasions." This is supported by the fee applications filed by the Advisors, which reveal more than 325 hours of ex parte meetings with the attorneys for various parties in the Five Asbestos Cases. . . . During the proceedings on remand, Judge Wolin acknowledged that he received extra-judicial information at the ex parte conferences.

The ex parte meetings were not limited to the parties and their attorneys. In the first half of 2002, Judge Wolin and the Advisors held a series of four ex parte meetings at which they discussed, in Advisor McGovern's words, "[j]ust whatever issue you can think of" . . . . The primary purpose of these meetings was to educate Judge Wolin on the issues likely to arise in the Five Asbestos Cases . . . .

One of these initial meetings was attended by Bob Komitor, a plaintiff's attorney. According to Advisor Dreier, Komitor described an expert, Dr. Peter Barrett, as "a charlatan" . . . Dr. Barrett had been previously engaged by USG Corp. While there is no official record of this meeting, notes taken by Advisor Gross suggest that some of the Advisors also expressed negative views about the positions taken by USG's expert and other USG Corp. defenses.

Following this series of initial meetings, Judge Wolin also held an ex parte meeting on November 19, 2002 with Advisors Gross, McGovern and Dreier to discuss certain issues in the Owens Corning bankruptcy. . . .

... At the November 19th meeting, the Advisors discussed some of the key issues contained in the proposed plan with Judge Wolin and explained their effects as well as what appear to be certain settlement figures that had been discussed with the parties.

At a conference held on November 21, 2002, Judge Wolin stated that he did not favor Owens Corning's proposed plan. In January 2003, Owens Corning filed a revised plan of reorganization that this time was supported by the tort claimants who had objected to the first draft plan.

During the course of the Five Asbestos Cases, Advisor Hamlin prepared a draft opinion in each of the Five Asbestos Cases, a role that Hamlin likened to that of a federal magistrate judge. At his deposition, Hamlin explained that he would normally receive a phone call from Judge Wolin's chambers informing him that an appeal had been taken from the Bankruptcy Court and that he was to prepare a draft opinion for Judge Wolin. The issues on which he drafted opinions included, among other things, bar dates for asbestos property claims, defenses by USG Corp. to asbestos personal injury claims, and proof of claim forms.

C. *The G-I Holdings Bankruptcy*

Two months before Judge Wolin appointed the Advisors in the Five Asbestos Cases, the Bankruptcy Court for the District of New Jersey (Chief Judge Rosemary Gambardella) had appointed Advisor Hamlin to serve as the "Legal Representative of Present and Future Holders of Asbestos-Related Demands" in still another asbestos-related bankruptcy case captioned *In re G-I Holdings Inc.* The *G-I Holdings* bankruptcy is not related to the Five Asbestos Cases, and Judge Wolin has played no role in the *G-I Holdings* proceedings. There is, however, a substantial likelihood and a tacit, if not express, agreement that some of the future claimants in *G-I Holdings* will also have claims against one or more of the debtors in the Five Asbestos Cases.

Less than one month after Judge Wolin appointed the five Advisors, Hamlin filed an application in *G-I Holdings* to engage Advisor Gross as his local counsel. Chief Judge Gambardella approved Gross as Hamlin's local counsel. . . .

D. *Kensington's Recusal Motion*

Almost two years later, Kensington filed a motion in the Bankruptcy Court seeking to recuse Judge Wolin from further participation in the Owens Corning bankruptcy. . . . [D.K. Acquisitions Partners, another creditor, then filed a motion to recuse Judge Wolin in the Owens Corning bankruptcy and the W.R. Grace bankruptcy. USG also filed a similar motion.]

[The court of appeals first found that it had jurisdiction to issue a writ of mandamus, and then found that Judge Wolin's decision not to recuse himself should be reviewed under an abuse-of-discretion standard.]

V. DISCUSSION

A. *Standard for Disqualification Under § 455(a)*

Whenever a judge's impartiality "might reasonably be questioned" in a judicial proceeding, 28 U.S.C. § 455(a) requires that the judge disqualify himself. The test for recusal under § 455(a) is whether a reasonable person, with knowledge of all the facts, would conclude that the judge's impartiality might reasonably be questioned. . . .

A party moving for disqualification under § 455(a) need not show actual bias because § 455(a) "concerns not only fairness to individual litigants, but, equally important, it concerns 'the public's confidence in the judiciary, which may be irreparably harmed if a case is allowed to proceed before a judge who appears to be tainted.'"

B. *Who is the Hypothetical Reasonable Person under § 455(a)?*

Judge Wolin's opinion . . . held that the reasonable person under § 455(a) is someone "with the professional skills and experience in mass-tort [asbestos-related] bankruptcies sufficient to understand the import of the facts presented," thus excluding "laypersons or attorneys not conversant with the basics of mass-tort bankruptcy practice." . . .

To the best of our knowledge, Judge Wolin's gloss on § 455(a)'s "reasonable person" standard has no precedent. It also appears to be in tension with our observation in *School Asbestos* that § 455(a) was enacted by Congress because "'people who have not served on the bench are often all too willing to indulge suspicions and doubts concerning the integrity of judges.'" [In re Sch. Asbestos Litig., 977 F.2d 764, 782 (3d Cir. 1992) (*supra* p. 607)] (quoting Liljeberg v. Health Servs. Acquisition Corp., 486 U.S. 847, 864-65 (1988)). Notably, the *School Asbestos* lawsuit was precisely the sort of complex, mass-tort litigation that Judge Wolin believed required a more nuanced definition of the reasonable person. . . .

No one disputes that asbestos bankruptcies are complicated, but the alleged perception of impropriety is fairly straightforward in this case. The gravamen of the Petitions is that Judge Wolin was tainted by the involvement of two court-appointed advisors who, at the same time that they were supposed to be giving neutral advice in the Five Asbestos Cases, represented a class of tort claimants in another, unrelated asbestos-driven bankruptcy and espoused views therein on the same disputed issues that are at the core of the Five Asbestos Cases.

We are confident that the average layperson could grasp this alleged impropriety and, after being fully informed of all the surrounding circumstances, could draw a conclusion about Judge Wolin's ability to render a fair and impartial decision. That being so, we perceive no reason to depart from the traditional "man on the street" standard.

Judge Wolin's definition of the hypothetical reasonable person is contrary to the goal of § 455(a) . . . ., which is "to promote public confidence in the integrity of the judicial process." Accordingly, . . . the hypothetical reasonable person under § 455(a) must be someone outside the judicial system because judicial insiders, "accustomed to the process of dispassionate decision making and keenly aware of their Constitutional and ethical obligations to decide matters solely on the merits, may regard asserted conflicts to be more innocuous than an outsider would."

C. *Did the Advisors [H]ave a Conflict of Interest?*

Before we can decide whether the reasonable person might question Judge Wolin's impartiality, we must determine if his Advisors had a conflict of interest. If not, then our inquiry comes to an end because the Petitioners will have failed to show that they have a clear and indisputable right to disqualification. On the other hand, if there was a conflict, then we must reach the question of whether that conflict might be perceived by the reasonable person as having tainted Judge Wolin. . . .

We conclude that two of the Advisors, Gross and Hamlin, did, in fact, operate under a structural conflict of interests at the same time that they served as Judge Wolin's Advisors. This conflict arose from the dual roles they played in the Five Asbestos Cases and the *G-I Holdings* bankruptcy.

On the one hand, Gross and Hamlin clearly had a duty to remain neutral in the Five Asbestos Cases and to provide objective, unbiased information to Judge Wolin. . . .

On the other hand, Advisors Gross and Hamlin also had a duty to act as zealous advocates for the future asbestos claimants in the G-I Holdings bankruptcy. . . . In those roles, Gross and Hamlin owed the future asbestos claimants in *G-I Holdings* a fiduciary duty to advance their interests and to see that they received the greatest possible share of the bankruptcy estate. . . . By their very position as representatives of the future asbestos claimants in *G-I Holdings*, Gross and Hamlin signaled to all that they could not be non-partisan, benign, or neutral. . . .

Given their dual roles, we find that Gross and Hamlin had a conflict of interest. The structural conflict arose primarily out of the close relationship between the future asbestos claimants and the issues in the Five Asbestos Cases and *G-I Holdings*. . . . [M]any of the same legal issues (e.g., bar dates, proof of claim forms, medical manifestations, etc.) either have arisen or will arise in both the Five Asbestos Cases and the *G-I Holdings* bankruptcy.

. . . [T]hese suspicions are heightened by the ex parte nature of the communications between Judge Wolin and his Advisors. We do not hold that ex parte communications alone — in the absence of any conflict of interest — require recusal. We emphasize that it is the *conflict of interest* and not the particular specialty of the neutral expert or advisor that concerns us. . . . Indeed, a judge may consult ex parte with a *disinterested* expert provided that the judge "gives notice to the parties of the person consulted and the substance of the advice, and affords the parties reasonable opportunity to respond." Code of Conduct for U.S. Judges Canon 3 § A(4) (2003). . . .

D. *Did the Advisors' Conflict Taint Judge Wolin?*

We turn now to the question of whether Gross's and Hamlin's conflict of interest irreversibly tainted Judge Wolin. We obviously do not equate this "taint" of Judge Wolin with any wrongdoing or bias on his part. We are fully aware that the § 455(a) standard asks only if a reasonable person knowing all the circumstances might question Judge Wolin's impartiality. . . .

Given the unique level of access and influence that Gross and Hamlin had, the length of their appointment, and the overlapping issues and clients, we find that the reasonable person, with familiarity of these circumstances, would conclude that their conflict of interest tainted Judge Wolin.

E. *The Ex parte Communications Contributing to Taint*

The extensive ex parte communications between Judge Wolin, on the one hand, and the Advisors and parties, on the other, further support disqualification under § 455(a). We have previously described ex parte communications as "anathema in our system of justice." *School Asbestos*, 977 F.2d at 789. One leading reason is that ex parte meetings are often, as they were here, unrecorded. Consequently, there is no official record of what was said during those meetings. Of even greater concern is the argument urged upon us by the Petitioners who, without knowledge of what was discussed at these meetings, contended that they could not respond to these "silent" facts. . . .

The other problem is that ex parte communications run contrary to our adversarial trial system. The adversary process plays an indispensable role in our system of justice because a debate between adversaries is often essential to the truth-seeking function of trials. If judges engage in ex parte conversations with the parties or outside experts, the adversary process is not allowed to function properly and there is an increased risk of an incorrect result. . . .

. . . Judge Wolin's ex parte meetings with the Advisors presented an even more egregious problem. The instant record reveals a conflict as to what the Advisors brought to the meetings from their extrajudicial experience and, in the case of Hamlin and Gross, from their advocate roles in *G-I Holdings*, and the extent of their influence on the entire process. We know, for instance, that someone at one of the meetings disparaged a possible expert witness and criticized a defense. Of equal concern is the record's disclosure that at a November 19, 2002 meeting attended by Advisors Gross, McGovern, and Dreier, matters of substance were discussed, but we have no knowledge about their content. . . .

Given all of these considerations, we are confident that the reasonable person would be troubled by the fact that so many communications between Judge Wolin and Gross or Hamlin took place outside the presence of the parties. If the structural conflict of interests gave Gross and Hamlin a motive to give Judge Wolin less-than-neutral advice, it was the ex parte meetings that gave them the opportunity. In the absence of the parties, Gross and Hamlin were in a position to influence Judge Wolin without concern about judicial constraints or independent challenges from those individuals or entities with a stake in the outcome of the Five Asbestos Cases. . . .

G. *Disqualification Under § 455(b)(1)*

. . . [T]he Petitioners also seek Judge Wolin's disqualification under § 455(b)(1) on the basis of his ex parte communications with the Advisors, parties, and attorneys. Because we have determined that Judge Wolin must be disqualified under § 455(a), there is no need to reach . . . the merits of § 455(b)(1). Section 455(b)(1) is embraced within the perception that a reasonable person might entertain that the judge's impartiality might reasonably be questioned. . . .

As to [the creditors] and USG Corp., who have asked us to issue a Writ of Mandamus disqualifying Judge Wolin from further presiding over the Owens Corning, W.R. Grace & Co. and USG Corp. bankruptcies, we will grant their request. . . .

■   FUENTES, Circuit Judge, dissenting. . . .

. . . Judge Wolin took admittedly extraordinary measures to manage an unprecedentedly large and complex asbestos bankruptcy proceeding. Although his methods were unconventional, none of them would inspire within the reasonable and informed observer legitimate questions regarding Judge Wolin's impartiality. I fear that in moving for Judge Wolin's recusal, Petitioners have employed a guerrilla tactic timed to serve their own economic interests in this case, rather than the interests of justice and judicial integrity. In the end, putting the stamp of judicial approval on this kind of litigious gamesmanship threatens to undermine the integrity of our judicial proceedings far more than any techniques employed by Judge Wolin. I must respectfully dissent.

JACK B. WEINSTEIN, INDIVIDUAL JUSTICE IN MASS TORT LITIGATION

50, 111-12 (1995)

The judge in mass tort as well as public institution cases has an obligation to assist both attorneys and clients. . . . But the court also needs to consider how what is done affects the larger community. Mass cases require us to rethink the obligation of the judge in our society. . . .

. . . Judges who remain passive and rely solely on the parties to drive the litigation and protect the rights of all those affected will be more likely to fail, I believe, in their duty to society as a whole as well as to the individual parties. Judges should reach out and embrace what competent and neutral help they can secure in the difficult task before them. . . .

This broadening of responsibility has its costs. In place of the relatively hard-edged and tested ethical rules of traditional one-on-one cases, the court has broader and less well-defined responsibilities. . . .

I have suggested that forms of communitarian and communicatarian ethics might help guide lawyer and judge through these largely uncharted waters. Since the law is both eclectic and pragmatic, all the traditional ethical rules and jurisprudential approaches, from Aristotelian to Posnerian, need to be mined for their wisdom and insights.

Notes

1. "To decide when a judge may not sit is to define what a judge is. To define what a judge is is to decide what a system of adjudication is all about." John Leubsdorf, *Theories of Judging and Judicial Disqualification*, 62 N.Y.U. L. REV. 237, 237 (1987). What theory of adjudication underlies *Kensington*? What theory underlies Judge Weinstein's proposals?

2. The purposes of recusal are to remove a judicial officer who is unduly biased or prejudiced against a particular party or proceeding, *see* Liteky v. United States, 510 U.S. 540 (1994), and to ensure public confidence in the integrity of the administration of justice, *see* Liljeberg v. Health Servs. Acquisition Corp., 486 U.S. 847 (1988). Three sources provide the rules and standards of judicial conduct. The first is the Due Process Clause (and, for state judges, similar provisions of the state constitution). *See* Caperton v. A.T. Massey Coal Co., 556 U.S. —, 129 S. Ct. 2252 (2009). Second, statutes may establish standards for recusal; in the federal system, the statutes are 28 U.S.C. §§ 144 and 455. Third, the applicable judicial code of conduct establish ethical norms whose violation might require recusal. In federal court, the determinative sources are usually §§ 144 and 455, which closely track judicial codes of conduct. In re Int'l Bus. Machs. Corp., 618 F.2d 923 (2d Cir. 1980); *see* In re Ronald Parr, 13 B.R. 1010, 1019 (E.D.N.Y. 1981) (stating that the Due Process Clause "may be invoked in situations where the statutes do not technically apply").

3. Section 455 and the Code of Conduct expressly apply to federal magistrate judges. Section 144 does not, but there is little doubt that magistrate judges fall within § 144. Likewise, all of the ethical strictures apply to law clerks. In re Allied-Signal, Inc., 891 F.2d 967 (1st Cir. 1989). Neither § 144 nor § 455 mentions special masters or technical advisors. Codes of judicial conduct usually mention masters (with exceptions not pertinent here), and one court has held that § 455 applies to masters. United States v. Conservation Chem. Co., 106 F.R.D. 210 (W.D. Mo.), *rev'd on other grounds*, 770 F.2d 103 (8th Cir. 1985). In a footnote edited out of the opinion, *Kensington* suggested that codes of judicial conduct do not apply to advisors, 368 F.3d at 312 n.20, but it did not address the applicability of the other sources of judicial ethics.

4. The law of recusal is similar to that of lawyer disqualification: Judicial disqualification occurs either when a judge commits an actual impropriety or when an appearance of partiality requires recusal. For federal judges, a list of actual improprieties is found in 28 U.S.C. § 455(b). Appearances of partiality fall under § 455(a).

(a) *Actual Impropriety.* Section 455(b) lists the situations in which judges must recuse themselves. These situations encompass nearly all of the actual improprieties which other statutes, judicial codes of ethics, and the Due Process Clause also reach:

- *"Where [a judge] has a personal bias or prejudice concerning a party, or personal knowledge of disputed evidentiary facts concerning the proceeding."* This language of § 455(b)(1) is nearly identical to the language of § 144.

- *Prior Representations.* Judges must recuse themselves when, in private practice, they or a lawyer associated with them represented a party in the present case, or were material witnesses. § 455(b)(2). With regard to prior government service, recusal is required when a judge acted as counsel, adviser, or material witness in a case, or expressed an opinion regarding its merits. § 455(b)(3).

- *Financial or Other Interest.* A judge with a financial interest in a case must be recused. § 455(b)(4); Aetna Life Ins. Co. v. Lavoie, 475 U.S. 813 (analyzing the question under the Due Process Clause). In addition, fiduciary and comparable interests (for instance, the judge's role as guardian of his or her children) require recusal.

- *Close Relationship.* A judge also must disqualify himself or herself when a spouse or a "person within the third degree of relationship to either of them, or a spouse of such a person," is a party; is an officer, director, or trustee of a party; is a lawyer in the case; is known to have an interest that could be substantially affected by the outcome; or is known to be a material witness. § 455(b)(5).

Complex litigation poses unique problems in the application of these situations. For instance, due to the need for case management, a judge is likely to form impressions and acquire knowledge about disputed facts at an early stage in the litigation. Does this activity create "personal bias" and "personal knowledge" within the meaning of § 455(b)(1)? Before *Liteky,* this question tended to be answered by referring to the "extrajudicial source doctrine," which held that a judge could be disqualified only when biases, prejudices, or knowledge derived from sources other than those to which the judge was exposed in performing his or her judicial duties. *Liteky,* however, thought that the "extrajudicial source" test was both too broad and too narrow: "[I]t would be better to speak of the existence of a significant (and often determinative) 'extrajudicial source' *factor,* than of an 'extrajudicial source' *doctrine,* in recusal jurisprudence." 510 U.S. at 554. *See* In re TMI Litig., 193 F.3d 613 (3d Cir. 1999), *amended,* 199 F.3d 158 (3d Cir. 2000) (refusing to disqualify a judge when the alleged bias resulted from his rulings and comments from the bench).

The commonsensical rule about recusing a judge with a financial or fiduciary interest can also create problems. For instance, a judge handling an antitrust case might benefit, as all consumers will, from the breakup of a monopoly. Addressing this reality, the rule is that a judge who benefits only as a member of the public need not be disqualified. *See* In re N.M. Natural Gas Antitrust Litig., 620 F.2d 794 (10th Cir. 1980). When a judge has greater interests — perhaps ownership of a few shares of stock in a company that will benefit from the breakup — the issue has proven more intractable. In *In re Cement Antitrust Litigation (MDL No. 296)*, 688 F.2d 1297 (9th Cir. 1982), *aff'd in absence of quorum*, 459 U.S. 1191 (1983), the court of appeals upheld the recusal decision of a judge whose wife owned stock in seven of the 210,000 class members, even though the judge had fairly managed the case for four years. *But see* In re Indus. Gas Antitrust Litig., 1985 WL 2869 (N.D. Ill. Sept. 24, 1985) (refusing to order recusal in a 172,000-member class action when the judge's husband owned stock in two class members, the husband divested himself of the stock after learning of the situation, and little activity had occurred in the case). In *Agent Orange*, plaintiffs who sought to continue litigating after a class settlement moved to recuse Judge Weinstein on the theory that Judge Weinstein's fiduciary obligations to the settlement fund created a conflict of interest. The Second Circuit held that "legally-imposed duties qua judge with regard to the settlement funds are not a 'fiduciary' obligation within the meaning of section 455(b)(4), and do not mandate disqualification from cases which may involve the fund." In re "Agent Orange" Prod. Liab. Litig., 996 F.2d 1425 (2d Cir. 1993).

Finally, strict enforcement of the rule that a judge's close relationship with a party or lawyer requires recusal can cripple some large-scale class actions, and the rule has been adjusted accordingly. *See* United States v. Ala., 828 F.2d 1532 (11th Cir. 1987) (judge not required to recuse himself even though his children were members of class action, when their interest in discrimination-free schools was no greater than that of other children).

(b) *Appearance of Partiality*. The Due Process Clause, judicial codes of ethics, and federal statutes all require recusal when an appearance of partiality exists. *See Lavoie*, 475 U.S. 813; ABA Code of Judicial Conduct, Canon 3(c); 28 U.S.C. § 455(a). Rather than creating an entirely new set of expectations for judges, this standard has acted largely as a penumbra around the specific instances of actual impropriety listed above. For instance, the Supreme Court has held that apparent biases created during the performance of judicial duties can, in rare cases, serve as grounds for recusal under § 455(a). *Liteky*, 510 U.S. 540.

In one area, courts have been willing to use § 455(a) despite the lack of a clear analogue in § 455(b): communications between the trial judge and the media about a matter before the court. The most famous example is the *Microsoft* antitrust litigation, in which the presiding judge held interviews during and after trial, and provided some media with access to his thinking about the credibility of witnesses. Although such extrajudicial comments do not easily fit within any of the strictures of § 455(b), they violate Canon

3(A) of the Code of Conduct for United States Judges. The court of appeals had no trouble concluding that this behavior might lead a reasonable person to question the impartiality of the judge, thus violating § 455(a). United States v. Microsoft Corp., 253 F.3d 34 (D.C. Cir. 2001). *See also* In re: Boston's Children First, 244 F.3d 164 (1st Cir. 2001) (recusing a judge for comments explaining her class-certification ruling to a reporter).

5. Perhaps because of their active case management, judges in complex cases see their fair share of recusal motions. Recusal motions premised on the overly activist nature of a judge are rarely successful. *See Allied Signal*, 891 F.2d at 972 (refusing to order recusal, in part because the "need for judicial management by the district court counsels caution prior to intervention by an appellate court" in "large, complex, and time consuming" cases). In *Agent Orange*, 996 F.2d at 1439, the court of appeals brushed aside the argument of the plaintiffs that Judge Weinstein should have recused himself because he possessed "some traits of megalomania, of having a 'systematic interest in retaining excessive judicial powers over mass tort cases,'" and praised Judge Weinstein for his "'innovations' and 'innovative managerial skills' in such large-scale litigation." On the other hand, some of these motions succeed. *Kensington* is one example. Another is *In re School Asbestos Litigation*, 977 F.2d 764 (3d Cir. 1992) (*supra* p. 697).

6. Even when a case does not meet the requirements for recusal, a court of appeals retains the authority to order that a case be assigned to a different judge for further proceedings. 28 U.S.C. § 2106; *see* United States v. Microsoft Corp., 56 F.3d 1448 (D.C. Cir. 1995); Haines v. Liggett Group Inc., 975 F.2d 81 (3d Cir. 1992). Appellate courts usually apply the substantive standards for disqualification to their decision to re-assign.

7. When grounds for disqualification exist, a secondary issue is whether remedies in addition to recusal are warranted — in particular, whether the judge's prior orders or judgment should be vacated. Because vacation reopens a judgment or settled rulings, it is rarely invoked. Three factors — "the risk of injustice to the parties in the particular case, the risk that the denial of relief will produce injustice in other cases, and the risk of undermining the public's confidence in the judicial process," *Liljeberg*, 486 U.S. 864 — determine the issue. *See also Allied-Signal*, 891 F.2d at 973 (1st Cir. 1989) (declaring a mistrial in a mass-tort case would needlessly "threaten to undo matters of considerable importance previously decided").

8. You might compare Judge Wolin's conduct in *Kensington* to that of other well-known judges. Begin with Miles Lord, who was one of the most colorful characters ever to occupy the federal bench. He was an early disciple of strong case management. In one antitrust case, Judge Lord aggressively questioned a witness at a deposition he attended, later opining on the truthfulness of the witness; attempted to block a settlement with the government because it upset his "'game plan' for managing the case"; solicited new class plaintiffs to continue the litigation when a settlement of the private class action appeared imminent; and called the Patent Office "the sickest institution . . . ever invented." The court of appeals thought

that Judge Lord's characterization of the Patent Office was "injudicious," but saw nothing in the case that manifested a personal bias or prejudice toward defendants. Pfizer Inc. v. Lord, 456 F.2d 532 (8th Cir. 1972).

Next, Judge H. Lee Sarokin had shepherded one of the first tobacco product-liability cases through trial and was turning his attention to others. In ruling on a discovery motion, Judge Sarokin's opinion opened with a three-sentence lamentation about the culture of concealment in American industry. He followed with this sentence: "As the following facts disclose, despite some rising pretenders, the tobacco industry may be the king of concealment." While refusing to order Sarokin's recusal, and praising him for his "magnificent abilities," the court of appeals held that the remarks created an appearance of partiality and exercised its supervisory powers under § 2106 to re-assign the case on remand. *Haines*, 975 F.2d 81.

Finally, Judge James McGirr Kelly was presiding over a series of complex asbestos cases. He attended, all expenses paid, a scientific conference planned largely by asbestos plaintiffs' lawyers. Unknown to Judge Kelly, settlement proceeds whose distribution he had approved partially funded the conference. The court of appeals ordered his recusal. *School Asbestos*, 977 F.2d 764.

If you were to rank the conduct of the four judges — Judge Kelly, Judge Lord, Judge Sarokin, and Judge Wolin — didn't Judge Lord commit the most "recusable" offense? Why was he the only one not removed?

9.   As with lawyers, the fundamental question is whether we should adjust judges' ethical standards in complex litigation. One way to answer this question is to consider the nature of adjudication. We can never allow judges to act in a way that jeopardizes their essential adjudicatory role, but we might compromise on the desirable features of an ideal judge when adequate cause exists. For example, if rational judgment is an essential component of adjudication, and if an adversarial approach is a desirable feature, we would never allow a judge who is biased to decide a case; but when the needs of a case are compelling, we might allow the judge to engage in conduct inconsistent with the judge's adversarial role. On the other hand, adversarial process is an essential aspect of adjudication, conduct inconsistent with the judge's adversarial role would be barred.

Is this analysis sound? If so, is an adversarial system essential or desirable? If it only desirable, it is incumbent on us, as Judge Weinstein says, to draft a code of conduct for judicial officers involved in complex cases. Until this code is developed, is it wise to allow judges to free-lance away from the ethical norms for the judge of the adversarial model?

CHAPTER EIGHT

NARROWING ISSUES AND DISCOVERING FACTS

In terms of readying a case for trial, a successful pretrial process must accomplish two things: It must define the claims and issues that will be tried, and it must develop factual information relevant to these claims and issues. A tension exists between these two functions. It is impossible to know whether the right claims and issues have been selected for trial until the relevant facts are discovered, but it is impossible to know what the relevant facts are until the claims and issues have been defined. Hence the "chicken and egg" problem of pretrial procedure.

Different systems of procedure feel this problem more or less acutely. In a civilian system, pretrial and trial intermingle, so that the tasks of issue definition, discovery, and issue resolution proceed together seamlessly. The Anglo-American system has traditionally had more difficulty. The common-law system, with its jury-trial process, saw a trial as a final phase to resolve all factual issues, distinct from the pretrial phase of defining issues and discovering facts. Common-law procedure handled the pretrial tasks of issue definition and discovery rather bluntly; it focused almost exclusively on narrowing a claim to a single issue by means of pleading rules and it provided no direct means for discovering facts (although common-law litigants could sometimes use a supplemental proceeding in equity to obtain some discovery). As a descendant of the civilian tradition, equity had less rigid pleading rules and permitted discovery, but it had a limited capacity to resolve disputed issues, and often had to rely on a supplemental common-law proceeding in which a jury determined disputed facts.

Our modern procedural system blended elements of the common law and equity. It kept the common-law ideal of a single, all-issues trial that strongly separated the pretrial and trial phases. In the pretrial stage, however, it swung strongly toward, and in some instances beyond, the looser pleadings and the generous discovery procedures of equity. Pleadings were intended to be short and plain, designed to give notice of the principal issues rather than to delineate and narrow them. A range of discovery devices — including interrogatories, requests for production, and depositions — allowed broad discovery of relevant facts. Although some devices for issue resolution (such as motions to dismiss and motions for summary judgment) were built into the pretrial process, defining and narrowing issues were secondary concerns; the expectation was that, once the issues were fully developed through discovery, lawyers would abandon claims and issues lacking merit. Discovery was seen as a technique for narrowing issues. The modern procedural system resolves the "chicken and egg" conundrum by coming down rather decidedly in favor of full discovery over issue narrowing.

For routine cases this system of procedure has worked reasonably well. Cases are usually decided on their merits rather than on procedural traps and technicalities. With good factual information, parties can make good judgments about the value of their cases and are better equipped to settle amicably. There are complaints about the costliness of discovery, the mean-spiritedness of lawyers, and the abuse of frivolous lawsuits. But in the main, the modern system seems superior to the processes that preceded it.

In complex cases, however, this modern system of pretrial does not function well. The relevant factual information is vast; the claims, issues, and party structures are sprawling and amorphous; the costs of pretrial are staggering; the temptation of well-funded adversaries to win by attrition is irresistible. Moreover, trial is no longer the end game for most complex cases. Whether the pretrial process should focus on resolving the sticking points that prevent a likely settlement — as opposed to discovering the issues that are the focus of an unlikely trial — is a critical question that a judge considering how to manage the pretrial process must consider.

In either event, it seems that complex cases require courts to become more active in defining and narrowing issues at an early point in the litigation than they need to be in more routine litigation. Do our modern rules gives the judge enough tools to accomplish this task? Do the judge's case-management powers adequately supplement any deficiencies in the existing tools? If we allow judges to narrow issues (and thus constrict discovery) at an earlier point, are we denying thousands of litigants access to the information that might change defeat into a victory, or a nuisance-value settlement into an appropriate one? What justifies different, possibly outcome-determinative treatment between plaintiffs in complex cases and plaintiffs in routine disputes? Can judges strike, on a case-by-case basis, the proper balance between issue definition and discovery? Didn't the common law try the approach of early issue narrowing already, and didn't it fail? Are there any middle paths that lessen the "chicken and egg" conundrum in complex litigation?

These are the questions we address in this chapter, as we examine the ways in which a managerial judge can push a complex case through the pretrial process. We begin by exploring the devices that the judge can use to define and narrow claims and issues, and then turn to the issues that can arise during discovery.

A. NARROWING ISSUES

Perhaps one way to understand what is at stake with issue-narrowing devices is to look in your library at the Federal Reporter, 2d series. There are 999 volumes in the series, totaling 1.25 million pages (give or take a few thousand). If you assume that you spent 6 seconds a page, which is enough time to scan the page and get a very rough sense of its contents, it would take you nearly 2,100 hours (an entire year's worth of billable hours!) to read the entire series. It is not unusual for a complex case to contain as many as 10 million pages of documents — in other words, eight complete sets of Federal Reporter, 2d Series, or eight years worth of quick scanning. Comprehension time, of course, would be extra.

Suppose now that available devices made it unnecessary for you to read three-quarters of the documents. You'd be all for it, wouldn't you? But suppose that somewhere in the reams of discovery that an issue-narrowing technique obviated is a smoking gun proving the defendant's liability. Suddenly issue-narrowing techniques act like the bad old rules of common-law procedure, cutting off inquiry into relevant matters and thwarting substantive justice.

That, in a sense, is what is at stake with regard to devices that define and narrow issues at an early stage: the benefits and costs of techniques that can forestall, and perhaps forever eliminate, vast amounts of discovery. Most of the devices that we study permanently eliminate claims or issues, making discovery regarding those issues unnecessary. Other devices, however, postpone certain issues in the hope that, after the initial exploration of some claims or issues, litigation on remaining claims and issues will be unnecessary or greatly abbreviated.

We begin by examining the ways in which judges can use the pleading process to streamline the pretrial process. From there, we move to post-pleading issue-narrowing techniques.

1. Pleading as a Means of Narrowing Issues

This subsection considers two pleading issues. The first is the judge's power to force parties to use the initial pleadings to define and narrow issues. The second is the judge's power to require plaintiffs or defendants to file a single, consolidated pleading to streamline the litigation.

a. Pleading Standards in Complex Cases

The basic pleading rule of the Federal Rules of Civil Procedure, Rule 8, is one of the linchpins of the modern procedural system. Rule 8(a) provides for *notice pleading*, under which a plaintiff is required to provide only a "short and plain statement" of jurisdiction, "a short and plain statement of the claim showing that the pleader is entitled to relief," and "a demand for the relief sought." The defendant is to respond similarly, stating "in short and plain terms" any defenses and "to admit or deny the allegations asserted" in the complaint. Fed. R. Civ. P. 8(b). Pleadings are to be "simple, concise, and direct. No technical form is required." Fed. R. Civ. P. 8(d)(1). Only with regard to some matters — most notably fraud and mistake — must a party "state with particularity" the nature of the allegations. Fed. R. Civ. P. 9(b). Moreover, Rule 18(a) permits a party to join "as many claims as it has against an opposing party," and Rules 13(a), -(b), and -(g) allow a party to assert all counterclaims and all transactionally related crossclaims as well.

These pleading rules are not designed to define and narrow the issues for trial. They are premised on the assumption that pleading technicalities should not stand in the way of resolving cases on their merits; rather, the discovery process can winnow the triable claims, defenses, and issues from the chaff. Whether this assumption holds true in complex cases is far from clear. Should the expectation for pleading change in complex cases, so that the pleadings serve, as they had at common law, important issue-defining and issue-narrowing functions?

NAGLER v. ADMIRAL CORP.

248 F.2d 319 (2d Cir. 1957)

■ CLARK, Chief Judge.

This is an antitrust and price-discrimination action for injunction and damages by thirteen retailers in the Greater New York area of radio, television, and electrical appliances. It is brought against twenty-six defendants, of whom twenty-four are "suppliers," i.e., manufacturers, wholesalers, and distributors, and two are retailers operating chain stores in this area. The case is founded upon the allegation that these two defendant-retailers, Davega Stores Corporation and Vim Television and Appliance Stores, Inc., received special price concessions from the supplier defendants. The complaint is in twenty-nine paragraphs and three counts, or "causes of action" as they are labeled. The first cause is for "Defendants' Discrimination Against Plaintiffs in Violation of the Robinson-Patman Act," 15 U.S.C. § 13; while the other causes, reincorporating the allegations of the first, are for violations of the Sherman Act, 15 U.S.C. §§ 1, 2. Ten of the defendants joined in a motion to dismiss for improper pleading . . . and for misjoinder of parties. [The district court dismissed the complaint as to all the defendants, and the plaintiffs appealed.]

The drastic remedy here granted for pleading errors is unusual, since outright dismissal for reasons not going to the merits is viewed with disfavor in the federal courts. . . . And this has been true generally in both English and American law and legal history, for cases are not finally disposed of on mere points of pleading alone. Courts naturally shrink from the injustice of denying legal rights to a litigant for the mistakes in technical form of his attorney. . . . We are clear, therefore, that the case must go back for some less final disposition at least permitting the plaintiffs to amend. But because of their practical importance in routine litigation, we think some elaboration of both the pleading and the joinder issues is desirable.

It is true that antitrust litigation may be of wide scope and without a central point of attack, so that defense must be diffuse, prolonged, and costly.   So many defense lawyers have strongly advocated more particularized pleading in this area of litigation; and recently the judges in the court below have treated it as accepted law that some special pleading — the extent is left unclear — is required in antitrust cases. But it is quite clear that the federal rules contain no special exceptions for antitrust cases. When the rules were adopted there was considerable pressure for separate provisions in patent, copyright, and other allegedly special types of litigation. Such arguments did not prevail; instead there was adopted a uniform system for all cases — one which nevertheless allows some discretion to the trial judge to require fuller disclosure in a particular case by more definite statement, Fed. R. Civ. P. 12(e), discovery and summary judgment, Fed. R. Civ. P. 26-35, 56, and pre-trial conference, Fed. R. Civ. P. 16. . . .

In asserting a special rule of pleading for antitrust cases, [some district judges have] in terms rejected the "modern 'notice' theory of pleading" as here insufficient and said that an antitrust complaint must "state a cause of action instead of merely stating a claim." But while these essentially nebulous concepts often creep into pleading discussions, they are no part of the rules themselves, but were in fact rejected for more precise formulations. It is well to go back to the rules themselves and their intended purpose. . . . "The intent and effect of the rules is to permit the claim to be stated in general terms; the rules are designed to discourage battles over mere form of statement and to sweep away the needless controversies which the codes permitted that served either to delay trial on the merits or to prevent a party from having a trial because of mistakes in statement. . . . It is accordingly the opinion of the Advisory Committee that, as it stands, the rule adequately sets forth the characteristics of good pleading; does away with the confusion resulting from the use of 'facts' and 'cause of action'; and requires the pleader to disclose adequate information as the basis of his claim for relief as distinguished from a bare averment that he wants relief and is entitled to it."

Turning to the complaint before us, we remark that in outward form at least it is an imposing document consisting of twelve or more printed pages. . . . The complaint is filled with the pleading of conclusions of both fact and law; it is far from that lean and terse allegation in sequence of events as they have happened which we have stressed. But we are not conducting exercises in pleading; we must look beyond the mere mountain of words to the meaning sought to be conveyed. So looking we can have no doubt that plaintiffs say the supplier defendants have given their favored customers Vim and Davega price discounts and other special favors (listed in some detail) which have lost sales to the plaintiffs, destroyed their capacity to compete, and forced some of them out of business.

In testing whether this is a sufficient statement of claim upon which to base a lawsuit, we ought practically to consider the alternatives, both what can be expected and asked of antitrust plaintiffs and what can be accomplished by compulsive orders. Here seems to be the rock upon which [cases that attempt] to achieve more particularized pleading have definitely foundered; for the judges' directions double the bulk without increasing enlightenment, while they delay the cause and exhaust the time of several judges. So in this case the district judge has stated several requirements which would seem either not feasible or not such as to advance the case toward adjudication. Most of them relate to details either not pertinent to the legal point or covered generally, such as addresses and location of defendants, the territory involved (the "Greater New York area"), the time (necessarily the period permitted by the applicable statutes of limitation to the date of filing of the complaint), and so on. Perhaps the nub of all this is the conclusion that by "stating the claims of all the plaintiffs against all the defendants collectively, they have deprived the defendants of notice of the precise nature of the claims that each will be required to meet." But we note that a similar order in a companion case has resulted only in a complaint doubled in length, with separate paragraphs of iteration in general form of action by individual plaintiffs against individual defendants — a formal compliance, with no gain in useful information that we can perceive.

It is to be noted that this complaint . . . does lack a direct allegation that the defendants conspired together, although it assumes the defendants' "combinations and conspiracies" and the resulting damage to plaintiffs. But as to this the trier of facts may draw an inference of agreement or concerted action from the "conscious parallelism" of the defendants' acts of price cutting and the like, as the Supreme Court recognizes. It would seem therefore that the plaintiffs have set forth a prima facie case which, if proved, will force the defendants to their proof in rebuttal.

In criticizing these complaints the trial judges have tended to see willful violations of precise instructions. We doubt if this is a profitable approach in any event; however willful seeming, lawyers must represent their clients in what they conceive the most effective way in the light of their knowledge, which must include that neither English nor American experience lends support to mere pleadings as a substitute for trial. But as we try to visualize practical substitutes we question the adverse implication. For actually this demand seems to come to a call for specific instances, as that Admiral made such and such a discount sale of specified goods to Davega on a particular day at a particular place. Anything short of this, as the practice below is demonstrating, will permit of the vagueness the judges are finding troublesome. And yet such pleading of the evidence is surely not required and is on the whole undesirable. It is a matter for the discovery process, not for allegations of detail in the complaint. The complaint should not be burdened with possibly hundreds of specific instances; and if it were, it would be comparatively meaningless at trial where the parties could adduce further pertinent evidence if discovered. They can hardly know all their evidence, down to the last detail, long in advance of trial.

The sad truth is that these cases are likely to prove laborious in any event and that there is no real substitute for trial, although pre-trial conferences and orders may greatly speed the result. But a considerable part of federal litigation is of a lengthy and burdensome nature and we are not justified in frowning on a Congressional policy so definitely cherished as is this, a policy which is, after all, the cause of our troubles. And while as appellate judges we would help our brethren at the crucial trial stage where we could, the experience, as generally noted, shows that attempts at special pleading are definitely not the remedy. . . . The real solution — so far as there is one short of trial — would appear to be . . . continuing pretrial conferences under the direction of a single judge who may thus avoid the duplicating efforts of various judges we have noted above.

[The court then held that plaintiffs had adequately alleged facts to permit joinder under Federal Rules 20 and 23.]

Reversed and remanded.

BELL ATLANTIC CORP. V. TWOMBLY

550 U.S. 544 (2007)

■ JUSTICE SOUTER delivered the opinion of the Court.

Liability under § 1 of the Sherman Act, 15 U.S.C. § 1, requires a "contract, combination . . ., or conspiracy, in restraint of trade or commerce." The question in this putative class action is whether a § 1 complaint can survive a motion to dismiss when it alleges that major telecommunications providers engaged in certain parallel conduct unfavorable to competition, absent some factual context suggesting agreement, as distinct from identical, independent action. We hold that such a complaint should be dismissed.

I

The upshot of the 1984 divestiture of the American Telephone & Telegraph Company's (AT&T) local telephone business was a system of regional service monopolies (variously called "Regional Bell Operating Companies," "Baby Bells," or "Incumbent Local Exchange Carriers" (ILECs)), and a separate, competitive market for long-distance service from which the ILECs were excluded. [Congress enacted the Telecommunications Act of 1996 (1996 Act), which withdrew the local monopolies enjoyed by the ILECs. A critical provision in the 1996 Act required each ILEC to share its network with certain competitors, known as "competitive local exchange carriers" (CLECs). The ILECs vigorously litigated the scope of this obligation during the ensuing decade.]

Respondents William Twombly and Lawrence Marcus (hereinafter plaintiffs) represent a putative class consisting of all "subscribers of local telephone and/or high speed internet services . . . from February 8, 1996 to present." In this action against petitioners, a group of ILECs, plaintiffs seek treble damages and declaratory and injunctive relief for claimed violations of § 1 of the Sherman Act . . . .

The complaint alleges that the ILECs conspired to restrain trade in two ways . . . . Plaintiffs say, first, that the ILECs "engaged in parallel conduct" in their respective service areas to inhibit the growth of upstart CLECs. . . .

Second, the complaint charges agreements by the ILECs to refrain from competing against one another. . . .

[The complaint contained these allegations, which we quote verbatim:

40. The failure of the [ILECs] to compete with one another would be anomalous in the absence of an agreement among the [ILECs] not to compete with one another in view of the fact that in significant respects, the territories that they service are non-contiguous. As reflected in Exhibit A hereto, SBC serves most of the State of Connecticut even though Verizon rather than SBC serves the surrounding states. SBC serves California and Nevada, even though Qwest serves the other surrounding states. . . . The failure of the [ILECs] that serve the surrounding territories to make significant attempts to compete in the surrounded territories is strongly suggestive of conspiracy, since the service of such surrounded territories presents the [ILECs] serving surrounding territories with an especially attractive business opportunity that such [ILECs] have not meaningfully pursued.

42. On October 31, 2002, Richard Notebaert[,] the former Chief Executive Officer of Ameritech, who sold the company to Defendant SBC in 1999 and who currently serves as the Chief Executive Officer of Defendant Qwest, was quoted in a *Chicago Tribune* article as saying it would be fundamentally wrong to compete in the SBC/Ameritech territory, adding "it might be a good way to turn a quick dollar but that doesn't make it right." . . .

46. The [ILECs] do indeed communicate amongst themselves through a myriad of organizations . . . .

47. Defendants have engaged in parallel conduct in order to prevent competition in their respective local telephone and/or high speed internet services markets. "They have refused to open their markets by dragging their feet in allowing competitors to interconnect, refusing to negotiate in good faith, litigating every nook and cranny of the law, and avoiding head-to-head competition like the plague." Consumer Federation of America, Lessons From 1996 Telecommunications Act: Deregulation Before Meaningful Competition Spells Consumer Disaster, February 2001, p. 1. Defendants also have engaged and continue to engage in unanimity of action by committing one or more of the following wrongful acts . . .: [Here the complaint listed 12 courses of action in which the defendants either discriminated against the CLECs in the provision or quality of services, or otherwise used their monopoly power to maintain a competitive advantage.] . . .

51. In the absence of any meaningful competition between the [ILECs] in one another's markets, and in light of the parallel course of conduct that each engaged in to prevent competition from CLECs within their respective local telephone and/or high speed internet services markets and the other facts and market circumstances alleged above, Plaintiffs allege upon information and belief that Defendants have entered into a contract, combination or conspiracy to prevent competitive entry in their respective local telephone and/or high speed internet services markets and have agreed not to compete with one another and otherwise allocated customers and markets to one another.]

The United States District Court for the Southern District of New York dismissed the complaint for failure to state a claim upon which relief can be granted. The District Court acknowledged that "plaintiffs may allege a conspiracy by citing instances of parallel business behavior that suggest an agreement," but emphasized that "while '[c]ircumstantial evidence of consciously parallel behavior may have made heavy inroads into the traditional judicial attitude toward conspiracy[, . . .] "conscious parallelism" has not yet read conspiracy out of the Sherman Act entirely.'" . . .

The Court of Appeals for the Second Circuit reversed . . . . Although the Court of Appeals took the view that plaintiffs must plead facts that "include conspiracy among the realm of 'plausible' possibilities in order to survive a motion to dismiss," it then said that "to rule that allegations of parallel anticompetitive conduct fail to support a plausible conspiracy claim, a court would have to conclude that there is no set of facts that would permit a plaintiff to demonstrate that the particular parallelism asserted was the product of collusion rather than coincidence."

We granted certiorari to address the proper standard for pleading an antitrust conspiracy through allegations of parallel conduct, and now reverse.

II

A

Because § 1 of the Sherman Act "does not prohibit [all] unreasonable restraints of trade . . . but only restraints effected by a contract, combination, or conspiracy," "[t]he crucial question" is whether the challenged anticompetitive conduct "stem[s] from independent decision or from an agreement, tacit or express." While a showing of parallel "business behavior is admissible circumstantial evidence from which the fact finder may infer agreement," it falls short of "conclusively establish[ing] agreement or . . . itself constitut[ing] a Sherman Act offense." Even "conscious parallelism," a common reaction of "firms in a concentrated market [that] recogniz[e] their shared economic interests and their interdependence with respect to price and output decisions" is "not in itself unlawful." . . .

Accordingly, we have previously hedged against false inferences from identical behavior at a number of points in the trial sequence. An antitrust conspiracy plaintiff with evidence showing nothing beyond parallel conduct is not entitled to a directed verdict; proof of a § 1 conspiracy must include evidence tending to exclude the possibility of independent action; and at the summary judgment stage a § 1 plaintiff's offer of conspiracy evidence must tend to rule out the possibility that the defendants were acting independently.

B

This case presents the antecedent question of what a plaintiff must plead in order to state a claim under § 1 of the Sherman Act. Federal Rule of Civil Procedure 8(a)(2) requires only "a short and plain statement of the claim showing that the pleader is entitled to relief," in order to "give the defendant fair notice of what the . . . claim is and the grounds upon which it rests," Conley v. Gibson, 355 U.S. 41, 47 (1957). While a complaint attacked by a Rule 12(b)(6) motion to dismiss does not need detailed factual allegations, a plaintiff's obligation to provide the "grounds" of his "entitle[ment] to relief" requires more than labels and conclusions, and a formulaic recitation of the elements of a cause of action will not do. Factual allegations must be enough to raise a right to relief above the speculative level, on the assumption that all the allegations in the complaint are true (even if doubtful in fact), *see, e.g.,* Swierkiewicz v. Sorema N. A., 534 U.S. 506, 508 n.1 (2002).

In applying these general standards to a § 1 claim, we hold that stating such a claim requires a complaint with enough factual matter (taken as true) to suggest that an agreement was made. Asking for plausible grounds to infer an agreement does not impose a probability requirement at the pleading stage; it simply calls for enough fact to raise a reasonable expectation that discovery will reveal evidence of illegal agreement.[4] And, of course, a well-pleaded complaint may proceed even if it strikes a savvy judge that actual proof of those facts is improbable, and "that a recovery is very remote and unlikely." In identifying facts that are suggestive enough to render a § 1 conspiracy plausible, we have the benefit of the prior rulings and considered views of leading commentators . . . that lawful parallel conduct fails to bespeak unlawful agreement. It makes sense to say, therefore, that an allegation of parallel conduct and a bare assertion of conspiracy will not suffice. Without more, parallel conduct does not suggest conspiracy, and a conclusory allegation of agreement at some unidentified point does not supply facts adequate to show illegality. Hence, when allegations of parallel conduct are set out in order to make a § 1 claim, they must be placed in a context that raises a suggestion of a preceding

---

4. Commentators have offered several examples of parallel conduct allegations that would state a § 1 claim under this standard. . . . The parties in this case agree that "complex and historically un- precedented changes in pricing structure made at the very same time by multiple competitors, and made for no other discernible reason" would support a plausible inference of conspiracy.

agreement, not merely parallel conduct that could just as well be independent action.

The need at the pleading stage for allegations plausibly suggesting (not merely consistent with) agreement reflects the threshold requirement of Rule 8(a)(2) that the "plain statement" possess enough heft to "sho[w] that the pleader is entitled to relief." A statement of parallel conduct, even conduct consciously undertaken, needs some setting suggesting the agreement necessary to make out a § 1 claim; without that further circumstance pointing toward a meeting of the minds, an account of a defendant's commercial efforts stays in neutral territory. An allegation of parallel conduct is thus much like a naked assertion of conspiracy in a § 1 complaint: it gets the complaint close to stating a claim, but without some further factual enhancement it stops short of the line between possibility and plausibility of "entitle[ment] to relief."

. . . So, when the allegations in a complaint, however true, could not raise a claim of entitlement to relief, "'this basic deficiency should . . . be exposed at the point of minimum expenditure of time and money by the parties and the court.'"

Thus, it is one thing to be cautious before dismissing an antitrust complaint in advance of discovery, but quite another to forget that proceeding to antitrust discovery can be expensive. As we indicated over 20 years ago in Associated Gen. Contractors of Cal., Inc. v. Carpenters, 459 U.S. 519, 528 n.17 (1983), "a district court must retain the power to insist upon some specificity in pleading before allowing a potentially massive factual controversy to proceed." *See also* MANUAL FOR COMPLEX LITIGATION, FOURTH, § 30, p. 519 (2004) (describing extensive scope of discovery in antitrust cases). That potential expense is obvious enough in the present case: plaintiffs represent a putative class of at least 90 percent of all subscribers to local telephone or high-speed Internet service in the continental United States, in an action against America's largest telecommunications firms (with many thousands of employees generating reams and gigabytes of business records) for unspecified (if any) instances of antitrust violations that allegedly occurred over a period of seven years.

It is no answer to say that a claim just shy of a plausible entitlement to relief can, if groundless, be weeded out early in the discovery process through "careful case management," given the common lament that the success of judicial supervision in checking discovery abuse has been on the modest side. And it is self-evident that the problem of discovery abuse cannot be solved by "careful scrutiny of evidence at the summary judgment stage," much less "lucid instructions to juries"; the threat of discovery expense will push cost-conscious defendants to settle even anemic cases before reaching those proceedings. Probably, then, it is only by taking care to require allegations that reach the level suggesting conspiracy that we can hope to avoid the potentially enormous expense of discovery in cases with no "reasonably founded hope that the [discovery] process will reveal relevant evidence" to support a § 1 claim.

Plaintiffs do not, of course, dispute the requirement of plausibility and the need for something more than merely parallel behavior . . ., and their main argument against the plausibility standard at the pleading stage is its ostensible conflict with an early statement of ours construing Rule 8. Justice Black's opinion for the Court in *Conley v. Gibson* spoke not only of the need for fair notice of the grounds for entitlement to relief but of "the accepted rule that a complaint should not be dismissed for failure to state a claim unless it appears beyond doubt that the plaintiff can prove no set of facts in support of his claim which would entitle him to relief." This "no set of facts" language can be read in isolation as saying that any statement revealing the theory of the claim will suffice unless its factual impossibility may be shown from the face of the pleadings; and the Court of Appeals appears to have read *Conley* in some such way when formulating its understanding of the proper pleading standard.

On such a focused and literal reading of *Conley*'s "no set of facts," a wholly conclusory statement of claim would survive a motion to dismiss whenever the pleadings left open the possibility that a plaintiff might later establish some "set of [undisclosed] facts" to support recovery. So here, the Court of Appeals specifically found the prospect of unearthing direct evidence of conspiracy sufficient to preclude dismissal, even though the complaint does not set forth a single fact in a context that suggests an agreement. It seems fair to say that this approach to pleading would dispense with any showing of a "'reasonably founded hope'" that a plaintiff would be able to make a case . . . .

Seeing this, a good many judges and commentators have balked at taking the literal terms of the *Conley* passage as a pleading standard.

. . . *Conley*'s "no set of facts" language has been questioned, criticized, and explained away long enough. To be fair to the *Conley* Court, the passage should be understood in light of the opinion's preceding summary of the complaint's concrete allegations, which the Court quite reasonably understood as amply stating a claim for relief. But the passage so often quoted fails to mention this understanding on the part of the Court, and after puzzling the profession for 50 years, this famous observation has earned its retirement. The phrase is best forgotten as an incomplete, negative gloss on an accepted pleading standard: once a claim has been stated adequately, it may be supported by showing any· set of facts consistent with the allegations in the complaint. *Conley*, then, described the breadth of opportunity to prove what an adequate complaint claims, not the minimum standard of adequate pleading to govern a complaint's survival.

III

When we look for plausibility in this complaint, we agree with the District Court that plaintiffs' claim of conspiracy in restraint of trade comes up short. To begin with, the complaint leaves no doubt that plaintiffs rest their § 1 claim on descriptions of parallel conduct and not on any independent allegation of actual agreement among the ILECs. Although in form a few stray statements speak directly of agreement, on fair reading these are merely legal conclusions resting on the prior allegations. . . .[10] The nub of the complaint, then, is the ILECs' parallel behavior, consisting of steps to keep the CLECs out and manifest disinterest in becoming CLECs themselves, and its sufficiency turns on the suggestions raised by this conduct when viewed in light of common economic experience.

We think that nothing contained in the complaint invests either the action or inaction alleged with a plausible suggestion of conspiracy. As to the ILECs' supposed agreement to disobey the 1996 Act and thwart the CLECs' attempts to compete, we agree with the District Court that nothing in the complaint intimates that the resistance to the upstarts was anything more than the natural, unilateral reaction of each ILEC intent on keeping its regional dominance. . . . The economic incentive to resist was powerful, but resisting competition is routine market conduct . . . .

Plaintiffs' second conspiracy theory rests on the competitive reticence among the ILECs themselves in the wake of the 1996 Act . . . .

But [this behavior] was not suggestive of conspiracy, not if history teaches anything. In a traditionally unregulated industry with low barriers to entry, sparse competition among large firms dominating separate geographical segments of the market could very well signify illegal agreement, but here we have an obvious alternative explanation. In the decade preceding the 1996 Act and well before that, monopoly was the norm in telecommunications, not the exception. The ILECs were born in that world, doubtless liked the world the way it was, and surely knew the adage about him who lives by the sword. Hence, a natural explanation for the noncompetition alleged is that the former Government-sanctioned monopolists were sitting tight, expecting their neighbors to do the same thing. . . .

. . . We agree with the District Court's assessment that antitrust conspiracy was not suggested by the facts adduced under either theory of the complaint, which thus fails to state a valid § 1 claim.[14]

---

10. If the complaint had not explained that the claim of agreement rested on the parallel conduct described, we doubt that the complaint's references to an agreement among the ILECs would have given the notice required by Rule 8. Apart from identifying a seven-year span in which the § 1 violations were supposed to have occurred (i.e., "[b]eginning at least as early as February 6, 1996, and continuing to the present"), the pleadings mentioned no specific time, place, or person involved in the alleged conspiracies. . . .

14. In reaching this conclusion, we do not apply any "heightened" pleading standard, nor do we seek to broaden the scope of Federal Rule of Civil Procedure 9, which can only be accomplished "'by the process of amending the Federal Rules, and not by judicial interpretation.'" Swierkiewicz v. Sorema N. A., 534 U.S. 506, 515 (2002). On certain subjects understood to raise a high risk of abusive litigation, a plaintiff must state factual allegations with greater particularity than Rule 8 requires. Fed. R. Civ. P. 9(b)-(c). Here, our concern is not that the allegations in the complaint were insufficiently "particular[ized]"; rather, the complaint warranted dismissal because it failed in toto to render plaintiffs' entitlement to relief plausible.

Plaintiffs say that our analysis runs counter to *Swierkiewicz v. Sorema N. A.*, 534 U.S. 506, 508 (2002) . . . . Even though *Swierkiewicz's* pleadings "detailed the events leading to his termination, provided relevant dates, and included the ages and nationalities of at least some of the relevant persons involved with his termination," the Court of Appeals dismissed his complaint for failing to allege certain additional facts that Swierkiewicz would need at the trial stage to support his claim in the absence of direct evidence of discrimination. We reversed on the ground that the Court of Appeals had impermissibly applied what amounted to a heightened pleading requirement by insisting that Swierkiewicz allege "specific facts" beyond those necessary to state his claim and the grounds showing entitlement to relief.

Here, in contrast, we do not require heightened fact pleading of specifics, but only enough facts to state a claim to relief that is plausible on its face. Because the plaintiffs here have not nudged their claims across the line from conceivable to plausible, their complaint must be dismissed.

* * *

The judgment of the Court of Appeals for the Second Circuit is reversed, and the cause is remanded for further proceedings consistent with this opinion.

■ JUSTICE STEVENS, with whom JUSTICE GINSBURG joins . . ., dissenting. . . .

. . . The Court and petitioners' legal team are no doubt correct that the parallel conduct alleged is consistent with the absence of any contract, combination, or conspiracy. But that conduct is also entirely consistent with the *presence* of the illegal agreement alleged in the complaint. . . . [T]he Federal Rules of Civil Procedure, our longstanding precedent, and sound practice mandate that the District Court at least require some sort of response from petitioners before dismissing the case.

Two practical concerns presumably explain the Court's dramatic departure from settled procedural law. Private antitrust litigation can be enormously expensive, and there is a risk that jurors may mistakenly conclude that evidence of parallel conduct has proved that the parties acted pursuant to an agreement when they in fact merely made similar independent decisions. Those concerns merit careful case management, including strict control of discovery, careful scrutiny of evidence at the summary judgment stage, and lucid instructions to juries; they do not, however, justify the dismissal of an adequately pleaded complaint without even requiring the defendants to file answers denying a charge that they in fact engaged in collective decisionmaking. More importantly, they do not justify an interpretation of Federal Rule of Civil Procedure 12(b)(6) that seems to be driven by the majority's appraisal of the plausibility of the ultimate factual allegation rather than its legal sufficiency. . . .

Rule 8(a)(2) . . . did not come about by happenstance and its language is not inadvertent. The English experience with Byzantine special pleading rules . . . made obvious the appeal of a pleading standard that was easy for the common litigant to understand and sufficed to put the defendant on notice as to the nature of the claim against him and the relief sought. . . .

Under the relaxed pleading standards of the Federal Rules, the idea was not to keep litigants out of court but rather to keep them in. The merits of a claim would be sorted out during a flexible pretrial process and, as appropriate, through the crucible of trial. . . .

Everything today's majority says would therefore make perfect sense if it were ruling on a Rule 56 motion for summary judgment and the evidence included nothing more than the Court has described. But it should go without saying . . . that a heightened production burden at the summary judgment stage does not translate into a heightened pleading burden at the complaint stage. The majority rejects the complaint in this case because — in light of the fact that the parallel conduct alleged is consistent with ordinary market behavior — the claimed conspiracy is "conceivable" but not "plausible." I have my doubts about the majority's assessment of the plausibility of this alleged conspiracy. But even if the majority's speculation is correct, its "plausibility" standard is irreconcilable with Rule 8 and with our governing precedents. . . . [F]ear of the burdens of litigation does not justify factual conclusions supported only by lawyers' arguments rather than sworn denials or admissible evidence.

This case is a poor vehicle for the Court's new pleading rule, for we have observed that "in antitrust cases, where 'the proof is largely in the hands of the alleged conspirators,' . . . dismissals prior to giving the plaintiff ample opportunity for discovery should be granted very sparingly." Moreover, the fact that the Sherman Act authorizes the recovery of treble damages and attorney's fees for successful plaintiffs indicates that Congress intended to encourage, rather than discourage, private enforcement of the law. It is therefore more, not less, important in antitrust cases to resist the urge to engage in armchair economics at the pleading stage.

The same year we decided *Conley*, Judge Clark wrote, presciently,

> I fear that every age must learn its lesson that special pleading cannot be made to do the service of trial and that live issues between active litigants are not to be disposed of or evaded on the paper pleadings, i.e., the formalistic claims of the parties. Experience has found no quick and easy short cut for trials in cases generally *and antitrust cases in particular*.

[Charles E. Clark,] *Special Pleading in the "Big Case"?*, *in* PROCEDURE — THE HANDMAID OF JUSTICE 147, 148 (Charles Alan Wright & Harry M. Reasoner eds. 1965) (emphasis added).

In this "Big Case," the Court succumbs to the temptation that previous Courts have steadfastly resisted. While the majority assures us that it is not applying any "heightened" pleading standard, . . . I have a difficult time understanding its opinion any other way.

Notes

1.   *Nagler* is an old case, but an influential one. Its author, Judge Clark, was a primary drafter of the Federal Rules of Civil Procedure, and an advocate for notice pleading. *See, e.g.*, Charles E. Clark, Handbook on the Law of Code Pleading (1928). *Nagler* was a practical application of Clark's fervent belief that "strict special pleading has never been found workable or even useful in English and American law" and that "in federal pleading no special exceptions have been created for the 'Big Case' or for any other particular type of action." Charles E. Clark, *Special Pleading in the "Big Case,"* 21 F.R.D. 45, 47-48 (1957).

2.   As you know from your course in Civil Procedure, the Supreme Court has recently veered away from the liberal notice-pleading approach established by Judge Clark and represented by *Conley v. Gibson*, 355 U.S. 41 (1957). *Conley* had two critical holdings. First it held that a complaint passes muster under Rule 8(a)(2) "short and plain statement" requirement if it gives defendant "fair notice of what the plaintiff's claim is and the grounds upon which it rests." *Id.* at 47. Second, a complaint meeting this requirement cannot be dismissed "unless it appears beyond doubt that the plaintiff can prove no set of facts in support of his claim which would entitle him to relief." *Id.* at 45-46. Of these two holdings, *Twombly* overturns only the latter; the former still remains good law. Although it was hardly written as a response to Judge Clark, *Twombly* seems to be a point-by-point refutation of *Nagler*'s reasoning.

3.   When *Twombly* first came out, courts were uncertain about its effect.   Some courts wondered whether *Twombly* stated a particular pleading rule just for antitrust cases — or at least just for "big" cases (i.e., complex cases) in which the costs of allowing a case to proceed into pretrial discovery were high. *Ashcroft v. Iqbal*, 556 U.S. —, 129 S. Ct. 1937 (2009), ended debate on the subject. In a slender 5-4 majority, *Iqbal* affirmed and even strengthened the Court's commitment to *Twombly*'s approach:

> Two working principles underlie our decision in *Twombly*. First, the tenet that a court must accept as true all of the allegations contained in a complaint is inapplicable to legal conclusions. Threadbare recitals of the elements of a cause of action, supported by mere conclusory statements, do not suffice. . . . Second, only a complaint that states a plausible claim for relief survives a motion to dismiss. Determining whether a complaint states a plausible claim for relief will . . . be a context-specific task that requires the reviewing court to draw on its judicial experience and common sense.   But where the well-pleaded facts do not permit the court to infer more than the mere possibility of misconduct, the complaint has alleged — but it has not "show[n]" — "that the pleader is entitled to relief." Fed. R. Civ. P. 8(a)(2). . . .
>
> Respondent first says that our decision in *Twombly* should be limited to pleadings made in the context of an antitrust dispute. This argument is not supported by *Twombly* and is incompatible with the

Federal Rules of Civil Procedure. Though *Twombly* determined the sufficiency of a complaint sounding in antitrust, the decision was based on our interpretation and application of Rule 8. That Rule in turn governs the pleading standard "in all civil actions and proceedings in the United States district courts." Fed. R. Civ. P. 1. Our decision in *Twombly* expounded the pleading standard for "all civil actions," and it applies to antitrust and discrimination suits alike. . . .

Respondent next implies that our construction of Rule 8 should be tempered where, as here, the Court of Appeals has "instructed the district court to cabin discovery . . . ." We have held, however, that the question presented by a motion to dismiss a complaint for insufficient pleadings does not turn on the controls placed upon the discovery process. [129 S. Ct. at 1949-50, 1953.]

4. Academic commentary on *Twombly* and *Iqbal* has been voluminous, most of it highly unfavorable. The lower-federal-court and state-court decisions wrestling with their implications are legion. It is likely to be years before a better understanding emerges about the amount of pleading that satisfies the new "plausibility" standard.

In addition, as of this writing, bills have been introduced in both the Senate and the House to overturn *Twombly* and *Iqbal*. Hearings on both bills have been conducted, but the fate of the legislation is uncertain. *See* S. 1504, 111th Cong. (2009); H.R. 4115, 111th Cong. (2009).

5. In the meantime, *Twombly* and *Iqbal* will have important effects in complex litigation. One evident effect is that plaintiffs in federal court will likely need to plead more facts to avoid dismissals of their claims. From the viewpoint of early issue definition and issue narrowing, this result is good. But Judge Clark and Justice Stevens both articulate important costs with this approach. Is the right analysis to ask whether the cost of premature and erroneous dismissals (a possible consequence of *Twombly* and *Iqbal*) outweighs the cost of allowing meritless cases to consume discovery resources? Judge Clark and Justice Stevens emphasize the first set of costs; the majorities in *Twombly* and *Iqbal* emphasize the latter. Why is it that no one tries to balance both sets of costs against each other? Is it because it is impossible to quantify either set of costs? But if the costs cannot be quantified, aren't arguments about the costs of either rigorous or lax pleading anything more than a smoke screen for arguments about whether we like plaintiffs or defendants?

Second, won't heightened federal pleading drive cases into state courts that retain a liberal approach to pleading? *See* Colby v. Umbrella, Inc., 955 A.2d 1082 (Vt. 2008) (rejecting *Twombly*). Some cases (like *Twombly* and *Iqbal*) lie within exclusive federal jurisdiction or can be removed to federal court. But in other cases, plaintiffs can gerrymander their allegations to hold onto a state forum. Will an untoward effect of *Twombly* and *Iqbal* be increased difficulty in aggregating cases in a federal forum?

6. *Twombly* and *Iqbal* involve insufficient allegations concerning the defendant's behavior. In complex litigation, however, a plaintiff often needs

to make allegations about co-plaintiffs' conduct even though the plaintiff might not have that information. (For instance, a complaint might need to describe the members of a class, their characteristics, and their behavior in relation to the defendant's actions.) Are allegations about co-parties subject to the more stringent requirements imposed by *Twombly* and *Iqbal*? For an argument that they should not be, see Robin Effron, *The Plaintiff Neutrality Principle: Pleading Complex Litigation in the Era of* Twombly *and* Iqbal, 51 WM. & MARY L. REV. — (forthcoming 2010).

7. In some common types of complex cases — securities-fraud claims, and often RICO or consumer-protection claims — heightened pleading is required either by Rule 9(b), which requires the allegations of fraud be stated with particularity, or by the Private Litigation Securities Reform Act of 1995 (PSLRA), which requires that "the complaint shall, with respect to each act or omission alleged to violate this chapter, state with particularity facts giving rise to a strong inference that the defendant" intended to defraud. 15 U.S.C. § 78u-4(b)(2). In *Tellabs, Inc. v. Makor Issues & Rights, Ltd.*, 551 U.S. 308 (2007), the Court contrasted the PSLRA's standard with the usual Rule 8(a)(2) standard, and held that "[t]o qualify as 'strong' . . . an inference must be more than merely plausible or reasonable — it must be cogent and at least as compelling as any opposing inference of nonfraudulent intent." 551 U.S. at 314. *Tellabs* did not cite *Twombly*, but its distinction between an insufficient "plausible" allegation and a sufficient "strong" one suggests that a "plausible" allegation is more than conceivably true but not necessarily more likely to be true than another possibility. On the other hand, some language in *Iqbal* suggests that a plausible allegation must also be "more likely" than any other inference. *See Iqbal*, 129 S. Ct. at 1951 (rejecting allegations of unconstitutional behavior because "given more likely explanations, they do not plausibly establish" an unconstitutional motive); *id.* at 1950 (describing *Twombly* as a case in which the defendants' conduct "was not only compatible with, but indeed was more likely explained by, lawful, unchoreographed free-market behavior"). If so, what is the distinction between basic pleading in Rule 8 and heightened pleading in Rule 9(b)?

Whatever the answer to that question, courts tend to agree that the heightened pleading of Rule 9(b) requires the pleader "to assert the 'who,' 'what,' 'where,' 'when,' and 'how' of fraud[ ]." Hopper v. Solvay Pharms., Inc., 588 F.3d 1318, 1327 (11th Cir. 2009); *see* Rao v. BP Prods. N. Am., Inc., 589 F.3d 389, 401 (7th Cir. 2009).

8. Beyond the specific contexts of Rule 9 and the PSLRA, should a federal court have the power to impose even more stringent pleading requirements for complex cases than those required for ordinary cases? A few courts indicate that such a power exists. *See* Tamayo v. Blagojevich, 526 F.3d 1074, 1083 (7th Cir. 2008) ("For complaints involving complex litigation — for example, antitrust or RICO claims — a fuller set of factual allegations may be necessary to show that relief is plausible."); Elec. Lab. Supply Co. v. Motorola, Inc., 1989 WL 113127, at *1 (E.D. Pa. Sept. 20, 1989) ("The more complex the litigation the greater the amount of detail

required in the pleadings."); *cf.* Associated Gen. Contractors of Cal., Inc. v. Cal. State Council of Carpenters, 459 U.S. 519, 528 n.17 (1983) ("Certainly in a case of this magnitude, a district court must retain the power to insist upon some specificity in pleading before allowing a potentially massive factual controversy to proceed.").

Some cases erect rules of heightened pleading for particular substantive claims often associated with complex litigation. For instance, in RICO cases, many district courts require a person asserting a RICO claim to file a "RICO case statement," which provides detailed information about the dates and events that allegedly establish a RICO violation. *See, e.g.,* Northland Ins. Co. v. Shell Oil Co., 930 F. Supp. 1069 (D.N.J. 1996) (holding that a court has the power to order a RICO case statement under the authority of the Civil Justice Reform Act, the power of courts to make local rules, and Rule 16(c)(2)(*l*), which authorizes the use of "special procedures for managing potentially difficult or protracted action"). The insistence on using RICO case statements rarely invokes negative comment on appeal. *See* Tal v. Hogan, 453 F.3d 1244 (10th Cir. 2006); Word of Faith World Outreach Ctr. Church v. Sawyer, 90 F.3d 118 (5th Cir. 1996); *but see* Commercial Cleaning Servs., L.L.C. v. Colin Serv. Sys., Inc., 271 F.3d 374 (2d Cir. 2001) (holding that a violation of a standing order requiring a RICO case statement could not serve as the basis for dismissal of a case when the case statement sought information in excess of that needed to establish a legally sufficient claim, the plaintiff had not been given time for discovery, and the failure to comply with the order was not egregious).

For antitrust claims, some courts have inverted an observation by the Supreme Court — "where a bona fide complaint is filed that charges every element necessary to recover, summary dismissal . . . can seldom be justified," United States v. Employing Plasterers Ass'n of Chicago, 347 U.S. 186, 189 (1954) — into a requirement that an antitrust complaint contain factual allegations on each element of a claim. *See* Faulkner Adver. Assocs., Inc. v. Nissan Motor Corp., 905 F.2d 769, 772 (4th Cir. 1990); *see also* Or. Nat'l Res. Council v. Mohla, 944 F.2d 531, 539 (9th Cir. 1991) (requiring heightened pleading when the antitrust allegations threatened to chill First Amendment rights). Some cases have also imposed heightened pleading in environmental cases. *See* Cash Energy, Inc. v. Weiner, 768 F. Supp. 892, 900 (D. Mass. 1991); *but see* Warwick Admin. Group v. Avon Prods., Inc., 820 F. Supp. 116, 121 (S.D.N.Y. 1993) (holding that there are no heightened pleading requirements in environmental cases). The *Manual for Complex Litigation* recommends that, in securities-fraud cases, courts consider using the equivalent of a RICO case statement to flesh out allegations of fraud. MANUAL FOR COMPLEX LITIGATION, FOURTH § 31.32 (2004).

In any event, with the exception of sometimes lengthy RICO case statements, most of the cases that have imposed heightened pleading have not insisted on a great deal more by way of pleading — certainly not enough to generate a significant amount of issue- and fact-narrowing in the pleading process. We discuss courts' power to require more specificity through post-pleading techniques *infra* pp. 804-67.

9.   Most of the world requires more specificity in pleadings than the American system does. The American Law Institute (ALI) and UNIDROIT together created the *Principles of Transnational Civil Procedure*, which were an attempt to synthesize common-law, civil law, and other procedural regimes into a set of concepts usable in international commercial disputes. In addition, the ALI created a set of rules to implement the principles more concretely. The principal pleading rule is Rule 12, which reads in part:

12.1   The plaintiff must state the facts on which the claim is based, describe the evidence to support those statements, and refer to the legal grounds that support the claim, including foreign law, if applicable.

12.2   The reference to legal grounds must be sufficient to permit the court to determine the legal validity of the claim.

12.3   The statement of facts must, so far as reasonably practicable, set forth detail as to time, place, participants, and events.

ALI/UNIDROIT PRINCIPLES OF TRANSNATIONAL CIVIL PROCEDURE 111 (2006). The drafters of this rule specifically contrasted it with the notice-pleading philosophy of American law.

b. Consolidating Pleadings

When multiple cases are consolidated in one proceeding, different complaints may name different defendants and allege different theories of recovery. The cacophony of complaints makes it difficult to keep track of who is suing whom, and for what. Responsive pleadings, in which different admissions might be made and different defenses might be raised to each complaint, increases the confusion. These problems, in turn, make it more difficult to manage the pretrial process: Figuring out which discovery is relevant to which complaint, who can attend which deposition, and who may file or respond to which motion can be a great headache.

It would often be far easier, more tidy, and more economical if the array of pleadings could be replaced by a single consolidated pleading for each side.   That simple solution, however, carries a significant drawback: Parties are no longer "masters of their complaints," and lose control of the proofs and arguments that they wish to make. In prior chapters we have seen that parties may be joined in a forum not of their choosing and may be represented by counsel not of their choosing. When they also lose the ability to control who they sue and on what theories, the assault upon the traditional adversarial model is nearly complete.

For a time after the Supreme Court's decision in *Johnson v. Manhattan Railway Co.*, 289 U.S. 479 (1933), it was believed that a federal court could not order consolidated pleadings. *Johnson* stated that the consolidation of cases "does not merge the suits into a single cause, or change the rights of the parties, or make those who are parties in one suit parties in another." *Id.* at 496-97. Thus, any consolidation of pleadings that added (or deleted) parties, claims, or defenses appeared to run afoul of *Johnson*. In 1975, however, *Katz v. Realty Equities Corp. of New York*, 521 F.2d 1354, 1355 (2d Cir. 1975), held that a district court's order "requiring the filing and service of a single consolidated complaint for pretrial purposes upon defendants in a number of related securities cases . . . was a proper exercise of the trial judge's authority in the management of complex multiparty litigation."

Katz upheld the authority over the objection of two peripheral defendants who had been sued by only two of the twenty-one plaintiffs. Because of the consolidated pleadings that the district court ordered, these two defendants now found themselves defending against the claims of twenty-one plaintiffs and the crossclaims of thirty-nine defendants. *Katz* emphasized that the consolidation was for pretrial purposes only, and, despite the increased burden to the two peripheral defendants,

> the overall economies in reducing the proliferation of duplicative papers warrant the trial judge's efforts in the present circumstances. . . . Directing discovery to one complaint, rather than to seventeen complaints, avoids the possible confusion and the possible problems stemming from the situation where each plaintiff pursues his individual complaint.
>
> . . . [E]ach case in which it may appear desirable to consolidate complaints in different actions must be evaluated on its own facts with close attention to whether the anticipated benefits of a consolidated complaint outweigh potential prejudice to the parties. [*Id.* at 1359-60.]

The following case discusses other issues that consolidated pleadings can raise.

IN RE PROPULSID PRODUCTS LIABILITY LITIGATION

208 F.R.D. 133 (E.D.La. 2002)

■ FALLON, District Judge.

[Plaintiffs filed more than thirty class actions claiming that a heartbeat-regulating medicine, Propulsid, had caused personal injuries to hundreds or thousands of users. The Judicial Panel on Multidistrict Litigation transferred all federal Propulsid cases to the Eastern District of Louisiana. The MDL judge appointed a plaintiffs' steering committee, which moved to certify a nationwide medical-monitoring class action. The committee did not seek certification of a damages class action.

[In ruling on the class-certification motion, the court began with the choice-of-law question.] It is a well established principle that a federal court sitting in diversity must apply the choice-of-law rules of the forum state in determining which state's substantive law to apply in the case. Klaxon v. Stentor Elec. Mfg. Co., Inc., 313 U.S. 487 (1941). In the MDL setting, the forum state is usually the state in which the action was initially filed before it was transferred to the court presiding over the MDL proceedings. In the present case the plaintiff filed a master complaint in the MDL proceeding on October 5, 2001 and simultaneously filed a nearly identical complaint in the U.S. District Court for the Southern District of Indiana. The Indiana complaint was subsequently transferred to this Court pursuant to 28 U.S.C. § 1407 to be included in the MDL proceeding. The Plaintiffs' Steering Committee seeks to utilize the Indiana suit as the basis for a choice-of-law analysis. Defendants, on the other hand, argue that the MDL master complaint should be used. Thus, as a threshold matter this Court must decide which complaint — the master complaint filed in Louisiana or the complaint filed in Indiana — should be used in the choice-of-law analysis.

Defendants note that although the master complaint and the Indiana suit were filed on October 5, 2001, the Indiana suit was not transferred to the MDL proceeding until December 31, 2001, nearly three months after plaintiff Jones's appearance in the master complaint. Defendants argue that since the master complaint was the first to be filed in the MDL proceeding, it should be used to determine the applicable choice-of-law rules. Accordingly, defendants urge this Court to apply Louisiana's choice-of-law rules in determining the substantive law applicable to the putative class action since the master complaint was filed in Louisiana.

Plaintiff correctly notes that the master complaint was filed pursuant to this Court's Pretrial Order No. 2. Plaintiff argues that the master complaint is nothing more than an administrative device used by the Court to streamline pleadings and motion practice. Therefore, as it is not a traditional complaint, according to plaintiff, Louisiana's choice-of-law rules do not come into play. Instead, plaintiff argues that Indiana's choice-of-law rules apply because that is where the true complaint was filed. The answer to this conundrum requires an analysis of the nature and origin of the master complaint in MDL proceedings. . . .

Master complaints are often used in complex litigation, although they are not specifically mentioned in either the Federal Rules of Civil Procedure or in any federal statute.[5] They seem to be grounded instead in the general provisions of Rule 42(a) of the Federal Rules of Civil Procedure. Rule 42(a) broadly authorizes district courts to consolidate actions pending before the court and to make such orders "as may tend to avoid unnecessary costs or delay."[*] Courts have interpreted Rule 42(a) to authorize the filing of a

---

5. The use of a master class action complaint is documented in cases such as *In re Bridgestone/Firestone, Inc. Tires Products Liability Litigation*, 155 F. Supp. 2d 1069 (S.D. Ind. 2001). However, in that case it was not necessary to address the nature of the master complaint as in this case.

In *Bridgestone/Firestone* a master complaint asserting a nationwide class action was filed in the Southern District of Indiana. In determining which state's choice-of-law rules would apply to the class, the court noted that "the parties agree that this Court should be treated as the forum court because Plaintiff filed their master complaint in this Court." Accordingly, the *Bridgestone/Firestone* court applied Indiana's choice-of-law rules. There is no such agreement in this case.

[*] The 2007 stylistic amendments changed the quoted language to the simpler "to avoid unnecessary cost or delay," and placed it in the newly constituted Rule 42(a)(3). — ED.

unified or master complaint in cases consolidated both for pretrial discovery and for trial. *See* Katz v. Realty Equities Corp. of N.Y., 521 F.2d 1354 (2d Cir. 1975); In re Equity Funding Corp. of Am. Sec. Litig., 416 F. Supp. 161, 175 (C.D.Cal. 1976). In both situations, consolidation is not supposed to "merge the suits into a single cause, or change the rights of the parties, or make those who are parties in one suit parties in another." Rather, consolidation is intended only as a procedural device used to promote judicial efficiency and economy.

Although the use of a consolidated or master complaint is mentioned as an option in a checklist found in the *Manual for Complex Litigation (Third)*, the manual does not address the ramifications or effects of master complaints on the future course of the litigation. Some commentators have astutely observed that master complaints in class actions may create substantive problems despite their intended purpose as an administrative vehicle to streamline the litigation. These concerns are well founded.

If the master complaint in the present case were to be treated as a traditional complaint, many significant and perhaps unintended consequences would follow. First, it would make applicable Louisiana's choice-of-law rules even though the class action for which class certification is sought was filed in Indiana. Second, it would complicate the matter of the subsequent remand of the individual MDL actions back to the transferor court by introducing confusion as to which court is the transferor court in light of the fact that two substantive complaints — one in Louisiana and one in Indiana — have been filed. Indeed, taking this to the extreme, a master complaint, if given the status of a traditional complaint, could be used to circumvent the remand requirement of 28 U.S.C. § 1407 by substituting itself for all individual actions filed in the MDL and thereby frustrate the intended effect of that statute as recognized in the Supreme Court's decision in *Lexecon, Inc. v. Milberg Weiss Bershad Hynes & Lerach*, 523 U.S. 26 (1998) [*supra* p. 162].[6] In light of these concerns the master complaint should not be given the same effect as an ordinary complaint. Instead, it should be considered as only an administrative device to aid efficiency and economy.

Having concluded that the master complaint filed . . . in this Court is merely a procedural device, the Court looks to the specific action brought before the Court for class certification, namely the Indiana complaint, to determine which state's choice-of-law rules apply. Since Indiana is the forum state, the Court must look to the Indiana choice-of-law rules to determine which state's substantive law applies to the putative class.

---

6. The *Lexecon* decision concerned the propriety of self-referrals of MDL consolidated cases to the MDL transferee court pursuant to 28 U.S.C. § 1404; however, the basis of the decision lies in the Court's resolution of the tension between a broad reading of the MDL court's pretrial authority and the Panel's remand obligation under § 1407(a) based on the statute's legislative history. In recognizing a limitation on the power of the transferee court to self-refer cases, *Lexecon*'s message is relevant to the use of a master complaint insofar as a master complaint filed in the MDL court may be used to replace all § 1407 transferred actions such that the transferee court becomes the trial court for all cases.

[Applying Indiana's *lex loci* rule, the district court held that the law of the state in which a plaintiff class member took Propulsid would determine that class member's claim. It then held that using the substantive law of multiple jurisdictions would make a class action unmanageable, and it denied the motion to certify the class.]

Notes

1.   Since *Katz*, courts have routinely authorized the use of consolidated pleadings. *See, e.g.*, In re Prudential Sec. Inc. Ltd. P'ships Litig., 158 F.R.D. 562 (S.D.N.Y. 1994); In re Wirebound Boxes Antitrust Litig., 128 F.R.D. 262 (D. Minn. 1989); In re Equity Funding Corp. of Am. Sec. Litig., 416 F. Supp. 161 (C.D. Cal. 1976). The use of these "master complaints" is so routine today that appellate and district courts mention them only in passing, without a thought that they might be problematic.

Curiously, the *Manual for Complex Litigation*, which many judges regard as the Bible for handling of complex litigation, makes little mention of consolidated complaints. The *Manual*'s prior edition had recommended their use in securities cases. *See* MANUAL FOR COMPLEX LITIGATION, THIRD § 33.32 (1995). The present edition deletes this reference, perhaps because the Private Securities Litigation Reform Act of 1995 often places the largest shareholder in the position of a lead plaintiff that then controls the pleading decisions. *See* MANUAL FOR COMPLEX LITIGATION, FOURTH § 31.32 (2004). The present *Manual* does recommend that judges consider the practice of automatically "deeming" that pleadings from earlier-filed actions apply to later-filed actions — at least unless later-filing parties specifically disavow those pleadings. *See* MANUAL, FOURTH, *supra*, § 11.32. In addition, some courts have established electronic "master long-form complaints," listing all jurisdictional bases and claims that can be asserted, and then have allowed plaintiffs to electronically check the boxes that correspond to the jurisdictional bases and claims that they wish to bring. The defendant is deemed to have denied all the allegations. *See* In re Diet Drugs (Phentermine/Fenfluramine/Dexfenfluramine) Prods. Liab. Litig., 2009 WL 1924441, at *1 (E.D. Pa. June 30, 2009). Other courts have allowed plaintiffs to sign a form adopting the master complaint in lieu of filing a separate pleading. In re Guidant Corp. Implantable Defibrillators Prods. Liab. Litig., 2008 WL 682174, at *3 (D. Minn. Mar. 7, 2008).

2.   Yet another approach, which we examined is Chapter Two, is that of *In re Avandia Marketing, Sales Practices and Products Liability Litigation*, 2008 WL 2078917 (E.D.Pa. May 14, 2008) (*supra* p. 71). In *Avandia* an MDL court permitted plaintiffs with unrelated claims to file a single complaint, as long as all plaintiffs resided in the same federal district. The court thought that this approach streamlined the pretrial process, but indicated that the cases might need to be tried separately.

3.   *Propulsid*'s approach — to treat the consolidated complaint as an administrative aid rather than a document that defines the parties' rights

on such matters as choice-of-law analysis — was subsequently adopted in *In re Vioxx Products Liability Litigation,* 239 F.R.D. 450 (E.D.La. 2006) (*supra* p. 645). As *Propulsid* notes, *In re Bridgestone/Firestone, Inc. Tires Products Liability Litigation,* 155 F. Supp. 2d 1069 (S.D. Ind. 2001), adopted the opposite approach, and treated the master complaint as a new filing that required adoption of the choice-of-law rules of the state in which the MDL forum sat. *In re Rezulin Products Liability Litigation,* 210 F.R.D. 61 (S.D.N.Y. 2002), dodged the issue by holding that, even under the *Bridgestone/Firestone* approach, the forum state's choice-of-law rules required the use of a sufficient number of state substantive laws that class-action treatment was not warranted. Cases have tended to favor the *Propulsid* approach. The various positions are analyzed in *In re Conagra Peanut Butter Products Liability Litigation,* 251 F.R.D. 689 (N.D.Ga. 2008) (refusing to apply the choice-of-law rules of the MDL forum state to a class-action master complaint filed in the MDL forum).

4.   Is the consolidation of complaints only a matter of administrative convenience? The two minor defendants in *Katz* that suddenly found themselves at the center of the litigation storm would beg to differ with that characterization of the consolidated complaint in *Katz.* In drafting a master complaint, doesn't the plaintiffs' lawyer have an incentive to throw in the kitchen sink? Aren't defendants that now face broad allegations that they might not have faced with more tailored complaints harmed?

5.   Likewise, aren't plaintiffs that would have preferred to proceed with more tailored allegations against some defendants harmed? In *Wirebound Boxes,* two plaintiffs in an MDL proceeding moved to dismiss a consolidated complaint that was filed by plaintiffs' lead counsel and that named them as parties. The plaintiffs complained that they would be prejudiced because the consolidated complaint "alleges a broader plaintiff class and names more defendants than do their individual complaints." 128 F.R.D. at 264. Judge Murphy refused to dismiss the complaint because the consolidated complaint's "anticipated, and already proven, benefits greatly outweigh any potential prejudice to the parties." *Id.* Judge Murphy stressed that the complaint operated only for pretrial purposes; she would "undertake appropriate measures to preserve for trial and judgment, if proper, the individual identities of these actions." *Id.; see also* In re Storage Tech. Corp. Sec. Litig., 630 F. Supp. 1072, 1074 (D. Colo. 1986) (allowing lawyers who objected to the consolidated complaint to "disavow the inclusion of their clients' claims within the amended consolidated complaint").

In considering the possibility of plaintiff harm, Professor Steinman has observed:

> . . . [D]ecisions [to file an amended consolidated complaint] will be beyond the control of claimants. This change is largely a function of the consolidation of large numbers of claims and of the typically concomitant appointment of lead counsel and executive or steering committees, whom the courts afford considerable freedom to act without regard to the wishes and directions of individual claimants whom counsel have been appointed to represent.

The forces that isolate parties from the lawyers handling their claims, which may first be manifest in connection with pleadings, continue to operate throughout the litigation. These indirect effects of consolidation change, if not the procedural rights of litigants, at least the realities of the litigation process for them.

Joan Steinman, *The Effects of Case Consolidation on the Procedural Rights of Litigants: What They Are, What They Might Be Part II: Non-Jurisdictional Matters*, 42 UCLA L. REV. 967, 974-75 (1995).

6   Finally, can't consolidated pleadings cause harm to the litigation process? Although shotgun pleadings reduce the upfront expense of preparing and arguing over the pleadings, their "kitchen sink" nature also expands rather than narrows issues during the pretrial process.

7. We should not, of course, overstate these harms to plaintiffs, defendants, and courts. The pleadings are drafted by a lawyer charged with the responsibility of representing a party's interests. Moreover, parties often consent to the filing of consolidated pleadings. *See* Diane E. Murphy, *Unified and Consolidated Complaints in Multidistrict Litigation*, 132 F.R.D. 597, 601-02 (1991) (recognizing that court order to consolidate pleadings is more problematic than consensual consolidation). Nonetheless, should courts attend more closely to the costs to defendants, plaintiffs, and the judicial system before they allow consolidated pleadings? *See* Murphy, *supra*, at 598, 603 (1991) (considering both the benefits and the costs of consolidated pleadings, questioning whether courts really could fashion pretrial orders "that would preserve the separate identity of consolidated cases for trial and judgment," and concluding that consolidated pleadings had "pros and cons as a case management device").

8. What is the source of the judge's power to order consolidated pleadings? The cases do not usually focus on the question. Some of the authority may derive from Fed. R. Civ. P. 42(a), which authorizes a court to consolidate cases and to "make such orders concerning proceedings therein as may tend to avoid unnecessary costs or delay." What about cases not consolidated under Rule 42(a) (for instance, cases consolidated under 28 U.S.C. § 1407)? Does the judge have an inherent power to order consolidated pleadings? What are the limits on this power?

Whatever the source of the power, the decision to order consolidated pleadings is typically regarded as a matter within the trial judge's discretion. *Equity Funding*, 416 F. Supp. at 175.

2. Narrowing Issues After the Pleadings

In this subsection of the chapter we examine post-pleading techniques that can narrow the factual and legal issues. As you will see, some of these devices are specifically designed to narrow the issues, and others narrow issues only indirectly. Some are party-initiated; others are judicially driven. Some derive from the text of the Federal Rules of Civil Procedure; others emanate from inherent judicial power.

Taken together, this group of devices constitutes the bulk of a judge's case-management authority. (We have already examined other aspects of a judge's case-management powers, such as appointing lead counsel or masters and ordering consolidated complaints; we will also examine a few other powers in the next section.) A judge will never employ all of these devices in one case; but it is likely that the judge will use some combination of these devices during the pretrial process. Their importance cannot be overstated. Even before pretrial commences, lawyers must be aware of these techniques, about different ways to combine and time their use, and about the effects that they might have, singly or in combination, on the outcome of the case. In turn, the judge's view on the effectiveness of these techniques, singly or in combination, will exercise an enormous influence over the judge's decision whether to aggregate a set of related cases.

In most cases, judges will embody the chosen case-management devices in a case-management order ("CMO") (also called a pretrial order ("PTO")) or in a series of CMOs or PTOs. As you consider these devices, ask whether they do an adequate job addressing the problems posed by complex cases, whether other devices not yet adopted might do better, and whether these devices grant too much (or too little) power to the managerial judge.

a. The Case-Management Order

The central feature of case management is the conference between the judge and the lawyers. *See* Fed. R. Civ. P. 16(a) (authorizing a court to hold pretrial conferences). Typically there are a number of pretrial conferences during the course of a complex case. The first few conferences are usually devoted to organizing party and counsel structures, establishing a schedule for such tasks as amending the pleadings and joining parties, and setting in place the case-management plan for narrowing the issues and conducting discovery. Decisions that emerge from these conferences are memorialized in CMOs. *See* Fed. R. Civ. P. 16 (b)(3) (describing the contents of a scheduling order), -(d) (stating that a judge should "issue an order reciting the action taken" after any pretrial conference). These CMOs "control[ ] the course of the action unless the court modifies it." Fed. R. Civ. P. 16(d); *see also* Fed. R. Civ. P. 16(b)(4) (permitting a scheduling order to be "modified only for good cause and with the judge's consent").

The following reading describes the breadth of the issues and the case-management techniques that might be discussed at a case-management conference. We examine a number of the specific techniques shortly.

MANUAL FOR COMPLEX LITIGATION, FOURTH

36-39 (2004)

The primary objective of the conference is to develop an initial plan for the "just, speedy, and inexpensive determination" of the litigation. This plan should include procedures for identifying and resolving disputed issues of law, identifying and narrowing disputed issues of fact, carrying out disclosure and conducting discovery efficiently and economically, and preparing for trial in the absence of settlement or summary disposition. The agenda should be shaped by the needs of the particular litigation. The following checklist of procedures could help in the development of case-management plans . . .:

- identifying and narrowing issues of fact and law . . .;
- establishing deadlines and limits on joinder of parties and amended or additional pleadings . . .;
- coordinating with related litigation in federal and state courts. . .;
- severing issues for trial . . .;
- consolidating of trials . . .;
- referring, if possible, some matters to magistrate judges, special masters, or other judges . . .;
- appointing lead, liaison, and trial counsel and special committees . . .;
- reducing filing and service requirements through a master file . . .;
- planning for prompt determination of class action questions . . .;
- managing disclosure and discovery, including establishing:
  — a process for preserving evidence . . .;
  — document depositories and computerized storage . . .;
  — procedures for the exchange of digital-format materials, such as databases, fax server files, PDA (personal digital assistant) files, E-mail, and digital voicemail;
  — informal discovery and other cost-reduction measures . . .;
  — protective orders and procedures for handling claims of confidentiality and privilege . . .;
  — sequencing and limitations, including specific scheduling and deadlines . . .;
- setting guidelines for the disclosure and exchange of digital evidentiary exhibits . . .;
- establishing procedures for managing expert testimony . . .;
- creating schedules and deadlines for various pretrial phases of the case and setting a tentative or firm trial date . . .;
- evaluating prospects for settlement . . . or possible reference to mediation or other procedures . . .;
- instituting any other special procedures to facilitate management of the litigation.

Federal Rule of Civil Procedure [16(d)] directs the court to enter an order reciting any action taken at the conference. The order . . . should memorialize all rulings, agreements, or other actions taken, and it should set a date for the next conference or other event in the litigation.

Notes

1. The *Manual* provides samples of standard case-management orders and of specialized orders on matters such as appointment of counsel. MANUAL, *supra*, §§ 40.2-.29.

2. In many ways the list of possible conference topics mentioned in the *Manual* mirrors the lists of topics found in Rules 16(b) and (c), which extend case management to all cases, not merely complex cases. Rule 16(b)(3)(A) requires judges to enter a scheduling order that fixes dates for joining parties, amending the pleadings, filing motions, and completing discovery. Rule 16(b)(3)(B) also allows this scheduling order to address other topics, principally concerning discovery, as well as "other appropriate matters." Rule 16(c)(2) contains a sixteen-item laundry list of matters that "the court may consider and take appropriate action on" at a pretrial conference. Among these matters are "formulating and simplifying the issues," Fed. R. Civ. P. 16(c)(2)(A); "obtaining admissions and stipulations about facts and documents," Fed. R. Civ. P. 16(c)(2)(C); "avoiding unnecessary proof and cumulative evidence," Fed. R. Civ. P. 16(c)(2)(D); "determining the appropriateness and timing of summary adjudication under Rule 56," Fed. R. Civ. P. 16(c)(2)(E); "referring matters to a magistrate judge or master," Fed. R. Civ. P. 16(c)(2)(H); and "ordering a separate trial under Rule 42(b) of a claim, counterclaim, crossclaim, third-party claim, or particular issue," Fed. R. Civ. P. 16(c)(2)(M).

Of particular interest is Rule 16(c)(2)(L), which authorizes the court to adopt "special procedures for managing potentially difficult or protracted actions that may involve complex issues, multiple parties, difficult legal questions, or unusual proof problems." Does Rule 16(c)(2)(L) act as a *carte blanche* to a judge to use any pretrial procedure that leads to a more efficient resolution in a complex case? If not, what are its limits? What procedural powers, if any, does Rule 16(c)(2)(L) provide to a judge that the more specific powers listed in Rules 16(b) and (c) do not already provide?

3. Rule 16(c)(2)(L) assumes that it is possible to distinguish between complex and non-complex cases, yet neither defines the term "complex." If special case-management principles and techniques (or at least special applications of those principles and techniques) are necessary for complex cases, shouldn't the establishment of a definition be a critical first step? The idea of "differential case management" likewise creates separate management "tracks" — and therefore different levels of case management — for cases that meet various criteria. One of the "tracks" is usually a "complex case" track, in which complexity is determined by judicial designation, by attorney designation, or by objective criteria such as the presence of a class action, a certain number of plaintiffs or defendants, or certain legal theories (such as products liability, securities fraud, or RICO).

See Maureen Solomon & Holly Bakke, *Case Differentiation: An Approach to Individualized Case Management*, 73 JUDICATURE 17 (June/July 1989); *cf.* JAMES S. KAKALIK ET AL., AN EVALUATION OF JUDICIAL CASE MANAGEMENT UNDER THE CIVIL JUSTICE REFORM ACT 47-50 (1996) (reporting generally unsuccessful results with differential case management). Do you agree that objective criteria can adequately distinguish complex from non-complex cases? Is it better to leave the decision about what is "complex" to the discretion of the judge, as Rule 16 seems to contemplate? Is the definition of "complexity" that we proposed (*see supra* p. 47) a better alternative?

4. In its empirical study of case-management practices, the RAND Corporation found that a court's early case management reduced cases' median time to disposition. For cases lasting nine or more months, the estimated reduction was 1.5 to two months. On the other hand early case-management was also associated with increased work hours per attorney, with the number of hours worked rising by about twenty hours. Not surprisingly, litigant costs also rose because of early case management. Attorney satisfaction with the process was unchanged, and litigant satisfaction showed mixed results. *See* KAKALIK, *supra*, at 52-55. What effect should these data have on the debate over case management?

5. Whatever the source of a court's case-management power and whatever its arguable costs and benefits, the *Manual* shows that the number of case-management tools that a court can and does employ is great. We have already explored several of these tools. In the remainder of this chapter we examine other tools to narrow issues and streamline discovery. As we examine them, ask yourself whether these tools are adequate to meet the demands of complex litigation and whether other case-management devices make more sense. Also keep in mind that various management techniques can often be used together, and ask yourself whether certain combinations of techniques depart too radically from the adversarial method.

b. Establishing Early, Firm Deadlines

A court's scheduling order, which is the first case-management order that the court is likely to enter, establishes deadlines for accomplishing various pretrial tasks. At best, imposing deadlines is an indirect means of narrowing issues. If they work, they force the parties to concentrate their attention on the issues and information that are critical to their case, and leave no time for the parties to chase every arguable dispute down a rabbit hole. To be successful, therefore, deadlines must be fairly short, and the must be strictly enforced. But such early, firm time limits threaten to preclude the development of relevant issues, they induce well-financed parties to "lawyer up" and throw more bodies at the case, and they might work to the disadvantage of parties who are not well-enough financed to afford a pretrial blitzkrieg or who need access to information in the other party's possession.

IN RE FINE PAPER ANTITRUST LITIGATION

685 F.2d 810 (3d Cir. 1982)

■ ALDISERT, Circuit Judge.

These consolidated appeals present several procedural issues arising from a complex antitrust proceeding. Ten states, plaintiffs below, appeal from judgments entered on a jury verdict in their actions for treble damages alleging a nationwide price-fixing conspiracy in violation of § 1 of the Sherman Act. The defendants did not offer any evidence at trial, but rested at the close of the plaintiffs' case; the jury then found in favor of all defendants. On appeal, the plaintiffs assert numerous procedural errors, generally contending that the district court unduly limited their opportunity to develop and present their case. We are not persuaded that the district court either abused its discretion or erred in its selection, interpretation, or application of the controlling legal precepts, and therefore we will affirm its judgment in all respects.

I.

This case has a complicated procedural history, owing in part to the number of parties. Named as defendants were manufacturers and merchants of "fine paper," which the states buy in large quantity. Some of the merchants are owned by the mills themselves and some are independent. Beginning in 1977, . . . several states and private plaintiffs brought a total of 37 individual actions alleging that the mills and merchants had participated in a nationwide price-fixing conspiracy. Pursuant to 28 U.S.C. § 1407, the Judicial Panel on Multidistrict Litigation transferred the cases to the Eastern District of Pennsylvania for coordinated pre-trial proceedings . . . .

The district court divided the plaintiffs into three groups: a class of private plaintiffs, "minority states," and "majority states." The minority states alleged only a horizontal conspiracy among the mill defendants; the majority states, the present appellants, alleged both a horizontal conspiracy among the mill defendants and vertical conspiracies involving mills and merchants. In addition to certifying a class of private plaintiffs, the court certified each minority state and its respective government entities as a separate plaintiff class, but it refused to do the same for the majority states because the added factor of vertical conspiracy made those actions less susceptible to generalized proof.

Following a pre-trial conference on March 7, 1979, the court established discovery deadlines and set a tentative trial date of January 2, 1980. The next few months were occupied with discovery and related motions. On September 27, 1979, plaintiffs asked for an extension of the trial date because of the number of depositions they wished to take, but the court expressed reluctance to deviate from its schedule. At a conference on December 4, 1979, the court rejected plaintiffs' proposal that trial not begin until October 1980, but it rescheduled the trial for the "certified plaintiffs" (the private plaintiffs and the minority states) to September 22, 1980, barring a "nuclear holocaust." The court did not fix a trial date for the majority states, but it established July 3, 1980, as the discovery cut-off date in all of the cases.

On January 15, 1980, the court decided it could resolve the litigation more efficiently if trial on the majority states' claims were conducted in advance of the certified plaintiffs' trial. It then set for the majority states a trial date of June 16, 1980, and a revised discovery deadline of May 30. Appellants vehemently protested that they still had 300,000 documents to review and more than 100 depositions to take, and that the court's revised schedule left inadequate time for discovery and trial preparation. The court denied their motion for reconsideration. . . .

In early June 1980, in contemplation of a June 16 trial, the majority states submitted a 200-page pre-trial memorandum. Defendants moved to dismiss, contending that the memorandum was unacceptable because it presented only conclusory allegations rather than the specific enumeration of facts the court had required. The court did not grant defendants' motion, but it ordered plaintiffs to prepare a memorandum by July 25 "which outlines the case chapter and verse as to each defendant." Plaintiffs moved for a continuance, again complaining that they had not been allowed enough time for discovery. The court stated that the majority states' actions would be tried with or after the certified plaintiffs' trial. It did not modify the discovery schedule, but it did allow some additional depositions.

The certified plaintiffs settled their cases shortly before trial. On September 25, 1980, the court announced that the majority states' trial would begin on October 6, 1980 — nine months after the tentative trial date and four months after the trial date set on January 15, 1980. Although they had been on notice since January 17, 1980, that the court wished to try the cases itself, the plaintiffs objected that they would have insufficient time to set up a Philadelphia office and to transport their files across the country. The court considered these arguments but concluded that October 6 was a realistic date.

On September 29, 1980, over plaintiffs' objections, the district court, pursuant to 28 U.S.C. § 1404(a), formally transferred all of the majority states' cases to the Eastern District of Pennsylvania for trial, which began on October 6, 1980. Following plaintiffs' four-week presentation, which consisted primarily of reading depositions to the jury, the defendants rested without offering any evidence. The jury returned a verdict in favor of all defendants on December 2, 1980. . . .

III.

Appellants' primary argument is that they were afforded too little time for discovery and trial preparation. Appellants have a heavy burden to bear, however, as matters of docket control and conduct of discovery are committed to the sound discretion of the district court. We will not interfere with a trial court's control of its docket "except upon the clearest showing that the procedures have resulted in actual and substantial prejudice to the complaining litigant." Similarly, we will not upset a district court's conduct of discovery procedures absent "a demonstration that the court's action made it impossible to obtain crucial evidence, and implicit in such a showing is proof that more diligent discovery was impossible."

We find no abuse of discretion by the district judge in his scheduling of discovery or of the trial. After considering all of appellants' contentions and examining the 16-volume appendix that they have supplied to this court, we are not persuaded that the pre-trial rulings of the district court prejudiced the preparation or presentation of their case. The trial of their antitrust claims followed fifteen months of discovery, including approximately 270 depositions and production of nearly two million documents. The trial commenced four months after conclusion of discovery and one month after the date appellants had earlier set as the date on which they would be ready for trial.

When discovery ended on May 30, 1980, the majority states sought a continuance and further discovery. The court allowed them to depose some additional witnesses and, relying on their representation that they would need until September 1 to prepare for trial, advised them that their trial would commence with or after the certified plaintiffs' trial, scheduled for September 22, 1980.

Upon settlement of the certified plaintiffs' cases, the court on September 25, 1980, notified appellants that their trial would commence on October 6. Appellants again requested a continuance, but the district court responded:

> Every time I set a deadline I get the same problem arising from the Majority States. They're never ready. They can't go to trial, the case is going to be prejudiced. The same thing happened in June, the same thing when I asked you to file answers to these interrogatories and you didn't have the time. The same thing happened when I asked you to file your pretrial memorandum. You said you didn't have the time, you needed more time, you wanted to supplement. I gave you time to supplement. It hasn't even been supplemented yet, except for a couple of states. It's just constant.

Having reviewed the record, we consider the district court's observations to be accurate. Moreover, we do not share the view expressed by appellants' counsel at oral argument that antitrust cases involving price fixing are generically complex. It has been our experience that the legendary complexity is due largely to the parties' inability or unwillingness to simplify their presentations. Our independent review of the record persuades us that the trial court in this case was firm but fair. It deferred the trial date from January 2 to June 16 to October 6, 1980, and it accommodated appellants' requests whenever feasible. The appellants have not shown that "the court's action made it impossible to obtain crucial evidence"; nor have they made a clear showing that the court's conduct "resulted in actual and substantial prejudice." We find no abuse of discretion.

[The court of appeals then rejected the majority states' argument that an MDL court could not transfer cases to itself for trial — a practice later halted by *Lexecon Inc. v. Milberg Weiss Bershad Hynes & Lerach*, 523 U.S. 26 (1998) (*supra* p. 162). It also rejected other arguments brought by the majority states concerning other rulings during pretrial and trial.]

The judgment of the district court will be affirmed.

Notes

1. Rule 16(b)(3) authorizes judges to set timetables for completing discovery and starting trial. These powers are appropriate and necessary. By themselves they are hardly case-management tools; a court needs to be able to set its own calendar. But establishing deadlines becomes a case-management tool when the deadlines are *early* and *firm*. Both adjectives are important. When discovery must be concluded and the trial is set to occur as early as possible, the parties' opportunity to develop evidence shrinks and the parties will (in theory, at least) come quickly to the heart of the case. When these dates are reasonably firm, the parties will focus on completing discovery and readying the issues for trial within the allotted time. If a judge establishes an early trial date that is not firm, or a firm trial date that is not early, the parties have less reason to cut to the chase.

Indirectly, therefore, setting an early, firm trial date and setting a firm discovery cutoff the potential to narrow issues. Indeed, both techniques have developed considerable support in the literature. *See, e.g.*, MANUAL FOR COMPLEX LITIGATION, FOURTH §§ 10.13, 11.422, 11.61 (2004); Wayne D. Brazil, *Pretrial Conferences; Scheduling; Management*, in 3 JAMES WM. MOORE, MOORE'S FEDERAL PRACTICE §16.13.[2][e][ii] (3d. ed. 2009) ("Nothing spurs litigants to more efficient pretrial work and to more serious consideration of settlement than an early, firm trial date"); REPORT TO THE PRESIDENT AND ATTORNEY GENERAL OF THE NATIONAL COMMISSION FOR THE REVIEW OF ANTITRUST LAWS AND PROCEDURES 28-30 (1979), *reprinted in* 80 F.R.D. 509, 534-36 (1979). Although aggrieved parties sometimes complain, courts generally agree with *Fine Paper*'s approach toward setting early, firm dates. *See, e.g.*, In re Air Crash Disaster, 86 F.3d 498, 517-18 (6th Cir. 1996) (court appropriately adhered to discovery cutoff when failure to do so would have forced change in established trial date); Whittaker Corp. v. Execuair Corp., 736 F.2d 1341, 1347 (9th Cir. 1984); Horn v. Kline, 2007 WL 4198167 (M.D. Pa. Nov. 26, 2007). For example, in one of the most complex antitrust cases of all time, *United States v. Microsoft Corp.*, the trial judge used short discovery and trial deadlines to good effect and brought the case to a quick resolution. For a discussion of the court's approach and copies of the court's orders, see Richard L. Schwartz, *Pretrial Preparation in Antitrust Cases: What Can One Learn from the* Microsoft *Case?*, 1152 PRACTISING L. INST. CORP. L. & PRAC. 17 (1999).

2.   In its empirical study of case-management practices, the RAND Corporation found that an early trial date significantly reduces median disposition times, and appeared to reduce slightly (but not to a statistically significant level) attorney hours as well. It also found that, unsurprisingly, that reducing the discovery cutoff by 60 days (from 180 days to 120 days) reduced the median time to disposition of cases by about 45 to 60 days; it also appeared to reduce attorney work by 17 hours, and had little impact on attorney or litigant satisfaction.   JAMES S. KAKALIK ET AL., AN EVALUATION OF JUDICIAL CASE MANAGEMENT UNDER THE CIVIL JUSTICE REFORM ACT 52-55, 63-65 (1996). These data make an early, firm trial date and discovery cutoff an almost irresistible combination: They shorten time to disposition, reduce attorney hours, and cause no dissatisfaction in the process. *See id.* at 91-92 (recommending this package of case-management reforms).

3.   So is there a credible case against early, firm trial dates or discovery cutoffs? Judge Schwarzer raises a number of difficulties:

> [T]ime limits restrict the ability of the parties to obtain information, to prepare for trial and to present their case at trial. Unless carefully fashioned, they may handicap one side more than the other. They should also be set and administered with due regard for each party's right to a fair trial.

WILLIAM W SCHWARZER, MANAGING ANTITRUST AND OTHER COMPLEX LITIGATION § 4-1 (1982). The *Manual for Complex Litigation* raises related concerns, noting that "standing alone [time limits] may be insufficient to control discovery costs" because "attorneys may simply conduct multitrack discovery, increasing expense and prejudicing parties with limited resources." MANUAL, *supra*, § 21.422. Other concerns also exist. For instance, in *Harleysville Mutual Insurance Co. v. Sussex County*, 831 F. Supp. 1111 (D. Del. 1993), *aff'd*, 46 F.3d 1116 (3d Cir. 1994) (Table), the district court refused to certify a critical question of state law to the Delaware Supreme Court for a definitive ruling. The court's only stated reason for denying certification was that it would take too long, thwarting the court's case-management goal to try all cases within 18 months.

Moreover, discovery cutoffs and early trial dates may not treat all cases fairly. A discovery cutoff of six months will give the parties plenty of time in a simple slip-and-fall case, but will make impossible the full development of issues in a massive antitrust case. Once a judge tries to tailor the cutoff to the type of case, however, other problems arise. For a cutoff to be a useful means of forcing the parties to cut to the chase, it must provide the parties with adequate time to address central issues but inadequate time to develop all issues. How much inadequacy should a judge tolerate in a slip-and-fall? How much inadequacy should a judge tolerate in an antitrust case? Do you like the idea of giving the judge the case-by-case power to decide the amount of time that is adequate? How can the judge make the judgment about which issues are central, and which are not?

4.   Another concern manifests itself in *Fine Paper*, which is perhaps the leading case on the enforcement of discovery and trial deadlines. The

plaintiffs' lawyers in *Fine Paper* had not yet completed discovery and had not been able to organize the issues adequately for trial. Assume that the reason for the lawyers' inability lay beyond their control; they were not lazy or acting strategically (perhaps the amount of evidence was voluminous or technical). In this circumstance, the discovery cutoff and early, firm trial date did not act as an aid to overcome the lawyers' inability to perform their adversarial role; they frustrated the adversarial process by reducing the time of the plaintiffs' lawyers to perform their responsibilities in defining and developing the issues. Discovery cutoffs and early, firm trial dates do little, in and of themselves, to cure problems of pretrial complexity that are unrelated to excessive cost or delay. Are speed and economy sufficient reasons not to allow the adversarial process to work? Should a judge ever be able to employ a case-management technique that creates lawyer dysfunction just to achieve other goals?

The judge does not assume the lawyers' adversarial tasks; she simply gives the lawyers less time within which to perform these tasks. When cutoffs and trial dates are used in cases that are complex for non-financial or non-time-sensitive reasons, must the judge also use positive case management techniques that will aid the lawyers in the discharge of their pretrial tasks? In other words, do such deadlines demand even greater judicial involvement at other points in the pretrial process?

5. The RAND study also made no effort to measure the value of short discovery cutoffs and early, firm trial dates as issue-narrowing devices, either in complex cases or in routine ones. To the extent that a reduced time to disposition is correlated with better issue-narrowing, then short discovery cutoffs and early, firm trial dates can help to narrow issues. But that correlation is far from clear. RAND was studying the effects of establishing early, firm discovery cutoffs and trial dates on expense, delay, and satisfaction, not on issue-narrowing.

6. What is the consequence for failing to comply with one of these deadlines? The consequence for failing to show up for trial is obvious, and too painful to consider. What if a lawyer continues to try to discover information after the discovery cutoff? Other parties can usually get a protective order against such discovery, and the court is also likely to preclude any evidence accumulated in the post-cutoff period. *See* Stewart v. Walbridge, Aldinger Co., 162 F.R.D. 29 (D. Del. 1995); *cf. Whittaker*, 736 F.2d 1341 (holding that a court improperly excluded post-cutoff evidence obtained during discovery in a related case; if discovery in the related case was being used to circumvent the discovery cutoff, the court in the related case could issue a protective order).

c. Bifurcating Pretrial Issues

The next case-management device we consider is an order that divides pretrial issues into some sequential order, and requires parties to complete proceedings on one issue before proceeding to the next. When the pretrial process is split into two, we often say that the pretrial process has been "bifurcated"; when split into three issues, "trifurcated"; and when split into more than three sets of issues, "polyfurcated." For convenience and in accordance with the usual convention, we will refer to any pretrial issue-splitting only as "bifurcation."

The theory underlying bifurcation is simple: The early development and resolution of certain critical issues may lead to a quicker disposition of the entire case (whether by settlement or motion). This resolution in turn eliminates the need to engage in discovery on the remaining issues, saving a significant amount of time and expense. Like early, firm discovery cutoffs and trial dates, bifurcation of issues does not directly narrow the issues for trial; but if the issues are divided and arranged wisely, bifurcation may avoid the need to develop and discover many issues. On the other hand, this device contains some very large "ifs." Suppose that the evidence on the initial issues fails to resolve the case; in this case, bifurcation may slow down rather than speed up the pretrial process. Or suppose that the issues that would logically come first are also the most complex and intractable; deciding these issues first will do little to overcome the problems of complexity that the case poses. Moreover, the judicial decision to bifurcate pretrial issues brings the judge into a task classically reserved to the advocate: how best to develop the proofs and arguments for trial.

Finding a source of the power to engage in pretrial bifurcation is tricky. Federal Rule of Civil Procedure 42(b) authorizes the "separate trial of one or more issues [or] claims," but it does not mention separating issues during pretrial. Rule 16(c)(2)(M) redundantly gives a judge the case-management authority to order "a separate trial under Rule 42(b)," but none of the case-management authorities mentioned in Rules 16(b) and -(c) specifically authorize pretrial bifurcation. Consider both this question of power and the question of when best to use this power as you read the following cases.

KOS PHARMACEUTICALS, INC. v. BARR LABORATORIES, INC.

218 F.R.D. 387 (S.D.N.Y. 2003)

■ MARRERO, District Judge.

Plaintiff Kos Pharmaceuticals ("Kos") commenced three separate actions in the instant matter, later consolidated by the Court into one case, alleging willful infringement by defendant Barr Laboratories, Inc. ("Barr") of five United States patents held by Kos pertaining to a sustained-release niacin product marketed by Kos under the brand name, Niaspan. Barr has filed Abbreviated New Drug Applications ("ANDAs") with the United States Food and Drug Administration ("FDA") challenging the validity of Kos's patents, and/or Kos's potential claims of infringement of the patents-in-suit, and seeking approval to produce and sell a generic form of Kos's niacin product, thereby prompting the litigation at hand. Now before the Court is Barr's motion, pursuant to Federal Rule of Civil Procedure 42(b), to bifurcate consideration of the action so as to address liability and willfulness issues in separate trials and to stay discovery with respect to willfulness. For the reasons discussed below, the motion is granted in part and denied in part.

I. BACKGROUND AND THE PARTIES' ARGUMENTS

This case presents a recurring debate uniquely pervasive in patent litigation. In countless reported cases, time after time the controversy features, as if in a familiar script from a set piece, defendants presenting the same arguments in favor of their requests for a bifurcation of the action into separate trials for liability and willfulness and/or damages, while plaintiffs predictably counter with their own customary reasoning against, each side propounding in turn why a trial so divided would or would not produce incalculable prejudice, inconveniences, delays, increased costs and untold other impositions and inefficiencies. In addressing these disputes, the courts have been no less divided; the reported rulings often mirror the divergence in the respective contentions advanced by the parties. The case at bar is no exception.

Barr asserts that in connection with its development of a generic version of Niaspan, it engaged counsel to assess issues concerning the validity and infringement of the Kos patents at issue and to advise on legal strategies for Barr to pursue in the event Kos instituted infringement litigation. In this connection, Barr obtained eight lengthy legal opinions, which Barr indicates encompass nearly 1200 pages and 19 volumes of appendices. Kos, having learned of the existence of these opinions through Barr's privilege log, served a notice seeking the deposition of Robert C. Millonig ("Millonig"), the attorney who prepared the opinions. . . . Barr points out that Millonig is one of its attorneys of record in the instant litigation. It contends that Barr would suffer extensive and irreparable prejudice if it were compelled at this point, long prior to trial on liability, to waive its attorney-client privilege and disclose the legal opinions in question. The harm that Barr asserts derives from the fact that the documents, some comprising attorney's work product, contain highly privileged legal analysis, strategies and theories that would reveal aspects of Barr's trial plans. To guard against this prospect, Barr moves the Court for an order bifurcating trial of the proceeding and staying discovery as to Kos's claim of willfulness of the alleged infringement until issues relating to liability are determined at trial by the factfinder.

Barr argues that the procedure it proposes would not only avoid prejudice to it, but serve the interest of judicial economy. Specifically, Barr maintains that, because it expended considerable resources seeking legal advice and relied on counsel's opinions in proceeding with the production of the allegedly infringing product, a finding of willful infringement here is highly unlikely, and that, in any event, if it were found not liable for infringement, the second trial as to willfulness would be unnecessary. Moreover, Barr cites to the complexity of the myriad issues, claims and defenses involved in the case and the voluminous record the litigation will generate for the liability phase alone. According to Barr, superimposing discovery pertaining to willfulness to a proceeding already so complicated and extensive, would demand considerable allocation of additional resources from the Court and the parties, inconvenience witnesses and occasion delays that will significantly prolong resolution of the merits.

In support of its request, Barr contends that courts routinely bifurcate willfulness from liability issues in patent infringement actions. For this proposition Barr cites to a string of recent cases from various districts.

Kos responds, with equal intensity, persuasiveness and weighty authority, that it is the bifurcation of this case as Barr proposes that would create undue delay, inconvenience the parties and witnesses, add expense and produce more cumbersome litigation, retard resolution of the merits of the dispute and thereby, to Kos's prejudice, facilitate Barr's ability to infringe Kos's Niaspan patents. . . . According to Kos, because the litigation at hand arises from ANDA proceedings and Kos has sought only equitable relief, a jury trial is not required, the case will be less complicated to try and thus Barr's fears of substantial prejudice are unfounded.

Moreover, Kos contends that in the absence of both damages claims and allegations of bad faith or misconduct on Kos's part, the litigation is less complex than Barr makes it out to be, and the case thus not one warranting the separate supplemental discovery and pretrial proceedings, the added trial before a different jury and the various other inefficiencies ordinarily associated with bifurcation.

II. DISCUSSION

Federal Rule of Civil Procedure 42(b) grants the district courts broad discretion to order separate trials of discrete issues or claims if the court finds that bifurcation would be ["[f]or convenience, to avoid prejudice, or to expedite and economize"]. The Rule is thus actuated by two central aims: fairness and efficiency. As formulated, the first objective is preventive — to avoid prejudice to the parties; the other is more affirmative — to foster more convenient, expeditious and economical administration of justice in the interest of all concerned.

Paradoxically, however, in the ordinary case, dividing the ultimate resolution of a dispute into separate trials equates to a formula that inevitably works against some or all of the very values of convenience, expedition, economy and avoidance of prejudice that Rule 42(b) prescribes as grounds to warrant bifurcation. Extending the adjudication into two or more proceedings necessarily implicates additional discovery; more pretrial disputes and motion practice; empaneling another jury or imposing more on the jurors who decide the earlier phase of the litigation; deposing or recalling some of the same witnesses; and potentially engendering new rounds of trial and post-trial motions and appeals. The inconveniences, inefficiencies and harms inherent in these probable consequences — to the parties and third parties, to the courts, and to the prompt administration of justice — weigh against separation of trials and suggest that, for those probable adverse effects to be overcome, the circumstances justifying bifurcation should be particularly compelling and prevail only in exceptional cases.

Nonetheless, because the court's discretion under Rule 42(b) is extensive and the governing criteria so general, application of the governing standards does not lend itself to uniform practice. In examining the many precedents that give expression to the Rule, the Court has found no coherent or consistent pattern, but rather a more prevalent inclination to a case-by-case approach that yields seemingly conflicting results . . . .

The Court is not persuaded that the complete bifurcation of the instant case into two distinct trials, as Barr advocates, is warranted by the circumstances prevailing here. Insofar as patent litigation goes, this case does not present any of the major complexities that on balance ordinarily might tip in favor of bifurcation. The dispute involves only two parties. While the case relates to five patents-in-suit, these derive from overlapping inventors and a common patent application and pertain to essentially the same product, varying only as to quantities. As stated above, no claims of damages are at issue here, a complication that generally raises sufficiently independent issues to support bifurcation. Nor does the action entail allegations of illegality or bad faith on the part of Kos, or ancillary issues such as antitrust or unfair competition, also typically associated with patent litigation justifying separate trials.

The claims that do remain to be adjudicated encompass issues pertaining to infringement, validity and willfulness. With regard to the application of Rule 42(b) to the resolution of these issues, the Court has found some divergence in the procedures followed by various courts. One view maintains that infringement and willfulness claims are sufficiently independent from each other and that trying them together holds the risk of confusing and prejudicing the jury.

Conversely, other courts hold that evidence of willful infringement is integrally related to issues concerning liability and that the two determinations cannot be facilely disentangled from one another.

Were this case one that involved claims of extensive damages from actual production and marketing of the infringed product, thus presenting a discrete issue that potentially might justify bifurcation, the question of willfulness arguably could be similarly deferred until the separate damages trial. In fact, most of the cases in which bifurcation of the willfulness issue has been found warranted have also entailed claims of damages and a finding by the court of a factual overlap between issues regarding willfulness and those pertaining to damages, which provided a distinct ground supporting a separate trial.

This Court, however, is persuaded that trial practicalities and the weight of authority tilt the application of Rule 42(b) against separation of willfulness from liability, absent a basis for bifurcation justified by damages claims. Consequently, the Court finds the better view to hold that the issue of willfulness is not sufficiently discrete and readily severable from matters of infringement, as the determination of damages is more often recognized to be. Evidence supporting both matters tends to be sufficiently interrelated that it is likely to rely on substantially the same witnesses and documentation. . . .

Contrary to Barr's contention, questions regarding infringement and willfulness cannot always be neatly disaggregated into distinct evidentiary foundations grounded on entirely different witnesses and documents. These matters are more commonly sufficiently interdependent as to render it probable that bifurcation would require a duplication of discovery proceedings, serial trials and, assuming the case were not tried by the Court, presentation of much of the same witness testimony and other evidence to different juries, consequently producing a source of unnecessary cost and inconvenience and undue delay.

Finally, the Court finds that, on balance, the delays, inconvenience and additional litigation costs attendant to bifurcation in this case would be more prejudicial to Kos. At issue here is not one patent, as was the case in some of the instances in which courts have bifurcated willfulness from infringement, but five, thus significantly affecting Kos's prospects of prevailing as to some of its claims. In the event Kos prevailed at the trial on liability on even one of its claims, the burdens associated with an entirely new round of pretrial proceedings and a second trial would fall predominantly on Kos. While the converse is also true that were Barr to succeed fully at the liability phase there would be no need for another trial at all, the Court is not convinced that on the basis of the sparse record before it sufficient evidence exists at this point, long before discovery is complete, to support a clear finding either that Barr did not infringe on the patents-in-suit or that if it did, it did not do so willfully, so as to justify a ruling in favor of bifurcation at this stage on the basis of such a tenuous forecast of Barr's likelihood of success.

Barr's principal assertion of substantial irreparable prejudice is grounded in its concern over being compelled at this point in the proceedings to choose between waiving its attorney-client privilege, and thus potentially prejudicing its liability case by disclosing the extensive counsel's opinion and voluminous accompanying appendices upon which it allegedly relied in deciding to undertake the production of its generic form of Niaspan, or to forego a defense of reliance on counsel's advice in response to Kos's charge of willful infringement and risk an adverse determination of that claim. . . .

The Court is mindful that the quandary . . . poses substantial risks to Barr, and that in this case, given the still relatively early stages of the litigation, it would be particularly constraining and prejudicial to Barr's preparation of its defense at trial if it were compelled to turn over to Kos the legal opinions at issue. Simply put, it may be premature at this time to force that choice.

However, that Barr should not be compelled at this stage to elect to disclose privileged documents or face other adverse consequences does not mean that, by that reason alone, the Court should accede to Barr's request to stay all discovery relating to willfulness and to bifurcate the trial. It is highly unlikely that the evidentiary basis Kos offers to bolster its claim of willful infringement would be rooted solely on what evidence Barr's legal opinions may or may not supply. To the contrary, it is likely that the grounds for any finding of willfulness would be supported by testimony and documentary proof generated by numerous other Barr witnesses. Thus, whatever recognized validity may sustain Barr's assertion of prejudice at this point as it relates to Barr's privileged opinions of counsel cannot be expanded to encompass deferring discovery from its other sources and witnesses.

The Court also recognized that some witnesses would have been unnecessarily inconvenienced in the event the issue of liability ultimately were adjudicated in Barr's favor, thereby altogether obviating the need to consider Kos's claims of willfulness. . . .

As a way to reconcile the diverse and overlapping interests colliding here, the Court contemplates, at least as a preliminary approach, the procedure described below. Barr's request to bifurcate the trial into liability and willfulness and stay all discovery as regards the latter will be denied at this point. Kos will be permitted to proceed with discovery and with preparation for a single trial as to all issues. However, Barr will not be required to provide discovery with regard to its legal opinions at this time. At trial, the Court will permit the parties to address all relevant issues of infringement, validity and willfulness. At the conclusion of the presentation of all the evidence pertaining to liability, however, the Court will divide the factfinding and charge the jury, on the premise that the case is so to be tried, to adjudicate liability and defer consideration of the willfulness claims. In the event the jury reaches a determination of validity and infringement, the Court will then direct the same panel, after a brief pause in the proceedings, to turn attention to a finding with regard to the claim of willfulness, on the basis of the evidence then on the trial record, but supplemented by limited additional discovery the Court will permit at that time strictly confined to Barr's legal opinions, should Barr then choose to waive its privilege.

. . . The Court has weighed carefully that the proposed procedure may require some interruption of the trial, which the court would contemplate extending to no more than two or three days, to accommodate the additional discovery and related preparation. Here, though Barr asserts that its legal opinions encompass 1200 pages and multiple volumes of accompanying materials, they were apparently all prepared by the same counsel. The additional discovery therefore would exclude collateral issues and witnesses, and be confined to what the attorneys advised the client, not to the wisdom or correctness of the opinions. . . .

For the reasons discussed above, it is hereby . . . ordered that adjudication of all matters now at issue shall proceed in a single trial, except insofar as consideration of the claim of willful infringement may be phased and determined separately as discussed above.

OCEAN ATLANTIC WOODLAND CORP.
V. DRH CAMBRIDGE HOMES, INC.

2004 WL 609326 (N.D. Ill. Mar. 23, 2004)

■   GUZMAN, District Judge.

Ocean Atlantic Woodland Corporation ("Ocean Atlantic") has sued DRH Cambridge Homes, Inc. ("Cambridge"), Cowhey, Gundmundson, Leder, Ltd. ("Cowhey"), and Pugsley & LaHaie, Ltd ("Pugsley") (collectively "defendants") alleging copyright infringement, unfair competition and deceptive trade practices, false designation of origin, conversion and unjust enrichment. . . . Defendants filed a joint motion for . . . bifurcation of discovery . . . .

DISCUSSION

. . .

On November 26, 2002, the defendants filed a motion pursuant to Rule 42(b) requesting the court to bifurcate liability and damages discovery. The defendants requested that the Court decline to allow the parties to enter into damages discovery until liability issues were determined. . . .

Whether to bifurcate discovery is a matter committed to the discretion of the trial court. Rule 42 specifies the factors to be weighed when considering whether or not to bifurcate: convenience, the avoidance of prejudice, expedition and economy.

The Court has the inherent power to control its docket. Separating the issues of liability and damages for the purposes of discovery will avoid unnecessary time and expense and further the interest of expedition by expediting the decision on liability. A verdict of no liability for infringement would render discovery on the damages issue unnecessary. In the instant case, this Court has already found . . . that, "[t]he record in this case . . . presents substantial issues which bear on Ocean Atlantic's likelihood of proving infringement . . . ." Thus, should plaintiff fail to establish liability in this case, the savings in time and costs with regard to discovery and discovery management would benefit both the parties and the Court.

It is clear, based on the breadth of the discovery requests, that the defendants would expend substantial amounts of time and resources responding to the discovery requests on damages. Continuation of discovery on the issue of damages would necessitate considerable operating costs in hiring accountants, researching, and calculating at a time when the development site is not even complete. Because, as noted above, the distinct possibility exists that the issue of damages will never be reached, bifurcating discovery as to liability from that of damages will serve the goals of convenience, expedition and economy. Moreover, evidence necessary to establish liability will nominally, if at all, overlap with evidence relating to damages and therefore the risk of duplication and delay is minimal.

Accordingly, the discovery of this case will be bifurcated into two phases. In the first, all discovery on liability will be completed. The defendants have already notified this Court that they will seek summary judgment as soon as discovery is complete. Therefore, discovery on damages is stayed pending resolution of the issue of liability. . . .

. . . The Court hereby orders bifurcation of discovery.

Notes

1.   There is no necessary correlation between pretrial and trial bifurcation. It is possible to divide the discovery pretrial process into discrete segments, but ultimately to try all issues at once. (We examine that idea, often called "phased discovery," later in this chapter. *See infra* p. 935.) Conversely, it is possible to bifurcate a case for trial, but to allow the pretrial process to be unitary. (We examine the costs and benefits of trial bifurcation in Chapter Ten. *See infra* p. 1033. You will learn there that trial bifurcation is controversial, and you will gain additional insight into the appropriateness of pretrial bifurcation.)

As *Kos* shows, however, there is typically a close relationship between bifurcating pretrial proceedings and bifurcating trial. In most cases, the best reason to bifurcate the pretrial issues is that the court has decided to bifurcate the trial; in these situations, it is logical, and often efficient, to conduct discovery just on the issues that will be tried first. The hope is that the first phase will narrow the case in a way that obviates the need to examine some or all of the later issues; as *Ocean Atlantic* describes, summary judgment on the liability issue eliminates the need to address subsequent issues. Unlike phased discovery, which is concerned more with efficiently conducting discovery, or trial bifurcation, which is concerned more with fairly and efficiently conducting the trial, here we are interested in using pretrial bifurcation as a means to narrow the issues.

2.   From an issue-narrowing perspective, a judge would love to find an issue that (1) is not complicated and does not require extensive discovery; (2) is completely severable from other issues in the case, so that no duplicative discovery will occur; (3) is highly likely to be resolved without need for trial; and (4) is highly likely to dispose of (or at least significantly narrow) the case. As you might imagine, however, such a perfect issue is hard to come by. When no perfect candidate emerges, how is the judge to choose among imperfect contenders that possess some but not all of these characteristics? In evaluating issues in light of these characteristics, isn't the judge's information imperfect (especially regarding factors (1)-(3))? When the judge selects a case-dispositive issue to be handled first, isn't there pressure on the judge to rule in a case-dispositive way that justifies the decision to bifurcate and avoids the inefficiency and delay that will occur if that first issue turns out not to be case-dispositive?

3. The answers to some of these questions might be found in empirical data about the effect of pretrial bifurcation on the outcomes of cases. We are unaware of any direct data that has addressed these matters. There are data, which we consider in Chapter Ten (*infra* p. 1042), suggesting that *trial* bifurcation results in a significantly higher chance for a defense verdict, but also leads to significant savings in terms of trial time. Although we have not data supporting this hypothesis, it seems plausible intuitively that pretrial bifurcation would change the litigation dynamics in a similar way: more defense-favoring results, but less expense. If this intuition is correct, how do we justify using outcome-determinative procedures in some, but not all, cases?

4. Bifurcating issues can help to achieve optimal aggregation. For instance, in *In re Sugar Industry Antitrust Litigation*, 427 F. Supp. 1018 (J.P.M.L. 1977), the Judicial Panel on Multidistrict Litigation "bifurcated" § 1407 transfers so that some parts of the cases were heard in one district, and other parts in another district. Likewise, in class actions, courts often bifurcate discovery so that discovery concerning class certification is handled before discovery on the merits of class or individual claims. *See, e.g.*, Harris v. Option One Mortgage Corp., 261 F.R.D. 98 (D.S.C. 2009). On the other hand, in *In re Rail Freight Fuel Surcharge Antitrust Litigation*, 258 F.R.D. 167 (D.D.C. 2009) (*infra* p. 939), the court refused to bifurcate class discovery and merits discovery. It held that the evidence concerning the propriety of certification and the merits was "closely intertwined," and that such bifurcation would require "ongoing supervision of discovery" and "needless disputes that would arise concerning the classification of each document as 'merits' or 'certification' discovery." *Id.* at 173, 174.

5. Although federal judges often bifurcate pretrial issues, the source of their power to do so remains unclear. The source is not Rule 42(b), which authorizes a court to order separate *trials*. Nor does Rule 16, the fountainhead of case-management authority, expressly mention pretrial bifurcation. Several of Rule 16's provisions, however, could be read to imply such a power. *See* Fed. R. Civ. P. 16(c)(2)(A) ("formulating and simplifying the issues"); -(c)(2)(L) ("adopting special procedures for managing potentially difficult or protracted actions"); -(c)(2)(M) ("ordering a separate trial"); -(c)(2)(N) ("ordering the presentation of evidence early in the trial"); -(c)(2)(P) ("facilitating in other ways the just, speedy, and inexpensive disposition of the action"). The best textual sources for bifurcation may be Rule 26(f)(3)(B) — which requires the parties' discovery plan to consider "whether discovery should be conducted in phases or be limited to or focused on particular issues" — in conjunction with Rule 26(c)(1)(B) — which authorizes a court to issue a protective order "specifying terms, including time and place, for the disclosure or discovery." But Rule 26 puts the onus for proposing bifurcated pretrial proceedings on the lawyers; if they do not agree in a Rule 26(f) discovery plan for bifurcated treatment, the court must tease out its authority to bifurcate from other sources. What might those sources be? Do courts possess an inherent power to order bifurcation, just like they seem to the inherent power to appoint lead counsel or order consolidated pleadings? What are the limits of this power?

6. The *Manual for Complex Litigation* seems to have a lukewarm attitude toward pretrial bifurcation. In its lists of techniques for case management and for narrowing issues during pretrial, bifurcation does not rate a mention. *See* MANUAL FOR COMPLEX LITIGATION, FOURTH §§ 11.211, 11.33 (2004); *cf. id.* § 11.632 (noting that a separate trial of an issue "early in the litigation . . . can affect . . . the scope of discovery"). In its discussion of discovery plans, it acknowledges pretrial bifurcation, *see id.* § 21.421, but it does not endorse the idea. Why the reluctance?

7. One of the differences between American and civil-law procedure is that the civil law lacks a definitive trial event; it proceeds through a series of hearings on discrete issues until the case is resolved. *See supra* p. 26. Pretrial bifurcation is a clear example of the shift in complex litigation away from the classic Anglo-American form of adversarial trial toward the civil-law tradition. Does this fact speak well or ill of pretrial bifurcation?

d. Post-Pleading Techniques to Narrow Factual and Legal Disputes

The rules of pleading require that the parties reveal basic information regarding the factual and legal nature of their claims and defenses, but the American theory of pleading does not expect the pleadings to narrow the issues in dispute. Might it be possible for a judge to develop post-pleading techniques by which the factual and legal issues are narrowed and meritless cases weeded out? We consider here three techniques: requiring the parties to provide additional disclosures designed to narrow the issues; developing a process by which the parties are required to stipulate to certain issues; and using expert medical panels.

i. Pretrial Disclosures

Federal Rules of Civil Procedure 26(a) contains three types of disclosure devices: the initial required disclosure of relevant lay witnesses and documents (Rule 26(a)(1)), the disclosure of expert witnesses (Rule 26(a)(2)), and the disclosure of trial witnesses and exhibits (Rule 26(a)(3)). These disclosures force the parties to reveal only basic information concerning the case, they do nothing directly to narrow the issues in dispute, and (except for Rule 26(a)(1)) they come fairly late in the pretrial process. Can a court, in the exercise of its case-management authority, do more?

ACUNA V. BROWN & ROOT INC.

200 F.3d 335 (5th Cir. 2000)

■ BENAVIDES, Circuit Judge.

. . . Plaintiffs-appellants . . . appeal the imposition of certain pre-discovery orders and argue, in the alternative, that they satisfied any burdens placed upon them and that their cases should not have been dismissed. As discussed below, we find that . . . dismissal of the cases was proper.

I. FACTS AND PROCEDURAL HISTORY

Crecension Acuna and other plaintiffs, in total numbering over one thousand, brought suit . . . against defendant companies for alleged personal injuries and property damage arising from defendants' uranium mining and processing activities. Rebecca Garcia and approximately 600 other plaintiffs brought suit alleging similar claims against a partially overlapping set of defendants, most of whom were also engaged in uranium mining activities in another area of Texas.

In both cases, plaintiffs alleged that they were exposed to and injured by the defendants' mining and processing activities. Some plaintiffs worked in uranium mines or processing plants, while others alleged exposure to radiation or uranium dust or tailings through contact with family members who worked in the mines or through environmental factors such as wind and groundwater. Plaintiffs alleged a range of injuries as well as durations and intensities of exposure. . . .

First in *Acuna* and then in *Garcia*, the court issued pre-discovery scheduling orders that required plaintiffs to establish certain elements of their claims through expert affidavits. Those affidavits had to specify, for each plaintiff, the injuries or illnesses suffered by the plaintiff that were caused by the alleged uranium exposure, the materials or substances causing the injury and the facility thought to be their source, the dates or circumstances and means of exposure to the injurious materials, and the scientific and medical bases for the expert's opinions.

In response to the order issued in *Acuna*, plaintiffs submitted just over one thousand form affidavits from a single expert, Dr. Smith. Those affidavits identified a series of illnesses and effects that can occur as a result of uranium exposure and stated that the relevant plaintiff suffered from some or all of them. The affidavits stated that Dr. Smith had reviewed the plaintiff's medical data and had come to the conclusion that exposure to uranium and its byproducts had reached clinically significant doses. The affidavits went on to list all of the mining facilities covered in the lawsuit as responsible for each plaintiff's exposure and routes of exposure as including inhalation, ingestion, and direct skin contact. The affidavits also included a list of scientific studies and materials.

The magistrate judge found that the affidavits did not comply with the scheduling order, reiterated some of the requirements of the order, and gave plaintiffs an additional month to comply. Plaintiffs then submitted additional affidavits by Dr. Smith and two other experts. Some individuals were identified in these affidavits as suffering from particular diseases but the other required information was not provided regarding their claims. The supplemental affidavits did not provide any new information regarding the specific claims of the vast majority of plaintiffs. The magistrate judge found that these additional affidavits still failed to meet the specificity requirements of the order and recommended that the case be dismissed. The district court issued a memorandum and order dismissing the case.

An identical pre-discovery order was issued some months later in *Garcia*. [Plaintiffs submitted only one affidavit by Dr. Smith, designed to cover all plaintiffs' claims. The district court dismissed the case for failure to comply with the order.] Plaintiffs in both cases appeal.

II. ANALYSIS

. . .

B. *Pre-trial Procedure in the District Court*

Plaintiffs contend that the pre-discovery orders requiring expert support for the details of each plaintiff's claim imposed too high a burden for that stage of litigation. In the alternative, they argue that they in fact complied with the orders and that their cases should be remanded for discovery and trial. The district court's dismissal of plaintiffs' claims in *Garcia* is reviewed for plain error, because plaintiffs did not make a timely objection to the magistrate judge's recommendation of dismissal. . . . Plaintiffs did file an objection in *Acuna*, and the district court therefore conducted a de novo review of the recommendation to dismiss. We review the district court's dismissal order under Fed. R. Civ. P. 16(f) for abuse of discretion. *See* Nat'l Hockey League v. Metro. Hockey Club, Inc., 427 U.S. 639, 642 (1976) . . . .

The pre-discovery orders in issue are of a type known as *Lone Pine* orders, named for *Lore v. Lone Pine Corp.*, No. L-33606-85 (N.J. Super. Ct. 1986). *Lone Pine* orders are designed to handle the complex issues and potential burdens on defendants and the court in mass tort litigation. In the federal courts, such orders are issued under the wide discretion afforded district judges over the management of discovery under Fed. R. Civ. P. 16.

In these two cases, treated as related in the district court, there are approximately one thousand six hundred plaintiffs suing over one hundred defendants for a range of injuries occurring over a span of up to forty years. Neither the defendants nor the court was on notice from plaintiffs' pleadings as to how many instances of which diseases were being claimed as injuries or which facilities were alleged to have caused those injuries. It was within the court's discretion to take steps to manage the complex and potentially very burdensome discovery that the cases would require.

The scheduling orders issued below essentially required that information which plaintiffs should have had before filing their claims pursuant to Fed. R. Civ. P. 11(b)(3). Each plaintiff should have had at least some information regarding the nature of his injuries, the circumstances under which he could have been exposed to harmful substances, and the basis for believing that the named defendants were responsible for his injuries. . . . The affidavits supplied by plaintiffs did not provide this information. The district court did not commit clear error or an abuse of discretion in refusing to allow discovery to proceed without better definition of plaintiffs' claims. . . .

. . . We therefore affirm the judgments of the district court.

IN RE DIGITEK® PRODUCT LIABILITY LITIGATION

264 F.R.D. 249 (S.D. W. Va. 2010)

■   GOODWIN, Chief Judge.

Pending is defendants' motion for entry of a *Lone Pine* case management order . . . . I deny the motions without prejudice.

I.

The plaintiffs in this multidistrict litigation ("MDL") are spread throughout the United States. [The defendants included companies that manufactured, marketed, tested, promoted, sold or distributed a cardiac glycoside known either as Digitek® or Digoxin. The drug was widely used to treat a variety of heart conditions. Digitek® had a "narrow therapeutic index"; in other words, there was a limited margin between effectiveness and toxicity. An excessive dose of the active ingredient could result in serious health problems or death.

[The United States Food and Drug Administration ("FDA") approved the drug, but issued a warning letter to the defendants in 2006 because they had failed to comply with reporting obligations, marketed drugs without proper clearance, and caused at least twenty-six adverse drug experiences ("ADEs") by failing to submit periodic safety reports. It issued another warning letter in 2007 due to deficiencies in the defendants' quality-control units. Finally, on April 25, 2008, the FDA issued a "Class I Recall" of the Digitek® manufactured by some of the defendants. A Class I Recall is instituted only when "there is a reasonable probability that the use or exposure to a violative product will cause serious adverse health consequences or death."]

The filing of various civil actions in state and federal courts across the country followed the recall, in which plaintiffs claimed injuries from alleged exposure to defectively manufactured Digitek®. On August 13, 2008, the Judicial Panel on Multidistrict Litigation entered an order establishing an MDL proceeding in this District consolidating federal Digitek® related actions for joint case management. The Master Complaint filed on February, 9, 2009, asserts the following claims: (1) Failure to Warn and Instruct; (2) Manufacturing Defect; (3) Design Defect; (4) Negligence; (5) Negligence Per Se; (6) Breach of Implied Warranty; (7) Breach of Express Warranty; (8) Negligent Misrepresentation; (9) Intentional Misrepresentation; (10) Fraud; (11) Constructive Fraud; (12) Violation of the West

Virginia Consumer Credit and Protection Act; (13) Other Unfair Trade Practice Act Violations; (14) Wrongful Death; (15) Survival Action; (16) Medical Monitoring; (17) Unjust Enrichment; (18) Medicare MSP Liability; (19) Loss of Consortium.

Defendants now seek the entry of a "limited" *Lone Pine* order requiring plaintiffs to produce an affidavit from a medical expert identifying case-specific evidence of digoxin toxicity as to [most plaintiffs]. Defendants request that the affidavit either (1) identify the specific portions of the medical records that, to a reasonable degree of medical certainty, constitute case-specific evidence (e.g., medical records that show elevated digoxin levels or references in the record showing a clinical concern about it), or (2) include medical records demonstrating that a treating physician diagnosed digoxin toxicity. The basis for the request is that "a substantial number of cases currently pending in the MDL are not supported by any case-specific evidence of digoxin toxicity." [In support of this motion, the defendants noted that "responses to Requests for Admission served by various Plaintiffs have revealed that many Plaintiffs' counsel had no medical records in their possession when they filed suit that established high digoxin levels. In even more cases (likely over a majority) there is simply no evidence of digoxin toxicity reflected by the medical records collected to date by a third party collection service since the inception of the lawsuit."]

Much of the preceding factual development is found in the Master Complaint. In the instant motion, defendants counter the allegations of that master pleading, in part, as follows:

The recall was initiated after nonconforming tablets were observed in one lot of the 0.125 mg tablets manufactured-Lot 70924A, manufactured in November 2007. The small number of larger-than-normal tablets were observed before shipment of Lot 70924A, and two comprehensive inspections followed. First, the entire lot, consisting of approximately 4.8 million tablets, was visually inspected pursuant to a protocol drafted by the Quality Assurance Department. [One of the defendants] discovered a total of 20 (0.00041 %) nonconforming tablets. The lot was then subjected to a second, rigorous sampling inspection, in which no nonconforming tablets were found. . . . The April 25, 2008 recall included all lots then in distribution, regardless of dose strength, and even though there was no evidence of any other nonconforming tablets.

No Plaintiffs counsel in any Digitek® case in any jurisdiction has produced a [larger-than-normal] tablet or provided test results from a certified lab that a tablet . . . was out of specification. . . . It has become increasingly clear that the publicity of the recall and aggressive advertising in follow-up to the recall is at the root of this litigation, not actual evidence of ingestion of a defective product. . . .

While the record collection process and evaluation described above has been underway, the FDA determined that there is a small likelihood that any recalled Digitek® caused injury to anyone. . . .

Defendants offer a number of additional contentions supporting the requested *Lone Pine* order. First, they assert that they have experienced "significant difficulties and inordinate delays" in the process of attempting to secure plaintiffs' fact sheets ("PFS") and related discovery. Second, they contend that responses to requests for admission "show repeated instances of filings without having any medical records in hand." Third, they note instances where medical records were in plaintiffs' possession at the time they instituted their civil actions but that the records revealed no elevated or toxic levels of digoxin were involved. Fourth, defendants state as follows:

> [D]epletion of insurance proceeds by defense costs incurred by defending meritless cases is an interest that all parties and this Court should recognize. . . . The parties have retained RecordTrak to obtain medical records. To date, RecordTrak has billed Defendants over $75,000 to obtain records and this figure will soon exceed $100,000. As indicated above, many of these records show no digoxin toxicity. . . . Absent the entry of a *Lone Pine* order, judicial resources will be expended considering numerous Rule 11 motions filed by Defendants in individual cases addressing the Plaintiffs' basic failure to conduct pre-filing factual investigation. . . .

II.

A *Lone Pine* order is designed to assist in the management of complex issues and potential burdens on defendants and the court in mass tort litigation, essentially requiring plaintiffs to produce a measure of evidence to support their claims at the outset. *See* Acuna v. Brown & Root Inc., 200 F.3d 335 (5th Cir. 2000); McManaway v. KBR, Inc.,— F.R.D. —, 2009 WL 4061581 (S.D. Ind. Nov. 20, 2009); In re Vioxx Prod. Liab. Litig., 557 F. Supp. 2d 741, 743 (E.D. La. 2008). As observed in *In re Vioxx*, however, "[i]n crafting a *Lone Pine* order, a court should strive to strike a balance between efficiency and equity."

It is of some consequence that no federal rule or statute requires, or even explicitly authorizes, the entry of *Lone Pine* orders. Nevertheless, *Lone Pine* orders have proven useful at times in complex litigation, and the courts citing authority for this type of extraordinary procedure typically rely upon the broad permission bestowed by Federal Rule of Civil Procedure 16. *See Acuna*, 200 F.3d at 340; *McManaway*, 2009 WL 4061581, at *1 ("*Lone Pine* orders are permitted by Rule 16(c)(2)(L) of the Federal Rules of Civil Procedure . . . .").

The propriety of entering a *Lone Pine* order appears to hinge on a number of factors, including (1) the posture of the action, (2) the peculiar case management needs presented, (3) external agency decisions impacting the merits of the case, (4) the availability and use of other procedures explicitly sanctioned by federal rule or statute, and (5) the type of injury alleged by plaintiffs and its cause.

The circumstance-specific nature of the decision to enter a *Lone Pine* order is perhaps best illustrated by the following analysis, undertaken by the Honorable Eldon E. Fallon, who presides over *In re Vioxx* . . .:

Lone Pine orders may not be appropriate in every case and, even when appropriate, they may not be suitable at every stage of the litigation. For example, in the present case, a *Lone Pine* order may not have been appropriate at an earlier stage before any discovery had taken place since little was known about the structure, nature and effect of Vioxx by anyone other than perhaps the manufacturer of the drug. But this case is no longer in its embryonic stage. It has existed in state courts for over seven years and in this Court for over three years, and much discovery has taken place. . . . [The defendant] has produced over 22 million pages of documents. Hundreds of depositions have taken place. [*In re Vioxx*, 557 F. Supp. 2d at 744.]

In addition to case posture and management needs, relevant external agency decisions, the availability and use of rule- and statutory-based procedures, and injury type and cause, case complexity and pleading defects are additional factors worth considering in advance of entering a *Lone Pine* order. . . . Overlying all of these factors, however, are the valid concerns expressed by some judges about the untethered use of the *Lone Pine* process . . . . Also, few *Lone Pine* orders have undergone federal appellate scrutiny. Concerns about the potential for misuse of the device have led at least one judge to observe that "[a] *Lone Pine* order should issue only in an exceptional case and after the defendant has made a clear showing of significant evidence calling into question the plaintiffs' ability to bring forward necessary medical causation and other scientific information." *McManaway*, — F.R.D. —, 2009 WL 4061582, at *5.

III.

Regarding the posture of the action, I received the first MDL transfer order on August 13, 2008. Accordingly, this action has not proceeded as far along as some other cases, such as *In re Vioxx*, where *Lone Pine* orders were deemed appropriate.

Regarding the peculiar case management needs presented, and the use of other procedures explicitly sanctioned by federal rule or statute, I have taken a number of measures, with the cooperation of counsel and my fellow judicial officers on the state bench, to put this litigation on track for a just, speedy, and efficient disposition. Some of these steps are worth noting. First, following preliminary case management efforts, including the appointment of lead and liaison counsel, federal and state coordination efforts, preliminary discovery orders, and various conferences, a case management and scheduling order, referred to as PTO 16, was entered on March 5, 2009. That detailed PTO was designed to address many of the concerns expressed by the defendants in support of the *Lone Pine* request. If that PTO is being violated, as it has in times past, defendants have remedies available to them, some of which are discussed below.

Second, I required the plaintiffs to file a Master Complaint. That document, which has withstood scrutiny under Rule 12(b)(6), has largely eliminated any concerns respecting pleading defects. It recites in detail the bases of liability asserted by the growing number of plaintiffs who have adopted it. Third, as noted, PTO 16 requires that the defendants receive from each plaintiff in this MDL a PFS, which is in essence treated as a formal discovery response. The PFS is governed by the standards applicable to written discovery under Rules 26 through 37 and must be answered essentially without objections. Plaintiffs are also required by PTO 16 to provide authorizations for release of medical records and to reimburse reasonable copying costs, which address some of the expense concerns presented by defendants. Plaintiffs are further required to produce any documents in their or their counsels' possession showing the fact and dates of Digitek® prescriptions, proof the prescriptions were filled, and re-filled, and medical records documenting the alleged injury suffered as a result of ingesting the drug. If a PFS is not timely or substantially completed, sanctions will result. . . . The procedure has been used successfully by defendants, and certain plaintiffs have dismissed a number of meritless cases. I have also used Rule 16 and the same PTO 16 process to begin the process of imposing monetary sanctions when appropriate. Additionally, in those cases where the PFS, while complete, has called into question the prefiling investigation performed by plaintiffs' counsel, defendants have sought sanctions under Rule 11. Both remedies are a further measure to alleviate the expenses defendants assert they have borne as a result of plaintiffs' noncompliance with existing discovery devices.

Given a choice between a *"Lone Pine* order" created under the court's inherent case management authority and available procedural devices such as summary judgment, motions to dismiss, motions for sanctions and similar rules, I believe it more prudent to yield to the consistency and safeguards of the mandated rules especially at this stage in this litigation. Claims of efficiency, elimination of frivolous claims and fairness are effectively being addressed using the existing and standard means. Resorting to crafting and applying a *Lone Pine* order should only occur where existing procedural devices explicitly at the disposal of the parties by statute and federal rule have been exhausted or where they cannot accommodate the unique issues of this litigation. We have not reached that point.

Regarding the impact of external agency decisions, one might properly characterize the setting as a mixed bag. . . . When viewed together, this is not a case, like some others, where the regulatory agency has sounded the "all clear."

Regarding the type of injury alleged and its cause, it is likely that substantial and highly contentious causation issues will arise collectively and individually as this action progresses. Indeed, much expert testimony is anticipated in this litigation as to the causal relationship between the allegedly defective Digitek® and the adverse outcomes allegedly suffered by the affected plaintiffs. I recently scheduled a *Daubert* hearing, roughly a year from now, that will aid in final resolution of those issues. It seems unwise to begin addressing causation issues, in a summary-judgment type fashion that defendants surely contemplate, at this somewhat early juncture when those issues might proliferate and become more complex as the case proceeds.

In sum, the factors that often coincide to warrant entry of a *Lone Pine* order are not presented at this time. This is not to say that, at a later point in the litigation, that the need for this type of case management tool within the discretion of the court, might not arise. At this point, however, it has not been shown that this action qualifies as "an exceptional case" justifying the extraordinary relief sought. Accordingly, I deny without prejudice defendants' motion for entry of a *Lone Pine* case management order . . . .

Notes

1.   Aside from *Lone Pine* orders, the principal device that courts have used to determine whether a sufficient factual basis exists to proceed with a claim is the RICO case statement (which has occasionally been adopted for use in non-RICO cases as well). We discussed RICO case statements *supra* p. 796, Note 8. Although the information requested in a *Lone Pine* order (essentially medical in nature) and RICO case statements (essentially the "who, what, when, where, and how" of fraud) differ, the impetus is the same: the desire to weed out claims that lack merit by ensuring, at an early stage in the pretrial process, that the plaintiffs have evidence to support their positions.

2.   There is one important distinction between *Lone Pine* orders and RICO case statements. *Lone Pine* orders seek disclosure of information uniquely within the possession of the plaintiff. RICO case statements often ask plaintiffs to reveal what they know about the defendants' conduct, even before discovery about that conduct commences. Does this distinction suggest that courts should more readily grant *Lone Pine* orders than require RICO case statements? Is the chance of an erroneous dismissal of a meritorious claim greater when a RICO case statement is required than when a *Lone Pine* disclosure are required?

On the other hand, many RICO claims involve allegations of fraud, for which heightened pleading is required. Fed. R. Civ. P. 9(b). Does that requirement give judges a toehold to require RICO case statements, even if *Lone Pine* orders are problematic?

3.   As we saw in our discussion of RICO case statements, and as the fault line between *Acuna* and *Digitek*® proves, using such devices is controversial. Because they impose disclosure obligations early in the pretrial process — indeed, the *early* disclosure of information designed to weed out meritless claims is their very point — these devices seem to be an extension of the pleading rules, and seek to force the parties to plead with far more specificity than our pleading rules demand. They also require disclosures not demanded by the initial required disclosures of Rule 26(a)(1). And they accelerate to the beginning of the pretrial process the summary adjudication of claims, even though summary judgment does not

usually occur until the parties have had "adequate time for discovery." *See* Celotex Corp. v. Catrett, 477 U.S. 317, 322 (1986). Whether they are therefore consistent with either the letter or the spirit of the Federal Rules is debatable.

4.   Indeed, as *Acuna* and *Digitek®* show, the debate over early pretrial-disclosure techniques to weed out meritless claims is in large measure a debate about the scope of a judge's case-management powers. The vague "eliminating frivolous claims" provision of Rule 16(c)(2)(A) and the capacious "special procedures" provision of Rule 16(c)(2)(L) are often cited as the basis for a court's case-management authority to employ such techniques. But neither provision expressly authorizes either RICO case statements or *Lone Pine* orders, and both contradict to some extent the more specific commitments of Rules 8, 9(b), 26(a)(1), and 56. Judges who employ these devices are therefore operating in the shadows of the Federal Rules — not completely beyond the Rules, so that the judges' actions are justifiable only on a theory of inherent power, but not squarely within the Rules either.

The ambiguous position of a judge's case-management power has been, and will continue to be, a central theme of case management: At what point must the desire to resolve a complex case give way to the demand to treat complex cases under the same rules as ordinary cases? Part of your answer to this question might come from your vision of the Federal Rules of Civil Procedure — whether they are strict rules or mere guidelines. Part of your answer might come from your view of what makes a case complex, and whether "off-book" judicial power can or should correct it. Part of your answer might come from the value that you place on the like procedural treatment of ordinary and complex cases.

5.   One of the more extended defenses of using a *Lone Pine*-type order is *Cottle v. Superior Court*, 5 Cal. Rptr. 2d 882 (Cal. Ct. App. 1992), in which the court argued that its authority derived from various provisions of the California code, from California's standards of judicial administration for complex litigation, and from the court's "inherent equity, supervisory and administrative powers." *Id.* at 887-88.

6.   One reason why *Digitek®* rejects the *Lone Pine* order is the set of other case-management techniques that the court has already put in place, including a master complaint and "plaintiffs' fact sheets." Let us make two observations about this rationale. First, as the court recognizes, case-management techniques are rarely adopted in isolation, and it is important to understand how all the case-management techniques fit together. It is not necessary that a single case-management technique do all the lifting.

Second, the technique of using "plaintiffs' fact sheets" is not uncommon in mass-tort litigation. In lieu of full discovery and depositions, plaintiffs provide basic factual information regarding exposure and illness; typically, they also sign releases so that the defendant can obtain medical and related records. Depending on the inclination of the judge and parties, the information can be provided in writing (as it apparently was in *Digitek®*) or it can be provided to third-party interviewers who are far less expensive to employ than attorneys. For one description of the interview process, which was conducted to determine eligibility for a settlement, see Francis E. McGovern & E. Allen Lind, *The Discovery Survey*, 51 LAW & CONTEMP. PROBS. 41 (Autumn 1988).

Such survey methods are usually designed to expedite the discovery process; hence, their consideration more properly belongs in the following section of the chapter, which examines techniques to streamline fact gathering in complex cases. But one common feature of such methods is to include a sanction that forces the parties to complete the written or oral surveys. The most common stick is to dismiss the claims of plaintiffs who fail to comply. Dismissals are justified under the sanction powers of Rules 16(f) and 37(b). Thus, plaintiff surveys have a claim-narrowing function — albeit an indirect one that hinges on a plaintiff's noncompliance.

7. *Lone Pine* orders have received a fair amount of judicial attention. *Digitek®* is an excellent source of authorities on both sides of the question. These orders have received only modest scholarly attention. *See* Elizabeth M. Schneider, *The Dangers of Summary Judgment: Gender and Federal Civil Litigation*, 59 RUTGERS L. REV. 705, 756 (2007). They have received far more attention in the practitioner literature; predictably, they receive more favorable treatment in the defense-side journals than in the plaintiff-side journals.

ii. Pretrial Stipulations

Another way to narrow the factual and legal issues is to develop mechanisms that force the parties to stipulate to certain factual or legal propositions in advance of trial. The Federal Rules of Civil Procedure contain one device to force stipulations: the request for admission (Rule 36). But a party can escape answering a request for admission if, after a reasonable inquiry, "the information [the party] knows or can readily obtain is insufficient to enable [the party] to admit or deny" the request. Fed. R. Civ. P. 36(a)(4). Moreover, the consequences for failing to admit a Rule 36 request — paying the opposing party's costs of proving the issue at trial in the event that the admission was of "substantial importance" and the refusal to admit was not based on a "reasonable ground," *see* Fed. R. Civ. P. 37(c)(2) — are not particularly ominous in a world in which few cases go to trial. As a result, requests for admission often work best at the end of the discovery process to narrow trial issues, rather than in the early stages of the discovery process to reduce pretrial issues; and even then, they work best to eliminate simple disputes such as the genuineness of documents.

The issue, therefore, is whether the judge enjoys a case-management authority independent of Rule 36 to force the parties to stipulate to factual or legal propositions to narrow the issues well in advance of trial. Once again, we find that the need for the efficient resolution of complex cases is pitted against fears of increased judicial power and the potential for dissimilar treatment of similar cases. Once again, we find that, in resolving this tension, judges claim the necessary power.

UNITED STATES V. AMERICAN
TELEPHONE & TELEGRAPH CO.

461 F. Supp. 1314 (D.D.C. 1978)

■ GREENE, District Judge.

The motions before the Court . . . raise fundamental issues concerning the discovery that should govern the future path of this antitrust litigation. . . .

The complaint was filed on November 20, 1974. It alleges violations of Section 2 of the Sherman Act, 15 U.S.C. § 2, by the American Telephone and Telegraph Company (AT&T), Western Electric Company, Inc. (Western Electric), and Bell Telephone Laboratories, Inc. (Bell Labs). . . .

The complaint explains that the defendants are violating the antitrust laws by various monopolistic practices . . . . Among other relief, the action seeks the divestiture by AT&T of all Western Electric stock; the separation of some or all of the Long Lines Department of AT&T from the Bell Operating Companies; the divestiture by Western Electric of its manufacturing and other assets sufficient to insure competition in the manufacture and sales of telecommunications equipment; and such relief against Bell Labs as the Court may find appropriate. . . .

Shortly after the filing of the complaint, in November of 1974, . . . the parties began to engage in discovery. Defendants served a request for production of documents upon the government, as well as a comprehensive set of interrogatories. The government, for its part, filed numerous discovery requests upon defendants and each of the operating telephone companies in which AT&T holds a majority interest, and it began fairly extensive third party discovery. Disputes arose almost immediately, however, with each side accusing the other of making unduly broad requests and of engaging in obstructive conduct in relation to opposing requests. [Discovery was stayed for about thirty-one months while the parties litigated jurisdictional issues as far as the Supreme Court.]

When the last certiorari petition was denied, and the stays were dissolved, the parties filed a number of proposed orders concerning pretrial discovery, and the Court, by its order of February 7, 1978, referred the case to Magistrate Lawrence S. Margolis to direct the preparation of a discovery schedule. [In addition, the court appointed two special masters, Professors Geoffrey Hazard and Paul Rice, to deal with claims of privilege. After dealing with preliminary matters, the court turned to "the future course of this action, including the scheduling of proceedings and the authority of the Magistrate and the Special Masters."]

IV

. . . During the infrequent periods lasting no more than a few months at a time when the proceedings were not under a stay order, relatively little discovery was being carried on. Thus, in spite of its age, this case has not come close to going to trial. . . .

However, in view of the Court's decision today on all major outstanding issues, the time is ripe for sketching out a procedural plan to move this litigation expeditiously along toward its disposition without doing violence to the legitimate rights of the parties. . . .

The complaint, as defendants have pointed out, is sweeping, broad, and vague. This has not only had the effect of making it difficult for defendants to formulate their defenses, but it has also been an obstacle to discovery. Absent greater precision and specificity with respect to the government's claims, discovery is likely to remain so unfocused as to be both unduly expensive and unmanageable. Moreover, it is generally agreed that one key to the swift disposition and firm management of cases such as this is a narrowing of the issues. Thus, it is essential that this relatively amorphous complaint be shaped as quickly as possible into specific allegations, and that a continuing mechanism be established for identifying and narrowing the issues and specifying the evidence to be relied upon by both plaintiff and defendants.

After considering defendants' request for greater specificity, plaintiff's offer to submit a preliminary order of proof, and the need for expeditious processing of this litigation and an appropriate limitation on discovery, an order to govern pretrial proceedings (Pretrial Order No. 12) is being entered this date.[98]

In essence, that order provides that the parties shall file four successive Statements of Contentions and Proof over the next eighteen months, each to become progressively more specific than the last, and each to be followed by a special pretrial conference. The filing of the final statements shall signal the close of discovery.

Thus, by November 1, 1978, plaintiff shall file a Statement of Contentions and Proof, in which it shall describe, with specificity, each of the government's legal and factual contentions, including the activities of the defendants it expects to rely upon to prove its charges of violation of § 2 of the Sherman Act. Under the heading of each factual contention, the statement shall list the witnesses and the documentary and other evidence which will be used to support the claim that such activity was carried on to effect unlawful combinations in violation of the antitrust laws, or which will otherwise support the allegations of the complaint. The statement shall describe the extent to which such evidence is presently in the possession of the plaintiff, or where, in the government's view, it may be found.

Defendants shall then have until January 1, 1979, to file their first Statement of Contentions and Proof in which they shall state their factual and legal contentions in response to plaintiff's claims, the factual and legal

---

98. The order is based on the Court's authority under Rules 16 and 26. At the same time, the Court recognizes that in a lawsuit of this magnitude, pretrial mecha- nisms must not merely follow the literal language of the Rules but should also take account of the logistics of dealing with proof of potentially enormous proportions. . . .

basis for their affirmative defenses, if any, and the documentary or other proof they expect to rely upon in support of each factual contention. Defendants' statement shall be organized in a manner similar to that of plaintiff and it shall be similarly detailed.

Within thirty days thereafter, a special pretrial conference shall be held before the Magistrate in accordance with Rule 16 and 28 U.S.C. § 636, for the principal purposes of narrowing and simplifying the issues, arriving at stipulations of uncontroverted facts, and reducing further unnecessary discovery.

Each of the parties shall file three additional Statements of Contentions and Proof, and three additional special pretrial conferences shall be held successively thereafter . . . . Some of these pretrial conferences, particularly the later ones, may be conducted by the Court rather than the Magistrate. On April 1, 1980, contemporaneously with the submission of the final statements, all discovery shall be closed.

If the issues are to be narrowed and this case is to be brought to trial within a reasonable period of time, it is essential that the parties be bound by their Statements of Contentions and Proof. Accordingly, after a party has filed a statement, it will be restricted to discovery within the limitations of the issues identified by that statement and the contemporaneous opposing statement. Likewise, with the exceptions noted below, subsequent statements may not enlarge upon or add to contentions previously made, and they will have as their purpose not the inclusion of matters neglected or overlooked in earlier statements, but the further narrowing and tightening of matters in dispute between the parties.

Discovery will also be restricted to data relevant to proof of propositions which are material, as distinguished from merely generally relevant conduct, periods of time, or areas, and proof at trial will be limited to the issues framed by the final statements and the last pretrial order.

To be sure, in the early stages of this process the parties may not be able to be fully definitive as to either the evidence or the specific contentions that will be based on that evidence. Accordingly, upon leave of the Magistrate, which will be freely granted with respect to a request based upon new discovery, the second statement may enlarge upon the first, either by broadening existing contentions or by adding new contentions. *Cf.* Fed. R. Civ. P. 15. Thereafter, however, the burden to justify a departure from previous statements shall become progressively heavier. After the parties file their second statements, an enlargement will be allowed only upon good cause shown, and after the third statements are filed, any amendment, other than by way of limitation, will be granted only to prevent manifest injustice. These procedures will be enforced and administered to achieve a narrowing of the issues, to apprise opponents and the Court of the status of the case, and to effect appropriate limitations on discovery.

To a substantial extent, the development of discovery and the definition and clarification of issues present a classic "chicken and egg problem," i.e., "to be manageable, discovery ought to be confined to framed issues, but to be framed carefully, issues must be based on concrete knowledge." The authorities differ on how this dilemma should be resolved, that is, in what sequence and by what methods discovery and issue definition should take place. Some writers advocate that, in order to avoid the unnecessary production of documents and the taking of depositions which ultimately may not prove to be helpful, all discovery should be stayed until the issues have been clearly specified. The highly respected *Manual for Complex Litigation*, on the other hand, takes the position that the issues cannot be defined until all discovery has more or less been completed.

In my judgment, in a suit of this magnitude it would be self-defeating either to let discovery continue on an almost unlimited basis, until the parties are prepared fully to define the issues, or to freeze discovery indefinitely in the illusory hope that the parties without the benefit of discovery will somehow acquire the capability to give concrete shape to the generalized issues raised by the complaint and the answer. Either course can lead only to procrastination. The short of the matter is that "the need to settle every conceivable dispute and to have every conceivable theory and fact presented must be balanced by the need for final resolution." The procedures specified herein are designed to move the case along while seeking to escape the adverse consequences inherent in the several contending methods of handling the pretrial process. Discovery and issue definition will go hand in hand. Initially this will entail a certain amount of discovery that will have to be disregarded later but as the issues are narrowed further, less and less irrelevant discovery should take place. Concomitantly the ongoing discovery process should provide the information necessary to narrow the issues.

If mutually fair, appropriately complete, and expeditious discovery is to be effected, and if the real issues are to emerge at an early date, it is essential that the parties cooperate in good faith with each other, the Magistrate, the Special Masters, and the Court. Counsel will be expected to meet informally with each other whenever appropriate to attempt to iron out discovery disputes, and only when controversies are so genuine and substantial that they cannot be resolved informally shall they be submitted to the Court.

The parties are in agreement that the details of discovery must be closely supervised by a judicial officer if this case is to move expeditiously to a disposition on the merits. There is some difference of opinion as to whether these supervisory functions would best be exercised by the Court, the Magistrate, or the Special Masters . . . .

[I]t appears that broadening the responsibilities of the Special Masters to include ruling on all discovery disputes, as suggested by defendants, would be inappropriate. The Special Masters will have an enormous responsibility, with respect to both volume and sensitivity, in passing upon claims of privilege advanced by defendants and many government departments. . . . The Magistrate, unlike the Masters, has his office in this courthouse where he may be deemed to be available both to the parties and to this Court at all times. Further, the legislation creating the post of Magistrate contemplated that persons occupying the position would undertake precisely such responsibilities.

For these reasons, the Magistrate is hereby designated to supervise pretrial discovery and to consider and deal with all discovery disputes, other than those matters which . . . have been delegated by the Court to the Special Masters, and except as may hereafter be ordered otherwise by the Court. . . .

Important substantive issues are raised in this action, and the parties are entitled to a judicial process which will fairly, impartially, and expeditiously resolve these issues. It is the Court's purpose to provide them with such a process.

Notes

1.   The *AT&T* case probably was the most complex two-party dispute in history. The allegations of antitrust conspiracy spread over decades and involved dozens of distinct courses of conduct. In spite of its radical-seeming nature, Judge Greene's response to *AT&T* established a framework that still let the parties develop the issues and proofs. In some ways, the stipulation process was a throwback to common-law pleading, in which the swapping of increasingly specific pleadings framed the issues for trial. One difference is that the parties also engaged in discovery to help refine the pleadings; the common law had no discovery devices; but Judge Greene's approach was essentially consistent with the adversarial model's traditional judicial role, in which the judge takes no active role in shaping the case for trial. So, in light of the nature of the case, was it radical enough?

2.   This is what happened. Shortly after the process commenced, it became apparent that a limited judicial role was inadequate. The linchpin of the plan was the Statement of Contentions and Proof, and the parties had bogged down. The second round of Statements yielded 1,872 pages filed by the plaintiff, and 2,147 pages filed by the defendants.   The Statements amounted to "a concatenation of conclusory allegations with ambiguous factual contentions. Hyperbole was rampant. . . . [The process of going through each allegation and its documentary support] generated thousands of pages of worksheets, required the expenditure of tens of thousands of man-hours over a six-month period of exchanges, and resulted in agreement on only a few paragraphs of factual contentions. And a substantial number of contentions had not even been addressed." Geoffrey C. Hazard, Jr. & Paul R. Rice, *Judicial Management of the Pretrial Process in Massive Litigation: Special Masters as Case Managers, in* WAYNE D. BRAZIL ET AL., MANAGING COMPLEX LITIGATION 103 (1983).

Consequently, in a larger departure from the adversarial ideal, Judge Greene put the stipulation process in the hands of the special masters, to whom he had initially declined to give this role. The masters convinced the parties to divide the case into episodes. The parties identified 82 discrete episodes at issue, many of which "constitute[d] major antitrust disputes in their own right." United States v. Am. Tel. & Tel. Co., 88 F.R.D. 47, 51 n.21 (D.D.C. 1980). The masters met on a regular basis with the lawyers to negotiate over the stipulations regarding each episode. The "negotiation process was long, arduous, and costly. It lasted for 13 months, ultimately involving 19 negotiating teams for each side and a heavy cost in manpower and supporting services." Hazard & Rice, *supra*, at 105.

Aside from this stipulation process, enormous discovery problems existed. Hundreds of depositions needed to be coordinated, and the information from these depositions and from millions of pages of documents needed to be digested for inclusion in the stipulations. At one point shortly before trial commenced, the government indicated that, just to complete its deposition program (in which multiple attorneys would take depositions simultaneously), it needed thirty-six more weeks. Judge Greene took an increasingly active role in managing the pretrial process, and ultimately set a firm trial date of January, 1981 — even though he realized that discovery could not possibly be completed by that time.

If efficiency is the measure of benefit, the stipulation process yielded some benefits. Many factual propositions — estimated by Professors Hazard and Rice at eighty to eighty-five percent — were agreed on. The United States agreed to abandon fourteen of the episodes, leaving a mere sixty-eight episodes for trial. The deposition testimony of witnesses became part of the Statements of Contention and Proof, so that direct examinations at trial were eliminated or drastically reduced.

Despite the limits placed on traditional party control of discovery, the trial itself lasted nearly a year. The government "presented close to one hundred witnesses, many thousands of documents, and additional thousands of stipulations. . . . [Defendants] presented approximately 250 witnesses and tens of thousands of pages of documents." United States v. Am. Tel. & Tel. Co., 552 F. Supp. 131, 140 (D.D.C. 1982). The parties settled before the conclusion of the trial, and entered into a consent decree in whose shadow we still live.

3. Even if the stipulation process was not particularly successful in narrowing pretrial issues, would the process be worthwhile if it simplified the trial? (As with pretrial bifurcation, a pretrial case-management technique might be justified not so much for its ability to resolve problems of pretrial complexity as for its ability to reduce problems of trial complexity.) Are reductions in pretrial and trial complexity worth the harm that the process caused to adversarial and trans-substantive ideals?

4. The special masters thought that the departure from the these ideals was not only warranted, but essential:

Historically judges have assumed a formal and distant roles in their relationship with the litigants and the management of the litigation. . . . [T]his judicial posture severely inhibits the type of supervision needed to resolve expeditiously, if not avoid altogether, the myriad disputes that give rise to delay. . . . [W]hat is needed is a new type of supervising judicial officer, possessing the power of the presiding judge but serving more in the role of judicial case manager — an intensely active and substantially less formal position. This is the role we assumed in the government litigation against AT&T, a role we have concluded is vital to the most successful management of litigation.

Hazard & Rice, *supra*, at 91.

One of *AT&T*'s lead attorneys was less sanguine; he noted problems with the informality of the process, frequent ex parte communications, counterproductive supervision of the stipulation process, costliness of the masters, and the possibility (not present in the *AT&T* case itself) of masters of marginal competence or commitment. His conclusion:

> Hazard and Rice may be attempting to draw universal conclusions from an unusual situation. . . . [A]ny attempt to impose such a system automatically in all or even most complex cases would be fraught with danger and could very easily increase the cost of complex litigation substantially without any concomitant improvement in quality.

Robert D. McLean, *Pretrial Management in Complex Litigation: The Use of Special Masters in* United States v. AT&T, *in* MANAGING COMPLEX LITIGATION, *supra*, 275, 279-80. Professor Sherman has raised still other questions with the stipulation procedure:

> Does this portend a move away from the traditional Anglo-American notion that oral testimony elicited through direct and cross examination of a witness observed by the factfinder is the preferred form of evidence? Does it mean that our trial process will move closer to the "dossier-trial" system of European continental countries, in which the entire case is put into a dossier on which the factfinders will base their conclusions? If so, how will this change the discovery and trial strategy of attorneys?

Edward F. Sherman, *Restructuring the Trial Process in the Age of Complex Litigation*, 63 TEX. L. REV. 721, 746 (1984).

5. It is hard to believe that each of the 68 episodes remaining for trial received the consideration it would have received if it had been the only allegation at stake; with only five months to try its case, the government needed to prove a major antitrust violation every other day (and that includes time for defendants' cross-examination). Would a better option have been to bifurcate for pretrial and trial a few of the critical episodes, to allow traditional discovery on those episodes, and to move along (if necessary) to other episodes as earlier ones were resolved? Of course, with that approach, the parties might have litigated the case into this century, and relevant information would have been lost, forgotten, or destroyed in the meantime. Which is worse: early but inadequate participation on all issues, or full participation on some issues and the risk of little to no participation on the rest?

6. Judge Greene refers to the "chicken and egg" problem of any pretrial management alternative: In order to streamline discovery and make it manageable, the lawyers and the court need to know which issues

are relevant, but they cannot know which issues are relevant until the facts have been discovered. By now it should be obvious that there is no easy answer to the problem. Judge Greene's stipulation plan created a fairly rigid pretrial procedure useful for identifying the issues, but it was far less helpful for discovering the facts. Judge Greene tried to compensate for this fact by allowing the second round of stipulations to expand on the first.

7. Another practical question also confronted Judge Greene: the source of his power to order pretrial stipulations. Ultimately he located the power in Rules 16 and 26 of the Federal Rules of Civil Procedure. At the time, this approach was utterly novel because the then-current versions of Rules 16 and 26 did not make even the remotest mention of such a power. Today Rule 16 contains several possible sources for this power: the "formulating and simplifying the issues" language of Rule 16(c)(2)(A), the "obtaining admissions and stipulations of facts" language of Rule 16(c)(2)(C), and the "special procedures" language of Rule 16(c)(2)(L). But this language again begs the question about how much power the judge has, in the absence of consent by the parties, to alter the ordinary course of issue and fact development during pretrial.

Similarly, the *Manual for Complex Litigation* recommends — both as an issue-narrowing device and as a trial-expediting device — that judges require parties to "present a detailed statement of their contentions, with supporting facts and evidence." MANUAL FOR COMPLEX LITIGATION, FOURTH § 11.33 (2004); *see id.* §§ 11.471, 11.641. This language is broad enough to include the *AT&T* approach, but could also include less rigorous approaches as well. *See also* WILLIAM W SCHWARZER, MANAGING ANTITRUST AND OTHER COMPLEX LITIGATION § 2-2(C)(3) (suggesting use of statements of contention and proof to "identify and clarify issues").

Few cases have used the *A&T* stipulation process — at least in pure form. The reported cases have tended to be antitrust actions, and none has explained in detail the reasons for adopting the procedure. *See, e.g.*, Greater Rockford Energy and Tech. Corp. v. Shell Oil Co., 790 F. Supp. 804 (C.D. Ill. 1992); Ralph C. Wilson Indus., Inc. v. Am. Broad. Co., 598 F. Supp. 694 (N.D. Cal. 1984); S. Pac. Commc'ns Co. v. Am. Tel. & Tel. Co., 556 F. Supp. 825 (D.D.C. 1982).

8. Courts are not bound by parties' stipulations. "A court, for example, is not bound to accept stipulations regarding questions of law, . . . nor may the parties create a case by stipulating to facts that do not exist. . . . A district court may also disregard a stipulation if it would be manifestly unjust to enforce the stipulation." Sinicropi v. Milone, 915 F.2d 66, 68 (2d Cir. 1990).

9. At the end of the pretrial process, there will usually be a final pretrial conference, for which the parties are typically required to submit a proposed final pretrial order. Fed. R. Civ. P. 16(e). This proposed order will contain the matters on which the parties agree, the legal issues remaining in dispute, the factual issues remaining in dispute, a list of the documents that each side will use to prove its case, and a list of the witnesses that each side will call. *See* MANUAL, *supra*, § 11.67. In the event

that there is no final pretrial order, Rule 26(a)(3) requires the parties to disclose trial witnesses and exhibits. According to Rule 16(e), the court can modify the final pretrial order "only to prevent manifest injustice." *See* Phoenix Can. Oil Co. v. Texaco, Inc., 842 F.2d 1466 (3d Cir. 1988) (enforcing pretrial orders is particularly important in complex litigation).

10. From the perspective of issue-narrowing, stipulations and final pretrial orders are weak devices. The native caution of counsel usually prevents early stipulations on issues of significance. The final pretrial order narrows issues, but it comes at the end of the discovery process. Its ability to streamline the trial is useful in dealing with problems of trial complexity, but it does not alleviate problems of pretrial complexity.

11. To some extent, all the case management devices we have explored harken back to a single question: If the case cannot be managed by the lawyers through the adversarial process, should the case be adjudicated at all? Here Professor Fuller's point about polycentrism is critical. *See supra* pp. 38-39. The breakup of AT&T was at least as polycentric a problem as the examples that Professor Fuller cited as instances that were improper for adjudication.

Justice Rehnquist noted a part of this problem when the *AT&T* consent decree came before the Supreme Court. Before entry of a consent judgment in an antitrust case like *AT&T*, 15 U.S.C. § 16(b) required the district court to "determine that the entry of such judgment is in the public interest." Judge Greene so found. The Supreme Court upheld this determination summarily. Justice Rehnquist dissented, suggesting that the role forced upon the judge was unconstitutional:

> The question assigned to the district courts by the Act is a classic example of a question committed to the Executive. . . . There is no standard by which the benefits to the public from a "better" settlement of a lawsuit than the Justice Department has negotiated can be balanced against the risk of an adverse decision, the need for a speedy resolution of the case, the benefits obtained in the settlement, and the availability of the Department's resources for other cases. . . . Even though Congress may by statute impose such a duty on the federal courts, they may not perform it.

Md. v. United States, 460 U.S. 1001, 1005-06 (1983) (Rehnquist, J., dissenting) (some paragraphing omitted).

iii.   Expert Panels

Complex cases almost invariably involve expert testimony. As part of their responsibility to streamline the discovery process, judges must develop ways to handle such testimony expeditiously. A related but distinct question is whether a judge can devise a way to narrow the scientific or technical issues in the case, thus obviating the need for extensive party presentation of expert witnesses. The following case constitutes a modest step in this direction. The portent of the decision is much greater.

HALL V. BAXTER HEALTHCARE CORP.

947 F. Supp. 1387 (D. Or. 1996)

■ JONES, District Judge.

I. INTRODUCTION

Currently pending in this court are a number of silicone breast implant cases brought by or on behalf of the plaintiffs against various breast implant manufacturers. Plaintiffs seek damages for injuries they claim to have suffered as a result of implantation with silicone gel breast implants.

Among other things, the plaintiffs assert that silicone from the implants has migrated and degraded in their bodies and has caused a systemic syndrome or illness, which they generally refer to as "atypical connective tissue disease" (ACTD). In essence, plaintiffs claim a "unique constellation of symptoms" consisting of hundreds of symptoms commonly experienced by the general population.

This opinion addresses the defendants' motions in limine to exclude testimony by plaintiffs' experts concerning any causal link between silicone breast implants and the alleged systemic disease or syndrome. To resolve these motions, the court, in its role as "gatekeeper" (*see* Daubert v. Merrell Dow Pharms., Inc., 509 U.S. 579 (1993) (hereinafter *Daubert I*)), initiated proceedings under Federal Rule of Evidence 104.[*] The process through which the court has endeavored to resolve the pending motions, a process the court believes to be unique in federal practice to date, is described below.

II. FACTS AND PROCEDURAL BACKGROUND

The breast implant cases at issue here were either filed initially in this court or removed from state court. The cases were then transferred to the Judicial Panel for Multidistrict Litigation, where they have been managed expeditiously under the watchful eye of the transferee judge, Chief Judge Sam C. Pointer, Jr. In 1995 and 1996, Judge Pointer remanded a number of cases to Oregon for trial.

All breast implant cases remanded to Oregon federal district court have been assigned to this judge. After a series of status conferences involving all interested parties and counsel, I determined that, at least initially, similar cases should grouped for trial. [The judge organized the claimants into three groups.]

After initial trial dates were set, the court instructed counsel for Groups 1 and 2 to provide a list of all lay and expert witnesses to be called at trial, together with a narrative statement of each witness' proposed testimony.

---

[*] Fed. R. Evid. 104(a) provides in part: "Preliminary questions concerning ... the admissibility of evidence shall be determined by the court ...." — ED.

The court also instructed counsel to summarize each expert witness' opinion, to identify all the materials upon which each expert would rely for his or her opinions, and to submit transcripts of any testimony given by the witness in similar cases.

Once the witness materials were duly filed, in July 1996, defendants jointly filed a series of motions in limine to exclude plaintiffs' experts' testimony concerning causation. To address these motions, I scheduled an integrated hearing under Rule 104(a) on the admissibility of the scientific evidence. . . .

In view of the complicated scientific and medical issues involved and in an effort to effectively discharge my role as "gatekeeper" under *Daubert I*, I invoked my inherent authority as a federal district court judge to appoint independent advisors to the court.[8] Pursuant to that inherent authority, I began a search to find technical advisors with the necessary expertise in the fields of epidemiology, immunology/toxicology, rheumatology, and chemistry to assist in evaluating the reliability and relevance of the scientific evidence. Dr. Richard Jones, M.D., Ph.D., assisted the court by screening dozens of potential appointees and ultimately selecting four totally unbiased and uncommitted experts in the necessary fields, which the court approved and appointed. The technical advisors and their fields of expertise are: Merwyn R. Greenlick, Ph.D. (epidemiology); Robert F. Wilkens, M.D. (rheumatology); Mary Stenzel-Poore, Ph.D. (immunology/toxicology); and Ronald McClard, Ph.D. (polymer chemistry). . . .

I structured the Rule 104 hearing according to subject matter, with plaintiffs presenting their experts in a particular field, followed by defendants' witnesses in the same field. All participating parties stipulated to the experts' qualifications under Rule 702. Because in proceedings pursuant to Rule 104(a) the court is not bound by rules of evidence, except those that pertain to privileges I ruled that no evidentiary objections would be permitted.

At the hearing, which spanned four intense days (August 5-8, 1996), experts on both sides were questioned by counsel, the court, and the technical advisors. The parties then submitted videotaped summations, which the court and all technical advisors reviewed. The court also asked the parties to submit proposed questions to guide the technical advisors in evaluating the testimony and preparing their reports. After considering the parties' proposed questions, the court prepared and submitted the following questions to the advisors:

1. Is the expert's opinion supported by scientific reasoning and methodology that is generally accepted in the expert's particular

---

8. To keep the advisors independent of any ongoing proceedings, I appointed them under Fed. R. Evid. 104, not Fed. R. Evid. 706, which requires court-appointed experts, in effect, to act as additional witnesses subject to depositions and testifying at trial. Although certain plaintiffs (in Group 3) moved to invoke Rule 706 procedures, I denied those motions.

scientific community or otherwise qualified as stated in [*Daubert v. Merrell Dow Pharmaceuticals, Inc.*, 43 F.3d 1311 (9th Cir. 1995)]?

2. Is the expert's opinion based upon scientifically reliable data?

3. If epidemiological studies have not been done or are inconclusive, what other data, such as animal studies, biophysical data, clinical experience in the field, medical records, differential diagnosis, preliminary studies, general scientific knowledge, and medical literature can justify, to a reasonable medical probability, a conclusion concerning the cause of the syndrome or disease at issue?

4. Do the methodology and data support the expert's conclusions?

5. Does the scientific data relied upon by the expert apply to the syndrome or disease in issue in these cases? For instance, are epidemiological studies directed at other typical or classical diseases relevant to an atypical disease?

The court also submitted almost all of the parties' proposed questions to the technical advisors for their consideration . . . .

The technical advisors submitted their reports to the court in September 1996, and on September 13, 1996, the court gave counsel on both sides an opportunity to question them. Following this hearing, the court expressed preliminary concerns that plaintiffs' position could not be sustained and asked defense counsel to submit proposed findings of fact and conclusions of law. Plaintiffs then filed objections and proposed alternative findings, and the defendants filed a further response.

Having fully reviewed the entire record and the reports of the advisors, I am now prepared to rule on the pending Rule 104 hearing motions in limine. For the reasons explained below, the defendants' motions in limine to exclude plaintiffs' expert testimony concerning causation of any systemic disease or syndrome are granted.

I note, however, that while this court was in the midst of the Rule 104 proceedings, Judge Pointer appointed a national panel of experts pursuant to Fed. R. Evid. 706 to assist in a similar evaluation of the scientific evidence in the MDL. . . . [I]t will probably be some time before the national panel completes its important work.

In view of the ongoing national proceedings and the potential for further scientific developments during their pendency, the court will defer the effective date of this opinion until the findings of the national Rule 706 panel are available. Depending on the court's evaluation of those findings, plaintiffs in these cases may seek reconsideration, if appropriate, of this decision. Plaintiffs' motion to add the national Rule 706 panel members to the witness lists in Groups 2 and 3 is also deferred pending completion of the panel's work.

[The court then discussed in detail the reasons to exclude the testimony of the plaintiffs' experts who tried to establish a causal connection between silicone-gel breast implants and certain systemic illnesses.]

Notes

1. *Hall* mentions the national panel of experts that Judge Pointer assembled in the related MDL proceedings. Judge Pointer's approach was slightly different. He first constituted a panel of experts to help him choose four neutral, leading experts in the fields of epidemiology, toxicology, immunology, and rheumatology. Once those four experts were identified, he then designated them as court-appointed experts under Fed. R. Evid. 706. His charge to this "Science Panel" was "to review, critique, and evaluate existing scientific literature, research, and publications — addressing such matters as the meaning, utility, significance, and limitations of such studies — on topics as, from time to time, may be identified by the Court as relevant in breast-implant litigation, particularly on issues of 'general causation.'" *See* Order No. 31, In re: Silicone Gel Breast Implant Prods. Liab. Litig. (MDL 926), No. CV 92-P-10000-S (N.D. Ala. May 30, 1996). They were then to prepare written findings, and to be subject to examination and cross-examination during the MDL process. Their testimony was to be recorded, so that it could be used in multidistricted cases after remand or in state-court litigation.

The Science Panel conducted hearings and, in 1999, concluded that it could find no clear evidence associating the plaintiffs' injuries with the breast implants. *See* Summary of Report of National Science Panel, available at http://www.fjc.gov/BREIMLIT/SCIENCE/summary.htm.

2. The approach of *Hall* (to use a panel of experts to rule on the admissibility of the parties' expert opinions) is different from the approach of the *Silicone Gel* MDL proceedings (to use a panel of experts to generate an opinion that stood along side of the parties' expert opinions, but that was arguably more trustworthy because of its neutrality). The *Silicone Gel* approach does little directly to narrow the issues during pretrial, although it probably creates significant settlement pressures on the party whose preferred opinions the panel treats unfavorably. The *Hall* approach narrows issues more directly, at least if the panel's conclusions convince the judge to strike certain opinions, as a result of which parties then dismiss or withdraw claims or defenses that hinge on those opinions. Of course, if the panel's conclusions validate the legitimacy of the opinions on both sides, then the approach does nothing to narrow the issues.

3. The idea of using panels of experts is discussed more in the literature than it is employed in practice. *See, e.g.,* In re Dow Corning Corp., 211 B.R. 545, 590-91 (Bankr. E.D. Mich. 1997) (declining to appoint a panel of experts to assist in the estimation process of the *Silicone Gel* bankruptcy case, in part because the Bankruptcy Rules gave bankruptcy judges no authority to appoint special masters). The *Manual for Complex Litigation* discusses both the benefits (including "reducing adversariness and potentially clarifying and narrowing issues") and the costs (including expense, delay, undue influence, and lack of neutrality) in using experts or panels of experts. MANUAL FOR COMPLEX LITIGATION, FOURTH § 11.51 (2004).

4. The *Manual* also points out the need to be clear about the nature of the appointment — whether the experts are appointed as experts under Fed. R. Evid. 706, as technical advisors within the court's inherent power, or pursuant to some other authority. The authority for the appointment and the terms of engagement can determine important matters such as whether the experts are able to testify and be deposed and whether they can have ex parte communications with the judge. *Id.*; *see supra* p. 766, Note 6 (discussing the use of and authority for court-appointed experts and technical advisors during pretrial); *infra* p. 1111 (discussing use of and authority for court-appointed experts during trial). Note that, although Judge Jones relied on Fed. R. Evid. 104 in appointing a panel of experts, the Rule says nothing about a judge's power to make such appointments.

5. Did Judge Jones step too far outside of the judge's role in an adversarial system by appointing a panel of experts? A judge's traditional role is to determine the admissibility of evidence; indeed, the Supreme Court's *Daubert* decision required him to exclude expert testimony that lacked sufficient reliability. Without a background in a particular scientific or medical field, how can a judge able to fulfill these responsibilities without expert assistance? Is Judge Pointer's use of a national science panel a greater departure from the adversarial ideal?

e. Adjudicating Disputed Issues

Until now, we have seen a number of case-management techniques that can narrow or eliminate claims, defenses, and issues in specific situations. Some of these techniques work directly; some are more indirect. Now we turn to the most significant and direct issue-narrowing power that a judge could possess: the power to adjudicate, and finally dispose of, claims, defenses, or issues during the pretrial process. Such a power blurs the line between pretrial and trial, and threatens the jury's role as factfinder if the claim, defense, or issue necessarily involves factual disputes that are triable to a jury. On the other hand, sometimes adjudicating a particular issue cuts the Gordian knot and sets up the resolution of the remainder of the case. Adjudicating claims, defenses, or issues during pretrial also moves our procedural system closer to the civil law's continuous-trial method, and away from the culminating common-law trial. So should the judge possess a power to adjudicate claims or defenses during the pretrial process? Relatedly but distinctly, should a judge have the power to determine not only claims and defenses, but also non-dispositive factual issues whose resolution will significantly narrow the remaining discovery and trial?

The existing pretrial adjudicatory mechanisms are few. There is the Rule 12(b)(6) motion to dismiss on the basis of the pleadings and the Rule 12(c) motion for judgment on the pleadings, but, as we have seen, both motions require the court to accept well-pleaded factual allegations as true. Other than dismissals as a sanction for violating discovery or case-management obligations (*see* Fed. R. Civ. P. 16(f), 37(b)(2)(A)(v)), the only other option is the Rule 56 motion for summary judgment.

The importance of Rule 56 in modern litigation practice — both in ordinary cases and in routine ones — cannot be overstated. A judge can grant a motion for summary judgment when "no genuine issue as to any material fact and that the movant is entitled to judgment as a matter of law." Fed. R. Civ. P. 56(c)(2).* In jury-tried cases, the Supreme Court has equated this standard with the standard under which a judge should grant judgment as a matter of law during or after trial: whether "a reasonable jury would not have a legally sufficient evidentiary basis to find for the party on that issue" and a claim or defense could be maintained "only with a favorable finding on that issue." Fed. R. Civ. P. 50(a)(1); Anderson v. Liberty Lobby, Inc., 477 U.S. 242, 248-51 (1986).

Summary judgment has certain constraints that make it less than ideal as an issue-narrowing device in complex litigation. First, and necessarily, it cannot short-circuit the trial of claims that involve factual issues in serious dispute. Second, in *Celotex Corp. v. Catrett*, 477 U.S. 317, 322 (1986), the Court held that summary judgment was proper only after the non-moving party has had "adequate time for discovery" — a restriction that limits summary judgment's utility as an early issue-narrowing device. Third, summary judgment requires that a moving party be entitled to *judgment*; in other words, it cannot generally be used to determine factual issues that do not dispose of a legal theory on which judgment can be granted. *Cf.* Fed. R. Civ. P. 56(d) (allowing summary judgment on the issue of liability, even if a trial on damages is required; also allowing a judge to establish "material facts . . . not genuinely at issue" in the event that the motion for summary judgment is denied).† Fourth, read literally, Rule 56 allows only the parties to move for summary judgment; it does not give a judge a sua sponte power to order summary judgment (although, as we will see *infra* p. 859, this has not proven a significant obstacle in practice).

Finally, some of the Court's earlier summary-judgment decisions were read to make the grant of summary judgment particularly difficult in complex cases. The most cited decision for this proposition was *Poller v. Columbia Broadcasting System, Inc.*, 368 U.S. 464 (1962), a 5-4 decision in an antitrust action involving allegedly monopolistic behavior in a local broadcast market. In overturning a summary judgment entered for the defendant, the Court observed:

> We believe that summary procedures should be used sparingly in complex antitrust litigation where motive and intent play leading roles, the proof is largely in the hands of the alleged conspirators, and hostile witnesses thicken the plot. It is only when the witnesses are present and subject to cross-examination that their credibility and the weight to be given their testimony can be appraised. Trial by affidavit is no

---

*   At the time of this writing, a proposal to move this language into a re-written Rule 56(a) is pending before the Supreme Court. — ED.

†   At the time of this writing, a proposal to change the quoted language to "material facts . . . not genuinely in dispute" and then to move the quoted language into a re-written Rule 56(g) is pending before the Supreme Court. — ED.

substitute for trial by jury which so long has been the hallmark of "even handed justice." [*Id.* at 473.]

Justice Harlan's dissent disputed the majority's view, arguing that:

. . . [T]he Rule does not indicate that it is to be used any more "sparingly" in antitrust litigation than in other kinds of litigation, or that its employment in antitrust cases is subject to more stringent criteria than in others. On the contrary, without reflecting in any way upon the good faith of this particular lawsuit, having regard for the special temptations that the statutory private antitrust remedy affords for the institution of vexatious litigation, and the inordinate amount of time that such cases sometimes demand of the trial courts, there is good reason for giving the summary judgment rule its full legitimate sweep in this field. [*Id.* at 478.]

The following case is often read as refuting *Poller* and paving the way for the more widespread use of summary judgment in complex litigation.

MATSUSHITA ELECTRIC INDUSTRIAL CO. V. ZENITH RADIO CORP.

475 U.S. 574 (1986)

■ JUSTICE POWELL delivered the opinion of the Court.

This case requires that we again consider the standard district courts must apply when deciding whether to grant summary judgment in an antitrust conspiracy case.

I

. . .

A

Petitioners, defendants below, are 21 corporations that manufacture or sell "consumer electronic products" (CEPs) — for the most part, television sets. Petitioners include both Japanese manufacturers of CEPs and American firms, controlled by Japanese parents, that sell the Japanese-manufactured products. Respondents, plaintiffs below, are Zenith Radio Corporation (Zenith) and National Union Electric Corporation (NUE). Zenith is an American firm that manufactures and sells television sets. NUE is the corporate successor to Emerson Radio Company, an American firm that manufactured and sold television sets until 1970, when it withdrew from the market after sustaining substantial losses. Zenith and NUE began this lawsuit in 1974, claiming that petitioners had illegally conspired to drive American firms from the American CEP market. According to respondents, the gist of this conspiracy was a "'scheme to raise, fix and maintain artificially *high* prices for television receivers sold by [petitioners] in Japan and, at the same time, to fix and maintain *low* prices for television receivers exported to and sold in the United States.'" These "low prices" were allegedly at levels that produced substantial losses for petitioners. The conspiracy allegedly began as early as 1953, and according to respondents was in full operation by sometime in the late 1960's. Respondents claimed that various portions of this scheme violated §§ 1 and 2 of the Sherman Act, § 2(a) of the Robinson-Patman Act, § 73 of the Wilson Tariff Act, and the Antidumping Act of 1916.

After several years of detailed discovery, petitioners filed motions for summary judgment on all claims against them. The District Court directed the parties to file, with preclusive effect, "Final Pretrial Statements" listing all the documentary evidence that would be offered if the case proceeded to trial. . . .

The District Court . . . found that the admissible evidence did not raise a genuine issue of material fact as to the existence of the alleged conspiracy. At bottom, the court found, respondents' claims rested on the inferences that could be drawn from petitioners' parallel conduct in the Japanese and American markets, and from the effects of that conduct on petitioners' American competitors. After reviewing the evidence both by category and *in toto*, the court found that any inference of conspiracy was unreasonable, because (i) some portions of the evidence suggested that petitioners conspired in ways that did not injure respondents, and (ii) the evidence that bore directly on the alleged price-cutting conspiracy did not rebut the more plausible inference that petitioners were cutting prices to compete in the American market and not to monopolize it. Summary judgment therefore was granted . . . .

B

The Court of Appeals for the Third Circuit reversed. . . .

. . . The court acknowledged that "there are legal limitations upon the inferences which may be drawn from circumstantial evidence," but it found that "the legal problem . . . is different" when "there is direct evidence of concert of action." . . . [T]he Court of Appeals concluded that a reasonable factfinder could find a conspiracy to depress prices in the American market in order to drive out American competitors, which conspiracy was funded by excess profits obtained in the Japanese market. . . .

II

We begin by emphasizing what respondents' claim is not. Respondents cannot recover antitrust damages based solely on an alleged cartelization of the Japanese market, because American antitrust laws do not regulate the competitive conditions of other nations' economies. Nor can respondents recover damages for any conspiracy by petitioners to charge higher than competitive prices in the American market. Such conduct would indeed violate the Sherman Act, but it could not injure respondents:

as petitioners' competitors, respondents stand to gain from any conspiracy to raise the market price in CEPs. Finally, for the same reason, respondents cannot recover for a conspiracy to impose nonprice restraints that have the effect of either raising market price or limiting output. . . . The Court of Appeals therefore erred to the extent that it found evidence of these alleged conspiracies to be "direct evidence" of a conspiracy that injured respondents.

Respondents nevertheless argue that these supposed conspiracies, if not themselves grounds for recovery of antitrust damages, are circumstantial evidence of another conspiracy that is cognizable: a conspiracy to monopolize the American market by means of pricing below the market level. The thrust of respondents' argument is that petitioners used their monopoly profits from the Japanese market to fund a concerted campaign to price predatorily and thereby drive respondents and other American manufacturers of CEPs out of business. Once successful, according to respondents, petitioners would cartelize the American CEP market, restricting output and raising prices above the level that fair competition would produce. The resulting monopoly profits, respondents contend, would more than compensate petitioners for the losses they incurred through years of pricing below market level. . . .

The issue in this case thus becomes whether respondents adduced sufficient evidence in support of their theory to survive summary judgment. We therefore examine the principles that govern the summary judgment determination.

III

To survive petitioners' motion for summary judgment, respondents must establish that there is a genuine issue of material fact as to whether petitioners entered into an illegal conspiracy that caused respondents to suffer a cognizable injury. This showing has two components. First, respondents must show more than a conspiracy in violation of the antitrust laws; they must show an injury to them resulting from the illegal conduct. Respondents charge petitioners with a whole host of conspiracies in restraint of trade. Except for the alleged conspiracy to monopolize the American market through predatory pricing, these alleged conspiracies could not have caused respondents to suffer an "antitrust injury," because they actually tended to benefit respondents. Therefore, unless, in context, evidence of these "other" conspiracies raises a genuine issue concerning the existence of a predatory pricing conspiracy, that evidence cannot defeat petitioners' summary judgment motion.

Second, the issue of fact must be "genuine." Fed. R. Civ. P. 56(c), (e). When the moving party has carried its burden under Rule 56(c), its opponent must do more than simply show that there is some metaphysical doubt as to the material facts. . . . Where the record taken as a whole could not lead a rational trier of fact to find for the non-moving party, there is no "genuine issue for trial." [Fed. R. Civ. P. 56(e)(2).]

It follows from these settled principles that if the factual context renders respondents' claim implausible — if the claim is one that simply makes no economic sense — respondents must come forward with more persuasive evidence to support their claim than would otherwise be necessary. . . .

Respondents correctly note that "[o]n summary judgment the inferences to be drawn from the underlying facts . . . must be viewed in the light most favorable to the party opposing the motion." . . . But antitrust law limits the range of permissible inferences from ambiguous evidence in a § 1 case. . . . To survive a motion for summary judgment . . ., a plaintiff seeking damages for a violation of § 1 must present evidence "that tends to exclude the possibility" that the alleged conspirators acted independently. Respondents in this case, in other words, must show that the inference of conspiracy is reasonable in light of the competing inferences of independent action or collusive action that could not have harmed respondents.

Petitioners argue that these principles apply fully to this case. According to petitioners, the alleged conspiracy is one that is economically irrational and practically infeasible. Consequently, petitioners contend, they had no motive to engage in the alleged predatory pricing conspiracy; indeed, they had a strong motive not to conspire in the manner respondents allege. Petitioners argue that, in light of the absence of any apparent motive and the ambiguous nature of the evidence of conspiracy, no trier of fact reasonably could find that the conspiracy with which petitioners are charged actually existed. This argument requires us to consider the nature of the alleged conspiracy and the practical obstacles to its implementation.

IV

A

A predatory pricing conspiracy is by nature speculative. Any agreement to price below the competitive level requires the conspirators to forgo profits that free competition would offer them. The forgone profits may be considered an investment in the future. For the investment to be rational, the conspirators must have a reasonable expectation of recovering, in the form of later monopoly profits, more than the losses suffered. . . . Moreover, it is not enough simply to achieve monopoly power, as monopoly pricing may breed quick entry by new competitors eager to share in the excess profits. The success of any predatory scheme depends on *maintaining* monopoly power for long enough both to recoup the predator's losses and to harvest some additional gain. . . . For this reason, there is a consensus among commentators that predatory pricing schemes are rarely tried, and even more rarely successful. . . .

Two decades after their conspiracy is alleged to have commenced, petitioners appear to be far from achieving this goal: the two largest shares of the retail market in television sets are held by RCA and respondent Zenith, not by any of petitioners. . . .

The alleged conspiracy's failure to achieve its ends in the two decades of its asserted operation is strong evidence that the conspiracy does not in fact exist. . . .

B

[C]ourts should not permit factfinders to infer conspiracies when such inferences are implausible, because the effect of such practices is often to deter procompetitive effect. . . . [M]istaken inferences in cases such as this one are especially costly, because they chill the very conduct the antitrust laws are designed to protect. . . .

V

. . . The Court of Appeals did not take account of the absence of a plausible motive to enter into the alleged predatory pricing conspiracy. It focused instead on whether there was "direct evidence of concert of action." The Court of Appeals erred in two respects: (i) the "direct evidence" on which the court relied had little, if any, relevance to the alleged predatory pricing conspiracy; and (ii) the court failed to consider the absence of a plausible motive to engage in predatory pricing.

The "direct evidence" on which the court relied was evidence of *other* combinations, not of a predatory pricing conspiracy. Evidence that petitioners conspired to raise prices in Japan provides little, if any, support for respondents' claims: a conspiracy to increase profits in one market does not tend to show a conspiracy to sustain losses in another. Evidence that petitioners agreed to fix *minimum* prices . . . for the American market actually works in petitioners' favor, because it suggests that petitioners were seeking to place a floor under prices rather than to lower them. . . .

That being the case, the absence of any plausible motive to engage in the conduct charged is highly relevant to whether a "genuine issue for trial" exists within the meaning of Rule 56(e). Lack of motive bears on the range of permissible conclusions that might be drawn from ambiguous evidence: if petitioners had no rational economic motive to conspire, and if their conduct is consistent with other, equally plausible explanations, the conduct does not give rise to an inference of conspiracy. . . . This conduct suggests either that petitioners behaved competitively, or that petitioners conspired to *raise* prices. Neither possibility is consistent with an agreement among 21 companies to price below-market levels. Moreover, the predatory pricing scheme that this conduct is said to prove is one that makes no practical sense: it calls for petitioners to destroy companies larger and better established than themselves, a goal that remains far distant more than two decades after the conspiracy's birth. Even had they succeeded in obtaining their monopoly, there is nothing in the record to suggest that they could recover the losses they would need to sustain along the way. In sum, in light of the absence of any rational motive to conspire, neither petitioners' pricing practices, nor their conduct in the Japanese market, nor their agreements respecting prices and distribution in the American market, suffice to create a "genuine issue for trial." Fed. R. Civ. P. 56(e)

On remand, the Court of Appeals is free to consider whether there is other evidence that is sufficiently unambiguous to permit a trier of fact to find that petitioners conspired to price predatorily for two decades despite the absence of any apparent motive to do so. . . . In the absence of such evidence, there is no "genuine issue for trial" under Rule 56(e), and petitioners are entitled to have summary judgment reinstated. . . .

■ JUSTICE WHITE, with whom JUSTICE BRENNAN, JUSTICE BLACKMUN, and JUSTICE STEVENS join, dissenting. . . .

The Court's initial discussion of summary judgment standards appears consistent with settled doctrine. . . . But other language in the Court's opinion suggests a departure from traditional summary judgment doctrine. . . . Such language suggests that a judge hearing a defendant's motion for summary judgment in an antitrust case should go beyond the traditional summary judgment inquiry and decide for himself whether the weight of the evidence favors the plaintiff. . . .

If the Court intends to give every judge hearing a motion for summary judgment in an antitrust case the job of determining if the evidence makes the inference of conspiracy more probable than not, it is overturning settled law. If the Court does not intend such a pronouncement, it should refrain from using unnecessarily broad and confusing language.

Notes

1. *Matsushita* was one of three cases — usually referred to as the "summary-judgment trilogy" — decided in the Court's 1985 term. The other two are *Anderson v. Liberty Lobby, Inc.*, 477 U.S. 242 (1986), and *Celotex Corp. v. Catrett*, 477 U.S. 317 (1986). Taken together, they are often read as the Court's endorsement of a broader use of summary judgment. As *Celotex* put it, "Summary judgment procedure is properly regarded not as a disfavored procedural shortcut, but rather as an integral part of the Federal Rules as a whole . . . ." 477 U.S. at 327.

2. In your Civil Procedure course, you undoubtedly examined the debate surrounding summary judgment. In its favor, as you can now appreciate, the Federal Rules of Civil Procedure lack significant issue-narrowing devices; the major available device is the motion for summary judgment. As a case-management tool, therefore, summary judgment is critical. On the other hand, summary judgment has attracted significant critics among those who support a strong right to jury trial and those who fear an apparent move toward civil-law — and away from common-law — procedure (even though the summary-judgment device was first developed in English common-law courts during the nineteenth century). The intuitively evident proposition that summary judgment also changes the economic incentive to litigate cases in a way that generally favors defendants — a fact that could, depending on your point of view, be an

argument for or against its use — has also been demonstrated both theoretically and empirically. *See* Samuel Issacharoff & George Loewenstein, *Second Thoughts About Summary Judgment*, 100 YALE L.J. 73 (1990) (using economic analysis to demonstrate the defense-favoring nature of summary judgment); Joe S. Cecil et al., *A Quarter-Century of Summary Judgment Practice in Six Federal District Courts*, 4 J. EMPIRICAL LEGAL STUD. 86 (2007) (noting that defendants are two-and-a-half times more likely to file summary-judgment motions); William P. McLauchlan, *An Empirical Study of the Federal Summary Judgment Rule*, 6 J. LEG. STUD. 427 (1977) (in an older study, noting that plaintiffs sought summary judgment in 21.7% of cases and defendants in 58.1%) .

Among those who favor summary judgment, there are also criticisms that the device does not go far enough. The summary-judgment motion has important limitations. First, its factual threshold — "no genuine issue as to any material fact" — is high. Second, its legal threshold — that the motion must lead to a judgment on a legal theory or claim — weakens it as an issue-narrowing device. Third, its practical threshold that courts cannot grant summary judgment until the parties have had an adequate time for discovery also limits its utility as an issue-narrowing device. Of the three criticisms, the first seems insurmountable in jury-tried cases due to the operation of the Seventh Amendment, although a more relaxed standard is possible in bench-tried cases. The second criticism has generated proposals to convert Rule 56 into an issue-adjudicating (as opposed to a claim-or-theory-eliminating) device. *See* Paul D. Carrington, *Making Rules to Dispose of Manifestly Unfounded Assertions: An Exorcism of the Bogy of Non-Trans-Substantive Rules of Civil Procedure*, 137 U. PA. L. REV. 2067 (1989). Despite proposals along this line and a few cases that seem to have endorsed such an approach, *see* Archer-Daniels-Midland Co. v. Phoenix Assurance Co. of N.Y., 936 F. Supp. 534, 536-37 (S.D. Ill. 1996), Rule 56 has not changed. *See* EDWARD J. BRUNET ET AL., SUMMARY JUDGMENT § 1.05 & n.109 (1994) (endorsing the use of summary judgment to resolve issues and collecting cases). The third criticism is tied to the question of how much issue narrowing is appropriate, or can fairly be expected, before fact development commences (the "chicken and egg" problem to which we have occasionally referred).

3.   Whatever the merits of these criticisms and calls for improvement, there is no question that summary judgment is an integral dimension of American pretrial practice. The issue here is whether the complexity of a case should or does affect the scope of summary judgment — whether it should (or is) used more or less in complex cases than in routine ones. If *Matsushita* were a simpler case — perhaps a car accident at the corner in which both parties died and there were no witnesses about who had the green light — do you think that the Court would have upheld a grant of summary judgment based on the assumption that the defendant was a rational economic actor, and rational economic actors always take proper care when approaching an intersection? If the Court would have regarded such a case as jury-triable, why is *Matsushita* different? Although the Court does not mention this fact in its decision, *Matsushita* was one of the

largest, most complex antitrust cases in history. In Chapter Nine, we examine a prior decision in the case, *In re Japanese Electronics Products Antitrust Litigation*, 631 F.2d 1069 (3d Cir. 1980) (*infra* p. 999), which gives a better sense of the case's complexity. In that opinion, the Third Circuit thought that the case was so complex that it would be a violation of the Due Process Clause to allow a jury to hear the case, and it struck the plaintiffs' jury-trial demand. Should — or did — this fact color *Matsushita*? Conversely, although it was an antitrust case, was *Poller* complex?

More generally, concerns for respecting the parties' jury-trial rights, which the Seventh Amendment guarantees, hang over the proper scope of the "no genuine issue" standard. In bench trials, courts may enjoy a broader power to grant summary judgment. *See* Johnson v. Diversicare Alton Oaks, LLC, 597 F.3d 673 (5th Cir. 2010) ("When deciding a motion for summary judgment prior to a bench trial, the district court 'has the limited discretion to decide that the same evidence, presented to him or her as a trier of fact in a plenary trial, could not possibly lead to a different result.'"). Assuming that *Japanese Electronics* is correct, and that courts can suspend the right of jury trial in complex cases, should the greater power to grant summary judgment in bench trials affect the decision to suspend the right to jury trial?

4. In thinking about these questions, consider *Eastman Kodak Co. v. Image Technical Services, Inc.*, 504 U.S. 451, 454 (1992), which the Court described as "yet another case that concerns the standard for summary judgment in an antitrust controversy." *Eastman Kodak* emphasized that antitrust determinations are not to be made on the basis of presumptions and legal fictions, but rather on the realities of market power. Judge Schwarzer, the district judge in *Eastman Kodak*, had granted summary judgment after limited discovery; the defendant had filed the motion prior to discovery, after which Judge Schwarzer had "permitted respondents to file one set of interrogatories and one set of requests for production of documents and to take six depositions." *Id.* at 459. Although its decision to reverse the entry of summary judgment did not hinge on the fact, the Court was troubled by the thin factual record. *See* William W Schwarzer & Alan Hirsch, *Summary Judgment After* Eastman Kodak, 45 HASTINGS L.J. 1, 14 (1993). *Eastman Kodak* can be read at least two different ways — either broadly as a cutback on *Matsushita* and a return to *Poller*, or narrowly as an unwillingness "to accept [defendant's] theory as a matter of law on a record based on only truncated discovery." *Id.* at 14.

You might also consider the following statement from the Court in an older decision, *Kennedy v. Silas Mason Co.*, 334 U.S. 249, 256-57 (1948): "summary procedures, however salutary where issues are clear-cut and simple, present a treacherous record for deciding issues of far-flung import, on which this Court should draw inferences with caution from complicated courses of legislation, contracting, and practice." *Silas* involved an issue of the method for paying contractors' employees under cost-plus contracts — an issue of considerable significance to the federal budget during World War II.

5.   You can find opinions on all sides about whether a case's complexity should affect the use of summary judgment. Some courts have argued that complexity makes some cases less susceptible to summary judgment. *See* Int'l Healthcare Mgmt. v. Haw. Coalition for Health, 332 F.3d 600, 604 (9th Cir. 2003) ("Summary judgment is only disfavored in complex antitrust litigation where motive and intent are important, proof is largely in the hands of the alleged conspirators, and relevant information is controlled by hostile witnesses.") (internal quotation marks omitted). Some courts have indicated that summary judgment should be granted more liberally in complex cases than in routine ones. *See* Collins v. Associated Pathologists, Ltd., 844 F.2d 473, 475 (7th Cir. 1988) ("Contrary to the emphasis of some prior precedent, the use of summary judgment is not only permitted by *Matsushita* but encouraged . . . in antitrust cases."). The typical interpretation of *Matsushita*, however, is represented by *Thompson Everett, Inc. v. Nat'l Cable Adver., L.P.,* 57 F.3d 1317, 1322 (4th Cir. 1995):

> While Rule 56 is to be applied to antitrust cases no differently from how it is applied to other cases, that is not to say that the summary judgment device is not an appropriate and useful tool for resolving antitrust cases. On the contrary, because of the unusual entanglement of legal and factual issues frequently presented in antitrust cases, the task of sorting them out may be particularly well-suited for Rule 56 utilization. The summary judgment practice does not become disfavored simply because a case is complex.

Is this just double-talk that tacitly admits the favored status of summary judgment? *Cf.* B.F. Goodrich v. Betkoski, 99 F.3d 505, 521 (2d Cir. 1996) (in CERCLA cases, summary judgment is a "powerful legal tool" that can "avoid lengthy and perhaps needless litigation," but the "showing required to survive summary judgment also remains the same"); *but see* MANUAL FOR COMPLEX LITIGATION, FOURTH § 11.34 (2004) (although "the standard for deciding a summary judgment motion is the same in all cases," the need for discovery on complicated issues may make complex cases "not as susceptible to resolution as issues in more familiar settings"). *See also* In re ATM Fee Antitrust Litig., 554 F. Supp. 2d 1003, 1010 (N.D. Cal. 2008) (noting that "any presumption against the granting of summary judgment in complex antitrust cases has now disappeared").

6.   Rule 56 is worded to permit the parties to bring a motion for summary judgment; it does not indicate that a court can issue summary judgment sua sponte. Such a power seems a useful case-management tool, but can judges employ it? *Celotex* presumed that a sua sponte power exists, but it did not address the question in detail. *See* 477 U.S. at 326 ("[D]istrict courts are widely acknowledged to possess the power to enter summary judgments sua sponte, so long as the losing party was on notice that she had to come forward with all of her evidence."). If the power exists, under what authority? Rule 56? Rule 16(c)(2)(A)? Inherent power? Is the same standard ("no genuine issue as to any material fact") to be used in handling factual disputes? Are there other limitations on the exercise of this power? Consider the following case.

PORTSMOUTH SQUARE, INC. V. SHAREHOLDERS PROTECTIVE COMMITTEE

770 F.2d 866 (9th Cir. 1985)

■ CANBY, Circuit Judge.

Portsmouth Square, Inc. appeals from an adverse judgment on its claim against the Shareholders Protective Committee — a group of Portsmouth Square minority shareholders — and the individual members of the Committee. Portsmouth Square seeks injunctive and declaratory relief under section 13(d) of the Securities and Exchange Act of 1934, 15 U.S.C. § 78m(d). After several years of litigation, the district court dismissed Portsmouth Square's suit sua sponte at the final pretrial conference. Portsmouth Square now challenges both the procedure by which the court entered judgment and the conclusion of law on which the judgment rests. We affirm the district court in all respects. . . .

We begin by addressing Portsmouth Square's attack on the procedure by which the district court dismissed its claim. At the final pretrial conference, Judge Schwarzer raised sua sponte the question whether the plaintiff had stated a section 13(d) claim. He did not specifically notify the parties in advance that he intended to raise the issue. At the conference, the court pressed counsel for Portsmouth Square to show how the facts set forth in the plaintiff's proposed Findings of Fact stated a section 13(d) claim. After a lengthy dialogue with plaintiff's counsel, the court denied a motion for a continuance and indicated that it would enter judgment for the defendant. In its Amended Order and Judgment, the court labelled its action a "judgment on the pleadings treated as a Motion for Summary Judgment under Rules 12(c) and 56 of the Federal Rules of Civil Procedure." For purposes of the judgment, the court accepted the plaintiff's proposed Findings of Fact as true. It concluded that neither those facts nor the evidence set forth in the pretrial conference materials established a cause of action under section 13(d).[1]

Portsmouth Square argues that the district court had no power to enter a summary judgment sua sponte. It also claims that the court violated Rule 56(c), which requires at least 10 days notice of a hearing on a summary judgment motion, and Local Rule 220-2 of the Northern District of California, which requires 28 days notice.[*] Furthermore, Portsmouth

---

1. The pretrial conference materials, submitted by both parties pursuant to a pretrial order, included trial memoranda stating the facts expected to be proved at trial and the law applicable to those facts. The parties also submitted statements summarizing the expected testimony of all witnesses; copies of all exhibits that they planned to introduce; and citations to relevant portions of interrogatories and deposition testimony.

[*] The 2009 amendments to Rule 56 eliminated the ten-day requirement. Rule 56(c)(1)(B) now provides the opposing party twenty-one days to file a response. As of this writing, a pending amendment to Rule 56, due to become effective later in 2010, will delete any timing requirement, presumably leaving the issue up to the district courts' local rules. — ED.

Square tells us, the court denied it an opportunity to respond with affidavits and other evidence in support of its claim. Portsmouth Square implies that the district court and opposing counsel have obscured the absence of due process by characterizing the result as a Rule 12(c) judgment on the pleadings treated as a summary judgment. We reject all of these arguments. We are satisfied that the district court proceedings met the requirements of the Federal Rules and the demands of due process.

Under certain limited circumstances a district court may issue summary judgment on its own motion. For example, sua sponte summary judgment is appropriate where one party moves for summary judgment and, after the hearing, it appears from all the evidence presented that there is no genuine issue of material fact and the *non-moving* party is entitled to judgment as a matter of law. . . . We have also allowed summary judgment where a district court, on its own initiative, converted a Rule 12 motion to dismiss into a summary judgment motion by considering pertinent documents that the parties had not presented . . . .

We believe that the district court has similar limited authority to grant summary judgment sua sponte in the context of a final pretrial conference. One purpose of the Rule 16 pretrial conference procedure is to promote efficiency and conserve judicial resources by identifying litigable issues prior to trial. If the pretrial conference discloses that no material facts are in dispute and that the undisputed facts entitle one of the parties to judgment as a matter of law, a summary disposition of the case conserves scarce judicial resources. The court need not await a formal motion, or proceed to trial, under those circumstances.

Where the district court grants summary judgment in the absence of a formal motion, we review the record closely to ensure that the party against whom judgment was entered had a full and fair opportunity to develop and present facts and legal arguments in support of its position. A litigant is entitled to reasonable notice that the sufficiency of his or her claim will be in issue. Reasonable notice implies adequate time to develop the facts on which the litigant will depend to oppose summary judgment. Having reviewed this record, we conclude that Portsmouth Square was afforded a full and fair opportunity to make its case.

Although it would have been preferable for the district court specifically to notify the parties that it intended to consider granting a summary judgment at the pretrial conference, Portsmouth Square was adequately notified that it might have to defend the sufficiency of its claim. The merits of the parties' claims and defenses are a legitimate subject of discussion at a pretrial conference. Throughout the course of this litigation the parties have disputed whether Portsmouth Square states a section 13(d) cause of action, and counsel should not have been surprised that the issue arose at the conference. Portsmouth Square also had a full opportunity to develop the facts in support of its case. Its discovery was complete at the time of the pretrial proceedings.

Moreover, Portsmouth Square had a full opportunity to present to the district court its section 13(d) theory and the facts supporting that theory.

The court made clear from the outset of the pretrial conference that it intended to explore the merits of the plaintiff's claim, and that it was specifically concerned about whether the corporation could establish a violation of section 13(d). In that connection the court considered all the evidence that Portsmouth Square planned to present at trial. It repeatedly pressed Portsmouth Square's counsel to show that a genuine issue of material fact remained for trial, or that the facts set forth in the proposed Findings stated a claim. The court reached its decision only when it had become clear that counsel could not make the necessary showing.

[The court then held that Portsmouth Square had not established a claim under section 13(d).]

The district court's judgment is affirmed.

Notes

1. *Portsmouth Square* was decided before *Celotex Corp. v. Catrett*, 477 U.S. 317 (1986), recognized the widespread practice of sua sponte grants of summary judgment. Since *Celotex*, courts have continued to claim this authority. Like *Portsmouth Square*, courts have placed clear limits on this authority, requiring that the parties be afforded the protections of party-initiated summary-judgment motions. As *Portsmouth Square* says, the first of these protections is adequate notice. *See also* Global Petromarine v. G.T. Sales & Mfg., Inc., 577 F.3d 839 (8th Cir. 2009) ("[A] determination of summary judgment sua sponte in favor of the prevailing party is appropriate so long as the losing party has notice and an opportunity to respond."); Massey v. Congress Life Ins. Co., 116 F.3d 1414 (11th Cir. 1997) (requiring adequate notice even when sua sponte summary judgment is entered against a party who moved for summary judgment in its favor).

The second of these protections is permitting an adequate time for discovery. As *Ramsey v. Coughlin*, 94 F.3d 71, 74 (2d Cir. 1996), statd:

> Where it appears clearly upon the record that all of the evidentiary materials that a party might submit in response to a motion for summary judgment are before the court, a sua sponte grant of summary judgment against that party may be appropriate if those materials show that no material dispute of fact exists and that the other party is entitled to judgment as a matter of law. Before granting summary judgment sua sponte, the district court must assure itself that following the procedures set out in Rule 56 would not alter the outcome. Discovery must either have been completed, or it must be clear that further discovery would be of no benefit. The record must, therefore, reflect the losing party's inability to enhance the evidence supporting its position and the winning party's entitlement to judgment.

See also Berkovitz v. Home Box Office, Inc., 89 F.3d 24 (1st Cir. 1996) (permitting Rule 16 dismissal of a claim lacking factual support only after ensuring both adequate opportunity for discovery and adequate opportunity to present evidence to the court). Obviously, this second protection makes sua sponte summary adjudication a less attractive case-management tool for the early resolution of disputed factual issues.

2.   Some courts have expressed a general reluctance to permit use of sua sponte summary adjudication. In *Goldstein v. Fidelity & Guaranty Insurance Underwriters*, 86 F.3d 749, 751 (7th Cir. 1996), the court noted:

> We do not want to encourage district courts to consider summary judgment sua sponte because the procedure warrants "special caution," and it's often inappropriate. It is also largely unnecessary, as a district court can always invite a nonmoving party to file a motion for summary judgment in its favor. But while we do not express resounding approval of sua sponte summary judgment, it is not always wrong for a district court to resolve certain cases in this fashion. It's just a bit risky.

3.   One of the few things that has divided the courts is the source of their sua sponte power. Some courts have located the power in Rule 56 (hence the imposition of Rule 56's notice requirements). Other courts have thought that the power emanates from Rule 16 — in particular from what is now Rule 16(c)(2)(A), which gives courts the case-management power to "formulat[e] and simplify[ ] the issues, and eliminat[e] frivolous claims or defenses." Rule 16(c)(2)(A) was first adopted in 1983, and was originally located in Rule 16(c)(1). According to the 1983 Advisory Committee Note:

> . . . [This rule] has been added in the hope of promoting efficiency and conserving judicial resources by identifying the real issues prior to trial, thereby saving time and expense for everyone. The notion is emphasized by expressly authorizing the elimination of frivolous claims or defenses at a pretrial conference. There is no reason to require that this await a formal motion for summary judgment. Nor is there any reason for the court to wait for the parties to initiate the process . . . .

The earliest case to suggest a sua sponte adjudicatory power in Rule 16, decided long before the adoption of the former Rule 16(c)(1), was *Holcomb v. Aetna Life Insurance Co.*, 255 F.2d 577 (10th Cir. 1958).

If Rule 16, rather than Rule 56, is the source of the sua sponte power, there is no necessary reason that a court is bound by the "no genuine issue" standard of Rule 56, by the specific time limits of Rule 56's notice requirements, or by Rule 56's "adequate time for discovery" limitation. But it would still be bound to respect constitutional concerns for jury trial and due process, so presumably there would be some limits on the sua sponte power; most significantly, because the "no genuine issue" standard equates with the "no reasonable jury" standard at trial, the Seventh Amendment seems to banish any notion that a court in a jury-tried case can sua sponte decide disputed factual issues when a "genuine issue" for trial remains. *Cf.* Fid. & Deposit Co. of Md. v. S. Utils., Inc., 726 F.2d 692, 693 (11th Cir. 1984) ("Rule 16 by its terms does not confer special powers to enter judgment not contained in Rule 56 or the other rules.").

Another important limitation on Rule 56 is the requirement that a motion be dispositive of a legal theory; summary judgment cannot resolve disputed issues unless that resolution results in judgment. *See supra* p.

855, Note 2. Moreover, constitutional limits likely limit the power of a court to adjudicate discrete issues in a jury-tried case. *Cf.* Gasoline Products Co. v. Champlin Refining Co., 283 U.S. 494 (1931) (holding that, "where the requirement of a jury trial has been satisfied by a verdict according to law upon one issue of fact, [the Seventh Amendment] does not compel a new trial of that issue even though another and separable issue must be tried again"). Basing a sua sponte power in Rule 16, rather than in Rule 56, could give a court the issue-adjudicating power that Rule 56 lacks and that would be a useful case-management tool in complex litigation. Despite much discussion about a court's power to grant sua sponte partial summary judgments, however, the cases have never focused on the adjudication of non-dispositive factual issues. *See* David L. Shapiro, *Federal Rule 16: A Look at the Theory and Practice of Rulemaking*, 137 U. PA. L. REV. 1969, 1989 (1989) (raising the question in passing).

4. The issue about the source of a sua sponte power may soon be moot. In an amendment to Rule 56 that is pending as of the time of this writing, a redrafted Rule 56(g) will give courts the power, "[a]fter notice and a reasonable time to respond," to "consider summary judgment on its own after identifying for the parties material facts that may not be genuinely in dispute." This power will presumably be subject to the "no genuine issue" standard, and to a "reasonable-notice" standard. Presumably as well, it will be subject to the "adequate time for discovery" standard. Whether this new language will be interpreted to give a court issue-adjudicating power when the determination of the issue does not entitle the moving party to judgment remains to be seen. In short, it appears that, from an issue-narrowing point of view, the sua sponte summary-judgment power will suffer from most of the deficiencies as the party-initiated device, and will fall somewhat short of the ideal early issue-narrowing device that a theory of case management desires. Would it have been better to retain more flexibility by keeping the sua sponte adjudicatory power in Rule 16?

5. One of the ways in which a court can determine a factual issue early in a case is to use the doctrine of issue preclusion, which bars a party from relitigating a factual issue that was litigated, decided, and essential to a prior judgment. In Chapter Two, we explored the idea of using preclusion doctrines to induce parties to join the first lawsuit. *See supra* p. 208. As we saw, the doctrine has important limitations — especially its inability to be invoked against nonparties to the prior case. Here we are considering using preclusion as a case-management tool to overcome pretrial complexity. Should these different uses lead to different interpretations of preclusion in the two contexts, or should the doctrine remain constant regardless of the use to which it is put? We know of no cases that suggest a differential interpretation for issue preclusion based on its proposed use.

6. Even if sua sponte summary adjudication is a weak vehicle for disposing of non-dispositive factual disputes before costly discovery, some courts use Rule 16 to determine a pure issue of law before discovery begins when the ruling will shape the pretrial proceedings. *See* United States v. Kramer, 953 F. Supp. 592 (D.N.J. 1997).

7. If our system moves toward a strong power of sua sponte issue adjudication to address the needs of complex litigation, how close have we drawn toward civil-law procedure? *Cf.* Wallace v. SMC Pneumatics, Inc., 103 F.3d 1394 (7th Cir. 1997) (Posner, J.) (noting that the trend toward increased use of summary judgment "must be resisted unless and until Rule 56 is modified (so far as the Seventh Amendment permits) to bring federal practice closer to the practice in the legal systems of Continental Europe"). Once again, complex litigation puts our procedural system between a rock and a hard place: either develop special rules for complex cases, thus creating two distinct systems of procedure for the routine and the complex, or move away from adversarial process in the routine cases in which it functions perfectly well. Do these choices make the option of handling of complex cases outside of the adjudicatory system more attractive?

f. Encouraging Settlement

Like most litigation, most complex cases settle. One way in which a judge can "narrow" the issues is to make their determination irrelevant — in other words, to foster a settlement between the parties that avoids the need to determine the merits of the case. Exploring and encouraging early settlement are often regarded as important case-management goals. *See* MANUAL FOR COMPLEX LITIGATION, FOURTH § 13.1-.24 (2004). Among the techniques that judges are encouraged to employ are some that we have already examined: early, firm trial dates; appointing counsel and either a special master or a magistrate judge specifically to handle the task of fostering settlement; consistently raising the prospect of settlement at the initial scheduling conference and at all later pretrial conferences; and bifurcating for early decision an issue or set of issues that are sticking points between the parties. *See id.* § 13.13. In addition, by law all federal courts must maintain a plan for alternative dispute resolution (ADR), *see* 28 U.S.C. §§ 651-58, so the court can employ one or more ADR mechanisms at its disposal or else create such a mechanism for a complex case. Among the mechanisms that have moved litigants away from adjudication and toward settlement or other resolutions of their disputes are court-sponsored arbitration and mediation, as well as devices such as summary jury trials. *See* FED. JUD. CTR., GUIDE TO JUDICIAL MANAGEMENT OF CASES IN ADR (2001).

Whether or not the judge's efforts to encourage settlement is effective is open to debate. As any lawyer will tell you, most judges are very good at "persuading" parties to do things "voluntarily" that the judge could not order them to do. A great deal of this persuasion is "an iron fist in a velvet glove"; as we have seen, judges have tremendous discretion to manage pretrial issues, and can make a recalcitrant party's life difficult. At the same time, it seems unlikely that a judge can force sophisticated parties to settle a case that they were otherwise unwilling to settle. At best, the judge might accelerate the process somewhat. The question is whether the reduction in pretrial complexity is worth the time and energy that the judge and the lawyers put into judicially-induced settlement or ADR processes.

The most extensive study to date shows that ADR provides no to very weak benefits in terms of reducing cost and delay. Overall ADR is a wash: It saves time and expenses in those cases in which it works, but adds time and expense in those cases in which it does not. *See* JAMES S. KAKALIK ET AL., AN EVALUATION OF JUDICIAL CASE MANAGEMENT UNDER THE CIVIL JUSTICE REFORM ACT 71-76 (1996); JAMES S. KAKALIK ET AL., AN EVALUATION OF MEDIATION AND EARLY NEUTRAL EVALUATION UNDER THE CIVIL JUSTICE REFORM ACT 52-55, 63-65 (1996). But this study did not look specifically at the costs and benefits of ADR in complex cases, in which the ratio of the benefits to costs of ADR might be somewhat greater. Even if there were savings in time or expense, some critics object that the push toward settlement weakens the rule of law and favors the party with the superior bargaining power. The classic article is Owen M. Fiss, *Against Settlement*, 93 YALE L.J. 1073 (1984); *see also* Rex R. Perschbacher & Debra Lyn Bassett, *The End of Law*, 84 B.U. L. REV. 1 (2004) (arguing that ADR weakens the clarity and force of legal rules). These concerns are also likely to be of greater import in complex litigation.

In this connection, let us mention a common but underanalyzed aspect of the trial judge's discretion: giving or withholding non-authoritative judicial "advice." It is often the case, and nowhere moreso than in complex litigation, that the parties need to know the judge's views on a legal, evidentiary, or factual issue in order to make certain strategic and tactical decisions. It is also likely that knowledge of the judge's views might help to promote a settlement in the case. At the same time, as we have seen, an authoritative ruling in the context of a motion to dismiss or a motion for summary judgment is often not possible.

One way to handle the matter is to let judges provide a preliminary, non-authoritative opinion. The authority for issuing preliminary opinions is not entirely clear. Rule 56 does not specifically authorize it; neither does Rule 16. But this power fits as easily within the penumbras of Rules 16(c)(2)(A), -(c)(2)(D), -(c)(2)(L), and -(c)(2)(P) as other case-management powers that we have seen judges assert. One of the original purposes of the pretrial conference authorized under Rule 16 was precisely to give the lawyers the opportunity to exchange ideas about the case's progress with the judge.

During conferences with the judge, this type of informal judicial guidance occurs all the time, in cases both complex and routine. Rarely does it come to the public eye. The judge's advice is almost never put into a published decision; indeed, the advice may not even be transcribed into the record. Only on a few occasions does one of these advisory opinions emerge into the limelight. *See, e.g.,* In re "Agent Orange" Prod. Liab. Litig., 580 F. Supp. 690 (E.D.N.Y. 1984) (*supra* p. 689) (issuing a "preliminary memorandum" on choice-of-law matters).

Conversely, on some occasions the best response is for the judge to keep the parties in the dark about the judge's views to give them a mutual incentive to settle the case on their own. Uncertainty often helps to foster settlements and can therefore be a significant case-management tool:

. . .[S]ome trial courts have successfully attempted to promote settlement of mass tort claims by *withholding* decisions on these crucial questions in order to maintain a high level of uncertainty — and, consequently, risk — for both sides of the litigation. . . .

The *Agent Orange* litigation offers repeated examples of the court's strategic manipulation of uncertainty. Throughout the litigation, Judge Weinstein avoided issuing final decisions on potentially dispositive issues. Instead, he issued statements of preliminary decisions or indications of how he might rule on those issues. Judge Weinstein finally ruled on critical issues . . . only after the litigation had been settled. Weinstein's opinion on the fairness of the settlement turned on his conclusion that plaintiffs' cases were so weak as to have little value. . . . If these opinions had been issued prior to the settlement, the defendants would have had no incentive for settling the litigation. . . .

Courts' attempts to decide . . . complicated issues entail hard intellectual labor, certain criticism, and the risk of reversal, all of which can be avoided if litigation is resolved by settlement before the court is forced to decide. Postponing resolution of these complicated questions pressures parties toward settlements, which may relieve the judge from ever having to decide the issues. In short, trial courts faced with mass tort lawsuits often find it in their interests to fail to articulate and address legal issues.

Mark A. Peterson & Molly Selvin, *Mass Justice: The Limited and Unlimited Power of Courts*, 54 LAW & CONTEMP. PROBS. 227, 240-41 (Summer 1991). This withholding of advice or decision is hardly an isolated phenomenon; in one study, no action was recorded with respect to 34% of the summary-judgment motions filed in three district courts during 1986. JOE S. CECIL & C.R. DOUGLAS, SUMMARY JUDGMENT PRACTICE IN THREE DISTRICT COURTS 5-6 (1987) (noting that, in many of these cases, "the case settled soon after the motion was filed").

The literature on case management rarely mentions — much less legitimates — the practice of refusing to rule. Indeed, principles of case management — such as the need for just, speedy, and inexpensive resolution of disputes, the need for prompt, firm, and fair judicial management, and the need to define and narrow factual and legal issues as soon as possible — point in the opposite direction. *See* MANUAL, *supra*, § 11.211 (urging early resolutions on jurisdictional and class-action issues); *id.* § 10.13 ("The judge decides disputes promptly, particularly those that may substantially affect the course or extent of further proceedings.").

The best-known case discussing the "failure to judge" issue took a dim view of the practice. In *In re School Asbestos Litigation*, 977 F.2d 764 (3d Cir. 1992) (*supra* p. 697), Georgia Pacific and W.R. Grace were among the more than fifty defendants sued by a plaintiff class in a massive asbestos case. Although it had set no deadline for filing motions for summary judgment, the trial court, based on its "discretionary powers," refused to entertain motions for summary judgment from the two defendants because consideration of the motions might unduly delay the upcoming trial, whose starting date had not yet been definitely scheduled. The defendants petitioned the court of appeals for writs of mandamus requiring the district court to decide their motions for summary judgment. The court of appeals noted that mandamus was an appropriate remedy because "a district court's failure to consider the merits of a summary judgment motion is a failure to exercise its authority when it has the duty to do so." *Id.* at 793. The court of appeals then turned to the merits of the petition:

> . . . [I]n this case the district court had set no explicit deadline for summary judgment motions, nor a specific trial date. These factors make all the difference. The district court may well have been correct that resolution of these motions in December 1991 would not have advanced the litigation from an overall perspective. [The initial trial] would still have had to proceed with the other defendants, and if the district court had had to deal with more than a handful of these motions, trial might have been delayed. But fairness to defendants is as much a policy of Rule 56 as are fairness to plaintiffs and the convenience to the district court. [*Id.* at 794.]

Would mandamus have been appropriate if, instead of denying the motions for summary judgment, the judge had failed to rule on them? Try to reconcile *School Asbestos* with the following observation:

> Neither do we suggest that the trial courts should act other than with caution in granting summary judgment or that the trial court may not deny summary judgment in a case where there is reason to believe that the better course would be to proceed to a full trial.

Anderson v. Liberty Lobby, Inc. 477 U.S. 242, 255 (1986).

B. DISCOVERING FACTS

The first section explored case-management techniques for narrowing issues during pretrial. You can now appreciate some of the concerns — such as efficiency, the costs and benefits of judicial discretion, the potential loss of the right to jury trial, the shift from adversarial or inquisitorial process, and the damage to the equalitarian ideal of treating like cases alike — that drive the debate about these case-management techniques. The same concerns surround the other half of the "chicken-and-egg" problem: the control of pretrial discovery.

Pretrial discovery, which had been available in a limited fashion in equity, became available in all civil actions after the adoption of the Federal Rules of Civil Procedure in 1938. The drafters of the Federal Rules hoped that the discovery rules would make the trial run efficiently and avoid "trial by ambush." Whether these goals were best accomplished by affording the parties nearly unlimited access to their opponents' storehouses of information is debatable. To some degree, the costliness of discovery has replaced trial by ambush with another merits-frustrating problem: the "blackmail" of strike suits in which a defendant settles a meritless case to avoid incurring discovery costs. Although these and other criticisms of discovery have continued unabated since 1938, discovery remains the central feature of modern American procedure.

We are interested not in the general debates over discovery, which you likely explored in Civil Procedure, but in the particular ways in which the demands of complex litigation intersect with discovery. Complex litigation often requires that the parties gather, sift, organize, and store massive quantities of potential evidence. This process can be extremely costly. Indeed, it was this fact that led us to search for early and effective issue-narrowing devices. As we have seen, however, issue-narrowing devices are often unavailable until some discovery has occurred.

These considerations suggest that we want to change our usual rules of discovery in complex cases. The changes can occur in various ways: techniques can be developed to process information and resolve discovery disputes more efficiently; restrictions can be placed on the quantity of information to which the parties have access; and the judge can become more active on discovery matters. These changes are not an unadulterated blessing. As access to information declines, the chance of reaching the correct decision declines. Moreover, without an adequate opportunity for discovery, devices such as summary judgment may no longer be available and the possibility of a crisply conducted trial disappears. Conversely, if the discovery rules are changed in such a way that the judge has more control over the development of proofs and arguments, a conflict with the system's adversarial ideal ensues. If similar steps are not taken in more routine cases, changes in discovery in complex litigation also create a two-tiered pretrial system in which a party's prospects for success might hinge on whether a court designates the case as "complex" or "routine."

These major issues occupy this subsection. We begin with a look at the concept of the discovery plan, which is an integral aspect of the overall case-management plan. We then examine adjustments that have been made in traditional discovery to accommodate the demands of complex litigation.

1. The Discovery Plan

Rule 26(f) requires parties "to develop a proposed discovery plan" before the court issues the initial scheduling order. The plan can contain various components, including proposed limitations on discovery, methods for handling privilege claims or other issues that might affect the scope of disclosure and discovery, the most effective timing and sequence of discovery, problems with the disclosure or discovery of electronically stored information ("ESI"), and proposals for case-management orders that the court might enter. *See* Fed. R. Civ. P. 26(f)(3). The parties then submit the plan to the court.

At that point, Rule 16(b) requires the judge to enter a scheduling order establishing the deadline within which the parties must complete discovery. *See* Fed. R. Civ. P. 16(b)(3)(A). The scheduling order can also address "the extent of discovery," "disclosure and discovery of electronically stored information," and "any agreements the parties reach for asserting claims of privilege or [work product]." *See* Fed. R. Civ. P. 16(b)(3)(B)(ii), -(iii), -(iv). Rule 16(c)(2)(F) further authorizes the court, at any pretrial conference, to "consider and take appropriate action on . . . controlling and scheduling discovery, including orders affecting disclosures and discovery pursuant to Rule 26 and Rules 29 through 37."

As these rules show, judges regard the development of a discovery plan as an essential aspect of their case-management responsibilities. Therefore, the issue is not whether the judge should be active in developing the discovery plan, but rather how active the judge should be.

MANUAL FOR COMPLEX LITIGATION, FOURTH

51, 53 (2004)

A discovery plan should facilitate the orderly and cost-effective acquisition of relevant information and materials and the prompt resolution of discovery disputes. The plan should reflect the circumstances of the litigation, and its development and implementation must be a collaborative effort with counsel. The judge should ask the lawyers initially to propose a plan, but should not accept joint recommendations uncritically. Limits may be necessary even regarding discovery on which counsel agree. The judge's role is to oversee the plan and provide guidance and control. In performing that role, even with limited familiarity with the case, the judge must retain responsibility for control of discovery. The judge should not hesitate to ask why particular discovery is needed and whether information can be obtained more efficiently and economically by other means. Regular contact with counsel through periodic conferences will enable the judge to monitor the progress of the plan, ensure that it is operating fairly and effectively, and adjust it as needed. . . .

Adoption of a discovery plan is a principal purpose of the initial conference. . . .

Discovery control in complex litigation may take a variety of forms, including time limits, restrictions on scope or quantity, and sequencing. The Federal Rules and the court's inherent power provide the court with broad authority.

Notes

1.   In the adversarial model, lawyers have responsibility for gathering evidence; in the inquisitorial model, judges do. The role set out in the *Manual* places the managerial judge in a spot somewhere between these two poles. The *Manual* does not propose to turn the judge into the chief evidence gatherer. At the same time, the judge is not leaving the task entirely to the lawyers. Is this position a tenable one for the judge? The

Manual admits that the judge will never possess the familiarity with the case that the lawyers acquire. Is it a good idea to put someone who is not as knowledgeable as the lawyers in control of discovery? If the lawyers can agree on the best way to gather evidence, what is the basis on which the judge can override that choice?

2.   The empirical evidence on the value of creating a discovery plan is mixed. For reasons we have discussed, one feature of a discovery plan — setting an early, firm discovery cutoff — has some benefits in terms of reducing delay without additional costs. *See supra* p. 813, Note 2. Beyond discovery cutoffs, however, the data revealed no effect on delay, cost, or attorney satisfaction associated with the development of joint discovery or trial plans. James S. Kakalik et al., An Evaluation of Judicial Case Management Under the Civil Justice Reform Act 52-55 (1996). This study specifically mentioned that discovery plans had no effect on litigation costs "even if we consider only complex cases." *Id.* at 54. It did not mention whether the same was true of cost or satisfaction levels in complex cases. *See also* Fed. Jud. Ctr., Discovery and Disclosure Practice, Problems, and Proposals for Change 31-32 (1997) (reporting that 60% of attorneys actually met to develop discovery plans, and that the majority of attorneys stated that these meetings had no effect "on litigation expenses, disposition times, fairness, or the number of issues in the case").

3.   When related cases cannot be consolidated in a single forum, one way to achieve many of joinder's advantages is to file a joint discovery plan in each relevant forum. For examples of such plans in the state-federal context, as well as for a sample order, see James G. Apple et al., Fed. Jud. Ctr. & Nat'l Ctr. for State Courts, Manual for Cooperation Between State and Federal Courts 18-19, 131-36 (1997).

Suppose, however, that the case is multidistricted to another forum after the entry of a discovery plan. Can the multidistrict judge amend the plan, or is it the law of the case? Likewise, suppose that the original discovery plan was adopted by a multidistrict judge after transfer. After completion of multidistrict proceedings and remand to the transferor forum, can the transferor judge amend the discovery plan, or is the plan the law of the case? *See* In re Multi-Piece Rim Prods. Liab. Litig., 653 F.2d 671, 676 (D.C. Cir. 1981) (holding that the MDL judge "has the power to set aside pretrial rulings of transferor courts, and courts performing auxiliary roles must be guided by the transferee judge's rulings").

2. Traditional Discovery: Problems and Solutions

In a general sense, the problems that a discovery plan must address fall into two categories. First, the fair and efficient exchange of information must be facilitated. Second, disputes regarding the scope of or entitlement to disclosure and discovery must be fairly and expeditiously handled. In the real world these problems sometimes overlap, and a single technique might address aspects of both problems. Moreover, although facilitating the exchange of information logically precedes handling disputes over this exchange, it is sometimes necessary to put dispute-avoiding provisions into a discovery plan even before the information-exchanging provisions are settled on. In the following subsections, therefore, we eschew a simplistic distinction between the exchange-facilitating and dispute-minimizing parts of a discovery plan. Rather, we proceed more or less sequentially through some of the most common provisions contained in discovery plans, with those issues that need to be addressed immediately being discussed first.

a. Documents and Electronically Stored Information

Cases that are complex in the pretrial sense almost invariably involve vast quantities of documents and electronically stored information ("ESI"). The expense of retrieving, examining, and storing such information — as well as the expense in litigating over the opposing parties' entitlement to such information — are usually the largest costs that parties incur. Finding ways to facilitate the exchange of documents and ESI, and to reduce the disputes that can arise regarding their production, are central tasks in most discovery plans. The following four subsections describe some of the mechanisms that the court can employ.

i. Preservation Orders

Due to the high cost of preserving documents and ESI, corporations and governments, which are often parties in complex cases, typically have information-destruction policies (sometimes euphemistically called "document-retention policies" or "document-preservation policies") that require employees to discard documents and automatically purge ESI after a certain date. The *Manual for Complex Litigation* recommends that, "[b]efore discovery starts, and perhaps before the initial conference," judges "consider whether to enter an order requiring the parties to preserve and retain documents, files, data, and records that may be relevant to the litigation." MANUAL FOR COMPLEX LITIGATION, FOURTH § 11.442 (2004); *see also id.* § 40.25 (providing a sample document-preservation order). These orders are sometimes referred to as "litigation holds."

UNITED STATES V. PHILIP MORRIS USA, INC.

327 F. Supp. 2d 21 (D.D.C. 2004)

■ KESSLER, District Judge.

The United States has filed a Motion for Evidentiary and Monetary Sanctions Against Philip Morris USA ("Philip Morris") and Altria Group Due to Spoliation of Evidence ("Motion"). Upon consideration of the Motion, the Opposition, the Reply, and the entire record herein, the Court concludes that the Motion should be granted in part and denied in part.

On October 19, 1999, this Court entered Order #1, First Case Management Order for Initial Scheduling Conference, requiring preservation of "all documents and other records containing information which could be potentially relevant to the subject matter of this litigation." Despite this Order, Defendants Philip Morris and Altria Group deleted electronic mail ("email") which was over sixty days old, on a monthly systemwide basis for a period of at least two years after October 19, 1999. In February, 2002, Defendants became aware that there was inadequate compliance with Order #1, as well as its own internal document retention policies, and that some emails relevant to this lawsuit were, in all likelihood, lost or destroyed. It was not until June 19, 2002, four months after learning about this serious situation, that Philip Morris notified the Court and the Government. Moreover, despite learning of the problem in February 2002, Philip Morris continued its monthly deletions of email in February and March of 2002.

The parties have set forth in great detail the facts pertaining to Philip Morris' policies for preservation of documents and emails. Such policies were created with and approved by its parent company, Altria Group. Despite the lengthy submissions and explanations, there is no question that a significant number of emails have been lost and that Philip Morris employees were not following the company's own internal procedures for document preservation. What is particularly troubling is that Phillip Morris specifically identified at least eleven employees who failed to follow the appropriate procedures, and that those eleven employees hold some of the highest, most responsible positions in the company. These individuals include officers and supervisors who worked on scientific, marketing, corporate, and public affairs issues that are of central relevance to this lawsuit. Specifically, they include, among others, the Director of Corporate Responsibility, the Senior Principal Scientist in Research Development and Engineering, and the Senior Vice President of Corporate Affairs. All but one of the eleven employees were noticed for deposition by the United States. . . .

. . . [I]t is astounding that employees at the highest corporate level in Philip Morris, with significant responsibilities pertaining to issues in this lawsuit, failed to follow Order #1, the document retention policies of their own employer, and, in particular, the "print and retain" policy which, if followed, would have ensured the preservation of those emails which have been irretrievably lost. Moreover, it must be noted that Philip Morris is a particularly sophisticated corporate litigant which has been involved in hundreds, and more likely thousands, of smoking-related lawsuits.

The only issue is what remedy is appropriate. As a practical matter, as this Court noted at the January, 2003 status hearing, "you cannot recreate what has been destroyed." Because we do not know what has been destroyed, it is impossible to accurately assess what harm has been done to the Government and what prejudice it has suffered. *See* In re Prudential Ins. Co., 169 F.R.D. 598, 616 (D.N.J. 1997).

The Government requests four different forms of relief. First, it seeks an adverse inference that Philip Morris "has researched how to target its marketing at youth and actively marketed cigarettes to youth through advertising and marketing campaigns that are intended to entice young people to initiate and continue smoking, manipulated the nicotine content of its cigarettes in order to create and sustain smokers' addiction, and failed to market potentially less hazardous cigarettes after October 19, 1999."

There is no doubt that the Court has the authority to impose such a sanction for a discovery violation as serious and as irremediable as Philip Morris' email destruction. However, the Court has concluded, in the exercise of its discretion and with knowledge of the breadth of issues involved in this lawsuit, that such a far-reaching sanction is simply inappropriate. In *Bonds v. District of Columbia*, 93 F.3d 801, 808 (D.C. Cir. 1996), the Court of Appeals emphasized that "[t]he choice of sanctions should be guided by the 'concept of proportionality' between offense and sanction." The sanction sought by the United States fails to meet this test and simply casts too wide a net.

Second, the Government requests that Philip Morris be precluded from calling Peter Lipowicz as a fact or expert witness at trial. That request is granted. Mr. Lipowicz, as well as any other individual who has failed to comply with Philip Morris' own internal document retention program, will be precluded from testifying in any capacity at trial.

[The court rejected a third form of relief — dismissal of one of the defenses — because a pretrial ruling on another matter had effectively granted this relief.]

Fourth and finally, the Government requests that Philip Morris and Altria Group pay a monetary sanction of $2,995,000 to the Court Registry as punishment for their egregious violation of Order #1. A monetary sanction is appropriate. It is particularly appropriate here because we have no way of knowing what, if any, value those destroyed emails had to Plaintiff's case; because of that absence of knowledge, it was impossible to fashion a proportional evidentiary sanction that would accurately target the discovery violation. Despite that, it is essential that such conduct be deterred, that the corporate and legal community understand that such conduct will not be tolerated, and that the amount of the monetary sanction fully reflect the reckless disregard and gross indifference displayed by Philip Morris and Altria Group toward their discovery and document preservation obligations. Consequently, Philip Morris and Altria Group will be jointly required to pay a monetary sanction of $2,750,000 into the Court Registry no later than September 1, 2004.[1] In addition, Phillip Morris and Altria Group will be required to reimburse the United States for the costs associated with a Fed. R. Civ. P. 30(b)(6) deposition on email destruction issues. Those costs are a minimal $5,027.48.

---

1. Philip Morris identified eleven corporate managers and/or officers who failed to comply with the "print and retain" policy. Each such individual is being sanctioned in the amount of $250,000.

Notes

1.   Because of the sheer size of the sanction, *Philip Morris* has already become one of the best-known cases on litigation holds. The most famous of these cases, which *Philip Morris* cites, is *In re Prudential Insurance Co. of America Sales Practices Litigation*, 169 F.R.D. 598, 616 (D.N.J. 1997). *Prudential* imposed a mere $1 million sanction. As *Philip Morris* shows, non-monetary sanctions are also possible. *See, e.g.*, Wachtel v. Health Net, Inc., 239 F.R.D. 81 (D.N.J. 2006) (appointing a discovery master to monitor the defendant's compliance with its discovery obligations after, *inter alia*, the defendant failed to preserve documents).

2.   The *Manual for Complex Litigation* recommends that the court initially order the parties to confer and to attempt to come to an agreement about the shape of a preservation order. The reason is the fear that such an order "may interfere with the normal operations of the parties and impose unforeseen burdens." MANUAL FOR COMPLEX LITIGATION, FOURTH § 11.442 (2004). The *Manual* also counsels against a "blanket preservation order" because of its burden and expense. It contemplates that the preservation order provide a means by which, after reasonable notice to the opposing party, a party can purge documents or ESI, and it recommends that the order exclude those categories of documents or ESI for which the cost of retention "outweighs substantially their relevance." *Id.* Can a judge make this determination early in the litigation?

3.   Do parties have an obligation to preserve documents and ESI independently of, and even antecedent to, a litigation hold? According to the increasingly prevalent view, "[t]he obligation to preserve evidence arises when the party has notice that the evidence is relevant to litigation or when a party should have known that the evidence may be relevant to future litigation." Fujitsu Ltd. v. Fed. Express Corp., 247 F.3d 423, 436 (2d Cir. 2001); *accord* Silvestri v. Gen. Motors Corp., 271 F.3d 583, 591 (4th Cir. 2001); Cache La Poudre Feeds, LLC v. Land O'Lakes, Inc., 244 F.R.D. 614, 625 (D. Colo. 2007).

A preservation order is still significant. First, it can specify and clarify the precise obligations that the parties must meet. Second, once an order exists, Rules 16(f) and 37(b) provide a court with the authority to impose sanctions for the order's violation. Without an order, the court needs to rely on more amorphous sanctioning authority, such as its inherent power or 28 U.S.C. § 1927.

4.   The prevalence of ESI complicates the preservation problem in many ways. The routine use of computers and their networks destroys information regularly. For instance, think about how you destroy, or at least make difficult to retrieve, ESI every time you push the "save" button on your word-processing program. Moreover, some companies have short-term backup systems for disaster recovery, but these systems regularly overwrite old information. Must each iteration of the disaster-recovery information be preserved? If so, the cost of disaster-recovery systems will rise significantly. *See* Zubulake v. UBS Warburg LLC, 220 F.R.D. 212, 218

(S.D.N.Y. 2003) ("As a general rule, [a] litigation hold does not apply to inaccessible back-up tapes . . . which may continue to be recycled on the schedule set forth in the company's policy.").

We will soon examine the more general problem of ESI discovery. *See infra* p. 901. But it is worth mentioning now that Rule 37(e) does not allow a court to impose sanctions "under these rules" if ESI is lost "as a result of the routine, good-faith operation of an electronic information system." The Advisory Committee Note that accompanies Rule 37(e) indicates that the existence of a duty to preserve the information and "the steps the party took to comply with a court order in the case or party agreement requiring preservation" are relevant considerations determining "good faith."

Rule 37(e) came into force in 2006, after the court's decision in *Philip Morris*. Would the result in the case have been different if Rule 37(e) had been in effect? Note that Rule 37(e) limits resort only to the sanctions available under the Federal Rules of Civil Procedure. Arguably the court might still have been able to sanction Philip Morris and Altria under its other sanctioning powers.

5.   Litigation holds do nothing to streamline the fact-gathering process — indeed, if anything, they increase the amount of information that the parties must wade through. They also can be costly to implement, and non-compliance can generate satellite litigation. Nonetheless, they avoid a major source of friction in the discovery process, as well as major satellite litigation about whether the party that destroyed evidence is liable for the tort of spoliation, by fixing the parties' duties to preserve evidence. But the basic sensibility of litigation holds is to assure that parties have access to the fullest information in preparing their cases.

ii. Document Identification and Depositories

Once the exchange of documents and ESI begins, the process must be handled efficiently. In a multiparty case, it might be far cheaper to place documents in a single clearinghouse than to provide copies to each party, who must then make its own provisions for storage. Likewise, because the parties will be using these documents for many purposes — for instance, in taking depositions or in making motions — it is also helpful if they have a common method of identifying them. These ideas are linked; placing documents in a single depository makes their identification according to a common standard easier to accomplish.

Left to their own devices, however, parties might not be able to agree on establishing a depository or a common method of identifying documents; nor might they agree on how to share the costs of this enterprise. Here is an opportunity for the judge to slice through the natural contentiousness of the parties and to forge an agreement that creates a document-handling system that is beneficial to all. But suppose that one or more of the parties refuses to agree? Can the court ram a document-handling system down the throat of an unwilling party? What is the source of such a power?

MANUAL FOR COMPLEX LITIGATION, FOURTH

71-72, 75-77 (2004)

. . . Efficient management during discovery and trial requires planning and ongoing attention to the documentary phase of the litigation by the attorneys and the judge from the outset.

11.441 Identification System

. . . Before any documents are produced or used in depositions, the court should direct counsel to establish a single system for identifying all documents produced (by any procedure) or used in the litigation. To reduce the risk of confusion, each document should be assigned a single identifying designation for use by all parties for all purposes throughout the case, including depositions and trial.

Counsel should be informed that consecutive numbering is usually the most practicable; blocks of numbers are assigned to each party in advance to make the source of each document immeditely apparent. Every page of every document is Bates-stamped consecutively. . . . To avoid later disputes, a log should record each document produced and should indicate by, to whom, and on what date production was made.

The court can also order an identification system for computerized data that complements or integrates into the system adopted for paper documents. At a minimum, computer tapes, disks, or files containing numerous E-mail messages or word-processed documents should be broken down into their component documents for identification. However, data bases containing millions of data elements, none of which are meaningful alone, can be difficult or impossible to break down and organize in a way directly analogous to conventional document collections. Special consideration should be given to their identification and handling. . . .

11.444 Document Depositories

Central document depositories can promote efficient and economical management of voluminous documents in multiparty litigation. Requiring the production of all discovery materials in common, computer-readable formats and insisting that these materials be made available on centrally generated computer-readable media (such as CD-ROM or DVD) or through a secure internal Web site or a dial-in computer network may reduce substantially the expense and burden of document production and inspection. A depository also facilitates determination of which documents have been produced and what information is in them, minimizing the risk of later disputes.

On the other hand, the cost of establishing and maintaining either a paper or computerized central document depository may be substantial; before ordering or approving one, the court must be sure that the cost is justified by the anticipated savings and other benefits. In consultation with counsel, the court should allocate costs fairly among the parties, considering their resources, the extent of their use of the depository, and the benefit derived from it. . . . The judge may consider special arrangements for less affluent or less technologically sophisticated parties to ensure fair access.

It may be necessary to appoint an administrator to operate the depository, with the cost allocated among the parties. . . .

To create and operate a depository, counsel and the judge should collaborate in establishing procedures for acquiring, formatting, numbering, indexing, and maintaining discovery materials. . . .

Counsel and the judge must agree on a computer service provider to administer the depository, although technologies such as CD-ROM and the Internet reduce the need for physical storage facilities, inspection, and copying.

IN RE THREE ADDITIONAL APPEALS ARISING OUT OF THE SAN JUAN DUPONT PLAZA HOTEL FIRE LITIGATION

93 F.3d 1 (1st Cir. 1996)

■ SELYA, Circuit Judge.

These appeals commemorate the latest flight of the phoenix that rises repeatedly from the ashes of the tragic fire that engulfed the San Juan Dupont Plaza Hotel a decade ago. . . .

I. BACKGROUND

. . .

The sprawling litigation that burst forth from the smoldering embers of the charred hotel encompassed wrongful death, personal injury, property damage, and other claims brought by more than 2,000 plaintiffs against more than 200 defendants. In an effort to tame this behemoth and to orchestrate the proceedings, the district court devised an innovative case-management system. The system included the appointment of liaison counsels (to facilitate interactions both between the court and the legion of lawyers linked to the litigation as well as among the lawyers themselves); the formation of a Joint Discovery Committee ("JDC") to coordinate discovery initiatives; and the creation of a Joint Document Depository ("JDD") as a resting place for all pleadings, discovery materials, and the like. To pay for this case-management system, the trial judge imposed mandatory assessments on all litigants.

The appellants (whom we shall call "the pre-fire insurers") comprise thirteen insurance companies that had issued liability policies to firms which eventually became defendants in the underlying litigation. The quondam insureds settled with various claimants and then sued the pre-fire insurers for indemnification . . . . Not to be outdone, the original plaintiffs joined the pre-fire insurers as direct defendants. Though they had been brought late into the fray, the district court levied an assessment against each pre-fire insurer for a standard "defendant's share" (which, over time, amounted to roughly $41,500). Like all such assessments, these funds were slated for use in defraying the expenses associated with the case-management scheme.

Fairly early in the game, the pre-fire insurers moved for summary judgment on all claims against them. After a lengthy interval, the district court granted their motions but ordered sua sponte that they bear their own costs. . . .

On appeal, the pre-fire insurers . . . complain that they did not receive any benefit from the case-management system, and that, therefore, the court improperly refused to relieve them from the standardized assessments.

II. DISCUSSION

Because the district court has spelled out an acceptable basis for its cost-sharing orders and for its refusal to grant a special dispensation to the pre-fire insurers, we affirm . . ., adding only a few amplificative comments.

. . . The pre-fire insurers have incorrectly identified the legal standard applicable to appellate review of [the order requiring the insurers to contribute a standard share]. They insist that plenary review is appropriate . . .

This issue is fact-sensitive . . . . Stripped of rhetorical flourishes, the pre-fire insurers' real complaint is not that the judge misunderstood the relevant factors but that he weighed them haphazardly. Emblematic of this focus is the undeniable fact that, at bottom, the appellants challenge the court's factbound conclusion that the pre-fire insurers actually benefitted from the elaborate network of case-management devices (like the JDD) that their payments helped to subsidize. So viewed, these appeals raise fact-sensitive disputes that invite discretionary judgments. In circumstances where, as here, a matter is committed to the trial judge's equitable discretion, deference is due. . . .

. . . The district court's finding that the pre-fire insurers did in fact receive a significant benefit from the existence of the case-management system withstands review under an abuse-of-discretion test. The pre-fire insurers assert that they received no benefit from the devices because (1) discovery already had been completed at the time they were brought into the case, (2) they were perfectly capable of doing for themselves what the JDD accomplished for them, and (3) they did not need to rely on the material in the JDD since they sought (and were granted) summary judgment as a matter of law on the claims lodged against them. We agree with the district court that these assertions stem from an overly simplistic view of the pre-fire insurers' situation. . . .

The fact that discovery had been concluded was a two-edged sword. While it meant that the pre-fire insurers did not have to use the JDD to keep track of ongoing discovery, it also meant that they "had available to them in a single location all pleadings, discovery, service lists, pretrial documents, records of all court proceedings, trial transcripts, evidence utilized at trials, memoranda, as well as docket reference[s] as to all that had transpired up to that time."

For another thing, it is of no moment that the pre-fire insurers might have preferred to go it alone. The case-management system that the district court so painstakingly devised could not have operated on a voluntary basis. It depended on the court's authority to order all parties both to participate and to share the associated costs. Since the court acted within the scope of its case-management powers in establishing the overall paradigm, we give short shrift to the notion that the pre-fire insurers would have been better off conducting their defense in more traditional surroundings.

Finally, the district court found specially that the materials in the JDD were of significant benefit to the pre-fire insurers. . . . This finding is also supportable. After all, the allegations against the pre-fire insurers developed during, and arose from the results of, the discovery process. Thus, materials in the JDD had to be searched, and some were directly relevant to the claims asserted and/or to the pre-fire insurers' defenses. As the district court put it, "upon being served with [a] copy of the claims asserted against them — two or three years after the initial complaint [in the underlying litigation] had been filed — [the pre-fire insurers] could, through the availability of a well-organized and efficient Joint Document Depository, ascertain the status of the proceedings and have readily available all documentation pertinent to their case." . . .

The proof of the pudding is in the pre-fire insurers' admission that their confidence knew certain limits. Faced with upward of $200,000,000 in claims, the pre-fire insurers undertook full-scale trial preparations notwithstanding the pendency of their dispositive motions. The preparations envisioned reopening discovery, and as a necessary prelude (under the terms of the applicable pretrial orders) entailed heavy use of the JDD, resulting, for example, in making copies of over 275,000 documents and ordering in excess of 110 computer disks that contained stored information. In light of these statistics, the "no benefit" claim rings hollow.

Furthermore, as the district court explained, previous litigation of other issues earlier in the trial (including extensive discovery) had framed the issues, thereby enabling the court to resolve the claims against the pre-fire insurers with relative ease. . . .

. . . [I]t is simply not practicable to contrive a clean matrix of benefits and burdens. The best that a trial court can do is to determine, as a matter of rough remedial justice, whether significant disparities in the distribution of benefits and burdens demand readjustment of a generic formula. . . .

Affirmed.

Notes

1.   Document depositories can streamline discovery. Parties operate under an agreement, or sometimes a court order, that placing documents in the depository acts as service on all other parties, who are responsible for checking the depository periodically to see if new documents have come in. Courts can also order the parties to tailor their document requests so as not to duplicate requests for information already contained in the depository. *See* In re Air Crash Disaster at Stapleton Int'l Airport, Denver, Colo., on Nov. 15, 1987, 1988 WL 243502 (D. Colo. Apr. 18, 1988). The existence of a depository can also lead a court to deny a request to discover information that could be gleaned from documents in the depository, and can defeat a claim that a party has not had adequate opportunity to conduct discovery. *See* City of Detroit v. Grinnell Corp., 495 F.2d 448 (2d Cir. 1974); City of N.Y. v. Exxon Corp., 697 F. Supp. 677 (S.D.N.Y. 1988).

2.   Technology has radically changed the world of document-control practices such as document identification and document depositories. As the *Manual* says, the standard approach to assigning a unique identifying number to each page of a document was the quaint practice of using a Bates stamp. (If you want to see what a Bates-stamp machine looks like, try this link: http://www.nextag.com/bates-stamp-machine/shop-html.) As *Three Appeals* shows, the standard approach to a document depository was to rent an old warehouse staffed with file clerks and filled with file cabinets.

The prevalence of ESI and the ability to scan hard-copy documents into electronic form have dramatically reduced the need for physically stamping each document with an identifying number and filing documents in a physical location. Computer programs can electronically Bates-stamp a unique number on each page of each stored or scanned document. Internet sites or computer disks allow documents to be accessed at an attorney's desk. Software makes it increasingly easy to search documents for key words or to organize them by date or witness.

3.   This technology is not necessarily cheap, and many litigation-support firms and computer-forensics experts make a nice living off of complex litigation. Maintaining good control of documents, being able to mine them for information, and being able to access them easily are vital skills for lawyers in complex cases — more vital than making spellbinding closing arguments to juries. Its necessity raises the possibility that each side will devise its own document-control system, and its costliness raises the possibility that a less well-funded party will be unable to compete effectively in managing the flow of information. The first possibility is inefficient; the second is arguably unjust. By inserting itself into the document-control process, the court seeks to avoid both possibilities.

Granting for now that the court should intervene to prevent inefficient spending on discovery, should it also intervene to help less well-financed parties obtain access to information? The *Manual* says that the court can order the parties to share the cost of document-control systems, and that a party's resources are a relevant concern in deciding how much of the cost of a system a party should bear. Is there any reason to let a party bear less than the proportional benefits that the party receives? Won't such a party be tempted to overuse the system? By removing a major cost from a less well-financed party, isn't the court effectively making it easier for that party to prevail (when compared to a non-case-management world in which each party would bear the expense of its own document-control system in the absence of an agreement with other parties)? Isn't the court effectively increasing the pressure on the better financed party to settle and skewing the value of the settlement in favor of the less well-financed party? In the absence of a party's agreement to share costs, can you justify a case-management power that has such an outcome-influencing effect?

4. *Three Appeals'* implicit response to these arguments is that, if the parties were left to seek a voluntary agreement, agreement (however desirable) would be unlikely; the parties there were locked in a contentious relationship, and the number of affected parties (more than 2,200 in *Three Appeals*) made bargaining very costly and the incentives to free-ride very high. Court intervention was necessary to achieve the bargain that the parties would likely have struck but for these impediments. So viewed, document-control measures like a common identification system and a single site for documents are in some ways (albeit not all) akin to a public good that benefits all but that no individual has a sufficient incentive to produce. According to one theory of the role of government, the role of the court in this context is to facilitate the production of such a good.

Assuming that this argument is plausible, can it be generalized? In other words, does it act as a source or an underlying theory of the scope of — as well as the limits on — a judge's case-management powers? Consider the other case-management powers that we have studied. How many of them can be justified under this "public good" rationale?

5. Does *Three Additional Appeals* satisfy you that a court has the authority to order parties to pay for a document depository? From what source does such authority derive? Certainly not from the Federal Rules of Civil Procedure (unless the penumbras of Rules 16(c)(2)(L) and -(c)(2)(P) cast their shadows this far). Prior to its amendment in 1993, Rule 26(f) gave district courts the authority to enter an order "determining such other matters, including the allocation of expenses, as are necessary for the proper management of discovery." In the first *Dupont Plaza* decision to deal with the allocation of case-management expenses, the First Circuit was uncertain about the source of the authority to allocate case-management expenses. Citing Rule 26(f), however, it observed that "we are skeptical that a district court's authority to impose reasonable cost-sharing orders in multi-district litigation is much in doubt." In re Recticel Foam Corp., 859 F.2d 1000, 1004 (1st Cir. 1988). When it considered the issue again, the First Circuit had convinced itself not only of the court's power to impose such costs but also to reallocate those costs at the end of discovery; it cited Rule 16 (which never mentions such expenses), Rule 26(f), and the court's inherent power. In re Two Appeals Arising out of the San Juan Dupont Plaza Hotel Fire Litig., 994 F.2d 956, 965-66 & n.15 (1st Cir. 1993).

The 1993 Federal Rules amendments, however, deleted the quoted language from Rule 26(f). It was not relocated (as other parts of Rule 26(f) were) to Rule 16. What inference should be drawn from this fact? *Recticel Foam* also relied, in part, on the multidistrict nature of the case. Do courts have the same authority in non-MDL cases? Do the 2006 amendments for handling ESI — in particular, the ability of a court to "specify the conditions for the [ESI] discovery," Fed. R. Civ. P. 26(b)(2)(B) — provide the requisite authority for sharing costs associated with ESI?

6. An indirect way to achieve cost sharing for a document depository, and to avoid free-riding, is to let some parties agree to share the cost, and then to deny access to parties that fail to enter the agreement. *See* Case v. Cont'l Airlines Corp., 1992 WL 201080 (10th Cir. Aug. 11, 1992). Can a court subsequently assess a portion of the cost to a party that refuses to enter an agreement, on the theory that the party indirectly benefitted from the work of those who had access? On the facts of the case, *Case* thought the argument "tenuous, conclusory, and without merit," and reversed an order assessing costs against a non-participating plaintiff. *Id.* at *4.

7. Note the related argument that the district court in *Three Appeals* made: It was proper to assess some of the depository costs against the insurers because the depository was useful to the court in framing and resolving the issues in the insurers' favor. Is this a good argument? Does it mean that a losing party should pay less? Even more problematically, the court contributed nothing to maintaining the depository, but it derived benefits from the depository. Isn't there a risk that a court will be tempted to order too much document control when it finds these controls beneficial to its work but it bears none of the costs of such controls? (Put differently, isn't it human nature to overuse something when we don't pay for it?)

8. Should the location of a document depository affect a decision about whether and where to transfer the venue of a case? *See* Armco Steel Co. v. CSX Corp., 790 F. Supp. 311 (D.D.C. 1991) (giving this factor little weight).

iii.   Umbrella Protective Orders

Under the Federal Rules of Civil Procedure, the parties are entitled to obtain through disclosure or discovery information that is relevant to any party's claims or defenses, as long as that information is proportional to the needs of the case and is not either privileged or otherwise protected from disclosure or discovery. Fed. R. Civ. P. 26(b)(1)-(2). In addition, parties can, for good cause and on court order, obtain proportional, non-protected information that is "relevant to the subject matter involved in the action." Fed. R. Civ. P. 26(b)(1). These limitations — relevance, proportionality, and privilege — are generally interpreted by courts in a way that gives the parties broad access to information in the possession of others. They are also the source of much dispute, with the party from whom disclosure or discovery is sought often claiming that particular requests run afoul of one or more of these limitations. In complex litigation, in which the quantity of information is vast and the cost of permitting discovery is great, parties often have an incentive to argue that particular disclosure or discovery is impermissible. Moreover, due to the potential consequences to a party that turns over documents or ESI containing privileged or protected material — they might be deemed to have waived the privilege or protection — battles over the scope of disclosure and discovery of documents and ESI are likely.

Therefore, the parties and the court must find mechanisms to deal with disputes over the proper scope of discovery. We examine the issue of ESI more generally *infra* p. 901. Because of its relationship to the discovery of documents and ESI, and because it is usually implemented as a part of the initial discovery plan, we examine now one important method to streamline the dispute-resolution process: the umbrella protective order.

IN RE SOUTHEASTERN MILK ANTITRUST LITIGATION

666 F. Supp. 2d 908 (E.D. Tenn. 2009)

■ GREER, District Judge.

[This multidistricted antitrust litigation alleged that the defendants conspired in refusing to compete for the purchase of raw Grade A milk produced, marketed, and processed in the southeastern United States.]

I. BACKGROUND

On April 14, 2008, a protective order, drafted and largely agreed to by the parties, was signed by United States Magistrate Judge Dennis H. Inman. The protective order "governs the use and handling of documents, electronic information in any form, testimony, interrogatory responses and other information . . . produced or given by any defendant, plaintiff, or other individual or entity . . . in pre-trial proceedings in this Litigation." The stated purpose of the protective order is to protect against the "inappropriate dissemination of documents and information produced in the course of discovery, which may include competitively sensitive and confidential information about pricing, budgets, forecasts, strategic plans, cost of production, inventory and other confidential commercial information."

Pursuant to the terms of the protective order, materials produced during discovery may be designated as "confidential" by the producing party if the producing party believes, in good faith, that the material "constitutes, contains, reflects or discloses confidential, non-public research and analysis, development or commercial information, or other information for which a good faith claim of need of protection from disclosure can be made under the Federal Rules of Civil Procedure and/or other applicable law . . . ." The producing party may designate as "highly confidential" non-public personal information or other material of an "extremely sensitive confidential and/or proprietary" nature which it believes in good faith "would compromise and/or jeopardize the Producing Party's business interests." The protective order places certain limitations on the disclosure of "confidential" or "highly confidential" material, absent written consent of the producing party, or order of the Court.

Of particular importance to the presently pending matters are the provisions of paragraph 9 of the protective order. . . . Pursuant to the terms of the protective order, if a party wishes to use confidential or highly confidential material in "any papers containing or making reference to the contents of such material or information, in a pleading or document filed with the Court in this Litigation, such pleading or document . . . shall be filed under seal . . . until such time as the Court orders otherwise, or denies permission to file under seal."

The instant controversy finds its origin in the filing of motions by the dairy farmer plaintiffs and the retailer plaintiffs to seal their motions and supporting documents for class certification. The motions to seal were granted by the Magistrate Judge on May 4, 2009. Thereafter, defendants moved to seal their responses in opposition to plaintiffs' class certification motions. Then, on July 23, 2009, the dairy farmer plaintiffs filed a motion to unseal their class certification filings and to modify the protective order. . . .

On July 1, 2009, this Court conducted a status conference with the parties. At that conference, . . . the [Court] expressed considerable dissatisfaction with the apparent practice of the parties of engaging in wholesale sealing of filed documents and his perceived abuse of the protective order.

On August 5, 2009, the Magistrate Judge denied the motions to seal and granted the motion to unseal and modify the protective order. . . . [D]efendants filed their objection to the Magistrate Judge's order on August 19, 2009. Objections to the order were also filed by [three] non-party producing parties . . ., all of which produced testimony, documents or materials pursuant to subpoena during discovery in this case. . . .

Then, on August 26, 2009, the [New York Times Company ("Times") and National Public Radio ("NPR")] moved for ". . . Leave to Intervene and For Unsealing Of Judicial Documents." The motion to intervene was unopposed and was orally granted on September 10, 2009. The motion of the Times and NPR seeks an order adopting and affirming the Magistrate Judge's August 5, 2009, order and is opposed by the defendants and the non-party producing parties. The retailer plaintiffs and the dairy farmer plaintiffs support the motion of the Times and NPR.

II. LEGAL STANDARD AND ANALYSIS

A. *Protective Orders*

Plaintiffs have chafed under the burden of the protective order entered in this case from the inception of the litigation in this Court and have repeatedly complained about the protective order orally during hearings, despite having consented, in large part, to the entry of the order. Plaintiffs have now moved to modify the protective order to allow named plaintiffs access to materials designated "highly confidential" under the protective order. Plaintiffs assert the public's right of access to court proceedings based on First Amendment principles of right of public access to court records. Although the Times and NPR also assert the right of public access, these organizations do not seek modification of the protective order.

Protective orders are authorized by Rule 26 of the Federal Rules of Civil Procedure, and are used frequently in cases such as the instant one. Rule 26(c) authorizes "[a] party or person from whom discovery is sought" to move for a protective order "to protect a party or person from annoyance, embarrassment, oppression, or undue burden or expense . . . ." Fed. R. Civ. P. 26(c)(1). The rule specifically permits the court, under appropriate circumstances, to limit the scope of disclosure, designate persons who may be present while discovery is conducted, seal depositions and other documents and information and prohibit trade secrets and other commercially sensitive information from being revealed. Fed. R. Civ. P. 26(c)(l)(D), -(E), -(F), -(G), and -(H).

It is not at all unusual in this or in other courts for a protective order to be entered by agreement of the parties . . . :

> Protective orders are also often obtained by agreement, particularly regarding confidential information and in litigation likely to involve a large volume of documents. Frequently these take the form of "umbrella" protective orders that authorize any person producing information to designate that which is confidential as protected under the order. One distinguished judge noted in 1981 that he was "unaware of any case in the past half-dozen years of even a modicum of complexity where an umbrella protective order . . . has not been agreed to by the parties and approved by the court. Protective orders have been used so frequently that a degree of standardization is appearing."

[CHARLES ALAN WRIGHT ET AL., FEDERAL PRACTICE AND PROCEDURE § 2035 (2d ed. 1994).] . . . [T]he *Manual for Complex Litigation*, used by virtually every court handling multidistrict litigation, contains a standardized form protective order. *See* MANUAL FOR COMPLEX LITIGATION, FOURTH § 40.27 (2004). The use of protective orders, in fact, has become standard practice in complex cases. Protective orders serve to facilitate and expedite discovery and are often essential to the proper functioning of civil discovery. Indeed, in the present case, all parties have benefitted from the protective order, which has allowed a large volume of documents to be produced without the burden of [protracted] litigation.

A protective order is always subject to modification or termination for good cause, *see* Public Citizen v. Liggett Group, Inc., 858 F.2d 775, 782-83 (1st Cir. 1988); In re "Agent Orange" Prod. Liab. Litig., 821 F.2d 139, 145 (2d Cir. 1987), even where the parties have consented to its entry. The modification of a protective order is left to the sound discretion of the district court. In this case, the protective order itself anticipates and allows the parties to seek modification of the order. The party seeking modification of the protective order has the burden of establishing cause for the modification. In deciding whether to modify an existing protective order the court must "balance the potential harm to the party seeking protection against the requesting party's need for the information and the public interest served by its release." MANUAL FOR COMPLEX LITIGATION, FOURTH § 11.432. Also important may be the disclosing party's degree of reliance on the protective order when the disclosure was made. *Id.*

As noted above, the plaintiffs seek to modify the protective order to allow named plaintiffs the ability to review and access material which has been designated highly confidential. The protective order currently forbids the named plaintiffs from accessing such material. Plaintiffs argue that this limitation hinders their ability to fully inform their clients of the basis, nature and evidence supporting the claims in this case. Plaintiffs point to what they perceive to be abuse of the protective order by the defendants who, they claim, have engaged in wholesale designation of documents as highly confidential. Plaintiffs argue that when they initially agreed to the protective order, it was with the assurance that defendants would not engage in such wholesale designations. At oral argument on this matter, plaintiffs asserted that defendants had designated approximately 3.5 million documents as either confidential or highly confidential.[7]

On the one hand, plaintiffs' claims that defendants have engaged in wholesale designation of documents as confidential or highly confidential, without a good faith basis for doing so, appears to have some merit and may be a sufficient reason for granting the modification request. On the other hand, non-party third parties have produced certain documents designated as highly confidential in clear reliance on the provisions of the protective order and the modification would potentially impair the business interests of those parties, who did not institute or initiate this litigation and are not involved in it. The Court is not, therefore, inclined to delete the restriction on named plaintiffs' access to highly confidential documents altogether. That does not mean, however, that named plaintiffs should not have access to at least some of the highly confidential documents and have the opportunity to review them with their counsel in order to facilitate their ability to prepare and prosecute their case.

At the Court's hearing on September 10, 2009, the Court expressed its view that some modification of the protective order was likely justified to facilitate the preparation and prosecution of this case by the plaintiffs and directed the parties to confer in an effort to reach some agreement that would accommodate the competing interests. . . . The Court will therefore reserve its decision on defendants' appeal of the Magistrate Judge's order granting the requested modification of the protective order until the parties have conferred and once again bring the matter to the Court's attention by the filing of an appropriate pleading.

---

7. Pursuant to the protective order, material designated confidential may be shared with a designated named plaintiff while material designated highly confi- dential may not. The Court is unaware of the number of documents designated highly confidential.

B. *Public Access to Judicial Documents*

There can be no doubt that the public has both a constitutional and a common law presumptive right of access to civil proceedings and judicial records. Brown & Williamson Tobacco Corp. v. Fed. Trade Comm'n, 710 F.2d 1165, 1179 (6th Cir. 1983). The public right of access, however, is not absolute. "[E]very court has supervisory power over its own records and files, and access has been denied where court files might have become a vehicle for improper purposes." Nixon v. Warner Commc'ns, Inc., 435 U.S. 589, 598 (1978). Once documents are filed with the Court, there is a "strong presumption that they should be open to the public." While sealing orders are permissible under the First Amendment, Seattle Times Co. v. Rhinehart, 467 U.S. 20 (1984), the "good cause" standard of Rule 26(c) does not apply; rather, the party seeking to seal must show "compelling reasons." Meyer Goldberg, Inc. v. Fisher Foods, Inc., 823 F.2d 159, 163 (6th Cir. 1987). Despite the Court's discretion, there are two broad exceptions to the "strong presumption" in favor of public access: "those based on the need to keep order and dignity in the courtroom and those which center on the content of the information to be disclosed to the public." *Brown & Williamson*, 710 F.2d at 1179.

Only the latter exception is at issue here. In discussing this exception, the Sixth Circuit has enumerated several interests which might justify the application of the exception: a criminal defendant's right to a fair trial, privacy rights of participants or third parties, trade secrets and national security. The defendants and non-party producing parties in this case rely only on their privacy rights and trade secrets and/or competitive sensitivity of the materials produced. Importantly, neither harm to reputation of the producing party nor conclusory allegations of injury are sufficient to overcome the presumption in favor of public access. "Only the most compelling reasons can justify non-disclosure of judicial records."

One other factor is important here. Third parties who were not responsible for the initiation of the litigation are protected by the terms of the protective order. As recognized by the Sixth Circuit, these individuals possess a "justifiable expectation of privacy that their names and financial records not be revealed to the public," and "[t]heir interests in privacy are sufficiently compelling to justify non-disclosure." When a third party has produced material in reliance on a protective order, "only 'extraordinary circumstances' or 'compelling need' warrant the reversal of a protective order."

There is no doubt that the use of sealed pleadings has been grossly abused in this case, as the Magistrate Judge found. The blame for that, however, rests as much with this Court as with the parties. Because of the burden placed on the Court by all the sealed pleadings filed in this case, most of which have been voluminous, the Court has likely failed at this point in assuring that all sealing was fully justified and that the public's right of access was guaranteed. Said more simply, the Court should have anticipated the issues that have now arisen and put in place at an earlier stage of this litigation a more specific procedure for weighing the competing interests of the litigants, non-party producing parties and the public. . . .

Paragraph 9 of the protective order provides that pleadings which contain or make reference to materials designated as confidential or highly confidential shall be sealed. Pursuant to these provisions of the protective order, the parties have sealed thousands of pages of pleadings and attachments to those pleadings. It goes without saying that not every line and every page of these pleadings was entitled to protection from public view. . . . In making these filings, the parties have ignored the spirit of Local Rule 26.2(b) which requires the parties to file redacted versions "where only a portion thereof is to be placed under seal." Rather than filing a redacted pleading making available for public inspection all but the confidential or highly confidential material contained in the pleading, the parties have employed a broad brush approach by seeking to seal the entire pleading. The protective order must be read in the context of the local rule. And, while it must be acknowledged that the task of preparing redacted pleadings may be a burdensome one given the voluminous nature of those pleadings, that burden rightly belongs with the parties. Once the necessary redactions are made, the burden of justifying continued sealing will be placed where it belongs — on the producing party. Then, the Court can make the determination necessary by weighing all the competing interests.

This litigation involves issues of considerable importance to the public and nondisclosure cannot be justified on the basis of the protective order alone. Except where a compelling interest of a party or a non-party producing party requires otherwise, these proceedings will be conducted in full public view. In making a determination that a document or reference in a pleading should be sealed from public view, this Court must balance the competing needs and interests of the litigants, non[-]party producing parties and the public and present a reasoned analysis explaining why. . . .

As a result of all this, the various motions to seal and/or unseal the pleadings relating to the class certification motions will be re-referred to the Magistrate Judge for the type of individualized, reasoned analysis necessary. . . . Within seven (7) calendar days of this order, any party which has filed a class certification motion, response or reply shall file with the Court a redacted version of the pleading which shall be available for public review . . . . [U]nless a party objects to the unsealing of material redacted within ten (10) business days, the entire pleading will be unsealed. . . . [T]he Magistrate Judge will then be able to determine whether or not continued sealing is justified under the law.

[The Court also referred the motion of the Times and NPR to permit unsealing to the Magistrate Judge.]

Notes

1.   Umbrella protective orders are also called umbrella confidentiality orders, blanket protective orders, or blanket confidentiality orders. The

Manual for Complex Litigation recommends that an order address a series of issues, including the categories of information included within the order, the procedure by which documents are designated and identified for protection, the persons who can access the material, the extent to which designated material can be used in related cases, the procedures by which a designation can be challenged, and the process under which the order can be terminated or modified. MANUAL FOR COMPLEX LITIGATION, FOURTH § 11.432 (2004). For a sample of such an order, see *id.* § 40.27.

2. *Southeastern Milk* gives a good sense of both the benefits and the drawbacks of umbrella protective orders. The prospect of reviewing 3.5 million documents on an individual basis is, to say the least, unappealing to most courts. The effort would consume a judge for years, and in the end it would be largely wasted because the parties would likely use only a small fraction of these documents in the litigation itself. Likewise, the costs to the parties of screening each document and litigating over the extent of its protection — especially when most of that cost will be wasted — are prohibitive. The umbrella protective order provides a means by which the court and the parties can kick the issue down the road; the parties can exchange documents now with assurance of their confidential treatment, and argue later about whether the documents that become critical to the litigation are in fact protected. As *Southeastern Milk* says, it is nearly unimaginable that, in any case involving large numbers of potentially sensitive documents, such an order would not be issued.

At the same time, these orders are controversial. One set of concerns relates to the parties' ability to abuse the system. Depending on the nature of the protective order, designating a document as confidential can mean that only the parties can have access to the information (in other words, the information is to be kept from the public's eyes), or that only certain of the parties' agents (usually the lawyers and experts) can have access; in the latter case, not even the parties can see the information. *Southeastern Milk* involved both types of confidentiality. Because the designation process runs without any significant judicial check (indeed, it is precisely to avoid individualized judicial determinations that the system is put in place to begin with), it is easy to understand how one or more parties will over-designate documents as confidential, thus shielding information from public view or the view of other parties. It is the judge's task to protect against unwarranted disclosure of documents, so the delegation of this function to parties with an incentive to overuse the system smacks of an abdication of the judicial function.

Another set of concerns involves the public's right to know about the workings of the judicial system — especially in large public controversies such as most complex cases. Many of the protective-order cases involve suits or motions brought by news agencies that are seeking access to documents designated as confidential under an umbrella protective order. The leading Supreme Court decision is *Seattle Times Co. v. Rhinehart*, 467 U.S. 20, 37 (1984), in which the Court held that the public has no First Amendment right to obtain documents disclosed during the pretrial process as long as the "protective order is entered on a showing of good cause as required by Rule 26(c), is limited to the context of pretrial civil discovery, and does not restrict the dissemination of the information if gained from other sources." *Seattle Times* did not involve an umbrella protective order, so the question of whether the savings in judicial resources that an umbrella order generates is a sufficient "good cause" to counter First Amendment concerns remains an open issue. Moreover, *Southeastern Milk* presented a problem that was in part beyond the confines of *Seattle Times*, because the parties kept confidential not only certain documents but also pleadings, motions, and briefs that they filed with the court. The public and First Amendment interests in having access to matters filed in court is evidently greater than in having access to private documents, most of which will never influence the judge's decision.

In a case famously critical of umbrella protective orders, Judge Posner tied together both concerns and balanced them against the benefits:

> [The judge] granted a virtual carte blanche to either party to seal whatever portions of the record the party wanted to seal. This delegation was improper. . . .
>
> . . . [T]he public at large pays for the courts and therefore has an interest in what goes on at all stages of a judicial proceeding. That interest does not always trump the property and privacy interests of the litigants, but it can be overridden only if the latter interests predominate in the particular case, that is, only if there is good cause for sealing a part or the whole of the record in that case. The determination of good cause cannot be elided by allowing the parties to seal whatever they want, for then the interest in publicity will go unprotected unless the media are interested in the case and move to unseal. The judge is the primary representative of the public interest in the judicial process and is duty-bound therefore to review any request to seal the record (or part of it).
>
> We are mindful of the school of thought that blanket protective orders . . . are unproblematic aids to the expeditious processing of complex commercial litigation because there is no tradition of public access to discovery materials. The weight of authority, however, is to the contrary. Most cases endorse a presumption of public access to discovery materials, and therefore require the district court to make a determination of good cause before he may enter the order. Rule 26(c) would appear to require no less. . . .
>
> We do not suggest that all determinations of good cause must be made on a document-by-document basis. In a case with thousands of documents, such a requirement might impose an excessive burden on the district judge or magistrate judge. There is no objection to an order that allows the parties to keep their trade secrets (or some other properly demarcated category of legitimately confidential information) out of the public record, provided the judge (1) satisfies himself that the parties know what a trade secret is and are acting in good faith in deciding which parts of the record are trade secrets and (2) makes

explicit that either party and any interested member of the public can challenge the secreting of particular documents. Such an order would be a far cry from the standardless, stipulated, permanent, frozen, overbroad blanket order that we have here.

Citizens First Nat'l Bank of Princeton v. Cincinnati Ins. Co., 178 F.3d 943, 945-46 (7th Cir. 1999).

3.   Another difficulty with umbrella protective orders is their inability to address certain types of confidential information — especially documents generated during the litigation for which a party might wish to claim work-product protection or attorney-client privilege. In theory, such documents could fall within the terms of an umbrella order, but in practice parties would never wish to have such sensitive strategic information in the hands of an opponent; there is also the concern that handing such information over to an opponent waives the privilege in present or future litigation. (On the general question of waiver, see *infra* pp. 957-69.) Although umbrella protective orders work well to minimize skirmishes over claims that documents are irrelevant, contain trade secrets, or involve technical proprietary information, they are no panacea for eliminating all disputes over the production of confidential information.

4.   Parties who enter umbrella protective orders should do so with their eyes open. As *Southeastern Milk* shows, they cannot always count on the fact that the documents will remain out of others' sight. To begin, other parties or the public can challenge a party's designation of a document as protected; in that instance, the party seeking protection bears the burden of proving that the document is in fact worthy of protection. *See* Cipollone v. Liggett Group, Inc., 785 F.2d 1108, 1122 (3d Cir. 1986); Uniroyal Chem. Co. v. Syngenta Crop Prot., 224 F.R.D. 53, 57 (D. Conn. 2004) ("The opposing party can designate specific documents it believes to be not confidential, and the movant would have the burden of proof in justifying the protective order with respect to those documents. The burden of proof remains at all times on the party seeking the protective order.")

Second, as *Southeastern Milk* shows, courts retain the power to modify umbrella protective orders during the litigation and even after the case concludes. The leading case is In re "Agent Orange" Product Liability Litigation, 821 F.2d 139 (2d Cir. 1987), in which a public advocacy group sought access to documents produced in the *Agent Orange* litigation. Although one of defendants' express conditions in entering a $180 million settlement was that all discovery materials produced to plaintiffs be returned, Judge Weinstein ordered the material unsealed. He also rejected the defendants' claim that they were entitled to renege on the settlement. The Second Circuit affirmed; it found that the public had a presumptive right to discovery material, that the order did not violate the settlement agreement, but that, if it did, the modification was merely "incidental." *See also* Phillips v. Gen. Motors Corp., 307 F.3d 1206 (9th Cir. 2002); Public Citizen v. Liggett Group, Inc., 858 F.2d 775 (1st Cir. 1988). *See generally* Arthur R. Miller, *Confidentiality, Protective Orders and Public Access to the Courts*, 105 HARV. L. REV. 427 (1991) (suggesting limits on modifying confidentiality orders); MANUAL, *supra*, § 11.432 (listing eight factors to consider when lifting confidentiality orders).

5.   It is not clear who bears the burden of proving that a modification is warranted. *See* SEC v. TheStreet.Com, 273 F.3d 222, 229 (2d Cir. 2001) ("Where there has been reasonable reliance by a party or deponent, a District Court should not modify a protective order granted under Rule 26(c) 'absent a showing of improvidence in the grant of [the] order or some extraordinary circumstance or compelling need.'"); Pansy v. Borough of Stroudsburg, 23 F.3d 772, 790 (3d Cir. 1994) ("The party seeking to modify the order of confidentiality must come forward with a reason to modify the order."); Bayer AG & Miles, Inc. v. Barr Labs., Inc., 162 F.R.D. 456, 465 (S.D.N.Y. 1995) ("'Umbrella' protective orders are disfavored, and on a motion for modification, the burden generally will be on the party seeking protection to show good cause. . . . Where, however, the modification motion is brought by a party who stipulated to a blanket protective order, the party should be held to its agreement and thus should have the burden of showing good cause for its modification request.").

The usual procedure for a nonparty seeking to modify or challenge an umbrella order is to permissively intervene in the case. *See* Beckman Indus., Inc. v. Int'l Ins. Co., 966 F.2d 470 (9th Cir. 1992).

6.   When one court enters a confidentiality order, are other courts required to abide by it? *Compare* Keene Corp. v. Caldwell, 840 S.W.2d 715 (Tex. App. 1992) (notions of comity and the Full Faith and Credit Clause required a state court to defer to the protective order of a federal court), *with* Baker v. Gen. Motors Corp., 522 U.S. 222 (1998) (full-faith-and-credit principles did not require a federal court to defer to a state-court injunction prohibiting the testimony of a witness).

7.   An alternative to the umbrella protective order is a particularized protective order to prevent the disclosure or dissemination of specific information. *See* MANUAL, *supra* § 11.432. The *Manual* points out that particularized orders "will reduce the burdensomeness of the order and render it less vulnerable to later challenge." For further discussion of the benefits and drawbacks of the particularized approach, in a case that ultimately supported the umbrella approach, see *Cipollone*, 785 F.2d at 1123:

> There may be cases in which the document-by-document approach adopted by the district court, which deters over-designation of confidentiality and imposes heavier costs on parties making the confidentiality designation, will be preferable. A case in which the district court has reason to believe that virtually all confidentiality designations will be spurious may be such a case. Our purpose in extending the discussion is to explain that the district court erred to the extent that it felt obliged to utilize the document-by-document approach to avoid shifting the burden of proof of confidentiality, and to commend the umbrella approach for consideration of the district courts in this circuit in complex cases.

iv. Discovery from Prior Litigation

Related lawsuits are common in complex litigation; aggregation in one suit is not always achievable (or even, perhaps, desirable). One way to reduce significantly the costliness of later lawsuits — and hence the costliness of our inability to aggregate — is to allow the parties to use documents and ESI produced during an earlier case.

UNITED STATES V. AMERICAN TELEPHONE & TELEGRAPH CO.

461 F. Supp. 1314 (D.D.C. 1978)

■ GREENE, District Judge.

[The United States alleged that AT&T had engaged in a long-standing pattern of seeking to monopolize the telecommunications industry. Several other companies — including MCI Communications Corp. and Litton Systems, Inc. — had also sued AT&T on antitrust grounds.]

III

Discovery Order No. 2, entered by Magistrate Margolis on April 27, 1978, requires inter alia that defendants produce for inspection and copying all microfilm copies of documents, transcripts, and exhibits produced in connection with a number of antitrust actions brought by private parties against AT&T in other districts. Defendants have appealed this order to the Court, contending that, for a number of different reasons, such a requirement is inconsistent with the spirit, if not the letter, of the Federal Rules of Civil Procedure.

It is appropriate initially to articulate precisely what is currently at issue between the parties with respect to Discovery Order No. 2. . . . [T]he question before the Court is whether defendants should be required in this proceeding to produce to plaintiff here copies of documents previously produced and selected for use in the lawsuits brought against defendants by Litton Systems, Inc. and MCI Communications Corp. in the Southern District of New York and the Northern District of Illinois, respectively. . . .

As a defendant in this litigation, AT&T's duty to produce is squarely resolved by Rules 26 and 34, Fed. R. Civ. P., which provide for the production of relevant documents within a party's possession, custody, and control. The documents here sought are, and always have been within defendants' possession, since they are defendants' own documents. Conceptually it makes no difference under the Rules whether as such they represent the product of some process of selection worked out between the parties in the other actions or whether that process never took place.

Defendants here do not and cannot dispute that in the normal course of discovery in this litigation the government would be entitled to production of the same 12 million pages of documents (subject to claims of relevancy and privilege) they produced in the *Litton* and *MCI* lawsuits. What plaintiff is seeking to do is to obtain some lesser number of documents, perhaps some 2.5 million,[75] by eliminating for purposes of production in this case all those which the attorneys for Litton and MCI have already determined to be irrelevant. The only effect of the procedure requested by plaintiff, then, is to exclude the bulk of the records from even being considered for production here. The Court can find no basis for concluding that AT&T is suffering legal injury as a result of such a narrowing of the volume of the documents to be produced.

If anyone would have a legitimate complaint concerning this procedure, it would be the plaintiffs in the private lawsuits, who could conceivably assert a work product privilege. Yet, not only have these plaintiffs not asserted that privilege, but they have affirmatively agreed with the procedure proposed by the government. Defendants have cited no authority for what would appear to be a startling proposition: that they may assert a work product privilege claim on behalf of their opponents in other lawsuits.

To be sure, to the extent that the government will not need to review the millions of documents generated by AT&T at the request of the private plaintiffs and may confine itself to the more limited number of records which those plaintiffs found useful, it will ease the government's discovery burden and speed this litigation along. But defendants have no legal interest in making the government's accumulation of proof more difficult or in delaying a trial on the merits. The intricacies of common law pleading and procedure, whereby a party could, through artifice, prolong litigation or avoid adjudications on the merits, have long given way to more sensible, merit-oriented processes. . . It would not advance but defeat the purpose of the Rules to require plaintiff in this case to proceed laboriously, and possibly at the cost of several years' delay, to duplicate the document selection process conducted by the plaintiffs in *Litton* and *MCI* when the fruits of that process are readily available and in the possession of a party to this very litigation, and when those who conducted the search do not object.

Defendants next argue that unspecified portions of the requested documents might be irrelevant to this litigation, or privileged, and that therefore the Court may not order their production until (1) the government has made specific designations of classes of documents in terms of their relevancy to this action, and (2) the defendants have screened the documents to eliminate privileged materials. These contentions will be considered seriatim. . . .

The only substantial difference between the claims and issues involved in the government's case here on the one hand, and those involved in the *Litton* and *MCI* cases on the other hand, is that the former subsume the latter. In effect, Litton and MCI each represent a separate and identifiable segment of the government's case here. Thus, a fortiori, the documents relevant to those actions would be relevant here; their relevancy is further assured by their having been thoroughly screened for relevancy in the private actions.

To be sure, neither the confluence of issues in the private lawsuit with those in this lawsuit, nor the findings of relevancy made in those private actions, are determinative, and some of the documents produced by AT&T in *Litton* and *MCI* may ultimately be found to be outside the range of relevancy within the meaning of this action. But the discovery rules do not require absolute precision, and no order of production can serve as a guarantee that every document produced will be relevant. If the purposes of the Rules, and of pretrial discovery generally are to be effectuated, actual discovery must be expected to be somewhat of a "fishing expedition," particularly in antitrust and similarly complex litigation.

It is difficult to envision what prejudice could ensue from the production of documents, a small number of which might turn out not to be relevant to this lawsuit. To the extent that any irrelevant documents are produced, defendants will be amply protected by this Court's protective order, which will maintain the confidentiality of all documents produced, and order the return of any irrelevant documents to the defendants.

. . . The Court clearly has the authority under the Federal Rules to order production of documents which are on any reasonable interpretation of that concept relevant, and through a process which fully protects the legitimate interests of defendants. There is no basis in the law or common sense to prescribe the more cumbersome procedure.

This, then, leaves only defendants' claims as to privilege. In this regard, defendants are entitled to a mechanism (1) for honoring appropriate claims of privilege and (2) for insuring, by means of an appropriate protective order, that any privileged documents produced to plaintiff will not be used improperly. . . .

Accordingly, the Court has this day entered Pretrial Order No. 11 which requires defendants to produce by November 1, 1978, all of the approximately 2.5 million documents produced by them in *Litton* and *MCI* and selected for use by those private plaintiffs. Documents as to which defendants wish to assert a claim of privilege are to be segregated and delivered to the Special Masters by that date. . . . Pretrial Order No. 11 further directs plaintiff to bring this Order to the attention of the U.S. District Court for the Southern District of New York and the U.S. District Court for the Northern District of Illinois, and to request leave from those courts for the production of such documents notwithstanding any protective orders that may have been entered therein.

Notes

1. Having access to discovery proceedings from other cases can significantly streamline the discovery process, as long as the allegations in the cases are closely related and the lawyers in the earlier cases are competent. *Cf.* In re Temporomandibular Joint (TMJ) Implants Prods.

Liab. Litig., 113 F.3d 1484, 1489 (8th Cir. 1997) (noting that district court had ordered the parties to use a document depository created in related litigation, and had permitted additional discovery only upon leave of court).

Are there any reasons not to allow the lawyers in later cases access to the earlier work? From the viewpoint of a litigant in AT&T's shoes, the answer may be "Yes" for at least four reasons. First, the litigant may want to impose delays and additional costs on the opponent, making it more difficult for the opponent to maintain the litigation. Second, the litigant may have handed over material in the prior litigation under the terms of a confidentiality order (*see supra* p. 882), and has a legitimate expectation of privacy in the documents or ESI that the second litigation might not honor. Third, the litigant may have been forced to turn over the documents after an adverse ruling from the first court, and may want a chance to convince the second court not to permit discovery or use of the previously disclosed material. Fourth, the litigant may be the subject of a grand jury or other governmental investigation; when the government is the opponent in the second case, the litigant might legitimately fear that granting access would become a shortcut in that investigation. From the viewpoint of the court, granting access might be problematic if this access makes parties in other cases less willing to enter into confidentiality orders. From the viewpoint of the parties that obtained the information in the prior litigation, granting access might be objectionable when it invades their work product or bestows a benefit without compensating them for their work in developing the material.

Which, if any, of these concerns are legitimate? How would a court balance any legitimate concerns against the interest in streamlining the discovery process? Note that Rule 26(c)(1) authorizes a court to tailor a protective order to accommodate some of these concerns; for instance, to deal with the free-rider issue, a court could presumably condition disclosure on fair compensation to the party that originally obtained the information. *Cf.* Johnson v. Bryco Arms, 222 F.R.D. 48, 50 (E.D.N.Y. 2004) (Weinstein, J.) ("This court has the power to require that the parties to a civil action reimburse a third party for its expenses in producing subpoenaed data.").

2. The lawyers for AT&T continued to resist the disclosure of the materials from the *Litton* and *MCI* litigations, ultimately pressing their arguments all the way to the Supreme Court. In *Litton*, AT&T sought a a writ of mandamus staying Judge Greene's order. When the issue reached the Supreme Court, the Chief Justice briefly granted a stay, but the Court vacated when it denied certiorari. *See* Am. Tel. & Tel. Co. v. United States, 439 U.S. 962 (1978).

In *MCI*, AT&T agreed to hand over the documents, but argued that the protective order in *MCI* should not be modified to permit disclosure of deposition transcripts and MCI's data analyses. The district judge handling the *MCI* litigation modified the protective order to permit the disclosure of all the material the government sought. The court of appeals affirmed:

... The exceptional considerations warranting the alteration of an agreed protective order exist in the present case. . . . [T]here is no showing that the government seeks to exploit *MCI v. ATT* in the prosecution of *USA v. ATT*. In addition, there is no showing that any claim of privilege was waived . . . . We are impressed with the wastefulness of requiring government counsel to duplicate the analyses and discovery already made.

Am. Tel. & Tel. Co. v. Grady, 594 F.2d 594, 597 (7th Cir. 1978). The Supreme Court again denied certiorari. 440 U.S. 971 (1979).

Subsequently, the Seventh Circuit thought that "exceptional considerations" was "an unfortunate choice of words," Wilk v. Am. Med. Ass'n, 635 F.2d 1295, 1300 (7th Cir. 1980), and modified the *Grady* test so that "where an appropriate modification of a protective order can place private litigants in a position they would otherwise reach only after repetition of another's discovery, such modification can be denied only where it would tangibly prejudice substantial rights of the party opposing modification," *id.* at 1299.

3. Is the *Wilk* reformulation a better test? Professor Marcus has worried that a near-automatic modification of protective orders in prior litigation will reduce parties' willingness to enter into such orders and "increases the risk that parties fearing repeated claims may fight discovery more vigorously." Richard L. Marcus, *Myth and Reality in Protective Order Litigation*, 69 CORNELL L. REV. 1, 43 (1983). His proposal would not allow a modification of a protective order "if all the parties to litigation number one oppose it, even though it may increase the nonparty's expenses" or, in the absence of "extraordinary circumstances," if the confidentiality orders were "entered in connection with settlements." *Id.* at 44.

4. The strongest cases denying access to discovery materials from prior litigation arise in the context of government investigations. In the leading case, *GAF Corp. v. Eastman Kodak Co.*, 415 F. Supp. 129 (S.D.N.Y. 1976), the Department of Justice sought to modify a protective order to obtain from GAF certain documents that GAF had received from Eastman Kodak in a private antitrust suit. The government's reason for wanting these documents was unclear, but it appeared that Eastman Kodak was the subject of an antitrust investigation. Judge Frankel began by citing dictum that "the discovery procedures 'are designed to be used solely for the purpose of obtaining information for use in the federal court action in which they are employed.'" *Id.* at 131 (quoting Beard v. New York Central Railroad Co., 20 F.R.D. 607, 609 (N.D. Ohio 1957)). He then observed that many documents had been given by consent and that "[t]here has been throughout an explicit understanding between the parties that discovery was being demanded and given solely for use in, and preparation of, this case." *Id.* Finally, he came to the heart of the matter: "The Government as investigator has awesome powers, not lightly to be enhanced or supplemented by implication. . . . [I]ts inquisitorial powers are great, and certainly as great as Congress has determined they should be." *Id.* at 132. The first two reasons suggest a very limited power to permit disclosure of materials obtained in prior litigation; the last suggests a power is limited only when the government is acting in an investigatory capacity.

GAF was subsequently limited by *United States v. GAF Corp.*, 596 F.2d 10 (2d Cir. 1979), in which the government again sought access to some of the same materials. In the meantime, its hand had been strengthened by legislation that broadened its power to issue "civil investigative demands" in antitrust cases. As a result, the Second Circuit held that the government was entitled to obtain the material that it sought — not by means of a modification of the discovery order but by means of a civil investigative demand. *Cf.* Martindell v. Int'l Tel. & Tel. Co., 594 F.2d 291 (2d Cir. 1979) (denying the government access to depositions given under a protective order when the government wished to use the testimony in a criminal investigation; leaving open the issue of the government's ability to seek the transcripts by means of a subpoena).

5.   Conversely, can a private litigant obtain files from the government's prior litigation? If the government is a civil litigant in the prior suit, and if no governmental privileges are at stake, materials in the government's possession should be accessible on the same terms as materials in a private litigant's possession. When the government acts as a prosecutor in the first case, however, different concerns apply. When the material is publicly available (such as transcripts or exhibits from a criminal trial), questions of access usually do not exist. *Cf.* MANUAL, *supra*, § 20.2 (suggesting that a criminal case should often take priority over a related civil case). But what happens when a party wants access to the government's investigatory files or the materials or testimony considered by a grand jury?

With respect to investigatory materials, a "law-enforcement privilege" may block disclosure in subsequent litigation unless a significant need for the material is demonstrated. *See* Black v. Sheraton Corp. of Am., 564 F.2d 531 (D.C. Cir. 1977); In re Dep't of Investigation of N.Y., 856 F.2d 481 (2d Cir. 1988); *cf. Johnson*, 222 F.R.D. at 50 (ordering the production of government data supplied under a protective order in a prior case when the law-enforcement privilege did not apply and no "benefit [to] criminals [or] detriment to law enforcement" could be shown from disclosure in the later case).

With respect to grand-jury materials, the matter is complicated. The workings of grand juries have historically been shrouded in secrecy. Today Federal Rule of Criminal Procedure 6(e)(2)(B) guards that secrecy, providing that government attorneys, grand jurors, and those assisting the investigation "must not disclose a matter occurring before the grand jury." Major exceptions include a prosecutor's disclosure to another grand jury; court-authorized disclosure "at the request of a defendant" seeking dismissal of an indictment "because of a matter that occurred before the grand jury"; court-authorized disclosure to appropriate state or foreign law-enforcement officials; and court-authorized disclosure "preliminarily to or in connection with a judicial proceeding." Fed. R. Crim. P. 6(e)(3)(C), -(E).

6.   The Supreme Court has considered the applicability of Rule 6(e) — and particularly the "judicial proceeding" exception presently located in Rule 6(e)(3)(E)(i) — in a series of cases in which a party in civil litigation has either sought access to grand-jury materials or claimed that the

government improperly disclosed grand-jury materials to government lawyers handling related civil litigation. *See, e.g.,* United States v. John Doe, Inc., I, 481 U.S. 102 (1987); United States v. Baggott, 463 U.S. 476 (1983); United States v. Sells Eng'g, Inc., 463 U.S. 418 (1983); Douglas Oil Co. of Cal. v. Petrol Stops Nw., 441 U.S. 211 (1979). The rules for disclosure of matters occurring before the grand jury seem to be: (1) Application for an order for access to grand jury information must be made before the court in which the grand jury sat, although this court may consult with the court in which the civil case is pending, *Douglas Oil*, 441 U.S. 211; (2) The disclosure must be "related fairly directly to some identifiable litigation, pending or anticipated"; "it is not enough to show that some litigation may emerge from the matter in which the material is to be used, or even that litigation is factually likely to emerge," *Baggott*, 463 U.S. at 480; (3) A government lawyer who handled the grand-jury investigation can use information obtained during these proceedings in a subsequent civil action as long as the lawyer is careful not to disclose the processes of the grand jury itself, *see John Doe*, 481 U.S. 102; and (4) Disclosure of information to any other person — whether to another government lawyer handling the civil litigation or to private litigants — can be made only upon a showing of "particularized need," *id.*; *Douglas Oil*, 441 U.S. 211.

Most of the attention in the Supreme Court and lower-court opinions has been directed at the issue of "particularized need." In *Douglas Oil*, 441 U.S. at 222, the Court suggested a three-part test:

> Parties seeking grand jury transcripts under Rule 6(e) must show that the material they seek is needed to avoid a possible injustice in another judicial proceeding, that the need for disclosure is greater than the need for continued secrecy, and that their request is structured to cover only material so needed. . . . [I]n considering the effects of disclosure on grand jury proceedings, the courts must consider not only the immediate effects upon a particular grand jury, but also the possible effect upon the functioning of future grand juries.

The burden of establishing "particularized need" rests on the person seeking disclosure. *Id.* at 223; *see Sells Engineering*, 463 U.S. at 443 (requiring "strong showing of particularized need"). It is generally easier for government attorneys to show "particularized need" than for private litigants to do so. *Sells Engineering*, 463 U.S. at 445; *John Doe*, 481 U.S. at 112-13. But this is not always true; a court can "take into account any alternative discovery tools available by statute or regulation to the agency seeking disclosure." *Sells Engineering*, 463 U.S. at 445; *John Doe*, 481 U.S. at 113. *John Doe* also emphasized that cost savings and reduced delay in the second litigation are valid considerations in permitting disclosure. 481 U.S. at 115-16; *see* In re Grand Jury Investigation, 55 F.3d 350, 354 (8th Cir. 1995) (same).

7. According to the wording of Rule 6(e), witnesses themselves can usually disclose their own grand-jury testimony. *Cf.* Butterworth v. Smith, 494 U.S. 624 (1990) (stating that witnesses have a First Amendment right to disclose their testimony after state grand-jury proceedings concluded).

In *Pillsbury Co. v. Conboy*, 459 U.S. 248 (1983), corporate officials had testified before a grand jury regarding an alleged price-fixing scheme. Their testimony, for which they were willing to invoke a Fifth Amendment privilege against self-incrimination, had been compelled by a grant of "use immunity." In related civil cases, the same officials continued to assert their Fifth Amendment privileges. As a result, the multidistrict judge found that the plaintiffs had demonstrated a "particularized need" for the grand-jury testimony. The plaintiffs then deposed the witnesses, reading back to them their grand-jury testimony in question form. After one of the witnesses again invoked his Fifth Amendment privilege, the district judge found him in contempt. *Conboy* held that the witness could not be compelled to give testimony. *Conboy* also noted in passing that "[t]he propriety of the District Court's release of grand jury materials to the civil parties is not before the Court." 459 U.S. at 250 n.1.

8. The Supreme Court's decisions deal with the discovery of testimony and other materials prepared specifically for a grand-jury proceeding. Should pre-existing documents or ESI produced to a grand jury be subject to the same showing of "particularized need"? In *In re Grand Jury Proceedings*, 851 F.2d 860, 863 (6th Cir. 1988), the court surveyed the positions of the federal courts, and found four answers: (1) A per se rule that such material is never "a matter occurring before the grand jury," and are always subject to disclosure; (2) An opposite per se rule that this material is "a matter occurring before the grand jury," and are subject to disclosure only on a showing of "particularized need"; (3) A rule that such documents are subject to disclosure unless the purpose of the discovery request is to find out what transpired before the grand jury; and (4) An individualized determination that determines if the effect (rather than the purpose) of disclosure will be to reveal grand jury secrecy. *Grand Jury Proceedings*, 851 F.2d at 866-67. It then adopted a fifth approach:

> The general rule . . . must be that confidential documentary information not otherwise public obtained by the grand jury by coercive means is presumed to be "[a matter] occurring before the grand jury" just as much as testimony before the grand jury. The moving party may seek to rebut that presumption by showing that the information is public or was not obtained through coercive means or that disclosure would be otherwise available by civil discovery and would not reveal the nature, scope, or direction of the grand jury inquiry, but it must bear the burden of making that showing, just as it bears the burden of showing that there is a "particularized need."

See also United States v. Rutherford, 509 F.3d 791, 795 (6th Cir. 2007).

9. The concern for disclosing documents and ESI from a prior case is most acute in cases in which the material in the first litigation was disclosed in secrecy. When secrecy does not exist, lawyers representing similar interests often collaborate and share information, and sometimes establish networks to share information. *See supra* p. 334 (discussing coordination of related cases). With some types of litigation, specialized media also cover developments in individual cases. When market forces

provide a free flow of information, should the judge ever step in to require disclosure in subsequent litigation?

v. Disclosure and Discovery of Electronically Stored Information

Electronically stored information is pervasive in modern life and in modern litigation. In prior subsections, we examined techniques that can be employed to make the disclosure and discovery of ESI more efficient. There we treated ESI as if its disclosure and discovery involved the same concerns as those presented by paper documents. In reality, however, ESI presents unique disclosure-and-discovery issues that a judge must manage. Indeed, in 2006, following attempts by courts to mold this new form of information into existing disclosure-and-discovery categories, the Federal Rules of Civil Procedure adopted specific rules regarding ESI. *See* Fed. R. Civ. P. 26(b)(2)(B), 34(a)(1)(A), 34(b)(2)(D)-(E), 37(e), 45(d)(1).

The first case, which was decided before the present ESI amendments, was enormously influential in shaping these amendments and continues to exercise influence today. The subsequent two cases address related ESI issues that courts in complex litigation frequently face.

Zubulake v. UBS Warburg LLC

217 F.R.D. 309 (S.D.N.Y. 2003)

■ SCHEINDLIN, District Judge.

The world was a far different place in 1849, when Henry David Thoreau opined (in an admittedly broader context) that "[t]he process of discovery is very simple." That hopeful maxim has given way to rapid technological advances, requiring new solutions to old problems. The issue presented here is one such problem, recast in light of current technology: To what extent is inaccessible electronic data discoverable, and who should pay for its production?

I. INTRODUCTION

The Supreme Court recently reiterated that our "simplified notice pleading standard relies on liberal discovery rules and summary judgment motions to define disputed facts and issues and to dispose of unmeritorious claims." Thus, it is now beyond dispute that "[b]road discovery is a cornerstone of the litigation process contemplated by the Federal Rules of Civil Procedure." The Rules contemplate a minimal burden to bringing a claim; that claim is then fleshed out through vigorous and expansive discovery.

In one context, however, the reliance on broad discovery has hit a roadblock. As individuals and corporations increasingly do business electronically — using computers to create and store documents, make deals, and exchange e-mails — the universe of discoverable material has expanded exponentially. The more information there is to discover, the more expensive it is to discover all the relevant information until, in the end, "discovery is not just about uncovering the truth, but also about how much of the truth the parties can afford to disinter."

This case provides a textbook example of the difficulty of balancing the competing needs of broad discovery and manageable costs. Laura Zubulake is suing UBS Warburg LLC, UBS Warburg, and UBS AG (collectively, "UBS" or the "Firm") under Federal, State and City law for gender discrimination and illegal retaliation. Zubulake's case is certainly not frivolous[8] and if she prevails, her damages may be substantial. She contends that key evidence is located in various e-mails exchanged among UBS employees that now exist only on backup tapes and perhaps other archived media. According to UBS, restoring those e-mails would cost approximately $175,000.00, exclusive of attorney time in reviewing the e-mails. Zubulake now moves for an order compelling UBS to produce those e-mails at its expense.

II. BACKGROUND

A. *Zubulake's Lawsuit*

UBS hired Zubulake on August 23, 1999, as a director and senior salesperson on its U.S. Asian Equities Sales Desk (the "Desk"), where she reported to Dominic Vail, the Desk's manager. At the time she was hired, Zubulake was told that she would be considered for Vail's position if and when it became vacant.

In December 2000, Vail indeed left his position to move to the Firm's London office. But Zubulake was not considered for his position, and the Firm instead hired Matthew Chapin as director of the Desk. Zubulake alleges that from the outset Chapin treated her differently than the other members of the Desk, all of whom were male. . . .

Zubulake ultimately responded by filing a Charge of (gender) Discrimination with the EEOC on August 16, 2001. On October 9, 2001, Zubulake was fired with two weeks' notice. . . .

B. *The Discovery Dispute*

Discovery in this action commenced on or about June 3, 2002, when Zubulake served UBS with her first document request. At issue here is request number twenty-eight, for "[a]ll documents concerning any communication by or between UBS employees concerning Plaintiff." The term document in Zubulake's request "includ[es], without limitation,

---

8. Indeed, Zubulake has already produced a sort of "smoking gun": an e-mail suggesting that she be fired "ASAP" after her EEOC charge was filed, in part so that she would not be eligible for year-end bonuses.

electronic or computerized data compilations." On July 8, 2002, UBS responded by producing approximately 350 pages of documents, including approximately 100 pages of e-mails. UBS also objected to a substantial portion of Zubulake's requests. . . .

. . . UBS never searched for responsive e-mails on any of its backup tapes. To the contrary, UBS informed Zubulake that the cost of producing e-mails on backup tapes would be prohibitive (estimated at the time at approximately $300,000.00).

Zubulake . . . objected to UBS's nonproduction. In fact, Zubulake *knew* that there were additional responsive e-mails that UBS had failed to produce because she herself had produced approximately 450 pages of e-mail correspondence. Clearly, numerous responsive e-mails had been created and deleted at UBS, and Zubulake wanted them. . . .

C. *UBS's E-Mail Backup System*

In the first instance, the parties agree that e-mail was an important means of communication at UBS during the relevant time period. Each salesperson, including the salespeople on the Desk, received approximately 200 e-mails each day. Given this volume, and because Securities and Exchange Commission regulations require it, UBS implemented extensive e-mail backup and preservation protocols. In particular, e-mails were backed up in two distinct ways: on backup tapes and on optical disks.

1. *Backup Tape Storage*

UBS employees used a program called HP OpenMail, manufactured by Hewlett-Packard, for all work-related e-mail communications. With limited exceptions, *all* e-mails sent or received by *any* UBS employee are stored onto backup tapes. To do so, UBS employs a program called Veritas NetBackup, which creates a "snapshot" of all e-mails that exist on a given server at the time the backup is taken. Except for scheduling the backups and physically inserting the tapes into the machines, the backup process is entirely automated. . . .

Once e-mails have been stored onto backup tapes, the restoration process is lengthy. Each backup tape routinely takes approximately five days to restore, although resort to an outside vendor would speed up the process (at greatly enhanced costs, of course). . . .

Fortunately, NetBackup also created indexes of each backup tape. Thus, [UBS] was able to search through the tapes from the relevant time period and determine that the e-mail files responsive to Zubulake's requests are contained on a total of ninety-four backup tapes.

2. *Optical Disk Storage*

In addition to the e-mail backup tapes, UBS also stored certain e-mails on optical disks. For certain "registered traders," probably including the members of the Desk, a copy of *all* e-mails sent to or received from outside sources (i.e., e-mails from a "registered trader" at UBS to someone at another entity, or vice versa) was simultaneously written onto a series of optical disks. Internal e-mails, however, were not stored on this system.

UBS has retained each optical disk used since the system was put into place in mid-1998. Moreover, the optical disks are neither erasable nor rewritable. Thus, UBS has *every* e-mail sent or received by registered traders (except internal e-mails) during the period of Zubulake's employment, even if the e-mail was deleted instantaneously on that trader's system.

The optical disks are easily searchable using a program called Tumbleweed. Using Tumbleweed, a user can simply log into the system with the proper credentials and create a plain language search. . . . For example, UBS personnel could easily run a search for e-mails containing the words "Laura" or "Zubulake" that were sent or received by Chapin [or certain other supervisors at UBS]. . . .

IV. DISCUSSION

A. *Should Discovery of UBS's Electronic Data Be Permitted?*

Under Rule 34, . . . "[e]lectronic documents are no less subject to disclosure than paper records." This is true not only of electronic documents that are currently in use, but also of documents that may have been deleted and now reside only on backup disks.

That being so, Zubulake is entitled to discovery of the requested e-mails so long as they are relevant to her claims, which they clearly are. As noted, e-mail constituted a substantial means of communication among UBS employees. To that end, UBS has already produced approximately 100 pages of e-mails, the contents of which are unquestionably relevant.

Nonetheless, UBS argues that Zubulake is not entitled to any further discovery because it already produced all responsive documents, to wit, the 100 pages of e-mails. This argument is unpersuasive for two reasons. First, because of the way that UBS backs up its e-mail files, it clearly could not have searched all of its e-mails without restoring the ninety-four backup tapes (which UBS admits that it has not done). UBS therefore cannot represent that it has produced all responsive e-mails. Second, Zubulake herself has produced over 450 pages of relevant e-mails, including e-mails that would have been responsive to her discovery requests but were never produced by UBS. These two facts strongly suggest that there are e-mails that Zubulake has not received that reside on UBS's backup media.

B. *Should Cost-Shifting Be Considered?*

Because it apparently recognizes that Zubulake is entitled to the requested discovery, UBS expends most of its efforts urging the court to shift the cost of production to "protect [it] . . . from undue burden or expense." Faced with similar applications, courts generally engage in some sort of cost-shifting analysis . . . .

The first question, however, is whether cost-shifting must be considered in every case involving the discovery of electronic data, which — in today's world — includes virtually all cases. In light of the accepted principle, stated above, that electronic evidence is no less discoverable than paper evidence, the answer is, "No." The Supreme Court has instructed that "the presumption is that the responding party must bear the expense of complying with discovery requests. . . ." Any principled approach to electronic evidence must respect this presumption.

Courts must remember that cost-shifting may effectively end discovery, especially when private parties are engaged in litigation with large corporations. As large companies increasingly move to entirely paper-free environments, the frequent use of cost-shifting will have the effect of crippling discovery in discrimination and retaliation cases. This will both undermine the "strong public policy favor[ing] resolving disputes on their merits," and may ultimately deter the filing of potentially meritorious claims.

Thus, cost-shifting should be considered *only* when electronic discovery imposes an "undue burden or expense" on the responding party. [Fed. R. Civ. P. 26(c).] The burden or expense of discovery is, in turn, "undue" when it "outweighs its likely benefit, taking into account the needs of the case, the amount in controversy, the parties' resources, the importance of the issues at stake in the litigation, and the importance of the proposed discovery in resolving the issues." [Fed. R. Civ. P. 26(b)(2)(iii).]*

Many courts have automatically assumed that an undue burden or expense may arise simply because electronic evidence is involved. This makes no sense. Electronic evidence is frequently cheaper and easier to produce than paper evidence because it can be searched automatically, key words can be run for privilege checks, and the production can be made in electronic form obviating the need for mass photocopying.

In fact, whether production of documents is unduly burdensome or expensive turns primarily on whether it is kept in an *accessible or inaccessible* format (a distinction that corresponds closely to the expense of production). In the world of paper documents, for example, a document is accessible if it is readily available in a usable format and reasonably indexed. . . . [I]n the world of electronic data, thanks to search engines, any data that is retained in a machine readable format is typically accessible.

Whether electronic data is accessible or inaccessible turns largely on the media on which it is stored. . . .

The case at bar is a perfect illustration of the range of accessibility of electronic data. As explained above, UBS maintains e-mail files in three

---

*   The 2006 ESI amendments and the 2007 restyling amendments to the Federal Rules of Civil Procedure slightly altered this language and moved it to a newly created subsection, Fed. R. Civ. P. 26(b)(2)(C)(iii). — ED.

forms: (1) active user e-mail files; (2) archived e-mails on optical disks; and (3) backup data stored on tapes. The active (HP OpenMail) data is obviously the most accessible: it is online data that resides on an active server, and can be accessed immediately. The optical disk (Tumbleweed) data is only slightly less accessible . . . . The e-mails are on optical disks that need to be located and read with the correct hardware, but the system is configured to make searching the optical disks simple and automated once they are located. For these sources of e-mails — active mail files and e-mails stored on optical disks — it would be wholly inappropriate to even consider cost-shifting. UBS maintains the data in an accessible and usable format, and can respond to Zubulake's request cheaply and quickly. Like most typical discovery requests, therefore, the producing party should bear the cost of production.

E-mails stored on backup tapes (via NetBackup), however, are an entirely different matter. Although UBS has already identified the ninety-four potentially responsive backup tapes, those tapes are not currently accessible. In order to search the tapes for responsive e-mails, UBS would have to engage in the costly and time-consuming process detailed above. It is therefore appropriate to *consider* cost shifting.

C. *What Is the Proper Cost-Shifting Analysis?*

. . .

In order to maintain the presumption that the responding party pays, the cost-shifting analysis must be neutral; close calls should be resolved in favor of the presumption. . . .

1. *The* Rowe *Test Is Incomplete*

[The court discussed and critiqued a leading case on shifting costs for the production of electronic data, *Rowe Entertainment, Inc. v. William Morris Agency, Inc.*, 205 F.R.D. 421 (S.D.N.Y. 2002). *Rowe* had created an eight-factor test to determine whether to shift costs.]

Set forth below is a new seven-factor test based on the modifications to *Rowe* discussed [above].

1. The extent to which the request is specifically tailored to discover relevant information;

2. The availability of such information from other sources;

3. The total cost of production, compared to the amount in controversy;

4. The total cost of production, compared to the resources available to each party;

5. The relative ability of each party to control costs and its incentive to do so;

6. The importance of the issues at stake in the litigation; and

7. The relative benefits to the parties of obtaining the information.

2. *The Seven Factors Should Not Be Weighted Equally*

Whenever a court applies a multi-factor test, there is a temptation to treat the factors as a check-list, resolving the issue in favor of whichever column has the most checks. But "we do not just add up the factors." When evaluating cost-shifting, the central question must be, does the request impose an "undue burden or expense" on the responding party? Put another way, "how important is the sought-after evidence in comparison to the cost of production?" The seven-factor test articulated above provide[s] some guidance in answering this question, but the test cannot be mechanically applied at the risk of losing sight of its purpose.

Weighting the factors in descending order of importance may solve the problem and avoid a mechanistic application of the test. The first two factors — comprising the marginal utility test — are the most important. These factors include: (1) The extent to which the request is specifically tailored to discover relevant information and (2) the availability of such information from other sources. . . .

The second group of factors addresses cost issues: "How expensive will this production be?" and, "Who can handle that expense?" These factors include: (3) the total cost of production compared to the amount in controversy, (4) the total cost of production compared to the resources available to each party and (5) the relative ability of each party to control costs and its incentive to do so. The third "group" — (6) the importance of the litigation itself — stands alone, and . . . will only rarely come into play. But where it does, this factor has the potential to predominate over the others. Collectively, the first three groups correspond to the three explicit considerations of Rule [26(b)(2)(C)(iii)]. Finally, the last factor — (7) the relative benefits of production as between the requesting and producing parties — is the least important because it is fair to presume that the response to a discovery request generally benefits the requesting party. But in the unusual case where production will also provide a tangible or strategic benefit to the responding party, that fact may weigh *against* shifting costs.

D. *A Factual Basis Is Required to Support the Analysis*

Courts applying *Rowe* have uniformly favored cost-shifting largely because of assumptions made concerning the likelihood that relevant information will be found. . . . But such proof will rarely exist in advance of obtaining the requested discovery. . . .

Requiring the responding party to restore and produce responsive documents from a small sample of backup tapes will inform the cost-shifting analysis laid out above. When based on an actual sample, the marginal utility test will not be an exercise in speculation — there will be tangible evidence of what the backup tapes may have to offer. There will also be tangible evidence of the time and cost required to restore the backup tapes, which in turn will inform the second group of cost-shifting factors. Thus, by requiring a sample restoration of backup tapes, the entire cost-shifting analysis can be grounded in fact rather than guesswork.

[V.] CONCLUSION AND ORDER

. . .

Accordingly, UBS is ordered to produce *all* responsive e-mails that exist on its optical disks or on its active servers (i.e., in HP OpenMail files) at its own expense. UBS is also ordered to produce, at its expense, responsive e-mails from any *five* backups tapes selected *by Zubulake*. UBS should then prepare an affidavit detailing the results of its search, as well as the time and money spent. After reviewing the contents of the backup tapes and UBS's certification, the Court will conduct the appropriate cost-shifting analysis. . . .

Notes

1. In another part of its opinion, the court mentioned that UBS had reported profits of $716 million in the third quarter of 2002, and that the case, if it had merit, was "potentially worth millions of dollars." Do these facts affect your judgment about whether the court decided the issue of electronic discovery correctly?

2. The sampling that *Zubulake* ordered uncovered about 600 e-mails mentioning the plaintiff, of which the court regarded 68 as relevant. Based on the sample, UBS determined that the cost of producing all the requested e-mails was $273,649.39 — $165,954.67 to restore and search the tapes and $107,694.72 in attorney and paralegal review costs. Applying its seven-factor test, the court thought that the first four factors "slightly" cut against cost-shifting, the fifth and sixth were neutral, and the seventh favored cost-shifting. Recognizing that "the precise allocation is a matter of judgment and fairness rather than a mathematical consequence of the seven factors," the judge ordered UBS to pay 75% of the cost of restoring and searching the tapes, and 100% of its attorney and paralegal review costs. Zubulake v. UBS Warburg LLC, 216 F.R.D. 280, 289 (S.D.N.Y. 2003). In the final chapter of the *Zubulake* saga, the defendant's employees willfully deleted relevant e-mails after a litigation hold had been put in place, and other e-mail correspondence was produced to the plaintiff tardily. Among other sanctions, the court stated that it would inform the jury of the missing e-mails and allow the jury to draw a negative inference from the defendant's conduct, and would not allow the defendant to use tardily produced e-mails at trial. Zubulake v. UBS, 229 F.R.D. 422 (S.D.N.Y. 2004).

3. The figures involved in the *Zubulake* discovery — something in the hundreds of thousands of dollars — are not unique. *Zubulake* was hardly a complex case, nor did it involve massive quantities of ESI or peculiar

problems of proprietary software or incompatibility among computer systems that can arise. You can perhaps now appreciate why ESI presents significant problems in complex litigation, and why the *Manual for Complex Litigation* encourages a judge to address issues of ESI early in the case and to "consider how to minimize and allocate the costs of production." MANUAL FOR COMPLEX LITIGATION, FOURTH § 11.446 (2004).

Perhaps self-evidently, the *Manual* observes that "[n]arrowing the overall scope of electronic discovery is the most effective method of reducing costs." *Id.* Doing so, however, comes at the price of ignoring potentially relevant information, and gives an incentive to parties to store damaging information in inaccessible formats. On the other hand, allowing unlimited access to ESI provides some parties with a tool for bludgeoning opposing parties that have significant amounts of ESI into unwarranted settlements. *Zubulake*'s idea of allowing discovery but shifting some or all of the costs onto the party seeking the production of ESI is a pragmatic, intermediate position that puts the decision about whether the ESI is worth its cost into the hands of the party that wants the information. Is it a sensible solution?

4. *Zubulake* carved its solution out of Rule 26(b)(2)'s concept of proportionality and Rule 26(c)'s power to grant protective orders to prevent "undue burden or expense." Soon afterwards, in 2006, the Federal Rules adopted amendments designed specifically for ESI. The principal ESI provision, Fed. R. Civ. P. 26(b)(2)(B), more or less followed *Zubulake*'s lead. It distinguished between ESI that is and is not "reasonably accessible because of undue burden or cost." When a party from whom production is sought identifies the ESI as not reasonably accessible, the ESI need not be provided; but if the party seeking the ESI moves to compel production, the party from whom production is sought must prove inaccessibility. Even when that showing is made, the court can order production "if the requesting party shows good cause, considering the limitations of Rule 26(b)(2)(C)," which bars cumulative, tardy, or disproportional discovery. In particular, Rule 26(b)(2)(C)(iii) bars discovery when "the burden or expense of the proposed discovery outweighs its likely benefit, considering the needs of the case, the amount in controversy, the parties' resources, the importance of the issues at stake in the action, and the importance of the discovery in resolving the issues." If the court orders production, "[t]he court may specify conditions for the discovery" — presumably including cost-shifting.

The Committee Note to Rule 26(b)(2)(B) did not define the terms "reasonably accessible" or "undue burden or cost." But the Note suggests that, in making the determination of "good cause," a court may consider:

(1) the specificity of the discovery request; (2) the quantity of information available from other and more easily accessed sources; (3) the failure to produce relevant information that seems likely to have existed but is no longer available on more easily accessed sources; (4) the likelihood of finding relevant, responsive information that cannot be obtained from other, more easily accessed sources; (5) predictions as to the importance and usefulness of the further information; (6) the

importance of the issues at stake in the litigation; and (7) the parties' resources.

The Note also acknowledges that one of the conditions that a court can impose is "payment by the requesting party of part or all of the reasonable costs of obtaining information from sources that are not reasonably accessible." But the Note does not describe the circumstances under which cost-shifting is appropriate.

Courts have tended to determine the meaning of "reasonably accessible because of undue burden or cost" as *Zubulake* did — by examining the storage medium and the ease with which documents can be retrieved in that medium. They have also tended not to order cost-shifting when the information is reasonably accessible, and to employ the seven *Zubulake* factors when deciding whether to allow cost-shifting if the ESI is not reasonably accessible. *See, e.g.*, Proctor & Gamble Co. v. S.C. Johnson & Son, Inc., 2009 WL 440543 (E.D. Tex. Feb. 19, 2009); W.E. Aubuchon Co. v. BeneFirst, LLC, 245 F.R.D. 38 (D. Mass. 2007); OpenTV v. Liberate Techs., 219 F.R.D. 474 (N.D. Cal. 2003).

5.   Isn't all of this too complicated and redundant? First, a court must determine if there is "undue burden or cost." Next, the court must decide if there is "good cause," which is determined with reference to whether "the burden or expense of the proposed discovery outweighs its likely benefit"(is this the same thing as whether the discovery is an "undue burden or cost"?) — and then supplements this inquiry with the five factors listed in Rule 26(b)(2)(C) and the seven, somewhat overlapping factors listed in the Committee Note. Finally, the court must determine whether to shift costs — an inquiry decided by *Zubulake*'s seven factors, which overlap significantly with the seven factors that the Note recommended using to determine "good cause." If ESI is not accessible because of *undue* burden or cost, is there ever good cause to permit its discovery? Is there a better way to write this rule to accommodate the various interests?

6.   The next three cases raise other issues that are emerging in ESI disclosure and discovery.

WILLIAM A. GROSS CONSTRUCTION ASSOCIATES, INC. V. AMERICAN MANUFACTURERS MUTUAL INSURANCE CO.

256 F.R.D. 134 (S.D.N.Y. 2009)

■ PECK, United States Magistrate Judge.

This Opinion should serve as a wake-up call to the Bar in this District about the need for careful thought, quality control, testing, and cooperation with opposing counsel in designing search terms or "keywords" to be used to produce emails or other electronically stored information ("ESI"). While this message has appeared in several cases from outside this Circuit, it appears that the message has not reached many members of our Bar.

FACTS

This case involves a multi-million dollar dispute over alleged defects and delay in the construction of the Bronx County Hall of Justice, also known as the Bronx Criminal Court Complex. The Dormitory Authority of the State of New York ("DASNY") was the "owner" of the project. Non-party Hill International is DASNY's current construction manager, and DASNY has agreed to produce Hill's project-related documents and ESI to the other parties to this suit. The issue before the Court is the production of Hill's emails, stored on its server at its New Jersey office, and how to separate project-related emails from Hill's unrelated emails.

DASNY's proposed search terms included "DASNY," "Dormitory Authority," and "Authority," and the names of the other parties to the action. DASNY also added "Court! in connection with Bronx," "Hall of Justice," and "Bronx but not Zoo" (since Hill worked on an unrelated project involving the Bronx Zoo). The other parties requested the use of thousands of additional search terms, emphasizing the construction issues they were involved in, such as "sidewalk," "change order," "driveway," "access," "alarm," "budget," "build," "claim," "delay," "elevator," "electrical" — you get the picture. DASNY correctly pointed out that use of such extensive keywords would require production of the entire Hill email database, since Hill's business is construction management, and those terms would be used for any construction project.

Hill's only contribution to the discussion was to agree that DASNY's search terms were probably too narrow but the other parties' terms were overbroad, and that Hill did not want to produce emails that did not relate to the Bronx Courthouse project. . . . [W]hile Hill was in the best position to explain to the parties and the Court what nomenclature its employees used in emails, Hill did not do so — perhaps because, as a non-party, it wanted to have as little involvement in the case as possible.

That left the Court in the uncomfortable position of having to craft a keyword search methodology for the parties, without adequate information from the parties (and Hill). The Court ruled at yesterday's conference that in addition to DASNY's proposed terms (including variations on and abbreviations of party names), the search should also include the names of the parties' personnel involved in the Bronx Courthouse construction.

DISCUSSION

This case is just the latest example of lawyers designing keyword searches in the dark, by the seat of the pants, without adequate (indeed, here, apparently without any) discussion with those who wrote the emails. Prior decisions from Magistrate Judges . . . have warned counsel of this problem, but the message has not gotten through to the Bar in this District. As Magistrate Judge Paul Grimm has stated:

> While keyword searches have long been recognized as appropriate and helpful for ESI search and retrieval, there are [well-known]

limitations and risks associated with them, and proper selection and implementation obviously involves technical, if not scientific knowledge. . . .

Selection of the appropriate search and information retrieval technique requires careful advance planning by persons qualified to design effective search methodology. The implementation of the methodology selected should be tested for quality assurance; and the party selecting the methodology must be prepared to explain the rationale for the method chosen to the court, demonstrate that it is appropriate for the task, and show that it was properly implemented.

Victor Stanley, Inc. v. Creative Pipe, Inc., 250 F.R.D. 251, 260, 262 (D. Md. 2008).

Magistrate Judge Facciola has taken the warning even further:

Whether search terms or "keywords" will yield the information sought is a complicated question involving the interplay, at least, of the sciences of computer technology, statistics and linguistics. Given this complexity, for lawyers and judges to dare opine that a certain search term or terms would be more likely to produce information than the terms that were used is truly to go where angels fear to tread. This topic is clearly beyond the ken of a layman and requires that any such conclusion be based on evidence that, for example, meets the criteria of Rule 702 of the Federal Rules of Evidence.

United States v. O'Keefe, 537 F. Supp. 2d 14, 24 (D.D.C. 2008);[3] see also, e.g., In re Seroquel Prods. Liab. Litig., 244 F.R.D. 650, 662 (M.D. Fla. 2007) ("[W]hile key word searching is a recognized method to winnow relevant documents from large repositories, use of this technique must be a cooperative and informed process. . . . Common sense dictates that sampling and other quality assurance techniques must be employed to meet requirements of completeness.").

Of course, the best solution in the entire area of electronic discovery is cooperation among counsel. . . .

CONCLUSION

. . . [W]here counsel are using keyword searches for retrieval of ESI, they at a minimum must carefully craft the appropriate keywords, with input from the ESI's custodians as to the words and abbreviations they use, and the proposed methodology must be quality control tested to assure accuracy in retrieval and elimination of "false positives." It is time that the Bar — even those lawyers who did not come of age in the computer era — understand this.

---

3. This Court need not now decide whether expert testimony is required; what is required is something other than a lawyer's guesses, without client input, and without any quality control testing to see if the search terms produce reasonably all the responsive ESI and limited "false positives."

AGUILAR V. IMMIGRATION AND CUSTOMS ENFORCEMENT DIVISION

255 F.R.D. 350 (S.D.N.Y. 2008)

■ MAAS, United States Magistrate Judge.

This civil rights class action is brought by more than thirty Latino plaintiffs ("Plaintiffs") who contend that the Immigration and Customs Enforcement Division of the United States Department of Homeland Security ("ICE") and certain of its employees (collectively, the "Defendants") subjected them to unlawful searches of their homes in violation of the Fourth Amendment. Because counsel failed to discuss the form of production for electronic documents early in the case, the Court now must resolve several issues concerning the discoverability of metadata. For the reasons set forth below, the Plaintiffs' application to compel the production of metadata is granted in part and denied in part.

I. RELEVANT FACTS

[The complaint alleged that ICE agents entered and searched the homes of Latinos without having previously obtained a search warrant or consent, in violation of the Fourth Amendment.] Pursuant to *Bivens v. Six Unknown Named Agents of Federal Bureau of Narcotics*, 403 U.S. 388 (1971), the Plaintiffs seek the damages they allegedly suffered as a result of these unconstitutional searches. The Plaintiffs also seek a permanent injunction barring ICE from continuing to conduct its searches in this manner. . . .

On December 7, 2007, the Defendants moved . . . to dismiss the claim for injunctive relief in the first amended complaint. The Defendants also sought a stay of discovery while the motion to dismiss was pending, except to the extent that the discovery related to the *Bivens* claims. Thereafter, at a discovery conference on January 15, 2008, Judge Koeltl urged the parties to resolve which elements of discovery should proceed and which should be stayed while the motion to dismiss the injunctive claim was pending. . . . At or about this time, the Defendants began to harvest the relevant documents from ICE employees.

During a Rule 26(f) discovery conference on January 18, 2008, the parties agreed that discovery would proceed with regard to the *Bivens* claims only . . . .

On February 15, 2008, the Plaintiffs served their first request for the production of documents. Their request did not specify the form in which they sought to have electronically stored information ("ESI") produced, nor did it mention the production of metadata.

The subject of metadata first arose on March 18, 2008, when the Plaintiffs apparently mentioned it "in passing." By this time, the Defendants had almost completed their document collection efforts.

The first formal discussion among the parties regarding metadata occurred on May 22, 2008, during a conference call to discuss the production of ESI. During the call (and by means of a subsequent letter), the Plaintiffs requested (1) that emails and electronic documents be produced in Tagged Imaged File Format ("TIFF") with a corresponding load file containing metadata fields and extracted text,[3] and (2) that spreadsheets and databases be produced in native format.[4] As noted above, by this date, the Defendants had already substantially completed their document collection efforts.

. . . On July 14, 2008, the Defendants objected, on relevance and burden grounds, to producing electronic documents in the form requested by the Plaintiffs, proposing instead to produce their ESI in the form of text-searchable PDF documents. To the extent that the Plaintiffs sought metadata, the Defendants stated that they would provide it if the Plaintiffs were able to demonstrate that the metadata associated with a particular document was relevant to their claims.

During a discovery conference on July 17, 2008, I directed counsel and their ESI experts to meet and confer in a renewed attempt to resolve their disputes regarding metadata. They did so on July 25 and 30, 2008, but were unable to resolve their differences. . . . I also scheduled a follow-up session with counsel and their ESI experts to be held in my courtroom [on September 8, 2008]. . . .

Although no formal motion has been made, the Plaintiffs' letters amount to a motion to compel the Defendants' production of (1) responsive emails and electronic documents (such as Word, PowerPoint, and Excel documents) in TIFF format with corresponding metadata, and (2) meaningful information about the metadata fields of ICE's hierarchical databases so that the Plaintiffs can determine which database metadata they should request.

II. DISCUSSION

A. *Metadata and Discovery*

"As a general rule of thumb, the more interactive the application, the more important the metadata is to understanding the application's output." Thus, while metadata may add little to one's comprehension of a word processing document, it is often critical to understanding a database application. "A spreadsheet application lies somewhere in the middle" and

---

3. TIFF is a static image format similar to a PDF that creates a mirror image of the electronic document.

A load file is a "file that relates to a set of scanned images or electronically processed files, and indicates where individual pages or files belong together as documents, to include attachments, and where each document begins and ends," and may also include "data relevant to the individual documents, such as metadata, coded data, text, and the like."

4. Native format is the "default format of a file," access to which is "typically provided through the software program on which it was created."

the need for its metadata depends upon the complexity and purpose of the spreadsheet. To understand why the importance of metadata varies, it is first necessary to explain what it is and distinguish among its principal forms.

1. *Types of Metadata*

Metadata, frequently referred to as "data about data," is electronically-stored evidence that describes the "history, tracking, or management of an electronic document." It includes the "hidden text, formatting codes, formulae, and other information associated" with an electronic document. Although metadata often is lumped into one generic category, there are at least several distinct types, including substantive (or application) metadata, system metadata, and embedded metadata.

a. *Substantive Metadata*

Substantive metadata, also known as application metadata, is "created as a function of the application software used to create the document or file" and reflects substantive changes made by the user. This category of metadata reflects modifications to a document, such as prior edits or editorial comments, and includes data that instructs the computer how to display the fonts and spacing in a document. Substantive metadata is embedded in the document it describes and remains with the document when it is moved or copied. A working group in the District of Maryland has concluded that substantive metadata "need not be routinely produced" unless the requesting party shows good cause.

b. *System Metadata*

System metadata "reflects information created by the user or by the organization's information management system." This data may not be embedded within the file it describes, but can usually be easily retrieved from whatever operating system is in use. Examples of system metadata include data concerning "the author, date and time of creation, and the date a document was modified." Courts have commented that most system (and substantive) metadata lacks evidentiary value because it is not relevant. System metadata is relevant, however, if the authenticity of a document is questioned or if establishing "who received what information and when" is important to the claims or defenses of a party. This type of metadata also makes electronic documents more functional because it significantly improves a party's ability to access, search, and sort large numbers of documents efficiently.

c. *Embedded Metadata*

Embedded metadata consists of "text, numbers, content, data, or other information that is directly or indirectly inputted into a [n]ative [f]ile by a user and which is not typically visible to the user viewing the output display" of the native file. Examples include spreadsheet formulas, hidden columns, externally or internally linked files (such as sound files), hyperlinks, references and fields, and database information. This type of metadata is often crucial to understanding an electronic document. For instance, a complicated spreadsheet may be difficult to comprehend without the ability to view the formulas underlying the output in each cell. For this reason, the District of Maryland working group concluded that embedded metadata is "generally discoverable" and "should be produced as a matter of course."

2. *Discovery of Metadata*

a. *Federal Rules*

Metadata is not addressed directly in the Federal Rules of Civil Procedure but is subject to the general rules of discovery. Metadata thus is discoverable if it is relevant to the claim or defense of any party and is not privileged. Fed. R. Civ. P. 26(b)(1). Additionally, "[f]or good cause, the court may order discovery of any matter [including metadata] relevant to the subject matter involved in the action." . . . The discovery of metadata is also subject to the balancing test of Rule 26(b)(2)(C), which requires a court to weigh the probative value of proposed discovery against its potential burden.

Although metadata is not specifically referenced, Rule 34 of the Federal Rules of Civil Procedure addresses the production of ESI. Under the Rule, a requesting party may specify a form of production and request metadata. (A typical request might be to produce Word documents in TIFF format with a load file containing the relevant system metadata.) The responding party then must either produce ESI in the form specified or object. If the responding party objects, or the requesting party has not specified a form of production, the responding party must "state the form or forms it intends to use" for its production of ESI. Fed. R. Civ. P. 34(b)(2)(D). . . .

If the requesting party does not specify a form for producing ESI, the responding "party must produce it in a form or forms in which it is ordinarily maintained or in a reasonably usable form or forms." Fed. R. Civ. P. 34(b)(2)(E)(ii). Although a party may produce its ESI in another "reasonably usable form," this does not mean "that a responding party is free to convert electronically stored information from the form in which it is ordinarily maintained to a different form that makes it more difficult or burdensome for the requesting party to use the information efficiently in the litigation." In particular, if the ESI is kept in an electronically-searchable form, it "should not be produced in a form that removes or significantly degrades this feature."

The Federal Rules also specify that a "party need not produce the same [ESI] in more than one form." Fed. R. Civ. P. 34(b)(2)(E)(iii).

b. *Sedona Principles*

The Sedona Conference ("Conference"), a nonprofit legal policy research and education organization, has a working group comprised of judges, attorneys, and electronic discovery experts dedicated to resolving electronic document production issues. Since 2003, the Conference has published a number of documents concerning ESI, including the *Sedona Principles*. Courts have found the *Sedona Principles* instructive with respect to electronic discovery issues. . . .

Weighing the advantages and disadvantages of different forms of production, the Conference concluded that even if native files are requested, it is sufficient to produce memoranda, emails, and electronic records in PDF or TIFF format accompanied by a load file containing searchable text and selected metadata. . . .

c. *Case Law*

There is a clear pattern in the case law concerning motions to compel the production of metadata. Courts generally have ordered the production of metadata when it is sought in the initial document request and the producing party has not yet produced the documents in any form. On the other hand, if metadata is not sought in the initial document request, and particularly if the producing party already has produced the documents in another form, courts tend to deny later requests, often concluding that the metadata is not relevant. . . .

B. *Application to Facts*

Metadata has become "the new black," with parties increasingly seeking its production in every case, regardless of size or complexity. In keeping with that trend, the Plaintiffs in this case argue that all metadata for all electronic documents should be produced, both because the metadata is relevant to their claims and because it will enable them to search and sort the documents more efficiently. In evaluating these assertions, the timing of the Plaintiffs' request is important. The first Rule 26(f) conference was held on January 18, 2008. Thereafter, the first request for production of documents was made on February 15, 2008. Throughout this time period, the Plaintiffs made no mention of metadata even though the Defendants had started to harvest their documents. Indeed, by the time the Plaintiffs first informed the Defendants of their desire for metadata (in passing on March 18 and formally on May 22, 2008), the Defendants' document collection efforts were largely complete and they had already produced many of their electronic documents in PDF format without accompanying metadata. In these circumstances, the Plaintiffs face an uphill battle in their efforts to compel the Defendants to make a second production of their ESI.

With this heightened burden in mind, I will turn to a review of the types of ESI for which the Plaintiffs have requested metadata.

1. *Emails*

One consequence of the Defendants' document production format is that the emails produced to date do not contain information about who was blind copied ("bcc'd") or the folders to which the emails were saved. The Plaintiffs allege that this information is relevant because it may help bolster their claim that certain defendants condoned a pattern and practice of unconstitutional home searches. The Plaintiffs also contend that the process of searching the emails would be more efficient if they had the underlying metadata. The Defendants concede that the metadata regarding "bcc" information is "arguably relevant," but contend that information about the folder to which an email was saved is not relevant because it does not indicate how an individual used the information contained in the email. . . .

The Defendants have produced a total of approximately 500 emails to the Plaintiffs in several tranches. They further have represented that their search for and production of responsive emails is largely complete. As part of their production on July 31, 2008, the Defendants turned over approximately 200 emails, "approximately three-quarters" of which were harvested in a manner that preserved the metadata. During the September 8th conference, the Defendants offered to re-produce the emails in that tranch to the extent that they were turned over . . . with the original metadata intact. They declined to undertake a review of the remaining emails to determine if metadata was available, citing the potential burden.
. . .

Here, the Defendants made a persuasive showing during the September 8th conference that the process of restoring and reviewing the back-up tapes generated by its decentralized email system would be extremely burdensome. Moreover, the Plaintiffs have not shown that there is a likelihood of recovering important information not previously disclosed. Accordingly, because the cost of this additional discovery is unquestionably high and the likely benefit low, the Defendants will not be required to review and produce any data regarding emails in ICE's back-up tapes.

2. *Word Processing Documents and PowerPoint Presentations*

The Plaintiffs seek system metadata, including the date created, date modified, and modified by fields, for all Word, Excel and PowerPoint documents. The Plaintiffs make two arguments why the production of this metadata should be required. First, they claim that they cannot efficiently search the documents without the metadata. Second, they argue that the metadata is relevant so that they can piece together "who knew what when." In particular, the Plaintiffs claim that this information will assist them in demonstrating that ICE employees (a) were inadequately trained and supervised, (b) engaged in or condoned a pattern or practice of unconstitutional home searches, or (c) lacked probable cause for the searches.

Although it undoubtedly is true that Word and PowerPoint documents could be searched more easily with metadata, the Plaintiffs have been provided with text-searchable PDFs. More importantly, this is not a case involving hundreds of boxes of documents in which the Plaintiffs' concern about their ability to search and sort the documents would carry some force. Rather, only about 5,200 pages of documents have thus far been produced, the equivalent of slightly more than one "banker's box" of documents. The Defendants also have represented that few additional documents remain to be produced. Given the limited universe of documents, the Plaintiffs should not encounter significant difficulty sorting and searching the word processing and PowerPoint files they have received.

Turning to the relevance argument, the Plaintiffs have failed to show that the "who" and "when" of document creation or modification is relevant to their *Bivens* claims that the home searches resulted in a deprivation of their constitutional rights. . . . [T]he information the Plaintiffs seek would be of limited relevance to the fundamental question posed by their *Bivens* claim: whether their constitutional rights were violated because the ICE agents did not seek their consent before entering their homes.

If establishing probable cause for the searches (or the lack thereof) were important, there might be a need to know what information each officer had learned by the time of a search. However, the Defendants have conceded that they lacked probable cause for the searches and that they engaged in the searches solely in the belief that they had obtained the voluntary consent of the occupants of the homes they searched. This admission largely eviscerates any need to consider whether the officers had probable cause. Accordingly, the Plaintiffs' justification for the production of metadata to determine probable cause is unpersuasive. . . .

. . . Nevertheless, because the metadata could potentially have some relevance and increase the utility of the documents (and in light of the new emphasis in the *Sedona Principles* regarding the need to produce metadata), I will grant the Plaintiffs' motion to compel the production of metadata for any Word and PowerPoint documents, but on the condition that the Plaintiffs pay all costs associated with a second production of these documents. Because the Plaintiffs will bear the cost of the production, they may wish to reexamine whether they, in fact, need this metadata and, if so, to what extent.

3. *Spreadsheets*

As noted above, the relevance of metadata to an Excel spreadsheet depends upon its complexity and purpose. When a spreadsheet relies on mathematical formulas, the metadata that discloses those formulas often is necessary for a thorough understanding of the spreadsheet. Here, however, the spreadsheets cited by the Plaintiffs are nothing more than lists that could have been created through a word processing program. The spreadsheets merely list the date of a particular operation, the field office that conducted the operation, the number of arrests made, and a breakdown of those arrests into different categories. While the spreadsheets appear to contain some embedded metadata that computes the total number of arrests in each category, the underlying formulas are not necessary to understand the spreadsheet. Moreover, absent some preliminary showing that these spreadsheets were fraudulently modified after the fact to conceal the true scope of the operation, the date the spreadsheets were created or modified is not relevant to the any claims or defenses in this action.

That said, the request for spreadsheet metadata evidently is not unduly burdensome. Indeed, during the September 8, 2008 conference, the Defendants expressed a willingness to re-produce the spreadsheets in native format. For this reason, the Court will so direct. . . .

III. CONCLUSION

This lawsuit demonstrates why it is so important that parties fully discuss their ESI early in the evolution of a case. Had that been done, the Defendants might not have opposed the Plaintiffs' requests for certain metadata. Moreover, the parties might have been able to work out many, if not all, of their differences without court involvement or additional expense . . . . Instead, these proceedings have now been bogged down in expensive and time-consuming litigation of electronic discovery issues only tangentially related to the underlying merits of the Plaintiffs' *Bivens* claims. Hopefully, as counsel in future cases become more knowledgeable about ESI issues, the frequency of such skirmishes will diminish.

In this case, for the reasons set forth above, the Plaintiffs' application to compel the production of metadata is granted in part and denied in part.

JOHN B. V. GOETZ

531 F.3d 448 (6th Cir. 2008)

■ ROGERS, Circuit Judge.

State defendants seek mandamus relief from two discovery orders issued by the district court during the course of this class-action litigation. [The class action was brought on behalf of children enrolled in state managed health system, the plaintiffs sought to enforce certain Social Security Act provisions requiring early and periodic screening, diagnosis, and treatment services. The plaintiffs and the state entered a consent decree. During implementation of the remedy, a discovery dispute arose regarding defendants' duty to preserve and produce electronically stored information relevant to the litigation. In response to a request for production, the defendants produced hard copies of documents that it had stored in electronic form. These documents proved incomplete, and the court eventually found that the defendants had failed to implement a court-ordered litigation hold for ESI during much of the litigation — resulting in destruction of relevant ESI — and had failed to produce relevant ESI in its possession. At one point the court ordered that the defendants production of ESI include all metadata and all deleted information on any computer of any of the designated custodians.

[After further skirmishing between the parties about the responsiveness of the defendant's production, the district court issued two orders, which together] directed plaintiffs' computer expert and a court-appointed monitor to inspect the state's computer system and the computers of 50 key custodians to ascertain whether any relevant information has been impaired, compromised, or removed. . . . [The orders] allow plaintiffs' computer expert to make forensic copies of the hard drives of identified computers, including not only those at the work stations of the state's key custodians, but also any privately owned computers on which the custodians may have performed or received work relating to the TennCare program. The orders also direct the U.S. Marshal, or his designated deputies, to accompany plaintiffs' computer expert to ensure full execution of the orders. . . .

It is axiomatic that "[m]andamus relief is an extraordinary remedy, only infrequently utilized by this court." . . . Indeed, for the writ to issue, petitioners must demonstrate a "clear abuse of discretion" on the part of the district court. . . .

. . . The provisions in the orders that require the forensic imaging of all computers containing responsive ESI constitute an abuse of discretion.

As a general matter, it is beyond question that a party to civil litigation has a duty to preserve relevant information, including ESI, when that party "has notice that the evidence is relevant to litigation or . . . should have known that the evidence may be relevant to future litigation." It is the responsibility of the parties to ensure that relevant ESI is preserved, and when that duty is breached, a district court may exercise its authority to impose appropriate discovery sanctions.

There is less clarity, however, surrounding the question of a district court's authority to compel the forensic imaging and production of computer hard drives as a means by which to preserve relevant electronic evidence. Because litigants are generally responsible for preserving relevant information on their own, such procedures, if at all appropriate, should be employed in a very limited set of circumstances. In this case, the district court ordered the forensic imaging predominantly for preservation purposes, explaining that "[t]hese Orders were to protect against the Defendants' destruction of responsive information in light of the Defendants' persistent refusals to produce ESI in violation of the Court's orders." In so doing, the district court committed a clear error in judgment.

To be sure, forensic imaging is not uncommon in the course of civil discovery. A party may choose on its own to preserve information through forensic imaging, and district courts have, for various reasons, compelled the forensic imaging and production of opposing parties' computers. Nevertheless, "[c]ourts have been cautious in requiring the mirror imaging of computers where the request is extremely broad in nature and the connection between the computers and the claims in the lawsuit are unduly vague or unsubstantiated in nature." . . . [M]ere skepticism that an opposing party has not produced all relevant information is not sufficient to warrant drastic electronic discovery measures. And the *Sedona Principles* urge general caution with respect to forensic imaging in civil discovery:

> Civil litigation should not be approached as if information systems were crime scenes that justify forensic investigation at every opportunity to identify and preserve every detail. . . . [M]aking forensic image backups of computers is only the first step of an expensive, complex, and difficult process of data analysis that can divert litigation into side issues and satellite disputes involving the interpretation of potentially ambiguous forensic evidence.

[THE SEDONA PRINCIPLES: BEST PRACTICES, RECOMMENDATIONS & PRINCIPLES FOR ADDRESSING ELECTRONIC DOCUMENT PRODUCTION 34, 37 (The Sedona Conference Working Group, 2d ed. 2007).] Thus, even if acceptable as a means to preserve electronic evidence, compelled forensic imaging is not appropriate in all cases, and courts must consider the significant interests implicated by forensic imaging before ordering such procedures.

The district court's compelled forensic imaging orders here fail to account properly for the significant privacy and confidentiality concerns present in this case. The district court has ordered plaintiffs' computer expert, accompanied by deputy U.S. Marshals, to enter state agencies, and the offices and homes of state officials, to make forensic images of hard drives and other devices, whether state-owned or privately owned, that contain information relevant to the instant litigation. As discussed, the media at issue will almost certainly contain confidential state or private personal information that is wholly unrelated to the litigation. Although the risk of improperly exposing such information, standing alone, might not preclude the employment of forensic imaging in all cases, the forensic imaging must be premised on an interest significant enough to override that risk. Such an interest is not demonstrably present in this case. . . .

. . . [T]he record lacks evidence that defendants have intentionally destroyed relevant ESI in the past, and nothing in the record indicates that defendants are unwilling, or will refuse, to preserve and produce all relevant ESI in the future. Furthermore, forensic imaging is not the only available means by which the district court may respond to what it perceives to be discovery misconduct. The district court maintains authority to impose sanctions for discovery violations under the federal rules and pursuant to its inherent powers. Although we take no position regarding the propriety of sanctions in this case, such measures can be less intrusive than forensic imaging, and it is not apparent from the record that the district court has exercised its sanctioning authority. . . .

Aside from these privacy and confidentiality considerations, this case raises other obvious issues that counsel against the forensic imaging procedures ordered by the district court. As directives to state officials, these orders implicate federalism and comity considerations not present in typical civil litigation. Many of the computers subject to the orders are in the custody of high ranking state officials, and these computers will contain information related to confidential state matters. Further, the orders call for federal law enforcement officers to accompany plaintiffs' computer expert into state agencies — and, in some cases, the homes and offices of state officials — to effect the imaging. . . .

Certainly, state officials are not immune from complying with federal discovery mandates. However, where less intrusive means are available to address the perceived discovery violations of state parties, those means should be employed before resorting to inherently intrusive measures like forensic imaging, especially in cases where there is no evidence of purposeful or intentional destruction of relevant ESI. In light of the significant confidentiality and federalism concerns present in this case, the district court's forensic imaging orders constitute the type of "demonstrable abuse of discretion" that warrants mandamus relief. . . .

[The court of appeals also found that other factors favored granting the writ.]

For the foregoing reasons, we grant defendants' petition for mandamus and set aside those provisions of the district court's November 15, 2007 and November 19, 2007 orders that require the forensic imaging of state-owned and privately owned computers, including the provisions that require the U.S. Marshal or his designee to assist plaintiffs' computer expert in the execution of the orders. We recognize that the two contested orders also contain provisions related to the inspection of defendants' computer system. We decline to address those provisions to the extent that those provisions can be executed in a manner consistent with this opinion and without undue intrusion.

■ COLE, JR., Circuit Judge, concurring. . . .

. . . The district court has thus far reserved the exercise of its wide discretion to hold Defendants in contempt or to impose monetary sanctions. If the district court resorts to such measures and Defendants nevertheless continue to disregard their undisputed duty to preserve and produce relevant ESI, the preservation order at issue in this case, in my view, may no longer be considered inappropriate.

Notes

1. Designing keyword searches, capturing metadata, imaging hard drives — these are the types of issues that confront the modern litigator, especially in complex litigation. The three cases that we have chosen represent just a slice of the struggles that come with ESI. You probably noticed that in *Aguilar* and *John B.*, the parties retained experts just on the subject of ESI; and *Gross Construction* acknowledged, without necessarily requiring the parties to accept, the increasing trend toward

demanding expert testimony when disputes arise over the proper scope of the parties' disclosure and discovery of ESI. The technical issues have indeed become daunting, and parties routinely retain consultants to design ESI searches and "mine" ESI for relevant information. Conferences, conventions, and trade shows on e-discovery abound. Blogs and websites are devoted to e-discovery issues; there are even websites that list other e-discovery blogs, websites, and resources. (For one such website, see http://www.ims-expertservices.com/newsletters/sept/guide-toe-discovery-resources-on-the-web-093008.asp#4.) Some have argued passionately that law schools should begin teaching e-discovery skills to law students. *See* William Hamilton, *The E-Discovery Crisis: An Immediate Challenge to Our Nation's Law Schools, available at* http://e-discoveryteam.com/school/the-e-discovery-crisis-an-immediate-challenge-to-our-nation%E2%80%99s-law-schools (Aug. 17, 2009).

ESI issues have also begun to percolate into ethics opinions. For instance, the Vermont Bar Association has issued an opinion that an attorney can ethically mine ESI for metadata, even when the metadata might contain privileged or confidential matters and the metadata was inadvertently disclosed. *See* Vt. Bar Ass'n Prof'l Responsibility Section, Ethics Opinion 2009-1 (2009). Undoubtedly the issue will receive more treatment in the future.

2. Unfortunately, this is not the course to explore these issues in depth. These issues are nonetheless highly relevant to our concern, which is the pressure that ESI places on complex litigation. At some point in the future, the technology might evolve to the point that the expense and technical issues in requesting and responding to e-discovery will become irrelevant, and the legal and ethical issues will be sorted out. But we do not yet live in that day. For now, as a general proposition, ESI makes discovery in complex litigation more expensive and difficult. As a result, it is a matter that judges in complex cases need to manage effectively.

3. Increasingly, requesting parties ask the responding party to run specific keyword searches suggested by the requesting party and to provide the ESI that these searches yield. The advantage of such a process is that it eliminates any argument that the responding party did not search properly for responsive documents. The disadvantages include the need for the requesting party to have some familiarity with the responding party's systems for storing ESI and the opportunity that this system creates for the disputes about the relevance and burden of each specific discovery request — disputes that can often be resolved only through expert testimony. One recent example is *In re Zurn Pex Plumbing Products Liability Litigation*, 2009 WL 1606653 (D. Minn. June 5, 2009). In this class action, the court initially bifurcated discovery so that class-certification issues would be handled first. The plaintiffs then requested that the defendant run searches using twenty-six search terms through two different hard drives on the defendant's servers and e-mail accounts of the computers of certain designated employees. The defendant estimated that a search of the employees' e-mails and just one of the two hard drives "will require

approximately seventeen weeks and cost $1,150,000, exclusive of vendor collection and processing costs, to review and process the data." *Id.* at *2. The defendant objected that this discovery was unduly burdensome, and was also irrelevant to the class-certification issue. The judge, who thought that the defendant's estimate of costs was high because it was rendered by an attorney rather than an ESI expert, began with a presumption that the discovery was relevant to the class-certification motion. The judge was more troubled by the issue of burden; she therefore limited ESI discovery to the employees' e-mails plus one hard drive, and further limited discovery to fourteen of the twenty-six search terms.

4.   *Zurn* indirectly points out one drawback to the tightening of class-certification standards that we examined in Chapter Four. *See supra* p. 361, Note 5; p. 463-64, Notes 1-2. When inquiries on the merits become intertwined with inquiries on class certification, it becomes difficult to avoid expensive ESI discovery at the preliminary stages of the case.

5.   In passing, *Zurn* also noted that, in order to frame its requests, the plaintiffs had taken depositions of some of the defendant's information-technology employees to determine what types of ESI the defendant had and how it was stored. Depositions of this type are now commonplace, and are another discovery cost that ESI uniquely imposes.

6.   *Aguilar* denied access to the defendant's metadata in large part because of the tardiness of the request, but it also showed doubt about the relevance of metadata under any circumstance. Other courts have also expressed doubts about the relevance of metadata, and have refused to give the requesting party access to it. *See* Dahl v. Bain Capital Partners, 655 F. Supp. 2d 146, 150 (D. Mass. 2009) (denying a blanket request for metadata, as opposed to a tailored request for specific types of documents, because of "the general uneasiness that courts hold over metadata's contribution in assuring prudent and efficient litigation"); Wyeth v. Impax Lab., Inc., 248 F.R.D. 169 (D. Del. 2006); Williams v. Sprint/United Mgmt. Co., 230 F.R.D. 640 (D. Kan. 2005).

7.   According to Rule 26(a)(1)(A)(ii), parties must disclose all documents, including ESI, ten days before the initial scheduling conference. In many complex cases, it is impossible to identify, much less to disclose, all relevant information at that point. Rule 26(e), which imposes a limited duty on parties to supplement or correct initial disclosures, eases some of the problems, and suggests that a good-faith effort is all that can be expected in the initial disclosure. *Cf.* In re TMI Litig. Cases Consol. II, 922 F. Supp. 997 (M.D. Pa. 1996) (discussing good-faith idea with regard to expert disclosures). Because the sanction for failing to make a required disclosure is often the exclusion of the evidence, *see* Fed. R. Civ. P. 37(c)(1), the stakes for providing the proper initial disclosure are high.

Should the process of initial disclosure therefore be suspended in complex litigation? The *Manual's* answer is "Quite possibly":

> The scope of disputed issues and relevant facts in a complex case may not be sufficiently clear from the pleadings to enable parties to

make the requisite disclosure. . . . To the extent the parties cannot agree during their [discovery-planning] conference, it sometimes helps to defer disclosure and fashion an order at the Rule 16 conference, defining and narrowing the factual and legal issues in dispute and establishing the scope of disclosure.

MANUAL FOR COMPLEX LITIGATION, FOURTH § 11.13 (2004).

But the *Manual's* advice seems to conflict with some cases — admittedly dealing with expert disclosures rather than initial disclosures — that have suggested that "[c]ompliance with the disclosure requirements is particularly important in complex cases." In re Ford Motor Co. Bronco II Prods. Liab. Litig., 1996 WL 28517, at *1 (E.D. La. Jan. 23, 1996) (striking experts for class-certification motion when non-disclosure occurred without "substantial justification"); *TMI*, 922 F. Supp. at 1005 (observing that, "[w]ere the instant action a less complex lawsuit, the court would be more inclined to find Plaintiffs' Rule 26 violations harmless").

b. Limits on Discovery

An evident way to cut the cost of discovery in complex cases is to limit the amount of discovery in which the parties can engage. The first subsection of this chapter examined a number of techniques, such as early and firm discovery deadlines and bifurcation, that indirectly had this effect. In this section we look at a couple of techniques that seek to influence more directly the amount of discovery in which parties can engage.

i. Limits on Quantity

The most common forms of discovery are interrogatories, requests for production, and depositions. The Federal Rules of Civil Procedure impose no limits in the number of requests for production, but they do impose limits on the number of depositions (ten per side, with no deposition to last more than seven hours) and interrogatories (twenty-five, including all subparts). Fed. R. Civ. P. 30(a)(1)(A)(i) and -(d)(1), 33(a)(1). The Federal Rules impose no limit on the number or extent of requests for production, although, as we saw in the last subsection, some special limits are imposed on the disclosure or discovery of electronically stored information. *See* Fed. R. Civ. P. 26(b)(2)(B), 45(d)(1)(C)-(D). In addition, discovery in all forms is subject to the requirement that it be proportional to the needs of the case. *See* Fed. R. Civ. P. 26(b)(2)(C)(iii) (barring discovery when "the burden or expense of the proposed discovery outweighs its likely benefit, considering the needs of the case, the amount in controversy, the parties' resources, the importance of the issues at stake in the action, and the importance of the discovery in resolving the issues").

Most complex cases (especially cases that are complex in the pretrial sense) cannot function within the constraints of twenty-five interrogatories and ten depositions per side. Likewise, a single deposition might need to last more than seven hours. *See* In re Natural Gas Royalties Qui Tam

Litig., 467 F. Supp. 2d 1117, 1152 (D. Wyo. 2006) (noting a thirty-day deposition). Under the Federal Rules, these limits are presumptions; a court can grant the parties leave to take more than ten depositions; it can also order, or the parties can stipulate, that the parties can propound more than twenty-five interrogatories. *See* Citgo Petroleum Corp. v. Ranger Enters., Inc., 2009 WL 2058213, at *1 (W.D. Wis. July 13, 2009) ("[T]he ten deposition limit is an advisory one that is particularly unadvisable in complex and large cases . . . ."). A common point of discussion at discovery-planning conferences and at pretrial conferences thereafter is the number of interrogatories and depositions that the parties need. One advantage of presumptive low limits on interrogatories and depositions is that these limits focus attention immediately on the parties' estimation of the likely amount of discovery; this estimation can become a baseline against which any future requests for departure can be measured. *But see* Griffin B. Bell et al., *Automatic Disclosure in Discovery — The Rush to Reform*, 27 GA. L. REV. 1, 39-40 (1992) (arguing that it is often impossible to know early in a case what the disputed facts are).

The following case raises an important recurring issue regarding limits on discovery, as well as an interesting solution.

SMITH V. LOWE'S HOME CENTERS, INC.

236 F.R.D. 354 (S.D. Ohio 2006)

■   KING, United States Magistrate Judge.

BACKGROUND

The named plaintiffs bring this action on behalf of themselves and other employees subject to Lowe's "Salaried Plus Overtime Eligible Compensation Plan" under the Fair Labor Standards Act of 1938 ("FLSA"), 29 U.S.C. § 216(b), and the Ohio Minimum Wage Act, ("OMWA"), O.R.C. § 4112.01 et seq. Plaintiffs allege that certain salaried employees . . . are not exempt from the overtime requirements of the FLSA and OMWA, are routinely required to work more than 40 hours per week, and are paid at a rate calculated using a federal regulation commonly known as the Fluctuating Workweek Method ["FWM"] of overtime compensation, 29 C.F.R. § 778.114.

An employer may use the FWM if four conditions are satisfied . . .

Plaintiffs allege that application of the FWM calculation of overtime to these non-exempt salaried employees is inappropriate because they [do not meet some of the conditions for using the FWM]. . . .

The action was brought as a collective action under the FLSA and as a class action under Fed. R. Civ. P. 23 on behalf of the following:

All current or former Lowe's Non-Exempt Salaried Employees, including, inter alia, employees holding the titles of Department Manager, Assistant Department Manager and Specialist in any Ohio stores who worked overtime while employed as Non-Exempt Salaried Employees and were compensated for such overtime work at an amount equal or less than one and one-half the employee's regular rate of pay based on a 40-hour workweek.

On May 11, 2005, the Court granted plaintiffs' motion to provide notice to potential opt-in plaintiffs pursuant to the provisions of 29 U.S.C. § 216(b). More than 1,500 individuals have opted in as plaintiffs in the collective action. Defendant anticipates filing a motion to de-certify the collective action following completion of discovery and plaintiffs anticipate filing a motion to certify a class of plaintiffs under Rule 23.

Defendant propounded interrogatories and requests for production of documents to each opt-in plaintiff. This matter is now before the Court on plaintiffs' motion for a protective order limiting the discovery to which defendant is entitled to a representative sample of 90 randomly selected individuals among the more than 1,500 opt-in plaintiffs. Defendant insists that it is entitled to the written discovery propounded by it to each of the 1,500 opt-in plaintiffs, but offers to limit its depositions to 10% of those parties, or 150 depositions.

STANDARD

Under Fed. R. Civ. P. 26, the Court may order, upon a showing of good cause, that certain matters not be inquired into or that the scope of discovery be limited to specific matters. In large or complex litigation, the Court may limit the scope of discovery to protect a party from unduly burdensome discovery requests.

COLLECTIVE ACTIONS UNDER THE FLSA

The FLSA authorizes an action "by any one or more employees for and in behalf of himself or themselves and other employees similarly situated." 29 U.S.C. § 216(b). It is generally recognized that, at trial, the testimony of "fairly representative employees" may form the basis for a determination of liability and back wages, even in the absence of testimony from all employees.

Courts are in general agreement that the certification of a collective action under the FLSA should proceed in two stages. The preliminary certification is intended to provide notice and opportunity to opt in. The named plaintiff's burden at this stage is "fairly lenient," and requires only "a modest factual showing" that he or she is similarly situated to the other employees sought to be notified. Thereafter, a defendant may file a motion for decertification, challenging the earlier preliminary determination that employees are sufficiently similarly situated.

At the de-certification stage, usually after discovery and shortly prior to trial, the Court determines whether or not the opt-in collective plaintiffs are "similarly situated" within the meaning of the FLSA. If the Court concludes that they are, the collective action proceeds to trial; if the claimants are not similarly situated, the district court de-certifies the class, the opt-in plaintiffs are dismissed without prejudice and the original named plaintiffs proceed to trial on their individual claims. Among the factors to be considered at the de-certification stage are "the disparate factual and employee settings of the individual plaintiffs; the various defenses available to the defendant which appear to be individual to each plaintiff; fairness and procedural considerations; and whether plaintiff made any required filings before instituting suit."

Plaintiffs contend that to permit discovery of all 1,500 opt-in plaintiffs would be unreasonably burdensome and would result in a duplication of discovery to an unwarranted degree. Instead, plaintiff propose the use of statistical sampling and limiting discovery to 90 opt-in plaintiffs. In response, defendant insists that the written discovery propounded to all 1,500 opt-in plaintiffs is necessary to establish, during de-certification proceedings, that not all members of the collective class are "similarly situated" within the meaning of the FLSA.

DISCUSSION

Whether opt-in plaintiffs in a collective action should be treated as ordinary party plaintiffs, subject to the full range of discovery, has been the subject of discussion. Some courts have permitted — if not required — individualized discovery addressed to all opt-in plaintiffs.

Other courts, however, have held that collective actions under the FLSA should be governed by the same standards as govern discovery in Rule 23 class actions and should be limited to only class wide and class based discovery. To permit individualized discovery, the reasoning goes, would undermine the purpose and utility of both class and collective actions. For example, some courts have limited discovery to only representative samples.

This Court agrees that limiting discovery to a statistically significant representative sampling, at this juncture, will both reasonably minimize the otherwise extraordinary burden imposed on the plaintiffs and their counsel and yet afford the defendant a reasonable opportunity to explore, discover and establish an evidentiary basis for its defenses. The Court will therefore limit the discovery appropriate to the de-certification and class certification proceedings to a statistically significant sample. However, if, after conducting the discovery of the representative sample, defendants can demonstrate to the Court that broader discovery is appropriate and necessary, the defendants can so move.

PLAINTIFFS' PROPOSAL

Relying on the opinions and recommendations of a statistician, Linda Volnino, Ph.D., plaintiffs propose utilizing a sample of 90 individuals. Defendant challenges the proposed statistical sampling and statistical model utilized by plaintiffs' expert.

The Court agrees that the proposed inquiry . . . fails to fully or even meaningfully address either defendant's concerns or the issues relevant to the anticipated motions to decertify and certify. The parties are therefore directed to confer with each other with a view to formulating an appropriate methodology for arriving at a meaningful sampling of the opt-in class for purposes of discovery. The parties must meet and confer prior to the next status conference . . . .

It is so ordered.

Notes

1. The *Manual* urges courts to consider ways to limit both discovery in general, *see* MANUAL FOR COMPLEX LITIGATION, FOURTH § 11.422 (2004), and depositions in particular, *see id.* § 11.45. Beyond this hortatory admonition, the *Manual* is somewhat short of specific advice. It recommends not imposing limits until hearing from the attorneys. It also recommends a variant of the process used in *Smith*: limiting discovery but then employing "statistical sampling techniques to measure whether the results of the discovery fairly represent what unrestricted discovery would have been expected to produce." *Id.* § 11.422. As for depositions, which "are often overused and conducted inefficiently, and thus tend to be the most costly and time-consuming activity in complex litigation," *id.* § 11.45, the *Manual* recommends that the judge considering whether to impose limits on depositions consider — whether at the macro level of the entire deposition program or the micro level of any given deposition the *Manual* declines to say — "the need for the proposed depositions, the subject matter to be covered, and the available alternatives." *Id.* § 11.451. Among the alternatives that the *Manual* mentions are informal interviews; taking depositions by telephone or video; deposition on written questions; and representative depositions, for which counsel can "stipulate that the testimony of other named witnesses would be the same." *Id.* § 11.452. Are both sides likely to agree to these alternatives?

2. Aside from outright restrictions on conducting discovery, courts can impose limits that make the discovery that is conducted run more smoothly. For instance, courts need to consider whether to limit attendance at depositions; whether and under what circumstances to permit second depositions of witnesses; and whether to require high-level (or "apex") corporate officials to testify. *See, e.g.,* MANUAL, *supra,* §§ 11.422, 11.451; Folwell v. Hernandez, 210 F.R.D. 169 (M.D.N.C. 2002) (permitting deposition of CEO of major company, but limiting the topics into which the deposition could inquire; rejecting the company's offer to let CEO answer written questions submitted by the plaintiff); In re Bridgestone/Firestone, Inc., Tires Prods. Liab. Litig., 205 F.R.D. 535 (S.D. Ind. 2002) (permitting a time-limited, coordinated deposition of the Chairman of the Board of Ford Motor Company in lawsuits arising in state courts and an MDL proceeding; requiring the deposing lawyers to submit for *in camera* review a list of the subjects to be covered in the deposition); Tri-Star Pictures, Inc. v. Unger,

171 F.R.D. 94, 100-03 (S.D.N.Y. 1997) (permitting a second deposition of the plaintiff's general counsel, but imposing severe restrictions).

3. Limiting the quantity of discovery has been highly influenced by the economic perspective on litigation. According to classical economic theory, discovery is efficient as long as the marginal expected benefit from the information exceeds the marginal cost of obtaining the information. *See* Robert Cooter & Daniel Rubinfeld, *An Economic Model of Legal Discovery*, 23 J. LEG. STUD. 435 (1994). The basic rule limiting discovery — the proportionality limit of Rule 26(b)(2)(C) — reflects this approach. This approach, which is a variant of the Hand Formula, assumes a rational decision-maker operating with perfect information. Does the managerial judge have adequate information about the parties' legal theories (which the parties often wish, for strategic reasons, to keep secret) and about the existing evidence to calculate exactly when the marginal cost exceeds the marginal benefit? Can the judge ever be expected to quantify marginal costs and benefits precisely enough that her ruling leads to an efficient level of discovery? Isn't such valuation particularly hard in complex cases?

4. Difficulty in measuring the benefits and costs of limiting discovery creates a risk that judges will use their general attitudes about resolving the merits versus the costliness and abuse of discovery to fill the empirical gap. For what they are worth, empirical studies of attorney satisfaction and their estimates of the cost of discovery in relation to the stakes of the case reflect little reason to limit discovery. In the most recent survey conducted by the Federal Judicial Center, plaintiffs' lawyers estimated that discovery accounted for 20% of their litigation costs and defense attorneys estimated that discovery amounted to 27% of their litigation costs. Median expenditures on discovery were about 1.6% of the reported stakes for plaintiffs' attorneys and 3.3% of the reported stakes for defense attorneys. Most thought that discovery costs were "just right" in relation to the stakes of the cases. The survey was highly consistent with a survey done in 1997. *See* EMERY G. LEE III & THOMAS E. WILLGING, FED. JUD. CTR., NATIONAL, CASE-BASED CIVIL RULES SURVEY 27-44 (2009), *available at* http://www.fjc.gov/public/pdf.nsf/lookup/dissurv1.pdf/$file/dissurv1.pdf. The prior study had found, among other things, that 69% of attorneys thought that discovery generated the right amount of information to resolve the case fairly, 9% thought that it generated too much, and 8% thought that it generated too little. (The rest had no opinion.) *See* Thomas E. Willging et al., *An Empirical Study of Discovery and Disclosure Practices Under the 1993 Federal Rule Amendments*, 39 B.C. L. REV. 525, 551 (1998). A contemporaneous RAND study focused more on attorney satisfaction regarding specific aspects of discovery, but did state that "subjective information from our interviews with lawyers also suggests that the median or typical case is not 'the problem.'" James S. Kakalik et al., *Discovery Management: Further Analysis of the Civil Justice Reform Act Evaluation Data*, 39 B.C. L. REV. 613, 636 (1998).

On the other hand, the 2009 study was conducted after the discovery limits in the present Federal Rules had been imposed. Moreover, none of the three studies examined specifically the costs of, or attorney attitudes about, discovery in complex litigation. Both of the studies in the 1990s suggested that a small minority of cases did present significant discovery problems. For instance, the 1997 FJC study reported that attorneys thought that 9% of discovery expenses, which constituted 4% of litigation expenses, were unnecessary due to problems in discovery.

5. Is the classical economic analysis of limitations on discovery even the right way to think about the problem? Operating from within an economic paradigm, Professor Hay believes that a case-by-case focus on the optimal amount of discovery neglects the social-welfare perspective. This perspective recognizes that the ultimate goal of a legal system is to minimize the sum of accident costs, accident prevention costs, and the costs of running the legal system. Bruce L. Hay, *Civil Discovery: Its Effects and Optimal Scope*, 23 J. LEGAL STUD. 481, 509 (1994). Professor Hay suggests that, while discovery might not be efficient from the perspective of a particular case, it might be efficient if the extra discovery leads to a more optimal level of precaution by potential wrongdoers *and* if the savings in terms of reduced injuries exceeds the combined costs of extra discovery plus extra costs of taking precautions. He concedes that it is often difficult to apply this test, or to know if it leads in concrete instances to a more efficient outcome than the case-specific test. When he considers the settlement-inducing effects of discovery, he becomes even more pessimistic, stating that even a "rule allowing an apparently ideal amount of discovery may backfire if it leads the parties to settle without undertaking discovery." *Id.* at 514. He concludes that "[f]inding the best approach to discovery control — a hardy perennial on the litigation reform agenda — will not be easy." *Id.* at 515.

Also using economic analysis, Professor Kaplow puts another spin on the discovery problem. He suggests that parties often have "an excessive incentive to provide information in adjudication." Louis Kaplow, *The Value of Accuracy in Adjudication: An Economic Analysis*, 23 J. LEGAL STUD. 307, 384 (1994). He therefore suggests that methods to reduce these incentives — including limits on the amount of discovery — are necessary to achieve efficiency.

6. Another problem with the economic paradigm for limiting discovery is that some costs of discovery are difficult to quantify. For instance, in *Marrese v. American Academy of Orthopaedic Surgeons*, 726 F.2d 1150 (7th Cir. 1984) *rev'd on other grounds and remanded*, 470 U.S. 373 (1985), two doctors rejected for membership in a medical association brought antitrust claims against the association, arguing that its membership decisions were made to restrict competition. The doctors requested discovery of all applications that the association had rejected in the past ten years. The district court ordered the discovery. A majority of the court of appeals overturned that order. Judge Posner stated that the defendant had, "if not a First Amendment right, at least a First Amendment interest, which the discovery sought by the plaintiffs would impair and which differentiates this case from the usual antitrust case." *Id.* at 1159. On the other hand,

"barring the plaintiffs or their counsel from all access to the membership files would probably make it impossible for them to prove their antitrust case." *Id.* at 1160. In striking the proper balance, Judge Posner stated:

> A motion . . . to limit discovery requires the district judge to compare the hardship to the party against whom discovery is sought, if discovery is allowed, with the hardship to the party seeking discovery if discovery is denied. He must consider the nature of the hardship as well as its magnitude and thus give more weight to interests that have a distinctively social value than to purely private interests; and he must consider the possibility of reconciling the competing interests through a carefully crafted protective order. [*Id.*]

Does this formula give adequate guidance to the judge faced with costs not readily quantified in monetary terms? Because the files of rejected memberships were voluminous, Judge Posner recommended that the court strike the compromise by examining *in camera* the defendant's files on the plaintiffs' cases to see if they reflected any anti-competitive concerns; if they did not, Judge Posner thought that there was no reason to go further. Would a better method have been for the judge to examine a randomly selected sample of the defendant's files? Judge Posner thought that looking at the defendant's files on the plaintiffs was sufficient in part because the case was not a class action in which the plaintiffs were suing on behalf of all rejected applicants. Is that reasoning sound?

7. Given its drawbacks, are there any alternatives to the economic approach to limiting discovery? One alternative is to analyze the situation in functional terms. We employ an adversarial system, which assigns the function of requesting and gathering information to the lawyers. As long as the lawyers are capable of (1) making decisions about which information to seek, (2) gathering that information, and (3) organizing it into proofs and arguments, there is no functional reason to change the system. Only when the lawyers are stymied in carrying out their functions — typically because of either the cost or quantity of information involved — does a reason for asserting judicial controls over discovery exist.

Carrying out this analysis, lawyers, even in complex cases, do not usually have difficulty during the information-seeking stage; their problems lie in the second and third stages of obtaining and assimilating information. To avoid problems in these stages, the judge must step into the process. Restricting the quantity of discoverable information is the obvious way in which the judge can do so. But the judge should not be able to restrict discovery concerning information that is useful to a lawyer's ability to present proofs and arguments unless rational adjudication of the merits of the case is impractical without such a restriction.

What are the drawbacks of this approach? Is the word "impractical" just a way of sneaking the cost-benefit analysis back in? If not, does this approach allow the parties to engage in an inefficient amount of discovery? How can this be justified? Because of the inherent value of the adversarial system and the individual autonomy it vindicates?

8. Throughout the past two chapters we have examined other techniques to enhance the pretrial process other than restricting the quantity of discovery. As we have seen, all of these methods have drawbacks. Does the difficulty of finding, and then applying, a workable test for limiting discovery increase the value of these other methods in your eyes? Or is a direct restriction on discovery preferable to these other methods?

9. *Smith* highlights a common problem in complex cases: the extent to which discovery should be permitted against unnamed class members. Sometimes defendants claim that they need to discover information from these plaintiffs. The great fear of allowing them to do so, of course, is that defendants are merely trying to impose costs on their opponents, either making it too costly for them to maintain the case as a class action or else securing the dismissal of the claims of class members that would prefer not to be involved in discovery.

The leading case is *Brennan v. Midwestern United Life Insurance Co*, 450 F.2d 999 (7th Cir. 1971), in which the district judge dismissed the claims of absent class members that ignored repeated efforts and court orders to answer interrogatories that the defendant had propounded. The court of appeals affirmed, noting that the "requests were not designed solely to determine the identity and amount of the class members' claims, but were also directed at obtaining information relating to certain defenses raised by Midwestern in the principal trial" and that "there is nothing in the record to suggest that the discovery procedures were used as a tactic to take undue advantage of the class members or as a stratagem to reduce the number of claimants." *Id.* at 1005. Then-Circuit Judge Stevens dissented, arguing that plaintiffs that did not wish to respond should have been given the opportunity to opt out. *Brennan* was arguably limited in its own circuit by *Clark v. Universal Builders, Inc.*, 501 F.2d 324 (7th Cir. 1974), in which the court both found that the requested discovery sought information already known to the defendants, and suggested that the requested discovery was a ruse to limit the size of the class. An even greater inroad on *Brennan*'s attitude toward class discovery is *Cox v. American Cast Iron Pipe Co.*, 784 F.2d 1546 (11th Cir. 1986). In *Cox*, the court thought that the requested discovery probably did not meet the *Brennan-Clark* test, but then went on to hold that the threat of dismissal effectively made answering discovery an "affirmative 'opt-in' device — that is, it requires passive class members to take positive action to stay in the suit. The Advisory Committee specifically rejected the practice of forcing absent class members to opt into a Rule 23 class action to secure its benefits." *Id.* at 1556.

10. Can a judge to whom MDL proceedings have been transferred for pretrial purposes enter an order that limits the number of witnesses that might be used at trial, once the cases have been remanded to the transferor forums? One MDL court has so held, slashing the number of potential expert witnesses that the defendant wished to place on the witness list from 137 to just 24. The court noted that this restriction was necessary to keep the pretrial deposition schedule in the case manageable. It further found

that "Rule 16 applies to multidistrict proceedings the same as it applies to individual cases, and the transferee court may exercise the authority granted under Rule 16(c)(4) [now Rule 16(c)(2)(D) — ED.] to limit the number of expert witnesses to be called at trial." In re Factor VIII or IX Concentrate Blood Prods. Litig., 169 F.R.D. 632, 637 (N.D. Ill. 1996). The court acknowledged that individual transferor judges might need to make adjustments to the list of 24 experts in particular cases. *Id.* at 637. If so, how effective is the transferee judge's power of limitation?

Obviously, if *Factor VIII* is right, the ability of an MDL judge to enter an order effectively limiting discovery in all of the consolidated cases is an important cost-containment advantage of the MDL process.

ii. Staged Discovery

A different way to limit discovery is to stage or sequence discovery in such a way that parties cannot conduct some discovery until other discovery is completed. The goal of such an approach, which in some variants bears a relationship to the idea of bifurcating pretrial issues that we discussed *supra* p. 814, is to stage discovery in such a way that it obviates the need for other discovery or makes that discovery run more efficiently. The following two cases explore aspects of staging discovery.

KLEIN V. KING

132 F.R.D. 525 (N.D. Cal. 1990)

■ BRAZIL, United States Magistrate.

[Plaintiffs, who were shareholders in a company called Informix, brought a class action against certain defendants after Informix merged with a company called Innovative. They alleged violations of federal securities laws. After a discovery-planning conference and hearing, the court entered the following order on September 14, 1990.]

1. *Class certification.*

A. Defendants shall have no more than *90 calendar days* from the date this Order is filed to complete all discovery related to class certification issues *and* to file and serve any objections/challenges/opposition to plaintiffs' motion for class certification. . . .

D. Without a stipulation from plaintiffs' counsel or an order from this court, defendants may take no more than three depositions, each of no longer than one day, as part of the discovery they conduct with respect to the class certification issues. . . .

E. Without a stipulation from plaintiffs' counsel or an order from this court, defendants may serve no additional interrogatories or document requests with respect to the class certification issues. . . .

4. *Staged discovery with respect to the core aspects of the case.*

The Court has considered carefully defendants' creative suggestions about staging discovery by time periods and about using 90 day interval iterations of issues to focus, discipline and limit the discovery process. . . . We decline to adopt the staging by time periods approach because we feel that there is considerable overlap in evidence, and sources of evidence, relating to the periods suggested, and because it is arguable that the center of the case rests in the second period, a period which the parties would not aggressively explore, under defendants' plan, for many months. We do not want to put exploration of the center of this case on hold. Instead, we want the parties to go to the center first and try to settle this case before they spend unjustifiable amounts of their clients' resources dotting every discovery "i" and crossing every discovery "t". The "issue iteration" proposal also carries several risks. It would require investment of considerable lawyering resources that might well be better spent finding out what the essential underlying facts are. While there is a lot of fancy verbiage about a case like this, in essence it is about facts: what was the state of the company at various points, and who knew or should have known what about that state. We want the parties to focus on these major factual matters, because once they are explicated good lawyers ought to have a pretty good idea about where the case is going to end up. The issue iteration proposal also would create a considerable risk of friction between lawyers and lots of unproductive and perhaps inconclusive satellite litigation. . . .

A. *A general outline of the Court's discovery plan.*

The plan the Court hereby imposes contemplates dividing discovery into two or three stages (the parties, at a juncture to be described, will have a great deal to say about whether there are two or three stages). The purpose of the first stage will be to get as efficiently on the table as possible the core information that the parties need in order to value the case sensibly for settlement purposes. In this stage we will focus primarily on documents, and on those documents that shed the most light on the most important facts. After core document production, and a limited number of depositions, the parties will participate in Court-ordered settlement negotiations, hosted by a special master or team of special masters of their choosing (assuming they can agree on nominees in whom the Court has confidence). The Court expects the parties to make a very hard run at settlement at this juncture. If that hard run fails, they will have two options. The first option would be to conduct limited additional discovery, for about two months, for the purpose of explicating matters that surfaced as obstacles to settlement in the negotiations held at the end of the first stage. That discovery would make up stage two of the pretrial process. It would be followed by another, final round of settlement negotiations, again hosted by the special master(s). If settlement could not be achieved, the parties would move into stage three of the pretrial period, during which they would be permitted to complete the document, deposition, and other discovery necessary to prepare the case for trial. If the parties, with inputs from the special master, conclude after the settlement negotiations at the end of stage one that there is no point in returning after two months or so of additional discovery for further settlement negotiations, they would skip what we are labelling stage two and move directly into the broader additional discovery necessary to dispose of the case by trial (what we are calling the final discovery stage). . . .

For the discovery in the final period, the Court will require submission of detailed discovery plans and will enter another discovery planning order.

Under this plan, no party will be permitted to file a motion for summary judgment or any motion under Rule 12 or Rule 16 until the completion of stage one discovery. This restriction is imposed for several reasons. First, we want all counsel to focus in this first period on learning the facts necessary to understand the center of the case and to value it for settlement. We do not want resources devoted during this early stage to motions that are unlikely to completely derail or substantially re-configure this case. Moreover, we believe that the discovery we contemplate for stage one would have to be done in any event before the Court is likely to be in a position to rule on a motion that would change the basic shape of this litigation. . . .

B. *Stage One.*

(1) *Documents.*

In this stage the discovery will focus almost exclusively on documents. Counsel for all parties shall work together to identify the documents (wherever located) that are most likely to shed light on the *facts* on which disposition of this litigation will turn. In particular, counsel are ordered to focus their initial document examinations and productions on the papers that show, at various junctures, how Informix and, to a lesser extent, Innovative, were in fact doing . . . .

There is no justification for forcing opposing counsel to use interrogatories to acquire basic information about the nature, organization, and location of discoverable documents; counsel shall work together to identify, at least by category, the documents most likely to provide reliable information about the factual matters that are at the center of this action. . . . *The initial productions by defendants shall be made no later than 60 days after the filing of this order.* The court does not expect these initial productions to be exhaustive, even as to "essential" or core documents. But the court does expect a substantial production. After this initial substantial production, defendants shall make additional productions, on a schedule whose specifics the court leaves to counsel to work out, of the remainder of the core documents, i.e., documents needed to sensibly value the case for settlement purposes. *The production of the stage one documents shall be complete by March 1, 1991.* . . .

Because the productions ordered here will be made on something of a fast track, the court hereby orders that inadvertent disclosure of documents protected by attorney-client privilege or the work product doctrine shall not be deemed a waiver of the right to invoke protection for either the documents inadvertently disclosed or other communications in the same subject area as long as counsel for the party who made the inadvertent disclosure is not dilatory thereafter in bringing the matter to the attention of other counsel.

Counsel are reminded that the court does not expect the stage one document production to be exhaustive. Additional opportunities to complete production of documents that are clearly less central to assessing the case for settlement purposes but that are necessary for trial will be afforded in stages two or three.

(2) *Interrogatories.*

During stage one, interrogatories may be used for only one purpose: to ascertain the "identity" of persons with knowledge of relevant matter. During this stage no party may serve more than 35 interrogatories . . . .

Any interrogatories used during stage one shall be served no later than January 15, 1991, and shall be answered fully within 30 days. The Court has selected these dates to give counsel an opportunity to use information learned in the first core document productions to frame interrogatories seeking the identity of individuals with knowledge of important matters disclosed in those documents. Counsel may want to depose some such people toward the end of stage one. . . .

(3) *Depositions.*

Unless the parties otherwise stipulate, plaintiffs will be permitted to take no more than 12 and defendants no more than 6 depositions during stage one. Absent stipulations to the contrary, none of these depositions may consume more than two days.

Because the purpose of discovery in this first stage is not to probe exhaustively every dimension of each area of knowledge that each deponent might have, but to get to the center of things efficiently, the Court does not expect counsel to "complete" each deposition noticed in this stage. Thus, if the parties fail to settle the case, or to dispose of it by motion, the Court will entertain requests by counsel to re-convene in the final stage of discovery some depositions that were taken in stage one. . . .

Counsel shall complete the taking of the depositions permitted here (stage one) by no later than May 1, 1991. . . .

(5) *Requests for Admission.*

No party may serve requests for admission during stage one. . . .

(7) *Settlement negotiations at the close of stage one.*

During May, 1991, the parties shall engage in intensive, good faith settlement negotiations. . . .

C. *Stage Two Discovery. (Optional)*

(1) As noted above, if the parties fail to reach a settlement during the negotiations at the close of stage one but feel that some limited, well-focused additional discovery (or other process of generating information) might improve appreciably the odds of reaching agreement, the Court will permit counsel to submit plans for developing or sharing the necessary information over a limited period, e.g., two months, to be followed promptly by a second intensive round of settlement negotiations. . . .

(3) At the close of this second stage, the parties again shall engage in intensive settlement negotiations. . . .

D. *Motions.*

Any party may file motions directed to the merits of the case, e.g., a motion for summary judgment or partial summary adjudication, at any time after the completion of stage one discovery, i.e., any time *after May 1, 1991*. . . .

E. *Final Stage Discovery.*

If neither settlement negotiations nor motions have resolved this case after the close of the first and second stages of discovery, the parties shall submit proposed plans for completing the discovery that is necessary to prepare for trial. . . .

The parties shall submit these plans either by June 17, 1991 (if the parties decide not to engage in second state discovery for purposes of follow-up settlement efforts) or by September 10, 1991 (if follow-up discovery and settlement are pursued).

IN RE RAIL FREIGHT FUEL SURCHARGE ANTITRUST LITIGATION

258 F.R.D. 167 (D.D.C. 2009)

■ FACCIOLA, United States Magistrate Judge.

Now pending before the Court is Defendants' Motion for Phased Discovery. Defendants propose a Case Management Order that provides for class discovery before class certification and merits discovery. Plaintiffs propose an alternative order that provides for class certification at the conclusion of all fact discovery.

The issue now before this Court is whether bifurcated discovery is appropriate.

I. BACKGROUND

Defendants are the four largest Class I railroads based in the United States. Plaintiffs are eighteen businesses from multiple districts that allege that defendants entered into a conspiracy in 2003 which they continued to enforce through 2007. [Plaintiffs alleged that defendants violated federal antitrust laws by fixing and maintaining the prices of rail freight transportation services through the use of Rail Fuel Surcharges. The plaintiffs' actions were consolidated by the Judicial Panel on Multidistrict Litigation. The plaintiffs sought class certification pursuant to Rules 23(b)(2) and 23(b)(3).] . . .

III. ANALYSIS

A. *Standard of Review.*

In resolving motions to bifurcate discovery at the pre-certification stage, district courts must "balance the need to promote effective case management, the need to prevent potential abuse, and the need to protect the rights of all parties." . . . The District of Columbia Circuit Court has not set a "bright line" test to determine the circumstances under which discovery should be bifurcated. Bifurcation, however, is generally permitted in cases in which it promotes "fairness and efficiency." Although some discovery is necessary to resolve certification issues, "pre-certification discovery is subject to the limitations which may be imposed by the court, and any such limitations are within the sound discretion of the court."

B. *Defendants' Proposal to Provide Plaintiffs with Voluntary Disclosures and Thereby Eliminate the Need for a Search into Their Data.*

Early certification of a class has significant advantages, so bifurcation of discovery into merits and class certification to facilitate early resolution has initial appeal. But, that appeal may prove superficial in any antitrust case, particularly one in which most of the discovery is going to be of ESI.

Defendants argue that it would be simple, in practice, to isolate the items that are relevant to class certification and the items that would be relevant to the merits of the case. Defendants identify three types of documents that they consider to be relevant to the issue of class certification, offer to produce those, and invite the plaintiffs to make good faith suggestions for other types of documents that plaintiffs deem relevant to the class certification issue.

First of all, defendants have to concede that they are asking plaintiffs (and therefore the Court) to accept their formulation of the certification question and their determination of what pertains to it. But, the whole purpose of discovery is to find not only those documents that defendants wish for plaintiffs to see but all documents that pertain to the certification issue that plaintiffs believe will advance their position. To limit plaintiffs to what defendants will give them is to, in effect, begin and end discovery with defendants' voluntary disclosures. But, unlike continental systems where discovery consists of what the parties voluntarily exchange, the American system expressly authorizes each party to independently demand relevant evidence from its opponent. While bifurcated discovery may have much to recommend it, defendants' assertions about the ease with which they can find responsive documents only apply if I limit plaintiffs to what defendants will give them. That approach in effect amends the Federal Rules of Civil Procedure to create a unique form of discovery for class actions.

To the extent that all documents of a certain type are relevant to class certification, it is relatively easy to see how the defendants could isolate all documents of that type and produce them without having to go through an expensive and time consuming review process. Things become infinitely more complicated, however, when we are confronted with the possibility that there will exist, within a given type of document — such as e-mails, memoranda, or meeting minutes — items that are relevant to class certification, items that are relevant to the merits, and items that aren't relevant to the case at all.

The creators of the pertinent ESI could not possibly have foreseen that it would some day prove important to discriminate and differentiate between information that pertained to a policy and information that pertained to the impact of that policy upon a discrete group of consumers. Moreover, the creation of means to search large databases is a work in progress and no one has suggested how the search of defendants' data could be refined so that a search engine of some sort could yield ESI that pertained to impact but not ESI pertaining to any thing else. While defendants blithely suggest that the lawyers in this case are skilled at searching and can therefore find what they need, they do not propose exactly how the lawyers will use this claimed expertise and create a search engine so refined and exquisite that it will yield information bearing on the certification question but not the merits.

C. *The Distinctiveness of "Merits-Based" and "Certification-Based" Evidence.*

Courts must consider the degree to which the certification evidence is "closely intertwined" with, and indistinguishable from, the merits evidence in determining whether bifurcation is appropriate. Here, the evidence plaintiffs need for certification purposes is closely intertwined with the merits evidence.

To certify the class, plaintiffs must establish that "the questions of law or fact common to class members predominate over any questions affecting only individual members and that a class action is superior to other available methods for fairly and efficiently adjudicating the controversy." Fed. R. Civ. P. 23(b)(3). To satisfy this "predominance" requirement, plaintiffs must secure evidence concerning "Defendants' adoption of the fuel surcharge program, how it was imposed, and the Defendants' purposes in doing so" which bears directly on the element of common impact. In essence, the scope of defendants' alleged conspiracy is indistinguishable from its operation. Plaintiffs need evidence concerning the operation of the conspiracy — evidence defendants classify as "merits-based" — to establish the scope of the conspiracy. In turn, plaintiffs need evidence of the scope of the conspiracy to prove common impact and thereby satisfy Rule 23's "predominance" requirement. . . .

D. *The Promotion of Judicial Economy and Efficiency.*

Bifurcated discovery fails to promote judicial economy when it requires "ongoing supervision of discovery." If bifurcated, this Court would likely have to resolve various needless disputes that would arise concerning the classification of each document as "merits" or "certification" discovery. Concurrent discovery is more efficient when bifurcation "would result in significant duplication of effort and expense to the parties." MANUAL FOR COMPLEX LITIGATION (FOURTH) § 11.213 [(2004)].

Furthermore, the continued need for supervision and the increased number of disputes would further delay the case proceedings. Such prevention of the "expeditious resolution of the lawsuit" would prejudice plaintiffs. A significant public interest exists in the "vigorous enforc[ement of] national anti-trust laws through the expeditious resolution of[ ] private antitrust litigation." This public interest is even greater in class actions. . . .

Even if plaintiffs' proposed class is not certified, discovery into merits-based evidence is not necessarily wasted; the information "may be valued circumstantial evidence" if litigation continues absent certification. At this stage, "there is no reason to believe that denial of class certification will terminate this litigation." Eighteen individual businesses from multiple districts have alleged claims against defendants. . . .

G. *Plaintiffs' Proposal for Full and Complete Discovery Before Certification.*

This discussion is not to say that untrammeled and unlimited discovery is appropriate before the issue of class certification is addressed. Plaintiffs will have to concede that what may be a king's ransom will have been spent on discovery that may never be used if Judge Friedman denies class certification or narrows the nature of the class. Settlements based solely on avoiding discovery costs are not the hallmark of a judicial system that is working fairly. Thus, I am obliged to create a means by which the merits discovery that I will permit is no greater than it has to be. Working from the principle that nothing concentrates a lawyer's mind like a deadline, I have rejected plaintiffs' attempt to postpone briefing of the class certification until all discovery is finished, and a date for dispositive motions is set.

Instead, I intend to allow an initial period of discovery, after which the parties will have to brief the certification issue.

I appreciate that this is a compromise but I can only hope that like any compromise it will displease both sides equally. It is my goal to avoid creating the new discovery disputes that would arise by instituting a new criterion — relevance to certification — on top of the requirements for discoverability outlined in the Federal Rules of Civil Procedure. . . . I find this a preferable solution to attempting to define the ineffable by attempting to identify in advance what ESI will bear on the certification issue and not the merits and what I view as the unacceptable solution of limiting plaintiffs to the information defendants deem relevant to the certification issue.

Accordingly . . ., I will order counsel to meet and confer in the next ten days to ascertain whether they can jointly agree to a schedule for all the remaining events to take place in the case, with the understanding that I will insist that any such schedule allow for briefing of the certification issue before the conclusion of discovery . . . . If the parties cannot agree, each side will have to file proposed schedules fourteen days from the date of this Order.

IV. CONCLUSION

For the reasons discussed herein, defendants' Motion will be denied.

Notes

1. Magistrate Judge (formerly Professor) Brazil is a well-known authority on case management. His discovery-planning order in *Klein* therefore makes an interesting study, as he blends several techniques and rejects others. In brief, this is what he does (and does not) order:

- He *targets* initial discovery at a particular issue — here, the class-certification issue.

- He *phases* discovery into two (possibly three) stages, with the hope of concluding the case after the first stage. He rejects, however, the idea of phasing discovery by time periods, instead relying on the next three discovery-control devices to prevent unbounded discovery.

- His timetable for first-stage discovery strongly encourages the parties to *sequence discovery according to form* — in other words, to engage in one form of discovery (document production) first, followed by another form of discovery (interrogatories), and then another form (depositions). As part of this sequencing, requests for admission are temporarily suspended.

- He limits the amount of second-wave (interrogatories) and third-wave (deposition) discovery permitted during the first stage. We examined imposing such limits on the quantity of discovery in the last subsection (*see supra* p. 926).

- He rejects the proposal to use "issue iteration," which sounds a lot like the *AT&T* stipulation method (*see supra* p. 835), to narrow issues. Instead, he keeps discovery from running amok by imposing another issue-narrowing device we have examined — stringent time limitations (*see supra* p. 808).

2. As *Klein* shows, judges often mix and match techniques in the attempt to strike the right balance between issue definition and discovery, and between full discovery and cost-effectiveness. (Note, for instance, Magistrate Judge Brazil's use of an umbrella protective order, which we discussed *supra* p. 882, to speed up the initial production of documents.) In this subsection, we examine the idea of staged discovery. "Staged discovery" is our umbrella term for more specific methods of ordering discovery to achieve efficiency: targeted discovery, phased discovery, and sequenced (or wave) discovery. Different people use these labels to mean different things, so let us be clear about our definitions.

(a) "Targeted discovery" refers to discovery that is directed toward particular legal issues. Often these issues will be critical issues that, once explored, will narrow the case or lead to dismissal or settlement. In this regard, a strong affinity exists between targeted discovery and bifurcation. There are also differences, among them the lack of a formal bifurcation order and the flexibility that the judge retains to adjust the case-management plan and permit discovery on legal issues other than those that are targeted.

(b) "Phased discovery" refers to discovery that is broken into a sequence of smaller segments. Targeted discovery is a special type of phased discovery; it segments discovery by legal issues. But discovery can be phased in other ways for other reasons. Phasing can be used, as in *Klein*, to facilitate settlement; it can be used to control the development of information according to time periods, geographical areas, conduct, or party; or it can be used to uncover the basic information necessary to determine how to structure further case-management and discovery plans.

(c) "Discovery sequenced according to form" refers to the seriatim use of each form of discovery. Typically, document production precedes interrogatories, which precede depositions, which precede requests for admission; but other orderings of discovery are also possible. A variant of formal sequencing is "wave discovery," in which the first wave is geared to identifying witnesses and relevant documents, and a second wave is geared to deposing witnesses and completing other discovery aimed at the merits.

4. The *Manual for Complex Litigation* endorses targeted, phased, and sequenced discovery as one option for limiting discovery. MANUAL FOR COMPLEX LITIGATION, FOURTH § 11.422 (2004). The *Manual* cautions, however, that these tailored discovery techniques also carry risks to which

the court must be sensitive, including the risk that such discovery devices will be inefficient. This is particularly true when discovery on certain targeted issues is intertwined with discovery on non-targeted issues; for instance, if *Klein* did not settle after the first two stages, the defendants would need to back through the same files to find "non-core" documents and some deponents might need to be re-examined. Relatedly, a principal reason that *Rail Freight* refused to adopt the defendants' plan for targeting discovery at the class-certification issue was the inability to divide discovery neatly between class-certification and merits issues. Likewise, forcing all document production to occur at the outset may be less efficient than permitting document production and deposition testimony to be woven together. As we have seen, production of ESI might not be possible until some depositions of information-technology personnel have been conducted. *See supra* p. 925, Note 5.

The caution of the *Manual* is born of experience. The original ancestor of the present *Manual* flatly asserted that, "in the absence of rare and exceptional circumstances," discovery should be conducted in two to three waves. MANUAL FOR COMPLEX AND MULTIDISTRICT LITIGATION §§ 0.5, 1.5, 2.3 (1970). But such a rigid rule did not adapt itself to all complex cases. The *Manual*'s successor therefore tempered this enthusiasm, stating only that "[d]iscovery generally proceeds in a more orderly fashion" if discovery is conducted in waves. MANUAL FOR COMPLEX LITIGATION (SECOND) § 21.421 (1985). The ideas of targeted and phased discovery did not even rate a mention in the 1970 and 1985 *Manuals*.

5. Speaking of experience, there is a dearth of data about the effect of these techniques on case outcomes. Some data shows that bifurcating issues for trial purposes decidedly skew results in the defendants' favor, *see infra* pp. 1042-45; thus, targeted discovery, to the extent that it acts to bifurcate issues, may be a pro-defense device. To our knowledge, phased, sequenced, and wave discovery have not been studied to determine what changes, if any, they might have on case outcomes.

These devices have been in use for fifty or more years. Does it concern you that courts use discovery-control devices without first developing data that analyze their effects on case outcomes?

6. Relatedly, is there a risk that using staged discovery becomes a self-fulfilling prophecy? In *Klein*, Magistrate Judge Brazil's decision to stage discovery is brilliant if the case settles quickly. If it does not, staged discovery is likely going to be less efficient. So the power and prestige of the court are now committed to a particular resolution of the case, and that resolution is now the likeliest to occur. But on what basis, at such an early stage in the case, can the court determine that settlement is the best outcome for all the participants in the case? Recall that one criticism of the managerial judge was the possibility that the judge's biases about how the case "should" come out can creep into decisions that set the case down the judge's preferred path.

On the other hand, is there any way to avoid bias? If the court refuses to stage discovery, as happens in *Rail Freight*, that decision also sets the case down a particular path. Is the difference between *Klein* and *Rail Freight* that the default approach of the Federal Rules of Civil Procedure is not to stage discovery, and departures from that default position should be justified only by very strong reasons?

7. Although the default rule of the Federal Rules of Civil Procedure is not to target, phase, or sequence discovery, the judge has clear textual authority to employ these techniques. *See* Fed. R. Civ. P. 16(b)(3)(ii), 16(c)(2)(F), 26(b)(2)(C), 26(c). The Civil Justice Reform Act, which was in effect during much of the 1990s and required courts to adopt case-management plans, authorized district courts to develop plans that "phase discovery into two or more stages" in complex cases. 28 U.S.C. § 473(a)(3)(C)(ii). Reported cases usually mention such controls in passing; they do not question the power of the court to adopt them. *See, e.g.,* In re "Agent Orange" Prod. Liab. Litig., 506 F. Supp. 762, 797 (E.D.N.Y. 1980) (ordering wave discovery within phased discovery).

8. Even granting the power to stage discovery, when should judges use it? Our anecdotal sense is that judges in complex cases rarely order targeted, phased, or sequenced discovery. When left to their own devices, lawyers typically engage in sequenced and wave discovery on an informal basis, obtaining documents before proceeding with depositions. Likewise, when grounds for a dispositive motion exist, lawyers on the other side often target their early discovery at this weak spot.

If these observations are true, why should a judge order targeted, phased, or sequenced discovery? From an efficiency perspective, shouldn't a judge be reluctant to impose these controls when lawyers are perfectly capable of determining, and indeed are in a better position to determine, the most efficient way to conduct discovery? The only occasions on which the court should need to act are cases of "market failure": when one party hopes to use uncontrolled (i.e., non-targeted, non-phased, or non-sequenced) discovery primarily to impose costs on an opposing party to extract an unjustified settlement, rather than to obtain information. Even then, the court will need to consider whether the party requesting such controls is seeking them to avoid disclosing information that would bolster the other side's case, thus skewing the outcome in the other direction.

Is efficiency the sole issue that should concern a court faced with the option of staging discovery? What other concerns might, or should, weigh into the balance? A general preference for adversarial procedure? The like procedural treatment of routine and complex cases? If the former is a relevant consideration, then using discovery controls such as targeting, phasing, and sequencing discovery makes sense only when the lawyers, left to their own devices, are unable to gather information in an orderly fashion and organize it into proofs and reasoned arguments. (For more on this point, see *supra* p. 933, Note 7.) But how frequently will such situations arise, and how frequently will staged discovery be the proper remedy for this "lawyer dysfunction"?

Was *Klein* a case of either lawyer dysfunction or abusive, impositional discovery? If not, then why formally stage discovery? Was staged discovery only a manifestation of the court's preference for settling the case quickly? On what information was such a preference based? Conversely, can we be sure that *Rail Freight* is not a case of lawyer dysfunction or impositional discovery?

There are no more reported decisions in *Klein*, so we cannot be sure whether staging discovery turned out to be the best approach. For what it is worth, one of the lawyers in the case reported to us that he did not think that *Klein*'s discovery controls were effective. His stated reason is that one set of lawyers balked at the system, and made it difficult for the plan to work as intended. The same participant said, however, that essentially the same plan had worked extremely well in other, more routine litigation.

9. Sometimes lawyers in complex litigation will refer to "discovery tracks." One meaning of this phrase is that lawyers conduct discovery on different issues simultaneously. Thus, one team of plaintiffs' and defense lawyers may be conducting discovery with regard to one time frame or one issue in the litigation, while another team of plaintiffs' and defense lawyers conduct discovery on another time frame or issue. In this sense, tracks are a form of staged discovery. Using tracks is most common, however, when parties are faced with a discovery cutoff too short to allow a single team of lawyers to conduct full discovery on all issues. The track system can be inefficient; it is often difficult for the lead lawyers to keep abreast of all the information that is being generated. The system also requires that each side have enough lawyers available to handle all the tracks. Because of these problems, and because tracks can be used to impose significant costs on less well-funded parties, judges may be required to approve the use of discovery tracks. *See* In re Multi-Piece Rim Prods. Liab. Litig., 464 F. Supp. 969, 974 (J.P.M.L. 1979) (noting that an MDL judge "has the authority to group the pretrial proceedings on different discovery tracks according to the common factual issues or according to each defendant if necessary for the just and efficient conduct of the litigation, and to schedule any discovery unique to particular parties, actions or claims to proceed in separate discovery tracks concurrently with the common discovery, thus enhancing the efficient processing of all aspects of the litigation"); *cf.* In re MGM Grand Hotel Fire Litig., 660 F. Supp. 522, 526 (D. Nev. 1987) (mentioning use of eleven discovery tracks to take 1,400 depositions).

c. Discovery Disputes

One of the *bête noires* of disclosure and discovery is resolving disputes about the proper scope of the parties' obligations. Efficiently handling these disputes is critical in all cases, but nowhere more so than in complex litigation, in which the opportunities for parties to object to disclosure and discovery are as vast as the amount of information that is discoverable. The Federal Rules of Civil Procedure contain a dispute-resolution process. *See* Fed. R. Civ. P. 26(c), 37, 45(c). A party from whom disclosure or discovery is sought can either move for a protective order preventing disclosure or discovery, or the party seeking information can move to compel disclosure or discovery. A nonparty wishing to resist discovery can move to quash the subpoena requiring the discovery. In all cases, the basic issue is the same. As a general matter, parties are entitled to obtain information that is relevant, proportional, and not privileged. Fed. R. Civ. P. 26(b)(1)-(2). The person resisting disclosure or discovery must show that one or more of these three limits applies.

The Federal Rules' approach, which is designed for ordinary litigation, is to resolve each dispute one by one. In complex cases, this retail-level approach could tie up a case for years, as a court examines each document or each deposition question to determine its conformity with Rules 26(b)(1) and -(b)(2). Thus, some mechanism to handle disputes in bulk must often be developed. We previously examined one such technique — the umbrella protective order — that courts employ in this context, but this approach does not so much resolve discovery disputes as punt them down the road. *See supra* p. 882. Unless the parties settle first, judges must at some point determine the evidence on which the parties can rely in shaping their proofs and arguments.

A related problem — and one that induces or intensifies many of the disputes that arise — is the doctrine of waiver. For most privileges, the traditional rule was that a party who discloses privileged information — whether intentionally or inadvertently — waives the privilege not only for that piece of information but for all other pieces of information covering the same subject matter. Thus, the inadvertent disclosure of a single piece of paper containing material protected by the attorney-client privilege forced the party to disclose all attorney-client material regarding that same representation. The harsh consequences of waiver has three possible effects. The first is the necessity of parties spending significant amounts of money screening documents before handing them over to an opponent. The second is the parties' use of broad privilege objections to categories of requested information to avoid the possibility of waiver. The third is a reluctance to work cooperatively with others who share common interests, for fear that sharing information with a co-party might be regarded as a waiver of work-product protection.

This subsection examines the ways in which courts have handled discovery disputes regarding mass quantities of information and minimized the negative effects of the waiver doctrine.

IN RE "AGENT ORANGE" PRODUCT LIABILITY LITIGATION

97 F.R.D. 427 (E.D.N.Y. 1983)

■ PRATT, Circuit Judge.

In this multidistrict litigation, plaintiffs, Vietnam war veterans and members of their families, seek to recover for injuries allegedly suffered as a result of the veterans' exposure to various herbicides, which defendants manufactured and supplied to the government for use in the Vietnam war. On April 29, 1982, the court appointed Sol Schreiber as special master pursuant to Fed. R. Civ. P. 53, to supervise all pretrial discovery for the Phase I trial on the government contract defense, scheduled to commence on June 27, 1983. . . .

Since most of the defendants' documentary discovery on the government contract defense centers on documents which are in the possession of various government agencies and which may be subject to executive privilege claims, the special master submitted to the court a report entitled "Recommended Procedures for Assertion of Executive Privilege" . . . . Defendants have submitted a letter with attached exhibits in support of their objection to portions of the special master's recommendation, and the government has submitted a memorandum in support of the recommendation with suggestions for two modifications. . . .

The government cannot be required to produce in litigation material which falls within the "deliberative process" privilege, Kinoy v. Mitchell, 67 F.R.D. 1, 10-11 (S.D.N.Y. 1975), or the "state secrets" privilege, United States v. Reynolds, 345 U.S. 1, 6 (1953). The former protects communications to the executive for purposes of decision making; the latter protects material which contains national security or state secrets. The special master recommended different procedures for handling these two categories of materials and discussed them separately in his report.

I.   *Deliberative Process Privilege*

In his report to the court, the special master thoroughly discussed the rationale for the deliberative process privilege and the factors to be considered in determining whether the privilege should apply. . . . Whether or not such a privilege will apply to particular documents or testimony must await the specifics of a particular claim, when and if it is made. As to the procedural side of the problem, now before the court, without expressing any view as to the scope or extent of the privilege, the court concludes that the special master has recommended a practical and efficient method for handling possible assertions of the privilege by the government, and the court adopts these procedures in full. . . .

1.   *Documents* — If the government objects to production of a document on the basis of the deliberative process privilege, it shall submit an affidavit by an official of the agency having custody of the document describing the document in general terms, why the privilege should apply, and the harm which would result from disclosure. In addition, the government shall make the document available to the special master for *in camera* inspection. The party seeking disclosure shall have seven days to submit to the special master and the government a statement of litigative need. After the special master has ruled on the privilege claim, the parties and the government may appeal his decision within ten days to this court.

2.   *Depositions* — If the government asserts the privilege with respect to a witness at a deposition, the party seeking a response has seven days to

submit to the government and the special master a copy of the unanswered questions, together with a detailed statement of litigative need. Seven days after that submission, the government must submit to the parties and the special master an affidavit by an official of the agency on whose behalf the privilege is asserted, stating why the privilege applies and what harm disclosure of the response would cause. In addition, the government must submit to the special master a detailed summary of the responses the witness would have made absent the privilege. The appeal procedure from the special master's ruling is the same as that with respect to documents.

No party has objected to the recommended procedures for assertion of the deliberative process privilege. However, the government recommends that the procedures be modified in two respects. First, it suggests that the special master determine whether a document is relevant to the litigation before requiring the government to assert the privilege formally. Second, it requests that the government be permitted to submit a more detailed affidavit to the special master in lieu of the requirement of automatic *in camera* review.

The special master considered the possibility of making a relevance finding prior to formal assertion of the deliberative process privilege and rejected it. In doing so, he noted that he will consider relevance in determining whether the privilege should apply, and the court agrees with his reasoning on this issue.

The court also concludes that the provision for automatic *in camera* inspection of a document at issue is fair. Courts have often employed this method to determine whether the privilege should apply. It enables the special master to make a speedy determination as to whether the document should be protected, thereby expediting discovery; at the same time, the government's burden is lessened because the affidavit it must submit in support of its claim of privilege need not be as detailed.

Because of the limited time remaining before the commencement of trial and because of the parties' need to conduct full discovery, the court concludes that *in camera* inspection provides the best method for determining whether the privilege is applicable. . . .

II. *State Secrets Privilege*

Material containing information concerning national defense, military secrets, or international relations is protected by the state secrets privilege. Unlike the deliberative process privilege, which is qualified and may be overcome by a showing that the interests in disclosure outweigh the interests in non-disclosure, the state secrets privilege is absolute and will not be overcome by a demonstration of litigative need. In addition, while *in camera* review of documents claimed to be protected by the deliberative process privilege is routinely utilized, *in camera* inspection is not routine in cases where the state secrets privilege is invoked. . . .

The special master . . . recognized that the case law indicates that, for assertion of the privilege, there must be a formal claim of privilege by the head of the department or agency in control of the matter after personal consideration by that officer, *United States v. Reynolds*, 345 U.S. at 7-8; he also recognized, that, in view of the large number of documents at issue here, a requirement that the government formally assert the privilege for all documents, including those which are not relevant to the litigation, may be oppressive and burdensome. In addition, he recognized, as do the government and all parties to the litigation, that the imminence of the trial date requires a speedy and efficient method of resolving privilege claims.

Briefly stated, the special master's recommended procedures for assertion of the state secrets privilege are as follows:

1. *Documents* — If the government believes that a document is protected by the privilege but is not relevant to the litigation, it shall supply to the parties and the special master an affidavit by one with knowledge of the document indicating why it is not relevant. The government shall also either (a) submit the document to the special master for *in camera* review, or (b) submit a more detailed affidavit on the issue of relevance. A party seeking disclosure has seven days to submit a statement showing why the document is relevant. If the special master determines that the document is relevant and the government asserts the privilege, it shall then submit to the parties and the special master an affidavit by the head of the agency having control over the matter describing the document in general terms, stating that the affiant has personally examined the documents and describing the harm which would result from disclosure. The party seeking disclosure has seven days to submit a statement of litigative need. The government may also submit the document to the special master for *in camera* inspection, or an affidavit describing it in more detail. After the special master rules on the privilege claim, the parties and the government may appeal his ruling to the court.

2. *Depositions* — If the government asserts the privilege with respect to a witness at a deposition, the party seeking a response has seven days to submit to the government and the special master a copy of the unanswered questions and a detailed statement of relevance and litigative need. The government has seven days to submit to the special master and the parties an affidavit of nonrelevance and a summary of the responses the deponent would have made if the privilege were not asserted. If the special master determines that the questions are relevant, and the government asserts the state secrets privilege, it has seven days to submit to the parties and the special master an affidavit by the head of the agency having control over the matter stating that the affiant has personally reviewed the questions and the responses, and stating the harm resulting from disclosure. The government may also submit to the special master a summary of the responses for *in camera* inspection. The parties and the government may appeal the special master's ruling on the privilege claim to the court.

Defendants object to the recommended procedures on the ground that the government as a nonparty has no standing to object to discovery requests on relevance grounds. They argue that the government should be required to assert the state secrets privilege formally with respect to all documents requested, whether or not relevant to the issues in this case. The government, on the other hand, argues that to require it to assert the privilege formally with respect to each and every document, whether or not relevant to this litigation, may be burdensome and oppressive. . . .

This argument [by the defendants] is disingenuous, to say the least. In its memorandum, the government outlined the procedures it is required to follow if it wishes to assert the state secrets privilege formally.   [The procedures involved a four-step review process by a privilege committee and high-ranking officials in two agencies.]

These procedures are obviously cumbersome and time consuming, but the issue now facing us is not the efficiency or validity of the government's established procedures. The issue, instead, is: how can this case be fairly and efficiently prepared for trial, given such governmental obstacles to releasing potentially relevant information? Requiring the government to follow these procedures for every document it believes should be protected by the state secrets privilege, whether or not relevant to this litigation would entail a much longer time than will be required by the special master's examination of the documents for relevance prior to formal assertion of the privilege. . . .

With respect to the defendants' argument that the government lacks standing to object to the relevance of requested discovery, the court agrees with the special master that, in view of the large number of documents at issue here, a prior determination of relevance will tend to decrease the burden on the government. In addition, all parties, if they have not done so already, should inform the special master, in detail, of the nature of the information they believe is relevant in order to assist him in making his relevance prior to formal assertion of the privilege. Contrary to defendants' position, the special master's recommended procedures are designed to enable defendants to obtain quickly all of the relevant documents and testimony not subject to privilege. . . .

The special master's recommended procedures provide an orderly method through which the defendants can obtain materials relevant to the Phase I trial without unduly burdening the government . . . . . The procedures . . . are adopted in full.

Notes

1.   The standing issue in *Agent Orange* — whether a nonparty can object on relevance grounds — has never been definitively resolved. Rule 45, which governs the subpoena of information from nonparties, underwent significant changes in 1991. These changes generally provided more protection for nonparties.   Rule 45(c)(3) requires a court to quash a subpoena when it "requires disclosure of privileged or other protected matter, if no exception or waiver applies," Fed. R. Civ. P. 45(c)(3)(A)(iii), or if disclosure "subjects a person to undue burden," Fed. R. Civ. P. 45(c)(3)(A)(iv). The Rule also permits a court to quash a subpoena that

requires disclosure of trade secrets or other confidential material. Fed. R. Civ. P. 45(c)(3)(B)(i). Curiously, however, the rule does not mention relevance as a ground for quashing subpoenas. Prior to the amendment, there were some cases that therefore suggested that nonparties could not assert a relevance objection. *See* Ghandi v. Police Dep't of Detroit, 74 F.R.D. 115 (E.D. Mich. 1977). Today, like *Agent Orange*, most cases permit nonparties to assert a relevance objection. *See* 9A CHARLES A. WRIGHT & ARTHUR R. MILLER, FEDERAL PRACTICE AND PROCEDURE § 2459 (3d ed. 2008). Some cases reason that a nonparty's relevance objection can be accounted for under the "undue burden" prong of Rule 45(c)(3)(A)(iv). *See, e.g.*, Snoznik v. Jeld-Wen, Inc., 259 F.R.D. 217, 222 (W.D.N.C. 2009); Am. Elec. Power Co. v. United States, 191 F.R.D. 132, 136 (S.D. Ohio 1999) ("Whether a subpoena imposes an 'undue burden' upon a witness is a case specific inquiry that turns on 'such factors as relevance, the need of the party for the documents, the breadth of the document request, the time period covered by it, the particularity with which the documents are described and the burden imposed.'").

2. *Agent Orange* demonstrates the range of issues that can arise in discovery disputes: relevance, privilege, and burden. Relevance and burden are often fact-specific inquiries about which it is difficult to generalize. For claims of privilege, some generalizations are possible.

(a) *Source of Privilege Law.* The Federal Rules of Civil Procedure do not themselves list the applicable privileges; that task is left to the Federal Rules of Evidence. The basic privilege rule is Fed. R. Evid. 501, but it is not particularly helpful. When state law provides the rule of decision, the privilege "shall be determined in accordance with State law"; in other cases, the privilege "shall be governed by the principles of the common law as they may be interpreted . . . in the light of reason and experience." What happens when a case involves both federal question and state-law claims? *See* von Bulow v. von Bulow, 811 F.2d 136 (2d Cir. 1987) (federal law of privilege controls).

(b) *Types of Privilege.* As *Agent Orange* shows, there are two basic structures to privileges: absolute privileges, which cannot be overcome, and qualified privileges, which can be overcome when a great enough need is shown. Among the absolute privileges are the attorney-client privilege, the doctor-patient privilege, the marital communication privilege, the clergy privilege, the state secrets privilege, and the Fifth Amendment privilege against self-incrimination. *See* JOHN W. STRONG, MCCORMICK ON EVIDENCE §§ 78-143 (4th ed. 1992); 23 CHARLES A. WRIGHT & KENNETH W. GRAHAM, JR., FEDERAL PRACTICE AND PROCEDURE §§ 5425-31 (1980). Among the qualified privileges are the deliberative-process privilege. In addition, certain protections are afforded to work-product material; in general, material prepared in anticipation of litigation is protected unless a requesting party shows substantial need and undue hardship, and even then, an attorney's mental impressions receive absolute or near-absolute protection. Fed. R. Civ. P. 26(b)(3); Upjohn Co. v. United States, 449 U.S. 383 (1981); Hickman v. Taylor, 329 U.S. 495 (1947).

Since the basic content of the absolute and qualified privileges does not vary with the complexity of the case, we leave to other courses the task of examining the details of these privileges.

3.   In attempting to resolve disputes about a potentially significant number of privilege claims, *Agent Orange* employs three techniques: entrusting decisions about disclosure to a judicial adjunct, using *in camera* screening, and forcing the parties to articulate more precisely their legal theories. A fourth common tactic is to require the party claiming protection to prepare an index that provides the basic identifying information and subject matter of each document withheld. A fifth technique is to require the party (or the court) to redact sensitive material from documents. A sixth is to use umbrella protective orders. Each tactic is used in complex litigation, sometimes in combination with other tactics; each has benefits and drawbacks. We have already examined the umbrella protective order, which is less of a dispute-resolving than a dispute-deferring technique. *See* *supra* p. 882. Here we examine the other five techniques.

(a) *Judicial Adjuncts.*   One of the most common uses of judicial adjuncts, such as masters or magistrate judges, is to resolve disputes about the disclosure of particular documents. Typically the court develops the framework under which the adjunct decides the claims of relevance, proportionality, or privilege; the adjunct then applies the framework to the specific documents. (Note, however, that in *Agent Orange* the master both developed and applied the framework. Is this wise?) This approach frees up the judge to work on larger case-management issues. It also keeps the judge from becoming too familiar with certain information in advance of trial — arguably maintaining the judge's neutrality.

On the other hand, judicial adjuncts may delay the litigation if the parties take a significant number of appeals from the adjunct's decisions, and they may also prevent the judge from getting a feel for the litigation that she is supposed to be managing. Moreover, a master may impose significant costs on the parties. Finally, using judicial adjuncts does not obviate the need for document-by-document review; it merely substitutes one reviewer for another. Other concerns regarding adjuncts, which we explored *supra* pp. 753-66, are also applicable.

(b) In Camera *Review.* *In camera* review allows the judge or adjunct to review contested documents in private. One problem with *in camera* inspection is that it may prejudice the judge, particularly in a non-jury case; indeed, the *Manual* recommends in such cases that another judge or judicial adjunct be used to review the documents. MANUAL FOR COMPLEX LITIGATION, FOURTH § 11.431 (2004). Moreover, with respect to some types of claims (such as a state-secrets privilege with respect to highly classified information), *in camera* inspection may not be an option. In *Agent Orange*, the special master received a security clearance from the government to avoid the problem. But the security classification of some documents may exceed the clearance of the judge or adjunct.

Moreover, *in camera* review does not preclude the need for document-by-document review; indeed, automatic *in camera* review is very labor-intensive. Selective *in camera* review of representative documents or particularly sensitive documents avoids some of the labor, but still requires the judge to find ways to deal with the remaining documents.

(c) *Detailing Legal and Factual Theories.* Forcing the parties to develop their legal and factual theories in detail is one of the least invoked powers for resolving discovery disputes. It makes particularly good sense with respect to relevance claims, but it would also be helpful in assessing the degree of need for qualified-privilege claims. This technique has the happy side-effect of acting as an issue-narrowing tool akin to the forced stipulation process explored *supra* p. 834. Unfortunately, document discovery, as well as the assertion of relevance or privilege claims, often occurs in the early stages of the litigation, just when the parties are least able to provide a helpful degree of detail concerning their cases. Waiting to rule on objections until more discovery has occurred may obviate that problem, but if the documents are ultimately released, a certain amount of discovery may need to be repeated.

(d) *Indexing.* Federal Rule 26(b)(5)(A)(ii) requires a party withholding information under a claim of privilege or work product to "describe the nature of the documents, communications, or tangible things not produced or disclosed — and to do so in a manner that, without revealing the information itself privileged or protected, will enable other parties to assess the claim." The idea of generating such lists of documents developed in the Freedom of Information Act context, in which the government was required to describe documents withheld pursuant to a FOIA request. *See* Vaughn v. Rosen, 484 F.2d 820 (D.C. Cir. 1973). The concept quickly spread into complex litigation; indeed, in complex cases, Rule 26(b)(5) merely codified an already common practice. Such a list, which usually contains the author and addressee of a document, its date, its title, and a brief description of the document, is commonly called a "privilege log" or "*Vaughn* index." *See* MANUAL, *supra*, § 11.431.

Indexing should, in theory, reduce the number of documents about which there will be legitimate disputes, and should provide the court with basic information concerning each document. Because indexing is expensive, it should also, in theory, discourage profligate objections. On the other hand, the process imposes a significant additional cost on a party legitimately entitled to withhold information.

(e) *Redaction.* Sometimes a document is objectionable only in part. In these situations, the party or the court can edit out the portions of a document that are privileged, and produce the remainder. From the court's viewpoint, it is usually preferable for the party to do the editing, although there is the problem that the party has an incentive to do a bit too much redaction. Redaction often occurs in conjunction with an *in camera* inspection of a privileged document; the court might order production only of a redacted version of the document it reviewed.

A leading example of redaction is *Equal Employment Opportunity Commission v. University of Notre Dame du Lac*, 715 F.2d 331, 337 (7th Cir. 1983), in which a university refused, in response to an administrative subpoena, to produce the personnel files of faculty members in a department that had allegedly made a discriminatory tenure decision. The court of appeals found that the identity and other revealing characteristics of the department's faculty members were subject to a qualified academic-freedom privilege (a position later rejected in *University of Pennsylvania v. EEOC*, 493 U.S. 182 (1990)). The court of appeals ordered the defendant to redact the personnel files to eliminate identifying information, and further ordered the district court to review the redactions *in camera* to ensure that the redactions were "reasonably necessary" to protect the faculty's identity. It allowed the plaintiff an opportunity to obtain more information from the files upon a showing of "substantial need." *Id.* at 337-38. We previously encountered redaction in *In re Southeastern Milk Antitrust Litigation*, 666 F. Supp. 2d 908 (E.D. Tenn. 2009) (*supra* p. 883), in which the court removed the umbrella protection given to filed materials that the parties denominated as confidential, and instead ordered the parties to redact any confidential portions of materials filed with the court. *Cf.* Roberts v. Heim, 123 F.R.D. 614 (N.D. Cal. 1988) (ordering sanctions against a lawyer who failed to produce the non-privileged aspects of a document after a special master ordered the lawyer to produce a redacted version).

Redaction has become a particular issue in court filings in financial, bankruptcy, and government-benefit cases; documents in these cases can contain sensitive information like social-security, taxpayer-identification, or financial-account numbers. Rule 5.2(a) requires parties to redact such information in filings.

4. The techniques mentioned in the last Note do not absolve the parties of the obligation to screen their documents to determine if disclosure or discovery is objectionable. Indeed, the indexing requirement forces parties to screen documents. In-house screening of documents prior to disclosure (or to making an objection) is often called a "privilege review." Privilege reviews can be extraordinarily expensive. For instance, in *Zubulake v. UBS Warburg LLC*, 216 F.R.D. 280, 283(S.D.N.Y. 2003), the estimated cost of restoring the ESI was $165,954.67, and the attorney- and paralegal-review cost to screen the documents for privileged material was $107,694.72 — a whopping 39% of the total cost of production. These numbers are not unique. According to a survey of 300 general counsel in both large and small corporations:

> So much of the cost of American litigation these days is driven by the page-by-page privilege review that those hapless contract lawyers are doing .... More than a quarter estimated that at least one-fifth of their annual litigation expense went toward a pre-production privilege review, including 16% for whom it represented at least 30% of litigation spending. Even for smaller companies, 30% said the pre-production process accounted for a fifth or more of overall litigation costs; for billion-dollar firms, it was 33% of annual spending — vivid reminders that companies might do well to revisit best practices for this critical task. One of our $1 billion+ respondents stated it had spent over $3 million on pre[-]production privilege review in a single matter!

Robert D. Owen, *Litigation Trends Survey Results* (Nov. 4, 2007), *available at* http://www.slaw.ca/2007/11/04/litigation-trends-survey-results.

Unless techniques to bring down this enormous cost are developed — and we know of none (other than outsourcing the matter to foreign vendors to perform such reviews more cheaply or hoping that artificial-intelligence programs might some day reduce the cost further) — a huge chunk of the pretrial cost in complex litigation is irreducible. Umbrella protective orders reduce the need to do some pre-production screening. As we have observed, however, these orders are better at addressing trade-secret or related confidentiality claims than they are at addressing privilege claims; no party is going to hand over work-product or attorney-client material, even if the opposing party agrees to treat it in confidence. *See supra* p. 891, Note 3. As long as documents must be reviewed for these privileges, umbrella orders save less money than you might have thought that they did.

5.   With mass document screenings being handled by "hapless" lawyers working by the hour for vendors, it is likely that at least a few privileged documents will slip through the screen. That possibility raises the issue of waiver, as well as the issue whether a party can get back and "re-privilege" the document. As you might expect, these issues have been often litigated.

COBURN GROUP, LLC v. WHITECAP ADVISORS LLC

640 F. Supp. 2d 1032 (N.D. Ill. 2009)

■   BROWN, United States Magistrate Judge.

Before the court is Defendant Whitecap Advisors LLC's Motion to Compel Return of Documents and to Strike Deposition Testimony. For the reasons set out below, . . . the motion is granted.

BACKGROUND

Coburn Group, LLC, ("Coburn") claims in this lawsuit that Whitecap Advisors LLC ("Whitecap") breached an oral contract to pay Coburn fees for referring investors to Whitecap. In the present motion, Whitecap originally requested an order requiring Coburn to return two documents totaling 16 pages that it claims are privileged and were inadvertently produced in its document production of approximately 40,000 pages. Whitecap also asked that the court strike any deposition testimony related to the documents and bar Coburn from using any information obtained from the documents. Coburn refused Whitecap's request to return the documents and opposes the motion. . . . The sole remaining issue is a half-page long e-mail that Whitecap employee Brian Broesder sent to Whitecap principal Eric Kamisher on September 26, 2007 (hereinafter, "the e-mail").

Whitecap claims that the e-mail is protected work product and was produced inadvertently despite the efforts of Whitecap and its counsel. Michael Hultquist, one of Whitecap's attorneys, states that, in order to respond to Coburn's discovery requests, Whitecap provided him with computer hard drives containing approximately 72,000 pages of potentially responsive documents. He assigned two experienced paralegals to review the documents and to separate them into categories for production or assertion of privilege, including attorney-client and work-product material. That review took five weeks. On March 6, 2008, Whitecap produced approximately 40,000 responsive documents to Coburn in hard-copy form. A CD with electronic copies of those documents was sent to Coburn in June 2008.

Mr. Hultquist states that he first realized that the e-mail had been produced to Coburn when Coburn's counsel began questioning Mr. Broesder about it at his deposition on July 14, 2008. Mr. Hultquist objected. The next day, at Mr. Kamisher's deposition, Mr. Hultquist told Coburn's counsel that the e-mail was privileged and work-product protected, and requested its return. . . . On August 5, 2008, Coburn's counsel wrote to Whitecap's counsel refusing to return the documents. . . . In that letter, Coburn's counsel . . . agreed to keep the documents secured until the court's decision, and requested that the parties try to work out an agreed briefing schedule in light of the lawyers' schedules. . . . Whitecap filed its motion on September 5, 2008.

. . . [Subsequently] Whitecap clarified that it is asserting only work-product protection, not attorney-client privilege. . . .

ANALYSIS

I. *Work-product protection*

. . .

The court's *in camera* review shows that the e-mail is work product. The e-mail was sent on September 26, 2007, more than four months after this lawsuit was filed. The subject line of the e-mail is "Requests on Coburn Filing." In it, Mr. Broesder provides Mr. Kamisher with information he gathered about Whitecap's dealings with Coburn, in order to respond to requests by attorneys who were already representing Whitecap. . . .

Thus, the e-mail is protected against disclosure unless Whitecap has waived the protection or Coburn has made the showing of "substantial need" required by Rule 26(b)(3)(A)(ii).

II. *Waiver*

Fed. R. Evid. 502, which became effective September 19, 2008, creates a new framework for managing disclosure issues in a cost effective manner in the age of large electronic document productions. Before Rule 502 was adopted, courts considering whether the unintended disclosure of a privileged document resulted in a waiver of privilege looked at the circumstances surrounding the disclosure and followed a "balancing approach" considering a number of factors. Rule 502 organizes those considerations into three steps:

> When made in a Federal proceeding or to a Federal office or agency, the disclosure [of a communication or information covered by the attorney-client privilege or work-product protection] does not operate as a waiver in a Federal or State proceeding if:
>
> (1) the disclosure is inadvertent;
>
> (2) the holder of the privilege or protection took reasonable steps to prevent disclosure; and
>
> (3) the holder promptly took reasonable steps to rectify the error, including (if applicable) following Federal Rule of Civil Procedure 26(b)(5)(B).

A. *Inadvertent disclosure*

Rule 502 does not define "inadvertent." Under the prior case law, reaching the conclusion that a document had been "inadvertently produced" required analysis of the circumstances surrounding the production, including the number of documents produced in discovery and the care with which the pre-production document review was performed. If the production was found to be inadvertent, the court used a "balancing approach" to determine whether the inadvertent disclosure waived the privilege. In that step, many of the same factors, such as scope of discovery and reasonableness of precautions taken, were reviewed again.

Some opinions determining the question of "inadvertent disclosure" under subpart (b)(1) of Rule 502 repeat the prior case law's process. *See, e.g.*, Heriot v. Byrne, 257 F.R.D. 645, 658-59 (N.D. Ill. 2009). In *Heriot*, for example, to determine whether the disclosure was inadvertent, the court considered "factors such as the total number of documents reviewed, the procedures used to review the documents before they were produced, and the actions of producing party after discovering that the documents had been produced." The court also applied the first two of these factors to the analysis under subpart (b)(2), considering whether the producing party took reasonable steps to prevent disclosure.

In this court's view, the structure of Rule 502 suggests that the analysis under subpart (b)(1) is intended to be much simpler, essentially asking whether the party intended a privileged or work-product protected document to be produced or whether the production was a mistake. To start, the parallel structure of subparts (a)(1) and (b)(1) of Rule 502 contrasts a waiver that is *intentional* with a disclosure that is *inadvertent*.[5]

---

5. Rule 502(a) provides that a disclosure that waives the attorney-client privilege or work-product protection extends the waiver to undisclosed communications only if:

(1) the waiver is intentional;

(2) the disclosed and undisclosed communications or information concern the same subject matter; and

(3) they ought in fairness to be considered together.

More importantly, subparts (b)(2) and (b)(3) separately address the reasonableness of the privilege holder's steps to prevent disclosure and to rectify the error. That they are set out as separate subparts distinct from the question of inadvertent disclosure strongly suggests that the drafters did not intend the court to consider for subpart (b)(1) facts such as the number of documents produced only to repeat the consideration of those same facts for subparts (b)(2) and (b)(3).

Here, there is no real dispute that Whitecap did not intend to produce a work-product protected e-mail, and that producing the e-mail was a mistake. The court finds that the production of the e-mail was inadvertent.

B. *Reasonable steps to prevent disclosure*

The factors used in prior case law are helpful in determining what are "reasonable steps to avoid disclosure" under subpart (b)(2) of Rule 502. According to the Judicial Conference Rules Committee, the rule "is really a set of non-determinative guidelines that vary from case to case. . . . [C]onsiderations bearing on the reasonableness of a producing party's efforts include the number of documents to be reviewed and the time constraints for production."

The scope of discovery is a logical starting point in many cases because "[w]here discovery is extensive, mistakes are inevitable and claims of inadvertence are properly honored so long as appropriate precautions are taken." As discussed above, Whitecap gave its attorneys computer hard drives containing approximately 72,000 pages of potentially responsive documents, from which 40,000 pages of documents were produced to Coburn. Those numbers substantially exceed the number of documents that have been characterized as "large."

Mr. Hultquist, one of Whitecap's lead counsel for this case, supervised the document production and submitted an affidavit about the document review process. He states that he implemented a protocol for two experienced paralegals with 17 and 16 years' experience, respectively, to follow in reviewing the documents received from Whitecap for production to Coburn. The protocol to govern the document review included [various] parameters [including to "identify and mark as privileged documents prepared by any employee of Whitecap in anticipation of or in preparation for litigation pursuant to request by Whitecap's outside counsel"]. The review took five weeks, during which Mr. Hultquist reviewed many documents that were marked as privileged, and other documents that the paralegals presented to him with questions.

Coburn criticizes Whitecap's use of paralegals for the document review. Although the experience and training of the persons who conducted the review is certainly relevant to the reasonableness of the review, this court joins with *Heriot* in declining to hold that the use of paralegals or non-lawyers for document review is unreasonable in every case. In light of the large number of documents to be reviewed, Whitecap's use of experienced paralegals who were given specific direction and supervision by a lawyer who is lead counsel in the case was not unreasonable.

Coburn also claims that the protocol described by Mr. Hultquist did not teach the paralegals what to look for in determining whether a document was "prepared in anticipation of litigation." Coburn argues that it is unreasonable to expect the paralegals to identify the e-mail at issue here as work product because it is not apparent on its face that it is work product and therefore the procedure was unreasonable.

Unquestionably, reviewing documents for work product can be challenging because sometimes there are subtleties to the determination. As Coburn points out, whether a document is work product can rest on facts not apparent from the face of the document, as in this case. . . . But the document review can not be deemed unreasonable solely because a document slipped through which in close examination and with additional information turns out to be privileged or work product. If that were the standard, Rule 502(b) would have no purpose; the starting point of the Rule 502(b) analysis is that a privileged or protected document was, in fact, turned over. . . .

The court finds that Whitecap took reasonable steps to prevent disclosure. That Whitecap made a mistake in producing the e-mail despite those steps is not fatal to its claim for protection.

C. *Reasonable steps to rectify the error*

Coburn cites two time periods as demonstrating that Whitecap failed to promptly take reasonable steps to rectify the error: the four month delay between the document production in March 2008 and Whitecap's counsel's discovery at the depositions in July 2008 that the e-mails had been produced, and the five weeks between Coburn's final refusal to return the documents on August 5, 2008 and Whitecap's filing the present motion.

Prior to Rule 502, courts in this circuit looked to the time between a party's learning of the disclosure and that party's taking action to remedy it, rather than the time that elapsed since the document was placed in the hands of the other party. The Committee's comment that Rule 502 does not require a post-production review supports this view that the relevant time under subpart (b)(3) is how long it took the producing party to act after it learned that the privileged or protected document had been produced.

In this case, there is no dispute that Whitecap was unaware that the e-mail had been produced until Coburn's counsel asked Mr. Broesder about it, and that Whitecap's counsel immediately objected to its use. The next day Whitecap's counsel requested its return and followed that up with a written request. There was no delay on Whitecap's part in trying to rectify the error once it was discovered.

As for the delay in filing the motion, the facts recited above show that counsel for both sides acted reasonably and civilly in dealing with the disputed documents and the associated deposition transcripts. The lawyers for both sides needed time to investigate the facts and law surrounding the documents, and the issues turned out to have some complexity. In light of the fact that Whitecap accommodated Coburn's counsel's request for additional time to formulate Coburn's position, and that Coburn agreed to "quarantine" the documents until the dispute was resolved, the time Whitecap took to file the actual motion was not unreasonable.

The court finds, pursuant to Rule 502, that Whitecap did not waive work-product protection for the e-mail.

III. *Substantial need*

The finding that the e-mail is protected work product and that Whitecap has not waived that protection does not end the inquiry. Coburn may still retain the e-mail if it demonstrates that it has "substantial need for the materials to prepare its case and cannot, without undue hardship, obtain their substantial equivalent by other means." Fed. R. Civ. P. 26(b)(3)(A)(ii).

Coburn argues that it should be able to retain the e-mail because, in its view, paragraph 4 in the e-mail (relating to Whitecap's Illinois investors and whether any were brought to Whitecap by Coburn) contradicts statements Whitecap made in 2007 when it moved to dismiss Coburn's complaint for lack of personal jurisdiction. Importantly, Coburn does not argue that it has not be able to get discovery about Whitecap's Illinois investors. Rather, it is the e-mail itself that Coburn wants, to seek sanctions and "show at trial a pattern of untruthfulness by Kamisher."

As requested by Coburn, the court has carefully compared Mr. Broesder's statement in paragraph 4 of the e-mail to the statements Whitecap made when moving to dismiss and in Mr. Kamisher's various declarations in support of Whitecap's motion. . . . Whitecap's statements to the court are not dramatically at odds with Mr. Broesder's approximation, and Mr. Kamisher may well have had other information in addition to Mr. Broesder's e-mail. . . . Accordingly, the court concludes that Coburn has not made the showing required by Rule 26(b)(3)(A)(ii).

Finally, relying on a 1999 advisory opinion by the Illinois State Bar Association, Coburn's attorneys argue that they have a right, indeed, perhaps a duty, to retain the e-mail in order to represent their client zealously. ISBA Advisory Opinion on Prof'l Conduct 98-04 (Jan. 1999). The advisory opinion concluded that a lawyer who, without notice of the inadvertent transmission, receives and reviews an opposing party's confidential materials through the error or inadvertence of opposing counsel, may use the information in such materials.

The advisory opinion did not purport to address a situation where, as here, the court has found that the document retains work-product protection. Rule 502 prevents inadvertent disclosure from waiving the assertion of privilege or protection if the privilege holder has acted reasonably. That rule applies in federal court even if state law provides the rule of decision. Fed. R. Evid. 502(f). Additionally, the advisory opinion did not have the force of law even when it was issued and the continuing validity of its conclusion is doubtful in light of the evolution of the law in the past decade. The recently revised Illinois Rules of Professional Conduct added a new subsection requiring a lawyer who receives a document that the lawyer knows was inadvertently sent to notify the sender promptly. Ill. R. Prof'l Conduct 4.4(b) (effective Jan. 1, 2010). The commentary states that the purpose of the notification is to allow the sender to take protective measures, although whether the privileged status of the document has been waived is beyond the scope of the rule. Requiring the receiving lawyer to notify the sending lawyer is clearly at odds with any purported duty on the part of the receiving lawyer to use the information for the benefit of his or her client. . . .

CONCLUSION

For the foregoing reasons, . . . Defendant Whitecap Advisor LLC's Motion to Compel Return of Documents and to Strike Deposition Testimony is granted. Plaintiff Coburn Group, LLC and its counsel shall return the e-mail, including any copies in any format, to Whitecap's counsel immediately and shall not use that document for any purpose.

Notes

1.   *Coburn* briefly describes — simplifies might be a better word — the rather messy state of the law that preceded the congressional enactment of Federal Rule of Evidence 502 in 2008. On the consequences of disclosure, courts varied. The classical waiver rule was that any disclosure — inadvertent or not — amounted to a waiver; and once waiver occurred, all communications relating to the same subject matter must be disclosed. *See*, *e.g.*, In re Sealed Case, 877 F.2d 976, 980-81 (D.C. Cir. 1989). In more recent years, in part driven by the harshness of this rule in complex cases in which some inadvertent disclosure of protectable information is almost inevitable, courts had developed other approaches. One of these was precisely the opposite of the classical rule; it held that inadvertent disclosure did not amount to waiver under any circumstances. *See* Georgetown Manor, Inc. v. Ethan Allen, Inc., 753 F. Supp. 936, 938 (S.D. Fla. 1991) (attorney-client privilege is held by the client and cannot be waived by the attorney's mistake). The third approach lay between the others; it eschewed per se rules in favor of a test that focused on whether the disclosing party took reasonable steps to prevent disclosure. This approach was the one that *Coburn* discussed; it was the law in the Seventh Circuit at the time. *See* Judson Atkinson Candies, Inc. v. Latini-Hohberger Dhimantec, 529 F.3d 371, 388-389 (7th Cir. 2008).

Under the intermediate approach, "reasonableness" was often determined by a balancing test that examined such factors as "(1) the reasonableness of the precautions taken to prevent inadvertent disclosure, (2) the time taken to rectify any error, (3) the scope of discovery, (4) the extent of the disclosure, and (5) overriding issues of fairness." *See* Bank Brussels Lambert v. Credit Lyonnais (Suisse) S.A., 160 F.R.D. 437, 443 (S.D.N.Y. 1995) (also noting that "[t]his regimen best reconciles the principles underlying the attorney-client privilege with the realities of document production in complex litigation"); *accord, Judson*, 529 F.3d at 388. As another way of avoiding the harsh consequences of waiver, some courts took the position that disclosure pursuant to court order was not "voluntary" and therefore not a waiver. *See* Transamerica Computer Co. v. Int'l Bus. Mach. Corp., 573 F.2d 646, 651 (9th Cir. 1978) (no voluntary waiver when judge imposed "extremely rigorous schedule for discovery" and significant measures to prevent inadvertent disclosure were taken).

2. In addition, 2006 amendments to the Federal Rules of Civil Procedure required (and still requires) a person who discloses privileged or protectable information to notify the party to whom it has been given; the latter party "must promptly return, sequester, or destroy the specified information and any copies," and cannot use the information until the court resolves the waiver issue. Fed. R. Civ. P. 26(b)(5)(B), 45(d)(2)(B). But these amendments stated only the procedures by which claims of waiver and re-capturing of information were decided; they assiduously avoided setting any standards for determining whether waiver occurred. In light of the disparity in the cases and the limits in the Federal Rules of Civil Procedure, Congress filled the gap with Fed. R. Evid. 502.

3. *Coburn* describes Rule 502, which fairly well follows the middle course that had emerged in some of the cases. Rule 502, which applies solely to attorney-client and work-product waivers, distinguishes between intentional and inadvertent disclosures. For an intentional disclosure, Rule 502(a) discusses the effect of a disclosure on undisclosed information, sometimes requiring the party also to disclose other attorney-client or work-product communications that "concern the same subject matter." The strong implication of Rule 502(a) is that a party cannot renege on an intentional disclosure and try to re-privilege the information.

With respect to inadvertent disclosures, Rule 502(b) opens a wider door to permit the re-privileging of information. It requires both reasonable efforts to prevent the disclosure and reasonable efforts to re-capture it after disclosure. As *Coburn* shows, the word "reasonable" is the key to Rule 502(b), and it is nowhere defined. The Advisory Committee Note likewise refused to pin down the definition, although it did suggest that the group of factors developed in cases like *Bank Brussels* and *Judson* were good guideposts. So far, the cases appear to be adopting these factors. *See* Rhoads Indus. Inc. v. Bldg. Materials Corp., 254 F.R.D. 216 (E.D. Pa. 2008).

4. In *Coburn*, the defendant conducted a document-by-document search (albeit by paralegals) for privileged material. Such manual reviews are expensive. Therefore, it is common for parties to rely as much as possible on electronic means — perhaps by searching their ESI for certain keywords (names of attorneys, etc.) and then manually reviewing only the documents that the electronic screening surfaces. Indeed, in truly massive, document-intensive cases, this approach is to some extent inevitable. Using

a keyword-search process, however, virtually guarantees some failures. (For instance, suppose that a memorandum misspells the attorney's name).

The issue that emerges, and that is likely to receive much attention in the future, is whether relying on electronic searching is a reasonable means to prevent disclosure. *Victor Stanley, Inc. v. Creative Pipe*, 250 F.R.D. 251 (D. Md. 2008), applied the five "reasonableness" factors, and determined that using only keyword searches to find protected material was not reasonable. The court relied heavily on the defendant's failure to randomly sample the results of the keyword search to determine if the results were reliable. *Stanley* noted that "all keyword searches are not created equal; and there is a growing body of literature that highlights the risks associated with conducting an unreliable or inadequate keyword search or relying exclusively on such searches for privilege review." *Id.* at 256-57.

5.   In some circumstances even an intentional disclosure of information does not result in waiver.

(a) Disclosure of attorney-client information to a consultant does not constitute a waiver if the consultant possesses expertise that helps the lawyer to provide advice to the client. *See* United States v. Kovel, 296 F.2d 918 (2d Cir. 1961). Similarly, disclosure of work-product material to consultants does not waive the protection. *See* In re Tri-State Outdoor Media Group, Inc., 283 B.R. 358 (Bankr. M.D. Ga. 2002).

But lawyers need to be careful with these disclosures. Although the matter is in some doubt in the cases and the literature, the dominant view is that, once a lawyer designates a consultant as a testifying expert, opposing parties are entitled to review all information with which the expert was provided. *See* Regional Airport Auth. v. LFG, LLC, 460 F.3d 697 (6th Cir. 2006) (adopting majority view; collecting cases on both sides); 8 CHARLES ALAN WRIGHT ET AL., FEDERAL PRACTICE AND PROCEDURE § 2016.5 (Supp. 2010) (arguing for disclosure of all material supplied to a testifying expert); *but see* Haworth, Inc. v. Herman Miller, Inc., 162 F.R.D. 289, 292-96 (W.D. Mich. 1995) (adopting minority view); 6 JAMES WM. MOORE ET AL., MOORE'S FEDERAL PRACTICE § 26.80[1][a], at 26-477 (3d ed. 2007) (arguing that exempting shared information from disclosure has benefits, including "(1) it does not favor wealthy parties who can afford to hire both testifying and non-testifying experts, [and] (2) it discourages the use of strained hypotheticals between expert and counsel in order to avoid disclosure"). The text of Rule 26(a)(2), combined with the 1993 Advisory Committee Note accompanying the Rule, favor the majority view. In any event, even on the minority view, a party must disclose information — including attorney-client or work-product information — on which the expert *relied* in forming an opinion.

(b) Many courts recognize a "common interest doctrine" or "joint defense privilege" when co-parties with a common legal position share work-product information concerning that common position. *See, e.g.,* Lugosch v. Congel, 219 F.R.D. 220, 239-41 (N.D.N.Y. 2003). Some courts limit the doctrine to the situation in which information is shared by parties represented by the same lawyer; other courts use the doctrine whenever the parties have a common interest in a joint defense; and still other courts arguably permit the doctrine to be invoked when the parties do not have a common legal strategy but do have a "community of interests." *See Bank Brussels*, 160 F.R.D. 437 (adopting middle position); Richard L. Marcus, *The Perils of Privilege: Waiver and the Litigator*, 84 MICH. L. REV. 1605, 1637-42 (1986).

Here is one example. When we last encountered the *AT&T* antitrust saga, the district court had permitted the United States to obtain documents that a private plaintiff, MCI, had culled from AT&T's 7.5 million pages of production in the *MCI* case. The district court in the *MCI* case also modified its umbrella protective order to allow the United States to access these documents, as well as depositions and exhibits. *See supra* p. 896; p. 896, Note 2. To pick up the story at this point, one of the items that the modified protective order allowed the United States to obtain was "any explanatory material or information which would be helpful to an understanding of the items produced." United States v. Am. Tel. & Tel. Co., 642 F.2d 1285, 1288 (D.C. Cir. 1980). Included within the explanatory material that MCI gave to the United States were documents describing the structure of its litigation-support system, which contained computerized abstracts of documents, deposition transcripts, and exhibits received from AT&T. AT&T requested that the United States produce these documents. MCI intervened, objecting that these documents were work product prepared in anticipation of litigation: If AT&T saw what MCI thought worthy to place in its database, it would have a good idea of MCI's litigation strategy. AT&T responded that MCI had waived the protection by sharing the documents with the United States, and MCI then countered that the waiver fell within the common-interest doctrine. The special masters and the district court ordered the production, but the court of appeals reversed:

> . . . Several [prior] decisions have turned on whether the transferor has "common interests" with the transferee. In applying this standard courts have held the work product privilege not to be waived by disclosures between attorneys for parties "having a mutual interest in litigation," or . . . or between attorneys representing parties "sharing such a common interest in litigation, actual or prospective," or between parties one of whose interests in prospective litigation may turn on the success of the other party in a separate litigation. The earlier opinions in this line of decisions tended to employ a narrow definition of "common interests," restricted to situations in which the relationship of the parties was similar to that between co-parties in a suit. . . .

> . . . The purpose of the work product doctrine is to protect information against opposing parties, rather than against all others outside a particular confidential relationship, in order to encourage effective trial preparation. A disclosure made in the pursuit of such trial preparation, and not inconsistent with maintaining secrecy against opponents, should be allowed without waiver of the privilege. We conclude, then, that while the mere showing of a voluntary disclosure to a third person will generally suffice to show waiver of the

attorney-client privilege, it should not suffice in itself for waiver of the work product privilege. . . .

. . . "[C]ommon interests" should not be construed as narrowly limited to co-parties. So long as transferor and transferee anticipate litigation against a common adversary on the same issue or issues, they have strong common interests in sharing the fruit of the trial preparation efforts. . . .

We recognize that the truth-finding process might be further enhanced in the short term in this particular case if AT&T gained access to the documents in question. In the long run, however, this would discourage trial preparation and vigorous advocacy and would discourage any party from turning over work product to the government. . . .

Finally, the work product privilege is a qualified privilege which may be overridden by a showing of substantial need by the requesting party. . . . On appeal AT&T has asserted the district court's discretion concerning the applicability of this qualified privilege, but AT&T has made no showing of substantial need on the record. [*Id.* at 1298-1300, 1302.]

6.   In *In re Motor Fuel Temperature Sales,* 2009 WL 959491, at *1 (D. Kan. Apr. 3, 2009), attorneys for defendants who were engaged in a joint defense had exchanged "tens of thousands of documents (primarily email communications)," and asked to be relieved of the Rule 26(b)(5) obligation of reviewing all these documents and providing a privilege index of each communication for which the privilege was claimed. (For discussion of this obligation, see *supra* p. 955, Note 3(d).) They estimated that creating this index would take more than 1,000 hours and cost more than $165,000 — all of which would be wasted because they were entitled not to disclose this information. The court split the difference, requiring the attorneys to review the documents to see if they contained protected information but not requiring them to produce a privilege index of the documents that did.

7.   An opposing party is entitled to examine attorney-client or work-product information that is shown to a witness to refresh the witness's recollection, when it does in fact refresh recollection. Fed. R. Evid. 612. On the other hand, when the documents do not actually refresh the witness's recollection, some cases hold that lawyer's selection of documents to show to a witness during preparation for a deposition is itself work product, and opposing lawyers can obtain these specific documents only by showing that the witness relied on them to refresh his recollection. *See* Sporck v. Peil, 759 F.2d 312 (3d Cir. 1985). *Sporck* has been much criticized. *See, e.g.,* Nutramax Labs., Inc. v. Twin Labs. Inc., 183 F.R.D. 458 (D. Md. 1998). But keep the *Sporck* issue distinct from other intentional disclosures; *Sporck* did not involve the disclosure of documents containing protected information, but rather asked whether the process of selecting documents to show to a witness is itself work-product-protected activity. If attorney-client or work-product material were contained in the documents selected to be shown to the witness, presumably the ordinary analysis of intentional disclosure

would apply to that material. (On the other hand, if the witness does not rely on such material and the court follows *Sporck*, so that the documents need not be revealed, the opposing party might have trouble proving that an intentional disclosure occurred.)

8. The effect of disclosing information to testifying experts, *AT&T*'s recognition that litigation-support systems can be work product, and *Sporck* combine to raise questions of great import to complex litigation. It is common in complex cases for parties to create (or hire a vendor that has created) proprietary, computerized litigation-support systems to search and organize documents, depositions, and exhibits, and to analyze data. These systems can be expensive. The first issue is whether opposing parties can discover these systems, thereby obviating the need to spend significant resources creating another system. The evident legal objections to such free-riding are trade-secret or proprietary-information protection and work-product protection. The former can be handled with confidentiality orders or protective orders requiring the requesting party to pay a share of the cost of the system. On the latter objection, disclosure of a computerized litigation-support system is proper when the system is not developed for or in anticipation of litigation. *See* Santiago v. Miles, 121 F.R.D. 636 (W.D.N.Y. 1988). (Indeed, if the rule were otherwise, parties could not gain access to ESI systems, but would need to rely on hard copies produced by an opponent.) When the system is created for or in anticipation of litigation, however, courts generally treat the system as protected; as *AT&T* reflects, the system is then discoverable only on a showing of substantial need and undue hardship. *Cf.* MANUAL FOR COMPLEX LITIGATION, FOURTH § 11.12 (2004) (suggesting that a court establish a master file at the start of the case); MANUAL FOR COMPLEX LITIGATION, THIRD § 34 (1995) (encouraging parties to share technology that is to be used at trial).

Granting that such litigation-support systems are usually work product, the next issue is whether a waiver of that protection occurs when a party uses the system to generate the documents that are shown to a witness or the data on which an expert relies. We can assume for now that the opposing parties are entitled to the documents or data themselves; the issue is whether they are also entitled to disclosure of the system, even though that system was not given to the witness or expert. In *Pearl Brewing Co. v. Jos. Schlitz Brewing Co.*, 415 F. Supp. 1122, 1134-41 (S.D. Tex. 1976), experts retained by the plaintiff in an antitrust suit developed a computer model. The computer experts themselves were not going to testify, but their model was going to be relied on by the expert economic witness that was going to testify. The plaintiff offered to make available the data that the model developed, but balked at providing the model itself. The defendant contended that, without the model, its expert could understand the data only by spending a great deal of time and money and that this process would further delay discovery. Finding that these facts were exceptional enough to override the work-product protection accorded to expert testimony and materials, the court held that the reliance of the plaintiff's expert economist on the computer model required its disclosure to the defendant. The court further required that the computer experts themselves be subject to limited depositions that would help interpret the computer program, and that the defendant should pay the costs of copying the program and deposing the experts. It did not, however, require that alternative model designs rejected by the computer experts be disclosed.

Somewhat more broadly, *National Union Electric Corp. v. Matsushita Electric Industrial Co.*, 494 F. Supp. 1257 (E.D. Pa. 1980), suggests that, at least in some circumstances, the disclosure of information obtained by using a litigation-support system might make portions of the system discoverable. *National Union* was one of the early skirmishes in the complex antitrust case that culminated in *Matsushita Electric Industrial Co. v. Zenith Radio Corp.*, 475 U.S. 574 (1986) *(supra* p. 850). The plaintiffs responded to the defendants' interrogatories with information in a computer-printout format. The plaintiffs generated the printout by using a litigation-support system specially prepared for the litigation. The underlying information that had been entered into the litigation-support system was factual in nature; no one disputed that it was discoverable. After receiving the printout, however, the defendants requested the information in a computer-readable format, so that they could save the expense of creating their own database. The defendants even offered to pay all the expenses of creating the tape. The plaintiff objected, stating that the database contained the mental impressions of the lawyers that made decisions about which information to collect, that they could not be forced under the Federal Rules to create a document (the computer tape) not already in existence, and that the defendants could create their own database from the information supplied.

How would you decide the case? Judge Becker ordered the plaintiff to create and supply the tape. *See also* Fauteck v. Montgomery Ward & Co., 91 F.R.D. 393, 399 (N.D. Ill. 1980) (ordering production of a computer analysis of the plaintiff class when"the judgments entailed in database compilation are essentially statistical in nature and that the methodology of computerizing personnel records for litigation purposes is well established in the field"; further ordering the plaintiffs to pay 50% of the defendant's costs of compilation).

9.   Do cases like *Pearl Brewing, National Union,* and *Fauteck* in effect give a judge a case-management power to force the parties to build a single litigation-support system and to share the expense? Is such a power consistent with an adversarial system? Even if it isn't, is a shared system the result that the parties would have negotiated ex ante, but for strategic behavior on one side? Should issues of waiver generally be analyzed in this same light: whether ordering disclosure overcomes strategic behavior that imposes needless costs; or whether, on the other hand, it threatens the core of adversarial process?

3. Non-Traditional Discovery

This subsection examines very briefly discovery techniques that lie beyond the standard methods. In 1985, the *Manual for Complex Litigation* urged courts to consider an array of "informal discovery" techniques and the lawyers to consider stipulations that amended the usual methods of conducting discovery. MANUAL FOR COMPLEX LITIGATION (SECOND) § 21.422 (1985). The present *Manual* continues the call for lawyers and judges to consider non-traditional discovery methods to reduce costs and delay. MANUAL FOR COMPLEX LITIGATION, FOURTH § 11.423 (2004); *see* Thomas H. Hart, III, *Case Preparation in Federal Court: Informal Discovery*, CASE & COMMENT 22 (July-Aug. 1987). Today such efforts can be critically important to the successful prosecution or defense of most complex cases.

All this is fairly obvious; the hard parts are figuring out what methods should be used to get the information, and then getting it. For instance, parties must never overlook the possibility of obtaining information from the government through Freedom of Information Act requests. The Internet is another treasure trove of information. This book is not the place to explore these issues in detail, but let us briefly mention two devices with some thematic importance.

a. Interviews in Lieu of Depositions

One method of discovering information is to use neutral persons that conduct interviews to garner information. Aside from providing initial directions to the interviewers, the lawyers are cut out of the information-gathering process. MANUAL FOR COMPLEX LITIGATION, FOURTH § 11.452 (2004). The most noteworthy example of an interview process occurred in a toxic tort containing 10,000 plaintiffs allegedly exposed to DDT. Rather than deposing each plaintiff, the parties negotiated a set of questions that interviewers asked each plaintiff at an interview center. The interviewers had limited discretion to ask follow-up questions. A plaintiff that missed two interview appointments was dismissed from the case.

Professor Francis McGovern, who designed the discovery-survey process as a special master, reported that it resulted in the dismissal of more than 3,000 plaintiffs. He also estimated that the process saved more than 52,000 hours of attorney time and $7,400,000. On the other hand, the case ended up settling before individual plaintiff discovery would have been necessary, thus necessitating a second, mailed survey for settlement purposes and largely mooting the first set of interviews. Professor McGovern reported that the quality and reliability of the interviews was comparable to that of a traditional interrogatory-and-deposition process, but that the mailed surveys were more disappointing. Attorney satisfaction with the discovery-survey process was reported to be high. For a complete analysis of the interview process, see Francis E. McGovern & E. Allen Lind, *The Discovery Survey*, 51 LAW & CONTEMP. PROBS. 41 (Autumn 1988).

Whatever its success, this informal interview process has never, to our knowledge, been replicated in any other mass tort. Why not? What does this lack of use say about the attitudes of lawyers and judges toward the parties' adversarial right to control the gathering of information?

The discovery survey in the DDT litigation resulted from a stipulation among the parties. *See* Fed. R. Civ. P. 29 (allowing the parties to stipulate to changes in discovery).   Getting parties to agree on changes to the ordinary course of discovery is evidently difficult.   Typically one party — usually the better-financed party — is advantaged by the status quo.   The carrots that induced the parties to agree in the DDT litigation were great cost savings to the less well-financed plaintiffs and the prospect of many dismissals of peripheral plaintiffs for the better-financed defendants.   Does the court have any sticks to force such a stipulation?   In *Crandall v. City and County of Denver*, 594 F. Supp. 2d 1245 (D. Colo. 2009), the plaintiffs lost at trial.   The court suggested that it might have refused to grant the defendant's request to impose as costs the witness fees for eighteen background witnesses that the court believed the defendant could have informally interviewed.   Because the plaintiffs frustrated any such efforts, however, the court granted the costs, which amounted to $521.   That amount — less than $30 per witness — is unlikely in and of itself to induce most parties to adopt the interview process.

Does a court have the power to impose an interview process even when the parties do not agree?   *Biben v. Card*, 789 F. Supp. 1001 (W.D. Mo. 1992), found the authority under Rule 23(d) to require class members to file proof-of-claim forms drafted by the parties before the damages phase of the case commenced.   *See* 7B CHARLES ALAN WRIGHT ET AL., FEDERAL PRACTICE AND PROCEDURE § 1793 (3d ed. 2005).   But the purpose of the forms in *Biben* was to obtain damages information for settlement purposes; and the request did not employ neutral third persons to gather the information.

b. Sampling in Lieu of Comprehensive Discovery

Interviews seek to obtain information from all witnesses, but at a lower cost.   Another way to lower costs is not to obtain information from all the sources, but to survey or sample those sources and then to extrapolate from those results to make claims about the group as a whole.   We have seen many uses of sampling in this chapter: determining whether to require disclosure and cost-shifting for ESI, *see supra* p. 908, Note 2; determining relevant characteristics of a class, *see supra* p. 927 & p. 930, Note 1; and ensuring that reasonable steps are taken to avoid disclosure of privileged ESI, *see supra* p. 964, Note 4.   The following case extends this idea to use statistical sampling as a means of proving a proposition of substantive law — a concept that could alter significantly discovery in aggregated litigation.

IN RE SIMON II LITIGATION

211 F.R.D. 86 (E.D.N.Y. 2002), *vacated and remanded,*
407 F.3d 125 (2d Cir. 2005) [*supra* p. 396]

■   WEINSTEIN, Senior District Judge.

[The facts of this litigation are fully described *supra* p. 396.   Briefly, plaintiffs included smokers or entities (insurers, unions, and asbestos trusts) that had paid medical expenses for those smokers.   Their theory was fraud: The defendant tobacco companies had misled smokers about the health consequences of cigarettes, the smokers had relied on these misrepresentations and started or continued smoking as a result, and the smokers and other plaintiffs had suffered losses. The plaintiffs sought punitive damages, and further sought class certification of a non-opt-out, Rule 23(b)(1)(B) class action based on a "limited-punishment" theory: that the total amount of punitive damages that could be awarded for the defendants' conduct was constitutionally limited.

[In this opinion, which was later reversed on appeal, Judge Weinstein certified the class. Other than the claims of the class representatives, no claims for compensatory damages were to be tried. In order to prove the claim of fraud on which punitive damages were based and to keep the punitive-damage award within a constitutionally permissible multiplier of compensatory damages, however, class members needed to show both compensable injuries and their amount. They proposed to do so by sampling of the class; the class's total injuries were to be extrapolated from the sample. In this excerpt, Judge Weinstein addressed this approach.]

One of the problems for claimants has been the enormous expense of trying the cases, making them unattractive to plaintiffs' attorneys suing for individual clients on a contingency fee basis. Class or consolidated actions for compensatory damages have been difficult to justify because of the varied individual circumstances of the smokers. Yet statistical analysis based upon the law of large numbers, together with extensive demographic and epidemiological data and sampling techniques, arguably provide a basis for computing an appropriate approximation of total compensatory damages that could be awarded were all those injured to sue as a single class. . . .

Plaintiff['s] use of aggregate proof does not violate defendants' Constitutional rights. It is consonant with New York law. . . . Three years of coordinated discovery among nine related tobacco cases and two full trials, has strengthened the conclusion that statistical proof combined with other evidence is a necessary, pragmatic and evidentiary approach that reflects full due process in this and many other massive tort cases. . . .

The idea that due process and jury trial rights require a particularized traditional form of evidence for each element would make this case and cases like it impossible to try. There is little harm in retaining a requirement for "particularistic" evidence of causation and damages in sporadic individual accidents where there are few medical histories and witnesses; such evidence is almost always available and convenient in such litigation. Even in such cases, of course, use of almost any experts, whether doctors or DNA masters, depend upon implied or express probabilistic underpinning of their professional judgments.

In mass exposure cases with hundreds of thousands or millions of injured the cost of one-on-one procedures is insuperable and unsuitable for either a jury or a bench trial. The consequence of requiring individual proof from each smoker would be to allow defendants who have injured millions of people and caused billions of dollars in damages, to escape almost all liability. As Professor Rosenberg noted almost a score of years ago . . .:

The concept of "particularistic" evidence suggests that there exists a form of proof that can provide direct and actual knowledge of [the parties' conduct]. "Particularistic" evidence, however, is in fact no less probabilistic than is the statistical evidence that courts purport to shun.

David Rosenberg, *The Causal Connection in Mass Exposure Cases: A "Public Law" Vision of the Tort System*, 97 HARV. L. REV. 851, 870 (1984). Many commentators agree.

The Federal Rules of Civil Procedure and the Federal Rules of Evidence grant district judges broad authority to shape the nature and scope of admissible evidence for trial. Scientific evidence — such as the sampling and statistical extrapolations — is well suited to mass tort actions. It is particularly appropriate in massive consumer fraud cases — so long as it passes the gatekeeping criteria described in the Federal Rules of Evidence and *Daubert v. Merrell Dow Pharmaceuticals, Inc.*, 509 U.S. 579 (1993) . . . .

. . . When, as in the case at bar, the plaintiffs are a widely spread group suffering injury from a common action of defendants, statistical analysis may provide a more accurate and comprehensible form of evidence than would the testimony of millions of individual smokers. Extrapolated claim yields in the aggregate can with appropriate approximations provide a reliable estimate of total health care costs based upon individual claims. Laurens Walker & John Monahan, *Sampling Liability*, 85 VA. L. REV. 329 (1999).

Resolving mass tort disputes on a case-by-case basis may create a systematic bias against plaintiffs because, "[w]hile defendants spread the risk of adverse judgments across all test trials, each trial decides the fate of each plaintiff party on a single roll of the dice." The defendant who successfully resolves a mass tort dispute with aggregate tools enjoys the economic benefit of a final resolution to all proceedings, not just a single case.

1. *Federal Rules of Civil Procedure and Evidence*

A trial court has wide discretion to manage pre-trial discovery. The Federal Rules of Civil Procedure grant a district court judge flexibility to shape the type and scope of information available before and during a complex trial. The Rules contemplate the trial or magistrate judge's setting time limits and restrictions on the quantity, scope, and the sequencing of discovery. *See* Fed. R. Civ. P. 1 (Rules to be construed and administered to secure "just, speedy, and inexpensive determination of every action"); Fed. R. Civ. P. 16(b) (limiting the time for, and other aspects of, discovery in pretrial conference); Fed. R. Civ. P. 26(b)(2) (court to limit "frequency or extent of use of discovery methods[ ]"); Fed R. Civ. P. 30(a) & 33 (establishing presumptive limits for depositions and interrogatories).

The *Manual For Complex Litigation* specifically recommends "limiting discovery that is cumulative, duplicative, more convenient or less burdensome or expensive to obtain from another source, or seeks information the party has had ample opportunity to obtain." MANUAL FOR

COMPLEX LITIGATION, THIRD § 21.421 [(1995)]. A balance must be struck between the burden and expense of discovery sought and its potential benefit. Limiting discovery under the Federal Rules confronts litigants with hard choices. Some discovery necessarily must be foregone or structured in complex litigation if massive cases are to be expeditiously resolved. The goal in a federal court should be to fairly decide claims based on the merits, not on informational costs associated with the deposition of millions of witnesses. . . . It is particularly important not to deny the courts the ability to take advantage of cost saving through modern scientific techniques for acquiring information.

The trial judge is a primary protector against excessive transactional costs in litigation. She or he has broad powers under the Federal Rules of Evidence to regulate the admission of expensive cumulative evidence at trial. *See* Fed. R. Evid. 403 (restricting cumulative evidence); Fed. R. Evid. 611(a) ("The court shall exercise reasonable control over the mode and order of interrogating witnesses and presenting evidence"); Fed. R. Evid. 1006 (allowing writings, recordings, or photographs which cannot be conveniently examined in court to be presented in the form of "chart[s], summar[ies] or calculation[s]").

Although the manner of presenting evidence is best left to counsel, Rule 611 of the Federal Rules of Evidence entrusts the trial judge with the "ultimate responsibility" for the efficient ascertainment of truth by authorizing the exercise of reasonable control over the presentation of evidence. The wording of Rule 611 is broad enough to authorize innovations in the presentation of evidence provided the court considers ways to limit prejudice to the parties. Trial court decisions under Rule 611 of the Federal Rules of Evidence are virtually immune from attack on the grounds of Constitutional due process — particularly in the civil context — and are only challengeable upon a finding that the abuse of discretion substantially denigrated a party's right to a fair trial.

2. *Appropriateness of Sampling and Survey Techniques*

Sampling and survey techniques are a well-accepted alternative for the trial judge facing crippling discovery and evidentiary costs. MANUAL, [*supra*,] § 21.422 ("statistical sampling techniques may be used to measure whether the results of the discovery fairly represent what unrestricted discovery would have been expected to produce"); [*id.*] § 21.493 ("The use of acceptable sampling techniques in lieu of discovery and presentation of voluminous data from the entire population, may produce substantial savings in time and expense."). In some cases sampling techniques may prove the only practicable way to collect and present relevant data.

Surveys and sampling techniques have been admitted in a large variety of actions to establish causation so long as they accord with *Daubert* and Rule 702 of the Federal Rules of Evidence. Castaneda v. Partida, 430 U.S. 482 (1977) (statistical data to prove discrimination in jury selection); Toys R Us, Inc. v. Canarsie Kiddie Shop, Inc., 559 F. Supp. 1189 (E.D.N.Y. 1983) (factors for examining the trustworthiness of a survey). The *Toys R Us* factors are whether:

> (1) the "universe" was properly defined, (2) a representative sample of that universe was selected, (3) the questions to be asked of interviewees were framed in a clear, precise and non-leading manner, (4) sound interview procedures were followed by competent interviewers who had no knowledge of the litigation or the purpose for which the survey was conducted, (5) the data gathered was accurately reported, (6) the data was analyzed in accordance with accepted statistical principles and (7) objectivity of the entire process was assured.

Toys R Us, 559 F. Supp. at 1205. "The *Toys R Us* criteria are typically used by courts to analyze the weight to be accorded a survey, not its admissibility under Rule 403." Friesland [Brands, B.V. v. Vietnam Nat'l Milk Co., 221 F. Supp. 2d 457, 460 n.1 (S.D.N.Y. 2002)].

Properly developed survey evidence is admissible subject to arguments regarding its weight and probative value. . . .

Greater reliance on statistical methods is required by the profound evolution in our economic communication and data compilation and retrieval systems in recent decades. Manufacturers now mass produce goods for consumption by millions using new chemical compounds and processes, creating the potential for mass injury. Modern adjudicatory tools must be adapted to allow the fair, efficient, effective and responsive resolution of the claims of these injured masses.

State legislatures, courts, and commentators have recognized that tools for aggregation are especially helpful in the context of consumer fraud, when the relatively low value of specific claims or the litigation advantages of a well-financed defendant can discourage individuals from pressing their claims in court. . . .

In the bulk of the third-party tobacco cases that contemplated discovery and trial, courts have properly limited the level of individual proof available.

Against this backdrop, the use of statistical evidence in the instant case violates neither the Constitutional guarantee of due process nor the Constitutional right to a jury trial. The Supreme Court has spoken favorably of the science behind sampling and statistical analysis. *See* Utah v. Evans, 536 U.S. 452 (2002) (noting extensive technical literature on sampling); United States v. Fior D'Italia, Inc., 536 U.S. 238 (2002) (using aggregate estimation).

3. *Due Process*

"'Due [p]rocess,' unlike some legal rules, is not a technical conception with a fixed content unrelated to time, place and circumstances." Cafeteria and Rest. Workers Union, Local 473 v. McElroy, 367 U.S. 886, 895 (1961) ("The very nature of due process negates any concept of inflexible procedures universally applicable to every imaginable situation."). Whether a procedural device utilized where a private party invokes state authority to deprive another person or entity of property comports with due process is determined by a balancing of interests:

> [F]irst, consideration of the private interest that will be affected by the [procedure]; second, an examination of the risk of erroneous deprivation through the procedures under attack and the probable value of additional or alternative safeguards; and third, . . . principal attention to the interest of the party seeking the [procedure], with, nonetheless, due regard for any ancillary interest the government may have in providing the procedure or forgoing the added burden of providing greater protections.

Conn. v. Doehr, 501 U.S. 1, 11 (1991).

Consideration of the private interests at issue counsels in favor of utilizing statistical methods. Tobacco companies admittedly have an interest in not paying for damages in excess of what alleged misconduct may have caused; that interest would be furthered by their confronting (before a jury) each of the hundreds of thousands of plaintiffs who suffered smoking-related illnesses with respect to their reliance on tobacco company misstatements and omissions, and about their discovery of their injuries (so as to precisely determine in each instance when the statute of limitations started to run).

Practical considerations temper the weight of tobacco companies' interest, however. If such an individualized process were undertaken, it would have to continue beyond all lives in being. Assuming tobacco companies were willing to expend the resources and monies necessary both in discovery and at trial to mount such an undertaking, the litigation costs in doing so would far exceed any monies saved by avoiding erroneous payments especially given appropriate statutes of limitations.

Transactional costs would be enormous. Much of these costs would be borne by the public through financing of a court system that would require expansion.

The interest of plaintiffs in avoiding the additional litigation costs that would arise if defendants were permitted to confront each possible plaintiff at trial is enormous. The necessary additional litigation costs plaintiffs would have to bear would consume much of any recovery from defendants, making continued pursuit of the litigation fruitless.

The interests of the injured plaintiffs must be considered. Requiring individual proof as to each claim would unnecessarily intrude on the lives of hundreds of thousands of people. Examining each grain of sand is too burdensome in a survey of a beach.

The second element of the due process balancing test — examination of the risk of erroneous deprivation through the procedures under attack and the probable value of additional or alternative safeguards — also supports allowance of the proffered statistical proof, subject to appropriate *Daubert* challenges. *Cf.* Int'l Bhd. of Teamsters, Local 734 v. Philip Morris Inc., 196 F.3d 818, 823 (7th Cir. 1999) ("Statistical methods could provide a decent answer — likely a more accurate answer than is possible when addressing the equivalent causation question in a single person's suit.").

Experts have developed appropriate modeling techniques for reaching statistically significant and reliable conclusions. . . .

In addition to statistical evidence, parties will be permitted to present to the jury relevant lay testimony, expert testimony, and documentary evidence — subject to the constraints of the Federal Rules of Evidence and the practical considerations of trial management.

The third due process consideration — regard for any interest the government may have in procedures — heavily weighs in support of allowing plaintiffs to rely on statistical evidence. A consolidated trial with full presentation of the individual facts of each of plaintiffs' claims relating to smoking-related illnesses before a single jury would be unmanageable. Hundreds-of-thousands of separate trials brought by individuals who suffered a smoking-related illness would prove unnecessarily burdensome; it would "clog the docket of the district court for years."

Under the balancing test set forth in *Doehr*, the use of statistical evidence (subject to satisfaction of the *Daubert* criteria) by plaintiffs does not violate due process strictures. . . .

4.   *Jury Right*

The use of aggregated proof in plaintiffs' claims does not violate the Seventh Amendment. A contrary view would require concluding that the Constitution establishes fixed limitations on the methods of proof a particular party may offer. Requiring such a horse and buggy interpretation for trials in a computer-guided-rocket age seems somewhat far-fetched. Courts cannot ignore and deny themselves what the rest of the world relies upon in fact-finding.

The Seventh Amendment of the Constitution . . . "was designed to preserve the basic institution of jury trial in only its most fundamental elements, not the great mass of procedural forms and details, varying even then so widely among common-law jurisdictions." *See* Galloway v. United States, 319 U.S. 372, 392 (1943); Ex parte Peterson, 253 U.S. 300, 309-12 (1920).

Over the past two centuries, the primary concern in interpreting the Seventh Amendment has been to preserve the jury's role as a finder of fact, without constitutionally freezing evidentiary and trial procedures. Justice Brandeis expounded on the necessity of adapting the jury trial right to contemporary realities in *Ex parte Peterson*:

> [The Seventh Amendment] does not prohibit the introduction of new methods for determining what facts are actually in issue, nor does it prohibit the introduction of new rules of evidence. . . . New devices may be used to adapt the ancient institution to present needs and to make of it an efficient instrument in the administration of justice. Indeed, such changes are essential to the preservation of the right. The

limitation imposed by the Amendment is merely that enjoyment of the right of trial by jury be not obstructed, and that the ultimate determination of issues of fact by the jury be not interfered with.

Id. at 309-10.

The historical record demonstrates that the framers' main objective in drafting the Seventh Amendment was to limit the ability of an appellate court to overturn a civil jury's finding of fact. There is no indication they intended to constrain the trial judge's substantial discretion to employ appropriate procedural mechanisms in managing a trial so as to permit the jury to arrive at the truth — or as near to the truth as time and humankind's limitations allow.

... [T]he jury has unquestionably had much of its fact-finding authority attenuated indirectly through various evolving "procedural devices." The increasing use of bench trials, *Daubert* hearings, summary judgments, and directed verdicts — as authorized by appellate courts — to limit fact finding and set aside verdicts poses a threat to the continued viability of the Seventh Amendment jury trial. The development of new fair procedures that accord with modern statistical and informational gathering techniques for making factual determinations does not.

Courts must be especially careful not to hobble the jury system by excluding potential evidence. Prematurely cutting off the flow of evidence to the jury generally favors defendants, who do not have the burden of proof on most issues, leading not only to a violation of the Constitution, but a tilting of the scales of justice. . . .

Many authorities have demonstrated that jury fact-finding is enhanced by the use of aggregating techniques. The essential protections of the Seventh Amendment are enhanced, not reduced, by procedures which streamline and focus jury fact-finding. The jurors in this district are generally educated and aware of current technology; they would justly feel insulted by being denied modern fact finding techniques. . . .

Excluding information on the ground that jurors are too ignorant to evaluate it properly may have been appropriate in England at a time when a rigid class society created a wide gap between royal judges and commoner juries, but it is inconsistent "with the realities of our modern American informed citizens and the responsibility of independent thought in a working society."

Enforcement of federal law in areas such as employment, copyright and patent law relies upon the appropriate use of statistical evidence. There is no reason under either federal or state law why statistical evidence should be prohibited in mass tort class actions. . . .

The equity in allowing statistical proof of reliance and causation is underscored by the massive nature of the fraud alleged. If plaintiffs' allegations are borne out, the defendants sought to mislead the whole of the American public by distorting the entire body of public knowledge on the lethal and addictive effects of smoking. By carrying out this alleged widespread scheme, it was the defendants themselves who made a claim-by-claim showing virtually impossible.

5. Erie

A decision to allow statistical proof is not in conflict with *Erie R. Co. v. Tompkins*, 304 U.S. 64 (1938). There is no ruling New York case which holds that state substantive law will not permit the use of modern aggregation forensic tools to support a massive fraud action. Aggregation is appropriate in light of New York Court of Appeals decisions on common law fraud. . . .

New York state courts' failure to fully embrace *Daubert* does not suggest that they would forego appropriate statistical sampling along with individual testimony to prove elements of consumer fraud. They have accepted such evidence in discrimination, tax assessment determinations, DNA sampling and criminal cases.

The New York Court of Appeals has not ruled that "individualized proof" is the only way to prove causation and damages. In *Stutman v. Chemical Bank*, 731 N.E.2d 608 (N.Y. 2000), the Court of Appeals underscored that a showing of causation could be satisfied by proving a "fraud-on-the[-]market," a theory friendly to modern sampling techniques . . . . While that case dealt with section 349 of the General Business Law, a consumer fraud statute, which does not apply in the instant case, there is good reason to believe that fraud-on-the-market is an equally valid way to approach common law fraud cases. . . .

The procedural use of sampling is consistent with New York state substantive law. No *Erie* question is presented with respect to evidentiary issues.

Notes

1. In arguing for statistical sampling, *Simon* relies on the desirability of class-action treatment and the manageability of trial as much as it does on streamlining the pretrial process. Many case-management techniques have this quality; they cut across the various manifestations of complexity. For instance, a technique that reduces pretrial or trial costs is also likely to make aggregation more desirable. To what extent, however, do these types of arguments put the cart before the horse? Even if we can streamline the pretrial and trial processes and thus make the aggregation of cases more attractive, should we?

2. Because statistical sampling is an especially powerful — and controversial — technique for reducing the length and complexity of trial, we return to this idea of "trial by statistics" in Chapter Ten. *See infra* p. 1058. *Simon* never reached trial; and its arguments for adopting a statistical method of proof relied on simplifying the discovery process as well. Hence, although we examine the idea of statistical sampling in much

greater detail later, the idea of using statistics is worth mentioning now —
if, for no other reason, because gathering statistical evidence for use at
trial, as well as eliminating the need to collect individual evidence, raise
pretrial concern, and significantly affect the structure of the pretrial
process.

3. In reversing Judge Weinstein's class-certification order in *Simon*,
the Second Circuit noted, but took no position regarding, the district court's
decision to use sampling in lieu of individual proof of reliance and damages:

> Defendant-appellants also contend the Certification Order runs
> afoul of the Rules Enabling Act, 28 U.S.C. § 2072(b), because, on a
> number of counts, it alters or abridges the parties' substantive rights.
> . . .
>
> Because we have held that certification is [inappropriate], we need
> not address whether the district court's proposed statistical aggregation
> of proof . . . would have been appropriate for a class-wide approximation
> of compensatory liability in this case, or for proof of any given element
> going toward actual liability in a conventional class action for
> compensatory and punitive damages.

In re Simon II Litig., 407 F.3d 125, 139-40 (2d Cir. 2005).

The Second Circuit's view on this matter has waffled. In a prior case,
Blue Cross & Blue Shield of N.J., Inc. v. Philip Morris, Inc., 178 F. Supp. 2d
198 (E.D.N.Y. 2001), Judge Weinstein permitted an insurer of smokers to
use statistical proof at trial to show its right to recover health-care costs
from the tobacco companies. (Indeed, *Simon* was nearly a verbatim recital
of the analysis in *Blue Cross*.) Although the Second Circuit ordered that
judgment be entered in the defendants' favor, *see* Blue Cross & Blue Shield
of N.J., Inc. v. Philip Morris USA Inc., 344 F.3d 211 (2d Cir. 2003); Empire
Healthchoice, Inc. v. Philip Morris USA, Inc., 393 F.3d 312 (2d Cir. 2004),
it upheld the decision to allow proof of loss through statistical sampling. In
doing so, it, rejected the defendants' arguments under the Due Process
Clause and the Seventh Amendment. *Blue Cross*, 344 F.3d at 225-28.

After *Simon*, Judge Weinstein certified yet another class, this time of
smokers who claimed that the tobacco companies' marketing of "light"
cigarettes was fraudulent and therefore a RICO violation. In language that
was again a near-verbatim recital of *Blue Cross* and *Simon* (less the *Erie*
analysis, which was irrelevant to the federal claims involved), Judge
Weinstein again allowed the plaintiffs to prove causation and loss with
statistical evidence; the plaintiffs intended to give each class member a pro
rata amount of the total damages. Schwab v. Philip Morris USA, Inc., 449
F. Supp. 2d 992 (E.D.N.Y. 2006). The Second Circuit reversed this
certification order. *See* McLaughlin v. Am. Tobacco Co., 522 F.3d 215 (2d
Cir. 2008) (*infra* p. 1076). Here, the court was skeptical of statistical proof:

> We reject plaintiffs' proposed distribution of any recovery they
> might receive because it offends both the Rules Enabling Act and the
> Due Process Clause. The distribution method at issue would involve an
> initial estimate of the percentage of class members who were defrauded

(and who therefore have valid claims). The total amount of damages suffered would then be calculated based on this estimate (and, presumably, on an estimate of the average loss for each plaintiff). But such an aggregate determination is likely to result in an astronomical damages figure that does not accurately reflect the number of plaintiffs actually injured by defendants and that bears little or no relationship to the amount of economic harm actually caused by defendants. This kind of disconnect offends the Rules Enabling Act, which provides that federal rules of procedure, such as Rule 23, cannot be used to "abridge, enlarge, or modify any substantive right." 28 U.S.C. § 2072(b)....

The district court's distribution scheme also raises serious due process concerns. . . . When fluid recovery is used to permit the mass aggregation of claims, the right of defendants to challenge the allegations of individual plaintiffs is lost, resulting in a due process violation. [522 F.3d at 231-32.]

Granting that *Blue Cross*, *Simon*, and *Schwab* used slightly different variants of statistical sampling to prove somewhat different points, can you explain the variations in the three opinions of the Second Circuit?

4.   As Judge Weinstein says, courts have used surveys and sampling in a variety of cases. Surveys are often conducted in the ordinary course of business, and as long as they are relevant and non-privileged, they can be used in the litigation. Surveys conducted for purposes of litigation also occur with some frequency. For instance, surveys based on representative sampling are sometimes used in areas such as trademark, securities, and antitrust. *See, e.g.*, Schering Corp. v. Pfizer Inc., 189 F.3d 218, 224-28 (2d Cir. 1999) (reversing a decision excluding surveys; collecting cases and analyzing issues under the Federal Rules of Evidence); Bath & Body Works, Inc. v. Luzier Personalized Cosmetics, Inc., 76 F.3d 743, 750 (6th Cir. 1996) (trademark survey conducted after discovery cutoff inadmissible); Piper Aircraft Corp. v. Wag-Aero, Inc., 741 F.2d 925 (7th Cir. 1984) (trademark survey admissible); Volkswagen AG v. Dorling Kindersley Publ'g, Inc., 614 F. Supp. 2d 793 (E.D.Mich. 2009) (limiting the weight given to a potentially biased trademark survey); In re Airline Ticket Comm'n Antitrust Litig., 918 F. Supp. 283 (D. Minn. 1996) (permitting sampling survey of a plaintiff class). Party control of these surveys is typical; the few examples of surveys not controlled by the parties were designed to obtain information on a class or aggregated group of plaintiffs. *See, e.g.*, Hilao v. Estate of Marcos, 103 F.3d 767 (9th Cir. 1996) (*infra* p. 1058) (permitting the use of a special master to review claim forms of a representative sample of 137 plaintiffs and to estimate damages for the class); In re Fibreboard Corp., 893 F.2d 706 (5th Cir. 1990) (rejecting the use of a special master that surveyed 3,031 plaintiffs and advised the jury of the demographics of the entire group).

5.   For a description of methodological concerns that surround the admissibility of sampling evidence, see MANUAL FOR COMPLEX LITIGATION, FOURTH § 11.493 (2004); *see generally* FED. JUD. CTR., REFERENCE MANUAL ON SCIENTIFIC EVIDENCE (2d ed. 2000).

PART THREE

TRIAL COMPLEXITY

An implicit assumption in the first two Parts of this book was that, after aggregation and pretrial management, the trial process could rationally resolve all the claims of all the claimants. Now we put that assumption to the test. The following two chapters explore issues that surround the trial of complex cases.

You might wonder whether this material is important. In American litigation, few cases come to trial. Complex cases are no exception to this rule; the amounts at stake and the difficulty of trying large cases create pressures that make non-trial resolutions attractive for lawyers and judges. Nonetheless, trial issues are significant for three reasons. First, trial is the default option when other dispute-resolution methods fail. Predicting whether a case will go to trial is nearly impossible early on, so every case must be prepared as if it were going to trial. Second, the form of trial influences the pretrial preparation in which the parties will engage. For instance, if the trial is a discrete event at which all issues will be decided once and for all by a jury, the pretrial process needs to develop all the issues, and at trial the evidence and the issues need to be packaged in a form comprehensible to lay persons. On the other hand, if the trial involves a judge as factfinder, the judge might be able to divide the trial into a series of discrete hearings, thus dictating a different pretrial process.

Third, and most important, we have seen that the manageability of a case is a significant factor in a judge's decision to aggregate cases or claims. In considering the question of manageability, the judge needs to consider both how to manage the pretrial process and — because the case might go to trial — how the case will be tried. Indeed, in many Rule 23(b)(3) class actions, the judge requires the lawyers seeking certification to submit a trial plan describing how the case will be tried; if the case cannot be tried, the judge is more likely to find the class action is unmanageable and deny certification. Hence, even if a case is unlikely to be tried, lawyers need to have an idea about how the trial process in a complex case might be structured. Hence, the trial issues that we discuss here are vital to understanding the aggregation and pretrial issues that arise in all cases.

It is useful to begin by asking what it means to say that a case is "complex" in terms of trial.   Consider the roles the adversarial system assigns to players at trial.   As with pretrial, the lawyers' role is central: They define the issues in dispute, present the evidence, and make the arguments. As with pretrial, the parties do little. Unlike pretrial, however, the adversarial system gives the decision-maker(s) important responsibilities during trial: They must rule on the admissibility of evidence, find the facts, declare the law, apply the law to the facts, and, if necessary, declare a remedy.   These functions can be accomplished by one person or it can be divided among various persons or groups.

Cases are "complex" in the trial sense when either the lawyers or the decision-maker(s) are incapable of performing adequately their expected functions.   Among the circumstances that make the lawyers and decision-maker(s) unable to perform their tasks are:

(1)   The information that the lawyer must marshal makes it impossible for the lawyer to formulate adequate proofs and arguments.   For instance, the information may be wide-ranging and extensive, costly to obtain, or, due to time lags, no longer in existence.

(2)   Lawyers who represent the same or similar interests may be unable to frame the facts and the issues in a way that clarifies the case for the decision-maker(s).

(3)   The factfinder may be unable to use reasoned judgment to resolve the case.   This incapacity can arise from different sources.   For example, the factfinder may lack the ability to understand the evidence, either because it is esoteric, technical, or overwhelmingly voluminous; the factfinder may be unable to understand the law; or the length of trial may put demands on the factfinder's ability to deliberate.

The first two concerns are nearly identical to two of the concerns that define pretrial complexity.   Indeed, although the correlation is not perfect, many cases that are complex in pretrial will be complex at trial.   The third issue is new, because it involves the factfinder.

Chapter Nine begins the exploration of these issues by examining the ability of the judge to change the counsel structure or to replace the factfinder (whether a jury or even the judge) in order to ensure the rational resolution of the dispute.   Chapter Ten examines non-traditional trial techniques that a judge might adopt to ensure rational adjudication.   As with pretrial complexity, the issues of who fills particular roles and what techniques can be used are integrally related; for instance, the use of some trial techniques (a Chapter Ten issue) might allow us to preserve the right to jury trial (a Chapter Nine issue).   Moreover, these issues are integrally related to those we have already studied.   For instance, the availability of jury trial has important consequences for parties and courts making aggregation and pretrial decisions.   Civil procedure is a seamless web.

CHAPTER NINE

DEFINING THE ROLES OF LAWYERS, JURIES, AND JUDGES AT TRIAL

The traditional trial process assigns various roles to the participants in litigation. Aside from providing evidence, the parties are passive. A judge is the lawgiver. A jury is the factfinder in cases at law, while the judge is the factfinder in suits in equity. Finally, the lawyer for each party is responsible for presenting proofs and arguments. For the most part, lawyers are the central figures at trial; judge and jury are a *tabula rasa* upon whom the lawyers write their stories.

This process ill suits cases with voluminous and often technical facts. Just as complexity forced the judge to make adjustments in the standard approaches to aggregation and pretrial, it forces judges to adjust the trial responsibilities of lawyers, judges, and juries.

A. SELECTING TRIAL COUNSEL

In Chapter Seven, we examined the power of the trial judge to appoint lawyers other than a party's own to represent the party. Our focus was the power of the court to appoint lead, liaison, or committees of counsel for pretrial; but we learned in passing that courts also claim the power to appoint counsel to try the case on behalf of a group of plaintiffs. Here we examine the power to appoint trial counsel in more detail. Our goal is limited. We do not address issues such as the selection process for trial counsel or disqualification of trial counsel. Those vital issues have already been addressed in Chapter Seven. This section focuses on the arguments for and against the judge's ability to alter one of the — if not *the* — fundamental rights of parties in an adversarial system: the right to have a lawyer of a party's own choosing present the party's proofs and arguments.

MANUAL FOR COMPLEX LITIGATION, FOURTH

137 (2004)

Appropriate procedures to minimize delay and confusion from the proliferation of counsel in multiparty cases can include the following:

- assigning primary responsibility for the conduct of trial to a limited number of attorneys, either by formal designation of trial counsel . . . or encouraging by informal arrangements among the attorneys, taking into account legitimate needs for individual representation of parties; . . .

- providing that objections made by one party will be deemed made by all similarly situated parties unless expressly disclaimed;

- permitting other counsel to add further grounds of objection, again on behalf of all similarly situated parties unless disclaimed . . . .

IN RE AIR CRASH DISASTER AT DETROIT METROPOLITAN AIRPORT ON AUGUST 16, 1987

737 F. Supp. 396 (E.D. Mich. 1989)

■ COOK, Chief Judge.

[The case arose out of an airline crash that killed more than 250 people. The Judicial Panel on Multidistrict Litigation consolidated all federal suits before Chief Judge Cook, who subsequently ordered the transfer of the cases to himself for trial. In this order,] this Court notified the parties that it intended to appoint the Plaintiffs' Steering Committee (PSC) to serve as the lead counsel for the purpose of prosecuting the joint liability trial which began on October 2, 1989. . . .

The only objection to the proposed lead counsel designation was submitted by the Plaintiff in [one consolidated case]. . . . [S]he essentially maintains that (1) this Court has no authority to appoint the PSC to serve as the lead counsel in a joint liability trial, and (2) such a designation would abridge her right to representation by counsel of her choice. . . .

In *In re Bendectin Litigation*, 857 F.2d 290, 297 (6th Cir. 1988) [*infra* p. 1034], the Sixth Circuit Court of Appeals upheld the lower court's decision to appoint a "lead counsel committee" that would serve as counsel for the plaintiffs in a multidistrict litigation case. Despite the protestations of some plaintiffs that such an appointment would "den[y] them the right freely to choose counsel," the *Bendectin* Court concluded that "[i]n complex cases, it is well established that the district judge may create a Plaintiffs' Lead Counsel Committee."

In addition, the Fifth Circuit Court of Appeals also determined that the district court has the authority to appoint lead counsel to conduct pretrial discovery and to litigate liability issues which are common to all plaintiffs.

In *In re Air Crash Disaster at Florida Everglades*, 549 F.2d 1006 (5th Cir. 1977), the district court appointed lead counsel to conduct all pretrial matters and to prosecute the issues of liability on behalf of all plaintiffs. In recognizing the authority of the trial court to make such an appointment, the *Florida Everglades* Court noted:

> The need for a court to exercise its inherent managerial powers as expressed in rule 42(a) may take precedence over desires of counsel. . . .

> It is not open to serious question that a federal court in a complex, consolidated case may designate one attorney or a set of attorneys to handle pre-trial activity on aspects of the case where the interests of all co-parties coincide. *MacAlister v. Guterma*, 263 F.2d 65 (2d Cir. 1958), is perhaps the leading case on the court's power to appoint and rely on lead counsel. . . .

Despite the Plaintiff's objections, this Court concludes that it does have the authority to appoint and designate the PSC to serve as lead counsel for the Plaintiffs for the purpose of prosecuting the common issues in a joint liability trial. *See also* Vincent v. Hughes Air West, Inc., 557 F.2d 759 (9th Cir. 1977) [*supra* p. 721].[6]

Roger H. Trangsrud, MASS TRIALS IN MASS TORT CASES: A DISSENT

1989 U. ILL. L. REV. 69, 74-76, 82-83, 87-88

Underlying our tradition of individual claim autonomy in substantial tort cases is the natural law notion that this is an important personal right of the individual. While much less celebrated than other natural rights, such as the right to practice one's own religion or to think and speak freely, the right to control personally the suit whereby a badly injured person seeks redress from the alleged tortfeasor has long been valued here and in England. . . .

This jealous protection of the individual's absolute right to control his own tort claim was respected for practical as well as philosophical reasons.

---

6. This Court further reasons that the source of authority which supports this appointment may emanate from (1) the inherent power of a federal district court to "'control the disposition of the causes on its docket with economy of time and effort for itself, counsel and for litigants,'" In re FTC Line of Bus. Report Litig., 626 F.2d 1022, 1027 n.29 (D.C. Cir. 1980) (quoting Landis v. N. Am. Co., 299 U.S. 248, 254 (1936)), or (2) the terms of Rule 42(a) of the Federal Rules of Civil Procedure.

This Court also notes that, contrary to the Plaintiff's position, it has not precluded non-PSC members from participating in the joint liability trial. Certainly, the non-PSC members may offer assistance and suggestions to lead counsel during the course of the proceedings. However, the conduct of this trial would become chaotic and totally unmanageable if the Court permitted the counsel for each Plaintiff to present his position or theory of the case to the jury.

. . . Unless control of such tort claims was left with the injured party, a "litigious person could harass and annoy others if allowed to purchase claims for pain and suffering and pursue the claims in court as assignees." There was also the risk of overreaching, deception, and other misconduct by the party seeking to acquire the right to bring a tort claim on another's behalf. These remain major concerns today, as evidenced by the methods used by attorneys to solicit clients in mass tort cases and to obtain control over the cases of nonclients by bringing class actions or becoming lead counsel in huge consolidated tort cases. . . .

Other traditional justifications for individual claim autonomy remain important today in mass tort cases. From a purely economic point of view, our system operates mainly on the assumption that economic decisions are best made by the true owner of property rather than by any other person. . . . If others assume control over their claim, then [the best outcome for a plaintiff] is less likely to happen because these strangers will often not be aware of the special circumstances attending this claim or will have a divided loyalty because the stranger will often be responsible for many other substantial tort claims as well.

Traditionally, our civil justice system avoided mass trials of mass tort claims for another reason grounded in efficiency. . . . Large numbers of plaintiffs and defendants often create a matrix of cross-claims, a web of choice-of-law issues, and a host of peripheral and satellite litigation that would never exist if the claims had been tried separately. . . .

Conflicts of interest . . . are particularly troubling in a mass tort case where a mass trial is ordered because the individual plaintiff is in a poor position to exercise influence over lead counsel for the plaintiff group or the course of the complex litigation. . . .

Our civil justice system owes a twelve-year-old girl born with foreshortened limbs after her mother took [Bendectin] the same due process it owes a thirty-two-year old man paralyzed when the brakes on his Chevrolet fail and his automobile slams into a tree. In the latter case, the man's claim would be tried in its entirety to one jury, in the venue of the man's choosing, represented by a lawyer of the man's choosing . . . . So long as we rely on private compensation to redress private wrongs and on juries to hear all the facts of a case and to do justice consistent with common sense and our community norms, we owe the young girl the same procedure we routinely afford the victims of the many automobile accidents that are tried every year.

Notes

1. *Detroit Metropolitan* is a very rare case. To our knowledge, it is the only published decision, state or federal, during the last thirty-five years in which a party squarely challenged the court's power to appoint trial counsel. In *In re Air Crash Disaster at Stapleton International Airport, Denver, Colorado, on November 15, 1987*, 720 F. Supp. 1505 (D. Colo. 1989),

a plaintiff who had received an unfavorable verdict on a liability issue challenged the court's trial plan. Under that plan, appointed trial counsel had presented liability and damages evidence for two plaintiffs and only liability evidence for the remaining plaintiffs. The objecting plaintiff did not squarely challenge the right of the court to appoint trial counsel; rather, the plaintiff attacked "the procedures applied pursuant to the trial plan." The trial court held that the "standard of review applied to determine whether trial procedures applied in complex litigation have combined to deny a party's rights to due process and fair trial is one of actual prejudice to the substantial rights of that party." *Id.* at 1513. Without specifically addressing the appointment of trial counsel, the court found no actual prejudice in the trial procedures.

2.   In class actions, the source of the power to appoint trial counsel lies in Rules 23(d)(1) and -(g)(1); Rules 23(g)(1) and -(g)(4) then provide the standards that this counsel must meet. But Rule 23 contains other protections — adequacy of representation, notice and opt-out rights in (b)(3) class actions, and Rule 23(c)(2)(B)(iv)'s right to class members who do not opt out to "enter an appearance through counsel," to name a few — that blunt some of the effects of this power and guarantee that class counsel will protect the rights of individual litigants. In cases consolidated for trial, the authority is thought to reside in Rule 42(a); but neither a specific power to appoint trial counsel nor any standard for such an appointment is found in Rule 42(a). *Detroit Metropolitan* locates the authority in the court's inherent power, but it does not state what the appropriate standard is. Should *Stapleton Airport*'s "denial of due process and fair trial" be the standard used to determine whether the appointment of trial counsel is appropriate in all non class-action disputes? *Cf.* AM. L. INST., PRINCIPLES OF THE LAW OF AGGREGATE LITIGATION § 1.05(b) & cmts. *b* & *c* (2009) (stating that judges who limit "control of aggregate proceedings" by appointing counsel for groups of litigants should "ensure that parties and represented parties are adequately represented"); Joan Steinman, *The Effects of Case Consolidation on the Procedural Rights of Litigants: What They Are, What They Might Be Part II: Non-Jurisdictional Matters*, 42 UCLA L. Rev. 967, 978 (1995) (stating that Rule 23's protections should be extended to counsel in consolidated cases).

3.   If *Stapleton Airport* is correct, how much of the adversarial model does the "denial of due process and fair trial" test incorporate? In *Mathews v. Eldridge*, 424 U.S. 319 (1976), the Supreme Court held that the Due Process Clause permitted departures from an adversarial approach when the benefits of non-adversarial process outweighed the losses in accuracy that a non-adversarial process entailed. But *Mathews* does not answer whether this cost-benefit calculation should be conducted at the individual level or at the global level (at which the net loss to an individual due to a less accurate non-adversarial procedure can be justified if the average per-litigant savings exceed the average per-litigant loss). Another view of the Due Process Clause is that it guarantees fair process (in other words, it protects rational adjudication). On this view, when individual trial counsel threatens rational adjudication, the court must have the power to override

an individual's right to choose counsel to protect the more fundamental interest in reasoned judgment. But in how many cases does the presence of multiple counsel make rational decision-making impossible?

On the other hand, Professor Fiss distinguishes between a right of participation and a right of representation. In contexts in which "particular individuals have been singled out," "the value of individual participation ranks very high, maybe even supreme. . . . But in structural litigation no individual is singled out . . . . Accordingly, the value of participation, understood in its individualist form, loses some of its force." Owen M. Fiss, *The Allure of Individualism*, 78 IOWA L. REV. 965, 978 (1993). In structural cases, due process requires "not a representation of individuals but a representation of interests. . . . If an individual's interest has been adequately represented then he or she has no further claim against the decree." *Id.* at 972.

4. Professor Trangsrud's article raises philosophical, economic, and pragmatic difficulties with the power to appoint trial counsel. One of his criticisms is the loss of trans-substantivity that use of trial counsel in some, but not all, cases entails. Why don't we afford litigants in complex cases the same adversarial rights that litigants in simpler cases enjoy? Which set of claimants (if either) deserves more vigorous individual representation?

In thinking about these questions, consider the potential outcome-determinative effects of appointing trial counsel. First, a single counsel can press only a single theory of the case. Details of individual litigants must be trimmed to fit a generic theory good enough to serve for all. Multiple counsel, on the other hand, can provide judge and jury with particularized perspectives that might positively affect the individual's chances of success. Second, using trial counsel almost invariably requires the trial of common issues first. In most cases, the common issues concern liability rather than damages. As we learn in the next chapter, trying liability issues first increases the chances of a defense verdict (*see infra* pp. 1042-45). Should courts consider these effects before they appoint trial counsel? Should they nonetheless appoint trial counsel if, on average, the savings from the appointment exceeds the losses that an individual litigant suffers? Is this cost-benefit standard too crassly utilitarian?

5. When the *Manual for Complex and Multidistrict Litigation* was published in 1970, it did not suggest trial counsel as a case-management option. Two years later, the revised *Manual* suggested trial counsel; soon thereafter, appointing trial counsel received its first appellate imprimatur. In re Air Crash Disaster at Fla. Everglades on December 29, 1972, 549 F.2d 1006, 1015 (5th Cir. 1977). Today such appointments are fairly routine. See, *e.g.*, In re San Juan Dupont Plaza Hotel Fire Litig., 768 F. Supp. 912 (D.P.R. 1991) ("Full participation by each individual plaintiffs' counsel would likely result in numerous attorneys each vying for the attention of the Court, zealously representing the interests of their individual cases and possibly leading to the presentation of confusing and conflicting theories. Clearly, this would be detrimental to the interests of the larger group of plaintiffs.").

The 1985 predecessor to the *Manual, Third* — the *Manual for Complex Litigation (Second)* — contained the following admonition: "Other counsel should be afforded an opportunity to conduct supplemental examination, particularly on matters unique to their clients not already covered in prior examination." The *Manual, Third* deleted this sentence, inserting in its place the softer instruction that judges "tak[e] into account legitimate needs for individual representation of parties." The *Manual, Fourth* maintains the latter position. Perhaps the change in language from the *Manual (Second)* to *Manual, Third* was more descriptive than normative: "[C]ourts sometimes have uttered reassurances about the ability of nonlead counsel to participate, but increasingly they have acknowledged the substantial disenfranchisement of nonlead counsel." Steinman, *supra*, at 976.

6.   Typically, a court issues an order to confirm a lawyer's status as trial counsel. What happens if the court never makes a formal designation, but an attorney acts as *de facto* trial counsel? In *Central Illinois Public Service Co. v. Allianz Underwriters Insurance Co.*, 633 N.E.2d 675 (Ill. 1994), two sets of insurers had identical interests with respect to certain dispositive issues. During pretrial, the insurers ran a single defense, fully participated in discovery, shared litigation expenses, and even agreed on the experts that would be presented at trial. The trial, however, involved only the first set of insurers. After a verdict against the first set, the trial judge bound the second set of insurers to the judgment on the theory that trial counsel's representation of the common interests made the first set of insurers the "virtual surrogate" of the second. The Illinois Supreme Court held that, because the second set of insurers had not participated in the trial, they could not be bound. A dissent argued that, although "perhaps it might have been more prudent if the trial court . . . had formally appointed . . . lead counsel or trial counsel," *id.* at 683, the control exercised by the second set of insurers bound them to the judgment.

B. SELECTING THE FACTFINDER

In an adversarial system, factfinding and lawgiving tasks are kept distinct from the task of presenting proofs and arguments. In the American version of the adversarial system, factfinding and lawgiving tasks often are subdivided. With respect to factfinding, a judge bears certain factfinding responsibilities, a jury bears others, and judicial adjuncts such as masters may bear still others. With respect to lawgiving, judicial officers dominate, but in jury cases, juries have an ability to decide mixed questions of law and fact and may also, due to the usual secrecy of their verdicts, refuse to follow legal rules with which they disagree.

In this section, we examine the task of factfinding. A case can be complex when the factfinding task cannot be performed adequately by the judge or jury entrusted with factfinding responsibility. Complexity can arise when the case might last a long time or else involve voluminous or sophisticated economic, scientific, or technical evidence. In these cases, does a trial judge possess the power to take the factfinding function away from the player who traditionally performs it and order it performed by another player more capable of the task? This question suggests a head-on collision with the Seventh Amendment's right to jury trial and Article III's requirement that an Article III judge perform essential judicial functions. The following materials sort out these tensions, first in the context of replacing a jury as factfinder and then in the context of delegating the factfinding task when the judge must find the facts.

1. The Power of the Trial Judge to Strike a Jury

Even in routine cases, trying to understand which player(s) are responsible for factfinding, and the precise scope of their responsibilities, is vexing. Start with the federal courts. The Seventh Amendment provides: "In suits at common law, where the value in controversy shall exceed twenty dollars, the right of jury trial shall be preserved, and no fact tried by a jury, shall be otherwise re-examined in any Court of the United States, than according to the rules of the common law." The first half of this amendment has been interpreted to require the use of juries in actions at common law, but not to require juries in suits in equity. But even if a jury is not constitutionally required, Congress can by statute provide for jury trials, and it has done so with regard to a few types of claims. The Supreme Court has never held that the Seventh Amendment applies to state courts; but every state except Louisiana and Wyoming has a constitutional provision comparable to the Seventh Amendment. In some states, the right to jury trial is even stronger than it is in the federal system.

Using juries to hear some but not all types of cases raises three concerns. First, some line of demarcation needs to be established between common-law matters and matters sounding in equity. But the line between the common law and equity was always fluid, and changed a fair amount during the course of Anglo-American history. Moreover, finding an answer to this historical question would do nothing to solve the problem of jury trial in cases involving modern statutory and administrative rights that have no ready analogue to common law or equity.

A second set of pressures arises from the modern ability to join multiple claims in one proceeding. It is possible that one case might involve both jury-tried issues and judge-tried issues. Some disputed facts are likely to be relevant to both sets of claims. The problem, then, is how to allocate factfinding responsibility in such cases.

Third, once we sort out factfinding responsibility both for claims and for overlapping facts within those claims, it becomes necessary to consider what controls, if any, should be placed on the factfinder.

Your basic course in Civil Procedure might have addressed aspects of the ways in which American courts have resolved these three issues. To take the issues in reverse order, the first issue is the extent of judicial control over the factfinding function. In the federal system, appellate courts act as a limited check on a judge's factfinding authority; a judge's findings of fact can be reversed when there is clear error, *see* Fed. R. Civ. P. 52(a)(6); a trial or appellate court can also order a new trial (*see* Fed. R. Civ. P. 59(a)(2)). A jury's findings of fact are subject to numerous controls, both direct and indirect. Directly, the trial judge can enter judgment as a matter of law (during or after trial) when she is convinced that no reasonable jury could find for a party on a particular issue. *See* Fed. R. Civ. P. 50(a)-(b). Indirectly, a judge can ask questions to elicit evidence (*infra* p. 1119), comment on the evidence to the jury (*see id.*), instruct the jury (*see* Fed. R. Civ. P. 51), and order a new trial when she believes that the jury's verdict is against the weight of the evidence (*see* Fed. R. Civ. P. 59(a)(1)). Most states have comparable controls.

It is fair to say that the vigor with which jury-control devices have been employed has varied over time, with the twentieth century easing the more stringent controls that occurred during the late nineteenth century. *See* Stephan Landsman, *The History and Objectives of the Civil Jury System*, *in* VERDICT 22 (Robert E. Litan ed. 1993). This general statement must be tempered with the qualification that summary judgment took root in the twentieth century; that judgment as a matter of law was widely used in twentieth century; and that the latter half of the century saw important changes (such as six-member panels, non-unanimous verdicts, and segmented verdicts) in the composition and function of the jury.

The second issue — allocating responsibility when factual issues in legal and equitable claims overlap — has been settled in the federal system by two cases, *Beacon Theatres, Inc. v. Westover*, 359 U.S. 500 (1959), and *Dairy Queen, Inc. v. Wood*, 369 U.S. 469 (1962). *Beacon Theatres* held that except perhaps "under the most imperative circumstances, circumstances which in view of the flexible procedures of the Federal Rules we cannot now anticipate, can the right to a jury trial of legal issues be lost through prior determination of equitable claims." 359 U.S. at 510-11. Even if the legal claim is "incidental" to the equitable one, the judge must let the jury find the common facts first, and must accept them in deciding the equitable part of a claim. *Dairy Queen*, 369 U.S. at 473.

There still remains the final judge-jury issue: determining the claims or issues that are "legal" (i.e., jury-tried) and those that are "equitable" (i.e., bench-tried). The modern discussion of the Seventh Amendment's scope — especially in complex litigation — necessarily begins with *Ross v. Bernhard*, 396 U.S. 531 (1970). *Ross* was a shareholders' derivative suit, in which the Court held that "the right to jury trial attaches to those issues in derivative actions as to which the corporation, if it had been suing in its own right, would have been entitled to a jury." *Id.* at 532-33.

This holding was significant in its own right because, in the days of common law and equity, a shareholders' derivative suit was equitable in nature, so that the case would have been decided without a jury. The Supreme Court's willingness to designate certain issues in such a case as jury-triable suggested a broadened role for juries. This fact is particularly important in complex litigation because, like shareholders' derivative suits, many joinder devices have their origin in equity. Had *Ross* come out differently, it is likely that no issues in class actions (at least those class actions traditionally associated with equity, and possibly even the modern Rule 23(b)(3) class action) would be triable to juries. The same would likely be true of claims in interpleader and claims in intervention, both of which had their origins in equity. The effect that bench trials would have had on the law of aggregation and on the pretrial management of complex cases could have been enormous. Instead, *Ross* seems to show that, if the issues in class members' underlying claims are jury-triable, they do not become bench-triable merely because they are packaged in a class action.

But *Ross* is best known for its footnote 10, which described the factors that a court must use in its Seventh Amendment analysis:

> As our cases indicate, the "legal" nature of an issue is determined by considering, first, the pre-merger custom with reference to such questions; second, the remedy sought; and, third, the practical abilities and limitations of juries. Of these factors, the first, requiring extensive and possibly abstruse historical inquiry, is obviously the most difficult to apply. [*Id.* at 538 n.10.]

Ross's first two factors — historical practice and the remedy sought — have become the backbone of the Supreme Court's Seventh Amendment analysis. The first factor requires an inquiry into jury-trial practices in 1791, when the Seventh Amendment was ratified. The second factor is straightforward: A claim seeking monetary relief points toward a jury; a claim seeking an injunction favors a bench trial. Of the two factors, the Court has said that "[t]he second inquiry is more important in our analysis." *See* Chauffeurs, Teamsters & Helpers Local No. 391 v. Terry, 494 U.S. 558, 565 (1990); *see also* Granfinanciera, S.A. v. Nordberg, 492 U.S. 33, 42 (1989) ("The second stage of the analysis is more important than the first."). Despite calls to "dispense with [the historical test] altogether," *see Terry*, 494 U.S. at 574 (Brennan, J., concurring), it has emerged as at least the equal of the remedial factor in recent cases. *See* City of Monterey v. Del Monte Dunes at Monterey, Ltd., 526 U.S. 687 (1999); *cf.* Markman v. Westview Instruments, Inc., 517 U.S. 370 (1996) (turning to functional jury-trial considerations only after an inquiry into historical practices provided no clear answer).

The intriguing factor in *Ross*, however, is the third: "the practical abilities and limitations of the jury." In cases before *Ross*, the Court used a combination of the first two factors to analyze the Seventh Amendment right. But the Supreme Court had never mentioned the third factor — at least not explicitly. It was not clear exactly what this factor meant, or how it should be weighed against the first two factors. Justice Stewart's dissent in *Ross* heightened the intrigue; in an opinion joined by Chief Justice Burger and Justice Harlan, he argued that shareholders' derivative suits were equitable, so that all issues should be bench-tried. In passing, Justice Stewart stated:

> Certainly there is no consensus among commentators on the desirability of jury trials in civil actions generally. Particularly where the issues in the case are complex — as they are likely to be in a

derivative suit — much can be said for allowing the court discretion to try the case itself. [396 U.S. at 545 n.5.]

Needless to say, *Ross*'s third factor did not escape notice. In a series of complex cases in the 1970s and early 1980s, litigants argued that juries could not comprehend voluminous or technical information, and they asked the judge to strike the jury. If this argument is ultimately correct, the repercussions throughout the law of aggregation, case management, and trial in complex litigation will be significant.

IN RE BOISE CASCADE SECURITIES LITIGATION

420 F. Supp. 99 (W.D. Wash. 1976)

■ SHARP, District Judge.

Before the Court are defendants' motions to strike plaintiffs' jury demands in this securities fraud litigation. The question before the Court is whether these jury demands may be stricken without conflicting with the Seventh Amendment. The Court is of the opinion that the answer is in the affirmative.

[The case arose out of the acquisition of West Tacoma Newsprint Co. (Newsprint) by Boise Cascade Corp. (Boise) in November, 1969. Newsprint stockholders received shares of Boise worth approximately $75 per share. In 1971 and 1972 Boise was forced to write down its assets, which resulted in a reduction in the price of Boise's shares to approximately $12. Several shareholders in Newsprint brought actions alleging violations of federal and state securities laws by Boise, its accountant, and its directors and officers. The Judicial Panel on Multidistrict Litigation consolidated the cases.

[During pretrial, counsel expended more than 50,000 hours, and produced more than 900,000 documents. The court granted motions by the plaintiffs to consolidate some of the multidistricted cases for trial. The defendants then moved to strike the plaintiffs' demand for a jury trial.

[The court began its analysis by listing a number of complicating factors presented by the consolidated trial. The first was the number of plaintiffs. According to the court, "each plaintiff has a different measure of reliance and . . . it will be necessary to contain the proof of each plaintiff to that particular plaintiff" — a complicated task because the burden of disproving reliance varied according to the context of the transaction.]

Other portions of the complaints present complicated concepts that will involve lengthy explanation and documentary evidence.

For example, the complaints allege that Boise failed to make proper provision for discount reserves with respect to its land sales. . . . The foundation for this will likely require proof that a market rate of interest existed with respect to the land sales in question; the rate or rates charged by Boise; the amount of time that the market rate exceeded the rate actually charged and the amount of interest outstanding at various times.

It may also be necessary to present evidence regarding the reasonableness of the rate or rates charged by Boise as well as proof relating to usury laws and state regulations, if any, of land sales and installment purchase contracts.

As another example, plaintiffs claim that Boise chose improper bases for the valuation of assets acquired in corporate acquisitions effected under 26 U.S.C. § 334(b)(2). As a result, it is alleged that Boise failed to note that it could be liable for up to $5,000,000 in federal income taxes. One of the issues here would be whether Boise properly accrued potential judgments resulting from litigation with the Internal Revenue Service . . . .

Other portions of the complaints which present unique and difficult accounting concepts are the following:

Boise improperly allocated unit land costs to the costs of goods sold so as to understate the costs of goods sold for more desirable lots, overstate the value of the remaining land inventory, and consequently to overstate profits derived from the sale of recreational land.

And also:

Boise's quarterly financial statements for the first three quarters of each year, including 1969, failed to recognize ratably and proportionately various adjustments made in the fourth quarter and therefore overstated net income for the first three quarters accordingly. The effect of said fourth quarter adjustments was concealed by the device of pooling the financial results of profitable companies acquired by merger during the year.

In addition to the complex accounting and proof questions, there is the very real possibility of substantial prejudice to the defendants due to evidence that Boise settled numerous civil actions . . . alleging improper land development and marketing practices. . . .

Finally, and most important, in order to determine whether liability exists, the fact finder will have to analyze the Boise accounting, not only of the accounts as they existed at the time of the merger, but as the plaintiffs claim they should have existed. It is anticipated that experts for each side will have to go through the accounting techniques and resulting figures in each of the areas complained of in [the complaint]. In all, assets and liabilities in excess of a billion dollars are involved and a period of more than five years will have to be examined.

. . . [T]he truth or falsity of many of the allegations may have to be determined in the light of economic conditions as they existed a decade ago.

Competing theories of accounting will be presented for all of these matters. It has been suggested that more than one "generally accepted accounting principle" can be applied to a particular booking problem but that not all of those principles fairly reflect the financial condition of the corporation.

In sum, it appears to this Court that the scope of the problems presented by this case is immense. The factual issues, the complexity of the evidence that will be required to explore those issues, and the time required to do so leads to the conclusion that a jury would not be a rational and capable fact finder.

III

There can be no doubt that jury trials are favored in civil litigation in this country. The combination of the Seventh Amendment and the merger of actions at law and in equity into a single civil action under the Federal Rules of Civil Procedure encourages the use of juries to determine facts. *See* Ross v. Bern[h]ard, 396 U.S. 531 [1970].

However broad this policy may be, the Supreme Court has recognized that the use of juries is not without limits. In *Ross v. Bern[h]ard*, the Court set forth three factors which determine the susceptibility of a claim to trial by jury:

> [First,] the pre-merger custom with reference to such questions; second the remedy sought; and third, the practical abilities and limitations of juries. *Id.* at 538 n.10.

No authority was cited for these three factors. As for the first two, Supreme Court precedent appears so clear as to be obvious. The third part is not explicit from previous opinions.

The procedural safeguards inherent in our legal system provide the impression and fact of fairness to the litigants and society. This is necessary in order to assure obedience to judgments and resort to the legal system as the only sanctioned means of settling disputes in a complex civilized society. Indeed, under the Fifth and Fourteenth Amendments, the legitimacy of government action is measured in terms of fairness.

Central to the fairness which must attend the resolution of a civil action is an impartial and capable fact finder. A properly selected panel of veniremen must generally be presumed to yield an impartial and capable jury. However, at some point, it must be recognized that the complexity of a case may exceed the ability of a jury to decide the facts in an informed and capable manner. When that occurs, the question arises as to whether the right and necessity of fairness is defeated by relegating fact finding to a body not qualified to determine the facts. The third part of the analysis in footnote 10 to the majority opinion in *Ross v. Bern[h]ard, supra,* directly recognizes this.

Of course, the point at which a jury's limitations exceed its abilities is not precise nor is it easy of definition. No single factor alone can dictate that a jury should not hear a case. As in this case, a number of factors must combine to convince the Court that a jury would be incapable of fairly deciding the case.

IV

It must be apparent that any jury chosen to hear this case will not be a fair cross section of the community at large because of the estimated trial time of four to six months. It would not be unreasonable to excuse prospective jurors from serving in this civil case if they believe that service for that period of time would impair their employment. At the outset, then, the availability of employed persons to serve on this jury is limited. This suggests that at least the appearance of fairness would be diminished, if not eliminated, when a lengthy civil action involving millions of dollars in potential damages in a commercial setting would be heard by jurors who have not had exposure to a contemporary commercial or business environment. This should not be taken to mean that a non-employed person is somehow less able to determine facts. Rather, a basic purpose of the jury, the determination of facts by impartial minds of diverse backgrounds, is defeated if a sizable and significant portion of the community must be excluded from service.

Pointing out the limits of a jury to hear an extended civil action does not answer the problems presented by a particular case unless it can be shown that trial to the Court would be superior.

In addition to the Court's experience in presiding over other complicated cases involving commercial matters, the Court has available to it tools that are unwieldy in the possession of a jury. Among these tools are review of daily transcripts; admission of depositions into evidence instead of reading relevant portions aloud; review of selected portions of testimony from the reporter's notes and flexibility in scheduling trial activities. In addition, the Court is able to study exhibits in depth and carry on colloquies with witnesses, expert and non-expert alike, in an orderly and systematic manner. Of course, this is in addition to the Court's knowledge of the litigation resulting from its review of the record since the cases were filed.

In the light of the limitation of a jury to determine the facts in an informed manner and the ability of the Court to hear and review the evidence in an efficient and effective manner, the Court believes that it would be more capable of fairly deciding the facts.

V

The Court is of the opinion that the third part to footnote 10 in *Ross v. Bern[h]ard, supra,* is of constitutional dimensions. . . . Furthermore, the Court is of the opinion that there is no conflict in this case with any statutory policy favoring trial by jury, 28 U.S.C. § 1861, or the Federal Rules of Civil Procedure.

The explosion of litigation in the past two decades in terms both of number of filings and the complexity and scope of many of those cases has led thoughtful minds to wonder whether the judicial system as we now know it can cope with some of these cases. . . .

With these thoughts in mind, the necessity for the appearance and fact of fairness dictate that the motions now before the Court be granted.

Because of the effect of this Order, the Court hereby certifies this question for appeal under 28 U.S.C. § 1292(b).

IN RE JAPANESE ELECTRONIC PRODUCTS ANTITRUST LITIGATION

631 F.2d 1069 (3d Cir. 1980)

■   SEITZ, Chief Judge.

This certified interlocutory appeal from a pretrial order of the district court raises an issue that currently is the subject of much debate: In an action for treble damages under the antitrust and antidumping laws, do the parties have a right to trial by jury without regard to the practical ability of a jury to decide the case properly?

I.

This litigation began in the District of New Jersey with the complaint of National Union Electric Corp. (NUE). . . . NUE was a major domestic producer of television receivers until February 1970. The following December, it filed the first complaint of this litigation, charging several of its Japanese competitors with violations of the antitrust laws and the laws governing competition in international trade. The complaint names as defendants the Mitsubishi Corp., which is a Japanese trading company, and seven Japanese television manufacturers: Matsushita Electric Industrial Co., Toshiba Corp., Hitachi, Ltd., Sharp Corp., Mitsubishi Electric Corp., Sanyo Electric Co., and Sony Corp. Nine subsidiaries of these companies also are named as defendants in NUE's action.

NUE alleges that the defendants have sought to drive American television producers out of the American market by selling televisions at artificially depressed prices. Charging that defendants have maintained lower prices for televisions sold in the United States than for comparable televisions sold in Japan, NUE asserts violations of the 1916 Antidumping Act, 15 U.S.C. § 72. NUE further alleges that these dumping practices are part of a large conspiracy in which defendants have agreed among themselves and have acted in concert with over 90 coconspirators around the world to maintain artificially low prices for Japanese televisions sold in the United States. Defendants allegedly have facilitated and financed this scheme by fixing high prices for televisions sold in Japan, a practice made possible by concerted action and protection afforded by the Japanese government. NUE asserts that this conduct violates §§ 1 and 2 of the Sherman Act, 15 U.S.C. §§ 1, 2, and § 73 of the Wilson Tariff Act, 15 U.S.C. § 8.

NUE seeks treble damages for injuries sustained between 1966 and 1970. . . . NUE also seeks injunctive relief.

[Zenith Radio Corp. filed a complaint in 1974, naming all of the defendants of the NUE action, a few additional subsidiaries, and two American companies: Motorola, Inc., and Sears, Roebuck, and Co. The *Zenith* complaint contained comparable allegations of dumping, conspiracy, and intent to destroy domestic competition, but was broader in the number of years covered (1968-77), in the products (televisions, phonographs, radios, tape and audio equipment, and electronic components) involved, and in the antitrust statutes that the defendants' conduct allegedly violated (the Clayton Act and the Robinson-Patman Act). Some of the defendants in *Zenith* then filed counterclaims alleging that Zenith and its distributors had violated various antitrust acts, and that Zenith and its 30 co-conspirators maintained a program of sham litigation against Zenith's competitors.

[The two suits were consolidated for pretrial proceedings in the Eastern District of Pennsylvania, and subsequently consolidated for trial.]

Both NUE and Zenith made timely demands for jury trial. Fourteen of the defendants moved to strike the demands, arguing that the case is too large and complex for a jury. The district court denied their motion, concluding that the seventh amendment does not recognize the complexity of a lawsuit as a valid reason for denying a jury trial. The court . . . certified its order for interlocutory appeal under 28 U.S.C. § 1292(b). We have permitted the appeal . . . .

II.

Appellants argue that the proof of foregoing claims will be too burdensome and complicated for a jury. They have cited several dimensions of complexity.

The district court accepted one of appellants' basic contentions: the trial will be protracted. The court predicted that the trial would last a full year. It noted that the parties are nearing the end of discovery, which after nine years has produced millions of documents and over 100,000 pages of depositions. The court did not estimate how much of this evidence will be introduced at trial.

Beyond these observations of the district court, we have only the parties' divergent predictions of the proof that appellees' claims call for. We understand their primary disagreements to concern four general sources of complexity: proof of the Antidumping Act claims, proof of the alleged conspiracy, resolution of a number of financial issues, and understanding of several conceptually difficult legal and factual issues.

Under the Antidumping Act, appellees must prove that the defendants made sales of articles in the United States at a price lower than the price of "such articles" in Japan. Appellants read the Act to permit price comparisons only for identical products sold in the two countries. During the relevant periods, defendants produced thousands of technically distinct models of the products covered by this litigation. They contend that to identify the products appropriate for price comparisons, the jury will have to review the technical features of thousands of different models and understand how differences between the models relate to cost of manufacture, product performance, and marketability. Appellees construe the Antidumping Act to permit price comparisons between functionally equivalent products, such as all portable color televisions with a particular screen size and VHF-UHF channel selection. They contend that a jury could identify such functionally equivalent products without massive or highly technical proof.

The conspiracy charged in this suit is massive. Appellees allege that it has lasted for at least 30 years, involved almost 100 firms around the world, and affected international trade in several consumer electronic products. Appellants argue that litigation of the existence and operation of this conspiracy will produce an enormous amount of evidence for the jury to consider. They see further difficulties in the fact that the alleged conspiracy involved Japanese businessmen and that its operations included restraint of trade in Japanese markets. Appellants fear that a jury might not understand the evidence due to the difficulty of understanding business practices and market conditions in Japan. Appellees respond that proof of the conspiracy and its operations will be simple because the facts are well established in unambiguous documentation. . . .

Some parts of the case will require the jury to resolve a series of financial issues. Appellants have highlighted three such parts. First, for the Antidumping Act claims, the jury will have to decide whether the price of an article sold in the United States is "substantially less than the actual market value or wholesale price" in Japan and whether a defendant has maintained differential pricing "commonly and systematically." This inquiry may be complicated by several influences on prices that might have to be factored out before comparing prices, such as currency fluctuations and different marketing techniques in the two countries. Second, appellees allege that the conspirators disguised their artificially low prices in the United States by a series of complicated rebate schemes. Appellants say that the jury will be able to test this allegation only by reviewing the circumstances surrounding thousands of separate transactions. Third, appellees intend to show injury by proving that they lowered their own prices in response to defendants' artificially low prices and that they lost sales to defendants. These allegations will require evidence of appellees' transactions and may raise issues regarding appellees' pricing policies and marketing techniques and the quality of appellees' products.

Appellants contend that litigation of these three parts of the case will produce an enormous mass of financial documentation for the jury to work through. They also contend that the jury will need the assistance of substantial amounts of expert testimony on accounting, marketing, and other technical matters. Appellees reject this prediction, arguing that all the relevant financial evidence can be submitted neatly in computer printouts with accompanying summaries. They do not foresee great problems in the jury's understanding of the evidence.

Finally, appellants argue that the complexity of the suit will be compounded by the presence of some issues that conceptually are very difficult. The claims under both the Antidumping Act and § 2 of the Sherman Act will require proof of predatory intent. On the § 2 claims and on Zenith's claims under § 7 of the Clayton Act, appellees will have to prove relevant product markets, relevant geographic markets, and market shares. Zenith's claims under the Robinson-Patman Act will raise issues of whether products sold to different customers are of a "like grade and quality" and whether any price differences are cost justified. . . .

IV.

. . .

Suits for treble damages under the antitrust and antidumping laws, as a class, are plainly legal in nature. They seek relief in a form traditionally associated with courts of law: compensatory and punitive damages caused by legal wrongs. Indeed, prior cases have always assumed that the seventh amendment guarantees a jury trial in antitrust suits.

Appellants dispute none of the foregoing . . . . They argue that the seventh amendment does not guarantee a right to jury trial when any particular suit, because of its extraordinary complexity, is beyond the ability of the jury to decide.

For the sake of clarity, we should state our understanding of complexity in this context. A suit is too complex for a jury when circumstances render the jury unable to decide in a proper manner. The law presumes that a jury will find facts and reach a verdict by rational means. It does not contemplate scientific precision but does contemplate a resolution of each issue on the basis of a fair and reasonable assessment of the evidence and a fair and reasonable application of the relevant legal rules. A suit might be excessively complex as a result of any set of circumstances which singly or in combination render a jury unable to decide in the foregoing rational manner. Examples of such circumstances are an exceptionally long trial period and conceptually difficult factual issues. . . .

The third prong of the [*Ross* v. *Bernhard*] test plainly recognizes the significance, for purposes of the seventh amendment, of the possibility that a suit may be too complex for a jury. . . .

The district court made no use of the *Ross* footnote, finding it too brief to authorize a major departure from the traditional construction of the seventh amendment. We also find it unlikely that the Supreme Court would have announced an important new application of the seventh amendment in so cursory a fashion. Yet, at the very least, the Court has left open the possibility that the "practical abilities and limitations of juries" may limit the range of suits subject to the seventh amendment and has read its prior seventh amendment decisions as not precluding such a ruling. With this understanding of *Ross*, we shall consider the merits of appellants' arguments for a complexity exception.

V.

Appellants' first argument relies on historical analysis to advance the proposition that the fact of extraordinary complexity renders a suit equitable in nature. Although complexity is not commonly recognized as a defining feature of equity, appellants argue that by the time of the adoption of the seventh amendment the chancellor's jurisdiction had extended to any suit that he found too complex for a jury. . . .

Whether or not [the chancellor used such power] is a question that may interest historians; we need not decide it here. We note that appellants' only support for the authority of a chancellor to remove difficult issues from juries in suits at law is a single decision of dubious authority[, *Clench v. Tomley*, Cary 23, 21 Eng. Rep. 13 (Ch. 1603)]. With this meager support, we cannot conclude that complexity alone ever was an established basis of equitable jurisdiction. . . .

. . . [The court then turned to an argument based on historical research by Patrick Devlin, a noted British Lord. According to this argument, in] England in 1791, the chancellor controlled the boundary between law and equity. He exercised this control with a measure of flexibility, removing suits from trial at common law when the procedures of law were inadequate to do justice in a particular case. . . . In essence, the argument is a deduction of the likely reaction of the English chancellor to a hypothetical complex suit filed in 1791. . . .

We choose not to pioneer in this use of history. If the developments since 1791 have so changed the character of a suit at law to make trial of particular suits to a jury unjust, then perhaps the historically recognized boundary between law and equity should not govern the extent of the seventh amendment right. If so, then deviations from this approach to the seventh amendment should be based on the current policies and present circumstances of the federal courts. We see no persuasive reason for incorporating into the seventh amendment the policies and probable actions of the English chancellor of 1791.

VI.

. . . [A]ppellants . . . offer a second constitutional argument. They contend that the due process clause of the fifth amendment prohibits trial by jury of a suit that is too complex for a jury. They further contend that this due process limitation prevails over the seventh amendment's preservation of the right to jury trial.

Although no specific precedent exists for finding a due process violation in the trial of any case to a jury, the principles that define the procedural requirements of due process would seem to impose some limitations on the range of cases that may be submitted to a jury. The primary value promoted by due process in factfinding procedures is "to minimize the risk of erroneous decisions." Greenholtz v. Inmates of the Neb. Penal & Corr. Complex, 442 U.S. 1, 13 (1979). *See also* Mathews v. Eldridge, 424 U.S. 319, 335 (1976). A jury that cannot understand the evidence and the legal rules to be applied provides no reliable safeguard against erroneous decisions. Moreover, in the context of a completely adversary proceeding, like a civil trial, due process requires that "the decisionmaker's conclusion . . . rest solely on the legal rules and evidence adduced at the hearing." Goldberg v. Kelly, 397 U.S. 254, 271 (1970). Unless the jury can understand the legal rules and evidence, we cannot realistically expect that the jury will rest its decision on them.

. . . [T]he law presumes that a jury will decide rationally; it will resolve each disputed issue on the basis of a fair and reasonable assessment of the evidence and a fair and reasonable application of relevant legal rules. We conclude that due process precludes trial by jury when a jury is unable to perform this task with a reasonable understanding of the evidence and the legal rules.

DPC grounds for striking jury trial

If a particular lawsuit is so complex that a jury cannot satisfy this requirement of due process but is nonetheless an action at law, we face a conflict between the requirements of the fifth and seventh amendments. In this situation, we must balance the constitutionally protected interests, as they are implicated in this particular context, and reach the most reasonable accommodation between the two constitutional provisions.

The due process objections to jury trial of a complex case implicate values of fundamental importance. If judicial decisions are not based on factual determinations bearing some reliable degree of accuracy, legal remedies will not be applied consistently with the purposes of the laws. There is a danger that jury verdicts will be erratic and completely unpredictable, which would be inconsistent with evenhanded justice. Finally, unless the jury can understand the evidence and the legal rules sufficiently to rest its decision on them, the objective of most rules of evidence and procedure in promoting a fair trial will be lost entirely. We believe that when a jury is unable to perform its decisionmaking task with a reasonable understanding of the evidence and legal rules, it undermines the ability of a district court to render basic justice.

The loss of the right to jury trial in a suit found too complex for a jury does not implicate the same fundamental concerns. The absence of a jury trial requirement in equitable and maritime actions indicates that federal courts can provide fair trials and can grant relief in accordance with the basic justice without the aid of a jury. Moreover, the Supreme Court has consistently refused to rule that preservation of civil jury trial is an essential element of ordered liberty required of the states by the due process clause of the fourteenth amendment.

. . . Because the jury is a representative of the community and can call upon the community's wisdom and values, the legal system has relied on it to perform two important functions. The first is "black box" decision-making. The jury issues a verdict without an opinion to explain or justify its decision. This feature allows juries to perform a type of "jury equity," modifying harsh results of law to conform to community values in cases where a judge would have to apply the law rigidly. The second function is to accord a greater measure of legitimacy to decisions that depend upon determinations of degree rather than of absolutes, such as whether particular conduct constitutes negligence. Certain decisions of this "line drawing" nature seem less arbitrary when made by a representative body like the jury.

In the context of a lawsuit of the complexity that we have posited, however, these features do not produce real benefits of substantial value. . . . [W]hen the jury is unable to determine the normal application of the law to the facts of a case and reaches a verdict on the basis of nothing more than its own determination of community wisdom and values, its operation is indistinguishable from arbitrary and unprincipled decisionmaking. Similarly, the "line drawing" function is difficult to justify when the jury cannot understand the evidence or legal rules relevant to the issue of where to draw a line.

The district court also noted that preservation of the right to jury trial is important because the jury "provides a needed check on judicial power." A jury unable to understand the evidence and legal rules is hardly a reliable and effective check on judicial power. Our liberties are more secure when judicial decisionmakers proceed rationally, consistently with the law, and on the basis of evidence produced at trial. If the jury is unable to function in this manner, it has the capacity of becoming itself a tool of arbitrary and erratic judicial power.

Therefore, we find the most reasonable accommodation between the requirements of the fifth and seventh amendments to be a denial of jury trial when a jury will not be able to perform its task of rational decisionmaking with a reasonable understanding of the evidence and the relevant legal standards. In lawsuits of this complexity, the interests protected by this procedural rule of due process carry greater weight than the interests served by the constitutional guarantee of jury trial. Consequently, we shall not read the seventh amendment to guarantee the right to jury trial in these suits.

VII.

The district court devoted most of its discussions of appellants' due process argument not to factors relevant to the balancing of interests set out in the foregoing section but to a number of practical objections to the argument. We shall consider those objections in this section.

First, the district court challenged the premise that a case could exceed a jury's ability to decide rationally and asserted that a jury was at least as able as a judge, the only alternative factfinder, to decide complex cases. The court noted that a jury possesses the wisdom, experience, and common sense of twelve persons. It has a greater effect than a judge in disciplining attorneys to present their cases clearly and concisely. Furthermore, its capabilities can be enhanced by special trial techniques like the preliminary charge and interim charges on the law contemplated by the district court in this case. On the basis of these observations, the court concluded that a jury "is brighter, more astute, and more perceptive than a single judge, even in a complex or technical case; at least it is not less so."

Any assessment of a jury's ability to decide complex cases should include consideration not only of a jury's particular strengths and the possible enhancement of its capabilities but also of the particular constraints that operate on a jury in complex cases. The long time periods required for most complex cases are especially disabling for a jury. A long trial can interrupt the career and personal life of a jury member and thereby strain his commitment to the jury's task. The prospect of a long trial can also weed out many veniremen whose professional background qualifies them for deciding a complex case but also prohibits them from lengthy jury service. Furthermore, a jury is likely to be unfamiliar with both the technical subject matter of a complex case and the process of civil litigation. The probability is not remote that a jury will become overwhelmed and confused by a mass of evidence and issues and will reach erroneous decisions. . . .

Given that a jury has both particular strengths and weaknesses in deciding complex cases, we cannot conclude *a priori* that a jury is capable of deciding a suit of any degree of complexity. A litigant might prove that a particular suit is too complex for a jury. Because of the important due process rights implicated, a litigant should have the opportunity to make that showing.

A general presumption that a judge is capable of deciding an extraordinary complex case, by contrast, is reasonable. A long trial would not greatly disrupt the professional and personal life of a judge and should not be significantly disabling. In fact, the judge's greater ability to allocate time to the task of deciding a complex case can be a major advantage in surmounting the difficulties posed by the suit. Although we cannot presume that a judge will be more intelligent than a jury or more familiar with technical subject matters, a judge will almost surely have substantial familiarity with the process of civil litigation, as a result of experience on the bench or in practice. This experience can enable him to digest a large amount of evidence and legal argumentation, segregate distinct issues and the portions of evidence relevant to each issue, assess the opinions of expert witnesses, and apply highly complex legal standards of the facts of the case. The judge's experience also can enable him to make better use of special trial techniques designed to help the factfinder in complex cases, like colloquies with expert witnesses. The requirement that a judge issue findings of fact and conclusions of law offsets the substantial tendency to overlook issues in order that a verdict might be reached in these difficult cases. Fed. R. Civ. P. 52(a). Finally, if after trial and during deliberation a judge finds himself confused on certain matters or unable to decide certain issues, he can reopen the trial for the purpose of obtaining clarification or additional evidence. Fed. R. Civ. P. 59(a).

A judge's abilities are, of course, not unbounded. It is conceivable that a case might be so complex that a judge could not decide it rationally and competently. However, the possibility of such a case cannot justify trial by jury, because the presence of a jury does not relieve the judge of the need to understand the issues disputed in a case and the relevance and strength of the evidence. . . .

The lawsuit that exceeds the ability of a judge to decide rationally and competently would challenge the basic capacity of our system of civil litigation to decide lawsuits by any means. It would call for adjustments far more fundamental than an allocation of issues between judge and jury. Prudence compels us to defer consideration of these adjustments until we face a real possibility of such a lawsuit. In the meantime, the best course to follow is to presume the judge's ability to decide a complex case and to focus inquiry on the jury's ability.

Finally, the district court feared that the authority to strike jury trial demands on case-by-case determinations of complexity would lead to the long-run dilution of the right to jury trial. . . .

We do not believe that a due process limitation allows the district courts a substantial amount of discretion to deny jury trials. Because preservation of the right to jury trial remains a constitutionally protected interest, denials of jury trial on grounds of complexity should be confined to suits in which due process clearly requires a nonjury trial. This implies a high standard. It is not enough that trial to the court would be preferable. The complexity of a suit must be so great that it renders the suit beyond of the ability of a jury to decide by rational means with a reasonable understanding of the evidence and applicable legal rules. Moreover, the district court should not deny a jury trial if by serverance of multiple claims, thoughtful use of the procedures suggested in the *Manual for Complex Litigation,* or other methods the court can enchance a jury's capabilities or can reduce the complexity of a suit sufficiently to bring it within the ability of a jury to decide. Due process should allow denials of jury trials only in exceptional cases. . . .

. . . [T]he district court has not ruled on whether this particular lawsuit is too complex for a jury to understand and decide rationally. . . . We shall vacate the court's order on the basis of our previous discussion and shall leave for consideration on remand the issue of the complexity of this lawsuit. . . .

■ GIBBONS, Circuit Judge, dissenting.

First, I agree that this case is complex. Three objective manifestations of complexity are present: the predicted length of trial; the multiplicity of factual issues which may have to be resolved; and the conceptual difficulty of the governing law. However, all three manifestations of complexity are for the most part products of the liberal joinder rules of the Federal Rules of Civil Procedure and of the district court's ruling consolidating two multi-count cases for trial. Neither the liberal joinder rules nor the rule permitting consolidation for trial are required by any provision of the Constitution. The seventh amendment guarantees a jury trial of any separate claim for relief which would have been tried to a jury at common law. It does not guarantee that a single jury will decide multiple separate claims. If by virtue of joinder and consolidation a case becomes too complex for a single jury to handle, the remedy mandated by the seventh amendment is separate juries, as at common law. Thus we should not even consider the constitutional issue which the majority undertakes to decide in the form in which it has been presented here, because we are considering not the actual constitutional issue, but a hypothetical construction of a series of procedural rulings.

I have, however, a more serious disagreement with the majority. . . . The majority opinion attempts to objectify the factors that bear upon complexity, but in the end the factors which are identified will permit the exercise of trial court discretion. I fear that the exercise of that discretion will sometimes be influenced by unarticulated sympathies for or hostilities toward the underlying policies sought to be advanced in the lawsuit. . . .

. . . It is often said that the judicial process involves the search for objective truth. We have no real assurance, however, of objective truth whether the trial is to the court or to a jury. The judicial process can do no more than legitimize the imposition of sanctions by requiring that some minimum standards of fair play, which we call due process, are adhered to. In this legitimizing process, the seventh amendment is not a useless appendage to the Bill of Rights, but an important resource in maintaining the authority of the rule of law. . . . Any erosion of citizen participation in the sanctioning system is in the long run likely, in my view, to result in a reduction in the moral authority that supports the process.

Notes

1. Many trees lost their lives in the wake of *Ross v. Bernhard* and lower-court cases like *Boise Cascade* and *Japanese Electronics*. The existence (or non-existence) of a "complexity exception" in the Seventh Amendment and the Due Process Clause became one of the most debated issues in the legal literature during the 1970s and 1980s. For some of the best research on eighteenth-century English and American practices, see Patrick Devlin, *Jury Trial of Complex Cases: English Practice at the Time of the Seventh Amendment*, 80 COLUM. L. REV. 43 (1980); Morris S. Arnold, *A Historical Inquiry into the Right to Trial by Jury in Complex Litigation*, 128 U. PA. L. REV. 829 (1980); James S. Campbell & Nicholas Le Poidevin, *Complex Cases and Jury Trials: A Reply to Professor Arnold*, 128 U. PA. L. REV. 965 (1980). For other helpful pieces, see *Developments in the Law — The Civil Jury*, 110 HARV. L. REV. 1408 (1997); Richard O. Lempert, *Civil Juries and Complex Cases: Let's Not Rush to Judgment*, 80 MICH. L. REV. 68 (1981); Montgomery Kersten, Note, *Preserving the Right to Jury Trial in Complex Civil Cases*, 32 STAN. L. REV. 99 (1979); Note, *The Right to a Jury Trial in Complex Civil Litigation*, 92 HARV. L. REV. 898 (1979).

2. For all the academic smoke, there has been remarkably little fire. Aside from *Boise Cascade* and *Japanese Electronic*, there were only four federal cases that either struck a jury trial due to the complexity of the case or suggested that the trial judge could do so. ILC Peripherals Leasing Corp. v. Int'l Bus. Machs. Corp., 458 F. Supp. 423, 444-49 (N.D. Cal. 1978) (granting motion for directed verdict; in dicta striking jury trial in the event of a remand); Bernstein v. Universal Pictures, Inc., 79 F.R.D. 59 (S.D.N.Y. 1978); In re U.S. Fin. Sec. Litig., 75 F.R.D. 702 (S.D. Cal. 1977); and an

unreported decision, Cotten v. Witco Chem. Corp., (E.D. La.). Of the six, *Cotten* and *U.S. Financial* were reversed on appeal, and *ILC* was affirmed on other grounds. Cotten v. Witco Chem. Corp., 651 F.2d 274 (5th Cir. 1981); In re U.S. Fin. Sec. Litig., 609 F.2d 411 (9th Cir. 1979); Memorex Corp. v. Int'l Bus. Mach. Corp., 636 F.2d 1188 (9th Cir. 1980). Because *ILC* and *Boise Cascade* predated the Ninth Circuit's opinion in *U.S. Financial*, they are no longer good law within their own circuit. Thus, only *Bernstein* and *Japanese Electronic* remain unblemished.

Aligned against these two "survivors" are a host of cases, federal and state, that have either declined to recognize a complexity exception to the right to jury trial, or found that the case was not complex enough. *See, e.g.,* Soderbeck v. Burnett County, 752 F.2d 285 (7th Cir. 1985); SRI, Int'l v. Matsushita Elec. Corp., 775 F.2d 1107 (Fed. Cir. 1985); Pinemont Bank v. Belk, 722 F.2d 232 (5th Cir. 1984); City of New York v. Pullman, Inc., 662 F.2d 910 (2d Cir. 1981); Brisk v. City of Miami Beach, 726 F. Supp. 1305 (S.D. Fla. 1989); Kian v. Mirro Aluminum Co., 88 F.R.D. 351 (E.D. Mich. 1980); Davis-Watkins Co. v. Serv. Merch. Co., 500 F. Supp. 1244 (M.D. Tenn. 1980), *affirmed on other grounds,* 686 F.2d 1190 (6th Cir. 1982); Kenney v. Scientific, Inc., 512 A.2d 1142 (N.J. Super. Ct. Law Div. 1986) (striking jury demand), *rev'd,* 517 A.2d 484 (N.J. 1986) (reinstating jury demand); S.P.C.S., Inc. v. Lockheed Shipbuilding & Constr. Co., 631 P.2d 999 (Wash. Ct. App. 1981). *Cf.* Loral Corp. v. McDonnell Douglas Corp., 558 F.2d 1130 (2d Cir. 1977) (affirming striking of jury trial demand when case would have exposed jury to classified information and parties arguably waived the right to jury trial in their contract).

3.   One reason that the interest in a "complexity exception" has cooled so dramatically is the Supreme Court's decision in *Granfinanciera, S.A. v. Nordberg,* 492 U.S. 33 (1989). In dicta *Granfinanciera's* footnote 4 limited *Ross's* third factor — "the practical abilities and limitations of juries" — to cases in which "Congress has permissibly entrusted the resolution of certain disputes to an administrative agency or specialized court of equity, and . . . jury trials would impair the functioning of the legislative scheme." 492 U.S. at 42 n.4. *Chauffeurs, Teamsters and Helpers Local No. 391 v. Terry,* 494 U.S. 558, 565 n.4 (1990), re-affirmed this dicta in more dicta. This dicta tied the third factor to a line of cases that had found no Seventh Amendment or other constitutional defect in delegating the factfinding function to administrative law judges in public-law cases. *Granfinanciera's* idea was that, if Congress can constitutionally delegate factfinding to an administrative agency without offending the right to a jury trial, it can delegate factfinding to a judge. It is not important that you understand exactly when the Constitution permits delegation of factfinding to an agency; it is enough to appreciate that this reading of *Ross's* third factor abolishes the idea of a general "complexity exception" in the Seventh Amendment — at least unless Congress creates a specialized court, with judicial factfinders, to handle complex cases. (If Congress ever did so, then the question whether such a delegation of factfinding was constitutionally permissible would arise.)

It is far from clear that *Granfinanciera* accurately describes *Ross*'s intended meaning for the third factor. But its interpretation of the third factor has, for the time, fairly well silenced arguments about a "complexity exception." *But see Terry*, 494 U.S. at 583 (Stevens, J., concurring) (determining if an issue was triable to jury in part by asking whether the facts "are typical grist for the jury's judgment").

4. Although *Granfinanciera* has tamped down efforts to take away all factfinding in complex cases from juries, the idea lives on in a more discrete form. In *Markman v. Westview Instruments, Inc.*, 517 U.S. 370 (1996), the Court held that an important factual issue in most patent cases — whether a patent claim should be construed broadly enough to cover the allegedly infringing product — should be determined by a judge, not a jury, even when the case sought damages. *Markman* began by examining eighteenth-century historical practice, but found little guidance. In deciding that the specific issue of claim construction was a judicial, not a jury, function, the Court relied on "both the relative interpretive skills of judges and juries and the statutory policies that ought to be furthered by the allocation" of the factfinding function. *Id.* at 384. These "functional considerations also play their part in the choice between judge and jury":

> The construction of written instruments is one of those things that judges often do and are likely to do better than jurors untrained in exegesis. . . . "The judge, from training and discipline, is more likely to give a proper interpretation to such instruments than a jury; and he is, therefore, more likely to be right, in performing such a duty, than a jury can be expected to be." . . .
>
> . . . [I]n these cases a jury's capabilities to evaluate demeanor, to sense the "mainsprings of human conduct," or to reflect community standards are much less significant than a trained ability to evaluate the testimony in relation to the overall structure of a patent. [*Id.* at 388-90.]

The Court also held that the important policy "of uniformity in the treatment of a given patent [was] an independent reason to allocate all issues of construction to the court." *Id.* at 390.

In patent cases, *Markman* has had an extraordinary effect. "*Markman* hearings," at which a judge usually hears evidence from lay and expert witnesses to determine the construction of a patent claim, are now *de rigeur* in patent cases. Thus far, however, *Markman* and its aftermath have not re-ignited a general movement to recognize a "complexity exception" to the Seventh Amendment right. *Cf.* Warner-Jenkinson Co. v. Hilton Davis Chem. Co., 520 U.S. 17 (1997) (indicating in dicta that applying the patent-law doctrine of equivalents was a jury issue despite concerns for the jury's competence).

5. Even if the Seventh Amendment and comparable state provisions do not recognize a "complexity exception," the issue of due process remains. The Due Process Clauses of the Fifth and Fourteenth Amendments do not mention rational adjudication. The Seventh Amendment, by contrast, is

specific on the issue of jury trial. How can it reasonably be thought that the former trumps the latter? *See SRI*, 775 F.2d 1107 (no due process trump); *U.S. Financial*, 609 F.2d 411 (same). One argument is that the trump is implicit in modern procedure. For instance, jury-control devices such as the power to order judgment as a matter of law and summary judgment can be justified on the ground that the notion of rational decision-making inherent in due process overrides the jury-trial guarantee of the Seventh Amendment. *See* Paul D. Carrington, *The Seventh Amendment: Some Bicentennial Reflections*, 1990 U. CHI. LEGAL F. 33, 44-47. Viewed in this light, the due process obligation to strike juries in complex cases is the logical endpoint of courts' long-standing responsibility to supervise the work of juries.

Remember, though, that jury trial advances not only the goal of rational and accurate adjudication but also the political objectives of American democracy. From this perspective, it isn't so easy to sacrifice the voice of average citizens to our desire for rational adjudication.

6. Rather than asking whether the Due Process Clause trumps the Seventh Amendment, as *Japanese Electronic* does, shouldn't the question be why the Federal Rules of Civil Procedure and other modern aggregation devices trump the Seventh Amendment? Recall that *Beacon Theatres* said that "only under the most imperative circumstances, circumstances which in view of the flexible procedures of the Federal Rules we cannot now anticipate, can the right to a jury trial of legal issues be lost"? Beacon Theatres, Inc. v. Westover, 359 U.S. 500, 510-11 (1959). Has the flexibility of modern aggregation rules created that which *Beacon Theatres* thought unimaginable? Or must the flexibility in aggregation devices be employed to preclude the joinder of related cases that create jury-endangering complexity? This was Judge Gibbons' point in his dissent in *Japanese Electronic*, and it is critical: Does the Seventh Amendment limit our ability to aggregate cases when the aggregated proceeding cannot be tried to a jury? The answer, which determines the permissible scope of aggregation, shows again how issues of aggregation and issues of trial seamlessly blend together.

7. Even if there is no "complexity exception" in either the Seventh Amendment or the Due Process Clauses, a case's complexity can still have an effect on other aspects of a right to a jury. For instance, in BCCI Holdings (Luxembourg), S.A. v. Khalil, 182 F.R.D. 335 (D.D.C. 1998), the defendant failed to demand a jury trial and filed an untimely request for a jury trial after the close of discovery. Analyzing the issue under Fed. R. Civ. P. 39(b), the district court denied the demand. One of the four factors that the court considered was the complexity of the case. After citing *Japanese Electronic*, the court continued:

> . . . In some complex cases, it may turn out that [the complexity] factor favors a jury trial because the parties are more likely to streamline their presentations to resonate with the common sense of jurors rather than to overcomplicate the case in their presentations to a single judge. In other complex cases, real efficiencies can be had in

trying the case to the Court rather than a jury because of the greater procedural flexibility available in a bench trial.

In this case, . . . a bench trial will be considerably more efficient because the Court can absorb the information at the speed of light (by reading the testimony) rather than at the slower speed of sound (by listening to the transcripts being read into the record). While a jury could no doubt comprehend the evidence to be adduced, this factor favors a bench trial because it will allow for a far more expeditious development of the record. [*Id.* at 339.]

Second, the complexity of a case has influenced some state courts in deciding whether a particular claim is jury-triable. For instance, breaking with the approach used in *Ross v. Bernhard*, the Iowa Supreme Court has held that shareholders' derivative actions are equitable in nature, so that no factual issues are tried to a jury. Weltzin v. Nail, 618 N.W.2d 293, 303 (Iowa 2000) ("To provide an avenue for shareholders to have a jury for their legal claims would prove inefficient and overly burdensome on the lower courts as well as untrained juries.").

8. Until now, the working assumption has been that juries do not perform well in complex cases; the issue has been whether a judge has the power to act on that assumption and to strike the jury. But, as *BCCI Holdings* says, juries are not necessarily a disadvantage in complex cases. One advantage of juries is that they force the lawyers to simplify evidence and think their arguments through clearly. Patrick Higginbotham, a federal judge who has served at both the trial and appellate levels, once observed: "I see the effect on the lawyers when the jury is out of the box. When the scalpel goes out, the shovel comes in." ABA ANTITRUST SECTION, EXPEDITING PRETRIALS AND TRIALS OF ANTITRUST CASES 135 (1979). Similarly, H. Blair White, a veteran trial lawyer, observed that "a civil antitrust suit tried to a judge . . . is the most uncontrolled, worst proceeding that can be conceived, and that's because the judiciary takes the attitude, let anything in. We will get it all, and it's going to be faster. In fact, it's much slower. If we let go of the jury in this context, we are really going to have two elephants trying to get into that Volkswagen." *Id.*

Moreover, research suggests that, across a range of civil and criminal cases, judges and juries agree on the result about eighty percent of the time; when they disagree, judges are on balance more disposed toward civil plaintiffs than juries are. *See* Harry Kalven, Jr., *The Dignity of the Civil Jury*, 50 VA. L. REV. 1055 (1964); R. Perry Sentell, Jr., *The Georgia Jury and Negligence: The View from the Bench*, 26 GA. L. REV. 85 (1991); Kevin M. Clermont & Theodore Eisenberg, *Trial by Jury or Judge: Transcending Empiricism*, 77 CORNELL L. REV. 1124 (1992); AUDREY CHIN & MARK A. PETERSON, DEEP POCKETS, EMPTY POCKETS (1985). In one field study of complex civil and criminal trials, judge-jury agreement fell significantly, down to about sixty-three percent, but neither the complexity of the trial nor the trial process used to address complexity was significantly related to the level of judge-jury agreement. Larry Heuer & Steven Penrod, *Trial Complexity: A Field Investigation of Its Meaning and Its Effects*, 18 LAW &

HUM. BEHAV. 29, 49 (1994) (noting that "our data do not support the proposition that judges and juries decide cases differently [or] that complexity influences the rationality of jury decision making"). At the same time, this field study, as well as another study using experimental subjects, reported that increased information decreased jurors' understanding and weakened their confidence in the accuracy of their verdict. *See id.*; Irwin A. Horowitz et al., *Effects of Trial Complexity on Decision Making*, 81 J. APPLIED PSYCHOL. 757 (1996). The field study also showed that, when they disagreed with juries, judges tended to be somewhat more pro-plaintiff. The experimental study also found that test subjects exposed to high-information conditions tended to perform worse in terms of assigning appropriate blame to the defendant and those exposed to complex-language conditions tended to have more difficulty distinguishing among plaintiffs' cases. One of the counterintuitive aspects of the experimental study was that the inclusion of a larger number of plaintiffs in the trial seemed to hurt the plaintiffs' chances of recovery — a result probably explained by the fact that the presence of more plaintiffs created a high-information condition under which jurors were less likely to assign responsibility to the defendant.

Other research also suggests that juries perform well under most conditions; it turns out that twelve heads are often better than one in terms of decision-making, although the group's decision isn't necessarily better than the decision to which the most competent member of the group would have come. One area in which juries perform horrendously is the comprehension of jury instructions: Jurors fail to comprehend adequately as many as half of the judge's instructions regarding the law. *See* Nancy S. Marder, *Bringing Jury Instruction into the Twenty-First Century*, 81 NOTRE DAME L. REV. 449 (2006). Another challenge for juries is understanding technical, scientific, or statistical evidence; the adversarial presentation of such evidence, usually through experts, often does little to clarify matters, and can lead to a jury's disregard of the testimony on both sides. But judges often make the same mistakes, and share the same misconceptions, regarding statistical and technical evidence. *Compare* William C. Thompson, *Are Juries Competent to Evaluate Statistical Evidence?*, 52 LAW & CONTEMP. PROBS. 9 (Autumn 1989) (juries tend to undervalue statistical evidence), *and* David L. Faigman & A.J. Baglioni, Jr., *Bayes' Theorem in the Trial Process: Instructing Jurors on the Value of Statistical Evidence*, 12 LAW & HUM. BEHAV. 1 (1988) (same), *with* Gary Wells, *Naked Statistical Evidence of Liability: Is Subjective Probability Enough?*, 62 J. PERSONALITY & SOC. PSYCHOL. 739 (1992) (judges demonstrate same fallacious statistical reasoning as juries), *and* Richard Lempert, *Civil Juries and Complex Cases: Taking Stock after Twelve Years*, in VERDICT 181, 215-217 (Robert E. Litan ed. 1993) (anecdotal evidence and inferences from data suggest that judges have equal difficulty assessing difficult scientific evidence).

In an article notable for its attempt to synthesize the results of a vast quantity of empirical jury research, one of the leading researchers on the American jury rendered the following verdict on the jury's performance under conditions of complexity:

[P]rocedural complexity probably does affect the process by which juries reach decisions and ultimately verdicts. Whether the changes are positive or negative depends on which perspective one takes, but they do raise the desirability of aids to assist the jury and, at the same time, caution about what additional consequences may result from changes in procedures.

Neil Vidmar, *The Performance of the American Civil Jury: An Empirical Perspective*, 40 ARIZ. L. REV. 849, 875 (1998). The following chapter examines a number of the aids to which Professor Vidmar refers. You might wish to reserve final judgment on the desirability of a judicial power to strike juries until you consider these devices.

9. For a sampling of the contributions to the empirical literature on juries either in complex cases or in general, see NEIL VIDMAR & VALERIE P. HANS, AMERICAN JURIES (2007); INSIDE THE JURY (Reid Hastie ed. 1993); VALERIE P. HANS & NEIL VIDMAR, JUDGING THE JURY (1986); HARRY KALVEN, JR. & HANS ZEISEL, THE AMERICAN JURY (1966); Symposium, *Is the Jury Competent?*, 52 LAW & CONTEMP. PROBS. 1 (Autumn 1989).

10. You might have wondered whether it might be possible to have your cake and eat it too by empaneling jurors who possess special or technical competence to decide the factual issues. For instance, in a securities-fraud case, a jury might consist of accountants and auditors; an antitrust case might use economists and CEOs. This idea of a "special jury" (also called a "blue-ribbon jury" or a "struck jury") is an ancient one in Anglo-American law. In 1351 a special jury composed of cooks and fishmongers tried a person accused of selling bad food. Special juries of merchants were often used in mercantile disputes. In 1730 Parliament declared every litigant's entitlement, whether in civil or criminal cases, to a special jury upon motion and a willingness to pay the jury's expenses. *See* James B. Thayer, *The Jury and Its Development (Part II)*, 5 HARV. L. REV. 295, 300-02 (1892). Lord Mansfield, Chief Justice of the King's Bench from 1756 to 1788, frequently used special juries, especially in commercial cases. *See* Note, *The Case for Special Juries in Complex Cases*, 89 YALE L.J. 1155, 1164-65 (1980). Blackstone's view was that special juries were available "when the causes were of too great nicety for the discussion of ordinary freeholders; or where the sheriff [who was ordinarily responsible for selecting jurymen] was suspected of partiality." 3 WILLIAM BLACKSTONE, COMMENTARIES *357.

Special juries have occasionally been employed in American states. *See* Jeannette E. Thatcher, *Why Not Use the Special Jury?*, 31 MINN. L. REV. 232, 251 (1947) (listing sixteen states that passed special-jury statutes, and two that used special juries without legislative authorization). The Supreme Court declared the special jury constitutional in criminal cases. *See* Moore v. N.Y., 333 U.S. 565 (1948); Fay v. N.Y., 332 U.S. 261 (1947). Delaware has one of the most interesting special-jury statutes:

> The court may order a special jury upon the application of any party in a complex civil case. The party applying for a special jury shall pay the expense incurred by having a special jury, which may be allowed as part of the costs of the case.

10 DEL. CODE ANN. § 4506. The statute never defines "complex civil case" and gives discretion to judges to determine when a special jury would be appropriate. *See* In re Asbestos Litig., 551 A.2d 1296 (Del. Super. 1988) (upholding the statute against a constitutional challenge).

It is unlikely that federal judges possess a similar power to constitute a special jury in complex cases. The usual view is that special juries must be statutorily authorized. The Jury Selection and Service Act of 1968 declares as "the policy of the United States that all litigants in Federal courts [are] entitled to trial by jury . . . selected at random from a fair cross section of the community." 28 U.S.C. § 1861. The Act disqualifies from service only those who are (1) not citizens; (2) are "unable to read, write, and understand the English language with a degree of proficiency sufficient to fill out satisfactorily the juror qualification form"; (3) are "unable to speak the English language"; (4) are "incapable, by reason of mental or physical infirmity, to render satisfactory jury service"; or (5) are charged with or have been convicted of a felony. *Id.* § 1865(b). The second, third, and fourth exceptions demonstrate a desire for rational jurors, but no case has constructed from these sections a license to constitute a special jury. *See* William V. Luneburg & Mark A. Nordenberg, *Specially Qualified Juries and Expert Nonjury Tribunals: Alternatives for Coping with the Complexities of Modern Civil Litigation*, 67 VA. L. REV. 887 (1981) (arguing for amendments to the Jury Selection and Service Act to allow special juries in complex cases); Louis Harris & Assocs., *Judges' Opinions on Procedural Issues: A Survey of State and Federal Trial Judges Who Spend at Least Half Their Time on General Civil Cases*, 69 B.U. L. REV. 731, 747-48 (1989) (reporting that 58% of federal and 66% of state judges rejected a minimal educational level for jurors in complex cases). *Cf.* Laura G. Dooley, *National Juries for National Cases: Preserving Citizen Participation in Large-Scale Litigation*, 83 N.Y.U. L. REV. 411 (2008) (arguing that using national juries in complex cases would increase the legitimacy and quality of jury decisions).

Granting that special juries may face a high hurdle as a statutory matter, could their use be required as a matter of due process?

A more modest solution might be to "salt" the jury with two or three persons with relevant experience; the remaining members could be drawn from a cross section of the community. So far, no cases have taken this step. *See generally* Jonathan D. Casper, *Restructuring the Traditional Civil Jury: The Effect of Changes in Composition and Procedures, in* VERDICT, *supra*, 414, 428-32 (noting that "[e]xtensive experience with the use of special juries and research on their impact are lacking"). In addition, the parties presumably can consent to a trial before a special jury. In *In re Richardson-Merrell, Inc. "Bendectin" Products Liability Litigation*, 624 F. Supp. 1212, 1217 (S.D. Ohio 1985), *aff'd*, 857 F.2d 290 (6th Cir. 1988), the court sought to convince the parties to use either a "blue ribbon jury" of people with greater formal education or a "blue, blue ribbon jury" of people knowledgeable in the relevant field. The defendant was willing, but the plaintiffs were not; the district judge therefore dropped the idea.

For a discussion of the English and American history of the special jury, ultimately arguing for the special jury's greater use in modern trials, see JAMES OLDHAM, TRIAL BY JURY (2006).

11. To some extent, criticisms of the jury are really criticisms about the way in which juries are picked. Lawyers seeking an adversarial edge have little incentive to seek an impartial jury; they are seeking a jury as partial to their viewpoints as they can empanel. Truly impartial or qualified jurors are often struck by means of peremptory challenges. One solution, which probably would require an amendment to 28 U.S.C. § 1870 (granting each party in a civil case three peremptory challenges), would be to eliminate peremptory challenges. A different solution would be to allow the judge to select the jury. *See* WILLIAM W SCHWARZER, MANAGING ANTITRUST AND OTHER COMPLEX LITIGATION § 7-2(B)(1) (1982) (describing an antitrust case in which the parties consented to allow a judge to excuse prospective jurors who lacked adequate qualifications).

2. The Power to Appoint an Alternate Factfinder in Bench Trials

Judges are not necessarily better equipped than juries to find the facts in the face of complex and technical evidence. Yet they act as factfinders in complex bench trials. In this section we examine the ability of the trial judge to assign all or part of this factfinding role to specialized judicial adjuncts. Such authority to delegate, should it exist, is important. Most obviously, the nature of the pretrial and trial process will be different if a specialized adjunct will determine the facts. In addition, if judges can delegate factfinding to uniquely qualified adjuncts, then bench trials can outperform jury trials in terms of factfinding — a result that might put pressure on judges to find some "complexity" exception or other doctrinal artifice to keep complex cases away from juries.

LA BUY V. HOWES LEATHER CO.

352 U.S. 249 (1957)

■ MR. JUSTICE CLARK delivered the opinion of the Court.

These two consolidated cases present a question of the power of the Courts of Appeals to issue writs of mandamus to compel a District Judge to vacate his orders entered under Rule 53(b) of the Federal Rules of Civil Procedure referring antitrust cases for trial before a master. . . .

History of the Litigation. — These petitions for mandamus, filed in the Court of Appeals, arose from two antitrust actions instituted in the District Court in 1950. [The two cases, *Rohlfing* and *Shaffer*, involved ninety-three plaintiffs that were either operators of independent retail shoe-repair shops or wholesalers of shoe-repair supplies. Each case involved six defendants, who were manufacturers, wholesalers, retail mail-order houses, and chain operators of shoe-repair stores. The complaints asserted a Sherman Act conspiracy "to monopolize and to attempt to monopolize" and fix the price of shoe-repair supplies in the Chicago area, and a price-discrimination charge under the Robinson-Patman Act.] Both complaints pray for injunctive relief, treble damages, and an accounting with respect to the discriminatory price differentials charged.

The record indicates that the cases had been burdensome to the petitioner. In *Rohlfing* alone, 27 pages of the record are devoted to docket entries reflecting that petitioner had conducted many hearings on preliminary pleas and motions. The original complaint had been twice amended as a result of orders of the court in regard to misjoinders and severance; 14 defendants had been dismissed with prejudice; summary judgment hearings had resulted in a refusal to enter a judgment for some of the defendants on the pleadings; over 50 depositions had been taken; and hearings to compel testimony and require the production and inspection of records were held. It appears that several of the hearings were extended and included not only oral argument but submission of briefs, and resulted in the filing of opinions and memoranda by the petitioner. It is reasonable to conclude that much time would have been saved at the trial had petitioner heard the case because of his familiarity with the litigation.

The References to the Master. — The references to the master were made under the authority of Rule 53(b) of the Federal Rules of Civil Procedure. The cases were called on February 23, 1955, on a motion to reset them for trial. *Rohlfing* was "No. 1 below the black line" on the trial list, which gave it a preferred setting. All parties were anxious for an early trial, but plaintiffs wished an adjournment until May. The petitioner announced that "it has taken a long time to get this case at issue. I remember hearing more motions, I think, in this case than any case I have ever sat on in this court." The plaintiffs estimated that the trial would take six weeks, whereupon petitioner stated he did not know when he could try the case "if it is going to take this long." He asked if the parties could agree "to have a Master hear" it. The parties ignored this query and at a conference in chambers the next day petitioner entered the orders of reference sua sponte. The orders declared that the court was "confronted with an extremely congested calendar" and that "exception [sic] conditions exist for this reason" requiring the references. The cases were referred to the master "to take evidence and to report the same to this Court, together with his findings of fact and conclusions of law." It was further ordered in each case that "the Master shall commence the trial of this cause" on a certain date and continue with diligence, and that the parties supply security for costs. While the parties had deposited some $8,000 costs, the record discloses that all parties objected to the references and filed motions to vacate them. Upon petitioner's refusal to vacate the references, these mandamus actions were filed in the Court of Appeals seeking the issuance of writs ordering petitioner to do so. [The appellate court issued the writs.]

The Power of the Courts of Appeals. — . . . Since the Court of Appeals could at some stage of the antitrust proceedings entertain appeals in these cases, it has power in proper circumstances, as here, to issue writs of mandamus reaching them. . . . We pass on, then, to the only real question involved, i.e., whether the exercise of the power by the Court of Appeals was proper in the cases now before us.

The Discretionary Use of the Writs. — It appears from the docket entries to which we heretofore referred that the petitioner was well informed as to the nature of the antitrust litigation, the pleadings of the parties, and the gist of the plaintiffs' claims. He was well aware of the theory of the defense and much of the proof which necessarily was outlined in the various requests for discovery, admissions, interrogatories, and depositions. He heard arguments on motions to dismiss, to compel testimony on depositions, and for summary judgment. In fact, petitioner's knowledge of the cases at the time of the references, together with his long experience in the antitrust field, points to the conclusion that he could dispose of the litigation with greater dispatch and less effort than anyone else. Nevertheless, he referred both suits to a master on the general issue. Furthermore, neither the existence of the alleged conspiracy nor the question of liability vel non had been determined in either case. These issues, as well as the damages, if any, and the question concerning the issuance of an injunction, were likewise included in the references. Under all of the circumstances, we believe the Court of Appeals was justified in finding the orders of reference were an abuse of the petitioner's power under Rule 53(b). They amounted to little less than an abdication of the judicial function depriving the parties of a trial before the court on the basic issues involved in the litigation.

The use of masters is "to aid judges in the performance of specific judicial duties, as they may arise in the progress of a cause," and not to displace the court. The exceptional circumstances here warrant the use of the extraordinary remedy of mandamus. . . .

. . . The record does not show to what extent references are made by the full bench of the District Court in the Northern District; however, it does reveal that petitioner has referred 11 cases to masters in the past 6 years. But even "a little cloud may bring a flood's downpour" if we approve the practice here indulged, particularly in the face of presently congested dockets, increased filings, and more extended trials. This is not to say that we are neither aware of nor fully appreciative of the unfortunate congestion of the court calendar in many of our District Courts. . . . But, be that as it may, congestion in itself is not such an exceptional circumstance as to warrant a reference to a master. If such were the test, present congestion would make references the rule rather than the exception. Petitioner realizes this, for in addition to calendar congestion he alleges that the cases referred had unusual complexity of issues of both fact and law. But most litigation in the antitrust field is complex. It does not follow that antitrust litigants are not entitled to a trial before a court. On the contrary, we believe that this is an impelling reason for trial before a regular, experienced trial judge rather than before a temporary substitute appointed on an ad hoc basis and ordinarily not experienced in judicial work. Nor does petitioner's claim of the great length of time these trials will require offer exceptional grounds. The final ground asserted by petitioner was with reference to the voluminous accounting which would be necessary in the event the plaintiffs prevailed. We agree that the detailed accounting required in order to determine the damages suffered by each plaintiff might be referred to a master after the court has determined the over-all liability of defendants, provided the circumstances indicate that the use of the court's time is not warranted in receiving the proof and making the tabulation.

We believe that supervisory control of the District Courts by the Courts of Appeals is necessary to proper judicial administration in the federal system.   The All Writs Act confers on the Courts of Appeals the discretionary power to issue writs of mandamus in the exceptional circumstances existing here. Its judgment is therefore affirmed.

■   [The dissenting opinion of MR. JUSTICE BRENNAN, with whom MR. JUSTICE FRANKFURTER, MR. JUSTICE BURTON, and MR. JUSTICE HARLAN joined, is omitted.]

REILLY V. UNITED STATES

863 F.2d 149 (1st Cir. 1988)

■   SELYA, Circuit Judge.

[Peter and Donna Reilly and their minor daughter, Heather, brought a medical malpractice action due to severe injuries that Heather suffered at birth. Liability was conceded.]

After discovery [on damages] was completed, a 7-day bench trial ensued. Both sides introduced expert testimony as to the calculation of damages for lost earning capacity.   Appellees also supplied expert testimony regarding expenses for Heather's future care, but "the government presented almost no factual argument against the necessity for and pecuniary valuation of the[se] itemized damages." The trial came to a halt on November 26, 1986 — but, as matters turned out, more evidence was to be taken at supplementary hearings.

During the interval between the trial and the resumed hearings, the district judge attempted to enlist an economist to assist him in respect to certain technical aspects pertinent to the calculation of a damage award. He approached several potential candidates . . . and one agreed to serve. The judge did not inform counsel of his search. By happenstance, the government learned of it . . . .

The [government's attorney] immediately requested a chambers conference. The session was held on April 10, 1987. The district judge recounted his conversations with the economists and made no bones about his intent to hire one as a technical advisor. He informed all counsel that he had already contacted the Administrative Office of the United States Courts to this end, and that he was awaiting approval from the Chief Judge of the First Circuit. The government voiced no contemporaneous objection to the procedure, did not ask the name of the economist whom the court intended to retain, did not ask that either the court's instructions to the expert or the expert's advice be reduced to writing, and did not request an opportunity to question him.

To make a tedious tale tolerably terse, the approvals were forthcoming, and the judge appointed Dr. Arthur Mead of the University of Rhode Island to act as a technical assistant to the court. The judge had two short conferences with Dr. Mead in the spring of 1987. During the same time frame, the court conducted supplemental evidentiary hearings on April 16 and May 5, 1987. On July 28, an opinion and order was issued awarding Heather Reilly $1,000,000 for pain and suffering, $1,104,641 for lost earning capacity, and $8,933,323 in respect to anticipated future care. . . .

II. APPOINTING A TECHNICAL ADVISOR

The United States concedes that a district court has inherent authority to appoint an expert as a technical advisor.[4] It maintains, notwithstanding, that (1) such power is strictly circumscribed by Fed. R. Evid. 706(a), a rule whose protocol the district court saw no need to obey; (2) the court abused its discretion in appointing an advisor at all in this case; (3) the court's appointee far exceeded the limited role of a technical advisor; and (4) the absence of meaningful procedural safeguards rendered utilization of the advisor fundamentally unfair. We examine these points seriatim.

A. *Rule 706*

Throughout its text, Fed. R. Evid. 706 refers not to "experts" generally, but to a more exclusive class: "expert witnesses." Because the plain language of a Civil Rule is the most reliable indicator of its meaning, we are constrained to conclude that the grasp of Rule 706 is confined to court-appointed expert witnesses; the rule does not embrace expert advisors or consultants. . . .

This conclusion is buttressed by the text of the advisory committee notes (Notes) accompanying Rule 706. As we read them, the Notes seem geared exclusively to expert witnesses as opposed to technical advisors. . . . Given the undeniable fact that, at common law, federal trial courts were empowered not only to designate expert witnesses, but to appoint technical

---

4. The court below held that it had both statutory and inherent authority to appoint a technical advisor. Because we agree that such power inheres generally in a district court, see, e.g., Ex parte Peterson, 253 U.S. 300, 312-13 (1920), we need not explore — and express no opinion on — the lower court's view of the statutory mosaic. By the same token, we need not analyze the suggestion (eschewed by all of the parties to this case) that Fed. R. Civ. P. 53, which deals with the naming of masters, may be a fertile source of judicial power to retain necessary technical assistance. See, e.g., Reed v. Cleveland Bd. of Educ., 607 F.2d 737, 746 (6th Cir. 1979) (authority to appoint "expert advisors or consultants" derives from either Rule 53 or court's inherent power) [*infra* p. 1028].

advisors as well, *see, e.g.*, Ex parte Peterson, 253 U.S. 300, 312-13 (1920) (Brandeis, J.), the omission of any language limitative of the latter power is, we think, telling. . . .

The substance as well as the language of Rule 706 comports with this interpretation. The rule establishes a procedural framework for nomination and selection of an expert witness and for the proper performance of his role after an appointment is accepted (e.g., advising the parties of his findings, submitting to depositions, being called to testify, being cross-examined). By and large, these modalities — though critically important in the realm customarily occupied by an expert witness — have marginal, if any, relevance to the functioning of technical advisors. Since an advisor, by definition, is called upon to make no findings and to supply no evidence, provisions for depositions, cross-questioning, and the like are inapposite. . . .

We conclude, therefore, that Rule 706, while intended to circumscribe a court's right to designate expert witnesses, was not intended to subsume the judiciary's inherent power to appoint technical advisors. The Civil Rules, after all, were never meant to become the sole repository of all of a federal court's authority.

B. *Abuse of Discretion*

The government's immediate fallback position is that, even if literal compliance with Rule 706 was not essential, the district court nevertheless abused its discretion in appointing a technical advisor at all. We concur wholeheartedly that such appointments should be the exception and not the rule, and should be reserved for truly extraordinary cases where the introduction of outside skills and expertise, not possessed by the judge, will hasten the just adjudication of a dispute without dislodging the delicate balance of the juristic role. *Cf.* La Buy v. Howes Leather Co., 352 U.S. 249, 255-57 (1957) (discussing appropriate occasions for employment of special masters) [*supra* p. 1016].

We wish to emphasize our strongly-held view that the appointment of a technical advisor must arise out of some cognizable judicial need for specialized skills. Appropriate instances, we suspect, will be hen's-teeth rare. The modality is, if not a last, a near-to-last resort, to be engaged only where the trial court is faced with problems of unusual difficulty, sophistication, and complexity, involving something well beyond the regular questions of fact and law with which judges must routinely grapple. Although a technical advisor can be valuable in an appropriate case, the judge must not be eager to lighten his load without the best of cause.

Despite the fact that the integument as we have shaped it is a narrow one, we believe that this litigation slips fittingly within it. The case involved esoterica: complex economic theories, convoluted by their nature, fraught with puzzlement in their application, leading to a surpassingly difficult computation of damages. Future-care expenditures and lost earnings had to be projected over a 70-year period — and for an infant with no proven financial track record. Plaintiffs' experts differed among themselves on some points. The stakes were demonstrably high. The government was of small help. Its submission on damages, amounting to little more than a lick and a promise, can best be characterized as feeble. The one-sidedness of the evidence itself lent encouragement to the use of a technical advisor to help the court understand the theories which were bruited about. All in all, the litigation was so far outside the mainstream that the judge, in our estimation, had good reason to energize his inherent power to bring a technical advisor on board. *Cf.* MANUAL FOR COMPLEX LITIGATION, SECOND § 21.54 (1985) (court may consider appointing confidential advisor in "complex litigation" and "when complicated issues are involved"). Mindful of the trier's discretion in this regard, the charge of abuse simply will not wash.

C. *The Technical Advisor's Role*

Our decision that this was a seemly case for nominating a technical advisor and that the district court was not bound to comply with the requirements of Rule 706 in making the appointment does not end this phase of our inquiry. The government argues that, whatever may be said of the need for the appointment or its mechanics, the district court permitted Dr. Mead to roam far beyond the precincts to which a technical advisor must properly be confined. In the end, the government hints, the judge abdicated the factfinding function in favor of Dr. Mead, relying on him to resolve the merits. We find that the district court's use of its expert in this case was limited to appropriate technical assistance, and therefore reject the government's plea.

We start with a restatement of the principle derived from a watershed case anent technical advisors. In *Ex parte Peterson*, 253 U.S. 300 (1920), the Supreme Court recognized that trial judges in the federal system possessed "inherent power to provide themselves with appropriate instruments required for the performance of their duties," including the power to "appoint persons unconnected with the court to aid judges in the performance of specific judicial duties, as they may arise in the progress of a cause." *Id.* at 312. Advisors of this sort are not witnesses, and may not contribute evidence. Similarly, they are not judges, so they may not be allowed to usurp the judicial function. *See* Kimberly v. Arms, 129 U.S. 512, 524 (1889) (court may not, through appointment of a master or otherwise, "abdicate its duty to determine by its own judgment the controversy presented"). A judge may not, for example, appoint a legal advisor to brief him on legal issues, since "determination of purely legal questions is the responsibility of the court itself." Reed v. Cleveland Bd. of Educ., 607 F.2d at 747 [*infra* p. 1028]. Neither may a court employ a technical advisor to "undertake an independent mission of finding facts" outside the record of the case. In fine, the advisor's role is to act as a sounding board for the judge — helping the jurist to educate himself in the jargon and theory disclosed by the testimony and to think through the critical technical problems.

In this case, it does not appear that the district judge stepped over the line. . . . [T]he judge wrote that he needed an expert in-house "to advise and instruct [him] on the myriad and arcane aspects of economic science necessary to a just adjudication of the . . . case." The judge reported to counsel at a chambers conference that he had explained to Dr. Mead the economist's role as being to function "in the nature of a law clerk," someone with whom the judge could engage in "freewheeling discussion." . . . It is readily apparent that the district court crafted the contours of the engagement with care. . . .

A second contention hawked by appellant is more troublesome. The government urges that because Dr. Mead received no written instructions and submitted no written report, it is unclear to what extent the district court may have allowed the boundaries to be overrun. We agree that it would have been better practice to document the interchange between jurist and advisor in some more readily retrievable fashion. Yet we perceive no fatal flaw. . . . Here, the record fully supports the judge's explanation of how he used Dr. Mead's services, and the government has offered no cogent reason to doubt this explanation. . . .

Appellant's complaint that it was deprived of any opportunity to cross-examine Dr. Mead appears asthenic. If, as the district court stated, the advisor was not an evidentiary source, there was neither a right to cross-question him as to the economics of the situation nor a purpose in doing so. And, to the extent that it might have profited the government to grill Dr. Mead about his role in the case, the short and simple response is that, after being informed at the April 10 chambers conference that the district court intended to hire a technical advisor, the [government's attorney] did not ask for written specification of the advisor's anticipated role or attempt to reserve a right of inquiry. . . . Having failed to raise that point below, the United States cannot raise it for the first time on appeal. . . .

D. *Procedural Safeguards*

Appellant has one remaining shot in its sling. It protests vigorously that, even where a technical advisor may appropriately be engaged by a trial judge outside the realm of Rule 706, fundamental fairness requires that the appointment be hedged about with a panoply of procedural safeguards. Among other things, appellant urges that the district court should have given advance notice to the parties of the expert's identity and how he was to be used; that written instructions should have been prepared regarding the expert's duties; and that Dr. Mead should have been required to file a written report. We are quick to acknowledge that these suggestions have some merit.

We think it advisable in future cases that the parties be notified of the expert's identity before the court makes the appointment, and be given an opportunity to object on grounds such as bias or inexperience. . . . We also think that there is much to commend the preformulation of a written "job description" for the advisor (or in lieu thereof, that the judge deliver comprehensive verbal instructions to the advisor, on the record, in the presence of all counsel). At the conclusion of his stint, the advisor should file an affidavit attesting to his compliance with the job description.[8] And we do not regard such matters as mere ritual; in an appropriate case, we would not hesitate to reverse if procedural safeguards were wholly inadequate.

Our belief in the value of such prophylactic measures, however, does not avail the government here. . . . [A]ppellant sat back and knowingly acquiesced in the court's unconditional hiring of an unidentified technical advisor. This was, we think, a waiver. . . .

[The court then ordered the award reduced by approximately $1 million for an unrelated reason.]

Notes

1.   According to briefs filed in *La Buy*, none of the parties awaiting trial had demanded a jury, which meant that Judge La Buy was the factfinder on all issues. Assuming that this had been a jury trial, could Judge La Buy have appointed a master to serve as an aid to a jury? In 1957 the answer was yes, but only in exceptional circumstances. After the 2003 amendments to Rule 53, however, the answer is no — unless the parties consent. *See* Fed. R. Civ. P. 53(a)(1)(B) (permitting non-consensual trial references only in non-jury cases, and only on a showing of "some exceptional condition" or "a difficult computation of damages" such as an accounting); *cf.* Turner Constr. Co. v. First Indem. of Am. Ins. Co., 829 F. Supp. 752 (E.D. Pa. 1993) (describing the consensual use of a special master to hear the evidence and find the facts).

2.   In a non-jury suit in which a reference is appropriate, the master usually submits a report, containing findings of fact and conclusions of law, to the judge. *See* Fed. R. Civ. P. 53(e)-(f). The parties can object to the report, and the judge must review all findings of fact and conclusions of law under a *de novo* standard (except that the parties can stipulate, with court approval, to the review of factual findings, under a clear-error standard). Fed. R. Civ. P. 53(f)(3)(A), -(f)(4). Hence, even if a reference for factfinding is appropriate, the judge retains important responsibility for factfinding.

3.   Is *La Buy* a constitutional holding, a holding about the scope of Rule 53's "exceptional condition" requirement, or both? Lower courts tend to treat *La Buy* more as a Rule 53 case, albeit one with significant Article III underpinnings. *See* In re Bituminous Coal Operators' Ass'n, 949 F.2d 1165

---

8.   We disagree with the suggestion that a technical advisor should be required, as a matter of course, to write a report. The essence of the engagement, requires that the judge and the advisor be able to communicate informally, in a frank and open fashion. Given the freewheeling nature of the anticipated discourse, and the fact that the advisor is not permitted to bring new evidence into the case, requiring a written report in every case would serve no useful purpose.

(D.C. Cir. 1991); United States v. Conservation Chem. Co, 106 F.R.D. 210 (W.D. Mo.), *rev'd sub nom.* In re Armco, Inc., 770 F.2d 103 (8th Cir. 1985); *but see* Stauble v. Warrob, Inc., 977 F.2d 690 (1st Cir. 1992) (analyzing Article III constraints inherent in Rule 53).

The question about the source of *La Buy*'s holding is more than an academic one. In considering pretrial references to masters in Chapter Seven, we encountered a respectable body of thought that courts retain an inherent power to appoint masters even when the reference does not comply with the terms of Rule 53. *See supra* p. 762, Note 1(b); Ex Parte Peterson, 253 U.S. 300 (1920) (federal courts have inherent power to appoint adjuncts that aid in the performance of judicial duties). If *La Buy* is grounded in an interpretation of Rule 53, then a judge arguably possesses inherent power to appoint a master for a non-jury trial even when that reference is inconsistent with *La Buy* or Rule 53. On the other hand, if *La Buy* is grounded in the Constitution, no such residual power exists.

4.   In addition to the issue of abdicating the factfinding role, all the pragmatic concerns about using masters that we examined in Chapter Seven — such as cost, delay, partiality, abuse of power, and the loss of trans-substantivity — play into the decision about whether to authorize a reference for trial. *See supra* p. 763, Note 1(d). When all these concerns are added together with Rule 53(a)(1)(B)(i)'s "exceptional condition" requirement, a reference to a master for factfinding at trial is, to use *Reilly*'s phrase, "hen's-teeth rare." In non-jury cases, masters are sometimes appointed to handle intricate matters of account or damages, or to help implement a court's remedies. *See* Fed. R. Civ. P. 53(a)(1)(B)(ii), -(C); 9C CHARLES ALAN WRIGHT & ARTHUR R. MILLER, FEDERAL PRACTICE AND PROCEDURE § 2605 (3d ed. 2008); *infra* pp. 1193-1204 (discussing the use of masters at the remedial stage). Trial references on liability issues almost never occur, and when they do, appellate courts have little trouble issuing writs of mandamus to prevent the reference. *See Bituminous Coal*, 949 F.2d 1165; *Armco*, 770 F.2d 103; *Stauble*, 977 F.2d 690; *In re United States*, 816 F.2d 1083 (6th Cir. 1987). All these cases involved references for, *inter alia*, a trial on liability issues; all agreed, in the words of *Bituminous Coal*, that "it is the function of the district judge, in a non-jury civil case, to decide dispositive issues of fact and law genuinely disputed by the parties. The judge may not impose on the parties . . . [a] master as a 'surrogate judge' to try the controversy and determine liability." 949 F.2d at 1169. *See also* United States v. Microsoft Corp., 147 F.3d 935, 955 (D.C. Cir. 1998) (issuing a writ of mandamus against a blanket reference to a master to handle pretrial, trial, and remedial issues; noting that "it is very doubtful that complexity tends to legitimate references to a master at all"); Liptak v. United States, 748 F.2d 1254, 1257 (8th Cir. 1984) (noting that, other than complicated pretrial matters, accountings, and damage calculations, "it is difficult to conceive of a reference of a nonjury case that will meet the rigid standards of the *La Buy* decision"); Irving R. Kaufman, *Masters in Federal Courts: Rule 53*, 58 COLUM. L. REV. 452, 459 (1958) ("With a few minor exceptions, references in non-jury cases run counter to the spirit and purpose of judicial administration in the federal courts.").

Among the few reported post-*La Buy* cases in which non-jury trial references were allowed are *United States v. Suquamish Indian Tribe*, 901 F.2d 772 (9th Cir. 1990) (arguably a reference for remedial matters); *Loral Corp. v. McDonnell Douglas Corp.*, 558 F.2d 1130 (2d Cir 1977); *Rogers v. Societe Internationale, S.A.*, 278 F.2d 268 (D.C. Cir. 1960); and *Olsen Assocs. v. United States*, 853 F. Supp. 396 (M.D. Fla. 1993). *Cf.* Datapoint Corp. v. Standard Microsystems Corp., 31 F.App'x 685 (Fed. Cir. 2002) (mentioning the trial court's use of a master to construe a patent claim at a *Markman* hearing, but not analyzing the legality of the reference).

5.   One of the reasons that *La Buy* rejected the reference to the master was that a knowledgeable judge was being replaced by a master who knew little of the case. Doesn't this reason suggest that the more active the judge is during pretrial, the less likely it is that the judge will be able to turn to judicial adjuncts at trial? Is this an argument against case management in cases likely to be complex at trial?

6.   A trial reference to a master becomes unnecessary if other devices can aid the judge's factfinding process. In the next chapter we examine a number of such aids that judges can employ while still retaining the entire onus of factfinding. Here we focus on two aids that substitute, to some extent, another factfinder for the judge. One is the advisory jury, permitted under Fed. R. Civ. P. 39(c). Advisory juries are just that — advisory; the judge is still the factfinder, giving no deference to the jury's advice. *See* 9 CHARLES A. WRIGHT & ARTHUR R. MILLER., FEDERAL PRACTICE AND PROCEDURE § 2335 (3d ed. 2008). If a judge could appoint a "blue ribbon" advisory jury composed of knowledgeable persons, then the advisory jury could be of great use. Rule 39(c) says nothing about the composition of advisory juries. Nor is it clear that the Jury Selection and Service Act applies to them. *See* 28 U.S.C. §§ 1861, 1862 (the Act applies to "grand and petit" juries). To our knowledge, no cases have addressed the point. *Cf.* MANUAL FOR COMPLEX LITIGATION, FOURTH § 11.54 (2004) (suggesting "use of an advisory jury of experts in a nonjury case," but failing to analyze the issue under the Jury Selection and Service Act and urging "[c]aution . . . in experimenting with such procedures"). *See generally* James A. Martin, *The Proposed "Science Court,"* 75 MICH. L. REV. 1058 (1977) (discussing pros and cons of advisory or binding scientific panels).

Second, as *Reilly* shows, a judge can appoint a technical advisor who can provide the judge with the insight needed to understand and deliberate on the evidence. Appointing a technical advisor is akin to appointing a court-appointed expert witness, which is a technique to increase factfinder comprehension that the following chapter explores (*see infra* p. 1111). Unlike an expert, however, the advisor can have ex parte communications with a judge, and is not a witness subject to the parties' examination and cross-examination. In this regard, a technical advisor lies somewhere between an expert witness who supplies helpful facts and a special master who actually finds the facts.

7.   As *Reilly* says, the fountainhead of authority for the use of technical advisors is *Ex Parte Peterson*, 253 U.S. 300 (1920). Justice Brandeis' dicta

in the case is broad, stating that "[c]ourts have (at least in the absence of legislation to the contrary) inherent power to provide themselves with appropriate instruments required for the performance of their duties." *Id.* at 312. *Peterson* involved an appointment of an auditor in a common-law case — a novel idea but hardly remarkable in light of the long history of using auditors in equity. Moreover, the auditor was supposed to narrow the disputed issues for trial, examine evidence and conduct a hearing on remaining disputed matters, and write a report with tentative findings of fact that were submitted to a jury. These tasks are rather different than the tasks assigned to the technical advisor in *Reilly*.

8. Assuming that the power to appoint an advisor exists, was *Reilly* sufficiently extraordinary to invoke the power? Making predictions about inflation, discount rates, worklife expectancy, and life expectancy are not simple tasks, but, as the Supreme Court has noted, the tasks need not become a "graduate seminar on economic forecasting." Jones & Laughlin Steel Corp. v. Pfeifer, 462 U.S. 523, 548 (1983). Judges and juries undertake this task in tort cases every day. If *Reilly*'s circumstance was sufficiently compelling, is there any complex case in which a technical advisor could not be appointed? An additional factor mentioned in *Reilly* was the failure of the United States to meet its adversarial obligation to provide proofs and arguments of its position. Should *Reilly* therefore be limited to cases in which the judge needs to "even up" the sides to preserve rational judgment?

9. The first complex case in which an advisor of the *Reilly* type appears to have been used was *United States v. United Shoe Machinery Corp.*, 110 F. Supp. 295 (D. Mass. 1953), *aff'd per curiam*, 347 U.S. 521 (1954), an antitrust case in which Judge Wyzanski employed an economist. Judge Wyzanski and the economist were later reported to have regretted the appointment, believing that the economist should have (1) been appointed as an expert witness or as a special master, (2) written a report, and (3) been subject to cross-examination. *See* Samuel R. Gross, *Expert Evidence*, 1991 WIS. L. REV. 1113, 1188 n.230. Nonetheless, the concept of a technical advisor took hold, was endorsed in the *Handbook of Recommended Procedures for the Trial of Protracted Cases, reprinted in* 25 F.R.D. 351, 420-21 (1960), and continues to receive a qualified recommendation in the present *Manual for Complex Litigation. See* MANUAL, *supra*, § 11.54 (stating that "consultation with a confidential adviser to the court may be considered," but, as with advisory juries, urging caution " in experimenting with such procedures" to avoid "displac[ing] the parties' right to a resolution of disputes through the adversary process").

10. In a noted decision that we examined in Chapter Eight, Judge Jones appointed a panel of expert advisors to assist him in conducting an evidentiary hearing concerning the admissibility of controversial expert testimony by plaintiffs. After the hearing and consultations with the expert advisors, Jones tentatively excluded nearly all of the plaintiffs' expert testimony regarding certain disease processes. *See* Hall v. Baxter Healthcare Corp., 947 F. Supp. 1387, 1392 n.8 (D. Or. 1996) (invoking Fed.

R. Evid. 104 to appoint advisors) (*supra* p. 844); *cf.* Note, *Improving Judicial Gatekeeping: Technical Advisors and Scientific Evidence* 110 HARV. L. REV. 941 (1997) (arguing for a greater use of technical advisors to assist judges in determining the admissibility of expert testimony). Is *Baxter* a useful precedent for the more general use of technical advisors?

11. Courts rarely appoint technical advisors. *See* Renaud v. Martin Marietta Corp., 972 F.2d 304, 308 n.8 (10th Cir. 1992) (toxic exposure); Burton v. Sheheen, 793 F. Supp. 1329, 1339 (D.S.C. 1992) (redistricting); Hemstreet v. Burroughs Corp., 666 F. Supp. 1096 (N.D. Ill. 1987) (patent); *cf.* Concilio de Salud Integral de Loiza, Inc. v. Perez-Perdomo, 551 F.3d 10 (1st Cir. 2008) (suggesting that the court might want to appoint a technical advisor in a complex Medicaid action); In re E. & S. Dists. Asbestos Litig., 151 F.R.D. 540 (E. & S.D.N.Y. 1993) (recognizing the inherent power to appoint an advisor, but choosing to treat a consultant as a court-appointed expert witness). Discussions of the proper scope of the advisor's authority are even rarer.

12. One of the reason that masters or technical advisors are thought necessary is that trial judges are usually generalists, without specialized technical expertise. Should the Senate confirm a certain number of federal judges who possess expertise in specialized fields? *See* Edward V. Di Lello, Note, *Fighting Fire with Firefighters: A Proposal for Expert Judges at the Trial Level*, 93 COLUM. L. REV. 473 (1993). Alternatively, should Congress or state legislatures create specialized courts with a limited subject matter in which judges could become expert? A number of expert courts exist in our country, including the Delaware Chancery Court, which handles a high volume of corporate litigation; the Tax Court; the Bankruptcy Court; and the Federal Circuit, which has exclusive appellate jurisdiction over patents and government contracts. *See* Symposium, *The Sixth Abraham L. Pomerantz Lecture*, 61 BROOK. L. REV. 1 (1995) (favorably evaluating specialized courts in terms of accuracy, efficiency, and due process).

C. SELECTING THE LAWGIVER

In the modern American adversarial model, the judge is responsible for declaring the legal principles. Given that judges, by virtue of their legal training, are expert in such matters, should a judge have the power to delegate the lawgiving task in the face of legal complexity?

REED V. CLEVELAND BOARD OF EDUCATION

607 F.2d 737 (6th Cir. 1979)

■ LIVELY, Circuit Judge.

This appeal is from an order of the district court making an interim allowance of fees to the special master and several experts appointed by the court in a school desegregation case. [A class action was filed, seeking a permanent injunction enjoining racial and economic segregation in the public schools of Cleveland, Ohio. After conducting a bench trial on the issue of liability, the district court found the defendants' operation of the school system violated the Constitution. Subsequently the district court appointed a special master, Daniel R. McCarthy, to assist with remedial issues. The court also appointed two "experts" to aid the master in his appraisal of various desegregation plans. One of the experts, Dr. Gordon Foster, was an expert in the field of school administration. The other expert, Edward A. Mearns, Jr., was a professor of constitutional law.

[Subsequently, the court ordered the defendants to pay the interim fees, which exceeded $500,000, of the masters and experts. Prof. Mearns' share of the fees was $66,330, representing 1105.5 hours of work. The defendants objected to the payment of the fees, and an appeal ensued.

[The court began by upholding the power of the district court to appoint expert advisors pursuant to either Rule 53 or its inherent powers. It then approved the fees for Dr. Foster.]

The appointment of Professor Mearns presents the court with a more complex problem. In explaining the selection of Mr. McCarthy as special master the district court pointed out that he was experienced in accounting, business and finance, skills which the court itself did not possess. This same reasoning would support the appointment of Dr. Foster, whose expertise in educational matters was not shared by the special master or the court. On the other hand, Professor Mearns is primarily a teacher of constitutional law, an area with which the experienced trial judge in this case has been involved throughout his career. The use of masters is permitted because they improve the judicial process by bringing to the court skills and experience which courts frequently lack. However, courts are presumed to be informed on legal issues, and the determination of purely legal questions is the responsibility of the court itself. The court is not without assistance in performing this duty. The attorneys in a given case are required to inform the court of their views of the controlling law. Each district judge is provided at public expense with a staff which includes qualified law clerks. In addition, the United States was designated as *amicus curiae* in the present case and participated actively in the remedy phase, appearing through attorneys in its Civil Rights Division.

It is difficult to determine from the record exactly what duties Professor Mearns actually performed. . . . The record discloses that Professor Mearns met with the court and the judge's law clerks on a number of occasions and that he wrote memoranda and drafted orders for the court. Our conclusion is that Professor Mearns functioned frequently as an advisor to the court on constitutional law issues. These activities and communications did not occur in open court and the parties had no opportunity to question Professor Mearns as a witness.

The use of masters in non-jury cases has been criticized on three main grounds: it causes delay in the proceedings, it adds to the expense of litigation and it often leads to an abdication of the judicial function. . . . The appointment of the master in this case does not appear to have caused delay. However, the appointment of two experts to advise the master has added significantly to the expense of this litigation. In view of Mr. McCarthy's lack of experience in educational matters, he clearly required the assistance of someone with Dr. Foster's qualifications. However, the same justifications did not exist for the appointment of Professor Mearns, and we do not approve the practice of appointing legal advisors to a master or the court. To the extent that the master was not qualified to make recommendations to the court because of a lack of experience in constitutional law, he should have submitted such legal issues to the court. The court could rely on his own experience and learning and the assistance of his staff and all counsel in the case. The District Judge clearly had no intention to abdicate his judicial responsibility in this case. Nevertheless, to the extent that he relied on advice received in chambers from a "legal expert" there was a partial abdication of his role. Whatever may have been the practice of Lord Mansfield the adversary system as it has developed in this country precludes the court from receiving out-of-court advice on legal issues in a case. He must depend on his own resources, which include the work of his staff and the offerings of counsel.

This court realizes that a case of the magnitude of the present one puts a severe strain on the resources of a district court. . . . In the absence of an express agreement by all the parties, however, a court may not avail itself of legal advice from one who is neither counsel in the case nor subject to the oath and discipline imposed on members of his staff. . . .

It is our conclusion that 322.5 hours [of Prof. Mearns's time] were spent on activities which . . . involved research for the court, meetings with the court and his staff and drafting orders and memoranda. These are not services for which defendant should be required to pay. . . . Thus, we conclude that Professor Mearns is entitled to be paid for 738 hours.[6]

Notes

1. *Reed* involved the appointment of a legal advisor for a remedial matter. As we shall see in more detail in Chapter Twelve, the rules for the appointment of judicial adjuncts in the remedial stages are often more lenient. Hence, it is fair to assume that the court of appeals in *Reed* would have been even more concerned with the use of a legal advisor to assist the court in its lawgiving tasks on trial issues.

2. Can you envision any circumstance in which the law is so complex that a court is incapable of rationally determining the applicable law? *Cf.* Fed. R. Civ. P. 44.1 (allowing judge to receive evidence and testimony regarding the law of foreign country). If you cannot, then you should expect to find that the trial judge has no power to shift the task of law determination to another person.

---

6. Since there was no objection to the appointment of Professor Mearns, all his work related to assisting the special master will be compensated. . . .

In fact, that expectation is largely fulfilled. Cases on the point are sparse, perhaps because the lawgiving function of the judge is taken for granted. *See* Crowell v. Benson, 285 U.S. 22 (1932) (Article III requires that responsibility for lawgiving be retained by Article III officials). The notion of using a legal advisor has fared badly in the few cases that have raised the idea. *See* Reilly v. United States, 863 F.2d 149, 157 (1st Cir. 1988) (stating in dicta that "judge may not, for example, appoint a legal advisor to brief him on legal issues") (*supra* p. 1019); Young v. Pierce, 640 F. Supp. 1476, 1485 n.9 (E.D. Tex. 1986) (appointing an advisor but giving advisor no authority to advise on "what is a constitutionally permissible remedy, since that is a legal issue best handled by the court").

The same reluctance to delegate the lawgiving task at trial exists for adjuncts other than legal advisors. Although magistrate judges render conclusions of law in cases referred to them, *see* 28 U.S.C. § 636(b)(1), the parties must consent to a trial reference, *see id.* § 636(c)(1). References to special masters for trial are very rare; even when a reference is permissible, the master's conclusions of law are entitled to no deference. *See* Fed. R. Civ. P. 53(4)(4). *Cf.* Amgen Inc. v. Hoechst Marion Roussel, Inc., 457 F.3d 1293, 1318 (Fed. Cir. 2006) (noting in passing, without negative comment, a trial court's appointment of a special master "to aid in researching the law, analyzing the issues, and drafting" a patent opinion).

3. In one trademark case, a judge sought to delegate the lawgiving (and factfinding) task to a special master with the following blunt assessment of his capabilities:

> I don't understand anything about the merits of any patent or trademark case. I'm not about to educate myself in that jungle. . . . I would have no confidence in my ability to do any justice in that thicket of patent and trademark, which I never understood when I was trying to practice law, and I wouldn't begin to understand it now.

The parties consented to the reference, one of them reluctantly so. On appeal, that party then sought to challenge the reference. The Second Circuit held that the party had waived its right to contest the reference because of its consent, but left no doubt about its views:

> We must express our firm disagreement with the district judge's concept of his duties. Having by his oath of office accepted the task of adjudicating all issues falling within the court's federal jurisdiction, he is obligated, whenever faced with unfamiliar factual or legal issues (including those involving trademark and copyright matters), to educate himself in those fields with the aid of counsel, colleagues on the bench, law clerks, and published texts and decisions. This has been the path traditionally followed by respected members of the federal judiciary.

Madrigal Audio Labs., Inc. v. Cello, Ltd., 799 F.2d 814, 818 & n.1 (2d Cir. 1986); *id.* at 821 n.2 ("[T]he fact that 'the case involves complex issues of law or fact is no justification for reference to a Master, but rather a [com]pelling reason for trial before an experienced judge.'").

CHAPTER TEN

TRYING A COMPLEX CASE

Once the trial counsel, the factfinder, and the lawgiver have been set into place, the trial can begin. But exactly what form should the trial take? In a routine case that is jury-triable, the jury is selected, the lawyers for the parties make an opening statement, the lawyer for the plaintiff presents all the plaintiff's evidence at once (interrupted only by cross-examination by the defendant's lawyer), the lawyer for the defendant does the same (subject to cross-examination by the plaintiff's lawyer), each lawyer makes a closing argument, and the judge instructs the jury. The jury retires to deliberate, and returns with a verdict on which judgment is entered.

In this trial the presentation of evidence and arguments is adversarial, in the sense that the parties (and their lawyers) determine what witnesses to call, what questions to ask, what documents to introduce, and what arguments to make. The jury and the judge sit stone-faced, absorbing the proofs and arguments. This trial is a single, culminating event; the jury decides all issues at one time. Judge-tried cases usually proceed in a similar way; without the constraint of a jury, however, judges sometimes feel more free to cut a trial into discrete segments, to depart from the rules of evidence concerning admissibility, and to ask questions of the witnesses.

We saw in the last chapter that the traditional trial — lay factfinder, single trial on all issues, adversarial presentation — created difficulties for a factfinder trying to comprehend the issues in a complex case. This chapter explores techniques to help the factfinder overcome the problems of comprehending factual and, in the case of juries, legal issues. The success of one or more of these techniques bears significantly on a number of issues in this book. Most immediately, the availability of comprehension-enhancing techniques affects whether we can expect juries or judges to resolve complex cases with an acceptable level of accuracy. If these techniques fail, a series of consequences tumble out: whether judges have the power to strike juries as factfinders; whether judges should instead dismiss these cases as not being adjudicable within our constitutional structure; and whether (in lieu of either of these options) judges should tolerate a concededly inadequate verdict to be rendered. None of these options is desirable, and their undesirability might lead judges to refuse to aggregate related cases that create trial complexity, despite the advantages that aggregation generates in terms of efficiency or fair treatment (and despite the fact that the cases are unlikely to be tried). Therefore, however rare trials in fact are, the availability of comprehension-enhancing trial techniques in many ways determines the fate of complex litigation.

Comprehension-enhancing techniques divide into two types. The first type limits the amount of information that the factfinder considers at one sitting. The other increases the factfinder's ability to comprehend whatever information is presented. To some extent these approaches are substitutes; to some extent they can work together. For conceptual purposes, this chapter treats each approach separately.

Most of the techniques that this chapter examines — regardless of whether they limit information or increase comprehension — invest more discretion in the trial judge. As a result, the judge has more ability to affect the outcome than a pure adversarial model would tolerate. At the same time, the techniques help to preserve the right to jury trial and seek to enhance reasoned decision-making in complex cases. You should ask whether these techniques are necessary (as opposed to being merely novel and chic), and, if they are, whether trial is the most sensible way to resolve the dispute. This is the great question of this chapter: Are the costs of preserving jury trial and reasoned judgment too high?

A. TECHNIQUES TO LIMIT INFORMATION AT TRIAL

Limiting the amount of information that the factfinder gets as a means of increasing comprehension contains certain risks. If a judge simply limits information (perhaps by allowing no witness to testify for more than ten minutes), the risk is that the factfinder will not understand the nuances of a problem and will therefore render a poor decision. The trick is to find ways to limit the factfinder's exposure to information without unduly distorting the nature of the dispute. The following subsections examine a number of techniques, beginning with the most common — splitting the case into discrete issues or claims that are decided seriatim — before moving to less common approaches that have been tried in some complex cases. Pay attention to the way in which limiting information might affect the decision that the factfinder renders.

1. Limiting Issues and Claims

The most obvious way to limit the factfinder's information is to limit the number of factual disputes that need to be resolved at one time. Thus, we could divide the case into segments, handling issues, claims, or parties seriatim. One advantage of this approach is that, if the judge chooses the early issues well, and if the decision on those issues comes out a certain way, later trials on the remaining issues might become unnecessary.

We already encountered this idea of dividing a case into segments when we studied pretrial bifurcation, in which a judge orders discovery into certain issues before permitting discovery into other issues. *See supra* p. 814. No necessary correlation exists between the division of issues during pretrial and the division of issues at trial. Issues could be discovered in stages, but tried together; conversely, issues could be discovered together, but tried separately. Moreover, during pretrial the judge is concerned with the problems faced by lawyers in accumulating and organizing evidence. Those concerns are still relevant to the decision whether to break up the at trial, but now two new concerns can arise: first, the concern that any division of issues be done in a way that enhances the factfinder's ability to comprehend the evidence; and second, when the factfinder is a jury, the concern that too fine a parsing of issues into mini-trials might contravene the nature of jury trial and hence run afoul of the Seventh Amendment.

IN RE BENDECTIN LITIGATION

857 F.2d 290 (6th Cir. 1988)

■ ENGEL, Chief Judge.

These actions were brought on behalf of children with birth defects against Merrell Dow Pharmaceuticals, Inc., alleging that their birth defects were caused by their mothers' ingestion during pregnancy of defendant's anti-nausea drug Bendectin. Immediately involved are eleven hundred eighty claims in approximately eight hundred forty-four multidistrict cases. These cases represent only a part of the Bendectin cases which have been brought in numerous federal and state courts around the nation. Although there are some differences among the complaints, most are virtually identical, requesting relief on the grounds of negligence, breach of warranty, strict liability, fraud, and gross negligence, and asserting a rebuttable presumption of negligence per se for defendant's alleged violation of the misbranding provisions of the federal Food, Drug and Cosmetic Act (FDCA), 21 U.S.C. § 301 et seq.

After twenty-two days of trial on the sole question of causation, the jury answered the following interrogatory in the negative: "Have the plaintiffs established by a preponderance of the evidence that ingestion of Bendectin at therapeutic doses during the period of fetal organogenesis is a proximate cause of human birth defects?" . . . Accordingly, the district judge entered judgment for defendant. . . .

I. BACKGROUND OF THE CASE

The unusually large number of individual cases involved here found their way to the United States District Court for the Southern District of Ohio in a variety of ways [including direct filings, removal, and multidistrict transfers. In all, nearly 2,300 cases were aggregated.]

. . . After the completion of discovery, on November 16, 1983, the district court consolidated under Rule 42(a) of the Federal Rules of Civil Procedure all Bendectin cases [originating in Ohio,] and set those cases for trial beginning June 4, 1984 on all common issues of liability. The original decision was to bifurcate the trial, and if the plaintiffs were successful in obtaining a verdict finding liability, the court would schedule individual damages trials. While consolidation for trial was mandated for all cases pending in federal court in Ohio, the trial judge also permitted consolidation upon the liability issues for any case which had been transferred to the Southern District of Ohio under MDL 486. 28 U.S.C. § 1404. Those cases would be returned to the originating district if the verdict in the first portion of the bifurcated trial was for the plaintiffs. The district judge indicated that under *Erie Railroad Co. v. Tompkins*, 304 U.S. 64 (1938), all claims which had been originally brought or removed to federal court in Ohio would necessarily be governed by Ohio law, and that plaintiffs who had originally filed in other districts and who voluntarily chose to participate in the common issues trial would consent to application of the law of Ohio by so agreeing to participate. A number of plaintiffs chose to leave the consolidated proceedings after the completion of discovery and this order, and the district court accordingly returned those suits to the district in which they had been originally filed. [In total, 557 Ohio cases and 261 cases from the MDL proceeding went forward to trial.]

Because the parties could not agree which issues should be tried during the first phase of trial, the court itself decided that the common issues to be tried . . . would be whether: (1) taken as prescribed, Bendectin caused any of a list of birth defects; (2) Bendectin was unreasonably dangerous as defined by Ohio courts; and (3) Merrell Dow provided to the medical profession adequate warnings of the danger of the product. On April 12, 1984, the district court amended this order. Rather than bifurcating the trial on issues of liability and damages, the court instead decided to trifurcate the case, or bifurcate the liability question into liability and causation. Initially, a jury determination would be made on the causation question. If plaintiffs prevailed on the causation question, the jury would then consider the other liability questions. Conversely, if defendant received a favorable verdict on the causation issue, the trial would cease. . . .

The trifurcated trial commenced in February, 1985. . . . Following trial, judgment was entered for defendant upon the jury's negative answer to the question whether plaintiffs had proven that ingestion of Bendectin proximately causes birth defects. . . .

IV. TRIFURCATION

The plaintiffs challenge the district judge's decision to trifurcate this case by trying only the issue of proximate causation. They maintain that trifurcation violates their due process rights and Seventh Amendment right to trial by jury, and thus renders the decision an abuse of discretion. . . .

Plaintiffs raise many different arguments to support their claim that the district court judge abused his discretion in ordering trifurcation. First, they maintain that under the law of proximate causation as applied in this case, causation is not an issue capable of separation from issues of defendant's fraud, wrongful conduct, or negligence. Second, they object to the ruling because: the court's trifurcation decision came as a surprise and only *after* discovery had been completed; a different jury would have heard later stages of trial; proximate cause was a particularly difficult and improper issue to be independently decided by a lay jury; and trifurcation resulted in a sterile trial removed from plaintiffs' actual injuries. Third and finally, plaintiffs assert that the trifurcation ruling resulted in the exclusion of evidence that was vital to the determination of the single, causation issue.

Of all the issues on appeal, the validity of the trifurcation ruling has been most troubling to us. We reiterate that the standard of review is abuse of discretion. . . . "The decision whether to try issues separately is within the sound discretion of the court. . . . Abuse of discretion exists only where there is 'definite and firm conviction that the court below committed a clear error of judgment in the conclusion it reached upon a weighing of the relevant factors.'"

The standards for separating issues is set forth in the language of Fed. R. Civ. P. 42(b) . . . . "The Advisory Committee Note to the 1966 amendment, though cryptic, suggests that . . . the changes in Rule 42 were intended to give rather delphic encouragement to trial of liability issues separately from those of damages, while warning against routine bifurcation of the ordinary negligence case." It cannot seriously be argued that this is a routine case.

The principal purpose of the rule is to enable the trial judge to dispose of a case in a way that both advances judicial efficiency and is fair to the parties. . . . Neither Rule 42(b) nor the textual elaboration cited gives any precise guidelines for the trial judge in considering the propriety of ordering separate trials, probably because of the wide variety of circumstances in which it might come into play. Consequently, courts have adopted a case-by-case approach. . . . Courts, including our own, have measured trial court decisions to try issues separately by whether fairness was advanced in the particular case . . . .

In our case this same test applies to whether the decision is to try only one or more than one issue separately. Our opinion in *In re Beverly Hills [Fire] Litigation*, 695 F.2d 207 (6th Cir. 1982), approving trifurcation on the causation question, did not indicate any different standard of review than that applicable to bifurcation nor has our research led us to authority suggesting such a distinction. While few cases appear to have been trifurcated on the issue of causation, there are nonetheless numerous cases that have tried an individual issue separately under circumstances that, had the issue been decided in favor of the plaintiff, the trial would have had more than two phases to it. . . . It follows, therefore, that a decision to try an issue separately will be affirmed unless the potential for prejudice to the parties is such as to clearly demonstrate an abuse of discretion. *Beverly Hills*, 695 F.2d at 216.

Of course, the subject for review is not the abstract question of trifurcation generally, but the appropriateness of trifurcation in the context of the litigation at hand. It is to the specific facts of this case that we must apply the 42(b) standards for separating issues.

A. *Proximate Causation as a Separable Issue*

Fundamental to plaintiffs' challenge of the trifurcation decision is their argument that the causation question in this case was not an issue which could be tried separately. In support of their claim, plaintiffs rely heavily on *Gasoline Products Co. v. Champlin Refining Co.*, 283 U.S. 494, 500 (1931). There, the Court held that "where the practice permits a partial new trial, it may not properly be resorted to unless it clearly appears that the issue to be retried is so distinct and separable from the others that a trial of it alone may be had without injustice." The Court noted that the issue in that case could not be submitted independently of the others without creating jury confusion and uncertainty that would "amount to a denial of a fair trial." Many courts consider the issue's ability to be tried separately, and without injustice, to be the standard for determining whether the Seventh Amendment has been violated by conducting a trial only on that one issue. Thus, they apply the *Gasoline Products* standard to initial determinations whether a district judge properly ordered a separate trial in the first instance. . . . We affirm the appropriateness of the *Gasoline Products* standard to the context of Rule 42(b).

Under this standard, many courts have upheld cases bifurcated between liability and damages because the evidence pertinent to the two issues is wholly unrelated, and as a logical matter, liability must be resolved before the question of damages. By the same token, courts have refused to permit even bifurcation of liability and damages where these issues could not be tried separately. . . .

In the present case, plaintiffs argue that the *Gasoline Products* standard is violated because under the current standards and presumptions set forth in Ohio law, the issue of causation cannot be separated from the issue of defendant's tortious conduct. In their assertion of the nonseparability of these two issues, plaintiffs cite various tort theories that shift the burden of proof to defendants before causation has been proven more probable than not or weaken plaintiffs' burden of proof with regard to causation.

First, plaintiffs contend that in cases involving multiple possible causes, the courts must abandon any "but for" causation test in favor of the "substantial factor" test to be applied where plaintiff seeks to prove that the defendant's wrongful act is only one of several substantial factors bringing about the injury. Thus, it is argued, because the determination of wrongdoing affects which standard plaintiffs need prove, liability must be tried either before or contemporaneously with the determination of causation. Moreover, plaintiffs argue that the court should have charged the jury that the plaintiff need only show that Bendectin is a substantial contributing factor in causing birth defects and the burden of proof would then shift to the defendant to prove that Bendectin was not such a substantial factor. . . .

[After surveying Ohio law, the court concluded] that even if the cited Ohio cases were applied to the present case, plaintiffs would still have to prove "but for" causation rather than some weaker "substantial factor" standard. . . .

B. *Trifurcation as a Potential Source of Unfair Prejudice*

. . .

The plaintiffs also challenge the trifurcation order because even had they won this stage of the trial, the court gave no assurance that the same jury that heard the evidence on causation, and rendered them a favorable verdict, would decide the question of liability. Plaintiffs' attorney Chesley specifically repeated this assertion at oral argument. The facts are otherwise. In Mr. Chesley's presence, the district judge indicated "that if the plaintiffs prevailed . . . the same jury [would] be used for the next phase of the trial." Judge Rubin did, however, offer to impanel a new jury if both sides so requested. No objection was raised to either comment, and, in fact Mr. Chesley explicitly indicated that it would "not [be] impossible to seat a new jury." Even had such a procedure been contemplated, and we emphasize that it was not, the party challenging such a procedure was willing to accept it below. . . . [T]here is no constitutional prohibition against trying these issues before different juries. . . .

Plaintiff[s] next challenge the decision to trifurcate on the proximate causation question because the issue trifurcated was the one which a lay jury would be least qualified to understand, evaluate, and decide. The district judge offered to try the case before a blue ribbon jury, but the plaintiffs rejected the idea. This was, of course, their right. In any event we conclude that if the issues were indeed difficult, their resolution was not rendered more difficult due to trifurcation. If anything, the narrowing of the range of inquiry through trifurcation substantially improved the manageability of the presentation of proofs by both sides and enhanced the jury's ability to comprehend the causation issue.

Plaintiffs' primary argument against trifurcation as unfairly prejudicial is that trying the question alone prejudiced plaintiffs by creating a sterile trial atmosphere. In *Beverly Hills*, we addressed similar concerns that trifurcation could possibly prevent the plaintiffs from exercising their right to present to the jury the full atmosphere of their cause of action, including the reality of injury:

> A strong argument can, it is true, be made against the bifurcation of a trial limited to the issue of causation. There is a danger that bifurcation may deprive plaintiffs of their legitimate right to place

before the jury the circumstances and atmosphere of the entire cause of action which they have brought into the court, replacing it with a sterile or laboratory atmosphere in which causation is parted from the reality of injury. In a litigation of lesser complexity, such considerations might well have prompted the trial judge to reject such a procedure. Here, however, it is only necessary for us to observe that the occurrence of the fire itself, a major disaster in Kentucky history by all standards, was generally known to the jurors from the outset. Further, the proofs themselves, although limited, were nonetheless fully adequate to apprise the jury of the general circumstances of the tragedy and the environment in which the fire arose. As a result, we hold that the trial judge did not abuse his discretion in severing the issue of causation here.

Judge Rubin considered this language when he denied the plaintiffs' motion for a new trial. On appeal plaintiffs also rely heavily on the same language. Sterility is not necessarily the inevitable consequence in a trifurcated trial merely because the jury may not hear the full evidence of defendant's alleged wrongdoing. It more properly refers to the potential danger that the jury may decide the causation question without appreciating the scope of the injury that defendant supposedly caused and without the realization that their duties involve the resolution of an important, lively and human controversy. It is with respect to this latter concern that the plaintiffs urge that they were unfairly prejudiced by the trifurcation. The record reveals that the district judge consciously worked to avoid the potential for unfair prejudice. For example, he instructed the jury:

> Let me suggest to you that what you are about to do may be one of the most important things you will ever do in your entire entire [sic] life. This is a significant case. It involves a lot of people. It involves not only the plaintiffs who are individuals, it involves people, scientists, people who have done experiments, people who are employees of the defendant company. The totality of this case involves people and while you will hear technical evidence, I do point out to you that at all times, you should keep in mind that on both sides, there are people involved.

The court was not alone in efforts to avoid the dangers of sterility. In his final argument, plaintiffs' attorney Eaton told the jury that the trial was not an academic exercise, and that the case involved many real people who sought justice, and who would, as children, be affected by the jury's verdict well into the next century.

Finally, plaintiffs argue that Judge Rubin failed to consider the caveats of Rule 42(b) in his trifurcation decision, and instead justified trifurcation only upon unsubstantiated claims of judicial efficiency, thus unduly prejudicing plaintiffs' case without good reason. We believe, however, that the district judge carefully made the necessary inquiry. In his final order the trial judge noted that Bendectin litigation could "substantially immobiliz[e] the entire Federal Judiciary. There have been only four cases involving Bendectin which have been individually tried. They required an average of 38 trial days." Judge Rubin calculated that if all 1100 cases were tried at that average length on an individual basis, they would be able to keep 182 judges occupied for one year. Contrary to the plaintiffs' claims that Judge Rubin never considered the language of Rule 42(b), he did correctly require plaintiffs to prove that the defendant's drug caused their injury, and would not allow plaintiffs to buttress a weak causation case with a strong negligence case. Thus, in line with the language of Rule 42(b), the trial judge considered the causation question to be a separate issue.

In reviewing the district court's decision to trifurcate we further note Rule 42 which "giv[es] the court virtually unlimited freedom to try the issues in whatever way trial convenience requires." Thus, a court may try an issue separately if "in the exercise of reasonable discretion [it] thinks that course would save trial time or effort or make the trial of other issues unnecessary." In this case, the district judge considered the time savings in trying this case in this fashion, and surmised that if the plaintiffs won on this issue, another eight weeks of trial would be necessary to resolve the other questions.

Many courts have in fact permitted separate issue trials when the issue first tried would be dispositive of the litigation. . . . Plainly, Judge Rubin had a massive case management problem to resolve, and chose to do so by trying the case on a separate issue that would be dispositive.

C. *Claims of Prejudice Resulting from Exclusion of Evidence Bearing on Causation*

While we have held that proximate causation is a separate legal question, that trifurcation did not unfairly prejudice more general aspects of plaintiffs' case, and that trifurcation furthered economy in this case, we must still consider whether trifurcation unduly prejudiced plaintiffs by restricting the evidence they could bring forth in proving the proximate causation issue. . . .

Probably the plaintiffs' most serious charge is that the trifurcation format prevented them from challenging the validity of various studies that the defendant relied on in support of its position that Bendectin did not cause birth defects. For example, at oral argument plaintiffs' counsel represented that while plaintiffs could attack part of [one] study defendant had used to justify the safety of Bendectin, most of the study could not be criticized because of limitations placed upon counsel by the court. Also, co-counsel alleged at oral argument that when the defendants relied on a particular study, the plaintiffs tried to cross-examine these studies' methodology and biases, but the district judge prevented this line of inquiry because of the trial's limitation to causation. These assertions would be potentially serious except that they are not supported by the record. . . .

. . . In sum, plaintiffs would have us hold that their failure to persuade the jury resulted from the district judge's improper preclusion of evidence. It did not. The issue of causation was thoroughly and skillfully presented by both sides.

D. *Conclusion*

To summarize, the three considerations we apply in reviewing a decision to try an issue separately are (1) whether the issue was indeed a separate issue, (2) whether it could be tried separately without injustice or prejudice, and (3) whether the separate trial would be conducive to judicial economy, especially if a decision regarding that question would be dispositive of the case and would obviate the necessity of trying any other issues. We hold that since the initial trial on the proximate causation issue was a separate issue, promoted efficiency, and did not unduly prejudice plaintiffs, trifurcating this case on the separate issue of proximate causation was proper. We need not decide whether this was the best or even the only good method of trying this case. We need only determine whether, under all of the circumstances before him, the trial judge's decision to trifurcate was an abuse of discretion.

While Ohio tort law does govern all suits originally filed in Ohio state courts or in federal courts located in Ohio, . . . it is not clear that Ohio tort law would apply to those claims filed initially in other states or federal courts outside of Ohio, which were subsequently transferred to Ohio. Based on the cases cited by plaintiffs and a thorough search of the literature on causation however, we are not persuaded that the law in any American jurisdiction would preclude separation of the issues of causation and culpability in such complex cases as the present one. Therefore, we conclude that the district judge did not abuse his discretion in determining to try causation as a separate issue as to all plaintiffs over which that court had jurisdiction. . . .

CONCLUSION

. . .

In upholding the result here to the extent we have, it is at least deserving of note that a careful examination of the trial record itself reveals the management of the trial by a judge who does not appear at any time throughout to have sought consciously or unconsciously to have unfairly tipped the scales in favor of one side or the other, but who instead in his rulings appeared to be genuinely concerned with producing a trial that was as fair and free from error as human endeavor could make it. While we must always be conscious of the potential danger of making the trial a sterile exercise of scientific investigation by limiting issues and evidence too narrowly, it is quite evident, through several thousand pages of testimony, that the jury was presented with and bound to appreciate the seriousness of a very real issue of great importance to the parties at suit. In fact, to have broadened the issues beyond that of causation would have occasioned a real risk of overencumbering the jurors and impairing their ability to reach a knowledgeable and intelligent verdict based upon the evidence and upon the law applicable under the appropriate instructions. . . .

The judgment of the district court is . . . affirmed.

■   JONES, Circuit Judge, concurring in part and dissenting in part. . . .

Although I have no problem with the approved trifurcation order in this court's *Beverly Hills* decision, I do become hesitant when that decision is applied, seemingly without reservation, to a case, such as this one, which is complex in nature. . . .

. . . [A]ll of the victims in the *Beverly Hills* litigation were affected by the same event, a disastrous and tragic fire. Thus, the issue of causation could, quite competently, be tried separately from the issues of liability and damages with only a small chance that the plaintiffs would be prejudiced. Individual facts about the individual plaintiffs would therefore, have had little significance in regard to the question of causation.

The *Bendectin* litigation, however, is quite different. Over eight hundred plaintiffs, whose mothers took the drug at different times and places and under different circumstances, are involved. . . . In tying all of these claims together, an argument could certainly be made as to prejudice. That is, by not allowing the plaintiffs to present evidence as to how they were individually affected by the drug could have resulted in prejudice to them in their attempt to establish the required elements of their case. . . . The majority opinion refers to the fact that the plaintiffs were not "unduly" prejudiced by the court's trifurcation order. I do not agree that this is the burden plaintiffs must meet to establish an abuse of discretion by the lower court with regard to a trifurcation order. Rather, my suggestion is that *any* prejudice to a plaintiff in the litigation of his or her case should be enough to hold that the lower court has abused its discretion. . . . Plaintiffs here simply failed to meet their burden to demonstrate any prejudice. That is, plaintiffs lost their case because they failed to establish any link between their birth defects and the drug Bendectin, not because of any prejudice to them resulting from the trifurcation order. . . .

Simply because a litigant shares his complaint with eight hundred other claimants is not a reason to deprive him of the day in court he would have enjoyed had he been the sole plaintiff. However, as the majority points out, a trifurcation order is authorized and necessitated at some point so as to allow a district court to manage and control the complexities and massive size of a case. The duty of this court, however, is to prevent such a case-management tool from becoming a penalty to injured plaintiffs seeking relief via the legal system.

Hans Zeisel & Thomas Callahan, SPLIT TRIALS AND TIME SAVING: A STATISTICAL ANALYSIS

76 HARV. L. REV. 1606, 1607-08, 1616-17, 1624-25 (1963)

The way in which separation of issues may save court time is clear. In the traditional form of trial, the damage issue must be litigated even where the verdict will ultimately reject liability; separation would eliminate the need for trying the damage issue in those cases, comprising roughly 40 per cent of all personal injury jury trials. . . . There remained, however, the possibility that these savings might well be offset by a number of countervailing factors not so immediately obvious. . . . The crucial question for this study was, therefore, not so much whether but rather *how much* time would be saved by the separation of issues. . . .

[One] table provides further insights into the means by which time is saved through the separation process: Table 6 compares the stage and mode of termination of regular and separated trials. . . .

TABLE 6

STAGE AND MODE OF DISPOSITION OF PERSONAL INJURY JURY TRIALS

Stage of Termination	Settled	Verdict for Defendant		Jury Verdict for Plaintiff on Liability and Damages	Total
		Directed Verdict	Jury Verdict		
A. Regular Trials					
During Plaintiff's Case	18%	. .	. .	. .	18%
At End of Plaintiff's Case	3%	1%	. .	. .	4%
During Defendant's Case	. .	. .	. .	. .	. .
After Full Trial	3%	2%	31%	42%	78%
Total	**24%**	**3%**	**31%**	**42%**	**100%**
B. Separated Trials					
During Liability Trial	10%	9%	. .	. .	19%
At End of Liability Trial	15%	4%	43%	. .	62%
During Damage Trial	4%	. .	. .	. .	4%
After Full Damage Trial	3%	. .	. .	12%	15%
Total	**32%**	**13%**	**43%**	**12%**	**100%**

* * *

Separation of issues will save, on the average, about 20 per cent of the time that would be required if these cases were tried under traditional rules. The saving derives from the fact that in many cases separation makes the litigation of damages unnecessary. This group includes all cases in which liability is denied, but also the majority of cases in which liability is affirmed, because two out of three of these cases are likely to be settled without trial of the damage issue. There is no evidence that this saving is offset by a change in the settlement ratio prior to trial, in the frequency of jury waivers, or in the proportion of hung juries, any one of which factors — if affected — could increase the court's trial load.

It is not possible to sort out effectively in advance the cases in which separation would prove futile. Therefore, if a court wants to realize the maximum of potential time saving through separation, it should separate as frequently as possible. . . .

The introduction of the separation rule . . . raised other questions beyond its efficacy as a delay remedy. These questions concern the possible effect of separation on the substance of the jury verdicts. By depriving the jury of its joint verdict, it is argued, subtle influences operate to affect the verdict, and should therefore be included in an overall appraisal of the rule. We are now in the process of collecting data which might have a bearing on this problem; if findings prove significant, they will appear in a subsequent report.

Notes

1.   Professor Zeisel and Mr. Callahan did not subsequently report any findings on the effects of trial-splitting on the substance of jury verdicts. They may, however, have overlooked the rather stunning effect shown in Table 6. In cases with all issues tried together, 33% of the 78% of trials that reached completion ended in a defense verdict, for a 44% success rate. In bifurcated cases, 47% of the 62% of cases resulted in a defense verdict, for a 76% success rate. (A less dramatic, but equally accurate, way of describing the statistics is to say that 34% of all single-trial cases resulted in a defense verdict, while 56% of bifurcated cases resulted in a defense verdict.) Other commentators have noted the outcome-changing effect suggested by these statistics.

Would you expect trifurcation of issues — especially trifurcation in which a "sterile" issue like scientific causation is tried first — to show an even more dramatic skew in defendants' favor? In one recent experiment, 25% of the mock juries that heard only causation found for plaintiffs, while a whopping 87.5% of the mock juries that heard all the evidence, but were asked to deliberate only on the causation question, found for the plaintiffs. The same study also showed, however, that the 25% of the plaintiffs who prevailed in the causation-only trial were awarded significantly higher damages than the 87.5% of the plaintiffs who prevailed in a full trial. *See* Irwin A. Horowitz & Kenneth S. Bordens, *An Experimental Investigation of Procedural Issues in Complex Tort Trials*, 14 LAW & HUM. BEHAV. 269 (1990).

Would you also expect an order of bifurcation or trifurcation to have a spill-over effect and to result in settlements more favorable to defendants?

2. If the statistics of Zeisel and Callahan or Horowitz and Borden are correct, under what circumstances would a trial judge be justified in using bifurcation or trifurcation? Are efficiency gains of 20 per cent enough? What if the efficiency gain is the avoidance of damages testimony for a 3,000 member class? What if the jury's ability to comprehend the case and render a reasonably accurate verdict was threatened without trial splitting? Some scholars have questioned whether splitting trials yields the efficiency gains that the method initially promises. Professor Landes has performed an extensive economic analysis of trial-splitting techniques, the conclusion of which was that

> a sequential [i.e., bifurcated] trial lowers the expected cost of litigation compared to a unitary trial for both the plaintiff and the defendant .... Consequently, a sequential trial (a) increases the plaintiff's incentive to sue, (b) increases the number of lawsuits, and (c) reduces the likelihood that the parties will settle out of court by narrowing the range of mutually acceptable settlements. Hence, sequential decision making may increase the aggregate cost of litigation even though it lowers the expected cost of litigating (as opposed to settling) a particular dispute.

William M. Landes, *Sequential Versus Unitary Trials: An Economic Analysis*, 22 J. LEGAL STUD. 99, 100-01 (1993) (italics omitted). Professor Landes did not determine whether the individual gains that typically result from trial splitting outweigh the aggregate losses, but opined that "a sequential trial may cost more than a unitary trial." *Id.* at 134. He also described a set of circumstances in which split trials gave incentives to parties to spend more than on a single trial, thus reversing the aggregate effects described above. *See also* George L. Priest, *Private Litigants and the Court Congestion Problem*, 69 B.U. L. REV. 527, 552-54 (1989) (using economic analysis to show that bifurcation does little to improve court congestion, but may encourage settlement).

3. Whatever the gain, can we justify the disparate treatment of similar Bendectin claimants, some of whom received the trifurcated procedure, and some of whom did not? Can we justify the disparate treatment of Bendectin plaintiffs and plaintiffs who are the victims of other torts? *See* Roger H. Trangsrud, *Mass Trials in Mass Tort Cases: A Dissent*, 1989 U. ILL. L. REV. 69, 80-82:

> Trifurcation of issues in a mass tort case is neither fair nor efficient. It is not fair because it robs the jury of its traditional flexibility in tort cases to balance uncertainties in the plaintiff's case on liability against strengths in the plaintiff's case on damages. Trifurcation of issues also inevitably leads to the sterile trial of technical issues related to causation divorced from the fact of the

plaintiff's injury and a full account of the defendant's role in the tragedy. . . .

. . . This Bendectin jury was deprived of the evidence most tort juries would routinely hear regarding the totality of circumstances surrounding the plaintiff's injury in a manner likely to affect their deliberations in a substantial way. . . .

If the Bendectin claims had been tried separately, it is possible that the defendant would have consistently prevailed. It is also possible, however, that juries presented with the entire case against the manufacturer of this drug would have awarded discounted damages to the plaintiffs before them, mindful of the serious character of the plaintiffs' injuries and the inconclusive evidence that the injuries were caused by the defendant's drug. Such an outcome would seem to be at odds with our current law of causation, but might anticipate reform of that law in the future. Perhaps the law is moving to allow a discounted recovery when a defendant's product increases the risk of disease or injury beyond natural levels, but strict causation cannot be proven due to the passage of time or the imperfect nature of our science.

In any event, it is wrong to take such options and flexibility away from those juries that hear mass tort trials and leave them only with the opportunity to give an opinion on an abstract question of causation. The plaintiffs in such cases are no less deserving of and entitled to full jury consideration of their case than are the victims of isolated torts.

4. Is bifurcation constitutional? *Bendectin* raises, and refutes, the standard argument: that splitting the case up impinges on the Seventh Amendment's right to jury trial. The argument derives from *Gasoline Products Co. v. Champlin Refining Co.*, 283 U.S. 494 (1931). *Gasoline Products* involved a somewhat different issue: whether the Re-Examination Clause of the Seventh Amendment required that a jury hear the entire case, as opposed to just the damages issues, when a judge ordered a new trial because of an erroneous instruction regarding the measure of a counterclaim defendant's damages. Hoping for a second bite at the apple, the defendant on the counterclaim argued that the Seventh Amendment required a retrial of the entire counterclaim. The Court said no: It was permissible to retry just the damages portion of the case because "the issue to be retried is so distinct and separable from the others that a trial of it alone may be had without injustice." *Id.* at 500.

After *Gasoline Products*, courts have tended to use the "distinct and separable" test to decide whether and how a case may be bifurcated for trial. Thus, in jury-tried cases, the usual view is that a court cannot bifurcate a case in such a way that a jury in the second trial would need to re-examine and find the facts that were already determined by the first jury. *See* Franchi Constr. Co. v. Combined Ins. Co., 580 F.2d 1 (1st Cir. 1978). In bench trials, no comparable restriction exists.

Borrowing from the holding of *Gasoline Products*, courts have had little difficulty finding that the bifurcation of damages from liability is constitutionally appropriate. Similarly, bifurcating an issue like the statute of limitations from other issues is normally unproblematic. What about bifurcating some liability issues from others? *Bendectin* indicates that the issue of factual causation can be bifurcated from the issue of negligence. On the other hand, in *In re Rhone-Poulenc Rorer Inc.*, 51 F.3d 1293, 1303 (7th Cir. 1995), Judge Posner argued that negligence could not be bifurcated from comparative negligence or proximate causation, and he struck down a class certification in part because it relied on a trial plan that called for such bifurcation:

> The first jury . . . will determine merely whether one or more of the defendants was negligent under one of the two theories. . . . Unless the defendants settle, a second (and third, and fourth, and hundredth, and conceivably thousandth) jury will have to decide, in individual follow-on litigation . . ., such issues as comparative negligence — did any class members knowingly continue to use unsafe blood solids after they learned or should have learned of the risk of contamination with HIV? — and proximate causation. Both issues overlap the issue of the defendants' negligence. Comparative negligence entails, as the name implies, a comparison of the degree of negligence of plaintiff and defendant. Proximate causation is found by determining whether the harm to the plaintiff followed in some sense naturally, uninterruptedly, and with reasonable probability from the negligent act of the defendant. It overlaps the issue of the defendants' negligence even when the state's law does not (as many states do) make the foreseeability of the risk to which the defendant subjected the plaintiff an explicit ingredient of negligence. A second or subsequent jury might find that the defendants' failure to take precautions against infection with Hepatitis B could not be thought the *proximate cause* of the plaintiffs' infection with HIV, a different and unknown blood-borne virus. How the resulting inconsistency between juries could be prevented escapes us.

Are these conclusions necessarily true? Couldn't the first jury determine the fact of negligence, and the second jury — after being instructed that the defendant was negligent — determine the quantum of that negligence in comparison to that of the plaintiff? Likewise, isn't the foreseeability of harm to the plaintiffs (the proximate-cause question) distinct from whether the defendant's negligence poses a foreseeable risk of harm to anyone (the negligence question)?

5.   One way in which courts have sought to avoid the Seventh Amendment issue is to retain the first jury for subsequent trials, so that the same jury will hear all the evidence. *See* In re Air Crash Disaster at Detroit Metro. Airport on Aug. 16, 1987, 737 F. Supp. 391, 395 (E.D. Mich. 1989) (using the same jury will prevent a sterile or laboratory atmosphere); Maenner v. St. Paul Fire & Marine Ins. Co., 127 F.R.D. 488, 491-92 (W.D. Mich. 1989) (leaving open until after the first trial whether the same jury would need to be recalled because issues were constitutionally intertwined). Does the use of the same jury for each trial meet the concerns in *Gasoline Products*? Will this solution work in sprawling complex litigation?

6. Given its outcome-influencing potential, another concern with bifurcating liability from damages is Rule 42(a)'s consistency with the Rules Enabling Act, 28 U.S.C. § 2072, which forbids the Federal Rules from "abridg[ing], enlarg[ing], or modify[ing] any substantive right." *Compare* Eubanks v. Winn, 420 S.W.2d 698, 701 (Tex. 1967) (holding that liability cannot be bifurcated from damages in tort cases because they are "elements of an indivisible cause of action"), *with* Rosales v. Honda Motor Co., 726 F.2d 259 (5th Cir. 1984) (in a Texas diversity case, holding that liability was properly divided from damages under Rule 42; bifurcation was procedural under the Rules Enabling Act), *and* Simpson v. Pittsburgh Corning Corp., 901 F.2d 277 (2d Cir. 1990) (holding that bifurcation was not required even when state courts traditionally use bifurcation for similar cases).

7   Assuming that bifurcation between liability and damages is both constitutional and not beyond the terms of the Rules Enabling Act, should courts still try to preserve the single-trial method whenever possible? *See* Jennifer M. Granholm & William J. Richards, *Bifurcated Justice: How Trial-Splitting Devices Defeat the Jury's Role*, 26 U. TOL. L. REV. 505 (1995). *See generally* Steven S. Gensler, *Bifurcation Unbound*, 75 WASH. U. L. REV. 705 (2000) (arguing that bifurcation should be used more broadly). In a somewhat dated survey, judges overwhelmingly supported bifurcation (94% of federal and 82% of state judges sometimes bifurcated cases, and 84% thought that it helped the process). Louis Harris & Associates, *Judges' Opinions on Procedural Issues: A Survey of State and Federal Trial Judges Who Spend at Least Half Their Time on General Civil Cases*, 69 B.U. L. REV. 731, 743-45 (1989).

8. Rule 42 permits courts to conduct separate trials in any manner that furthers convenience or avoids prejudice; it does not require a court to use the liability-damage or one-liability-issue-first divisions that arguably stack the deck against the plaintiff. Consider the following alternative as a way to divide the issues. Does it better meet the goals of limiting the jury's exposure to large quantities of information at the first trial, providing information that might avoid future trials, and avoiding the outcome-affecting potential of traditional bifurcation?

IN RE CHEVRON U.S.A., INC.

109 F.3d 1016 (5th Cir. 1997)

■ PARKER, Circuit Judge.

Chevron U.S.A., Inc. ("Chevron") petitions this Court for a Writ of Mandamus seeking relief from an order of the district court dated December 19, 1996, containing a trial plan for this litigation. We deny the petition as it relates to the scheduled trial of the thirty selected plaintiffs referenced in the district court's order, but grant the petition as it relates to utilization of the results of such trial for the purpose of issue or claim preclusion.

UNDERLYING FACTS AND PROCEDURAL HISTORY

This controversy arose out of the alleged injuries suffered by over 3,000 plaintiffs and intervenors ("Plaintiffs"), who claim damages for personal injuries, wrongful death, and property contamination allegedly caused by Chevron's acts and omissions. . . . The Plaintiffs contend that their subdivision was constructed on land used in the 1920's by Chevron for a crude oil storage waste pit. . . . Later, Chevron sold the property for residential development knowing that the land was contaminated. . . .

[The Plaintiffs sued Chevron in state and federal court. After removal of the state cases and their consolidation with the federal cases, the district court approved a trial plan. This plan provided for a "unitary trial" on the issues of "general liability or causation" on behalf of all plaintiffs, as well as a trial of individual causation and damage for thirty (30) "bellwether" plaintiffs — fifteen (15) to be chosen by the plaintiffs and fifteen (15) to be chosen by Chevron. The "unitary trial" was to determine Chevron's liability and, if it was found liable, to establish bellwether verdicts for settlement purposes.] It is this selection process which Chevron argues will not result in a representative group of bellwether plaintiffs.

Chevron filed with the district court the affidavit of Ronald G. Frankiewicz, Ph.D. which evaluated the district court's trial plan for selecting the thirty plaintiffs, concluding that such a plan was "not representative." Instead, Frankiewicz detailed the "stratified selection process" which should be used by the district court in selecting the bellwether group which would result in a representative group of plaintiffs. The district court however struck Frankiewicz's affidavit as untimely filed and redundant in substance. On January 7, 1997, the district court denied Chevron's request to certify an interlocutory appeal. This Petition for Writ of Mandamus ensued.

DISCUSSION

1.   *Standard of Review*

Our review of a trial court's plan for proceeding in a complex case is a deferential one that recognizes the fact that the trial judge is in a much better position than an appellate court to formulate an appropriate methodology for a trial. . . . We have historically reserved the issuance of the writ for "extraordinary" cases, and will issue the writ where the petitioner has met its burden of proving a clear and indisputable abuse of discretion or usurpation of judicial power by a trial judge.

Our traditional reluctance to meddle in the formulation of a district court's trial plan is tempered by the demands placed upon judicial resources and the extraordinary expense to litigants that typically accompanies mass tort litigation. We, therefore, as we proceed, do so mindful of the admonition contained in Rule 1 — that what we do should serve the compelling interests of justice, speed, and cost-containment. . . .

2. *The Plan*

The trial court has in our view quite properly categorized this litigation as complex. . . .

This case is a classic example of a non-elastic mass tort, that is, the universe of potential claimants are either known or are capable of ascertainment and the event or course of conduct alleged to constitute the tort involved occurred over a known time period and is traceable to an identified entity or entities. When compared to an elastic mass tort where the universe of potential plaintiffs is unknown and many times is seemingly unlimited and the number of potential tortfeasors is equally obtuse, the task of managing the non-elastic mass tort is infinitely less complex. In the non-elastic context, the necessity for the obtainment of maturity as reflected by a series of verdicts over time is not required in order to test the viability of plaintiffs' claims or the defendant's defenses.

The district court, after designating the case as complex, then articulated the goals of its trial plan as seeking to achieve the greatest efficiency and expedition in the resolution of all issues involved in the case. . . .

Initially, we note the obvious. The trial plan, while clearly designed to resolve the issue of liability on the part of Chevron to all the plaintiffs by referring to a unitary trial on the issues of general liability or causation, does not identify any common issues or explain how the verdicts in the thirty (30) selected cases are supposed to resolve liability for the remaining 2970 plaintiffs. It is impossible to discern from the district court's order what variables may exist that will impact on both the property and personal injury claims in this litigation. Similar litigation typically contains property issue variables that are related to time, proximity, and contamination levels of exposure to any pollutants that may be present, and personal injury claims that contain a mix of alleged exposure related maladies that also may be affected by time, proximity, and exposure levels. We, however, may not speculate on the homogeneity of the mix of claims, the uniformity of any exposure that may have existed and what diseases, if any, may be related to that exposure. Instead our review is restricted to the record and to an examination of the district court's order.

3. *A Bellwether Trial*

The term bellwether is derived from the ancient practice of belling a wether (a male sheep) selected to lead his flock. The ultimate success of the wether selected to wear the bell was determined by whether the flock had confidence that the wether would not lead them astray, and so it is in the mass tort context.

The notion that the trial of some members of a large group of claimants may provide a basis for enhancing prospects of settlement or for resolving common issues or claims is a sound one that has achieved general acceptance by both bench and bar. References to bellwether trials have long been included in the *Manual for Complex Litigation*. *See* MANUAL FOR COMPLEX LITIGATION §§ 33.27-.28 (3d ed. 1995). The reasons for acceptance by bench and bar are apparent. If a representative group of claimants are tried to verdict, the results of such trials can be beneficial for litigants who desire to settle such claims by providing information on the value of the cases as reflected by the jury verdicts. Common issues or even general liability may also be resolved in a bellwether context in appropriate cases.

Whatever may be said about the trial contemplated by the district court's . . . order, one thing is clear. It is not a bellwether trial. It is simply a trial of fifteen (15) of the "best" and fifteen (15) of the "worst" cases contained in the universe of claims involved in this litigation. There is no pretense that the thirty (30) cases selected are representative of the 3,000 member group of plaintiffs.

A bellwether trial designed to achieve its value ascertainment function for settlement purposes or to answer troubling causation or liability issues common to the universe of claimants has as a core element representativeness — that is, the sample must be a randomly selected one of sufficient size so as to achieve statistical significance to the desired level of confidence in the result obtained. Such samples are selected by the application of the science of inferential statistics. The essence of the science of inferential statistics is that one may confidently draw inferences about the whole from a representative sample of the whole. The applicability of inferential statistics have long been recognized by the courts.

The selected thirty (30) cases included in the district court's "unitary trial" are not cases calculated to represent the group of 3,000 claimants. Thus, the results that would be obtained from a trial of these thirty (30) cases lack the requisite level of representativeness so that the results could permit a court to draw sufficiently reliable inferences about the whole that could, in turn, form the basis for a judgment affecting cases other than the selected thirty. While this particular sample of thirty cases is lacking in representativeness, statistical sampling with an appropriate level of representativeness has been utilized and approved. As recognized by the Ninth Circuit, "[i]nferential statistics with random sampling produces an acceptable due process solution to the troublesome area of mass tort litigation." In re Estate of Marcos Human Rights Litig., 910 F. Supp. 1460, 1467 (D. Haw. 1995), *aff'd* sub. nom. Hilao v. Estate of Marcos, 103 F.3d 767 (9th Cir. 1996) (holding that the random sampling procedures used by the district court do not violate due process) [*infra* p. 1058].

We, therefore, hold that before a trial court may utilize results from a bellwether trial for a purpose that extends beyond the individual cases tried, it must, prior to any extrapolation, find that the cases tried are representative of the larger group of cases or claims from which they are selected. Typically, such a finding must be based on competent, scientific, statistical evidence that identifies the variables involved and that provides a sample of sufficient size so as to permit a finding that there is a sufficient level of confidence that the results obtained reflect results that would be obtained from trials of the whole. . . . Without a sufficient level of confidence in the sample results, no inferences may be drawn from such results that would form the basis for applying such results to cases or claims that have not been actually tried.

We recognize that in appropriate cases common issues impacting upon general liability or causation may be tried standing alone. However, when such a common issue trial is presented through or along with selected individuals' cases, concerns arise that are founded upon considerations of due process. Specifically, our procedural due process concerns focus on the fact that the procedure embodied in the district court's trial plan is devoid of safeguards designed to ensure that the claims against Chevron of the non-represented plaintiffs as they relate to liability or causation are determined in a proceeding that is reasonably calculated to reflect the results that would be obtained if those claims were actually tried. Conversely, the procedure subjects Chevron to potential liability to 3,000 plaintiffs by a procedure that is completely lacking in the minimal level of reliability necessary for the imposition of such liability.

Our substantive due process concerns are based on the lack of fundamental fairness contained in a system that permits the extinguishment of claims or the imposition of liability in nearly 3,000 cases based upon results of a trial of a non-representative sample of plaintiffs. Such a procedure is inherently unfair when the substantive rights of both plaintiffs and the defendant are resolved in a manner that lacks the requisite level of confidence in the reliability of its result. . . .

The elements of basic fairness contained in our historical understanding of both procedural and substantive due process therefore dictate that when a unitary trial is conducted where common issues, issues of general liability, or issues of causation are coupled with a sample of individual claims or cases, the sample must be one that is a randomly selected, statistically significant sample.

We express no opinion on whether the mix of claims that collectively make up the consolidated case lend themselves to the sampling techniques required to conduct a bellwether trial or whether this is an appropriate case for a stand-alone, common-issue trial.

We are sympathetic to the efforts of the district court to control its docket and to move this case along. We also are not without appreciation for the concerns a district court might have when it concludes that some of the issues raised may be motivated by delay tactics. However, our sympathies and our appreciation for the efforts of the district court in this case do not outweigh our due process concerns.

CONCLUSION

The petition, therefore, for mandamus as it relates to the trial of the thirty (30) selected cases is denied. Whether the district court wishes to proceed with that trial, to secure thirty (30) individual judgments, is a matter within the discretion of the trial court. Likewise, whether the trial judge wishes to attempt to structure a common-issues trial or conduct a bellwether trial based on a properly selected sample are matters also within the discretion of the district court. . . .

The petition for mandamus is granted insofar as it relates to utilization of the results obtained from the trial of the thirty (30) selected cases for any purpose affecting issues or claims of, or defenses to, the remaining untried cases.

■   JONES, Circuit Judge, specially concurring.

I agree with Judge Parker's conclusions that mandamus must be granted in this case, that the district judge's method of selecting "bellwether" cases is fatally flawed, and that the most expeditious remedy is, without interfering with the setting of these cases, to deprive them of preclusive consequences. . . . I also have serious doubts about the major premise of Judge Parker's opinion, i.e., his confidence that a bellwether trial of representative cases is permissible to extrapolate findings relevant to and somehow preclusive upon a larger group of cases. . . .

The only case cited in the *Manual for Complex Litigation* concerning a bellwether strategy was tried by Judge Parker when he sat on the district court.   Cimino v. Raymark, 751 F. Supp. 649, 653, 664-65 (E.D. Tex. 1990)
. . . .

The use of statistical sampling as a means to identify and resolve common issues in tort litigation has . . . been severely criticized. Among other things, the technique may deprive nonparties of their Seventh Amendment jury trial right. . . . That is, even if the bellwether jury found liability on the part of Chevron, later juries could be called upon to reassess that decision when faced with questions of comparative causation or comparative negligence. . . . Additionally, . . . there is a fine line between deriving results from trials based on statistical sampling and pure legislation. Judges must be sensitive to stay within our proper bounds of adjudicating individual disputes. We are not authorized by the Constitution or statutes to legislate solutions to cases in pursuit of efficiency and expeditiousness.   Essential to due process for litigants, including both the plaintiffs and Chevron in this non-class action context, is their right to the opportunity for an individual assessment of liability and damages in each case. Nowhere did the district court explain how it was authorized to make the results of this bellwether trial unitary for any purposes concerning the 2,970 other plaintiffs' cases pending before him.

Notes

1.   The trial judge's plan in *Chevron* blended elements of traditional bifurcation, in which the liability issues for all claims are determined, with the traditional trial process, in which all elements of a plaintiff's claim are

---

*   At the time that *Chevron* was decided, *Cimino* was pending before the Fifth Circuit. The court of appeals subse- quently reversed *Cimino*. We consider that decision shortly. *See infra* p. 1066. — ED.

tried at once. From the plaintiffs' perspective, one of the benefits of this method is its avoidance of the "sterile laboratory atmosphere" that, some believe, infects liability-damages bifurcation. Now the jury gets to see the effect of the defendant's conduct on real people.

Obviously, the plaintiffs that the plaintiffs' lawyer most want the jury to see are those who are most drastically injured. In a number of cases in which courts wanted to put a human face on the case by combining the liability trial for all plaintiffs with the full trial for a few selected plaintiffs, courts essentially countenanced this practice. For instance, some courts used class representatives as "exemplar" or "bellwether" plaintiffs. *See* Maenner v. St. Paul Fire & Marine Ins. Co., 127 F.R.D. 488 (W.D. Mich. 1989) (using class representatives as bellwether plaintiffs); In re Air Crash Disaster at Stapleton Int'l Airport, Denver, Colo., on Nov. 15, 1987, 720 F. Supp. 1455 (D. Colo. 1988); *see also* In re Copley Pharm., Inc., 161 F.R.D. 456 (D. Wyo. 1995) (rejecting the use of randomly selected plaintiffs when this method would have delayed trial and class representatives already served as bellwethers); Affiliated Ute Citizens v. United States, 406 U.S. 128, 140 (1972) (mentioning the use of "bellwether plaintiffs" without describing the manner of their selection). Needless to say, defendants often protested this approach, so some courts developed the practice of letting them pick an equal number of plaintiffs. The trial court in *Chevron* followed this approach, which was not uncommon in the 1990s.

If the two sides pick well, the chosen cases will be outliers; they won't say much about the ordinary or typical cases. To sidestep that evident problem, the idea of using a sufficient number of randomly selected plaintiffs to get a bead on the "typical" case caught on. *Chevron* was among the first cases to insist on the use of a randomly selected group if the trial court intended to afford preclusive effect to the decision. The idea of randomly selecting bellwether plaintiffs has now become widely accepted: "Over the last decade, bellwether trials have become more common in large actions, and, in particular, mass tort actions." In re Methyl Tertiary Butyl Ether (MTBE) Prods., 2007 WL 1791258, at 1 (S.D.N.Y. June 15, 2007); *see generally* Alexandra D. Lahav, *Bellwether Trials*, 76 GEO. WASH. L. REV. 576 (2008) (discussing the use of such trials).

2.   The critical point of *Chevron* is the need for random selection of the bellwether cases *if* the court affords preclusive effect to the bellwether trial. *Chevron* allows the trial court to proceed with "best and worst" bellwethers as long as the court does not extend those findings to other plaintiffs. The lack of preclusive effect certainly diminishes the value of a "best and worst" trial, but in some cases, courts might still think that such a trial will provide the parties with enough information about the relative strengths of their cases that the method is worth it. Using bellwethers in this way might be especially necessary when the number of bellwether cases needed to achieve statistical confidence in the results is high.

But stop for a minute to question the assumption of *Chevron*: that only trials with a statistically sufficient number of randomly selected plaintiffs are entitled to preclusive effect. *Chevron* grounds this rule in the Due

Process Clause. Why? In Section E of Chapter Two, we examined issue preclusion in complex cases. Although those cases imposed other limits on the use of offensive collateral estoppel, they did not insist that the judgment be rendered in a case involving representative plaintiffs. Indeed, in the case in which the Supreme Court first recognized offensive collateral estoppel, the plaintiff in the first case was the Securities and Exchange Commission, which certainly did not have claims that were representative of the plaintiffs in the second case. *See* Parklane Hosiery Co. v. Shore, 439 U.S. 322 (1979). Similarly, when a case is bifurcated on liability issues only and the liability decision is applied to all cases (as in *Bendectin, supra* p. 1034), representativeness is not a requirement. Why is it constitutional to bifurcate the liability issues of all the plaintiffs so that *no* plaintiffs get their complete individual cases before the jury, but not constitutional to bifurcate liability from damages when *some* plaintiffs have their cases heard by the jury? The strongest argument for random sampling is that it is necessary if the court intends to afford preclusive effect to the determination of damages — an issue addressed in the next subsection. But that was not the point of the trial plan in *Chevron*.

3.   Even if *Chevron* went too far in its constitutional claim, courts recognize that often the best practice is to select the bellwether plaintiffs randomly. For a thorough review of the issues involved in using bellwether plaintiffs, co-authored by the judge in the *Vioxx* MDL litigation in which the bellwether trials were effectively used to provide information on which the parties could base a subsequent settlement, see Eldon E. Fallon et al., *Bellwether Trials in Multidistrict Litigation*, 82 TUL. L. REV. 2323 (2008).

4.   Aside from liability-damages bifurcation and bellwether trials, other possibilities to split the trial into more digestible bites include:

(a)   *Reverse Bifurcation*. Courts in some mass torts, especially asbestos cases, have used "reverse bifurcation" (or "reverse trifurcation"), in which damage and causation issues are tried before liability issues. The rationale for such a procedure is that, in mature mass torts like asbestos, the parties have excellent information about the likelihood of success on liability; the real sticking points in settlement are the individual issues of causation and damage. Furthermore, by reversing the usual order, some of the "sterility" problems of liability-first bifurcation are removed, although the same jury will need to hear the liability case in order to overcome the problem altogether. *See* Angelo v. Armstrong World Indus., Inc., 11 F.3d 957 (10th Cir. 1993); United States v. Kramer, 770 F. Supp. 954 (D.N.J. 1991); *but see* Coates v. AC and S, Inc., 844 F. Supp. 1126, 1138 (E.D. La. 1994) (refusing to reverse bifurcate when plaintiff had prepared for single trial and reverse bifurcation had not, in court's experience, facilitated settlements).

(b)   *Wave Trials*. In multi-plaintiff cases a court might try one set of plaintiffs or one type of claim first, and if necessary, another and then another. *See* In re Shell Oil Refinery, 136 F.R.D. 588, 596 (E.D. La. 1991). Akin to bellwether trials, but without any pretense that the selected cases are representative or exemplary of others, these "wave trials" have two purposes. One is to make the factfinding task, which would be difficult if all of the cases of all of the plaintiffs were tried at once, more manageable. If the early cases are chosen wisely, a second purpose of wave trials is to provide the general range of likely verdicts so that the parties can settle the latter cases without trial.

(c) *Other Forms of Claim Bifurcation.* Other types of claim bifurcation are also possible. For instance, one asbestos case divided the trials according to the types of asbestos products to which the plaintiffs had been exposed. *See* Adams-Arapahoe Sch. Dist. No. 28-J v. GAF Corp., 959 F.2d 868 (10th Cir. 1992). Likewise, legal theories can be segregated. For instance, federal claims can be tried before state claims; patent claims before antitrust claims; or principal claims before counterclaims.

(d) *Background and Blueprint Trials.* Plaintiffs have sometimes proposed trials in which the first jury would decide the "background" issues that would then establish the factual framework for later discovery and trials. Other plaintiffs have suggested "blueprint" trials, in which the first jury would leave to later triers of fact only ministerial questions of fact. For instance, in a case like *Bendectin*, the first jury would decide not only whether Bendectin caused the injuries, but also what injuries and in what dosages. The only thing that later juries would need to decide would be whether the specific plaintiff was exposed to Bendectin, what the dosage was, and whether the plaintiff had a Bendectin-related injury.

Thus far, courts have not been overly receptive to either background or blueprint trials. *See* United States v. Am. Tel. & Tel. Co., 83 F.R.D. 323, 335-36 (D.D.C. 1979) (declining to adopt a background trial, in part because the parties could not agree on what was a background, and what was a central, issue); Payton v. Abbott Labs, 83 F.R.D. 382, 395 (D. Mass. 1979) (holding that a blueprint trial would lead to "confusion and uncertainty, which would amount to a denial of a fair trial"); *but see* Union Carbide & Carbon Corp. v. Nisley, 300 F.2d 561, 589 (10th Cir. 1961) (approving antitrust trial plan in which the first jury established the formula for damages recovery for class members).

5.   No studies comparable to the Zeisel and Callahan study have been performed on bellwether trials or these other trial-splitting devices, so their time saving and outcome-determinative effects are unknown.

6.   A decision whether to split issues into separate trials will have not only a dramatic effect on trial strategy, but also on pretrial strategy, since discovery and issue-narrowing devices are often tailored to the ultimate form of trial. Moreover, the possibility and nature of separate trials also has an effect on joinder decisions. For instance, in ruling on a class certification decision, many courts consider the possibility of bifurcating the trial. *See, e.g.,* McCarthy v. Kleindienst, 741 F.2d 1406, 1415 (D.C. Cir. 1984) (holding that a "district court should, of course, ordinarily consider such well-established methods as bifurcating the trial into liability and damages phases before denying class certification"); *Maenner*, 127 F.R.D. at 490-91 ("[I]n complex cases with complex issues, justice is often best served if issues are separated."). Similarly, the possibility of using bellwether plaintiffs can affect aggregation decisions. *Compare* Boughton

v. Cotter Corp., 65 F.3d 823 (10th Cir. 1995) (holding that it is not an abuse of discretion to refuse to certify a class and instead to use bellwether plaintiffs), *with* Cook v. Rockwell Int'l Corp., 151 F.R.D. 378 (D. Colo. 1993) (using bellwether plaintiffs rather than a class action would be wasteful).

In short, trial splitting is more than a method by which information can be made more digestible for the factfinder. It is also a case-management tool that can reduce or eliminate joinder and pretrial complexity, and consequently might be useful even when trial complexity is not present.

7. Courts differ somewhat on the standards under which trial-splitting should occur. One of the most comprehensive lists of factors is found in *Kimberly-Clark Corp. v. James River Corp. of Virginia*, 131 F.R.D. 607, 608-09 (N.D. Ga. 1989):

> In addition to the more general factors set forth in Rule 42(b); i.e., (1) convenience; (2) prejudice; (3) expedition; and (4) economy; a court reviewing a motion for separate trials may properly consider (5) whether the issues sought to be tried separately are significantly different; (6) whether they are triable by jury or the court; (7) whether discovery has been directed to a single trial of all issues; (8) whether the evidence required for each issue is substantially different; (9) whether one party would gain some unfair advantage from separate trials; (10) whether a single trial of all issues would create the potential for jury bias or confusion; and (11) whether bifurcation would enhance or reduce the possibility of a pretrial settlement.

Some courts also look to the enhancement of juror comprehension of complex issues, the possibility that bifurcation may make the presentation of lengthy evidence unnecessary, and the lack of unfair prejudice. *See* Barr Labs., Inc. v. Abbott Labs., 978 F.2d 98 (3d Cir. 1992); *see also* In re Air Crash Disaster at Detroit Metro. Airport on Aug. 16, 1987, 737 F. Supp. 391 (E.D. Mich. 1989) (also mentioning the distinctness of the separated issues and the lack of objection by the parties).

8. Trial splitting is hardly automatic; courts and litigants have cited a host of practical problems. Among them are: (1) the exclusion of relevant evidence, the dissimilarities among plaintiffs, and, if one jury hears general liability issues and another hears plaintiff-specific defenses, the inability of a single jury to obtain a complete picture of the case, *see* Rosen v. Reckitt & Colman Inc., 1994 WL 652534 (S.D.N.Y. Nov. 17, 1994); (2) the possibility of inconsistent verdicts, *see* Lempel & Son Co. v. Boden, 1993 WL 256711 (S.D.N.Y. July 7, 1993); (3) the problem that evidence may need to be introduced and witnesses may need to testify twice, *see* Miller v. N.J. Transit Auth. Rail Operations, 160 F.R.D. 37, 40 (D.N.J. 1995); (4) the unfairness of requiring a party to reveal its theory of the case during the first trial, *see* Yung v. Raymark Indus., Inc., 789 F.2d 397, 400-01 (6th Cir. 1986); (5) relatedly, the damage that trial splitting might do to a case-management plan or to a party's trial strategy, *see* Refac Int'l, Ltd. v. Mastercard Int'l, 758 F. Supp. 152 (S.D.N.Y. 1991); and (6) the ability of a party to use inconsistent legal theories in the two trials, thus maximizing their chance of recovery, *see* Angelo, 11 F.3d at 965.

9. A few procedural points on trial splitting:

(a) *Burden of Proof.* The party who requests separate trials bears the burden of proving the need for the separation. Lowe v. Philadelphia Newspapers, Inc., 594 F. Supp. 123 (E.D. Pa. 1984).

(b) *Waiver.* A party can waive its right to object to a judge's trial-splitting decision. Sanford v. Johns-Manville Sales Corp., 923 F.2d 1142, 1145-46 (5th Cir. 1991).

(c) *Standard of Review.* A decision to separate issues for trial lies within the judge's discretion. In re Master Key Antitrust Litig., 528 F.2d 5 (2d Cir. 1975); *Lowe*, 594 F. Supp. at 125. The decision is not appealable of right until the litigation is complete. *Master Key*, 528 F.2d at 14.

2. Trial by Statistics

Trial splitting does not avoid the factfinder's ultimate obligation to consider the individual liability and damages issues of individual claimants. Hence, even though trial splitting can limit the information that the factfinder must consider in one trial, it does not limit the information that the factfinder needs to consider overall (at least if plaintiff prevails). In this section we examine a controversial method in which the overall information that the factfinder needs to consider can be limited. That method is often called, sometimes disparagingly, "trial by statistics." The basic idea of this trial is that the court surveys or tries a representative sample of the plaintiffs' claims and allows the factfinder to extrapolate, based on the survey data or the bellwether cases, the appropriate remedy for the entire group of claimants. Sound fair? Read on.

HILAO V. ESTATE OF MARCOS

103 F.3d 767 (9th Cir. 1996)

■ FLETCHER, Circuit Judge.

The Estate of Ferdinand E. Marcos appeals from a final judgment entered against it in a class-action suit after a trifurcated jury trial on the damage claims brought by a class of Philippine nationals (hereinafter collectively referred to as "Hilao") who were victims of torture, "disappearance", or summary execution under the regime of Ferdinand E. Marcos. . . .

PROCEDURAL HISTORY

Shortly after Marcos arrived in the United States in 1986 after fleeing the Philippines, he was served with complaints by a number of parties seeking damages for human-rights abuses committed against them or their decedents. . . . The Judicial Panel on Multidistrict Litigation consolidated the various actions in the District of Hawai'i.

In 1991, the district court certified the Hilao case as a class action, defining the class as all civilian citizens of the Philippines who, between 1972 and 1986, were tortured, summarily executed, or "disappeared" by Philippine military or paramilitary groups; the class also included the survivors of deceased class members. Certain plaintiffs opted out of the class and continued, alongside the class action, to pursue their cases directly. . . .

The district court ordered issues of liability and damages tried separately. In September 1992, a jury trial was held on liability; after three days of deliberation, the jury reached verdicts against the Estate and for the class and for 22 direct plaintiffs and a verdict for the Estate and against one direct plaintiff. . . .

The district court then ordered the damage trial bifurcated into one trial on exemplary damages and one on compensatory damages. The court ordered that notice be given to the class members that they must file a proof-of-claim form in order to opt into the class. Notice was provided by mail to known claimants and by publication in the Philippines and the U.S.; over 10,000 forms were filed.

In February 1994, the same jury that had heard the liability phase of the trial considered whether to award exemplary damages. After two days of evidence and deliberations, the jury returned a verdict against the Estate in the amount of $1.2 billion.

The court appointed a special master to supervise proceedings related to the compensatory-damage phase of the trial in connection with the class. In January 1995, the jury reconvened a third time to consider compensatory damages. . . .

IX. METHODOLOGY OF DETERMINING COMPENSATORY DAMAGES

The Estate challenges the method used by the district court in awarding compensatory damages to the class members.

A. *District Court Methodology*

The district court allowed the use of a statistical sample of the class claims in determining compensatory damages. In all, 10,059 claims were received. The district court ruled 518 of these claims to be facially invalid, leaving 9,541 claims. From these, a list of 137 claims was randomly selected by computer. This number of randomly selected claims was chosen on the basis of the testimony of James Dannemiller, an expert on statistics, who testified that the examination of a random sample of 137 claims would achieve "a 95 percent statistical probability that the same percentage determined to be valid among the examined claims would be applicable to the totality of claims filed." Of the claims selected, 67 were for torture, 52 were for summary execution, and 18 were for "disappearance."

1. *Special Master's Recommendations*

The district court then appointed Sol Schreiber as a special master (and a court-appointed expert under Rule 706 of the Federal Rules of Evidence). Schreiber supervised the taking of depositions in the Philippines of the 137 randomly selected claimants (and their witnesses) in October and November 1994. These depositions were noticed and conducted in accordance with the Federal Rules of Civil Procedure; the Estate chose not to participate and did not appear at any of the depositions. (The Estate also did not depose any of the remaining class members.)

Schreiber then reviewed the claim forms (which had been completed under penalty of perjury) and depositions of the class members in the sample. On the instructions of the district court, he evaluated

(1) whether the abuse claimed came within one of the definitions, with which the Court charged the jury at the trial . . ., of torture, summary execution, or disappearance; (2) whether the Philippine military or paramilitary was . . . involved in such abuse; and (3) whether the abuse occurred during the period September 1972 through February 1986.

He recommended that 6 claims of the 137 in the sample be found not valid.

Schreiber then recommended the amount of damages to be awarded to the 131 claimants. . . . [H]e applied Philippine, international, and American law on damages. . . . The recommended damages for the 131 valid claims in the random sample totalled $3,310,000 for the 64 torture claims (an average of $51,719), $6,425,767 for the 50 summary-execution claims (an average of $128,515), and $1,833,515 for the 17 "disappearance" claims (an average of $107,853).

Schreiber then made recommendations on damage awards to the remaining class members. Based on his recommendation that 6 of the 137 claims in the random sample (4.37%) be rejected as invalid, he recommended the application of a five-per-cent invalidity rate to the remaining claims. He then performed the following calculations to determine the number of valid class claims remaining:

	Torture	Summary Execution	Disappearance
Claims Filed	5,372	3,677	1,010
Facially Invalid Claims	-179	-273	- 66
Remaining Claims	5,193	3,404	944
Less 5% Invalidity Rate	-260	-170	- 47
Valid Claims	4,933	3,234	897
Valid Sample Claims	- 64	- 50	- 17
Valid Remaining Claims	4,869	3,184	880

He recommended that the award to the class be determined by multiplying the number of valid remaining claims in each subclass by the average award recommended for the randomly sampled claims in that subclass:

	Torture	Summary Execution	Disappearance
Valid Remaining Claims	4,869	3,184	880
x Average Awards	$51,719	$128,515	$107,853
Class Awards	$251,819,811	$409,191,760	$94,910,640

By adding the recommended awards in the randomly sampled cases, Schreiber arrived at a recommendation for a total compensatory damage award in each subclass:

	Torture	Summary Execution	Disappearance
Class Awards	$251,819,811	$409,191,760	$94,910,640
Sample Awards	$3,310,000	$6,425,767	$1,833,515
TOTALS	$255,129,811	$415,617,527	$96,744,155

Adding together the subclass awards, Schreiber recommended a total compensatory damage award of $767,491,493.

2. *Jury Proceedings*

A jury trial on compensatory damages was held in January 1995. Dannemiller testified that the selection of the random sample met the standards of inferential statistics, that the successful efforts to locate and obtain testimony from the claimants in the random sample "were of the highest standards" in his profession, that the procedures followed conformed to the standards of inferential statistics, and that the injuries of the random-sample claimants were representative of the class as a whole. Testimony from the 137 random-sample claimants and their witnesses was introduced. Schreiber testified as to his recommendations, and his report was supplied to the jury. The jury was instructed that it could accept, modify or reject Schreiber's recommendations and that it could independently, on the basis of the evidence of the random-sample claimants, reach its own judgment as to the actual damages of those claimants and of the aggregate damages suffered by the class as a whole.

The jury deliberated for five days before reaching a verdict. Contrary to the master's recommendations, the jury found against only two of the 137 claimants in the random sample. As to the sample claims, the jury generally adopted the master's recommendations, although it did not follow his recommendations in 46 instances.[9] As to the claims of the remaining

---

9. The jury awarded more than recommended to six torture claimants and less than recommended to five torture claimants; more than recommended for lost earnings to two execution claimants and less than recommended for lost earnings to nineteen execution claimants; more than recommended for pain and suffering to three execution claimants and less than recommended to one execution claimant; less than recommended for lost earnings to six "disappearance" claimants; and more than recommended for pain and suffering to one "disappearance" claimant and less than recommended for three "disappearance" claimants.

class members, the jury adopted the awards recommended by the master. The district court subsequently entered judgment for 135 of the 137 claimants in the sample in the amounts awarded by the jury, and for the remaining plaintiffs in each of the three subclasses in the amounts awarded by the jury, to be divided pro rata.[10]

B. *Estate's Challenge*

The Estate's challenge to the procedure used by the district court is very narrow. It challenges specifically only "the method by which [the district court] allowed the validity of the class claims to be determined": the master's use of a representative sample to determine what percentage of the total claims were invalid.

The grounds on which the Estate challenges this method are unclear. It states that to its knowledge this method "has not previously been employed in a class action". This alone, of course, would not be grounds for reversal, and in any case the method has been used before in an asbestos class-action case, the opinion in which apparently helped persuade the district court to use this method. *See* Cimino v. Raymark Indus., Inc., 751 F. Supp. 649, 659-667 (E.D. Tex. 1990).

The Estate also argues that the method was "inappropriate" because the class consists of various members with numerous subsets of claims based on whether the plaintiff or his or her decedent was subjected to torture, "disappearance", or summary execution. The district court's methodology, however, took account of those differences by grouping the class members' claims into three subclasses.

Finally, the Estate appears to assert that the method violated its rights to due process because "individual questions apply to each subset of claims, i.e., whether the action was justified, the degree of injury, proximate cause, etc." It does not, however, provide any argument or case citation to explain how the methodology violated its due-process rights. Indeed, the "individual questions" it identifies — justification, degree of injury, proximate cause — are irrelevant to the challenge it makes: the method of determining the validity of the class members' claims. The jury had already determined that Philippine military or paramilitary forces on Marcos' orders — or with his conspiracy or assistance or with his knowledge and failure to act — had tortured, summarily executed, or "disappeared" untold numbers of victims and that the Estate was liable to them or their survivors. The only questions involved in determining the validity of the class members' claims

---

10. Although never expressly explained by the district court, the mechanics of this division, as represented by Hilao, are as follows: The 135 random-sample claimants whose claims were found to be valid would receive the actual amount awarded by the jury; the two sample claimants whose claims were held invalid would receive nothing. All remaining 9,404 claimants with facially valid claims would be eligible to participate in the aggregate award, even though the aggregate award was calculated based on a 5% invalidity rate of those claims.

were whether or not the human-rights abuses they claim to have suffered were proven by sufficient evidence.

Although poorly presented, the Estate's due-process claim does raise serious questions.   Indeed, at least one circuit court has expressed "profound disquiet" in somewhat similar circumstances. In re Fibreboard Corp., 893 F.2d 706, 710 (5th Cir. 1990). . . . [*Fibreboard*] granted the petitions for mandamus and vacated the trial court's order, but it did so not on due-process grounds but because the proposed procedure worked a change in the parties' substantive rights under Texas law that was barred by the *Erie* doctrine.[14]

On the other hand, the time and judicial resources required to try the nearly 10,000 claims in this case would alone make resolution of Hilao's claims impossible. The similarity in the injuries suffered by many of the class members would make such an effort, even if it could be undertaken, especially wasteful, as would the fact that the district court found early on that the damages suffered by the class members likely exceed the total known assets of the Estate.

While the district court's methodology in determining valid claims is unorthodox, it can be justified by the extraordinarily unusual nature of this case. "'Due process,' unlike some legal rules, is not a technical conception with a fixed content unrelated to time, place and circumstances." Cafeteria & Rest. Workers Union, Local 473 v. McElroy, 367 U.S. 886, 895 (1961). In *Connecticut v. Doehr*, 501 U.S. 1, [11] (1991), a case involving prejudgment attachment, the Supreme Court set forth a test, based on the test of *Mathews v. Eldridge*, 424 U.S. 319 (1976), for determining whether a procedure by which a private party invokes state power to deprive another person of property satisfies due process:

> [F]irst, consideration of the private interest that will be affected by the [procedure];   second, an examination of the risk of erroneous deprivation through the procedures under attack and the probable value of additional or alternative safeguards; and third, . . . principal attention to the interest of the party seeking the [procedure], with, nonetheless, due regard for any ancillary interest the government may have in providing the procedure or forgoing the added burden of providing greater protections.

The interest of the Estate that is affected is at best an interest in not paying damages for any invalid claims. If the Estate had a legitimate concern in

---

14. *Cimino*, the district court case upon which the district court appears to have relied in choosing the procedure it followed here, was decided after *Fibreboard* by the same district judge whose order had been vacated in *Fibreboard*. The main difference between the procedures disapproved in *Fibreboard* and those used in *Cimino* appears to be that while the *Fibreboard* process would have presented the 41 cases of the class representatives and allegedly "illustrative" class members to the jury and used those cases to determine an aggregate damage award for the class, the *Cimino* process presented to the jury a statistically significant random sample of class claims and awarded each of the non-sample claims the average of the damages awarded in the sample claims. . . .

the identities of those receiving damage awards, the district court's procedure could affect this interest. In fact, however, the Estate's interest is only in the total amount of damages for which it will be liable: if damages were awarded for invalid claims, the Estate would have to pay more. The statistical method used by the district court obviously presents a somewhat greater risk of error in comparison to an adversarial adjudication of each claim, since the former method requires a probabilistic *prediction* (albeit an extremely accurate one) of how many of the total claims are invalid. The risk in this case was reduced, though, by the fact that the proof-of-claim form that the district court required each class member to submit in order to opt into the class required the claimant to certify under penalty of perjury that the information provided was true and correct. Hilao's interest in the use of the statistical method, on the other hand, is enormous, since adversarial resolution of each class member's claim would pose insurmountable practical hurdles. The "ancillary" interest of the judiciary in the procedure is obviously also substantial, since 9,541 individual adversarial determinations of claim validity would clog the docket of the district court for years. Under the balancing test set forth in *Mathews* and *Doehr*, the procedure used by the district court did not violate due process. . . .

The judgment of the district court is therefore affirmed.

■   RYMER, Circuit Judge, concurring in part and dissenting in part.

Because I believe that determining causation as well as damages by inferential statistics instead of individualized proof raises more than "serious questions" of due process, I must dissent from Part IX of the majority opinion. Otherwise, I concur.

Here's what happened: Hilao's statistical expert, James Dannemiller, created a computer database of the abuse of each of the 10,059 victims based on what they said in a claim form that assumed the victim's torture. Although Dannemiller would have said that 384 claims should be examined to achieve generalizability to the larger population of 10,059 victims within 5 percentage points at a 95% confidence level, he decided that only 136 randomly selected claims would be required in light of the "anticipated validity" of the claim forms and testimony at the trial on liability that the number of abuses was about 10,000.

He selected three independent sample sets of 242 (by random selection but eliminating duplicates). Hilao's counsel then tried to contact and hold hearings or depositions with each of the claimants on the first list, but when attempts to contact a particular claimant proved fruitless, the same number in the next list was used. . . .

The persons culled through this process went to Manilla to testify at a deposition (which Dannemiller thought was "remarkable"). He opined that "this random selection method in determining the percentage of valid claims was fair to the Defendant" as "[a] random selection method of a group of 9541 individuals is more accurate than where each individual is contacted." Further, the statistician observed that "[t]he cost and time required to do 9541 would be overwhelming and not justified when greater precision can and was achieved through sampling." Finally, he concluded that "the procedures followed conformed to the standards of inferential statistics and therefore . . . the injuries of the 137 claimants examined are representative of the 9541 victims."

In accordance with the "computer-generated plan developed by James Dannemiller," the Special Master oversaw the taking of the 137 depositions in the Philippines. Based on a review of the deposition transcripts of the 137 randomly selected victim claims, and a review of the claims, the Special Master found that 131 were valid within the definitions which the court gave to the jury; the Philippine military or para-military were involved in the abuse of the valid claims; and the abuse occurred during the period 1972 through February 1986. As a result, he recommended the amount of compensatory damages to be awarded to the valid 131 claimants, and for the entire class based on the average awards for torture, for summary execution . . ., and disappearance . . . . His report indicates that "for all three categories, moral damages as a proximate result of defendants' wrongful acts or omissions, PHIL. CIV. CODE §§ 2216, 2217 were weighed into the compensation."

Thus, causation and $766 million compensatory damages for nearly 10,000 claimants rested on the opinion of a statistical expert that the selection method in determining valid claims was fair to the Estate and more accurate than individual testimony; Hilao's counsel's contact with the randomly selected victims until they got 137 to be deposed; and the Special Master's review of transcripts and finding that the selected victims had been tortured, summarily executed or disappeared, that the Philippine military was "involved," that the abuse occurred during the relevant period, and that moral damages occurred as a proximate result of the Estate's wrongful acts.

This leaves me "with a profound disquiet," as Judge Higginbotham put it in *In re Fibreboard Corp.*, 893 F.2d 706, 710 (5th Cir. 1990). Although I cannot point to any authority that says so, I cannot believe that a summary review of transcripts of a selected sample of victims who were able to be deposed for the purpose of inferring the type of abuse, by whom it was inflicted, and the amount of damages proximately caused thereby, comports with fundamental notions of due process.

Even in the context of a class action, individual causation and individual damages must still be proved individually. . . . Sterling v. Velsicol Chem. Corp., 855 F.2d 1188, 1200 (6th Cir. 1988).

. . . If due process in the form of a real prove-up of causation and damages cannot be accomplished because the class is too big or to do so would take too long, then (as the Estate contends) the class is unmanageable and should not have been certified in the first place.

. . . I think that due process dictates the choice: a real trial. I therefore dissent.

CIMINO V. RAYMARK INDUSTRIES, INC.

151 F.3d 297 (5th Cir. 1998)

■ GARWOOD, Circuit Judge.

Before us are appeals and cross-appeals in personal injury and wrongful death damage suits against several manufacturers of asbestos-containing insulation products and some of their suppliers, the district court's jurisdiction being based on diversity of citizenship and the governing substantive law being that of Texas. This is the same set of cases addressed in *In re Fibreboard*, 893 F.2d 706 (5th Cir. 1990), but the judgments now before us result from a trial plan modified following that decision. Principally at issue on this appeal is the validity of that modified trial plan.

The district court originally consolidated the some 3,031 such cases then pending in the Beaumont Division of the Eastern District of Texas for trial of certain common issues under Fed. R. Civ. P. 42(a) and also certified a class action under Fed. R. Civ. P. 23(b)(3), the class generally consisting of the insulation and construction workers, their survivors and household members . . . . [T]he trial plan ultimately implemented after *Fibreboard* consisted of three phases, generally described as follows. Phase I comprised a complete jury trial of the entire individual cases of the ten class representatives and also a class-wide determination of issues of product defectiveness, warning, and punitive damages (including a multiplier as to each defendant). Phase II, which was to address exposure on a craft and job site basis, was dispensed with on the basis of a stipulation. In phase III, 160 different individual cases ("sample cases"), some from each of the five different allegedly asbestos-related diseases included in the entire group of underlying cases, were tried to two other juries to determine only each of those individual sample case plaintiffs' respective actual damages from their asbestos-related disease. Thereafter, and following a one-day bench hearing on the basis of which the district court determined that in each disease category the 160 sample cases were reliably representative of the cases involving the like disease among the remaining some 2,128 cases,[2] the court ruled that each of these remaining 2,128 cases (the "extrapolation cases") would be assigned by the court to one of the five disease categories and each would be entitled to judgment based on an amount of actual damages equal to the average of the verdicts rendered in those of the 160 sample cases involving the same disease category. Punitive damages in each case would be essentially based on the phase I verdict.

By the time of the [appeal, most defendants had either settled or gone into bankruptcy. Only Pittsburgh Corning Corp. (Pittsburgh Corning) and Asbestos Corporation, Limited (ACL) remained.]

Judgment was entered against ACL in only two of the ten class representative cases (and in none of either the phase III sample cases or the

---

2. By the time of the phase I trial, the original 3,031 total cases had been reduced to 2,298 by settlement, severance, or dismissal.

extrapolation cases). Judgment was actually entered against Pittsburgh Corning in a total of 157 cases, consisting of 9 of the class representative phase I cases, 143 of the phase III sample cases, and 5 of the extrapolation cases (1 from each of the 5 different diseases included in the class). In these 157 cases, Pittsburgh Corning has been cast in judgment for a total of approximately $69,000,000.[6] ...

Pittsburgh Corning's appeal ... challeng[es] the implemented *Cimino* trial plan as a whole, particularly its asserted failure to properly try and determine individual causation and, in the five extrapolation cases, damages also, as to any plaintiffs other than the class representatives, assertedly contrary to our decision in *Fibreboard* and Texas substantive law and in derogation of Pittsburgh Corning's Seventh Amendment and Due Process rights . . . .

I.

PITTSBURGH CORNING APPEAL

. . .

1. *Trial Plan*

[The *Cimino* trial plan initially adopted by the district court, which *Fibreboard* rejected, called for three phases. In phase I, the jury was to decide general issues of liability, such as defectiveness and negligence. In phase II, the same jury was to decide the percentage of plaintiffs in the class exposed to each defendant's products and the percentage of claims barred by limitations and other defenses, and was then to determine a lump sum amount of actual damages for each disease category for all plaintiffs in the class. The jury in this phase was also to determine liability and damages for each of the eleven class representatives individually, as well as for thirty illustrative plaintiffs, fifteen chosen by the defense and fifteen by plaintiffs. It was also to hear expert testimony regarding the total actual damages of the class; the expert testimony was to be based, among other things, on questionnaires filled out by all class members and other discovery, including forty-five-minute oral depositions of class members taken by defendants. In phase III, to be non-jury, the court would distribute the awarded damages among the individual class members.

[*Fibreboard* found "no impediment to the trial of Phase I," 893 F.2d at 712, but it invalidated the balance of the plan invalid because it "infringe[d] upon the dictates of *Erie* that we remain faithful to the law of Texas, and upon the separation of powers between the judicial and legislative

6. Pittsburgh Corning asserts, without dispute, that the orders for judgment in the remaining some 2,123 extrapolation cases (in which judgments have not been entered) call for judgments against Pittsburgh Corning in the approximate total amount of $1,300,000,000 for actual damages only, excluding prejudgment interest and punitive damages.

branches," *id.* at 711. *Fibreboard* noted that, under Texas law, proof of individual causation was required. But "statistical estimates deal only with general causation, for 'population-based probability estimates do not speak to a probability of causation in any one case; the estimate of relative risk is a property of the studied population, not of an individual's case.'" *Id.* at 712.

[After remand, the district court went back to the drawing board, essentially retaining the phase I trial, but adding in the claims of the ten class representatives. After an eight-week trial, a jury found the appellants liable in phase I, and further found that Pittsburgh Corning should pay a multiplier of three times actual loss in punitive damages. The jury also found that, for each of the nine class-representative cases resulting in a plaintiffs' verdict, Pittsburgh Corning's causation should be fixed at 20%, with the remainder divided among the other defendants or the plaintiffs' contributory negligence.

[After the phase II trial became unnecessary when the parties stipulated that some of their products had been used at each of twenty-two worksites during some of the relevant time periods, the trial court moved to phase III. Having determined that, if it conducted a series of wave trials (with ten in each wave per week), trial of all the remaining cases would require four-and-a-half years to complete, the trial court therefore submitted individual damage cases of a statistically significant, randomly selected sample from each of the five disease categories known to be associated with asbestos. The court determined that 160 plaintiffs in total (with more of the cases selected from the more serious but less common disease categories) constituted a representative sample.

[The trial judge used two juries, each of which heard five common days of medical testimony and then heard specific evidence in about eighty cases. The juries were instructed to assume that the plaintiffs had sufficient exposure to asbestos; for the most part, evidence of any individual claimant's actual exposure to Pittsburgh Corning's asbestos or the amount of that exposure was not allowed, and the issue of whether a given plaintiff's exposure to Pittsburgh Corning's asbestos was a cause of injury was neither litigated nor determined. Nor were any matters concerning any individual sample plaintiff's past connection with any particular worksite or craft either litigated or determined.

[The phase III trial lasted three months, involved more than 560 witnesses and 6,100 exhibits totaling 577,000 pages, and generated more than 25,300 pages of transcripts. Four judges and three magistrate judges were involved. The phase III jury verdicts included 12 zero verdicts, and the district court ordered remittiturs in 35 of these cases. Each of the 160 sample plaintiffs then received as his or her damages the amount of the jury's verdict. The trial judge observed at the end of these trials that, "[i]f all that is accomplished by this is the closing of 169 cases, then it was not worth the effort and will not be repeated." Cimino v. Raymark Indus., Inc., 751 F. Supp. 649, 653 (E.D. Tex. 1990).

[Therefore, after a one-day hearing, the district court decided to extrapolate the results of these judgments to the remaining 2,128 cases.

After factoring in the zero verdicts and the remittiturs, he then calculated the average of the award granted to the sample cases in that category: mesothelioma, $1,224,333; lung cancer, $545,200; other cancer, $917,785; asbestosis, $543,783; and pleural disease, $558,900. He then proposed to assign each of the 2,128 cases to one of these categories, to award the average amount for that category to each plaintiff, to reduce the award to 20% (to account for Pittsburgh Corning's causal contribution, and to multiply the result by three to determine Pittsburgh Corning's punitive damages. In order to set up the issue for appeal, he entered judgment in the cases of the 10 class representatives, the 160 sample cases, and 5 of the 2,128 extrapolation cases. Pittsburgh Corning filed appeals; in total, 143 individually tried and 5 extrapolation cases remained alive on appeal.

[Counsel for the plaintiffs consented to the trial procedure.]

2. *Analysis*

As noted, Pittsburgh Corning attacks the *Cimino* trial plan, as it did at all times below, principally on the basis that it fails to properly try and determine individual causation, and in the extrapolation cases also fails to properly try and determine individual damages, as to any plaintiffs other than the ten class representatives whose individual cases were fully tried in phase I. Pittsburgh Corning asserts in this connection, among other things, that these aspects of the trial plan are contrary to *Fibreboard*, impose liability and damages where they would not be imposed under Texas substantive law, and invade its Seventh Amendment and due process rights. Although we do not separately address the due process contention as such, we conclude that the *Cimino* trial plan is invalid in these respects, necessitating reversal of all the phase III sample case judgments as well as the five extrapolation case judgments before us.

We begin by stating some very basic propositions. These personal injury tort actions for monetary damages are "a prototypical example of an action at law, to which the Seventh Amendment applies." The Seventh Amendment applies notwithstanding that these are diversity cases. But because these are diversity cases, the Rules of Decision Act, 28 U.S.C. § 1652, and *Erie R.R. v. Tompkins*, 304 U.S. 64 (1938), with its seeming constitutional underpinning, mandate that the substantive law applied be that of the relevant state, here Texas. . . .

None of the foregoing is or can be altered by the utilization of Fed. R. Civ. P. 23(b)(3) or Fed. R. Civ. P. 42(a). . . . [T]his Court has long held that the applicability of the Seventh Amendment is not altered simply because the case is Rule 23(b)(3) class action. *Ala. v. Blue Bird Body Co., Inc.*, 573 F.2d 309, 318 (5th Cir. 1978).

Similarly, use of Rule 23(b)(3) or 42(a) does not alter the required elements which must be found to impose liability and fix damages (or the burden of proof thereon) or the identity of the substantive law — here that of Texas — which determines such elements. We squarely so held in *Fibreboard*. And the [R]ules [E]nabling [A]ct, 28 U.S.C. § 2072 likewise mandates that conclusion. As we said in *Blue Bird Body Co.*, 573 F.2d at 317-18:

> This Circuit has also explained that the meaning of liability for antitrust purposes does not change simply because a trial is bifurcated under Fed. R. Civ. P. 42(b). . . . [B]ifurcation in no way diminishes the requirement that a plaintiff show some evidence that a violation caused him injury before a defendant is found liable. . . .

> Just as the meaning of liability does not vary because a trial is bifurcated, the requisite proof also in no way hinges upon whether or not the action is brought on behalf of a class under Rule 23. It is axiomatic that a procedural rule cannot "abridge, enlarge, or modify any substantive right."

Nor is deviation from these settled principles authorized because these are asbestos cases whose vast numbers swamp the courts. . . .

When, after *Fibreboard*, the district court adopted the present trial plan, it initially justified doing so on the basis of its conclusion that "the Texas Supreme Court, if faced with the facts of this case, would apply a collective liability theory, such as the Court's plan, to an asbestos consolidated action." . . . We are compelled to reject the district court's conclusion . . . . To begin with, it is contrary to *Fibreboard*, which plainly holds that under Texas substantive law causation of plaintiff's injury by defendant's product and plaintiff's resultant damages must be determined as to "individuals, not groups." . . . No Texas appellate decision or statute subsequent to *Fibreboard* casts doubt on the correctness of its reading of Texas law. . . .

Thus, the question becomes: did the implemented trial plan include a litigated determination, consistent with the Seventh Amendment, of the Texas-law mandated issues of whether, as to each individual plaintiff, Pittsburgh Corning's product was a cause of his complained-of condition and, if so, the damages that plaintiff suffered as a result.

We turn first to the phase III plaintiffs. In these cases, the trial plan was adequately individualized and preserved Seventh Amendment rights with respect to each individual's actual damages from an asbestos-related disease. However, it was not designed or intended to, and did not, provide any trial or any determination of whether a Pittsburgh Corning product was a cause of that disease. It was strictly a damages trial as to those individual plaintiffs. The stipulation — not entered into until midway through phase III — established merely that "some" individuals working in each of the listed crafts, "during" each of the four decades 1942-1982 and at each of the twenty-two worksites, "were exposed to asbestos" with "sufficient length and intensity to cause pulmonary asbestosis of varying degrees" and that "an asbestos-containing product of Pittsburgh Corning Corporation was present during the decades 1962-1982 at the specified worksites." It was expressly not stipulated "that any members of the various crafts at the various worksites had the same exposure to any products," or "that any such individuals had the same susceptibility to asbestos-related diseases in the various crafts and worksites," or that "any individual plaintiff was in fact exposed to injurious quantities of asbestos from the products of any defendant." Phase III did not litigate or determine whether or to what extent any of the one hundred sixty individual plaintiffs was exposed to Pittsburgh Corning's — or any other defendant's — asbestos, or was exposed to asbestos at any of the twenty-two worksites, or whether any such exposure was in fact a cause of that plaintiff's illness or disease. Nor did phase III litigate or determine either any individual plaintiff's past connection with any particular worksite or craft, or whether or to what extent such individual was exposed to asbestos otherwise than at any of the specified worksites. Indeed, for the most part exposure evidence was not allowed and the jury was instructed to assume sufficient exposure. Nor did phase III either litigate or determine whether or to what extent asbestos exposure, either generally or to the product of any particular defendant, was uniform or similar for members of any given craft at any one or more of the specified worksites.

. . . Pittsburgh Corning tendered evidence that [some of the worksites covered] several square miles and indicating that at refineries, shipyards, and other installations asbestos exposure levels were not uniform at the site or throughout a craft or within a decade or between decades, and that most individuals employed at the twenty-two worksites did not have sufficient exposure to cause asbestosis. Also so tendered was evidence indicating that exposure to asbestos below some level would not produce asbestosis and even above that level risks remain very low until a multiple of five or ten or twenty times the threshold level is reached; that not all those exposed to asbestos in substantial quantities and for protracted periods of time develop asbestosis; that asbestosis develops in "a relatively small percentage of patients with significant asbestos exposure"; and, that although there is a dose response relationship — the more exposure the more risk, the less, the less risk — respecting asbestosis, nevertheless the effect of the same exposure is not the same as between different individuals and "two similarly exposed asbestos workers with exactly the same asbestos historical exposure can go on to have in one case asbestosis and the other case no lung problems." . . .

The district court . . . justified its trial plan by reliance on *Pettway v. American Cast Iron Pipe Co.*, 494 F.2d 211, 258-63 (5th Cir. 1974), where, in a Title VII Rule 23(b)(2) class action, we stated that back pay could be awarded on a class-wide basis, using average rates of pay and approximations, and did not require an individual plaintiff by individual plaintiff approach. However, *Pettway* is inapplicable here, for each of several reasons. In the first place, Title VII actions are entirely equitable actions and back pay awards therein are strictly equitable remedies . . . . Thus, in *Pettway* there was no Seventh Amendment right to jury trial. Here, by contrast, we have personal injury damage suits, the protypical Seventh Amendment case. In the second place, *Pettway* involved only federal law, and hence this Court was not constrained by the Rules of Decision Act and *Erie*, as it is here. . . .

Nor do we consider that *In re Chevron U.S.A., Inc.*, 109 F.3d 1016 (5th Cir. 1997) [*supra* p. 1048], justifies the instant trial plan. . . . While the majority opinion (one judge specially concurred) contains language generally looking with favor on the use of bellwether verdicts when shown to be statistically representative, this language is plainly dicta, certainly insofar as it might suggest that representative bellwether verdicts could properly be used to determine individual causation and damages for other plaintiffs. To begin with, no such question was before this Court, as the trial plan contemplated that individual causation and damages issues would not be controlled by the thirty individual bellwether verdicts, which would be used to encourage settlement. Moreover, what we did — our holding — was to prevent any preclusive use of the unitary trial results (whether for general causation or individual causation or otherwise) in cases other than those of the thirty selected plaintiffs. . . . Finally, the majority opinion in *In Re Chevron U.S.A.* does not even cite *Fibreboard*, or the Seventh Amendment (or discuss the right to jury trial), and does not refer to the Texas substantive law elements of liability and damages in the matter before it. . . .

In *Hilao v. Estate of Marcos*, 103 F.3d 767 (9th Cir. 1996) [*supra* p. 1058], a divided panel of the Ninth Circuit in a rule 23(b)(3) class action permitted recoverable tort damages to be determined in a lump sum for the entire class. *Hilao* was a suit under the Alien Tort Claims Act, and the Court essentially applied substantive principles of federal or international "common law." The majority distinguished *Fibreboard* on the basis that there "the proposed procedure worked a change in the parties' substantive rights under Texas law that was barred by the *Erie* doctrine." By the same token, *Hilao* is distinguishable here; it did not operate under the constraints of the Rules of Decision Act or *Erie*; the present case, by contrast, does operate under those constraints. If *Hilao* is not thus distinguishable it is simply contrary to *Fibreboard*, which binds us and which in our opinion is in any event correct. Further, *Hilao* did not address — and there was apparently not presented to it any contention concerning — the Seventh Amendment. Finally, we find ourselves in agreement with the thrust of the dissenting opinion there.

In sum, as *Fibreboard* held, under Texas law causation must be determined as to "individuals, not groups." And, the Seventh Amendment gives the right to a jury trial to make that determination. There was no such trial determination made, and no jury determined, that exposure to Pittsburgh Corning's products was a cause of the asbestos disease of any of the one hundred sixty phase III plaintiffs. Nor does the stipulation determine or establish that. Accordingly, the judgments in all the one hundred forty-three phase III cases before us must be reversed and remanded.

We turn now to the extrapolation cases. As to the matter of individual causation, it is obvious that the conclusion we have reached in respect to the phase III cases applies a fortiori to the extrapolation cases. In the extrapolation cases there was no trial and no jury determination that any individual plaintiff suffered an asbestos-related disease. Indeed, in the extrapolation cases there was no trial at all — by jury or otherwise — and there was no evidence presented. So, our holding as to the phase III cases necessarily requires reversal of the judgments in the five extrapolation cases before us.

As to the matter of actual damages, the extrapolation cases are likewise fatally defective. Unlike the phase III cases, in the extrapolation cases there was neither any sort of trial determination, let alone a jury determination, nor even any evidence, of damages. The district court considered that these deficiencies were adequately compensated for by awarding each extrapolation case plaintiff who alleged an asbestos-related disease an amount of actual damages equal to the average of the awards made in the phase III cases for plaintiffs claiming the same category of disease. This plainly contravenes *Fibreboard*'s holding that under the substantive law of Texas recoverable damages are the "wage losses, pain and suffering, and other elements of compensation" suffered by each of the several particular plaintiffs as "individuals, not groups." We also observe in this connection that none of the experts at the extrapolation hearing purported to say that the damages suffered by the phase III plaintiffs in a given disease category (whether as disclosed by the phase III evidence or as found by the jury) were to any extent representative of the damages suffered by the extrapolation plaintiffs in the same disease category. The procedure also violates Pittsburgh Corning's Seventh Amendment right to have the amount of the legally recoverable damages fixed and determined by a jury. The only juries that spoke to actual damages, the phase I and III juries, received evidence only of the damages to the particular plaintiffs before them, were called on to determine only, and only determined, each of those some one hundred seventy particular plaintiffs' actual damages individually and severally (not on any kind of a group basis), and were not called on to determine, and did not determine or purport to determine, the damages of any other plaintiffs or group of plaintiffs. We have held that "inherent in the Seventh Amendment guarantee of a trial by jury is the general right of a litigant to have only one jury pass on a common issue of fact." *Blue Bird Body Co.*, 573 F.2d at 318. This requires that if separate trial are ordered, the separately tried issues must be "distinct and separable from the others." *Id.* By the same token, where the issues to be separately tried are separable and distinct, the Seventh Amendment rights of the parties are preserved as to both sets of issues. . . . It necessarily follows from these principles that the jury's phase III findings of the actual damages of each of the individual phase III plaintiffs cannot control the determination of, or afford any basis for denial of Pittsburgh-Corning's Seventh Amendment rights to have a jury determine, the distinct and separable issues of the actual damages of each of the extrapolation plaintiffs.

We conclude that the extrapolation case judgments, as well as the phase III judgments, are fatally flawed, are contrary to the dictates of *Fibreboard*, and contravene Pittsburgh-Corning's Seventh Amendment rights. We do not act in ignorance or disregard of the asbestos crises. In *Amchem Products, Inc. v. Windsor*, 521 U.S. 591, 598 (1997) [*supra* p. 493], the Supreme Court called attention to the report of the Judicial Conference's Ad Hoc Committee on Asbestos Litigation, stating that "Real reform, the report concluded, required federal legislation creating a national asbestos-dispute resolution scheme." . . . Nevertheless, the Court refused to stretch the law to fill the gap resulting from congressional inaction. As we said in *Fibreboard*, federal courts must remain faithful to *Erie* and must maintain "the separation of powers between the judicial and legislative branches." . . .

We accordingly reverse the judgments before us in all the one hundred forty-three phase III cases and in all the five extrapolation cases, and those one hundred forty-eight cases are remanded for further proceedings not inconsistent herewith.

[The court then held that the award of punitive damages against Pittsburgh Corning in the class-representative cases was warranted, and addressed other issues raised by Pittsburgh Corning, the plaintiffs on a cross-appeal, and the appeal of ACL.]

■ GARZA, Circuit Judge, specially concurring.

. . . [A]lthough the procedure outlined above does not satisfy the demands of Texas law requiring individual determinations of damages, the parties should take notice of these figures as representative of an appropriate settlement range within each disease category. Such notice is particularly advisable for Pittsburgh Corning, against whom the phase I jury awarded a three to one punitive damages multiplier (i.e., $3.00 of punitive damages for every $1.00 of actual damages).

Notes

1. The concept of trial by statistics is, in our opinion, one of the central matters in this book. It assures the like (indeed, the identical) treatment of similarly situated claimants, but it does so without any individualized participation in the lawsuit that determines the plaintiffs' rights and without any accommodation of the unique positions of individual parties. It suggests the single most promising way in which large numbers of cases can be tried, thus making aggregation in a single proceeding feasible. Whether this result is a good one can depend on your perspective about the value of aggregation; conversely, your perspective on aggregation likely helps to shape your view about trial by statistics.

2. In a pair of cases decided between *Fibreboard* and *Cimino*, the Fifth Circuit seemed to backtrack on the spirit, if not the letter, of *Fibreboard*. In *Watson v. Shell Oil Co.*, 979 F.2d 1014 (5th Cir. 1992), the court allowed a jury to determine the proper ration of punitive damages to compensatory damages for a class of 18,000 based on the trial of twenty sample cases. The Fifth Circuit granted rehearing en banc in *Watson*, 990 F.2d 805 (5th Cir. 1993), but the case settled. *See* In re Shell Oil Refinery, 155 F.R.D. 552 (E.D. La. 1993). Then, as we have seen, *In re Chevron U.S.A., Inc.*, 109 F.3d 1016, 1021 (5th Cir. 1997) [*supra* p. 1048], suggested

in dicta that preclusive effect could attach to the findings of a trial that contained a representative sample of the plaintiffs. *Chevron* was authored by Judge Parker, who had designed the *Cimino* trial plan before he was appointed to the Fifth Circuit. (*Cimino* was pending in the court of appeals for more than seven years.) *Cimino* rather decisively closed the door on the extrapolation approach, at least for state-law claims involving juries.

3. Also intervening between *Fibreboard* and *Cimino* was *Hilao*, which upheld a trial plan that was based on the trial plan in *Cimino*. In several ways, however, the *Hilao* plan was more radical than *Cimino*'s plan: It used a judicial adjunct to advise the jury on appropriate damage awards, it authorized a lump-sum jury award to non-sample plaintiffs, and it accepted a 95% (as opposed to 99% for most categories in *Cimino*) confidence level that the actual verdicts would have fallen within the sample's range.

4. *Hilao* and *Cimino* are ships passing in the night. *Hilao* addressed only the question of due process; *Cimino* addressed only the questions of the Seventh Amendment and *Erie*. Because *Hilao* involved federal law, the estate could not make an *Erie* challenge, and it abandoned on appeal the Seventh Amendment challenge that it made in the district court. *See* In re Estate of Ferdinand E. Marcos Human Rights Litig., 910 F. Supp. 1460, 1468-69 (D. Haw. 1995) (rejecting the Seventh Amendment argument).

5. The due process analysis in *Hilao* was influenced by a well-known article. *See* Michael J. Saks and Peter David Blanck, *Justice Improved: The Unrecognized Benefits of Aggregation and Sampling in the Trial of Mass Torts*, 44 STAN. L. REV. 815, 827 (1992). Professors Saks and Blanck strongly advocated aggregate procedures because they better comported with both the instrumental values in the due process clause and non-instrumental values such as the appearance of fairness, equality, predictability, transparency, rationality, revelation, and participation. The authors further argued that aggregate procedures are more accurate and more likely to provide both distributive and procedural justice to long queues of claimants than individual trials. *Id.* at 826-39. To ensure that these goals are met, they recommended that the random sampling be performed accurately, that the sampling groups be designed appropriately, and that attention be paid to the appropriate number of juries to use in order to assure a more accurate set of verdicts. *Id.* at 841-50. In this regard they were critical of *Cimino*'s award of the actual verdicts to the 160 randomly selected plaintiffs; they thought that these plaintiffs should have received the average award for the entire subgroup. *Id.* at 849.

Hilao picks up on only one strand of this multi-layered analysis: the *Mathews v. Eldridge* test for due process. The *Mathews* test is essentially an economic-efficiency calculus; it ignores a range of other values that are also often understood to inhere in the idea of "due process" — including the notion of individual, adversarial participation at trial. Is a judge capable of balancing the plaintiffs' due process interest in a remedy, the plaintiffs' and defendant's due process interest in accurate individualized outcomes, and the court's interest in expeditious resolutions? Are these judgments better made through the legislative and administrative processes? How different are the trial plans in *Cimino* and *Hilao* from the mass-tort equivalent of an administrative worker's compensation system?

6.   How strong is the Seventh Amendment argument in *Cimino*? Does the jury-trial right contain not only a guarantee of a lay factfinder but also a guarantee of a trial method consonant with the individualized adversarial approach of the common law?

7.   *Hialo* and *Cimino* are far from the last words on using statistical sampling to prove issues that would be difficult or impossible to prove on an individualized basis. Consider the following three cases.

IN RE SIMON II LITIGATION

211 F.R.D. 86 (E.D.N.Y. 2002), *vacated and remanded,*
407 F.3d 125 (2d Cir. 2005) [*supra* p. 396]

See supra p. 971

McLAUGHLIN V. AMERICAN TOBACCO CO.

522 F.3d 215 (2d Cir. 2008)

■   WALKER, Circuit Judge.

While redressing injuries caused by the cigarette industry is "one of the most troubling . . . problems facing our Nation today," not every wrong can have a legal remedy, at least not without causing collateral damage to the fabric of our laws. Plaintiffs' putative class action suffers from an insurmountable deficit of collective legal or factual questions. Their claims are brought as based in fraud under the Racketeer Influenced and Corrupt Organizations Act (RICO), 18 U.S.C. §§ 1961-1968, but under RICO, each plaintiff must prove reliance, injury, and damages. . . . Rule 23 is not a one-way ratchet, empowering a judge to conform the law to the proof. We therefore reverse the order of the district court and decertify the class.

BACKGROUND

Plaintiffs, a group of smokers allegedly deceived — by defendants' marketing and branding — into believing that "light" cigarettes ("Lights") were healthier than "full-flavored" cigarettes, sought and were granted class certification. Schwab v. Philip Morris USA, Inc., 449 F. Supp. 2d 992 (E.D.N.Y. 2006) (Weinstein, J.). Plaintiffs' suit is brought under RICO, with mail and wire fraud as the necessary predicate acts. The gravamen of plaintiffs' complaint is that defendants' implicit representation that Lights were healthier led them to buy Lights in greater quantity than they otherwise would have and at an artificially high price, resulting in plaintiffs' overpayment for cigarettes. Plaintiffs allege claims arising from their purchase of Lights from 1971, when defendants first introduced Lights, until the date on which trial commences.

[The plaintiffs sought to certify a Rule 23(b)(3) class action. The plaintiffs needed to prove reliance, causation, injury, and damages for each smoker in the class. Without a way to determine these issues in an aggregated fashion, a (b)(3) class action was in trouble; common questions did not predominate, and the class action was not as manageable. *Schwab* solved the problem by adopting a statistical-sampling methodology to prove each of these elements. Its argument for sampling was almost identical to the analysis that Judge Weinstein had used in two prior tobacco cases, *Blue Cross* and *Simon*, that we examined. *See supra* p. 971; p. 980, Note 3.]

DISCUSSION

I. *Elements of a Civil RICO Claim and the Predominance Requirement*

[The court of appeals held that the plaintiffs could not prove reliance, causation, or injury on a class-wide basis. Reliance required individualized proof because there was no indication that misrepresentations of the health properties of light cigarettes affected the market price of the companies that made the cigarettes; without such a "fraud on the market," "reliance is too individualized to admit of common proof." With respect to causation, the plaintiffs argued that they paid more for the cigarettes than they would have if they had known the true health properties of light cigarettes; and that the amount of overpayment could be determined from sampling the class. But the price of light cigarettes had not fallen after the true health effects of light cigarettes became known. Hence, although the plaintiffs' theory might apply to some class members, the court of appeals concluded that "the issue of loss causation, much like the issue of reliance, cannot be resolved by way of generalized proof." Finally, with respect to injury, the court of appeals said that "out-of-pocket losses cannot be shown by common evidence because they constitute an inherently individual inquiry: individual smokers would have incurred different losses depending on what they would have opted to do, but for defendants' misrepresentation." The court rejected two alternative theories to avoid this problem, noting that the dashed expectations of class members — in other words, the deprivation of the benefits of their bargains with the tobacco companies — were not an injury to "business or property," as RICO required. The court then turned to *Schwab*'s proposal to determine damages by means of a class action.]

II. *Calculation of Damages*

The district court concluded that plaintiffs could prove collective damages on a class-wide basis, and individual plaintiffs would then claim shares of this fund [based on the number of "light" cigarettes purchased in the relevant geographical area and time]. . . . But such "fluid recovery" has been forbidden in this circuit since *Eisen v. Carlisle & Jacquelin*, 479 F.2d

1005, 1008 (2d Cir. 1973). And while the fact that damages may have to be ascertained on an individual basis is not, standing alone, sufficient to defeat class certification, it is nonetheless a factor that we must consider in deciding whether issues susceptible to generalized proof "outweigh" individual issues.

We reject plaintiffs' proposed distribution of any recovery they might receive because it offends both the Rules Enabling Act and the Due Process Clause. The distribution method at issue would involve an initial estimate of the percentage of class members who were defrauded (and who therefore have valid claims). The total amount of damages suffered would then be calculated based on this estimate (and, presumably, on an estimate of the average loss for each plaintiff). But such an aggregate determination is likely to result in an astronomical damages figure that does not accurately reflect the number of plaintiffs actually injured by defendants and that bears little or no relationship to the amount of economic harm actually caused by defendants. This kind of disconnect offends the Rules Enabling Act, which provides that federal rules of procedure, such as Rule 23, cannot be used to "abridge, enlarge, or modify any substantive right." 28 U.S.C. § 2072(b).

Roughly estimating the gross damages to the class as a whole and only subsequently allowing for the processing of individual claims would inevitably alter defendants' substantive right to pay damages reflective of their actual liability. *See, e.g.,* In re Hotel Tel. Charges, 500 F.2d 86, 90 (9th Cir. 1974) (rejecting a fluid recovery argument because "allowing gross damages by treating unsubstantiated claims of class members collectively significantly alters substantive rights," in violation of the Rules Enabling Act); *Eisen,* 479 F.2d at 1019 ("[P]ossible recoveries run into astronomical amount [and] generate more leverage and pressure on defendants to settle . . . ."); *Schwab,* 449 F. Supp. 2d at 1272 ("A question under the Rules Enabling Act is posed by the danger of overcompensation inherent in the plaintiff's fluid distribution plan. It is possible that some claimants will benefit from the plaintiff class' recovery despite the fact that they did not rely on defendants' alleged misrepresentations regarding 'light' cigarettes and were not, therefore, injured in their business or property by defendants' actions."). We disagree with the district court's conclusion that "[t]he risk of . . . overcompensation can be limited by requiring proof through claim forms from claimants concerning the extent of their reliance during the distribution stage." *Schwab,* 449 F. Supp. 2d at 1272. Given that any residue would be distributed to the class's benefit on the basis of cy pres principles rather than returned to defendants, defendants would still be paying the inflated total estimated amount of damages arrived at under the first step of the fluid recovery analysis. Thus, even if defendants were able to avoid overcompensating individual plaintiffs, they would still be overpaying in the aggregate.

Moreover, in this case, the district court determined that "evidence of the percentage of the class which was defrauded and the amount of economic damages it suffered appears to be quite weak." It further concluded that "determin[ing] the impact of the fraud on the size of the market and its nature for damage purposes is a daunting enterprise even with the many proffered experts holding up their statistical lanterns to help in the search for the truth." Nevertheless, the district court believed that "the proof of acts of defendants and the various experts' opinions permit[ ] a finding of damages to the class with sufficient precision to allow a jury award." For the reasons stated above, we disagree, and we further note our skepticism that if statistical experts cannot with accuracy estimate the relevant figures, a jury could do so based on the testimony of those experts.

The district court's distribution scheme also raises serious due process concerns. As we explained in *Eisen*,

> if the "class as a whole" is or can be substituted for the individual members of the class as claimants, then the number of claims filed is of no consequence and the amount found to be due will be enormous. . . . Even if amended Rule 23 could be read so as to permit any such fantastic procedure, the courts would have to reject it as an unconstitutional violation of the requirement of due process of law.

479 F.2d at 1018. When fluid recovery is used to permit the mass aggregation of claims, the right of defendants to challenge the allegations of individual plaintiffs is lost, resulting in a due process violation. The Third Circuit properly observed in *Newton v. Merrill Lynch, Pierce, Fenner & Smith, Inc.* that "actual injury cannot be presumed, and defendants have the right to raise individual defenses against each class member." 259 F.3d 154, 191-92 (3d Cir. 2001). To be sure, this does not mean that defendants are "constitutionally entitled to compel a parade of individual plaintiffs to establish damages." In re Antibiotic Antitrust Actions, 333 F. Supp. 278, 289 (S.D.N.Y. 1971). However, when fluid recovery is used, as here, to mask the prevalence of individual issues, it is an impermissible affront to defendants' due process rights. . . .

In sum, because we find that numerous issues in this case are not susceptible to generalized proof but would require a more individualized inquiry, we conclude that the predominance requirement of Rule 23 has not been satisfied. We recognize that a court may employ Rule 23(c)(4) to certify a class as to common issues that do exist, "regardless of whether the claim as a whole satisfies Rule 23(b)(3)'s predominance requirement." Nevertheless, in this case, given the number of questions that would remain for individual adjudication, issue certification would not "reduce the range of issues in dispute and promote judicial economy." Certifying, for example, the issue of defendants' scheme to defraud, would not materially advance the litigation because it would not dispose of larger issues such as reliance, injury, and damages. We therefore decline plaintiffs' request for issue certification.

CONCLUSION

For the foregoing reasons, we reverse the judgment of the district court and order the class decertified.

IN RE PHARMACEUTICAL INDUSTRY AVERAGE WHOLESALE PRICE LITIGATION

582 F.3d 156 (1st Cir. 2009)

■ HOWARD, Circuit Judge.

AstraZeneca Pharmaceuticals LP ("AstraZeneca") appeals from the judgment of the district court, entered after a lengthy bench trial, of liability for unfair and deceptive business practices in violation of Massachusetts General Laws Chapter 93A ("Chapter 93A"). The district court found that AstraZeneca had caused the publication of false and inflated average wholesale prices ("AWPs"), a price used as a benchmark for various reimbursement plans, for its physician-administered drug Zoladex (goserelin acetate), thereby creating a windfall for the appellant's physician customers and causing injury to the government, insurers, and patients who were forced to pay inflated prices. AstraZeneca now brings a panoply of challenges to the district court's reasoning and result. Discerning no material factual or legal infirmity in the district court's disposition of the case, we affirm.

[This nationwide class action was a part of a multidistrict litigation composed of nearly one hundred AWP cases brought against more than forty pharmaceutical defendants. Plaintiffs included consumers, third-party payors ("TTPs"), and several states, counties, and cities. To manage the litigation, the district court structured the master consolidated class action into two separate tracks for purposes of class certification, summary judgment and trial. AstraZeneca was placed into "Track 1," the first group to proceed through trial. The district court then certified three classes: (1) a nationwide class of Medicare beneficiaries who made co-payments for Medicare Part B drugs ("Class 1"); (2) a Massachusetts class of third-party payors that provided MediGap insurance that reimbursed Medicare beneficiaries for their co-payments ("Class 2"); and (3) a Massachusetts class of customers and third-party payors that made payments based on AWP for (non-Medicare Part B) physician-administered drugs ("Class 3"). Only the latter two classes were involved in the appeal.

[At the summary-judgment stage, the district court found that AstraZeneca had inflated the AWP for Zoladex, whose price exceeded actual physician acquisition costs by as much as 169%, and then marketed these "mega-spreads" between the physician's acquisition costs and the AWP reimbursement benchmark to induce doctors to buy its drug based on the drug's profitability rather than its therapeutic benefits. The district court then awarded aggregate, class-wide damages to both Class 2 and Class 3. In a later order, the district court found that AstraZeneca's conduct as to Class 2 was knowing and willful, and awarded multiple damages; it declined, however, to make the same finding as to Class 3. The award against AstraZeneca was nearly $13,000,000.

[After holding that the district court was correct to find liability, the court turned to the propriety of awarding class-wide damages.]

VII. CLASS-WIDE JUDGMENT

The final issue presented by this appeal is whether the district court erred in entering a class-wide judgment, a decision that AstraZeneca argues impermissibly abridged its substantive rights and violated due process by depriving AstraZeneca of its opportunity to raise individual defenses against each class member. *See* Amchem Prods., Inc. v. Windsor, 521 U.S. 591, 612-13 (1997) (citing the Rules Enabling Act, 28 U.S.C. § 2072(b) for the proposition that Fed. R. Civ. P. 23 may not be used to "abridge, enlarge or modify any substantive right") [*supra* p. 493]. . . .

B. *Absent Class Members*

The gravamen of AstraZeneca's second challenge to the class-wide judgment is its contention that the district court erred in addressing only the knowledge of the named class representatives, particularly [Blue Cross Blue Shield of Massachusetts ("BCBS-MA")], when examining the TPPs' knowledge and expectations as to AWP inflation. Pointing to the "fact-specific" nature of the district court's analysis of the class representatives' knowledge and expectations, AstraZeneca argues that the district court should also have analyzed — and permitted discovery and inquiry by AstraZeneca into — the knowledge and expectations of absent class members, who AstraZeneca maintains may have had more knowledge than BCBS-MA did of Zoladex pricing. . . .

This argument, of course, is a familiar one in the context of class action lawsuits. It is beyond question that, under some circumstances, constitutional principles prohibit a court from relying on proof relating to the class representatives to make class-wide findings. But it is equally obvious that class-action litigation often requires the district court to extrapolate from the class representatives to the entire class . . . . The district court in this case determined that the class was adequately represented when it certified the class, and it carefully examined the representatives' knowledge and expectations as to spreads. As a general matter, this is precisely the kind of analysis that Rule 23 was designed to permit, and it would quickly undermine the class-action mechanism were we to find that a district court presiding over a class action lawsuit errs every time it allows for proof in the aggregate.

More specifically, the district court's aggregate determination as to knowledge and expectations was permissible and appropriate for two reasons. First, AstraZeneca . . . [was] allowed ample opportunity to depose TPPs prior to trial — in all, these defendants deposed roughly fifty TPPs, and multiple representatives from many of those. Despite this extensive discovery, AstraZeneca marshals no specific evidence on appeal to suggest that absent class member TPPs had knowledge or expectations that differed substantially from class representative BCBS-MA. . . .

Second, the district court's conclusions about industry knowledge and expectations were based on a careful analysis of the class representatives and on expert testimony that was properly admitted, and therefore it did not exhibit any of the evils paraded in AstraZeneca's brief with references to cases such as *Broussard v. Meineke Discount Muffler Shops, Inc.*, 155 F.3d 331, 343 (4th Cir. 1998) (reliance on a fictitious, composite plaintiff "divorced from any actual proof of damages" whereas North Carolina law required "reasonable certainty" about lost profits awards), and *Cimino v. Raymark Industries, Inc.*, 151 F.3d 297 (5th Cir. 1998) (extrapolating damages from personal injuries and death from a set of sample cases) [*supra* p. 1066].

Nor are we persuaded that this case has individualized circumstances similar to those at issue in *McLaughlin v. American Tobacco Co.*, 522 F.3d 215 (2d Cir. 2008), where the Second Circuit cast doubt on the use of common proof to establish reliance and causation among a class of smokers who had purchased "light" cigarettes over a thirty-seven year period. In that case, the Second Circuit expressed its concern that the class-member consumers may have chosen the product for a variety of reasons, such as personal preference, unrelated to the alleged misrepresentations implied in the term "light." Here, however, we harbor no such concerns about intractably payor-specific issues. The evidence in the record relating to the knowledge and expectations about AWP inflation and Zoladex pricing among TPPs is voluminous, and . . . the portions of the record cited by AstraZeneca as cause for concern contain strikingly consistent evidence as to each of the TPPs. We thus are not persuaded that the evidence of variation across the class members as to their knowledge and expectations about AWP inflation and Zoladex pricing demonstrates the existence of significant individualized issues in the first place, much less variations so significant as to raise concerns of a constitutional dimension.

C. *Aggregate Damages*

AstraZeneca's third challenge to the entry of a class-wide judgment is that the district court awarded aggregate damages "without any individualized determination of damages as to a single class member (including the named plaintiffs)," thereby violating AstraZeneca's "fundamental right" to defend against each class member's claim of injury and damages. In support of its argument that a "rough estimate" of damages is insufficient, AstraZeneca cites . . . *McLaughlin* for the proposition that the plaintiffs should have been required to prove that each class member was harmed by AstraZeneca's pricing practices. Requiring such proof, the company argues, ensures that AstraZeneca will pay damages reflective of its actual liability.

As to whether the plaintiffs adequately proved the class members' claims of injury, AstraZeneca [criticizes the methodology of Dr. Hartman, the plaintiffs' expert. This methodology was used to determine the size of the spreads that might trigger liability. The methodology], which included an examination of TPPs' (including class representative BCBS-MA's) testimony, data, and contracts, sufficiently incorporated individualized information about the class members to support the district court's decision to adopt it for the entire class.

AstraZeneca's criticisms of Dr. Hartman's damages calculation, however, merit further discussion. AstraZeneca alleges that Dr. Hartman's calculation fails to account for five factors: i) that fourteen Massachusetts TPPs and 23,000 consumers opted out of the class; ii) that those persons with flat co-payments were defined out of the class; iii) that some TPPs did not always reimburse based on AWP during the class period; iv) that some physicians did not bill patients for the co-payments; and v) that some physicians did not collect the co-payments that were billed. AstraZeneca asks us to review the district court's damages methodology for a violation of the company's due process rights, and of Federal Rule of Civil Procedure 23.

The use of aggregate damages calculations is well established in federal court and implied by the very existence of the class action mechanism itself. There is nothing about this case to suggest a contrary conclusion. Thus, to the extent that AstraZeneca argues that the district court's decision to use an aggregate damages methodology violated Rule 23 or the company's due process rights, AstraZeneca's challenge fails in the starting gate.

To the extent that AstraZeneca's arguments instead go to the question of whether Dr. Hartman's methodology was sufficiently reliable, *see* Daubert [v. Merrell Dow Pharms., Inc., 509 U.S. 579, 597 (1993)], we review the district court's ruling for an abuse of discretion, but we find none here. To begin, we note that none of AstraZeneca's first three purported errors in Dr. Hartman's damages calculations is severe enough to suggest that the district court abused its discretion in relying on it. As to the various parties who opted out of the class action, the number of opt-outs was a small fraction of the number of notices mailed: according to a signed declaration from the Notice and Administration Manager of Complete Claim Solutions, LLC, which was appointed as the Litigation Administrator below, nearly 45,000 notices were mailed to TPPs, and nearly 950,000 notices were mailed to consumers. In the scope of a gargantuan mailing effort such as this, the number of opt-outs, while large, clearly represents a very small percentage of the class. Even assuming arguendo that Dr. Hartman's analysis did indeed fail to account for parties who opted out, any imprecision that resulted was likely to be small. . . .

Similarly, we are unable to ascertain from AstraZeneca's brief (or from the record) how Dr. Hartman's alleged failure to take into account persons who paid a flat co-payment could have affected the reliability of his damages calculation. . . .

As to AstraZeneca's claim that some TPPs did not always reimburse based on AWP, the district court found to the contrary . . . .

Finally, AstraZeneca's two remaining challenges — that some physicians did not bill patients for co-payments, and that some physicians did not collect the co-payments that were billed — are also insufficient to prove an abuse of the district court's discretion. AstraZeneca provides no argument explaining how many co-payments went unbilled or uncollected, or what impact the resulting imprecision would have on the ultimate damages calculation. . . . [T]he district court was mindful of potential imprecision in the aggregate damages methodology when it imposed its award, yet decided that the imprecision, if any, was negligible. . . .

VIII. CONCLUSION

. . . Consequently, the rulings of the district court are affirmed.

Notes

1.   In *Simon*, Judge Weinstein rejected the defendants' due process, Seventh Amendment, and *Erie* arguments, which were also the arguments pressed in *Hialo* and *Cimino*. *See supra* p. 1075, Note 4. While also considering the due process argument, *McLaughlin* and *AWP Litigation* introduced another argument into the trial-by-statistics mix: the fidelity of such procedures to the Rules Enabling Act when sampling is joined with a Rule 23 class action to achieve an aggregation that results in greater exposure to liability than individual litigation would have achieved. Among the five principal cases concerning trial by statistics (*Hialo, Cimino, Simon, McLaughlin,* and *AWP Litigation*), there is disagreement regarding the validity of each and every one of these arguments.

2.   The Second Circuit overturned the class certification in *Simon* on grounds other than Judge Weinstein's decision to use sampling to prove the existence of fraud and its amount, and specifically declined to address the propriety of the sampling approach. In re Simon II Litig., 407 F.3d 125, 139-40 (2d Cir. 2005). It had previously upheld the decision to use sampling in another of Judge Weinstein's cases, in which insurers were seeking reimbursement for smoking-related medical expenses from the tobacco defendants. Blue Cross & Blue Shield of N.J., Inc. v. Philip Morris USA Inc., 344 F.3d 211, 225-28 (2d Cir. 2003).

In many ways, *AWP Litigation* is like *Blue Cross* because it involves claims by insurers who paid on vast numbers of claims; in other ways, it is like *McLaughlin* because it involves deceptive-practice claims by individual consumers. Should there be a difference in a court's receptivity to statistical sampling based on the character of the plaintiffs as large-scale market participants or single individuals?

3.   Can you distinguish *McLaughlin* from *AWP Litigation*? To test your distinction, consider that Judge Weinstein, undeterred by *McLaughlin*, has again resorted to sampling in a class action (composed of consumers and third-party payors) alleging overpayments for an antipsychotic drug. In re Zyprexa Prods. Liab. Litig., 253 F.R.D. 69, 188-91 (E.D.N.Y. 2008). One way in which Judge Weinstein sidestepped *McLaughlin* was to point out that a subsequent Supreme Court decision appeared to reject one of *McLaughlin*'s arguments regarding the need for proof of individual reliance in RICO cases. *See* Bridge v. Phoenix Bond & Indem. Co., 553 U.S. 639 (2008). In addition, Judge Weinstein indicated that the case involved an ascertainable actual loss (the difference between the amount paid for a

prescription and the amount that should have been paid), and that "fluid recovery" relief would be unnecessary in *Zyprexa* because each plaintiff could prove the amount of damages owed. Persuaded? If so, can you describe the rule that distinguishes a permissible trial by statistics to determine damages from an impermissible one?

4. Most courts continue to approach the trial-by-statistics idea with caution. For instance, *Arch v. American Tobacco Co.*, 175 F.R.D. 469, 493 (E.D. Pa. 1997), refused to certify a class because it was unmanageable. The district court rejected the *Hilao* approach as means of avoiding unmanageability because defendants did not consent to the use of a statistical approach and because the plaintiffs' injuries varied significantly. It further distinguished *Hilao* because the damages sought in *Hilao* exceeded assets of defendant. Note that each of *Arch*'s distinction of *Hilao* suggests a different rationale for its scope.

Likewise, in *Leverence v. PFS Corp.*, 532 N.W.2d 735 (Wis. 1995), occupants of 222 defective homes sued the company that negligently inspected the homes. Since the amount at stake in each case was small, the trial court adopted the *Cimino* plan of trying a sample of cases that generated a 95% confidence level and then applying the average verdict of the sample to the remaining cases. The Wisconsin Supreme Court reversed:

> [T]he aggregative procedure cannot be used, as it was here, in place of a party's right to a trial, unless all parties to the litigation consent. . . . [T]he right to a jury trial guaranteed by Art. 1, § 5 of the Wisconsin Constitution is not contingent upon (a) the amount of damages at stake in a given case or (b) the burden the litigation might place upon the court system. [*Id.* at 740.]

See also Kpadeh v. Emmanuel, 261 F.R.D. 687 (S.D. Fla. 2009) (rejecting *Hilao*).

On the other hand, the Ninth Circuit has recently suggested that *Hilao*'s trial-by-statistics approach could be used in a massive employment-discrimination claim seeking back pay. Dukes v. Wal-Mart, Inc., 509 F.3d 1168, 1191-93 (9th Cir. 2007), *reh'g granted*, 556 F.3d 919 (9th Cir. 2009).

5. The *Manual for Complex Litigation, Third* had suggested a series of approaches for resolving individual issues in mass-tort cases, one of which sounds a great deal like the lump-sum damage award rejected in *Fibreboard* and another of which was exactly the average-verdict approach of *Cimino*. It also recommended an approach akin to the *Hilao* plan, in which "a stipulated procedure [is used] to resolve individual claims according to a formula or by a hearing before an arbitrator, special master, or magistrate judge." MANUAL FOR COMPLEX LITIGATION, THIRD § 33.28 (1995). The most recent version of the *Manual*, however, takes a more cautious view of such approaches. MANUAL FOR COMPLEX LITIGATION, FOURTH § 22.93 (2004).

6. To what extent is the reluctance to use the trial-by-statistics approach substance-specific? Aggregate procedures for the award of relief

are more common in areas other than mass torts, especially in class actions. The oldest case of which we are aware is Union Carbide & Carbon Corp. v. Nisley, 300 F.2d 561, 589 (10th Cir. 1961), an antitrust case in which the trial plan called for a jury to decide liability issues as well as the formula for determining the damages suffered by each class member (i.e., the number of cents per pound that the defendants' conduct had caused the price of ore to drop). The trial judge then appointed a special master to determine the amount owed to each class member (calculated by multiplying the jury's formula times the amount of ore that, according to defendant's records, each class member sold to the defendant). In approving the plan, the court emphasized that any questions regarding the identity of class members or the amount of money due them would be resolved by a jury empaneled for that purpose. *Cf.* Tull v. United States, 481 U.S. 412 (1987) (holding that the Seventh Amendment does not require a jury to determine the amount of a statutory fine).

Likewise, in Long v. Trans World Airlines, Inc., 761 F. Supp. 1320 (N.D. Ill. 1991), which involved a labor dispute, the court limited discovery on damages to a sampling of class plaintiffs, despite the defendant's argument that it was entitled to individual discovery from each plaintiff. The court held that, because a class-wide damage award could be given, discovery of a random sample of plaintiffs was adequate. It distinguished *Fibreboard* in three ways: individual issues of causation predominated in *Fibreboard*, Texas law required individual proof, and the 41 plaintiffs in *Fibreboard* were not a random sample. *See also* Daniel v. Quail Int'l, Inc., 2010 WL 55941, at *1 (M.D. Ga. Jan. 5, 2010) (refusing to permit sampling of the damages of 15% of the members of an opt-in FLSA case when the entire class consisted of thirty-nine members and the plaintiffs "point to nothing in the record to demonstrate that [15%] is statistically significant" or that "individualized discovery of the Plaintiff class would raise sufficient efficiency concerns to justify representative discovery").

7. As we discussed in Chapter Eight, *see supra* pp. 971-81, statistical evidence is often introduced in American courts. Usually statistical evidence is used to prove a defendant's wrongful conduct (for instance, statistics used to prove a pattern of racial discrimination) or causation (for instance, statistics used to prove the cancer-causing potential of a chemical). This form of statistical evidence helps answer a critical issue that is in dispute ("Was there discrimination?" or "Was there causation?"). In cases like *Cimino* and *Hilao*, however, statistics are not used to answer a question in dispute; they are used to avoid answering the critical questions in dispute ("Is *this* plaintiff entitled to damages, and, if so, how much?"). Until "the average verdict" is the legal standard for the award of damages to all plaintiffs, the statistics in *Cimino* and *Hilao* answer no legally relevant question.

Granting this to be true, what is wrong with using procedural devices to push the substantive law in bold new directions? A trial by statistics would be a "real trial" if the relevant issue were group, rather than individual, harm. Besides, what is a "real trial," other than a bunch of procedures created by people long since dead to resolve a type of dispute that does not resemble modern mass controversies? Once we clear our head of nostalgia and tradition, don't aggregate procedures based on valid statistical methods make the most sense?

8.   Is it possible to form an adequate opinion about this last question without turning to core procedural values? Two of the values we have discussed throughout this book are adversarialism and equality. From an adversarial viewpoint, the lack of individual participation and control makes aggregate procedures dubious. From an equality viewpoint, the reaction is mixed. Trans-substantivism, which is one form of procedural equality, requires only that the same procedures be applied to all types of cases; it does not demand that the substantive outcome be identical in all cases. Moreover, although the similarity of procedural treatment accorded claimants in a trial by statistics meets the requirement of procedural equality, so do procedures that guarantee each plaintiff a one-on-one trial. What is troubling to the equalitarian assumption is the use of disparate procedures that result in different outcomes for similarly situated persons. Thus, Judge Parker's disparate treatment of the sample cases (which received their actual verdicts) and the remaining cases (which received the average of all verdicts) is difficult to defend. More broadly, the fact that other asbestos plaintiffs who could recover under Texas law received different procedures than the *Cimino* class plaintiffs is problematic.

9.   Procedural developments in complex litigation are often harbingers of developments in routine litigation. Are we about to enter a brave new world of collective trials in all cases? After all, we have (or could generate) excellent information about the average verdicts in cases involving car accidents, slip-and-falls, and medical malpractice. Why not award every plaintiff this average amount (perhaps periodically adjusting for inflation or by means of a few sample trials each year)? If we won't do that, then why would we allow trial by statistics?

10. Until now we have assumed that the factfinder is capable of understanding statistical evidence. Empirical data suggest that factfinders — including highly educated factfinders such as judges — routinely misunderstand statistical evidence even when it has been accurately explained to them. *See* William C. Thompson, *Are Juries Competent to Evaluate Statistical Evidence?* 52 LAW & CONTEMP. PROBS. 9 (Autumn 1989); Laurence H. Tribe, *Trial by Mathematics: Precision and Ritual in the Legal Process*, 84 HARV. L. REV. 1329 (1971) (stating that juries may overvalue statistical evidence); Michael J. Saks & Robert F. Kidd, *Human Information Processing and Adjudication: Trial by Heuristics*, 15 LAW & SOC'Y REV. 123 (1980-81) (critiquing Professor Tribe's argument and suggesting that juries undervalue or ignore statistical evidence). That's a telling argument against a trial by statistics, isn't it?

11. *AWP Litigation* briefly points out a critical matter in any statistical sampling: Such sampling requires expertise, and the testimony of the experts who sample or interpret the data must pass muster under Federal Rules of Evidence 702 and 703.

12. Trial by statistics has generated significant commentary. For a non-random sample of articles, see Laurens Walker & John Monahan, *Sampling Evidence at the Crossroads*, 80 S. CAL. L. REV. 969 (2007); Laurens Walker & John Monahan, *Sampling Liability*, 85 VA. L. REV. 329 (1999); Laurens Walker & John Monahan, *Sampling Damages*, 83 IOWA L. REV. 545 (1998); Robert G. Bone, *Statistical Adjudication: Rights, Justice, and Utility in a World of Process Scarcity*, 46 VAND. L. REV. 561 (1993).

3. Time Limits on Trial

In Chapter Eight, we encountered the use of early, firm deadlines on discovery as a way of keeping the discovery of information during the pretrial process within bounds. *See supra* p. 808. Here we consider the equivalent idea: imposing time limits on trial as a way of limiting the amount of information to which the factfinder is exposed.

MCI COMMUNICATIONS CORP. V. AMERICAN TELEPHONE AND TELEGRAPH CO.

708 F.2d 1081 (7th Cir. 1983)

■ CUDAHY, Circuit Judge.

In this extraordinary antitrust case, defendant American Telephone and Telegraph Company ("AT&T") appeals from a judgment in the amount of $1.8 billion, entered on a jury verdict, in a treble damage suit brought by plaintiffs MCI Communications Corporation and MCI Telecommunications Corporation (collectively "MCI") under section 4 of the Clayton Act, 15 U.S.C. § 15 (1976).

I. FACTS

. . .

The case was tried to a jury between February 6 and June 13, 1980. After completion of MCI's case in chief, the district court directed a verdict in favor of AT&T on seven of the twenty-two alleged acts of misconduct. The remaining fifteen charges — all based on section 2 of the Sherman Act — were submitted to the jury. A special verdict form required the jury to make a separate finding of liability as to each of the fifteen charges, but permitted the jury to award damages in a single lump sum, without apportioning MCI's claimed financial losses among AT&T's various lawful and unlawful acts. The jury found in favor of MCI on ten of the fifteen charges submitted, and awarded damages of $600 million . . . . The district court trebled this damage award, as required by section 4 of the Clayton Act, resulting in a judgment of $1.8 billion, exclusive of costs and attorneys' fees. . . .

VII. THE CONDUCT OF THE TRIAL

AT&T argues that the manner in which the district court presided over the case amounted to a denial of due process. AT&T complains of the court's . . . imposition of a time limit upon the parties' presentations . . . .

We . . . reject AT&T's argument that the district court did not allow AT&T sufficient time to present its case in an intelligible manner. Originally, AT&T predicted that it would take approximately eighteen months to try the case. Understandably chagrined, the district court directed the parties to submit lists of their witnesses and a summary of the testimony of each, together with a more precise estimate of the time required for trial. MCI's list named seventeen witnesses and predicted that it would require twenty-six days to present its case-in-chief. AT&T's list, by contrast, named 162 witnesses and described a minimum of twenty-one more by category. At that time, AT&T predicted that trial of the entire case would take eight to nine months. The district court reviewed those materials and only then imposed a twenty-six day time limit on the presentation of each side's case-in-chief.[130] The district court did not place a limit on the time allotted for rebuttal or surrebuttal. . . . On appeal, AT&T argues that the limits which were imposed were wholly arbitrary and amounted to a denial of due process. We cannot agree.

Litigants are not entitled to burden the court with an unending stream of cumulative evidence. As Wigmore remarked, "it has never been supposed that a party has an absolute right to force upon an unwilling tribunal an unending and superfluous mass of testimony limited only by his own judgment and whim. . . ." Accordingly, Federal Rule of Evidence 403 provides that evidence, although relevant, may be excluded when its probative value is outweighed by such factors as its cumulative nature, or the "undue delay" and "waste of time" it may cause. Whether the evidence will be excluded is a matter within the district court's sound discretion and will not be reversed absent a clear showing of abuse.

The time limits ordered by Judge Grady had the effect of excluding cumulative testimony, although in setting those limits the district court apparently fixed a period of time for the trial as a whole. This approach is not, per se, an abuse of discretion. This exercise of discretion may be appropriate in protracted litigation provided that witnesses are not excluded on the basis of mere numbers. Moreover, where the proffered testimony is presented to the court in the form of a general summary, the time limits should be sufficiently flexible to accommodate adjustment if it appears during trial that the court's initial assessment was too restrictive.

The limits set by the district court were not absolute. As Judge Grady stated in his order, "[t]hese limits are subject to change if events at the trial satisfy the court that any limit is unduly restrictive. It is my intention to

---

130.   . . . The record indicates that much of AT&T's proposed testimony would in fact have been repetitive. . . . AT&T also predicted that it would require between twenty-two and forty-six days to cross-examine MCI's witnesses who, by MCI's estimate, could be directly examined in twenty-six days.

allow each party sufficient time to present its case; I have no interest in speed for the sake of speed." . . . After MCI completed presentation of its case in fifteen and one-half days, the court expressed an unwillingness to permit AT&T to exceed its twenty-six day limit, yet it later tempered this by reminding the parties, "I want to make it very clear that nobody is being pushed to do anything that is inconsistent with what he perceives to be the best interest of his client." We cannot say that the district court was prepared to adhere strictly to its preliminary time limits without regard to possible prejudice to either party.

Insisting that the twenty-six day limit was too restrictive, AT&T cites *SCM Corp. v. Xerox Corp.*, 77 F.R.D. 10 (D. Conn. 1977), where the court imposed a six-month limit on the plaintiff's presentation when the plaintiff had failed to make a prima facie showing of liability after fourteen weeks of trial. AT&T in effect suggests that whenever time limits are imposed in a complex case, the limits should involve months, not days. Although there may be some validity to this suggestion in most complex cases, we cannot say that it should necessarily control in the case before us. Obviously, there must be specific attention to the substance of the testimony and the complexity of the issues, but it does not follow that several weeks for each side will never suffice. The circumstances of each individual case must be weighed by the trial judge, who is in the best position to determine how long it may reasonably take to try the case. MCI was confident that it could establish liability in twenty-six days, and in fact finished eleven days ahead of schedule. We recognize, as did the district court, that presentation of a competent defense may require more time than presentation of a plaintiff's case-in-chief. In light of the substance of AT&T's proffered testimony, however, and the district court's considered view that an efficient, yet effective, presentation of AT&T's defense would take no longer than the time MCI used to present its case, we conclude that the district court did not manifestly abuse its discretion in limiting the time for AT&T's case-in-chief.

Notes

1. Reducing the amount of time reduces the amount of information. That, in turn, makes it easier for the factfinder to remember the evidence and come to a judgment. According to Judge Leval, who ordered a time limit in the "vast" *Westmoreland v. CBS* libel trial, there are other benefits:

> . . . It requires counsel to exercise a discipline of economy choosing between what is important and what is less so. It reduces the incidence of the judge interfering in strategic decisions. It gives a cleaner, crisper, better-tried case. It gives a much lower cost to the clients. Finally, it will save months of our lives.

> All counsel in the *Westmoreland* trial have told me they believe they tried their case better as a result of the time limit, and that it was shorter by a half than it would have been.

Pierre N. Leval, *From the Bench*, 12 LITIGATION 7, 8 (Fall 1985).

2.   There are several ways to impose trial limits. One way is to limit time for direct and cross examination on a witness-by-witness basis. *See* Rohrbaugh v. Owens-Corning Fiberglas Corp., 965 F.2d 844 (10th Cir. 1992) (30 minutes for direct, 45 minutes for cross, of each expert). A second way is to impose a limit on the number of days within which a party must rest its case. Under this approach, the plaintiff's case, including direct, cross-examination, re-direct, and so forth may take no more than X days (in *MCI*, 26 days). The third way is to allocate to each side X hours, which the party may use as it sees fit — in direct, cross-examination, re-direct, and so forth. There is no limit (other than the outside limit of X hours) within which the party must rest its case. If it does so quickly, it has more time for cross-examination of the other party's case. If it does so slowly, it may have little or no time left to contest the opponent's case.

Judge Leval thought that the third method was far preferable to the second. Because the evidence of each side is not necessarily of the same quantity, especially if the plaintiff has laid a good foundation, the "X days for each party's case" approach may leave too much time for defendants in relation to plaintiffs. More significantly, this approach creates an incentive for each side to linger over its cross-examinations, making it difficult for the party to get in its evidence on direct. But the "X hours for each party" approach creates its own disincentives; a plaintiff may use most of its time on its case-in-chief and call lots of witnesses, trying to force the defendant to run out of time before it can even present its case-in-chief. *Cf.* Duquesne Light Co. v. Westinghouse Electric Corp., 66 F.3d 604 (3d Cir. 1995) (judge switched from "X hours" to "X days for each side's case" approach when judge thought that the plaintiff was not moving quickly enough). Could the three approaches be combined? *See* CRS Sirrine, Inc. v. Dravo Corp., 445 S.E.2d 782 (Ga. Ct. App. 1994) (limiting cross examinations to 4 hours each and defendant's overall trial time to 3 weeks). Isn't it an inevitable side effect of the adversarial system that any set of rules, however reasonable, will be exploited by parties seeking a private advantage?

3.   How is the judge to determine how many hours are appropriate for the trial? A judge who has had little contact with the case during pretrial is not likely to have enough of a feel for the case to know how many hours are correct, and will need to rely on the estimates of counsel. A judge who manages a case during pretrial would get a better feel of the required time, but the case manager can develop biases or predispositions. Will the judge be able to put these opinions aside when she allots the trial time?

4.   How is the judge to divide the time fairly among the parties? It is often true that one side needs longer to present its case than the other. A judge, however, is hard pressed to allot more time to one side than the other, since it seems unfair. Thus, the judge is likely to give each side the same amount of time, even though equal allocations can advantage one party. The reported decisions overwhelmingly use equal time allocations rather than time allocations tailored to achieve substantive fairness. *See* *Duquesne Light*, 66 F.3d at 608-09 (140 trial hours apiece, switched to 11

trial days apiece); Gen. Signal Corp. v. MCI Telecomms. Corp., 66 F.3d 1500 (9th Cir. 1995) (28 hours apiece); Monotype Corp. PLC v. Int'l Typeface Corp., 43 F.3d 443 (9th Cir. 1994) (9 trial days, divided equally); Deus v. Allstate Ins. Co., 15 F.3d 506 (5th Cir. 1994) (3 days apiece); Tabas v. Tabas, 166 F.R.D. 10 (E.D. Pa. 1996) (30 hours apiece); *but see* Flaminio v. Honda Motor Co., 733 F.2d 463 (7th Cir. 1984) (18 hours for plaintiff, 15 for defendant); McKnight v. Gen. Motors Corp., 908 F.2d 104 (7th Cir. 1990) (11 hours for the plaintiff, 10 for the defendant). How should multiple plaintiffs, defendants, or third-party defendants affect the allocation?

5. Was it really possible to present all the evidence necessary to determine AT&T's liability in a $1.8 billion case in just 52 days? Consider the concern expressed in *McKnight*:

> . . . [I]n this age of swollen federal caseloads district judges must manage their trials with an iron hand . . . . But to impose arbitrary limitations, enforce them inflexibly, and by these means turn a federal trial into a relay race is to sacrifice too much of one good — accuracy of factual determination — to obtain another — minimization of the time and expense of litigation. [908 F.2d at 115.]

See also Newton Commonwealth Prop., N.V. v. G + H Montage GmbH, 404 S.E.2d 551, 552 (Ga. 1991) (limiting trial time in complex case was erroneous when the limit had "the effect of prejudicing the parties and preventing a full and meaningful presentation of the merits of the case"). Do time limits inhibit, rather than advance, rational adjudication? Perhaps it depends on what "rational adjudication" means. If it means the ability to apply reason to a set of given facts and to make inferences from those facts, then rational adjudication can occur within short time frames. On the other hand, if it means the ability to apply reason to the complete universe of relevant information to ensure an outcome that is accurate, then rational adjudication is threatened by short time frames. Doesn't a judge with a crowded docket have an incentive to value comprehension (i.e., brevity) more than accuracy? *See* United States v. Reaves, 636 F. Supp. 1575, 1580 (E.D. Ky. 1986) ("Setting a reasonable time limit forces counsel to conform their zeal to the need of the court to conserve its time and resources."); Patrick E. Longan, *The Shot Clock Comes to Trial: Time Limits for Federal Civil Trials*, 35 ARIZ. L. REV. 663 (1993) (arguing that parties and courts value marginal costs and benefits of additional evidence in different ways).

6. *MCI* says that the use of time limits does not violate due process. But its due process analysis is quite thin. It never identifies the due process values at stake, much less analyze those values in terms of relevant precedent. Does the last note convince you that a credible due process claim exists? *See General Signal*, 66 F.3d at 1507-09 (rejecting due process argument because time limits were "reasonable," "sufficiently flexible," and did not "sacrifice justice in the name of efficiency").

7. From what source does the power to order time limits derive? *Duquesne Light*, 66 F.3d at 609, thought that the power derived from a combination of the court's inherent power; from Federal Rule of Civil

Procedure 1, which requires courts to construe the Federal Rules of Civil Procedure "to secure the just, speedy, and inexpensive determination of every action and proceeding"; from Federal Rule of Evidence 102, which requires the Federal Rules of Evidence to be "construed to secure . . . elimination of unjustifiable expense and delay"; and from Federal Rule of Evidence 403, which allows judges to exclude relevant evidence because of "considerations of undue delay, waste of time, or needless presentation of cumulative evidence." *See also Reaves,* 636 F. Supp. at 1578 (citing Fed. R. Evid. 611 as an additional source of power). What about Federal Rule of Civil Procedure 16(c)(2)(O), which permits a court to "take appropriate action" with respect to "establishing a reasonable limit on the time allowed to present evidence"? In *United States v. DeCologero,* 364 F.3d 12, 23 (1st Cir. 2004), the court stated that the power to impose time limits resided in "the district court's inherent authority." *DeCologero* was a criminal case, so the Federal Rules of Civil Procedure did not apply. Should a court continue to possess inherent power when a textual authority exists?

8. What happens when a party's time runs out? The answer may depend on the judge, and on her opinion of how well you have been trying your case. In *McKnight* the defendant had only 49 minutes left to put on the four witnesses in its case-in-chief. The judge gave the defendant an extra thirty minutes, but no more — a ruling which led to the spectacle of witnesses literally running to and from the stand to save time. 908 F.2d at 115. Likewise, in *General Signal,* the plaintiff used all of its time presenting its case-in-chief. It asked for additional time for cross-examination and for a rebuttal case. The court gave no time for rebuttal, and a whopping five minutes to do each cross-examination. It may not have helped the plaintiff that its attorney had earlier insisted on rigid enforcement of time limits against the defendant, and had ignored the judge's suggestion to save time for cross-examination with the comment that he asked only five questions of witnesses on cross. 66 F.3d at 1509.

9. Appellate courts seem most troubled by time limits when they detect a lack of flexibility on the trial judge's part. That concern, however, does not seem to translate into reversals. *See Flaminio,* 733 F.2d at 473 ("disapprov[ing] of the practice of placing rigid hour limits on a trial," but nonetheless upholding limits in case); *McKnight,* 908 F.2d at 115 (indicating that it would have reversed district judge for sticking rigidly to time allocations if defendant had preserved issue for appeal); *Monotype,* 43 F.3d at 451 (waiver when party failed to request additional time); Johnson v. Ashby, 808 F.2d 676 (8th Cir. 1987) (waiver of the issue when a party failed to object or to make an offer of proof regarding the evidence that was excluded). An aggrieved party must also show prejudice — in other words, that the excluded evidence might have made a difference. *Flaminio,* 733 F.2d at 473; *McKnight,* 908 F.2d at 115 (no reversible error when defendant failed to "show what it would have done with" extra time); *Duquesne Light,* 66 F.3d at 611; *General Signal,* 66 F.3d at 1510.

10. Whatever the method used for time limits, time-keeping issues always arise. One issue is whether and how to count jury selection, opening

and closing statements, rebuttal, objections, sidebar arguments, court breaks, partial trial days, and so on. *Compare Duquesne Light*, 66 F.3d at 608-09 (time included opening and closing arguments; partial trial days counted as full day), *with General Signal*, 66 F.3d at 1504 (time included rebuttal; breaks and delays charged equally to both sides), *and Tabas*, 166 F.R.D. at 12-13 (time included rebuttal, but not jury selection or opening and closing statements). When the "X hours" approach is used, someone constantly needs to be keeping track of the time, starting and stopping the clock depending on whose time is charged for various matters — a "method that [makes] the computation of time almost as complicated as in a professional football game." *Flaminio*, 733 F.2d at 473.

11. Witnesses running to and from the stand, timekeepers with stopwatches who must decide when and how to allocate time, lawyers managing their cases like football coaches nursing a lead as the clock winds down — is this a trial? Maybe the problem is that lawyers have forgotten how to try cases — how to achieve the optimal blend of accuracy and comprehension. Would a better solution be to create a barrister system, in which a small cadre of truly skilled lawyers handled complex cases?

4. Presenting Evidence in Summary or Narrative Form

A final method of limiting trial information is to require that evidence be submitted in condensed or summary form. One form of evidence that lends itself to summary presentation is the deposition. The traditional practice concerning deposition testimony has been for the lawyer (often assisted by another reader) to read the questions and answers from the deposition to the jury. Unless you have Tom Cruise and Jack Nicholson playing the two roles, transcript reading is tedious; and it puts the testimony at the mercy of the theatrical talents of the readers. Today this problem is often solved by using edited videotaped depositions in which the most salient aspects are played back. But this approach does not always shorten the trial or the amount of information the factfinder hears; it simply shifts testimony from the stand to the computer monitor. Consider the following approach to condensing information at trial.

OOSTENDORP V. KHANNA

937 F.2d 1177 (7th Cir. 1991)

■ FLAUM, Circuit Judge.

Plaintiff Debra Oostendorp sued the defendants for negligence following gall bladder surgery in 1986. The jury found for the defendants. Oostendorp appeals, citing as error . . . the district court's order that the parties summarize in five pages or less any deposition testimony they wished to present at trial . . . .

. . . Plaintiff's counsel objected to this procedure before trial, and refused to summarize the depositions of two witnesses, Doctors Michael Sarr and Myron Denney, he intended to present at trial. The district court therefore barred Oostendorp from introducing their deposition testimony at trial, a ruling she claims contravenes Fed. R. Civ. P. 32(a)(3)(B), the due process clause of the fifth amendment, and her seventh amendment right to a jury trial.

To begin, we note that Oostendorp did not attempt to comply with the district court's procedure. She made no attempt to show why the district court's requirement was unreasonable as applied to the depositions she wished to offer in this case, nor did she offer any objections to the content of the deposition summaries prepared by the defendants. . . . Plaintiff's beef, then, is not with the district court's application of the rule but with the rule itself; she makes a facial challenge to the district court's deposition summary procedure. Although we might question the validity of an overly rigid application of the district court's requirement (the district court should be willing to consider increasing the five-page limit in appropriate cases), we have not been presented with such a claim here. At oral argument, plaintiff's counsel rejected our invitation to cast the claim in terms of an abuse of discretion and we must therefore consider not whether it was reasonable to require Oostendorp to summarize the Sarr and Denney depositions in five pages, but only whether the district court may require such summaries as a general matter.

In this focus, plaintiff's claim is without merit. Rule 32 of the Federal Rules of Civil Procedure permits the use of depositions in civil cases, but contrary to the plaintiff's assertion that deposition testimony must be admitted when offered, the decision to admit deposition testimony is within the sound discretion of the district court. It follows that the court may control the manner in which deposition testimony is presented; indeed, trial courts are charged to "exercise reasonable control over the mode and order of interrogating witnesses and presenting evidence so as to (1) make the interrogation and presentation effective for the ascertainment of the truth [and to] avoid needless consumption of time . . . ." Fed. R. Evid. 611(a). The district court adopted its rule to serve these objectives, and we agree that requiring deposition summaries can be a reasonable means of implementing the mandate of Rule 611. We therefore conclude that the district court's requirement was not an abuse of its discretionary authority to regulate the conduct of civil trials.

Plaintiff's attempt to ground her objection in the Constitution borders on the frivolous. Neither the due process clause nor the seventh amendment requires courts to admit deposition testimony; indeed, the more common argument is that the Constitution forbids the substitution of depositions for the live testimony of witnesses. . . . [The plaintiff] was not denied the right to call witnesses; rather, she opted to present deposition testimony rather than testimony from a witness in court. . . . The due process clause gives parties to litigation the right to present evidence; the seventh amendment gives them the right to do so in front of a jury. Neither provision, however, gives litigants license to prolong trials needlessly; neither deprives courts of their authority to regulate the conduct of the trial. As long as the procedures utilized by the trial courts are fair, there is no conflict with either constitutional provision. Since there is nothing inherently unfair in requiring the parties to summarize deposition testimony . . . we hold that the rule imposed by the district court in this case does not offend the due process clause or the seventh amendment.

The judgment for the defendants-appellees . . . [is] affirmed.

Notes

1.   Narrative summaries of testimony change the nature of trial from a dialectic (question-and-answer) approach to a didactic (lecture) approach. As you have noted in law school, a lecture approach is more efficient at conveying information, but a question-and-answer approach may lead to a deeper understanding of difficult points. Which approach seems more appropriate for complex cases?

Maybe the answer is a compromise: that some routine, fairly non-controversial information can be best conveyed in a didactic fashion, while other, more critical information is best conveyed in a dialectic fashion. This was the solution used in *In re Air Crash Disaster at Stapleton International Airport, Denver, Colorado, on November 15, 1987*, 720 F. Supp. 1493 (D. Colo. 1989). The trial judge limited the use of narrative summaries to the presentation of "corroborative testimony on various issues, lessening the delay of repetitive testimony. Because the applicability of summary testimony is tempered by the court's preference for oral testimony in open court, the parties were neither requested nor allowed to present the testimony of key witnesses in summary form." 720 F. Supp. at 1503. How can the judge know which witnesses are central and which are peripheral?

2.   One important way in which *Stapleton International* is broader than *Oostendorp* is that the judge in *Stapleton International* ordered narrative summaries even of witnesses who could have appeared live at trial; in *Ooostendorp*, the doctors were apparently unavailable for trial. What is the source of the court's authority to order summaries of testimony from witnesses who can testify in court? The few courts to consider the issue have found the authority either in Fed. R. Evid. 611(a) or (once again) in the court's inherent power to control cases. Walker v. Action Indus., Inc., 802 F.2d 703, 713 (4th Cir. 1986); United States v. Young, 745 F.2d 733, 761 (2d Cir. 1984); *Stapleton International*, 720 F. Supp. at 1481; Nigh v. Dow Chem. Co., 634 F. Supp. 1513, 1519 (W.D. Wis. 1986). The first source, Rule 611(a), allows a court to "exercise reasonable control over the mode and order of interrogating witnesses and presenting evidence." The Advisory Committee Notes state that Rule 611(a) "restates in broad terms the power and obligation of the judge as developed under common law principles," including "such concerns as whether testimony shall be in the form of a free narrative or responses to specific questions." The Notes seem to

contemplate that the *witness* will be doing the narrating; it does not suggest that the *lawyer* can narrate or summarize testimony on a witness's behalf. *But see* Charles R. Richey, *A Modern Management Technique for Trials Courts to Improve the Quality of Justice: Requiring Direct Testimony to be Submitted in Written Form Prior to Trial*, 72 GEO. L.J. 73, 80 (1983) ("rule 611(a) read in light of rule 102 gives the trial judge authority not only to *control* but also to *devise* a *mode* of interrogation"). Is the court's inherent power a sufficient basis for letting the lawyers narrate?

We keep running across this inherent power, which seems to act as a reserve of authority allowing courts to do things that the rules of procedure and evidence do not exactly allow. What are the limits of this inherent power, anyway? What is the point of having rules if they can be superseded so easily? *See* Edward R. Becker & Aviva Orenstein, *The Federal Rules of Evidence after Sixteen Years — The Effect of "Plain Meaning" Jurisprudence, The Need for an Advisory Committee on the Rules of Evidence, and Suggestions for Selective Revision of the Rules*, 60 GEO. WASH. L. REV. 857, 903 (1992) (since "neither [Rule 611] nor the accompanying Advisory Committee notes encourages [narrative] statements," the Federal Rules of Evidence should be amended to permit them).

3. *Stapleton International* used two different forms of narrative summaries. The court described the two methods as follows:

> The primary method of summary testimony involves summarization of the relevant portions of a deposition in a one or two page narrative, prepared by the offering attorney. Opposing counsel is given an opportunity to review the summary and the deposition for accuracy. The offering attorney then reads a stipulated narrative summary to the jury.

> The second method of summary testimony involves the reading of a narrative statement of a witness's direct testimony while the witness is in court, under oath. The presenting attorney reads a summary of direct examination. The witness is then asked to supplement or correct the attorney's statement, under oath, again in narrative form. Testimony then proceeds through traditional cross and redirect examination. This method of presenting evidence is most useful in presenting the testimony of witnesses who appear to corroborate the testimony of key witnesses. [720 F. Supp. at 1503-04.]

The first technique is equivalent to the one used in *Oostendorp*. In some ways the first technique is more worrisome than the second; the deposition witness is not present in court to correct statements or to be subject to cross-examination. But the second technique is also problematic; there may be good reason to require summaries of the testimony of witnesses who cannot be present, but to require a summary for a witness sitting on the stand deprives the court and jury of an opportunity to hear the story in the witness's own words and might make the cross-examination appear stronger or weaker than it should. *Cf.* Traylor v. Husqvarna Motor, 988 F.2d 729, 734 (7th Cir. 1993) (describing the potential prejudicial effect of allowing witness to testify live on direct examination but through videotape on cross-examination).

Nonetheless, the second technique has often been used. The most notable example is the *United States v. AT&T* antitrust litigation, in which the direct testimony of most of the 350 witnesses called was submitted in writing. No background or preliminary questioning was allowed. *See* United States v. Am. Tel. & Tel. Co., 83 F.R.D. 323, 339-40 (D.D.C. 1979). As a result, the largest antitrust trial in history "took less than a year. That's not bad." *See* Geoffrey C. Hazard, Jr. & Paul R. Rice, *Judicial Management of the Pretrial Process in Massive Litigation: Special Masters as Case Managers, in* WAYNE D. BRAZIL ET AL., MANAGING COMPLEX LITIGATION 77, 107-08 (1983). *See also* Saverson v. Levitt, 162 F.R.D. 407 (D.D.C. 1995) (ordering use of narrative direct testimony and citing cases). *Cf.* Fed. R. Civ. P. 43(a) (requiring testimony to be taken in open court).

4. *Oostendorp* was not a complex case, at least as we use that term. Should a court have greater authority to use narrative or summary techniques in complex cases? *See Stapleton International*, 720 F. Supp. at 1504 ("Development of techniques for the summary presentation of evidence is recommended in complex litigation."); *cf.* Lynne ForsterLee et al., *The Cognitive Effects of Jury Aids on Decision-Making in Complex Civil Litigation*, 19 APPLIED COGNITIVE PSYCHOL. 867 (2005) (finding that summary statements, when combined with juror notetaking, enhanced mock jurors' cognition).

5. Is there more to plaintiff's due process and jury-trial arguments than *Oostendorp* acknowledged? The Chancellor sitting in equity never heard testimony; he relied on written summaries of testimony and evidence. In comparison, the strength of the common-law trial lay in the immediacy and drama of live testimony; it is impossible to believe that a common-law court would have permitted narrative summaries in 1791, when the Due Process Clause and the Seventh Amendment were enacted.

Once again in this chapter, we confront a fundamental question: How much of the historical form of common-law trial is constitutionally enshrined? More specifically, is the ability of the jury to hear the testimony of witnesses a matter of constitutional stature? *Cf.* Ex parte Peterson, 253 U.S. 300, 310-11 (1920) (Brandeis, J.) ("New devices may be used to adapt the ancient institution [of jury trial] to present needs and to make of it an efficient instrument in the administration of justice. Indeed, such changes are essential to the preservation of the right.").

Suppose that we pile novel procedure on novel procedure, so that we have a bifurcated trial-by-statistics with time limits and narrative summaries for witnesses. Have we finally crossed the constitutional line? Does the Seventh Circuit's test — that no Seventh Amendment issue exists as long as the procedures are "fair" — adequately describe the constitutional concern or the constitutional limit? *See Stapleton International*, 720 F. Supp. at 1481 n.14; 720 F. Supp. at 1504 (summarily dismissing argument that summaries violate the right to jury trial).

6. Are the due process and jury-trial concerns as acute with the second technique, which permits cross-examination of the witnesses?

7. In bench trials, the jury-trial concerns about narrative summaries disappear, but due process concerns remain. *Compare* In re Burg, 103 B.R. 222, 225 (9th Cir. BAP 1989) ("[E]ssential [due process] rights of the parties may be jeopardized by a [narrative direct testimony] procedure where the oral presentation of evidence is not allowed, where the bankruptcy court's ability to gauge the credibility of a witness or evidence is questionable and where rulings on objections to the admissibility of all direct evidence, may be unclear"), *with* In re Adair, 965 F.2d 777, 780 (9th Cir. 1992) ("We disagree with the *Burg* panel that [a "trial by affidavit"] procedure raises significant due process concerns"). *See also* Kuntz v. Sea Eagle Diving Adventures Corp., 199 F.R.D. 665 (D. Haw. 2001) (upholding the use of a "declarations procedure" in all civil non-jury trials); WILLIAM W SCWHARZER, MANAGING ANTITRUST AND OTHER COMPLEX LITIGATION § 7-3(A) (recommending narratives for non-controversial testimony in bench trials).

8. The summary technique can be applied to evidence other than testimony. In complex cases, it is not unusual for thousands of lengthy documents to be admitted. The salient points of these documents can often be succinctly stated, either through redaction of the original text or through a summary of the document's contents. Courts encourage summaries, and believe them authorized by Federal Rule of Evidence 611(a). *Nigh*, 634 F. Supp. at 1518; *see also* MANUAL FOR COMPLEX LITIGATION, FOURTH §§ 11.492, 12.32 (2004) (recommending use of summaries for voluminous or complicated data and for other exhibits).

9. A somewhat different technique is to require the lawyers to provide the jurors with the relevant portions of the deposition transcripts, and to let the jurors read the transcripts on their own time. Thus far, however, the practice of giving juries this type of homework has been disapproved. *See* Stine v. Marathon Oil Co., 976 F.2d 254, 267 (5th Cir. 1992).

10. A party can waive its objections to the use of a narrative summary. *See Walker*, 802 F.2d at 712; *Stapleton International*, 720 F. Supp. at 1504 (considering objection in spite of untimeliness).

11. On appeal, a judge's decision regarding the use of narrative summaries is reviewed for abuse of discretion. *Young*, 745 F.2d at 761.

B. TECHNIQUES TO MAKE INFORMATION MORE COMPREHENSIBLE AT TRIAL

In the last section we examined ways to limit the amount of information that a factfinder must consider. A different way to make the factfinder's task of adjudication easier is to make the information more comprehensible. In this section we examine some comprehension-enhancing techniques that have been employed in complex cases. Our basic concerns remain the same. Do these techniques unduly infringe on the parties' rights to adversarial presentation, due process, and jury trial? Do they skew results in predictable ways?   Can we justify using these procedures in some but not all cases? Do the changes so distort the process of trial that the game of complex litigation is no longer worth the candle?

1. Amending the Usual Order and Structure of Trial

MANUAL FOR COMPLEX LITIGATION, FOURTH

146-47 (2004)

Jury recollection and comprehension in lengthy and complex trials may be enhanced by altering the traditional order of trial. Techniques that have been used include the following:

• *Evidence presented by issues.* Organizing the trial in logical order, issue by issue, with both sides presenting their opening statements and evidence on a particular issue before moving to the next can help the jury deal with complex issues and voluminous evidence, but may result in inefficiencies if witnesses must be recalled and evidence repeated. . . .

• *Arguments presented by issues/sequential verdicts.*   If it is impractical to arrange the entire trial in an issue-by-issue format, it may still be helpful to arrange closing arguments by issue, with both sides making their closing on an issue before moving to the next.   The entire case may be submitted to the jury at the conclusion of all argument, or the issues may be submitted sequentially . . . . The latter procedure may be advantageous if a decision on one issue would render others moot or if the early resolution of pivotal issues will facilitate settlement; on the other hand, it can lengthen the total time for deliberations and requires recurrent recesses while the jury deliberates.

• *Interim statements and arguments.* In a lengthy trial, it can be helpful if counsel can intermittently summarize the evidence that has been presented or can outline forthcoming evidence. Such statements may be scheduled periodically (for example, at the start of each trial week), or as the judge and counsel think appropriate, with each side allotted a fixed amount of time. . . . (Interim jury instructions . . .and reminders to the jury about the difference between evidence and counsel's statements may also be helpful.)

Notes and Questions

1.   The judge's power to change the usual structure of trial derives from Federal Rule of Evidence 611(a). We return to the concept of the

sequential verdict in a later section. *See infra* p. 1132. Do the remaining ideas seem sensible?

2. Start with the idea of presenting all the evidence on one issue before proceeding to the next issue. If the judge instructed the jury and asked for a verdict on the first issue before proceeding to the next, we would have, of course, bifurcation, whose advantages and disadvantages we have already considered. *See supra* pp. 1033-48. Issue-by-issue trial organization might soften some of the pro-defendant effects of bifurcation while still achieving some of bifurcation's benefits. Is it an experiment worth pursuing? On the other hand, does the inability of this procedure to end the litigation after the trial of a single dispositive issue make this procedure both less attractive than bifurcation and less efficient than a regular trial?

We are unaware of empirical studies that have directly addressed the issues raised in issue-by-issue trial organization. *Cf.* SCM Corp. v. Xerox Corp., 463 F. Supp. 983 (D. Conn. 1978), *aff'd*, 645 F.2d 1195 (2d Cir. 1981) (judge who used this method in conjunction with special verdicts at end of each issue thought that procedure eliminated introduction of unnecessary evidence, promoted organized consideration of evidence, and reduced chance of retrial). In a potential relevant study, Professors Horowitz and Borden examined the effects on outcomes and damage awards under various forms of unitary and bifurcated trials. One of the things that they did was to switch the order of evidence; some juries heard the plaintiffs' evidence in the order of liability, causation, and damage, followed by the defendant's evidence on those issues, while others heard causation first, then liability and damages. The study found that the order of evidence presentation in both unitary and bifurcated trials had significant effects: In unitary trials in which causation was heard first, juries that returned verdicts for the plaintiffs "rendered higher average compensatory awards than juries hearing liability first," and in bifurcated trials, while defendants won most cases, the juries that did find the defendant liable awarded "significantly higher [compensatory damage awards] than their unitary counterparts." Irwin A. Horowitz & Kenneth S. Bordens, *An Experimental Investigation of Procedural Issues in Complex Tort Trials*, 14 LAW & HUM. BEHAV. 269, 281 (1990). While this study does not squarely address the issue-by-issue trial plan, it appears that the order in which the judge arranges the issues *may* have an effect on the substantive outcome of trial and *will* have an effect on the amount of damages awarded. For a bibliography of psychological studies on the effect of order of presentation of evidence on a jury, see WALTER F. ABBOTT ET AL., JURY RESEARCH 29, 183-85 (1993). *Cf.* United States v. Real Prop. Known as 77 East 3rd St., N.Y., N.Y., 1994 WL 4276, at *3 (S.D.N.Y. Jan. 4, 1994) (Sotomayor, J.) (declining to switch the order of proof to allow defendant to present its case first, but suggesting that the court had power to do so when it was "logical and more efficient").

3. Interim arguments seem logical enough an idea: Let the lawyers put the past and upcoming evidence into context, thus helping the jury better focus on and comprehend the issues in the case. Interim arguments

work particularly well in conjunction with an issue-by-issue trial plan. Does the idea have as much utility in a standard unitary trial? We know of no empirical studies considering whether interim arguments increase comprehension, or whether they have undesired side effects.

In one asbestos case, the court allowed the plaintiff and defendant 30 minutes of interim argument each week, and the cross-claim defendants 10 minutes, to be used however they wished. The defendants eventually objected when it became apparent that the plaintiff was using the time to argue for punitive damages, trying to sway the jury before the defendants' evidence came in. Because it found that punitive damages were unavailable for other reasons, the appellate court declined to reverse the decision to allow interim arguments. ACandS, Inc. v. Godwin, 667 A.2d 116, 152-54 (Md. 1995). *Cf.* United States v. Yakobowicz, 427 F.3d 144, 154 (2d Cir. 2005) (in a criminal case, finding "a structural error" when the district court "systematically allowed argumentative summations after each witness without any showing of particularized need based on length of the trial or complexity of the issues, without any authorization in a rule of criminal procedure, and without any attempt to limit the argumentative aspects of the interim summations").

For cases authorizing interim arguments, see Informatica Corp. v. Bus. Objects Data Integration, Inc., 2007 WL 607792 (N.D. Cal. Feb. 23, 2007) (allowing interim arguments based on the parties' agreement; deducting the length of any argument from the total time each side was allotted for trial); In re E. & S. Dists. Asbestos Litig., 772 F. Supp. 1380, 1386 (E. & S.D.N.Y. 1991), *rev'd in part on other grounds*, 971 F.2d 831 (2d Cir. 1992); In re N.Y. Asbestos Litig., 149 F.R.D. 490, 499 (S.D.N.Y. 1993), *but see* Gray v. Phillips Petroleum Co., 1990 WL 62074 (D. Kan. Apr. 19, 1990) (declining to permit weekly interim arguments). *See also* BROOKINGS INST., CHARTING A FUTURE FOR THE CIVIL JURY SYSTEM 17 (1992) (recommending "mini-opening statements" throughout trial); William W Schwarzer, *Reforming Jury Trials*, 132 F.R.D. 575, 595-96 (1991) (discussing pros and cons).

4. The touted benefits of pre-instructions and interim instructions are the establishment of an appropriate legal framework for the evidence and the multiple opportunities that the jury receives to understand the law in the case (such understanding being one of the jury's weakest points (*see supra* p. 1013; *infra* p. 1130)). The potential drawbacks are that the instructions may conform poorly to the evidence presented, that they may create prejudgment or bias in the jury, and that the judge might direct jurors toward testimony the judge finds relevant and away from testimony the jury finds relevant. *See* Larry Heuer & Steven D. Penrod, *Instructing Jurors: A Field Experiment with Written and Preliminary Instructions*, 13 LAW & HUM. BEHAV. 409 (1989); Robert MacCoun, *Inside the Black Box: What Empirical Research Tells Us about Decisionmaking by Civil Juries*, *in* VERDICT 137, 151-52 (Robert E. Litan ed. 1993) (describing research suggesting increased comprehension due to preliminary instructions); *cf.* Crivelli v. Gen. Motors Corp., 40 F. Supp. 2d 639 (W.D.Pa. 1999), *rev'd on other grounds*, 215 F.3d 386 (3d Cir. 2000) (noting that errors in the court's

preliminary instructions were harmless when the final instructions corrected them).   Professors Heuer and Penrod found no evidence of harmful consequences and some limited evidence of better comprehension of legal standards. Their research did not allow them to explore some of the more serious possible drawbacks of pre-instruction (such as the creation of initial biases), and also did not show strong positive effects. *See* Heuer & Penrod, *supra*, at 426-27, 429-30. One study of criminal cases found that "pre-instruction produces more not guilty verdicts because it predisposes jurors to favor the defendant," but another study "found that pre-instructions had no effect on patterns of overall verdicts in criminal trials." *See* Jonathan D. Casper, *Restructuring the Traditional Civil Jury: The Effects of Changes in Composition and Procedures, in* VERDICT, *supra*, at 414, 445-46. More recent experimental studies have shown strong positive benefits from instructions read before the beginning of the evidence. *See* Lynne ForsterLee & Irwin A. Horowitz, *The Effects of Jury-Aid Innovations on Juror Performance in Complex Civil Trials*, 86 JUDICATURE 184, 186-87 (Jan.-Feb. 2003). *See generally* Phoebe C. Ellsworth & Alan Reifman, *Juror Comprehension and Public Policy: Perceived Problems and Proposed Solutions*, 6 PSYCH., PUB. POL'Y & LAW 788, 814-15 (2000) (citing bar recommendations to use interim instructions).

5.   Courts have long experience with interim instructions in multi-defendant criminal cases, in which the court often needs to caution a jury to disregard evidence of other defendants' guilt. Pre-instructions have been similarly used in multi-plaintiff trials consolidated under Rule 42(a) to ensure that the jury focuses on each plaintiff individually. *See* Johnson v. Celotex Corp., 899 F.2d 1281, 1285 (2d Cir. 1990) ("When considering consolidation, a court should also note that the risks of prejudice and confusion may be reduced by the use of cautionary instructions . . . ."); *Eastern & Southern Districts Asbestos*, 772 F. Supp. at 1386. They have also been proposed as a means of "provid[ing] ongoing education for the jury as to the contentions of the parties and the applicable legal principles" in an antitrust trial expected to last a year. Zenith Radio Corp. v. Matsushita Elec. Indus. Co., 478 F Supp. 889, 953 (E.D. Pa. 1979), *vacated on other grounds*, 631 F.2d 1069 (3d Cir. 1980).

The *Manual for Complex Litigation* recommends that the court caution the jury about their interim nature, and tell it that final instructions will be given prior to deliberations. MANUAL, *supra*, § 12.433.

2. Using Computer-Generated Evidence

Seeing is believing.   A diagram, model, or computer animation can communicate in a second information that hours of testimony could not convey as clearly.   Today the technology to create charts, diagrams, graphics, and even computer animation sits on every lawyer's desk.   Not surprisingly, litigation guides advocate the use of glossaries, indexes, time lines, charts, diagrams, data summaries and compilations, enlargements, and the like. *See, e.g.*, MANUAL FOR COMPLEX LITIGATION, FOURTH § 12.3

(2004); LARRY S. KAPLAN, COMPLEX FEDERAL LITIGATION §§ 25.01-26.22 (1993). But such technology is not an unadulterated good. What can lead to a true understanding can also mislead and obfuscate. The technology can be expensive, resulting in the possibility that an undeserving litigant can buy a verdict with a dazzling technical display. The new era that this technology presages — a world of virtual reality disconnected from the events in dispute — may also make traditionalists uncomfortable.

HINKLE V. CITY OF CLARKSBURG

81 F.3d 416 (4th Cir. 1996)

■   RUSSELL, Circuit Judge.

[Plaintiffs sued the City of Clarksburg and various police officers for violating the civil rights of their decedent, Bea Wilson. Among the claims was that one police officer, Officer Lake, had used excessive force when he shot and killed the decedent. At trial, the judge allowed the defendants to introduce a computer-animated videotape showing their expert's opinion of the events leading up to the shooting. The videotape showed the decedent raising his gun first, and the officer firing in self-defense. It then showed how the officers' version of the event was consistent with the physical evidence by concluding with a depiction of the trajectory of Officer Lake's bullet that lined up with the wounds to Wilson's forearm, chest, back, and the bullet hole in the wall of the room.

[The jury returned a verdict for the defendants. Plaintiffs appealed.]

Appellants contend the district court erroneously admitted a computer-animated videotaped demonstration of the Appellees' theory of the case . . . .

We review a district court's decisions whether to admit or exclude evidence for abuse of discretion. . . .

Typically, demonstrations of experiments used to illustrate principles forming an expert's opinion are not required to reflect conditions substantially similar to those at issue in the trial. Gladhill v. Gen. Motors Corp., 743 F.2d 1049, 1051 (4th Cir. 1984). We have, however, recognized the unique problems presented by the introduction of videotapes purporting to recreate events at the focus of a trial. In *Gladhill*, we noted the potential prejudicial effect of such evidence because the jury viewing a recreation might be so persuaded by its life-like nature that it becomes unable to visualize an opposing viewpoint of those events. Hence, we established a requirement that video taped evidence purporting to recreate events at issue must be substantially similar to the actual events to be admissible.

Obviously, the requirement of similarity is moderated by the simple fact that the "actual events" are often the issue disputed by the parties. Nonetheless, to the extent the conditions are not a genuine trial issue, they should be reflected in any videotaped recreation. . . .

We have not previously applied the requirement of "substantial similarity" to computer-animated videotapes that purport to recreate events at issue in trial. We fail to see a practical distinction, however, between a real-life recreation and one generated through computer animation; both can be a particularly powerful recreation of the events. Nonetheless, we need not explicitly decide this issue because we are satisfied the jury here fully understood this animation was designed merely to illustrate Appellees' version of the shooting and to demonstrate how that version was consistent with the physical evidence. The district court carefully instructed the jury on this point . . . .

Although there is a fine line between a recreation and an illustration, the practical distinction "is the difference between a jury believing that they are seeing a repeat of the actual event and a jury understanding that they are seeing an illustration of someone else's opinion of what happened." The jury understood that the very thing disputed in this trial was the condition under which the shooting occurred. In light of this fact and the court's cautionary instruction, there was no reason for the jury "to credit the illustration any more than they credit the underlying opinion."

We are convinced Appellants suffered no undue prejudice as a result of this computer animation, and we will not disturb the broad discretion afforded trial judges in this area. In reaching this holding, however, we are not unmindful of the dramatic power of this type of evidence; hence, we encourage trial judges to first examine proposed videotaped simulation evidence outside the presence of the jury to assess its foundation, relevance, and potential for undue prejudice. . . .

Accordingly, . . . the entering of judgment for the Appellees after a jury trial . . . is affirmed.

IN RE AIR CRASH DISASTER

86 F.3d 498 (6th Cir. 1996)

■   BOGGS, Circuit Judge.

[After the crash of a Northwest Airlines jet, the Judicial Panel on Multidistrict Litigation transferred all cases to the Eastern District of Michigan. The main defendants in the case, Northwest and McDonnell Douglas, settled with all plaintiffs, but retained claims against each other for contribution and equitable apportionment. One of the main points in dispute was whether the pilots had turned off a circuit breaker for a warning beeper that would have alerted them to the problem that caused the crash. After an eighteen-month trial, the jury found Northwest 100% at fault for the crash, and awarded McDonnell Douglas damages on its equitable apportionment claim. Northwest appealed, citing numerous errors, including the introduction of a computer animation.]

. . . [W]e now turn to Northwest's challenges to rulings that admitted evidence. Our standard of review is [that the] trial court has broad discretion, and we will not reverse a judgment unless we believe that errors at trial had a substantial effect on the final result. . . .

Northwest claims that the court erred in allowing Exhibit 3096, McDonnell Douglas's circuit breaker videotape, to be shown to the jury. Exhibit 3096 is a six-minute computer-animated videotape that depicts the operation of a TI 7274-55 circuit breaker. The videotape was used during the testimony of circuit breaker expert John Bryan Williamson to demonstrate the circuit breaker's inner workings. According to Northwest, the court's admission of the videotape . . . was inadmissible under Rule 403 of the Federal Rules of Evidence. . . .

. . . Northwest argues that the videotape was inadmissible under Rule 403 because it suggested a similarity to actual events and illustrated MDC's argument that the crew pulled the circuit breaker. We agree that it did both of these things — but do not agree that it was improper. Use of the videotape was limited to demonstration, and the court instructed the jury about the limited basis of its admission. The district court found, and we cannot disagree, that the probative value of the videotape was not substantially outweighed by its prejudicial effect.

The videotape was not, as Northwest contends, offered to simulate what had happened to the circuit breaker in the accident or to simulate the results of Williamson's examination of that circuit breaker. Northwest has not objected on appeal to the Williamson testimony that was the subject of Exhibit 3096. As McDonnell Douglas points out, Williamson could have drawn the same information on a sketch pad in front of the jury. Moreover, no less than six witnesses testified in defense of the circuit breaker design. The use of the tape was entirely proper. . . .

The judgment of the district court is affirmed.

RACZ V. R.T. MERRYMAN TRUCKING, INC.

1994 WL 124857 (E.D. Pa. Apr. 4, 1994)

■ TROUTMAN, Senior District Judge.

[Plaintiff brought a wrongful-death action for an accident in which one of the defendant's drivers allegedly veered into another lane. Whether the driver actually did so was hotly disputed. The defendant's accident-reconstruction expert developed a computer-animated reconstruction of the scene. The plaintiff moved to preclude the animation under Fed. R. Evid. 403.]

Relying upon the old adage, "seeing is believing," we conclude that the jury may give undue weight to an animated reconstruction of the accident. . . . The apparent decision of the accident reconstructionist to discount the testimony of a witness who reported seeing the trailer portion of the truck encroach into the decedent's lane of travel is magnified and given enhanced credibility when such decision becomes part of the data upon which an animated visual representation is based.   It would be an inordinately difficult task for the plaintiff to counter, by cross-examination or otherwise, the impression that a computerized depiction of the accident is necessarily more accurate than an oral description of how the accident occurred. Because the expert's conclusion would be graphically depicted in a moving and animated form, the viewing of the computer simulation might more readily lead the jury to accept the data and premises underlying the defendant's expert's opinion, and, therefore, to give more weight to such opinion than it might if the jury were forced to evaluate the expert's conclusions in the light of the testimony of all of the witnesses, as generally occurs in such cases.

Based upon our conclusion that the relevance of the computer animation is outweighed by the danger of confusion and prejudice, we will grant plaintiff's motion to preclude the computer simulation.

Notes

1.   A range of high-tech and low-tech evidence exists: live or videotaped simulations, videotaped reconstructions of events, charts, diagrams, models, mock-ups, enlargements, and the like.   As a general matter, the use of such evidence is beyond question, at least as long as it portrays the matter being described with some semblance of fairness. Colgan Air, Inc. v. Raytheon Aircraft Co., 535 F. Supp. 2d 580 (E.D. Va. 2008); Verizon Directories Corp. v. Yellow Book USA, Inc., 331 F. Supp. 2d 136 (E.D.N.Y. 2004) (Weinstein, J.). In-court simulations also enjoy a broad latitude of admissibility and, in many jurisdictions, need not be substantially similar to the actual events at issue; because the jury and the opposing lawyers can observe the test, the risk of bamboozling the jury is limited. *See* Veliz v. Crown Lift Trucks, 714 F. Supp. 49 (E.D.N.Y. 1989) (allowing live demonstration using fork lift that differed from the fork lift at issue in significant ways; the judge gave precautionary instructions). Out-of-court simulations, whether live-action or computer-generated, create greater concerns about bamboozlement. *Hinkle* reflects the general rule that out-of-court reconstructions must be substantially similar to the events at issue in order to be admissible. *See also* Champeau v. Fruehauf Corp., 814 F.2d 1271, 1278 (8th Cir. 1987) ("Admissibility, however, does not depend on perfect identity between actual and experimental conditions. Ordinarily, dissimilarities affect the weight of the evidence, not its admissibility."); *id.* (noting that the defendant proffered a list of similarities and differences between experimental and actual conditions to jury); *but see* Ingram v. ABC Supply Co., Inc., 2009 WL 5205970, at *6 (D.S.C. Dec. 29, 2009) ("The court is not persuaded that the conditions in the videotape are sufficiently close to those of the accident to make its probative value outweigh its prejudicial effect.").

2.   Out-of-court live-action or computer-animated tapes come in two flavors. They are either a "reconstruction," in which the demonstration visually depicts a person's opinion of what occurred, or a "simulation," in

which data or formulas pertaining to an event are fed into a computer, which analyzes the data and draws conclusions about what must have occurred (or might occur in the future). *See* Lorraine v. Markel Am. Ins. Co., 241 F.R.D. 534, 559-60 (D. Md. 2007); State v. Sayles, 662 N.W.2d 1, 9 (Iowa 2003). Because most live-action and computer-animated reconstructions are demonstrative in nature, they are not ordinarily admitted as substantive evidence over a party's objection. *See, e.g.*, Datskow v. Teledyne Cont'l Motors Aircraft Prods., 826 F. Supp. 677, 685-86 (W.D.N.Y. 1993). It is not unusual, however, for computer simulations to be used as substantive evidence of what occurred or might occur. *See, e.g.*, Comm. Union Ins. Co. v. Boston Edison Co., 591 N.E.2d 165 (Mass. 1992) (model used to determine how much a utility had overcharged consumers for heat); PPG Indus., Inc. v. Costle, 630 F.2d 462 (6th Cir. 1980) (model used to predict the future concentrations of pollutants). The line between "reconstruction" and "simulation" can be thin, and appellate courts normally defer to the trial judge's discretion. *See* Fredric I. Lederer, *Technology Comes to the Courtroom, and . . .*, 43 EMORY L.J. 1095, 1117 (1994).

3.   The admissibility of any live-action test or computer animation begins with relevance; it must have probative value under Federal Rules of Evidence 401 and 402, and that probative value must outweigh the potential for undue prejudice under Rule 403. *See* Carlo D'Angelo, *The Snoop Doggy Dogg Trial: A Look at How Computer Animation Will Impact Litigation in the Next Century*, 32 U.S.F. L. REV. 561 (1998). When the evidence will be used as substantive proof rather than as a demonstrative aid, additional evidentiary hurdles must be overcome. First, the underlying data on which the evidence is based must either be admissible (hearsay and authentication are often the stumbling blocks), be the expression of an expert's opinion or the grounds for the expert's opinion, or be regarded as data derived from a method used and accepted within the relevant scientific or other community. Second, a ground for admitting the evidence itself (the usual route being Federal Rules of Evidence 702 and 703, concerning expert testimony) must be found. *See* LARRY S. KAPLAN, COMPLEX FEDERAL LITIGATION §§ 26.06-.11 (1993); Mario Borelli, Note, *The Computer as Advocate: An Approach to Computer-Generated Displays in the Courtroom*, 71 IND. L.J. 439 (1996). Third, an adequate foundation for the evidence must be laid. *Cf.* Bledsoe v. Salt River Valley Water Users' Ass'n, 880 P.2d 689, 692 (Ariz. Ct. App. 1994) (counsel could not use computer animation in closing argument when it had never been used during trial, no foundation had been laid for admissibility, and no opportunity for cross-examination existed). *See generally* Steven Goode, *The Admissibility of Electronic Evidence*, 29 REV. LITIG. 1, 22-23, 37-39 (2009) (analyzing admissibility of computer animations and computer simulations).

4.   Should computer animation, which can isolate (and possibly distort) aspects of an event to a greater degree than a live-action videotape, be held to a higher standard than "substantial similarity"? Using a mock case in which the victim fell from a rooftop, Professors Kassin and Dunn created a pro-plaintiff version of the fall and a pro-defendant version of the fall, and developed a computer animation that accurately depicted each

version. Using a control group that heard only oral testimony and experimental groups that were exposed to a computer animation that correctly depicted the fall, the results of the experiment "clearly supported the hypothesis that a computer-animated reconstruction can facilitate decision making by increasing the extent to which jurors render verdicts consistent with the physical evidence." Saul M. Kassin & Meghan A. Dunn, *Computer-Animated Displays and the Jury: Facilitative and Prejudicial Effects*, 21 LAW & HUM. BEHAV. 269, 276 (1997). Then they flipped the experiment, and showed a computer animation that inaccurately depicted the fall. In this condition, jurors rendered decisions contrary to the physical evidence at a greater rate when shown the misleading animation than when they heard only oral testimony. The authors hypothesized that both positive and negative effects would be more pronounced in cases involving "complex physical events that the average juror does not understand as a matter of common sense" and in lengthy trials in which oral testimony tends to recede from jurors' memories. *Id.* at 279-80; *see also* Linda C. Morell, *New Technology: Experimental Research on the Influence of Computer Animated Displays on Jurors*, 28 SW. U. L. REV. 411, 414 (1999) (reporting that "animation makes cognitive tasks more concrete by supplying visual motion to coincide with verbal cues").

5.   Computer animation and other high-tech evidence give the parties creative control over the images and message presented at trial. But there are also disadvantages to this type of evidence. Aside from the possibility that the medium may overpower the truth, other concerns include the high cost of computer animation; the need for a "guide" to lead the factfinder through the animation program; the biases that animation, as a product of the human mind, can create; and the need to establish an adequate foundation for both the underlying data and the computer program. *See* MANUAL FOR COMPLEX LITIGATION, THIRD § 34.32 (1995); Betsy S. Fiedler, Note, *Are Your Eyes Deceiving You?: The Evidentiary Crisis Regarding the Admissibility of Computer Generated Evidence*, 48 N.Y.L. SCH. L. REV. 295, 311-12 (2003-04) (suggesting that the technological limitations of computer animation can subtly distort reality; that the production process can introduce subliminal messages; and that human error in constructing the animation may further increase the possibility of unfair prejudice).

Another concern is that the traditional form of trial, with its emphasis on live witnesses, will erode. *See* Van Houten-Maynard v. ANR Pipeline Co., 1995 WL 317056 (N.D. Ill. May 23, 1995), at *12 (excluding a computer animation in part because other parties had not been given notice of its use and in part because of undue prejudice under Federal Rule of Evidence 403; noting that "we believe that computer animation evidence, by reasons of its being in a format that represents the latest rage and wrinkle in video communications and entertainment, may well have an undue detrimental effect on other more reliable and trustworthy direct-type evidence."). Is this such a bad thing? Judge Marvin Frankel, a staunch critic of the adversarial system, would not think so. His observations on the use of television in the courtroom seem equally applicable to computer animation:

The miracle of television, if it became widely known in American courts, could spare us some of the pressures and misfortunes of the live, continuous trial. . . . When both sides have recorded all their witnesses and other evidence, the jury can be selected and the entirety of the trial submissions can be given to the assembled jurors without recurrent delays and interruptions, combining the taped accounts of witnesses with the "live" offerings of counsel, documents, other evidence, and the judge's instructions. The process would consume a fraction of our standard trial time. The worries we have about prejudicial evidence inadvertently revealed will be eliminated by the TV "editor" (the editor being in this case the judge, resolving in standard manner of ruling on objections what should and what should not be placed before the jury).

MARVIN F. FRANKEL, PARTISAN JUSTICE 110 (1978). *See also* WALTER F. ABBOTT ET AL., JURY RESEARCH 224-29 (1993) (describing empirical research, generally favorable, on jury trials that used videotape and computer graphics). Is the TV trial, with liberal use of computer animation to aid understanding, the way to save the adversarial system while assuring rational adjudication? Will the great advocates of the twenty-first century be the Steven Spielbergs and James Camerons of the legal world? Is this new world just a little too brave?

6. Should the complexity of the case be a factor in a judge's decision whether to admit high-tech evidence? Which way does complexity cut — in favor of such evidence or against?

7. Suppose that a lawyer chooses not to use high-tech evidence that would enhance factfinder comprehension. Can the trial judge require the lawyer to use it? Is the source of this authority Federal Rule of Evidence 611? The court's inherent power? The *Manual for Complex Litigation* walks a fine line, recognizing that "presentation of evidence is normally controlled by counsel's strategies and tactics," but also stating that "[t]he judge should encourage or even direct the use of techniques to facilitate comprehension and expedition, . . . [including] use of visual and other aids." MANUAL FOR COMPLEX LITIGATION, FOURTH § 12.3 (2004). This amounts to a more ambitious role for the judge than the role outlined in one of the *Manual*'s predecessor, which stated that "[a]ctive involvement by the judge . . . need not and should not alter counsels' primary responsibility for collecting, organizing, and presenting the evidence." MANUAL FOR COMPLEX LITIGATION (SECOND) § 22.24 (1985).

8. How is a judge to know when computer-generated evidence is an aid and when it is a ruse? Must the judge seek the guidance of a technical advisor? *See supra* p. 1019. An alternative is to let the adversarial process work, and to let opposing parties object to the use of misleading evidence. To make this approach work, the opposing parties must have notice of the use of the evidence and lead time to examine the evidence and its method of production. *See* MANUAL, *supra*, § 11.643. In Maryland, the issue is dealt with by rule. *See* Md. Rule 2-504.3 (requiring that, in most cases, notice be given to other parties of an intended use of computer-generated

evidence at least 90 days before trial; providing an opportunity for other parties to view, conduct discovery on the production of, and object to the evidence); *see also* Dean A. Morande, *A Class of Their Own: Model Procedural Rules and Evidentiary Evaluation of Computer-Generated "Animations,"* 61 U. MIAMI L. REV. 1069 (2007) (proposing a model rule).

9.   One issue that has been litigated with increased frequency, with some split in the cases, is whether the expense of computer-generated evidence can be taxed to a losing party as a cost. *See, e.g.,* Summit Tech., Inc. v. Nidek Co., Ltd., 435 F.3d 1371 (Fed. Cir. 2006) (refusing to tax as costs more than $96,000 for trial exhibits, including $80,000 for computer animations and $16,000 for videos, PowerPoint presentations, models, and graphic illustrations).

3. Using Court-Appointed Experts and Masters as Aids for the Factfinder

Nearly all complex cases involve difficult scientific and technical issues that lie beyond the knowledge of lay factfinders. The usual approach to this problem is to allow each side to call expert witnesses to render opinions that assist the factfinder. In an adversarial system, some built-in incentives can lead to abuse of the expert-witness system. One side might have a reason to cloud the scientific or technical issues rather than to clarify them. Likewise, a wealthy party might be able to buy up all the best experts in the field, or else buy the testimony of "hired gun" experts who will arrive at whatever opinion the holder of the checkbook desires. These tendencies are magnified in complex litigation, in which the stakes are high.

Much has been written on the subject of using expert witnesses in complex litigation: how you pick them, how you prepare them, how you persuade the jury to accept their opinions on direct examination, how you poke holes in their opinions on cross-examination. For the most part, these issues are not dramatically different in simple and complex cases, and they are better addressed in evidence and trial advocacy courses. Instead, our focus will be, as it has been throughout, on the judge's power to influence the standard operation of the adversarial system. This focus leads us to examine a court's power to appoint its own experts or to use special masters to present evidence to the factfinder.

IN RE HIGH FRUCTOSE CORN SYRUP ANTITRUST LITIGATION

295 F.3d 651 (7th Cir. 2002)

■ POSNER, Circuit Judge.

The plaintiffs appeal from the grant of summary judgment for the defendants in an antitrust class action charging price fixing in violation of section 1 of the Sherman Act, 15 U.S.C. § 1. The defendants are the principal manufacturers of high fructose corn syrup (HFCS) . . . . The plaintiffs represent a certified class consisting of direct purchasers from the defendants. . . .

The plaintiffs claim that in 1988 the defendants secretly agreed to raise the prices of HFCS, that the conspiracy was implemented the following year . . . . Billions of dollars in treble damages are sought . . . . The suit was brought in 1995 and though an enormous amount of evidence was amassed in pretrial discovery, the district judge concluded that "no reasonable jury could find in [the plaintiffs'] favor on the record presented in this case without resorting to pure speculation or conjecture." The soundness of this conclusion is the basic issue presented by the appeal.

[The court of appeals examined the circumstantial and direct evidence of conspiracy, and concluded that the evidence of the defendants' liability was weak, "but not so weak as to justify summary judgment in their favor."]

The upshot of our analysis of the evidence is that unless this opinion provides enough guidance to the parties to enable them to converge in their estimates of the likely outcome of a trial to the point at which settlement is feasible, there must be a trial; and we are naturally concerned about the practicability of a jury trial (the plaintiffs want and are entitled to a jury) in a case with such a staggeringly large record — the sealed exhibits alone fill 14 large boxes — that includes so much highly technical statistical material. We want to be realistic about the absorptive capacities of judges and juries. But actually the complexity of the case is largely illusory and a streamlined trial strikes us as eminently feasible. So far as the nonstatistical evidence is concerned, it is remarkable how little is in dispute. Most of the facts that we have recited in this opinion are not denied by the defendants; their quarrel with the plaintiffs is merely over the inferences to be drawn both from individual pieces of evidence and from the evidence considered as a whole. . . . When basic facts of the who-said-or-did-what-to-whom kind are agreed upon and only the inferences to be drawn from those facts are in dispute, the judge can streamline the trial by requiring the parties to stipulate to the undisputed facts and present the stipulations to the jury, rather than allowing the lawyers to bore everyone by eliciting uncontradicted facts by means of protracted direct examination and cross-examination of witnesses, as if they were dentists pulling teeth the old-fashioned way. *See* FED. JUD. CTR., MANUAL FOR COMPLEX LITIGATION § 21.47 (3d ed. 1995).

Turning to the technical statistical evidence (not the data themselves, which for the most part are uncontested, but the inferences drawn from them by the use of statistical methodology), we recommend that the district judge use the power that Rule 706 of the Federal Rules of Evidence expressly confers upon him to appoint his own expert witness, rather than leave himself and the jury completely at the mercy of the parties' warring experts. *See* MANUAL FOR COMPLEX LITIGATION, *supra*, § 21.51. The main objection to this procedure and the main reason for its infrequency are that the judge cannot be confident that the expert whom he has picked is a genuine neutral. The objection can be obviated by directing the party-designated experts to agree upon a neutral expert whom the judge will then appoint as the court's expert. The neutral expert will testify (as can, of course, the party-designated experts) and the judge and jury can repose a degree of confidence in his testimony that it could not repose in that of a party's witness. The judge and jurors may not understand the neutral expert perfectly but at least they will know that he has no axe to grind, and so, to a degree anyway, they will be able to take his testimony on faith.

No doubt in view of the complexity of the case the judge will also want to bifurcate the trial, that is, to have a trial on liability first and only if the jury finds that the defendants violated the law to conduct a trial to determine the plaintiffs' damages.

If these suggestions are followed, we think the case can be tried in a reasonable amount of time and be made comprehensible to a jury. . . .

Reversed and remanded.

GATES V. UNITED STATES

707 F.2d 1141 (10th Cir. 1983)

■ PER CURIAM.

This is an appeal from the judgment of the district court dismissing plaintiff's action against the United States for personal injury allegedly caused by the swine flu vaccination administered during the National Swine Flu Immunization Program of 1976, 42 U.S.C. § 247b(j)-(l) (1976). The sole issue was whether the swine flu vaccine received by plaintiff (Fae L. Gates) was the proximate cause of the Guillain-Barre Syndrome ("GBS") she suffered in the fall of 1977. The district court held that plaintiff had failed to prove causation by a preponderance of the evidence. . . .

In advance of [the non-jury] trial, the district court appointed a panel of three medical experts to assist the court in resolving the complex medical issues involved. The panel submitted its findings to the court in a report which was admitted into evidence. . . .

On appeal plaintiff raises . . . [w]hether the trial court's appointment of a panel of experts was error . . . .

Plaintiff challenges the make-up of the panel of experts appointed to assist the trial court because, plaintiff argues, the panel of three experts consisted of two specialists in neurology and one expert witness with a strong predilection to a neurological bias.

The panel consisted of C.H. Milliken, M.D., professor of neurology at the University of Utah; Stanley H. Appel, M.D., professor of neurology at Baylor College of Medicine; and Leonard T. Kurland, M.D., professor of epidemiology and medical statistics at the Mayo Clinic. All members of the panel had had previous experience in diagnosing GBS. The panel was empowered to conduct physical examinations of plaintiff, consider medical literature submitted by the parties, and review past medical records of plaintiff. Two members of the panel conducted separate examinations of plaintiff. The panel was unanimous in its conclusion that plaintiff suffered from GBS but that the time interval between the inoculation and onset of GBS, which the panel determined to be approximately eleven months, was too great for a causal nexus to exist.

Plaintiff argues that the diagnosis and treatment of GBS crosses a broad spectrum of medical disciplines and, therefore, the appointment of a panel of experts consisting of two neurologists and one epidemiologist was erroneous in that the experts' backgrounds in neurology constituted a bias in their conclusions and findings.

The trial judge has broad discretion in regulating trial procedure, including the appointment of a panel of experts to assist the trial court in understanding complex matters. Federal Rule of Evidence 706(a) provides in relevant part that

> [t]he court may on its own motion or on a motion of any party enter an order to show cause why expert witnesses should not be appointed and may request the parties to submit nominations. The court may appoint any expert witnesses agreed upon by the parties, and may appoint expert witnesses of its own selection.

Before the appointment of the advisory panel, the trial court directed the parties to discuss whether such a panel should be appointed. The parties were allowed to offer a proposed order for appointment and to suggest up to five potential panel members. The panel members were required to be available for trial and for deposition. Plaintiff deposed two of the panel members, and the depositions were admitted into evidence.

The diagnosis and treatment of GBS is primarily committed to specialists in neurology. . . . The experts appointed by the trial court are well qualified in their fields. Moreover, plaintiff has failed to show the existence of any bias on the part of this panel. Under these circumstances, we find no abuse of discretion in the trial court's appointment of the panel.

We affirm the judgment of the district court.

Joe S. Cecil & Thomas E. Willging, ACCEPTING *DAUBERT*'S INVITATION: DEFINING A ROLE FOR COURT-APPOINTED EXPERTS IN ASSESSING SCIENTIFIC VALIDITY

43 EMORY L.J. 995, 1004, 1041, 1043-45, 1069-70 (1994)

Many commentators have mentioned that the use of court-appointed experts appears to be rare, an impression based on the infrequent references to such experts in published cases. To obtain an accurate assessment of the extent to which court-appointed experts have been employed, we sent a one-page questionnaire to all active federal district court judges. . . .

[E]ighty-six judges, or 20% of those responding to the survey, revealed that they had appointed an expert on one or more occasions. The figures indicate that, taken together, these judges made approximately 225 appointments, far more than suggested by the paucity of published opinions dealing with the exercise of this authority. . . .

Our interviews revealed that juries and judges alike tend to decide cases consistent with the advice and testimony of court-appointed experts. We asked, "Was the disputed issue resolved in a manner consistent with the advice or testimony of the 706 expert?" Of fifty-eight responses, only two indicated that the result was not consistent with the guidance given by the expert. Both of these cases involved bench trials in which the judge pursued a legal analysis that was independent of the technical issues. [In five other cases, the expert either did not render an opinion or was regarded merely as useful in shaping a resolution.]

In the remaining fifty-one cases, including seven jury trials, the outcome was consistent with the expert's advice or testimony. Whether the advice of the expert influenced the outcome is, of course, another matter. Twenty-one of the judges who indicated consistent outcomes also volunteered the information that the experts' opinions were not the exclusive, or even the most important, factor in determining the outcome of their cases. . . .

One final question when the case involved a jury trial was, "Did the testimony of the court-appointed expert appear to overwhelm the expert testimony offered by the parties?" In a dozen jury cases, it appears that the testimony of court-appointed experts dominated the proceedings. . . .

We are wary of overstating the strength of these findings in light of the inability of social psychologists to demonstrate greater deference to appointed experts by jurors in controlled laboratory settings. . . .

. . . Nonetheless, the central finding is clear: judges who appointed an expert indicated that the final outcome on the disputed issue was almost always consistent with the testimony of the appointed expert. . . .

Appointment of an expert by the court represents a striking departure from the adversarial process of presenting information for the resolution of disputes. But such an appointment should not be regarded as showing a lack of faith in the adversarial system. We learned that judges who appointed experts appear to be as devoted to the adversarial system as those who made no such appointments. Most appointments were made after extensive efforts failed to find a means within the adversarial system to gain the information necessary for a reasoned resolution of the dispute. Appointment of an expert was rarely considered until the parties had been given an opportunity and failed to provide such information. We find it hard to fault judges for failing to stand by a procedure that had proved incapable of meeting the court's need for information; to insist, in such a circumstance, that the court limit its inquiry to inadequate presentations by the parties is a poor testament to the adversarial system and the role of the courts in resolving disputes in a principled and thoughtful manner.

Notes

1. Two different judicial adjuncts can assist the factfinder: a special master or a court-appointed expert witness. Chapters Seven and Nine examined other uses to which a special master could arguably be put — as an assistant case manager, *see supra* p. 756, or as a substitute factfinder or lawgiver, *see supra* pp. 1016, 1028. Here we see yet another possible role for the master: aiding the factfinder's comprehension by recommending findings of fact. Before 2003, examples of masters who were used in this fashion was rare. *See* In re Estate of Ferdinand E. Marcos Human Rights Litig., 1994 WL 874222 (D. Haw. Jan. 3, 1995) (noting the appointment of a single person as a master for some trial tasks and as a court-appointed expert for others); *but see* Hiern v. Sarpy, 161 F.R.D. 332 (E.D. La. 1995) (refusing to appoint a person as either a special master or an expert). After the 2003 amendments to the Rule 53, the technique has become even rarer. The court's ability to use a special master to recommend findings of fact to juries (the type of thing that the special master did in the trial-by-statistics portion of the *Marcos* trial (*supra* p. 1058)) was intentionally eliminated in the present Rule 53(a)(1); the only circumstance in which a special master can now make recommendations to a jury is when the parties consent to the procedure. Fed. R. Civ. P. 53(a)(1)(A). In non-jury trials, a judge can appoint a master to recommend findings of fact when there exists "some exceptional condition" or complex damages calculations.

Therefore, most of the focus lies on court-appointed experts. Chapter Eight examined the pretrial uses of such experts. *See supra* p. 843. There, court-appointed experts helped the judge narrow the issues for trial. In the trial context, a court-appointed expert aids a factfinder's comprehension. In terms of function, therefore, the difference between the use of a special master as a witness at trial and the use of a court-appointed expert as a witness at trial is trivial. But the standard under which an appointment can be made, in either a jury or a non-jury trial, is a simple showing of "cause." Fed. R. Evid. 706(a). In reality, however, as the research of Messrs. Cecil and Willging suggest, judges are reluctant to appoint experts unless the parties have failed in their adversarial task or else a court-appointed expert is seen as necessary to reasoned decisionmaking. Thus, the use of court-appointed experts is also somewhat exceptional.

Assuming that a master is available, the end-products of masters and court-appointed experts are somewhat different. A master writes a report, *see* Fed. R. Civ. P. 53(e); an expert gives testimony, *see* Fed. R. Evid. 706(a). But this formal difference can be overstated; masters can testify at trial, *cf.* Crateo, Inc. v. Intermark, Inc., 536 F.2d 862 (9th Cir. 1976) (not reversible error not to require a master to read findings or to be subject to cross-examination), and experts often prepare written reports that form the basis of their testimony, *see* Cecil & Willging, *supra*, at 1035-36.

2. Despite these differences, there are strong similarities between special masters and court-appointed experts in terms of the specific function that we consider here — making the factfinder's task of

comprehension easier. Should there be a single set of standards and procedures for these "comprehension assistants," rather than two? If so, should the standard be the high threshold of the master's reference or the nominally lower threshold of the expert's appointment?

3. In previous chapters we explored some of the problems, including cost, delay, bias, and dissimilar treatment of like cases, that masters generate. How many of those problems carry over to the master as a "comprehension assistant"? Would the same problems infect the court-appointed expert? *See* MANUAL FOR COMPLEX LITIGATION, FOURTH § 11.51 (2004) (stating that disadvantages of court-appointed expert include cost, delay, potential harm to neutrality of court, lack of neutrality of expert, and undue influence of the expert; advantages are "great tranquilizing effect" on contentious experts of parties, facilitation of settlement or issue narrowing, and increase in comprehension).

4. Unsurprisingly, courts take different views on the wisdom of appointing expert witnesses. In *Contini v. Hyundai Motor Co.*, 149 F.R.D. 41, 41-42 (S.D.N.Y. 1993), Judge Broderick explained why he expected to appoint an expert in a products liability case:

> Concern about the impact of presentation to lay juries (who cannot study background written materials and ask extensive questions of experts to assure understanding of complex concepts) of testimony given by biased experts is increasing. This reflects the-ever-more technical nature of issues presented in product liability and similar intricate litigation.
>
> This phenomenon may be especially troubling where, for example, a significant part of the livelihood of an expert is drawn from testimony favorable to a particular side of a controversy, or where an expert is dependent upon income from an industry closely connected to the interests of one side or another. Requiring the fullest disclosure of potential sources of partiality of expert witnesses represents an important if incomplete response to this problem.
>
> With proper cross-examination generalist factfinders may be able to assess experts' credibility. This does not assure generalists' ability to reach correct affirmative conclusions with respect to controverted obscure technical issues, a challenge deserving of continuing attention.

See also In re Joint E. & S. Dists. Asbestos Litig., 830 F. Supp. 686, 693 (E.& S.D.N.Y. 1993) (noting that appointment "is not commonplace," but that the "work of such experts is especially critical in dealing with complex mass tort problems such as" complex and interdependent scientific issues, thousands of parties, equitable treatment, and strong and conflicting interests in character of relevant data).

On the other hand, in *Kian v. Mirro Aluminum Co.*, 88 F.R.D. 351, 356 (E.D. Mich. 1980), Judge Gilmore refused to appoint an expert in jury trial when facts "are within the comprehension of laypersons" and "[t]he presence of a court-sponsored witness, who would most certainly create a strong, if not overwhelming, impression of 'impartiality' and 'objectivity,' could potentially transform a trial by jury into a trial by witness." *See also* J & M Turner, Inc. v. Applied Bolting Tech. Prods., Inc., 1997 WL 83766, at *19 (E.D. Pa. Feb. 19, 1997) (declining to appoint an expert to help a jury interpret a complicated engineering standard when the parties could retain own experts and court appointment would cloak one expert with "an imprimàtur of judicial approval").

5.   The title of the Cecil and Willging article refers to the Supreme Court's decision in *Daubert v. Merrell Dow Pharmaceuticals, Inc.*, 509 U.S. 579 (1993), which held that expert testimony was admissible as long as it was relevant and scientifically valid but which then suggested that, in deciding whether to admit such testimony, the judge "should also be mindful of other applicable rules [including] Rule 706." *Id.* at 595. *Cf.* In re Joint E. & S. Dists. Asbestos Litig., 151 F.R.D. 540, 545 (E. & S.D.N.Y 1993) (Weinstein, J.) (suggesting that *Daubert* requires "trial court to take an active role in the presentation of expert evidence").

6.   The Cecil and Willging article that we excerpted is a condensed version of their manuscript on court-appointed experts. JOE S. CECIL & THOMAS E. WILLGING, COURT APPOINTED EXPERTS (1993). This manuscript contains a great deal of additional information on court-appointed experts, including (1) how judges pick experts (usually from nominations from the parties, but not always); (2) in what kinds of cases experts are useful (patent cases topped the list, followed by product liability and antitrust cases); (3) when appointments are made (usually early in the litigation, but many were appointed on the eve of trial); (4) how experts are used (frequently to testify, but often to perform advisory or other non-testimonial functions, including to aid in settling a case); (5) how experts are paid (usually the cost is split equally among parties, with the possibility that the judge will award the prevailing party its share of the fee as a cost of litigation under 28 U.S.C. § 1920(6)); and (6) whether the jury is told of the expert's court-appointed status (almost always).

7.   Like special masters, court-appointed experts have a long history in Anglo-American procedure. Court-appointed experts appear to have been used as early as 1345, and by the 1600s their use seems to have become routine. *See* Learned Hand, *Historical and Practical Considerations Regarding Expert Testimony*, 15 HARV. L. REV. 40, 42-47 (1901); Hart v. Cmty. Sch. Bd. of Brooklyn, 383 F. Supp. 699, 762-63 (E.D.N.Y. 1974) (Weinstein, J.). Prior to the creation of Rule 706, federal courts claimed that they possessed an "inherent power" to appoint expert witnesses. Scott v. Spanjer Brothers, Inc., 298 F.2d 928 (2d Cir. 1962).

How do you feel about this non-adversarial application of judicial power? Is it generally justifiable? Is it at least justifiable in complex cases? Does your answer depend on whether an expert or master might increase the accuracy of the verdict or judgment?

8.   As *Gates* shows, a court appointment is not limited to one person; a panel of experts with different relevant areas of expertise can sometimes be appointed. *See Asbestos Litigation*, 151 F.R.D. 540 (expert panel on

remedial issue); In re Swine Flu Immunization Prods. Liab. Litig., 495 F. Supp. 1185 (W.D. Okla. 1980).

9.   In *Young v. Pierce*, 640 F. Supp. 1476, 1478 (E.D. Tex. 1986), a judge appointed a special master who was specifically authorized to seek the advice of a court-appointed expert.   Can the Rule 706 appointment power be exercised by judicial adjuncts?

10. Judges also enjoy a power to call and interrogate fact witnesses. Fed. R. Evid. 614(a) (stating that a court "may, on its own motion or at the suggestion of a party, call witnesses, and all parties are entitled to cross-examine witnesses thus called"). This power is rarely invoked in civil trials.

4. Questions and Comments by Judge and Jury

An obvious solution to comprehension problems is to let the person who is having difficulty in comprehension either ask questions of the persons providing information or make comments that reflect the present level of understanding. We do this every day in class, at home, and at work. In an adversarial system, which hinges on party control of the information that the decision-maker hears, this obvious solution also has drawbacks.

IN RE INTERNATIONAL
BUSINESS MACHINES CORP.

618 F.2d 923 (2d Cir. 1980)

■   MULLIGAN, Circuit Judge.

More than a decade ago, on January 17, 1969, the United States of America, by its attorneys, acting under the direction of the Attorney General, filed a complaint in the United States District Court for the Southern District of New York which alleged that International Business Machines Corporation (IBM), commencing in or about 1961, had monopolized and attempted to monopolize the market for general purpose electronic digital computers in violation of Section 2 of the Sherman Act (15 U.S.C. § 2).... On January 26, 1972, Hon. David N. Edelstein, Chief Judge of the Southern District, assumed control of the case.   After extensive pretrial discovery, the bench trial was commenced on May 19, 1975. Counsel for the Government estimated that its case would take two to three months and IBM's counsel predicted that its defense would take six to eight months.

These estimates in fact proved to be grossly erroneous.   The Government's direct case lasted for almost three years, ending on April 26, 1978. IBM's defense began on that date and it continues as of this writing. Eleven years have elapsed since the filing of the initial complaint, pre-trial depositions commenced some eight years ago, and more than four and one-half years of trial time have been consumed. A mammoth record of trial transcript and exhibits has been assembled. To the best of our knowledge no litigation has taken so much time and involved such expense.

On July 19, 1979, IBM filed an application requesting Chief Judge Edelstein to recuse himself on the grounds that he has a "personal bias and prejudice against IBM and in favor of plaintiff, that his impartiality in this action may reasonably be questioned, that he has a bent of mind that will prevent impartiality of judgment, and that his bias and prejudice could not have come from any source other than an extrajudicial source." IBM therefore urged his recusal under 28 U.S.C. §§ 144, 455 and the due process clause of the Fifth Amendment. In addition IBM argued that resumption of the trial before a new judge would be inappropriate until the record has been "purged of the effects of the Chief Judge's bias."

On September 11, 1979, Chief Judge Edelstein filed a written opinion in which he denied the request for recusal as both untimely and legally insufficient.... On September 13, 1979 IBM filed in this court a Petition for a Writ of Mandamus .... Argument on the merits of the petition was heard in this court on October 16, 1979. As of that time more than 90,000 pages of testimony had been transcribed, almost 9,000 documents had been received into evidence, several hundred witnesses deposed, and some seventy trial witnesses called. In the argument counsel for IBM suggested that the case might take five more years of trial time to complete, putting the case into 1984, an appropriately Orwellian denouement. . . .

IBM's petition recognizes that the alleged prejudice of the trial judge must be extrajudicial, that it must arise by virtue of some factor which creates partiality arising outside of the events which occur in the trial itself. . . .

IBM has not shown and does not purport to establish or identify any personal connection, relationship or extrajudicial incident which accounts for the alleged personal animus of the trial judge. IBM's claim of prejudice is based completely on Chief Judge Edelstein's conduct and rulings in the case at hand. These we have repeatedly held form no basis for a finding of extrajudicial bias. . . .

. . . Chief Judge Edelstein is the sole finder of the fact here. His role is not that of a passive observer. His obligation is to determine the facts in a field which is exceedingly complex and technical. . . .

We have examined the affidavits of the nine IBM witnesses, all of whom state that his conduct demonstrates an unidentified personal bias. Much of this is not discernible from the record. Many complain of his "stares," "glares" and "scowls." One urges that the Chief Judge "would often glower at me, scowl and then turn and make bold notes on a pad of paper, as if threatening me with the contents."

There is no question but that these witnesses have felt that the judge's conduct was intimidating. However, the burden of IBM is to establish clearly and convincingly that his attitude can only be attributed to his personal prejudice. . . . [T]he trial judge has the obligation to form judgments as to the veracity of the witnesses before him. His asperity and incivility may well be due to his feeling that a witness is not forthright, that he is trying to protect a position, or is otherwise attempting to obfuscate the fact finding process.   IBM complains, for example, that Chief Judge Edelstein has asked its witnesses too many questions, has required them to draw meaningless charts and diagrams, to answer questions "yes" or "no" when they are not susceptible to such simplistic solutions.   He has, we are assured, interrupted plaintiff's 52 witnesses "only 846 times and has interrupted IBM's first 19 witnesses over 1200 times."   Accepting all of these contentions at face value we do not find them to be of the stuff upon which one can sensibly premise extrajudicial bias.

What may be a simple technical issue to the expert witness or even to IBM counsel, who have been given technical training in preparation for this litigation, may well be arcane to the jurist.   His questioning, his interruption, his insistence on clarification may well be prompted by his struggle to determine the truth in a field in which he is not sophisticated.   His asperity may well be prompted by a feeling that the witnesses for IBM (three are long time employees) are dissembling.   We do not know and cannot on this record determine whether his conduct has been guided by what he has learned during the trial, in which case his reaction is licit, or whether it is due to a personal prejudice which is clearly impermissible.   The point is that IBM has not met its burden of showing that the Chief Judge is personally biased against the petitioner.

There is of course another factor at play here — the seemingly interminable length of the trial.   The IBM witnesses did not begin to testify until almost three years of trial time had elapsed.   Even the most stoic might well lose patience in these circumstances.   The judge's allegedly hostile attitude to IBM witnesses as compared to Government witnesses may be due to the natural factor of fatigue in a case of this difficulty and duration. . . .

The petition for the writ of mandamus is denied.

DeBenedetto v. Goodyear Tire & Rubber Co.

754 F.2d 512 (4th Cir. 1985)

■ MICHAEL, District Judge.[*]

Deborah Samluck Drier and Melissa E. DeBenedetto (by her guardian ad Litem, Frances DeBenedetto) appeal from the jury verdict in favor of the defendant Goodyear Tire & Rubber Company (Goodyear) in these consolidated product liability cases. . . .

The second assignment of error is based on the trial court's decision allowing jurors to question witnesses.[1]   Appellants maintain that since the

---

[*]   James H. Michael, Jr., United States District Judge for the Western District of Virginia, sitting by designation.

[1]   In his opening comments to the jury, the trial judge expounded his policy of permitting questions by jurors.   After

Federal Rules of Evidence do not explicitly permit this practice, it is error for a trial court to permit it. . . .

The Federal Rules of Evidence neither explicitly allow nor disallow the practice of permitting jurors to question witnesses. The only guidance to be found is in Fed. R. Evid. 611(a) which instructs the court to "exercise reasonable control over the mode and order of interrogating witnesses . . . ." Those courts considering the propriety of juror questions have concluded that it is a matter within the discretion of the trial judge. . . .

While we agree that allowing juror questions is a matter within the discretion of the trial court, we do not agree that such questions are analogous to or even comparable to questioning of witnesses by the judge. Suffice it to say that the judge is not "an umpire or . . . moderator at a town meeting," but he sits "to see that justice is done in the cases heard before him." United States v. Rosenberg, 195 F.2d 583, 594 (2d Cir. 1952) . . . . One simply cannot compare the questioning by the trial judge — who is trained in the law and instructed to "see that justice is done" — with the questioning by members of the jury — who are untutored in the law, and instructed to sit as a neutral fact-finding body. Thus, we believe that juror questioning and questioning by the trial judge are clearly and properly distinguishable, although both forms of questioning are matters within the trial court's discretion.

Notwithstanding our belief that juror questioning is a matter within the trial court's discretion, we believe that the practice of juror questioning is fraught with dangers which can undermine the orderly progress of the trial to verdict. Our judicial system is founded upon the presence of a body constituted as a neutral factfinder to discern the truth from the positions presented by the adverse parties. The law of evidence has as its purpose the provision of a set of rules by which only relevant and admissible evidence is put before that neutral factfinder. Individuals not trained in the law cannot be expected to know and understand what is legally relevant, and perhaps more importantly, what is legally admissible.

Since jurors generally are not trained in the law, the potential risk that a juror question will be improper or prejudicial is simply greater than a trial court should take, absent such compelling circumstances as will justify the exercise of that judicial discretion set out above.

While the procedure utilized in the trial below permitted screening of the questions before an answer was given, the statement of the question itself was in the hearing of the other jurors, bringing with it the unknown, and perhaps unknowable, mental reactions of those other jurors. In the case where such a question is rejected, not only the questioning juror but the other jurors are likely to retain whatever mind-set has been generated by the question, leaving the court and counsel to ponder, under the stress

counsel completed their examination of a witness, the court allowed jurors to direct questions to the bench. If the trial judge deemed the question proper, he instructed the witness to answer it. Counsel were given the opportunity to re-question each witness after all inquiries from the jury were resolved.

of trial, how much influence a juror question, answered or unanswered, may have had on the perceptions of the jury as a whole.

Although the court can take remedial steps once such an improper or prejudicial question is asked, it is questionable how effective remedial steps are after the jury has heard the question, as noted *supra*. More importantly, the remedial steps may well make the questioning juror feel abashed and uncomfortable, and perhaps even angry if he feels his pursuit of truth has been thwarted by rules he does not understand. Under the tension and time pressure of a trial, such a reaction is all the more likely. Of course, under the worst case, a juror question may emerge which is so prejudicial as to leave only a declaration of mistrial as an appropriate remedial step, with all the waste that flows from a mistrial.

One further aspect of this practice deserves comment. Human nature being what it is, one or two jurors often will be stronger than the other jurors, and will dominate the jury inquiries. Indeed, this appears to have happened in this case, as discussed *infra*. Moreover, since these questions are from one or more jurors, the possibility that the jury will attach more significance to the answers to these jury questions is great. Every trial judge has noted the development in most lengthy trials of a cohesiveness in the jury as the trial goes on, coming eventually almost to a spirit of camaraderie, in which the actions and reactions of any individual juror are perceived by the jurors as those of the whole jury. In such a setting, the individual juror's question, and the answer elicited, almost certainly will take on a stronger significance to the jury than those questions and answers presented and received in the normal adversarial way.

To the extent that such juror questions reflect consideration of the evidence — and such questions inevitably must do so — then, at the least, the questioning juror has begun the deliberating process with his fellow jurors. Certainly, this is not by design, but stating the question and receiving the answer in the hearing of the remaining jurors begins the reasoning process in the minds of the jurors, stimulates further questions among the jurors, whether asked or not, and generally affects the deliberative process.

With these concerns in mind, we examine the record to determine whether in this instance appellants were prejudiced by the jurors' questions.

There were some 95 questions by jurors during this three-week trial; over half of the questions were asked by the foreman. As noted *supra*, the foreman's number of questions indicates that he was one of the stronger, more vocal members of the jury. Appellants claim that if nothing else, the sheer volume of juror questions indicates a loss of control by the court, thereby prejudicing the appellants' rights.

We have examined carefully each of the questions propounded by jurors and we perceive no bias in any of the questions. The vast majority of the juror questions were technical in nature and reflect a commendable degree of understanding and objectivity by the jury. That such a salutary conclusion is to be reached in this case does not by any means assure that the same or a similar result would come about with other juries.

Because we detect no prejudice to any party, and because appellants did not object to the procedure at the time of trial, we do not find error in the use of juror questions in this case. However, for the reasons set out above, such juror questioning is a course fraught with peril for the trial court. No bright-line rule is adopted here, but the dangers in the practice are very considerable. . . .

For the reasons stated, we affirm.

Notes

1.   The power of the judge to ask questions is not in doubt. *See* Fed. R. Evid. 614(b) ("The court may interrogate witnesses, whether called by itself or a party."). Indeed, judicial questioning "was never doubted at common law. . . . One of the natural parts of the judicial function, in its orthodox and sound recognition, is the judge's power and duty to *put to the witnesses* such *additional questions* as seem to [the judge] desirable to elicit the truth more fully." 3 WIGMORE'S EVIDENCE § 784 (James H. Chadbourn ed. 1970). The dangers of judicial questioning are similar to the dangers of the court's appointment of an expert in a jury-tried case: The judge's questions may exert an undue influence on the jury, they may suggest to the jury that the judge is leaning in a particular way, and they may hamper the ability of the parties to control the proofs and arguments. In addition, there is no guarantee that such questions will aid the jury's comprehension, since the judge has no greater knowledge of the jury's level of comprehension than the parties and their lawyers do. On the other hand, judicial questioning is a useful check on the tendency of the adversary system to devalue truth. It can also assist the orderly presentation of evidence and prevent unnecessary repetition.

Judicial questioning of witnesses in jury trials is a common practice, both in criminal and in civil cases. *See* United States v. Evans, 994 F.2d 317, 323 (7th Cir. 1993) (clarifying questions may be particularly useful in "lengthy and complex trial" or when lawyers cannot competently perform adversarial tasks); Warner v. Transamerica Ins. Co., 739 F.2d 1347, 1351 (8th Cir. 1984) (judge may "take active role in . . . developing the evidence," but may not "assume the role of advocate"). Reversals for inappropriate judicial questioning are exceedingly rare, although they do occur. *See* Champeau v. Fruehauf Corp., 814 F.2d 1271 (8th Cir. 1987) (new trial proper when a judge interrupted and questioned defendant's expert 145 times). It is advisable for the court to instruct the jury that it should draw no inferences from the judge's questions. Van Leirsburg v. Sioux Valley Hospital, 831 F.2d 169 (8th Cir. 1987); William W Schwarzer, *Reforming Jury Trials*, 132 F.R.D. 575, 591-93 (1991) (providing a sample instruction).

2.   A more difficult question is whether the judge or the jury, when acting as factfinder, should be entitled to ask questions of the witnesses.

The reasons to allow the factfinder do so, which are detailed to some extent in *IBM*, are obvious. The risks, which are described in *DeBenedetto*, are equally obvious. Your attitude about factfinder questioning is likely to be shaped by your views on the merits of the adversarial system. If you believe that truth-seeking at trial is paramount, and if you doubt that the adversarial system finds the truth with any degree of regularity, then questioning by the factfinder is not problematic. *See* United States v. Gray, 897 F.2d 1428, 1429 (8th Cir. 1990) ("A trial is a search for truth . . . Trial judges must have substantial latitude in overseeing this search . . . ."). On the other hand, if you believe that party control of proofs and arguments is a critical value, or if you think that the adversarial system is an effective engine of truth-seeking, you will be skeptical of factfinder questioning. United States v. Johnson, 892 F.2d 707, 713 (8th Cir. 1989) (en banc) (Lay, C.J., concurring) ("The fundamental problem with juror questions lies in the gross distortion of the adversary system and the misconception of the role of the jury as a neutral factfinder in the adversary process.").

3.   Are there unique concerns when a judge who is the factfinder asks questions? As *IBM* shows, the judge likely has been intimately involved in shaping and managing the case. If biases begin to develop during the case-management process, doesn't question-asking make it even harder for the judge to resolve factual disputes neutrally? *See also* Reserve Mining Co. v. Lord, 529 F.2d 181 (8th Cir. 1976) (recusing judge who called and questioned his own witnesses during remedial proceedings after becoming convinced that the defendant's witnesses were lying at trial).

4.   Even if we allow judges to ask questions when they are the factfinders, should we allow juries to ask questions when they are the factfinders? A judge has certain institutional advantages (knowing the law, knowing the rules of evidence, and having experience as a lawyer and presider at trial) that juries lack. Many of the concerns with jury questioning are discussed in *DeBenedetto*. *See also Johnson*, 892 F.2d at 715 (Lay, C.J., concurring) ("When the jury becomes an advocate or inquisitor in the process, it forsakes its role of arbiter between the government and its citizens."). *Johnson* was a criminal case. Is the concern equally applicable in civil cases? *See* Spitzer v. Haims & Co., 587 A.2d 105 (Conn. 1991) (rejecting constitutional arguments).

5.   In trying to assess the merits of these concerns, we are not without helpful data points. One set of information is comparative: Many procedural systems around the world use an inquisitorial mode in which the factfinder (usually a judge) asks questions. Another set is historical: In suits in equity, the Chancellor or his deputies solicited evidence by asking questions of witnesses.

Finally, we have empirical information. Using actual trials, Professors Heuer and Penrod created two sets of trial conditions, one in which jurors were instructed that they could ask questions and one in which they were not allowed to do so. In the former set, judges filled out forms analyzing each question, and in both sets jurors, lawyers, and judges were surveyed after trial. Jurors asked a total of 88 questions in 33 cases (2.7 questions per trial); 67% of the questions were directed toward the witnesses of the plaintiff (or prosecution); 18% were objected to by the lawyers for one or both sides. The surveys revealed that juror questions (1) did not "uncover important issues in the trial," (2) did not "increase the jurors' satisfaction with the procedure," (3) did "serve to alleviate juror doubts about trial testimony," (4) did "provide[ ] the lawyers with feedback about the jurors' perception of the trial," (5) did not "slow the trial," (6) did not "upset the lawyers' strategy," and (7) did not become "a nuisance to the courtroom staff." In addition, lawyers were not embarrassed to object to questions, and jurors did not report feeling embarrassed or angry when their questions were objected to. Lawyers reported that the juror questions had no great benefit, but seemed to do no harm. The study did not examine whether "[j]uror questions would cause the jurors to become overinvolved in the trial, thus losing their objectivity." *See* Larry Heuer & Steven Penrod, *Increasing Jurors' Participation in Trials: A Field Experiment with Jury Notetaking and Question Asking*, 12 LAW & HUM. BEHAV. 231 (1988).

More recent studies have come to similar conclusions. Shari Seidman Diamond et al., *Juror Questions During Trial: A Window into Juror Thinking*, 59 VAND. L. REV. 1927, 1965 (2006) ("The juror questions in Arizona required only a modest commitment of court time and nearly all of the questions reflected attempts by jurors to fill in and check their understanding of the evidence, rather than to attack or defend a particular position or side, to obtain information rather than to prove a point."); Nicole Mott, *The Current Debate on Juror Questions: "To Ask or Not to Ask, That is the Question,"* 78 CHI.-KENT L. REV. 1099, 1119-21 (2003) (analyzing 2,271 juror questions asked in civil and criminal cases in state and federal court; concluding that jurors used questions to enhance their roles as neutral fact-finders, not to become advocates, and that questions improved juror comprehension and clarified the issues).

6.   The general run of academic commentary cautiously favors the use of questioning by factfinders. *See, e.g.*, MANUAL FOR COMPLEX LITIGATION, FOURTH § 12.423 (2004); VALERIE P. HANS & NEIL VIDMAR, JUDGING THE JURY 123-24 (1986); Schwarzer, *supra*, at 591-93.

7.   Today judicial questioning of witnesses is taken for granted when the judge is the factfinder. *See* United States v. Witt, 215 F.2d 580 (2d Cir. 1954). With regard to juror questioning, at least ten federal circuits allow the practice, as do most states that have considered the issue — although a few states do not permit juror questioning either in all cases or at least in criminal cases. *See* State v. Doleszny, 844 A.2d 773, 778-79 (Vt. 2004) (collecting and discussing cases). A number of states permit juror questioning by statute or rule. *See, e.g.*, FLA. STAT. ANN. § 40.50(3) (in civil cases, "[t]he court shall permit jurors to submit to the court written questions directed to witnesses or to the court"); Ind. R. Evid. 614(d) ("A juror may be permitted to propound questions to a witness by submitting them in writing to the judge, who will decide whether to submit the questions to the witness for answer, subject to the objections of the parties . . . ."). Although they often permit juror questions, the federal cases, many

of them decided in the criminal context, reflect the cautious attitude toward juror questioning that *DeBenedetto* does. *See, e.g.,* United States v. Cassiere, 4 F.3d 1006, 1018 (1st Cir. 1993) (allowing questions but warning that "the practice should be reserved for exceptional situations, and should not become the routine, even in complex cases"). But the tide may be turning toward a broader use. *See* SEC v. Koenig, 557 F.3d 736, 742 (7th Cir. 2009) ("Now that several studies have concluded that the benefits exceed the costs, there is no reason to disfavor the practice.").

8. Because of the concerns about questioning, most courts have adopted certain precautions to accompany their use. Some of the standard precautions are "(1) the questions should be factual, not adversarial or argumentative, and should only be allowed to clarify information already presented; (2) the questions should be submitted to the court in writing; (3) counsel should be given an opportunity to object to the questions outside of the presence of the jury; (4) the trial judge should read the questions to the witness; and (5) counsel should be allowed to ask follow-up questions." State v. Graves, 907 P.2d 963, 967 (Mont. 1995). For additional suggested precautions, see *Cassiere,* 4 F.3d at 1018. Because the trial judge has broad discretion over factfinder questioning, courts of appeal have upheld the process even in the absence of one or more of these safeguards. *See, e.g.,* United States v. Groene, 998 F.2d 604 (8th Cir. 1993) (affirming conviction even when jurors asked questions directly). A party can waive the issue by failing to object seasonably during trial to factfinder questioning. *Id.* at 606 (a party must show prejudice or plain error to overcome lack of objection).

9. Related to the notion of judicial or jury questioning is the judge's ability to comment on or summarize the evidence. Comments are a two-edged sword. They interject the judge's impression of evidence that has been received, and can therefore act as an aid to the factfinder in the process of comprehension. On the other hand, comments may also lead to premature judgment.

The power of a judge to comment on, and thereby to seek to bring the jury around to her view of, the evidence has been an integral part of the common-law system of trial for centuries. Nonetheless, American judges have always been far more loathe to comment on or summarize the evidence than their British counterparts. *See* Jack B. Weinstein, *The Power and Duty of Federal Judges to Marshall and Comment on the Evidence in Jury Trials and Some Suggestions on Charging Juries,* 118 F.R.D. 161, 162 (1988). The leading case on judicial commentary remains *Quercia v. United States,* 289 U.S. 466, 468 (1933), in which the Supreme Court reversed a conviction when the trial judge said that a witness's demeanor meant that nearly everything the witness said "was a lie." The Supreme Court said that a judge commenting upon testimony "may not assume the role of a witness. He may analyze and dissect the evidence, but he may not either distort or add to it." *Id.* at 470.

Judicial commentary or summary is authorized in federal court, *see, e.g., Van Leirsburg,* 831 F.2d at 173, but it is rarely used. Many states forbid judicial comments on or summaries of the evidence, believing that these devices unduly impinge on the right to jury trial. *See* Weinstein, *supra*, at 169 & nn. 17-18 (listing twenty states that do not permit comment or summary, and seventeen that permit only summary). Judge Weinstein finds the American reluctance to comment on the evidence "unfortunate, . . . particularly in complex and technically oriented trials which are difficult for juries to follow." According to Judge Weinstein, "a judge's summary and comment on the evidence can increase the jury's ability to understand the proceedings it has attended, and thus increase the accuracy of verdicts." *Id.* at 166.

10. In the famous jury-trial study by Professors Kalven and Zeisel, the authors found that, when summaries and commentary were not used, judges disagreed with the jury verdict in 4% to 26% of all cases. When summaries or commentary were used, disagreement dropped to less than 1%. Their conclusion was that "the jury's revolt [against the law] is never enough to carry the jury beyond both the evidence and the judge." HARRY KALVEN, JR. & HANS ZEISEL, THE AMERICAN JURY 417-27 (1966). In a field experiment on complex cases, Professors Heuer and Penrod found that judicial comments and summaries were not helpful to jurors, and that "judges' efforts were least helpful when the evidence was particularly complex." Larry Heuer & Steven Penrod, *Trial Complexity*, 18 LAW & HUM. BEHAV. 29, 50 (1994). Their conclusion, which was tentative due to a small sample size, was that "judges are exercising sound discretion in their reluctance to comment or summarize." *Id.*

11. Should jurors be allowed to comment on the evidence directly? This technique could increase comprehension by signaling areas of confusion or uncertainty to the lawyers. Traditionally, jurors have not been allowed to comment on or discuss the evidence until they enter the jury room for deliberation; the reason for this prohibition was to protect the jury from external influence and premature judgment. There has been some discussion of moving away from this rule, particularly in complex cases. *Compare* Schwarzer, *supra*, at 594 (supporting the idea), *with* State v. Hays, 883 P.2d 1093, 1101-02 (Kan. 1994) (finding jury deliberations that resulted in jury asking questions of witnesses to be "troubling"). *Cf. Spitzer*, 587 A.2d at 109 (mentioning constitutional prohibition). Will this proposal increase factfinder comprehension?

5. Jury Notetaking

Another way to increase comprehension is to allow the factfinder to take notes during the trial. In bench trials this idea is hardly novel; judges have long taken notes when they are factfinders. Traditionally courts were reluctant to extend this privilege to jurors. Numerous reasons have been cited: Undue emphasis might be placed on the notes by jurors who take them; jurors might make errors in their notes, and trust their notes excessively; notetaking jurors might exert an undue influence in jury deliberations; notetaking jurors might be less willing to change their minds or to engage in discussions with other jurors; notetaking might favor plaintiffs, since juries might tire of notetaking as the trial goes on; notetaking might be distracting to other jurors, the lawyers, and the judge; and notetaking might make the juror miss other, crucial information. *See* Larry Heuer & Steven Penrod, *Juror Notetaking and Question Asking During Trials: A National Field Experiment*, 18 LAW & HUM. BEHAV. 121 (1994); William W Schwarzer, *Reforming Jury Trials*, 132 F.R.D. 575, 590-91 (1991); Larry Heuer & Steven Penrod, *Increasing Jurors' Participation in Trials: A Field Experiment with Jury Notetaking and Question Asking*, 12 LAW & HUM. BEHAV. 231, 234-36 (1988).

Studies on the effectiveness of notetaking have come to different conclusions. Professors Heuer and Penrod examined actual trials, some of which permitted jurors to take notes and some of which did not. Their conclusions were that notetaking did not increase juror comprehension or serve as a useful memory aid, but that none of the feared drawbacks materialized either. Because notetaking increased (weakly) the level of juror satisfaction, and because judges and lawyers seemed favorably disposed to the idea, the authors concluded that notetaking "deserve[d] serious consideration by the judicial system." Heuer & Penrod, *Increasing Jurors' Participation, supra*, at 257. Although the studies did not single out complex cases in particular, the second study by Heuer and Penrod involved a fairly large number of cases that the authors considered complex. *See* Heuer & Penrod, *Juror Notetaking, supra*, at 149.

In another study, Professors Heuer and Penrod reported some counter-intuitive data on juror notetaking in complex federal cases. Although the judges in the complex federal cases did not perceive any difference between notetaking and non-notetaking juries, notetaking jurors in complex cases reported feeling less well-informed than jurors who were not allowed to take notes; notetaking juries also reported more difficulty in reaching a verdict. *See* Larry Heuer & Steven D. Penrod, *Trial Complexity*, 18 LAW & HUM. BEHAV. 29 (1994); *see also* Richard Lempert, *Civil Juries and Complex Cases: Taking Stock After Twelve Years*, in VERDICT 181, 225-26 (Robert E. Litan ed. 1993) (suggesting as an alternative that jurors be provided with daily transcripts of testimony).

A stronger endorsement of juror notetaking is Lynne ForsterLee et al., *Effects of Notetaking on Verdicts and Evidence Processing in a Civil Trial*, 18 LAW & HUM. BEHAV. 567 (1994). Using a simulated complex tort case and mock jurors, the authors found that notetaking jurors were better at correctly differentiating weak cases from strong ones, and at awarding appropriate levels of compensation. They concluded that notetaking in complex cases "holds some promise as a competence enhancing aid for jurors." *Id.* at 577. *See also* Irwin A. Horowitz and Lynne ForsterLee, *The Effects of Notetaking and Trial Transcript Access on Mock Jury Decisions in a Complex Trial*, 25 LAW & HUM. BEHAV. 373 (2001) (finding that notetaking was more efficacious than providing access to the transcript in terms of enhancing mock jurors' competence); *see generally* Valerie P. Hans, *Empowering the Active Jury: A Genuine Tort Reform*, 13 ROGER WILLIAMS U. L. REV. 39, 55-61 (2008) (summarizing studies). One intriguing study suggested that notetaking might have an outcome-influencing effect; six-person mock juries awarded lower amounts of punitive damages in one-plaintiff and multiple-plaintiff cases when they were allowed to take notes. In explaining this conclusion, the authors hypothesized that a smaller jury size, when combined with a lack of notetaking, put information-load pressures on the jury, which responded with higher punitive-damage awards. *See* Irwin A. Horowitz & Kenneth S, Bordens, *The Effects of Jury Size, Evidence Complexity, and Notetaking on Jury Process and Performance in a Civil Trial*, 87 J. APPLIED PSYCHOL. 121 (2002).

Many commentators have jumped on the notetaking bandwagon. *See, e.g.*, MANUAL FOR COMPLEX LITIGATION, FOURTH § 12.42 (2004). In the real world, notetaking is now common, both in complex cases and in routine ones. *See, e.g.*, FLA. STAT. ANN. § 40.50(2) (allowing jury notetaking in civil cases lasting more than five days); Mass. Eye and Ear Infirmary v. QLT, Inc., 495 F. Supp. 2d 188, 198 n.4 (D. Mass. 2007), *aff'd in part and vacated in part on other grounds*, 552 F.3d 47 (1st Cir. 2009). But notetaking is far from universally endorsed; many of its potential drawbacks worry judges who either refuse to allow notetaking or place restrictions on its use. *See* United States v. Darden, 70 F.3d 1507, 1536 (8th Cir. 1995) (notetaking is "not a favored procedure," especially in complex cases; judge properly let jury take notes on exhibits, but not on testimony); United States v. Baker, 10 F.3d 1374, 1403 (9th Cir. 1993) (finding no abuse of discretion when a district court denied juror notetaking due to concerns that notetaking would distract jurors from paying attention to the evidence).

6. Fashioning Comprehensible Jury Instructions

Although juries, by and large, perform their factfinding task well, one area in which juries are demonstrably weak is the comprehension of jury instructions. *See* Nancy S. Marder, *Bringing Jury Instructions into the Twenty-First Century*, 81 NOTRE DAME L. REV. 449 (2006). Two separate problems are presented. One is recall: The jury is expected to remember instructions orally read by the judge when they retire to the jury room. According to one study, individual jurors recalled half or less of the jury instructions, and jurors as a whole were able to recall the instructions with about 80% accuracy. *See* REID HASTIE ET AL., INSIDE THE JURY 78, 81 (1983); *see also id.* at 137 (jurors who had not completed high school recalled only 25% of some instructions). The second problem is the ability of the jury to understand the instructions they have remembered. A great deal of psychological and linguistic evidence suggests that "given the convoluted language and special legal terms, jurors' comprehension of instructions is often very low." *See* VALERIE P. HANS & NEIL VIDMAR, JUDGING THE JURY 121 (1986). One study of criminal instructions suggests that juries correctly referred to the law only 51% of the time, and incorrectly or unclearly referred to the law the other 49%. Deliberation did nothing to clear up these errors; some jurors who began with the correct understanding of the law changed to an incorrect one during deliberation. *See* Phoebe C. Ellsworth, *Are Twelve Heads Better Than One?*, 52 LAW & CONTEMP. PROBS.

205, 218-23 (Autumn 1989). Indeed, in one famous study, juries that received no jury instruction on the issue of negligence performed exactly as well as juries that received the pattern jury instruction. Amiriam Elwork et al., *Juridic Decisions: In Ignorance of the Law or in Light of It?*, 1 LAW & HUM. BEHAV. 163 (1977); *cf.* JOE S. CECIL ET AL., JURY SERVICE IN LENGTHY CIVIL TRIALS 33-34 (1987) (finding that jurors in lengthy trials were more likely to find judge's instructions difficult to understand).

In theory, the judge can solve the problem of recall without any damage to the adversarial system through a number of devices: by delivering the instructions in an interesting and informative way, *see* WILLIAM W SCHWARZER, MANAGING ANTITRUST AND OTHER COMPLEX LITIGATION § 7-2(C)(2) (1982); by letting the jury take notes on the instructions, *see* United States v. Porter, 764 F.2d 1, 12 (1st Cir. 1985); or by providing the jury with copies of the instructions, *see* MANUAL FOR COMPLEX LITIGATION, FOURTH § 12.434 (2004). This last option has attracted some attention. One study found that written instructions did not help the jury better understand, remember, or apply the judge's instructions; did not make the jury more satisfied with the process; did not decrease jury deliberation time; and did not reduce the number of disputes regarding the meaning of instructions. On the other hand, the use of written instructions did not have any drawbacks, such as jurors spending too much time reading them, jurors not focusing on the evidence, or judicial personnel being burdened. *See* Larry Heuer & Steven D. Penrod, *Instructing Jurors: A Field Experiment with Written and Preliminary Instructions*, 13 LAW & HUM. BEHAV. 409 (1989); *cf.* United States v. Quilty, 541 F.2d 172, 177 (7th Cir. 1976) (decision to use written instructions rests in judge's sound discretion). This study involved civil and criminal cases, most of which were not complex.

Providing written instructions cannot solve the more serious problem of juror comprehension. The obvious solution — to rewrite the jury instructions in a simpler, clearer form tailored to the case at hand — is problematic. First, judges are not linguists, and there is no guarantee that clearer instructions will emerge. Second, institutional pressures favor pattern jury instructions; the judge knows that reading the pattern instruction approved by the court of appeals will not result in reversal. Third, even simple stylistic changes often will change, perhaps subtly, the meaning of the substantive law. Finally, some evidence suggests that clearer instructions in criminal cases favor the prosecution, making the writing of clearer instructions a potentially outcome-influencing event. *See* Stephen A. Saltzburg, *Improving the Quality of Jury Decisionmaking*, *in* VERDICT 341, 356 (Robert E. Litan ed. 1993) (describing objections to simplified instructions); Jane Goodman & Edith Greene, *The Use of Paraphrase Analysis in the Simplification of Jury Instructions*, 4 J. SOC. BEHAV. & PERSONALITY 237 (1989) (suggesting that clarification of jury instructions may raise conviction rates).

Despite these concerns, field research suggests that jurors who receive clearer instructions perform better. *See* Elwork et al., *supra*. Indeed, one study of complex federal cases reported that jurors had less confidence in their verdicts when the judge stuck closely to the pattern jury instructions. Larry Heuer & Steven D. Penrod, *Trial Complexity*, 18 LAW & HUM. BEHAV. 29 (1994). As a result, there has been a strong academic movement in the direction of creating simpler jury instructions. *See, e.g.,* Saltzburg, *supra,* at 355-58; SCHWARZER, *supra,* § 7-2(C)(2) (describing rules to follow in drafting such instructions); *see also* ROBERT MACCOUN, IMPROVING JURY COMPREHENSION IN CRIMINAL AND CIVIL TRIALS (1995) (endorsing the idea in theory, but recognizing the need for more empirical research). Thus far, the movement has played less well in the courts.

7. Changing the Deliberation Process: General Verdicts with Interrogatories, Special Verdicts, and Sequential Verdicts

Another mechanism for enhancing comprehension is to reshape the jury's deliberation process in a way that makes it focus on discrete issues. Three devices are sometimes employed. The first is the special verdict, in which the jury answers only the factual questions propounded to it; the judge then uses the jury's answers to assess liability or damages. *See* Fed. R. Civ. P. 49(a). Second is the general verdict accompanied by answers to written questions; here, the jury renders a verdict on the ultimate issues, but is again asked a series of questions whose answers reflect (in theory, at least) the factual bases for its decision. *See* Fed. R. Civ. P. 49(b). Third, the "periodic segmented special verdict" (or sequential verdict) allows a court to ask a jury to render a special verdict on some factual issues first, then to return to the courtroom to hear more evidence and render more special verdicts on other issues later. Obviously, depending on the answers given in the special verdicts, later trial proceedings may be unnecessary. This last approach is not specifically countenanced in the Federal Rules of Civil Procedure or Evidence, but some judges believe that the power to order a periodic segmented special verdict derives from Federal Rule of Evidence 611. For a balanced presentation of all three devices, including their benefits and drawbacks, see Jonathan D. Casper, *Restructuring the Traditional Civil Jury: The Effects of Changes in Composition and Procedures, in* VERDICT 414, 432-44 (Robert E. Litan ed. 1993); *see also* Larry Heuer & Steven Penrod, *Trial Complexity*, 18 LAW & HUM. BEHAV. 29 (1994) (reporting on a field experiment in which special verdict forms were found useful in some, but not all, complex cases; forms were most useful in cases with large quantities of information).

Aside from the segmented special-verdict procedure, none of these devices is a means to limit trial information. Their strongest claim for adoption, then, is that they increase juror comprehension of the evidence. Can special verdicts or general verdicts with interrogatories increase the level of jury comprehension, when they are not even provided to the jury until after the evidence has been heard?

The segmented special-verdict procedure limits trial information, and might enhance juror comprehension because all of the testimony on a particular point is heard within a shorter time frame. But this procedure falls prey to the outcome-determinative concerns that we studied in the context of bifurcation. *See supra* pp. 1042-45. One possibility would be to treat each segmented verdict as preliminary, subject to reconsideration when the jury retires for final deliberations. Of course, if the verdict is treated merely as preliminary, one of the great advantages of segmenting — that some of the later testimony can be eliminated — will no longer exist.

The general verdict with interrogatories preserves a measure of jury discretion while providing a measure of jury control. A practical drawback of this procedure, which arises with some frequency, is that the jury's general verdict is not always consistent with its answers to interrogatories. In such cases Rule 49(b) instructs the trial court either to enter judgment in accordance with the answers, to return the case to the jury for further consideration, or to order a new trial. When the answers are also inconsistent with each other, Rule 49(b) permits only the latter two options. Trial and appellate courts, however, sometimes go to great lengths to make answers consistent. For instance, in *Watkins v. Fibreboard Corp.*, 994 F.2d 253 (5th Cir. 1993), a jury found in answer to one interrogatory that plaintiff's exposure to asbestos products had caused no disease, but then went on to answer another interrogatory that plaintiff should be compensated for his injuries resulting from asbestos exposure. The court of appeals said that, due to somewhat different definitions of "disease" and "injury" in the judge's instructions, the jury could have legitimately understood "disease" and "injury" to be different things.

Sometimes, however, even inventive interpretation cannot create consistency, leaving a judge with the choice between further deliberation or a new trial. If a new trial is ordered, can the judge limit the trial just to those aspects on which there was an inconsistency? In *In re New York Asbestos Litigation,* 155 F.R.D. 61 (S.D.N.Y. 1994), a jury found that one defendant's asbestos was a proximate cause of harm, but then allocated 0% of the responsibility to that defendant. The trial judge ordered a new trial limited just to the issue of the relative percentage of that defendant's responsibility. Does such a limited trial pass Seventh Amendment scrutiny? *See* Gasoline Prods. Co. v. Champlin Refining Co., 283 U.S. 494 (1931).

Special verdicts or general verdicts with interrogatories have enjoyed many champions, including judges such as Jerome Frank and John Brown; other judges, such as Charles Clark and Learned Hand, were more cautious. *See* 9B CHARLES ALAN WRIGHT & ARTHUR R. MILLER, FEDERAL PRACTICE AND PROCEDURE § 2505 (3d ed. 2008). Commentators tend to endorse the idea, especially in complex cases. *See, e.g.,* MANUAL FOR COMPLEX LITIGATION, FOURTH § 12.451 (2004). But these devices are not frequently used, even in complex cases. *See* 9B WRIGHT & MILLER, *supra,* §§ 2502, 2505; William W Schwarzer, *Reforming Jury Trials*, 132 F.R.D. 575, 586 (1991).

Not surprisingly, the decision to use special verdicts or general verdicts with interrogatories, as well as the form of the questions, lie within the discretion of the trial judge. *See* 9B WRIGHT & MILLER, *supra*, §§ 2505, 2508, 2511-12.

C. CONCLUDING THOUGHTS

One of the main purposes of this chapter was to explore techniques by which both the demand for rational adjudication and the right to jury trial could be preserved. You have now seen a wealth of alternative trial structures and formats. There are many other ideas — such as juror notebooks, providing daily transcripts or glossaries of terms to jurors, creating juror orientation materials, and so on — on which we did not touch or touched only briefly. Imaginative lawyers and judges will always be coming up with new ideas and new technologies; perhaps you have come up with a few of your own.

These various devices can often be used in conjunction with each other. If they all were used, the result would be a trial that resembles the trial of our common law tradition in name only. *See* Sims v. ANR Freight Sys., Inc., 77 F.3d 846, 849 (5th Cir. 1996) (suggesting that the combination of detailed stipulations of fact, judicial comment on evidence and questioning of witnesses, and setting rigorously enforced time limits "adversely impacted on the comprehensibility of the evidence to the point that [plaintiff] was denied a trial," but nonetheless finding the error harmless). Maybe a new form of trial is not a bad thing: "Fundamentally, trial procedures and evidentiary rules should be changed and simplified to embrace modern communication methods as well as modern knowledge of how we, as human beings, think and make decisions." BROOKINGS INST., CHARTING A FUTURE FOR THE CIVIL JURY SYSTEM 16 (1992). Are you willing to make compromises with tradition to keep alive the aspirations of reasoned decision-making and jury trial?

If you are not willing to make the sorts of compromises that this chapter suggests, would it be better to eliminate the jury? Would it be better not to have aggregation and discovery rules that put these enormous pressures on our trial system? Would it be better to handle complex cases through an administrative system?

Although aggregation and pretrial issues logically precede trial, and an administrative solution seems to raise issues distinct from the judicial system's method for trial, a procedural system's trial structure dictates logically antecedent and seemingly independent procedural and substantive choices. In choosing trial procedure, you dictate an entire procedural and substantive world.

PART FOUR

REMEDIAL COMPLEXITY

The parties have been aggregated, pretrial proceedings have finished, and the settlement or trial has concluded. Assuming that the defendants are not absolved of responsibility, the case now enters its final phase — the remedial phase. In many ways, this phase is the most important. Plaintiffs and their lawyers don't often litigate to obtain empty victories; they litigate to obtain a concrete remedy. If, for some reason, that remedy cannot be obtained or can be obtained only with undue difficulty, it is unlikely that most plaintiffs will bother to litigate in the first place. Furthermore, in many large-scale cases, the remedial phase is often more protracted and contested than the liability phase. For instance, in *Brown v. Board of Education*, the liability phase lasted only a few years, and was essentially over by 1954. The remedial phase lasted more than forty years. Likewise, in latent-injury mass torts, the settlement or judgment often comes after three to five years of litigation; implementation of the remedy may last for twenty to thirty years.

In the American system, the basic principle for providing a remedy is, to use Professor Laycock's term, "restoring the plaintiff to his rightful position." *See* Douglas A. Laycock, Modern American Remedies 11 (3d ed. 2002). Whether through damages for harm that has already occurred or through an injunction to prevent harm that has not yet occurred, the principle attempts to place the plaintiff in the position that he or she would have enjoyed in a counterfactual world without wrongful behavior. A nice corrective correspondence exists between the plaintiff and the defendant; the defendant did a wrong to the plaintiff, and now must provide a remedy to that plaintiff. Plaintiffs' rights and defendants' remedies are mirror images.

That nice correspondence between plaintiff and defendant — between right and remedy — does not exist in litigation that is complex in the remedial sense. The defendant may be a large institution that engaged in a long-standing pattern of wrongdoing, so that it is impossible either to match the wronged plaintiffs and the wrongdoing defendants or even to know exactly what the rightful position is. The costs of providing the traditional one-to-one remedy may be so high that the delivery of the remedy will leave plaintiffs with little to no compensation. Nonparties may exert such influence that the parties may be unable to implement the remedy effectively.

The following two chapters examines problems in determining and administering equitable and monetary remedies in complex cases. In some ways, these chapters mark a shift in approach. The three prior forms of complexity — joinder, pretrial, and trial — involved situations in which the cause of complexity was often the lawyers' inability to perform the tasks that the adversarial system had assigned to them. In the final stage of litigation — the remedial stage — the lawyers' role is different. Lawyers might negotiate the shape of the remedy, and they need to enforce it according to their clients' interests. But the central players in the remedial stage are the court, which must declare and enforce the remedy, and the parties, who must implement the remedy. Although Chapter Eleven looks briefly at the important practical question of attorneys' fees, the emphasis in these chapters is on the court, the parties, and their dysfunction.

Nonetheless, common themes run through this Part and the three prior Parts. Throughout the book we have seen that complex litigation makes it difficult for the relevant "player" to fulfill his or her function in the rational adjudication of the dispute; assigning portions of that function to a more powerful judge, however, permits rational adjudication to proceed. In the same way, remedial complexity exists in situations in which either the judge of the adversarial model is unable to perform her adversarial responsibility in determining the remedy, or else the parties are unable to perform their responsibility in implementing the remedy.

These forms of dysfunction can be overcome at the price of taking power away from the parties or lawyers and providing it to the judge. Whether and in what circumstances an increase in judicial power can either help the judge to declare the remedy or help the parties to implement the remedy are central questions in the following chapters. At the same time, several subsidiary themes emerge: Should we maintain a dual system of remedial principles — one for ordinary litigation and another for complex cases? Does the more powerful judge accord with our notions of the judicial function in American society? Given that many complex remedies involve federal courts, does the judge's more powerful role accord with our notions of the appropriate scope of *federal* power? If the price of complex litigation is the creation of remedial bureaucracies akin to administrative agencies, should complex litigation be handled through non-adjudicative means? How much does the scramble for fees affect the nature and scope of aggregated litigation?

Remedies are litigation's bottom line. Therefore, remedial issues may lie at the end of a complex case, but the answers to these questions necessarily affect and define all that comes before.

CHAPTER ELEVEN

DETERMINING REMEDIES: JUDGMENTS, SETTLEMENTS, AND ATTORNEYS' FEES

This chapter examines problems associated with determining the scope of the remedies in a complex case. The first section explores the difficulties that judges and juries have in declaring remedies — whether injunctive or monetary — in cases that end in a trial. In part because of these difficulties and in part because of the riskiness of trial, however, most complex cases end by settlement. The next section therefore examines some of the issues that arise when the parties settle. Whether the remedy is fixed by judgment or by agreement of the parties, a subsidiary remedial issue is the award of attorneys' fees. Although attorneys' fees are rarely a cause of remedial complexity, they drive so many of the issues in complex litigation that the process of awarding fees merits consideration here.

A. DETERMINING THE REMEDY AFTER TRIAL

Declaring the remedy after a trial that finds the defendant responsible may seem to be one of the easiest tasks in a complex case. Under the "rightful position" principle (or, as Professor Fiss calls it, the "tailoring principle"), the remedy follows ineluctably from the wrong — the wrongdoer places the plaintiff in the position that the plaintiff would have enjoyed but for the wrong. In some cases, the rightful position requires a court to issue an injunction to prevent future harmful consequences from an actual or threatened wrong. In other cases, money is required to compensate plaintiffs for harms that have already occurred. In either event, with the guidance of the lawyers' proofs at trial, the judge or jury should in theory be able to declare the remedy with some ease. And sometimes that is the case; however complex the case might have been in its aggregation, pretrial, or trial phases, the remedial phase is fairly straightforward. In other cases, however, placing the plaintiffs in the rightful position is a difficult — perhaps an impossible — task. The question becomes what a court should do about that fact. Provide no remedy? Abandon the "rightful position" principle in favor of some other principle? What other principle?

1. Injunctive Relief

Injunctive remedies either try to bar illegal behavior before it occurs (these are sometimes called preventive injunctions) or try to prevent the harmful future consequences of past illegal behavior (these are sometimes called reparative injunctions). When the plaintiffs seek an injunction against a government agency or major corporation and the injunction seeks to force a significant restructuring of the operations of that institution (such as desegregating a school system or changing hiring practices), these injunctions are often called structural injunctions. Structural injunctions can be either preventive or reparative, but they are typically reparative. Complex cases involving structural reparative injunctions can pose unique problems in determining the appropriate scope of the remedy.

BRADLEY V. MILLIKEN

540 F.2d 229 (6th Cir. 1976), *aff'd*, 433 U.S. 267 (1977)

■ PHILLIPS, Chief Judge.

When this school desegregation case was filed in August 1970, Ronald Bradley, one of the black plaintiffs, had been assigned to enter the kindergarten of a Detroit school whose enrollment was 97 per cent black. There have been numerous court proceedings since that time, culminating in the opinion of the Supreme Court in *Milliken v. Bradley*, 418 U.S. 717 (1974) . . . . The Supreme Court remanded with directions for "prompt formulation of a decree directed to eliminating the segregation found to exist in Detroit city schools, a remedy which has been delayed since 1970."

This court now reviews appeals and cross-appeals from various orders and decisions of the District Court . . . .

In September 1976 Ronald Bradley is scheduled to enter the sixth grade of the Clinton School, which now is more than 99 per cent black. The decisions of the District Court which we now review do nothing to correct the racial composition of the Clinton School. They grant no relief to Ronald Bradley nor to the majority of the class of black students he represents.

Nevertheless, this court finds itself in the frustrating position of having to leave standing the results reached by the District Judge on the issue of assignment of students, although we disagree with parts of his opinions and orders. Our affirmance is found to be necessary for the simple reason that reversal would be an exercise in futility under the situation now existing in the Detroit school system and the law of this case as established by the Supreme Court in *Milliken v. Bradley*. . . .

II. The Remedy

It is the law of this case that both the State of Michigan and the Detroit Board of Education have committed acts which have been causal factors in creating the de jure segregation which exists in the public schools of Detroit. The principal question to be resolved on the present appeal involves the remedy. . . .

a) Previous Efforts to Effect a Remedy

After his finding of de jure segregation, Judge Roth grappled with the problem of fashioning a remedy in accordance with *Swann v. Board of Education*, 402 U.S. 1 (1971), and *Brown v. Board of Education*, 349 U.S. 294 (1955). Initially he contemplated a "Detroit only" solution. A motion was made to add other school districts as parties defendant. Judge Roth reserved a decision on this motion pending submission and consideration of desegregation plans. . . .

Judge Roth required the school board defendants, Detroit and State, to develop and submit plans of desegregation, "designed to achieve the greatest possible degree of actual desegregation, taking into account the practicalities of the situation." Three "Detroit only" desegregation plans were submitted by the plaintiffs and by the Detroit Board of Education. Judge Roth found that:

> . . . none of the plans would result in the desegregation of the public schools of the Detroit school district. . . . [Relief] of segregation in the Detroit public schools cannot be accomplished within the corporate geographical limits of the city. . . .

[On interlocutory appeal from this decision, the court of appeals] held that it would be within the equity power of the District Court to adopt a plan of desegregation extending beyond the boundaries of the Detroit School District. . . .

The Supreme Court reversed the decision of this court, holding that no remedy involving any school district other than Detroit would be within the equitable power of the District Court without evidence that the suburban district or districts had committed acts of de jure segregation. . . .

b) The Remedy at Issue on Present Appeals

District Judge DeMascio[, who handled the case after Judge Roth's death,] was faced with an extremely difficult (if not impossible) assignment, confronted as he was with the responsibility of formulating a decree which would eliminate the unconstitutional segregation found to exist in the Detroit public schools, without transgressing the limits established by the Supreme Court. . . .

The plan adopted by the District Court became effective as of the beginning of the winter-spring semester, 1976. As of September 26, 1975, the Detroit public schools enrolled 247,774 students, 75.1 per cent of whom were black. In broad outline the plan adopted by the District Court required the reassignment of 27,524 students, of whom 21,853 would require bus transportation. The plan changed the racial balance in 105 schools out of approximately 300 zoned schools in the system. Prior to the implementation of the plan approximately 80 schools had enrollments of a majority of white students. Under the District Court's plan, 67 of these schools received black students through transportation and rezoning. The result of the student reassignments is that no school in Detroit, with two marginal exceptions, will have an enrollment of less than 30 per cent black students. Moreover, 47 of the previously white schools have become more than 40 per cent black.

In addition, 38 schools, the majority of which previously were at least 80 per cent black, received white students via transportation and rezoning. Under the plan 25 of these schools became 45 to 55 per cent black. Furthermore, at least 23 of Detroit's schools, enrolling approximately 22,599 students, contain a substantial mix of black and white students without any student reassignment. . . .

Finally, the District Court ordered the closing of certain antiquated schools, the establishment of vocational centers available on a non-racial basis to all qualifying students, and certain Educational Components . . . .

Although some improvements have been accomplished by the District Court, the plan contains glaring defects that could never pass constitutional muster and would not be countenanced by this court in a different factual situation. . . .

Notwithstanding the reassignments effected by the District Court, the percentage of black students in each of the eight regions remains substantially unchanged under the adopted plan. Only twelve of the 157 zoned schools with previous enrollments over 90 percent black have become under 90 percent black. Approximately half of Detroit's schools remain more than 90 percent black. Moreover, the three regions which contain the highest concentration of black students, regions 1, 5 and 8, remain virtually untouched. This means that approximately 83,000 students are granted no relief from unconstitutional de jure segregation. . . .

We recognize that the overwhelming number of black students in Detroit and their concentration in the inner city undoubtedly makes some one-race schools unavoidable under any "Detroit only" remedy. However, when the Detroit School Board virtually eliminated regions 1, 5 and 8 from both its initial plan and the plan finally adopted, it assumed the heavy burden of justifying its elimination of the schools located in these three regions. . . .

The Board's burden of justification is particularly heavy in this case because the three regions which the Board has left untouched, in the inner city, are in the area most affected by the acts of de jure segregation of which both the Detroit and State defendants have been found guilty.

The records discloses no adequate justification for excluding regions 1, 5 and 8 from the plan. The principal testimony pertaining to the reasons for excluding the inner city from student reassignments came from Merle Henrickson, Director of Planning and Building Studies for the Detroit Board. Mr. Henrickson stated that the inner city "was beyond the limits of possible treatment." Exclusion of the inner city was necessary, in his view, in order to maintain "the racial mix of desegregated schools." The result of desegregating the inner city, he predicted, would be white flight. . . .

Even though we do not approve of that part of the District Court's plan which fails to take any action with respect to schools in Regions 1, 5 and 8, this court finds itself unable to give any direction to the District Court which would accomplish the desegregation of the Detroit school system in light of the realities of the present racial composition of Detroit. . . .

Recognizing the absence of alternatives, we affirm the judgment of the District Court on the issue of assignment of students in areas other than Regions 1, 5 and 8. . . . We must, however, remand the case for further consideration in regard to the three central regions of the City of Detroit which both the school board and the District Judge excluded from their proposed remedial plans. We cannot hold that where unconstitutional segregation has been found, a plan can be permitted to stand which fails to deal with the three regions where the majority of the most identifiably black schools are located.

We recognize that it would be appropriate for us at this point to supply guidelines to the District Judge as to what he should do under this remand. Omission of such guidelines is not based on any failure to consider the problem in depth. It is based upon the conviction which this court had at the time of its [prior] opinion in this case — and for the reasons carefully spelled out therein — that genuine constitutional desegregation can not be accomplished within the school district boundaries of the Detroit School District. . . .

The case is remanded to the District Court for further proceedings not inconsistent with this opinion.

Notes

1. The Supreme Court subsequently affirmed portions of the district court's proposed remedial plan in *Bradley*. Milliken v. Bradley, 433 U.S. 267 (1977). It did not review the student re-assignment portions of the plan. On remand, the district court sought to follow the court of appeals' instructions to do something about the student re-assignment portion of the plan, but finally held that there were no lingering effects of de jure segregation in Detroit because the few neighborhoods in which intentional segregation had once occurred were now entirely African-American. Hence, the district court concluded, there was nothing left to remedy.

The court of appeals reversed as clearly erroneous the finding of no lingering effects. Again it ordered that the inner-city regions be integrated, but said that it might be enough to integrate a few of the inner-city schools by bringing in white students from other regions. Bradley v. Milliken, 620 F.2d 1143 (6th Cir. 1980). Further remedial issues, efforts by interested parties to intervene, and questions of attorneys fees occupied the Sixth Circuit until 1990 — nineteen years after the case was filed. *See* Bradley v. Milliken, 585 F. Supp. 348 (E.D. Mich. 1984), *vacated*, 772 F.2d 266 (6th Cir. 1985) Bradley v. Milliken, 828 F.2d 1186 (6th Cir. 1987); Bradley v. Milliken, 918 F.2d 178 (Table), 1990 WL 177183 (6th Cir. Nov. 14, 1990).

2.   If you were the plaintiffs' lawyer in *Bradley*, would you have taken the case if you knew that the most severely disadvantaged students (those discriminated against in Regions 1, 5, and 8) would receive virtually no remedy? Ethically you should explain the risks as well as the benefits of litigation to your client. Would your client be likely to press the case if you said that practical problems like those described in *Bradley* might preclude an effective remedy?

3.   Obviously, if we shake our allegiance to the rightful-position principle, we can avoid the problem of declaring a remedy that haunts *Bradley*. Eliminating reliance on the rightful position was one of Professor Chayes's main points: In public-law litigation, courts no longer conceived of remedies as retrospective, two-party affairs that precisely corrected past wrongs. *See supra* p. 39.   Professor Chayes appeared to replace the rightful-position principle with a principle of "equity" (in the modern and not in the historical sense; even in its heyday, equity aimed to keep plaintiffs in the rightful position). Yet Professor Chayes's notion of "doing good for the polity" is not without its problems.

(a) The first problem is a legal one. Although the Supreme Court has occasionally waffled on the issue, it has generally been firmly committed to the rightful-position principle in constitutional adjudication. The waffling is nicely captured in *Swann v. Charlotte-Mecklenburg Board of Education*, 402 U.S. 1, 15, 28 (1971), in which the Court observed that "the scope of a district court's equitable powers to remedy past wrongs is broad, for breadth and flexibility are inherent in equitable remedies" and that

> [t]he remedy for such segregation may be administratively awkward, inconvenient, and even bizarre in some situations and may impose burdens on some; but all awkwardness and inconvenience cannot be avoided in the interim period when remedial adjustments are being made to eliminate the dual school systems.

At the same time, however, *Swann* stated that "[a]s with any equity case, the nature of the violation determines the scope of the remedy." *Id.* at 16.

Later cases more clearly committed the Court to the view that the rightful position was the *maximum* remedial principle for federal courts in institutional-reform litigation.   Milliken v. Bradley, 418 U.S. 717, 746 (1974) ("[T]he remedy is necessarily designed, as all remedies are, to restore the victims of discriminatory conduct to the position they would have occupied in the absence of such conduct."); Dayton Bd. of Educ. v. Brinkman, 433 U.S. 406, 420 (1977) (holding that a desegregation order should correct only the "incremental segregative effect" of illegal discrimination). In *Milliken v. Bradley*, 433 U.S. at 280-81, the Court adopted a three-factor test, the last of which limits rightful-position relief:

> In the first place, like other equitable remedies, the nature of the desegregation remedy is to be determined by the nature and scope of the constitutional violation. *Swann*, 402 U.S. at 16. The remedy must therefore be related to "the condition alleged to offend the Constitution . . . ." *Milliken*, 418 U.S. at 738. Second, the decree must indeed be remedial in nature, that is, it must be designed as nearly as possible "to restore the victims of discriminatory conduct to the position they would have occupied in the absence of such conduct." *Id.* at 746. Third, the federal courts in devising a remedy must take into account the interests of state and local authorities in managing their own affairs, consistent with the Constitution.

Accord Missouri v. Jenkins, 515 U.S. 70, 88 (1995).

The constraints suggested by the third factor— separation-of-power and federalism concerns that limit federal-court interference with the operation of a state's executive and legislative functions — may prevent courts from restoring plaintiffs to their rightful position. *Cf. Jenkins*, 515 U.S. at 102 ("[T]he District Court must bear in mind that its end purpose is not only 'to remedy the violation' to the extent practicable, but also 'to restore state and local authorities to the control of a school system that is operating in compliance with the Constitution.'"); Bd. of Educ. of Okla. City Pub. Sch. v. Dowell, 498 U.S. 237, 248 (1991) (permitting dissolution of desegregation decrees in part due to "[c]onsiderations based on the allocation of powers within out federal system").

(b) There are also practical difficulties with abandoning a rightful-position approach in favor of "do good" remedies:

> Chayes's approach[ ] would put the judge in a difficult personal position. The judge in street clothes is in principle an equal of the parties. What justifies the power of the judge in robes is that the judge speaks of the law. Regarding findings of liability, judges can readily respond to a defendant's rebuke "how dare you find me liable" with "the law made you liable." This answer is inadequate, however, when the defendant challenges the judge's authority to issue an injunction because the judge must exercise discretion in shaping the injunction to fit the case. . . . [B]y turning the judge into a policy maker, Chayes's approach fails to offer constraints to both legitimate the exercise of equitable discretion and allow the judge to cast at least some of the blame for the injunction's consequences onto the law.

David Schoenbrod, *The Measure of an Injunction: A Principle to Replace Balancing the Equities and Tailoring the Remedy*, 72 MINN. L. REV. 627, 656-57 (1988). Aside from these questions of legitimacy, won't whatever principle we select to replace the rightful position — whether it be Professor Chayes's "do good" concept or some other notion — have its own problems in terms of defining and delivering a fair and practical remedy?

4. The rightful-position principle is highly consonant with an adversarial approach to litigation, in which each plaintiff controls her own claims and is entitled to receive only as much remedy as she personally deserves. Is the rightful-position principle normatively required by the form of adjudication? Professor Fuller's classic article on the adversarial system, to which Professor Chayes's article is the classic point-by-point critique, has often been read to make such an argument. *See supra* p. 36.

5. Even if the rightful-position principle is not normatively required, is it nonetheless required by Article III or the Due Process Clause, which embody fundamental norms of federal-court adjudication?

6. If the rightful-position is neither normatively nor constitutionally compelled, should we abandon it in complex cases, just as we have seen courts abandon other adversarial principles when faced with problems of complexity and dysfunction? Indeed, the rightful-position principle is one of the causes of dysfunction in the aggregation area, for the inability of the court to "do good" means that early-filing claimants seeking a remedy restoring them to their rightful positions might disadvantage late-filing claimants seeking a remedy restoring the late filers to their rightful positions. Now we see that the principle can also cause dysfunction at the remedial phase by making it impossible, at least in some cases, to declare a remedy. It can also create constitutional friction.

7. Assuming that the trial court could have overcome the practical impossibility of declaring a remedy, was a desegregation remedy in *Bradley* adequate under the rightful position? The generations of African-American school children who graduated from Detroit schools before a desegregation remedy was put in place received no benefits from the remedy. Shouldn't the judge attempt to undo the many consequences of an inferior education in terms of employment and missed opportunities? Is this even possible? If not, might the provision of "extra" benefits to the next generation of children be "fair" — a rough-and-ready effort to approximate the rightful position on a global scale? Might the provision of extra benefits be justified on the theory that Detroit spent less on African-Americans' education for generations, and the provision of extra benefits disgorges the unjust enrichment that the taxpayers of Detroit enjoyed? Might it be possible to reach across the Detroit city boundary on the same theory — that the white flight caused by illegal patterns of discrimination artificially swelled the tax bases of suburbs, and it is unjust for the suburbs to retain these benefits?

8. A court guided by the rightful-position principle must discontinue the use of its injunctive power as soon as it is no longer necessary. The Court has discussed the showing necessary to dissolve an injunction in several cases. *See* Horne v. Flores, 557 U.S. —, 129 S. Ct. 2579, 2593-94 (2009) (holding that, despite the high showing usually required to modify an injunction, a "flexible approach" to modifying an injunction is necessary in institutional-reform cases; noting that "[f]ederalism concerns are heightened when, as in these cases, a federal court decree has the effect of dictating state or local budget priorities"); Freeman v. Pitts, 503 U.S. 467 (1992); Rufo v. Inmates of Suffolk County Jail, 502 U.S. 367 (1992).

2. Monetary Relief

To the extent that the harmful consequences of the defendant's illegal behavior have manifested themselves in injuries to the plaintiffs, our legal system awards damages. Unless the defendant's conduct caused a purely monetary loss, giving plaintiffs money for their injuries can never precisely restore plaintiffs to the positions they would have occupied but for the illegal conduct, but it is the best that we can do (or at least the best that we have done) in the American legal system.

Determining a monetary remedy poses difficulties that determining injunctive relief usually does not. The principal difficulty arises from the individualization of relief that is typical in cases of monetary compensation. Because the extent of each plaintiff's injury is unique, each plaintiff's award is usually unique as well. Unlike most injunctions, which can issue broadly to protect the rights of groups of plaintiffs, the court must therefore engage in an individualized inquiry to determine whether each plaintiff deserves compensation and, if so, how much compensation. Making this inquiry is costly — in some cases, more costly than the loss that the plaintiff suffered. Moreover, in mass torts, individualized judicial tailoring of the damages for each plaintiff might take years.

In Chapter Ten, we encountered one (decidedly not rightful-position friendly) solution to this problem: trial by statistics, in which each plaintiff receives an award equal to the average recovery awarded to a sample of plaintiffs after discounting for the number of meritless claims in the sample. *See supra* p. 1058. Here we examine other issues and solutions.

DOUGHERTY V. BARRY

869 F.2d 605 (D.C. Cir. 1989)

■ RUTH BADER GINSBURG, Circuit Judge.

[Plaintiffs were eight white firefighters alleging reverse discrimination by the District of Columbia Fire Department and its former Administrator, Elijah B. Rogers. Plaintiffs argued that the Department had discriminated on the basis of race by promoting two black firefighters to deputy fire chief. Five of the plaintiffs brought suit under 42 U.S.C. § 1981 and Title VII; three filed only under Title VII. The district court held that the defendants had violated both § 1981 and Title VII. It awarded each plaintiff an amount of backpay and benefits to compensate for the full value of the promotion.]

I.

. . .

. . . [T]he district court . . . explained why an order directing promotion of any or all of the plaintiffs to deputy chief would be inappropriate. Only two positions had been open, meaning six plaintiffs definitely would not have been promoted even absent discrimination; promotions were based on subjective as well as objective factors, which made it difficult to evaluate plaintiffs against each other; and plaintiffs did "not comprise the entire group of officers eligible for promotion to deputy" at the time.

Nevertheless, the court awarded full monetary relief to each plaintiff in the form of back pay and an annuity adjustment, i.e., for monetary award purposes, each plaintiff was to be recompensed as though he had been promoted to one of the two deputy positions. The court reasoned that defendants could not show "that any particular plaintiff would not have been promoted absent discrimination." Dividing the monetary value of the two promotions eight ways would not make plaintiffs whole, the district court believed, for they had lost the opportunity to gain a large, albeit intangible, benefit — the "pride and respect of one's colleagues which accompany a hard-earned promotion." The District of Columbia and Rogers appealed, challenging the district court's decision only with regard to the timeliness of the Title VII claim and the scope of the relief granted.

II.

[The court concluded that the Title VII action should be dismissed because it was not timely filed and that the three firefighters who were party only to the Title VII action were not entitled to any relief. The five other firefighters who filed claims under § 1981 remained.]

III.

Turning to the question of monetary recovery, we reject appellants' argument that appellees are not entitled to any relief because two other whites [not party to this suit], Joseph R. Granados and Harry H. Shaffer, would have gotten the promotions absent discrimination. As the district court held, once appellees proved they had been subjected to disparate treatment, the burden shifted to appellants to show by clear and convincing evidence that each appellee was not entitled to relief because he would not have received one of the promotions even absent discrimination.[8] Appellants failed to carry that burden in this case. . . .

---

8. A court may impose classwide relief for a group of individuals subjected to discrimination where it is impossible to determine which particular individual would have received the benefit but for the discrimination without falling "into 'a quagmire of hypothetical judgments.'" Once the group establishes liability, as the district court found appellees did, there is a presumption that each member is entitled to relief; the burden is on the defendant to "rebut that presumption in each individual case." Although this case does not involve a class action, the same principles apply because all of the appellees were eligible for the promotion, and the district court was unable to determine which of them would not have been promoted. Furthermore, although cases establishing this allocation of burdens generally involve Title VII, we see no reason — and neither party offers any — to treat section 1981 differently in this regard. Dismissing the Title VII claim therefore does not affect the allocation of burdens.

Although appellees are entitled to monetary relief, the extent of that relief granted by the district court was overly generous. We are unaware of any support for the district court's decision to award full recompense to each appellee as though each had been promoted. Rather, precedent favors dividing the monetary value of the two promotions among appellees pro rata.

Dividing the value of the promotions among appellees more closely approximates the goal of " 'recreat[ing] the conditions and relationships that would have been had there been no' unlawful discrimination." If the district court had been able to determine with certainty which two of the appellees would have received the promotions, the proper course would have been to award those two appellees full relief and the others none. Because the court was unable to do so, however, one must assume that each appellee enjoyed less than a one hundred percent chance of being promoted. By awarding each appellee full back pay, however, the district court treated each as though he possessed a one hundred percent chance of receiving one of the promotions, counter to that court's own conclusion that one could not determine for certain which appellees, if any, would have been promoted. Thus, in order to restore appellees to the position they would have occupied absent discrimination, the district court should have awarded each appellee a fraction of the promotions' value commensurate with the likelihood of his receiving one of the promotions.

Because the relief awarded by the district court thus put appellees in a better position than they would have occupied absent discrimination, we vacate the award and remand the matter to the district court. The district court has already stated that it is unable to evaluate appellees against one another; on remand, then, the district court may simply divide the monetary value of the two promotions equally among appellees.[10]

. . . Accordingly, we vacate the judgment of the district court in part and remand for calculation of the monetary relief due appellees Dougherty, Buckler, Watts, Ford, and Flaherty.

KYRIAZI V. WESTERN ELECTRIC CO.

465 F. Supp. 1141 (D.N.J. 1979), *aff'd*, 647 F.2d 388 (3d Cir. 1981)

■   STERN, District Judge.

At the conclusion of "Stage I" of this Title VII litigation — the liability phase — this Court found that Western Electric discriminated against its

---

10. We need not consider the thornier question of whether the fraction due each appellee should in fact be smaller because other battalion chiefs not party to this suit were eligible for the promotions. Appellants have made no claim that the other qualified battalion chiefs should be considered in devising the share due each appellee, and appellants' counsel specifically conceded at oral argument that if we rejected the argument that Granados and Shaffer would have received the promotions, the value of the two promotions should be divided among appellees.

female employees, applicants and former employees in the areas of hiring, promotion, participation in job training programs, layoffs, wages and opportunities for testing. We now enter "Stage II", the damage phase. Stage II requires adjudication of the claims of thousands of class members. . . .

1.   *Burden of Proof*

The Supreme Court has made clear that once there has been a finding of class-wide discrimination, the burden then shifts to the employer to prove that a class member was not discriminated against; that is, a finding of discrimination creates a rebuttable presumption in favor of recovery. . . .

Accordingly, the sole burden upon class members will be to demonstrate that they are members of the class, that is, that now or at any time since June 9, 1971, they were either employed by Western, applied for employment at Western or were terminated by Western. . . . [O]nce an individual demonstrates that she is a class member, the burden will then shift to Western to demonstrate that the individual class member was not the victim of discrimination. . . .

3.   *Computation of Back Pay Awards*

The courts have adopted a number of approaches in connection with the computation of back pay awards. One approach, the "pro rata" formula . . ., looks to the difference between the salary of the class members computed collectively and that received by employees of comparable skills and seniority, not the victims of discrimination. The class member then receives his pro rata share of that collective difference, based upon his salary differential and the number of competitors for the position. Another approach is the "test period" approach, . . . in which the court awards class members the difference between the pay they receive after implementation of the Title VII decree and the pay they received while the discriminatory policies were in force. . . .

The Court finds none of these approaches appropriate here. As we found in connection with Stage I, we deal with discrimination which manifests itself in a number of ways. . . . It is, therefore, apparent that a backpay award must take into account the fact that a male and a female entering Western with comparable skills would, over a period of time, take dramatically divergent paths.

While this approach will not yield an exact measure of damages, neither could any other approach. However, the law is clear that where one has been damaged by the wrong of another, the victim is not to be denied any recompense merely because the exact measure of damages is uncertain. The approach we adopt at least gives individual consideration to each claimant and, if not precise, it is no more imprecise than lumping claimants into groups and extracting averages, or otherwise depersonalizing victims of discrimination by running them through a mathematical blender. . . .

... According to Western, if there were three women who should have been considered for one promotion and none were, and if we cannot now determine which of the three women should have received the promotion, then each one receives one-third of the benefits. As Western notes, this approach does shield Western from having to pay three increases when only one was actually possible, but it also unjustly penalizes the one woman who was entitled to *all* — not just one-third — of the benefits of that promotion. Under Western's approach, two of the claimants get a windfall while the actual victim receives only one-third of the back pay to which she is statutorily entitled. If we know that all three claimants were discriminated against in that they were not considered for promotion but that only one — which, we do not know — would have actually received the promotion, then all three should get the full benefit of the promotional opportunity. Where it is proved that an employer unlawfully disregarded women for promotion, it is better that it pay a little more than to permit an innocent party to shoulder the burdens of the guilty. Western *will* be permitted to demonstrate that the promotion would have gone to one class member, rather than the others. However, if Western cannot demonstrate which claimant would have received the promotion, Western cannot divide the benefits of the one job. It is no more unreal to construe three promotions out of one, than to divide the salary increase of one promotion among three prospects. Either smacks of some artificiality but the latter protects the wrongdoer at the expense of the innocent.

[Because there were as many as 10,000 claimants, the court then referred the implementation of the remedy to a special master.]

Notes

1. Is it equitable to give the individual plaintiff who would have been promoted absent discrimination only a partial remedy because the defendant's misconduct has made it difficult to determine which individual would have been promoted? Is it equitable to the defendant to pay the value of five promotions when only two were available? Can the difference between *Dougherty* and *Kyriazi* be explained by the courts' different conceptions of the victim — the group (*Dougherty*) or the individuals in the group (*Kyriazi*)? Can it be explained by a difference in emphasis between optimal deterrence (*Dougherty*) and full compensation to the victim (*Kyriazi*)? To what extent should substantive preferences for optimal deterrence limit the rightful-position principle? *Cf.* United States v. City of Warren, 138 F.3d 1083, 1099 (6th Cir. 1998) (distinguishing *Dougherty* and awarding full backpay when it was likely that an African-American applicant would have been selected for position).

2. Should the amount of backpay distributed among the *Dougherty* plaintiffs be discounted because some of the white firefighters eligible to compete for the promotion were not before the court? *Dougherty* leaves this "thornier" question open. Suppose that no discount occurs. Would a white firefighter be precluded from proving that he or she would have gotten the

promotion in a subsequent lawsuit? If preclusion occurs, don't we have the classic form of dysfunction that we studied in Part I? On the other hand, if the defendant's assets are sufficient to satisfy both claims, there is no dysfunction if the later lawsuit is permitted to proceed. But, using the rightful-position principle as our lens, it seems unfair to the defendant to pay twice for the same promotion. Does *Kyriazi* convince you that the defendant's wrongfulness, plus its ability to prove that the later-filing plaintiff didn't deserve the remedy, should assuage our concern for this unfairness? *See* Meredith v. Beech Aircraft Corp., 18 F.3d 890 (10th Cir. 1994) (holding that a later-filing plaintiff could not be precluded from litigating her entitlement to the promotion based on a judgment entered in favor of an earlier-filing claimant because she was not a party to earlier suit).

Of course, this particular "thorny" issue disappears if our procedural rules mandated the joinder of all interested parties in one lawsuit. But complete joinder still would not solve the declaration problem faced in *Dougherty* and *Kyriazi*.

3.   The risks of inequitable distribution of remedies among plaintiffs and unfairness to the defendant become magnified in class actions. Should courts consider this fact when deciding whether to certify class actions?

4.   Comparable problems of determining the proper monetary remedy can arise with regard to the allocation of punitive damages. Some courts have suggested that an absolute limit exists on the amount of punitive damages and the number of times that punitive damages might be used to punish a defendant for the same conduct. *See* Juzwin v. Amtorg Trading Corp., 705 F. Supp. 1053 (D.N.J. 1989), *vacated in part*, 718 F. Supp. 1233 (D.N.J. 1989); *contra* Dunn v. HOVIC, 1 F.3d 1371 (3d Cir. 1993), *modified on other grounds*, 13 F.3d 58 (3d Cir. 1993). Some states have passed statutes that permit punitive damages to be awarded in only one case. *See* GA. CODE ANN. § 51-12-5.1(e)(1) (limited to products-liability cases); *cf.* MO. STAT. ANN. § 510.263(4) (providing a credit for any punitive-damage awards paid in prior cases involving the same conduct). How should a court respond to the problem of determining and distributing a single punitive-damage award among a large group of plaintiffs? Should it certify a mandatory class action? *See supra* pp. 396-401.

5.   One advantage of *Dougherty*'s approach over *Kyriazi*'s approach is that it eliminates part of the costly endeavor of individualizing the remedy. Once the total amount of damage is determined, the award is neatly split among the claimants. This tidy solution was also one of the central features of the trial-by-statistics approach.

More generally, should the costliness of restoring plaintiffs to their rightful position act as a constraint on using the rightful-position principle in mass litigation? Suppose that, in a consumer-fraud case, there are 2,000 plaintiffs. Half of the plaintiffs suffer an injury of $500 and half suffer an injury of $50. The costs of determining eligibility for an award, determining the amount of the award, and distributing the award is $100. It makes no sense to spend $100 to deliver a $50 remedy, does it? Suppose that the court deducts $75 in benefits from each of the $500 awards to cover the cost of giving the $50 claimants $25 in relief, in addition to deducting the $100 necessary to determine and distribute the awards to the $500 claimants? Under this approach, some plaintiffs get $325 and some get $25. The total amount given to all the plaintiffs would be $350,000. Is this a fair approach? On the other hand, if the court gave nothing to the $50 claimants, the $500 claimants would receive $400 apiece, or $400,000 in total. So it's more efficient to give the $50 claimants nothing. Does the rightful-position principle compel a court to be inefficient? (Note that the inefficiency would remain even if we required the defendant to absorb the cost of determining and distributing the remedy; in any event, the law has never required the defendant to absorb these costs.) Conversely, does the principle compel that some plaintiffs get nothing?

6. Do the questions in these Notes, as well as the similar questions posed about injunctive relief, convince you that we should abandon the rightful-position principle in complex litigation? With what should we replace it? The damage-averaging principle found in the trial-by-statistics method and derided as a "mathematical blender" in *Kyriazi*? But even this approach is not costless. In any event, in light of the Supreme Court's adherence to the rightful-position principle in constitutional adjudication involving injunctive relief, *see supra* p. 1042, Note 3(a), is it possible for federal courts to abandon the principle in cases seeking damages?

7. What effect would abandoning the principle have on the problems of aggregation, pretrial, and trial complexity? Put differently, how many of the problems of complex litigation does the rightful-position principle spawn?

B. SETTLEMENT

The bulk of cases, including the bulk of complex cases, settle. There are many good reasons for the parties to settle, such as eliminating the uncertainty of liability exposure, obtaining a certain remedy, avoiding further litigation costs, providing the parties with some measure of control over important decisions affecting their welfare, and moving on with the parties' lives and business plans. From the court's perspective, settlement saves scarce judicial resources, often increases litigant satisfaction with the litigation process, and, as we have seen in the last section, avoids some intractable problems of calculating and delivering a remedy. All of these benefits seem heightened in complex litigation. As a result, it should be no surprise that "[t]he compromise of complex litigation is encouraged by the courts and favored by public policy." 4 WILLIAM B. RUBENSTEIN ET AL., NEWBERG ON CLASS ACTIONS § 11:41 (4th ed. 2002).

At the same time, settlements in complex cases, which often involve important public controversies, raise significant concerns. We worry that the plaintiffs' lawyers, lured in by the large fees that a settlement promises, will settle the case in their own best interests rather than in the interests of the plaintiffs they represent. We also worry that, unless the settlement provides only group relief or else specifies the individualized relief that each plaintiff can obtain, some plaintiffs may end up being treated better than others. (This is a great concern in cases in which money is awarded, because the settlement is usually for a lump sum; distribution of exact awards comes later, after the settlement concludes.) Finally, we worry that no one — not the plaintiffs' lawyers, not the defense lawyers, and not the court — has any incentive to derail a bad settlement.

In a class action, the court must approve the settlement. In injunctive cases in which the settlement is enforced by means of a consent decree (in essence, an agreed-to judgment), the court's entry of judgment gives the court the opportunity to examine the terms of the settlement. But no comparable protections necessarily exist in other aggregate settlements, including mass-tort or other monetary settlement. Courts regard the monetary settlement of a simple cases (for instance, a case between a pedestrian and a driver) as a private contractual affair whose terms are of little concern to the court; rightly or wrongly, courts have usually viewed non-class aggregate settlements in the same light.

This section examines some of the issues that arise in class-action and other aggregate settlements.

1. Class-Action Settlements

The standard for approving a class settlement requires the court to determine, after notice to class members and a hearing at which objecting class members can appear, that the settlement is "fair, reasonable, and adequate." Fed. R. Civ. P. 23(e)(1)-(2). The following case explores some of the issues that courts encounter in approving class settlements.

WAL-MART STORES, INC. v. VISA U.S.A., INC.

396 F.3d 96 (2d Cir. 2005)

■   WESLEY, Circuit Judge.

Appellants challenge the district court's approval of a class action settlement . . . . The class action involved approximately five million merchants and alleged, inter alia, that defendants Visa U.S.A. Inc. and MasterCard International Inc. tied merchant use of defendants' debit products to use of defendants' credit cards, in violation of the Sherman Act. Plaintiffs contended that Visa and MasterCard used their power in the credit card market to force merchants to accept an artificially-inflated transaction fee when accepting payment from consumers using debit cards operated by Visa or MasterCard. Plaintiffs further alleged that defendants employed a scheme of anti-competitive conduct to bar competition in the debit card market. In this bitterly contested lawsuit fought by expert counsel on all sides, the parties agreed to settle just before trial commenced.

The resulting settlement was the largest in the history of antitrust law. As part of the settlement, defendants agreed not to tie their debit and credit products together and to pay more than $3 billion to plaintiffs in exchange for the release of any and all claims that were or could have been filed against defendants or their member banks (non-parties in this action) based on the conduct alleged.

On appeal, appellants contest . . . the adequacy of class representation, the adequacy of notice, [and] the fairness of settlement . . . . We affirm the district court's order in all respects.

BACKGROUND

This case involves a clash of commercial titans. Plaintiffs, a class of merchants approximately five million strong led by Wal-Mart, the world's largest retailer, and several other large and sophisticated merchants, including The Limited, Sears, and Safeway, filed suit on October 25, 1996 against Visa U.S.A. Inc. and MasterCard International, Inc. ("Visa" and "MasterCard," respectively), seeking damages amounting to tens of billions of dollars for alleged violations of Sections One and Two of the Sherman Act, 15 U.S.C. §§ 1, 2. First, plaintiffs claimed that the defendants' "Honor All Cards" policy, which forced merchants who accepted Visa and MasterCard credit cards to accept Visa and MasterCard debit cards, was an illegal "tying arrangement" that violated Section One of the Sherman Act.[3] Second, plaintiffs alleged that defendants used their Honor All Cards policy in conjunction with other anti-competitive conduct to monopolize the debit market, in violation of Section Two of the Sherman Act. As a consequence, plaintiffs claimed that they incurred supra-competitive "interchange fees" (described in the next subheading) during every debit and credit transaction made between October 1992 and June 2003. . . .

A. *Visa and MasterCard Transactions*

Essentially, every debit or credit card transaction using a Visa or MasterCard product involves five entities: (1) Visa or MasterCard, (2) a "card-issuing" bank, (3) an "acquiring" bank, (4) a consumer, and (5) a merchant. At the outset, either Visa or MasterCard, each an association, grants a license to a member bank to issue credit and debit cards with its brand name. A "card-issuing" member bank then issues a credit or debit card to a cardholder with either the Visa or MasterCard brand name. An "acquiring" bank, a member of Visa and MasterCard, contracts with a merchant to accept payment through Visa and MasterCard. When a cardholder makes a purchase with either a Visa or MasterCard product, the acquiring institution reimburses the merchant for the cardholder's purchase, less a "discount fee." The discount fee is determined by the

---

3. "A tying arrangement is 'an agreement by a party to sell one product but only on the condition that the buyer also purchases a different (or tied) product.'" *Yentsch v. Texaco, Inc.*, 630 F.2d 46, 56 (2d Cir. 1980).

acquiring institution. The card-issuing bank charges an "interchange fee" each time it provides funds to the acquiring bank as payment to a merchant for the cardholder's purchase. Visa and MasterCard set the interchange fee that all card-issuing banks charge. Economics demands that the discount fee be greater than the interchange fee the acquiring institution must pay to the card-issuing institution. . . .

B. *Procedural History*

Plaintiffs originally filed their complaint on October 26, 1996. The district court certified plaintiffs as a class in February 2000. The class includes "all persons and business entities who have accepted Visa and/or MasterCard credit cards and therefore have been required to accept Visa[ ]Check and/or MasterMoney debit cards under the challenged tying arrangements during the fullest period permitted by the applicable statute of limitations," which is the period from October 25, 1992 through June 21, 2003. Plaintiffs' discovery included "a review of approximately five million pages of documents, almost 400 depositions, discovery from roughly 200 non parties, 54 expert reports, and 21 expert depositions." In June 2002, plaintiffs sent a notice of pendency to all class members. On April 30, 2003, "after complete and exhaustive discovery, summary judgment proceedings, and substantial mediation," Visa and MasterCard each signed a memorandum of understanding setting forth a preliminary settlement agreement with plaintiffs. The final settlement agreements were signed on June 4, 2003. Later that month, the district court approved the notice of settlement, which described the terms of settlement and quoted the Settlement's release verbatim. Eighteen merchants, in this class of approximately five million, filed objections to the Settlement and the allocation plan. In September 2003, the district court held a fairness hearing during which it offered each objector the opportunity to be heard. On December 19, 2003, after considering these objections, the district court issued a Memorandum and Order . . . approving the proposed settlement agreements between plaintiffs and Visa and MasterCard and the plan of allocation to distribute funds to class members . . . . The court entered final judgments on January 30, 2004. Each appellant filed a timely appeal.

C. *The Settlement*

The Settlement is the culmination of approximately seven years of hard-fought litigation and represents "the largest antitrust settlement in history." [In addition to a $3.05 settlement fund, the settlement required the defendants to cease using their"Honor All Cards" rules; to create clear, conspicuous and uniform visual identifiers on Visa and MasterCard debit cards so merchants and consumers can distinguish these products from credit cards; and to lower by roughly one third the interchange rates on debit products for the period from August 1, 2003, through December 31, 2003. In return, Visa and MasterCard received releases for themselves and their member banks from claims arising out of the conduct at issue prior to

January 1, 2004. The district court retained continuing jurisdiction to ensure compliance with the settlement.]

D. *Issues on Appeal*

[One of the objecting class members, Pasta Bella, initiated a class action (known as the *Reyn's* case) against Visa, MasterCard, and three member banks in the United States District Court for the Northern District of California in 2002. The principal claim was that the *Reyn's* defendants fixed credit-card interchange fees charged by issuing banks to acquiring banks, which, in turn, set merchant discount fees charged by acquiring banks to merchants. The District Court for the Northern District of California dismissed *Reyn's* with prejudice, finding that the settlement in this case released the *Reyn's* defendants from further liability.

[Likewise, NuCity initiated a putative class action (called the *Membership Rules* case) in the United States District Court for the Southern District of New York in 2001. This case arose out of an antitrust enforcement action by the United States (called the *Government's Membership Rules* case). In the government's case, the United States] established that Visa and MasterCard's "exclusionary rules" (also known as "membership rules"), which prohibited member banks from issuing competing payment cards, such as American Express or Discover, constituted an illegal boycott and an unreasonable restraint of trade in the credit card market. NuCity filed *Membership Rules* on behalf of merchants injured by the boycott proven in *Government's Membership Rules*. Pursuant to an order by the district court in that case, *Membership Rules* remains in limbo pending the outcome of this appeal. . . .

DISCUSSION

. . .

I. THE RELEASE WAS VALID

Broad class action settlements are common, since defendants and their cohorts would otherwise face nearly limitless liability from related lawsuits in jurisdictions throughout the country. Practically speaking, "[c]lass action settlements simply will not occur if the parties cannot set definitive limits on defendants' liability." Stephenson v. Dow Chem. Co., 273 F.3d 249, 254 (2d Cir. 2001), *aff'd in part by an equally divided court and vacated in part*, 539 U.S. 111 (2003) [*supra* p. 536].

Plaintiffs in a class action may release claims that were or could have been pled in exchange for settlement relief. Plaintiffs' authority to release claims is limited by the "identical factual predicate" and "adequacy of representation" doctrines. Together, these legal constructs allow plaintiffs to release claims that share the same integral facts as settled claims, provided that the released claims are adequately represented prior to settlement. Adequate representation of a particular claim is established mainly by showing an alignment of interests between class members, not by proving vigorous pursuit of that claim. . . .

A. *Identical Factual Predicate Doctrine*

The law is well established in this Circuit and others that class action releases may include claims not presented and even those which could not have been presented as long as the released conduct arises out of the "identical factual predicate" as the settled conduct. . . .

. . . When considering the permissibility of a release, the overlap between elements of *claims* is not dispositive. Class actions may release claims, even if not pled, when such claims arise out of the same factual predicate as settled class claims.

. . . [T]he district court did not abuse its discretion by concluding that the claims in *Membership Rules* are based on the identical factual predicate as the claims in this case. . . .

Even though the *Reyn's* claims may be released with respect to Visa and MasterCard, Pasta Bella objects to the release of the member banks, since they were not parties to this action. However, "class action settlements have in the past released claims against non-parties where, as here, the claims against the non-party being released were based on the same underlying factual predicate as the claims asserted against the parties to the action being settled." The district court did not, therefore, err by finding that the non-party banks could be released from liability for conduct premised on the identical factual predicate of claims alleged in this action.

The banks' settlement contributions further support the district court's conclusion. The banks "not only contributed to the Settlement[ ], but virtually all of the relief comes from them." . . .

B. *Due Process Requires that Released Claims be Adequately Represented*

A determination that all of the settled claims arose from the same factual predicate does not necessarily end the inquiry. Claims arising from a shared set of facts will not be precluded where class plaintiffs have not adequately represented the interests of class members. On appeal, Pasta Bella interprets the adequacy of representation doctrine to require that "settled claims of absent class members [be] adequately represented as a matter of fact before they can be barred." Consequently, Pasta Bella presses that the Settlement inadequately represents the *Reyn's* claims because it does not require payment from the member banks who were defendants in *Reyn's*. In the same vein, NuCity argues that *Membership Rules* seeks damages for billions of dollars stemming from the boycott of credit cards, whereas the Settlement is based merely on damages stemming from alleged tying arrangements in the debit card market and the concomitant effect on interchange rates. Respondents counter that these arguments amount to baseless allegations that the plaintiffs "left significant claims on the table." We agree. Adequate representation is not solely an assessment of effort. Rather, an examination of the interests of the settling plaintiffs and of the Settlement's effect on those who would be bound by it leads us to the conclusion that lead plaintiffs, who are also members of the classes led by Pasta Bella and NuCity, adequately represented the claims asserted in *Reyn's* and *Membership Rules* in this case. . . .

We agree with respondents that due process does not require that all class claims be pursued. Instead, where different claims within a class involve the identical factual predicate, adequate representation of a particular claim is determined by the alignment of interests of class members, not proof of vigorous pursuit of that claim. Thus, the district court did not err in ruling that plaintiffs' release of the *Reyn's* and *Membership Rules* claims did not violate due process, where plaintiffs are members of the *Reyn's* and *Membership Rules* classes and the release was part of the consideration necessary to obtain the largest antitrust settlement in history.

. . . Pasta Bella and NuCity seek greater compensation for the claims asserted in their respective lawsuits. Their contention that they were inadequately represented is more appropriately cast as a challenge to the Settlement's fairness than as a due process claim, since their positions are grounded in the notion that the Settlement resulted in a class recovery that was too low.

II. NOTICE TO CLASS MEMBERS WAS ADEQUATE

The standard for the adequacy of a settlement notice in a class action under either the Due Process Clause or the Federal Rules is measured by reasonableness. There are no rigid rules to determine whether a settlement notice to the class satisfies constitutional or Rule 23(e) requirements; the settlement notice must "fairly apprise the prospective members of the class of the terms of the proposed settlement and of the options that are open to them in connection with the proceedings." Notice is "adequate if it may be understood by the average class member."

A. *Pasta Bella Received Adequate Notice*

Since the class notice did not name the banks as parties and the settlement notice did not specifically inform class members that the *Reyn's* claims would be included in the Settlement, Pasta Bella argues that it was denied due process because class members were not given the opportunity to opt out after the settlement notice was issued. . . . The Ninth Circuit's decision in *Class Plaintiffs v. City of Seattle*, 955 F.2d 1268 (9th Cir. 1992), is directly on point. . . . Since the parties had been given notice of the action, the opportunity to opt out, notice of the proposed settlement, and the opportunity to object, the court [in *Class Plaintiffs*] held that it was not required to grant those who objected to the proposed settlement a second opportunity to opt out.

Here, although the member banks were not named as defendants, the complaint described "[a]pproximately 4,400 banks that have issued Visa and/or MasterCard credit cards and also issued Visa Check and/or MasterMoney debit cards" as co-conspirators. The notice of pendency, which incorporated the allegations in the complaint, alleged a conspiracy between Visa, MasterCard, and "their member banks." Attempting to distinguish the *Reyn's* claims from those in the instant action, Pasta Bella's amended complaint in *Reyn's* states, "Plaintiffs do not contest in this action, as averred in other litigation, any tying arrangement, of the VISA and MASTERCARD debit charges with other charges." Yet, Pasta Bella's attempt to distinguish the claims in *Reyn's* from the claims in the instant action does not alter the fact that the claims in both cases arise out of the identical factual predicate. Indeed, Pasta Bella's artful language belies its recognition of the potential for overlap between the two lawsuits. Thus, Pasta Bella cannot reasonably argue that it was not on notice of the possibility that, pursuant to settlement in this action, the banks would be released from future claims. Pasta Bella was required to opt out at the class notice stage if it did not wish to be bound by the Settlement.

B. *NuCity Received Adequate Notice*

NuCity argues that the settlement notice denied the *Membership Rules* class due process because it failed to disclose:

1. the judgment against Visa and MasterCard in *Government's Membership Rules*;

2. the pending claims in *Membership Rules*;

3. the prospect that the Settlement's contemplated release would extinguish all claims in *Membership Rules*;

4. the value attributed by plaintiffs' counsel to the *Membership Rules* claims; and

5. the value received by the class in exchange for release of the *Membership Rules* claims.

NuCity points to the notice of settlement in [*In re Auction Houses Antitrust Litigation*, 2001 WL 170792 (S.D.N.Y. Feb. 22, 2001)] and argues that the settlement notice in this case comes up short. In *Auction Houses*, the notice explicitly informed class members that the settlement would permanently bar them from pursuing claims based on auctions held outside the U.S., and that class members with potential claims arising out of foreign auctions "should consider whether or not to forego the benefits of the proposed settlement." In this case, NuCity asserts that the need to include cautionary language in the settlement notice was especially great, since the notice of pendency also lacked an explanation of the action's impact on *Membership Rules*. NuCity further asserts that since the *Membership Rules* class was not yet certified, claimants could not have been expected to intuit that their *Membership Rules* claims would be released by the Settlement. Thus, NuCity contends class members did not know they were releasing live claims in an already-filed action seeking billions in damages when they neglected to opt out of the class or object to the Settlement. . . .

In this case, the settlement notice quoted verbatim the Settlement's release. Respondents argue that (1) the law does not require parties to describe pending actions covered by a release in a proposed settlement notice, and, in any event, (2) quoting a release word for word in the settlement notice is sufficient to inform class members of the scope and effect of the release. . . . Since the release was quoted in its entirety, the [district] court concluded that "the expansive reach of the release[ ] could not have been clearer. This is all that was required." We agree with the district court and do "not believe that due process requires further explanation of the effects of the release provision in addition to the clear meaning of the words of the release." . . .

III. THE SETTLEMENT IS FAIR

A. *The Settlement Is Entitled to a Presumption of Fairness*

A court may approve a class action settlement if it is "fair, adequate, and reasonable, and not a product of collusion." Joel A. [v. Giuliani, 218 F.3d 132, 138 (2d Cir. 2000)]. A court determines a settlement's fairness by looking at both the settlement's terms and the negotiating process leading to settlement. A "presumption of fairness, adequacy, and reasonableness may attach to a class settlement reached in arm's-length negotiations between experienced, capable counsel after meaningful discovery." MANUAL FOR COMPLEX LITIGATION, THIRD, § 30.42 (1995). We are mindful of the "strong judicial policy in favor of settlements, particularly in the class action context." In re PaineWebber Ltd. P'ships Litig., 147 F.3d 132, 138 (2d Cir. 1998). "The compromise of complex litigation is encouraged by the courts and favored by public policy."

In the instant case, the district court rightly praised the efforts of plaintiffs' lead counsel. "Constantine & Partners is a premiere plaintiffs' litigation firm, specializing in antitrust litigation particularly and complex commercial litigation generally." Counsel for the class took and defended approximately 400 depositions, including 21 expert depositions, and reviewed more than 5 million pages of documents during approximately seven years of litigation. Clearly, counsel conducted meaningful discovery. Of course, "the quality of representation is best measured by results." Here, plaintiffs' counsel "produced the largest antitrust settlement ever." The Settlement includes $3,383,400,000 in compensatory relief, plus additional injunctive relief valued at $25 to $87 billion or more. According to settlement mediator Eric Green, "the court system and the mediation process worked exactly as they are supposed to work at their best; a consensual resolution was achieved based on full information and honest negotiation between well-represented and evenly balanced parties." Concluding that "there could not be any better evidence of procedural integrity" than the aggressive litigation spanning nearly a decade and the impassioned settlement negotiations that produced an agreement on the brink of trial, the district court affirmed Green's sentiments by finding that "[c]ollusion or coercion could not conceivably have tainted the process."

We agree with this assessment and conclude that the district court did not abuse its discretion in determining that a presumption of fairness arose.

B. *The Settlement Is Substantively Fair*

When reviewing a district court's approval of a settlement, a "trial judge's views are accorded 'great weight . . . because he is exposed to the litigants, and their strategies, positions and proofs. . . . Simply stated, he is on the firing line and can evaluate the action accordingly.'" *Joel A.*, 218 F.3d at 139 (quoting City of Detroit v. Grinnell Corp., 495 F.2d 448, 454 (2d Cir. 1974)).

In this Circuit, courts examine the fairness, adequacy, and reasonableness of a class settlement according to the " *Grinnell* factors." The factors are:

(1) the complexity, expense and likely duration of the litigation;

(2) the reaction of the class to the settlement;

(3) the stage of the proceedings and the amount of discovery completed;

(4) the risks of establishing liability;

(5) the risks of establishing damages;

(6) the risks of maintaining the class action through the trial;

(7) the ability of the defendants to withstand a greater judgment;

(8) the range of reasonableness of the settlement fund in light of the best possible recovery;

(9) the range of reasonableness of the settlement fund to a possible recovery in light of all the attendant risks of litigation.

1. *Complexity, Expense and Likely Duration of Litigation*

Federal antitrust cases are complicated, lengthy, and bitterly fought."Few areas of federal antitrust law are more confusing than the law that governs tying arrangements." The district court concluded that this case would have taken three months to try and several years for appellate review. None of the appellants argue that this case was uncomplicated or would have resulted in a short trial.

2. *Reaction of the Class to the Settlement*

On the whole, the class appears to be overwhelmingly in favor of the Settlement. Only eighteen class members out of five million objected to the Settlement. "If only a small number of objections are received, that fact can be viewed as indicative of the adequacy of the settlement." This Court is certainly aware that "[l]ack of objection by the great majority of claimants means little when the point of objection is limited to a few whose interests are being sacrificed for the benefit of the majority." But here, the absence of substantial opposition is indicative of class approval, since every member of the class in *Reyn's* and *Membership Rules* is also a member of the instant class.

3. *Stage of Proceedings and Amount of Discovery Completed*

"If all discovery has been completed and the case is ready to go to trial, the court obviously has sufficient evidence to determine the adequacy of settlement." Here, plaintiffs entered into settlement only after a thorough understanding of their case. As noted earlier, extensive discovery proceedings spanning over seven years and millions of pages of documents preceded the Settlement. The parties also underwent summary judgment proceedings and mediation before they struck a deal at the courthouse steps. Certainly, a substantial amount of work had been completed, leaving relatively few unknowns prior to trial.

4. *Risks of Class Prevailing (Establishing Liability, Establishing Damages, Maintaining the Class through Trial)*

Characterizing the defendants' "Honor All Cards" policy as having at least some pro-competitive features, the district court concluded that establishing liability "was no sure thing" for the plaintiffs. "Indeed, the history of antitrust litigation is replete with cases in which antitrust plaintiffs succeeded at trial on liability, but recovered no damages, or only negligible damages, at trial, or on appeal." *See, e.g.*, United States Football League v. Nat'l Football League, 644 F. Supp. 1040, 1042 (S.D.N.Y. 1986) ("[T]he jury chose to award plaintiffs only nominal damages, concluding that the USFL had suffered only $1.00 in damages as a result of the NFL's unlawful conduct."), *aff'd*, 842 F.2d 1335, 1377 (2d Cir. 1988). That said, we must acknowledge that the Government's successful prosecution of *Government's Membership Rules* improved plaintiffs' likelihood of success in this case. Yet, on balance, it is certainly fair to conclude that even if the plaintiffs had prevailed in establishing their tying claim, they would have faced significant challenges in proving damages.[24]

5. *Ability of Defendants to Withstand a Greater Judgment*

The compensatory relief provided in the Settlement constitutes "the largest settlement ever approved by a federal court." Additionally, the injunctive relief — valued at approximately $25 to $87 billion or more — adds great value to the Settlement. Yet, Pasta Bella insists that a settlement requiring payment from the banks could have been substantially

---

24. The record does not include evidence concerning the likelihood of maintaining the class through trial, though decertification is always possible as a case progresses and additional facts are developed.

higher. We cannot agree with this argument. It is hardly surprising that the district court did not make explicit findings with respect to the ability of the member banks to withstand a significantly greater damages award, since the banks are not defendants in this case. Even if such a finding were helpful, our concern about financial resources of member banks would be assuaged by the district court's finding that virtually all of the relief in the Settlement already comes from the banks.

6. *Range of Reasonableness of Settlement Fund in Light of Best Possible Recovery and Attendant Risks of Litigation*

[T]here is a range of reasonableness with respect to a settlement — a range which recognizes the uncertainties of law and fact in any particular case and the concomitant risks and costs necessarily inherent in taking any litigation to completion — and the judge will not be reversed if the appellate court concludes that the settlement lies within that range.

Newman v. Stein, 464 F.2d 689, 693 (2d Cir. 1972). Here, the statistics concerning the Settlement are staggering: the compensatory relief by itself constitutes the largest settlement ever approved by a federal court; the injunctive relief will save the class $25 to $87 billion or more. Since the district court found that experienced and able counsel fought this litigation "aggressively" and "negotiated feverishly," and that "virtually all of the relief comes from" the banks, there is little reason to believe that additional money would have been put into the settlement pot had the banks been named as parties. The banks' participation in the settlement speaks volumes of their stake in the litigation. Moreover, given that the *Reyn's* and *Membership Rules* plaintiffs are substantially similar to the instant plaintiffs, it cannot be said that the settlement fund was unreasonably small or particularly unfair to a subset of plaintiffs.

Indeed, the favorable reaction of the overwhelming majority of class members to the Settlement is perhaps the most significant factor in our *Grinnell* inquiry. Having considered this factor along with the others, we conclude that the district court did not err in finding the Settlement substantively fair.

C. *NuCity Is Not Entitled to Discovery*

NuCity appeals the district court's denial of its motion for limited discovery to examine whether the Settlement included consideration for claims asserted in *Membership Rules*, the value attributed to claims foregone, and the justification for such valuation. Generally, such a discovery request depends on "whether or not the District Court had before it sufficient facts intelligently to approve the settlement offer. If it did, then there is no reason to hold an additional hearing on the settlement or to give appellants authority to renew discovery." *Grinnell*, 495 F.2d at 462-63.

As noted by the *Grinnell* analysis described above, the district court possessed an abundance of facts to make a fairness determination. Plaintiffs were not required to bargain separately for relief in exchange for the *Membership Rules* claims. "No part of the consideration on either side is keyed to any specific part of the consideration of the other. Each side gives up a number of things. This is the way settlements usually work." Thus, the district court did not abuse its discretion in denying NuCity's discovery motion. . . .

We affirm the district court in all respects.

Notes

1. The *Grinnell* factors that *Wal-Mart* uses to determine the fairness, reasonableness, and adequacy of the settlement are fairly typical of the factors that other courts use in evaluating a settlement. The *Manual for Complex Litigation* provides a somewhat more comprehensive list, along with some guidance on the weight that should be given to each factor in different circumstances. *See* MANUAL FOR COMPLEX LITIGATION, FOURTH § 21.62 (2004). In the end, does *Wal-Mart* boil down to the fact that the settlement was the biggest settlement of all time? Does that fact prove the settlement's fairness, though? Does it prove that the representation was adequate? The court of appeals goes to some lengths to argue that a class representative's adequacy of representation cannot be measured only by the outcome achieved. How much weight should a large bottom line be given? Suppose that the defendants' potential exposure to damages was $300 billion. Does the $3 billion settlement look as good in that situation? Shouldn't the court consider the size of the defendants' potential exposure as well as the size of the settlement itself?

2. Perhaps the most famous case rejecting a class settlement is *In re General Motors Corp. Pick-Up Truck Fuel Tank Products Liability Litigation*, 55 F.3d 768 (3d Cir. 1995). Judge Becker rejected as unfair and inadequate a settlement in which plaintiffs who had suffered economic loss from a defect in their pick-up trucks received a $500 or $1,000 coupon for the future purchase of another pick-up from the same manufacturer. Applying the same nine factors as *Grinnell*, the court found that some class members (individuals as opposed to fleet owners) were unable or unlikely to use the coupons. The court noted that "[o]ne sign that a settlement may not be fair is that some segments of the class are treated differently from others," *id.* at 808; that restrictions on their use and the lack of a secondary market in which the coupons could be bought and sold rendered them of little value, *id.* at 809-10; that other alternatives, such as a retrofit or recall, were not pursued, *id.* at 810-11; and that the case settled without significant discovery or factual development, *id.* at 813-14.

3. Coupon settlements, in which lawyers collect hefty fees for coupons that are nearly worthless, are something of an urban legend in class-action practice. They are often cited as one of the most abusive aspects of class

actions, and as a reason to abolish the class-action rule. The Class Action Fairness Act of 2005 (CAFA) contained provisions specifically addressing coupon settlements. 28 U.S.C. § 1712. Among other limitations, § 1712(a) limits contingency-fee awards in coupon settlements just to the value of the coupons that are redeemed, and § 1712(e) requires that the court hold "a hearing to determine whether, and mak[e] a written finding that, the settlement is fair, reasonable, and adequate for class members." Aside from the requirement of a writing, this latter provision essentially the same as that already required under Rule 23(e).

In reality, there seem to be few of these line-the-lawyers'-pockets coupon settlements. One study "did not show recurring situations where (b)(3) actions produced nominal class benefits in relation to attorneys' fees." THOMAS E. WILLGING ET AL., FED. JUD. CTR., EMPIRICAL STUDY OF CLASS ACTIONS IN FOUR FEDERAL DISTRICT COURTS 77 (1996); *see id.* at 184-85 Tbl. 46 (describing details of the settlements of the twelve cases in which (b)(3) class actions yielded no monetary distribution to the class).

4.   CAFA contains other provisions designed to enhance the quality of class-action settlements. 28 U.S.C. §§ 1713-15. For instance, a court cannot approve a class settlement in which a class member ends up with a net loss after paying attorneys' fees unless that member receives non-monetary relief that "substantially outweigh[s] the monetary loss." § 1713. Moreover a defendant proposing to settle a class action must notify the "appropriate" federal or state official (usually the relevant Attorney General) of the terms of the settlement; no class settlement can become final until ninety days after the notice is received. § 1715. Presumably, the relevant official can use this period to examine the fairness of the settlement to those citizens within the official's jurisdiction, and to object to the settlement on their behalf if the settlement is unfair.

5.   Also contrary to popular lore, class actions usually do not result in blockbuster judgments. In one study, "the median level of average recovery per class member ranged from $315 to $528." WILLGING ET AL., *supra*, at 13. In later work, the same group of researchers found that the median recovery per class member in cases filed in state court was $300 and in federal court $517; the absolute median value of state-court class actions was $850,000 in cases removed but later remanded to state court and $300,000 in cases removed to federal court and retained there. Thomas E. Willging & Shannon R. Wheatman, *Attorney Choice of Forum in Class Action Litigation: What Difference Does It Make?*, 81 NOTRE DAME L. REV. 591, 639-40 (2006).

6.   In *Wal-Mart* the objecting class members resisted the settlement not only on substantive fairness grounds, but also on the procedural grounds of lack of notice and inadequate representation. On the latter issues, we provided only a short excerpt from the opinion; we already examined *Wal-Mart*'s view regarding adequacy more fully *supra* p. 542, Note 5. As we saw, the last word on this adequacy issue has yet to be written. The take-away from *Wal-Mart*, however, is that a settlement can be attacked for both substantive and procedural reasons.

7. Objections are often strategic rather than principled. Parties who opt out can sometimes extract larger payments than they could have from remaining in the class action. *See* Reed R. Kathren & Hagens Berman Sobol Shapiro, *Opt-Outs, MFNs and Game Theory: Can the High Multiples Achieved by Opt-Outs in Recent Mega-Fraud Settlements Continue, A Discussion Draft*, 1620 PRACTISING L. INST./CORP. 583 (Sept.-Oct. 2007) (discussing numerous securities-fraud cases in which opt-out institutional investors received settlement awards that were numerous multiples larger than the settlement awards received by class members). Similarly, objectors often extract an additional payment in return for withdrawal of the objection. One solution to stop this behavior is to include a "most favored nation" clause in a class settlement, so that class members get the same award that the defendant gives to any opt-out or objector. *See id.* But it is not always in the interest of class counsel or the defendant to negotiate such an agreement. Should courts insist on such a clause as a condition of approving a class settlement as fair, reasonable, and adequate?

8. One "advantage" of most settlements is that they avoid the need for the court to individualize monetary relief. For instance, *Wal-Mart* settled for a lump sum, and left to another day the question of how much each of the five million class members deserved. Put differently, in a settlement the parties define for themselves the rightful position, obviating the court's difficult task of determining the remedy. But two problems emerge from this approach. The first is implementation of the settlement: How are the distributions to be made? We consider this issue in more detail in Chapter Twelve, when we examine the implementation of remedies. *See infra* p. 1197. For now, however, it is important to ask how a court can approve a settlement without having some sense of what the distribution will look like. To take *Wal-Mart* as an example, what if Wal-Mart, Sears, and The Limited agreed to take the entire $3.05 billion, leaving the other five million class members with nothing? Presumably such a settlement would be regarded as wildly unfair as a substantive matter, and both the class representatives and class counsel would be regarded as woefully inadequate as a procedural matter. Why doesn't *Wal-Mart* focus on this issue?

A second problem with lump-sum settlements is ethical: How is the class counsel, who owes a duty of loyalty to each class member, to divide up the fund fairly? Unless the settlement covers all claims in full (which seems unlikely), counsel will need to make judgments about a distribution scheme; and this scheme invariably will favor some clients over others. Is there any way to escape from this ethical conflict? *See* Charles Silver & Lynn Baker, *I Cut, You Choose: The Role of Plaintiffs' Counsel in Allocating Settlement Proceeds*, 84 VA. L. REV. 1465, 1468-69 (1998) ("There being no way to eliminate conflicts [of interest] from multiple-claimant representations, the only question is how to deal with them.").

9. One way to avoid these problems, at least in part, is eschew a lump-sum settlement in favor of scheduled benefits. For instance, in a mass tort, the defendant could agree to pay so much per claim (say $100,000 for every claim involving Injury A, $200,000 for every claim involving Injury B, and

so on). *See* JAY TIDMARSH, FED. JUD. CTR., MASS TORT SETTLEMENT CLASS ACTIONS 36-37, 52-54, 65-66, 79-80, 93-94 (1998) (describing different approaches to scheduled payments). Likewise, in *Wal-Mart*, the defendants could have paid some percentage (say, 50%) of the amount they overcharged each merchant that submitted a claim. This method makes the ultimate size of the settlement depend on the number and type of claims that are ultimately filed; sometimes defendants retain a right to renege on the settlement if the number of claims results in greater exposure than they had anticipated. Although the scheduled-benefits approach is not uncommon, it is less typical than straight lump-sum settlements. Should courts insist on scheduled benefits, or at least some comparable indicator of the value that individual class members will receive, as a condition of approving a settlement? On the other hand, doesn't the scheduled-benefits approach simply shove the ethical problem up to an earlier point in the process, when the class counsel is negotiating over how much each category of injury should receive?

2. Aggregate Settlements

By "aggregate settlements," we mean simply non-class settlements. In theory, individuals in non-class aggregation are represented by their own lawyers, and each individual gives fully informed consent to the settlement of his or her claim. The court does not approve settlements in aggregate litigation or examine them for substantive or procedural fairness; the terms of the settlements are a matter for the parties and their lawyers alone. Indeed, the approval requirement in class settlements was a substitute for the individual consent that adversarial theory requires. In a non-class setting, the requirement of individual consent remains.

Does this model of the fully informed client individually consenting to a settlement bear any relationship to the world of modern aggregated litigation, in which plaintiffs are represented by lead counsel chosen by the court, the cost of obtaining thousands of individual consents is prohibitive, and binding the clients to the terms of the settlement is necessary to complete the deal? On the other hand, without a mechanism like court approval of the substantive and procedural fairness of a settlement, how do we protect individuals in aggregate litigation from being overrun?

THE TAX AUTHORITY, INC. V. JACKSON HEWITT, INC.

898 A.2d 512 (N.J. 2006)

■ JUSTICE WALLACE, JR. delivered the opinion of the Court.

The issue presented is whether our Rule of Professional Conduct (RPC) 1.8(g) prohibits an attorney who represents more than one client from entering into an aggregate settlement of the clients' claims without each client consenting to the settlement after its terms are known. In the present case, an attorney agreed to represent 154 individual franchisee-plaintiffs in their claims against franchisor-defendant Jackson Hewitt, Inc. Each plaintiff entered into an identical retainer agreement that provided for settlement of the matter if a weighted majority of plaintiffs approved the settlement. A Steering Committee of four plaintiffs was established to represent the interests of all 154 individual plaintiffs. After the Steering Committee negotiated a settlement in principle, a weighted majority of plaintiffs approved it, but eighteen others did not. Defendant sought to enforce the settlement against all plaintiffs, and the motion court granted that application. The Appellate Division held that the fee agreement violated RPC 1.8(g) because it required advance consent to abide by the majority's decision and reversed. We hold that RPC 1.8(g) forbids an attorney from obtaining advance consent from his clients to abide by the majority's decision about the merits of an aggregate settlement. However, . . . we apply this decision prospectively. We reverse and remand.

I.

[The individual franchisees believed that Jackson Hewitt breached the franchise agreement by failing to issue rebates for certain loans that the franchisees advanced to their customers.] Because the franchise agreement prohibited the franchisees from filing a class action lawsuit against Jackson Hewitt or its affiliates, the franchisees collectively retained attorney Eric H. Karp (Karp) . . . to represent the group in a mass lawsuit. As part of that representation, each of the 154 plaintiffs entered into an identical attorney-client retainer agreement with Karp. Plaintiffs agreed that the matter would be pursued on a collective basis with fees being shared by each plaintiff on a [per-loan] basis. Each retainer agreement provided that

> [t]he Client agrees that the Matter may be resolved by settlement as to any portion or all of the Matter upon a vote of a weighted majority of the Client and all of the Co-Plaintiffs. Each Plaintiff shall have one vote for each funded [loan] for the 2002 Tax Season. The Client will be eligible to vote only if current in all payments required under this agreement. . . . A quorum for such vote shall be sixty percent (60%) of the votes eligible to be cast.

In addition to the majority-rules provision, the agreement provided that a four person Steering Committee would make the decisions regarding "all strategic and similar procedural matters other than the decision to settle the matter." The members of the Steering Committee were Robert Phillips, Robert Schiesel, George Alberici, and Kenneth Leese. Leese is the owner and president of the sole plaintiff herein, The Tax Authority.

The retainer agreement also specified that settlement proceeds would be apportioned according to each plaintiff's proportionate share of the [loan] reserve. . . . Formulas to calculate net proceeds, client contributions, and other necessary figures were also included. Prior to signing the retainer agreement, each plaintiff had an opportunity to consult with outside counsel. . . .

In August 2002, Karp filed a single complaint against Jackson Hewitt, naming each of the 154 franchisees as individual plaintiffs. Thereafter, the parties agreed to mediate their dispute. During mediation, Jackson Hewitt and the . . . Steering Committee represented by Karp negotiated a settlement in principle . . ., which was conditioned on approval by plaintiffs and by Jackson Hewitt's Board of Directors.

Karp had previously established a password-protected website to inform plaintiffs of developments in the case. In response to questions from various plaintiffs regarding the JAMS Settlement, on July 15, 2003, Karp posted an eleven-page document on the website that included a spreadsheet showing the calculation of each plaintiff's estimated net participation in the cash portion of the settlement. . . .

Leese helped to arrange a telephone conference call among most of the plaintiffs for the next day. During the conference call, which lasted approximately three hours, Karp attempted to answer any questions plaintiffs had about the JAMS Settlement. . . .

At some point, Leese began to challenge Karp concerning the settlement. . . . Leese then resigned from the Steering Committee on August 7, 2003 . . . .

Ultimately, a weighted majority of plaintiffs approved the JAMS Settlement. Counsel prepared a more detailed, formal settlement agreement. . . . On November 21, 2003, Karp emailed every plaintiff and posted a notice to the website stating that any plaintiff who did not submit a response by December 1, 2003, would be presumed to have declined the settlement. That communication also indicated that Karp would ask the court for leave to withdraw as counsel for parties declining the agreement due to a conflict between those plaintiffs who had signed the settlement agreement and those who had not. . . .

On December 2, 2003, Karp filed the promised motion, originally seeking relief from representation of twenty-six of the 154 plaintiffs. The following day, Jackson Hewitt filed a motion to enforce the settlement agreement against all plaintiffs. . . .

By the time the trial court heard argument on the motions, only eighteen plaintiffs had not yet signed the settlement agreement. . . . They asserted that Karp violated RPC 1.8(g) by obtaining advance consent to abide by any settlement approved by a majority of plaintiffs, and that therefore, they should not be bound by the settlement.

The trial court granted both Karp's motion to withdraw as counsel for the non-signing plaintiffs and Jackson Hewitt's motion to enforce the settlement agreement. . . .

The Tax Authority was the sole plaintiff to appeal. The Appellate Division reversed . . . .

We granted defendant's petition for certification. Defendant informed us at oral argument that except for The Tax Authority, the settlement has been executed and the appropriate monies disbursed to all other plaintiffs.

II.

Defendant's main argument is that the Appellate Division incorrectly interpreted RPC 1.8(g) to preclude parties from agreeing to settle in any manner other than by unanimous consent. It asserts that "the Appellate Division relied almost exclusively on non-New Jersey authority applying [former Disciplinary Rule (DR) 5-106 of the American Bar Association's (ABA) Model Code of Professional Responsibility (1980) (Model Code)], rather than authority interpreting RPC 1.8(g), notwithstanding the textual differences" between the two rules. Defendant also contends that the judgment below undermines New Jersey's strong public policy in favor of settling disputes. Alternatively, defendant urges that this is an issue of first impression, so if this Court affirms the judgment, the ruling should be applied prospectively only.

In contrast, The Tax Authority contends that the Appellate Division properly interpreted RPC 1.8(g). It maintains that a majority-rules mechanism to govern settlement creates an inherent conflict of interest between the parties and their counsel. The Tax Authority further argues that RPC 1.8(g) is necessary to safeguard the individual interests of each client, and that because the safeguards of court oversight for class actions are not present, each client must individually consent to a settlement agreement after the terms of the settlement are made known.

III.

Pursuant to the New Jersey Constitution, the Supreme Court has "jurisdiction over the admission to the practice of law and the discipline of persons admitted." In discharging that responsibility, this Court has sought to maintain "public confidence in the judicial system." In re LiVolsi, 428 A.2d 1268 (N.J. 1981). "Given the critical importance of the constitutional power of this Court over the practice of law," *ibid.*, this Court has promulgated Rules of Professional Conduct that govern attorneys in New Jersey. Those rules "serve as a road map for the conduct of attorneys to guide them in their relationships with their clients, other attorneys, the courts, and the public."

The "[a]greements between attorneys and clients concerning the client-lawyer relationship generally are enforceable, provided the agreements satisfy both the general requirements for contracts and the special requirements of professional ethics."

When contracting for a fee, . . . lawyers must satisfy their fiduciary obligations to the client. The lawyer must explain at the outset the basis and rate of the fee. In addition, the lawyer should advise the client of potential conflicts, the scope of representation, and the implications of the agreement. A retainer agreement may not provide for unreasonable fees or for the unreasonable waiver of the clients' rights. [Cohen v. Radio-Elecs. Officers Union, 679 A.2d 1188 (N.J. 1996).]

An agreement that violates the ethical rules governing the attorney-client relationship may be declared unenforceable.

In 1984, New Jersey adopted the ABA's Model Rules of Professional Conduct (1983) (Model Rules). At the time the conduct in the present case took place, RPC 1.8(g) provided that

> [a] lawyer who represents two or more clients shall not participate in making an aggregate settlement of the claims of or against the clients, or in a criminal case an aggregated agreement as to guilty or no contest pleas, unless each client consents after consultation, including disclosure of the existence and nature of all the claims or pleas involved and of the participation of each person in the settlement.

The precursor to that rule was DR 5-106. It is necessary to review the evolution of DR 5-106 and the case law interpreting it to better understand the meaning of RPC 1.8(g).

In 1969, the American Bar Association adopted the Disciplinary Rules of the Model Code, and in 1971, New Jersey adopted the Model Code. Under the Model Code, DR 5-106 governed the settlement of multi-party litigation and provided that

> [a] lawyer who represents two or more clients shall not make or participate in the making of an aggregate settlement of the claims of or against his clients, unless each client has consented to the settlement *after being advised of the existence and nature of all the claims involved in the proposed settlement, of the total amount of the settlement, and of the participation of each person in the settlement.*

(Emphasis added.) That rule is commonly referred to as the "aggregate settlement" rule.

The seminal case interpreting DR 5-106 is *Hayes v. Eagle-Picher Industries, Inc.*, 513 F.2d 892 (10th Cir. 1975). There, the eighteen plaintiffs retained a single lawyer to file an action against the defendant. On the eve of trial, the parties reached a settlement agreement, which thirteen of the eighteen plaintiffs approved. The following day, in open court, the trial court inquired whether any of the plaintiffs were opposed to the settlement. After receiving no objections, the court entered a judgment of settlement. Thereafter, two members of the plaintiff group claimed they did not hear the court's question and challenged the settlement. After initially vacating the judgment, the trial court reconsidered and reinstated the settlement.

The Tenth Circuit reversed, finding that an agreement that authorized settlement of a case "contrary to the wishes of the client and without his approving the terms of the settlement is opposed to the basic fundamentals of the attorney-client relationship." The court was troubled by the majority-rules provision, stating that

> [i]t is difficult to see how this could be binding on non-consenting plaintiffs as of the time of the proposed settlement and in the light of the terms agreed on. In other words, it would seem that plaintiffs

would have the right to agree or refuse to agree *once the terms of the settlement were made known to them.* (Emphasis added).

The court also found that the agreement posed an ethical problem for attorneys under DR 5-106 of the Kansas Code of Ethics. In the court's view, that rule "requires the attorney to refrain from participating in a settlement on behalf of two or more clients unless each of them consents to it." The court reasoned that "it was untenable for the lawyer to seek to represent both the clients who favored the settlement and those who opposed it." As a result, the court concluded that "in a non-class action case such as the present one," an arrangement that allows a majority to control the rights of the minority "is violative of the basic tenets of the attorney-client relationship in that it delegates to the attorney powers which allow him to act not only contrary to the wishes of his client, but to act in a manner disloyal to his client and to his client's interests." . . .

. . . [O]n July 12, 1984, this Court adopted . . . RPC 1.8(g)[2] in place of DR 5-106.

Recently, the Louisiana Supreme Court reached the same result under RPC 1.8(g) as had *Hayes* under DR 5-106. In re Hoffman, 883 So.2d 425, 433-34 (La. 2004). . . .

Most scholars and commentators agree that a majority-rules provision is forbidden under RPC 1.8(g). *See, e.g.,* Howard M. Erichson, *A Typology of Aggregate Settlements,* 80 NOTRE DAME L. REV. 1769 (2005); Nancy J. Moore, *The Case Against Changing the Aggregate Settlement Rule in Mass Tort Lawsuits,* 41 S. TEX. L. REV. 149 (1999); Charles Silver & Lynn A. Baker, *Mass Lawsuits and the Aggregate Settlement Rule,* 32 WAKE FOREST L. REV. 733 (1997).

Obviously, in adopting a model rule promulgated by the ABA, we give great weight to . . . the ABA's interpretation of the rule. . . . [I]n discussing RPC 1.8(g), the *ABA/BNA Lawyers' Manual on Professional Conduct* makes it clear that a "lawyer may not seek advance consent or consent by way of a majority vote of the lawyer's multiple clients."

We are in accord with the position expressed by the Appellate Division that any textual differences between the former DR 5-106 and RPC 1.8(g) are without significance. The underpinning of both rules is that when a lawyer represents more than one client, each client has the right to accept or reject the settlement after the terms are known. Simply stated, RPC

---

2. RPC 1.8(g) was modified effective January 1, 2004, to include the term "informed consent." As modified, the rule provides:

A lawyer who represents two or more clients shall not participate in making an aggregate settlement of the claims of or against the clients . . . unless each client gives informed consent after a consultation that shall include disclosure of the

existence and nature of all the claims . . . and of the participation of each person in the settlement.

"Informed consent" is defined as "the agreement by a person to a proposed course of conduct after the lawyer has communicated adequate information and explanation about the material risks of and reasonably available alternatives to the proposed course of conduct."

1.8(g) imposes two requirements on lawyers representing multiple clients. The first is that the terms of the settlement must be disclosed to each client. The second is that after the terms of the settlement are known, each client must agree to the settlement.

We conclude that RPC 1.8(g) forbids an attorney from obtaining consent in advance from multiple clients that each will abide by a majority decision in respect of an aggregate settlement. Before a client may be bound by a settlement, he or she must have knowledge of the terms of the settlement and agree to them.

IV.

. . . Defendant . . . asserts that even if the majority-rules provision is invalid, this Court "should determine that such decisions on issues of first impression should only apply prospectively and that [The Tax Authority] remains bound by the settlement agreement."

The general rule is that judicial decisions will be applied retroactively. Even so, "[o]ur tradition is to confine a decision to prospective application when fairness and justice require." . . . [P]rospective application is "appropriate when 'a court renders a first-instance or clarifying decision in a murky or uncertain area of the law . . .,' or when a member of the public could reasonably have 'relied on a different conception of the state of the law.'"

Such is the case here. This is the first opportunity for this Court to interpret RPC 1.8(g). Plaintiffs' counsel represented plaintiffs that were from many different states and successfully sought to have all plaintiffs agree in advance to be bound by a weighted majority. That effort was a plausible, although incorrect, interpretation of RPC 1.8(g). In addition, defendant was led to believe that plaintiffs had agreed among themselves to be bound by a weighted majority vote and relied on that in reaching the settlement. The Tax Authority's president, Leese, was a member of the Steering Committee, assisted in reaching the JAMS Settlement, and signed it. Subsequently, he was actively involved in negotiating the voting mechanism for plaintiffs' approval of the settlement but ultimately rejected the final settlement. All of the other plaintiffs have consented to the settlement, and defendant has satisfied its terms with all other plaintiffs.

On balance, we conclude that prospective application of our holding, and thus enforcement of the settlement against The Tax Authority, is the appropriate and equitable disposition of this matter.

V.

Lastly, we recognize that some commentators have proposed that RPC 1.8(g) be changed to accommodate mass lawsuits. Professors Charles Silver and Lynn Baker suggest the rule should be amended to permit litigants to agree to abide by majority rule. They agree that "[b]ecause the stakes are so large and the issues so complex, settlement is both more urgent and more difficult in mass lawsuits than in other litigation, and the aggregate settlement rule is a complication that often gets in the way." The complications they refer to include generating expense and delay, preventing defendants from obtaining finality, invading plaintiffs' privacy, and allowing a single claimant to hold out or block an entire settlement.

In light of those and other concerns advanced in favor of permitting less than unanimous agreement in multi-plaintiff mass litigation, we refer this issue to the Commission on Ethics Reform for its review and recommendation to the Court.

VI.

The judgment of the Appellate Division is reversed. The case is remanded to the trial court to reinstate the judgment to enforce the settlement.

AMERICAN LAW INSTITUTE, PRINCIPLES OF
THE LAW OF AGGREGATE LITIGATION

(2009)

3.17   Circumstances Required for Aggregate Settlements to Be Binding

(a) A lawyer or group of lawyers who represent two or more claimants on a non-class basis may settle the claims of those claimants on an aggregate basis provided that each claimant gives informed consent in writing. Informed consent requires that each claimant be able to review the settlements of all other persons subject to the aggregate settlement or the formula by which the settlement will be divided among all claimants. Further, informed consent requires that the total financial interest of claimants' counsel be disclosed to each claimant.

(b) In lieu of the requirements set forth in subsection (a), individual claimants may, before the receipt of a proposed settlement offer, enter into an agreement in writing through shared counsel allowing each participating claimant to be bound by a substantial-majority vote of all claimants concerning an aggregate-settlement proposal (or, if the settlement significantly distinguishes among different categories of claimants, a separate substantial-majority vote of each category of claimants). An agreement under this subsection must meet each of the following requirements:

(1) The power to approve a settlement offer must at all times rest with the claimants collectively and may under no circumstances be assigned to claimants' counsel. . . .

(2) The agreement among the claimants may occur at the time the lawyer-client relationship is formed or thereafter, but only if all

participating claimants give informed consent. Informed consent requires that the claimants' lawyer fully disclose all the terms of the agreement to the claimants to facilitate informed decisionmaking regarding

(A) Whether to enter into the agreement;

(B) Whether to subsequently challenge the fairness of the settlement agreement under subsections (d) or (e);

(C) Whether to subsequently challenge the compliance of the settlement agreement with the requirements set forth in subsections (b) and (c); and

(D) The desirability of seeking, along with a reasonable opportunity to seek, the advice of independent legal counsel.

(3) The agreement must specify the procedures by which all participating claimants are to approve a settlement offer. The agreement may also specify the manner of allocating the proceeds of a settlement among the claimants or may provide for future development of an appropriate allocation mechanism.

(4) Before claimants enter into the agreement, their lawyer or group of lawyers must explain to all claimants that the mechanism under subsection (a) is available as an alternative means of settling an aggregate lawsuit under this Section. A lawyer or group of lawyers may not terminate an existing relationship solely because the claimant declines to enter into an agreement under subsection (b) and the lawyer must so inform the client. . . .

(c) An agreement pursuant to subsection (b) is permissible only in cases involving a substantial amount in controversy, a large number of claimants, and when the agreement requires approval by a substantial majority of claimants, with the foregoing minimum criteria to be determined by the applicable legislative or rulemaking body.

(d) The enforceability of an agreement under subsection (b) should depend on whether, based on all facts and circumstances, the agreement is fair and reasonable from a procedural standpoint. Facts and circumstances to be considered include the timing of the agreement, the sophistication of the claimants, the information disclosed to the claimants, whether the terms of the settlement were reviewed by a neutral or special master . . ., whether the claimants have some prior relationship, and whether the claims of the claimants are similar.

(e) In addition to the requirements of subsection (d), the enforceability of a settlement approved through an agreement under subsection (b) should depend on whether, under all the facts and circumstances, the settlement is substantively fair and reasonable. Facts and circumstances to be considered include the costs, risks, probability of success, and delays in achieving a verdict; whether the claimants are treated equitably (relative to each other) based on their facts and circumstances; and whether particular claimants are disadvantaged by the settlement considered as a whole. . . .

3.18   Limited Judicial Review for Non-Class Aggregate Settlements

(a) Any claimant who is subject to a settlement entered into pursuant to § 3.17(b) is entitled, within the time period set by the legislature or rulemaking body, to challenge the settlement on the grounds that the settlement does not satisfy some or all of the requirements of § 3.17(b) and § 3.17(c), or is not procedurally and substantively fair and reasonable pursuant to § 3.17(d) and § 3.17(e). Such a challenge may be brought in the court in which the claimant's case is or was pending or, if no case is or was pending, in any court of competent jurisdiction.

(b) Any claimant who contests the amount of his or her share of a settlement approved under § 3.17(b)-(e) is entitled, within the time period set by the legislative or rulemaking body, to challenge the fairness of the settlement. Such a challenge may be brought in the court in which the claimant's case is or was pending or, if no case is or was pending, in any court of competent jurisdiction.

Notes

1. The "aggregate settlement rule," which requires that each client in an aggregated case give individual, fully informed consent to a settlement, is followed in some form in every American jurisdiction. Many states have adopted Rule 1.8(g) of the Model Code, others have retained DR 5-106 of the Model Rules, and others have drafted a comparable provision. *See* Howard M. Erichson, *A Typology of Aggregate Settlements*, 80 NOTRE DAME L. REV. 1769, 1781 (2005). Despite having adopted such rules to deal with "aggregate settlements," states have not defined what an "aggregate settlement" is. Professor Erichson's article is the most comprehensive such effort. Except on one small matter (i.e., informed consent being satisfied by reviewing and consenting to the formula for distribution), § 3.17(a) of the *Principles of the Law of Aggregate Litigation* restates the current "aggregate settlement" rule.

2. You can appreciate the difficulties of the traditional rule that each client must give fully informed consent in an aggregated proceeding. In ordinary litigation, the lawyer can discuss settlement values and ranges with the client, and have a pretty good sense during negotiations about what the client is willing to take. In an aggregated proceeding, the lawyer might never have met the client; if the numbers are great enough, the communication between lawyer and each client to feel out what each client would take is impractical. Hence, when striking the deal, the lawyer cannot be sure that the client will go along. (Indeed, the deal might be for a lump sum, and the lawyer doesn't even know yet how much any client will receive.) From the defendant's viewpoint, clients' refusals to take the deal

is highly undesirable; it creates a "Russian style" dynamic in negotiation, in which the defendant must lay its cards on the table but the plaintiffs' lawyer can always escape by saying his superior (the client) refuses to accept the bargain. The defendant is unlikely to want to bargain in this environment; it wants a clear indication that the plaintiffs will accept the deal. The clients' acceptance is likely: The plaintiffs' lawyer holds a strong hand in terms of negotiating with clients, because the lawyer possesses expertise and the information about the case. If the lawyer says that the deal is a good one, few plaintiffs are in a position to disagree. But that outcome is never assured; some plaintiffs might say no.

3. One of the tools that the lawyer in *Tax Authority* used to force clients into the settlement was the threat of withdrawal from continued representation of the client who did not accept the deal. This threat is a powerful weapon. If withdrawal is successful, the non-settling clients now need to find a new lawyer (or proceed pro se). Getting a new lawyer willing to come up to speed and willing to work for whatever fee the case promises (remember, because most of the plaintiffs have settled, the economies of scale won't be as strong and the value of the claims on which the fee will be based is less) is an uncertain proposition.

The court must approve a motion to withdraw. As we saw in Chapter Seven, success on this motion is not guaranteed. *See supra* p. 751, Note 10. But is it even ethical to withdraw, or at least threaten to withdraw, in this circumstance? Doesn't the lawyer have a duty of loyalty to each client; if the client chooses not to follow the lawyer's advice, that isn't automatically grounds for the lawyer to end the relationship, is it? Note that the trial court in *Tax Authority* permitted the withdrawal (and note that all the holdout plaintiffs except Tax Authority thereafter took the deal). Note as well that § 3.17(b)(4) of the *Principles* does not countenance withdrawal in a representation governed by a majority-voting process, but it says nothing about the right to withdraw in cases governed by the traditional aggregate-settlement rule.

3. Even silver-tongued counsel and threats of withdrawal cannot make every plaintiff sign on the dotted line. For some, this result is not problematic; the client is the boss, and we must respect that autonomy even when it gums up a mass settlement of claims. For others, the aggregate-settlement rule is too costly; it makes global settlements hard to negotiate and achieve. *Tax Authority* rehearses these arguments when it refers the matter to the New Jersey ethics commission to consider whether to overthrow the aggregate-settlement rule in New Jersey.

Following the work of Professors Silver and Baker, the ALI's *Principles* (for which Professor Silver was an associate reporter) create § 3.17(b) as an alternative to the aggregate-settlement rule. Section 3.17(b) is likely to be controversial because it does an end-run around the rule by allowing a lawyer to secure up front (i.e., before the settlement is known, and even as early as the first meeting with the client) an agreement that the client will be bound by a vote of a substantial majority of the aggregated plaintiffs to accept the settlement. In essence, individual consent to a settlement is replaced with consent to a democratic process before the terms of the settlement are known. (The choice between consent and voting recalls, once again, the observation of Professor Fuller that, aside from adjudication, the two basic forms of ordering in a society are either negotiation (contract) or managerial direction (voting). *See supra* p. 36.) The rest of § 3.17 and § 3.18 then create certain protections for class members to ensure that they are not overrun by the will of the majority.

Is this limited consent to a process, plus the protections that the *Principles* provide to ensure a fair settlement, an adequate trade-off for the individual consent contemplated by the aggregate-settlement rule? In answering this question, is it relevant that the lawyer's superior knowledge and threat of withdrawal already cut deeply into the meaningfulness of the individual consent contemplated by the rule? Note that § 3.17(b) does not define how substantial the majority must be, apparently leaving the issue to each legislature or ethics committee. Would you want to know the exact percentage of the majority — how about 90%, or maybe only 51%? — before you passed judgment on the proposal? Or is the number irrelevant because each plaintiff ought to retain the right to consent to the settlement?

4.   In *Tax Authority*, it appears that a simple majority vote of the plaintiffs was sufficient to bind the entire group to accept the settlement, but that the vote was weighted by the number of claims each plaintiff could assert. Presumably, the bigger plaintiffs got a bigger say in the voting. The *Principles* requires use of a one-plaintiff, one-vote rule. Would *Tax Authority* have been as reluctant to bind non-approving plaintiffs to the result of the voting process if a substantial majority had been required? If the process was based on a one-plaintiff, one-vote principle?

5.   Thus far, § 3.17(b) has been criticized by a number of leading legal ethicists, some of whose work is cited in *Tax Authority*. *Tax Authority*'s refusal to apply its holding retrospectively and its referral of the issue to the ethics commission suggest that it too thought the issue difficult.

6.   Sections 3.17(b)-(e) and 3.18 incorporate some of the protections afforded to class members in a class action. Indeed, in its requirement that a substantial number of plaintiffs vote to accept the settlement, § 3.17(b) goes beyond the protections given to class members, and is more analogous to voting rights given to creditors in bankruptcy. Should class members be afforded a right to vote on a settlement? Or is the requirement of adequate representation a sufficient substitute for voting?

7.   Although § 3.18 provides for limited judicial review of settlements enforced through majority voting, it does not recognize a role — akin to the power to approve a settlement in a class action — for a court to approve a traditional settlement in the aggregate context. Some courts have claimed authority to approve (or disapprove) aggregate settlements. *See, e.g.,* Miryea Navarro, *Judge Rejects Deal on Health Claims of Workers at Ground Zero,* N.Y. TIMES, Mar. 20, 2010, at A12 (rejecting as inadequate a settlement valued between $575 million and $657 million for 10,000 rescuers who responded to the World Trade Center attacks; the settlement had required approval of 95% of the plaintiffs). The source of a court's

authority to reject an aggregate settlement is unclear. Would the court's inherent power do the job?

C. ATTORNEYS' FEES

Determining the amount of the attorneys' fees for the plaintiffs' lawyers is almost always part and parcel of determining the remedy itself. In aggregated cases, the fee is usually a matter of contract — set by the initial agreement between attorney and client. In these cases, the court does not become involved in fee awards unless a dispute arises. In other cases, however, an award of attorneys' fees in favor of a prevailing party is required by statute or rule; here courts become involved in either setting the amount of the award or, if the parties have agreed on the fee, approving the award. Although proceedings to determine the fee award usually occur after approval of the settlement, the amount of the fees is often negotiated as part of a settlement.

Determining the amount of the fees is not itself a complex affair in most cases. The court often needs to examine expense and time reports, and sometimes to make hard calls about whether certain services merit the compensation requested; but this activity is no more difficult than most of a judge's work. Nonetheless, it is worth spending some time considering the issue of attorneys' fees for two reasons. First, although most lawyers would not admit it in public, the prospect of significant attorneys' fees undoubtedly drives (or at least influences) many of the strategic and tactical decisions that lawyers make in complex litigation — none more so than the decision whether to recommend a settlement to the lawyer's clients. Second, the fear that a lawyer's desire for a huge fee will overbear (or has overborne) a lawyer's commitment to the best interests of the clients is a constant refrain in complex litigation. In Chapter Seven, we analyzed this problem as a type of agency cost. *See supra* pp. 731-33, Notes 7-10. Therefore, even though the award of attorneys' fees is not itself a complex matter, the importance of fees in shaping complex litigation warrants a very brief study of the mechanics by which fees are awarded.

WAL-MART STORES, INC. V. VISA U.S.A., INC.

396 F.3d 96 (2d Cir. 2005)

■ WESLEY, Circuit Judge.

[The facts in this massive antitrust case are set out *supra* p. 1152. Briefly, the plaintiff class consisted of merchants that claimed an illegal tying arrangement between the defendants' debits cards and credit cards, forcing the merchants to pay too high a fee when customers used debit cards. After seven years of litigation, the case settled for $3.05 billion (payable in installments over ten years), plus an agreement from the defendants to stop tying their credit and debit products. This agreement, which was to be enforced by means of an injunction, was valued somewhere between $25 billion and $87 billion. The court of appeals upheld the settlement against various procedural and substantive challenges made by objectors. It then turned to the issue of the proper attorneys' fee.]

PART IV

THE DISTRICT COURT'S FEE AWARD IS REASONABLE

At the district court, lead counsel for the plaintiffs sought a fee of $609,012,000 — approximately 18% of the present value of the Settlement's compensatory relief, 2.14% of the present value of the Settlement (inclusive of injunctive relief), and 9.68 times the lodestar figure of $62,940,045.84. Seventeen merchants objected to counsel's fee petition. The court found the fee petition excessive despite the excellence of plaintiffs' representation. Assessing the fee petition with a careful eye for the interests of all class members, the court awarded fees in the amount of $220,290,160.44 plus an additional $18,716,511.44 in costs and expenses. [One class member, Leonardo's Pizza by the Slice (Leonardo's),] argues that the district court's fee award was too high, while Constantine & Partners ("C&P"), plaintiffs' lead counsel, contends that the fee award was too low.

A. *"Percentage of the Fund" Is an Appropriate Method*

The district court utilized the "percentage of the fund" method to calculate attorneys' fees. Courts may award attorneys' fees in common fund cases under either the "lodestar" method or the "percentage of the fund" method. *See* Goldberger [v. Integrated Res. Inc., 209 F.3d 43, 50 (2d Cir. 2000)]. The lodestar method multiplies hours reasonably expended against a reasonable hourly rate. Courts in their discretion may increase the lodestar by applying a multiplier based on factors such as the riskiness of the litigation and the quality of the attorneys. The trend in this Circuit is toward the percentage method, which "directly aligns the interests of the class and its counsel and provides a powerful incentive for the efficient prosecution and early resolution of litigation." In contrast, the "lodestar create[s] an unanticipated disincentive to early settlements, tempt[s] lawyers to run up their hours, and compel[s] district courts to engage in a gimlet-eyed review of line-item fee audits."

B. *The* Goldberger *Factors Confirm the Reasonableness of the Fee Award*

Irrespective of which method is used, the "*Goldberger* factors" ultimately determine the reasonableness of a common fund fee. They include:

(1) the time and labor expended by counsel;

(2) the magnitude and complexities of the litigation;

(3) the risk of the litigation . . .;

(4) the quality of representation;

(5) the requested fee in relation to the settlement; and

(6) public policy considerations.

Goldberger, 209 F.3d at 50. Recognizing that economies of scale could cause windfalls in common fund cases, courts have traditionally awarded fees for common fund cases in the lower range of what is reasonable. *Goldberger*, 209 F.3d at 52; *see also* In re Indep. Energy Holdings PLC, 2003 WL 22244676, at *6 (S.D.N.Y. Sept. 29, 2003) ("[T]he percentage used in calculating any given fee award must follow a sliding-scale and must bear an inverse relationship to the amount of the settlement. Otherwise, those law firms who obtain huge settlements, whether by happenstance or skill, will be over-compensated to the detriment of the class members they represent.").

The district court concluded that the *Goldberger* factors compel an "extraordinary" fee under these circumstances: lead counsel devoted tremendous time and labor to this case for seven years; antitrust cases, by their nature, are highly complex; this case was especially large and complicated, involving almost every U.S. bank and more than five million U.S. merchants; the risk of the litigation was very high; lead counsel devoted 52% of its legal staff to work on a case that spanned seven years without any guarantee of recovery; plaintiffs' counsel achieved extraordinary results; plaintiffs' counsel did not have the benefit of "piggybacking" off of a previous case — instead, the Government piggybacked off of plaintiffs' counsel's work by using it in [a related enforcement proceeding]; even a very large fee award would be a small percentage of the settlement fund; and the Settlement produced "significant and lasting benefits for America's merchants and consumers." Asserting its jealous regard for absent class members, the court sought to compensate plaintiffs' counsel handsomely and at the same time limit the percentage of the award so that plaintiffs' counsel would not receive a windfall detrimental to the class . . . . C&P argues that the district court's fee award was insufficient because (a) the fee award provides a meager percentage of the settlement fund and (b) the fee award reduces the incentive to class lawyers to seek maximum relief.

1. *The Fee Award Is Based on a Reasonable Percentage of the Fund*

C&P cites *In re Linerboard Antitrust Litigation*, 2004 WL 1221350 (E.D. Pa. June 2, 2004), in support of its argument against a declining percentage approach to large fee awards. In that case, the court found that "the sliding scale approach is economically unsound." The *Linerboard* court explained that it is especially important to provide appropriate incentives to attorneys pursuing antitrust actions because public policy relies on private sector enforcement of the antitrust laws. C&P contends that not only was the court's percentage award low, but also the court did not adequately compensate counsel for the substantial injunctive relief it obtained for the class. Thus, C&P argues that the district court's fee award severely inhibits the strong public policy articulated in *Linerboard* that favors providing incentives to attorneys to pursue maximum relief for their clients.

We need not dispute whether the sliding scale approach is economically rational in the context of ensuring competent and committed counsel. Public policy concerns oftentimes redefine the focus of the court. In this case, the district court's decision in favor of protecting the instant class from an excessive fee award militates against awarding attorneys' fees based purely on economic incentives. Satisfied that its ruling would not deter plaintiffs' attorneys from pursuing similar claims, the district court remarked, "If [this fee award] amounts to punishment, I am confident there will be many attempts to self-inflict similar punishment in future cases." We agree.

While courts in megafund cases often award higher percentages of class funds as fees than the district court awarded in this instance, the sheer size of the instant fund makes a smaller percentage appropriate. As a "cross-check" to a percentage award, courts in this Circuit use the lodestar method. *Goldberger*, 209 F.3d at 50. Here, the lodestar yields a multiplier of 3.5, which has been deemed reasonable under analogous circumstances.[27] *See* In re Cendant Corp. PRIDES Litig., 243 F.3d 722, 742 (3d Cir. 2001) (finding lodestar multiplier of 1.35 to 2.99 common in megafunds over $100 million); [In re] NASDAQ Market-Makers [Antitrust Litig., 187 F.R.D. 465, 489 (S.D.N.Y. 1998)] ("multipliers of between 3 and 4.5 have become common"). Thus, the district court did not abuse its discretion in awarding plaintiffs' counsel a generous fee based on a somewhat low percentage of the fund.

2.   *The District Court Was Not Required to Adhere to the Fee Agreement Between Plaintiffs' Counsel and Lead Plaintiffs*

Plaintiffs' counsel argues that the district court was aware that class counsel had negotiated a fee arrangement with five of the nation's largest merchants that exceeded the 18% fee class counsel requested from the court and far exceeded the fee the court awarded. Thus, class counsel argues that the district court ignored the *Goldberger* proviso that "market rates, where available, are the ideal proxy for [class counsel's] compensation." As further proof of class satisfaction with counsel's fee request, counsel argues that none of the large and sophisticated merchants in this class action objected to its fee petition. *But see Goldberger*, 209 F.3d at 53 ("[Class members] have no real incentive to mount a challenge that would result in only a

---

27. . . . [T]he lodestar method calculates attorneys' fees by multiplying hours reasonably expended against a reasonable hourly rate; courts may use their discretion to increase the lodestar by applying a multiplier based on factors such as the riskiness of the litigation and the quality of the attorneys. Here, the lodestar calculation yields $62,940,045.84, which is approximately 29% of the district court's award of $220,290,160.44 to class counsel.

minuscule pro rata gain from a fee reduction."). For the reasons discussed in the prior subsection, we cannot say that the district court abused its discretion merely because it chose not to heed the terms of an agreement purportedly reached between lead plaintiffs and their counsel when settlement payments to approximately five million absent class members are at stake.

A final word is in order here. Measuring the difficulties of a large antitrust action and the degree of success by counsel in forging a settlement is not an easy task. In our view, the district court carried out its responsibility with admirable care and thoroughness, and with an eye to a just result. There is no doubt this case dominated the lives of all involved for many years. In approving the district court's fee award, we recognize the sacrifice and commitment plaintiffs' counsel made to its clients while preserving as much as possible for those who were harmed. . . .

. . . The district court's fee award is reasonable, as confirmed by the *Goldberger* factors.

We affirm . . . .

Notes

1. In class actions, the court "may award reasonable attorney's fees and non-taxable costs that are authorized by law or by the parties' agreement." Fed. R. Civ. P. 23(h). Class counsel must apply for an award, class members may object, the court may hold a hearing, and the court must enter findings of fact and conclusions of law on the fee. Fed. R. Civ. P. 23(h)(1)-(3). Rule 23 does not define what a "reasonable fee" is or what method should be used to calculate this fee.

2. As *Wal-Mart* says, courts have typically chosen one of two methods for calculating a reasonable fee. The first is the lodestar method; the other is the percentage-of-recovery method. The lodestar method, in which a lawyer receives an hourly rate that is determined by multiplying the market rate for comparable lawyers by some "multiplier" that accounts for the risk of loss and the quality of the outcome. (Generally, the multiplier exceeds 1.0, but the multiplier can be less than 1.0 if the representation or the result is poor. *See* Hensley v. Eckerhart, 461 U.S. 424, 436 (1983).) In cases in which injunctive relief or coupons are a large component of the class award, some variant of the lodestar approach is almost inevitable, because the litigation does not generate a monetary fund out of which class counsel can be paid. *See* MANUAL FOR COMPLEX LITIGATION, FOURTH § 14.121 (2004). Similarly, when fees are awarded to a prevailing party under a fee-shifting statute, the usual approach is to use a lodestar. *Id.* § 14.13. Because many of our fee-shifting statutes involve civil-rights-type claims in which injunctive relief often figures prominently, the reasons to use a lodestar approach overlap.

On the other hand, in cases in which a settlement or judgment creates a common fund, the percentage-of-recovery method is more common. *See*

THOMAS E. WILLGING ET AL., FED. JUD. CTR., EMPIRICAL STUDY OF CLASS ACTIONS IN FOUR FEDERAL DISTRICT COURTS 69-74 (1996) (finding that the percentage-of-recovery method was more common in three of four federal district courts). The shift to this method has been pronounced in recent years. One of the cases leading the charge was *In re General Motors Corp. Pick-Up Truck Fuel Tank Products Liability Litigation*, 55 F.3d 768 (3d Cir. 1995), which involved a coupon settlement. *GM Pick-Up* argued that coupon settlements are more akin to common-fund than statutory-fee cases, and that the percentage-of-recovery method better aligned class counsel's incentives with that of the class. *Wal-Mart* adopted this approach and reasoning, even though it was a hybrid of common-fund and injunctive relief. As *Wal-Mart* shows, however, courts do not entirely abandon the lodestar approach; they still use it as a cross-check on the reasonableness of the amount awarded under the percentage-of-recovery method.

In a few cases, courts have used other methods. The most common is the sliding-scale method mentioned in *Wal-Mart*. Here, the lawyer receives a percentage of the recovery, but the percentage declines as the lawyer brings more money into the fund. For instance, a court might award 30% of the first $1 million, 25% of the next $4 million, and 15% of the amounts over $5 million. The method was designed to avoid huge windfalls of the *Wal-Mart* variety when a flat percentage is used; the criticism of this method is that it gives a lawyer less and less incentive to wring that last penny out of the defendant in a judgment or settlement. Sliding-scale recoveries were common in the heyday of auctions for the class-counsel position; some counsel would bid on the job by using a sliding-scale fee structure, and sometimes the court would select such a bid. *See* In re Oracle Sec. Litig., 132 F.R.D. 538 (N.D. Cal. 1990). As we saw in Chapter Seven, however, the bidding approach to selecting class counsel has fallen off the table in recent years. *See supra* p. 732, Note 8.

3. In selecting the proper method, the question is usually one of incentive: What method gives the lawyer the best incentive to work for the best interests of the class, rather than for his or her own financial welfare? No method is perfect. The lodestar method gives an incentive to drag out the case and run up the bill. The percentage-of-recovery approach induces the lawyer to pursue monetary relief rather than (perhaps) more desirable injunctive remedies, and it can result in huge windfalls. The sliding-scale approach gives a disincentive to secure awards above a certain size.

It is more than vaguely troubling that we cannot count on lawyers to act in the best interests of their clients rather than in their own best interest. On the other hand, one complex case can consume an enormous portion of a lawyer's professional career, the lawyer passes up other lucrative opportunities, and the amounts of money involved are too staggering to expect any person to be impervious to their lure.

4. When the percentage-of recovery method is used, an important question is how to calculate the size of the recovery. For instance, some settlements require plaintiffs to use coupons or file claims. Is the value of the class's recovery the amount that class members could have claimed, or

the amount that they did claim? *See* Masters v. Wilhelmina Model Agency, Inc., 473 F.3d 423 (2d Cir. 2007) (possible claims) (*infra* p. 1216); In re TJX Cos. Retail Sec. Breach Litig., 584 F. Supp. 2d 395 (D. Mass. 2008) (arguing for actual claims, but using possible claims under the facts of the case).

5.   Repudiating *Masters*, the American Law Institute has taken the position that attorneys' fees should be based on the actual value of a judgment or settlement.   AM. L. INST., PRINCIPLES OF THE LAW OF AGGREGATE LITIGATION § 3.13(a) (2009). It also rejects the lodestar approach in favor of the percentage-of-recovery approach, except in cases involving injunctive relief or fee-shifting statutes that require a lodestar calculation. *Id.* § 3.13(b)-(c).

6.   In non-class mass aggregations, the court has less control over the fees paid to counsel.   When a court appoints lead counsel to represent a group of litigants in a multidistrict or consolidated proceeding that produces a common fund, courts assert that they have some control over the fees paid to lead counsel. *See, e.g.*, Vincent v. Hughes Air West, Inc., 557 F.2d 759 (9th Cir. 1977) (*supra* p. 721); *but see* Charles Silver & Geoffrey P. Miller, *The Quasi-Class Action Method of Managing Multi-District Litigation: Problems and a Proposal*, 63 VAND. L. REV. 107 (2010) (questioning the validity of this assertion).   As a general matter, however, fees are set by the attorney-client contract — a private agreement that lies outside of the purview of the court.

Should courts exercise more control over fee awards in mass aggregations? Under what authority? Perhaps its inherent power? *See* In re Vioxx Prods. Liab. Litig., 650 F. Supp. 2d 549 (E.D. La. 2009) (holding that an MDL proceeding's status as a quasi-class action and the court's inherent power gave the court the authority to cap attorneys' fees at 32%).

7.   Fee awards in class actions appear to be less than they are in aggregated cases. *See* WILLGING, *supra*, at 69 (noting that the median recovery rate for class counsel was 27-30%, and the "fee-recovery rate infrequently exceeded the traditional 33.3% contingency fee rate").   This finding slays one of the myths of class actions: that class actions benefit no one but class counsel.   It also raises ethical issues when a lawyer who is representing both individually aggregated clients and class clients negotiates on behalf of both of them at the same time.   Will the lawyer seek to negotiate better deals for the individual clients than for the class clients because the fees will be greater?   This question was contested in the *Amchem* litigation, although the Supreme Court ducked the issue in its decision. *See* Georgine v. Amchem Prods., Inc., 157 F.R.D. 246 (E.D. Pa. 1994) (*supra* p. 739), *rev'd on other grounds*, 83 F.3d 610 (3d Cir. 1996), *aff'd sub nom.* Amchem Prods., Inc. v. Windsor, 521 U.S. 591 (1997) (*supra* p. 493); Susan P. Koniak, *Feasting While the Widow Weeps:* Georgine v. Amchem Products, Inc., 80 CORNELL L. REV. 1045 (1995).

8.   In *Wal-Mart* the fee that counsel negotiated was 18%, far less than a standard 33.3% to 40% contingency fee that is common today.   Counsel negotiated this fee with Wal-Mart and other major retailers — hardly an unsophisticated bunch powerless to strike a hard bargain.   A significant

recovery was far from guaranteed; the fee looks huge only in retrospect. In this situation, why depart from the ex ante bargain struck by both sides?

9.   Sometimes a settlement negotiates the attorneys' fee separately; the class or aggregated clients are guaranteed to receive a certain amount, and the defendant agrees to set aside a separate amount for attorneys' fees. Often the deal is structured so that the defendant agrees not to oppose the plaintiffs' attorney's request to receive the full amount of the fee, and any amounts that the court decides not to award are returned to the defendant rather than added to the class's recovery. It is obvious to see why this is a good deal from the perspective of the plaintiffs' lawyer (the judge has little incentive not to give the amount requested, because it won't affect the amount that the plaintiffs get) and the defendant (there is some chance that the court will reduce the fee request of the plaintiffs' lawyer, resulting in a windfall to the defendant). But is this a good deal for the plaintiffs? Is it unethical for the plaintiffs' lawyer to agree to this fee structure?

10. Lawyers are also reimbursed for their costs from the common fund. As *Wal-Mart* shows, these costs can be enormous. In many cases, especially when the plaintiffs have limited means, the lawyer fronts these costs in the hope that a judgment or settlement will cover them. Often counsel needs to borrow the money or to include as part of the litigation team law firms willing to invest in the case. Obviously, the debt that the lawyer incurs in pursuing the case can weigh mightily on the lawyer's decisions whether to settle and whether to steer the negotiations toward monetary rather than other forms of relief. Is there any way to avoid this problem?

In an important development associated with the rise of class-action practices elsewhere in the world, a new industry has arisen in several countries: third-party financing of litigation. Foreign venture capitalists and hedge funds have been obtaining nice returns by providing money to lawyers in return for taking a pre-negotiated percentage of any recovery that the lawyer obtains on behalf of a class. To avoid concerns for champerty, these firms claim not to control the lawyers' tactical decisions in litigation; they are merely passive investors. As of this writing, some major lobbyists, such as the Chamber of Commerce, are scrambling to nip this practice in the bud. *See News Briefs*, L. OFFICE MGMT. & ADMIN. REP. (Jan. 2010). Whether this practice comes to the United States, and how much it will affect the course of complex litigation, bear watching.

11. We have only scratched the surface of the legal and ethical issues surrounding the award of attorneys' fees and costs. Nonetheless, we hope to have conveyed the important influence that issues about how (and how much) a lawyer gets paid can exercise on complex litigation. *See In re Fidelity/Micron Sec. Litig.*, 167 F.3d 735, 736 (1st Cir. 1999) ("In certain types of complex litigation, the lawyers' monetary interests often comprise a tail that wags the dog.") The adversarial system is premised on the assumption that lawyers will vigorously and selflessly pursue the interests of their clients. If that assumption is untrue, what is the argument for using the adversarial system in complex litigation?

CHAPTER TWELVE

IMPLEMENTING REMEDIES

In the adversarial system, implementing the declared remedy is the losing party's responsibility. The court possesses some tools — contempt for failures to comply with injunctions and proceedings supplemental (writs of execution, attachment, and garnishment) for failures to pay the judgment — to force the losing party to comply with a judgment; a breach-of-contract claim is available against a party that fails to comply with a settlement. *See* Kokkonen v. Guardian Life Ins. Co. of Am., 511 U.S. 375 (1994).

In complex litigation, however, implementing the remedy can be more difficult. In institutional-reform litigation, the court's injunction often requires significant funding and changes to settled structures. Resistance to the remedy from legislative and executive officials and other powerful actors is common. The judge's political position is delicate; for the remedy to be implemented, the judge must often oversee lengthy negotiations that bring the principal players to the point of supporting the remedy. In mass-injury litigation, a lump-sum judgment or settlement leaves difficult questions of distribution undetermined. Mechanisms must be established to determine who is entitled to compensation and how much they are entitled to. In both injunctive and monetary cases, sometimes parties who are not before the court hold the key to making the remedy work. Whether the court can bring these players into the litigation poses an additional difficulty.

This chapter explores these issues. As you read these materials, you will realize that, in many cases, getting to the point of a remedy is only half the battle. In mass torts, for instance, the risks and pressures on both sides are so great that, once aggregation by class action or another mechanism occurs, a settlement is almost inevitable. *See* Richard A. Nagareda, *Aggregation and its Discontents: Class Settlement Pressure, Class-Wide Arbitration and CAFA*, 106 COLUM. L. REV. 1872, 1879-95 (2006). Everyone knows this fact as the case proceeds to its almost inevitable denouement, and the pretrial process is more about shaping the litigation landscape to achieve the best settlement than about winning at trial.

As you read these materials, you will also see the role that the judge takes on in the implementation phase: less of an adjudicator and more of an administrator. Indeed, as some scholars have noted, complex cases blur the line between a court and an administrative agency. *See* Richard A. Nagareda, *Class Actions in the Administrative State: Kalven and Rosenfield Revisited*, 75 U. CHI. L. REV. 603 (2008); Martha Minow, *Judge for the Situation: Judge Jack Weinstein, Creator of Temporary Administrative Agencies*, 97 COLUM. L. REV. 2010 (1997). Therefore, this chapter inevitably returns to basic themes about the institutional legitimacy of using courts to resolve mass controversies.

A. IMPLEMENTING INJUNCTIVE REMEDIES

Injunctive remedies in complex litigation often involve significant expenditures. They also involve ongoing efforts to assure that defendants are complying with sometimes extensive obligations that they must undertake — often grudgingly — to remedy their wrongdoing. Unless something can be done to deliver effective relief, the plaintiffs' victory will be pyrrhic. The following two cases give some sense of the issues that courts confront, the powers they possess, and the limits within which they work.

MISSOURI V. JENKINS

495 U.S. 33 (1990)

■ JUSTICE WHITE delivered the opinion of the Court.

The United States District Court for the Western District of Missouri imposed an increase in the property taxes levied by the Kansas City, Missouri, School District (KCMSD) to ensure funding for the desegregation of KCMSD's public schools. We granted certiorari to consider the State of Missouri's argument that the District Court lacked the power to raise local property taxes. For the reasons given below, we hold that the District Court abused its discretion in imposing the tax increase. We also hold, however, that the modifications of the District Court's order made by the Court of Appeals do satisfy equitable and constitutional principles governing the District Court's power.

I

In 1977, KCMSD and a group of KCMSD students filed a complaint alleging that the State of Missouri and surrounding school districts had operated a segregated public school system in the Kansas City metropolitan area. The District Court realigned KCMSD as a party defendant, and KCMSD filed a cross-claim against the State, seeking indemnification for any liability that might be imposed on KCMSD for intradistrict segregation.

After a lengthy trial, the District Court found that KCMSD and the State had operated a segregated school system within the KCMSD.

The District Court thereafter issued an order detailing the remedies necessary to eliminate the vestiges of segregation and the financing necessary to implement those remedies. . . .The court concluded, however, that several provisions of Missouri law would prevent KCMSD from being able to pay its share of the obligation. . . .

The District Court believed that it had the power to order a tax increase to ensure adequate funding of the desegregation plan, but it hesitated to take this step. It chose instead to enjoin the effect of [one state law] to allow KCMSD to raise an additional $4 million for the coming fiscal year. The court ordered KCMSD to submit to the voters a proposal for an increase in taxes sufficient to pay for its share of the desegregation remedy in following years.

. . . KCMSD's efforts to persuade the voters to approve a tax increase . . . failed, as had its efforts to seek funds from the Kansas City Council and the state legislature. [The district court then approved and expanded the magnet-school program as a way to achieve integration. After holding that the State and KCMSD were 75% and 25% at fault, respectively, for the segregation of Kansas City schools, it ordered them to share the cost of the desegregation remedy in that proportion.]

Three months later, the District Court adopted a plan requiring $187,450,334 in further capital improvements. By then it was clear that KCMSD would lack the resources to pay for its 25% share of the desegregation cost. . . . The District Court declined to impose a greater share of the cost on the State, but it accepted that KCMSD had "exhausted all available means of raising additional revenue." Finding itself with "no choice but to exercise its broad equitable powers and enter a judgment that will enable the KCMSD to raise its share of the cost of the plan," and believing that the "United States Supreme Court has stated that a tax may be increased if 'necessary to raise funds adequate to . . . operate and maintain without racial discrimination a public school system,'" the court ordered the KCMSD property tax levy raised from $2.05 to $4.00 per $100 of assessed valuation through the 1991-1992 fiscal year. KCMSD was also directed to issue $150 million in capital improvement bonds. . . .

The State appealed, challenging the scope of the desegregation remedy, the allocation of the cost between the State and KCMSD, and the tax increase. [The court of appeals upheld the scope of the desegregation order and the allocation of costs. The court of appeals also rejected the argument that a federal court lacks the judicial power to order a tax increase.]

Although the Court of Appeals thus "affirm[ed] the actions that the [District] [C]ourt has taken to this point," it agreed with the State that principles of federal/state comity required the District Court to use "minimally obtrusive methods to remedy constitutional violations." The Court of Appeals thus required that in the future, the District Court should not set the property tax rate itself but should authorize KCMSD to submit

a levy to the state tax collection authorities and should enjoin the operation of state laws hindering KCMSD from adequately funding the remedy. . . .

III

We turn to the tax increase imposed by the District Court. The State urges us to hold that the tax increase violated Article III, the Tenth Amendment, and principles of federal/state comity. We find it unnecessary to reach the difficult constitutional issues, for we agree with the State that the tax increase contravened the principles of comity that must govern the exercise of the District Court's equitable discretion in this area.

It is accepted by all the parties, as it was by the courts below, that the imposition of a tax increase by a federal court was an extraordinary event. In assuming for itself the fundamental and delicate power of taxation the District Court not only intruded on local authority but circumvented it altogether. Before taking such a drastic step the District Court was obliged to assure itself that no permissible alternative would have accomplished the required task. We have emphasized that although the "remedial powers of an equity court must be adequate to the task, . . . they are not unlimited," and one of the most important considerations governing the exercise of equitable power is a proper respect for the integrity and function of local government institutions. Especially is this true where, as here, those institutions are ready, willing, and — but for the operation of state law curtailing their powers — able to remedy the deprivation of constitutional rights themselves.

The District Court believed that it had no alternative to imposing a tax increase. But there was an alternative, the very one outlined by the Court of Appeals: it could have authorized or required KCMSD to levy property taxes at a rate adequate to fund the desegregation remedy and could have enjoined the operation of state laws that would have prevented KCMSD from exercising this power. The difference between the two approaches is far more than a matter of form. Authorizing and directing local government institutions to devise and implement remedies not only protects the function of those institutions but, to the extent possible, also places the responsibility for solutions to the problems of segregation upon those who have themselves created the problems. . . .

The District Court therefore abused its discretion in imposing the tax itself. The Court of Appeals should not have allowed the tax increase to stand and should have reversed the District Court in this respect. . . .

IV

We stand on different ground when we review the modifications to the District Court's order made by the Court of Appeals. . . .

. . . [T]he State argues that an order to increase taxes cannot be sustained under the judicial power of Article III. Whatever the merits of this argument when applied to the District Court's own order increasing

taxes, a point we have not reached, a court order directing a local government body to levy its own taxes is plainly a judicial act within the power of a federal court. We held as much in *Griffin v. Prince Edward County School Bd.*, 377 U.S. [218, 233 (1964)], where we stated that a District Court, faced with a county's attempt to avoid desegregation of the public schools by refusing to operate those schools, could "require the [County] Supervisors to exercise the power that is theirs to levy taxes to raise funds adequate to reopen, operate, and maintain without racial discrimination a public school system . . . ." *Griffin* followed a long and venerable line of cases in which this Court held that federal courts could issue the writ of mandamus to compel local governmental bodies to levy taxes adequate to satisfy their debt obligations.

The State maintains, however, that even under these cases, the federal judicial power can go no further than to require local governments to levy taxes as authorized under state law. In other words, the State argues that federal courts cannot set aside state-imposed limitations on local taxing authority because to do so is to do more than to require the local government "to exercise the power that is theirs." We disagree. . . . .

It is therefore clear that a local government with taxing authority may be ordered to levy taxes in excess of the limit set by state statute where there is reason based in the Constitution for not observing the statutory limitation. . . . Here, the KCMSD may be ordered to levy taxes despite the statutory limitations on its authority in order to compel the discharge of an obligation imposed on KCMSD by the Fourteenth Amendment. To hold otherwise would fail to take account of the obligations of local governments, under the Supremacy Clause, to fulfill the requirements that the Constitution imposes on them. However wide the discretion of local authorities in fashioning desegregation remedies may be, "if a state-imposed limitation on a school authority's discretion operates to inhibit or obstruct the operation of a unitary school system or impede the disestablishing of a dual school system, it must fall; state policy must give way when it operates to hinder vindication of federal constitutional guarantees." North Carolina Bd. of Education v. Swann, 402 U.S. 43, 45 (1971). Even though a particular remedy may not be required in every case to vindicate constitutional guarantees, where (as here) it has been found that a particular remedy is required, the State cannot hinder the process by preventing a local government from implementing that remedy.

. . . The case is remanded for further proceedings consistent with this opinion.

■ JUSTICE KENNEDY, with whom THE CHIEF JUSTICE, JUSTICE O'CONNOR, and JUSTICE SCALIA join, concurring in part and concurring in the judgment.

. . . [T]he District Court exceeded its authority by attempting to impose a tax. . . .

In my view, however, the Court transgresses these [the basic principles defining judicial power] when it goes further, much further, to embrace by

broad dictum an expansion of power in the Federal Judiciary beyond all precedent. Today's casual embrace of taxation imposed by the unelected, life-tenured Federal Judiciary disregards fundamental precepts for the democratic control of public institutions. . . . The Court's statements, in my view, cannot be seen as necessary for its judgment, or as precedent for the future, and I cannot join Parts III and IV of the Court's opinion. . . .

Article III of the Constitution states that "[t]he judicial Power of the United States, shall be vested in one supreme Court, and in such inferior Courts as the Congress may from time to time ordain and establish." The description of the judicial power nowhere includes the word "tax" or anything that resembles it. This reflects the Framers' understanding that taxation was not a proper area for judicial involvement. "The judiciary . . . has no influence over either the sword or the purse, no direction either of the strength or of the wealth of the society, and can take no active resolution whatever." THE FEDERALIST No. 78, p. 523 (J. Cooke ed. 1961) (A. Hamilton). . . .

The confinement of taxation to the legislative branches, both in our Federal and State Governments, was not random. It reflected our ideal that the power of taxation must be under the control of those who are taxed. This truth animated all our colonial and revolutionary history. . . .

The operation of tax systems is among the most difficult aspects of public administration. It is not a function the Judiciary as an institution is designed to exercise. . . .

. . . In pursuing the demand of justice for racial equality, I fear that the Court today loses sight of other basic political liberties guaranteed by our constitutional system, liberties that can coexist with a proper exercise of judicial remedial powers adequate to correct constitutional violations.

Notes

1. *Missouri v. Jenkins* has to some degree been superseded by the Court's subsequent decision in the same case, holding that the remedial measures that the district court was attempting to fund exceeded the rightful position. Missouri v. Jenkins, 515 U.S. 70, 88 (1995). Nonetheless, the first *Missouri v. Jenkins* is significant. In some cases, a defendant institution might not be able to fund the remedy required under the rightful-position principle. The court must then face the question about the extent of its powers to implement the remedy.

2. The traditional power of the court to deal with the problem of a party that failed to implement an injunctive decree was contempt. *See* Int'l Union, United Mine Workers of Am. v. Bagwell, 512 U.S. 821 (1994). When the party itself holds the key to implementing the remedy, contempt can often be effective, although sometimes the contempt sanction needs to be draconian and punitive to make an institution act. *See* Spallone v. United States, 493 U.S. 265 (1990). In a remedially complex case like *Missouri v. Jenkins*, however, holding the school district in contempt is unlikely to

accomplish very much, since they were perfectly willing, but legally unable, to implement the remedy ordered by the court.

In this situation, how much power should a court have? Does your answer depend on whether the court is a state court as opposed to a federal court? On whether the defendant is a private actor or a public institution? On whether the defendant is attempting to act in good faith, or instead is intransigent? On whether the court is seeking to exercise powers that are typically performed by other branches of government?

3.   It is difficult to generalize about the exact scope of a court's power to assure adequate implementation of a remedy; it may depend on the facts and the fine balance of factors present in each case. Does the form of adjudication require that the court have the authority to remove stumbling blocks to implementation? If so, is this power grounded in the Due Process Clause's guarantee of rational adjudication? If so, how do we balance the constitutional concern for due process against constitutional concerns for separation of powers and federalism? *See* Donald L. Horowitz, *Decreeing Organizational Change: Judicial Supervision of Public Institutions*, 1983 DUKE L.J. 1265.

4.   Of course, the existence of a power to remove stumbling blocks to the implementation of a decree does not mean that the court must use the power. There are all sorts of reasons to hold at least some of the power in reserve. As a pragmatic matter, isn't the majority in *Missouri v. Jenkins* right that the court should apply less power rather than more as long as it appears that less power will do the job? But, by relying on the political process, is it as likely that the remedy will be effective? Isn't it a bit odd to rely so heavily on a wrongdoer to remedy the wrong? Will the judge accept something less than the rightful position from the defendant in order to make some remedy work? *See* Owen M. Fiss, *Foreword: The Forms of Justice*, 93 HARV. L. REV. 1 (1979).

5.   The traditional adversarial approach might not always be the best way to overcome implementation problems. In some institutional-reform cases, judges have entered into negotiations with the parties, met with legislators or others that hold the key to implementation, appointed a receiver to run an institution, commissioned remedial experts as officers of the court, and appeared at public forums to garner support. Do these departures from the judge's traditionally neutral and passive role seem appropriate? *See, e.g.*, Bradley v. Milliken, 620 F.2d 1143 (6th Cir. 1980) (refusing to order the recusal of a judge who commissioned officers and appeared at public forums in a desegregation case, but expressing concern about the judge's conduct).

6.   There is a wealth of literature — ranging from the anecdotal to the highly theoretical — on the problems of implementing consent decrees. For a small sampling, see OWEN M. FISS & DOUG RENDLEMAN, INJUNCTIONS 1-58, 528-827 (2d ed. 1984); OWEN M. FISS, THE CIVIL RIGHTS INJUNCTION (1978); DONALD L. HOROWITZ, THE COURTS AND SOCIAL POLICY (1977); Barry Friedman, *When Rights Encounter Reality: Enforcing Federal Remedies*, 65 S. CAL. L. REV. 735 (1992); Susan P. Sturm, *A Normative Theory of*

Public Law Remedies, 79 GEO. L.J. 1355 (1991); Special Project, *The Remedial Process in Institutional Reform Litigation*, 78 COLUM. L. REV. 784 (1978); Note, *Implementation Problems in Institutional Reform Litigation*, 91 HARV. L. REV. 428 (1977). *See generally* FISS & RENDLEMAN, *supra*, at 827-30 (bibliography of literature on structural injunctions).

RUIZ V. ESTELLE

679 F.2d 1115 (5th Cir. 1982), *amended in part and vacated in part on other grounds,*
688 F.2d 266 (5th Cir. 1982)

■   RUBIN, Circuit Judge.

[In a class action brought on behalf of the 33,000 prisoners housed in prisons operated by the Texas Department of Corrections (TDC), the district court found that prisoners were confined in violation of the Eighth and Fourteenth Amendments. It ordered a series of remedial measures to correct the violations. Among the orders was the appointment of a special master and monitors to ensure that the TDC was implementing the remedy. The court of appeals affirmed most of the findings of constitutional violation and of the remedy. It then turned to the district court's decision to use a master and monitors.]

The district court's order of reference appoints a special master and provides for the appointment of "several monitors" to help the special master. It imposes on the special master the responsibility of seeing that the district court's decree is implemented, and empowers him to hold hearings, find facts, and make recommendations to the district court concerning TDC's compliance with the decree. As authority for the appointment the district court invoked both Fed. R. Civ. P. 53 and its inherent power as a court of equity.

TDC contends that the appointment of a special master was improper because the district court failed to comply with rule 53, which, according to TDC, codifies and limits a court's authority to appoint a special master. . . . Rule 53(b) states that a district court may appoint a special master "only upon a showing that some exceptional condition requires" the appointment.[*]

The district court stated several reasons for its decision to make the appointment: the difficulty of superintending the implementation of "a comprehensive, detailed plan for the elimination of the unconstitutional conditions found to exist in the Texas prison system"; TDC's "record of intransigence toward previous court orders requiring changes in TDC's practices and conditions"; the "strained" working relations between TDC's lawyers and the plaintiffs' lawyers; TDC's failure to acknowledge even "completely evident" constitutional violations; and TDC's failure to conform

---

[*]   Amendments to Rule 53 in 2003 and 2007 changed the standard for post-trial appointments of special masters from the "exceptional condition" requirement, and Rule 53(a)(1)(C) now permits a reference for "post-trial matters that cannot be effectively and timely addressed by an available district judge." — ED.

its actual practices to its written policies and procedures. The district court did not, as TDC implies, simply rely on the "mere complexity" of the case. Moreover, the court was not required to await the failure or refusal of TDC to comply with the decree before appointing an agent to implement it. Noncompliance may constitute one "exceptional condition" under rule 53, but it is not exclusive.

Furthermore, rule 53 does not terminate or modify the district court's inherent equitable power to appoint a person, whatever be his title, to assist it in administering a remedy. The power of a federal court to appoint an agent to supervise the implementation of its decrees has long been established. Such court-appointed agents have been identified by "a confusing plethora of titles: 'receiver,' 'Master,' 'Special Master,' 'master hearing officer,' 'monitor,' 'human rights committee,' 'Ombudsman,'" and others. The function is clear, whatever the title.

. . . [W]e have previously approved the appointment of such agents to oversee compliance with continuing court orders. Insofar as the special master is to report on TDC's compliance with the district court's decree and to help implement the decree, he assumes one of the plaintiffs' traditional roles, except that, because he is the court's agent, he can and should perform his duties objectively. . . .

The special master is also given powers that are quasijudicial. He is permitted to hold hearings and is directed to find facts "concerning the defendants' compliance with the provisions of the Court's Orders and the need, if any, for supplemental remedial action." The order also establishes rules of procedure: the monitors are to make reports of factual observations and to submit them to the special master and the parties. If any party objects, the special master is to hold a hearing, then make his report to the district court. No objection may be filed to the special master's report that could have been filed to the monitor's report preceding it. The special master's findings of fact are to be accepted by the court unless clearly erroneous. . . .

To fulfill his responsibilities, the special master is given sweeping powers, including "unlimited access" to TDC premises and records as well as the power to conduct "confidential interviews" with TDC staff members and inmates, and to require written reports from any TDC staff member. These powers are unconfined save by the following instructions: he is not to intervene in the administrative management of either TDC or any of its units and he is not to direct the defendants or any of their subordinates to take or to refrain from taking any specific action to achieve compliance.

The order of reference does not make clear that, in conducting investigations and hearings, the special master and the monitors are not to consider matters that go beyond superintending compliance with the district court's decree. Such an express constraint is appropriate because of the danger that the special master or the monitors may entertain inmate complaints that convert the remedial process into a surrogate forum for new § 1983 actions. In the interests both of prison administration and sound judicial procedure, it should be made clear to the plaintiffs, the special master, the monitors, and the TDC staff that the special master is not an inmate advocate or a roving federal district court. As we have pointed out before, the powers of the court's appointed agents should not intrude to an unnecessary extent on prison administration.

In one respect, the order of reference is too sweeping. It permits the special master to submit to the district court "reports based upon his own observations and investigations in the absence of a formal hearing before him." This not only transcends the powers traditionally given masters by courts of equity, but denies the parties due process.

Accordingly, the order of reference shall be amended as follows: (1) it should be made clear that the special master and the monitors do not have the authority to hear matters that should appropriately be the subject of separate judicial proceedings, such as actions under § 1983, and that their duties are restricted to those set forth in the order of reference; and (2) unless based on hearings conducted on the record after proper notice, the reports, findings, and conclusions of the special master are not to be accorded any presumption of correctness and the "clearly erroneous" rule will not apply to them.

Finally, the reduction in the scope of the district court's decree directed by this opinion should occasion further inquiry by the district court to determine whether or not there is a continuing need for a staff of six monitors to assist the special master.

The district court's order of reference is affirmed [as modified] . . . .

Notes

1. *Ruiz v. Estelle* is one of the most famous cases regarding the use of masters and adjuncts such as monitors to implement institutional-reform injunctions. Although the use of masters in the implementation phase is a fairly recent occurrence, today it is generally accepted that, in appropriate circumstances, masters and other adjuncts can be used for this purpose. *See* Hoptowit v. Ray, 682 F.2d 1237, 1263 (9th Cir. 1982); AM. L. INST., PRINCIPLES OF THE LAW OF AGGREGATE LITIGATION § 3.09 (2009).

There are, however, instances in which courts thought that the use of monitors intruded too deeply into the prerogatives of an institutional defendant. The most well-known may be *Newman v. Alabama*, 559 F.2d 283, 288-90 (5th Cir. 1977), in which the Fifth Circuit (which later decided *Ruiz*) held that the district court had abused its discretion when it appointed a 39-member "Human Rights Committee" to monitor compliance. Among other things, the Court noted that the committee members had not been shown to have expertise in monitoring, the number of members made the committee unwieldy, the mandate of the committee was too broad, and the committee had apparently functionally taken over the administration of the prison. *See also* Women Prisoners of the D.C. Dep't of Corr. v. D.C., 93 F.3d 910, 930 (D.C. Cir. 1996) (reversing order that authorized monitors to "perform the functions of local authorities" and therefore "effectively usurp[ed] the executive functions of the District").

2.   In structural reform litigation, masters can play other roles than an enforcer. For instance, masters have been appointed to "to cope with anticipated resistance to the decree; . . . to negotiate with actors whose cooperation would be necessary to secure implementation; to advise and assist the defendant organization; to monitor the conduct of the organization and provide intelligence to the judge about its behavior; to be alert to the need to amend the decree; and to resolve disputes over the meaning of the decree." Donald L. Horowitz, *Decreeing Organizational Change: Judicial Supervision of Public Institutions*, 1983 DUKE L.J. 1265, 1298.

3.   Some federal courts have found that the appointment of a master to monitor compliance can be grounded in the All Writs Act, 28 U.S.C. § 1651. *See* Nat'l Org. for the Reform of Marijuana Laws v. Mullen, 828 F.2d 536 (9th Cir. 1987).

Assuming that the power to make the appointment exists, what factors should a court use in determining whether to appoint a judicial adjunct? One of the factors that often weighs heavily in the determination of an "exception" is the lack of the defendant's prior good-faith compliance, *see id.*; presumably, because of the size of the institution, it may be difficult for a court alone to monitor the defendant's future compliance. What other factors should enter into the decision? Does the answer depend on the function that the adjunct is being asked to perform? For instance, in *Ruiz v. Estelle*, why can't the district court adjudicate complaints of non-compliance? If the logic of *La Buy v. Howes Leather Co.*, 352 U.S. 249 (1957) (*supra* p. 1016) applies to appointments in the implementation phase, the mere complexity of the task or the burden on the court is not an adequate reason to pass off the job. Would reducing the judge's ability to appoint remedial masters and monitors make judges less willing to order sweeping relief?

4.   Professor Horowitz, a staunch critic of much institutional-reform litigation, sees problems with the use of masters:

> Precisely because masters sense the need to act unconventionally, they test the boundaries of judicial propriety. They sometimes engage in what would clearly be improper ex parte communications if engaged in by the judge. If they rely more heavily on one side or the other for information or for cooperation in drafting a plan, they risk the appearance or the reality of lost neutrality. If they hire subordinate personnel, they delegate some part of their function, thus removing the judge a second step from the action taken. If they use their power to interview staff members, to recommend staff changes, or to give orders to staff on operational matters, they may intrude unduly into administration and raise questions of organizational accountability and lines of authority. If, in monitoring a decree, they commit themselves to a certain view of who is responsible for shortfalls in implementation, they risk partisan commitment, in which they may also entangle the

judge if he accepts their view of the matter, even after a formal hearing. [Horowitz, *supra*, at 1298-99.]

B. IMPLEMENTING MONETARY REMEDIES

Implementation issues in cases involving monetary remedies usually arise after a trial or settlement results in a lump-sum award, although they can also arise when a settlement provides a schedule of benefits for various types of claims. In both situations, the eligibility of each claimant for an award must be determined and the awards must also be disbursed to the deserving; in the former situation, a method for allocating the amount of each award must also be chosen. How is the plaintiffs' lawyer to accomplish this task? Should the judge be involved? Must they give each claimant an amount proportional to the amount that the claimant would have received at trial? Can they obtain assistance in disbursing funds? In the first section, we examine these problems of disbursement.

In some cases, funds are left over because fewer people file valid claims than expected; in other cases, funds remain because it is too costly to engage in individualized claim determinations. What should the lawyer and the court do with the excess? Give it back to the defendant? Give more to claimants with valid claims? Give it to some organization that does good work? The second section explores these questions, which raise more difficult and controversial issues than it might initially appear.

1. Distributing Money

Obviously the plaintiffs' lawyer and the judge cannot handle the issues of disbursement alone; what the lawyer and the judge need is a staff of people with expertise in claims administration. But how much authority does the judge have to establish and monitor the work of claims-resolution facilities and to require plaintiffs to process their claims through such facilities? In a class action, presumably the requirement of court approval gives the judge some say in the disbursement process; but when the case is an aggregate rather than a class settlement, the authority of the judge to be involved in any disbursement matters is uncertain.

IN RE COMBUSTION, INC.

978 F. Supp. 673 (W.D. La. 1997), *aff'd*, 159 F.3d 1356 (Table),
1998 WL 698997 (5th Cir. Sept. 18, 1998)

■   HAIK, District Judge.

[Plaintiffs worked at or lived near a waste oil recycling site that operated for 18 years. After significant environmental contamination was discovered on and around the site, plaintiffs filed tort and environmental cases in Louisiana state court. The state court certified a class action, and the case was removed to federal court. Ultimately the case contained more than 10,000 plaintiffs and 450 defendants. After eleven years of litigation, all but one defendant settled for more than $20 million. The settlement did not provide a method of allocating the settlement among plaintiffs. After the court preliminarily approved the settlement as fair, reasonable, and adequate, it ordered a special master to establish specific criteria for distributing the settlement to class members. The master submitted a report recommending a distribution plan for the 10,000 claimants.]

On August 15 and 18, 19 and 22, 1997, this Court conducted a hearing ("Hearing") that represented the culmination of more than five month's work by the Special Master and his staff, the Plaintiff Steering Committee (PSC), and this Court toward the ultimate goal of disbursing funds to the Claimants. The purpose of the Hearing was to consider the recommendations of the Special Master and the Court-appointed-disbursing-agent, ("CADA"), regarding the allocation process and Claimant allocation schedule, to consider individual objections, and in general, to clear the last major hurdle in the long-awaited disbursement of funds.

For the reasons stated below, the Court adopts the Report of the Special Master . . . and the amended Claimant allocation schedule submitted under seal as CADA # 3.

Each Claimant who elected to maintain his objection after consideration by the Special Master and then by the Court at the Hearing was issued an individual Final Judgment, entered by the Clerk of Court at that time. By the Final Judgment issued in conjunction with this Ruling, the Court dismisses all objections by Claimants who timely filed but failed to appear at both the Special Master's conferences and before the Court at the Hearing, by claimants who filed timely objections and appeared before the Court but did not show just cause for failing to follow the Special Master's protocol and failing to appear at the Special Master's conferences, by Claimants who maintained their objections after the Special Master's conferences but who failed to appear at the Hearing, and by Claimants who failed to timely object but who appeared at the Hearing and did not show just cause for such derelict behavior. Finally, the Court dismisses all other claims asserted by Class members who appeared at the Hearing.

BACKGROUND

. . .

. . . [T]he Special Master enlisted a staff of attorneys and a medical expert board certified in pathology and internal medicine to assist evaluating all the reports of the medical and toxological experts filed in this case, and in reviewing each Claimant's file, including all medical records and property claims. Only after an exhaustive review of the information available to him did the Special Master recommend to the Court a methodology upon which individual allocations were based and a schedule of the individual allocation for each Claimant. . . .

METHODOLOGY

The cornerstones of the Special Master's methodology were exposure and medical problems. Using expert reports and the state court's geographical class definition, the Special Master determined that the site had no impact on people living beyond 3 miles from a center point lying between two portions of the site. Thus, personal injury recovery was limited exclusively to Claimants who lived, worked, or attended school within the 3 mile radius. Enhancement factors were proximity, duration, and degree of lethal activity at the site during the Claimant's time within the creditable radius. Once a Claimant's exposure points were calculated, each point was valued at $3.00, with the product yielding a total exposure award.

To this award was added the compensation for medical problems determined by the medical expert to be associated with the site. The expert evaluated and classified each Claimant's medical problem by studying the symptoms, the age of the Claimant, and the date of diagnosis. Enhancing factors included the nature and severity of the condition, the probability of a causal link to the site. the relationship of the medical claims to each other, and the effect on the life of the Claimant. Categories A, B, C, and D classified diseases or clinical courses according to severity from "unusual or unexpected major diseases and/or clinical courses" to "chronic effects to include birth defects and deformities." Other categories were used simply as a formality, but only these four classifications earned dollar credits.

The maximum awards for these four categories ranged from $1,000,000 to $15,000. After it was determined that a claimant belonged in category A, for example, that Claimant's maximum possible medical award was tapered to fit his actual circumstance.

First, the Special Master set up four "rejection of medical claim" categories. Medical claims were not allowed for Claimants who were diagnosed prior to January 1, 1968, or who moved from the site prior to January 1, 1968, or who were diagnosed after moving outside the 3 mile radius.

Causation was factored into the medical award for the claims that survived the rejection threshold. The actual medical award was the product of the maximum dollar amount for that Claimant's illness category and the ratio of that Claimant's actual exposure points to his maximum possible exposure points calculated as if he had lived at the site throughout all relevant time beginning with his date of birth. The sum of the medical award and the exposure point award was each Claimant's personal injury allocation.

Minimum compensation awards ranging from $250-$20,000 were allotted to Claimants whose exposure points fell into one of six categories but whose corresponding total allocation was lower than the corresponding minimum amount set by the Special Master. As a baseline rule, an allocation of $250 was allotted to the Claimants who lived outside the three mile radius and never attended school or worked within the radius and who had no other creditable exposure or property damage but who participated in the Class action as instructed by the many newsletters and legal notices.

Property damage was determined in increments of one-quarter mile from the site up to one mile from the site. The dollar amount was based on the Assessor's rolls for Claimants who owned the property when the suit was filed in July 1986. Reimbursement ranged from 100% to 25% of "actual value," calculated to be greater [than] the assessed value by the factor of ten.

Other categories were compensated. Business losses were considered on a case by case basis because of the relatively few claims of this nature. Compensation to class representatives, bellwether plaintiffs, and other claimants who participated in depositions, medical examinations, and generally contributed to the development of the case was awarded because of the extra time and effort and work of these Claimants during the course of the law suit.

In addition to individual awards to the Claimants, the Special Master also recommended establishing a medical monitoring fund for annual medical check-ups, including blood work, for five years free of charge to the Class members. He recommended $1.5 million for this service. This service had been requested by claimants in letters to the Court in conjunction with the April 18, 1997 hearing. Finally, the Special Master reported the intervention by the State of Louisiana asserting liens for recovery of medical and related expenses incurred by the State hospital facilities.

PROTOCOL

On June 26, 1997, the Court gave preliminary approval to [the special master's report] and allocation schedule and ordered a hearing pursuant to Federal Rule of Civil Procedure 23(e). The individual allocation letters and the Important Notice of Hearing were mailed to each Claimant beginning June 26, 1997. Incorporated in the Important Notice of Hearing was the procedure that dissatisfied Claimants were ordered to follow to object to their allocations. The notice also included the methodology to be used by the Special Master and his staff to review each objection. . . .

Approximately 1600 objections were received timely. Each objector's file was studied and re-evaluated. The Special Master scheduled individual appointments for every objector and notified each one of the appointment in writing and by phone. . . .

For eleven days, beginning July 29 through August 12, 1997, the Special Master and his staff held individual conferences with each objector who appeared in person, beginning at 8:00 a.m. and continuing until 9:00 or 10:00 p.m., in an effort to satisfy each Claimant's concerns. [More than $1 million in adjustments were made as a result of the conferences. Those still dissatisfied could then appeal their allocation to the court.]

COURT HEARING

Claimant's who maintained their objections, including several who received upward adjustments but wished to present their case in Court, appeared at the Hearing. For each objection presented, the Court read and reviewed that objector's complete file, the transcript of his conference with the Special Master, and an additional evaluation of the claimant's medical records provided by the court-appointed physician. The objector was given another opportunity to present to the Court additional evidence not presented to the Special Master.

As each Claimant appeared and after consideration of additional evidence introduced to the Court by the Claimant, the Special Master presented his revised recommendation. The Court then ruled on each objection from the bench. Those objectors who maintained their objections after the ruling by the Court were issued Final Judgments pursuant to FRCP 54(b). The individual Judgments were entered by the Clerk of Court on the dates they were issued.

In addition, Claimants who had not complied with the objection process but appeared at the Hearing and presented to the Court just cause for not complying with the Special Master's protocol were allowed to present their objections to the Special Master or an attorney on his staff and proceed through the same process at that time. . . .

A total of $1.6 million in adjustments was made as a result of this extraordinary effort by the Special Master and his staff and by the Claimants. . . . After considering almost 1,800 objections, the Court issued only sixty-three (63) Final Judgments, less than 4% of the original number [of objections] filed.

ANALYSIS

A district court shall accept the report of a master unless clearly erroneous. This Court finds no clear error in either of the reports submitted by the Special Master.

As repeatedly stressed by the Special Master in the conferences and in Court, the thesis of his methodology was fairness and parity to the Class as a whole, "an imperative consideration in a case of this kind." The Court whole-heartedly agrees and applauds the tireless efforts of the Special Master and his staff for holding firm to the equity touchstone of the distribution model and for taking the time to explain the methodology to every single objector who attended a conference.

The Court now focuses on several key findings made by the Special Master, as these determinations form the cornerstones of the Special Master's methodology. First is his determination that claims recovery should be limited to a radius of 3 miles from the site. This conclusion was based on his knowledge of the case through the tens if not several hundred settlement conferences he conducted, through the exhaustive review he made of the reports of the plaintiffs' and defendants' medical and toxicological experts, and through the extensive consultations he had with the court-appointed physician.

Further, the Court has not received credible evidence to the contrary. . . .

However, in keeping with equitable considerations, the Special Master set a minimum award of $250 for Class member who filed a valid proof of claim but who had no creditable exposure within the 3 mile radius. The purpose of this award was to account for considerations such as inconvenience, fear, fright, and medical conditions of these Claimants.

The Court will not repeat the lengthy analysis on causation set out in the Ruling of June 4, 1997, except to state that establishing a causal link between the chemicals at the site and the various personal injury claims alleged by Class members was the acknowledged Achilles Heel of the Plaintiffs' case. Defendants' experts concluded that harmful exposure, if any, expended only a matter of yards from the site. . . . The Court finds no clear error with the 3-mile radius determination or with the $250 minimum award for Claimant's having no other creditable points. . . .

The Special Master also found that no credit would be given for lost wages or medical expenses. This latter decision was based on the extreme subjectivity and difficulty with proof that chemical exposure caused a missed day of work during the time period from 1968-1994. In addition, almost every Claimant listed medical expenses in the proof of claim form. The Special Master determined that reimbursement of these expenses together with the expense required to verify each claim would itself exhaust the Claimant's fund. Therefore, the decision to eliminate recovery for medical expenses was due to the limited amount of time, personal, and funds available. Furthermore, . . . inclusion of these expenses as a consideration distinct from the exposure point considerations "would skew the allocation in such a way that would be generally unsatisfactory to the large majority of persons involved." The Court finds no clear error in this decision. . . .

The Special Master's recommendation that $1.5 million be set aside for medical monitoring to Class members free of charge for five years has been requested by Claimants and is wholeheartedly supported by the Court. . . . .

For the reasons stated above, the Court adopts the Report of the Special Master . . . .

Notes

1.   Can distribution schemes like *In re Combustion* be reconciled with the rightful-position principle? Is equity and fairness to the class the appropriate touchstone for disbursement of relief? What if *In re Combustion* was not a class action? How should the lawyer make the distribution decisions? What if the lawyer made the same decisions that the special master did? Could a client sue the lawyer for failing to represent the client

faithfully? If so, can *In re Combustion* be justified? If not, must the lawyer adopt a process like *In re Combustion* to defeat allegations of ethical impropriety? What should the standard for judging the lawyer's behavior be? Even though mass aggregations are not bound to respect the adequacy-of-representation requirement of class actions, is there any way to judge the lawyer's behavior except on some comparable adequacy standard?

2.   To what extent is the implementation problem in *In re Combustion* created by the lack of scientific evidence indicating a causal relationship between the injuries of plaintiffs and the toxic substances? To what extent is the problem caused by the parties' decision to settle for a lump sum without working out the details of the distribution? Doesn't the lump-sum settlement create inevitable conflicts of interest among different groups of claimants? Why should the court, rather than the parties, be forced into the role of resolving these conflicts and determining in the first instance the proper amount of the settlement for individual claimants?

From the viewpoint of defendants, sometimes there is an advantage in settling for a sum certain, rather than negotiating a payment schedule under which its obligations might remain uncertain. Should that reality be factored in by the court in deciding whether to take on the parties' usual role of allocating settlement proceeds? Should it make a difference that the case would present intractable problems of structural, pretrial, or trial complexity if the case were not settled? If so, why should a court have greater allocational powers in complex cases than in cases that are not complex? Was *In re Combustion* complex?

3.   In perhaps the most famous mass-tort disbursement decision, Judge Weinstein ordered the distribution of the $180 million *Agent Orange* settlement to Vietnam veterans that had died or were totally disabled; veterans with less than total disability received no awards. To receive an award, a veteran needed to show only that they had served in units known to be in areas in which herbicides had been sprayed. *See* In re "Agent Orange" Prod. Liab. Litig., 689 F. Supp. 1250 (E.D.N.Y. 1988). Among the problems that faced Judge Weinstein were the lack of good evidence of duration or amount of exposure and the lack of scientific evidence that Agent Orange and other herbicides caused any injuries whatsoever. Do the solomonic solutions in *Agent Orange* and *In re Combustion* convince you that providing the judge with the power to make distributional decisions is wise? Or do they convert the court into a social-service agency?

Both *Agent Orange* and *In re Combustion* simplify the eligibility determination by using a rough surrogate (location within a contaminated area and a certain type of injury) for factual causation. As the criteria to determine eligibility to a settlement's proceeds more closely model the criteria that courts use to evaluate causation, the distribution process more closely resembles an adjudicated solution. As the criteria depart from those that determine causation, the distribution process is less likely to give each plaintiff the "right amount" (where "right" is determined with reference to the strength of the individual's case in adjudication). In theory, we want the amount received through the distribution process to match up with this "right amount," but in practice, building more factors into the distribution criteria means that the distribution process becomes more expensive and complicated to operate. What is the right balance to strike between accuracy and simplicity in the distribution of settlement proceeds?

4. The modest claims-administration bureaucracy set up in *In re Combustion* pales in comparison to the bureaucracies that have been set up to deal with some of the larger mass torts, such as *Agent Orange, Dalkon Shield*, and asbestos. Some of these bureaucracies exist for more than a decade, cost millions of dollars to operate, and employ a staff of dozens. For a series of articles examining the operations of these claims-resolution facilities, see Symposium, *Claims Resolution Facilities and the Mass Settlement of Mass Torts*, 53 LAW & CONTEMP. PROBS. 1 (Autumn 1990). One of the articles in the symposium did a comparative study of the operation and costs of several such facilities, and concluded that they worked best when "modest money is given to claimants who have legally questionable claims." Conversely, "[t]he success of claims facilities is more clouded when their objectives are more ambitious, that is, where the facility has been substituted for litigation of great stakes to claimants." Mark A. Peterson, *Giving Away Money: Comparative Comments on Claims Resolution Facilities*, 53 LAW & CONTEMP. PROBS. 113, 135 (Autumn 1990). Claims facilities often differ in numerous ways, including the amount of evidence that must be presented to prove eligibility, the procedures under which claimants can appeal adverse decisions, and the ability of claimants to opt out of the resolution process. *See id.*; JAY TIDMARSH, FED. JUD. CTR., MASS TORT SETTLEMENT CLASS ACTIONS (1998); Francis E. McGovern, *The What and Why of Claims Resolution Facilities*, 57 STAN. L. REV. 1361 (2005).

Are the creation of such bureaucracies appropriate? Assuming that the creation of a claims-resolution bureaucracy is appropriate, should courts strive to routinize the process, so that claimants in different settlements do not receive markedly different methods of claims handling? Should the legislature prescribe a uniform approach? In the absence of legislative authorization, is the entire enterprise of creating judicial bureaucracies to implement monetary recoveries illegitimate? Are the alternatives to such bureaucracies — dismissal of claims or endless re-litigation of related claims — worse than the problems that the bureaucracies create?

5. Typically the organizations best equipped to deal efficiently with the demands of processing thousands of claims are insurance companies, some of which have developed significant expertise in handling mass-tort settlements. Even if a claims administrator handles claims efficiently, it is still likely to be true (as it was in *In re Combustion*) that some claims are worth less than the money it takes to process them. Should these claims be denied? Likewise, because looking at a claim is costly, sometimes it is cheaper (as it was in *In re Combustion*) to give a minimal amount of money to every claimant, but to reserve greater payments to those who provide some individualized proof of eligibility and injury. Does it seem fair to give money to people just for filing a claim?

2. Fluid Recovery and Cy Pres Relief

Sometimes it is too costly or cumbersome to distribute relief to claimants. Sometimes fewer people claim against a fund than anticipated. In both cases, money remains in the fund. What should happen to it?

SCHWAB V. PHILIP MORRIS USA, INC.

449 F. Supp. 2d 992 (E.D.N.Y. 2006), *rev'd* sub nom.
McLaughlin v. American Tobacco Co., 522 F.3d 215 (2d Cir. 2008) [*supra* p. 1076]

■ WEINSTEIN, Senior District Judge.

[A class of smokers sued manufacturers of "light" cigarettes. The plaintiffs alleged that they smoked light cigarettes because the defendants falsely represented that these cigarettes had fewer health consequences than regular cigarettes, and that as a result they suffered injuries to their "business or property" within the meaning of RICO. In a decision destined to be reversed (*see supra* p. 1076), Judge Weinstein held that the case could be certified as a Rule 23(b)(3) class action. One roadblock in certifying a class action was manageability: The case presented numerous individual issues, including damages. The following excerpt adopts a fluid-recovery approach for distributing damages. We excerpt from the opinion not because it is the law — the Second Circuit specifically rejected this part of the opinion — but because it constitutes an excellent summary of the law of fluid recovery and cy pres, two related doctrines that can ease the burden on the court and the plaintiffs' lawyer to distribute monetary remedies to claimants.]

. . . Plaintiffs plan to prove defendants' liability to the class on an aggregate basis, and to distribute the total damages among individual class members through a proof of claim procedure. Damages would be allocated among class members based on the number of "light" cigarettes purchased by each within the relevant geographic area and time.

Describing this proposed litigation scheme as a form of "fluid recovery," defendants contend it is illegal, requiring denial of certification and dismissal. They argue that the use of a fluid recovery is foreclosed by the Court of Appeals for the Second Circuit's decisions in *Eisen v. Carlisle & Jacquelin*, 479 F.2d 1005 (2d Cir. 1973), *vacated on other grounds*, 417 U.S. 156 (1974), and *Van Gemert v. Boeing Co.*, 553 F.2d 812 (2d Cir. 1977), *aff'd on other grounds*, 444 U.S. 472 (1980).

For reasons described below, the plaintiffs' proposed use of fluid recovery is permissible. It does not require denial of certification and dismissal. Although the Court of Appeals for the Second Circuit has appeared from time to time in individual cases to deny the power of courts in this circuit to use what have been characterized as a wide variety of forms of fluid recovery, it is not the rule of the circuit or of the nation to deny fluid recovery in every case. Such a rule could not be the law under present societal conditions. *Cf.* STEPHEN BREYER, ACTIVE LIBERTY 57 (2005) (writing that "principle must be implemented against the backdrop of a highly complex net of technology-based social problems").

1. *Fluid Recovery*

a. *Nature and use*

The phrase "fluid recovery" has been used to refer to a number of different methods of "indirect distribution of unclaimed funds of a class monetary recovery." In addition, it refers to "the entire procedure of classwide calculation of damages and distribution of the aggregate amount or any unclaimed balance . . . to injured class members or to others under cy pres . . . or other doctrines." Recoveries described as "fluid" include distribution of damages through price reductions rather than by cash to individual plaintiffs; distribution of settlement or damage funds left unclaimed by individuals to nonprofit organizations or to states for uses intended to benefit class members; and distribution of damages calculated on a classwide basis to individual plaintiffs or through various indirect means. Because the phrase is used with such imprecision, care must be taken to determine whether the "fluid recovery" approved or disapproved in a particular case is at all similar to the distribution system proposed in the case at hand.

What all the cases on fluid recovery have in common is their attempt to grapple with some of the realities of modern mass litigation. In today's "complex modern economic system," a single harmful act may have an adverse effect on large numbers of consumers. That adverse effect is often small on the individual but large in the aggregate. Typical is a defendant's price-fixing scheme raising prices no more than a few cents or dollars per item, but allowing the defendant to reap a "substantial wrongful gain."

Mass cases present complex problems for courts in terms of damage calculation and damage distribution. If the defendant's liability is determined on a plaintiff-by-plaintiff basis, the court will be required to "compel a parade of individual plaintiffs" to appear before it for near-identical damage calculations. When the individual claims are small, "traditional methods of proof [may not be] worthwhile," since many consumers are unlikely to "retain records of small purchases for long periods of time." And even when the defendant's total liability may be calculated easily — as in a settlement or under a law with statutorily fixed damages provisions — distribution to all of the affected consumers may prove impossible.

Fluid recovery often provides a reasonable and fair means to litigate these complex claims and distribute damages without an intolerable burden on courts and litigants.

These mechanisms were first used as a means of distributing settlement monies where individual class members would be difficult to identify or unlikely to come forward. By distributing settlement amounts for uses that indirectly benefit members of the class, courts are able to promote the deterrent and compensatory policies of substantive laws in situations where recovery would otherwise be impracticable.

This type of fluid recovery is more precisely referred to as a "cy pres" remedy, in reference to the "trust doctrine that if funds in a charitable trust can no longer be devoted to the purpose for which the trust was created, they may be diverted to a related purpose." Key examples of cy pres remedies include distribution of damages through the market, as by price or rate reduction schemes; distribution to nonprofit organizations whose goals are related in some way to the subject of the litigation; and distribution to one or more states for uses benefit[t]ing class members. In the discussion that follows, cases using the phrase "cy pres" are treated as fluid recovery litigations when that is appropriate.

As fluid recovery practice has evolved, it has been used in situations where liability has been decided by the court as well as in settlements. In decided cases, fluid recovery generally involves three steps. First, defendant's aggregate liability is determined in a single, class-wide adjudication and paid into a class fund. Second, "individual class members are afforded an opportunity to collect their individual shares," usually through a simplified proof of claim procedure. Third, any residue remaining after individual claims have been paid is distributed to the class' benefit under cy pres or other doctrines. This three-step procedure eliminates the need for repetitive litigation of individual damage claims, while allowing courts to hold defendants liable for the full harm caused by them, and compensating those harmed. Without this use of fluid recovery, "some class actions . . . would neither compensate nor deter, for to allow the defendant to insist upon proof of individual claims [would] enable it to benefit from the cumbersome nature of legal proceedings and the lack of sophistication and indolence of the consumer, and [would] reward [its] foresight in stealing from the multitude in small amounts."

b. *Interaction with procedural and substantive law*

Fluid recovery is consistent with the text and spirit of Rule 23 of the Federal Rules of Civil Procedure controlling class actions. The class action rule "stems from equity," and Rule 23(b)(3), in particular, is designed to provide justice on an equitable basis to injured parties whose cases would be impractical or impossible to litigate if handled individually.

While courts must stay within the bounds of due process and avoid altering substantive law in violation of the Rules Enabling Act when shaping the remedies in Rule 23(b)(3) actions, the Rule provides desirable flexibility and grants the courts broad equitable powers in litigation management.

Whether or not fluid recovery should be employed in a particular class action is determined by reference to the need to vindicate the substantive law at issue. While fluid recovery is not an appropriate remedy in all Rule 23(b)(3) actions, it is sometimes the only practicable way to implement the goals of the substantive law under which a federal mass litigation case is prosecuted.

"The general inquiry is whether the use of . . . [fluid recovery] is consistent with the policy or policies reflected by the statute violated." This approach can be particularized into an assessment of the extent to which "the statute embodies policies of deterrence, disgorgement, and compensation," and of the "strength and scope of the statute's concern" for those policies. The application of fluid recovery is particularly appropriate where a corporate defendant "illegally profits" through violation of a common law principle or "a statute which was intended to regulate socially opprobrious conduct such as that reflected in the antitrust or securities laws." It is least appropriate where there may be a danger of overdeterrence.

c.   *General law*

Fluid recovery in appropriate cases has received wide support from courts and commentators. *See, e.g.*, Simer v. Rios, 661 F.2d 655, 676-78 (7th Cir. 1981) (fluid recovery should be used when it would promote statutory goals of deterrence, disgorgement, and compensation); Cal. v. Levi Strauss & Co., 715 P.2d 564, 571 (Cal. 1986); *Developments in the Law — Class Action*, 89 HARV. L. REV. 1454 (1976). It has been used by federal and state courts in both decided and settled cases.

Some federal appellate courts have evinced concern about fluid recovery. In particular cases the Second, Third, Fourth, Eighth, and Ninth Circuit Courts of Appeals have all expressed opposition to the use of fluid recovery. The Second, Fourth, and Ninth Circuit Courts of Appeals have made a few sweeping statements that have been misunderstood by some commentators as wholesale rejections of the concept. *See Eisen*, 479 F.2d at 1018 (in dicta, describing fluid recovery as "illegal, inadmissible . . . and wholly improper"). While the Court of Appeals for the Seventh Circuit has explicitly endorsed the use of fluid recovery in appropriate cases, *see* Simer 661 F.2d at 676-77, recent dicta from that court described some cy pres forms of recovery as "purely punitive." Mirfashi v. Fleet Mortg. Corp., 356 F.3d 781, 784 (7th Cir. 2004) [*infra* p. 1213].

Courts that have declined to approve fluid recovery have been concerned that such mechanisms might violate the due process clause, *see Eisen*, 479 F.2d at 1018, or that they might alter substantive law in violation of the Rules Enabling Act. *See Eisen*, 479 F.2d at 1014. Others have expressed concern that fluid recovery might deprive defendants in class actions of their Seventh Amendment right to trial by jury. Because appellate courts have often been oracular in their discussion of fluid recovery, it can be difficult to determine the precise source and dimensions of their anxiety. Objections appear to arise primarily out of the perception that fluid recovery "relieve[s] plaintiff classes of the burden of individual proof of damages," and therefore violates the due process clause and the Seventh Amendment by denying the defendant an opportunity to challenge the plaintiffs' claims on an individual basis before the jury. Insofar as "individual" proof of damages is thought to be an essential element of a claim, any perceived lessening of the plaintiffs' burden on this point may be said to "eliminat[e] or erod[e]" traditional or statutory requirements and thereby to alter substantive law in violation of the Rules Enabling Act.

Despite these occasional misgivings, fluid recovery has been accepted in a wide variety of contexts by nearly all federal circuits that have considered it. It is most commonly employed by federal courts for damage distribution in settled cases. But courts have also utilized fluid recovery in decided cases. . . .

Most federal courts that have approved the use of fluid recovery have not found it necessary to discuss the constitutional issues. . . .

Of the eleven states that have confronted the issue, at least nine have endorsed the use of fluid recovery. . . . Three states — California, New Jersey, and North Dakota — have procedural rules explicitly permitting the use of fluid recovery in class actions.

State courts have embraced fluid recovery as a means of fulfilling the promise of class actions as a consumer protection device and as a way of ensuring that corporate wrongdoers do not retain "ill gotten gains" simply because of the administrative difficulties associated with proving and distributing small individual damage claims. A significant percentage of fluid recovery cases in the state courts are brought under state antitrust and consumer protection laws. Fluid recovery has also been approved in a number of state common law contract and conversion actions to recover overcharges by corporations.

A number of state courts have addressed the possible due process issues raised by fluid recovery. Assuming that courts' unexplained due process objections to fluid recovery must rest upon concerns about aggregate proof of damages, the Michigan Court of Appeals concluded that defendants "hardly seem[ ] prejudiced by being restricted to only one hearing on common issues. Even though the calculation of damages might involve issues on which a hearing would . . . be required[,] . . . it has never been thought that due process required multiple hearings when there was one full and fair adjudication of the merits." Cicelski [v. Sears, Roebuck & Co., 348 N.W.2d 685, 690 (Mich. Ct. App. 1984)]. The California Court of Appeals has persuasively explained that "[u]p until the time when damages are distributed, a class action with fluid class recovery is the same as any other . . . The class is certified the same way, the burden of proof . . . is no different, and the calculation of the total amount of damages is accomplished in no less precise a manner." Bruno [v. Superior Court, 179 Cal. Rptr. 342, 346 (Cal. Ct. App. 1981)]. As the court observed, a "class action which affords due process of law . . . through the time when the amount of [the defendant's] liability is calculated cannot suddenly deprive him of his constitutional rights because of the way the damages are distributed." *Id.* at 129. So long as the trial plan provides for an accurate means of assessing a defendant's liability, that defendant has no grounds to object to the absence of individual proceedings or to the way in which damages are distributed once they have been determined. . . .

3. *Application of Law to Facts*

The plaintiffs' proposed use of fluid recovery in this case would effectuate the policies of civil RICO, a law which was enacted both to provide compensation to injured people and to increase enforcement of federal law through the creation of "private attorneys general."

While the class members' estimated individual damages are significantly higher than those in *Eisen*, they are still low enough to make individual lawsuits cost-prohibitive. If the members of this class are to have a fair chance of receiving compensation for their alleged economic injuries — and if they are to hold responsible those corporations whose deliberate actions allegedly caused those injuries — they must make use of the Rule 23(b)(3) class action device. And, as in many large-scale consumer class actions, classwide damage determination and fluid distribution are necessary in order to effectively and fairly administer this litigation. Given the size of plaintiffs' purported class and the nature of the purchases involved — cigarettes are, like many other consumer products, relatively inexpensive and repeatedly consumed and replaced — "traditional methods of proof [may not be] worthwhile." *Levi Strauss & Co.*, 715 P.2d at 570. If plaintiffs' allegations regarding the defendants' actions are proved, then to "allow the defendant[s] to insist upon proof of individual claims [would] enable [them] to benefit from the cumbersome nature of legal proceedings and the lack of sophistication and indolence of the consumer," and would "reward [their] foresight in stealing from the multitude in small amounts." *Bruno*, 179 Cal. Rptr. at 346.

The application of fluid recovery in this case does run the risk of overcompensating some and undercompensating other members of the class who relied differently on the "lights" designation and acted differently and for diverse reasons. In terms of damage calculation, these important factual issues can be resolved by a jury with the aid of experts and statistical proof. In terms of distribution, concerns about over- and undercompensation may be at least partially allayed through requiring claimants to submit affidavits regarding their understanding of the health issues surrounding "light" cigarettes and their reliance on the "lights" descriptor in addition to information regarding their cigarette purchases. While a court must be alert to issues of due process and must not value efficiency over fairness to both parties, illegally injured plaintiffs should not be fobbed off on the basis of real and imagined management problems that can be circumvented in a fair adjudication.

a. Eisen *and* Van Gemert

. . . Given a sensible view of what is necessary for a viable and fair administration of the instant litigation, the fluid recovery proposed by the plaintiffs in this case is not barred by *Eisen*. . . .

. . . [T]he class members in this case are in fact "likely . . . to share in an eventual judgment," as opposed to those in *Eisen*. In *Eisen*, very few members of the class were expected to come forward to claim their share of the total damages, and the Court of Appeals thought it likely that many of the class members would receive no benefit at all from the recovery, while many new traders who were not members of the class would receive some benefit from the proposed reduction in trading costs. Although class members' estimated recoveries in the present case may be too low to justify the cost of individual litigation, they are significantly higher than the average damage claim of three dollars and ninety cents predicted in *Eisen*. As a result, a large number of class members can be expected to come forward to claim damages. Furthermore, while there are legitimate concerns about over- and undercompensation of class members because of individual reliance on the defendants' alleged misrepresentation, these concerns can be dealt with through requiring the kind of affidavit from claimants described above.

For much the same reason, the fluid distribution proposed in the present case does not run afoul of the Court of Appeals' decision in *Van Gemert*. In *Van Gemert*, class members who had already received their share of a total damage recovery requested that the court allow distribution of the unclaimed residue to them on a per capita basis. The Second Circuit Court of Appeals rejected this as an impermissible "windfall" to the claiming plaintiffs and an "expropriation" of the claims of the silent class members, who would receive no benefit at all from the distribution. In the present case, no such windfall will occur. Damages can be distributed to claiming class members on the basis of the number of "light" cigarettes purchased in the relevant geographic locations during the relevant time period. The residue — if any — can be distributed on the basis of cy pres principles to be determined at a later time.

b. *Due process and Seventh Amendment issues*

The plaintiffs' proposed use of fluid recovery would not deprive the defendants of their right to due process or of their Seventh Amendment right to a trial by jury, for all of the reasons set forth by [*In re Antibiotic Antitrust Actions*, 333 F. Supp. 278 (S.D.N.Y. 1971)], and by the Michigan and California courts of appeals in *Cicelski*, 348 N.W.2d 685, and *Bruno*, 179 Cal. Rptr. 342. The defendants are not "constitutionally entitled to compel a parade of individual plaintiffs to establish damages." *Antibiotic Antitrust Actions*, 333 F. Supp. at 289. Rather, they are entitled to a full and fair hearing — by a jury if they so request — of all of the issues relevant to their liability to the plaintiff class.

Aggregate determination of the plaintiff class' damages would provide adequate protection. In an aggregate determination, defendants would be able to challenge the plaintiffs' offers of proof regarding the extent of reliance by class members and the amount of their economic damages. If the jury does not find that the plaintiffs have proved the economic damages they allege the defendants caused them, the defendants will not be held liable. And if defendants are held liable, they will, as required by federal substantive law, be held liable for no more than treble the amount of the economic damages proved to have been caused by their actions. The fact that the proof is on a classwide rather than individual basis would not change this result.

Fluid distribution poses no due process or Seventh Amendment concerns. . . . If the defendants are held liable to the plaintiffs, they will be held liable only to extent of the "aggregate loss fairly attributable to their . . . conduct." The method by which the damages are then distributed has no bearing on the defendants' constitutional rights.

c. *Rules Enabling Act*

The plaintiffs' proposed use of fluid recovery would not alter the substantive requirements of RICO, and would not, therefore, violate the Rules Enabling Act. . . . [T]he plaintiff class will be held to exactly the same standard of proof as in individual trials.

The rights of the plaintiff class members are not enlarged by the classwide nature of the damage determination. If the defendants' liability is established, total damages should be equivalent to what they would be if each class member were required to come forward and prove his or her damages separately. Nor are the rights of the class members abridged by classwide adjudication. By submitting a claim, each individual member of the class will be able to receive his or her treble damages, "just as if he [or she] had brought an individual action."

A question under the Rules Enabling Act is posed by the danger of overcompensation inherent in the plaintiffs' fluid distribution plan. It is possible that some claimants will benefit from the plaintiff class' recovery despite the fact that they did not rely on defendants' alleged misrepresentations regarding "light" cigarettes and were not, therefore, injured in their business or property by defendants' actions. The risk of such overcompensation can be limited by requiring proof through claim forms from claimants concerning the extent of their reliance during the distribution stage. . . .

Ultimately, the risk of some overcompensation cannot be determinative. . . . It would be paradoxical if civil RICO — a law which was enacted by Congress both to compensate victims and to increase enforcement of federal laws against organizations acting illegally — could not be applied precisely where defendants' fraud caused the broadest harm.

. . . The fact that a relatively few uninjured individuals may also benefit from that distribution "should no more make such relief improper than does the fact that third parties may benefit from injunctions make that relief improper."

4. *Conclusion on Fluid Recovery*

The use of fluid recovery is appropriate in the instant case. It alone does not merit denial of certification and dismissal. The detailed methods of fixing damages and distribution, if necessary, will be left to determination after a jury verdict.

MCLAUGHLIN V. AMERICAN TOBACCO CO.

522 F.3d 215 (2d Cir. 2008)

See supra p. 1076

MIRFASHI V. FLEET MORTGAGE CORP.

356 F.3d 781 (7th Cir. 2004)

■ POSNER, Circuit Judge.

Class members have appealed, challenging the class- action settlement approved by the district judge. . . .

The suit was brought on behalf of approximately 1.6 million persons whose home mortgages were owned by Fleet Mortgage Corporation. It charges that without their permission Fleet transmitted information about their financial needs that it had obtained from their mortgage papers to telemarketing companies which then, in conjunction with Fleet, used that information and deceptive practices to sell those customers financial services they didn't want. The unauthorized transmission of the information to the marketers is alleged to have violated the federal Fair Credit Reporting Act along with state consumer protection laws plus state common law protections against invasion of privacy, while the use of the information to trick people into buying from the telemarketers is alleged to have violated both the federal Telemarketing and Consumer Fraud and Abuse Prevention Act and state consumer protection laws. There are thus two plaintiff classes, a "pure" information-sharing class of 1.4 million customers of Fleet whose financial information Fleet transmitted to the telemarketers but who did not buy anything from them, and a telemarketing class . . . consisting of 190,000 class members who were victims of the telemarketers. As far as we can determine, no lawyer represents only members of the pure information-sharing class. . . .

A settlement was negotiated that the judge approved and this appeal challenges. The challenge focuses on the fact that one of the classes, namely the pure information-sharing class, received absolutely nothing, while surrendering all its members' claims against Fleet. Of course, if their claims were worthless (more precisely, worth too little to justify a distribution — a qualification that we elaborate on below), they lost nothing. But the district judge did not find that their claims were worthless, and it would be surprising if they were. The allegedly unauthorized transmittal of information to the telemarketers may have violated state consumer protection statutes that authorize the victims of the violation to obtain damages; it may also have infringed state common law protections of privacy, including financial privacy. . . . Such a claim would not be a sure bet, but colorable legal claims are not worthless merely because they may not prevail at trial. A colorable claim may have considerable settlement value (and not merely nuisance settlement value) because the defendant may no more want to assume a nontrivial risk of losing than the plaintiff does.

The members of the telemarketing class received something in the settlement. Fleet agreed to disgorge the profits of its allegedly unlawful conduct. These profits, it appears, had actually come from the members of the information class, but because the total profits were only $243,000, so that the per capita recovery for the 1.4 million members of the class would amount to less than 20 cents, the settlement transferred the profits to the telemarketing class. Fleet further agreed to set aside $2.4 million (roughly 10 times the profits) for payments ranging from $10 to a maximum of $135 per transaction with a telemarketing class member, depending on the character of his transaction with the telemarketers. The part of the $2.4 million that is not claimed will revert to Fleet, and it is likely to be a large part because many people won't bother to do the paperwork necessary to obtain $10, or even a somewhat larger amount. The district judge has approved a handsome fee for the class lawyers, $750,000, despite the meagerness of the relief agreed to in the settlement.

Fleet, joined by the class counsel, argues that the members of the pure information-sharing class didn't really receive nothing in exchange for giving up their claims; they received the emotional satisfaction of knowing that Fleet had been forced to give up its profits. That is a preposterous argument. Supposing that each of the 1.4 million members of the information-sharing class could expect a damages award of, say, $25, the total damages of the class would be $35 million. The idea that a rational fiduciary would surrender a claim worth $35 million in exchange for the satisfaction of knowing that his wrongdoer had been forced to pay $243,000 to members of another class staggers the imagination. . . .

Fleet and the class counsel contend that the information-sharing class obtained a "cy pres" remedy. The reference is to the trust doctrine that if the funds in a charitable trust can no longer be devoted to the purpose for which the trust was created, they may be diverted to a related purpose; and so the March of Dimes Foundation was permitted to reorient its activities from combating polio to combating other childhood diseases when the polio vaccine was developed. The doctrine, or rather something parading under its name, has been applied in class action cases, but for a reason unrelated to the reason for the trust doctrine. That doctrine is based on the idea that the settlor would have preferred a modest alteration in the terms of the trust to having the corpus revert to his residuary legatees. So there is an indirect benefit to the settlor. In the class action context the reason for appealing to cy pres is to prevent the defendant from walking away from the litigation scot-free because of the infeasibility of distributing the proceeds of the settlement (or the judgment, in the rare case in which a class action goes to trial) to the class members. There is no indirect benefit to the class from the defendant's giving the money to someone else. In such a case the "cy pres" remedy (badly misnamed, but the alternative term — "fluid recovery" — is no less misleading) is purely punitive.

The class counsel and Fleet point out that if the $243,000 in restitution due the members of the information-sharing class were spread evenly across the 1.4 million members of that class, each member would receive an amount smaller than the cost of postage; therefore the telemarketing class should receive it (as part of the $2.4 million) because it has fewer members. The argument founders on the fact that restitution is merely an alternative remedy to damages. The aggregate damages of the information-sharing class might, as we said, be as high as $35 million (or even higher), and then there would be no reason for thinking distribution to the class members infeasible. . . .

Would it be too cynical to speculate that what may be going on here is that class counsel wanted a settlement that would give them a generous fee and Fleet wanted a settlement that would extinguish 1.4 million claims against it at no cost to itself? The settlement that the district judge approved sold these 1.4 million claimants down the river. Only if they had no claim — more precisely no claim large enough to justify a distribution to them — did they lose nothing by the settlement, and the judge made no finding that they had no such claim.

Because class actions are rife with potential conflicts of interest between class counsel and class members, district judges presiding over such actions are expected to give careful scrutiny to the terms of proposed settlements in order to make sure that class counsel are behaving as honest fiduciaries for the class as a whole. Unfortunately the district judge's decision approving the settlement does not discuss the settlement's questionable features — not only the one we've stressed, namely the denial of any relief to an entire class . . ., but also the reversion of unclaimed refunds to the putative wrongdoer and the fact that the class that was denied relief did not have separate counsel from the counsel for the favored class. Also not discussed is the failure of the notice of settlement to inform members of the information-sharing class (who, remember, were being told that their share of the settlement was a big fat zero) of a pending case in a Massachusetts state court seeking monetary relief on behalf of residents of that state who were members of the information-sharing class and whose rights would be extinguished if the settlement in the present case was approved, unless they opted out of it.

All these were warning signs, no more; we do not suggest that deletion of the reversion provision, or notice of the Massachusetts suit, or even the award of some relief for the information class, were per se requirements of an acceptable settlement. A reversion provision might encourage a more generous settlement offer. Notice of a pending suit that might offer only remote prospects of success might confuse class members and precipitate imprudent opting out. Even the denial of all relief to the information class might be justified if careful scrutiny indicated that the class had no realistic prospect of sufficient success to enable an actual distribution to the class members. But these were matters to be considered, not assumed. The last is the most important, especially in view of the fact that the information class did not have separate counsel. . . . The district judge in this case made no estimate of the value of the legal claims of the information-sharing class. . . .

. . . The judgment is therefore reversed and the case is remanded for further proceedings consistent with this opinion.

MASTERS V. WILHELMINA MODEL AGENCY, INC.

473 F.3d 423 (2d Cir. 2007)

■   MINER, Circuit Judge.

Plaintiffs-appellants, members of a class of present and former professional models, and their counsel appeal from two orders entered in the United States District Court for the Southern District of New York approving settlements and awarding attorneys' fees in a class action brought against defendant modeling agencies for conspiracy to fix commissions charged to members of plaintiff class, in violation of the Sherman Act. . . . The appellants contend that the District Court erred in . . . ordering the distribution of settlement proceeds in excess of recognized losses to various charities rather than to the class members as treble damages and prejudgment interest [and] applying the wrong standard in awarding counsel fees, with the result that the fee allowance to counsel for plaintiffs-appellants is inadequate.

For the reasons that follow, we vacate the orders appealed from insofar as they relate to the distribution of settlement proceeds and the award of counsel fees and remand the case to the District Court for reconsideration of those matters . . . .

BACKGROUND

[The plaintiffs claimed that the leading New York modeling agencies, acting in concert since the mid-1970s, had exceeded the 10% commission rate cap imposed on "employment agencies" under New York law and had charged a "standard rate" for model commissions of 20%. The plaintiffs brought a class action; after dismissal of state-law claims, only federal antitrust claims remained. With the threat of the defendants' bankruptcy looming over the negotiations, all of the defendants eventually settled. A sticking point in the negotiations was the disposition of unclaimed or unpaid funds (the "Excess Funds") that might remain after payment to the class members of their actual losses. Eventually the parties settled. Defendants agreed to stop charging more than 10%, and also agreed to pay the class $21,855,000, which was to be distributed to class members based on the amount of commissions paid by each member in excess of 10%, plus interest. Plaintiffs were required to submit claim forms indicating the amounts of their injuries. If the total of the plaintiffs' claims exceeded the amount of the settlement fund, then members' claims were to be paid on a pro rata basis. On the other hand, if funds were left over after all claims were submitted, the settlement agreement provided that "the Court shall, in its discretion, determine the disposition of the [Excess Funds] after hearing the views of the parties hereto as to such disposition."

[The district court approved the settlement. The 16,512 notices mailed to potential class members, however, yielded only reimbursable claims of $9,338,958.29. The district court chose to award class counsel fees of $3,759,583.16 (40% of the reimbursed claims) rather than its requested $7,285,000 (33.33% of the fund of $21,855,000).]

The Court determined to distribute the Excess Funds under the Cy Pres Doctrine. The Court met with representatives of various organizations designated by the parties and others to identify charities that would directly or indirectly benefit members of the class with the least administrative costs. The District Court chose the following organizations to receive the residual funds and provided a brief description of their purposes and goals and the manner of allocation of the funds to be distributed: Beth Israel Medical Center's Continuum Women's Cardiac Care Network; Columbia Presbyterian Medical Center's Eating Disorders Program; Columbia Presbyterian Medical Center's Division on Substance Abuse; Columbia Presbyterian Medical Center's Ovarian Cancer Repository; New York University Medical Center; Civil Division of the Legal Aid Society; and The Heart Truth.

[Class counsel moved the court to reconsider its rulings.] In reaffirming the decision to distribute Excess Funds under the Cy Pres Doctrine, the Court noted that the Settlement Agreement included a specific provision allowing for the Court to distribute such funds in the exercise of its discretion. The District Court also noted that "[p]laintiffs' counsel gave at least tacit approval to the distribution scheme by proposing charitable organizations of his own." The Court denied the motion for reconsideration . . . .

ANALYSIS

. . .

II. *Of the Distribution of Remaining Funds*

The Settlement Agreement approved by the District Court clearly contemplated the need to provide for the distribution of any Excess Funds that might remain after all class members were fully compensated for their actual losses. . . . Of course, it was not certain at the time the Agreement was entered into whether there would be Excess Funds, and the Agreement accordingly provided that if Total Recognized Losses exceeded the Net

Settlement Fund, the class members would receive distribution on a pro rata basis.

In support of their contention that the Excess Funds should be applied toward treble damages rather than allocated to charities under the Cy Pres Doctrine, plaintiffs bring to our attention the Supreme Court's observation that "the antitrust private action was created primarily as a remedy for the victims of antitrust violations. Treble damages 'make the remedy meaningful by counter-balancing the difficulty of maintaining a private suit' under the antitrust laws." Am. Soc'y of Mech. Eng'rs, Inc. v. Hydrolevel Corp., 456 U.S. 556, 575 (1982). We have noted that "[f]ull restitution of plaintiffs' losses is a no less central objective of the treble damage provision than the encouragement of private antitrust enforcement." . . .

While it is true that the Settlement Agreement reposes discretion in the District Judge as to the disposition of Excess Funds, that discretion is not absolute. Where we find an abuse of discretion in our review of the allocation of funds derived from class settlements, the scheme adopted by the District Court will not be upheld. In re Agent Orange Prod. Liab. Litig. VI, 818 F.2d 179, 181 (2d Cir. 1987). We have concluded that a district court abuses its discretion when "(1) its decision rests on an error of law (such as application of the wrong legal principles) or a clearly erroneous factual finding, or (2) its decision — though not necessarily the product of a legal error or a clearly erroneous factual finding — cannot be located within the range of permissible decisions." Zervos v. Verizon N.Y., Inc., 252 F.3d 163, 169 (2d Cir. 2001). In its original Opinion approving settlement, the District Court considered only the following dispositions: (i) the return of excess settlement funds to the defendants on a pro rata basis; or (ii) in the exercise of its equitable powers, distribution of the funds to charitable organizations. The court stated: "Having adopted the charitable route for these funds, it is my view that wherever possible, the cy pres doctrine should be invoked." The court then went on, in accordance with the Cy Pres Doctrine, to allocate the funds to those charities thought to benefit the class, either directly or indirectly.

We are not yet prepared to say that the District Court abused its discretion in allocating the Excess Funds under the Cy Pres Doctrine. It does appear, however, that the District Court was not aware of the extent of its discretion, failing to recognize that it was empowered to allocate funds to the members of the class as treble damages. The District Court ultimately held that the terms of the Settlement Agreement barred it from even considering such an alternative. . . .

. . . [A] treble damages award did lie within the ambit of the District Court's discretion and should be considered on remand.

In exercising its discretion, the District Court should bear in mind that the purpose of Cy Pres distribution is to "put[ ] the unclaimed fund to its next best compensation use, e.g., for the aggregate, indirect, prospective benefit of the class." Cy Pres means "as near as possible," and "[c]ourts have utilized Cy Pres distributions where class members are difficult to identify, or where they change constantly, or where there are unclaimed funds." In this connection, we take note of the recent Draft of the *Principles of the Law of Aggregate Litigation* by the American Law Institute. With respect to the approval of settlements providing for a Cy Pres remedy, the Draft proposes a rule limiting Cy Pres "to circumstances in which direct distribution to individual class members is not economically feasible, or where funds remain after class members are given a full opportunity to make a claim." This proposed rule is consonant with the observation of our sister circuit that "[f]ederal courts have frequently approved [the Cy Pres] remedy in the settlement of class actions where the proof of individual claims would be burdensome or distribution of damages costly." Six (6) Mexican Workers v. Ariz. Citrus Growers, 904 F.2d 1301, 1305 (9th Cir. 1990). In the case before us, neither side contends that a Cy Pres distribution is appropriate because it would be onerous or impossible to locate class members or because each class member's recovery would be so small as to make an individual distribution economically impracticable. We are confident that the district court, fully aware of the breadth of its discretion, will see to an appropriate distribution of the funds remaining after the models have been compensated for their actual losses.

[The court then held that the district court abused its discretion in awarding attorneys' fees based on the amount claimed rather than on the full value of the settlement.]

CONCLUSION

The . . . case is remanded to the District Court for further proceedings in accordance with the foregoing.

Notes

1. Because Judge Weinstein proposed to prove the defendants' liability and the extent of the plaintiffs' losses by means of statistical proof, and then to compensate the plaintiffs according to their actual losses, *Schwab* (and *McLaughlin*, which reverses *Schwab*) implicate the idea of trial-by-statistics more than they implicate fluid recovery or cy pres; for that reason, we studied *McLaughlin* in Chapter Ten (*supra* p. 1076). We excerpted from *Schwab* in this chapter because Judge Weinstein's decision in *Schwab* is the single most comprehensive judicial treatment of fluid recovery and cy pres, including the arguments and authorities both for and against. For the sake of length, we edited out most of *Schwab*'s citations to cases and literature; the full opinion is a wonderful resource for research on fluid recovery and cy pres.

Likewise, you might have noticed strong connections among fluid recovery, cy pres, and cases departing from the rightful-position principle like *Dougherty* and *Kyriazi*, which we studied in Chapter Eleven (*supra* pp. 1145-51). Whether fluid recovery and cy pres are departures from the rightful-position principle or merely aids in a court's implementation of a remedy is an interesting question that hinges in part on whether the relief involved is fluid recovery or cy pres, and in part on whether the relief occurs in a settlement or a judgment. But in truth, the question is really academic. We have spread the opinions regarding trial by statistics, departures from the rightful position, fluid recovery, and cy pres across three chapters, fitting each one in at the point where it seemed most logical to treat a particular piece of the issue as a pedagogical matter.

In the real world, however, issues do not often present themselves with pedagogical precision. The fundamental problem that all these doctrines address is this: Sometimes it is far easier to prove how much damage the defendant caused in the aggregate than it is to prove the damage that the defendant caused to each person within the aggregate. Trial by statistics approaches the quantum-of-damages issue from the plaintiffs' viewpoint, extrapolating from a sample to calculate the total damage caused to all. Fluid recovery and cy pres often approach the quantum-of-damages issue from the defendants' viewpoint, in which damages are awarded at trial or negotiated as a lump sum. The fact and amount of damage are clear, but the identity of the victims is not. For instance, in *Masters* it is easy enough to figure out the total amount of damage that the defendants caused (basically, half of the modeling commissions that the defendants took in — a number that should be determinable from the defendants' balance sheets) even if it is difficult to determine how much any given plaintiff lost.

2. As Judge Posner says, neither the term "fluid recovery" nor the term "cy pres" precisely captures the nature of the problem that these doctrines address. "Fluid recovery" usually refers to the idea of giving certain individuals the benefit of a settlement or judgment, even though those individuals might overlap only partially with the victims of the wrongdoing. A classic example is *Democratic Central Committee of the District of Columbia v. Washington Metropolitan Area Transit Commission*, 84 F.3d 451 (D.C. Cir. 1996), in which the transit authority overcharged bus riders in the 1960s. The case eventually settled. Trying to compensate the bus riders from the 1960s was too expensive; the proof problems for any individual's eligibility and amount of ridership were insurmountable. After considering other options (such as an escheat of the funds to the government or the establishment of a consumer trust fund), the court of appeals held that the best option was to give the money back to the transit authority to improve bus transportation. Its theory was that the present bus riders were the "next best" class to the bus riders in the 1960s.

Cy pres is slightly different. As *Masters* describes, this doctrine allows a court to award a settlement or judgment fund to charitable or educational organizations that work on issues that might be of benefit to the original victims. For instance, the district court in *Masters* gave some of the settlement proceeds to eating-disorder and women's health programs on the theory that these programs would benefit, at least in part, the class of models that were victims of the defendants' wrongdoing.

3. Thus understood, *Mirfashi* is a fluid-recovery case, and *Masters* is a cy-pres case. Although fluid recovery and cy pres can distinguished in

this fashion, they have a common bond. Both arise when a court permits (or the parties negotiate) a lump-sum award. Both provide substitutionary relief that is most appealing (and most justifiable) when the class of original victims and the beneficiaries of the fluid-recovery or cy-pres relief have an identity of interest, even if they are not precisely the same group. *Cf.* Six (6) Mexican Workers v. Ariz. Citrus Growers, 904 F.2d 1301, 1307 (9th Cir. 1990) (permitting cy-pres recovery, but rejecting the district court's cy-pres award when it "benefit[ted] a group far too remote from the plaintiff class. Even where cy pres is considered, it will be rejected when the proposed distribution fails to provide the 'next best' distribution."). Both theories also emphasize the deterrence aspect of damages (not letting defendants profit from wrongdoing) over the compensatory aspect (restoring plaintiffs to their rightful positions). Indeed, most of the criticism of fluid recovery and cy pres ultimately derives from this emphasis on deterrence.

Finally, both fluid recovery and cy pres have a common cause: the inability to award individual rightful-position recoveries because such recoveries are either too expensive to implement or are unclaimed by the victims. *Mirfashi* represents (at least on the class counsel's theory) the first situation; *Masters* represents the second situation. Reasonably enough, *Mirfashi* insists that the costs of implementing a remedy must in fact exceed the amount that the plaintiffs can rightfully expect by way of recovery — but this expectation must be measured by the claims' true value and not the amount received in the settlement. Equally reasonably, *Masters* insists that a cy-pres award to a charity cannot occur unless the plaintiffs who can readily be compensated receive full value for their claims.

4. *Masters* mentions the ALI's endorsement of cy-pres relief in its *Principles of the Law of Aggregate Litigation*, which was still in draft form when *Masters* was decided. Although the provision provoked much controversy, the final version of the *Principles* supported cy-pres relief in essentially the form that *Masters* described: that cy-pres relief should be available in aggregate litigation when providing individual relief to some or all of the plaintiffs is not economically justified (a *Mirfashi*-type situation) and when all of the plaintiffs' claims have been fully satisfied (a *Masters*-type situation). AM. L. INST., PRINCIPLES OF THE LAW OF AGGRE-GATE LITIGATION § 3.07 (2009).

The *Principles* suggest that courts should have the authority to approve a cy-pres remedy provided for in a settlement "even if such a remedy could not be ordered in a contested case." *Id.* § 3.07(a). Is *Masters* wrongly decided under this principle? How much of a factor should the parties' consent (or conversely, lack of consent) to a cy-pres remedy be?

On the other hand, § 3.07(b) states that, when class members receive individual awards, the "presumptively" correct method of distributing excess funds is to give them to these class members (presumably, even if the distribution results in super-compensatory awards). In this regard, the *Principles* appear to endorse the approach recommended in *Masters*.

5. Most cases that consider fluid recovery or cy pres are class actions. This connection is understandable, because fluid recovery and cy pres can

ease the manageability hurdle in Rule 23(b)(3) class actions. *Cf.* Nelson v. Greater Gadsden Hous. Auth., 802 F.2d 405, 409 (11th Cir. 1986) ("The objections to fluid recovery appear to relate to the use of this system to relieve plaintiff classes of the burden of proving individual damages or to avoid the dismissal of unmanageable class actions."). But there is no necessary connection between these forms of relief and the form of aggregation. *Democratic Central Committee*, for instance, was not a class action. The *Principles* are somewhat unclear on the point; § 3.07 does not mention class actions when it allows a court to approve an award of cy-pres relief by agreement, but such approval usually occurs only in class actions, and § 3.07 uses the words "class" or "class action" repeatedly in the remainder of the text and in the subsequent comments.

6. *Mirfashi* and *Masters* describe some of the dark underbelly of fluid recovery and cy pres. Some plaintiffs' lawyers want to maximize the fee they receive, perhaps to the detriment of the class. Fluid recovery can mask a poor settlement. Fluid recovery and cy pres also inflate the value of the recovery, and justify a request for a larger fee. You can therefore appreciate the antipathy that fluid recovery and cy pres generates among those who believe that class actions and other aggregate litigation exist principally to line the pockets of the lawyers who bring them.

7. To what extent can the injunctive remedies in school-desegregation and other institutional-reform cases be viewed as a type of fluid recovery? For example, even though the persons most seriously harmed by segregation were the generations of African-Americans educated in the "separate but equal" days, the impossibility of providing a remedy for these persons could mean that an enhanced remedy could be provided to the "next best" group — the present children in the school system. On this theory, a case could be made for remedies that exceed the rightful position of the present children. In determining the scope of injunctive remedies in institutional-reform cases, can we borrow fluid-recovery principles and permit non-rightful-position injunctive relief when it is too costly to provide relief to all of the victims and the identity of interest between the victims and the beneficiaries of the relief is great?

8. *Schwab* makes the best case for fluid recovery, but it admits that most federal courts of appeal have opposed the idea, at least under the facts that were presented in the cases under consideration. *McLaughlin*'s strong rejection of the theory (in a case in which fluid recovery was not precisely at issue) demonstrates the difficult uphill climb. On the other hand, a recent empirical study shows that the practice is on the rise. Between 1974 and 2000, approximately one federal court per year awarded cy-pres relief. Since 2001, approximately eight cases per year have awarded this relief. *See* Martin H. Redish et al., *Cy Pres Relief and the Pathologies of the Modern Class Action: A Normative and Empirical Analysis*, 61 FLA. L. REV. — (forthcoming 2010). The authors of this article also argue trenchantly against cy-pres recovery on theoretical grounds.

9. In the best known example of cy-pres relief, Judge Weinstein directed that one-quarter of the $180 million settlement in the *Agent*

Orange litigation, which was commenced on behalf of a class of 2.4 million service members who fought in the Vietnam War, be given to a "class assistance foundation" that would serve to mobilize Vietnam veterans and others to deal with the veterans' medical and related problems. Among the foundation's permissible activities were "[p]rotection and advocacy services" for children of veterans born with birth defects; "[a] public hotline and referral service"; "[g]rants to hospitals and clinics"; "insurance programs"; "vocational training projects"; "grants to establish peer support groups to enable children with birth defects to discuss their problems openly among themselves'" "[g]rants or loans . . . to families in grave financial need to help pay for essential medical services"; monitoring of the former Veterans Administration to ensure its responsiveness to the needs of class members"; and other aid to "help members of the class become a more integrated part of society." *See* In re "Agent Orange" Prod. Liab. Litig. MDL No. 381, 818 F.2d 145, 158-59 (2d Cir. 1987). (Note that *Agent Orange* proposed to use a portion of the actual settlement proceeds to establish the foundation, rather than only the unclaimed amounts.)

Although noting that this distribution avoided the concerns that led the Second Circuit to bar fluid recovery in *Eisen*, 479 F.2d 1005, and *Van Gemert*, 553 F.2d 812, the court of appeals nonetheless reversed:

> . . . We perceive no assurance that the "self-governing and self-perpetuating" board of directors of the class assistance foundation . . . will possess the independent, disinterested judgment required to allocate limited funds to benefit the class as a whole. . . .

> Moreover, we are concerned that the broad mandate given the class assistance foundation, which must remain an arm of the court however loosely connected, would permit settlement proceeds to be expended on activities inconsistent with the judicial function. For example, activities to "help class member veterans better obtain and utilize VA services" and to "increase public awareness of the problems of the class," might include political advocacy. We do not believe that the proceeds of a court-administered settlement ought to be used for such a purpose.

In re "Agent Orange" Prod. Liab. Litig. MDL No. 381, 818 F.2d 179, 185-86 (2d Cir. 1987). On remand, the district court allocated $40 million to a "Class Assistance Program" administered and monitored by the court. In re "Agent Orange" Prod. Liab. Litig., 689 F. Supp. 1250 (E.D.N.Y. 1988). Do such foundations or programs take the court too far afield from its traditional adversarial role?

10. As a lawyer, what are your ethical obligations with respect to a request for fluid recovery? Must you advise your client at the outset that you might be seeking relief that benefits other people, and might leave the client undercompensated? What would the client's likely response be?

11. The Supreme Court has yet to stake out a position on fluid recovery or cy pres. But a problem related to fluid recovery is the "passing-on" doctrine in antitrust litigation. Under this doctrine, when a distributor or

retailer passes on the cost of a good sold to it under anti-competitive conditions, and thus suffers no economic harm, the Court has declined to permit the distributor or retailer to obtain recovery for the violation. *See* Hanover Shoe, Inc. v. United Shoe Mach. Corp., 392 U.S. 481 (1968); W. Va. v. Chas. Pfizer & Co., 440 F.2d 1079 (2d Cir. 1971). If they did obtain a recovery, distributors and retailers could presumably pass along the savings to a "next best" class — the present purchasers of comparable products. What does the Supreme Court's unwillingness to permit "passing-on" recovery suggest about its attitude toward fluid recovery and cy pres more generally?

Conversely, state attorneys general are often able to maintain *parens patriae* actions on behalf of their citizens that are victimized by a defendant's conduct. The Supreme Court has long recognized *parens patriae* relief. *See* S.C. v. N.C., 558 U.S. —, 130 S. Ct. 854, 862, 868 (2010). Isn't recovery by a state attorney general a form of fluid recovery, in which the court delegates to the "next best" attorney general the task of distributing a settlement or judgment fund to individuals?

C. OVERCOMING THIRD-PARTY INTRANSIGENCE

Sometimes the parties' ability to implement a remedy is threatened by other parties or nonparties whose actions can disrupt the remedy. What should be the extent of the court's power to prevent third parties from thwarting the remedy? In yet another context, we face the problem of the court's power over persons that are not parties to the litigation, but that nonetheless hold a key to the court's ability to resolve the case.

UNITED STATES V. HALL

472 F.2d 261 (5th Cir. 1972)

■ WISDOM, Circuit Judge.

This case presents the question whether a district court has power to punish for criminal contempt a person who, though neither a party nor bearing any legal relationship to a party, violates a court order designed to protect the court's judgment in a school desegregation case. We uphold the district court's conclusion that in the circumstances of this case it had this power, and affirm the defendant's conviction for contempt.

On June 23, 1971, the district court entered a "Memorandum Opinion and Final Judgment" in the case of *Mims v. Duval County School Board*. The court required the Duval County [Jacksonville], Florida school board to complete its desegregation of Duval County schools, in accordance with the Supreme Court's decision in *Swann v. Charlotte-Mecklenburg Board of Education*, 402 U.S. 1 (1971), by pairing and clustering a number of schools which had theretofore been predominantly one-race schools. This order culminated litigation begun eleven years before . . . . The district court retained jurisdiction to enter such orders as might be necessary in the future to effectuate its judgment.

Among the schools marked for desegregation under the plan approved by the district court was Ribault Senior High School, a predominantly white school. The plan directed pairing of Ribault with William E. Raines Senior High School, a predominantly black school, so that the black enrollment would be 59 percent at Raines and 57 percent at Ribault. After the desegregation order was put into effect racial unrest and violence developed at Ribault, necessitating on one occasion the temporary closing of the school. On March 5, 1972, the superintendent of schools and the sheriff of Jacksonville filed a petition for injunctive relief in the *Mims* case with the district court. This petition alleged that certain black adult "outsiders" had caused or abetted the unrest and violence by their activities both on and off the Ribault campus. The petition identified the appellant Eric Hall, allegedly a member of a militant organization known as the "Black Front", as one of several such outsiders who, in combination with black students and parents, were attempting to prevent the normal operation of Ribault through student boycotts and other activities. As relief the petitioners requested an order "restraining all Ribault Senior High School students and any person acting independently or in concert with them from interfering with the orderly operation of the school and the Duval County School system, and for such other relief as the court may deem just and proper."

At an ex parte session on March 5, 1972, the district court entered an order providing in part [that students at Ribault "and other persons acting independently or in concert with them and having notice of this order" could not obstruct or prevent the attendance of students and faculty or "commit[ ] any other act to disrupt the orderly operation of Ribault Senior High School or any other school of the Duval County School System." The order further barred any "person" (other that students, faculty, staff, parents, those with business interests, and law-enforcement personnel) from "enter[ing] any building of the Ribault Senior High School or go upon the school's grounds."] The order went on to provide that "[a]nyone having notice of this order who violates any of the terms thereof shall be subject to arrest, prosecution and punishment by imprisonment or fine, or both, for criminal contempt under the laws of the United States of America. . . ." The court ordered the sheriff to serve copies of the order on seven named persons, *including Eric Hall.* Hall was neither a party plaintiff nor a party defendant in the *Mims* litigation, and in issuing this order the court did not join Hall or any of the other persons named in the order as parties.

On March 9, 1972, four days after the court issued its order, Hall violated that portion of the order restricting access to Ribault High School by appearing on the Ribault campus. When questioned by a deputy United States marshal as to the reasons for his presence, Hall replied that he was on the grounds of Ribault for the purpose of violating the March 5 order. The marshal then arrested Hall and took him into custody. After a nonjury trial, the district court found Hall guilty of the charge of criminal contempt and sentenced him to sixty days' imprisonment.

On this appeal Hall raises two related contentions. Both contentions depend on the fact that Hall was not a party to the *Mims* litigation and the fact that, in violating the court's order, he was apparently acting independently of the *Mims* parties. He first points to the common law rule that a nonparty who violates an injunction solely in pursuit of his own interests cannot be held in contempt. . . . Second, he contends that Rule 65(d) of the Federal Rules of Civil Procedure prevents the court's order from binding him, since Rule 65(d) limits the binding effect of injunctive orders to "parties to the action, their officers, agents, servants, employees, and attorneys, and . . . those persons in active concert or participation with them who receive actual notice of the order by personal service or otherwise."[*] We reject both contentions.

I.

For his first contention, that a court of equity has no power to punish for contempt a nonparty acting solely in pursuit of his own interests, the appellant relies heavily on the two leading cases of *Alemite Manufacturing Corp. v. Staff*, 42 F.2d 832 (2d Cir. 1930), and *Chase National Bank v. City of Norwalk*, 291 U.S. 431 (1934). In *Alemite* the district court had issued an injunction restraining the defendant and his agents, employees, associates, and confederates from infringing the plaintiff's patent. Subsequently a third person, not a party to the original suit and acting entirely on his own initiative, began infringing the plaintiff's patent and was held in contempt by the district court. The Second Circuit reversed in an opinion by Judge Learned Hand, stating that "it is not the act described which the decree may forbid, but only that act when the defendant does it." In *Chase National Bank* the plaintiff brought suit against the City of Norwalk to obtain an injunction forbidding the removal of poles, wires, and other electrical equipment belonging to the plaintiff. The district court issued a decree enjoining the City, its officers, agents, and employees, "and all persons whomsoever to whom notice of this order shall come" from removing the equipment or otherwise interfering with the operation of the plaintiff's power plant. The Supreme Court held that the district court had violated "established principles of equity jurisdiction and procedure" insofar as its order applied to persons who were not parties, associates, or confederates of parties, but who merely had notice of the order.

This case is different. In *Alemite* and *Chase National Bank* the activities of third parties, however harmful they might have been to the plaintiffs' interests, would not have disturbed in any way the adjudication of rights and obligations as between the original plaintiffs and defendants. Infringement of the *Alemite* plaintiff's patent by a third party would not

---

[*]   As a result of the 2007 restyling amendments, the quoted language has been slightly altered. The new language, now found in Fed. R. Civ. P. 65(d)(2), does not affect the meaning of the language quoted in the text. — ED.

have upset the defendant's duty to refrain from infringing or rendered it more difficult for the defendant to perform that duty. Similarly, the defendant's duty in *Chase National Bank* to refrain from removing the plaintiff's equipment would remain undisturbed regardless of the activities of third parties, as would the plaintiff's right not to have its equipment removed by the defendant. The activities of Hall, however, threatened both the plaintiffs' right and the defendant's duty as adjudicated in the *Mims* litigation. In *Mims* the plaintiffs were found to have a constitutional right to attend an integrated school. The defendant school board had a corresponding constitutional obligation to provide them with integrated schools and a right to be free from interference with the performance of that duty. Disruption of the orderly operation of the school system, in the form of a racial dispute, would thus negate the plaintiffs' constitutional right and the defendant's constitutional duty. In short, the activities of persons contributing to racial disorder at Ribault imperiled the court's fundamental power to make a binding adjudication between the parties properly before it.

Courts of equity have inherent jurisdiction to preserve their ability to render judgment in a case such as this. This was the import of the holding in *United States v. United Mine Workers of America*, 330 U.S. 258 (1947). There the district court had issued a temporary restraining order forbidding a union from striking, though there was a substantial question of whether the Norris-LaGuardia Act had deprived the district court of jurisdiction to issue such an order. The Supreme Court upheld the defendants' contempt conviction for violation of this order. As an alternative holding the Court stated that the contempt conviction would have been upheld even if the district court had ultimately been found to be without jurisdiction. This holding affirmed the power of a court of equity to issue an order to preserve the status quo in order to protect its ability to render judgment in a case over which it might have jurisdiction.

The integrity of a court's power to render a binding judgment in a case over which it has jurisdiction is at stake in the present case. In *Mine Workers* disruptive conduct prior to the court's decision could have destroyed the court's power to settle a controversy at least potentially within its jurisdiction. Here the conduct of Hall and others, if unrestrained, could have upset the court's ability to bind the parties in *Mims*, a case in which it unquestionably had jurisdiction. Moreover, the court retained jurisdiction in *Mims* to enter such further orders as might be necessary to effectuate its judgment. Thus disruptive conduct would not only jeopardize the effect of the court's judgment already entered but would also undercut its power to enter binding desegregation orders in the future.

The principle that courts have jurisdiction to punish for contempt in order to protect their ability to render judgment is also found in the use of in rem injunctions. Federal courts have issued injunctions binding on all persons, regardless of notice, who come into contact with property which is the subject of a judicial decree. A court entering a decree binding on a particular piece of property is necessarily faced with the danger that its judgment may be disrupted in the future by members of an undefinable class — those who may come into contact with the property. The in rem injunction protects the court's judgment. The district court here faced an analogous problem. The judgment in a school case, as in other civil rights actions, inures to the benefit of a large class of persons, regardless of whether the original action is cast in the form of a class action. At the same time court orders in school cases, affecting as they do large numbers of people, necessarily depend on the cooperation of the entire community for their implementation.

As this Court is well aware, school desegregation orders often strongly excite community passions.   School orders are, like in rem orders, particularly vulnerable to disruption by an undefinable class of persons who are neither parties nor acting at the instigation of parties. In such cases, as in voting rights cases, courts must have the power to issue orders similar to that issued in this case, tailored to the exigencies of the situation and directed to protecting the court's judgment. The peculiar problems posed by school cases have required courts to exercise broad and flexible remedial powers. *See Swann,* 402 U.S. at 6, 15. Similarly broad applications of the power to punish for contempt may be necessary, as here, if courts are to protect their ability to design appropriate remedies and make their remedial orders effective.

II.

The appellant also asserts that Rule 65(d) of the Federal Rules of Civil Procedure prevents the court's order from binding him. He points out that he was not a party to the original action, nor an officer, agent, servant, employee, or attorney of a party, and denies that he was acting in "active concert or participation" with any party to the original action.

In examining this contention we start with the proposition that Rule 65 was intended to embody "the common-law doctrine that a decree of injunction not only binds the parties defendant but also those identified with them in interest, in 'privity' with them, represented by them or subject to their control." Literally read, Rule 65(d) would forbid the issuance of in rem injunctions. . . . But courts have continued to issue in rem injunctions notwithstanding Rule 65(d), since they possessed the power to do so at common law and since Rule 65(d) was intended to embody rather than to limit their common law powers. . . .

Similarly, we conclude that Rule 65(d), as a codification rather than a limitation of courts' common-law powers, cannot be read to restrict the inherent power of a court to protect its ability to render a binding judgment. . . . We hold that Hall's relationship to the *Mims* case fell within that contemplated by Rule 65(d). By deciding *Mims* and retaining jurisdiction the district court had, in effect, adjudicated the rights of the entire community with respect to the racial controversy surrounding the school system. Moreover, as we have noted, in the circumstances of this case third parties such as Hall were in a position to upset the court's adjudication.

This was not a situation which could have been anticipated by the draftsmen of procedural rules. In meeting the situation as it did, the district court did not overstep its powers.

We do not hold that courts are free to issue permanent injunctions against all the world in school cases. Hall had notice of the court's order. Rather than challenge it by the orderly processes of law, he resorted to conscious, willful defiance. *See* Walker v. Birmingham, 388 U.S. 307 (1967).

It is true that this order was issued without a hearing, and that ordinarily injunctive relief cannot be granted without a hearing. But we need not hold that this order has the effect of a preliminary or permanent injunction. Rather, the portion of the court's order here complained of may be characterized as a temporary restraining order, which under Rule 65(b) may be issued ex parte. . . . Hall's violation occurred within four days of the issuance of the order, well within the ten-day limitation period for temporary restraining orders. . . .

We hold, then, that the district court had the inherent power to protect its ability to render a binding judgment between the original parties to the *Mims* litigation by issuing an interim ex parte order against an undefinable class of persons. We further hold that willful violation of that order by one having notice of it constitutes criminal contempt. The judgment of the district court is affirmed.

IN RE U.S. OIL AND GAS LITIGATION

967 F.2d 489 (11th Cir. 1992)

■   HATCHETT, Circuit Judge.

In this case of first impression in this circuit, we affirm the district court's imposition of a settlement bar order and establish the standard of review to be abuse of discretion.

FACTS AND PROCEDURAL HISTORY

In the late 1970s, the U.S. Oil and Gas Corporation, Eagle Oil and Gas Corporation, and the Stratford Company (the Companies) began selling an advisory service to investors seeking to bid on federal oil and gas leases. . . . The investments were extremely high risk . . . In an effort to serve customers who were willing to pay more for lower risk, the Companies developed a "money back guarantee" program. Essentially, the program required the purchase of a master insurance policy for participating investors.

The Companies contacted an insurance broker, Alexander and Alexander, Inc. (A & A). After domestic insurance companies refused to participate in the program, A & A obtained a policy from Pinnacle Reinsurance Company, Ltd. (Pinnacle), a Bermuda corporation. Pinnacle issued a $1 million annuity contract in exchange for a $525,000 premium.

By 1983, the Companies had sold their services to some 8,000 customers. They had also attracted the attention of United States postal authorities and the Federal Trade Commission (FTC). The FTC filed an enforcement action against the Companies in the United States District Court for the Southern District of Florida, and the court appointed a receiver to protect the interests of the Companies' customers. In 1985, the receiver filed a complaint on his behalf and instituted a class action on behalf of the customers alleging securities fraud and RICO violations.

The complaints named A & A, Pinnacle, and ninety-four others as defendants. As the plaintiffs state, the litigation became "breathtakingly complex." Between 1984 and 1990, the court held 50 hearings, the plaintiffs attended 260 depositions, and discovery produced hundreds of thousands of relevant documents. As trial approached, plaintiffs stipulated that more than 700 issues of fact remained unresolved.

Near the end of 1990, the possibility of a long, complicated, and expensive trial began to produce settlements. The Morgenstern defendants, a group which had provided legal services to the Companies, entered into the first major settlement with the plaintiffs. On January 26, 1991, pursuant to the settlement agreement, the district court entered a series of orders. These orders approved the fairness of the Morgenstern settlement, dismissed the receiver's and the class's claims against the Morgenstern defendants, and barred "all claims" by non-settling defendants against settling defendants, or by settling defendants against non-settling defendants, related to the subject matter of the litigation. This last order, the Morgenstern settlement bar, drew no serious objections from Pinnacle, which had no cross-claims pending against the settling defendants.

Pinnacle did, however, object to the settlement bar order which is the subject of this appeal. In 1988, Pinnacle filed a cross-claim against A & A alleging indemnity, breach of fiduciary duty, fraud, and negligence. Pinnacle claimed that A & A knew of the Companies' fraudulent activities, but wrongfully withheld that information from Pinnacle when it brokered the annuity contract. Throughout the litigation, Pinnacle sought to preserve this claim against A & A, even while it sought settlement with the plaintiffs.

Pinnacle's desire to preserve its cross-claim eventually conflicted with the plaintiffs' desire to achieve a favorable settlement with A & A. . . . When Pinnacle and plaintiffs agreed to settle for $500,000, a settlement bar order was not part of the bargain.

A & A, however, was still engaged in settlement negotiations with plaintiffs and was not willing to settle its liability without a bar order protecting it from Pinnacle's pending cross-claim. Although A & A and plaintiffs disputed in the district court whether a settlement bar order was a condition precedent to the effectiveness of their settlement agreement, they both agreed that the district court should enter such an order. Plainly, A & A was unwilling to disburse an eight and a half million dollar [$8,500,000] settlement without the assurance that it would be protected from further claims for contribution or indemnity. Even more plainly, plaintiffs weighed A & A's eight and a half million dollar settlement against Pinnacle's five hundred thousand dollar settlement and saw the light of supporting A & A's insistence on a bar order.

By the beginning of 1991, the plaintiffs and a large number of defendants had entered into settlement agreements. On January 30, 1991, the district court conducted a hearing to resolve outstanding issues among the settling parties. Chief among these outstanding issues was A & A's insistence on a settlement bar order, plaintiffs' support of such an order, and Pinnacle's opposition to it. The court afforded each party an opportunity to fully argue its position on the settlement bar issue. The court asked Pinnacle whether it sought to withdraw from its settlement with plaintiffs now that plaintiffs and A & A were jointly urging the court to adopt a settlement bar order. Pinnacle stated emphatically that it did not seek to withdraw from the settlement. . . .

On April 12, 1991, the district court entered a settlement bar order extinguishing all claims related to the litigation against the settling defendants. The court . . . concluded that the order was justified: "If litigation of cross-claims were allowed, the resources of the court, class members, class members' counsel, and defendants' counsel would continue to be expended, because it would be impossible to try cross-claims without addressing the complex facts underlying this litigation. . . . Settlements in complex cases cannot satisfy their ultimate purposes unless they conclude the litigation in its entirety." . . .

ISSUES

The issues presented are: (1) whether the district court erred in entering the settlement bar order; and (2) whether the district court denied Pinnacle due process in entering the order.

DISCUSSION

The Bar Order

Public policy strongly favors the pretrial settlement of class action lawsuits. Complex litigation — like the instant case — can occupy a court's docket for years on end, depleting the resources of the parties and the taxpayers while rendering meaningful relief increasingly elusive. Accordingly, the Federal Rules of Civil Procedure authorize district courts to facilitate settlements in all types of litigation, not just class actions. *See* Fed. R. Civ. P. 16(a), (c). Although class action settlements require court approval, such approval is committed to the sound discretion of the district court.

Modern class action settlements increasingly incorporate settlement bar orders such as the one at issue in this case. *See, e.g.*, In re[ ] Jiffy Lube Sec. Litig., 927 F.2d 155 (4th Cir. 1991). The reason for this trend is that bar orders play an integral role in facilitating settlement. Defendants buy little peace through settlement unless they are assured that they will be protected against codefendants' efforts to shift their losses through cross-claims for indemnity, contribution, and other causes related to the underlying litigation. Thus, in the present case, A & A expressed a strong unwillingness to pay eight and a half million dollars to the plaintiffs unless it was assured that Pinnacle's cross-claims would not subject it to further liability. In short, settlement bar orders allow settling parties to put a limit on the risks of settlement.

We believe that these principles strongly support the district court's decision to enter a settlement bar order in this case. We note, however, that this case involves unique features which distinguish it from the precedents cited above. In particular, this case presents a settling defendant's challenge to a settlement bar order. In all of the cases previously cited, nonsettling defendants challenged the bar order as prejudicial to their rights. In the typical case involving a nonsettling defendant, the court is concerned with calculating the proper "offset" to ensure that plaintiffs do not enjoy a double recovery against nonsettling defendants in any subsequent litigation of outstanding claims. *See, e.g., Jiffy Lube,* 927 F.2d at 160-62. We express no opinion in this case regarding the proper method to be applied in calculating such "offsets." Because Pinnacle agreed to settle, it risked no further liability from plaintiffs. Thus, the district court was not faced with the difficult task of determining the proper offset to ensure that plaintiffs did not gain a "double recovery" in subsequent judgments against nonsettling defendants.

A second distinctive feature about this case, related to the first, is the severability of the settlement bar order. At oral argument and in its brief, A & A repeatedly questioned Pinnacle's right to appeal the bar order. We agree that in many cases, a settling defendant's appeal of a bar order would be problematic. To the extent that the bar order is an integral part of the settlement, the settling defendant may have waived the right to object to it. Where the parties have stipulated that the bar order is integral to the settlement, this court may not consider the order in isolation. . . . Thus, as a general rule, we may not consider an appeal of a bar order separately from the entire settlement.

In the present case, however, Pinnacle preserved its right to challenge and appeal the bar order, despite its agreement to the settlement as a whole. . . . Because Pinnacle carefully reserved its rights, it was entitled to both the benefit of the settlement and a continuing challenge to the bar order on appeal.

We now address the merits of Pinnacle's specific challenge. Seeking to distinguish this case from the numerous precedents upholding the validity of settlement bar orders, Pinnacle argues that the district court erred as a matter of law when it barred Pinnacle's claims for indemnity, fraud, and negligence against A & A. According to Pinnacle, settlement bar orders have been entered only in cases where a nonsettling defendant sought to preserve contribution claims against settling defendants. Pinnacle argues that independent claims and indemnity claims cannot be precluded through a settlement bar order.

Pinnacle . . . offers this court not a shred of logic upon which we could base a principled distinction between bar orders against contribution, on the one hand, and orders against indemnity or so-called "independent claims," on the other. Pinnacle places primary reliance instead upon its argument that most, if not all, of the prior federal cases supporting bar orders dealt exclusively with contribution claims.

Pinnacle's legal argument is unavailing. First, several federal courts have approved of settlement bars against indemnity claims. *See, e.g., Jiffy Lube*, 927 F.2d at 158. In addition, as the district court noted, the substantive weakness of Pinnacle's indemnity claim supported the entry of the settlement bar against it. Indemnification claims are not cognizable under the Securities Acts of 1933 and 1934. Because Pinnacle's cross-claim was largely an attempt to seek indemnity from A & A for the federal securities law violations alleged against Pinnacle in the complaints, it was unlikely to survive even the most cursory adjudication on the merits.

The settlement bar order is also effective against Pinnacle's allegedly independent causes of action for fraud and negligence. These claims were not, in fact, independent of Pinnacle's or A & A's liability to the plaintiffs. . . . Pinnacle's fraud and negligence claims "are nothing more than claims for contribution or indemnification with a slight change in wording." Because Pinnacle's fraud and negligence claims were integrally related to plaintiffs' claims against both A & A and Pinnacle, the district court properly extinguished those claims in the settlement bar order.

The propriety of the settlement bar order should turn upon the interrelatedness of the claims that it precludes, not upon the labels which parties attach to those claims. If the cross-claims that the district court seeks to extinguish through the entry of a bar order arise out of the same facts as those underlying the litigation, then the district court may exercise its discretion to bar such claims in reaching a fair and equitable settlement. That is precisely what the district court did in this case.

Due Process

. . .

Our review indicates that . . . by the time the district court entered the bar order several months later, Pinnacle was fully aware that the order had become part of the settlement. . . .

A district court may issue a settlement bar order against a nonsettling defendant after it makes a reasoned determination that it is fair and equitable to do so. Surely, then, the district court may enter a settlement bar order against a defendant who has participated fully in settlement negotiations and utilized every opportunity to preserve its rights within those negotiations. In the end, Pinnacle has gotten exactly what it had a right to expect in this case: a binding settlement with plaintiffs and a full opportunity to challenge, at both the trial and appellate levels, the propriety of the settlement bar order.

CONCLUSION

For the foregoing reasons, the judgment of the district court is affirmed.

Notes

1. The Supreme Court has cited *Hall* with apparent approval on several occasions. See, *e.g.*, Golden State Bottling Co. v. NLRB, 414 U.S. 168, 180 (1973); Wash. v. Wash. State Commercial Passenger Fishing Vessel Ass'n, 443 U.S. 658, 693 n.32 (1979) (noting that respondents were "probably subject to injunction under . . . the rule that nonparties who interfere with the implementation of court orders establishing public rights may be enjoined; citing *Hall* and *Golden State Bottling*). On the other hand, in *Spallone v. United States*, 493 U.S. 265 (1990), the district court faced a city that refused to abide by an agreement requiring integrated housing. One of the reasons for the refusal was that the city council did not pass the necessary implementing legislation. The district court held both the city and the legislators, who were not parties to the litigation, in contempt. After a standoff of several weeks, during which the city was driven into bankruptcy by the increasing fines and the recalcitrant council members were threatened with imprisonment, one of the members of the council changed his vote, and the legislation passed. In an opinion heavily laced with concerns for federalism and separation of powers, the Court held that the district court had erred in acting against the nonparty legislators. The Court hinted that such action might have eventually been appropriate had the direct sanctions against the city not worked.

2. The logic of *Hall* should be very familiar by now: The parties' ability to obtain a meaningful remedy is threatened by the actions of nonparties, and the court must have the power to deal with the problem. This is precisely the logic that we have suggested throughout this book is a compelling ground for departure from a standard adversarial model, under which the court can act only on the parties before it. Taken out of the specific context that gave rise to its holding, does *Hall* suggest that courts possess — or should possess — a power to guarantee an effective remedy for the parties when standard adversarial processes cannot? Or is *Hall* limited, as *Washington State Commercial Passenger* suggests, just to public-law litigation? Is all complex litigation "public-law litigation"? Should we maintain different procedural rules for different cases, or should we strive to hold onto our modern aspiration to treat all cases alike?

3. One way to test some of these questions is to consider *U.S. Oil and Gas*. The case is not a public-law case, at least in the typical understanding of that phrase, but it is a complex case. Nor does it present a situation in which Pinnacle, who was a nonparty to the relevant settlement agreement,

threatened the ability of the plaintiffs to obtain any remedy at all. Do these facts mean that *U.S. Oil and Gas* is wrong? *See* TBG, Inc. v. Bendis, 36 F.3d 916, 924 (10th Cir. 1994) (disagreeing with *U.S. Oil and Gas* "that the interest in settlement can give courts the power to bar statutory contribution claims"; although "[c]ourts may not extinguish such rights in order to facilitate settlement unless the statute authorizes them to do so," noting that the All Writs Act, 28 U.S.C. § 1651, may provide a source of authority to enter bar orders in appropriate cases); *see also* In re Heritage Bond Litig., 546 F.3d 667 (9th Cir. 2008) (overturning a bar order that sought to release claims other than contribution and indemnity claims); AAL High Yield Bond Fund v. Deloitte & Touche, LLP, 361 F.3d 1305 (11th Cir. 2004) (limiting *U.S. Oil and Gas* to claims for contribution and indemnity, not independent claims); Gerber v. MTC Elec. Techs. Co., 329 F.3d 297 (2d Cir. 2003) (same).

Although the court's logic in *U.S. Oil and Gas* does not seem to limit itself to this fact, Pinnacle was a party in the case. Should that make a difference? Moreover, the equities in *Hall* and *U.S. Oil and Gas* are different; in *Hall*, the nonparty was attempting to disrupt the remedy, while in *U.S. Oil and Gas* Pinnacle had obtained a comparable bar order itself. Should that make a difference? In both cases, the "nonparty" (Hall and Pinnacle) had knowledge of the relevant order that sought to effectuate the remedy. Does this knowledge, combined with the desirability of obtaining a litigation-ending remedy for present parties, justify the result in *U.S. Oil and Gas*? What are the limits of this power?

4.   These questions — what is the court's power to deal with those who sit on the sidelines, what is the relevance of notice and opportunity to participate, can a court act in a non-adversarial manner when there exists a threat to rational adjudication, what about the need to prevent needless relitigation of claims, what about the like procedural treatment of like claims — return us full circle to the place where this book began. Complex civil litigation is truly a seamless web. Like all webs, there are no easy solutions that permit a quick escape. Ultimately, complex litigation is the story of a procedural system wrestling with the unavoidable difficulties that its chosen rules have caused. This quest for an unattainable justice gives complex litigation both its fascination and its peculiar bite.

INDEX